Microsoft®
Office 2013
Bible

Microsoft®
Office 2013
BIBLE

Lisa A. Bucki

John Walkenbach

Faithe Wempen

Michael Alexander

Dick Kusleika

WILEY

Microsoft® Office 2013 Bible

Published by
John Wiley & Sons, Inc.
10475 Crosspoint Boulevard
Indianapolis, IN 46256
www.wiley.com

Copyright © 2013 by John Wiley & Sons, Inc., Indianapolis, Indiana

Published simultaneously in Canada

ISBN: 978-1-118-48809-6
ISBN: 978-1-118-75046-9 (ebk)
ISBN: 978-1-118-76676-7 (ebk)

Manufactured in the United States of America

10 9 8 7 6 5 4 3 2 1

For general information on our other products and services please contact our Customer Care Department within the United States at (877) 762-2974, outside the United States at (317) 572-3993 or fax (317) 572-4002.

Wiley publishes in a variety of print and electronic formats and by print-on-demand. Some material included with standard print versions of this book may not be included in e-books or in print-on-demand. If this book refers to media such as a CD or DVD that is not included in the version you purchased, you may download this material at http://booksupport.wiley.com. For more information about Wiley products, visit www.wiley.com.

Library of Congress Control Number: 2013934762

To homeless and neglected pets everywhere, in the hope that you will find a better life and the loving care that you deserve. And to the many compassionate people involved in animal rescue work, in thanks for the selfless work that you do.

About the Authors

Lisa A. Bucki is an author, trainer, and consultant and has been writing and teaching about computers and software for more than 15 years. Also author of *Microsoft Word 2013 Bible* and contributing author for two prior editions of Office 2013 Bible, she wrote *Teach Yourself Visually Microsoft Office PowerPoint 2007*; *Microsoft Office Project 2007 Survival Guide*; *Learning Photoshop CS2*; *Dell Guide to Digital Photography: Shooting, Editing, and Printing Pictures*; *Learning Computer Applications: Projects & Exercises* (multiple editions); and *Adobe Photoshop 7 Fast & Easy*. Along with Faithe Wempen, Lisa also co-wrote *Windows 8* (brief and expanded editions) for educational publisher Paradigm Publishing. Lisa has written or contributed to dozens of additional books and multimedia tutorials covering a variety of software and technology topics, including FileMaker Pro, iPhoto, Fireworks and Flash from Adobe, Microsoft Office applications, and digital photography. She also spearheaded or developed more than 100 computer and trade titles during her association with the former Macmillan Computer Publishing (now a division of Pearson).

John Walkenbach is a bestselling Excel author and has published more than 50 spreadsheet books. He lives amid the saguaros, javelinas, rattlesnakes, bobcats, and gila monsters in Southern Arizona — but the critters are mostly scared away by his clayhammer banjo playing. For more information, Google him.

Faithe Wempen, MA, is an A+ Certified hardware guru, Microsoft Office Specialist Master Instructor, and software consultant with over 120 computer books to her credit. She has taught Microsoft Office applications, including PowerPoint, to over a quarter of a million online students for corporate clients, including Hewlett Packard, CNET, Sony, Gateway, and eMachines. When she is not writing, she teaches Microsoft Office classes in the Computer Technology department at Indiana University-Purdue University at Indianapolis (IUPUI), does private computer training and support consulting, and owns and operates Sycamore Knoll Bed and Breakfast in Noblesville, Indiana (www.sycamoreknoll.com).

Michael Alexander is a Microsoft Certified Application Developer (MCAD) and author of several books on advanced business analysis with Microsoft Access and Microsoft Excel. He has more than 15 years of experience consulting and developing Microsoft Office solutions. Mike has been named a Microsoft MVP for his ongoing contributions to the Excel community. In his spare time, he runs a free tutorial site, www.datapigtechnologies.com, where he shares Excel and Access tips.

Dick Kusleika has been awarded as a Microsoft MVP for 12 consecutive years and has been working with Microsoft Office for more than 20. Dick develops Access- and Excel-based solutions for his clients and has conducted training seminars on Office products in the United States and Australia. Dick also writes a popular Excel-related blog at www.dailydoseofexcel.com.

About the Technical Editor

Justin Rodino began his technical instructional career working as a guest lecturer while also attending Purdue University as an undergraduate. After graduation, he worked overseas for Tias Business School doing educational design for online delivery, by creating one of the first online eLearning platforms. Later, Justin joined Altiris/Symantec and was one of their lead Microsoft Consultants in the EMEA region where he became an expert in Microsoft Technologies, received his MCSE, and became an MCT. He has been an MCT for the past five years and in that time was also awarded the coveted MVP award two years in a row before joining Microsoft as a Technical Program Manager. In the past three years Justin has worked with Microsoft to help define their lab strategy as well as operationalize and run the internal eLearning platform. Over the years he has served as the technical editor on numerous books such as the Office 2010 and Office 2013 Bibles. As well as editing books, Justin speaks at numerous Microsoft Events, runs Square Baboon, a consulting company specializing in IP Telephony and IT services, and is a volunteer firefighter and EMT.

Credits

Acknowledgments

Thanks to Mariann Barsolo for signing me (Lisa A. Bucki) on for many months of adventure pulling together the contents of this Bible as well as rewriting the Word 2013 Bible. Mariann, you always know just when an author needs a good cheering section. I also appreciate the ongoing support that I've received from my friend Jim Minatel at Wiley.

Thanks also to Adaobi Obi Tulton, Senior Project Editor. Adaobi, it's time to promote you from superhero to Goddess. Thank you for helping a mere mortal through a massive project like this.

The authors who contributed chapters from their individual Bible books provided the granite from which this edifice was built. Thanks to these folks for their excellence and expertise:

- John Walkenbach, *Microsoft Excel 2013 Bible*
- Michael R. Groh, Michael Alexander, and Dick Kusleika, *Microsoft Access 2013 Bible*
- Faithe Wempen, *Microsoft PowerPoint 2013 Bible*

I thank Technical Editor Justin Rodino for lending his MVP experience in making this a better book. Justin, I appreciated the many thoughtful and informative comments you contributed over the course of so many chapters.

Contents

Contents

Contents

Contents

Part VII: Managing Information with Access and OneNote   1163

Contents

Introduction

Welcome to *Microsoft Office 2013 Bible*. This book provides the information you need to get up and running with the applications in the latest version of the Microsoft Office 2013 suite. Inside, you get coverage of these members of the various versions of the Office Suite:

- Microsoft Word 2013
- Microsoft Excel 2013
- Microsoft PowerPoint 2013
- Microsoft Outlook 2013
- Microsoft Publisher 2013
- Microsoft Access 2013
- Microsoft OneNote 2013

This book brings together chapters from the new versions of the Word, Excel, PowerPoint, and Access *Bibles*. You get the best information from experts in each program so that you can get to work and be productive quickly.

Who Should Read This Book

Office 2013 adds some terrific new features in Word, Excel, PowerPoint, Access, Outlook, Publisher, and OneNote. As a result, even experienced Office users can use this book to get up to speed with using the new features and other tricks quickly. Because this book presents information using the friendly, accessible *Bible* format that combines straightforward steps and concise reference information, beginners with Office can use it to learn Office quickly and expand their skills beyond the basics.

How This Book Is Organized

Microsoft Office 2013 Bible organizes information into several parts. In most cases, a part focuses on a particular application in the suite, so you can jump right to the part for the application you're currently using.

Part I: Common Office Features

The chapters in this part provide the first introduction to the new user interface in the major Office applications, as well as show how to perform fundamental operations, such as working with files.

Part II: Creating Documents with Word 2013

This part covers using the Microsoft Word 2013 word processing program to create and format text-based documents. In addition to learning how to format words, paragraphs, and pages, you get a shot at working with more sophisticated features such as tables and mail merge, and even the new SmartArt diagrams. You also see how document security settings can help protect information.

Part III: Making the Numbers Work with Excel 2013

The chapters here show you how to use the spreadsheet program Microsoft Excel 2013 to organize and calculate data. After getting a preview of the new features in the program, you learn how to enter, format, and calculate information. You also see how to create powerful charts that tell a story about your data, summarize data with data bars, sparklines, and conditional formatting.

Part IV: Persuading and Informing with PowerPoint 2013

In this part, you learn how to get the word out with the Microsoft PowerPoint 2013 presentation graphics program. This part explains how to add information, charts, SmartArt diagrams, and graphics to slides. You also see how to animate and automate a slide show and get expert tips about going live with your presentation.

Part V: Organizing Messages, Contacts, and Time with Outlook

The basics for using Microsoft Outlook 2013 appear in this part. Learn to set up an e-mail account; compose, send, and respond to messages; organize messages and deal with junk mail and security issues; manage your contacts, appointments, and to-do list.

Part VI: Designing Publications with Publisher

This part introduces you to the Microsoft Publisher 2013 page layout and design program. Learn how to not only create great-looking publications with Publisher's flexible tools but also prep your publications for professional printing.

Part VII: Managing Information with Access and OneNote

If you manage detailed lists — with customer or product data, for example — Microsoft Access 2013 and this part's chapters are for you. Get a roadmap here for designing a good database. Learn how to create tables, fields, and forms, and how to select and present data with queries and reports. Also get an overview about using OneNote 2013 to track notes and project details,

Part VIII: Sharing and Collaborating in the Cloud and Applications

This part explains not only how to share information between Office applications, but also how to use Office 2013 applications with SkyDrive.

Conventions and Features

As you work your way through the text, be on the lookout for these icons that bring your attention to important information:

CAUTION

This information is important and is set off in a separate paragraph with a special icon. Cautions provide information about things to watch out for, whether simply inconvenient or potentially hazardous to your data or systems.

TIP

Tips generally are used to provide information that can make your work easier—special shortcuts or methods for doing something easier than the norm.

NOTE

Notes provide additional, ancillary information that is helpful but somewhat outside of the current presentation of information.

The text also uses specific shortcuts for choosing commands:

- **Mouse:** When the text instructs you to choose a command from a menu or the Ribbon (in the new interface), the command is presented like this: Choose Home ⇨ Clipboard ⇨ Copy. That means to click the Home tab on the Ribbon, look in the Clipboard group, and click the Copy choice. These Ribbon tab name ⇨ group ⇨ command sequences help you navigate through the Ribbon to find and choose the appropriate command. When referencing contextual tabs, where the first part of the tab name appears on an upper row and the subtab name appears on the lower row along with the normal tabs, an arrow will also appear between the upper part of the contextual tab name and the subtab, as in Picture Tools⇨Format. After the first mention in a chapter, the text may refer to the contextual tab by its subtab name only, that is, Format rather than Picture Tools⇨Format.

- **Keyboard:** Any keyboard shortcuts appear like this: Ctrl+C. That means to press the Ctrl key and C key simultaneously and then release them.

Where to Go from Here

Microsoft has released several versions of the Microsoft Office 2013 suite, with different versions including different applications. You can jump right to the parts that offer coverage for the applications offered in the flavor of Office that you own.

Part I

Common Office Features

The new version of Microsoft Office brings some changes that even seasoned Office users will appreciate. Besides a more modern look and style, Office includes new tools, new views, new navigational tricks, and more. Chapter 1 provides your first look at the new Office, including introducing just a few of its new features. Chapter 2 shows you the basics for finding and using tools and commands in Office applications, including using task panes, dialog boxes, and options. It even introduces you to the touch gestures you can use if you're working with Office on a touch-enabled system or tablet. Chapter 3 summarizes common tasks such as creating and printing files, finding and replacing information, going to a location, working with the new user accounts feature, or even a brief introduction to working in the cloud.

Welcome to Microsoft Office 2013

IN THIS CHAPTER

Reviewing the core Microsoft Office business applications

Looking at additional Office applications

Getting a first look at new features in Office 2013

Starting and closing an application

Finding a file

Browsing and finding Help

M icrosoft Office 2013 provides a comprehensive toolkit for tackling day-to-day productivity and communication tasks for business or personal purposes. This chapter introduces the individual Office applications and teaches you skills for getting started using them.

Learning about Office Applications

Microsoft Office 2013 offers a robust set of applications, each tailor-made to provide the best tools for a particular job. For example, if you're creating a letter, you may need to work with commands for formatting text. If you need to total sales figures, you'll need an automated way to sum the numbers.

Office provides applications that enable you to handle each of those aforementioned scenarios and more. Read on to learn which Office applications to use for creating text-based documents, manipulating numbers, presenting your ideas, or even communicating with others.

Microsoft offers several different versions of the Microsoft Office 2013 software suite, including the Home & Student, Home & Business, and Professional retail versions. In addition, some plans for the Office 365 subscription service will include licensed copies of the different versions of the Office software, including a Professional Plus version, with the version varying depending on the subscription. Each version includes a different combination of the individual Office programs. Only Word 2013, Excel 2013, and PowerPoint 2013 are included in all versions. Therefore, depending on the Office version you've purchased, you may not have all of the applications described in this chapter and further throughout the book. Office 2013 also comes in both 32-bit and 64-bit releases. If you have a 64-bit computer system and are running a 64-bit operating system, you could choose a 64-bit Office release for enhanced functionality.

NOTE

This book focuses primarily on the Word, Excel, PowerPoint, Outlook, Access, and OneNote applications found in Office 2013 Professional and all the Office 365 suites.

Microsoft also offers free Office web apps: web-browser-based versions of Word, Excel, PowerPoint, and OneNote, helping eliminate the need for the software to be installed locally on your computer, subsequently enabling online file sharing and collaboration. (Some of the Office 365 subscriptions also enable you to offer other Office web apps.) Using Office web apps enables you to store your files in an online location, in the "cloud," in a SkyDrive account; if you have Office installed on your computer, you also can download from a web app to the local app. Access to Office web apps is included free with your Microsoft account, with a limited amount of storage available for free. This book focuses on the locally installed desktop versions of the Office applications, but you can explore Office web apps and online storage options if you require remote capabilities of either specific office applications or your data.

Finally, Office 2013 will include a version optimized for Windows RT — the version of Windows 8 optimized for tablet and other portable devices.

Word

Word processing — typing, editing, formatting letters, reports, fax cover sheets, and so on — is perhaps the most common activity performed on a computer. Whether you need to create a memo at the office or a letter at home, using a word processing program can save you time and help you achieve polished results.

Microsoft Word has long been the leading word processing program. As one of the core applications in the Office suite, Word provides a host of document-creation tools that have been refined to be easy to use, yet have comprehensive feature sets should you wish to extend your document beyond the basics. Using Word to apply a minor bit of text formatting and a graphic can make even a simple document, such as the meeting agenda shown in Figure 1.1, have more impact and appeal than just plain text alone.

FIGURE 1.1

Microsoft Word 2013 enables you to create appealing documents.

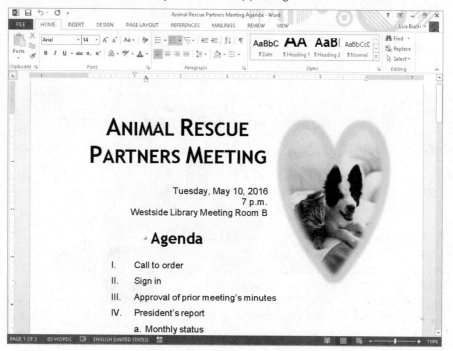

Word enables you to do more than just make your documents look great. Its features can help you enhance your document text more easily and furthermore create sophisticated elements such as footnotes, endnotes, and more. You'll learn about these powerful Word features, among others, later in this book:

- **Templates:** A *template* is a starter document that supplies the document design, text formatting, and, often, placeholder text or suggested text. Add your own text and your document is finished!

- **Styles:** If you like a particular combination of formatting settings that you've applied to text, you can save the combination as a style that you can easily apply to other text.

- **Tables:** Add a table to organize text in a grid of rows and columns to which you can then apply terrific formatting. In Word 2013, you can add a title and a summary to a table to better describe its contents.

- **Graphics:** You can add all types of pictures to your documents and even create diagrams like the one in Figure 1.2 using the SmartArt feature. Some SmartArt layouts even enable you to insert pictures as shown in Figure 1.2.

FIGURE 1.2

SmartArt diagrams illustrate information in a document.

- **Mail Merge:** Create your own, customized "form letter" wherein each copy is automatically customized for a particular recipient (or list entry). Word's Merge feature even enables you to create matching envelopes and labels.

- **Document Security and Review:** Word enables you to protect a document against unwanted changes, as well as to track changes made by other users. Using these features, you can control the document content through a collaboration process.

Excel

Spreadsheet programs — which provide formulas and functions that make it easy to calculate numerical data — made a critical technology leap in business computing. Business people no longer need to rely on adding machines, scientific calculators, or accountants to perform detailed sales or financial calculations. Even a beginning salesperson could insert numbers into a spreadsheet, type a few formulas, and have the data automatically calculated. Even better, spreadsheet programs give you the ability to represent data graphically, which communicates the impact of the data more effectively. Microsoft Excel 2013, shown in Figure 1.3, performs the spreadsheet duties in the Microsoft Office suite.

FIGURE 1.3

Use the Microsoft Excel 2013 program to organize and calculate numerical data.

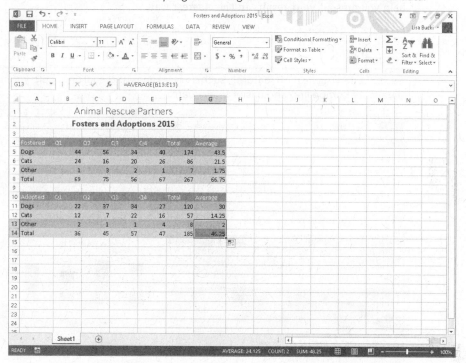

Excel 2013 enables you to build a calculation by creating a formula that specifies the values to calculate and which mathematical operators to use to perform the calculation. Excel also offers functions — predesigned formulas that perform more complex calculations, such as calculating accrued interest. Excel not only provides tools to assist you in building and error-checking spreadsheet formulas, but it also gives you many easy choices for formatting the data to make it more readable and professional. You'll learn these Excel essentials later in the book, as well as more about these key Excel features:

- **Worksheets:** Within each file, you can divide and organize a large volume of data across multiple worksheets or pages of information in the file.

- **Ranges:** You can assign a name to a contiguous area on a worksheet so that you can later select that area by name, or use the name in a formula to save time.

- **Number and Date Value Formatting:** You can apply a number format that defines how Excel should display a cell's contents, indicating details such as how many decimal points should appear and whether a percentage or dollar sign should be included. You can also apply a date format to determine how the date appears.

- **Charts:** Translate your data into a meaningful image by creating a chart in Excel (as shown in Figure 1.4). Excel offers dozens of chart types, layouts, and formats to help you present your results in the clearest way.

FIGURE 1.4

Excel's data visualization features, such as sparklines and charting, help you make data more compelling and easier to evaluate.

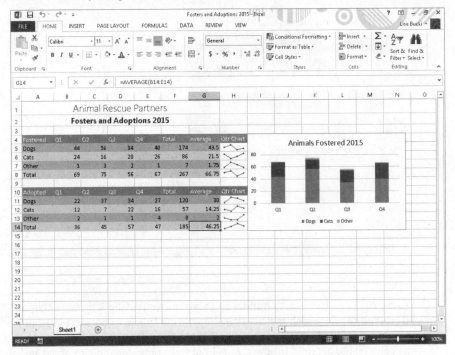

- **Specialized Data Formatting:** Sometimes it's more expedient to use cell formatting to help data have more visual impact rather than creating a separate chart. Excel offers *conditional formatting,* a tool that enables it to apply specialized formatting for selected cells based on the results of the formulas in those cells or the contents of the cells. For example, if you have a spreadsheet calculating grade averages, you can set up the cells to be formatted in one color for a passing average and another for a failing average. The conditional formats include data bars, color scales, icon scales, and more. Excel 2013 offers a sparklines feature that enables you to create a small chart within a cell. Refer to Figure 1.4 to see examples under Qtr Chart.

PowerPoint

To achieve positive outcomes in situations such as persuading customers to buy; convincing your company's leadership to invest in developing a new product you've conceived; training members of your team to follow a new operating procedure; or making sure that a group of volunteers understands program requirements — you must deliver your message in a clear, concise, convincing, and often visual way. A presentation graphics program helps you inform your audience in situations like those just described, and more.

The Microsoft PowerPoint 2013 presentation graphics program (see Figure 1.5) enables you to communicate information and ideas via an on-screen slide show or by printing the pages as handouts. Each slide should present a key topic that you want to convey, along with a few supporting points or a graphical reinforcement, such as a chart or picture. In this way, PowerPoint helps you to divide information into chunks that audience members can more easily absorb.

FIGURE 1.5

Use PowerPoint to present your message in informative slides.

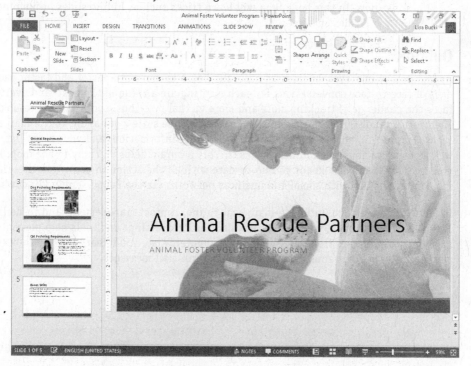

Later in the book, you will learn how to create the basic presentation structure and add information as well as use the following PowerPoint features to help reinforce your message:

- **Layouts, Themes, and Masters:** These PowerPoint features control the content that appears on a slide and how the content is arranged, as well as the appearance of all of the slides. You can quickly redesign a single slide or the entire presentation.

- **Tables and Charts:** Similar to Word and Excel, PowerPoint enables you to arrange information in an attractively formatted grid of rows and columns. PowerPoint works with Excel to deliver charted data, so the Excel charting skills you build make developing charts in PowerPoint even easier.

- **Animations and Transitions:** You can set up the text and other items on slides to make a special entrance, such as appearing to fly onto the screen, when you play them in a slide show. In addition to applying animations on objects, you can apply a transition that animates how the overall slide appears and disappears from the screen, such as dissolving or wiping in and away.

- **Live Presentations:** PowerPoint offers several different ways in which you can customize and control how the presentation looks when played as an on-screen slide show. In this book, you will learn tricks such as hiding slides or jumping between slides on-screen.

Outlook

As technology improves, businesses naturally begin to move at a faster and faster pace. The days of face-to-face conversations for each meeting are a thing of the past, and everyone faces the challenge of tracking more and more virtual meetings, contacts, and to-dos. The Microsoft Outlook 2013 program in the Microsoft Office suite can handle your e-mail messages (Figure 1.6), appointment scheduling, contact information, and your to-do list, as well as other various communication tasks. This program helps you stay in the loop, keeps you organized, and also keeps you up-to-date with all the action in your work life, including connecting you with social and business networks via the People app in Windows 8.

In addition to learning Outlook e-mail, scheduling, contact management, and to-do list basics later in the book, you will learn which Outlook settings and tools help prevent messages with viruses from infecting your computer. Also, you'll learn how Outlook can automatically manage annoying yet pervasive junk mail messages.

FIGURE 1.6

Send and receive e-mail messages in Microsoft Outlook.

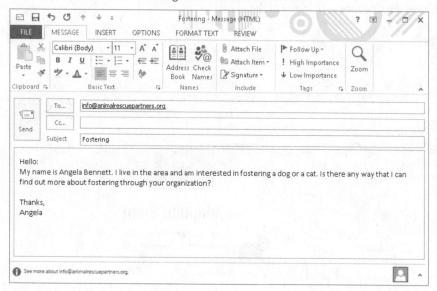

Taking Advantage of Other Office Applications

You may be a user whose needs extend beyond letter writing and number crunching. If you routinely take on special tasks such as creating printed publications or tracking extensive customer data, you may find yourself working with some of the other applications that are part of certain editions of Microsoft Office 2013. This section gives you a snapshot of those other applications; later chapters of the book revisit these topics.

Publisher

Microsoft Publisher 2013 enables you to create publications, which have a greater emphasis on design than a word processing program typically offers. To help the creative process, Publisher includes attractive publication designs and templates with placeholders for text and images, as well as other features, including decorative rules and backgrounds already in place, as shown in Figure 1.7.

FIGURE 1.7

Microsoft Publisher provides placeholders and design elements so that you can create eye-catching publications with minimal design effort.

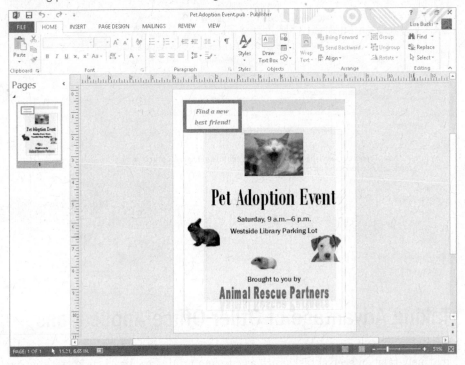

> **TIP**
>
> The distinction between documents and publications often is a very gray area; however, think of a *document* as something printed from a personal printer, either at home or in the office. This usually is something like a report or proposal. On the other hand, a *publication* is something typically printed professionally, like business cards or brochures and flyers. Typically, for example, you wouldn't use Word to prepare a brochure for professional printing, because many professional print shops require a more comprehensive page setup and design features such as those found in Publisher.

A later chapter shows you how to handle Publisher's basics of choosing a publication design and then adding the text and graphics. You'll also learn how to add effects such as drop caps and design gallery objects, and even how to prepare a publication for professional printing.

Access

The Microsoft Access 2013 database program can certainly do heavy lifting when it comes to managing detailed mountains of data such as customer detail, stock inventory, and order lists that may have hundreds or thousands of entries. The file that holds such lists is called a database. Each Access database file actually can hold multiple lists of data, each usually stored in a separate table, such as the Current Foster Animals table shown in Figure 1.8.

FIGURE 1.8

A Microsoft Access database organizes lists of information in tables.

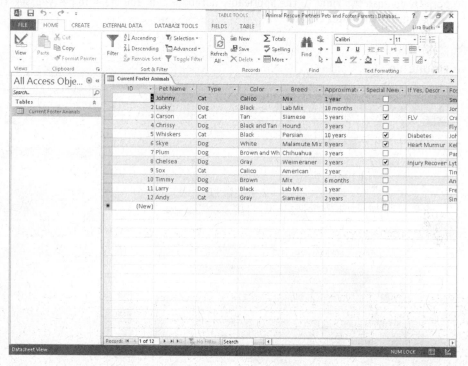

Access enables you to enter and view data using various forms. You also can set up queries to retrieve data that matches certain criteria out of your database tables. These queries can be used to generate reports that consolidate and analyze your data. Later chapters introduce you to these Access skills.

OneNote

It's a risky proposition to track your professional or educational life via notes scribbled on various scraps of paper or notebook pages. As the notes pile up, it becomes harder and harder to find relevant information, making it look as though you can't keep up. If you lose a scrap of paper containing a critical piece of information, you can put a project in jeopardy.

Microsoft OneNote 2013 as seen in Figure 1.9, serves as a type of electronic scrapbook for notes, reference materials, and files related to a particular activity or project. This way, when you need to find all the relevant material related to a specific topic or a particular project, you can flip right to the applicable notebook tab. You learn to get yourself together with OneNote in a later chapter.

FIGURE 1.9

Organize notes, files, pictures, and other material in a OneNote notebook.

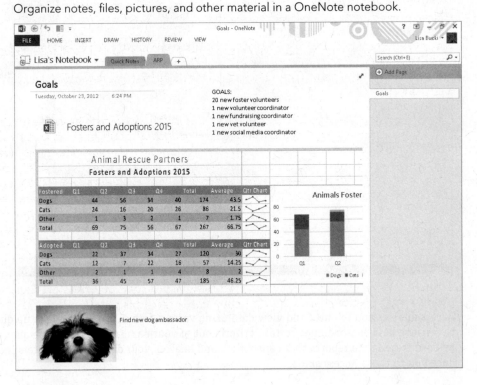

1

Previewing New Features

If you've worked with previous versions of the Office applications, then the previous figures showing the applications covered in this book just gave you a clue to one overall change for Office. The tabs and other screen elements now sport a streamlined, 2-D appearance. This makes it easier to identify the tools you want to use and to focus on the content you're creating. Some new features appear in nearly all of the applications, and from there, each application sports its own unique improvements. You'll learn about key new features throughout the book.

A number of the applications feature a new Start screen that appears by default when you start the program. From this screen, you can select a theme or template, search for templates, or open one of your recently used files. This helps you get on task in the application more quickly.

Many of the improvements across applications streamline your ability to work with the look of a document or work with graphics. For example, both Word and PowerPoint now have a Design tab offering updated choices, such as Style Sets in Word and theme variants in PowerPoint. Microsoft freshened up the themes and specific formatting styles found on Design contextual tabs. You can use live layout and alignment guides to help align graphics and other objects in Word and PowerPoint. A number of the applications enable you to search for and insert online pictures, including ones from an extensive royalty-free clipart collection on Office.com, or even audio and video from online sources. And when you select many different types of objects, one or more buttons appear on the right; click that type of button to open a flyout with contextual formatting and other choices such as toggling settings for a selected item on and off. Figure 1.10 shows an example of this new style of pane, in this case for applying a new style or color to a selected chart in Excel. (You might see this new style of pane referred to as a Format Object task pane.)

FIGURE 1.10

New "flyouts" offer contextual formatting choices or toggles.

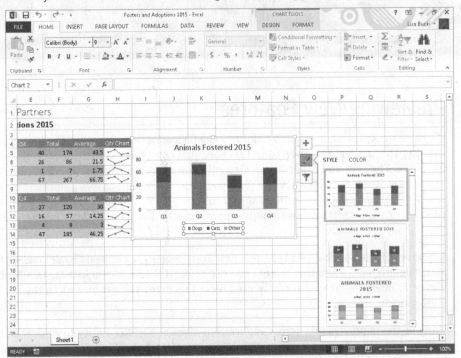

Office 2013 introduces new views in some applications, such as the new Read Mode in Word. This mode hides the Ribbon and other screen tools, so that you can see more of the document in the current view and flip through pages in a natural way. In Word's Read Mode and PowerPoint's Slide Show view, you can now zoom in on objects or parts of the slide. Both PowerPoint and Word now include a Resume Reading feature; when you reopen a document, you can go to the last slide or page you were working on by clicking the pop-up that appears.

The Office applications now help you work smoothly in the cloud. You can save directly to your online SkyDrive folder, or when you have SkyDrive for Windows also installed, you can save to a local SkyDrive folder that automatically syncs with your SkyDrive storage online in the cloud. This means you can sync files between devices. In addition, because you now sign into the Office applications with a user account, Office also can sync your settings across devices. Plus, you can install Apps for Office to add cloud-based capabilities and services within some Office applications, such as adding dictionaries to provide definitions in Word.

Beyond those positive new additions to Office 2013, you'll find new features such as these spread among the applications:

- **Word:** PDF editing with the PDF Reflow feature enabling you to open PDF files directly in Word and enhanced comments with Simple Markup view
- **Excel:** Recommended Chart suggestions for charting, Quick Analysis suggestions for analyzing and presenting selected data, Flash Fill, new functions, ability to embed data in an online web page, and enhanced data labels and other tools for charts
- **PowerPoint:** Improved Presenter view, enhanced ways to share a presentation online, Merge Shapes tool, and enhanced comments
- **Outlook:** Integration with the Windows 8 People app, Weather Bar on the calendar
- **OneNote:** Enhanced cloud integration and syncing between devices and accounts

Starting an Application

When you launch any of the Office applications, that program and its respective tool set will be loaded into your computer's RAM (working memory) so that you can begin working. Office 2013 only runs on the Windows 7 and Windows 8 operation systems. (It also runs on Windows Server 2008 R2 and Windows Server 2012, but this book limits coverage to using Office on the end user versions of Windows.) This book assumes that you're using Windows 8 in its default configuration. If you're using Windows 7, some actions won't apply, and the text will point them out along the way. Because of the significant changes made to the user interface in Windows 8, the start-up method you'll use will vary heavily depending on your operating system.

When you install Office 2013 in Windows 8, a *tile* for each Office program automatically appears on the Windows 8 Start screen, the screen that appears after you start your computer and sign in to your user account. The Start screen is the central location for accessing programs like Word and Windows 8 apps, and the fastest way to return to the Start screen at any time is to press the Windows logo key on the keyboard. You also can point to the lower-left corner of the Windows desktop — which retains much the same appearance in Windows 8 that it had in Windows 7 — until a Start tile appears, and then click it. Here's how to start an Office 2013 program from the Windows 8 Start screen:

1. **If needed, press the Windows logo key to go to the Start screen.**

2. **Depending on your screen resolution, you may need to point to the bottom of the screen to display a scroll bar and then scroll right to display the tiles for the Office 2013 applications.** Figure 1.11 shows the tiles.

FIGURE 1.11

Tiles for the Office 2013 programs appear on the Start screen.

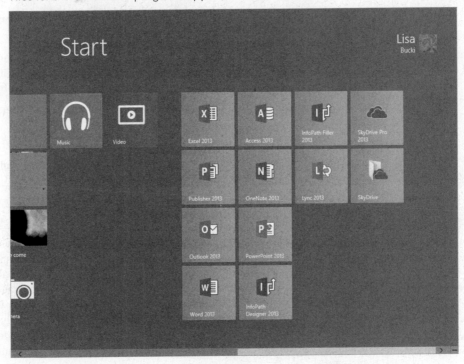

3. **Click the tile for the Office 2013 application to start.** The application opens on the Windows desktop, usually displaying its Start screen by default.

> **NOTE**
> Neither Outlook nor OneNote have an application Start screen, so you can start working immediately in them without having to select or create a file.

In Windows 8, you can sign on using two account types: a local account or a cloud-connected Microsoft account. (Microsoft accounts can be set up to work with your Outlook.com, Windows Live, G-mail account, or other e-mail account.) If you want to take full advantage of an Office application's online, social, and collaboration features, sign on to Windows with a Microsoft account. Then, the first time you start an Office application, it will use your Microsoft account as your Word account, and you should enter that account's information if prompted to activate the program. As described later in Chapter 39, "Collaborating in the Cloud with SkyDrive," you also can sign in to your Office applications with your Office 365 sign-in information to access Office 365 features.

TIP

Click File ⇨ Account in most Office applications to see the Sign out and Switch Account settings, along with other settings for working with your account in Office.

In Windows 7, you find and start the Office programs in the Start menu:

1. **Click the Start button at the left end of the Windows taskbar.** The taskbar appears along the bottom of the Windows 7 desktop. The Start menu opens.

2. **Click All Programs.** A list of available programs appears in the left column of the Start menu.

3. **Click Microsoft Office.** The available Office programs appear.

4. **Click the desired Office program.** The program window appears on-screen.

NOTE

If the Office application tile doesn't appear on your Windows Start screen, select the Search charm, scroll right to find it under Microsoft Office 2013, and then click the program's tile to start the program; you could also right-click the program's tile and then click Pin to Start or Pin to taskbar to add it back to the Start screen or the Windows desktop taskbar. In Windows 7, you can pin a program to the taskbar by starting the program, right-clicking its taskbar icon, and clicking Pin this program to taskbar.

Closing an Application

When you finish your work in an application, shutting the application down removes it from system memory, freeing that memory for other uses. Closing the application also provides the benefit of closing any possibly sensitive open files to prevent unwanted viewing by others.

Some Office programs enable you to have multiple files open at any given time. You have to shut down all of the files to shut down the program itself. You can use one of three methods to shut down any files and the program:

- **Press the Alt and F4 keys simultaneously (Alt+F4).** Repeat for each open file in the application.

- **Click the File tab in the upper-left corner of the program window; then click Close.** Repeat for each open file in the application.

- **Click the X in the upper-right corner, which denotes that you'd like to close the program.** Repeat for each open file in the program.

If you see a message box similar to the one in Figure 1.12, it means that you haven't saved all your changes to the file. Click Yes to save your changes.

FIGURE 1.12

A prompt appears to remind you to save file changes.

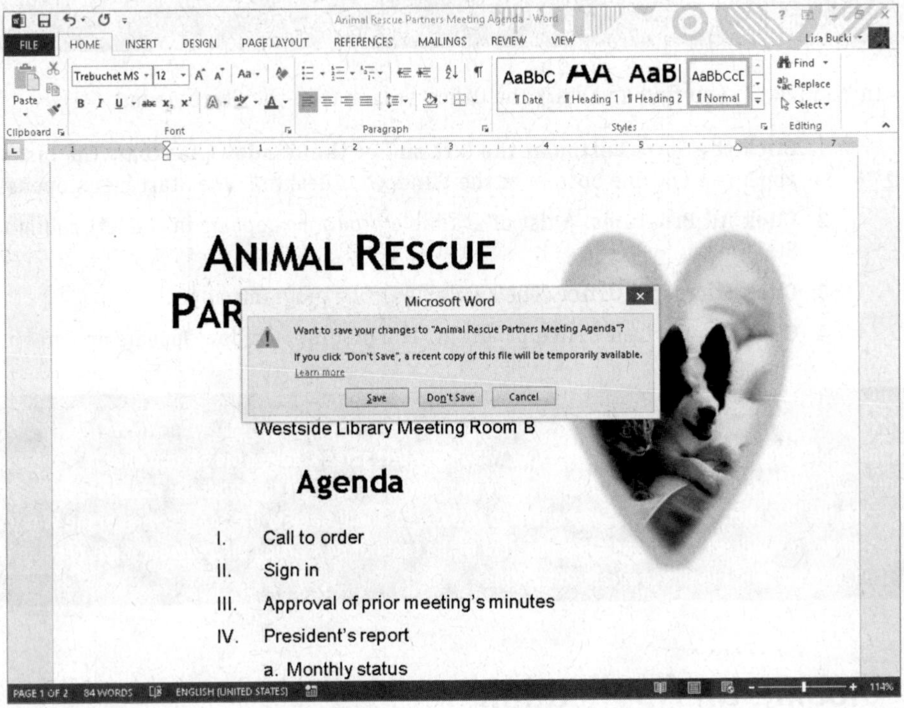

Finding Files

Searching through folders on a computer's hard drive to try to find the file you want to work with sure can waste valuable time you often don't have.

You can work in the Open dialog box for any Office program to search for a file. Use these steps when you're already working in the application used to create the file:

1. **Click the File tab** and then click **Open.** In Windows 7, the Open dialog box appears, and you can skip to Step 3.

2. **Click Computer under Open, and then click the Browse button in the right pane.** You also could click the listed Current Folder or one of the choices under Recent Folders if the specified folder is closer to the location you want to search.

3. **Use the folder tree in the pane at the left to select the folder that you think holds the file to find.**

TIP

If you're not sure even of what folder holds the file, choose a higher-level folder or even a disk icon. Doing so will search more locations, but this means that the search may take more time.

4. **Type the name of the file to search for in the Search or Search Documents textbox in the upper-right corner of the dialog box.** As you type, the Open dialog box lists files with matching names or contents, as shown in Figure 1.13. Also notice that for this example, All Files has been selected as the file type so you see more results. Depending on the application you're using and what type of files it can open, you may want to leave this set to the default for the application or choose another file type.

FIGURE 1.13

You can search for a file in the Open dialog box for any Office application.

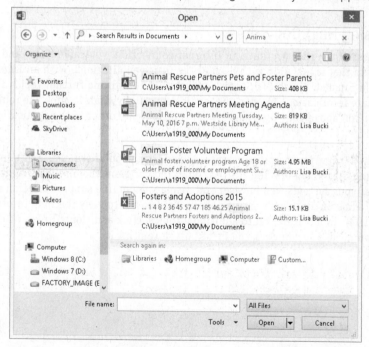

5. **Double-click on the name of the file to open.** The file appears in the application.

NOTE

If you want to search from outside an Office application, in Windows 8, select the Search charm by pointing to the bottom-left corner of your screen, and then clicking the top charm that appears. Click Files in the Search pane at left, type all or part of the file name in the text box, click the Search button if needed, and then click the name of the file to open at left. In Windows 7, click the Start button and then click Search programs and files in the left column of the menu. Then type the name of the file to find. In the list of matches that appears, click the file to open.

Getting Help

Program features sometimes can seem a little obscure, and because the interface has been heavily redesigned in the Microsoft Office 2013 applications, you may get stuck from time to time when you're trying out a feature that you don't use every day. If you don't have this book handy, it's time to turn to another resource — the Help system for the application that you're using.

Browsing Help Contents

Regardless of whether you have an Internet connection, you can explore and browse the basic Help that is installed with each of the Office applications. With an Internet connection, you can also search Office.com, a repository containing further topics as well as more up-to-date information. To open the application's Help window, click the round question mark button above your user name in the upper-right corner of the application window or press F1.

The Help window for the program appears and lists popular searches and a few general help categories under Getting started. (Clicking the More button to the right of this title launches your system's web browser and displays an online support location you can search.) Click on a category such as Learn Word basics to view the Help information (see Figure 1.14). To move around to additional topics, click additional links. When you see the topic you need, you can click the Print button to print it.

FIGURE 1.14

Browse by clicking on categories, subcategories, and topics.

When you finish working in the Help window, click the window's Close button to finish.

Searching Office.com

You can search for help about a particular topic or question using the Search online help text box near the top of the Help window. If your system is connected to the Internet, simply type the topic to search for into the text box and press Enter.

However, if you see OFFLINE displayed near the Help window title, you might need to double-check your connection to ensure you can search online Help. To go back online and search help:

1. **Click the drop-down arrow to the right of Help and click Word Help from Office.com (Figure 1.15).** Assuming your system is connected to the Internet, Help should now be able to work online.

FIGURE 1.15

You can request that Office go back online for Help.

2. **Type the search topic into the Search online help text box.**

3. **Press Enter.** The list of matching Help topics appears.

4. **Click on the desired topic.** The Help for the topic appears in the Help window.

NOTE

Whether you browse for Help while already connected to the Internet or forced the Help window to search online, in certain cases clicking on a Help topic link will launch your system's web browser and display the Help and resources there, rather than in the Help window.

Summary

This chapter introduced the programs that are part of the Microsoft Office 2013 system that will be covered in this book. You learned about core features in the Word (word processing), Excel (spreadsheet), PowerPoint (presentation graphics), and Outlook (e-mail scheduling and collaboration) programs. You also learned that you can perform more specialized business functions with Publisher (publication design), Access (database), and OneNote (information management). The chapter also previewed key new features throughout Office and within specific applications. In addition, you should now know how to:

- Start an Office application from Windows 7 or Windows 8.
- Close an Office application.
- Find a file from the Open dialog box.
- Use Help to find answers about applications.

1

Navigating in Office

IN THIS CHAPTER

Taking a look at the new Office

Locating and using tools in Office applications

Understanding the Start screen and File tab (Backstage)

Managing the Ribbon

Learning about new touch gestures

Reviewing application option settings

Working with a dialog box

The Microsoft Office 2013 programs have been retooled and updated to help you get things done faster. Underneath its streamlined new look, Office integrates smoothly with the new features built into the Windows 8 operating system and Windows 8 devices, though you can use Office on a Windows 7 system, too. (It also runs on Windows Server 2008 R2 and Windows Server 2012, but this book limits coverage to using Office on the end user versions of Windows.)

Office 2013 keeps the Ribbon interface found in the 2007 and 2010 versions. Its significant improvements show up elsewhere within individual applications. Even if you know the Ribbon, there's a lot to discover about Office in this book. This chapter kicks it off with leading you through a tour of common operations you'll need to perform in any Office application.

The Office Look

In redesigning Windows 8, Microsoft incorporated a sleeker look that would be at home on either tablets or PCs, added greater integration with cloud-based features such as SkyDrive, and built in even more social media functionality. You don't have to spend much time working in the new Office to find that it follows the lead of Windows 8:

- **Sleeker look:** As shown in Figure 2.1, the application window's title bar has eliminated the previous 3-D look in favor of flat tabs and a customizable Office Background graphic. The status bar likewise is strictly 2-D and easier to read. The upper-right corner of the screen has an icon you can click to see Ribbon Display Options; for example clicking Auto-hide the Ribbon puts away all of the on-screen tools and shows you your document head on. Similarly, a new Read Mode in Word displays a document in a format more comfortable for "paging" through it rather than editing. (The Ribbon Display Options are discussed later in the chapter in the section called "Controlling the Ribbon Display.")

- **Cloud integration:** The upper-right corner of Figure 2.1 also illustrates that the Microsoft account (or other applicable account type such as an Office 365 account) you use to sign in to an Office application appears, along with any picture assigned to the account. This means you can save and open documents directly to and

FIGURE 2.1

The sleek new look in Office applications helps you focus on your documents.

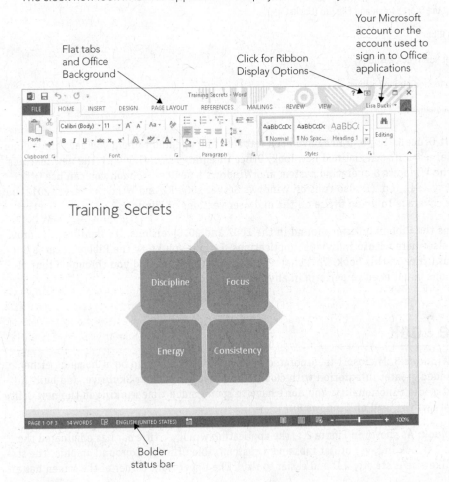

from the account's SkyDrive, a feature you'll learn more about in Chapter 3 and Chapter 39, "Collaborating in the Cloud with SkyDrive." Other new features tie into the cloud independent of your account. For example, the new Insert Online Pictures feature in Word, PowerPoint, and other applications enables you to find and add images from Office.com Clip Art, Bing Image Search, or your SkyDrive to a document. Chapters 9 and 24 cover the details of this more flexible way to find document images.

■ **Social media functions:** The Insert Online Pictures feature also enables you to insert pictures from a Flickr account associated with your Microsoft account. Just make the connection when prompted, and pictures you've shared to Flickr will be available for use in Office documents. And you can more easily share a document saved to your SkyDrive and present a document online, making collaboration with your contacts a seamless and productive experience. Later chapters delve into these social and collaboration features.

Your Interface to Faster File Creation

If you're like most users, when you begin a letter or a report, the first thing you do is check whether you've ever created a similar letter or report. If you have written and formatted a similar document, then you very likely will open it and use it as a starting point.

However, even if you have a document to use as a starting point, you are only recycling the same look and feel you've used before. Instead, you could take advantage of an existing template in the Microsoft Office ever-expanding online repertoire. You can either select one of the more popular templates or search for a template using a description such as letter, resume, budget, or sales presentation. Chapter 3 explains how you can find and use a template to create a document that has a professional appearance, even if you have no document design background.

If you also do not want to use a template, you can start with the clean slate of a blank document. Even with that starting point, you can choose from a collection of designs and tools to save time and guesswork. The Office applications include built-in *galleries* of already formatted options. For example, if you create a table, rather than formatting the text, borders, and fills separately, you can apply a single table style to format all the table elements with an attractive combination of settings. Most galleries work with the *Live Preview* feature. Simply move the mouse pointer over a choice in a gallery, and the selected text or object temporarily morphs in the document to show you how the gallery choice would look when applied. You can either click that choice to select it or move the mouse pointer along to preview other gallery choices. Some galleries even present special elements you can add to a document page. For example, when you insert a text box into a document, you have the option of inserting a box formatted as a pull quote or sidebar to add design interest to your document. You'll learn about the numerous galleries throughout later chapters in the book.

Office continues to streamline the number of tools on-screen at any time to help you achieve results quickly, rather than combing through myriad tabs and commands to discover possibilities. Depending on what you select on-screen, one or more new *contextual tabs* of options appears. For example, if a picture is selected, the Picture Tools' Format subtab appears on the Ribbon, as shown in Figure 2.2. It offers among other tools a gallery of Quick Styles for formatting the selected picture, and a preview of the style under the mouse pointer appears for the selected picture. Details about the various contextual tabs appear where applicable throughout the book.

FIGURE 2.2

The Picture Tools ⇨ Format contextual tab or subtab presents picture formatting options, including Picture Styles (Quick Styles).

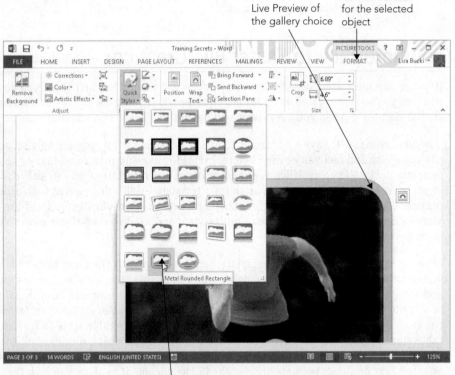

Live Preview of the gallery choice

Contextual tab for the selected object

Mouse pointer over a gallery choice

Finally, Office 2013 retains the most powerful design tool of all: themes. The theme defines the color scheme, fonts, and effects for a document (or in the case of Access, a database object). Changing the theme changes the look of the entire document. Various chapters later in the book provide the details about working with themes in different Office applications.

Using an Application Start Screen

When you first start most of the Office 2013 applications, you'll see a new feature called the Start screen. The Start screen is basically divided into two panes. At the left, you can click a file in the Recent list — which contains files you've worked with in recent work sessions — to open it immediately. Or, you can click Open Other Documents (the link name varies depending on which application you're using) below the recent list to navigate to various storage locations and open an existing file. See "Opening a file" in Chapter 3. Finally, you can use the gallery of templates at right to choose a template, as described in "Creating a file from a template" in Chapter 3. For now, if you're interested in seeing the application's tools, you can click the Blank choice (Blank document, Blank workbook, and so on, depending on which application you've started) in the templates at the top to open a blank file and look around.

> **TIP**
>
> If you want to turn the Start screen off, click the File tab on the Ribbon, and then click Options. Leave the General tab selected in the list at the left, and under Start up options, click to remove the check beside Show the Start screen when this application starts. Click OK to apply the change.

Touring an Office Application Screen

This chapter has already pointed out a few elements of Office application screens that you'll use to create and enhance your documents. Now it's time to review all the tools available via the screen in an Office application, several of which are identified in Figure 2.3. Office 2013 retains many of the same elements of the 2007 and 2010 versions of the programs. If you're new to Office, this section presents the essential roadmap to help you around the screen. Users of all levels can have an Aha! moment or two via the tips and notes found in the next few pages.

FIGURE 2.3

Office screen elements

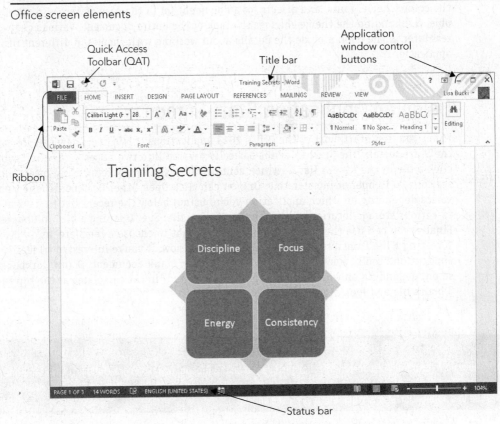

Quick Access Toolbar (QAT)

Title bar

Application window control buttons

Ribbon

Status bar

Title bar

The *title bar* at the top of the application window shows the name of the current document and the program, as in Figure 2.3. In addition to identifying the working document, the title bar enables you to control the size of the application window. Double-clicking the title bar toggles the current Office application between *maximized* (full screen) and *restored* (less than full screen) states. If you've set your screen to a fairly high resolution and have used the Windows Snap feature to snap a screen to full size or half-screen size, double-clicking the title bar also returns the window to its prior size.

The three application control buttons at the far-right end of the title bar (see Figure 2.3) also enable you to work with the window size. The left one, Minimize, collapses the current Word window down to a button on the Windows Desktop taskbar. The middle button toggles between being a Maximize and Restore down button, and works just like double-clicking the title bar. Finally, the Close button at the far right closes the current document and shuts down the application if that's the only open document. Pressing Alt+F4 also closes the document window. You also can right-click the title bar to see commands for sizing the window. And, if the window is less than full-screen size, dragging a window border resizes the window.

> **TIP**
>
> Use the Snap feature in Windows 7 and 8 to resize a restored down window. Drag the window by its title bar toward the top of the screen, and when you see a full-screen preview outline, release the mouse button to maximize the window. Or, drag the window to the left or right edge of the screen until you see a half-screen preview outline, and then release the mouse button to resize the window to half screen size. You also can press the Windows logo key along with the Left Arrow, Right Arrow, or Up Arrow keys to snap the active window. These features only work in Windows 8 when your screen is set to a 1366 × 768 or higher resolution.

The far-left button at the right end of the title bar is the Help button, with the question mark on it. Clicking it opens the application Help function, as described in Chapter 1. The button beside the Help button is the Ribbon Display Options button, which you'll learn about later in this chapter.

Ribbon

The *Ribbon* appears just below the title bar and is organized to put the tool you need where you need it when you need it. When you click one of the major *tabs* on the Ribbon, the tools you need for specific tasks related to the tab name appear. For example, in a few Office applications, you click the Insert tab to find commands for inserting tables, pictures, and other graphics into a file. In Word and Excel, click the Page Layout tab to find choices for setting up the document overall. Most Office applications include the View tab, used to change views and find other screen settings, and so on. The tabs offer buttons for commands, as well as drop-down menus of settings such as formatting choices and galleries of styles, and other formatting options, as have already been touched on in this chapter.

Each Ribbon tab further offers groups containing related commands. For example, in Word all of the commands for formatting paragraphs appear in the Paragraph group on the Home tab. Groups help you drill down to the command you need more rapidly, so you can click and move on to the next task.

Exactly what you see in any given Ribbon tab is determined by a number of factors, including your screen resolution, the orientation of your monitor, the size of the current window, and whether you're using Windows' display settings to accommodate low vision. Hence, what *you* see might not always be what is pictured in this book. If your screen is set to a fairly high resolution, you will see the entirety of the Home tab of the Ribbon, shown in the top of Figure 2.4. The bottom image shows the Ribbon at the lower 1024×768 resolution used for the screen shots in this book. You'll notice in the top image that the Home tab shows the Format Painter label in the Clipboard group and more styles in the Styles gallery. At an even higher resolution and/or with Word stretched across multiple monitors, the Home tab would show even more labels and styles.

FIGURE 2.4

At a high resolution, the Ribbon displays additional gallery options and text labels (top) not seen at lower resolutions (bottom).

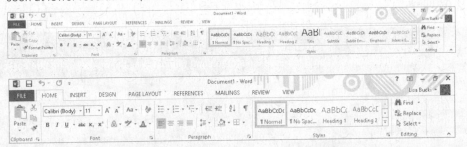

> **TIP**
>
> You can press Ctrl+F1 or click the arrow button at the lower-right corner of the Ribbon to collapse and expand the Ribbon. You also can double-click a Ribbon tab to collapse and re-expand it. At times the Ribbon might seem large or distracting when you're simply reading a document or when you're trying to see a graphic and write about it at the same time. And if you are fluent in the keystrokes you need to perform basic formatting, you don't necessarily need the Ribbon on-screen at all times. When the Ribbon is collapsed, you can click any tab once to turn it back on temporarily. In that case, you'll see a pin button at lower-right where the arrow previously appeared. Clicking the pin button expands the Ribbon so that it stays on-screen. You'll learn more about controlling the Ribbon in "Controlling the Ribbon Display" later in the chapter.

Note that you can customize the tabs that appear on the Ribbon. For example, if you want to create macros to handle certain document formatting tasks for you, you would need to display the Developer tab. Or you may want to hide tabs that you seldom use, such as the Mailings or Review tab in Word. To customize the Ribbon, right-click any Ribbon tab, and click Customize the Ribbon. Check and uncheck items in the Main Tabs list to control which tabs appear, or use the left list and the Add button to add commands to a tab. Click OK to apply your changes.

To see what any individual control or command on a Ribbon tab does, simply move the mouse pointer over it. A ScreenTip pops up with a description of the tool. Move the mouse pointer away from the button to hide the ScreenTip.

Ribbon groups

At the bottom of the Home tab shown in Figure 2.4, note the names Clipboard, Font, and Paragraph. These labels identify the command *groups*. Each contains individual tools or controls.

You can customize the groups that appear on any Ribbon tab. For example, you might want to add a group that collects all of your most-used commands in a single location.

> **NOTE**
>
> Throughout this book, you may see command shortcuts such as Insert ⇨ Header & Footer ⇨ Header. These Ribbon tab name ⇨ group ⇨ command sequences help you navigate through the Ribbon to find and choose the appropriate command. When referencing contextual tabs, where the first part of the tab name appears on an upper row and the subtab name appears on the lower row along with the normal tabs, an arrow will also appear between the upper part of the contextual tab name and the subtab, as in Picture Tools ⇨ Format. After the first mention in a chapter, the text may refer to the contextual tab by its subtab name only, that is, Format rather than Picture Tools ⇨ Format.

Contextual tabs

Along with the default set of main tabs, additional context-sensitive or *contextual tabs* or subtabs appear depending on what you are working on in the document. For example, if you change to Outline view, the Outlining toolbar, with commands for changing outline levels and more, automatically appears to the left of the Home tab. In other instances, a contextual tab might appear when you select part of a document or an object such as a table. For example, if you choose Insert ⇨ Header & Footer ⇨ Header in Word 2013 and insert a header from the Header gallery, the Header & Footer Tools ⇨ Design contextual tab appears, as shown in Figure 2.5.

FIGURE 2.5

When you work with the header in Word, the Header & Footer Tools ⇨ Design contextual tab and its commands appears.

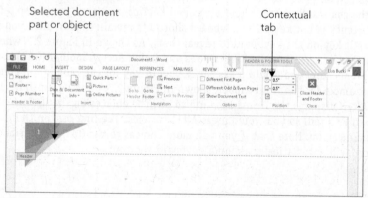

35

Notice that the right end of the contextual tab in Figure 2.5 has a Close group with a button for closing the tab. Some contextual tabs have such a button, and you have to use it to close the contextual tab. In the case of the Design subtab in Figure 2.5 and many other contextual tabs related to a selected object, you also can deselect or click outside the object, which closes the contextual tab automatically.

In some cases, multiple contextual tabs might appear. For example, when you select a table in a Word document, the Table Tools appear, with Design and Layout subtabs, as shown in Figure 2.6. In this instance, click a subtab to display its tools. For example, click the Design contextual tab to find the table design choices, or click the Layout contextual tab to find commands for changing the table's layout.

FIGURE 2.6

Selecting some objects, such as tables in Word, displays multiple contextual tabs.

Command keyboard shortcuts or KeyTips

While many users can move fluidly between using the mouse or the keyboard, for the best typists, doing so can actually be a hindrance that slows them down. For such users, shortcut key combinations provide a way to handle formatting tasks and select commands without taking their hands off the keyboard.

In Office 2013 the command shortcut keys are called *KeyTips*, and some users also refer to keyboard shortcuts as hot keys. The keyboard shortcuts remain hidden until you need them. Press the Alt key on the keyboard to reveal them. As shown in Figure 2.7, when you press Alt the letters for selecting the Ribbon tabs and Quick Access Toolbar (QAT) commands appear. From there, you would press the keyboard key for the Ribbon tab you want to display. For example for the Word Ribbon shown in Figure 2.7, pressing Alt+H displays the Home tab, Alt+N displays the Insert tab, and so on. The choices on the QAT are numbered rather than lettered, so you would press Alt+1 to select the first button there, Alt+2 the second one, and so on. Note that if you add more choices to the QAT as described later in the book, Word will automatically assign a keyboard shortcut.

FIGURE 2.7

Press the Alt key to display command keyboard shortcuts.

Notice that Figure 2.7 also shows the Table Tools Design and Layout contextual tabs. Each has a two-letter shortcut key. To display the Design contextual tab, you would need to press Alt+JT. (For example, press Alt+J, then T.) Pressing Alt+JL displays the Layout contextual tab.

After you press Alt + a letter to select a tab, a new set of letters and (sometimes) numbers appears. These identify the keys you need to press to choose a command from the displayed Ribbon tab. For example, if you press Alt+P to display the Page Layout tab, the shortcuts shown in Figure 2.8 appear. From there, you could press O if you want to change page Orientation, M to change page Margins, IL to add an Indent, and so on.

FIGURE 2.8

After you press Alt + a letter to select a Ribbon tab, press the next shortcut key(s) to select a command.

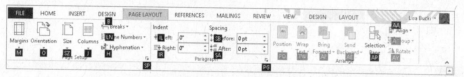

> **TIP**
>
> After you press Alt and then a letter to select a Ribbon tab, you can press Tab and Shift+Tab to move forward and backward between the commands on that tab. When you've highlighted the command you want to use, press either the Spacebar or Enter key.

If you decide not to use a shortcut after you've displayed the keys on-screen, no problem. Just press Alt again, click a blank area with the mouse, or press the Esc key once or twice to remove them from the screen.

> **NOTE**
>
> Word and the other applications also include an extensive collection of keyboard shortcuts for navigating in a file and selecting text and more. You'll learn about these in various chapters throughout the book.

Quick Access Toolbar

I mentioned earlier that you can add a group to the Ribbon to collect all your favorite commands in a single easy-access location. Another and perhaps even faster way to accomplish this goal is to add your favorite commands to the *Quick Access Toolbar*, or *QAT*. The QAT remains on-screen no matter which Ribbon tab is displayed, so any commands on the QAT are available at all times.

By default, the QAT has buttons for three commands: Save, Undo, and Redo. In Figure 2.9, I've moved the QAT below the Ribbon, so you can see these default buttons from left to right respectively. Note that the Redo button is unavailable (grayed out) until you perform an action that Word can repeat. Also, if you move the mouse pointer over the Undo and Redo buttons to see a ScreenTip, the ScreenTip name of each of those buttons changes depending on your last action. For example, the Redo button ScreenTip might read "Repeat Typing."

FIGURE 2.9

The Quick Access Toolbar (QAT) always appears, no matter which Ribbon tab you've selected.

As shown in Figure 2.9, clicking the Customize Quick Access Toolbar button at the right end of the QAT opens a menu of options for setting up the QAT. You can use the choices above the line on the menu to toggle commands on and off, choose More Commands to access all of the Word commands, or determine whether the QAT appears above or below the Ribbon.

You can add any item from the Ribbon — individual tools, groups, and even dialog box launchers — to the QAT without opening the Customize Quick Access Toolbar menu. For example, right-click Bold in the Font group of the Home tab and choose Add to Quick Access Toolbar. If you add a command such as Bold to the QAT and want to remove it later, right-click it and click Remove from Quick Access Toolbar.

> **TIP**
>
> If you click the Customize Quick Access Toolbar button, you'll see a new command called Touch/Mouse Mode. Click it to add a button for toggling Touch Mode on and off in an Office application. When enabled, this mode adjusts the Ribbon buttons and other areas of the application interface to make them easier to select by tapping a touch-enabled screen. Touch Mode can be a good option for people who have large fingers or who have cold hands and therefore have to tap harder to make a selection.

Galleries and Live Preview

In the Office applications, a *gallery* is a set of formatting results or preformatted document parts. Virtually every set of formatting results or document parts in Word 2013 (indeed, in all of Office 2013) might be called a gallery, although the applications themselves do not use the word *gallery* to refer to every feature set. Some, such as the list of bullets in Word, may be called *libraries* instead, and the drop-down galleries for selecting colors also may be called *Color Pickers*.

Word includes galleries for text styles, themes, headers, footers, page colors, tables, WordArt, equations, symbols, and more. The other Office applications include their own specific galleries, such as the Transitions and Animations galleries in PowerPoint. In most cases, you click a button or drop-down arrow to open a gallery, and then click the gallery choice to apply to the selected text or object. Galleries often work hand in hand with the Live Preview feature.

Live Preview temporarily applies the highlighted gallery choice to the current document selection, enabling you to instantly see the results without actually having to apply that formatting, as shown in Figure 2.10. Move the mouse pointer over the different gallery options to display the formatting on the document selection instantly.

FIGURE 2.10

Live Preview showing the Quote style applied to the selected paragraph in a Word document

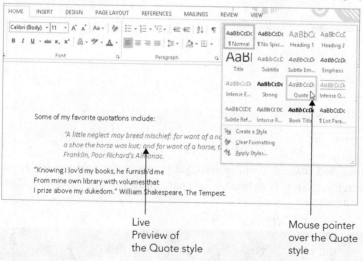

Note that not all galleries and formatting options have Live Preview enabled. For example, on the Page Layout tab in Word, none of the Page Setup items produces live previews, nor do its Paragraph group settings. Another time you won't see Live Preview is when working with dialog boxes, such as the Paragraph dialog box. Many of those offer internal Preview areas but do not take advantage of Office 2013's Live Preview capability.

A gotcha in all this newfangled functionality is that sometimes the gallery itself covers up all or part of the Live Preview. This gets old quickly and can negate much of Live Preview's functionality, unless you're blessed with lots of screen real estate.

Fortunately, some galleries and controls have draggable borders that enable you to see more of what you're trying to preview, as shown in Figure 2.11. A handle with four dots indicates when you can resize a control's border by dragging up. If a gallery has three dots in the lower-right corner, that means you resize both its height and width by dragging diagonally.

FIGURE 2.11

Some galleries can be resized to reveal the Live Preview that otherwise would be covered.

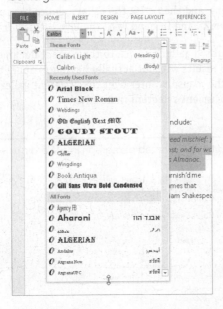

Once you've determined through Live Preview that you want to apply particular formatting, click the choice in the gallery. If necessary, you can always use the venerable Ctrl+Z (Undo) if you don't like the result.

> **CAUTION**
>
> When using Live Preview, it's easy to forget to click the desired gallery or formatting command when you come to it. Particularly in extensive lists (such as lists of fonts, colors, or styles), it's possible to get exactly the right effect without noticing what it's called. In the case of colors, you usually don't even have a name to use as a guide. Sometimes, the hand really is quicker than the eye. Once you move your mouse away from your selection, it's lost. You might have to re-inspect that entire list to find exactly what you already found, so once you find what you're looking for, don't forget to click! Ctrl+Z is your friend!

The MiniBar or Mini Toolbar

Another feature in some Office 2013 applications is the *MiniBar,* more formally known as the *Mini Toolbar*. The Mini Toolbar is a set of formatting tools that appears when you first select text. It is not context-sensitive, and it always contains an identical set of formatting tools. There is no Mini Toolbar for graphics and other nontext objects.

When you first select text, the Mini Toolbar appears above and to the right of the mouse pointer, as shown in Figure 2.12. If you move the mouse pointer off the selection, the MiniBar disappears.

FIGURE 2.12

The Mini Toolbar appears when text is first selected.

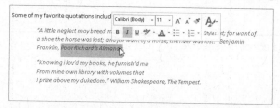

> **NOTE**
>
> Once the Mini Toolbar disappears, you cannot redisplay it by hovering the mouse over the selection. You can, however, redisplay the Mini Toolbar and a shortcut menu for the selection by right-clicking the selection. Note also that only the mouse triggers the Mini Toolbar. If you display the pop-up context menu by pressing Shift+F10 or by tapping the Menu button on a Windows keyboard, the Mini Toolbar will not appear.

When the Home tab is selected, the Mini Toolbar might seem superfluous, as all of the Mini Toolbar's commands also appear on that tab. However, consider for a moment how far the mouse has to travel to access the Ribbon commands. With the Mini Toolbar, you only have to move the mouse less than an inch or so to move the pointer to the command you need. For those with repetitive motion injuries, this can save a lot of wear and tear on the wrist.

If you decide that the Mini Toolbar gets in the way, you can turn it off. Even when it is turned off, however, you can still summon it by right-clicking the current selection. If you want to turn the Mini Toolbar off, click the File tab on the Ribbon, and then click Options. Leave the General tab selected in the list at the left, and under User Interface options, click to remove the check beside Show Mini Toolbar on selection. Click OK to apply the change.

> **NOTE**
>
> Unlike many Ribbon tools, the Mini Toolbar tools do not produce Live Previews of formatting and other effects. If you need to see a Live Preview, use the Ribbon instead.

Shortcut menus and contextual command buttons

If navigating through an Office application's Ribbon tabs still seems like a lot of work to you, *shortcut menus*, also called contextual or pop-up menus, remain. To display a shortcut menu, just select text, cells, or an object such as a picture in the file, and right-click or press the menu key on your keyboard. As shown in Figure 2.13, the shortcut menu offers the commands you're most likely to use next for the selected item.

FIGURE 2.13

When you right-click a selection, a context-sensitive shortcut menu appears, along with the Mini Toolbar.

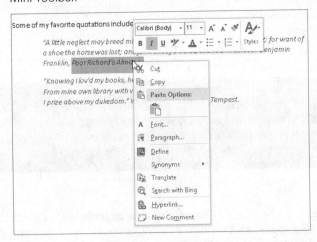

Office 2013 adds a new form of contextual tools to speed your work with some document objects, particularly on a touch-enabled system. When you select some types of objects, such as a chart, one or more contextual buttons will appear to the right of the object. Clicking some of these buttons opens a flyout gallery of formatting options for the selection, as shown in the example in Figure 2.14. Clicking other buttons opens a flyout list of choices that you can click to toggle on and off, as shown in Figure 2.15. Simply click the desired choice in either type of flyout, or deselect the object to hide the buttons.

FIGURE 2.14

New contextual command buttons appear when you select certain objects, such as a chart.

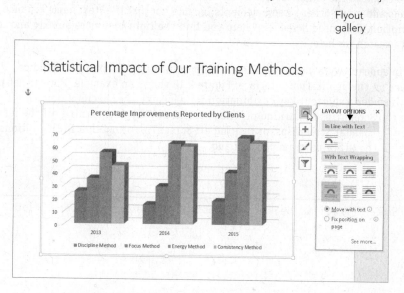

FIGURE 2.15

Clicking some of the buttons opens a gallery, as shown in the prior figure, or a list of toggled options, as shown here.

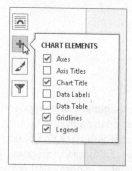

TIP

Some of the Office 2013 apps more optimized for touch also include compact radial menus that you can tap to expose the commands you need.

Enhanced ScreenTips

Office 2013 includes the enhanced ScreenTips feature. By default, the ScreenTips for the Ribbon tools and many other screen elements include not just the item name but also a feature description. Enhanced ScreenTips help you find the right tool more quickly and reduce the need to search for help.

A ScreenTip appears when you hover the mouse pointer over a Ribbon command or other choice on the application interface. Figure 2.16 shows an example. Notice that the ScreenTip includes a shortcut key combination for choosing the specified item. You can customize the ScreenTips by turning off the shortcut key display, turning off the feature description for smaller ScreenTips, or turning off ScreenTips altogether in the Options dialog box for the Office program you're using.

FIGURE 2.16

Enhanced ScreenTips include the name and description for a command or other tool.

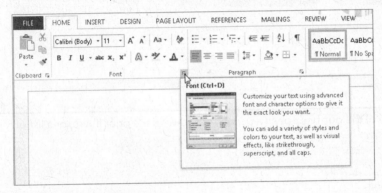

Dialog boxes and launchers

To the right of some group names, a small box button with a diagonal arrow appears. This button is a *dialog box launcher*. Clicking a dialog box launcher opens a dialog box with more detailed options for the commands in the group. For example, if you click the dialog box launcher for the Word Home tab's Paragraph group, the Paragraph dialog box opens. Point to any dialog box launcher to display a ScreenTip explaining what it does, as illustrated in Figure 2.16 in the previous section.

Clicking the dialog box launcher shown in Figure 2.16 opens the Font dialog box shown in Figure 2.17. Dialog boxes offer scrolling lists, drop-down lists, text boxes, check boxes, option buttons, command buttons, and other controls familiar to most computer users. You can click Cancel to close a dialog box without applying settings, or OK to finalize and apply your choices.

FIGURE 2.17

Dialog boxes enable you to refine formatting and other commands using familiar controls.

Task panes or panes

Similar to dialog boxes, *task panes* (now in Office 2013 more often simply referred to as *panes*) appear on-screen to help you navigate, perform research, apply formatting, and more. Think of them as dialog boxes that enable you to type while they're on-screen. Some of the panes open when you select a particular command such as the Thesaurus, while you toggle others such as the Navigation pane on and off as you work in an application. Still others appear when you select certain items for formatting, such as when you double-click a chart title. Figure 2.18 shows the Format Chart Title task pane in Word.

FIGURE 2.18

Office task panes make commands available while still enabling you to type and make selections in the document.

Some panes appear docked on the left or right side of the document window, whereas others automatically appear undocked. You can undock a task pane by pointing to its title until you see a four-arrow move mouse pointer, and then drag it to the desired location with the mouse. Double-click a floating pane's title to return it to its docked position. You can display and size multiple task panes on-screen at any time. To close a pane, you can click its Close (X) button at the upper right, or in some cases reselect the command you used to toggle it on.

Other Word features that manifest as task panes include the Navigation pane, the Mail Merge Wizard, Restrict Editing, Dictionary, the Clipboard, and the Reviewing Pane, among others. Some of these task panes also appear in the other Office applications, and the other applications also include their own unique panes, such as the Animation Pane in PowerPoint. Later chapters of the book introduce the various panes and when they come into action.

Status bar

Now we turn to the status bar. Shown in Figure 2.19, the status bar is the bar at the bottom of the Office application window. In Word, the status bar provides more than 20 optional pieces of information about the current document. Right-click the status bar in any Office application to display its configuration options.

FIGURE 2.19

Customize the status bar and control several features with the status bar shortcut menu.

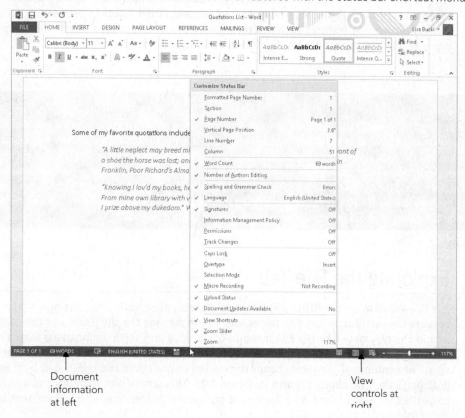

Document
information
at left

View
controls at
right

Do you need to keep track of the word count? Not only does Word update the word count continuously, but if you select text, it tells you how many words are selected, with one of the indicators near the left end of the status bar changing to read *39 OF 69 WORDS* or something similar. In other Office applications, the status bar offers similar features. For example, if you select a range of cells with numbers in Excel, the status bar by default shows the sum of those numbers. In PowerPoint, the status bar enables you to display and hide notes and comments.

To display the configuration choices shown in Figure 2.19, right-click the status bar. At the top and bottom of the shortcut menu, you can choose options to specify what indicators appear at the left and what view controls appear at the right. In between, it presents choices for turning features such as Track Changes or Overtype on and off. Then close the menu to apply your changes by clicking in the document or pressing Esc.

NOTE

The status bar shortcut menu stays on-screen until you click somewhere else in the application window. That means that you can enable or disable as many options as you want without having to repeatedly right-click the status bar. Notice also that the menu displays the current status too, so if you just want to quickly refer to it to find out what section of the document you're working in — but don't really want Section on the status bar — you don't have to put it on the status bar and then remove it. Note additionally that the status items aren't just pretty pictures. For example, clicking the Page Number (PAGE X OF X) item on the Word status bar opens the Navigation pane. Clicking the Macro Recording item on the Word or Excel status bar opens the Record Macro dialog box.

Exploring the File Tab

The File tab in all of the Office 2013 apps works a bit differently than the other tabs. That's because the settings on the File tab enable you to manage the file itself, not the contents within the file, more like the File menu in Office 2003 and other applications with a menu-based interface. When you click the File tab, it displays what is sometimes called *Backstage view*. The contents of the view change depending on the command selected at left; initially it displays the Info choices shown in Figure 2.20. This screen lets you view and add file properties, as well as work with document protection, hidden properties, document issues, and versions.

NOTE

Backstage view is also sometimes just called the "File tab."

FIGURE 2.20

Manage your file with the File tab choices.

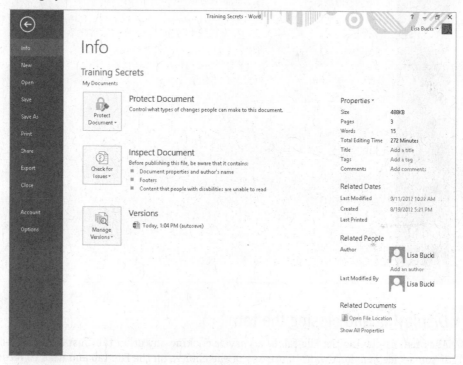

Clicking most of the commands along the left side of the File tab — Info, New, Open, Save, Save As, Print, Share, Export, Close, Account, and Options — causes the right pane of the screen to display the choices for that category. For example, if you click Share in the Word Backstage, as shown in Figure 2.21, options for presenting and publishing a document in the cloud appear.

FIGURE 2.21

Discover digital options on the Share tab.

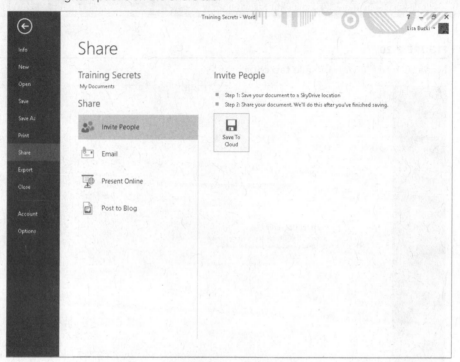

Displaying and closing the tab

As noted, displaying the File tab is as easy as clicking any other tab. Just click the tab itself. If you decide you don't want to use any of the choices on the File tab and need to return to editing your document, click the Back (left arrow) button at the upper left, or press Esc.

CAUTION

If you click the Close (X) button in the upper-right corner, the application not only closes the File tab, but closes itself too, which is probably not what you want.

Finding recent documents and pinning

Some users might have documents that they want to open and revise or reread frequently. For example, if you have a hot project for a new client and your work on the project is due in the near future, you'll want those documents at your fingertips rather than having to navigate around your hard disk or network to find them.

Most Office applications gather the files you've most recently opened into a Recent Documents list. (The list name changes depending on the application.) You can simply display that list via the File tab, and click a file to open it. However, the Recent Documents list updates itself based on the files you open. To ensure quick access to a particular document, you can *pin* it to the Recent Documents list on the File ⇨ Open screen. To do that:

1. **Click the File tab, and click Open at the left.**

2. **Move the mouse pointer over the file you want to pin until you see the horizontal Pin this item to the list icon, shown in Figure 2.22.**

FIGURE 2.22

Pinning a file in Recent Documents gives you fast access.

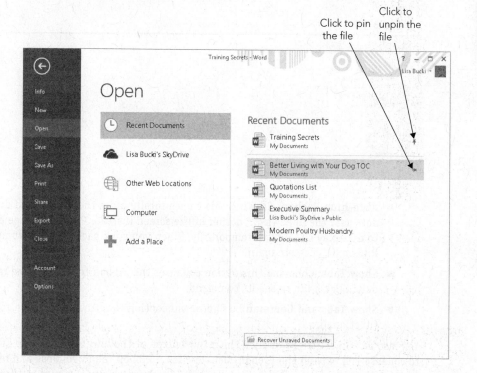

3. **Click the Pin this item to the list icon.** The file moves above the line separating pinned and unpinned files, and the pin icon changes to a vertical Unpin this item from the list icon.

Chapter 3 provides more information about using the File menu to open an existing file.

Controlling the Ribbon Display

You can choose whether or not to display the Ribbon in views other than Read Mode. Figure 2.23 shows the Ribbon Display Options button, visible in certain working views in Office applications. Clicking it opens a menu of options for controlling Ribbon display.

FIGURE 2.23

Ribbon display options

- **Auto-hide Ribbon:** Clicking this choice totally hides the Ribbon and displays three dots near the upper-right corner of the screen instead. Click the three dots button to redisplay the Ribbon temporarily. When you click back in the document, the Ribbon hides itself again.

- **Show Tabs:** Choosing this option collapses the Ribbon to a row of the tab names only. Click a tab to see its command.

- **Show Tabs and Commands:** Choose this option to return the Ribbon to its normal functionality.

You also can press Ctrl+F1 or click the arrow button at the lower-right corner of the Ribbon to collapse and expand the Ribbon. Double-click a Ribbon tab to collapse and re-expand the whole Ribbon. When the Ribbon is collapsed, you can click any tab once to turn it back on temporarily. In that case, you'll see a pin button at lower-right where the arrow previously appeared. Clicking the pin button expands the Ribbon so that it stays on-screen.

Gestures and Touch Navigation

The 2013 version of the Office applications now can be used effectively on touch-enabled devices in addition to desktop and laptop computers. Although your desktop or notebook computer will likely remain your primary Office 2013 platform for now, the new convenience and flexibility of using Office on a touch-enabled device like a tablet makes that platform a viable choice for road trips and extra work at home. Here's a brief introduction to the touch gestures and their basic uses in Office 2013:

- **Tap:** This is the equivalent of a mouse click. Move your finger over the desired item, and then touch and release, as when pressing a keyboard key. Tap to select buttons and other interface features and position the insertion point.

- **Tap-hold:** This is the equivalent of right-clicking. Move your finger over the desired item, and then touch and hold as when holding down a keyboard key. For example, tap-hold a QAT button to display the menu for customizing the QAT.

- **Double-tap:** This is the equivalent of double-clicking. Move your finger over the desired item, and touch and release twice. For example, you can double-tap to zoom in on graphics in some new views.

- **Pinch:** Drag your thumb and forefinger together on the screen. Use this action to zoom out in a document.

- **Stretch:** The opposite of pinch, in this gesture you drag your thumb and forefinger apart on the screen. Use this action to zoom in.

- **Slide:** Tap-hold, and then drag your finger. The tap-hold generally selects an object, and then dragging moves it into position.

- **Swipe:** Quickly drag your finger on screen, then lift it off. This action also can be used for scrolling and selecting.

Touch-enabled systems also give you the ability to display an on-screen keyboard for entering text. Tapping the Touch Keyboard button on the taskbar opens the keyboard. Tap its Close (X) button to close it when you've finished entering information.

> **TIP**
> Help has a topic called Office Touch Guide that provides even more specifics about navigating and working via touch.

> **NOTE**
> There are some differences in the touch interface, such as the number of default QAT buttons. The screenshots in this book show the nontouch versions of the Office applications, so your screen may look different if you are using touch.

Setting Application Options

Office 2013 offers a centralized dialog box for changing the options for each application. Most beginning users don't need to dive into customizing their Office setup. However, because chapters throughout this book refer to various options, take a moment now to familiarize yourself with where the options are and how they are organized. To open the Options dialog box in an Office application, choose File ➪ Options to open the dialog box shown in Figure 2.24.

FIGURE 2.24

The Options dialog box groups options by category.

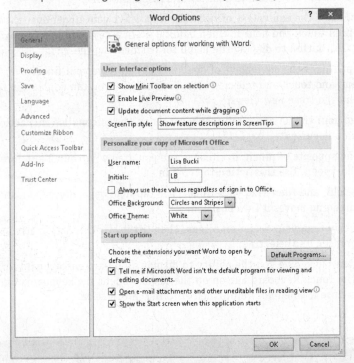

Finding the option you want

Each Office application Options dialog has several sections, or tabs, on the left. Do not be misled by the labels. Note that one of the tabs is called Advanced. Microsoft's idea of *advanced* might not be the same as yours. What's optional for someone else might be essential for you.

Microsoft's logic is to try to put at the top of the list the controls and options it thinks you are most likely to want to change. The first set, General, is therefore the group it thinks will matter most to the typical user. If you're reading the *Office 2013 Bible*, however, you might not be a typical user. Keep this in mind as you look at the available tabs.

Another caveat is that the labels aren't even objectively accurate. For example, there is a tab labeled Display. If you don't find the display option you're looking for there, don't give up. Some display options actually reside in General, such as Show Mini Toolbar on selection, Enable Live Preview, and Open e-mail attachments and other uneditable files in reading view.

A number of display options are also sheltered under the Advanced umbrella for most of the applications, including great favorites such as the Show document content options and the Display options (duh!) in Word, and Provide feedback with animation (under General). If you're keeping track, in Word Options there's a General tab, and there's a General section within the Advanced tab. Options are covered in more detail in Appendix A, but you can also discover a lot of options simply by taking a little time to explore the various tabs.

> **TIP**
>
> If an information icon (an *i* in a circle) appears to the right of one of the options, you can point to the icon to display a ScreenTip with more information about the option.

Advanced...versus not advanced?

The Advanced tab of the Word Options dialog box, partially shown in Figure 2.25, has 13 major sections. Also depending on how you count, the Advanced tab offers more than 150 different settings, including the Layout options. The other Office applications feature numerous Advanced choices, too.

FIGURE 2.25

Word's Advanced options contain over 150 settings.

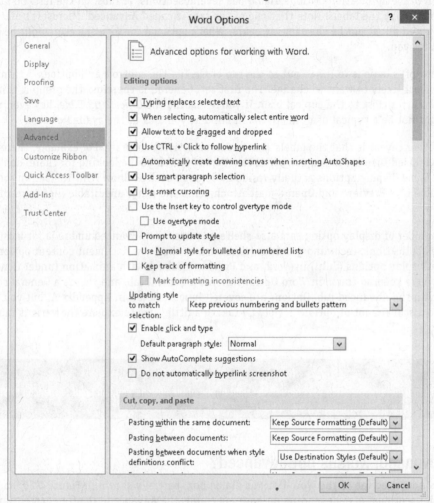

Scroll down the Advanced tab a bit, and you can see both the Save and Preserve fidelity when sharing this document sections at the same time. While "Prompt before saving Normal template" seems pretty clear as an option name, others such as "Embed linguistic data" might trip most people up. You can press F1 or click the ? icon at the upper-right corner of the window to use the Help system to search for more information about an option. A section in Chapter 1, "Getting Help," explains how to use Help.

Working with Dialog Boxes

Many Office commands display a dialog box, which is simply a way of getting more information from you. For example, if you choose Review ➪ Changes ➪ Protect Sheet in Excel, the program can't carry out the command until you tell it what parts of the sheet you want to protect. Therefore, it displays the Protect Sheet dialog box, shown in Figure 2.26.

FIGURE 2.26

Many Office applications use a dialog box to get additional information about a command.

Excel dialog boxes vary in how they work. You'll find two types of dialog boxes:

- **Typical dialog box:** A *modal* dialog box takes the focus away from the file. When this type of dialog box is displayed, you can't do anything in the worksheet until you dismiss the dialog box. Clicking OK performs the specified actions, and clicking Cancel (or pressing Esc) closes the dialog box without taking any action. Most Excel dialog boxes are this type.

- **Stay-on-top dialog box:** A *modeless* dialog box works in a manner similar to a toolbar. When a modeless dialog box is displayed, you can continue working in the Office application, and the dialog box remains open. Changes made in a modeless dialog box take effect immediately. An example of a modeless dialog box is the Find and Replace dialog box. You can leave this dialog box open while you continue to use your worksheet. A modeless dialog box has a Close button but no OK button.

Most people find working with dialog boxes to be quite straightforward and natural. If you've used other programs before Office, you'll feel right at home. You can manipulate the controls either with your mouse or directly from the keyboard.

Navigating dialog boxes

Navigating dialog boxes is generally very easy — you simply click the control you want to activate.

Although dialog boxes were designed with mouse users in mind, you can also use the keyboard. Every dialog box control has text associated with it, and this text always has one underlined letter (a *hot key* or an *accelerator key*). You can access the control from the keyboard by pressing Alt and then the underlined letter. You can also press Tab to cycle through all the controls on a dialog box. Pressing Shift+Tab cycles through the controls in reverse order.

> **TIP**
> When a control is selected, it appears with a dotted outline. You can use the Spacebar to activate a selected control.

Using tabbed dialog boxes

Several Excel dialog boxes are "tabbed" dialog boxes: That is, they include notebook-like tabs, each of which is associated with a different panel.

When you select a tab, the dialog box changes to display a new panel containing a new set of controls. The Format Cells dialog box from Excel, shown in Figure 2.27, is a good example. It has six tabs, which makes it functionally equivalent to six different dialog boxes.

Tabbed dialog boxes are quite convenient because you can make several changes in a single dialog box. After you make all your setting changes, click OK or press Enter. Some dialog boxes, such as the Word Options dialog box shown earlier in the chapter, may have tabs along the left rather than across the top.

FIGURE 2.27

Use the dialog box tabs to select different functional areas of the dialog box.

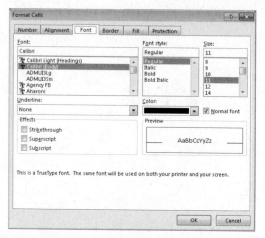

TIP

To select a tab by using the keyboard, press Ctrl+Page Up or Ctrl+Page Down, or simply press the first letter of the tab that you want to activate.

Summary

This chapter gave you your first tour of Office 2013. You've seen how Office has been updated with a sleek, modern look that mirrors other newer Windows 8 apps, while retaining familiar commands and functions like the Ribbon and File tab. The chapter helped you find program options for the first time, and at this point, you should be able to:

- Work with the various on-screen controls, including the Ribbon, Quick Access Toolbar (QAT), galleries, task panes, the status bar, and more.
- Select and use the File tab.
- Set whether or not the Ribbon appears.
- Use basic touch gestures if you have a touch-enabled system.
- Navigate and make selections in a dialog box.

Mastering Fundamental Operations

IN THIS CHAPTER

Understanding the file formats used by Office applications

Creating, saving, opening, and closing files

Choosing page and printer settings

Previewing and printing a file

Opening, selecting, and arranging windows

Undoing and redoing actions

Using Find and Replace, Go To, and spell checking

Using formatting and correction shortcuts

Previewing and applying styles

Switching between user accounts

Years ago, computer program developers began to standardize commands and functions, even in programs with significantly different purposes. Microsoft's Office suite was a pioneer in meeting the needs of users by standardizing names for menus and commands and by placing familiar tools in all of their applications. This chapter discusses features, commands, and tasks that many of the Microsoft Office 2013 applications have in common.

Working with Files

Computer files are part of a framework for managing data created and stored on a computer. When you create information in a program, such as a letter, you save that information in a file and assign the file a memorable name. When you want to work with the file at a later time, you can identify the file by its name and subsequently open the file in the program. Although the ins and outs of creating and using files can differ among Office programs, after you have learned to work with files in one Office application, you should be able to work with files in any other Office application. The skills you learn next will come in handy when you need to work with files in various Office programs.

Understanding Office 2013 file formats

Every program saves data in a particular file format that reflects how the program identifies, organizes, and interprets the information contained within the file. You can typically identify which program was used to create a file in one of two ways:

■ The file's icon in a Windows folder window or a dialog box, such as the Open dialog box, identifies the program used to create the file. All files created in a particular program use the program's icon. Figure 3.1 shows the file icons for some of the key Office programs. (The size and appearance of the icons vary depending on the view selected in Windows or the dialog box.)

FIGURE 3.1

A file's icon reflects the program used to create the file.

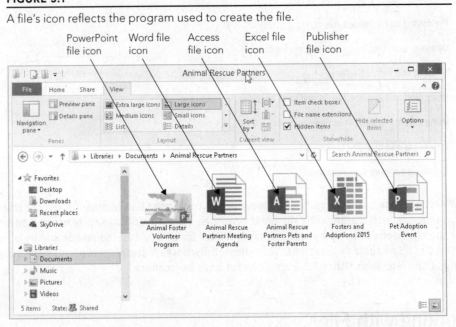

■ A three- to five-letter file name extension (such as .docx for Word 2013 files) also identifies the program used to create the file. Although file name extensions often are hidden, you may see the extension when viewing the properties of a file or browsing to find a file in Windows.

The file formats for the 2007 releases of Word, Excel, and PowerPoint dramatically changed to use the Microsoft Office Open XML Formats, and the Office 2010 and 2013 versions retain the XML formats. The Microsoft Office Open XML format is based on a wider standard called *eXtensible Markup Language* (XML), a method of describing data that was designed to facilitate sharing data between different systems. To signify their XML roots, the file name extensions for Word, Excel, and PowerPoint now include an *x*: .docx for Word documents, .xlsx for Excel workbooks, and .pptx for PowerPoint presentations. The change to XML-based file formats enables the applications to create smaller, more secure files that can be shared more easily.

NOTE

If an Office file from recent versions including 2013 has been saved in a special macro-enabled format, it will have the .docm (Word), .xlsm (Excel), or .pptm (PowerPoint) file name extension and its file icon will include an explanation point on a yellow page.

Access 2013 also retains the .accdb database file format rather than the older .mdb file format for versions prior to 2007. The Access file format and the database engine that drives it give tighter integration with SharePoint and Outlook 2013. There are also some special variations of the Access file format, including an execute-only database file (.accde) and a runtime version (.accdr). Although Access can read tables from database files created in earlier Access versions for backward compatibility, older Access versions cannot read tables from an Access 2013 database file. Publisher 2013 files continue to use the .pub file name extension.

The Office 2013 Word, Excel, and PowerPoint applications also can save and open files based on the Open Document Format (ODF) standard. The specific file format names vary depending on the application — OpenDocument Text (*.odt) for word processing, OpenDocument Spreadsheet (*.ods), and OpenDocument Presentations (*.odp). Support of these formats means that Office applications can work with files created using an OpenOffice application, further reducing barriers to collaboration. The primary Office 2013 applications also can save files in the portable XPS (XML Paper Specification) and PDF (Portable Document Format) file types. You can double-click an XPS document in a folder window to open it in XPS Viewer (Windows 7) or the Reader app (Windows 8). Viewing a PDF file in Windows 7 requires the free Adobe Reader application that you can download from any number of locations online, while the Reader app in Windows 8 enables you to view PDF files.

Creating a new, blank file

When you start some of the Office applications — such as Word, Excel, and PowerPoint — the application Start screen appears and gives you the choice of creating a new, blank file by clicking the choice for a new blank file. You can then begin adding and formatting the content you want to preserve for yourself or other readers or viewers.

If you're working with an existing file and need to create another blank file, you can do so at any time, using one of the following two methods:

- Press Ctrl+N. The blank file appears immediately.
- Click the File tab in the upper-left corner of the program window and then click New. The Backstage view appears and presents new file options, like the one for Excel shown in Figure 3.2. Click the Blank document type icon, which closes the Backstage view and immediately opens the new document on-screen.

FIGURE 3.2

You can create a blank file using the New command in Backstage view.

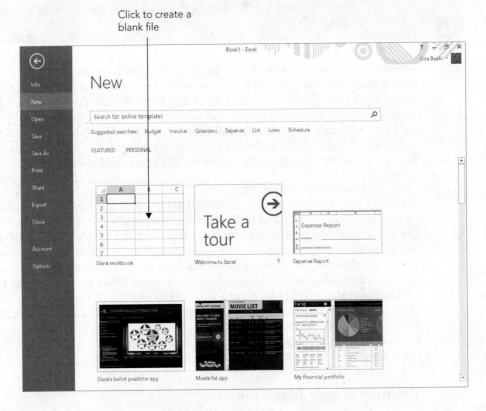

Because of its more complicated file structure, Access requires you to take a few more setup steps when you create a new database file. If you click the Blank desktop database icon after starting Access or choosing the New command, Access prompts you to enter a name for the file. After you click Create (Figure 3.3), you then must set up the first table that will hold the data you'll enter. Chapter 34 covers the process for creating an Access table.

FIGURE 3.3

Access prompts you to enter a file name immediately.

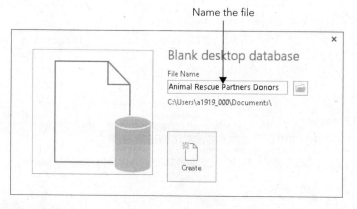

Name the file

Blank desktop database

File Name

Animal Rescue Partners Donors

C:\Users\a1919_000\Documents\

Create

NOTE

As you learned in Chapter 2, "Navigating in Office," by default you see a Start screen when you launch the core Office applications, and can choose to make a blank file or choose a template on that screen.

TIP

Outlook doesn't use files, so you'll learn how to work with its messages and information when we cover Outlook. Both the Publisher and OneNote programs have a somewhat unique process for setting up a new file, and you'll learn about each process in the applicable chapters.

Creating a file with a document template

You can avoid starting from scratch when creating a file by selecting a template. A *template* includes predefined content and attractive formatting, both of which you can adapt for your own uses. For example, when your system is not online or you are not signed in to Excel with your user account to enable its online features, it includes a limited number of templates, including a Loan Amortization template that includes all the formulas required to calculate payments on a loan; you plug in the loan terms, and it will finalize the results. The worksheet presents you with precise principal and payment information for any payment date in the life of the loan. When you are signed in and your system is connected to the Internet, Excel includes a greater selection of templates among the Featured templates. As shown in the template for tracking blood pressure and glucose levels shown in Figure 3.4 , all the templates include the formatting needed to organize and highlight your information.

FIGURE 3.4

Templates include starter information and formatting.

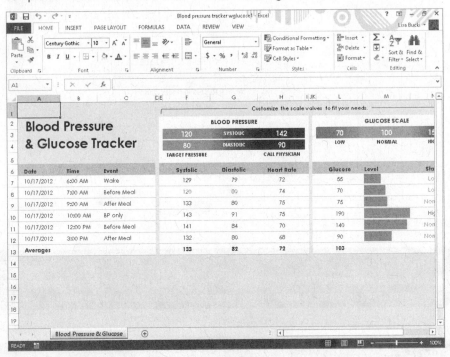

Some templates install on your system's hard disk when you install Office. When your system is connected to the Internet and you are signed in with your user account, the Office applications also enable you to browse and download templates stored online at Office .com, giving you the opportunity to take advantage of new templates as Microsoft adds them to the site.

Whether you choose an installed template or download a new template, the process for using a template to create a new file is roughly the same:

1. **Choose File ⇨ New.** The Backstage view appears, showing choices for creating files.

2a. **Click FEATURED or PERSONAL.** Note that you will only see these choices if you have saved your own custom templates.

   OR

2b. **Click on one of the Suggested searches under the Search for online templates text box.** You can use the filters that appear at the pane at the right to limit the matches found.

   OR

2c. **Click in the Search for online templates text box, type a search term or phrase, and click the Start searching button at the far right.**

3. **Click on a template thumbnail.** As shown in Figure 3.5, a window with a preview and description of the template appears.

FIGURE 3.5

The Office application displays a preview of the selected template.

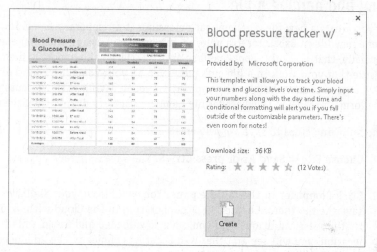

4. **Click Create.** If you selected a template installed on your system, the new file appears. An online template may take a few seconds to a few minutes to download, and then the new file will appear.

NOTE

PowerPoint also enables you to create a file by applying a design theme. Although themes don't include any content, they do provide attractive, consistent formatting for all the slides in a presentation. When you choose File ⇨ New, the PowerPoint Backstage displays themes; use one of the methods to search online (Steps 2b and 2c above) to find templates rather than themes.

Saving and naming a file

When you create a new file, the application assigns it a temporary name. If you create more than one new file in Excel, for example, the program will assign the temporary file names sequentially, that is, *Book1*, *Book2*, and so on. To replace the temporary file name and to make sure that your work in a file gets preserved on your computer's hard disk or a network drive, you need to *save* the file. The application you're saving with will automatically apply the file format extension to whatever file name you specify during the Save process.

Use the following steps to save a newly created file:

1. **Choose File ⇨ Save As or press Ctrl+S.** The Save As screen appears in Backstage view.

2. **Click Computer in the middle pane.** You could leave your SkyDrive selected, and save the file there. Chapter 39, "Collaborating in the Cloud with SkyDrive" describes that process. Additionally if you have downloaded and saved a file from an online location, you will see an Other Web Locations choice in the middle column and can use it to return to a prior location from which you saved an online file.

3. **Under Computer, click a folder, or the Browse button.** Any choice displays the Save As dialog box shown in Figure 3.6.

4. **Navigate to the desired folder using the Navigation pane at the left side of the Save As dialog box or by double-clicking subfolder icons in the list of files.** In the Navigation pane, double-click a higher-level location such as Computer or Network to open its tree, and then navigate down through the tree by clicking the white triangles that appear beside computer, disk, and folder names to open those locations. Click the folder or subfolder that holds the file you want to open when you see it in the tree.

5. **Select the contents of the File name text box by dragging over them with the insertion point if needed, and then type the desired file name.**

6. **Press Enter or click the Save button.** Word saves the file and returns to it on-screen.

TIP

Use the New folder button above the list of files in the Save As dialog box to create a new folder within the current folder. After clicking the button, type a folder name and press Enter. You can add a folder to the Favorites list in the Navigation pane by dragging it from the file list to the Favorites section.

FIGURE 3.6

Choose a save location and enter a file name.

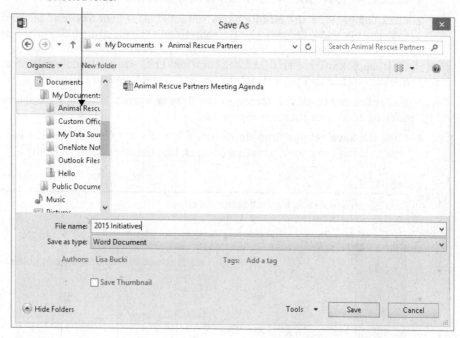

As you continue working with a file, you should save it periodically to ensure that your latest changes are included in the stored version. That way, in the event of a power surge or problem with your computer, you won't lose much work. Saving every 10 minutes proves good insurance for your file. To save your latest changes, click the Save button on the Quick Access toolbar or press Ctrl+S. If you must, you can click the File tab and then click Save, but why choose two steps when you can choose one?

Files created in the 2013 versions of Word, Excel, PowerPoint, and Access cannot be opened with versions of those programs prior to the 2007 versions by default. You can download and install a compatibility pack to handle the files; at this time, the latest version of the Compatibility Pack is at `http://www.microsoft.com/en-us/download/details .aspx?id=3`, but it's possible an update could be released at a later time. If that's the case, you also can go to the main Office download website at `http://www.microsoft .com/en-us/download/default.aspx`. Click in the Search Download Center text box at the top, type **Compatibility Pack**, and press Enter. Check the Search results for "Microsoft Office Compatibility Pack for Word, Excel, and PowerPoint File Formats," and download it.

If a user running an older version of one of these applications needs to open one of your files, you may need to save a copy of the file in a compatible format. Here's how:

1. **Click File ➪ Save As.** The Save As screen appears in Backstage view.

2. **Click Computer in the middle pane.** You could leave your SkyDrive selected, and save the file there. Chapter 39, "Collaborating in the Cloud with SkyDrive" describes that process. Additionally if you have downloaded and saved a file from an online location, you will see an Other Web Locations choice in the middle column and can use it to return to a prior location from which you saved an online file.

3. **Under Computer, click a folder, or the Browse button.** Any choice displays the Save As dialog box shown in Figure 3.6.

4. **Click the Save as type drop-down list.** A list of other file formats that you can select for the copy you're creating appears, like the one shown in Figure 3.7.

FIGURE 3.7

Choose an alternative format for the file copy.

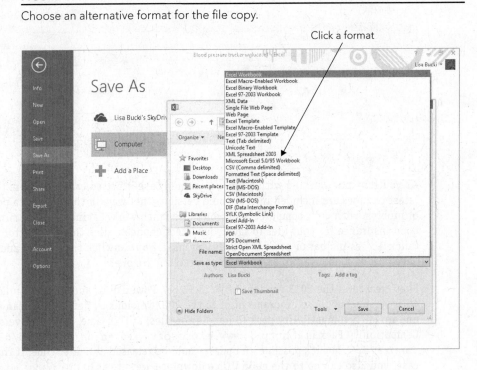

70

5. **Click the desired Save As format.**

6. **Specify a save location and file name in the Save As dialog box.** The process works just as described in the previous set of steps about saving a new file.

7. **Click Save.**

Opening a file

In every field you revisit your work to edit and improve it. You might make changes to the wording in a contract you've written using Word, update sales figures in an Excel workbook or PowerPoint presentation, change a quote in a Publisher publication, or add and delete records in a database. To perform these kinds of activities and more, you need to reopen a file that you've previously created and saved.

If you choose File ⇨ Open, most of the Office applications display a list of Recent Documents (the list name varies by application) at the right, which you can pin or unpin for faster access. The left pane of the Start screen for most applications displays the list of Recent files as well, and you can also pin and unpin files there by clicking the pushpin icon that appears when you point to the right side of the file name.

As you might guess, you can open an existing file by clicking it in the Recent files list on either the Start screen or the Open screen.

> **TIP**
>
> In addition to recent files, the Start screen may show other files listed under Recovered. These are files that may have been open when some sort of error was experienced. You can click Show Recovered Files to view and work with the files.

However, the Recent files list is dynamic, so if your file no longer appears there, you will need to navigate to it and open it from the location where you saved it. You can save files to and open them from one of two overall locations from the Open screen:

- **Computer:** Clicking Computer displays Recent Folders that have been used for storing documents, which is by default set as your user My Documents folder (part of the Documents library by default) and Desktop folder (files on the desktop). If you click either of those folders or the Browse button, the Open dialog box appears, as shown in Figure 3.8. You can use it to navigate to other locations, including shared folders on your local network.

FIGURE 3.8

You can open files stored on your computer or network.

Click to use your SkyDrive

Default folders for documents

Click to use the Open dialog box to find another folder, disk, or location

Even select another location on your network

■ **SkyDrive:** Microsoft hosts SkyDrive cloud storage. When you create a Microsoft account to sign in to Windows, your account automatically includes your own SkyDrive storage. To take advantage of that storage from within Office, sign in to Office with your Microsoft account information, and click your SkyDrive in the middle list shown in Figure 3.8. If you have installed the SkyDrive for Windows client application in Windows, that process sets up SkyDrive folders on your system that automatically sync with your SkyDrive storage in the cloud, so you can access those files from another computer or device if needed. Chapter 39 will show you how to set up and use SkyDrive. You can jump ahead to that chapter if you want to use SkyDrive in the near future.

NOTE

As mentioned earlier, if you've downloaded a file directly from the web, the Open list of places also includes an Other Web Locations choice. Click it to see websites from which you've downloaded files listed as Recent Folders at the right. If clicking a folder doesn't reconnect with the website as expected, right-click a choice and click Copy path to clipboard. You can then paste the path into your web browser's address bar and press Enter to return to the site from which you downloaded the file.

For now, use these steps to open a file that's not on the Recent files list:

1. **From the application Start screen, click Open Other Documents; within the application, select File ⇨ Open.**

2. **Under Recent Folders, click My Documents, Desktop, or another listed folder, or the Browse button.** All these choices display the Open dialog box, the difference being that both My Documents and Browse initially show the Documents library, whereas Desktop shows your user Desktop folder and clicking another listed folder shows that folder.

3. **If needed, further navigate to the desired folder using the Navigation pane at the left side of the Open dialog box or by double-clicking subfolder icons in the list of files.** In the Navigation pane, double-click a higher-level location such as Computer or Network to open its tree, and then navigate down through the tree by clicking the white triangles that appear beside computer, disk, and folder names to open those locations. Click the folder or subfolder that holds the file to open when you see it in the tree.

4. **Click the name of the file to open in the main file list, and then click the Open button.** Or simply double-click the file name when you see it.

TIP

You can still directly open an Office file by double-clicking it in a File Explorer (Windows 8) or Windows Explorer (Windows 7) window on the desktop. Use the Search box in the upper-right corner of a folder window in either operating system to search for a file. In Windows 8, you also can point to a right screen corner, click the Search charm, click Files in the right pane, and then type a file to search for in the text box under Search; if the desired file name appears, click it.

3

Closing a file

Closing a file that you've finished working on removes the file from the system's working memory. Only a few years ago, closing a file was a necessity because most computers had limited amounts of working memory. Today's powerful computers make that less of an issue, but there are some other equally important reasons to close a file after you finish making changes. For example, you may want to close a file so that it's not visible on-screen for security or privacy reasons. Closing a file also reduces the chance of the file being corrupted by a power fluctuation or a system error; it also gives you a reminder to save your changes to the file if you haven't already done so.

Because each file now opens in its own instance of the applicable Office application, the window offers a single Close (X) button near the upper-right corner of the window. Clicking the Close button closes the file and that instance of the Office application. You also can close the current file by clicking the File tab and then clicking Close. The keyboard short-cut Alt+F+C will close the current file as well in some Office applications.

If you haven't saved your most recent changes to the file being closed, a reminder message like the one shown in Figure 3.9 appears.

FIGURE 3.9

Click Save to save the file before closing it.

Microsoft Word

Want to save your changes to "Grand Canyon Report"?

If you click "Don't Save", a recent copy of this file will be temporarily available.
Learn more

[Save] [Don't Save] [Cancel]

Printing a File

With the crisp, vibrant output produced by today's cheap color printers, who would want a paperless office? Although the Internet and faster computer networks have made electronic transmission a common and accepted means of sharing documents, many circumstances still call for — if not require — that information be shared on paper:

- Legal documents such as contracts that need to be signed, initialed, dated, nota-rized, or otherwise stamped are still largely handled on paper. Standards for digital signatures are still evolving, and most users still print a hard copy of a contract or agreement for official filing.

- When a reader or viewer won't have a computer or connection at hand and will need to take notes, you need to provide a hard copy. For example, participants in semi-nars typically don't bring along a notebook and prefer to take their notes on a hard copy of a presentation.

- When you want to make a strong impression, hard copy is still preferred. Although e-mail is increasingly accepted as a standard business practice for many commu-nications, sometimes it doesn't measure up. For example, it might be acceptable to e-mail a proposal to a potential new client, but hand-delivering a hard copy and then following up by e-mail shows that you still care enough to make a personal effort to get the business.

- When you need a fresh perspective on a document, you can get it by working from hard copy. Reading through a printed copy of a document can help you catch text and formatting mistakes you previously missed, while also enabling you to make additional notes and engage in proofreading tricks such as reading the document backward.

- When you want to provide a more constant, visible reminder, you need a hard copy. Whether it's putting up a flyer at the grocery store about a found cat or giving a recognition certificate to a valued volunteer, hard copy is still the only useful format.

With all the great documents you can create in Office, you'll be proud to publish and share hard copies. This section explains how to set up and print your files.

> **NOTE**
>
> This section on printing assumes that a printer is installed on your system or network, and that the printer is powered on and has ample paper and ink or toner in it.

Performing a basic preview and print

Previewing and printing used to be separate operations in previous versions of Office applications. The Backstage view in Office 2013 enables you to preview the printout and select print settings, so you can adjust the document as needed without having to go back and forth between the preview and a separate setup dialog box. You can preview and print the document using the current settings for the printer with only a few mouse clicks if you want to use the default print settings. (Note that when you download an online file, it typically opens in Protected View, and you have to click Enable Editing in the Message Bar to be able to work with and print it.)

Viewing a preview and printing the document is easy:

1. **Click File ⇨ Print.** The Backstage view shows the preview and printing settings, as shown in Figure 3.10.

2. **Use the Zoom slider to adjust the preview zoom as desired.** The Zoom slider appears in the lower right of the preview. You also can use the Zoom Out and Zoom In buttons at either end of the slider to adjust the view.

3. **Use the Previous Page and Next Page buttons to move between pages if the document has multiple pages.** These buttons appear at lower left below the preview.

4. **Click Print.** The document prints.

TIP

If you prefer the keyboard to the mouse, you can use this rather long keyboard shortcut for performing a quick print: Alt+F+P+P.

TIP

You can add a Quick Print button to the Quick Access Toolbar. Clicking that button then prints the current file directly. To add the button, click the Customize Quick Access Toolbar drop-down arrow at the right end of the Quick Access toolbar; then, click Quick Print.

FIGURE 3.10

Preview the printout and choose print settings in Backstage view.

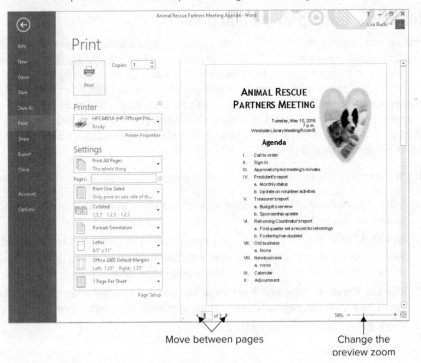

Move between pages   Change the preview zoom

Understanding page design settings

Some document settings affect the overall page design not only in terms of looks but also in making the document print correctly from the printer. The most important page settings you need to specify when it comes to printing fall into three categories:

- **Margins:** The *margin* is the white space between the edge of the paper and the information printed on the page. Most printers require at least 0.25 inches of margin on each edge of the document. If you specify a smaller margin than required by your printer, you could cause some of the printed information to appear "cut off." In some cases, you need to specify special-purpose margins such as *mirrored margins,* for which the inside (center) margins of each two-page spread are wider to allow for binding the pages.

- **Orientation:** You can choose to present information from a file in *Portrait* (tall) or *Landscape* (wide) format. When you choose a portrait orientation such as that used for a typical letter, the printer prints the text parallel to the shorter edges of the paper. When you choose a landscape orientation such as that often used for worksheets or presentation slides, the printer rotates the information and prints horizontal to the longer edges of the paper.

- **Size:** If you want to print on paper other than standard-sized sheets, you need to choose that paper size for the document's page design or setup. This choice automatically adjusts the document contents to fit within the margins on the specified sheet size.

Because page design settings vary quite a bit between applications, it's not possible to cover each and every choice here. Later chapters detail some of the settings that pertain to particular Office applications. So, here's an idea of where you can find the page settings you need to check or change before sending a file to the printer:

- **On the Page Layout or Design tab of the Ribbon:** The tab can be used to format the page or design and typically includes a Page Setup section with the options for changing crucial page settings. Clicking on a choice here typically displays a menu or gallery, as shown in Figure 3.11, of specific settings; click on the one you want to apply to the document.

- **In the Backstage view after you click Print:** As shown in Figure 3.10, the Settings area offers settings for orientation and margin. These settings work just like the corresponding settings found on the Ribbon.

3

FIGURE 3.11

The Page Layout or Design tab of the Ribbon offers page design settings.

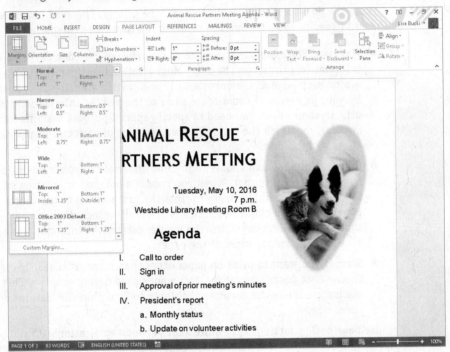

- **In the Page Setup dialog box:** The Page Setup dialog box for an application offers general page formatting options such as margin settings, as well as choices specific to the application that you're using. For example, the Page Setup dialog box for Excel includes a Sheet tab, on which you can indicate such details as whether gridlines should print (Figure 3.12). To open the Page Setup dialog box, you can click the dialog box launcher for the Page Setup group on the Page Layout or Design tab of the Ribbon (Figure 3.13). After you make your choices in the dialog box, click OK to apply them to the document.

FIGURE 3.12

Page Setup options vary from application to application.

FIGURE 3.13

Click the dialog box launcher for the Page Setup group.

Dialog box
launcher

Choosing print settings and printing

As opposed to being specific to the design of the pages of the document being printed, additional settings pertain to the nature of the hard copy being produced. These settings include which printer to use, which pages of the file to print, how many copies to print, what print quality to use, and so on. You choose all these types of settings in the Backstage view after clicking Print at the left side of the view.

Although settings such as which pages to print and how many copies to print are the same in most circumstances, other choices vary depending on the application or the selected printer. For example, Excel has additional options for enabling you to print only the current worksheet or the entire workbook file. And choosing an inkjet printer generally enables you to select whether you want to print in just black ink or in full color.

Despite those types of differences, the process for choosing a printer and print settings and finishing the print job is about the same in every application:

1. **Click File ⇨ Print or press Ctrl+P.** The Backstage view appears with its associated print settings.
2. **Select the printer to use from the Printer drop-down list.** The printer becomes the current or active printer (Figure 3.14).

FIGURE 3.14

Choose printout settings in the Backstage view after clicking Print.

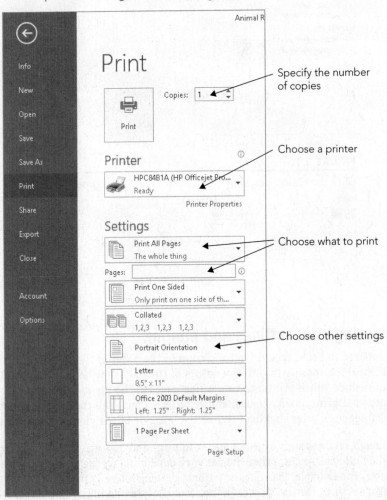

3. **Specify what pages to print in the Pages text box under settings.** You also can use the drop-down list above the text box to choose one of the available settings for the current application, such as printing the Document Properties for a Word document.

4. **Specify how many copies to print in the Copies box.** In some cases, you also can choose to collate the printed pages.

5. **Choose other print settings as desired.** For example, you might change zoom settings or print to a file rather than paper.

6. **Click the Printer Properties link below the selected printer.** The dialog box that appears has additional print settings, as in the example shown in Figure 3.15.

FIGURE 3.15

Properties for the selected printer enable you to fine-tune the print job even further.

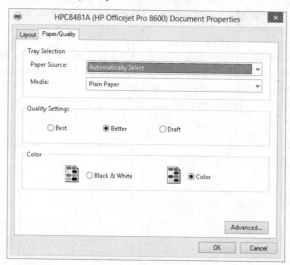

7. **Choose settings in the printer's Properties dialog box as needed, and then click OK.** The Print dialog box reappears.

8. **Click Print.** The application prints the file to the specified printer.

> **TIP**
>
> If you prefer to e-mail a file rather than print it, you can send it from right within some of the Office applications. Select File ⇨ Share ⇨ Email, and then click on the desired sending format to continue the process.

Working with Multiple Windows

Every time you open another file in an Office application, the file opens in its own file window. You can have multiple programs and files open to help you multitask — to jump between different jobs you're working on and to look at information stored in a number of different files and applications.

The taskbar is a band or bar that appears by default along the bottom of the Windows desktop. A button for programs that you open appears on the taskbar in Windows 7 or 8. The Office applications work with Windows to provide you with multiple options for navigating between open file and application windows, including using the taskbar.

Switching to another file or application window

Switching to another open file makes it the active file in its application. When you use the taskbar to switch between open files, Windows switches to the application for that file, if applicable. You can use one of the following techniques to navigate to another file or application in Office and Windows:

- **View tab on Ribbon:** To switch to another open file window in an application, click the View tab on the Ribbon, click Switch Windows in the Window group, and then click on the name of the file to select, as shown in the example in Figure 3.16. The selected file becomes the active file.

FIGURE 3.16

Using the Ribbon to switch between open files.

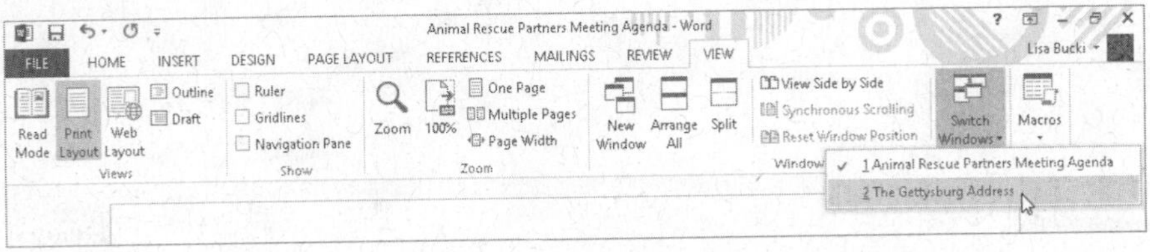

- **Taskbar:** If a single file for the application is open, click the taskbar button for the file to open, which immediately makes the file appear in its application. If the taskbar button represents more than one open file, move the mouse pointer over it. Windows 7 and 8 display a thumbnail of each open file. Click the thumbnail for the file you want to open to select it.

- **Keyboard shortcut combination:** If you press and hold the Alt+Tab keyboard shortcut, a task-switching box with an icon for each open file, as well as for the Windows desktop, appears. Continue holding down the Alt key as you press and release the Tab key until you've highlighted the desired file icon; then, release both keys. The last file you selected opens on-screen in its application.

Arranging windows

Arranging windows sizes all the open files in an application and positions them so that the files fill the available space in the application window without overlapping. (Word and PowerPoint actually size multiple instances of the application window to fill the screen.) This feature enables you to review and compare the information in multiple files more easily, or to perform an action such as moving or copying information from one file to another, as described in the next section.

The View tab of the Ribbon includes an Arrange All button in the window group. Click that button to arrange the open file windows, as in the example shown in Figure 3.17. Note that some applications also include Cascade, which stacks the open windows so that you can switch to another window by clicking on its title bar. You also can press the Windows logo key plus Left Arrow or Right Arrow to snap the current file window to the left or right half of the screen, respectively.

FIGURE 3.17

Arranging file windows makes file contents more accessible.

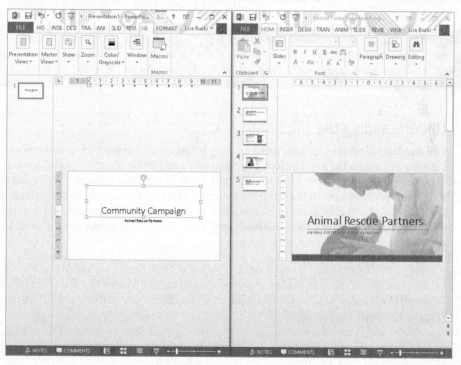

To arrange all the open file and program windows on the Windows desktop, right-click on a blank area of the taskbar (not a taskbar button) and then click Show Windows side by side.

Moving and Copying Information

A template can save you time by providing starter content for a document, but that starter content is not your own, unique information. When needed, you can reuse information you've created in one file in a new file by moving or copying that information.

Microsoft has dedicated significant effort over time to ensure that the Office applications can accept information from one to another so that users can build documents that integrate content created from different applications. For example, you can use an Excel worksheet to perform complicated calculations and then reuse that information in Word or PowerPoint.

This section shows you how simple techniques enable you to work quickly and have consistent content by moving or copying information.

> **NOTE**
>
> See Chapter 40, "Integrating Office Application Information," to learn more specifics about reusing information between applications.

Understanding the Clipboard

The Windows Clipboard enables users to copy information between virtually any two applications, as long as the applications are relatively compatible in terms of the file formats they use. Windows transfers information you copy or cut from a file to the Clipboard, a temporary holding area in the system's working memory. You can paste the information from the Clipboard into another location in the same file or into another file altogether. The information stays on the Clipboard until you copy or paste something else or shut down the computer.

Many Microsoft Office applications actually work with Office's own version of the Clipboard, called the Office Clipboard, which improves on the capabilities of the Windows Clipboard. Whereas the Windows Clipboard can hold only one copied or cut item, the Office Clipboard (Figure 3.18) can hold up to 24.

FIGURE 3.18

Multiple cut or copied items appear on the Office Clipboard for pasting.

Selecting information

Before you can copy or cut information to place it in the Clipboard, you have to *select,* or highlight, the information. Most users today prefer to use the mouse to select text or other on-screen content by clicking on it or dragging over it. Although selection methods can vary between Office applications, here are some basic techniques to know:

- In Word, drag over text to select it. Word also offers a variety of shortcut techniques, such as double-clicking on a word to select it, or triple-clicking on a paragraph to select the whole paragraph.

- In applications that use text placeholders, such as PowerPoint and Publisher, click on the placeholder to select or activate it, and then drag over the specific text to select.

- In Excel worksheets and Access tables, drag diagonally over cells to select the group of cells. For example, in Figure 3.19, you can see that the range A4:E8 is selected because the heavy black cell selector appears around the selected range, and the row and column headings for the selected cells appear highlighted.

FIGURE 3.19

Drag diagonally to select worksheet cells.

	A	B	C	D	E	F
1			Animal Rescue Partners			
2			**Fosters and Adoptions 2015**			
3						
4	Fostered	Q1	Q2	Q3	Q4	Total
5	Dogs	44	56	34	40	174
6	Cats	24	16	20	26	86
7	Other	1	3	2	1	7
8	Total	69	75	56	67	267
9						

- To select another type of item such as a graphic, simply click on it. Black selection handles and a selection box appear around the object. You can Shift+click or Ctrl+click additional objects to add them to the selection.

Copying

Copy a selection when you want to reuse information from one location in one or more other locations. Copying a selected item leaves the original intact and places a duplicate on the Clipboard. You can use one of three methods to copy a selection that you've already made:

- Press Ctrl+C.
- Click the Home tab on the Ribbon, and then click the Copy button in the Clipboard group. Figure 3.20 shows the Ribbon buttons for copying, cutting, and pasting.
- Right-click on the selection, and choose Copy in the shortcut menu.

FIGURE 3.20

The Home tab has tools for copying and moving a selection.

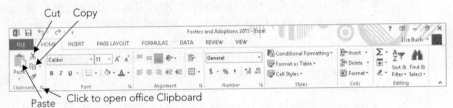

86

NOTE

After you copy or cut a range of cells in Excel, an animated marquee appears around the selected range to remind you to paste. Press Esc to clear the marquee if you decide not to paste the information. This also removes the data from the Clipboard, as does making a new cell entry without pasting.

Cutting

Cutting also places the selection on the Clipboard but removes the selection from its original location rather than make a duplicate. So, when you want to move information from one file to another, you first cut the selection from its original location and then paste it into position in another file.

As with copying, you can use one of three methods to cut:

- Press Ctrl+X.
- Click the Home tab on the Ribbon, and then click the Cut button in the Clipboard group.
- Right-click on the selection, and click Cut in the shortcut menu.

CAUTION

After you cut information from a text document or placeholder, be sure to take a look at the location from which you cut. In many instances, you might need to delete extra line spaces or add new spaces between words.

3

Pasting

Pasting places an item from the Clipboard into a new location within the same file or in a completely different file or application. For example, Figure 3.21 shows the selection from Figure 3.19 pasted from Excel onto a PowerPoint slide. Pasting finishes the overall activity of either copying or moving information between locations. The method you use to paste in Office depends on whether you need to use the Office Clipboard, which enables you to paste multiple selections or a selection other than the most recent item you cut or copied.

FIGURE 3.21

Pasting to finish copying and moving text enables you to deliver a powerful, consistent message by combining information you've developed in a variety of applications.

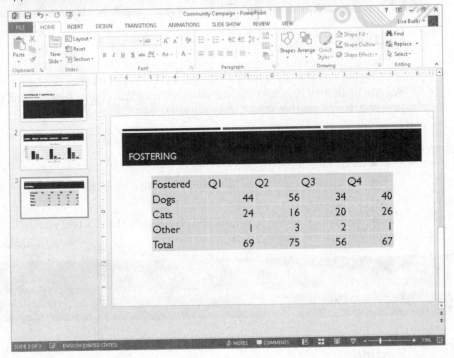

To paste directly:

1. **Click to position the insertion point at the location in which you want to paste the item.** Switch to the file first, if needed. In some cases, you might have to click within a text placeholder first. In Excel, click the upper-left cell in the range to paste to.

2. **Perform the paste.** As when copying or cutting, you can use one of three techniques to issue the Paste command:

   ■ Press Ctrl+V.

   ■ Click the Home tab on the Ribbon, and then click the top portion of the Paste button in the Clipboard group.

   ■ Right-click on the location where you want the selection inserted, and then click on one of the buttons under Paste Options in the shortcut menu.

3. (Optional) **Click the Paste Options button, which appears at the lower-right corner of the pasted selection, and choose one of the formatting or other options that appears.**

TIP

In Excel, you also can press Enter to paste after selecting a destination cell. This method clears the animated marquee from the copied or cut material, in contrast to the three techniques listed in the previous step.

Using the Office Clipboard enables you to take advantage of multiple selections that you've copied or cut. To paste using the Office Clipboard:

1. **Click to position the insertion point at the location in which you want to paste the item.** Again, switch to the destination file first, if needed.

2. **Click the Home tab on the Ribbon.**

3. **Click the dialog box launcher button in the Clipboard group.** The Clipboard pane opens at the left side of the window.

4. **Click on the item to paste in the pane.** As shown in Figure 3.22, the pasted item appears in the destination location. You can then resize and format it as needed in the destination.

FIGURE 3.22

Use the Office Clipboard to paste multiple selections.

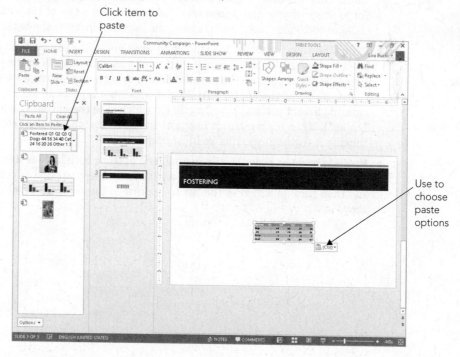

89

5. (Optional) **Click the Paste Options button that appears at the lower-right corner of the pasted selection, and choose one of the formatting or other options that appears.**

6. **Select additional paste locations and paste additional selections as needed.**

7. **Click the Close (X) button on the task pane window to close the pane.**

> **TIP**
>
> If you plan to use the Office Clipboard to paste multiple selections in a document, copy or cut all the selections before opening the Clipboard and pasting. Doing so can save you time moving back and forth between files.

Undoing and Redoing Actions

Figure 3.22 and other earlier figures show the Quick Access Toolbar. By default, the QAT has buttons for three commands: Save, Undo, and Redo. As their names suggest, Undo and Redo enable you to rescue your progress if you inadvertently slip up while working. Here's how they work:

- **Undo:** Click the Undo button or press Ctrl+Z immediately to rescind a prior action. For example, if you mistakenly delete some text, the name of the Undo button changes to "Undo Clear," and clicking the button reinstates the text.

- **Redo:** The Redo button is unavailable (grayed out) until you perform an action that Word can repeat. When it's active, click it or press Ctrl+Y to Redo the prior action. Note that the shape and the name of this button change. When it's a round arrow shape, it's called the Repeat button, and clicking it repeats an action such as entering a word you just typed again (in which case the button name is "Repeat Typing"). When it's the mirror image of the Undo button, it's the Redo button and clicking it redoes any action you just undid.

- **Multiple undo or redo:** The Undo and Redo buttons both include drop-down list buttons. Click the button to display a list of previously undone or redone actions, and then click an action in the list to undo/redo that action and all the ones listed above it.

Finding and Replacing

Lengthy, complex business files can hold a ton of information, and who wants to spend all day using the Page Down key and scrolling to try to find one bit of information? Luckily, you can use the Find feature to search for a particular word or phrase. For example, if you need to find the section of a construction contract that deals with site remediation, you can find the phrase "site remediation." Even better, you can use the Replace feature to correct words you've misspelled or to change phrases or names. For example, if you've mistakenly spelled *Artur Consulting* as *Arthur Consulting* throughout a proposal for a new client, you can replace all instances of the spelling boo-boo with the correction.

Find and Replace work in a very similar fashion, so you can use the following steps for either operation:

1. **Press Ctrl+Home.** This step moves the insertion point to the beginning of the document so that the Find or Replace operation starts from the top.

2. **Click the Home tab on the Ribbon.**

3. **Click Replace in the Editing group.** The Find and Replace dialog box appears. The Replace tab that appears for a find includes a Find what text box and a Replace with text box.

> **NOTE**
>
> In Excel, click the Find & Select button in the Editing group on the Home tab, and then click Replace. In Word, clicking Find opens the Navigation pane at the left; type a term to find in the text box at the top, and Word highlights all matches in the document. In most Office applications, you also can press Ctrl+F to start a find. The Find and Replace dialog box varies in appearance from application to application.

4. **Type the entry to find in the Find what text box.**

5. **Type the replacement entry, if any, in the Replace with text box.**

6. **Specify additional options, if needed.** The available options vary depending on the application. For example, in Word, you can click the More button and then specify choices such as matching case or matching a prefix or suffix.

7. **Click Find Next.** The application highlights the first matching instance of the search word or phrase, as shown in Figure 3.23.

FIGURE 3.23

The found match is selected (highlighted).

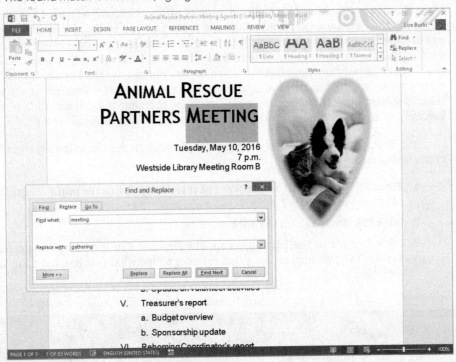

8. **Click on a button for replacing the found text, if applicable:**

   - **Replace:** Replaces only the highlighted instance of the matching word or phrase.

   - **Replace All:** Replaces all instances of the matching word or phrase.

   - **Find Next:** Skips to the next match without making a replacement.

9. **Repeat Steps 7 and 8 as needed to proceed through the find or replace operation.**

10. **Click OK in the message that tells you that the search has been completed.**

TIP

Some Office applications offer special methods for finding information. For example, Outlook enables you to find messages from a particular sender or having a particular subject. Access enables you to save and reuse a query, which finds information matching one or more criteria.

> **NOTE**
>
> Both the Navigation pane and the Find and Replace dialog box are *non-modal or modeless*. This means that you can click in the text and edit the file while the pane or dialog box is still on-screen, which is more handy than repeatedly closing and reopening either the pane or the dialog box.

Using Go To

Word, Excel, and Publisher offer a Go To feature that enables you to navigate to different locations, which can be handy when you're working in a long document. To use Go To, you can press Ctrl+G. The dialog box that appears varies and works differently in each of the applications, so here's an introduction for each:

- **Go To in Word:** In Word, the Find and Replace dialog box appears with the Go To tab selected. Make a selection in the Go to what list at the left, such as Page or Bookmark, then give the detail about where to go in the text box or list that appears at the right. For example, if you click Page, you would enter the page number in the Enter page number text box, or if you clicked Bookmark, you could select a bookmark from the Enter bookmark name drop-down list. After choosing your settings, click Go To. In Word, Home ➪ Editing ➪ Find ➪ Go To also starts the process.

- **Go To in Excel:** The Go To dialog box appears in Excel. Type a cell reference or range name in the Reference box or select a named range in the Go to list, and then click OK. Or, click the Special button in the Go To dialog box to open the Go To Special dialog box, which you can use to select specific items in the selected range, such as Formulas or Blanks. After choosing what type of item to go to, click OK. In Excel, Home ➪ Editing ➪ Find & Select ➪ Go To or Go To Special also starts the process.

- **Go To in Publisher:** Publisher enables you to move between pages, so Go To won't be active if a publication only has one page. Starting Go To opens the Go To Page dialog box. Enter the desired page number in the Go to page text box, and then click OK. In Publisher, Home ➪ Editing ➪ Find ➪ Go To Page also opens the Go To Page dialog box.

Spell Checking

Typos have no place in professional business documents, whether delivered electronically or in hard-copy form. You always want to put your best foot forward and make sure that your files are attractive, clear and easy to follow, and typo free.

By default, many of the Office applications quietly check your spelling for you as you type. If you see a telltale red squiggle appear underneath a word, that means that the application thinks you've misspelled the word — according to the application's own dictionary, anyway. If you see a wavy red underline underneath a word, right-click on the word. As shown in Figure 3.24, you can then click on a correction in the shortcut menu that appears to replace the typo with the correction, or click Add to Dictionary so that the word is no longer flagged as a misspelling.

FIGURE 3.24

Right-click on any word with a red wavy outline and then click on a correction.

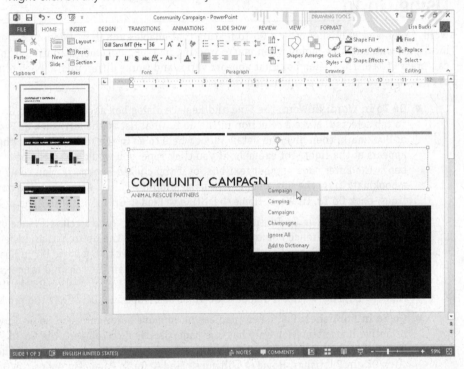

If you've finished creating the document and have moved on to the fine-tuning stage, you should always run a complete spell check to catch any typos that you might have missed earlier. Use these steps to run the check, and use the most common options for dealing with potential misspellings:

1. **Press Ctrl+Home.** This step moves to the beginning of the document so that the spell-checking operation will start from there.

2. **Click the Review tab on the Ribbon.**

3. **Click Spelling & Grammar (Word) or Spelling (other apps) in the Proofing group.** The Spelling pane appears with the first potential misspelling highlighted, as shown in Figure 3.25. Some applications enable you to start a spelling check simply by pressing F7.

FIGURE 3.25

The spelling check highlights the suspected word and displays suggested replacements in the Spelling pane.

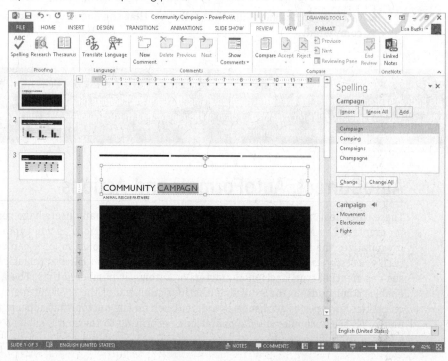

NOTE

Word can check grammar in addition to spelling every time you run a spell check. A green squiggle may appear under any potential grammar error in the document. Appendix A explains where you can find the settings for controlling how spelling and grammar checking behave in Word.

4. **Click on a button to tell the spelling check how to proceed:**

- **Ignore:** Skips only the currently found instance of the suspected word without replacing it.

- **Ignore All:** Skips all instances of the suspected word without replacing it.

- **Change:** Replaces only the currently found instance of the suspected word with the current selection in the Suggestions list. (Click on another suggestion before clicking on this button, if needed.)

- **Change All:** Replaces all instances of the suspected word with the current selection in the Suggestions list. (Click on another suggestion before clicking on this button, if needed.)

- **Add:** Adds the suspected word to the dictionary so that it will be skipped in future spelling checks.

5. **Repeat Step 4 as needed to proceed through the spelling check.**

6. **Click OK in the message that tells you that the spelling check has been completed.**

> **TIP**
>
> It's critical to proofread your files even after spell checking. No spell checker can pick up on every wrong word choice — such as when you use *then* instead of *than* or *their* instead of *there*. Therefore, you still need to apply your own intelligence in perfecting your documents.

AutoCorrect, AutoFormat, and Actions

These three features provide a trio of conveniences that many users have come to take for granted. The AutoCorrect feature makes certain corrections as you type. For example, it capitalizes the first word of a sentence if you've failed to do so, or it can change a typo such as *acessories* to *accessories*. The AutoFormat feature supplies automatic formatting, such as creating true fraction characters or automatic numbered lists. The Actions feature enables commands on the Additional Actions submenu of the shortcut menu when you click on particular types of data such as a date. Click on the button that appears with the data, and you'll see a menu of special operations pertaining to that data, such as seeing your calendar or finding an address.

Most users will want to keep these features working as they were originally installed. However, in other cases, you may want to turn off one or more aspects of these features, such as whether AutoFormat converts web or e-mail addresses to hyperlinks or whether the Actions feature flags dates.

You can access the settings for all three of these features in the AutoCorrect dialog box. To display the dialog box, click the File tab, and then click Options. Click the Proofing category in the list at the left side of the Options dialog box that appears and then click the AutoCorrect Options button. The AutoCorrect dialog box appears.

Change settings on each of the tabs as needed and then click OK to apply your changes. Here's a look at the tabs and the changes you might want to make:

- **AutoCorrect:** Clear the check box beside any of the standard corrections that you want the program to stop making. If you want to add your own correction to the list of typos that AutoCorrect fixes, type entries in the Replace and With text boxes (see Figure 3.26), and then click Add.

- **AutoFormat as You Type:** On this tab (Figure 3.27), clear the check box beside any of the formatting changes to disable that change.

FIGURE 3.26

You can create a new typo correction for AutoCorrect.

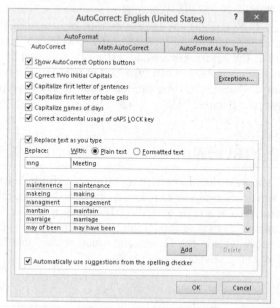

FIGURE 3.27

Choose which AutoFormatting changes the application will make.

- **Actions:** As on the other two tabs, clear or check boxes as needed to disable or enable Actions features. The Enable additional actions in the right-click menu check box turns actions on and off altogether.

- **Math AutoCorrect:** Word enables you to type certain keystroke combinations to insert characters not found on the keyboard, many of which are mathematical symbols. The majority of the keystrokes are a backslash (\) followed by two or more additional letters. For example, you can type **infty** to insert the (infinity) symbol. Use this tab to learn what symbols you can insert and to add keystroke combinations for other symbols if applicable.

Styles and Live Preview

Word, Excel, PowerPoint, and Publisher, in particular, offer powerful formatting choices loosely known as *styles*, which are typically found on a contextual Design tab that appears when you select an element such as a table on-screen. The styles might be found in a Ribbon group or gallery named "Styles" or something similar. For example, Figure 3.28 shows the gallery of styles available in the Table Styles group of the Table Tools ⇨ Design tab that you can use when you've selected a table in Word.

FIGURE 3.28

Click on a style to apply all its formatting choices to the selected object.

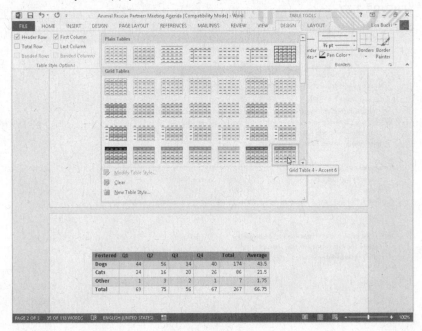

Style choices work with an Office feature called *Live Preview*. When you move your mouse pointer over a choice in a gallery like the one shown in Figure 3.28, the selected object temporarily changes to show you how it would look if you applied the highlighted style. In this way, you can quickly "try on" various looks for the selected item. When the Live Preview shows you the look you want, you can click the selected style to apply it to the selected item.

> **TIP**
>
> If you prefer not to use the Live Preview feature, you can turn it off. Click the File tab and click Options, and then clear the Enable Live Preview check box in the General options.

Working with User Accounts

As you learned in Chapter 1, Office is set up to work with the Microsoft account you use to sign on to Windows 8 (or an Office365 account) so that you can take full advantage of cloud features such as SkyDrive and be able to access your information no matter what device you're using. If you're using Windows 7, you should still sign in to your Office applications with an account, even though one is not needed for signing in to your operating system user account.

You may need to work with multiple online accounts in Office to access different storage locations, e-mail accounts, or social media accounts. Or you may want to have separate accounts for work and personal information. Here's a brief description of how to add and select accounts in Office.

Even if you have Windows 8 (or even Windows 7) set up with multiple user accounts, Office by default only uses the one that you were first signed on to when you started and set up the program. If you have other Microsoft accounts already set up with Outlook.com or Live .com and need to switch the account you're using in Office for the first time, follow these steps:

1. **Click your user name at the upper-right corner of the Office window, and then click Switch account.**

2. **In the Sign in to Office box, click either Personal or Organization or School.** If you need to sign in with your Office365 user name, click Organization or School. As discussed in Chapter 39, signing in with your Office365 credentials enables you to sync files with a SkyDrive Pro online library or access your Office365 team SharePoint online.

3. **Enter your user name and password at the Sign in screen that appears, and then click Sign in.** Your new account information appears.

After you switch accounts the first time during a work session, Office "remembers" the previous account you used and makes switching easier. When you click your user name and click Switch account, Office displays an Account window with your Current account and a list of Other accounts. Click the desired account under Other accounts to switch back to that account without having to re-enter your sign-in information.

Summary

You now should have a good grounding in tasks common to most of the Office applications. At this point, you should know how to:

- Create, save, open, and close files.
- Check out how a file will look when printed, how to tweak page and printer settings, and how to print.
- Work in multiple files and applications, move easily between different files and programs, and how to move or copy information from one file or program to another.
- Polish a document by replacing text, spell checking, making automatic corrections and formatting changes, and viewing and using the sophisticated styles offered in some Office 2013 applications.
- Switch user accounts.

Part II

Creating Documents with Word 2013

P art II teaches you about the essentials for creating documents in Word 2013. You will learn what it takes to create a new document, as well as the appropriate formatting to use for different types of text and different situations. You'll learn to take control of your documents through smarter use of features such as styles and sections. From there, you'll see how to use tables and graphics to clarify and highlight key information in a document, or just add interest and appeal. The part concludes by teaching you how to create personalized documents with mail merge, as well as how to work with collaboration-centric features such as security, comments, and change tracking.

Diving Into Document Creation

IN THIS CHAPTER

Making a new blank file or using a template

Reopening a saved document

Saving a document

Reviewing file formats and compatibility issues

Navigating in a document and selecting text

Using Word's various views

When a coach teaches someone a new sport, he or she starts with the fundamentals. Eager students often want to skip the basics — especially when in a rush to be productive with new software — and what they miss out on learning now can trip them up later. This chapter starts with the essential skills that will serve you well every time you work with Word 2013. If you're new to Word, this chapter makes getting started painless. If you've been using Word for years, you may not only pick up some tricks you previously missed, but also get an introduction to a few new features in the latest version of Word. You also explore creating files, saving and reopening files, navigating in the text and making selections, and viewing variations.

Creating a Blank File

When you start the Word 2013 application, the upper-left choice in the collection of templates that appears is Blank document. Selecting it creates a new, blank document file by default for you. (The actual name of the template applied to new, blank files is Normal.dotm.) This document file has the placeholder name *Document1* until you save it to assign a more specific name, as described later in the chapter. You can immediately start entering content into this blank document.

If you need another blank document at any time after starting Word, you can create it by following these steps:

1. **Select File ⇨ New.** The New Document dialog box appears.
2. **Click the Blank Document tile.** See Figure 4.1.

Clicking Ctrl+N also creates a new, blank file directly.

FIGURE 4.1

Click this tile or icon to create a blank file.

Blank document

Typing text

When you create a new, blank document, you can begin typing text to fill the page. As you type, each character appears to the left of the blinking vertical insertion point. You can use the Backspace and Delete keys to delete text, the Spacebar to enter spaces, and all the other keys that you're using for typing.

Word also enables you to start a line of text anywhere on the page using the Click and Type feature. To take advantage of Click and Type, move the mouse pointer over a blank area of the page. If you don't see formatting symbols below the I-beam mouse pointer, click once. This enables Click and Type and displays its special mouse pointer. Then, you can double-click to position the pointer on the page and type your text. Figure 4.2 shows snippets of text added to a page using Click and Type.

FIGURE 4.2

Double-click and type anywhere on the page.

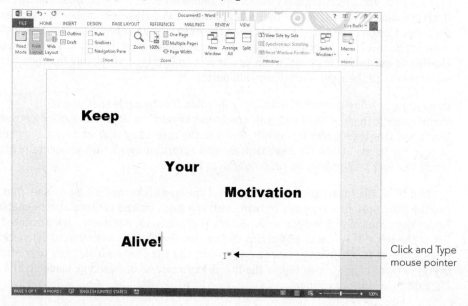

NOTE

Click and Type only works in the Print Layout view, so to learn more about that view, see the section called "Choosing the Right Word View for the Task at Hand" later in this chapter. Changing to another view does not remove the Click and Type text positioning, even though it might appear in a view such as Outline view. The document will look the same when you change back to Print Layout view.

Using word wrap

By default, the margins for a blank document in Word 2013 are 1 inch on the left and the right. When you type enough text to fill each line, hitting the right margin boundary, Word automatically moves the insertion point to the next line. This automated feature is called *word wrap*, and it's a heck of a lot more convenient than having to make a manual carriage return at the end of each line.

If you adjust the margins for the document, word wrap always keeps your text within the new margin boundaries. Similarly, if you apply a right indent, divide the document into columns, or create a table and type in a table cell, word wrap automatically creates a new line of text at every right boundary. Just keep typing until you want or need to start a new paragraph (covered shortly). Later chapters cover changing margins and indents and working with tables and columns.

Inserting versus overtyping

Like its prior versions, Word 2013 offers two modes for entering text: Insert mode and Overtype mode. In Insert mode, the default mode, if you click within existing text and type, Word inserts the added text between the existing characters, moving text to the right of the insertion point farther right to accommodate your additions and rewrapping the line as needed. In contrast, when you switch to Overtype mode, any text you type replaces text to the right of the insertion point.

Overtyping is a fine method of data entry — when it's the mode that you want. Unfortunately, in older Word versions, the Insert key on the keyboard toggled between Insert and Overtype modes by default. Because the Insert key is often found above or right next to the Delete key on the keyboard, many a surprised user would accidentally hit the Insert key and then unhappily type right over his text.

In Word 2013, the Insert key's control of Overtype mode is turned off by default. You can use the Word Options dialog box to turn Overtype mode on and off, and also to enable the Insert key's control of Overtype mode. Select File ➪ Options, and then click Advanced in the list at the left side of the Word Options dialog box. Use the Use overtype mode check box (Figure 4.3) to toggle Overtype mode on and off, and the Use the Insert key to control overtype mode check box to toggle the Insert key's control of Overtype mode on and off. Click OK to apply your changes.

FIGURE 4.3

The Word Options dialog box enables you to turn Overtype mode on and off.

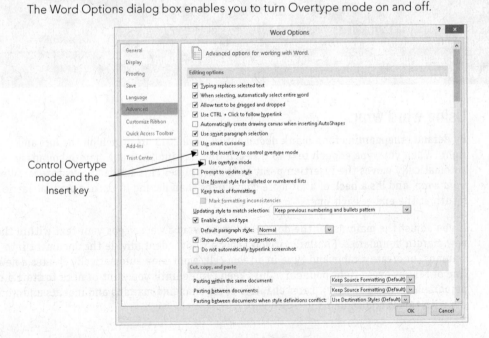

Using default tabs

Every new, blank document has default tab stops already set up for you. These tabs are set at 1/2-inch (0.5-inch) intervals along the whole width of the document between the margins. To align text to any of these default tab stops, press the Tab key. You can press Tab multiple times if you need to allow more width between the information that you're using the tab stops to align.

TIP

To display the rulers so that you can better work with text alignment features like tabs in a document, click the View ⇨ Show ⇨ Ruler check box to check it.

Making a new paragraph

In legacy versions of Word, when you wanted to create a new paragraph in a blank document, you had to press the Enter key twice. That's because the default body text style didn't provide for any extra spacing after a paragraph mark, which is a hidden symbol inserted when you press Enter.

Starting with Word 2007, pressing Enter by default not only inserts the paragraph mark to create a new paragraph, but also inserts extra spacing between paragraphs to separate them visually and eliminate the need to press Enter twice. As shown in Figure 4.4, when you press Enter after a paragraph, the insertion point moves down to the beginning of a new paragraph, and Word includes spacing above the new paragraph.

FIGURE 4.4

Press Enter to create a new paragraph in Word.

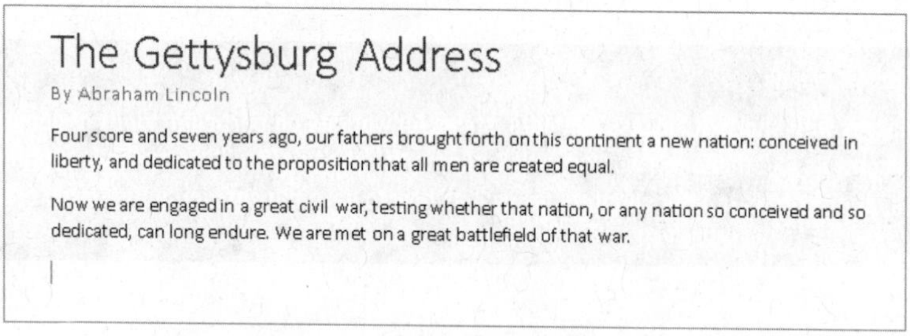
The Gettysburg Address

By Abraham Lincoln

Four score and seven years ago, our fathers brought forth on this continent a new nation: conceived in liberty, and dedicated to the proposition that all men are created equal.

Now we are engaged in a great civil war, testing whether that nation, or any nation so conceived and so dedicated, can long endure. We are met on a great battlefield of that war.

Creating a File from a Template

Every new document you create in Word 2013 — even a blank document — is based on a *template* that specifies basic formatting for the document, such as margin settings and default text styles. When you create a blank document, Word automatically applies the default global template, `Normal.dotm`.

While a document *theme* supplies the overall formatting for a file, a template takes that a step further. A template may not only include particular text and document formatting selections, but also has placeholders and example text as you saw when you created your first document earlier in the chapter. Templates also can contain automatic *macros* that swing into action each time you create, open, or close a document, as well as other macros you can use to perform tasks for building the document.

Using templates can dramatically reduce the amount of time you spend thinking about your document's content and formatting, because someone else has already invested the time to answer those questions. For example, a home repair company might set up a template for written estimates, job contracts, and change orders. Rather than starting every such document from scratch, the project manager could simply create a new document using the applicable template, and fill in the information pertinent to the current client.

In that type of scenario or in your business and personal life, using templates offers the following benefits:

- The documents produced will be consistent, even when they are produced by different people.

- If the templates are carefully developed and reviewed, using them ensures that your documents will be complete with all the needed information, every time.

- Setting up templates with your company logo and contact information ensures that information will appear on every document you create, which helps with branding and promoting your organization.

- For longer documents like reports or newsletters, the benefit of using a template increases, because designing all the formatting in such documents can be time consuming.

Take a look at the templates available to you via Word now.

> **NOTE**
> Templates can contain macros with shortcut key assignments, styles for working on particular kinds of documents, and even custom content controls like those you worked with earlier in the chapter. You'll learn about creating your own styles, macros, fields, and controls in later chapters, as well as how to save the custom features you create in your own templates.

Reviewing available document templates

When you start Word 2013 or click File ⇨ New, the right pane of the screen displays a selection of templates, shown in Figure 4.5. You can scroll down this screen to see a selection of suggested templates. Note that the available templates will vary depending on whether your computer is connected to the Internet and you are signed in to Word with your account information to enable online features.

FIGURE 4.5

Starting Word or clicking File ⇨ New shows you Word's templates.

Blank document and pinned templates

The Blank document template always appears among the templates. Selecting it creates a new document based on Normal.dotm. Figure 4.5 also shows a Letterhead and envelope template. Once you download and use a template, it will appear the next time you choose File ⇨ New, because Word automatically includes recently used templates in the list. If you look carefully at Figure 4.5, you'll see a small pushpin icon to the right of the Welcome to Word template name. That means that item is *pinned* to stay on the list of templates. To pin or unpin a template, point to its thumbnail, move the mouse pointer over the pushpin icon, and click the icon to toggle it to be pinned or unpinned.

Common templates you might want to pin to the list include:

- **Blog post:** This creates a new document based on Blog.dotx, a special template that's designed for blog entries.
- **Single spaced (blank):** This creates a new document based on the Single spaced.dotx template, with a Normal style that lacks extra spacing after paragraphs. If you choose this template, you have to press Enter twice to create paragraphs, as in older versions of Word.

To create a blank document based on Normal.dotm, you could simply press Ctrl+N, bypassing the need to choose the New command.

> **NOTE**
>
> It is possible to update the Normal.dotm template file on your system with custom content and text, but most experts don't recommend doing so. Keeping Normal.dotm clean and lean enables you to always start with a clean document slate when you need to.

Online templates

Virtually all of the templates in Word 2013 exist in the cloud rather than being installed on your computer. In addition to the suggested templates shown when you click File ➪ New, you can scroll down to see and select additional templates. Any template that you select is downloaded to your system and stored there for future use.

If you don't see a template that suits your needs, you can search online for additional templates. You can type a search word or phrase in the Search online templates text box above the templates and press Enter to begin a search. Or you can click one of the Suggested searches links below the Search online templates text box, such as Cards. After the search runs, scroll down to view additional results, or use the Filter by list at the right (see Figure 4.6) to refine the results.

FIGURE 4.6

You can refine the Cards search by clicking the Avery (or another) category under Filter by in the right pane.

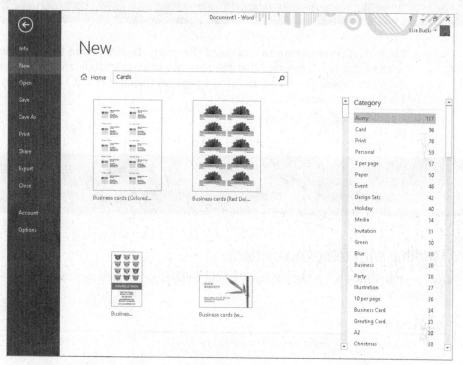

Creating the file from the template

Now that you're familiar with what templates do and where to find them, follow these steps when you want to create a new document based on a template:

1. **Select File ⇨ New.**

2. **To search for a template, type a search word or phrase in the Search online templates text box and press Enter, or click one of the Suggested searches links.**
   (If you don't need to search for a template, skip to Step 4.) Thumbnails or tiles and names for the matching templates appear in the middle section of the screen.

3. **To narrow the list of templates shown, click a category under Filter by in the right pane.**

4. **Click the thumbnail for the desired template.** Documents for the three direct templates discussed earlier will open immediately. For other templates, a preview for the template appears in its own window.

> **NOTE**
>
> When you see FEATURED and PERSONAL above the template thumbnails, it means you have saved a custom template. Click PERSONAL to find and select one of your custom templates.

5. **Click the Create button to download the template and create the new file.** The window displays a message that the template is downloading, and then the new document opens on-screen, showing a page for the envelope at top, and then a page for the letter itself.

The new document appears on-screen.

> **NOTE**
>
> Some of the templates available via `Office.com` were created in earlier Word versions. Those documents will open in Compatibility mode, which is described later in this chapter.

Working with template content

As shown in Figure 4.7, a template might hold a variety of sample contents and placeholders.

FIGURE 4.7

Replace template placeholders with your own content.

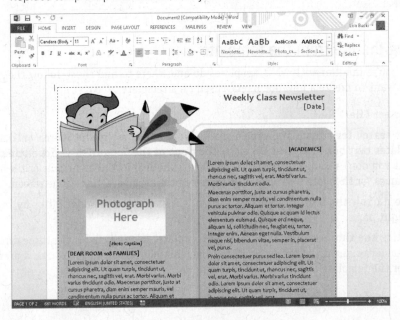

You can work with these placeholders and other contents as follows to finish your document:

- **Graphics placeholders:** The box in Figure 4.7 that says *Photograph Here* is a placeholder for a graphic. Click the placeholder to select it, click the Insert tab on the Ribbon, and then click the Pictures or Online Pictures choice in the Illustrations group to select a replacement item. Chapter 9, "Adding Tables and Graphics to a Document," provides more information about working with artwork in your Word documents.

- **Labels for text:** Some templates include lists of items with a colon after each. Clicking to the right of the colon for any of the label item places the insertion point at a precise position, ready for you to enter the text to go with the label.

- **Bracketed or gray field placeholders:** Template text that appears with square brackets and sometimes gray shading, such as the [Date], [Photo Caption], and other such fields shown in Figure 4.7, may be either content controls or text form fields. Clicking one of these placeholders selects the entire placeholder, and then any text you type replaces the placeholder contents.

- **Content controls:** These types of controls may feature automation such as a date picker, graphic selector, or linked entries. Click the control and make a selection or type to use it.

- **Other text:** You can supplement the template's contents by adding your own text anywhere in the document.

- **Styles:** Templates also include predefined styles (formatting) that you can apply to text that you add. See Chapter 7, "Using Styles to Create a Great Looking Document," to learn more about applying styles to text.

Opening an Existing File

Even the best writers revisit their work to edit and improve it. You will typically work on a given Word document any number of times, whether to correct spelling and grammar errors, rearrange information, update statistics and other details, or polish up the formatting.

You learned in Chapter 2 that you can choose File ⇨ Open to display a list of Recent documents, which you can pin or unpin for faster access. The left pane of the Word 2013 Start screen displays the list of Recent documents as well, and you can also pin and unpin files there by clicking the pushpin icon that appears when you point to the right side of the file name.

As you might guess, you can open an existing file by clicking it in the Recent files list on either the Word Start screen or the Open screen.

4

However, the Recent files list is dynamic, so if your document no longer appears there, you will need to navigate to it and open it from the location where you saved it. (The next section covers saving.) You can save documents to and open them from one of two overall locations from the Open screen:

- **Computer:** Clicking Computer displays Recent Folders that have been used for storing documents, which is by default set as your user My Documents folder (part of the Documents library by default) and Desktop folder (files on the desktop). If you click either of those folders or the Browse button, the Open dialog box appears, as shown in Figure 4.8. You can use it to navigate to other locations, including shared folders on your local network.

FIGURE 4.8

You can open files stored on your computer or network.

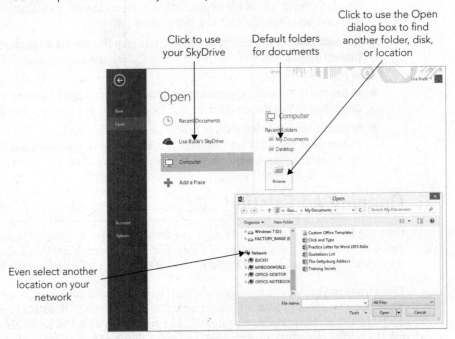

Click to use your SkyDrive

Default folders for documents

Click to use the Open dialog box to find another folder, disk, or location

Even select another location on your network

- **SkyDrive:** Microsoft hosts SkyDrive cloud storage. When you create a Microsoft account to sign in to Windows, your account automatically includes your own SkyDrive storage. To take advantage of that storage from within Word, sign in to Word with your Microsoft account information, and click your SkyDrive in the middle list shown in Figure 4.8. If you have installed the SkyDrive for Windows client application in Windows, that process sets up SkyDrive folders on your system that automatically sync with your SkyDrive storage in the cloud, so you can access those files from another computer or device if needed. Chapter 39, "Collaborating in the Cloud with SkyDrive," will show you how to set up and use SkyDrive. You can jump ahead to that chapter if you want to use SkyDrive in the near future.

NOTE

As mentioned in Chapter 2, if you've downloaded a Word file directly from the web, the Open list of places also includes an Other Web Locations choice. Click it to see websites from which you've downloaded files listed as Recent Folders at the right. If clicking a folder doesn't reconnect with the website as expected, right-click a choice and click Copy path to clipboard. You can then paste the path into your web browser's address bar and press Enter to return to the site from which you downloaded the file.

For now, use these steps to open a file that's not on the Recent files list:

1. **From the Word Start screen, click Open Other Documents; within Word, select File ⇨ Open.**

2. **Under Recent Folders, click My Documents, Desktop, or the Browse button.** All three choices display the Open dialog box, the difference being that both My Documents and Browse initially show the Documents library, whereas Desktop shows your user Desktop folder.

3. **Navigate to the desired folder using the Navigation pane at the left side of the Open dialog box or by double-clicking subfolder icons in the list of files.** In the Navigation pane, double-click a higher-level location such as Computer or Network to open its tree, and then navigate down through the tree by clicking the white triangles that appear beside computer, disk, and folder names to open those locations. Click the folder or subfolder that holds the file to open when you see it in the tree.

4. **Click the name of the file to open in the main file list, and then click the Open button.** Or simply double-click the file name when you see it.

TIP

You can still directly open a Word file by double-clicking it in a File Explorer (Windows 8) or Windows Explorer (Windows 7) window on the desktop. Use the Search box in the upper-right corner of a folder window in either operating system to search for a file. In Windows 8, you also can point to a right screen corner, click the Search charm, click Files in the right pane, and then type a file to search for in the text box under Search; if the desired file name appears, click it.

4

Saving and File Formats

As long as you see "Document1" in Word's title bar, you run the risk of losing your investment of time and creativity if a power surge zaps your computer or Word crashes. Even for previously saved files, you should save your work often to ensure that you won't have to redo much work should something go wrong. Saving in Word works as it does in most other apps, with a few variations based on how you want to use or ultimately share the document.

Saving as a Word file

The first time you save any file, even one created from a template, you will choose the location where you want to save it, and give the file a meaningful name. Word will suggest a name that's based on the first line of text in the document, but chances are it won't provide the benefit of making the file easy to find when you need to reopen it. I always recommend establishing a consistent file-naming system, particularly when you create many similar files. Including the date and client or contact person name in the file name are two tricks. For example, Smith Systems Marketing Plan 12-01-15 is more descriptive than Smith Marketing or even Smith Marketing v1. When viewing dated file names, you can easily see which one's the latest and greatest. Word automatically adds the .docx extension to every file saved in the default format. This section and the next present more ins and outs concerning file formats.

Here's how to save a file for the first time:

1. **Choose File ⇨ Save As or press Ctrl+S.** The Save As screen appears.
2. **Click Computer in the middle pane.** As noted earlier, you could leave your SkyDrive selected if installed, and save the file there. Chapter 39 describes that process.
3. **Under Computer, click a folder, or the Browse button.** Any choice displays the Save As dialog box, which is similar to the Open dialog box shown in Figure 4.8.
4. **Navigate to the desired folder using the Navigation pane at the left side of the Save As dialog box or by double-clicking subfolder icons in the list of files.** In the Navigation pane, double-click a higher-level location such as Computer or Network to open its tree, and then navigate down through the tree by clicking the white triangles that appear beside computer, disk, and folder names to open those locations. Click the folder or subfolder that holds the file you want to open when you see it in the tree.
5. **Select the contents of the File name text box by dragging over them with the insertion point if needed, and then type the desired file name.**
6. **Press Enter or click the Save button.** Word saves the file and returns to it on-screen.

After you've named the file, you can press Ctrl+S or choose File ⇨ Save to save the current document.

If you want to create a copy of the file, save it, and then choose File ⇨ Save As. This reopens the Save As dialog box. You can choose another save location and enter another file name, and then click Save to create the file copy. Changes you make to the copy appear only there. Save As is a quick and dirty alternative to setting up a template. The upside is that you may have less text to replace than with a template. The downside is that you may forget to update text that needs changing that otherwise would not have been in the template.

Converting to another format

Not every user immediately upgrades to the latest version of a particular program or uses the same platform as each of us. Nearly every Word user experiences a situation where they need to convert a document to another file format so someone else can open it on their computer or other device. And there may be instances where you need to save a document as a web page for addition to a website, as a PDF file that can be opened on an iPad, and so on. Word can handle other file formats for both incoming and outgoing files.

Converting a file from an earlier Word version

When you open a file in Word 2013 that was created in an earlier version of Word, [Compatibility Mode] appears in the title bar to the right of the file name. In this mode, some of the latest features in Word are disabled so that you can still use the file easily in an older Word version. In some cases, you may prefer to convert the file to the current Word format to take advantage of all Word's features. The only caution is that this can result in some layout changes to the document. If that's worth it to you, then by all means, convert the file. Even though Word 2007 and Word 2010 files use the same .docx file name extension as for Word 2013, the formats are not precisely identical, so even files from those versions may need to be converted.

1. **Choose File ⇨ Info.** The Info screen appears, with options for finalizing the current document file. As shown in Figure 4.9, a Convert button appears beside Compatibility Mode in the list of choices.

4

FIGURE 4.9

Convert a file to the current Word format and leave Compatibility Mode.

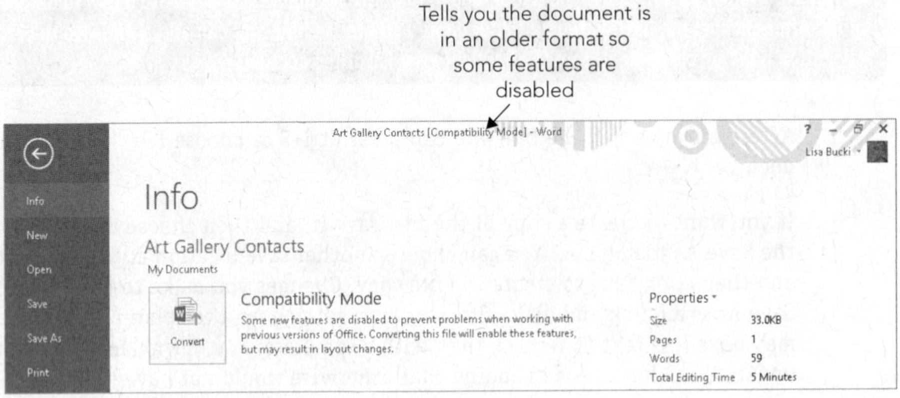

Tells you the document is
in an older format so
some features are
disabled

2. **Click Convert.** A message box appears, telling you that the document will be upgraded to the newest file format.

3. **Click OK.** Word changes the document to the Word 2013 .docx format and removes [Compatibility Mode] from the title bar.

4. **Save the file.**

CAUTION

Once converted, the previous version of the file is gone forever. If you think you might need the file in that previous version, such as to share it with other users, make a copy of the file or save the file under a new name *before* clicking Convert. The Convert option renames the original file — the .doc version will be gone. The first time you convert, Word does alert you to what it's doing, but if you're like most users you won't read the fine print and you'll click "Do not ask me again about converting documents." If you do happen to click that option, in the future there will be no warning — and if you're like me, you will forget it was there the first time.

When you convert, Word converts the document currently displayed to the Word 2013 .docx format. At this point you can still recover the original file by closing the file without saving the changes. Until you save, the converted file exists only in the current window.

Using Save As

The Save As dialog box includes a Save as type drop-down list directly below the File name text box. After you choose File ⇨ Save As, click Save as type to display the choices shown in Figure 4.10. Click a choice in the list, specify the file name, and then click Save. Word saves the file in the designated format, adding the file name extension for that format.

You might notice added behavior in the Save As dialog box when you select certain file types. For example, if you click Word Template, the folder specified for the save changes automatically. This is because storing your Office templates in a centralized location makes them easier to use. In an example like this, it's usually best to stick with the change suggested in the Save As dialog box and just click Save.

FIGURE 4.10

Use the Save as type drop-down to select another file format.

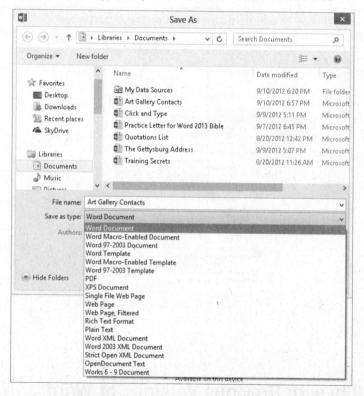

Using Export

If you need to save a file in another common format, you might choose to use the File ⇨ Export ⇨ Change File Type command instead. As shown in Figure 4.11, choosing this command opens an Export screen with a Change File Type list at the right. Word gives a small description of each of the file types there to make it easier to select the right one. Click the format to use, and then click Save As. Word opens the Save As dialog box with the specified format already selected for Save as type. From there, specify a file name and save location as usual, and click Save.

FIGURE 4.11

Learn more about and choose an alternate save format on the Export screen.

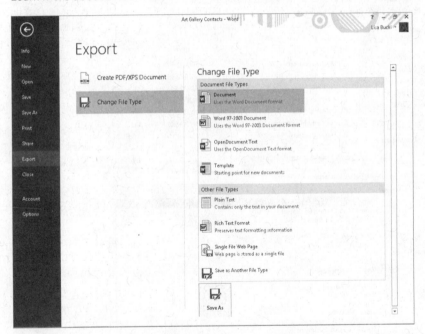

Compatibility with Previous Versions of Word

Between the 97 and 2003 versions of Word, the .doc file format remained basically unchanged. Feature enhancements, such as document versioning and floating tables, necessitated some modifications to the file format.

Even so, you can still open most Word 2003 files in Word 97 and the documents will look basically the same. Only if you use newer features will you see a difference, and usually that just means reduced functionality rather than lost data or formatting. However, when it comes to post-2003 versions of Word, file format changes introduce meaningful differences.

Understanding .docx

Word 2013, Word 2010, Word 2007, and Word 2003 users will continue to see interoperability. However, Word 2013's, 2010's, and 2007's "native" format is radically different — and better — than the old format. The new format boasts a number of improvements over the older format:

- **Open format:** The basic file is a ZIP format, an open standard, which serves as a container for .docx and .docm files. Additionally, many (but not all) components are in XML format (Extensible Markup Language). Microsoft makes the full specifications available free, and they may be used by anyone royalty-free. In time, this should improve and expand interoperability with products from software publishers other than Microsoft.

- **Compression:** The ZIP format is compressed, resulting in files that are much smaller. Additionally, Word's "binary" format has been mostly abandoned (some components, such as VBA macros, are still written in binary format), resulting in files that ultimately resolve to plain text and that are much smaller.

- **Robustness:** ZIP and XML are industry-standard formats with precise specifications that offer fewer opportunities to introduce document corruption. Hence, the frequency of corrupted Word files should be greatly reduced.

- **Backward-compatibility:** Though Word 2013, 2010, and 2007 have slightly different formats, they still fully support the opening and saving of files in legacy formats. A user can opt to save all documents in an earlier format by default. Moreover, Microsoft makes available a *Compatibility Pack* that enables Word 2000–2003 users to open and save in the new format. In fact, Word 2000–2003 users can make the .docx format their default, providing considerable interoperability among users of the different versions.

- **Extensions:** Word 2013 has four native file formats: .docx (ordinary documents), .docm (macro-enabled documents), .dotx (templates that cannot contain macros), and .dotm (templates that are macro-enabled, such as Normal.dotm).

Calling the x-file format "XML format" actually is a bit of a misnomer. XML is at the heart of Word's x format; however, the files saved by Word are not XML files. You can verify this by trying to open one using Internet Explorer. What you see is decidedly not XML. Some of the components of Word's x files, however, *do* use XML format.

Using the Compatibility Checker

Word runs an automatic compatibility check when you attempt to save a document in a format that's different from the current one. You can, without attempting to save, run this check yourself at any time from Word 2013. To see whether features might be lost in the move from one version of Word to another, open the document in Word 2013. Choose File ➪ Info ➪ Check for Issues ➪ Check Compatibility.

For the most part Word 2013 does a good job of checking compatibility when trying to save a native .docx file in .doc format. For example, if you run the Compatibility Checker on a Word 2013 document containing advanced features, you will be alerted, as shown in Figure 4.12.

4

FIGURE 4.12

Using the Compatibility Checker to determine whether converting to a different Word version will cause a loss of information or features.

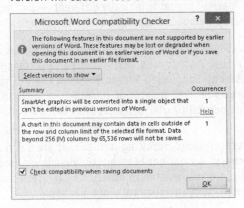

When moving in the other direction — checking a Word 2003 (or earlier) document for compatibility with Word 2013 — the checker usually will inform you that "No compatibility issues were found." Note, however, that the Compatibility Checker doesn't check when you first open a document formatted for Word 2003 (or earlier). It's not until you try to save the file that it warns you about any unlikely issues.

Choosing between .doc and .docx

Word's options enable you to choose to save in the older .doc format by default. A person may opt to do this, for example, if the majority of users in his or her organization still use Word 2003 or earlier. That's certainly a plausible argument, but consider one occasional down side to Word's binary .doc format. With a proprietary binary file format, the larger and more complex the document, the greater the possibility of corruption becomes, and it's not always possible to recover data from a corrupted file.

Another issue is document size. Consider a simple Word document that contains just the phrase "Hello, Word." When saved in Word 97–2003 format, that basic file is 26K. That is to say, to store those 11 characters it takes Word about 26,000 characters!

The same phrase stored in Word 2013's .docx format requires just 11K. Make no mistake: That's still a lot of storage space for just those 11 characters, but it's a lot less than what's required by Word 2003. The storage savings you get won't always be that dramatically different, but over time you will notice a difference. Smaller files mean not only lower storage requirements but faster communication times as well.

Still another issue is interoperability. When a Word user gives a .doc file to a user of WordPerfect or another word processor, it's typical that something is going to get lost in translation, even though WordPerfect claims to be able to work with Word's .doc format. Such documents seldom look identical or print identically, and the larger and more complex they are, the more different they look.

With Word's adoption of an open formatting standard, it is possible for WordPerfect and other programs to more correctly interpret how any given .docx file should be displayed. Just as the same web page looks and prints nearly identically when viewed in different web browsers, a Word .docx file should look and print nearly identically regardless of which program you use to open it (assuming it supports Word's .docx format).

Persistent Save As

If, despite the advantages of using the new format, you choose to use Word's .doc format, you can do so. Choose File ⇨ Options ⇨ Save tab. As shown in Figure 4.13, set Save files in this format to Word 97–2003 Document (*.doc).

FIGURE 4.13

You can tell Word to save in any of a variety of formats by default.

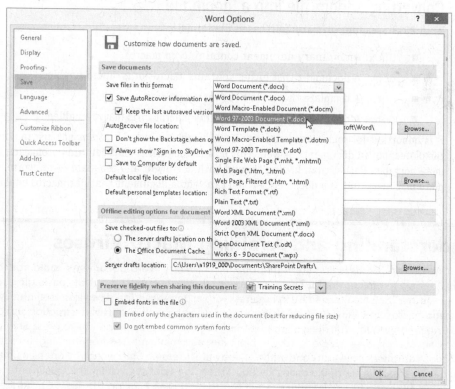

Note that even if you set .doc or some other format as your default you can still override that setting at any time by using Save As and saving to .docx or any other supported format. Setting one format as the default does not lock you out of using other formats as needed.

Microsoft Office Compatibility Pack

As of this writing, users of legacy versions of Word such as Word 2003 could open Word 2007, 2010, and 2013 files after installing a Compatibility Pack. While the Compatibility Pack was not developed specifically for Word 2013 files, in my testing, I was able to open a Word 2013 file in Word 2003 with the Compatibility Pack installed. The Compatibility Pack is a free downloads found at http://www.microsoft.com/en-us/download/details .aspx?id=3. Or, go to www.microsoft.com/en-us/download/default.aspx. Click in the Search Download Center text box at the top, type **Compatibility Pack**, and press Enter. Check the Search results for "Microsoft Office Compatibility Pack for Word, Excel, and PowerPoint File Formats," and download it. At this time, that was the latest version of the Compatibility Pack available, but it's possible an update could be released at a later time.

Converting a .docx file into a .docm file

Word 2013 uses four primary XML-based file formats:

- .docx: An ordinary document containing no macros
- .docm: A document that either contains macros or is macro-enabled
- .dotx: A template that does not contain macros
- .dotm: A template that either contains macros or is macro-enabled

It is important for some purposes for users to be able to include macros not just in document templates, but in documents as well. This makes documents that contain automation a lot more portable. Rather than having to send both document and template — or, worse, a template masquerading as a document — you can send a document that has macros enabled.

Understanding and Avoiding Macro Viruses

When Word macro viruses first started appearing, ordinary Word documents could not contain macros — only templates could. Therefore, one of the most popular ways of "packaging" macro viruses was in a .dot file that had been renamed with a .doc extension. The virus itself often was an automatic macro (typically AutoExec) that performed some combination of destruction and propagation when the rogue .dot file was first opened. A common precaution was to press Shift as you opened any Word file — .doc or .dot — to prevent automatic macros from running. In fact, even with various advances in security and antivirus software, pressing Shift when you open an unfamiliar Word document is still not being overly cautious. It's a good policy to check the Trust Center macro settings by choosing File ➪ Options ➪ Trust Center and then clicking the Trust Center Settings button. Make sure that Macro Settings is selected at the left side of the menu and that the Disable all macros with notification option is selected. With this setting enabled as it is by default, you will be prompted about whether to enable macros when you open a file that has them, as shown here.

Because Word 2003 documents can contain legitimate macros, there is no outward way to know whether any given .doc document file contains macros. If someone sends you a .doc file, is opening it safe?

Though it's not clear that the new approach — distinct file extensions for documents and templates that are macro-enabled — is going to improve safety a lot, it does provide more information for the user. This is true especially in business environments, where people don't deliberately change file extensions. If you see a file with a .docm or .dotm extension, you know that it likely contains macros, and that it might warrant careful handling.

If you want to convert a .docx file so that it can contain macros, you must use Save As and choose Word Macro-Enabled Document as the file type. You can do this at any time — it doesn't have to be when the document is first created. You can also remove any macros from a .docm file by saving it as a Word document (*.docx).

Even so, you can create or record a macro while editing a .docx file, and even tell Word to store it in a .docx file. There will be no error message, and the macro will be available for running in the current session. However, when you first try to save the file, you will be prompted to change the target format or risk losing the VBA project. If you save the file as a .docx anyway and close the file, the macro will not be saved.

Navigation and Selection Tips and Tricks

Bible readers already know the basics of using the Windows interface, so this book skips the stuff that I think every Windows user already knows about, and instead covers aspects of Word you might not know about. In our great hurry to get things done, ironically, we often overlook simple tricks and tips that might otherwise make our computing lives easier and more efficient.

Selecting text

When you want to make a change in Word, such as formatting text, you have to select it first. This limits the scope of the change to the selection only. Word lets you take advantage of a number of selection techniques that use the mouse or the mouse and keyboard together.

Dragging

Dragging is perhaps the most intuitive way to select text, and it works well if your selection isn't limited to a complete unit such as a word or sentence. Simply move the mouse pointer to the beginning of what you want to select, press and hold the left mouse button, move the mouse to extend the selection highlighting, and release the mouse button to complete the selection.

Triple-clicking

When you triple-click inside a paragraph, Word selects the entire paragraph. However, *where* you click makes a difference. If you triple-click in the left margin, rather than in a paragraph, and the mouse pointer's shape is the arrow shown in Figure 4.14, the entire document is selected.

FIGURE 4.14

A right-facing mouse pointer in the left margin indicates a different selection mode.

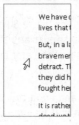

Is triple-clicking in the left margin faster and easier than pressing Ctrl+A, which also selects the whole document? Not necessarily, but it might be if your hand is already on the mouse. In addition, if you want the MiniBar to appear, the mouse method will summon it, whereas Ctrl+A won't.

Ctrl+clicking

Want something faster than triple-clicking? If you just happen to have one hand on the mouse and another on the keyboard, Ctrl+click in the left margin. That also selects the entire document and displays the Mini Toolbar.

If you Ctrl+click in a paragraph, the current sentence is selected. This can be handy when you want to move, delete, or highlight a sentence. As someone who sometimes highlights as I read, I also find that this can help me focus on a particular passage when I am simply reading rather than editing.

Alt+clicking

If you Alt+click a word or a selected passage, that looks up the word or selection using Office's Research pane. This method of displaying the Research pane can just be a little faster than selecting one of the Proofing group options on the Review tab.

Alt+dragging

You can use Alt+drag to select a vertical column of text — even if the text is not column oriented. This can be useful when you are working with *monospaced* fonts (where each character has the same width) and there is a de facto columnar setup. Note that if the text uses a *proportional font* (where character widths vary), the selection may appear to be irregular, with letters cut off as shown in Figure 4.15.

FIGURE 4.15

With the Alt key pressed, you can drag to select a vertical swath of text.

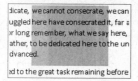

Shift+click

Click where you want a selection to start, and then Shift+click where you want it to end. You can continue Shift+clicking to expand or reduce the selection. This technique can be useful if you have difficulty dragging to highlight exactly the selection you want.

Multi-selecting

A few versions of Word ago, it became possible to make multiple noncontiguous selections in a document. While many know this, many more don't. To do it, make your first selection. Then, hold down the Ctrl key to make additional selections. Once you've made as many selections as you want, you can then apply the desired formatting to them, copy all of the selections to the Clipboard, paste the contents of the Clipboard over all of the selections, and so forth.

Using the Navigation pane

You can press Page Up or Page Down to scroll a document a screen at a time, but that can become tedious for a lengthy document such as a report or book chapter. Word includes a Navigation pane that enables you to use three quick methods for navigating in a document. To display the Navigation pane, check the View⇨Show⇨Navigation Pane check box visible in Figure 4.16.

FIGURE 4.16

Use the Navigation pane to move around a long document quickly.

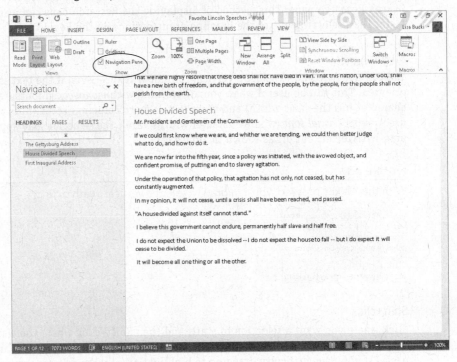

Once you've displayed the pane, here's how to use it:

- **Move between headings:** Click HEADINGS under the Search document text box, and then click the heading to jump to in the document. For example, in Figure 4.16, I've jumped to the "House Divided Speech" heading. Click the top bar to go back to the beginning of the document.

- **Move between pages:** Click PAGES to display page-by-page thumbnails of the document in the pane, scroll down the thumbnails, and then click the thumbnail for the page to go to.

- **Search and move between results:** This technique involves searching for text, displaying the RESULTS, and navigating to the found matches.

Clear the Navigation Pane check box or select the pane's Close (X) button to close the Navigation pane.

Keyboard shortcuts

Word 2013 continues to offer you the option of performing many tasks via keyboard short-cuts. If you're a highly skilled typist, using keyboard shortcuts can save time over using the mouse, because you never have to lift your hands off the keyboard. For example, say you're typing and want to underline a word for emphasis. Just before typing the word, press Ctrl+U to toggle underlining on. Type the word, and then press Ctrl+U again to toggle the underlining back off.

In addition to keyboard shortcuts for applying formatting, Word enables you to use keyboard shortcuts to navigate in a document, perform tasks such as inserting a hyperlink, or select commands from the Ribbon (using KeyTips, as described in Chapter 2). This section helps to round out your knowledge of keyboard shortcuts in Word 2013.

Creating a list of built-in keyboard shortcuts

Word boasts a broad array of keystrokes to make writing faster. If you've been using Word for a long time, you very likely have memorized a number of keystrokes (some of them that apply only to Word, and others not) that make your typing life easier. You'll be happy to know that most of those keystrokes still work in Word 2013.

Rather than provide a list of all of the key assignments in Word, here's how to make one yourself:

1. **Press Alt+F8.** The Macros dialog box appears.
2. **In the Macro name text box, type** listcommands.
3. **Click the Run button or press Enter.** The List Commands dialog box opens.
4. **Leave the Current keyboard settings options selected, and click OK or press Enter.** Word creates a new document with a table showing all of Word's current keyboard shortcuts.
5. **Save and name the file as desired.**

If you've reassigned any built-in keystrokes to other commands or macros, your own assign-ments appear in place of Word's built-in assignments. If you've redundantly assigned any keystrokes, all assignments will be shown. For example, Word assigns Alt+F8 to ToolsMacro. If you also assigned Ctrl+Shift+O to it, your commands table would include both assign-ments. The table also shows those assignments and commands you haven't customized.

> **TIP**
> If you want a list of Word's default built-in assignments, open Word in safe mode (hold down the Ctrl key as Word is starting and then click Yes) and run the listcommands macro again as just described.

Office 2003 menu keystrokes

One of Microsoft's aims was to assign as many legacy menu keystrokes as possible to the equivalent commands in Word 2007, 2010, and 2013, so if you're used to pressing Alt+I,B to choose Insert ➪ Break in Word 2003, you'll be glad to know it still works. So does Alt+OP, for Format ➪ Paragraph.

Now try Alt+HA for Help ➪ About. It doesn't work. In fact, none of the Help shortcuts work, because that Alt+H shortcut is reserved for the Ribbon's Home tab. Some others don't work, either.

Some key combinations can't be assigned because the corresponding commands have been eliminated. There are very few in that category. Some other legacy menu assignments haven't been made in Word 2013 because there are some conflicts between how the new and old keyboard models work. There are, for example, some problems with Alt+F because that keystroke is used to select the File tab. For now at least, Microsoft has resolved to use a different approach for the Alt+F assignments. Press Alt+I and then press Alt+F to compare the different approaches.

Custom keystrokes

You can also make your own keyboard assignments. To get a sneak peek, choose File ➪ Options ➪ Customize Ribbon, and then click the Customize button beside Keyboard shortcuts under the left-hand list.

If you prefer to highly customize the keyboard shortcuts, you can assign Alt+K (it's unassigned by default) to the `ToolsCustomizeKeyboard` command. Then, whenever you see something you want to assign, pressing Alt+K will save you some steps. To assign Alt+K to that command:

1. **Choose File ➪ Options ➪ Customize Ribbon.** The Customize Ribbon choices appear in the Word Options dialog box.

2. **Click the Customize button to the right of Keyboard shortcuts, below the left list.** The Customize Keyboard dialog box opens.

3. **Scroll down the Categories list, and click All Commands.**

4. **Click in the Commands list, and press the T key to skip to the Ts.**

5. **Scroll down and click ToolsCustomizeKeyboard.**

6. **Click in the Press new keyboard shortcut key text box, and then press Alt+K (or whatever other assignment you might find preferable or more memorable).** Make sure that the Save changes in drop-down list has Normal selected, so the keyboard shortcut change will be saved to the default document template.

7. **Click Assign, and then click Close, and click Cancel to dismiss the Word Options dialog box.** If you've told Word to prompt before saving changes in `Normal.dotm`, make sure you say Yes to saving this change (when prompted).

Choosing the Right Word View for the Task at Hand

To expand the ways of working with documents, Word offers a number of different environments you can use, called *views*. For reading and performing text edits on long documents with a minimum of UI (user interface) clutter, you can use the Read Mode view. For composing documents and reviewing text and basic text formatting, you can choose a fast-display view called Draft view.

For working with documents containing graphics, equations, and other nontext elements, where document design is a strong consideration, there's Print Layout view. If the destination of the document is online (Internet or Intranet), Word's Web Layout view removes paper-oriented screen elements, enabling you to view documents as they would appear in a web browser.

For organizing and managing a document, Word's Outline view provides powerful tools that enable you to move whole sections of the document around without having to copy, cut, and paste. An extension of Outline view, Master Document view enables you to split large documents into separate components for easier management and workgroup sharing.

Change to most of the views using the Views group of the Ribbon's View tab.

Print Layout

Print Layout is Word 2013's default view, and one that many users will be comfortable sticking with. One of Word 2013's strongest features, Live Preview, works only in Print Layout and Web Layout views.

Print Layout view shows your document exactly as it will print, with graphics, headers and footers, tables, and other elements in position. (One exception: Although you can see comments in this view, they do not print by default.) It presents an accurate picture of the margin sizes and page breaks, so you will have a chance to page through the document and make design adjustments, such as adding manual page breaks to balance pages or using shading and paragraph borders to set off text. Figure 4 .17 shows this workhorse view.

4

FIGURE 4.17

Print Layout view reproduces how the printed document will look.

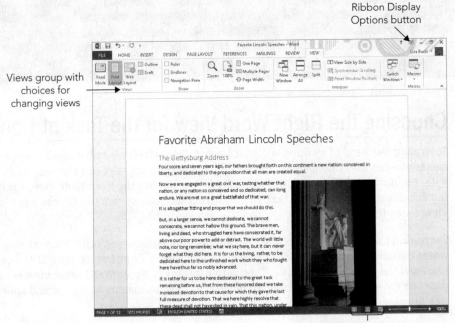

Ribbon Display Options button

Views group with choices for changing views

Read Mode, Print Layout, and Web Layout buttons

Change back to this view at any time with View ⇨ Views ⇨ Print Layout, or click the Print Layout button on the status bar, near the zoom slider.

Draft view

When you want to focus on crafting the text of your document, you can turn to Draft view. Choose View ⇨ Views ⇨ Draft to flip your document to this view. Draft view hides all graphics and the page "edges" so that more text appears on-screen. By default, it continues to display using the styles and fonts designated in the document.

You can further customize Draft view to make the text even plainer. Choose File ⇨ Options. In Word's Options dialog box, click Advanced at the left, and then scroll down to the Show document content section. Near the bottom of the section, notice the option to Use draft font in Draft and Outline views. Check this option to enable it, and then use the accompanying Name and Size drop-downs to select the alternate text appearance. Click OK to apply the changes. For an example, Figure 4.18 shows Draft view customized to use 10 pt. Courier New font for all styles.

FIGURE 4.18

You can customize Draft view to use a plainer font.

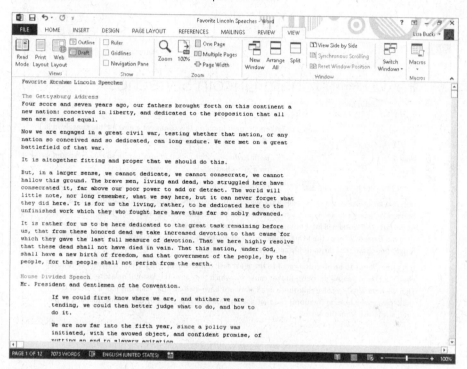

Read Mode and object zoom

Read Mode, new in Word 2013, displays a limited number of tools, zooms the document to a larger size, and repaginates it for reading. You can't edit document text in this view, but you can move and resize other objects, such as pictures. Use the arrow buttons to the left and right of the text to page through the text. (This latter functionality seems tailor made for touch-enabled devices.) Use this mode's View menu to change some of the on-screen features. For example, as shown in Figure 4.19, you can choose another page background color to make your eyes more comfortable while reading. You also can display and hide the Navigation pane or Comments, change Column with, or change the overall Layout of the view. The Tools menu enables you to find document contents or search the web with Microsoft's Bing for a highlighted text selection.

FIGURE 4.19

Kick back and enjoy your document's contents in Read Mode.

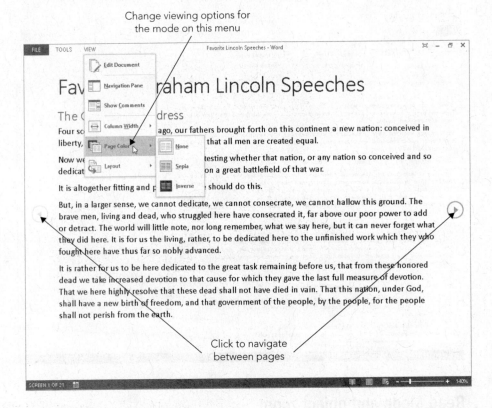

Change viewing options for the mode on this menu

Click to navigate between pages

One great feature of the Read Mode view is that it enables you to zoom in on graphics in the document. Double-click a graphic to display the zoomed version of it, as shown in Figure 4.20. Clicking the button with the magnifying glass at the upper-right corner of the zoomed content zooms in one more time. To close the zoomed object, press Esc or click outside it on the page.

If you want, you can use the Auto-hide Reading Toolbar button at the upper-right to hide even the few menus in the view. From there, you can click the three dots near the upper-right to temporarily redisplay the tools, or click Always Show Reading Toolbar to toggle them back on.

FIGURE 4.20

Double-click a graphic to zoom in on it in Read Mode.

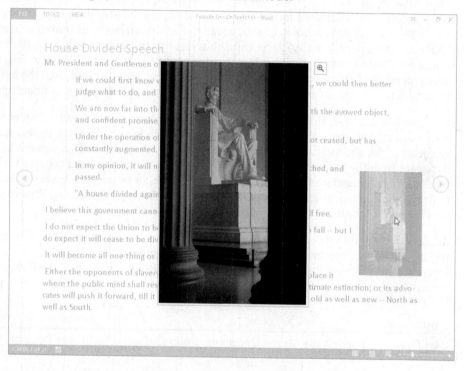

To exit Read Mode, you can click the Print Layout view button on the Status bar, or press Esc. In some cases, when Always Show Reading Toolbar is not toggled on, you may need to press Esc twice to exit Read Mode.

TIP

In addition to the arrow buttons on the screen, Read Mode offers a variety of ways to scroll the document pages: Page Down/Page Up, Space/Shift+Space, Enter/Shift+Enter, Right/Left arrow keys, Down/Up arrow keys, and the scroll wheel on your mouse.

Web Layout

Web Layout is designed for composing and reviewing documents that will be viewed online rather than printed. Hence, information such as page and section numbers is excluded from the status bar. If the document contains hyperlinks, they are displayed underlined by default. Background colors, pictures, and textures are also displayed.

Outline (Master Document tools)

The final distinct Word view is Outline (View ➪ Views ➪ Outline). Outlining is one of Word's most powerful and least-used tools for writing and organizing your documents. Using Word's Heading styles is one way to take advantage of this tremendous resource. Heading levels one through nine are available through styles named Heading 1 through Heading 9. You don't need to use all nine levels — most users find that the first three or four are adequate for most structured documents. If your document is organized with the built-in heading levels, then a wonderful world of document organization is at your fingertips.

As an outline manager, this view can be used on any document with heading styles that are tied to outline levels. (If you don't want to use Word's built-in Heading styles, you can use other styles and assign them to different outline levels. Additionally, you can build a document from the headings found in Outline view. You can expand and collapse text to focus on different sections of the document as you work, or to see an overview of how the topics in your document are flowing. Click Outlining ➪ Close ➪ Close Outline View to finish working with outlining.

As suggested by the title of this section, Outline view has a split personality, of sorts. Outline view's other personality includes the Master Document tools. As shown in Figure 4.21, if you click Show Document in the Master Document group of the Outlining Ribbon tab, additional tools appear.

FIGURE 4.21

Click Show Document in the Master Document group to display the Master Document tools.

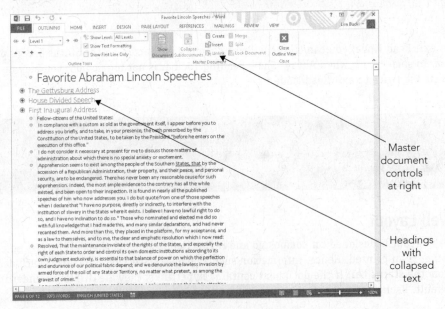

Resume Reading

Word 2013 includes a new Resume Reading feature. When you reopen a document you were previously editing, and the insertion point was on a page beyond page 1 when you closed the file, a prompt appears at the right side of the screen asking if you want to go back to the page you were last working on, as shown in Figure 4.22. Click the pop-up to go to the specified location. If you don't initially click the message, it shrinks to a smaller pop-up with a bookmark icon on it. You can move the mouse over it or click it to redisplay the message, and then click to jump to the later spot in the document. Scrolling the document makes the pop-up disappear.

FIGURE 4.22

Click the pop-up to return to the page you were last working on before you close the document.

Showing and hiding rulers

Another sometimes-overlooked tool is the ruler. It's useful for aligning and positioning text and other objects, which you'll learn about in later chapters. The ruler toggles on and off via the View ⇨ Show ⇨ Ruler check box.

Splitting the view

Choose View ⇨ Window ⇨ Split to divide the document window into two equal panes.

This feature comes in handy when you need to look at a table or a figure on one page of a document while you write about it on another page.

As another example, you might want to have one view of your document in one pane while using another view in the other, as shown in Figure 4.23. When viewing a document in two split panes, note that the status bar reflects the status of the currently active pane. Not only can you display different views in multiple panes, but you can display them at different zoom levels as well.

4

FIGURE 4.23

Split panes can display different views.

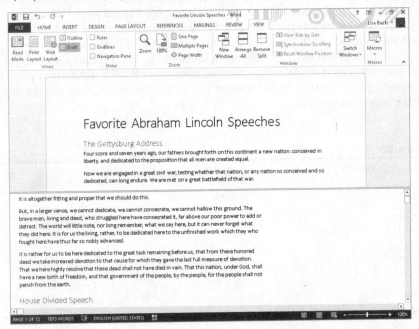

You can remove the split by dragging it up or down to the top or bottom of the screen, leaving the desired view in place, or double-clicking anywhere on the split line. Alternatively, Choose View ⇨ Window ⇨ Remove Split.

Summary

In this chapter you've learned basic yet essential skills for creating and working with document files, using file formats, navigating a document, and more. Putting it all together, you should now have no problem doing the following:

- Creating a document using a blank template or one with predefined content.
- Opening a document you've already saved.
- Saving a document or copy, including choosing another format.
- Navigating issues of file formats and compatibility.
- Selecting text and moving between pages and headings.
- Using Word's views and view tools.

Font/Character Formatting

In some early word processors, users applied text formatting by inserting formatting codes. For example, you had to add a code to turn on bold formatting, and add a second code to turn bold off later. Text between the codes was bold. This method of relying on a pair of codes often tripped up users. Accidentally delete one code in the pair, and you inadvertently changed the formatting for half the document.

Rather than letting you turn formatting on or off for a string of characters, Word uses an object-oriented formatting approach. In Word, you format objects such as letters, words, paragraphs, tables, pictures, and so on.

Another way to think about formatting is in *units*. Formatting can be applied to any unit you can select. The smallest unit that can be formatted is a single character. Discrete units larger than characters are words, sentences, paragraphs, document sections, and the whole document. Some types of formatting apply only to certain type of units. For example, you can't indent a single word; indention is a paragraph-level setting that applies to some or all of the lines in a paragraph.

Reviewing the Ways You Can Format Text in Word

Word has four levels of formatting: character/font, paragraph, section, and document. Character or font formatting includes bold, italic, points, superscript, and other attributes. You can apply character formats to a unit as small as a single character. Later chapters cover the other levels of formatting.

Font formatting might suggest for many people just changing from one font or typestyle design (for example Calibri, Times New Roman, Arial, or Tahoma) to another. The term *character formatting* used in this book more broadly encompasses all the formatting settings you can change for characters, but because Word positions all of these settings in a group called Font, as shown in Figure 5.1, font formatting and character formatting have come to be used interchangeably. It helps, however, to think in terms of character formatting, as a character is the smallest thing you can format in Word.

FIGURE 5.1

Find many character or font formatting settings in the Home tab's Font group.

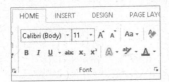

> **NOTE**
>
> You also may see the term *text level formatting* in the Word interface; this term means the same thing as character formatting.

Note also that the Font group in the Home tab does not offer all the available character-level formatting. For example, the Font group doesn't include a tool for changing character spacing. In addition, the Font group's Change Case button (its menu has Sentence case, lowercase, and other commands) doesn't change formatting at all. Changing capitalization is distinct from applying the Small caps and All caps character formatting settings to text.

Formatting Characters Directly or with Styles

Word includes paragraph styles and character styles. *Paragraph styles* can be applied only to a whole paragraph. *Character styles* provide formatting flexibility so that users can apply a style to characters within a paragraph. For example, you can create a style for all the article titles used within a document, or all the phone numbers, or all the web page addresses. Character styles enable you to distinguish one type of formal text from the surrounding paragraph text, and to do so consistently throughout the document.

A third type of style is a *linked style*. A linked style can behave like either a character or paragraph style, depending on the circumstances. If you have one or more entire words selected, selecting a linked style applies the style's character formatting to the selected words within the paragraph only. (Paragraph formatting such as line spacing is ignored.) The rest of the paragraph retains its original paragraph formatting. If you select the entire paragraph or merely place the insertion point within the paragraph without selecting any words, then an applied linked style behaves like a paragraph style, formatting the text with both the character and paragraph settings of the linked style. A number of the default styles in the `Normal.dotm` default template, including the heading styles, are linked styles.

The alternative to applying a character style is applying character formatting directly. As you're typing along, it's quite easy to use the Font group choices or shortcut keys to apply bold, italic, or underlining to text. That's called *direct formatting*, and often this is the easiest and fastest way to format text, particularly within a paragraph.

Word's default document template includes dozens of built-in styles, and Word gives you clues to help identify paragraph styles versus character styles, linked styles that you can use both ways, and direct formatting applied to text. Use the Styles pane (task pane) and Style Inspector to learn more about the styles and formatting applied to the selected text and also the styles that are available.

1. **Select the text that has the formatting you want to examine.**

2. **Click the dialog box launcher in the Styles group of the Home tab.** The Styles task appears. As shown in Figure 5.2, a symbol appears to the right of each style name. These symbols identify the type of style:

   - **Paragraph symbol:** A paragraph style that can only be applied to whole paragraphs.

   - **Lowercase a character:** A character style that that can be applied to selected text within a paragraph without changing the entire paragraph's formatting.

   - **Both a paragraph symbol and a lowercase a character:** A linked style you can use either as a paragraph or character style. With the insertion point in the paragraph, applying the style formats the whole paragraph. With text selected in the paragraph, applying the style formats only the selected text.

3. **Click the Style Inspector (middle) icon at the bottom of the Styles pane.** The Style Inspector, also shown in Figure 5.2, opens. As you can see in Figure 5.2, this pane identifies the styles and formatting applied to the selected text:

   - **Paragraph formatting:** Shows the applied paragraph style, Normal in this example.

   - **Text level formatting:** Shows the applied character style, if any. In this example, the Subtle Emphasis style is also applied to the selected word within the paragraph.

   - **Plus: boxes:** Lists any direct character formatting applied in addition to the applied styles.

5

FIGURE 5.2

Examine the styles and formatting applied to selected text in the Styles pane and Style Inspector.

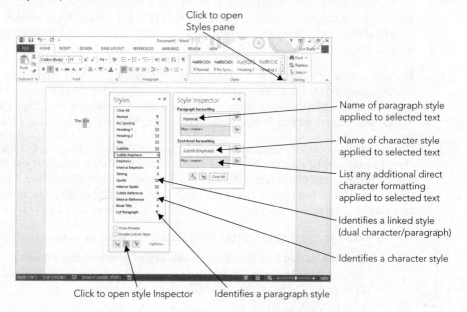

Click to open Styles pane

Name of paragraph style applied to selected text

Name of character style applied to selected text

List any additional direct character formatting applied to selected text

Identifies a linked style (dual character/paragraph)

Identifies a character style

Click to open style Inspector

Identifies a paragraph style

4. Click the Close (X) button on the Style Inspector and Styles pane to close them.

Given that creating and applying styles involves more thought, preparation, and work than using direct formatting, compare the pros and cons of each with regard to speed and functionality when creating and updating a document. Say you are creating a marketing document for your company's new product, and you want the product name to appear in bold throughout the document. You could apply the bold formatting directly by pressing Ctrl+B (for bold), typing the product name, and then pressing Ctrl+B again to toggle bold off each time you type the product name.

Next your boss decides the product name should appear in bold and small caps. Because chances are you've also bolded other text in the document, you would have to manually find and reformat each instance of the product name to include the new small caps direct format.

If instead you had created a new character style named Product Name and applied it to each instance of the product name, you could simply modify the Product Name style to include the small caps formatting, and all product name instances would immediately display the new formatting.

The commandment is this: *If the formatting is something you will need to repeatedly apply to certain categories of text (such as book titles, programming commands, product names, jargon, and so on), create a character style and use it.*

If conversely the use is *ad hoc* and not something for which you'll have a recurring need, then go ahead and use direct formatting. For example, when you're writing a letter or memo, you may want to use bold or italics for emphasis. In those cases, using direct formatting fits the bill.

> **TIP**
>
> To streamline using styles, you can assign keyboard shortcuts to some of them. From Word Options (File ⇨ Options), select the Customize Ribbon tab and click the Customize button beside Keyboard shortcuts. Choose Styles in the Categories list. Click the desired style in the Styles list, click in the Press new shortcut key text box, press the desired keys (the exact combination you want to assign, such as Alt+9 or Ctrl+Shift+F7), and then click Assign. Click Close to close the Customize Keyboard dialog box, and then click OK to close the Word Options dialog box.

Applying Character Formatting

There are at least six ways of directly applying various kinds of character formatting:

- Using the Font group on the Home tab of the Ribbon
- Using the Font dialog box (Ctrl+D or Ctrl+Shift+F, or click the Font group dialog box launcher)
- Using the Mini Toolbar (hover the mouse over selected text)
- Using keyboard shortcuts (See Table 5.1 later in this chapter or the topic Keyboard shortcuts for Microsoft Word in Word Help to learn about shortcuts beyond those presented in this chapter.)
- Using the Font group's tools or buttons added to the Quick Access Toolbar (QAT)
- Using the Language tool on the status bar

This section describes these methods and gives a sense of which ones to use. A lot depends on your working style, but your choice can also depend on what you happen to be doing. On any given day many users may take advantage of at least five of the six methods.

Formatting techniques

To apply character formatting, you have three basic options:

- **As you go method:** Apply formatting before you start typing a word or passage, and then turn it off when you're done. For example, click the Bold button in the Font group of the Home tab, type a word, and then click the Bold button again.

5

- **Selection method:** Select the text you want formatted and then apply the formatting.
- **Whole-word method:** Click anywhere in a word and then choose the desired formatting.

It would be redundant to repeat the basic steps for each and every formatting type. The techniques described here apply to all character formatting described in this chapter.

Repeating formatting (F4)

You can save a lot of time in Word by using the Repeat or Redo command keyboard shortcut, F4. Pressing F4 will repeat whatever you just did, from typing what you just typed again to repeat formatting.

Suppose for example that you're scanning a newsletter looking for people's names, which need to be made bold. You see the name John Smith, so you select it and press Ctrl+B. Thereafter, however, it might be faster to position one hand on the mouse and the other on the F4 key. From there, you can repeat the formatting on individual words or phrases. For example, if Jane Doe is the next name you find after John Smith, you could double-click on Jane, press F4, double-click on Doe, and press F4 again. Or, you could drag over Jane Doe to select both the first and last name, and then press F4. The F4 key enables you to temporarily forget about pressing Ctrl+B, right-clicking, or traveling to the top of the Word menu in search of a formatting tool.

Note that F4 and Ctrl+Y both can reapply formatting. Which you use is your choice. Many prefer F4 because it can be pressed with one finger. Others prefer Ctrl+Y because it doesn't involve as much of a stretch as F4. If you use Ctrl+Y, just make sure that you don't perform any other action after applying formatting, as Ctrl+Y redoes the most recent action.

Copying formatting

If you don't want to use a character style but still need to apply numerous formatting settings to selected text, you can use one of two common methods for copying formatting: the Format Painter and the shortcut key combinations for copying and pasting formatting. Note that these tools aren't limited to direct formatting. They'll work with style formatting as well.

Format painter

To use the Format Painter, click or drag to select the text with the formatting you want to copy. If you want to clone that formatting just once, click the Format Painter button in the Clipboard group on the Home tab, shown in Figure 5.3. If you want to apply that formatting multiple times, double-click the Format Painter. The mouse pointer changes to include a paintbrush.

FIGURE 5.3

Use the Format Painter in the Clipboard group to copy formatting.

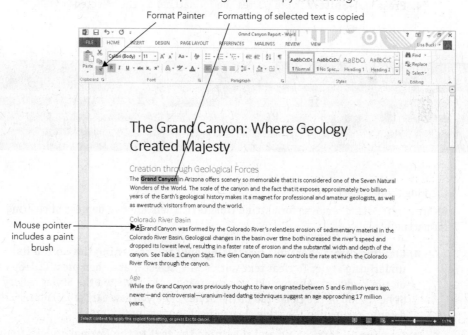

To copy the formatting to a single word, double-click the word. Otherwise, drag over the destination text to format. If you double-clicked the Format Painter, repeat making selections until you're done applying the copied formatting. Press Esc or click the Format Painter again to deactivate it.

Keyboard method

If you prefer to use keyboard shortcuts for your formatting work where possible, use this method to copy and paste formatting:

1. **Select the text with the formatting to copy.**
2. **Press Ctrl+Shift+C.** This keyboard shortcut copies the formatting of the selected text.
3. **Select the text on which you want to paste the copied formatting.**
4. **Press Ctrl+Shift+V.** Word pastes the formatting on the selected text.

Clearing formatting

Clearing formatting removes formatting from text. There are two degrees of clearing formatting:

- **Clearing direct character formatting only and returning the text to its underlying style:** To clear text in this way, select it and then press Ctrl+Spacebar on the keyboard. Alternately, you can reapply the style via the Styles gallery in the Styles group of the Home tab or the Styles pane you saw earlier in Figure 5.2. By default, reapplying the style clears direct formatting.

- **Clearing all formatting and returning the text to the Normal style:** After you select the text to return to the Normal style, click the Clear Formatting button in the Font group of the Home tab, shown in Figure 5.4. You also can click Clear All at the top of the Styles pane. Using these commands is the equivalent of copying a selection to the Clipboard and then using Home ⇨ Clipboard ⇨ Paste arrow ⇨ Paste Special ⇨ Unformatted Text to paste it back into the document.

FIGURE 5.4

The Clear Formatting tool removes not only direct formatting, but also paragraph and style formatting.

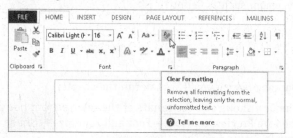

Using the Font group on the Home tab

Figure 5.5 shows you the Font group of the Home tab. It includes more than a dozen direct formatting tools on two rows. Figure 5.5 identifies some of the tools in the group that offer formatting options you may not have considered previously, beyond the typical bold, italics, and underlining.

FIGURE 5.5

The Font group puts character formatting choices a mouse click away.

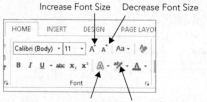

The pictures on some of the buttons in the Font group—such as Bold, Italic, and Underline—make their purpose obvious. The other buttons might call for more clarification. Hover the mouse pointer over each of the controls to see what it does. Notice that for many of the controls, shortcut keys are indicated in the ScreenTip. Some tools, for whatever reason, might not show shortcuts. Jump ahead to the "Character formatting keyboard shortcuts" section later in this chapter if you're just dying to know what's assigned to what.

A number of the Font tools offer a Live Preview to help you make the best formatting selection:

- Font (the overall type design, such as Calibri)
- Font Size
- Text Highlight Color
- Font color
- Text Effects and Typography (which you'll see later in the chapter)

As shown in Figure 5.6, Live Preview shows you the results of the selected (but not yet applied) formatting. Two of the Live Preview controls—Font and Font Size—can be rolled up and out of the way, as shown in Figure 5.6. The others cannot.

FIGURE 5.6

Live Preview shows how the selected font would look when applied.

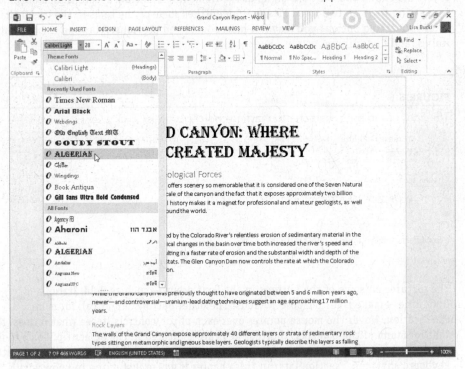

As shown in Figure 5.5, there's also the Font dialog box launcher, in the lower-right corner of the Font group. Clicking it opens the Font dialog box, which you'll learn more about later in the chapter.

Font

As noted earlier, the font defines the overall appearance or style of text lettering. The fonts you apply are key to a document's appearance, formality, and readability. Windows includes dozens of built-in fonts you can apply in your documents, and you can find literally thousands more online that you can buy and install.

Use the Font drop-down list at the left end of the top row of the Font group of the Home tab to apply another font to selected text. Click the control's down arrow, scroll to display the available fonts, point to a font to see a Live Preview (refer to Figure 5.6), and then click the font to apply.

TIP

Limit the number of fonts used in a document to two or three to achieve a consistent look. Generally speaking, use one font for headings, one for body text, and one for special elements that you might want to emphasize, such as quotes or sidebars.

NOTE

If you have purchased or other acquired unique fonts and installed them on your system, keep in mind that other users with whom you share documents may not have those fonts. When a document uses such a font, the text formatted with that font may not display or print correctly on other users' systems. To help avoid such problems, you can embed the fonts used in a document when saving. To turn on font embedding, choose File ⇨ Options ⇨ Save. Under Preserve fidelity when sharing this document, click the Embed fonts in the file check box to check it. To embed only needed characters, also check Embed only the characters used in the document (best for reducing file size). You also can leave Do not embed common system fonts checked. Click OK to apply the settings change.

Font size

Font or Point Size controls the height of the font, generally measured in points. A point is 1/72 of an inch, so 12 points would be 12/72 (or 1/6) of an inch. For Word, a font set's point size is the vertical distance from the top of the highest ascending character to the bottom of the lowest descending character.

Use the Font Size drop-down list just to the right of the Font control in the Font group of the Ribbon to choose a size for selected text. You aren't limited to the range of sizes you see in the Font Size drop-down list. Word can go as low as one point and as high as 1,638 points. Plus, you can set the height in increments of half a point. Hence, a point size of 1637.5 is perfectly valid. To apply a size not included in the drop-down list, select the number shown in the Font Size control, type a new size, and press Enter.

5

NOTE

The ScreenTips for the Font and Font Size controls give shortcut key combinations of Ctrl+Shift+F and Ctrl+Shift+P, respectively, for the tools. These shortcut key combos do not activate the tools on the Ribbon. Instead, the shortcuts open the Font dialog box and you can select the applicable formatting setting there.

Increase font size and decrease font size

You also can change text size with the Increase Font Size and Decrease Font Size tools (which are the two A buttons immediately to the right of the Font and Font Size tools in Figure 5.5). If you hover the mouse pointer over these you'll also learn that they both have shortcuts, Ctrl+Shift+. (the period character) and Ctrl+Shift+' (the apostrophe character), respectively.

NOTE

The ScreenTips actually identify the shortcut key combinations as Ctrl+> and Ctrl+<, and technically that's right because > and < are a shifted period and comma, respectively. Presenting them both ways here will help you know exactly what keys to press.

If you click the drop-down arrow next to the Font Size tool, you'll notice that the font sizes listed do not consistently increase by twos. Instead, they go from 8 to 12 in increments of one, then from 12 to 28 in increments of two, and then leap to 36, 48, and 72. The Increase and Decrease Font Size tools follow the listed increments.

If you want a finer degree of control (for example, when you're trying to make text as large as possible without spilling onto an additional page), you should know about two additional default shortcut keys: Ctrl+[and Ctrl+]. These two commands shrink or enlarge the selected characters by one point. The extra granularity often is just what you need to find the largest possible font you can fit inside a given space, such as a page, table, or text box.

Working with text color

Word has three color settings that you can apply at the character level:

- **Font Color:** The color of the characters themselves
- **Shading:** The color of the background immediately behind the text
- **Text Highlight Color:** The electronic equivalent of those neon-colored felt markers you use to focus your attention on key points buried within text

Font color

The Font Color setting determines the colors of the lettering for the selected text. Click the Text Color drop-down arrow in the Font group of the Home tab to open a palette or gallery of colors, as shown in Figure 5.7.

FIGURE 5.7

Changing text color

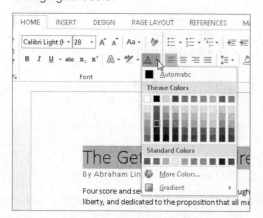

The theme applied to the document determines the available colors shown under Theme Colors in the gallery. The Automatic choice at the top can be black or white, and is based on the shading applied to the text. If the shading is so dark that black text can't be read without difficulty, Word automatically switches the Automatic color to white. The Standard Colors choices are the same no matter what theme is applied. You can click one of the colors under Theme Colors or Standard Colors to apply it to the selected text, or you can use the More Colors or Gradient choices to apply custom colors of blends of colors to the text.

Shading

Given that the Shading tool appears in the Paragraph group of the Ribbon, you might be tempted to believe that shading is paragraph-level formatting. Indeed, with nothing selected, your Shading choice applies to the entire current paragraph holding the insertion point.

However, if you select a single word or character, Shading suddenly acts like a character-formatting attribute. In reality, that's what it is. Because people seldom vary the shading within any given paragraph, Word includes it with the other paragraph formatting settings. And yet, just like font, font/point size, bold, and italic, shading is a character attribute.

As shown in Figure 5.8, the combination of the Shading and Font Color settings both contribute to the readability of the text. There needs to be adequate contrast between the two in order for the document to remain readable.

FIGURE 5.8

Despite its position in the Paragraph group of the Home tab, shading can be applied to a selection of characters.

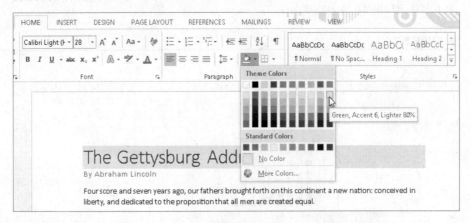

Text Highlight Color

The Text Highlight Color control — more generally known as the *highlighter* — is shown just to the left of the Font Color control in Figure 5.7. It actually has four modes of operation. Most people are aware of one mode or another, but not all four.

One method is to select text and then click the Text Highlight Color button in the Font group. This method, which directly applies the currently selected highlight color to the selected text, is the one that most users know and use. To change the highlight color, click the drop-down arrow and click a color in the gallery.

> **TIP**
>
> If you use this first highlight method, Word undoes the selection after you apply highlighting. This can be irritating if you use the wrong color, but if you immediately press Ctrl+Z or click Undo, Word not only undoes the highlighting, it also reselects that section of text so you can take another stab at highlighting it.

A second method is to select the first area of text to highlight and then turn the highlighter on by double-clicking the Text Highlight Color button; and then to use the mouse to drag over additional areas you want highlighted. The highlighter mouse pointer applies the currently selected highlight color and stays active until you click the Text Highlight Color button again, or until you press the Esc key.

A third method can be used to apply highlighting to all occurrences of a given word or phrase in a document, using the most recently applied highlighting color:

1. **Click the arrow for the Find button in the Editing group of the Home tab, and click Advanced Find.** The Find dialog box opens.

2. **Type the word or phrase to highlight in the Find what text box.**

3. **Click Reading Highlight⇨Highlight All, as shown in Figure 5.9.** The figure also illustrates the result of applying the reading highlight to the specified word, nation. Several instances of the word are highlighted throughout the document. Note that you can use the Clear Highlighting choice on the Reading Highlight drop-down to remove the highlighting from the specified word or phrase.

FIGURE 5.9

Use Find to apply a reading highlight to every occurrence of a word or phrase in your document.

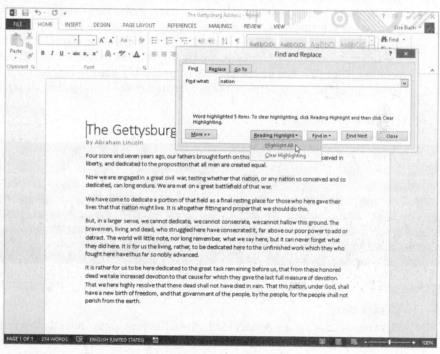

4. **Click Close.** The Find and Replace dialog box closes.

A fourth highlighting method might be even more useful than the Reading Highlight feature. It works from the Replace dialog box. Press Ctrl+H (Replace). In the Find what text box, type the word or phrase you want to highlight. Clear the contents of the Replace with text box, but make sure that the insertion point remains in the text box. Click the More >> button, and in the lower-left corner choose Format ➪ Highlight. Click Replace All to apply highlighting to all occurrences of the word or phrase in the Find what text box. Click the Close button to close the dialog box. Highlighting applied this way is more robust than highlighting inserted via the Reading Highlight feature and will not disappear if you choose to manually manipulate highlighting.

Note that when the Replace with text box is blank but has associated formatting, the formatting is applied to text that matches the Find what text box. If both formatting and Replace with text are absent, Replace deletes all occurrences of the matching text.

By default, highlight formatting appears when you print the document. You can choose not to print highlighting, giving you the best of both worlds. You can mark up a document for your own benefit, and then — if you wish — print it out without the highlighting. Not only is this good for keeping internal guides private, it also saves money on yellow ink. To prevent the printing (or displaying) of highlighting, choose File ➪ Options, select the Display tab, and remove the check next to Show highlighter marks. If you hover over the information while you're here, the tip informs you that this controls both display and printing. Click OK when you're done. Of course, you'll need to repeat this process and check Show highlighter marks after printing to redisplay the highlighting on-screen.

> **NOTE**
>
> You may be wondering what the difference between text shading and highlight coloring is, as the two look very similar, and you use similar methods for applying them. The key difference is that the colors for the Text Highlight Color tool work the same as the Standard color choices or any custom colors you apply using another color gallery or palette: The applied text highlight color doesn't change when you change the document theme. In contrast, if you use one of the Theme Colors choices in the Shading gallery in the Paragraph group, the shading color does update when you change the document theme.

Change case

The Change Case button doesn't really fit in the Font group, but that's precisely why I'm including it. Case is not formatting. Case is a choice of what capitalization to use — uppercase, lowercase, or some combination thereof. Why does Microsoft put it in the Font group? Probably because it can affect groups of characters, so it makes more sense here than anywhere else. And the Change Case setting for text is not saved as part of any style you create or update. You can apply a case option to selected text via the Change Case button in the Font group:

- **Sentence case.** capitalizes the first word in the selected text.
- **lowercase** removes all capitalization from the selection.
- **UPPERCASE** converts all letters of the selected text to uppercase.
- **Capitalize Each Word** capitalizes the first letter of each word.
- **tOGGLE cASE** reverses the case of each letter in the selection.

> **TIP**
>
> The formal method of capitalizing documents and section headings is called *title case*. You can easily achieve title case in your documents by applying the Capitalize Each Word setting and then converting prepositions, articles, and conjunctions back to lowercase, leaving only the major words capitalized.

> **TIP**
>
> When you need to distinguish between an uppercase i (I), a lowercase L (l), the number one (1), and the vertical line segment (|, usually typed with Shift+\ on most U.S. keyboards), one font that makes the distinction clearest is Comic Sans. It's also a very comfortable and readable font, its nonprofessional-sounding name notwithstanding. If after applying Comic Sans you're still uncertain as to what's what, try toggling the case. Properly distinguishing among these characters, as well as between 0 (zero) and O (capital o), can make a world of difference when you are trying to convey part numbers, serial numbers, usernames, and passwords.

Language

By default, Word is set up to edit and perform spelling and grammar checks in a single language. To work with editing and formatting choices for a second language, you have to install the language in the Word Options dialog box. Choose File ⇨ Options, and select the Language tab. Under Choose Editing Languages, open the [Add additional editing languages] drop-down list, click the language to add, and click Add. Click OK, and then restart Word when prompted so that the new editing language will take effect.

Even after that, language settings do not appear in the Home tab's Font group nor the Font dialog box, which you'll see shortly. So how do you know language is a character-formatting attribute? Two reasons: It can be applied to a single character in a document, and it can be included in a character style definition, as shown in Figure 5.10.

5

FIGURE 5.10

Language is included among the attributes associated with a character style.

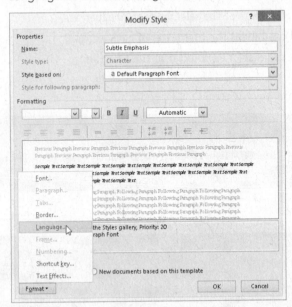

In many cases, Word correctly recognizes text from an installed language and formats it as such, but if not, you can set the language for selected text using the Language tool on the status bar. If you don't see the tool on the status bar, then right-click the status bar, click to enable Language, and then press Esc.

To open the Language dialog box to change settings for the selected text, click the language displayed on the status bar. Among the Language tool's more useful features is the Do not check spelling or grammar setting (see Figure 5.11), which you can apply to text. This can be handy for technical jargon and programming keywords that you might not want checked.

Conversely, the Detect language automatically check box can be a real troublemaker. With that setting turned on, it's possible for text to unintentionally be tagged as some other language, resulting in large sections of text being flagged as misspelled. If the corresponding proofing tools are not installed, the text is not checked at all. This can leave large sections of text unintentionally unchecked. You should turn that setting off unless you actually need it. It is enabled by default!

FIGURE 5.11

The Do not check spelling or grammar setting can be useful for technical writers. Detect language automatically can cause problems for chronically bad spellers.

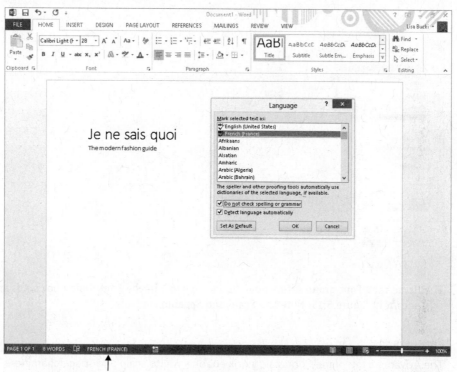

Shows the language applied to selected text; click to open the Language dialog box

To set the default for all documents based on the current template, choose the desired language as well as the desired settings for the last two options, and then click Set As Default. Confirm the settings by clicking Yes. Note that even though the confirmation box doesn't mention the latter two settings, they are included in the changes made to the underlying template.

Formatting via the Font dialog box

The Font tab of the Font dialog box, shown in Figure 5.12, can be a useful tool when you're applying multiple character format changes at the same time. Note, however, that the Font dialog box and the Font group on the ribbon do not provide identical capabilities. The Font dialog doesn't provide a full Live Preview and instead has a smaller preview area. On the other hand, it offers settings not available in the Font group, such as Underline color, Double strikethrough, Small caps, All caps, and Hidden. It also enables you to access detailed Text Effects settings.

5

FIGURE 5.12

The Font tab of the Font dialog box offers additional formatting choices beyond the Home tab's Font group.

The Home tab's Font group offers none of the controls in the Font dialog box's Advanced tab, shown in Figure 5.13. Note the Scale and Spacing controls.

FIGURE 5.13

The Advanced tab of the Font dialog box enables you to scale and space characters.

Use the Scale setting to stretch or compress the selected characters. You may want to do this to make text fill a particular amount of space in the document to create balance or to add emphasis or a modern appearance. The Spacing setting expands or condenses only the spacing between characters. Scaling and spacing expansion are demonstrated on the text shown in Figure 5.14. The bottom copy of the text was scaled to 150% and its Spacing set to Expanded By 2.8 pt. (That means an additional 2.8 points of spacing was inserted between each character.) In this example, the applied settings cause the bottom sample to span the width of the page.

FIGURE 5.14

Scaling and horizontal spacing can give text with the same basic font settings very different appearances.

The Gettysburg Address

The Gettysburg Address

The Position setting raises or lowers the selected characters by a specified number of points. Unlike spacing, which can vary by as little as .1 points, position's smallest gradation is .5 points. This tool is sometimes used to adjust subscripts and superscripts if the built-in versions don't accomplish the desired effect or you need the subscripts and superscripts to be the same size as the surrounding text.

Kerning is an advanced typography control that adjusts the space between certain letter pairs when they appear together and are formatted in a proportional font (with varying letter widths). For example, in the letter pair Wa, kerning removes a little bit of space so that the a tucks in under the right side of the W, yielding a more attractive and readable appearance. Overall, kerning visually balances out the spaces between various letter combinations. Kerning is turned on by default for font sizes above 14 points, as the effects of kerning are more obvious the larger the font size. You can turn kerning off by clearing the Kerning for fonts check box on the Advanced tab of the Font dialog box, or you can change the accompanying font size to determine when kerning takes effect.

5

TIP

If you have a chronic need to adjust subscripts and superscripts, you might consider creating a character style that gives you the desired formatting.

Understanding OpenType features

Figure 5.13 also shows the OpenType Features settings on the Advanced tab. Developed largely by Microsoft, OpenType is the successor to TrueType fonts, which helped in making fonts scalable. OpenType adds additional features that allow you to manipulate some of the more intricate aspects of fonts and number spacing. For example, if you have problems aligning numbers in numbered lists, you might try a different Number spacing choice under OpenType features.

Many OpenType fonts include *ligatures* at certain sizes. When a ligature occurs, similar stroke components of adjoining characters are joined, so that the characters form a new *glyph*, or typographic character. This happens frequently for the lowercase letter f, as shown in Figure 5.15. You can turn ligatures off by choosing None from the Ligatures drop-down list of the Font dialog box, or use one of the other choices beside it and Standard Only to increase the number of ligatures that Word automatically applies. You also can change settings for OpenType Number forms and Stylistic sets.

FIGURE 5.15

The f and t are joined in the top two examples, but not the bottom one.

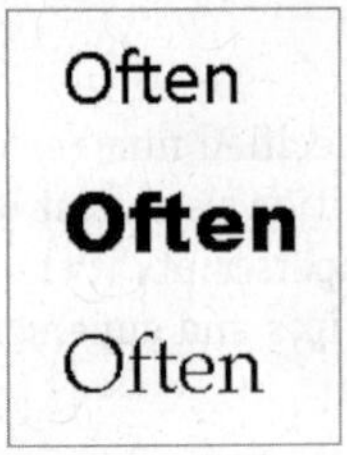

The Mini Toolbar

Yet another tool for applying formatting is the Mini Toolbar. This feature is fully explained in Chapter 2, "Navigating in Office." Shown in Figure 5.16, the Mini Toolbar has a sampling of character-formatting tools from the Font group of the Home tab.

FIGURE 5.16

The Mini Toolbar has a sampling of character-formatting tools from the Font group of the Home tab.

The Mini Toolbar's singular but important claim to fame for many users will be its ergonomic utility. When you need something on it, it's right there, close to the text. Many of its tools are easily accessible via direct keystrokes, as you'll see in the next section in this chapter.

Text Effects and Typography

Even though the Text Effects and Typography gallery is in the Font group of the Home tab and it does apply character formatting, its settings are so many and varied that it warrants separate discussion. You can use the tools found on this gallery to apply formatting that makes regular text look like a WordArt object. (To learn how to create WordArt, see Chapter 9, "Adding Tables and Graphics to a Document.") As in the example shown in Figure 5.17, you can use one of the choices at the top of the gallery to apply a WordArt-like overall appearance to selected text.

FIGURE 5.17

The Text Effects and Typography gallery in the Font group of the Home tab enables you to apply WordArt-like formatting and effects to regular text.

Choose an overall look for text

Click one of the listed effects to see a subgallery

Live Preview of an effect, in this case a glow

5

In addition, you can reopen the gallery and click any of the effects listed at the bottom of the gallery to see a subgallery of specific effects choices, as in the example in Figure 5.17. In most cases, the selected text will display a Live Preview of any effect you move the mouse pointer over. The available effects are:

- **Outline:** Displays a gallery where you can apply a theme or standard color for the text outline, as well as Weight and Dashes choices you can use to alter the outline style.

- **Shadow:** Make a choice from the Outer, Inner, or Perspective categories to add a text shadow, or click the choice under No Shadow to remove any existing shadow.

- **Reflection:** Use a choice to add a text reflection, which is a partial mirror image of the text.

- **Glow:** Click one of the Glow Variations choices (see Figure 5.17) to surround the selected text with a colored glow.

- **Number styles:** If your text includes numbers, select a formatting variation here. The subgallery includes a description of each choice.

- **Ligatures:** When the text includes letter pairs that can be optionally joined with a ligature, make a choice here to determine whether Word applies some or all of the ligature types. The subgallery includes a description of each choice.

- **Stylistic sets:** Click a choice here to add interest to the letter appearance. For example, one of the styles may size lowercase letters the same height as uppercase without changing letter shape.

> **TIP**
>
> As with other types of document formatting, resist the temptation to apply too many effects to document text. Doing so can reduce readability and even look a bit too gaudy.

Character formatting keyboard shortcuts

You can apply many of the character formatting settings discussed in this chapter via built-in keyboard shortcuts. Longtime Word users typically have many of these shortcuts committed to memory. Newcomers, however, might need a quick guide. As you navigate your way through Word 2013, keep your eyes open. Quite often, Word will show you its built-in key assignments. To make sure this happens, do the following:

- In File ⇨ Options ⇨ General, set ScreenTip style to something other than Don't show ScreenTips.

- In File ⇨ Options ⇨ Advanced, scroll down to the Display section, and enable the Show shortcut keys in ScreenTips check box.

Table 5.1 provides a quick reference of keyboard shortcuts related to character formatting. This list might not be exhaustive.

TABLE 5.1 **Default Character Formatting Keyboard Shortcuts**

Command	Keystroke
All Caps	Ctrl+Shift+A
Bold	Ctrl+B, Ctrl+Shift+B
Copy formatting	Ctrl+Shift+C
Font dialog box	Ctrl+D, Ctrl+Shift+F
Highlighting	Alt+Ctrl+H
Hyperlink	Ctrl+K
Italics	Ctrl+I
Paste formatting	Ctrl+Shift+V
Font/Point size	Ctrl+Shift+P
Font/Point size: decrease by one point	Ctrl+[
Font/Point size: decrease to next preset	Ctrl+ <
Font/Point size: increase by one point	Ctrl+]
Font/Point size: increase to next preset	Ctrl+ >
Remove non-style character formatting	Ctrl+Space
Small caps	Ctrl+Shift+K
Subscript	Ctrl+=
Superscript	Ctrl+Shift+=
Symbol font	Ctrl+Shift+Q
Toggle case of selected text	Shift+F3
Underline	Ctrl+U
Word underline	Ctrl+W

Summary

For most of us, our words form the most important thing about the documents we create. Judiciously used character formatting can help our words convey greater meaning by highlighting important words and phrases in a document. In this chapter you've seen the variety of formatting changes you can make on words and characters. You should now be able to:

5

- Apply character formatting to a text selection of any size, from a single character up to a complete document.
- Choose whether to apply formatting directly or to use a character style.
- Distinguish between character formatting and characters.
- Decide, from among the variety of formatting tools, which one to use in any given formatting situation.
- Remove unwanted character formatting.
- Explore advanced character formatting settings, such as the use of OpenType ligatures and WordArt-like effects.
- Save time by using keyboard shortcuts and shortcut techniques.

Paragraph Formatting

IN THIS CHAPTER

Working with paragraph styles or direct formatting

Finding and applying paragraph formatting tools

Indenting and aligning paragraphs

Adding spacing around and within paragraphs

Lining up text with tabs

Applying numbering, bullets, shading, and borders to emphasize paragraphs

Everything you type in Word exists in paragraphs. Even if you type nothing at all every Word document—even one that you believe is completely empty—contains at least one blank paragraph that already has formatting settings assigned to it. You can think of each paragraph as another type of formatting unit.

This chapter goes into detail about the numerous paragraph formatting choices available in Word, including indentation, alignment, spacing, list formats, shading, and borders. You'll also learn about the interaction between selected Word options and the nuances of paragraph formatting.

Choosing between Styles and Paragraph Formatting

When it comes to document design and formatting, you can often achieve a similar look using totally different tools in Word 2013. For any given paragraph, however, only one way is the most efficient. After you learn about the various ways to format paragraphs, developing the habit of using the most efficient tools will serve you well, especially when much of your workday involves creating documents.

As with character formatting, when you are formatting paragraphs, you have to choose between applying direct formatting and using paragraph styles. Many users simply ignore the existence of styles and use all direct formatting. But whether they realize it or not, every blank document created using the default Normal.dotm template contains a single paragraph style, called Normal, and a single character style, called Default Paragraph Font.

Generally speaking, paragraph styles can save a lot of time, because you can apply several new formatting settings to a paragraph in only a couple of mouse clicks. And when you update any style, either character or paragraph, Word updates all the text in the document with the new style settings.

Despite the obvious advantages of using paragraph styles, such as the ability to find and replace styles, you may not find a style that includes all the formatting that you want to apply to a given paragraph. In such a case, you will need to apply direct formatting. That's the reason why this chapter takes the time to highlight the various direct paragraph formatting settings.

For a one time ad hoc need, direct paragraph formatting is entirely appropriate. For example, if you're creating a centered title on a one-page flyer you're going to tack to a bulletin board, feel free to simply press Ctrl+E or click the Center button in the Paragraph group to align the text.

On the other hand, if it's formatting that you're going to need again and again, then use a paragraph style, even if you have to modify an existing style or create a brand-new style. For example, if you are formatting a number of headings in a newsletter you will be writing monthly for the next five years, either adapt and start applying the built-in heading styles (Heading 1, Heading 2, and so on), or create and use your own custom heading styles. The more work styles can do for you, the less time you're going to have to spend applying and reapplying direct paragraph formatting.

Finding Paragraph Formatting Tools

Word stores each paragraph's formatting in its paragraph mark. Say you have two paragraphs with different line spacing settings applied. If you click at the beginning of the second paragraph and press Backspace to combine the paragraphs, suddenly the combined paragraphs use the same line spacing. (They use the spacing of the top paragraph, which is a little counterintuitive.)

Similarly, say you create a double-spaced paragraph and then press Enter to start a new paragraph, creating a paragraph mark on a line by itself. Then, you cut a few sentences from a single-spaced paragraph elsewhere in the document and paste them just to the left of the new paragraph mark. Word reformats the pasted single space text with the double-spaced formatting setting stored in the paragraph mark.

That's just two examples of why you may need to see the paragraph marks when formatting and editing a document, especially when you're cutting or copying and pasting text. Pressing Ctrl+Shift+8 (Ctrl + *) or clicking the Show/Hide button in the Paragraph group of the Home tab toggles the paragraph marks and other nonprinting characters on and off as needed.

> **NOTE**
>
> The paragraph mark is also called a *pilcrow* or an *alinea*. Remember that if you show nonprinting characters and any of them, such as the paragraph marks, do not appear, you can control their display in Word Options. Choose File ➪ Options ➪ Display, make sure that Paragraph marks and any other character types you want are checked under Always show these formatting marks on the screen, and then click OK.

In Figure 6.1, all of numbered item 1 is a single paragraph. The character that you see after "Train yourself, too." is called a *manual line break*, which is the type of line return you create when you press Shift+Enter. Because a manual line break does not create a paragraph mark, text before and after a manual line break is within the same paragraph, as you see in the numbered item in Figure 6.1. To Word, the only thing that distinguishes one paragraph from another is the paragraph mark. A single sentence or short phrase with a paragraph mark after it, as for a list of items, is considered to be a complete paragraph. Similarly, a paragraph mark that contains no associated text at all is also considered to be a paragraph.

FIGURE 6.1

A paragraph is everything between two paragraph marks.

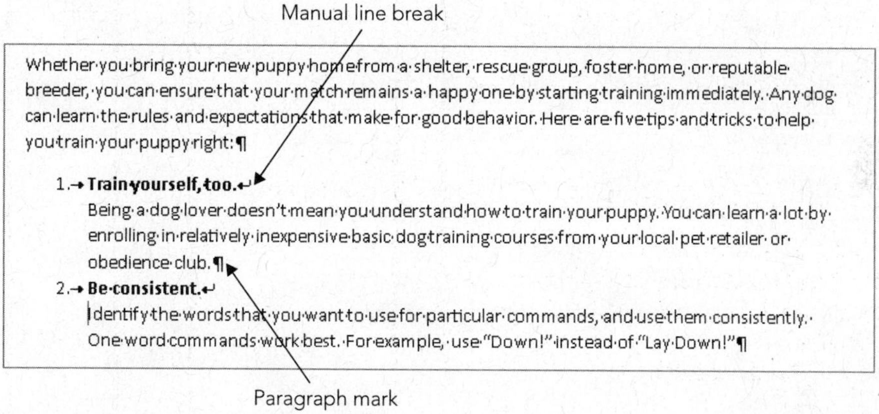

Many new Word users find the display of nonprinting characters (such as paragraph marks, manual line breaks, spaces, and tabs) distracting. However, displaying them can give you essential clues about what's going on in a document.

Sometimes it's useful to use a manual line break within a paragraph while still keeping it as a single paragraph. This most often is done within numbered or bulleted paragraphs, as shown in Figure 6.1. That way any paragraph formatting you do to any part of the paragraph is done to the entire paragraph (such as the main indentation and numbering). If the paragraphs are numbered or bulleted, a manual line break prevents a new number or bullet from being assigned while keeping all the text pertaining to that topic or item together as a single paragraph.

You also can use the Reveal Formatting pane shown in Figure 6.2 as a formatting diagnostic aid. You display it by pressing Shift+F1. It shows all the formatting that's applied to the selected text or the word holding the insertion point. It has four segments: Font (character formatting), Paragraph, Bullets and Numbering, and Section. It also displays the selected text, if any, using the current common formatting. If the insertion point is beside a paragraph mark without any text, the Reveal Formatting pane displays the words "Sample Text" using common current formatting.

FIGURE 6.2

Press Shift+F1 to open the Reveal Formatting pane. It shows all the formatting in effect for the selection.

Why do I say that it displays the common formatting? That's because the selected text might not be formatted homogeneously. Say the selected sentence was "It was a **dark** and *stormy* night." Because some formatting (bold and italic in this case) might not be common to the entire selection, you have to bear in mind that Reveal Formatting may not list all the formatting applied in a given selection.

You can use the triangles beside the section names in the Reveal Formatting pane to expand and collapse the formatting information. Clicking a black triangle collapses the formatting details, whereas clicking a white triangle expands and reveals formatting details. When you finish using the pane, click its Close (X) button to close it.

TIP

The Reveal Formatting command does not appear on the Ribbon. If you can't remember the Shift+F1 shortcut for displaying it, you can add a button for it to the Quick Access Toolbar. Right-click the QAT and choose Customize Quick Access Toolbar. Select Commands Not in the Ribbon from the Choose commands from list. Click in the list and tap the S key to accelerate to that part of the alphabet, and then press the Up Arrow key as needed to select Revel Formatting. Click Add, and then OK.

Paragraph formatting attributes

You can apply paragraph formatting using a wide variety of paragraph attribute buttons and tools. Many of those attribute controls, but not all, can be found in the Paragraph group in the Home tab, shown in Figure 6.3. Indent and Spacing, both of which are paragraph attributes, are located on the Paragraph group in the Page Layout tab, also shown in Figure 6.3. A number of attributes missing from the Ribbon are on the horizontal rulers: left and right indent, hanging and paragraph indent, and tab settings.

FIGURE 6.3

The Paragraph sections in the Home and Page Layout tabs contain a number of paragraph-formatting controls.

Paragraph group
on Home tab

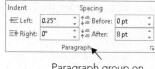

Paragraph group on
Page Layout tab

Many paragraph attributes — but again, not all — are also found in the Paragraph dialog box, shown in Figure 6.4. You can display the Paragraph dialog box by clicking the dialog box launcher in the lower-right corner of either Paragraph group, by double-clicking any of the indent controls on the horizontal ruler, or by pressing the legacy keystrokes Alt+O and then Alt+P or just Alt+O and then P.

FIGURE 6.4

The Paragraph dialog box contains controls for most, but not all, of Word's direct paragraph formatting attributes.

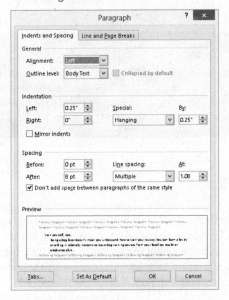 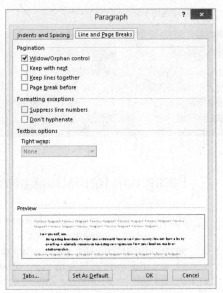

You have to open other dialog boxes to find additional paragraph formatting settings. For example, click the Tabs button in the lower-left corner of the Paragraph dialog box to open the Tabs dialog box. To find border and shading formatting choices, click Borders and Shading in the bottom of the Border tool's list of settings (on the Home tab), shown in Figure 6.5.

FIGURE 6.5

Open the Borders and Shading dialog box by clicking Borders and Shading at the bottom of the Borders menu in the Paragraph group of the Home tab.

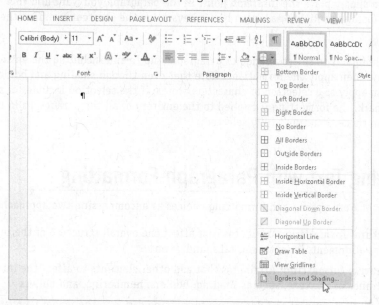

You might be wondering from all this how to determine whether a setting is a paragraph-formatting attribute. One way is to see whether the attribute can be applied to a paragraph without the whole paragraph's being selected. For example, if you click anywhere inside a paragraph and click the Center button in the Paragraph group of the Home tab, Word centers the whole paragraph. The same anywhere-in-the-paragraph rule is true for each of the other alignment options. The same applies to borders, shading, indentation, bullets, numbering, and line spacing.

Note, however, that two "paragraph-formatting" attributes behave according to the *if nothing is selected, format the whole paragraph* rule, but behave differently if part (but not all) of a paragraph is selected. These two are shading and borders. While they generally are considered paragraph formatting, they also can be character formatting.

Paragraph formatting techniques

You can use either of two techniques to apply paragraph formatting attributes. As noted, you can simply place the insertion point in the paragraph you want and then choose the attribute (using the Ribbon, a dialog box, a keystroke, the shortcut menu, or the Mini Toolbar).

The other technique is to select a range of paragraphs (up to and including the entire document), and then apply the formatting. Note that even though shading and border formatting can apply to a selection of characters/words, if the selection includes or spans a paragraph mark, the formatting is applied to the entirety of all the paragraphs in the selection, even those that aren't fully selected.

Structuring Text with Paragraph Formatting

You can think of Word's paragraph formatting choices as encompassing two approaches:

- **Structural formatting:** Attributes that affect the overall structure of the text, such as alignment, indentation, tabs, and so on
- **Decorative formatting:** Attributes that add other elements to affect the interior appearance of the text, such as shading, borders, numbering, and bullets

Used properly, both structural and decorative formatting can help the reader navigate the document more easily or find important information. This section deals with structural formatting. The subsequent section covers decorative formatting.

Adding indentation

Indentation refers to adding extra space between one or more lines of a paragraph and the left and/or right margins. You typically use indentation for automatically indenting the first line of paragraphs, indenting quotes relative to both the left and right page margins, and setting up hanging indentation for bulleted or numbered text. Add or remove indentation in preset half-inch increments by clicking the Decrease Indent or Increase Indent button in the Paragraph group of the Home tab.

You can also add indentation using the Indent Left and Indent Right controls in the Paragraph group of the Page Layout tab. For example, most report styles call for all lines in quotations to be indented .5 inches from the left or right margins, but you may want to use .75 inches instead. As shown in Figure 6.6, you can enter the desired indent settings for the selected paragraph in the Indent Left and Indent Right text boxes.

FIGURE 6.6

Set custom left and right paragraph indentation in the Paragraph group of the Page Layout tab.

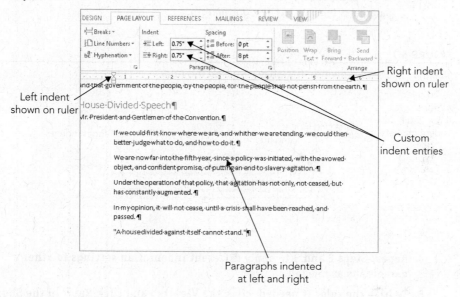

Paragraphs indented
at left and right

Indenting with the Ruler

The horizontal Ruler provides a mouse-based way to create indents and is especially easy for creating first line and hanging indents. A *first line indent* indents only the first line of a paragraph. A *hanging indent* indents all lines except the first line, as for the numbered and bulleted lists you see throughout this book.

This method also enables you to see how the text will change as you drag, so that you can judge as you go how much indentation to apply.

1. **To display the ruler if needed, click the View tab and click Ruler in the Show group.** The Ruler check box controls the display of the ruler within the current document only, so you may need to turn it on and off frequently.

2. **Select the paragraphs to indent.**

3. **Drag the indent symbols on the ruler as needed to apply the desired indentation.** Refer to Figure 6.7 to see what each of these symbols looks like:

   - **First Line Indent:** Drag to the right to indent the first line or to the left to reduce or remove indentation.

   - **Hanging Indent:** Drag to the right to indicate the amount of indentation to apply to all but the first line of the paragraph.

- **Left Indent:** Drag right or left to add or remove indentation for all lines of the paragraph relative to the left margin.
- **Right Indent:** Drag left or right to add or remove indentation for all lines of the paragraph relative to the right margin.

FIGURE 6.7

Use the mouse to drag indentation controls on the ruler.

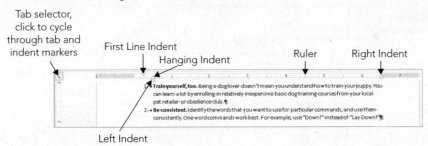

4. **Repeat Steps 2 and 3 to apply different indentation settings to other paragraphs as needed.**
5. **To hide the ruler if needed, click the View tab and click Ruler in the Show group.**

TIP

If you have trouble dragging the ruler's tiny indent controls with the mouse, you can use the tab selector control at the left end of the horizontal ruler. Click the (usually) L-shaped control to cycle through the different tabs and indents and stop at either the First Line Indent or the Hanging Indent marker. With that control displayed, you can now set a first-line or hanging indent by clicking the desired position on the ruler.

If you press the Alt key while dragging the indent controls on the ruler, Word displays the measurement as shown in Figure 6.8, allowing for more informed positioning.

FIGURE 6.8

Press Alt while dragging indent controls on the ruler to see precise measurements.

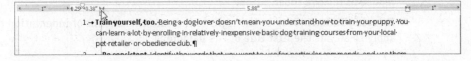

Custom and mirror indents

Many users still prefer to set indents in the Indentation section of the Indents and Spacing tab of the Paragraph dialog box, shown in Figure 6.9. For example, clicking the up and down arrow buttons for Left or Right increments those settings by .1 inch. You can choose either First Line or Hanging from the Special list to immediately set up either of those types of indents, or click the Mirror indents check box so that you can create indents to accommodate book style printing. When Mirror indents is enabled, the Left and Right text boxes become Inside and Outside, as shown in Figure 6.9.

FIGURE 6.9

Use the Paragraph dialog box to enter precise indent settings or add mirror indents.

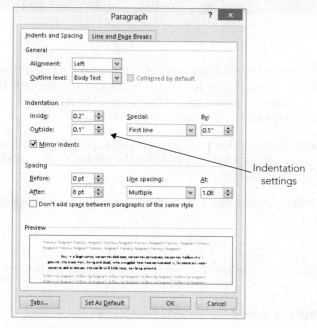

Indentation settings

Changing text alignment

Horizontal alignment determines how any given paragraph is oriented between the left and right margins. The Paragraph group of the Home tab includes four alignment buttons. Click a button or use its shortcut key to apply the specified alignment to the selected paragraph(s):

- **Align Left (Ctrl+L):** Starts the left side of each line of text at the left margin, leaving a ragged right paragraph edge.

- **Center (Ctrl+E):** Centers each line in a paragraph between the left and right margins, giving both sides of the paragraph a ragged appearance.

- **Align Right (Ctrl+R):** Moves each line of the paragraph over to the right, so the right side aligns at the right margin, leaving a ragged left edge.
- **Justified (Ctrl+J):** Adds additional spacing between letters to align the left and right side of each line of text to its respective margin, giving straight left and right paragraph edges.

CAUTION

Justified alignment can cause an unpleasant appearance when used in combination with a font size that's too large. With a large font size, fewer words fit on each line, and Word therefore might have to add large amounts of white space to justify the text, creating a distracting amount of white area within the text. If you notice this effect when using justified alignment, experiment with applying a smaller font size to fix the problem.

Changing spacing

You also may need to change the paragraph spacing settings for various documents to improve readability or conform with document formatting styles and requirements. For example, most academic reports require double-spaced formatting, whereas most business letters use single-spaced or a limited amount of space between lines.

By default the Normal paragraph style includes extra spacing after the paragraph. Pressing Enter once at the end of a paragraph automatically includes the needed spacing between the current paragraph and the next paragraph.

Use the Line and Paragraph Spacing drop-down list in the Paragraph group of the Home tab to change paragraph spacing.

Between lines

By default, the Normal paragraph style is set to 1.08 line spacing. To change to another line spacing setting:

1. **Select the paragraphs to change.**
2. **Click the Paragraph and Line Spacing button in the Paragraph group of the Home tab.** A menu with preset spacing settings and other commands appears.
3. **Move the mouse pointer over one of the spacing choices.** A Live Preview of the spacing appears in the document, as shown in Figure 6.10.

FIGURE 6.10

Changing line spacing within the second paragraph of the document.

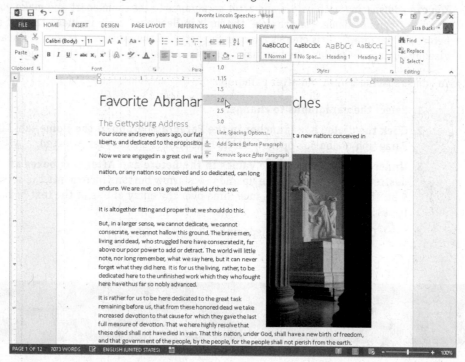

4. **Click the spacing to apply.**

If you click Line Spacing Options in the menu in Figure 6.10, Word opens the Paragraph dialog box, with its Indents and Spacing tab displayed. You can use the Line Spacing choice there to apply Single, 1.5 lines, or Double spacing. You also can use the At least, Exactly, or Multiple choices and make an entry in the At text box to set line spacing by smaller increments such as the 1.08 default for Word 2013's Normal paragraph style.

> **NOTE**
>
> When you install Word 2013 for the first time on a system, the Normal style's line spacing will be 1.08 and spacing after will be 1.08 and 8 pt, as described above and below. However, if you upgrade a prior version of Office, your Normal paragraph style may use the default settings from the prior version, 1.15 and 10 pt, respectively. If this is not what you want, you can edit the Normal style to match the new settings as described in "Modifying an existing style" in Chapter 7. Another more drastic workaround would be to delete the `Normal.dotm` file so that it will rebuild when you start Word; however, use that technique with caution, because you would also lose any other style modifications or custom macros stored in the default template.

Before and after paragraphs

The Normal paragraph style also includes 8 pt of extra spacing after each paragraph. You can add spacing both before and after paragraphs to set them apart and make your document more readable. For example, the built-in Heading 1 style includes 12 pt of spacing before the paragraph. This creates a larger gap between the preceding text and a heading, visually cueing the reader that one major topic is ending and another beginning.

To adjust spacing before and after paragraphs:

1. **Select the paragraphs to change.**
2. **Click the dialog box launcher in the Paragraph group of the Home tab.** The Paragraph dialog box opens with its Indents and Spacing tab selected.
3. **Under Spacing, change the values in the Before and After text boxes as desired.** Clicking one of the up and down arrow buttons increments the setting by 6 pt. If that's too large a change, drag over the entry of one of the text boxes and type the desired size.
4. **Click OK to apply the new spacing.**

> **TIP**
>
> The Add Space After Paragraph command on the Line and Paragraph spacing menu adds 12 pt of space after the selected paragraph. Remove Space Before Paragraph sets the space before the paragraph to 0 pt.

Setting and using tabs

Computer users increasingly have been using tables rather than tabs for aligning lists of text within a document. Although both formatting methods can give similar results and derive from the same root word, tabulation, tables give better control, more flexibility, and more formatting options than tabs. Still, there are many instances where using tabs on the fly provides a faster document formatting solution.

By default, a new document includes default preset tabs every 0.5 inch. When you set your own tab, all the built-in preset tabs to the left of the one you set are removed, leaving the manually inserted tab and all remaining preset tabs to the right.

Tabs versus tables

If you can use tabs, and you can use tables, when should you use which? There are times when tabs give you precisely what you want, and in a way that a table either can't or can't without your jumping through hoops. For example, if you want lines connecting two tabbed items, while there are other ways to accomplish the same effect, it's almost always faster and easier to use tab leaders.

6

If you need to create an underscored area for a signature or other fill-in information on a paper form, the solid tab leader line is definitely the way to go, even though you could draw lines where you want them instead, using Insert ➪ Shapes ➪ Line (holding down the Shift key as you draw to keep the line perfectly horizontal, of course). However, graphical lines have a way of not always staying where you put them, so you'll usually find that it's much more efficient and predictable to just use a leader line, as described shortly under "Working with tab leaders."

TIP

Word includes a new feature for creating a formal document signature line rather than a basic fill-in area. For more, see "Adding a signature line" in Chapter 11.

Another situation in which tabs give you what you want is with simple document headers. The default header for Word 2013 documents contains a center tab and a right tab. This enables you to easily create a header with text to the left, centered text, and right-aligned text, simply by separating those three components with tabs. Tabs also can be useful inside actual tables for aligning numbers at the decimal point. (To insert a tab inside a table, press Ctrl+Tab.)

However, for more complex presentations of information, particularly when you might need organizational control (copying and moving rows and columns), you'll save time and work by creating a table. Chapter 9, "Adding Tables and Graphics to a Document," covers how you can quickly build and format tables in a document.

Setting tabs in a dialog box

If you prefer the precision of typing in the tab measurements you want or if you need to include a leader, use the Tabs dialog box shown in Figure 6.11 to create your tabs. With the Tabs dialog box, you also can specify a tab alignment. Figure 6.12 shows examples of the various alignments.

FIGURE 6.11

Use the Tabs dialog box to set and clear tabs, set the default tab stop interval, and set a tab leader.

FIGURE 6.12

The first three lines show left, center, and right tabs; the number lines show a decimal tab; and the final lines show a bar tab.

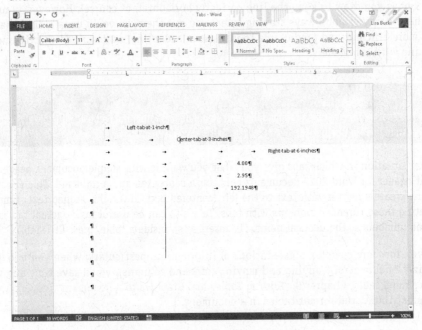

1. **Select the paragraphs to change.**

2. **Click the dialog box launcher in the Paragraph group of the Home tab.** The Paragraph dialog box opens with its Indents and Spacing tab selected.

3. **Click the Tabs button in the lower-left corner.** The Tabs dialog box appears.

4. **To set a tab, click in the Tab stop position text box, type the tab measurement, click the desired choices under Alignment and Leader, and click Set.**

5. **To remove a tab, click it in the Tab stop position list, and click Clear.**

6. **Click OK to close the dialog box.**

Working with tab leaders

Tab leaders are dashed or solid lines typically used to help the reader visually line up information separated by tabs. Tab leaders often are used in tables of contents and indexes, such as the one shown in Figure 6.13. You choose the type of leader to add when setting the tab, as noted in Step 4 above. The Leader section of the Tabs dialog box (Figure 6.11) offers four leader settings. The first removes any previously-applied leader for the tab selected in the Tab stop position list. The next three choices create a dotted, dashed, or underline leader, respectively, for a new or existing tab.

180

FIGURE 6.13

Tab leaders are visual aids that help the reader better track content separated by tabs.

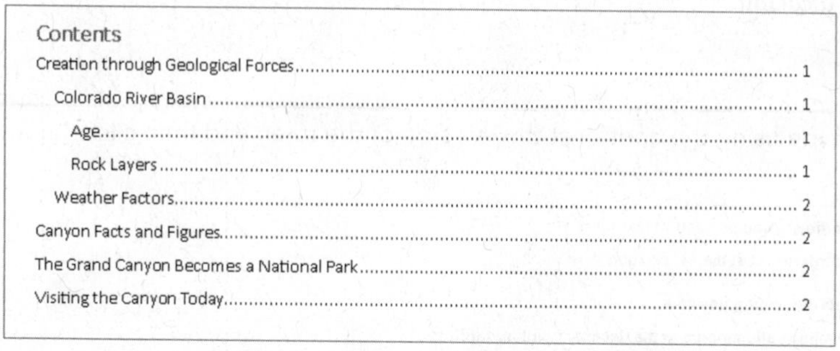

Contents

For example, to create a signature or other fill-in area for a printed form, type and format the prompt (Name:, Phone:, and so on). Open the Tabs dialog box, enter the desired Tab stop position value, click Right under alignment, and then click the Leader option 4 (solid underscore). Click OK, and then click to the right of your prompt and press Tab. This creates something like what is shown in Figure 6.14.

FIGURE 6.14

Tab leader lines are ideal for creating underscored fill in areas for paper forms.

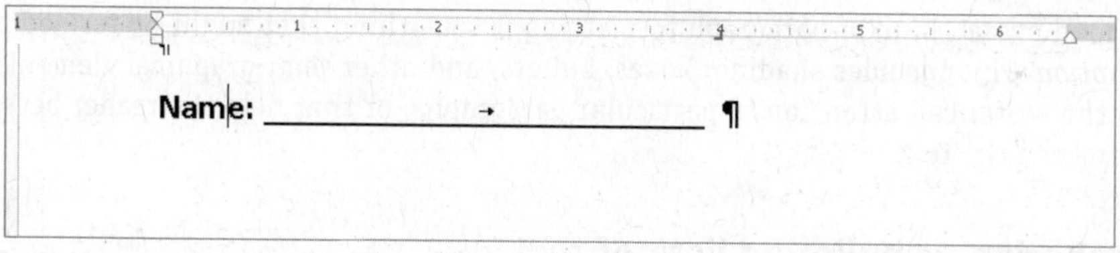

Name: _____ → _____ ¶

> **NOTE**
>
> To change a tab leader, click the tab in the Tab stop position list of the Tabs dialog box, click the desired style under Leader, and then click Set. Similarly, you can click a tab in the Tab stop position list, and then click Clear to remove the tab stop. When you finish working with Tabs, click OK to close the Tabs dialog box.

Setting tabs with the ruler

You can set tabs using the horizontal ruler as well. First display the ruler if needed by checking Ruler in the Show group of the View tab. Then determine the tab type by clicking the tab selector control at the left end of the ruler. (Refer to Figure 6.7 for its location.) As indicated earlier, this control cycles among Word's five built-in tab types, as well as First Line Indent and Hanging Indent controls. Figure 6.15 shows the markers or buttons for the five built-in tab types. When the desired tab type appears on the control, click the lower portion of the ruler (below the eighth-inch hash marks) to set the desired tabs. Drag a tab marker along the ruler to correct its placement; holding the Alt key while dragging shows you the exact location.

FIGURE 6.15

Choose a tab type using the control at the left side of the ruler, and then click the ruler to set the tab.

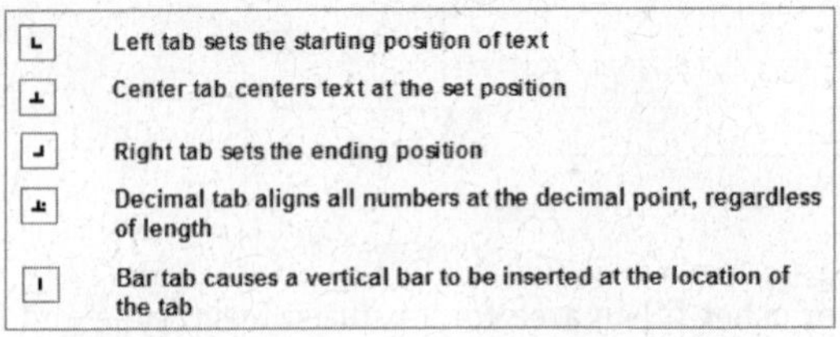

L	Left tab sets the starting position of text
⊥	Center tab centers text at the set position
⌐	Right tab sets the ending position
⊥.	Decimal tab aligns all numbers at the decimal point, regardless of length
I	Bar tab causes a vertical bar to be inserted at the location of the tab

To remove a tab from the ruler, simply drag the tab marker down and away from the ruler until the mouse pointer is no longer in the ruler area.

Setting Off Text with Paragraph Decoration

A second overall kind of paragraph formatting is something that might be termed *paragraph decoration*. This includes shading, boxes, bullets, and other semi-graphical elements that help the writer call attention to particular paragraphs, or that help the reader better understand the text.

Numbering or bulleting lists of text

Automatic numbering and bulleting helps clarify the nature of the lists in your document, as well as saving you the trouble of having to insert numbers and bullets manually, set tab stops and a hanging indent, adjust the spacing between paragraphs, and apply all the other paragraph formatting settings needed for a list. Another benefit of using Word's numbered list tool is that if you need to change the order of the items in the list, all you have to do is drag or cut and paste them. The list then automatically renumbers itself.

Traditionally, you create a numbered list to show steps in a process and a bulleted list for a nonchronological list of items. Numbered lists are also useful when you want to count the items in a list, such as when you are providing a "Top 10" list.

You can apply numbering or bullets to selected paragraphs by clicking the Numbering or Bullets button in the Paragraph group of the Home tab. Each paragraph in the list becomes a separate numbered or bulleted item.

You also can click the Numbering or Bullets tool and just start typing a brand-new list. When you're done with your list, simply press Enter twice to stop the numbering or bulleting. If you create additional indent levels in the list by pressing the Tab key, Word automatically uses different and appropriate numbering or bullet schemes for each level.

NOTE

If Automatic bulleted lists or Automatic numbered lists are enabled, then you don't even need to click the Numbering or Bullets tool. To begin a numbered list, simply type 1. (1 followed by a period) and press the Spacebar, and Word automatically replaces what you typed with automatic number formatting. Other variations work, too, such as 1<Tab>. To begin a bulleted list, simply type * and press the Spacebar. When you want to end either kind of list, press Enter twice.

You can change the number or bullet style by clicking the arrow for either the Numbering or Bullets tool. As shown in Figure 6.16, when you move the mouse pointer over a new bullet or numbering style, a Live Preview appears in the selected list. Click the desired format in the gallery to apply it to the list.

FIGURE 6.16

Live Preview shows the new numbering or bullet style.

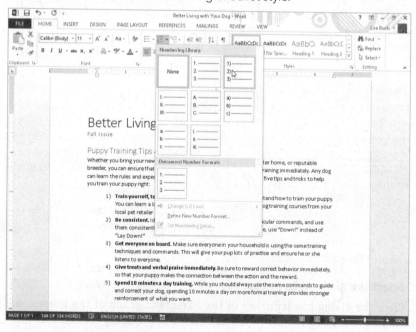

The Multilevel list button to the right of the Numbering button in the Paragraph group of the Home tab enables you to create an outline-style multilevel list. Its default format uses 1. (level 1), a. (level 2), i (level 3) style academic formatting, but it too offers a gallery of other formal and informal styles. Use Tab or Shift+Tab at the beginnings of lines to build the multilevel outline.

Line and page break controls

Figure 6.17 shows the Line and Page Breaks tab of the Paragraph dialog box, which offers additional paragraph-level formatting controls. Some of the settings found here are particularly useful for long documents with abundant headings, because they enable you to control what text stays together without the need for you to insert manual page breaks that you'd have to remove or move later if you edit the document.

FIGURE 6.17

Control how paragraphs behave around page breaks here.

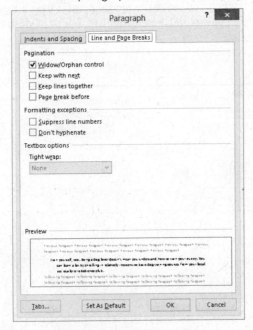

To set Line and Page Breaks options:

1. **Select the paragraphs to change.**
2. **Click the dialog box launcher in the Paragraph group of the Home tab.** The Paragraph dialog box opens with its Indents and Spacing tab selected.

3. **Click the Line and Page Breaks tab.**

4. **Click to check (enable) or uncheck (disable) the desired options under Pagination:**

   - **Widow/Orphan control:** Prevents a solitary paragraph line from being "stranded" on a page by itself without the rest of the paragraph. Widows precede the main portion of the paragraph and thus appear alone at the bottom of a page above the page break, whereas orphans follow the rest of the paragraph and appear alone at the top of the page below the page break).

   - **Keep with next:** Forces a paragraph to appear with the paragraph that follows. Use this setting to keep headings together with at least the first few lines of the first paragraph under that heading. You can also enable this setting to keep captions and pictures, figures, tables, and so on, on the same page.

   - **Keep lines together:** Prevents a paragraph from breaking across two pages.

   - **Page break before:** Forces an automatic page break before the paragraph. For example, you could enable this check box to force each chapter to begin on a new page.

5. **Click to check (enable) or uncheck (disable) the desired options under Formatting exceptions:**

   - **Suppress line numbers:** Enable this check box to temporarily hide line numbers that you've previously set up. Hiding the line numbers is faster than removing and reapplying them.

   - **Don't hyphenate:** Instructs Word not to perform hyphenation in the selected paragraphs. This often is done by those trying to reproduce a quote and maintain its integrity with respect to the words and position of the original being quoted.

6. **Click OK to close the dialog box.**

What's That Dot?

As you are working with various paragraph formatting choices you may notice a square dot appear at times to the left of some paragraphs. The square dot appears to the left of a paragraph when any of these attributes are assigned to that paragraph:

- Keep with next
- Keep lines together
- Page break before
- Suppress line numbers

The dot will not print, but provides a visual reminder that you have applied special line and page break formatting.

Shading paragraphs

You can shade paragraphs as well as individual words with the Shading drop-down in the Paragraph group of the Home tab. As shown in Figure 6.18, after you open the control, point to a color to see a Live Preview on the selected text; or, if no text is selected within a paragraph, Word applies the shading to the entire paragraph holding the insertion point. When you find the color you want, click it to apply it.

FIGURE 6.18

Word applies the shading to selected text or the whole paragraph holding the insertion point.

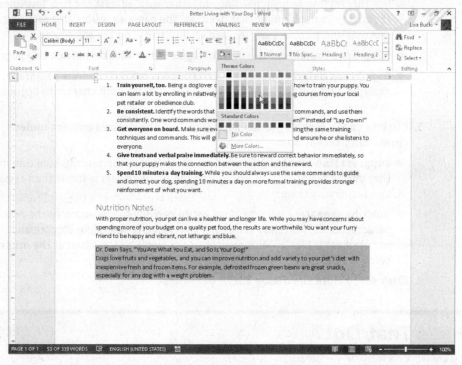

The Shading tab of the Borders and Shading dialog box offers additional shading options. To display the Borders and Shading dialog box, click the drop-down arrow next to the Border tool in the Paragraph group of the Home tab, and click Borders and Shading (at the bottom of the list). As shown in Figure 6.19, open the Style drop-down list under Patterns, and scroll down to view the various opacity and pattern settings that can be applied to the shading. Click the one you want, check its appearance in the Preview area at right, and then click OK to apply the change. Patterns often are more useful when you're preparing documents for grayscale printing in which shading variations might be too subtle.

FIGURE 6.19

Change opacity or apply a pattern to a shaded selection.

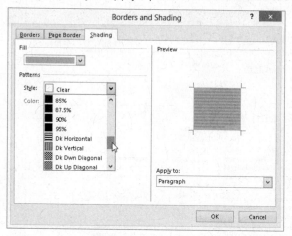

Borders and boxes

You can apply borders above and below or beside selected paragraphs for emphasis, or to set off one or more paragraphs from the rest of the text by boxing it. The Borders gallery in the Paragraph group of the Home tab offers several preset border types that you can preview with Live Preview. For example, as shown in Figure 6.20, after you click the Borders drop-down list arrow, pointing to Inside Borders displays lines between the paragraphs in the selected numbered list. Click a preset in the menu to apply it. Using Live Preview helps in this instance because the resulting box or border applied depends on how many paragraphs you've selected and how they're otherwise formatted.

Click the Borders and Shading command at the bottom of the drop-down list shown in Figure 6.20 to open the Borders and Shading the dialog box with the Borders tab selected, as shown in Figure 6.21. To use the dialog box to apply a border:

FIGURE 6.20

Preview and apply a border or box preset.

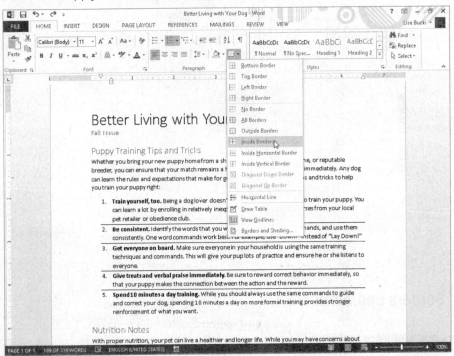

FIGURE 6.21

The Borders and Shading dialog box provides complete control over a paragraph's border.

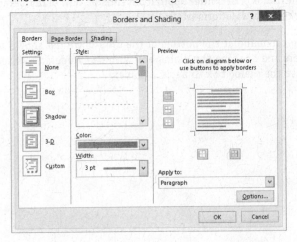

1. Click the Border drop-down arrow in the Paragraph group of the Home tab, and then click Borders and Shading.

2. Make a selection from the Style list.

3. Click the Color box and click the border color to use.

4. Open the Width drop-down and click a width.

5. Then, either click one of the presets under Setting to apply that style of box to the selected paragraph (Figure 6.20 shows the Shadow style of box selected), or click the four sides of the Preview box at right as needed to apply or remove the border on the specified side.

6. Make sure Paragraph is selected from the Apply To drop-down.

7. Click OK.

Additionally, you can adjust the distance between the border and paragraph text by clicking Options in the lower-right corner of the dialog box. You can individually adjust the distance for any of the four sides.

> **CAUTION**
>
> Note that the Border button in the Paragraph group of the Home tab changes to the last border preset that you applied. This does not apply if the last option you picked was Borders and Shading.

Caveats for printing and viewing

With formatting tools that are so easy to use, it's always tempting to think that more is better. Sometimes more is just more. And sometimes more can create issues for readers of your documents, whether they are printing them or viewing them on-screen. Before you wrap up that document and send it to the printer or e-mail it to another user, review your document for these potential problems:

- **Lack of spacing between paragraphs:** Applying bold and italic character formatting to create "headings" often doesn't break up the text enough. Use paragraph styles or insert spacing above and below heading paragraphs to give your reader's eyes a break. Adding a border below every heading also helps.

- **Lack of spacing between lines:** Make sure you understand the intended purpose of a document, and set line spacing accordingly. If your instructor or boss wants you to double-space the text in your report, make sure that you've done so.

- **Shading that's too dark for printing:** If you apply navy shading behind black text, chances are it won't be readable when printed, especially if your color printer does a poor job rendering color or you are printing to a black and white printer. Choosing the Lighter 60% or Lighter 80% variations of the right six accent colors under Theme Colors in the Shading pallet usually is safer than choosing one of the deeper variations on the rows below.

- **Shading that's not optimized for on-screen viewing:** If you believe most users will be reading your document online or if you plan to convert it to a PDF, keep in mind that it's sometimes easier to read light text on a dark background on-screen. This means that you might consider changing to a white text fill and dark shading for paragraphs you want to emphasize.

Summary

In this chapter we've explored the ins and outs of direct paragraph formatting. You should have also started to develop a better sense of when to use direct paragraph formatting, and when to take it to the next level and create your own style, one of the skills you'll learn in Chapter 7. You should now be able to do the following:

- Decide when to use direct formatting, and when to use a style.

- Distinguish between paragraph-formatting attributes and other kinds of attributes.

- Properly indent and align any paragraph, as well as determine how to find and use the appropriate tools.

- Adjust line spacing in a paragraph and spacing before and after paragraphs.

- Decide when to use tabs versus when to use a table.

- Apply and remove bullets and numbering.

- Use shading and boxes to highlight paragraphs.

Using Styles to Create a Great Looking Document

IN THIS CHAPTER

Working with the tools in the Styles group

Using, creating, and modifying styles

Updating the document using a Style Set

Creating and modifying Style Sets

Managing styles

Finding style inconsistencies

S tyles combine power and flexibility to serve as Word's most important formatting method. Some users hesitate to take advantage of styles because they can seem like an intimidating "advanced" feature with a dizzying array of options.

This chapter gives you a handle on which style tools to use for what in Word 2013 so that you can format new documents and update the look of older ones with ease. You will learn various ways to apply, clear, create, and modify styles. The chapter also introduces Style Sets, the Style Inspector, and methods for managing styles.

Using the Styles Group to Apply Styles

It's hard to overstate the value that styles deliver when creating and formatting a document. Not only do styles help a document look more lively and consistent, they give the reader a road map to understanding the relative priority of the text. Applying heading styles helps your readers identify major topics and their subtopics, and you can use other styles to emphasize special content, such as quotations and sidebars. Figure 7.1 compares a basic document that uses the default Normal style for all text to an improved version with title and heading styles applied.

FIGURE 7.1

Styles not only enhance the look of a document but also improve document readability.

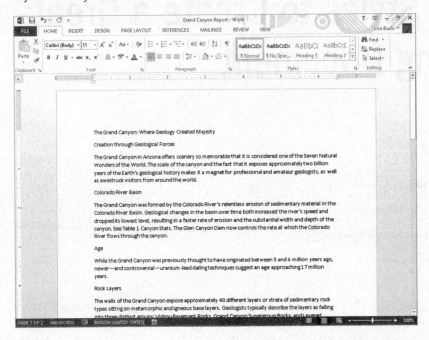

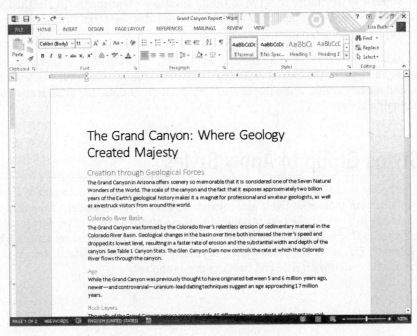

The Styles group on the Home tab of the Ribbon contains the primary set of commands and choices for applying and working with styles. On its face are three controls, shown in Figure 7.2: the Style gallery, the More button for expanding the gallery, and the Styles pane launcher. Note that in the gallery, a highlight appears around the name of the style applied to the paragraph holding the insertion point.

FIGURE 7.2

The Styles group is the command and control center for styles.

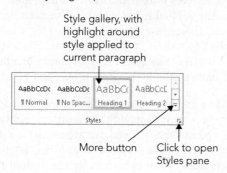

Style gallery, with
highlight around
style applied to
current paragraph

More button   Click to open
Styles pane

The number of styles that initially appear in the gallery depends on your screen resolution. As Figure 7.2 illustrates, at a very low screen resolution, the Style gallery might only display a handful of styles. To see all the available styles, click the More button to open the full gallery, as shown in Figure 7.3. If there are still more styles in the gallery, you can access them using the vertical scroll bar or by dragging the lower-right corner control to expand or shrink the size of the gallery.

FIGURE 7.3

Click the More button to open the Style gallery and see all the available styles.

> **NOTE**
>
> Word 2007 and 2010 sometimes called text formatting styles "Quick Styles" and the Style gallery the "Quick Styles gallery." This confusing terminology appears to have been eliminated when it comes to text formatting, but you might notice the term "Quick Style" applied to the galleries for formatting other types of objects, such as WordArt or SmartArt.

Notice also the Colors and Fonts controls. These tools work with themes, which aren't the same thing as styles. You can change the theme applied to the document to dramatically update its appearance. Unlike styles, however, themes are tied to the use of theme elements such as theme colors and effects applied to objects in your document. One way to think about themes is as design elements that affect the aesthetic appearance of a document. Styles, on the other hand, are geared more to the formatting of text and paragraphs.

In a moment you'll learn how to use the gallery and other mouse-oriented methods for applying styles. Word includes built-in shortcut keys for applying the most commonly used styles. Using only the keyboard shortcuts listed in Table 7.1, you can accomplish a significant amount of style formatting in a typical report or similar document. Move the insertion point into the paragraph to format, and press the keyboard shortcut for the desired style.

TABLE 7.1 Keyboard Shortcuts for Applying Built-In Styles

Press this keyboard khortcut	To apply this style
Ctrl+Shift+N	Normal
Alt+Ctrl+1	Heading 1
Alt+Ctrl+2	Heading 2
Alt+Ctrl+3	Heading 3

Applying styles from the Style gallery

When you first start typing in any new Word document, Word automatically applies the default Normal style to the text. As you create different types of content in the document, you should consider applying an appropriate style. For example, if you type a heading, consider applying a heading style to it, such as Heading 1, 2, or 3. The Normal.dotm template also includes built-in styles for the titles, subtitles, quotes, sidebars, emphasizing text, and more. To apply a style:

1. **Click in the paragraph to format, or select the text to format.** Whether you need to select the text depends on whether the style is a paragraph style, character style, or linked style. This is explained further in Step 3. (The section called "Formatting Characters Directly or with Styles" in Chapter 5 explained what paragraph, character, and linked styles are and the differences in how they work.)

2. **If needed, click the More button to open the Style gallery.**

3. **Move the mouse button over a style to display a Live Preview of how the selected text would look with the style applied.** See Figure 7.4. If you've just moved the insertion point to the paragraph rather than selecting text, Live Preview shows the style you've pointed to applied to the entire paragraph when it's a paragraph or linked style. For a character-only style, the style preview appears for only the word holding the insertion point. If you find that you need to apply a character style to more than just the current word, move the mouse pointer off the gallery and click in a blank area of the document. Then select the text and start over.

FIGURE 7.4

Point to a style in the Style gallery to see a Live Preview in the current paragraph or selection.

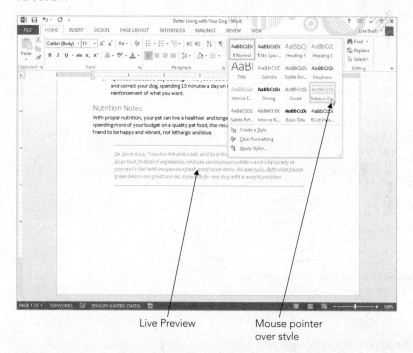

Live Preview   Mouse pointer
                      over style

4. **Click the style in the gallery to apply it and close the gallery.**

> **NOTE**
>
> `Normal.dotm` contains many different styles, and one of them happens to be named Normal. In fact, every Word template contains a style named Normal, so the actual formatting of this style will vary depending on whether you used an alternate template to create the document. You can think of the Normal style as the base or body style, which are other traditional terms for the body text in a document.

Applying styles using the Styles pane

Word 2013 continues to offer the Styles pane (or task pane), which you can use to view even more styles than appear in the Style gallery, and which offers additional commands for working with styles. You can either click the dialog box launcher in the lower-right corner of the Styles group of the Home tab or press Ctrl+Alt+Shift+S to open the Styles pane, shown in Figure 7.5. The pane by default lists only Recommended styles, and the style applied to the text holding the insertion point has a rectangular selection box around it (the Intense Quote style in Figure 7.5). See the "Recommended styles" section later in the chapter to learn more about what they are and how to work with them.

FIGURE 7.5

Click the Styles group dialog box launcher or press Alt+Ctrl+Shift+S to open the Styles pane.

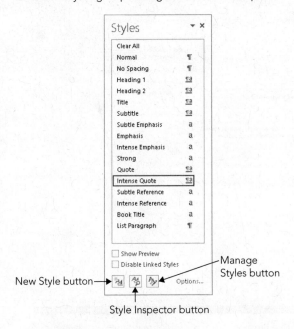

The basic method for applying a style from the Styles pane is similar to that for the Style gallery:

1. **Click in the paragraph to format, or select the text to format.** Whether you need to select the text depends on whether the style is a paragraph, linked, or character style.

2. **Click the style in the Style pane to apply it and close the gallery.**

This method doesn't enable you to get a Live Preview of the style before you apply it, but you can get information about a style prior to applying it in the Styles pane. You can do either of the following:

- Move the mouse pointer over the style to display a ScreenTip with information about the style's Font formatting settings, Paragraph formatting settings, and Style-related settings.

- Click the Show Preview check box below the list of styles in the pane. As shown in Figure 7.6, the styles listed in the pane preview their formatting settings. Also notice that this may make the basic list of styles too long to display in the pane, depending on your system's screen resolution. When that's the case and you move the mouse pointer over the list of styles, a scroll bar appears, and you can use it to scroll to the style choices you want.

FIGURE 7.6

Check Show Preview to see how each style looks in the Styles pane.

Select some text holding a particular style in the document, and then move the mouse pointer over that style in the Styles pane, and a drop-down list arrow appears to the right of it. Click the arrow to open a menu of commands for working with the style, as shown in Figure 7.7. (You also can right-click the style in the Style gallery of the Styles group of the Home tab to see the same menu.) The commands available on the menu vary depending on the type of style and whether you've selected any text in the document. The two most useful ones for working with the style formatting are:

- **Select All/Select All # Instance(s):** Click Select All to select all instances of the style in the document if it's the first time you're selecting the style during the current work session; after that the command changes to Select All # Instance(s). You can then reopen the drop-down list to see the number of locations in the document where you've applied the selected style. You can then select another style to apply to all the selected areas of text, quickly changing from one style to another throughout the document. If you've previously selected and then deselected all instances of the style, you can reopen the menu and choose Select All # Instance(s) to reselect them.

- **Remove All/Clear Formatting of # Instance(s):** Click this option to clean up a document's extraneous formatting. If you have not selected instances of the style in the current Word work session, the command that appears is Remove All. That command changes to Clear Formatting of # instances after you've selected all the instances of the style using one of the options noted in the prior bullet. Remove All/Clear Formatting of # Instance(s) does not delete the text in question. Instead, it removes the style wherever it is used, and resets the formatting of those occurrences to the default style for the current document, usually Normal.

FIGURE 7.7

Open the style's menu to access helpful commands.

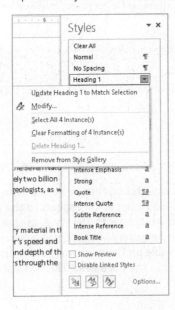

Applying Styles with the Apply Styles Pane

You can also display the Apply Styles pane (shown here) by pressing Ctrl+Shift+S. It has some of the same tools as the Styles pane. You can select a style to apply from its scrollable Style Name drop-down list, or use its Reapply and Modify buttons to work with style settings. It's just a matter of preference whether you want to use the Styles pane or the Apply Styles pane.

Reapplying or resetting a style

After you apply a style, you can apply direct formatting such as bold, italic, paragraph spacing changes, and so on. If you later decide to remove the added formatting, you don't have to backtrack setting by setting. Instead, you can reapply the style or reset the text to the style to remove the extra formatting settings all at once. Use any of these three methods to get the job done after selecting the text to reset:

- Click the style again in the Styles pane.
- Click Reapply in the Apply Styles pane.
- Press Ctrl+Spacebar.

Clearing all styles from selected text

You can clear all style formatting from selected text, which returns the text to the default Normal style. As for some of the other aspects of dealing with styles, Word 2013 provides many ways to handle this task in addition to using the Clear Formatting of # Instance(s) command in the Styles pane as described earlier:

- Click the Style gallery More button, and then click Clear Formatting at the bottom. (Refer to Figure 7.4.)
- In the Styles pane, click the Clear All choice at the top.
- On the Home tab of the Ribbon, click the Clear Formatting button in the upper-right corner of the Font group.

Modifying and Creating Styles

Despite the variety of styles available in most document templates, you may not find the exact style to give your document the appearance you want. The font or point size might be wrong, or the spacing might be off. No problem. Change it. Or, if you still need the existing style but want a slightly different version for another purpose, create a new style.

Modifying an existing style

When you've already applied a style throughout a document, you might want to modify that existing style to adjust the look of the already formatted text rather than applying a different style. You might need to make only a slight change to the style, such as adjusting its font size or spacing. To change an existing style:

1. **Right-click the style in the Style gallery or open the style's menu in the Styles pane, and click Modify; you also can select the style and click the Modify button in the Apply Styles pane.** Any of the methods opens the Modify Style dialog box shown in Figure 7.8.

2. **Make the desired formatting changes to the style.** The Formatting section of the dialog box includes a number of the settings found in the Font and Paragraph groups on the Home tab of the Ribbon. If the formatting you need to change isn't shown, click the Format button in the lower-left corner and click one of the choices there, such as Numbering or Text Effects, to open a dialog box with additional formatting settings. Click Close or OK to finish working in that additional dialog box.

FIGURE 7.8

Use the Modify Style dialog box to make changes to a style.

3. **Click OK to close the Modify Style dialog box.** Word updates the formatting for all text with the style applied in the document.

> **WARNING**
>
> Keep the Automatically update check box in the Modify Style dialog box turned off (unchecked) unless you absolutely need it. When that check box is enabled, each time you make changes to text using a specific style, those changes are automatically incorporated into the style's definition. All other text in the document formatted with that style will automatically change to reflect the changes in the style's definition. That might be just what you want if you've used the style in just one way in the document. On the other hand, if you've used the style in various ways (for example, say you have used Heading 3 for headings, table titles, sidebar titles, and so on) you might want formatting changes to apply in some of those instances but not others. In such a case, having Automatically update checked would work against you, because it would likely update text that you wanted to remain as is. Note that for this reason, there is no Automatically update option when you select the Normal style and open the Modify Style dialog box. You are so likely to apply other formatting to Normal text that any automatic updating would create an endless loop of updates to the Normal style.

A second way to update a style is to use the controls in the Font and Paragraph groups in the Home tab of the Ribbon to reformat some text to which you previously applied the style. When the text looks the way you want, click the style's drop-down arrow in the Styles pane, and then click Update *Style Name* to Match Selection.

If you find you frequently update style formatting, remember that you can enable Prompt to update style in Word's Advanced options. Then, any time you make formatting changes to styled text (except for the Normal style, which can't be automatically updated by any method) and then click the style's name in the Styles pane, Word displays the prompt dialog box shown in Figure 7.9. The Update the style to reflect recent changes option will add the new formatting to the style's definition, whereas the Reapply the formatting of the style to the selection option will revert the style. Leave the former option selected and then click OK to finish changing the style. To enable Prompt to update style, choose File ⇨ Options ⇨ Advanced, and in the Editing options section, click to check Prompt to update style. Click OK.

FIGURE 7.9

If you've enabled Prompt to update style, Word asks you to confirm whether you want to update or reapply the style.

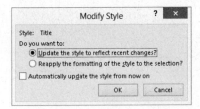

Creating a style from scratch

There are a couple of different ways you can create a new style. In general, every new style you create will be based on an existing style. So you will want to start from a style that's similar to the type of style you need to create. For example, if you want to create a Body Text style, start by reformatting some Normal text. Or, if you want to create a new heading style, start from the existing heading style that's closest to the look you want.

Here's how to use the Create New Style from Formatting dialog box to save a new style:

1. **Select some text that uses a style similar to the one you want to create, and apply desired formatting.** Leave the text selected.

2. **Click the new Style button in the lower-left corner of the Styles pane.** The Create New Style from Formatting dialog box shown in Figure 7.10 appears.

FIGURE 7.10

Set up a completely new style in this dialog box.

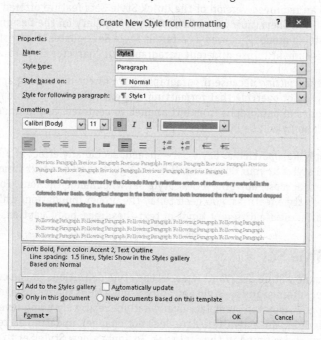

3. **Type a name for the style in the Name text box.**

4. **Make further adjustments to the style settings as needed.** For example, use the Style type drop-down list to indicate whether the style is a Paragraph, Character, Linked (paragraph and character), or another type of style. If you leave Paragraph selected as the style, use the Style for following paragraph drop-down to choose which style Word automatically applies to any new paragraph you create by pressing Enter. For a heading style, you would want this to be a Normal or body text style in many cases. Also apply any additional formatting changes as needed.

5. **Leave Add to the Styles gallery checked to provide access to the style via that control on the Home tab of the Ribbon.**

6. **Click OK to finish creating the style.**

You can also use the Modify Style dialog box to create a new style. Just change the entry in the Name text box in addition to making any formatting changes, and when you click OK Word creates the new style.

Changing the Whole Document via Style Sets

Word 2013 offers an improved version of the Quick Style Sets feature offered in prior Word versions. You can find them, now called Style Sets, in a gallery on the Design tab, in the Document Formatting group. Applying a different Style Set updates all the style formatting throughout the document to use different paragraph and character style formatting.

I emphasize *style formatting* because if paragraphs have direct formatting applied, applying a Style Set does not override that formatting. For example, if you manually change the alignment of a series of paragraphs from left aligned to centered, any alignment formatting in a Style Set you apply will be ignored.

The impact of applying a particular Style Set—indeed, seeing any effect at all—depends on your having used styles in your document. If you simply left all the text formatted with the Normal style, then, at most, applying a new Style Set will change the font. For maximum benefit from Word's style features, you need to lay the proper foundation, which means using styles to differentiate different kinds of text (headings, body, captions, and so on).

Applying a Style Set

When you apply a new Style Set, Word replaces the style definitions in the current document with those contained in the Style Set's `.dotx` file. (More about this shortly.) It effectively overlays a new document template over what you're already using (even though the name of the underlying document template does not change), updating all text that uses any corresponding styles found in the Style Set. To apply a new Style Set to the document:

1. **Click the Design tab on the Ribbon.**
2. **If needed, click the More button to open the Style Set gallery in the Document Formatting group.**
3. **Move the mouse button over a Style Set to display a Live Preview of how the selected text would look with the style applied.** See Figure 7.11.
4. **When you find the Style Set you want to use, click it to apply it to the document.**

Creating and deleting Style Sets

You create your own Style Sets to give yourself even more power and flexibility to format your documents with just the styles you want. Word stores each Style Set in a `.dotx` (not macro-enabled) template. When you create a Style Set, Word automatically suggests saving it in the `C:\Users\user name\AppData\Roaming\Microsoft\QuickStyles` folder. Leave this folder selected so that your custom Style Set will be automatically included in the Style Set gallery. Follow this process to create and save a Style Set:

1. **Apply a Style Set, if needed, and modify the document styles as desired.** The modified document styles will be stored in the new Style Set.

2. **Click the Design tab, click the More button in the Document Formatting group to open the Style Set gallery, and then click Save as a New Style Set.** The Save as a New Style Set dialog box shown in Figure 7.12 appears.

3. **Type a name for the Style Set file in the File name text box.**

4. **Click Save.**

FIGURE 7.11

Point to a Style Set in the gallery to see a Live Preview of the potential new document styles.

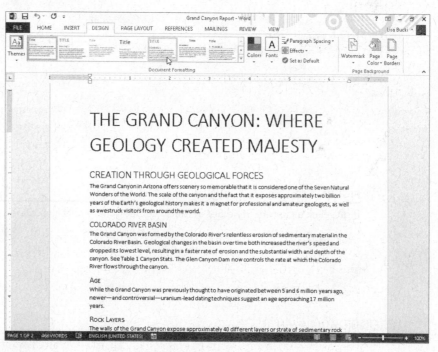

When you display the Style Set gallery after creating at least one custom Style Set, the gallery includes your style set in the new Custom category. If you want to delete a custom style set, right-click it in the gallery as shown in Figure 7.13, and click Delete. Click Yes in the dialog box that prompts you to confirm the deletion.

FIGURE 7.12

Word automatically suggests a specific folder to hold your new Style Set file.

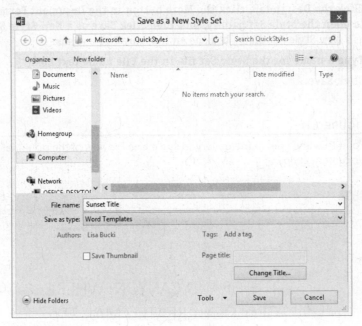

FIGURE 7.13

Right-click a custom Style Set in the Style Set gallery and click Delete to remove it.

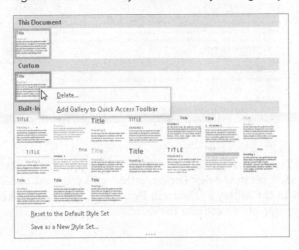

TIP

Do you have customized styles in your `Normal.dotm` file? If so, before working with Style Sets, protect your original `Normal.dotm` Style Set by saving it as a unique Style Set. To do this, press Ctrl+N to create a new document window based on `Normal.dotm`. Click the Design tab, and in the Document Formatting group, click the More button to open the Style Set gallery. Click Save as a New Style Set. In the File name text box, specify a name that's unambiguous, such as `My normal.dotm styles` and then click Save.

Word stores each of its default Style Set files in the `C:\Program Files (x86)\Microsoft Office\office15\1033\QuickStyles` (32-bit version) or `C:\Program Files\Microsoft Office\office15\1033\QuickStyles` (64-bit version) folder, as shown in Figure 7.14. The default Style Sets are stored as Word template (`.dotx`) files. In theory, you can apply one of the Style Sets to a blank document, modify the styles, and then use the Save as a New Style dialog box to navigate to the folder holding the default Style Set files, and enter the name of one of those files to save over it, thus modifying it. In practice, though, leaving the default Style Set files undisturbed and creating your own Style Set files gives you the choice to continue using the default styles in the future along with your custom sets.

FIGURE 7.14

The default Style Sets are stored as Word template files.

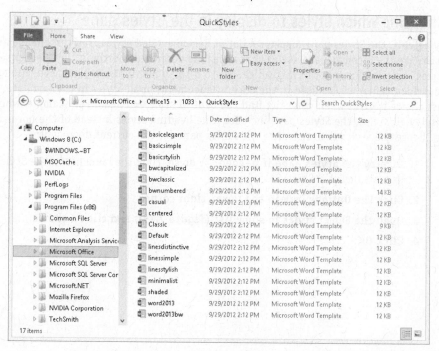

> **NOTE**
> The default .dotx files contain no text or other formatting, but only style information for dozens of built-in styles. To see a list of these styles, double-click one of the .dotx files in a folder window to open a blank document based on it in Word. Display the Styles pane, and then display all styles as described later in this chapter.

Changing your mind

If you've been experimenting with Style Sets but now want to revert to the styles of the document's underlying template, in most cases you can. Click the Design tab, and in the Document Formatting group, click the More button to open the Style Set gallery. Click Reset to Default Style Set near the bottom of the gallery to reset the styles immediately.

Managing Styles

You have control over numerous other aspects of how and where styles appear and behave in Word. Cleaning up or expanding the style listings can make you much more efficient when you're taking on the task of formatting your document. This section covers the most important style management features you need to know about.

Choosing which styles to display in the Styles pane

By default, the Styles pane displays a list of Recommended styles. You can change and prioritize the recommended styles that appear as described shortly in the "Recommended styles" section. But you can instead choose to display just in use styles (used throughout your documents), styles used in the current document, or all styles in the template. The last choice is great when you can't find the type of style you need. For example, when you display all styles, the Styles pane includes nine heading styles instead of the normal three. To choose the styles that appear in the Styles pane for the current document:

1. **Display the Styles pane if needed.** To do so, click the launcher in the Styles group or press Ctrl+Alt+Shift+S.
2. **Click the Options link in the lower-right corner.**
3. **Open the Select styles to show list (Figure 7.15), and click a choice.**
4. **Click OK.**

FIGURE 7.15

Choose how many styles Word lists in the Styles pane.

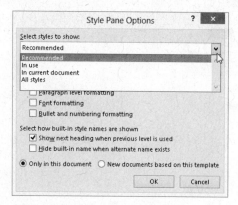

Removing a style from the gallery

Depending on how avidly you create and use your own styles, your Style gallery could rap-idly fill with styles, making it more cumbersome to use than it otherwise would be. You might want to trim the styles that appear in the gallery for certain documents, so you can more readily work with the styles you prefer. Removing a style from the Style gallery does not remove the style from the document; it only removes it from the gallery listing.

Use the Styles pane to control a style's inclusion in the Style gallery. Click the style's drop-down arrow, and then click Remove from Style Gallery to remove it. To reinstate the style in the gallery, display its menu again, and then click Add to Style Gallery.

You also can remove a style from the Style gallery by right-clicking the style and clicking Remove from Gallery.

Recommended styles

Word includes a Manage Styles dialog box that enables you to perform advanced style man-agement operations. Though there's not room to cover all the options exhaustively, you can get familiar with some key options here. To open the dialog box, click the Manage Styles button at the bottom of the Styles pane.

The Recommend tab, shown in Figure 7.16, controls which styles show up on the list of recommended styles. A *recommended style* shows up in each of the style-related task panes and the Style gallery. Click a style in the list at the top, and then click the desired button under Set whether style shows when viewing recommended styles. Clicking Show ensures the style will be displayed, or you can select Hide until used or Hide. It's a great way to focus the options when you want to exercise strong control over document formatting.

FIGURE 7.16

Use the Recommend tab to control what styles show up when you restrict style controls to displaying recommended styles.

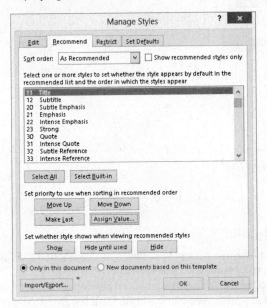

In the list of styles at the top of the dialog box, you can apply your changes one at a time or by using standard Windows selection techniques to select multiple styles. Note the Select All and Select Built-in buttons, too, which enable you to quickly distinguish between Word's standard styles and user-created styles.

Use the Move Up/Move Down/Make Last/Assign Value tools to determine the recommended order. You can even alphabetize them, if that makes more sense to you. Click OK to apply your changes when finished.

Restricted styles

For even stronger style enforcement, the Restrict tab of the Manage Styles dialog box enables you to limit which styles can be used. This is a good tool for designing templates and forms in which you want extremely tight control over the content formatting. It's also useful in setting up training classes for Word, when you might want to tame the options a bit to avoid overwhelming the novice user.

Additionally, if you want to enforce the use of only styles—and not direct formatting—the restricted styles capability provides a way to do it. Check Limit formatting to permitted styles, shown near the bottom of Figure 7.17, to accomplish this feat.

FIGURE 7.17

The Restrict tab enables you to make direct formatting off-limits.

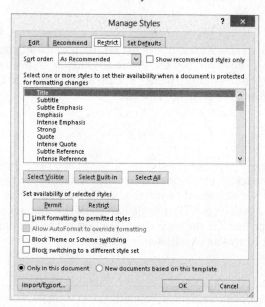

By restricting formatting only to styles, you effectively prevent the use of direct formatting tools. As shown in Figure 7.18, when formatting is restricted to Normal and Heading 1 through Heading 5, most of the Ribbon Font and Paragraph controls are grayed out (dimmed) as unavailable.

FIGURE 7.18

Limiting formatting to the use of styles turns off many of the direct formatting tools on the Home tab of the Ribbon.

To control the availability of a particular style, click it in the list on the Restrict tab, and then click either Permit or Restrict under Set availability of selected styles. Note that not only can you limit formatting only to permitted styles; you can also enable Block Theme or Scheme switching. If you want to tame "artistic" tendencies of users whose mission statement apparently includes using up all the colored ink or toner in the company printer, this provides an avenue of attack.

When you finish making your choices, click OK. A Start Enforcing Protection dialog box prompts you to enter and confirm a password. Do so, and then click OK.

Deleting a style

You can delete a style from the Styles pane. As mentioned earlier, Word won't let you delete certain built-in styles such as Normal. However, you can delete any custom style you create if you decide not to use it. Point to the style in the pane, click its down arrow, and then click Delete *Style Name*. At the confirmation prompt, click Yes.

Style Inspector

The Style Inspector enables you to quickly determine whether the formatting for selected text consists of a style alone, or a style and direct formatting. In Figure 7.19, notice that under the Paragraph formatting and Text level formatting (character), the first box identifies the applied style, and the second box has the word Plus:. The text to the right of the Plus: identifies any potential direct formatting applied over the style.

FIGURE 7.19

The Style Inspector can help you diagnose where direct formatting has been applied to styled text.

To use the Style Inspector, select the text to diagnose, and then click the Style Inspector button at the bottom of the Styles pane.

Summary

In this chapter you explored a variety of features that can help you format a document faster and more consistently through styles. You should also be able to do the following:

- Use the Style gallery, Styles pane, and other methods to apply, create, and modify styles.
- Use the Styles pane to quickly select all occurrences of any given style.
- Reapply a style's formatting.
- Update the look of the whole document by applying a Style Set.
- Create and delete a custom Style Set.
- Control which styles appear in the Styles pane and the Style gallery.
- Use the Manage Styles dialog box to hide and restrict styles and direct formatting.
- Use the Style Inspector to solve formatting mysteries.

7

Controlling Document Appearance with Sections and More

IN THIS CHAPTER

Adjusting basic page setup

Working with section breaks and section formatting

Understanding the header/footer layer

Navigating and designing headers and footers

Including page numbers

Creating and changing columns

Applying page borders

Working with themes

This chapter examines some concepts that might be a bit challenging if you're new to Word, perhaps even if you're not new to Word. Grasping these concepts, however, enables you to organize and vary the overall setup in your documents as needed.

The chapter starts out by identifying how to use basic Page Setup choices. From there, you learn how to use section breaks to change the page setup as needed for different parts of the document. Next you learn how to add a header or footer to identify document or section contents and number pages. Finally, the chapter shows you how to use columns to make text more readable in common publications such as newsletters, how to add a page border, and how to work with themes.

Changing Basic Page Setup

The Page Setup group on the Page Layout tab of the Ribbon offers the key settings you might need to change when determining the overall layout of a document. In a basic document without section breaks, most of the Page Setup group choices apply to the entire document. Once you start adding section breaks, as described later in the chapter, you can adjust the Page Setup choices within each individual section as needed.

Using the Page Setup dialog box

Unlike some other features in Word 2013 where traditional dialog boxes have been replaced with panes, Word still offers a Page Setup dialog box that you can use to fine-tune page formatting for the overall document (or current section, if applicable). To open the Page Setup dialog box, click the Page Layout tab, and then click the Page Setup group dialog box launcher. Figure 8.1 shows the Page Setup group choices and the Page Setup dialog box. Work on the various tabs of the dialog box as described throughout this chapter, and then click OK to apply your changes and close the dialog box.

FIGURE 8.1

The Page Setup group of the Page Layout tab enables you to make key document design choices and to open the Page Setup dialog box.

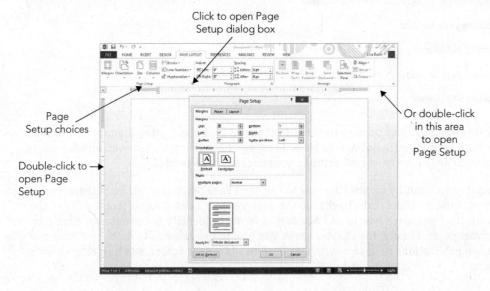

Click to open Page Setup dialog box

Page Setup choices

Double-click to open Page Setup

Or double-click in this area to open Page Setup

TIP

If the Page Layout tab isn't showing, you can also open the Page Setup dialog box by double-clicking the vertical ruler, if it's displayed, or even by double-clicking outside the left and right margins on the horizontal ruler.

Margins

Click Margins in the Page Setup group of the Page Layout tab to display the gallery of choices shown in Figure 8.2. You can apply one of the available preset margin settings by clicking it. If the document contains multiple sections, the presets will be applied only to the current document section if nothing is selected, or only to the selected sections if multiple sections are included in the selection.

FIGURE 8.2

The Margins gallery offers a selection of preset margins.

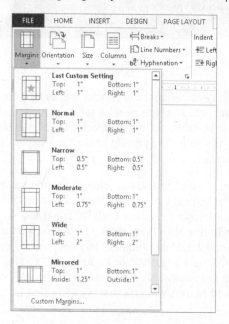

If you want more precise control, choose click Custom Margins, which opens the Page Setup dialog box to the Margins tab, shown back in Figure 8.1. From here you can control all margins as needed and apply the change where you want, which you'll learn more about later in the chapter. You can also adjust the top and bottom margins by dragging the boundary between the shaded and unshaded areas in the vertical ruler at the left side of the document window as shown in Figure 8.3. To increase the top margin, drag the top border down. To increase the bottom margin, draw the bottom border up. In either case, press the Alt key to display the margin setting as you're dragging. You can similarly drag to resize the left and right margins on the horizontal toolbar, but you may need to move the indention controls out of the way.

FIGURE 8.3

Drag the vertical ruler to change top and bottom margins.

Dragging to resize the top margin

> **TIP**
>
> Often you will choose Margin settings before adding any text to your document. But you can change margins later, and Word will rewrap the text in the document as needed.

Orientation

Orientation refers to whether the page is laid out horizontally (landscape) or vertically (portrait — the default orientation). You might sometimes need to rotate a document to landscape in order to fit wider pictures, charts, tables, or other objects. To change the document orientation, click Orientation in the Page Setup group of the Page Layout tab, and click either Landscape or Portrait as needed.

If you only have one object or page that has content that is too wide to fit, you can keep the orientation as portrait and rotate the table, chart, or picture instead. For pictures and charts, rotation isn't challenging. With Wrapping (Picture Tools⇨Format tab, in the Arrange group) set to anything other than In line with text, simply rotate the picture or chart 90 degrees by dragging the top center rotation handle, or by choosing Picture Tools⇨Format⇨Arrange⇨Rotate Objects⇨Rotate Right 90° or Rotate Left 90°. (For shapes and some other objects, the command is on the Drawing Tools⇨Format contextual tab.) If you rotate only the object, the headers and footers will still display according to the Portrait orientation.

Tables are a bit more challenging, but you have several options. If you're just now creating the table, select the entire table and in the Table Tools⇨Layout tab in the Alignment group, click Text Direction to rotate the text so that it can be read if you tilt your head to the right or left. Keep in mind that columns and rows are reversed. It's not necessarily easy to work this way, but it can be done, as shown in Figure 8.4.

Another option would be to copy a finished table to the Clipboard, choose Paste⇨Paste Special in the Clipboard group of the Home tab, and paste the table into the document as a picture. Because it's now a picture, you can choose any floating wrapping style and then

FIGURE 8.4

With all text in a table rotated 90 degrees, it's possible to create a sideways table, rather than have to change page orientation within a document.

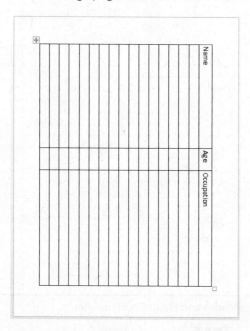

rotate the table as needed so that it fits comfortably, but sideways, in a portrait-oriented Word document page. Headers and footers will display in portrait mode because you haven't changed the paper orientation. The downside is that sometimes the graphics resolution of this technique isn't perfect. You'll have to decide if it's acceptable and legible. Plus, to make changes in the table, you need to maintain a copy of the actual table and remake the conversion as needed.

NOTE

The Page Setup group of the Page Layout tab also contains Hyphenation, which you can turn on document wide.

Size

The Size choice in the Page Setup group of the Page Layout tab refers to paper size. Click the Size button display a gallery of preset standard sizes, shown in Figure 8.5. Clicking More Paper Sizes displays the Paper tab in the Page Setup dialog box as shown in Figure 8.6. To create your own paper size, open the Paper size drop-down list at the top and click Custom size. Enter the desired sizes in the Width and Height text boxes; the maximum entry for each is 22 inches. Make sure your printer supports the measurements you enter, and then click OK to apply the size change to the document.

FIGURE 8.5

Click a preset paper size, or click More Paper Sizes to display the Paper tab in the Page Setup dialog box.

FIGURE 8.6

Choose Custom size and then enter new Width and Height measurements.

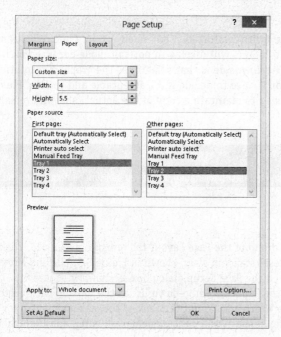

Note that you also can change the Paper source settings on the Paper tab of the Page Setup dialog box, as shown in Figure 8.6. For example, if the first page of the document prints on letterhead and the rest prints on plain paper, choose the applicable sources from the First page and Other pages lists.

> **TIP**
>
> In most cases, you will use the Manual Feed Tray to print envelopes. Even when you've inserted an envelope page or section in a document, it's usually easiest to print that page separately from the rest of the document so that you can be careful when feeding the blank envelope into the tray.

Section Formatting

Word uses *section breaks* to separate distinctly formatted parts of a document. Most documents, in fact, start off with and have just a single section. But a more complex document like a product brochure might need different sections if, for example, you want the product description text to appear in two columns on one page and the product specifications to appear in three columns on another page. You have to create new sections when you want to vary the following kinds of formatting within one document:

- **Headers and footers:** Includes changes in page numbering style (except for Different First Page settings)
- **Footnotes:** Can be set to be numbered continuously or set to restart numbering on every new page or section
- **Changes in line numbering style:** Except for suppression on a paragraph-by-paragraph basis
- **Margins:** Indentation can vary within a section, but not margins.
- **Orientation:** Landscape versus portrait
- **Paper size:** 8.5 × 11 (letter), 8.5 × 14 (legal), 7.25 × 10.5 (executive), A4 (210.03 × 297.03 mm), and so on
- **Paper source:** Upper tray, envelope feed, manual feed, and so on
- **Columns:** Snaking newspaper-style columns, the number of which cannot vary within a document section

> **NOTE**
>
> To work more effectively with sections, make sure that you can see section breaks and other nonprinting formatting characters. Press Ctrl+Shift+8 (Ctrl+*) to toggle them on and off, or click the Show/Hide button in the Paragraph group of the Home tab of the Ribbon. You also may need to show and hide the rulers from time to time with View⇨ Show⇨ Ruler. From here on out in this chapter, it's assumed that you have nonprinting characters turned on so you can see section marks and have the rulers on when needed.

Section breaks overview

Word uses four kinds of section breaks. What kind of break you use depends on why you're breaking the text:

- **Next Page:** Causes the new section to begin on the next page
- **Continuous:** Enables the current and next section to coexist on the same page. Not all kinds of formatting can coexist on the same page, so even if you choose Continuous, Word will sometimes force the differently formatted content onto a new page. Section formatting that can be different on different parts of the same page includes the number of columns, left and right margins, and line numbering.
- **Even Page:** Causes the new section to begin on the next even page. If the following page would have been odd, then that page will be blank (unless it has header/footer content, which can include watermarks).
- **Odd Page:** Causes the new section to begin on the next odd page. If the following page would have been even, then that page will be blank, except as noted for the Even Page break.

If you set up a letter in which the first page is to be printed on letterhead but subsequent pages are to be printed on regular stock (using different paper feed methods), the first page should be in a separate document section, because you will probably not want it to display any header or footer information that might overprint the preprinted letterhead contents. If you set up a letter for which the first or last page is an envelope, the envelope must be in a separate section — for multiple reasons, because envelopes typically use a different printer paper source, different orientation (landscape), and different margin settings.

Inserting or deleting a section break

To insert a section break:

1. **Click to position the insertion point at the location where you want the break to appear.**
2. **In the Page Setup group of the Page Layout tab, click Breaks.** As shown in Figure 8.7, Word displays a variety of kinds of breaks, including the four types of section breaks under Section Breaks at the bottom.

FIGURE 8.7

The icons next to the four section break types provide a graphic hint of what the different breaks do.

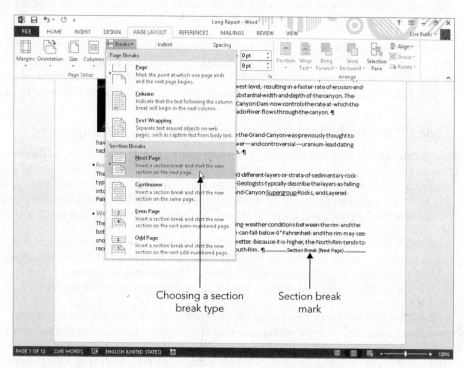

Choosing a section break type

Section break mark

3. **Click the desired section break.** Word adds the section break into the document, and adds one or more new pages as needed depending on the type of break. If nonprinting characters are displayed, you will also see the section break mark in the document.

To delete a section break, press Ctrl+Shift+8 (Ctrl+*) or click the Show/Hide button in the Paragraph group of the Home tab of the Ribbon to toggle the display of nonprinting formatting characters, such as the section break mark shown in Figure 8.7. Click just to the left of the section break you want to delete to position the insertion point there, press Shift+Right Arrow to select the mark, and then press Delete. If this results in an extra empty paragraph, delete it.

Automatic section breaks

Because some kinds of formatting require a section break in order to vary within a document, Word automatically inserts one or more section breaks when you apply "qualifying" formatting to selected text. Sometimes it gets those breaks right, sometimes not. You'll have to be vigilant if you're going to rely on this feature.

For example, suppose you want an interior set of paragraphs to be formatted in three columns, while the adjacent areas are formatted as a single column. Select the paragraphs you want to differentiate and then set up the columns as described later in this chapter. Word automatically inserts Continuous section breaks before and after the selected text to cordon it off for the distinct formatting.

Sometimes, but not always, Word will insert the wrong kind of section break before and/or after the selected text. It's never quite clear why, but when that happens the best recourse is to press Ctrl+Z to undo the attempt, bracket the target text with the desired type of section breaks, and then apply the formatting to the section you want formatted differently.

Styles, section formatting, and paragraph formatting

Styles can contain font and character- and paragraph-formatting attributes. However, they cannot contain section-formatting attributes. Therefore, for example, you cannot create a style that would enable you to format a given selection with three columns and 1.5-inch left and right margins. Stand by for a few minutes, however, and you'll see how you can indeed effectively create a style for section formatting, although it's not really a style.

Recall that in Chapter 6, "Paragraph Formatting," you learned that the paragraph mark is the repository of paragraph formatting. Similarly, the section break is the repository of section formatting. If you delete a section break, the current section adopts the formatting of the section that follows — that is, the section whose section break is still intact.

Where is the section break in a document that has only one section? In fact, most documents have only a single section, so this is a serious and valid question. There is an implied section break at the end of the document, so if you insert a section break into a single-section document, the formatting for section one resides in that section break, and the formatting for section two effectively resides in the permanent paragraph mark at the end of the document. (If you create a new, blank document with nonprinting characters displayed, you'll see that it contains a paragraph mark you cannot delete.)

Saving section formatting for reuse

If section formatting can't reside in a style, then how can you save it for later use? Suppose you often use a precise set of section formatting attributes — margins and columns, for example — and want to save them for use in other documents. There is a way, but it doesn't involve using what's traditionally called a style. Instead, use a Quick Part or a Building Block. To do this:

1. **Create a new blank document.**

2. **Insert a Continuous or Next Page section break, as needed — to bracket the area to be formatted.** Leave the formatting prior to that first section break as vanilla or typical as possible. This first section break will shield existing text from the new formatting when the Building Block or Quick Part is inserted into an existing document. If it's inserted at the beginning of a document, the first section break can then be deleted.

3. **Press Enter twice or more, and insert another section break of the desired type.** You don't have to insert text between the section breaks because section formatting resides in the section break mark, but you can add text if you want.

4. **Format the area between the section breaks as needed.** (More on section formatting is to come later in the chapter.)

5. **Select both section breaks and whatever you've placed between them.**

6. **Choose Insert ⇨ Text ⇨ Quick Parts ⇨ Save Selection to Quick Part Gallery.** The Create New Building Block dialog box shown in Figure 8.8 appears.

7. **Enter the name and other pertinent information about the new building block.** If you'll need this item frequently, save it to the Quick Parts gallery by choosing Quick Parts from the Gallery drop-down list. Or, if you choose AutoText as the Gallery drop-down list choice as shown in Figure 8.8, you'll be able to insert it by typing the beginning of the name and pressing F3 or pressing Enter after the ScreenTip appears to insert it; I've left the space out between 3 and Columns in the Name text box because that will make the AutoText entry more distinct and easier to use. You can use the Category drop-down list to assign another category if desired, and use the Save in choice to save the Quick Part in the current file rather than the default Normal template.

FIGURE 8.8

Save a Building Block to create reusable section "styles."

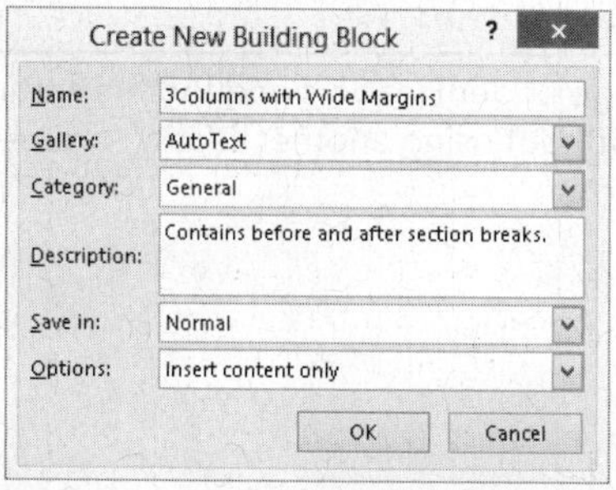

Create New Building Block	?	×

Name:	3Columns with Wide Margins
Gallery:	AutoText
Category:	General
Description:	Contains before and after section breaks.
Save in:	Normal
Options:	Insert content only

OK   Cancel

> **TIP**
>
> If you want to create a custom category for the section building block, open the Category drop-down list and click Create New Category. In the Create New Category dialog box, type a category name in the Name text box, and click OK to return to the Create New Building Block dialog box.

8. **Click OK to finish creating the building block.**

Now, whenever you want this particular kind of formatting, it's there waiting for you. Choose Insert ⇨ Text ⇨ Quick Parts, and if it's in the Quick Parts gallery, click it to insert it. If it's in AutoText, point to AutoText and click it. Or, if it's elsewhere, choose Building

8

Blocks Organizer to find and insert it. Or, if the first part of the name is unique like the example in Figure 8.8 and you saved it to the AutoText gallery, type it and press F3.

Page layout within a section

You're already seen the Margins and Paper tabs in the Page Setup dialog box. Click within the section where you want to change the settings, and then make choices from the Margins and Paper tabs as described earlier. After you click OK to close the Page Setup dialog box, the changes will apply in the current section only.

> **NOTE**
>
> It should be emphasized, however, that making a single-page landscape carries some consequences. Consider page numbers and other header and footer content. If the whole page is changed to landscape, then the header and footer now rotate as well. To get the orientation correct, you might consider putting the header and footer material into a text box that you can position as needed, or rotate the object with the page still in Portrait orientation, as described earlier.

The Page Setup dialog box also includes a Layout tab, visible in Figure 8.9, that houses additional settings that are vital for section setup. The choices under Headers and footers enable you to control whether a section uses all the same header/footer information, or whether the footer information is different. See the discussion of headers and footers later in the chapter to learn more about this. The other type settings on this tab will be described shortly.

FIGURE 8.9

The Different odd and even and Different first page under Headers and footers settings enable you to set different headers and footers without using another section break.

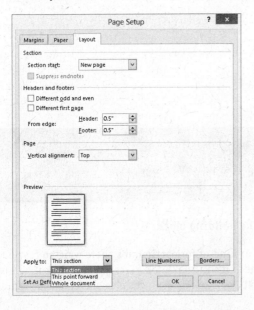

All three tabs of the Page Setup dialog box include an Apply to drop-down list. If you haven't added any additional section breaks to the document, by default this setting is set to Whole document, although you can open the drop-down list and click This point forward instead. If you've created a section, by default, Apply to displays This section, which is why the Page Setup choices apply only to the current section as noted earlier. If you've selected text in one or more sections, the list changes to include Selected sections or Selected text options. The bottom line is that you need to pay attention to the Apply to setting on any of the Page Setup dialog tabs to ensure you've specified the right document location for applying the Page Setup changes.

Fixing or changing a section break

The Section start setting shown in Figure 8.9 is a bit cryptic and confusing to many users, but it can be extremely useful. Have you ever ended up with the wrong kind of section break? For example, suppose you want a Continuous section break, but you have a New Page, Odd, or Even section break instead. This can happen either because *you* inserted the wrong kind of break, or because Word inserted the wrong kind of break automatically.

The ordinary impulse is to delete the wrong one and insert the kind you want. Sometimes, however, despite your best efforts, you still end up with the wrong kind of break. This is exactly the situation where you need to use Section start. Click to put the insertion point in the section that is preceded by the wrong kind of break. Open the Page Setup dialog box using any of the techniques described earlier. Click the Layout tab, open the Section start drop-down list, click the kind of section break you want, and click OK.

Vertical page alignment

Another often-unnoticed feature in Word is the Vertical alignment setting under Page near the center of the Layout tab of the Page Setup dialog box. By default, Word sets the vertical alignment to Top, and most users never discover the additional options, which include Center, Bottom, and Justified (which adds line and paragraph spacing to help the text fill the page vertically between the top and bottom margins). For example, the document in Figure 8.10 has been centered vertically to create a more balanced appearance. Because it is a section-formatting attribute, you can set vertical alignment for the whole document or just for selected sections.

Vertical alignment can be extremely useful for particular parts of a publication — such as the title page for a formal report, booklet, or book — as well as for short letters, brochures, newsletters, and flyers. For title pages, setting the vertical alignment to Centered is almost always more efficient than trying to insert the right number of empty paragraphs above the top line, or trying to set the Spacing Before: to just the right amount in the Paragraph group of the Page Layout tab. For one-page notices, vertical alignment is also often just what the doctor ordered.

8

FIGURE 8.10

Center a page vertically to balance the white space at the top and bottom of the page.

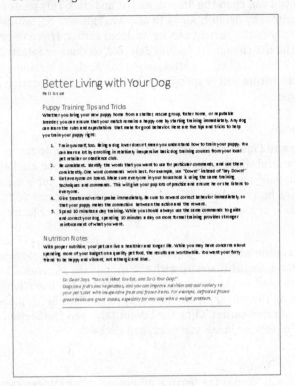

For some newsletters and other page-oriented publications, setting the alignment to Justified serves a couple of purposes. Not only does it make the most use of the whole sheet of paper, but it also adjusts line spacing to do it. Hence the appearance is smoother than it might be otherwise. This setting also lets you optimize the point size if you want to make the font as large as possible without spilling onto another page.

Numbering lines in legal or academic documents

Line numbering, which is different from numbered lists, often is used in legal documents, such as affidavits. The numbering allows for ready reference to testimony by page and line number. Line numbering itself, however, is not a paragraph-formatting attribute. It is a section-formatting attribute. Turn line numbering on with the Line Numbers tool in the Page Setup group of the Page Layout tab, or click Line Numbers in the Layout tab of the

Page Setup dialog box to open the Line Numbers dialog box, shown in Figure 8.11. Choose the desired settings in the dialog box, and click OK.

FIGURE 8.11

Line numbering is a section-formatting attribute controlled by this dialog box or the Line Numbers choice in the Page Setup group of the Home tab.

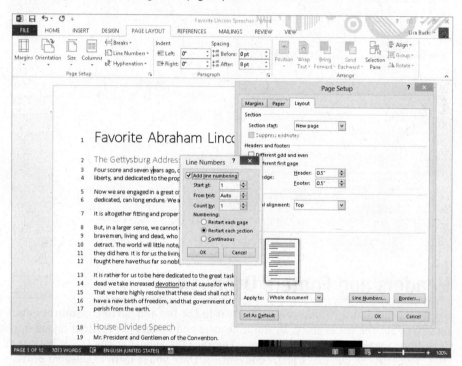

Although line numbering isn't a paragraph attribute, suppressing line numbering *is* a paragraph attribute, as shown in Figure 8.12. (Note that line numbers do not display in Draft or Outline view.) To suppress line numbering in any given paragraph, put the insertion point in that paragraph, display the Paragraph dialog box (click the Paragraph Group dialog box launcher), and enable the Suppress line numbers check box under Formatting exceptions in the Line and Page Breaks tab, as shown in Figure 8.12. Then click OK. Another way to turn off numbering for one or more paragraphs is to select the paragraph(s). Click Page Layout ⇨ Page Setup ⇨ Line Numbers, and then click Suppress for Current Paragraph.

FIGURE 8.12

Suppress line numbers on a paragraph-by-paragraph basis.

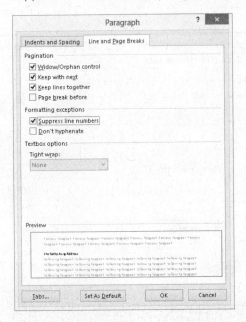

Headers and Footers Overview

Seemingly, headers and footers are the areas in the top and bottom margins of each page, but that's not the whole story. In Word, headers and footers are distinct layers in your document, usually behind the text area. They usually appear at the top or bottom of the page, respectively, but that's just a convention. Once you're in Word's header or footer layer, you can place text and graphics anywhere on the page. (See "Adding side margin material" later in this chapter for more information.)

This means that in addition to titles, page numbers, dates, and other essential bits of information, headers and footers can contain things such as watermarks, logos, or side margin material.

A second area of misunderstanding concerns how headers and footers are inserted into your Word documents. They aren't inserted — they've been there right from the start. When you "insert" or "create" a header, you're really doing neither. Instead, you're merely adding content to a previously empty or unused area.

The Header and Footer layer

When you're working in Print Layout view, any text in the header and footer layer usually shows up as grayish text at the top, bottom, or side of your document. To access those areas, double-click where you want to edit — even if you don't see any text there. This brings the header and footer areas to the surface, as shown in Figure 8.13. When you finish working with the header or footer, click Close Header and Footer in the Close group of the Header & Footer Tools⇨Design tab.

FIGURE 8.13:

Header and Footer tabs clarify what and where headers and footers are. With headers and footers open for editing, the document body text turns gray.

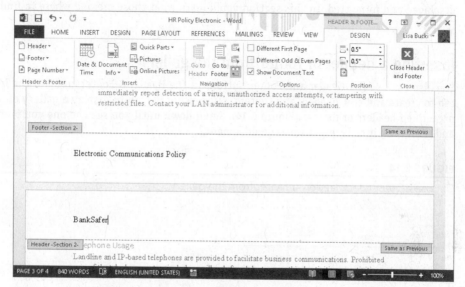

Headers and footers also display in Print Preview. There, however, because the view is supposed to represent what you'll see when the document is printed, the header and footer areas aren't gray and isolated. The same is true in Read Mode. Note that in Print Preview and Read Mode, you cannot perform normal editing — neither to normal text nor to text in headers and footers. In Read Mode view, however, you can insert comments. This chapter assumes that you are working in Print Layout view so that all kinds of editing are possible. If you don't see what's shown in the screen shots, then check your view setting.

Coordinating headers and footers and document sections

Figure 8.13 indicates the document section number in the header and footer tabs at the left end of each area. Word documents can be single-section or multi-section. You might use multiple sections for a variety of reasons, particularly in long documents. Some users place each chapter of a document in a separate section, with additional sections being used for front matter (tables of contents, tables of figures, foreword, and so on) and back matter (index, glossary, and so on).

Section formatting enables you to use different kinds of numbering for different sections. It also allows different header and footer text in different sections. For example, the header or footer might include the name of each chapter, or the word *Index* or *Glossary*.

Header and Footer Navigation and Design

Word provides a number of tools that enable you to control the way headers and footers are displayed and formatted. In this section you'll learn what those are and where to find them in Word 2013.

Inserting a header or footer from the gallery

You also can use the Header and Footer buttons in the Header & Footer group of the Insert tab to create and edit headers and footers. Click either button to display a gallery of predefined headers or footers (Figure 8.14). Scroll down until you see the one you prefer, and then click it to insert it into the document.

FIGURE 8.14

Choose a predefined header or footer from the gallery.

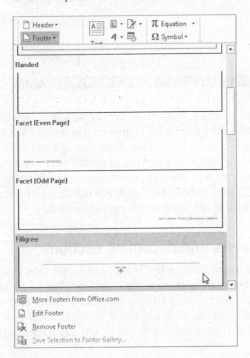

Editing in the header and footer areas

When the header or footer area is active, the main set of editing controls appears in the Header & Footer Tools⇨Design tab, shown in Figure 8.15. To display the Design tab, double-click the header or footer area in a document. Or, in the Insert tab Header & Footer group, choose Header⇨Edit Header (or Footer⇨Edit Footer). Once the header/footer layer is open for editing, either the header or the footer can be edited, as can items inserted into the side area (for example, page numbers in the side margins) as well as watermarks.

FIGURE 8.15

The Header & Footer Tools⇨Design tab provides complete control over headers and footers.

Notice the Go to Header and Go to Footer commands in the Navigation group of the tab. You can use those commands to quickly switch back and forth between the header and footer areas, but, as suggested by Figure 8.13, both areas are equally accessible. You do not need to click Go to Header or Go to Footer — you can simply click where you want to edit.

> **NOTE**
>
> While header and footer material can reside in the side margins, you cannot open the header or footer area for editing by double-clicking in the side margins. The double-click method for opening headers and footers works only in the top and bottom margin areas.

Using header and footer styles

If you are creating a header or footer from scratch rather than inserting one from the gallery, Word's headers and footers use built-in paragraph styles named Header and Footer. Each is formatted with a center tab and a right-aligned tab to facilitate placement of text and other items. This enables you to have three distinct components, one each at the left, center, and right within the header or footer, without having to resort to using a table, text box, or other device (although tables and text boxes are perfectly acceptable in headers and footers).

For example, to create a header with a left-adjusted document name, a centered date, and a right-adjusted author's name, you would enter the document name, press Tab, enter the date, press Tab, and finally type the author's name, as shown in Figure 8.16.

FIGURE 8.16

The default header style makes three-part headers easy.

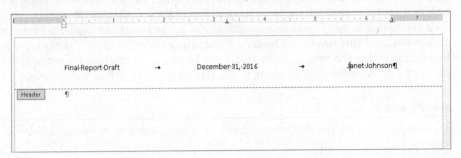

When editing the header/footer layer of a document, you can use the mouse or keyboard keys to navigate as needed. As long as you don't double-click in the text area of the document, the header and footer area remain open for business.

In a long document that contains many sections, however, scrolling can be tedious and imprecise. For greater control and precision you can use the Previous Section and Next Section tools in the Navigation section of the Header & Footer Tools⇔Design tab.

Link to Previous

Different document sections can contain different headers and footers. When Link to Previous is selected for any given header or footer, that header or footer is the same as that for the previous section. By default, when you add a new document section, its headers and footers inherit the header and footer settings of the previous section.

To unlink the currently selected header or footer from the header or footer in the previous section (which will allow the current section to maintain a distinct header or footer), click Link to Previous in the Navigation group of the Design tab to toggle it off.

Note that headers and footers in any section have independent Link to Previous settings. While Link to Previous initially is turned on for all new sections that are created, when you turn it off for any given header, the corresponding footer remains linked to the previous footer. This gives you additional control over how document information is presented.

Different First Page

Most formal reports and indeed many other formal documents do not use page numbers on the first page. To keep users from having to make such documents multi-section, Word lets you set an exception for the first page of each document section. To enable this option for any given document section, display a header or footer in that section, and click the Different First Page option in the Options group of the Design tab (refer to Figure 8.15).

Unlike with the Link to Previous option, Different First Page cannot be different for header and footer. You cannot suppress just one. To accomplish that you would need distinct document sections (separated by a section break).

Different Odd & Even Pages

You can, without using section breaks, instruct Word to maintain different headers and footers on odd and even pages. This feature is often used in book/booklet printing, where the header/footer always appears closest to the outside edge of the paper — on the left for left-hand pages, and on the right for right-hand pages. To control whether this feature is enabled, click the Different Odd & Even Pages check box, also in the Options group of the Design tab. Like the Different First Page option, this option applies to both headers and footers in the section, not individually for each header and footer. As Figure 8.17 illustrates, you can set up the headers or footers to mirror one another, such as placing the page numbers to mirror one another on the outside corners of the page.

FIGURE 8.17

Use Different Odd & Even pages to set up mirrored headers or footers for booklet or bound document printing.

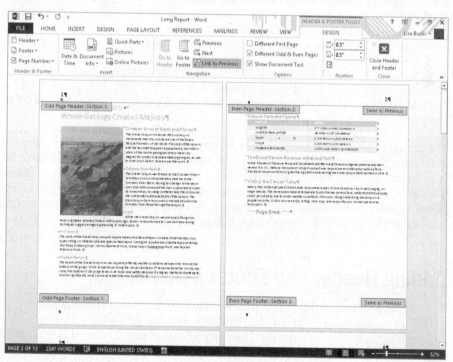

Show Document Text

Sometimes having document text showing is useful and helps provide a frame of reference for headers and footers. At other times, however, it can be distracting and can make it harder to identify header and footer text, particularly if you're actually using gray fonts in the header or footer area. Displayed text also can make it difficult to access graphics that are stored in the header or footer layer.

By default, Show Document Text in the Options group of the Header & Footer Tools ⇨ Design tab is enabled. To hide document text, click to remove the check next to that option.

Setting the distance from the edge of the page

Headers and footers are printed in the margin area. The margin is the area between the edge of the paper and the edge of the text layer in the body of the document. If the header or footer is too "tall" for a given page, Word reduces the height of the text layer on the fly so that the header or footer can be printed. That is, it will be printed if the distance between the top of the header or the bottom of the footer and the respective edge of the paper does not spill into the nonprintable areas of the paper.

Printers have a nonprintable area around the perimeter of the paper (usually 0.25 inches for most printers). This is an area in which it is mechanically impossible for a given printer to print. Windows' printer drivers do a good job of calculating the margin so that the printer does not try to print in the nonprintable region. When the margin is too small, Word will warn you.

Word does not warn you, however, if the header or footer extends too far into the margin. When this happens, all or part of the header or footer is cut off. Everything might look fine in Print Preview, and there is no warning, but part of the footer or header will be cut off in the printout.

You can rein the document in using the Header Position from Top and Footer Position from Bottom settings in the Design tab's Position group. If you find that the header or footer is being cut off, determine how much is being cut off and make that much additional allowance. For example, if 0.25 inches of text is being cut off the footer, then increase Footer Position from Bottom by that amount. You also can use the From edge settings on the Layout tab of the Page Setup dialog box to make these adjustments.

Adding Header and Footer Material

You can put a variety of things into headers and footers, ranging from file names and various other document properties (author, title, date last printed/modified, and so on) to page numbers and even watermarks. Inserting most text and graphics that will actually be printed in the top or bottom margin is straightforward. There are some special cases, however, such as page numbers, side margin matter, and background images and watermarks, that require special attention.

Page numbers

A common use for headers and footers is to display page numbers. To include page numbers in Word 2013, several methods are available — some new as of Word 2007, and some "legacy." This section focuses mostly on the new ways because they provide extraordinary ease, flexibility, and variety not found in pre-Ribbon Word. When the legacy ways are best, however, you'll learn about those.

Inserting page numbers

Inserting page numbers in Word has never been easier. First, decide where you want the page numbers to appear (top, bottom, or side margin). Then click anywhere on the first page in the document section where you want the number to appear. As noted earlier, documents can contain multiple sections, and each section can have independent headers and footers, which means they also can be numbered independently.

In the Insert tab's Header & Footer group, click Page Number to open its drop-down list, as shown in Figure 8.18, and choose Top of Page, for example. Scroll down the choices as needed, and click the one to insert. Word opens the header and footer layer and displays the inserted page number. Note that you also can use the Page Number button in the Header & Footer group of the Header & Footer Tools ⇨ Design tab to insert a number when you're already working with the header or footer.

FIGURE 8.18

Word 2013 has extensive galleries with a variety of page number formats from which to choose.

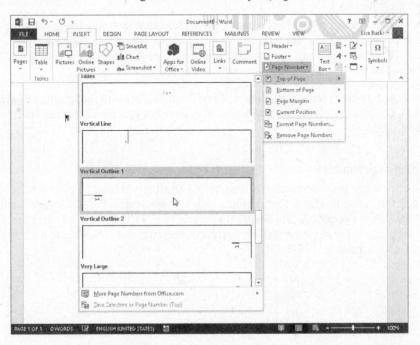

The Page Number menu enables you to select the option that corresponds to where you want the page number to appear:

- Top of Page
- Bottom of Page
- Page Margins (See "Adding side margin material" a little later in this section.)
- Current Position (Use this option when the insertion point is already exactly where you want the page number to appear.)

The bottom of the page is the most common choice for word processing documents, but there are times when the top or side works better for a particular document. Select the desired destination. Word displays a number of preset page number options.

When you find a page number gallery item that suits your fancy, click it to insert the page number into the header or footer (according to which option you chose to get here).

> **NOTE**
>
> To see additional choices for working with a preset listed on any gallery, right click the preset. For example, you can click Edit Properties to work with more detailed settings for the specified page number.

Deleting page numbers

To delete page numbers, move to the document section that contains the numbering you want to remove. In the Header & Footer group of the Insert tab, click Page Numbers ⇨ Remove Page Numbers. You also can remove page numbers via the Header & Footer group of the Header & Footer Tools ⇨ Design tab.

Remove Page Numbers removes all page numbers from headers and footers in the current section — including those in the side margins. It does not remove page numbers from other document sections.

Formatting page numbers

You can choose the page numbering format before or after you insert a page number. On the Insert tab in the Header & Footer group, choose Page Number ⇨ Format Page Numbers (or use the same command in the Header & Footer group of the Header & Footer Tools ⇨ Design tab), to display the Page Number Format dialog box, shown in Figure 8.19. Options are explained in Table 8.1.

FIGURE 8.19

Word provides flexible page numbering options.

TABLE 8.1 Page Number Options

Option	Purpose
Number format	Specifies numbering scheme: 1, 2, 3; A, B, C; a, b, c; I, II, III; or i, ii, iii. Provides an additional option to bracket Arabic numbers with dashes (to bracket others, edit the header or footer directly.)
Include chapter number	Applies a chapter numbering scheme such as I-1, II-5, III-43, where I, II, and III are chapter numbers, and chapters are formatted in a Heading 1 through Heading 9 style, with numbering included in the style definition.
Chapter starts with style	Available only if Include chapter number is enabled. For this option to work, chapter numbers must be formatted in a Heading 1 through Heading 9 style, and numbering must be included in the style.
Use separator	Specifies the separator to use between chapter and page numbers.
Continue from previous section	Indicates whether the current section's numbering is connected with that of the previous section. Use this option when distinct sections are being used for a reason other than to create distinct numbering, such as when switching sections to accommodate changes from portrait to landscape and back again.
Start at	Use this to specify a starting number other than 1.

Additional options that affect page numbers, such as whether headers or footers are displayed on the first page of a document or document section, are discussed earlier in this chapter, in the section "Different First Page."

Adding document information

Word 2013 makes it easier to add key information about the document directly into the header or footer. In previous versions of Word, you had to use field codes to insert such information as the document name, author, or title at the insertion point in the header or footer. Now, it's this easy:

1. **Double-click the header or footer area to open it for editing.**
2. **Click to position the insertion point where you want to insert the document information.**
3. **Click Header & Footer Tools ⇨ Design ⇨ Insert ⇨ Document Info.**
4. **Click the desired choice in the menu, shown in Figure 8.20.**

FIGURE 8.20

Inserting document information

Adding side margin material

Textual material inserted in the side margins of a document is inserted in either the header or footer layer. The "trick" is to use something like a non-inline text box to serve as a container for the text. You can use an existing page number preset item that inserts text into the side margin. Or you can insert a text box manually by double-clicking the header or footer area, selecting Insert ⇨ Text ⇨ Text Box ⇨ Draw Text Box, and drawing a text box of the desired shape and size in either the left or right margin. Then insert the page number or other matter there as shown in Figure 8.21. In the document in Figure 8.21, I inserted a circle shape, and then added text to it to make a page number bubble that spills over into the margin.

FIGURE 8.21

Add side margin material by editing the header or footer.

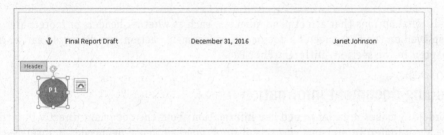

Adding header and footer graphics

Just as you can add a margin text box or graphic on the header and footer layer, you can insert graphics such as a company logo, WordArt, a watermark message such as Not For Distribution, and so on. The graphic will have a "washed out" appearance when you close the header or footer area (as shown in Figure 8.22), but it will print on every specified page for the document or section, depending on the header and footer settings for the section where you inserted it. Use the process just outlined in the previous section for adding a margin text box to add a graphic into the document header or footer.

FIGURE 8.22

Example WordArt added into a header

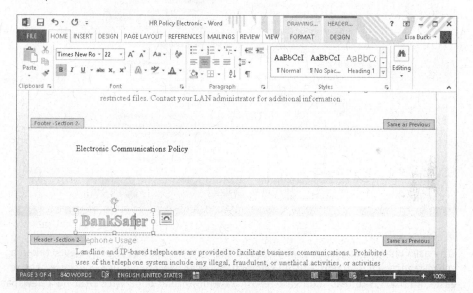

Changing the Number of Columns

You can divide the text in a document into *columns*. Tables have columns, but that's not what we're talking about here. You can also create the appearance of columns by setting up tabs. That's not what this section is about, either.

Here, *column formatting* refers to dividing the text so that it flows in columns across the page, as shown in Figure 8.23. This kind of formatting sometimes is called *newspaper columns* or *snaking columns,* and is a common format used in journals, newsletters, and magazines, although it's unlikely that those publications use Word's columns feature to accomplish their columnar formatting. Such publications likely use page layout programs because of the precise way in which they feature text, graphics, and advertising.

FIGURE 8.23

Column formatting is sometimes called *snaking columns* because of the way text zigzags from the bottom of one column to the top of the next.

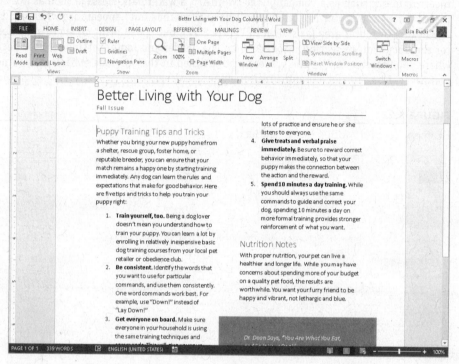

Why use columns? If you've ever analyzed the way you read or if you've ever taken a speed-reading course, you already know the answer. We use columns because they're easier and faster to read. Contrast reading a wide-format book with reading a newspaper. In a wide-format book each column of text (usually the whole page) is 5 or more inches wide. In a newspaper, columns typically are only a couple of inches across. We also use columns for a variety of other reasons, such as to utilize space more efficiently or for aesthetic reasons.

The truth is that whether you want columns or not, you already have at least one in every Word document, so the real question is *How many columns do you want?* To answer the question, you should consider the nature of what you're writing, how it will be printed or published, and who will be reading it. Text-dense documents benefit from columns, just as they benefit from graphics. Anything that helps the reader become more engaged with the text is good.

Column formatting is a section formatting attribute. Any part of a document that has a different number of columns must be "sectioned off" with section breaks. To insert a section break, choose the desired kind of break by selecting Page Layout ➪ Page Setup ➪ Breaks, as described earlier in the chapter.

> **NOTE**
>
> Notice that Column is listed under Page Breaks, not under Section Breaks. Technically, a column break is neither a page break *nor* a section break. To create different numbers of sections in different parts of the same document you must separate them by one of the four breaks listed in the section "Inserting or deleting a section break," earlier in the chapter.

To change the number of columns for the current section (or selected sections or selected text), select Page Layout ➪ Page Setup ➪ Columns. The current column formatting (Two, in this case) is highlighted, as shown in Figure 8.24. Remember that if you select a single column of text and format it in multiple columns, Word inserts section breaks as needed.

FIGURE 8.24

Word offers five preset column setups, or choose More Columns to design your own.

If you don't want any of the default preset column formatting, for additional control click More Columns, which displays the Columns dialog box, shown in Figure 8.25. This dialog box shows the same set of five preset column formats as the Columns drop-down tool, but you can insert as many as two columns per inch of horizontal space between the left and right margins, up to a maximum of 44 columns. For standard paper 8.5 inches wide with one-inch left and right margins, you can have up to 13 columns. To get the maximum of 44 columns you would need paper at least 22 inches wide, assuming no margins and a pretty unusual printer. Note that the Width and spacing controls provide access to only three sets of columns at a time. If there are more than three columns, a vertical scroll bar appears in the Columns dialog box, providing access to additional column settings. When you finish setting up columns, click OK to apply your changes.

FIGURE 8.25

Design your own columns here.

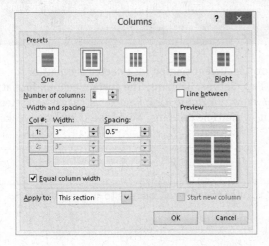

Adding a line between columns

In Figure 8.25, notice the Line between option. Check this option to draw a vertical line between columns. If columns are closely spaced, this can help in maintaining the visual separation of the columns, thereby improving readability. When you're using ragged-right text edges rather than justified text, adding a vertical line can create the appearance of straighter edges and better visual balance.

Formatting columns using the horizontal ruler

You can format column width and spacing using the horizontal ruler. In Figure 8.26, notice that the Left and Right Indent controls can appear in only one column at a time. This doesn't mean that you get those controls only in a single column. It simply means that they are shown only for the active column. To change the width of columns, drag the darker and lighter boundaries between the column spacing and width areas. When you drag to make a column larger, the adjoining space gets smaller, and vice versa. When Equal column width is checked in the Columns dialog box, dragging the boundaries of any column expands or contracts all columns at the same time. The minimum column spacing is 0. Select text in a column to format it individually. For example, in Figure 8.26, I selected the numbered list so I could drag the left indent setting and help its items fill the column better.

FIGURE 8.26

Left and Right Indent controls appear above the active column.

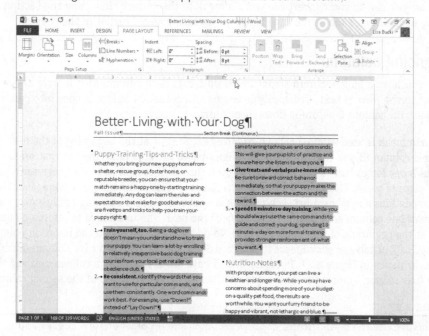

Changing columns using section breaks

If you want part of a document to have three columns and another part to have a single column, those two parts must reside in different sections. Consider the common newsletter format shown back in Figure 8.26. Notice that there is a section break between the top section, which is a single column, and the material that follows, which is in two columns.

One way to create this kind of format is to separate the *masthead* (the big title and other matter that goes with it) from the body using a Continuous section break, as shown in Figure 8.26. Move the insertion point to the beginning of where you want the multi-column formatting to begin, and choose Break ⇨ Continuous in the Page Setup group of the Page Layout tab. Now use the Columns tool or the Columns dialog box to apply the desired column formatting to the new section.

If there's a point at which you want the multi-column formatting to change the number of columns again, insert additional section breaks (choosing Continuous, Next Page, Even, or Odd as needed), and apply the desired column formatting to those additional sections.

Alternatively, let Word insert section breaks automatically. Select the part of the document to which you want a given number of columns applied, and then apply the column formatting. You can do this using the Columns tool or the Columns dialog box, but you will get more consistent and predictable results if you use the dialog box. For some unknown reason Word sometimes inserts Next Page section breaks instead of Continuous section breaks. If this happens, you can always convert the section break to the correct kind using the Section Start setting in the Layout tab of the Page Setup dialog box, covered earlier in the chapter.

Balancing columns

When you have a multi-column structure, Word treats each column as if it were a page with respect to the flow of text. Ordinarily text must fill column 1 before it goes into column 2, and must fill column 2 before it flows into column 3, and so on.

A column break is used *within* a column to force text to start at the beginning of the next available column. If you think of columns as mini-pages within a page, then in that sense a column break forces text to the next "page," even though that next page isn't necessarily on a new piece of paper. Problems happen when a column breaks awkwardly. For example, if the column contains a numbered list, you might not want a numbered paragraph to begin at the bottom of one column and continue at the top of the next. The solution is to insert a column break at the beginning of the numbered item. To do so, click to position the insertion point, click the Page Layout tab and click Breaks in the Page Setup group, and then click Column under page breaks, as shown in Figure 8.27. In Figure 8.27, I have already inserted a column break at the end of the first column to force the next numbered item to begin at the top of the second column.

FIGURE 8.27

You can use column breaks to control how columns line up or where text breaks at the bottom of the column.

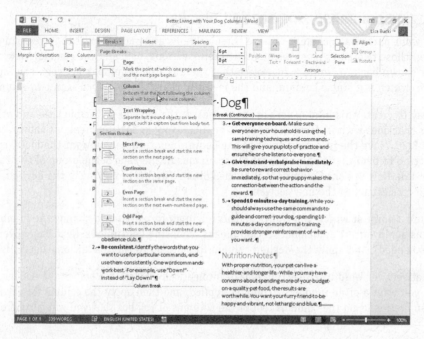

You also can force Word to balance the columns (make them approximately the same height) by inserting a Continuous section break at the end of the last column. When you do that, Word tries to optimize document space to accommodate what comes next, even if nothing comes next. In some cases the columns won't balance perfectly. That's because of other constraints, such as widows and orphans. Nonetheless, symmetrically speaking, it's usually an improvement.

Adding and Removing Page Borders

A page border is a line, a set of lines, or decorative artwork that appears around the perimeter of the page. You see them a lot on title pages as well as on flyers and brochures. Borders can be formal, discretely colored lines of various weights, or colorful graphics, as in the border for the flyer in Figure 8.28.

FIGURE 8.28

For page borders, you can insert a variety of lines or choose from dozens of built-in art borders.

To insert a page border:

1. **Click the Design tab, and then click Page Borders in the Page Background group.** (Refer to Figure 8.28). The Borders and Shading dialog box shown in Figure 8.29 appears. The dialog box offers the same options you saw earlier on the Borders tab in Chapter 6, "Paragraph Formatting," in the "Borders and boxes" section. In addition, however, the Page Border tab includes Art options you can use to create decorative borders, although some of these might not look sophisticated enough for many types of documents.

FIGURE 8.29

Choose page border settings in the Page Border tab of the Borders and Shading dialog box.

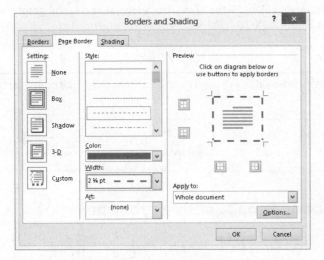

2. **Click an overall border type under Setting at the left.**

3. **In the center of the dialog box, pick a border Style, Color, and Width; alternately, open the Art drop-down list, scroll to find the style of border art to use, and click it.**

4. **To remove the border from any side, click that side in the border Preview.**

5. **To control which pages in the document have the border, make a choice from the Apply to drop-down list.** For placing a border around a title page, choose This section — First page only. Other options on the list include Whole document, This section, and This section — All except first page.

6. **To control the placement of the page border with respect to the edge of the text or paper, click Options.** The Border and Shading Options dialog box shown in

Figure 8.30 appears. Note that when you're setting page borders, paragraph-related options are grayed out.

7. **Make a choice from the Measure from drop-down list to set the distance of the page border either from the Text or from the Edge of page.**

8. **Adjust the Top, Bottom, Left, and Right distance values as desired.**

9. **Click OK twice to close the two open dialog boxes and apply the page border settings.**

FIGURE 8.30

Use Border and Shading Options if your page border crowds the text too much.

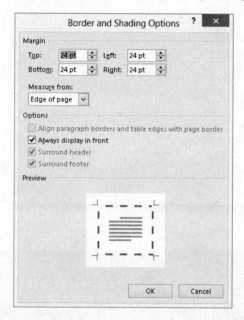

Working More Effectively with Themes

Like many other Word features, Themes work with Live Preview. Unless a document explicitly uses theme-based formatting, such as styles relying on colors and fonts specified by the theme, changing themes will appear to have no effect. Themes are housed at the left end of Word 2013's Design tab, shown in Figure 8.31. The rest of the tab's Document Formatting group contains other theme-related features that you'll learn more about in the following sections.

FIGURE 8.31

Theme settings color-coordinate document contents and change other overall features.

> **NOTE**
>
> Note also that the Themes feature set does not work in Compatibility Mode. There is no mechanism for storing Word 2013 theme information in the standard Word 97–2003 document format, even though Word 2003 has its own different brand of theme formatting.

Understanding and applying themes

Themes are coordinated sets of colors, fonts, table formats, and other graphic elements used to change the overall look of a document while leaving its content unchanged. Word comes with numerous built-in themes, some of which are shown in Figure 8.31. Although the applied theme's impact hinges on using certain Word 2013 formatting features such as styles and theme colors, themes are not part of style formatting. There is no way to associate or assign a theme with a particular style. Themes are applied to the entire document, wholly apart from styles, and affect many different aspects of document formatting.

To apply a theme:

1. **Click the Design tab, and in the Document Formatting group, click Themes.**

2. **Move the mouse pointer over the various themes — Facet, Integral, Ion, Ion Boardroom, Organic, and so on — to see a Live Preview of the theme on the document.**

3. **When you see the theme you want, click it to apply it.**

A template provides the base level of formatting through styles, page setup, and so on. The theme applies the next level of formatting on top of the template. The theme includes theme colors, theme fonts, and theme effects, each of which you'll learn more about later in this section.

The best way to understand themes and what they bring to the document design table is to use them on documents designed with themes specifically in mind. Follow these steps as a practice example to see how a theme impacts a document:

1. **Press Ctrl+N to create a new blank document.**

2. **Type** Heading 1**, and apply the Heading 1 style from the Styles gallery of the Home tab.**

3. **Type** Heading 2**, and apply the Heading 2 style from the Styles gallery of the Home tab.**

4. **Click the Insert tab, click Shapes in the Illustrations group, click Oval under Recently Used Shapes at the top of the gallery, and then click in the document to insert a circle in the default size.**

5. **With the circle still selected, click Shape Effects in the Shape Styles group of the Drawing Tools ⇨ Format tab, point to Preset, and click Preset 5 (second row, first column).**

6. **Click a blank area of the document.**

7. **Click the Themes button in the Document Formatting group of the Design tab (refer to Figure 8.31), and note the names of the themes — Facet, Integral, Ion, Ion Boardroom, Organic, and so on.**

8. **Click Integral.** Note the changes in the example document. The text formatted with heading styles changes color and font, and the circle color change as well. Figure 8.32 shows the example document with the new theme applied.

8

FIGURE 8.32

The Integral theme applies new heading fonts and more in the quickie practice document.

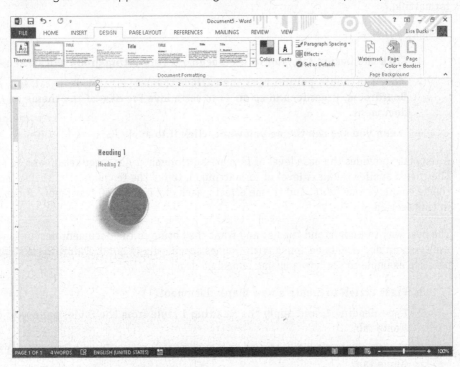

9. **Close the document without saving changes, or if you want to save it for future practice feel free to do so.**

Theme elements or components

Themes consist of three elements:

- Theme colors
- Theme fonts
- Theme effects

By modifying theme elements, you can apply a new overall look for the document. By creating a new combination of any of these three elements, you effectively create a new theme that you can save. Here's more about each of these three settings for an applied theme.

Theme colors

While each of the named themes that come with Word has a preassigned set of theme colors, there's no reason you have to stick with that set of colors. If you want the Organic theme but prefer the Slipstream theme colors set rather than the default colors, you can change the theme colors.

To change color sets, in the Design tab, click the Colors button in the Document Formatting group to display the gallery shown in Figure 8.33. Drag the mouse over the various color sets to see a Live Preview, and then click a color set when you see the colors you want.

FIGURE 8.33

After applying a theme, you can apply a different set of theme colors.

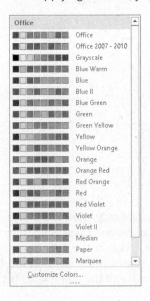

8

> **TIP**
>
> When you create a style or other template feature with a color other than Automatic, make sure the color you apply is one of the Theme Colors, not one of the Standard Colors in the color gallery. The Theme Colors will change as desired when you change themes, but the Standard Colors won't change.

If you click Customize Colors at the bottom of the gallery shown in Figure 8.33, the Create New Theme Colors dialog box shown in Figure 8.34 appears, where you can customize the colors and create your own theme colors. Click the various color buttons to display the color gallery, and click alternate colors as desired. Enter the theme colors set name in the Name text box, and then click OK. The file will be saved in .xml format in C:\Users\ *user name*\AppData\Roaming\Microsoft\Templates\Document Themes\Theme Colors. (This folder is created the first time you save a theme.)

FIGURE 8.34

Create a custom set of theme colors here.

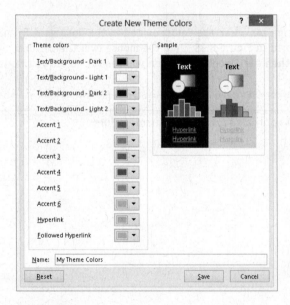

Theme fonts

Theme fonts are a bit simpler to understand because there are only two components: the heading font and body text font. Click the Fonts button in the Document Formatting group of the Design tab to change theme fonts. Notice in Figure 8.35 that the Arial Black-Arial theme fonts are selected. For each theme, the larger font shown is the one that will be applied to Heading styles (Heading 1, Heading 2, and so on), and the smaller one is the one that will be applied to body text.

FIGURE 8.35

For each theme, the Theme Fonts gallery shows the fonts used for headings and body text.

TIP

The theme fonts for the currently applied theme appear in the Theme Fonts group at the top of Font drop-down list in the Font group of the Home tab.

As for theme colors, you can create new theme font sets. Click Theme Fonts in the Document Formatting group of the Design tab, and then click Customize Fonts below the gallery choices, as shown in Figure 8.35. In the Create New Theme Fonts dialog box, shown in Figure 8.36, choose the Heading font and Body font, enter an informative name, and click Save. The theme font will be saved in .xml format in C:\Users*user name* \AppData\Roaming\Microsoft\Templates\Document Themes\Theme Fonts.

FIGURE 8.36

When you create new theme fonts, it's useful if the name you choose either describes the purpose for the fonts or includes the font names.

Theme effects

Theme effects are a bit harder to grasp than other theme elements, mostly because they're used a good deal less often by the average user. In the Design tab, click the Effects button in the Document Formatting group to display the gallery of options shown in Figure 8.37. If you study the different theme effects, you will see sometimes subtle and sometimes not-so-subtle differences among the elements shown. For example, the Office set looks soft-edged and perhaps a little blurred with shadows at the edges. Grunge has mottled fills applied. (It's unlikely you can see this in the picture in the book, so look on-screen.)

FIGURE 8.37

Apply theme effects to SmartArt, WordArt, Charts, and Shapes.

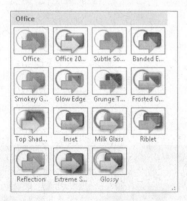

The easiest way to see theme effects in action is to create an example shape or graphic and use Live Preview to see the various effects.

You have seen how to save custom theme colors and theme fonts. The Word 2013 interface does not provide a built-in, direct way for you to save custom theme effects. You can indirectly save them, however, by saving the whole theme, as shown shortly.

Style sets and paragraph spacing

The Document Formatting group of the Design tab includes a couple of additional settings along with all the theme settings. Chapter 7 discussed Style Sets, which enable you to change the style fonts used throughout the document. Although they are not technically a component of the applied theme, the fonts in the available style sets do change when you apply a different theme to the document. Change style sets using the Style Sets gallery in the Document Formatting group of the Design tab.

That group also includes a Paragraph Spacing gallery, shown in Figure 8.38. Choose one of the presets from the gallery to apply the combination of line and paragraph spacing that looks appropriate in the current document. For example, you may want to use the Relaxed preset to space out the paragraphs and lines in a flyer document to fill the page better.

FIGURE 8.38

Change overall document paragraph spacing with the Paragraph Spacing choices on the Design tab.

Saving custom themes

Using the Colors, Fonts, and Effect controls in the Document Formatting group of the Design tab, it's possible to create sets of theme elements that you want to preserve for future use. As indicated, you can save custom colors and fonts. In addition, you can save entire themes. To save a custom theme, in the Document Formatting Group of the Design tab, choose Themes⇨Save Current Theme. In the Save Current Theme dialog box, shown in Figure 8.39, type a descriptive name and click Save.

FIGURE 8.39

Overall themes, theme colors, theme fonts, and theme effects are saved in the same folder set by default.

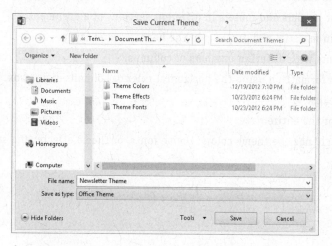

Alternatively and additionally, you can include other elements, such as text, styles, prebuilt headers and footers, and other document elements, and save the entire setup as a template. When you do that, any custom themes employed automatically become part of the saved template.

Setting the default theme

In previous Word versions, changing the default theme was a hassle. In Word 2013, open a new blank document, display the Design tab, choose a theme from the Themes gallery in the Document Formatting group, and then click Set as Default in the same group. To change the default theme for a particular template file, open the template file, change the theme, and then save and close the template.

Summary

In this chapter you've learned about the basic page setup choices, what section formatting is, and how the two interact. You also learned what headers and footers are, what they're used for, and how to create them with sections. Finally, you learned about creating columns in a document, and working with page borders and themes. You should now be able to do the following:

- Add the right type of section break at the desired location.
- Convert a Next Page section break into a Continuous section break, and vice versa.
- Vertically align page text in a section of a document.
- Change the paper size and paper feed for the section.
- Create headers, footers, and page numbers in your documents.
- Edit headers and footers.
- Set up different headers and footers in different sections of a document.
- Add side-margin material and graphics in the header/footer layer.
- Create documents with differing numbers of columns.
- Change column formatting using the horizontal ruler or Columns dialog box.
- Use column breaks.
- Add a border for the entire page.
- Apply themes; change the theme colors, theme fonts, or theme effects; and save a custom theme.

Adding Tables and Graphics to a Document

IN THIS CHAPTER

Creating tables

Using table styles and applying other table formatting and design settings

Handling tables, rows, columns, and cells

Adding shapes

Including and formatting pictures in your document

Creating WordArt

Adding and formatting SmartArt

Arranging graphics

Using the Selection Pane to work with object visibility

Tables and SmartArt enable you to illustrate data and processes in documents. They're extremely flexible and easy to create and manipulate. You can further illustrate a document with shapes, WordArt, and pictures, including thousands of royalty-free images offered online at Office.com. Thanks to numerous galleries, it's easy to create professional graphics of all sorts quickly and with minimal effort. Live Preview also comes into play when you work with table and graphic formatting. This chapter teaches you about these features in Word.

Getting a Quick Start with Quick Tables

The quickest way to create a table in Word is to use one that already exists. It might not be exactly what you want, but it often will be closer to what you want and save you a lot of formatting and setup versus creating a table from scratch. It helps if you can see a picture, of course, and Word 2013 includes a Quick Tables gallery from which you can select a predefined table to insert in the current document. After you click to position the insertion point at the location where you want to insert the table, click the Insert tab. Click the Table button in the Tables group of the Insert tab, and then point to Quick Tables. The gallery shown in Figure 9.1 appears.

FIGURE 9.1

The Quick Tables Gallery offers a number of preformatted tables.

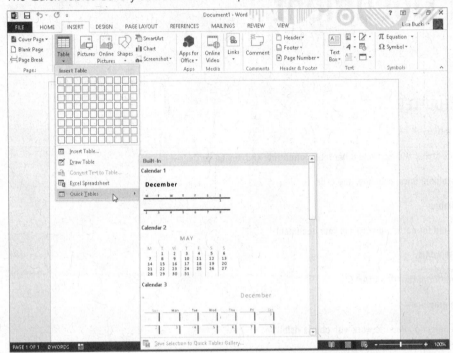

Scroll through the gallery to see if there's a table design you like — something that compares favorably with the table you envision. If there is, click on it. If it has too many rows, you can delete the ones you don't need. If it has too few columns, you can add a few more. If the proportions and other attributes aren't quite right, you can use Word's table tools to make them right. The point is that you hit the ground running.

Table Basics

One way to think about a table is as a container for information. The container consists of horizontal rows and vertical columns. If someone speaks of a five-by-four (5 × 4) table, by convention and agreement this refers to a table that's five columns high and four rows wide.

If the terminology is foreign to you, think of rows as you would the windows across each floor of a skyscraper. Think of columns as the vertical columns of windows on the same skyscraper building. Rows go across, and columns go up and down.

Inserting a table from scratch

There are three basic methods for creating a table from scratch. One is to use the Table tool to select the numbers of rows and columns you want. In the Insert tab click Table in the Tables group. Drag the mouse pointer down through the Insert Table grid. As you move the mouse, the selected table dimensions change, and Word shows a Live Preview in the document window, as shown in Figure 9.2. Click the mouse when the table has the number of rows and columns you want.

FIGURE 9.2

When a 6 × 4 table is selected in the Insert Table grid, a 6 × 4 Live Preview appears in the document window.

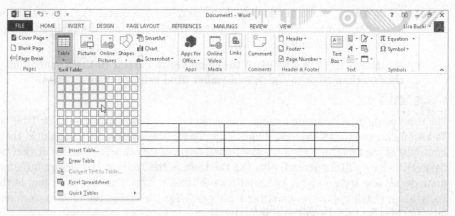

A second method for creating a table from scratch is by using the Insert Table dialog box, as follows:

1. **On the Insert tab, click Table in the Tables group, and click Insert Table.** The Insert Table dialog box shown in Figure 9.3 appears.

FIGURE 9.3

The Insert Table dialog box enables you to choose the number of columns and rows and specify additional settings when creating a table.

2. **Enter or use the spinner buttons to specify entries for the Number of columns and Number of rows.**

3. **Select an option under AutoFit behavior.** You can specify a Fixed column width or choose AutoFit to contents or AutoFit to window to make the table adjust to other elements of the document.

4. **(Optional) If you'd like Word to remember to default to the dimensions you choose, then click to check Remember dimensions for new tables.**

5. **Click OK.**

The third method for inserting a table from scratch is to draw it using the Draw Table tool. To begin, choose Insert ➪ Tables ➪ Table ➪ Draw Table. Drag a rectangle to establish the outer boundary of the table, and then use the Draw Table tool (which will be active at that point by default) to draw out the desired cells. Use the tools in the Table Tools ➪ Design tab's Borders group to set line style, weight, and color for the table borders. Use the Eraser tool in the Table Tools ➪ Layout tab to remove unwanted table parts. See the "Using the table eraser" section later in this chapter for additional information.

Cell markers and gridlines

When nonprinting formatting marks are displayed (Ctrl+Shift+8 [Ctrl+*] or Home ➪ Paragraph ➪ Show/Hide), cell markers display in each cell, showing where the cells are, as indicated in Figure 9.4. You might wonder why cell markers are needed if the table borders show the location of cells. That's because not every table has borders. If a borderless table's gridlines aren't displayed, you might not even know a table is there. Toggling the nonprinting cell markers provide visibility for the table cells. Cell markers, incidentally, display whenever paragraph marks do.

When a table has no borders, it's a good idea to display table gridlines. These are nonprinting marks that show the cell's dimensions. To display gridlines, click the View Gridlines choice in the Table group at the left end of the Table Tools ➪ Layout tab. See Figure 9.4.

FIGURE 9.4

Show hidden characters to display cell markers.

Click to display gridlines
for a table without borders.

Cell marker

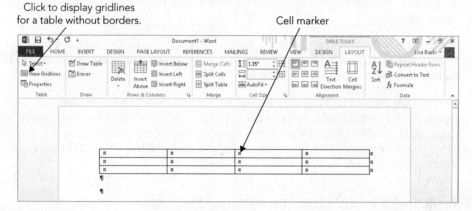

Managing AutoFit behavior

Notice the AutoFit behavior options shown in the Insert Table dialog box in Figure 9.3. These same AutoFit options are also available when you move the mouse pointer over the table, right-click the table move handle that appears at the upper left, and then point to AutoFit, as shown in Figure 9.5. The AutoFit settings enable you to size the table and its columns automatically.

FIGURE 9.5

Right-click the table move handle to display a shortcut menu with table options, including AutoFit.

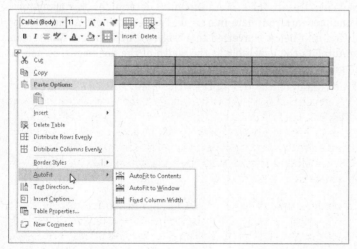

9

When you choose the Fixed Column Width option, the column widths remain fixed unless you explicitly change them by dragging or by using the Table Properties dialog box. Note that *fixed* is not the same as *equal*. The column widths might be equal also, but that's a different concept.

The AutoFit to Contents command causes a table to automatically resize as you add or remove material. It's not a temporary setting, so table columns widths continue to change when you add or remove text in existing cells.

Think of the AutoFit to Window command as "AutoFit to left and right margins." This option means that the table will remain as wide as the document text itself. If you add text disproportionately to any given column, that column will automatically resize, making the other columns correspondingly narrower. But the table itself will maintain the width of the document text.

Inserting a table based on existing content

There is a correspondence between the word *tab* and the word *table*. Although the proportion of the word processing population that was raised on typewriters is rapidly dwindling, those who took typing classes learned how to fashion tables using the tab stops and the Tab key. Tab stops are metal hardware on a typewriter that literally stop the carriage when you press the tab key. Because you can use tab stops to create a table-like arrangement, Word can readily convert your tab-delineated tables into real tables, and it even can convert information delimited with other characters such as commas. If for some reason you want to convert a table back to text, Word can perform that transformation, too.

Converting text to a table

If the text is set up with tabs between the "columns," you can use the Insert Table command to convert to a table immediately. Select the text, and then in the Tables group of the Insert tab click Table⇨Insert Table. Word instantly determines how many rows and columns there are and presents your data in a table. Figure 9.6 shows some selected tabbed text, and a copy of that text below converted to a table with the Insert Table command. Word automatically AutoFits the new table to the width of the document, so you might need to resize columns.

FIGURE 9.6

Word easily converts a tabbed "table" into an actual Word table.

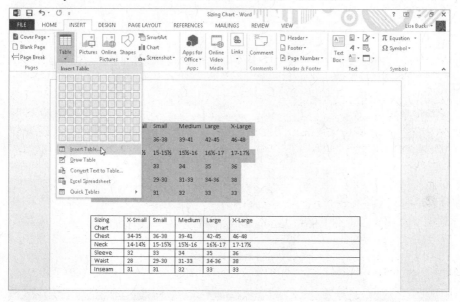

Sizing Chart	X-Small	Small	Medium	Large	X-Large
Chest	34-35	36-38	39-41	42-45	46-48
Neck	14-14½	15-15½	15½-16	16½-17	17-17½
Sleeve	32	33	34	35	36
Waist	28	29-30	31-33	34-36	38
Inseam	31	31	32	33	33

> **NOTE**
>
> To size the columns in the new table to better fit the text, move the mouse pointer over the table, right-click the table move handle, and choose AutoFit ⇨ AutoFit to Contents.

If you want control over the number of rows or columns or have text that's delimited by something other than tabs, you can use the Convert Text to Table dialog box to perform the conversion. For example, you might have a document exported from a spreadsheet or database program as a .csv (comma-separated values) or .txt (plain text) file using delimiters. Or someone may have manually delimited a list with another character, such as an asterisk. Here's how to make sure Word cleanly converts this type of content to a table:

1. **Select the list of text or data to be converted.** You can usually open a comma-separated values file or plain text file directly in Word, but you may have to import other types of files.

2. **Click Insert ⇨ Tables ⇨ Table ⇨ Convert Text to Table.** This displays the Convert Text to Table dialog box, shown in Figure 9.7.

9

FIGURE 9.7

The Convert Text to Table dialog box guesses how many rows and columns you want to create.

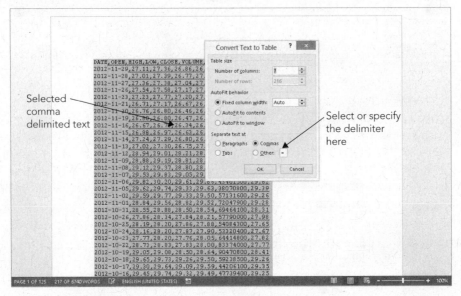

3. **Adjust the Number of columns or Number of rows settings as needed.** These settings will only be active when Word evaluates that there may be more than one way to divide the data.

4. **Choose an option under AutoFit behavior.**

5. **Specify the proper delimiter under Separate text at.** You can choose Paragraphs (for the paragraph mark), Tabs, or Commas; or you can click the Other option and type the custom delimiter character in the accompanying text box.

6. **Click OK.** Word performs the conversion and displays the table.

> **NOTE**
>
> If you opened a `.csv` or `.txt` file directly in Word, after you create the table, you'll need to use the Save As command and choose Word Document as the Save as type. If you simply tried to resave the existing file, you'd lose the table formatting, because those file formats don't support it.

The Convert Text to Table dialog box can be a useful diagnostic tool when the simple text to table method presented earlier (Insert ⇨ Tables ⇨ Table ⇨ Insert Table) yields unexpected results, such as more or fewer columns than you expected. When you get the wrong table dimensions, press Ctrl+Z, investigate the data, make any corrections, and try again.

You can get the wrong number of columns if there are too many tabs (sometimes obscured as a result of formatting issues) or if some rows use spaces instead of tabs to achieve the table "look." Display nonprinting formatting characters by clicking Show/Hide in the Paragraph group of the Home tab. You might for example find instances where multiple tabs were typed between columns. This confuses Word, which assumes there are more columns than needed. When this happens dismiss the dialog box, find and remove the extra tabs, and try again. Don't worry about setting a properly aligned tab, because you're converting the tabbed data into a table anyway; the table will handle the alignment for you.

Converting tables to text

Sometimes it's necessary or useful to convert an existing table to text. You might want to do this if the data needs to be provided to someone else in a different form. Some statistical programs will accept .csv data, but not Word tables. Or you might simply find it easier to manipulate the data in text form, and then transform it back into a table. Whatever the reason, it's easy:

1. **Save your document.**
2. **Move the mouse pointer over the table you want to convert, and then click the table move handle when it appears.** Word selects the entire table and the Table Tools contextual tabs appear.
3. **Click the Table Tools ⇨ Layout contextual tab, and click Convert to Text in the Data group.** The Convert Table to Text dialog box appears, as shown in Figure 9.8.

FIGURE 9.8

The Convert Table to Text dialog box prompts you to specify a delimiter for text.

4. **Choose the desired delimiter, and then click OK.** Note that if the table contains nested tables, then the Convert nested tables option will be available.

Selecting, copying, and moving in tables

As with plain text in Word, when working with a table you need to be able to make selections so that you can format or manipulate the contents. With a table, it's common to need to select entire columns or rows so that you can apply uniform formatting to them. You also might want to move or copy information in the table, which requires a few special techniques.

Selecting tables, rows, and columns

Word offers multiple techniques for making selections in tables. For example, when you want to select an entire table, you can use one of these quick methods:

- Move the mouse pointer over the table to display the table move handle, and then click it.

- Click anywhere in the table to reveal the Table Tools contextual tabs, shown in Figure 9.9. Click the Layout tab, and then click Select ➪ Select Table in the Tables group.

FIGURE 9.9

Use the Layout contextual tab to access a number of table selection and manipulation tools.

There is also a keyboard method for selecting tables, but it's tough to remember and to use. With the insertion point anywhere in the table, and Num Lock engaged, press Alt+Shift+5 on the numeric keypad. If Num Lock isn't engaged, press Shift+5 on the number pad instead. You also can click in the table and use KeyTips: Press Alt, and then press JLKT, one key at a time. Another method is to use the arrow keys to move the insertion point to the upper-left cell. Press and hold Shift, and use the Down Arrow and Right Arrow keys to extend the selection highlight over all table cells.

Another table selection method involves dragging from outside the table after clicking in the table. Dragging from a location diagonally above and to the left of the table move handle down over the lower-right cell selects the entire table. Or, you can drag from outside the lower-right corner to the upper-left cell until all cells are highlighted.

To select a row without using the Ribbon, move the mouse pointer into the margin to the left of the row until it changes to a right-tilting arrow as shown in Figure 9.10, and click. Drag to expand the selection to include contiguous rows, or Ctrl+click using the Select Row pointer to select additional noncontiguous rows.

FIGURE 9.10

Word's mouse pointer changes shape to indicate what action a click will perform.

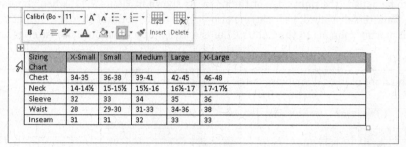

To select a column without using the Ribbon, move the mouse pointer just above the column so that it turns into a down-pointing black arrow, and click. Again, drag to expand the selection to include additional contiguous columns, or Ctrl+click to select additional discrete/noncontiguous columns.

You also can use the Select drop-down list in the Table Group of the Table Tools ⇨ Layout contextual tab. As shown in Figure 9.9, the menu includes Select Column and Select Row commands that you can choose to select the table column or row that currently holds the insertion point.

Copying table matter

You use the same copy and paste choices to copy a table selection as you would use for regular text. Use Copy and Paste in the Clipboard group of the Home tab, or use the Ctrl+C and Ctrl+V shortcuts.

When copying all or part of a table from one table to another, you need to consider the dimensions of the source and the target. Sometimes when you paste into the new table, the whole table is pasted into a single cell rather than individual rows or columns.

As a general rule, when you're pasting table matter, the receiving table dimensions should match the source dimensions. If you're trying to paste a 4 × 5 set of cells into a table whose dimensions are 6 × 8, copy the 4 × 5 source to the Clipboard, select the desired 4 × 5 location in the receiving table, and then paste. Pasting without first selecting sometimes works, but sometimes it doesn't. The situation can get even weirder when you're pasting between Word and Excel, so have that Ctrl+Z (Undo) command standing by.

To control what happens with respect to formatting, see the File ⇨ Options ⇨ Advanced ⇨ Cut, copy, and paste section. Use the top four pasting options to specify what happens when you paste under a variety of circumstances. If necessary, temporarily enable the desired behavior, perform the paste, and then go back to reset the defaults.

Moving and copying columns

To move one or more adjacent columns within a table, select them and then drag to the desired column. Release the mouse button anywhere in the destination column. The selected column(s)

9

will move to the position of the destination column, which will scoot to the right. To move one or more selected columns to the right of the rightmost column, drop the selection at what appears to be outside the right edge of the table. As shown in Figure 9.11, when you have non-printing characters displayed, cell markers also appear to the right of the table's right boundary. When moving columns to the right side of the table, drop them on those exterior markers.

FIGURE 9.11

Drag to the right of the cell markers outside the table to move a column there.

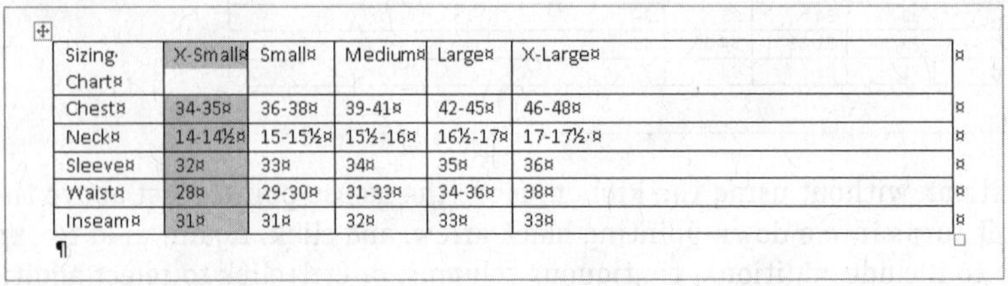

Sizing Chart¤	X-Small¤	Small¤	Medium¤	Large¤	X-Large¤		¤
Chest¤	34-35¤	36-38¤	39-41¤	42-45¤	46-48¤		¤
Neck¤	14-14½¤	15-15½¤	15½-16¤	16½-17¤	17-17½·¤		¤
Sleeve¤	32¤	33¤	34¤	35¤	36¤		¤
Waist¤	28¤	29-30¤	31-33¤	34-36¤	38¤		¤
Inseam¤	31¤	31¤	32¤	33¤	33¤		¤

¶

To copy one or more columns, hold the Ctrl key as you drop. The selection will be inserted at the drop point, using the same location rules that apply when you're moving columns.

When moving a column between tables, it's probably easier to use the Cut and Paste commands in the Clipboard group of the Home tab (or use Ctrl+X and Ctrl+V).

Moving and copying rows

You can move and copy rows in the same way as columns, except with respect to the last row. The last row does not have exterior cell markers. If you drop a selection of one or more rows onto the last row of a table, the selection will be placed above the last row. If you drop it after the last row, the selection will be appended to the table, but the formatting will often change.

Instead, when you want to move rows after the last current row, drop them on the last row. Then put the insertion point anywhere in the last row and press Alt+Shift+Up Arrow to move the stubborn last row up to where you want it.

> **TIP**
>
> Any time you want to move table rows around, Alt+Shift+Up Arrow and Alt+Shift+Down Arrow can be used to push the current row up or down in the table. If you're moving a single row you don't need to select anything. If you're moving multiple contiguous rows, select them first.

Changing table properties

If you need to set precise table settings, click Properties in the Table group of the Table Tools ⇨ Layout contextual tab, or right-click a table and choose Table Properties to display the dialog box shown in Figure 9.12. Use the Table tab to control overall layout and behavior; use the other tabs or the mouse to control row, column, and cell characteristics.

FIGURE 9.12

Use Table Properties to control overall alignment, indentation, and positioning of tables.

Preferred width

Check Preferred width and enter a measurement in the accompanying text box to set a target width for the table. The preferred width can't be absolute, however, because tables contain text and data, and are further constrained by paper and margin settings. Note that AutoFit settings override the Preferred width.

Alignment

Table alignment affects the entire table with respect to the current left and right margins. If the table extends from the left margin to the right margin, which is the default for tables inserted in Word, then the alignment controls seemingly will have no effect. This makes it easy not to notice if they're changed. If you later narrow the table, its placement on the page might suddenly seem askew. You can be sure you're centering a table by choosing Center under Alignment on the Table tab of the Table Properties dialog box.

The Indent from left setting on the tab controls how far the table is from the left margin. There is no Ribbon control for this setting, and it cannot be set with the ruler line.

Note that Indent from left is available only when Text wrapping is set to None and Alignment is set to Left. When Around text wrapping is enabled, use Positioning to set the distance from the left, as shown in the section that follows.

Text wrapping and moving a table

You can insert a table in line with other text, or if it is smaller than the full document width, you can move or drag it into position so that text outside the table wraps around it, as shown in Figure 9.13. To have this flexibility, change the Text wrapping setting in the Table tab of the Table Properties dialog box to Around. Dragging a table into a new position using the table move handle automatically changes the Text wrapping setting from None to Around.

FIGURE 9.13

Wrap text around tables for a more integrated appearance.

Clicking the Positioning button opens a Table Positioning dialog box. You can choose Horizontal and Vertical Position settings, and set the Distance from surrounding text for each side of the table. The Move with Text option controls whether the table's vertical position is governed by the paragraph to which it is anchored. If Move with Text is enabled, the vertical position can be relative to only paragraph. Use this setting if the paragraph's content and the table's content are interrelated so that the table would not make sense except when near that paragraph. This often is the setting you want for research reports.

Turn off Move with Text if the location of the table is not logically tied to a particular paragraph. This setting might be more in keeping with the design of a brochure or a newsletter in which the table's contents are relevant to the entire document and should appear in a particular location for aesthetic reasons.

> **TIP**
>
> When you paste a table with Ctrl+V or the Paste button in the Clipboard group of the Home tab, you can click the Paste Options button and choose a format for the pasted table.

Sizing a table, row, or column

Word tables feature several kinds of handles and mouse pointers that enable you to manipulate and select cells, rows, columns, and entire tables, for example:

- If you point to the lower-right corner of a table, the mouse pointer changes to a two-headed diagonal arrow. Drag it to resize the table.

- If you point to the bottom gridline or border for a table row, the mouse pointer changes to a resizing pointer, with a double black horizontal bar and up and down arrows. Drag when you see that pointer to resize the row height. Resizing rows is not usually necessary, because they will automatically change height when you change the font size for the text in the row.

- If you point to the right gridline or border for a table column, the mouse pointer changes to a resizing pointer, with a double black vertical bar and left and right arrows. Drag when you see that pointer to resize the column width.

TIP

Double-click the right column border with the resizing pointer to automatically fit the column width to its contents.

In other instances, you might need to be more precise about row and column sizes. For example, if you have a document such as an annual report or a product quality testing report, it's desirable to make column widths fairly consistent to make the report look more orderly. When that's the case, you can use the Row and Column tabs in the Table Properties dialog box to change the size for the selected row or column:

- **Row tab:** Leave Specify height checked, and enter a size in the accompanying text box. If you want to make the size more permanent, change the Row height is setting from At least to Exactly. Use the Previous Row and Next Row buttons to move to other rows to format, and click OK when done.

- **Column tab:** Leave Preferred width checked and enter a specific width (Figure 9.14). Use the Previous Column and Next Column buttons to choose the settings for other columns as desired, and click OK when finished.

FIGURE 9.14

Enter precise row and column heights on the Row and Column tabs.

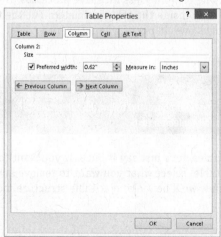

Working with Table Layout and Design

Word 2013's Table Tools⇨Design and Layout contextual tabs provide you with most of what you need to create tables that are both aesthetically appealing and functional. The Design tab tools enable you to improve the table's appearance. The tools on the Layout tab help you ensure that the table presents information in a logical way that is meaningful to the reader.

So far we've looked at a number of basic tools that help you achieve the right structure for your tables. In this section we're going to look at how to mold tables into shape and then polish them for your audience.

> **NOTE**
>
> Many of the Ribbon commands described in this section are also available in the right-click shortcut menu.

Modifying table layout

We all know that situations, ideas, and data change. Let's look at how to cope with changes that impact the structure of data in a table.

All references to the Layout tab in this section refer to the Table Tools⇨Layout contextual tab to keep the descriptions brief. None of the Layout tab tools provide Live Preview, so carefully review the impact of any layout change and use Ctrl+Z to undo a change immediately if it doesn't have the desired impact.

Deleting table, row, column, and cell contents

Sometimes you need to trim your tables by deleting rows or columns. Sometimes you have to delete the entire table, which is one of Word's less intuitive processes. If you select a table and press the Delete key, the data inside the table is deleted, but the table rows and columns remain. The same thing sometimes happens when you try to delete a cell, a row, or a column.

> **TIP**
>
> If the table is part of a larger selection of text with text both above and below the table selected, then pressing Delete does remove the table as well as the additionally selected text.

Rather than say this a half dozen times, let's just say it once. If you want to remove the contents of a cell, row, column, or table, select what you want to remove and press the Delete key. In the sections that follow we'll be looking at table structure, not contents.

Deleting a table

You can use any of the following methods to delete an entire table:

- Click anywhere in the table, and in the Layout tab click Delete in the Rows & Columns group, and click Delete Table, as shown in Figure 9.15. Word deletes the table immediately.

FIGURE 9.15

Delete the current cell, column, row, or table using the Layout tab's Delete menu.

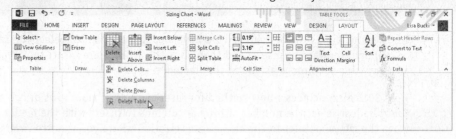

- Move the mouse pointer over the table, right-click the table move handle, and then click Cut.
- Select the table using the method of your choice, and then press Backspace.

Deleting rows, columns, and cells

To delete the current row or column, use techniques similar to deleting the table. Select the row(s), column(s), or cell(s) and press Backspace, or choose Layout ➪ Delete ➪ Delete Rows, Layout ➪ Delete ➪ Columns, or Layout ➪ Delete ➪ Cells.

When deleting cells, Word needs a little more information. The Delete Cells dialog box shown in Figure 9.16 prompts you to specify how to shift remaining cells or whether you in fact really mean to delete the row or column. Make your selection and click OK.

FIGURE 9.16

Word prompts to find out how to handle the rest of the column or row when you delete a single cell.

Inserting rows, columns, and cells

To insert a row or column into a table, click in the row or column adjacent to where you want to insert, and then click Insert Above, Insert Below, Insert Left, or Insert Right in the Rows & Columns group of the Layout tab (refer to Figure 9.15), depending on where you want the new row or column to appear.

> **TIP**
>
> To add a new row to the end of an existing table, place the insertion point at the end of the entry in the bottom-right cell and press the Tab key. To add a new interior row, click outside the right side of the table above where you want the new row to appear, and press Enter.

To insert multiple rows or columns you have a couple of options. Select the number of rows or columns you want to insert, and then click the appropriate insert tool. Word will insert as many rows or columns as you have selected.

Word 2013 also includes a new method for inserting one or more rows or columns — *Insert Controls*. Just select the number of rows or columns to insert with the mouse, and then move the mouse pointer to the side of the selection where you want to insert the new rows or columns. (Move the pointer to the left of the selected row or above and to the right of the selected column.) As shown in Figure 9.17, the Insert Control (which looks like a divider with a plus button) appears. Click the plus to insert the specified number of rows or columns at the divider. In the example in Figure 9.17, because two columns are selected and the divider is to the right of the selection, clicking the plus would insert two new columns to the right of the selection.

FIGURE 9.17

Click the plus button that appears to insert new rows or columns in the specified position.

Sizing Chart	X-Small	Small	Medium	Large	X-Large
Chest	34-35	36-38	39-41	42-45	46-48
Neck	14-14½	15-15½	15½-16	16½-17	17-17½
Sleeve	32	33	34	35	36
Waist	28	29-30	31-33	34-36	38
Inseam	31	31	32	33	33

To insert cells, select the cell(s) adjacent to where you want the new one(s) to appear, and click the dialog box launcher in the bottom-right corner of the Rows & Columns group in the Layout tab. You'll see a dialog box containing the identical options shown in Figure 9.16. Choose your desired action and click OK.

Controlling how tables break

Sometimes you don't particularly care how tables break across pages, but sometimes you do. When you need to keep certain rows together on a page:

1. **Select the rows in question.**

2. **Click Properties in the Table group of the Layout tab (or right-click the selection and choose Table Properties from the shortcut menu).**

3. **Click the Row tab, and under Options uncheck the Allow row to break across pages check box.**

4. **Click OK.**

To force a table to break at a particular point, move the insertion point to anywhere in the row where you want the break to occur, and then press Ctrl+Enter. Note that this doesn't simply force the table to break at that point; it actually breaks the table into two tables. If the Repeat as header row at the top of each page setting on the Row tab of the Table Properties dialog box is enabled for the first row(s) of the original table, it won't be inherited by the "new" table. You'll have to copy the heading row to the new table and reinstate the setting, if needed.

Merging table cells

Sometimes you need to merge columns, rows, or cells. For example, it's common to merge the cells in the top row of a table to create one larger cell to hold a title for the table. Merging cells is easy. Select the cells you want to merge and click Merge Cells in the Merge group of the Layout tab (refer to Figure 9.15).

> **TIP**
>
> You also can use the table eraser in the Layout tab's Draw group. Click the Eraser tool, and then click on the table gridline or border segment to remove. To turn the eraser off, click its Ribbon button again, or press the Esc key.

Word can't really merge rows or columns. Suppose you need to merge the cells from two columns into a single column on each row. What you want to end up with is the same number of rows with one less column. If you select both columns and click Merge Cells, however, Word treats that as a request to merge all the cells in the selection, and you end up with one big cell with the entries jumbled together. This is illustrated in Figure 9.18. The HIGH and LOW columns were merged, resulting in one big cell of useless data. There is no way around this. To get the desired result, you would have to select the HIGH and LOW column entries on each row and merge them individually.

9

FIGURE 9.18

Word cannot merge into multiple cells.

DATE	OPEN	HIGH	CLOSE	VOLUME	ADJ CLOSE
2012-11-29	27.11	LOW	26.95	69551400	26.95
2012-11-28	27.01	27.36	27.36	53018400	27.36
2012-11-27	27.36	26.86	27.08	45018600	27.08
2012-11-26	27.54	27.39	27.39	85198700	27.39
2012-11-23	27.23	26.77	27.70	57845700	27.70
2012-11-21	26.71	27.38	26.95	66360300	26.95
2012-11-20	26.76	27.04	26.71	47070400	26.71
2012-11-19	26.80	27.58	26.73	57179300	26.73
2012-11-16	26.67	27.17	26.52	64083300	26.52
2012-11-15	26.88	27.77	26.66	50955600	26.66
2012-11-14	27.24	27.20	26.84	76086100	26.84
2012-11-13	27.02	27.17	27.09	131689200	27.09
2012-11-12	28.94	26.67	28.22	61112300	27.99
2012-11-09	28.88	26.80	28.83	43291200	28.60
2012-11-08	29.12	26.46	28.81	49841800	28.58
2012-11-07	29.53	26.80	29.08	57871800	28.84
2012-11-06	29.82	26.47	29.86	43401500	29.62
2012-11-05	29.62	26.70	29.63	38070800	29.39
2012-11-02	29.59	26.34	29.50	57131600	29.26
2012-11-01	28.84	26.97	29.52	72047900	29.28
2012-10-31	28.55	26.63	28.54	69464100	28.31
2012-10-26	27.86	27.29	28.21	57790000	27.98
2012-10-25	28.19	26.80	27.88	54084300	27.65
2012-10-24	28.16	27.30	27.90	53320400	27.67
2012-10-23	27.77	26.75	28.05	64414800	27.82
2012-10-22	28.73	29.01	28.00	83374000	27.77
2012-10-19	29.05	28.21	28.64	90470800	28.41
2012-10-18	29.65	29.19	29.50	59238500	29.26
2012-10-17	29.30	28.81	29.59	44206100	29.35
		29.37			

ENGLISH (UNITED STATES)

> **NOTE**
>
> If you are also an Excel user, you could use Excel to merge columns of data as in the previous example. Excel has functions that enable you to join text from two separate cells into a single entry.

Splitting cells, rows, and columns

At first it seemed that one cell, row, or column was fine, but later you decide that the logic of the table layout calls for two (or more) cells where there once was one. If you split a cell that holds text, the text will remain in the left or upper-left cell in the split group. In Figure 9.19, the cell with X-Large in it was split into three cells, as illustrated by the settings in the Split Cells dialog box.

To perform a split, select the cell(s) to split, click Split cells in the Merge group of the Layout tab, make Number of columns and Number of rows entries as needed in the Split Cells dialog box, and click OK.

FIGURE 9.19

When you split cells, specify how many rows and columns you want to create.

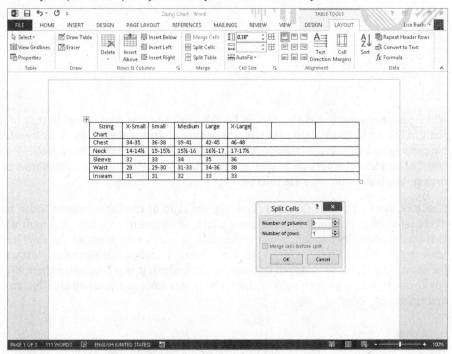

Horizontal splits or splits where you start by selecting multiple rows or columns are often harder to control. The trick is to make sure that items are horizontally displayed and separated either by at least two spaces or by a tab (press Ctrl+Tab to insert a tab inside a table). It can still be tedious, but it's a bit more direct than using the dialog box, and you have more control and precision.

Cell size

When you're using a table to lay out a fill-in form, cell measurements sometimes have to be precise, especially when you're trying to align a Word document with preprinted forms. When cell height and width need to be controlled precisely, click the Table Row Height or Table Column Width boxes in the Cell Size group on the Layout tab, shown in Figure 9.20. Note that cell height cannot vary for any cell within any given row.

FIGURE 9.20

Use the Cell Size group on the Layout tab to specify the precise height and width of rows and columns.

When you need rows to have a uniform height, click the Distribute Rows button to the right of the Table Row Height text box. If rows are of different heights — as sometimes happens when you're converting part of an Excel spreadsheet into a Word table — this command determines the optimal height and equalizes the height of all selected rows or of all rows in the table if no rows are selected.

Similarly, click Distribute Columns (found to the right of the Table Column Width text box) to set selected or all columns to the same width. If different rows have different widths, this command will not equalize the whole table. It works only when all the rows have the same width. If any differ (for example, if row two is 4 inches and all the other rows are 3.5 inches, giving the table a ragged left and/or right edge), it won't equalize them all. To remedy this, drag the right border(s) of shorter or longer rows so that they all align on the left and right.

Alignment

The Alignment group of the Layout tab offers nine cell alignment options, as shown at the left in Figure 9.21. To change how the contents align horizontally or vertically within any cell, click in or select the cells you want to change, and then click the desired tool. As noted elsewhere, many users confuse cell alignment with table alignment. With the whole table selected, this tool will at most set the individual alignment of each cell and won't have any effect on table alignment. Instead, select the whole table and use the Paragraph group alignment tools in the Home tab, or use the Alignment setting in the Table Properties dialog box.

FIGURE 9.21

Word offers nine options for cell alignment, as well as the ability to change text direction and cell margins.

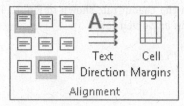

Text direction

To control text direction in selected table cells, click the Text Direction tool in the Alignment group of the Layout tab. This command toggles the text between the normal horizontal layout, to text vertically aligned at the right side of the cell, to text vertically aligned at the left side of the cell. For example, you may prefer to change to one of the vertical alignments when the titles in the top row of the table are wider than the rest of the entries in the column, and you're having trouble fitting the table horizontally on the page. Formatting the titles vertically would enable you to make the columns narrower to better fit the table on the page.

Cell margins and cell spacing

Word provides several kinds of controls for cell margins. *Cell margin* is the distance between cell contents and cell walls. Proper margins can keep cells from becoming too crowded and unreadable. Additional spacing can also prevent data from printing over the borders when you're using a table to format data for printing on preprinted forms. To set cell margins and cell spacing, click Cell Margins in the Alignment group of the Layout tab, shown in Figure 9.21. This displays the Table Options dialog box shown in Figure 9.22.

FIGURE 9.22

If your table is too crowded, increase the default cell margins.

Despite the name of the Default cell margins section of the dialog box, it does not set the *default* cell margins or spacing for tables. It sets the cell margins only for the currently selected table, and the settings you enter apply to all cells in the table.

The Allow spacing between cells setting under Default cell spacing in the Table Options dialog box can be used to create the effect shown in Figure 9.23. This gives the table the appearance of having a distinct box inside each table cell.

FIGURE 9.23

Cell spacing can give tables a dramatic appearance.

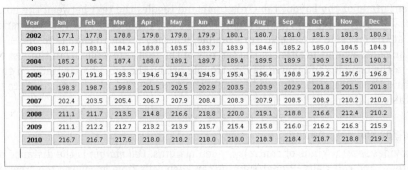

Year	Jan	Feb	Mar	Apr	May	Jun	Jul	Aug	Sep	Oct	Nov	Dec
2002	177.1	177.8	178.8	179.8	179.8	179.9	180.1	180.7	181.0	181.3	181.3	180.9
2003	181.7	183.1	184.2	183.8	183.5	183.7	183.9	184.6	185.2	185.0	184.5	184.3
2004	185.2	186.2	187.4	188.0	189.1	189.7	189.4	189.5	189.9	190.9	191.0	190.3
2005	190.7	191.8	193.3	194.6	194.4	194.5	195.4	196.4	198.8	199.2	197.6	196.8
2006	198.3	198.7	199.8	201.5	202.5	202.9	203.5	203.9	202.9	201.8	201.5	201.8
2007	202.4	203.5	205.4	206.7	207.9	208.4	208.3	207.9	208.5	208.9	210.2	210.0
2008	211.1	211.7	213.5	214.8	216.6	218.8	220.0	219.1	218.8	216.6	212.4	210.2
2009	211.1	212.2	212.7	213.2	213.9	215.7	215.4	215.8	216.0	216.2	216.3	215.9
2010	216.7	216.7	217.6	218.0	218.2	218.0	218.0	218.3	218.4	218.7	218.8	219.2

Tables that span multiple pages

When a table spans multiple pages, Word can automatically repeat one or more heading rows to make the table more manageable. When the need arises, select the target table's heading rows (you can have multiple heading rows), and click Repeat Heading Rows in the Data group of the Layout tab. The selected heading rows are then repeated where necessary. The setting can be toggled on or off for each individual table. Because the number of heading rows can vary, this setting cannot be made the default for all tables, nor incorporated into a style definition.

> **NOTE**
>
> If you are preparing a document for the web and working in Web Layout view, the Repeat Heading rows command has no effect, because web pages are seamless and do not have page breaks in concept.

Sorting table rows

Word provides a flexible and fast way to sort data in tables. To sort a table, select the first column (field) to sort by, and click the Sort button in the Data group of the Layout tab. Word displays the Sort dialog box, shown in Figure 9.24. If the table has headings in the first row at the top of each column, selecting the Header Row option under My list has does two things. First, it provides labels in the Sort by and Then by drop-down lists. Second, it excludes the header row from the sort.

FIGURE 9.24

The Sort command lets you sort by up to three fields.

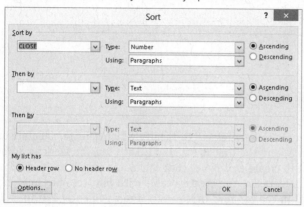

If you did not select a column before opening the Sort dialog box, select the first sort field from the Sort by drop-down list. Open the Type drop-down list and click Text, Number, or Date to match up with the type of data stored in the sort column. Choose Ascending or Descending depending on whether you want to sort from A to Z, or lowest to highest, or most recent to least recent — or vice versa for any of those. To sort by additional fields, open the two Then by drop-down lists and click a field name to include up to two of them, and set the additional type and sort order settings. Click Options to determine additional settings, including how fields are delimited (for non-table sorts), whether to make the sort case-sensitive, and the sorting language. Click OK to close Sort Options, and then click OK to apply the sort.

Adding table calculations

Word can perform some calculations using the Formula button in the Data group of the Layout tab (refer to Figure 9.19). To use it, first create a cell or row where you want to include formulas, and then select the first cell in which to enter a formula. Note that you only can select multiple cells when the formula will be the same in each one, such as summing all the cells above the selection. Click Formula in the Data group of the Layout tab. Edit the contents of the Formula text box. Or you can click to the right of the equals sign (=) in the Formula text box and use the Paste function drop-down list to paste in one of the predefined functions and indicate what cells to calculate between the parentheses. If needed, choose a format from the Number format drop-down list; the selection shown in Figure 9.25 formats the number with two decimal places. Click OK to insert the formula in the cell.

9

FIGURE 9.25

These Formula settings calculate an average and set it to display with two decimal places.

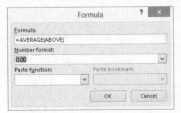

As with Excel, you also can use "cell addresses" to specify which cells to calculate on in a table; the column is column A, and the first row is row 1. Let's say you work as a freelance personal assistant and want to create an invoice that calculates your billing based on various rates you charge for various tasks. You create a table with four columns and enter **Task**, **Hours**, **Rate**, and **Item Total** in the top row. In the second row you enter **Filing**, **3.25**, and **10** in the first three cells. You then click in the fourth cell of the second row and display the Formula dialog box (Layout contextual tab, click Formula in the Data group). Edit the Formula text box entry to read **=B2*C2**, because you want to multiply the values in the second and third columns (Hours times Rate) to get the Item Total for the row. Choose a format with the dollar sign and two decimals from the Number format drop-down list, and click OK. The correct total of $32.50 displays for that row. In the next row, you could enter the next Task, Hours, and Rate values, and then use the Formula dialog box to create a formula in the fourth column that calculates **=B3*C3**, incrementing the row number in the formula for each new row. Then, to create an overall total in the final row, you can enter **Total** in the third column, and in the fourth column use the Formula dialog box to enter an =SUM(ABOVE) formula, formatted as currency like the formulas above it.

Unfortunately, you cannot copy or fill formulas across a row or down a column and have the addresses increment (as relative cell addresses in Excel do); you have to insert a new formula in each individual table cell, or copy a formula with Excel-style cell addressing and then edit the field and change the cell addresses. If you use Word for math, double-check all calculations using a calculator or Excel. But if you have Excel and you need complex math in tables, then use Excel. You can then link the results to Word.

As you might imagine if you've done any work with Excel, you can create more complicated formulas in Word by using parentheses to group multiple functions and calculations. To redisplay the Formula dialog box to edit a calculation, click in the calculation so you see gray shading behind it. And use Layout ➪ Data ➪ Formula to redisplay it.

> **NOTE**
>
> If you change the values that a table is using to perform calculations, then you will need to recalculate the table. The table formulas are inserted as fields, and unlike the formulas in Excel, they do not recalculate automatically. The safest way to ensure that a table's calculations are up to date is to click a table cell, click the table move handle to select the whole table, and then press F9.

Modifying table design

Word 2013 provides a number of powerful tools to help you quickly enhance the look and feel of your tables. One of these tools, Table Styles, features Live Preview. In this section we'll look only at the features contained in the Table Tools⇨Design contextual tab, shown in Figure 9.26.

FIGURE 9.26

The Design contextual tab provides access to six Table Style Options and a gallery of Table Styles.

Applying a table style

Word 2013's refreshed and updated preset table styles enable you to change the look of any table with just a few clicks. Table styles provide a wide variety of formatting that you can preview live in your table. You can use styles to ensure a consistent, professional look when you include multiple tables within a single document. You can also modify a table style and save the modified versions for later use.

To apply a table style, click anywhere in the table to format, and then click the Table Tools⇨Design contextual tab (from here referred to as the Design tab for simplicity). In Table Styles, hover the mouse over various styles and observe the changes to your table. As you move the mouse, tooltips display the name of the selected table style (such as Plain Table 1), as shown in Figure 9.27.

FIGURE 9.27

As you move the mouse over various table styles, the currently selected table displays a Live Preview of the formatting.

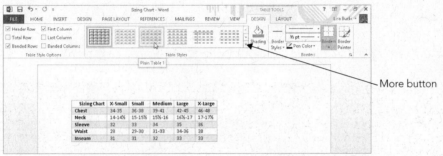

More button

If you see a style you like, click it to apply it to your table. If it's not perfect you can modify it. If you don't see a style you like, click the More button to the right of the table styles. Word displays the full Table Style Gallery, showing Plain Tables, Grid Tables, and (if you scroll down) List Tables categories of table styles, as shown in Figure 9.28. Move the mouse pointer over additional styles to preview their look on your table, and then click the style to apply. Note that you can click Clear near the bottom of the gallery to remove a previously applied table style.

FIGURE 9.28

The Table Styles gallery enables you to test-drive dozens of built-in table styles.

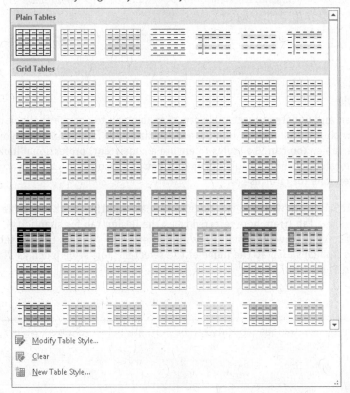

Choosing table style options

The Table Style Options group at the left end of the Design tab provides access to six options, shown in Figure 9.26, that you can apply to your table. For some of these to work, you have to apply a table style that includes shading rather than trying to use them with the plain Table Grid style that is the default for newly inserted tables. After you apply an overall table style, click to check to apply Table Style Options to your tables, or remove checks to turn the corresponding features off:

- **Header Row:** Applies special formatting to the entire top row in your table.
- **First Column:** Applies special formatting to the entire first column.
- **Total Row:** Applies special formatting to the last row, generally a double border above the row as for traditional accounting formatting for numeric totals. The formatting may be omitted for the first cell.
- **Last Column:** Applies special formatting to the last column, except for the top cell.
- **Banded Rows:** Alternates shading in rows to create a horizontal striping effect. This helps the reader focus on specific rows.
- **Banded Columns:** Alternates shading in columns to create vertical stripes, focusing the reader on columnar comparisons.

Shading cells

You can apply shading (a background fill color) to individual cells, rows, columns, or to a complete table. You can use shading sometimes to draw attention to one or more elements of a table. For example, if you added a row with calculated averages to the bottom of a table, you might want to call attention to that data with special shading. It's also common to use shading to set off a title row or column.

Select the cells, rows, or columns to shade, and then click Shading in the Table Styles group of the Design tab. Live Preview works with the Shading gallery, as shown in Figure 9.29. Move the mouse pointer over a color to preview it on the selection, and then click when you're ready to apply a color. Figure 9.29 shows light shading applied to the left column of a table, with darker shading being previewed in the top row. Note that when you apply Theme Colors as your shading choices, those colors automatically update whenever you apply a new theme to the document. Use the More Colors command to apply colors that won't change when you change the theme.

9

FIGURE 9.29

Live Preview works with the Shading choices.

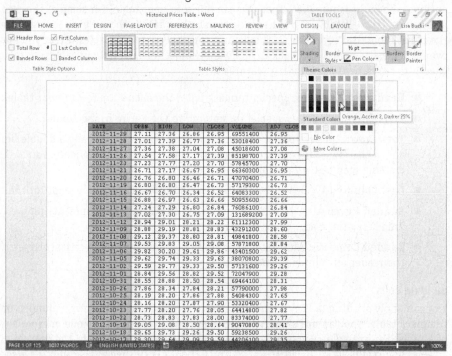

Modifying and saving a table style

To modify the table style applied to the selected table:

1. **Open the Table Styles gallery and click Modify Table Style near the bottom the gallery.** The Modify Style dialog box shown in Figure 9.30 appears.

2. **Type or edit the name in the Name text box if you want to rename the style.** You can use the Modify Style dialog box to apply style formatting, as described in Chapter 7, "Using Styles to Create a Great Looking Document."

FIGURE 9.30

Use the Modify Style dialog box to make changes to a table style.

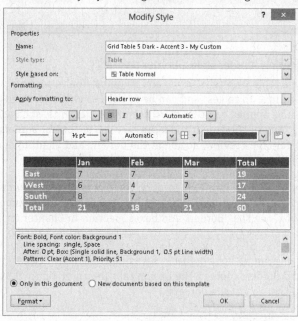

3. **Open the Apply formatting to drop-down list and choose the part of the table for which you want to change formatting.**

4. **Use the formatting choices above the preview to format the selected item.**

5. **Repeat Steps 3 and 4 to change additional parts of the style.**

6. **Check an option to store the style Only in this document or in New documents based on this template.**

7. **Click OK.**

If you want to create a new style rather than modify one of the existing ones — which is a good choice when you want to keep all the original table styles intact — click the New Table Style choice at the bottom of the Table Styles gallery. The Create New Style from Formatting dialog box that appears has the same settings as those in the Modify Style dialog box shown in Figure 9.30. Enter a table Name, and then open the Style based on the drop-down list to choose an existing table style to serve as the model or base for your new style. Make formatting adjustments as described in Steps 3 and 4 here, choose where to store the file, and then click OK to finish creating your new style. The new style will appear in a category named Custom at the top of the Table Styles gallery.

9

Borders and table drawing (border styles, border painter)

Border lines separate a table into cells, rows, and columns. You've seen in other chapters that borders are not unique to tables, and can be applied to characters and paragraphs as well. They also can be applied to other Word document elements, such as text boxes, frames, and graphics. Any of the border tools can be used to control borders in tables. None of the border tools offer Live Preview, although the Borders and Shading dialog box does provide a generic preview.

You have two strategies for working with borders. You can launch the Borders and Shading dialog box. For a detailed description of how to apply borders using the Borders and Shading dialog box, see the "Borders and boxes" section in Chapter 6, "Paragraph Formatting."

The second strategy uses an ad hoc approach, by using the Border Styles, Line Style, Line Weight, Pen Color, and Borders tools in the Design tab, shown in Figure 9.31. Use the border formatting tools together to change borders:

FIGURE 9.31

Use the Borders Styles tool and its friends to make ad hoc changes to table borders.

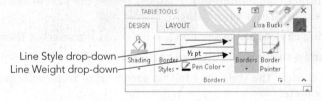

1. **Select the cells, rows, or columns to which you want to apply borders.**

2. **In the Borders group of the Design contextual tab, choose the settings you want from the Line Style, Line Weight, and Pen Color drop-downs; or click the Border Styles button and click a border style in the gallery.**

3. **Click the Borders button down arrow, and then click to specify where you'd like to apply the borders.** Click Outside Borders to put borders all around the selection, for example.

Once you've applied a border style you like to selected cells, you can use Word 2013's new Border Painter tool to copy it to other selections, as shown in Figure 9.32. Click Border Painter, and then drag the painter mouse pointer to apply the specified border to cell, row, and column boundaries. Press Esc to turn the Border Painter off when finished.

FIGURE 9.32

When the Border Painter is active, drag to copy border settings to other table locations.

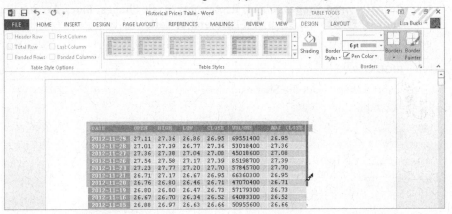

> **TIP**
>
> Remember that if you remove all table borders, you may want to turn on table gridlines so that you can see cell boundaries. The View Gridlines setting is in the Table group of the Table Tools ⇨ Layout tab.

Using the table eraser

The table eraser removes parts of tables. It doesn't merely remove border lines; it deletes the cell boundaries in a table where you specify. You can use the table eraser to turn interior cells into a larger interior cell. Be careful, though. If you try to delete a table's upper-left cell, you might instead delete the whole top row of the table.

To use the table eraser, click in a table and then click Eraser in the Draw group of the Table Tools ⇨ Layout tab. Click on cell boundaries to remove as needed. (Remember to press Ctrl+Z immediately if you inadvertently click the wrong border.) To dismiss the eraser, either click the Eraser tool again to toggle it off, or press Esc. The eraser also deactivates if you click outside a table (in regular text).

Adding a Shape

In addition to adding a table and inserting other types of graphics such as pictures (which you'll learn about next) into a document, you can insert a predefined shape. To add a shape to the current page of the document:

1. **Click the Insert tab, and in the Illustrations group, click Shapes.**

2. **In the Shapes gallery (see Figure 9.33), click a shape in one of the categories: Recently Used Shapes, Lines, Rectangles, Basic Shapes, Block Arrows, Equation Shapes, Flowchart, Stars and Banners, or Callouts.**

FIGURE 9.33

Insert a shape from the Shapes gallery.

3. **Add the shape to the document using one of two methods:**
   - Click to insert the shape at its default size.
   - Drag on the page to specify the size that you want for the shape.

NOTE

Generally speaking, you can combine Flowchart shapes along with the Lines shapes to create flowchart-like graphics. (Group the shapes after sizing and positioning them.) However, if you often need to create complex, professional flowcharts, a program such as Visio may be more appropriate for your needs.

Formatting a shape resembles formatting a picture and other types of graphics, which you'll learn more about later in the chapter. The key difference is that the commands for formatting a shape are found on the Drawing Tools⇨Format contextual tab rather than the Picture Tools⇨Format tab. One big difference in formatting options has to do with the overall composition of the shape. In most cases, when you insert a shape and select it by clicking it, one or more yellow handles appear along with the regular selection handles. You can drag these handles to redefine the proportions of individual aspects of the shape within the overall shape boundary. For example, Figure 9.34 shows three copies of the same shape. The left one shows how the shape appeared when originally inserted. It is selected, and the yellow smart handle appears at the left side of the circular center. In the middle copy I dragged the smart handle as far toward the center as possible. In the right copy, I dragged the smart handle as far away from the center as possible.

FIGURE 9.34

Use any yellow smart handles that appear to redefine the internal proportions of the shape.

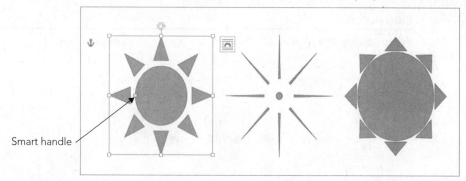

Smart handle

Inserting a Picture from a File

You can insert pictures in Word in several ways, using pictures from a variety of graphics formats. If you have pictures on removable media — such as SD (secure digital), CF (compact flash), CD, DVD, or USB drive — it's usually best to copy those pictures to your hard drive before you proceed. Although you can insert directly from such sources, or from a network location or over the Internet, you have more options available to you if the files are on your own computer in a location that is always accessible.

You might also have pictures available from a webcam, another camera, or a scanner connected to your computer. To use pictures from these types of devices, save the images to your hard drive first.

Though it's not necessary, you often can save time when pictures, sounds, and other files are where Word and other programs expect them to be. In the case of pictures, the expected location is your Pictures Library (or the My Pictures folder, which the Pictures library in Windows 7 or 8 integrates by default).

> **NOTE**
>
> This book assumes that you're working with a Word 2010 or Word 2013 .docx file, and not a Word 97–2003 Compatibility Mode file. This matters because in Compatibility Mode, picture file linking is accomplished with the INCLUDEPICTURE field. In a Word 2013 file, linking is accomplished with XML relationships.

Adding the picture

To insert a picture at the current insertion location in a document:

1. **Click Pictures in the Illustrations group of the Insert tab.** The Insert Picture dialog box appears as shown in Figure 9.35, by default showing the contents of your Pictures library.

FIGURE 9.35

When you insert a picture, the Pictures Library contents appear first.

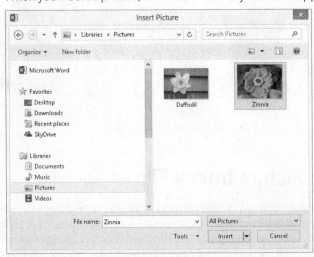

2. **If the picture is in an alternate location, navigate to it.**

TIP

Notice in Figure 9.35 that SkyDrive appears as a choice under Favorites. This choice appears when you have the SkyDrive for Windows application installed. When you copy a picture to your local SkyDrive Pictures folder and then sign in to SkyDrive.com, or upload a picture to your SkyDrive Pictures folder, the local and online Picture folders sync to have the same contents. In the Insert Pictures dialog box, click SkyDrive and then double-click Pictures to access the local copies of your synced image files.

3. **Once you've found the picture to insert, you can either double-click it to insert it immediately or click it once and choose an insert method from the Insert button drop-down list.** The options for inserting pictures are:

   - **Insert:** The picture is embedded in the current document. If the original is ever deleted or moved, it will still exist in your document. If the original is ever updated, however, your document will not reflect the update. The document file will be larger because the original image is stored in the .docx file. If neither file size nor updates are important, this is the best option.

   - **Link to File:** A link to the picture is inserted, and the picture is displayed in the document. The document file will be smaller — often dramatically smaller — because the image is external to the Word document. If the original file is moved or deleted, it will no longer be available for viewing in the document, and you will see the error message shown in Figure 9.36 (see the Caution that follows for more information). On the other hand, if the image is modified or updated, the update will be available and displayed in Word. If file size is an issue but the availability of the image file is not, then this is the best option.

FIGURE 9.36

If you rename, move, or delete a linked picture file, Word will not be able to display it.

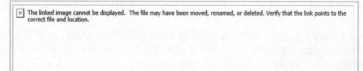

   - **Insert and Link:** The image is both embedded in the document and linked to the original file. If the original file is updated, the picture in the document will be updated to reflect changes in the original. Because the file is embedded, the document will be larger than it would be if only linked. However, the document will not be larger than it would be if only inserted. If file size is not an issue but updates are, this is the best option.

CAUTION

If a link is broken, you can find the name of the missing file, which can help you replace the file, if needed. To discover the name, choose File ⇨ Info ⇨ Edit Links to Files. (The link is near the bottom-right corner of the Info page in Backstage.) In the Links dialog box, the name of the file appears next to Source file. Note the Update Now button. If you restore a missing file and click Update Now, in theory the picture should replace the red X and error message. It does not always work, however — nor does pressing F9. What does usually work, however, is to save and close the file, and then reopen it. When opening files, Word does a better job of checking and restoring links than the Update Now button does.

Supported picture file formats

If the picture you want doesn't appear in Word's Insert Picture dialog box but you know it should be in the current folder, click the All Pictures button in the lower-right corner, and in the list of choices shown in Figure 9.37 click the desired picture (graphic) file format to narrow the list of displayed pictures to ones that match the selected type.

FIGURE 9.37

Word supports a number of popular graphics file formats.

The most popular picture format, used by most digital cameras, is JPEG, which stands for Joint Photographic Experts Group (so if you didn't know before, you do now). Word 2013 comes with a converter that supports JPEG files, which can have a `.jpg` or `.jpeg` file name extension. Other Word 2013–supported popular formats include Graphics Interchange Format (`.gif`), which is heavily used on the Internet due to its support for transparent backgrounds, which makes such images better suited for web page design; Portable Network Graphics (`.png`), also heavily used on the web due to its support for transparency; Tagged Image File Format (`.tif` or `.tiff`); Windows Metafile (`.wmf`); Enhanced Metafile (`.emf`); and Windows Bitmap (`.bmp`).

NOTE

A default Word installation includes all the available graphics filters (converters). To make sure all the graphics filters are installed, open Control Panel and click Uninstall a program under Programs. Click the Microsoft Office 2013 choice (the name may vary depending on your version of Office), and click Change. Type an administrator password when prompted, and then click Yes. Leave Add or Remove Features selected in the installation dialog box that opens, and click Continue. In the Installation Options tab, click the plus (+) icon beside Office Shared Features. Click the plus (+) icon beside Converters and Filters. Click the plus (+) icon beside Graphics Filters. Click the drop-down beside any converter you need to make sure it is installed, and click Run from My Computer if that option is not selected. Then click Continue to continue with the installation update, and close Control Panel when you finish. You may be prompted for an installation DVD, depending on how you set up Word.

If your file format isn't supported natively by Word 2013, your best bet might be to open it in the program originally used to create it, if available, and use Save As to convert it to a graphic file format that Word supports, such as JPEG. This is especially true if you created the image in a relatively esoteric type of design/drafting software or something like that. You could also search the web for a freeware or low-cost graphics editing program that can convert the desired file format; check the program's capabilities carefully before buying. The freeware program Gimp (www.gimp.org) can open and save to a number of different graphics file formats, as can IrfanView (download.cnet.com/IrfanView/), another freeware graphic program.

Adding an Online Picture

Prior versions of Word included a locally stored collection of clip art images that you could insert through a Clip Art pane or gallery. Word 2013 does away with that functionality, replacing it with a streamlined Online Pictures tool that enables you to find and insert pictures and clipart from Office.com, Bing Image Search, your SkyDrive, or Flickr. (It wouldn't be surprising to see other social media/sharing services added in future updates.)

This section shows you how to search for and select an image from Office.com. The benefit of choosing Office.com over Bing Image Search is that Office.com offers royalty-free images for use in your projects free of charge. (According to 8.1 in the Microsoft Services Agreement, http://windows.microsoft.com/en-US/windows-live/microsoft-services-agreement, you simply can't resell the pictures or any project that relies primarily on them. For example, you might get into trouble if you downloaded an image from Office.com, made 8 × 10 color printouts of it, and then tried to frame them and sell them as art.) Images on Bing Image Search are released under the Creative Commons licensing scheme. This means that the owner of each image or illustration determines the particular licensing. For example, a Creative Commons Attribution-Share-Alike 3.0 License requires that you give credit (attribution) as specified by the creator anywhere you use the image or illustration, and that you share any derivatives or alterations of the work under the same license. When you select a picture or illustration after using Bing Image Search,

9

the information should include a link that you can click to find out about the Creative Commons licensing for the selected item. The Flickr choice enables you to connect with images you've stored in your flickr.com account.

Here's how to find and insert an image from Office.com in a document:

1. **Make sure you are signed in and your system is connected to the Internet, and click to position the insertion point where you want to insert the picture.**

2. **Click the Insert tab, and then click Online Pictures in the Illustrations group.** The Insert Pictures window shown in Figure 9.38 appears.

FIGURE 9.38

Use the new Insert Pictures feature to find and download images from Office.com and more.

3. **Type a search term in the text box to the right of Office.com Clip Art, and then click the Search (magnifying glass) button at the right. Insert Pictures finds and displays matching pictures.**

4. **Scroll down to preview additional pictures, if needed; click the one you want to insert, as shown in Figure 9.39; and then click Insert.** Word downloads the image or illustration and displays it at the insertion point.

FIGURE 9.39

Select the image or illustration you want to insert, and then click Insert.

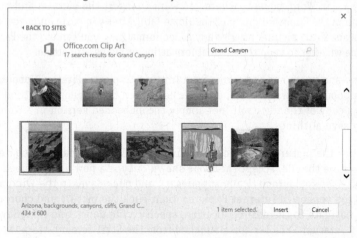

The process for finding a picture with Bing Image Search is similar to the above, except in Step 3 you would type the search term in the text box to the right of Bing Image Search, instead. Then run the search. To insert a picture from your SkyDrive from the Insert Pictures window, make sure you are signed in to Word using your Microsoft account. Open Insert Pictures, and click Browse to the right of your SkyDrive. The window displays the folders in your SkyDrive, including the Pictures folder. Click a folder to display its items, click an image to insert, and then click the Insert button.

> **TIP**
>
> The first time you click the Flickr button at the bottom of the Insert Pictures window, you'll see a prompt to connect to your account. Click Connect, and then enter your account sign-in information when prompted.

Pasting or Snapping a Picture

It may not always be the case that the source image is one stored on your hard disk. You may want to grab an image out of a document you've received from another user and reuse it yourself, or you may have downloaded a PDF file with an image you'd like to reuse. Or you may want to take a picture of what you're doing in another Office program to include in the current document. Let's see how that works.

Pasting a picture

You can also insert pictures from the Clipboard and from your Internet browser (usually, but not always). To use the Clipboard, display the picture in any Windows program that supports graphics, and use that program's controls to select and copy the picture to the Clipboard. If all else fails, try selecting the picture, right-clicking it, and choosing Copy or Copy Picture. Then, in Word, move to where you want to insert the picture, and press Ctrl+V (or click Paste in the Clipboard group of the Home tab). After you paste an image, a Paste Options button appears; if the picture includes any added formatting, you can use the Paste Options to determine whether to keep the original formatting or merge formatting.

Sometimes the copy-and-paste method works from Internet Explorer, Firefox, Google Chrome, and other popular browsers — other times not. When the Clipboard method fails, or when you want a copy of the file itself (not simply the embedded version in a Word document), you can try several things.

In Firefox, right-click the picture and choose Save Image As. In Save Image, navigate to where you want to store the file, accept the name shown or type a new one (no need to type an extension — Firefox automatically supplies it), and click Save. In the Windows 7 or Windows 8 Desktop version of Internet Explorer, right-click the picture and choose Save picture as. Again, navigate to the desired location, specify a file name, and click Save. In the new Windows 8 Internet Explorer app (launched from the Start screen), start the process by right-clicking the picture and clicking Save to picture library.

> **TIP**
>
> Before reusing pictures from the Internet, however, please make sure that you have a right to do so. Many pictures on the Internet are copyright protected.

There are a number of ways to find pictures on the Internet, from surfing to explicitly searching. Google itself has an Image Search feature. From Google's home page, click Images. In the Image Search page, type the search text (enclose in quotes to search for a whole name), and click Search Images. Another common technique is to include the word "gallery" in the search, although these days you'd probably find a lot of Office 2013 gallery hits! In addition to enabling you to store your own pictures, Flickr enables users to share pictures and make them available for download. It even has a special section of images released under the Creative Commons licensing scheme at http://www.flickr.com/creativecommons/.

Taking a screen shot

Windows itself has long offered the built-in ability to copy a picture of what's on-screen to the Clipboard via the Print Screen or Shift+prnt scr shortcut keys. Word 2013 (and some of the Office applications) builds on this feature by enabling you to insert a screen shot of other open Office file windows — including Help windows — directly into Word. You might want to take advantage of this feature if you are writing how-to instructions about a task for a colleague, or if you want to show data from an Excel workbook and don't feel that you need to be fussy about copying and pasting specific cells. To snap a screen shot in Word:

1. **After opening the desired application window and switching back to Word, click to position the insertion point where you want to insert the picture.**

2. **Click the Insert tab, and then click Screenshot in the Illustrations group.** The gallery of Available Windows to shoot appears as shown in Figure 9.40.

FIGURE 9.40

Insert a picture of another open Office window in the current document.

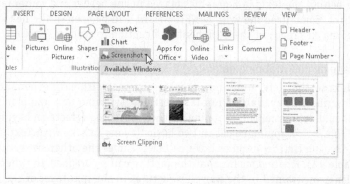

3. **Click the window to shoot.** A picture of the window appears at the insertion point.

> **TIP**
>
> If you want to crop the screen when you insert it, close all open Office windows except the current Word document and the one you want to insert. (Or, you can switch to the application that you want to take a screen shot of and then switch to Word; the key is the application you want to shoot has to be the last one that was active before you switched to Word.) Choose Insert ⇨ Screenshot, and then click Screen Clipping below the gallery. Drag on the shaded version of the window that appears to specify what portion will appear in Word. Or you can crop the screen shot after inserting it into Word as described later in this chapter.

9

Manipulating Inserted Pictures (and Other Graphics)

After you insert a picture or other graphic into the document, you can use a plethora of tools in Word 2013 to position, style, and otherwise work with the image to integrate it into your document in the most attractive way possible. For example, this section covers the various text wrapping options and their implications.

Controlling picture positioning

Wrapping is the term used to classify the various ways in which pictures (as well as other graphics) appear relative to the text in a Word document. It helps to understand that a

Word document has several different *layers*. Where you normally compose text is called the *text layer*. There are also *drawing layers* that are both in front of and behind the text layer. A graphic inserted in front of the text layer will cover text up, unless the graphic is semi-transparent, in which case it will modify the view of the text. Graphics inserted behind the text layer act as a backdrop, or background, for the text.

Additionally, there is the *header and footer layer*. This is where headers and footers reside. This area is behind the text area. If you place a graphic into a header or footer, the graphic will appear behind the text. Dim graphics placed in the header and footer layer often serve as watermarks. Sometimes the word CONFIDENTIAL will be used in the header and footer layer, branding each page of the document as a caution to readers.

Setting wrapping and wrapping defaults

The Wrap Text setting determines how graphics interact with each other and with text. Table 9.1 describes the available Wrap Text settings. Knowing how you plan to position a picture should determine the wrapping setting. Wrapping effects and typical uses are shown in Table 9.1. Wrapping comes in two basic flavors: In Line with Text (in the text layer) and floating (in the graphics layer, which includes the other six wrapping formats listed in Table 9.1). *Floating* means that the picture can be dragged anywhere in the document and isn't constrained in the way that pictures in the text layer of the document are.

TABLE 9.1 Wrap Text Setting

Wrapping setting	Effect/application
In line with text	Inserted into text layer. Graphic can be dragged, but only from one paragraph marker to another. Typically used in simple presentations and formal reports.
Square	Creates a square "container" in the text where the graphic is. Text wraps around the graphic, leaving a gap between the text and the graphic. The graphic can be dragged anywhere in the document. Typically used in newsletters and flyers with a fair amount of white space.
Tight	Effectively creates a "container" in the text where the graphic is, of the same shape as the overall outline of the graphic, so that text flows around the graphic. Wrapping points can be changed to reshape the "hole" that the text flows around. The graphic can be dragged anywhere in the document. Typically used in denser publications in which paper space is at a premium, and where irregular shapes are acceptable and even desirable.
Behind text	Inserted into the bottom or back drawing layer of a document. The graphic can be dragged anywhere in the document. Typically used for watermarks and page background pictures. Text flows in front of the graphic. Also used in the assembling of pictures from different vector elements.

In front of text	Inserted into the top drawing layer of a document. The graphic can be dragged anywhere in the document. Text flows behind the graphic. Typically used only on top of other pictures or in the assembling of vector drawings, or when you deliberately need to cover or veil text in some way to create a special effect.
Through	Text flows around the graphic's wrapping points, which can be adjusted. Text is supposed to flow into any open areas of the graphic, but evidence that this actually works is in short supply. For all practical purposes, this appears to have the same effects and behavior as Tight wrapping.
Top and bottom	Effectively creates a rectangular "container" the same width as the margin. Text flows above and below, but not beside, the graphic. The picture can be dragged anywhere in the document. Typically used when the graphic is the focal point of the text.

To set the wrapping behavior of a graphic, click it and then click the Wrap Text button in the Arrange group of the Picture Tools ➪ Format tab. Choose the desired wrapping from the list menu, as shown in Figure 9.41. The Square wrap setting was previously applied to the selected picture in Figure 9.41.

FIGURE 9.41

Wrapping behavior determines where you can position a picture or graphic in Word.

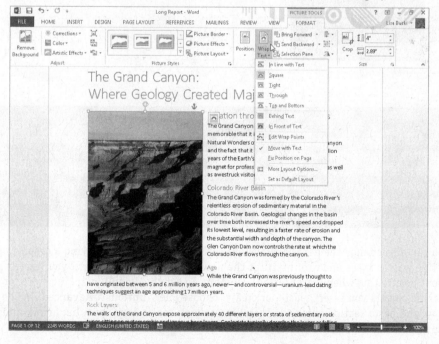

In Word 2013, you also can click the Layout Options button that appears to the right of a selected picture or graphic to access Text Wrapping settings in a flyout, as shown in Figure 9.42. You can click one of the wrap settings under In Line with Text or With Text Wrapping to change the wrapping. Clicking See more opens the Layout dialog box; you can use the settings on the Position tab to set a precise Horizontal and Vertical location on the page for the selected graphic, or the Text Wrapping tab to set more general wrapping options. For example, you can use the Distance from text settings to control the white space between the wrapped graphic and surrounding text.

FIGURE 9.42

The Layout Options button also enables you to work with text wrapping.

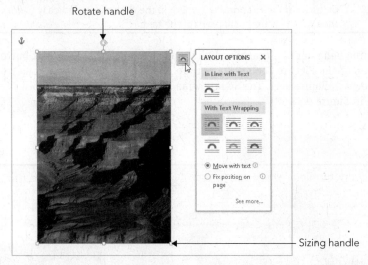

NOTE

Both the Wrap Text button menu and the Layout Options flyout include Move with text and Fix position on page options (with different capitalization, however). Choosing Move with text, the default, means the graphic will stay with its surrounding text, moving up or down as needed when you delete or add text earlier in the document. The Fix position on page option keeps the graphic in the same position, unless so much text is added or deleted that the paragraph it's anchored to moves to the next or prior page; in that case, the graphic moves with its anchor to the new page. Figure 9.42 shows the anchor icon at the upper left of a selected picture.

You can also change the default Wrap Text setting. In most cases, having a graphic appear in line wastes space and can interrupt the flow of the text, especially if you weren't precise about positioning when you inserted a graphic. To set the default wrapping style for most graphic objects you insert, paste, or create, choose File ➪ Options ➪ Advanced. In the Cut, copy, and paste section, click the Insert/paste pictures as drop-down list arrow, and click the desired default Wrap Text setting. Then click OK.

You should note that when you insert shapes, Word applies the In Front of Text Wrap Text setting by default. If you copy a picture from one part of a document and paste it elsewhere, the copy inherits the wrapping style of the original picture, and won't use your default.

Changing wrap points

When you've applied some of the Wrap Text settings to a picture or an object, you can change the *wrap points*. The wrap points are special handles that enable you to alter the wrapping boundaries for a graphic. Moving the wrap points further away from the graphic puts more space between the graphic and the text. For example, you might move the top corner wrap points for a photo up to add white space above the photo. To edit the wrap points for a graphic:

1. **Click the picture or graphic (you might need to click twice), to select it, and then apply the desired text wrapping setting if needed.**

2. **Choose Wrap Text ⇨ Edit Wrap Points in the Arrange group in the Picture Tools ⇨ Format tab (or from the applicable contextual tab for the selected object).** The object border changes color and the wrap point handles appear.

3. **Drag the wrap point handles to the desired position, as shown in Figure 9.43.** As you can see in the figure, the mouse pointer also changes when the wrap points are active.

FIGURE 9.43

Move wrap points to change the way text flows around a picture.

4. **Click outside the selected object to deactivate the wrap points.**

Choosing a position

The Position gallery in the Arrange group of the Picture Tools ⇨ Format tab (or the Drawing Tools ⇨ Format tab) enables you to skip moving a picture or graphic and setting wrapping on your own and just have Word handle it for you. Select the object to move into position, and then click Position in the Arrange group. A gallery of choices appears. Click one of the choices under With Text Wrapping to move the picture to the specified location on the current page.

Moving a graphic

You can move any graphic by dragging it, and some graphics can be dropped anywhere in the document. Graphics with Wrap Text (from the Arrange group in the Format contextual tab) set to In Line with Text, however, can be dropped only at a paragraph mark. All other graphics (in other words, those with wrapping settings that enable them to "float") can be dragged and dropped anywhere. To drag a graphic, click to select it, and then drag it where you want it to go.

> **NOTE**
>
> Word won't let you drag a picture or other graphic into position when Wrap Text is set to In Line with Text, because that wrap setting anchors the graphic to its original inserted location. If you find you can't move a picture to a new location as desired, check the Wrap Text setting and make sure it's set to an option that enables you to move the graphic.

Dragging a graphic with live layout and alignment guides

Word 2013 now provides a more real time preview of how your document will look as you move and resize objects. The *live layout* feature causes text to reflow around a wrapped graphic as you move it around. For example, this can be important if you have automatic hyphenation turned on and want to choose a position for the graphic that causes the least hyphenation. Live layout works hand in hand with the new *alignment guides* feature. One or more alignment guides appear when you drag a graphic and it reaches a position where it lines up with text, such as the top of a paragraph as shown in Figure 9.44, or the left margin, right margin, or center point of the page. If you release the mouse button when an alignment guide appears, chances are the graphic will land in a more pleasing position than you might achieve if purely aligning by eyeball. This method is also faster than using the Layout dialog box to align to the left or right margin.

FIGURE 9.44

Alignment guides appear as you drag a graphic to enable you to align it precisely with text or other graphics.

Alignment guide

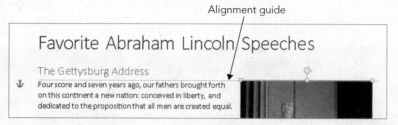

CAUTION

You can control live layout in Word Options. Choose File ⇨ Options. On the General tab, check or clear Update document content while dragging. The option also appears on the Advanced tab under Display. Click OK to apply the change.

Nudging

You can also *nudge* a selected floating graphic. Select it, and then use the arrow keys on the keyboard to move it a small distance in any of the four directions. Nudging works well for precise alignments, but alignment guides do not appear when you use this feature, so you will have to go by eye.

To drag in discrete steps using Word's built-in alignment gridlines, hold the Alt key as you drag, and drag slowly. You will see the graphic jump in small increments as it snaps to the grid. If you display the gridlines by checking Gridlines in the Show group of the View tab, however, Alt-dragging works in reverse, making Word ignore the grid. With the grid displayed, arrow key nudging also changes. Now the arrow keys move the picture in grid increments. Press the Ctrl key to nudge in smaller gradations.

The vertical and horizontal gridlines are an eighth of an inch apart, so nudging in any direction with the gridline displayed moves the graphic 1/8 inch at a time. Note that when gridlines are displayed, they will display in all open documents.

Resizing, rotating, and cropping a picture

Resizing changes the physical dimensions of the picture or other graphic as it is displayed in your document. Resizing in Word will not make the associated file (or the image stored in the .docx file) any larger or smaller. If you make it smaller and then later make it larger, you still retain the original file resolution.

Cropping refers to blocking out certain portions of a picture by changing its exterior borders. You can crop out distracting or unnecessary details. Again, cropping in Word does not affect the actual picture itself, only the way it is displayed in Word. The fact that Word doesn't change the actual image is a big plus, because you can undo the cropping if you later change your mind.

> **CAUTION**
>
> Resizing and cropping a picture file in a graphics editing program does change the picture itself. Keep this distinction in mind. Once you've saved a cropped or resized picture in a graphics program, you can't get the original back. If you want to crop graphics outside of Word to keep the file sizes more limited, always make a copy of each picture file and crop the copy.

Resizing and rotating

You can resize a picture by typing the measurements or by dragging. To resize by dragging, click on the picture and then move the mouse pointer so that it's over one of the eight sizing handles (refer to Figure 9.42). The mouse pointer changes into a double arrow. Drag until the picture is the desired size and then release the mouse button. Note that dragging the corner handles maintains the aspect ratio of the picture, whereas dragging the side handles can be used to stretch or compress the picture.

Hold down the Ctrl and/or Alt keys while dragging to modify the way resizing occurs:

- To resize symmetrically from the center point of the picture or graphic, causing the picture to increase or decrease by the same amount in all directions, hold down the Ctrl key while dragging.

- To resize in discrete steps, snapping to the alignment gridlines while hidden, press and hold down the Alt key while dragging and drag slowly, so that you can see each size increment as you go; if gridlines are displayed, the Alt key's behavior is reversed, as indicated earlier.

You can combine these options. For example, holding down the Alt and Ctrl keys at the same time while dragging a sizing handle slowly forces Word to resize in discrete steps while resizing from the center.

To specify an exact picture or graphic size, select the entry in the Shape Height and/or Shape Width text boxes in the Size group at the right end of the Picture Tools ⇨ Format tab (or Drawing Tools ⇨ Format tab) of the Ribbon. Type a new value, and press Enter. By default, these settings maintain the aspect ratio automatically, so if you enter a new Height and press Enter, the Width adjusts accordingly. To be able to change the picture proportions via the Size group settings, click the dialog box launcher in the Size group. Remove the check next to Lock aspect ratio on the Size tab of the Layout dialog box, and then click OK. (Note that for shape graphics, Lock aspect ratio is turned off by default, so the default setting differs depending on the selected object.)

Use the rotate handle with the circular arrow icon above the top center resizing handle (refer to Figure 9.42) to rotate a picture. Select the picture and drag the handle in the direction in which you want to rotate the picture. You also can rotate a selected picture using arrow key shortcuts. Pressing Alt+left or right arrow rotates the picture. If you add Ctrl key and press Ctrl+Alt+left arrow or Ctrl+Alt+right arrow, the rotation happens in smaller increments.

If you click the Position tab of the Layout dialog box, additional options of interest include the following:

- **Move object with text:** Associates a picture or graphic with a particular paragraph so that the paragraph and the picture will always appear on the same page. This setting affects only vertical position on the page. Although Word will allow you to check this option and Lock anchor at the same time, once you click OK the Move object with text option is cleared.

- **Lock anchor:** This setting locks the picture's current position on the page. If you have trouble dragging a picture, verify that it is set to one of the floating wrapping options (anything but In line with text), and that Lock anchor is turned off. Pictures that have been positioned with any of the nine Position gallery presets will also resist dragging.

- **Allow overlap:** Use this setting to allow graphical objects to cover each other up. One use for this is to create a stack of photographs or other objects. This feature is also needed for layered drawings.

- **Layout in table cell:** This setting enables you to use tables for positioning graphics on the page.

Cropping

To crop a picture, click the Crop button in the Size group in the Picture Tools ⇨ Format tab. Cropping handles appear on the selected picture. Move the pointer over any of the eight cropping handles, and when it changes shape to match the handle, drag to remove the part of the picture you want to hide. Click outside the picture to finish applying the crop. Note that pressing the Alt key while dragging slowly crops in discrete steps.

Clicking the down arrow on the bottom of the Crop button reveals other options for customized cropping. You can click Crop to Shape and then click one of the shapes in the gallery that appears to crop the picture to fit within the specified shape, as in the star example in Figure 9.45. Use the Aspect Ratio option to crop the image to standard proportions, such as 1:1 to square the image or 3:5 for a portrait (tall) image. Cropping all the images in a document to the same aspect ratio can lend a more consistent appearance. You can also use the Fill and Fit commands to resize the image within the current picture area. Fill generally snaps the picture back to its original aspect ratio, which may undo the crop depending on how it was applied, and Fit shrinks the picture so previously cropped areas redisplay at a smaller size within the picture area.

9

FIGURE 9.45

Crop to hide part of a picture or to change its overall shape.

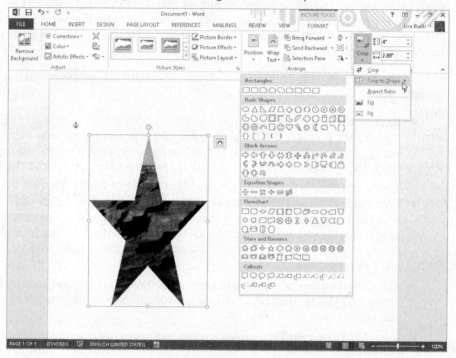

Formatting a picture or shape

You don't have to settle for a picture's original appearance when you insert it into a document. Word offers a variety of tools for making formatting adjustments. Applying uniform styles and effects to the pictures and other graphics in a document creates a unified look. This is the kind of approach that graphic designers use to create the brand identity for a magazine, for example. Here you learn how to find the settings you need to update the appearance of pictures and other graphics in your documents. Word offers dozens of changes that you can apply, so much so that every feature cannot be covered in detail here. Taking the time to explore the settings introduced here can help you make a document's graphics even more interesting.

Applying picture styles

Double-clicking one of the items in the Picture Styles of the Format tab enables you to apply any of a number of preset styles to the selected picture. The styles include various combinations of frames or borders, cropping, glows, shadows, and more. After selecting the picture, click the More button to display all of the gallery's choices. You can move the mouse over each style to see a Live Preview of it on the selected picture (or pictures). Note that the speed of Live Preview may be heavily affected by the size of the graphic file. If the picture is 2 MB, Live Preview is going to be a lot slower than if the file were only 50 KB. When you find the style that you prefer, click it to apply it to the picture.

> **NOTE**
>
> Note that for shapes, the Drawing Tools ➪ Format tab has a Shape Styles group with a Shape Styles gallery. The choices in that gallery enable you to apply different combinations of fills and borders, based on the applied theme, to the selected shape.

Applying a border or picture effects

You can apply a basic color border to a selected picture using the Picture Border button in the Picture Styles group of the Picture Tools ➪ Format tab. (For a shape, you would use the Shape Outline tool in the Shape Styles group of the Drawing Tools ➪ Format tab.) You have the option of using the drop-down that appears to change three settings for the border:

- **Color:** Click one of the Theme Colors or Standard Colors, or click More Outline Colors to choose a custom color. Keep in mind that when you use a theme color, the border color will update if you change the document theme.

- **Weight:** Click this option and then click a border width in the submenu that appears.

- **Dashes:** Click to display a submenu of border styles, and then click the desired style.

Click the No Outline choice in the Picture Border drop-down to remove any previously applied outline.

You can apply and refine additional effects with the Picture Effects tool, also located in the Picture Styles group. You can choose one of the Preset choices that combines effects, or apply any combination of individual effects that you prefer. In Figure 9.46, the picture already has a Reflection choice and a Bevel choice applied, and the Live Preview shows a potential Glow effect.

9

FIGURE 9.46

Apply any combination of Picture Effects to achieve the look you want.

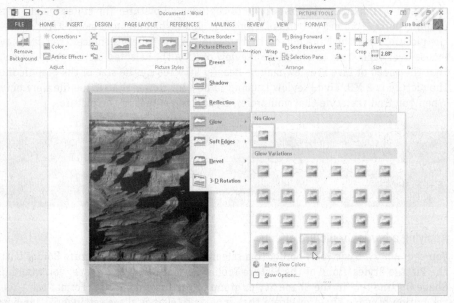

TIP

Use the Picture Layout choice in the Picture Styles group of the Picture Tools ➪ Format tab to convert a picture to a SmartArt object.

Applying other picture adjustments

Word also features seven tools for adjusting picture attributes in the Adjust group of the Picture Tools ➪ Format tab shown in Figure 9.46. Use the tools to accomplish a number of common tasks:

- **Remove Background:** Lets you automatically/selectively remove portions of a picture based on color patterns. For example, this feature can remove everything from a picture except for a single object, such as a flower or a car. After you click this tool, use the Mark Areas to Remove, Mark Areas to Keep, and Remove Mark buttons in the Refine group of the Background Removal tab to determine which portions of the image to remove and keep, and then click Keep Changes.

- **Corrections:** Clicking this button displays a gallery of preset corrections you can use to Sharpen/Soften or adjust the Brightness/Contrast of the selected picture for better printing or on-screen presentation. Move your mouse over the presets to preview their impact on the selected image, and then click the desired preset.

- **Color:** Open this gallery to see Color Saturation and Color Tone correction presets, as well as a variety of Recolor options for changing the overall color of the image. For example, you can apply Grayscale, Sepia, or Washout, or recolor the image using one of the theme colors. Use the mouse to preview a choice on the selected image, and then click it.

- **Artistic Effects:** This gallery provides more than a dozen special presets that you can use to transform the selected picture's overall appearance, such as Chalk Sketch, Paint Strokes, and Film Grain. Use your mouse to Live Preview an effect, and then click it.

- **Compress Picture:** Use this tool to reduce the size of the pictures stored in the file to the minimum needed for a given output. Clicking this tool displays the Compress Pictures dialog box. Under Compression Options, clear the Apply only to this picture check box if you want to compress all pictures in the document. Choose a resolution under Target output, and then click OK. If you will need to make high quality printouts of your document, be cautious when using this feature. Compressing picture size can reduce the image quality, and because the feature discards information during the process, you can't undo it later.

- **Change Picture:** Clicking this tool opens the Insert Pictures window, where you can choose to replace the selected picture with a different one. You can either use Insert from file to select a locally stored replacement image file or search online for a replacement. Picture Styles and Effects applied carry over to the replacement picture, as do changes applied with other tools in the Adjust group. Cropping and resizing, however, do not.

- **Reset Picture:** Removes formatting applied with Picture Styles, Picture Effects, and other Adjust tools (except for Change and Compress). If you open the menu for this option, as noted earlier, you can Choose Reset Picture & Size to restore a cropped picture.

Using the Format Picture pane

If you click the dialog box launcher in the Picture Styles group of the Picture Tools ⇨ Format tab, the Format Picture pane shown in Figure 9.47 appears at the right. You also can display this pane by right-clicking a selected picture and clicking Format Picture. The Format Picture pane in Word 2013 replaces the Format Picture dialog box found in previous Word versions and offers settings for you to fine-tune presets and other format changes made to a selected picture. Click one of the icons at top to choose an overall category of settings, click an arrow to expand particular settings, and then change the detailed settings. For example, Figure 9.47 shows the detailed settings for working with the Reflection preset applied to the selected image. The category icons at the top of the pane include:

9

313

FIGURE 9.47

Find more detailed settings in the Format Picture pane.

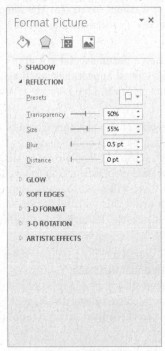

- **Fill & Line:** Use to change the settings for any interior Fill or Line (border) applied to the picture.
- **Effects:** Select to work with detailed Shadow, Reflection, Glow, Soft Edges, 3-D Format, 3-D Rotation, and Artistic Effects settings for the selected image.
- **Layout & Properties:** The Text Box settings here generally are not active for pictures, but you can use the Alt Text choices to add accessibility information.
- **Picture:** Make changes here to Picture Correction, Picture Color, and Crop settings.

> **NOTE**
>
> The Format Shape pane that appears when you click the dialog box launcher for the Shape Styles group of the Drawing Tools ⇨ Format tab offers similar choices for reformatting a selected shape or other graphic such as a text box.

> **NOTE**
>
> For some types of objects, you can display a pane with formatting or other settings by double-clicking, but this technique doesn't work with image files.

Creating WordArt

If there's something creative you need to do to text, and Word's normal text tools don't even come close to what you need, then WordArt probably has what you're looking for. WordArt enables you to get creative if you need to accomplish unique tasks like these:

- Stretch text diagonally across the page so you can make a CLASSIFIED watermark.
- Make a fancy banner headline for a newsletter or flyer.
- Rotate text to any angle.
- Place text in a circle for making a button.

9

Creating WordArt from scratch

The WordArt tool makes it surprisingly simple to create decorative text. Here's how to insert a new WordArt object into your document:

1. **Click to position the insertion point where you want to insert the WordArt.**
2. **Click the Insert tab, and then click the Insert WordArt button in the Text group.** Word presents you with the WordArt Style gallery, shown in Figure 9.48.

FIGURE 9.48

Click a style in the WordArt gallery.

3. **Click a style in the gallery.** Word applies the style to the placeholder phrase Your Text Here in the WordArt object.
4. **Type your text.**
5. **(Optional) Select the text in the object and apply additional formatting as desired.** This step is optional because you also can reselect the WordArt later to change its formatting.
6. **Click Outside the WordArt object to finish it.**

The wrap setting applied to a new WordArt object varies depending on whether the document already has text or not. If you insert WordArt in a blank document or one with only other objects, the new WordArt graphic appears in the upper-left corner of the document (although not in the header), formatted with wrapping set to In Front of Text. You can change the wrapping as desired using the Wrap Text choices in the Arrange group of the Drawing Tools⇨Format tab, and drag the WordArt text box where you want it.

If you positioned the insertion point in some text or have selected some text before adding the WordArt, it is inserted at the beginning of the current paragraph, also formatted with the In Front of Text wrapping style. You can change the wrapping style to create a decorative effect at the beginning of the paragraph, as shown in Figure 9.49.

FIGURE 9.49

Use WordArt to draw attention to the beginning of the paragraph or create wrapped titles.

Creation through Geological Forces The Grand Canyon in Arizona offers scenery so memorable that it is considered one of the Seven Natural Wonders of the World. The scale of the canyon and the fact that it exposes approximately two billion years of the Earth's geological history makes it a magnet for professional and amateur geologists, as well as awestruck visitors from around the world.

NOTE

When you insert WordArt within text, Word anchors it to the current paragraph's paragraph mark. Deleting the paragraph mark that "owns" the WordArt deletes the WordArt as well. Note also that WordArt text boxes are *not* inserted with the default wrapping style (set in File ⇨ Options ⇨ Advanced ⇨ Cut, Copy, and Paste ⇨ Insert/paste pictures as).

Creating WordArt from selected text

If you've already entered all the text for a document or have received a document to format from another person, the text that you want to format as WordArt may already be included in the document. If that's the case, select the text, and then select the WordArt type as described in Steps 2 and 3 in the previous section. The selected text appears in the WordArt object. Unlike in Word 2007 and earlier, the 10-word/200-character limit for WordArt text no longer exists, so it's possible to format entire paragraphs as WordArt. You might want to do this to create a flyer or a pull quote.

Formatting WordArt text

Because WordArt is integrated into Word's main graphics engine, Word displays the Drawing Tools ⇨ Format contextual tab when you select a WordArt object by clicking it and then clicking its border. As shown in Figure 9.50, the tab offers the same text-formatting tools that are available for text boxes and the same shape-formatting tools that are available for all Word shapes. You will also notice that there is also a lot of overlap of applicable tools when you're working with pictures.

FIGURE 9.50

Word displays the Drawing Tools ⇨ Format tab for formatting WordArt.

> **TIP**
>
> In general, you do not have to select the text within a WordArt object to change the formatting. In fact, if you click within the text rather than clicking the border to select the entire object, the changes you make will apply only to the word holding the insertion point. On the other hand, you are free to select part of the contents of a WordArt object and apply different formatting to that text if it meets your design needs to do so.

> **NOTE**
>
> If you have difficulty achieving correct centering of text inside a WordArt text box, take a look at standard formatting settings, such as the Paragraph groups alignment, indentation, before and after spacing, and line spacing choices on the Home tab.

Use the tools in the WordArt Styles and Text groups to format text. Any of these formatting tools can be applied letter by letter if that is what is required. In addition, you can use the normal settings in the Font and Paragraph groups of the Home tab to make changes to the selected WordArt text. Here are ways that you can format WordArt:

- **Moving, sizing, and rotating WordArt:** WordArt shapes can be formatted like any other picture or shape in Word. The techniques for moving, sizing, rotating, and so on described earlier in this chapter work the same for WordArt. WordArt text can be rotated to any angle using the rotate handle above the top center selection handle. You're not limited to the settings offered with the Text Direction tool in the Text group of the Drawing Tools ⇨ Format tab. Also, you can reverse WordArt both horizontally and vertically — by dragging top over bottom, side over side, and corner over corner, essentially flipping the object and the text it contains. You can use this method, or you can use the Rotate Objects choice in the Arrange group to rotate and flip the selected WordArt.

> **NOTE**
>
> When you paste cut or copied Word Art into a new location in Word and some other Office applications, a Paste Options button appears, and you can choose Keep Source Formatting (K) or Picture (U) to determine whether or not you want to edit it later. Also note that a Layout Options button appears at the upper-right corner of the WordArt object so you can adjust wrap settings for its new location as needed.

- **Changing WordArt styles:** To see the gallery of WordArt styles so that you can apply another one to a selected WordArt object, click the Quick Styles button in the WordArt Styles group (if your screen is at a low resolution), or if the gallery appears in the group, click its More button. The available styles are the same as those shown in Figure 9.48. Simply click an alternate style to apply it. The WordArt Styles group also contains the Text Fill, Text Outline, and Text Effects tools. Clicking Text Fill then enables you to click a new color to use as the fill for the WordArt text.

Text Outline and Text Effects enable you to change the WordArt text outline and effects, and work just as described earlier for pictures under "Applying a border or picture effects."

- **Changing 3-D rotation:** While there are a number of Effects choices you may want to apply to WordArt, 3-D Rotation is one that can make the WordArt really pop from the page. Click Text Effects ⇨ 3-D Rotation to use Live Preview to select a rotation setting, and then click it.

- **Changing the WordArt background:** While the tools in the WordArt Styles group of the Drawing Tools ⇨ Format tab apply to the text within a WordArt object, the tools in the Shape Styles group enable you to change the fill and outline for the WordArt object's surrounding box, creating a rectangular background for the WordArt graphic. By combining text formatting and overall shape formatting, you can create interesting effects and special objects such as a newsletter title.

- **Shaping and transforming WordArt:** Another important formatting change most users want to know about is how to change the overall shape of a WordArt object. There are two ways to do this: with the Format Shape pane or with the Transform tools. If you click the dialog box launcher for either the Shape Styles or WordArt Styles groups in the Drawing Tools ⇨ Format tab, the Format Shape pane appears at right. You also can right-click a selected WordArt object and click Format Shape to display the pane. The Format Shape pane works just like the Format Picture pane described earlier under "Using the Format Picture pane." One exception appears at the top of the pane, where you see Shape Options and Text Options choices. Click these as needed to flip between formatting the overall WordArt shape and the text in the shape. To find the 3-D Rotation Options for the shape text, click Text Options at the top of the pane. The X, Y, and Z Rotation controls let you rotate the text within the object in three dimensions. This allows you to, among other things, rotate text to any angle, as well as to rotate the text vertically and horizontally. (If you selected Shape Options at the top of the pane, rotation changes appear differently.) Click the pane's Close button when you finish choosing settings. If using the Format Shape pane doesn't give you the effect you are looking for, you can use the Transform tools. With the WordArt object selected, select Text Effects ⇨ Transform, and point to the different transformations provided. As shown in Figure 9.51, Live Preview shows how the effect would look if applied. When you click a choice, Word applies the new shape and also adds one or more additional controls, which appear as little purple diamonds. You can use these controls to further shape or warp the text inside. Drag one of the controls, and as you drag a diagram appears showing a preview of the shape. When you like what you see, release the mouse button.

9

FIGURE 9.51

Use Transform to warp WordArt text.

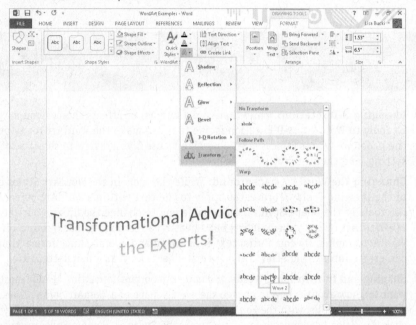

Inserting SmartArt

SmartArt provides you with a much wider selection of diagrams to illustrate processes, relationships, organizational hierarchies, and more. SmartArt also features 3-D formatting that's so dimensional it looks like it took hours for a graphic artist to create it.

Here are the basic steps for inserting SmartArt. I'll elaborate on some of the details after the steps:

1. **Click to position the insertion point at the location where you want to insert SmartArt.**

2. **Click the Insert tab on the Ribbon, and click SmartArt in the Illustrations group.** The Choose a SmartArt Graphic dialog box appears. It lists eight categories, plus All, which enables you to peruse all the graphic types.

3. **Click a category, and then click one of the graphic thumbnails that appears.** A larger preview and description appear at the right.

4. **When you find a graphic that looks appropriate, either double-click it or click it and then click OK.** Word inserts the shape into your document with the text pane ready to accept information, as shown in Figure 9.52.

FIGURE 9.52

Enter text to appear in the various shapes in a SmartArt graphic.

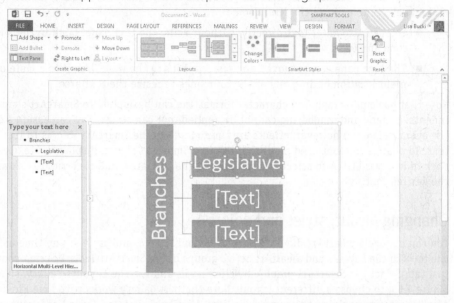

TIP

If the text pane doesn't appear, click Text Pane in the Create Graphic group of the SmartArt Tools ⇨ Design contextual tab. Click the choice again if you want to hide the text pane after you finish entering text for the graphic.

5. **Click each [Text] placeholder in the text pane at the left.** As you type, the text appears in the corresponding SmartArt shape on the right.

6. **Click outside the graphic when you finish working with it.**

There are a variety of ways to enter and format text in the text pane. The following list, though not exhaustive, offers a number of methods that work. Note that some actions can also be performed via the Create Graphic group in the SmartArt Tools ⇨ Design tab.

- To move to the next item, press the down arrow. Use the other arrow keys to navigate in the text entry box as well.

- To add a new item to the list, press Enter, either at the end of the list of items or above an existing item.

- To demote the current item, if possible, press the Tab key.

- To promote the current item, press Shift+Tab.

- To delete an item, select it, and press the Backspace key.

- To change the font for an item, select the text you want to change, mouse over the selection, and use the Mini Toolbar.

- You can also enter text directly, without using the text pane. Click in the SmartArt item and type.

- The text pane can be moved and resized if it's in the way: Drag it to a more convenient location or drag any of the four sides to resize the text area.

Note that basic paragraph and character formatting can be applied to SmartArt shapes. Indents, bullets, and numbering cannot be applied, nor can styles. You can assign a style to the overall diagram; however, effects are limited unless the SmartArt item is In line with text. To change the font used in all the text in a SmartArt object, display the text pane, click in it, press Ctrl+A to select the contents of the text area, and then right-click and set the desired font.

Changing layout, style, and colors

You can change a SmartArt diagram's overall layout, colors, and style at any time using the tools in the Layouts and SmartArt Styles groups of the SmartArt Tools ⇨ Design contextual tab. Select the SmartArt graphic by clicking it, and use the Layouts Gallery, shown in Figure 9.53, to choose a different layout. Note that the gallery works with Live Preview. You aren't limited to applying the same class (List, Hierarchy, Process, Cycle,) of layout, either. SmartArt will adapt the different designs using the relationship levels currently applied.

FIGURE 9.53

You can apply any layout to any SmartArt list.

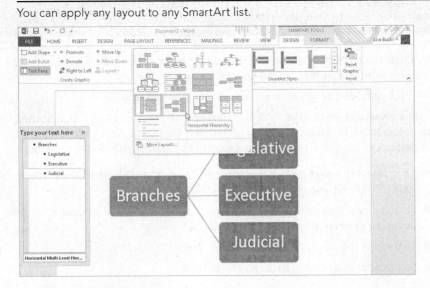

SmartArt Styles enable you to apply a variety of preset formatting to the selected SmartArt diagram. Click the More button to open the gallery and point to any choice — again, Live Preview helps you to make a selection. The styles offer both 2-D and 3-D options, as well as a variety of sophisticated surface treatments.

Open the Change Colors gallery beside the SmartArt styles to preview and select from a variety of color schemes you can apply to the selected SmartArt graphic.

NOTE

When the entire SmartArt graphic is selected, a Layout Options button appears at the right. Click it and then click the setting to use to wrap text around the graphic.

Adding a shape

You have to add and remove shapes in a SmartArt graphic to control the content that appears. You can do so in the text pane as noted earlier. Or you can click the SmartArt diagram to select it, click a shape within the diagram to which the new shape will relate, and then click the Add Shape drop-down list arrow in the Create Graphic group of the Design tab. The choices that appear are Add Shape After, Add Shape Before, Add Shape Above, and Add Shape Below. (Depending on the nature and position of the shape you initially selected, not all of these choices may be active.) Click the desired shape location, and then type the text for the new shape. You also can right-click a shape and use the Add Shape submenu of the shortcut menu to insert a shape.

TIP

If you have a list — hierarchical or not — that you would like to convert into a SmartArt object, select the list and copy it to the Clipboard before choosing the SmartArt tool. Once your SmartArt object appears, click in the text pane. Press Ctrl+A to select the placeholder list, and then press Ctrl+V to paste the list over the placeholder.

Changing shape styles and other formatting

SmartArt provides a number of additional tools for formatting individual shapes within a selected SmartArt object. After clicking the SmartArt diagram, click a shape to select it, and then use the applicable tools in the SmartArt Tools ⇨ Format tab, shown in Figure 9.54.

FIGURE 9.54

Formatting tools are found in the Shapes, Shape Styles, and WordArt Styles groups of the Format tab.

Use the Shapes group tools as follows:

- **Edit in 2-D:** When you click a shape, a 2-D version appears for more direct editing.
- **Change Shape:** Change the selected shape into any of dozens of Word's shapes.
- **Larger or Smaller:** Expand or shrink the selected shape.

The Shape Styles group includes these choices for formatting a selected shape:

- **Shape Style Gallery:** Choose from three dozen different patterns of outlines and fill.
- **Shape Fill:** Choose your own custom fill for the selected shape.
- **Shape Outline:** Choose a custom outline for the selected shape.
- **Shape Effects:** Choose from a variety of effects — shadow, reflection, glow, soft edges, bevel, and 3-D — to change individual shapes.

> **NOTE**
>
> When the entire SmartArt graphic is selected, some of the above settings apply to the background for the whole shape. For example, you can apply a Shape Fill to the background for the SmartArt object.

The settings in the WordArt Styles group change the appearance of the text in the selected shape.

> **NOTE**
>
> Use the Chart choice in the Illustrations group of the Insert tab to add a chart in Word. Charts in Word work much like charts in other Office applications, so to learn about charting, refer to Chapter 18, "Getting Started Making Charts," and Chapter 23, "Working with Tables and Charts."

Arranging Pictures and Other Objects

In addition to the Position and Wrap Text tools described earlier in the chapter, the Arrange group of the Picture Tools➪ and Drawing Tools➪ Format tabs has tools for working with the layering, alignment, grouping, and rotation of various types of Word graphics. These additional tools are:

- **Bring Forward:** When layering objects, moves the selected object one layer forward. Click the arrow to choose the Bring to Front (brings to the top layer) or Bring in Front of Text choices.
- **Send Backward:** When layering objects, moves the selected object one layer backward. Click the arrow to choose the Bring to Back (moves to the bottom layer) or Send Behind Text choices.

- **Align Objects:** Gives you choices for aligning selected objects relative to one another (when Align to Margin is selected). For example, click Align Center to align all objects relative to their center points. You also can choose Distribute Horizontally or Distribute vertically to space the objects equally.

- **Group Objects:** Allows you to group and ungroup selected objects. Grouping objects enables you to move them as a unit.

- **Rotate Objects:** Enables you to rotate or flip the selected object by selecting a preset rather than using the rotate handle

> **TIP**
>
> To select multiple graphic objects before aligning or grouping them, select the first object, and then use Shift+click or Ctrl+click to select more.

For example, you could layer a WordArt object over a picture. Apply Bring to Front to the WordArt and Send to Back for the Picture. Then select both objects and use Align Objects ➪ Align Center and then Align Objects ➪ Align Top to position them. Finally, group the objects. Techniques such as this enables you to compose more complex graphics within Word and other Office applications with similar graphics tools.

Using the Selection Pane

In Word 2013, you can format graphic objects as invisible, as long as they have a Wrap Text setting other than In Line with Text. To determine whether or not an object is set as invisible, open any .docx document that contains graphics with the right Wrap Text settings. In the Editing group of the Home tab, choose Select ➪ Selection Pane.

Each object with an applicable Wrap Text setting appears in the selection tab with an eye icon to its right. Clicking the icon makes the associated object invisible. In Figure 9.55, the top Picture objet has been marked as invisible, and the bottom Text Box object remains visible, as indicated by the eye icon still being visible. Use the Show All and Hide All buttons in the pane to show and hide all graphics.

FIGURE 9.55

Use the Selection pane to control visibility for floating (not inline) graphic objects.

You can use this feature to hide shapes, text boxes, SmartArt, and charts. You cannot unbundle parts of a chart or SmartArt object — it's all or nothing. Click the pane's Close (X) button to close it.

Summary

In this chapter, you've learned the essentials you need to know about tables, shapes, pictures, WordArt, and SmartArt. You should now be able to do the following:

- Insert a table, shape, picture, WordArt graphic, or SmartArt graphic into a document.
- Copy material from one table into another, even if the dimensions don't match.
- Use styles and other formatting settings to add zest and color to your tables and other graphics.
- Create tables from existing non-tabular data.
- Use the smart handle to change a shape.
- Change WordArt style or add a background fill.
- Add and format the text for a SmartArt diagram.
- Change a diagram's layout, style, and colors.
- Add shapes where needed.
- Layer and group objects.
- Use the Selection Pane.

Data Documents and Mail Merge

IN THIS CHAPTER

Reviewing data sources you can use with Word

Formatting source data

Attaching a data source to a data document

Editing data

Assembling a data document

Merging to a printer

Using the Mail Merge Wizard

This chapter shows you how to create specialized types of documents — such as envelopes, labels, form letters, mass e-mail, catalogs, and directories — by combining a main document with a list called a data source. Merging can save a lot of time once you are familiar with the process, but it does require careful setup for both the data source and the main document. This chapter covers how to bring your data and document together without errors so you can save time and let Word do some of the heavy lifting for you.

Previewing the Mail Merge Process

Let's say you need to send a letter about a new product to 20 clients, and you already have the client names and addresses typed into Excel. Rather than manually retyping each name and address into a separate copy of the letter, you can write the letter, specify where the name and address information from the list should go, and perform the *mail merge* to create 20 versions of the letter — each personally addressed for a specific recipient. Even better, you can quickly create a matching set of addressed envelopes or labels to use for the mailing.

You also can use mail merge to create updateable versions of other long documents. For example, let's say you maintain a directory of contact information for your department at work. You have access to the main employee database from the HR department, but you only need to list the employees for your department. During the merge process, you can select which items to use based on certain criteria, so Word easily pulls out just the list of colleagues from your department for the merge into the main directory document you've set up.

Setting up a mail merge *main document* and *data source* and merging them together involves a number of steps, some of which must be done before others can happen:

1. **Set the document type for the main document: letter, e-mail, envelope, labels, and directory.**

2. **Associate a data source with the document: new, Outlook contact, or some other source.** The data source file holds the *records* of information, such as one recipient's name and address, that will be inserted into the main document at specified locations.

3. **Design your main document by combining ordinary document features with Word *merge field codes*.** Each merge field corresponds to a *field* in the data source document, such as Fname, Lname. In this way, Word customizes each copy of the main document with information from a single record of the data source.

4. **Preview the finished document by testing to see how it looks with different data records.**

5. **Finish the process by merging the data document with the data source, creating a printed result, a saved document, or an e-mail document.**

Data Considerations

It might seem odd to discuss the data source first, but the data source is often the most important consideration for a merge and typically receives the least attention. Once you've identified and correctly set up your data source, the rest of the merge process is made much easier.

Some data considerations, such as usability (does the data set contain what you need?) and accuracy pretty much go without saying. Other considerations are equally important, such as whether the data source will be available when you need it, the ease of updating the data source, and access to the data source both for other data users as well as data creators.

Sometimes, your computer isn't the only device that needs to access data. For some documents, you will need access to data in other places — for example, on a laptop (notebook), for a presentation while traveling, on a different desktop computer at home, or elsewhere.

You can take several approaches to solving the need to either access data from another location or take the data with you. For the former, especially if the data source is large, unwieldy, or nonportable for other reasons, some kind of server solution will provide the answer. This might take the form of a data file residing on a SharePoint or other server, or you might place it in your SkyDrive so you can download it and reattach it as needed from any location. To see what's involved with using your SkyDrive, see Chapter 39, "Collaborating in the Cloud with SkyDrive." If you work in an enterprise, your company might have other kinds of server facilities that can serve as data sources for Word.

For portability, the answer often will be to extract a portion of a full data set — either a limited number of data records or a sample containing just the data fields you need. Every database has some unit or focus, such as individuals (for example, contact records) or products. Each person or product in a given database is called a *data record*.

Each piece of information about a person or product is called a *data field*. For example, a person's name, telephone number, address, e-mail address, and date of birth each would be data fields. For a product, data fields typically include name, SKU, shipping weight, price, color, description, and cost.

Unless a data set was constructed explicitly for a single purpose, most data sets will contain more records than you need, as well as more data fields than you need for a specific data-driven Word document. Often, it's possible to extract just what you need and take it with you. You have a variety of ways of doing that, as you see in this chapter.

> **TIP**
>
> To extract a portion of a larger database for use at a remote or inaccessible location, create a directory document using the mail merge feature, specifying only the records and fields you need. When you complete the merge, the resulting directory (or data document) will become the input data you need for associating with another data document.

Reviewing Data File Formats

Word enables you to use data from a variety of formats. You can create a data source directly from Word as part of the mail merge process or use an existing source. If you use an existing data source document, your options include the following:

- Outlook contacts
- Office Database Connections (`*.odc`)
- Access 2010 and later Databases (`*.accdb`, `*.accde`)
- Access 2007 Databases (`*.mdb`, `*.mde`)
- Microsoft Office Address Lists (`*.mdb`)
- Microsoft Office List Shortcuts (`*.ols`)
- Microsoft Data links (`*.udl`)
- ODBC File DSNs (`*.dsn`)

10

- Excel Files (*.xlsx, *.xlsm, *.xlsb, *.xls)
- Web Pages (*.htm, *.html, *.asp, *.mht, *.mhtml)
- Rich Text Format (*.rtf)
- Word Documents (*.docx, *.doc, *.docm, *.dot)
- Text Files (*.txt, *.prn, *.csv, *.tab, *.asc)
- Database Queries (*.dqy, *.rqy)
- OpenDocument Text Files (*.odt)

> **NOTE**
>
> Several older file formats are not directly supported in Word 2013, including Microsoft Works Databases (*.wdb), Outlook Personal Address Books (*.pab), Lotus 1-2-3 files (*.wk?, *.wj?), Paradox files (*.db), and dBASE files (*.dbf). Note that if you still have the old software, you can often export from those formats to a delimited *.txt or *.csv file that you can then use for the merge.

Using most of the data source formats works in a similar fashion, so there's no need to go through each and every type in detail. However, this chapter will cover the most common formats. Keep in mind that although the chapter examples repeatedly use names and addresses, you're by no means limited to those. Your list could be a list of products, an inventory, planetary information for a school project, and more. The idea is to use Word to present and format data in some fashion; it doesn't matter to Word what the data pertains to.

To begin, on the Mailings tab in the Start Mail Merge group, click the Select Recipients tool, exposing the options shown in Figure 10.1.

FIGURE 10.1

When selecting a data file, you can create it from Word, use a variety of other formats, or select data from Outlook Contacts.

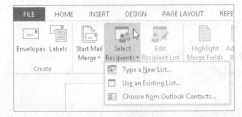

> **NOTE**
>
> This section explains how to set up the various types of data source files. You'll learn how to attach the data source during the merge process later in the chapter.

Typing a new list

To create a new list (a somewhat generic euphemism for "data document") in Word for a mail merge document:

1. **Click the Mailings tab, and in the Start Mail Merge group, choose Select Recipients⇨ Type New List.** The New Address List dialog box shown in Figure 10.2 appears.

FIGURE 10.2

Build your merge data source in this dialog box.

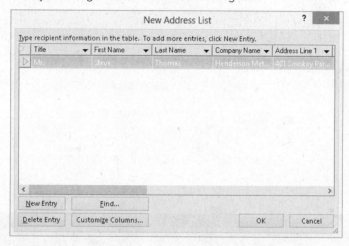

2. **Type your data into the fields shown, tabbing or clicking to get to the next entry field.**

3. **To accept the current entry and enter a new record, click New Entry.**

4. **To remove an entry, click it and then click Delete Entry.**

5. **When you're finished entering data, click OK.** The Save Address List dialog box prompts you to save the file as a Microsoft Office Address Lists file, as shown in Figure 10.3. Note that this is the only Save as type option.

> **NOTE**
>
> Also notice that Word automatically assumes you want to place the list file in the My Data Sources folder. Whereas some users prefer to keep all merge data source files in a single location for simplicity, others prefer the approach of storing the data source file in the same location as the merge document file that uses the data source to make it easier to copy both files to another location when needed.

6. **Type a name in the File name text box and click Save.**

FIGURE 10.3

Word saves new data source lists in the Microsoft Office Address Lists format.

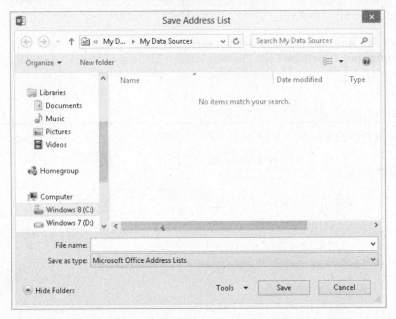

> **NOTE**
>
> After you click Save, behind the scenes, Word associates the new file with the current document. If you didn't set a document type using Start Mail Merge, Word sets it to Letters. You learn more about selecting or changing the main document type later in the chapter.

While you're working in the New Address List dialog box, if you've entered a lot of data and need to find a particular entry, click Find to display the Find Entry dialog box shown in Figure 10.4. Type the search text into the Find field. To search in a particular field, click the This field option button and select the desired field from the accompanying drop-down list. Click Find Next to find the next entry that matches the Find text in the field(s) specified. When the last matching entry is found, click OK to close the message. Click Cancel at any time to dismiss the Find Entry dialog box.

FIGURE 10.4

Once your data set is a bit larger, you might need some help finding a record.

If you want to create a list that consists of data other than a name and address list, click the Customize Columns button near the bottom of the New Address List dialog box. As shown in Figure 10.5, you can use the tools in the Customize Address List dialog box that appears to change the fields in your list.

- **To add a field select the field above where you want to add the new field, and click Add; type the field name in the Add Field dialog box that appears, and click OK. To delete a field select the field and click Delete; click Yes in the dialog box that prompts you to confirm the deletion.**

- **To rename a field, select it, click Rename, type a new name in the To text box of the Rename Field dialog box, and click OK.** (To add a field at the beginning, select the first field and click Add, as before. The added field will be second on the list, not first. Select the added field and then click Move Up.)

FIGURE 10.5

Use Customize Address List to specify your own fields for a merge data source.

TIP

To save time, rather than delete all of the existing fields and create new ones, rename the existing fields. They are not tied to particular types of data, so it doesn't matter what they're called.

10

- **To rearrange the fields, click a field you want to move, and then click Move Up or Move Down, as needed.**

When you're done customizing the list fields, click OK. Then you can make entries in the list as described earlier.

Word and text files

You can also use a Word document as your data source. Using a Word file as the data source usually works best when the data is stored in a table, but that's by no means essential. You can use a plain Word document in which the fields are separated by tabs, commas, slashes, or another delimiter. Plain text (`*.txt`) or comma-separated value (`*.csv`) files also should be delimited. Regardless of how the data file is formatted, Word assumes that the data file contains a header row or a header line containing the field names. The header itself should be formatted the same way the data is formatted — separated by tabs, commas, in a table row, and so on.

Figure 10.6 shows a merge data source properly entered as a table in Word. Notice that the first row of the table is the header row with the field names. Each column holds a single field (such as Restaurant), and each row holds a single record (all the fields for one restaurant).

FIGURE 10.6

A merge data source document created as a Word table

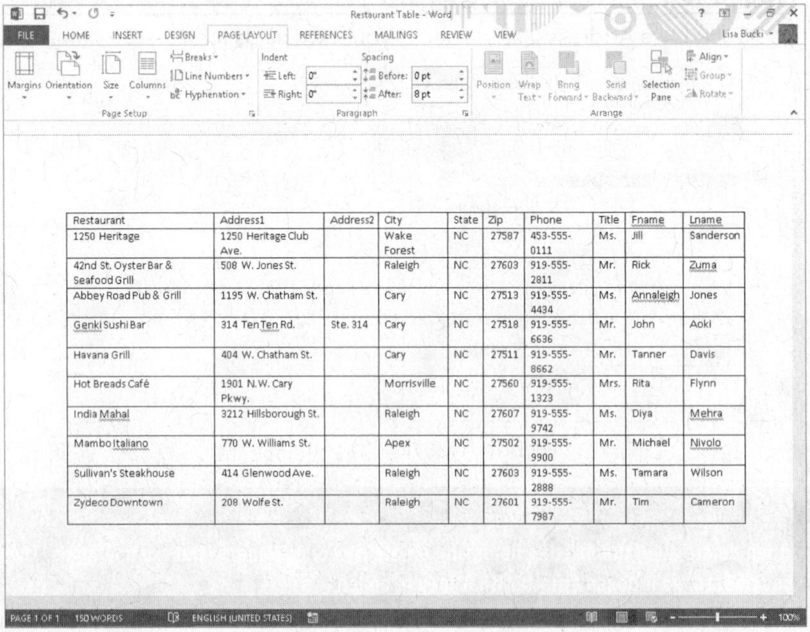

Restaurant	Address1	Address2	City	State	Zip	Phone	Title	Fname	Lname
1250 Heritage	1250 Heritage Club Ave.		Wake Forest	NC	27587	453-555-0111	Ms.	Jill	Sanderson
42nd St. Oyster Bar & Seafood Grill	508 W. Jones St.		Raleigh	NC	27603	919-555-2811	Mr.	Rick	Zuma
Abbey Road Pub & Grill	1195 W. Chatham St.		Cary	NC	27513	919-555-4434	Ms.	Annaleigh	Jones
Genki Sushi Bar	314 Ten Ten Rd.	Ste. 314	Cary	NC	27518	919-555-6636	Mr.	John	Aoki
Havana Grill	404 W. Chatham St.		Cary	NC	27511	919-555-8662	Mr.	Tanner	Davis
Hot Breads Café	1901 N.W. Cary Pkwy.		Morrisville	NC	27560	919-555-1323	Mrs.	Rita	Flynn
India Mahal	3212 Hillsborough St.		Raleigh	NC	27607	919-555-9742	Ms.	Diya	Mehra
Mambo Italiano	770 W. Williams St.		Apex	NC	27502	919-555-9900	Mr.	Michael	Nivolo
Sullivan's Steakhouse	414 Glenwood Ave.		Raleigh	NC	27603	919-555-2888	Ms.	Tamara	Wilson
Zydeco Downtown	208 Wolfe St.		Raleigh	NC	27601	919-555-7987	Mr.	Tim	Cameron

Headerless data files

After you attach a data source file, you can check it by clicking Edit Recipient List in the Start Mail Merge group of the Mailings tab. (You'll learn more about editing a data source later in the chapter.)

Word assumes that the first row of data contains the column headers. If your data source file doesn't include column headers in the first data record, you'll run into problems, as shown in the Mail Merge Recipients dialog box in Figure 10.7. And if a field in the top record is empty, Word displays AutoMergeField as the field title.

FIGURE 10.7

Beware of data files that don't contain a header row!

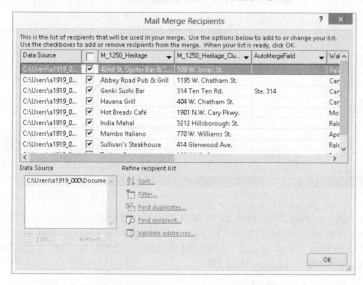

If the recipient list doesn't look as expected, click OK to close the Mail Merge Recipients dialog box. Open your data source document, and add the missing header row. Then return to the main document and reattach the file.

Understanding delimited files

Figure 10.8 shows a comma-separated value (`*.csv`) file opened in Word. The first row has the field names separated by commas, and each subsequent row contains one record, with the record's field entries separated by commas. Note that if a field is empty, two commas appear to keep the fields properly synchronized. When you attach a delimited file, you may be prompted to convert the file and confirm the encoding to use. In most cases, you can simply click OK to continue.

10

FIGURE 10.8

A delimited data source file can use commas, tabs, or another type of separating character.

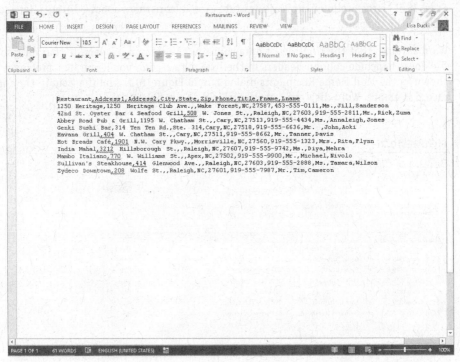

If your data file is not properly delimited or Word is unclear on the delimiter used, the Header Record Delimiters dialog box shown in Figure 10.9 appears when you attempt to attach the data source file. If not, select the proper delimiters from the Field delimiter and Record delimiter drop-down lists, and click OK.

FIGURE 10.9

If the data file doesn't contain a table, Word asks you to confirm the nature of the field and record delimiters (separators).

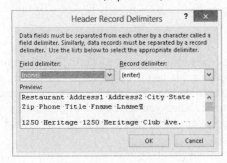

CAUTION

It's been my experier.ce that when the Header Record Delimiters dialog box appears, chances are the file wasn't delimited properly. If you see that dialog box, click the Edit Recipient List button in the Start Mail Merge group of the Mailings tab to check the fields.

NOTE

Only use the comma delimiter when the field contents themselves don't contain commas. For example, if your data includes commas in company names (as in Widgets, LLC or Widgets, Inc.) use another type of delimiter. If you need to include a field that may be blank in some instances, such as a suite/apartment number, consecutive commas indicate the blank field in the delimited file, as in "2424 Main St..," versus "2424 Main St., Apt. 3,".

Outlook

You can use contacts that you've entered in Outlook to perform a merge. To use data from Outlook, click Select Recipients in the Start Mail Merge group and select Choose from Outlook Contacts. The first time you do so, the Choose Profile dialog box may appear. Select a Profile Name and click OK. In Select Contacts, shown in Figure 10.10, if multiple contact folders are displayed, click the one you want to use and click OK.

FIGURE 10.10

When you select an Outlook contact folder, Word imports it.

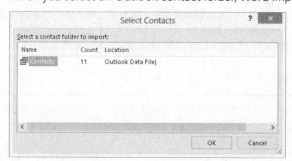

After you click OK, the Mail Merge Recipients list appears, as shown in Figure 10.11. Notice in the lower-left corner that the Data Source list shows Contacts as the source for the records. See the later section "Selecting recipients" to learn how to select and limit which contacts you use from the list.

10

FIGURE 10.11

Imported Outlook contacts display correctly.

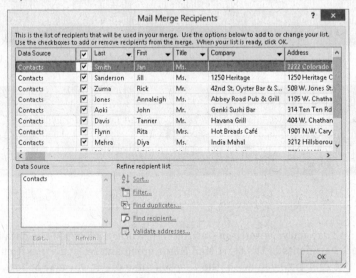

Excel

As in a Word table used for a data source, each column should hold one field and each row a single record; if you would like to include field names in row 1 as the header row, you can, but this is optional with Excel. If the workbook file has multiple tabs, the Select Table dialog box shown in Figure 10.12 appears. Click to select the table containing the data you want, and check or uncheck First row of data contains column headers as applicable.

FIGURE 10.12

Before attaching an Excel data source to a Word document, select the table you want to use.

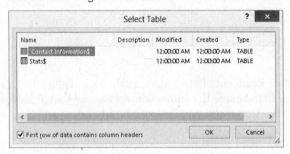

Access

As for Outlook contacts, when you select an Access file or another type of database as the data source, generally Word will have no trouble interpreting the data, as it's by definition set up correctly. Similar to when you attach an Excel data source, when you attach an Access data source, you will need to select the table or query that holds the records to merge. In the Select Table dialog box, click a table or query, and then click OK.

HTML files

When working with HTML files as data sources, note that they cannot reside on the Internet. You must first save the file to your local hard drive (or at least somewhere on your LAN or in your workgroup).

In addition, using HTML files as data sources almost never works unless the data has been carefully formatted. For best results, the data should be in a table and should contain a header row, and there should be no information above the table. If there is, the Header Record Delimiters dialog box shown in Figure 10.9 will appear, cuing you that the data won't import correctly.

Another problem occurs if Word can't recognize a consistent data pattern in the file or when the data source is inconsistently formatted, such as when some rows (records) contain different numbers of columns (data fields). When that is the case and you try to attach the file, an error message like the one shown in Figure 10.13 appears. Unfortunately, when this happens, the only recourse might be to edit the file to fix the problem, which ultimately means that the original data source is probably not going to be a reliable source of additional data or updates.

FIGURE 10.13

Word displays this message when different data records contain different numbers of data fields.

Choosing the Data Document Type

After you're sure you've properly set up your data source file, you can move on to work with the main data document. Either open the document to use or start a new blank file. To choose the type of data document, in the Mailings tab click Start Mail Merge in the Start Mail Merge group, as shown in Figure 10.14. Some of the options are obvious; others are not. There are basically two kinds of data documents you can design. For one kind, each data record in the data source will result in a personalized copy of the data document, such as a form letter, a mass e-mail, a product specification sheet, or an invoice. For the other kind, a single document is produced in which multiple records can appear on any given page. This approach is needed for creating directories, catalogs, and sheets of labels.

FIGURE 10.14

Letters, e-mail messages, and envelopes use one record per output document, whereas labels and directories use multiple records for each output document.

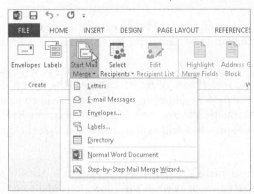

Contrast, for example, using an envelope (with a different address on each envelope) with using a sheet of labels (with a different address on each label). If you have only one address and want to print only one envelope or label, you don't need a data document, you can create an envelope within the current document by clicking Envelopes in the Create group of the Mailings tab, specifying address information in the Envelopes and Labels dialog box, and then clicking Add to Document. When you plan to crank out stacks of envelopes, each with a different address, or sheets of labels for which no two contain the same information, you need the approach described next.

As shown in Figure 10.14, Word offers five flavors of the two basic types of data documents:

- **Letters:** Use this option for composing and designing mass mailings for which only the recipient information varies from page to page. Use this approach too when you're preparing sheets containing product or other item specifications with one piece of paper per product or item. You might use this approach, for example, not only when sending out a form letter or invoices, but also when producing a job manual wherein each page describes a different job title, and job information is stored in a database.

- **E-mail Messages:** This is identical in concept to the form letter, except that it is geared to paperless online distribution. Contrast this with using multiple e-mail addresses in the To, Cc, or Bcc field. Using E-mail merge, each recipient can receive a personalized e-mail. Using multiple addresses, each recipient receives the identical e-mail.

- **Envelopes:** This is also identical in concept to the form letter, except that the resulting document will be envelopes. As a result, when you choose this option, Word begins by displaying the Envelope Options dialog box.

- **Labels:** Use this option to print to one or more sheets of labels. This combines Word's capability to print to any of hundreds of different label formats with the capability to associate a database with a document, printing many addresses (data records) on the same page, rather than the same address on each label.

- **Directory:** This is similar in concept to labels, in that you print from multiple data records on a single page. Use the directory approach when printing a catalog or any other document that requires printing multiple records per page.

To specify the kind of document, choose Start Mail Merge in the Mailings tab, and click the kind of document you want to create.

If you want step-by-step guidance through the process, note an additional option at the bottom of the Start Mail Merge list — Step-by-Step Mail Merge Wizard. Use this option if you're unfamiliar with the mail merge process. The Mail Merge Wizard process is described later in this chapter.

Restoring a Word document to Normal

Sometimes, by accident, temporary need, or whatever, a Word document becomes associated with a data file, and you want to restore the document to normal non–mail-merge status. To restore a Word document to normal, in the Mailings tab, choose Start Mail Merge in the Start Mail Merge group, and then click Normal Word Document. Note that when you restore a document to normal status, a number of tools on the Mailings toolbar that were formerly available become grayed out as unavailable. If you later decide that you need to again make the document into a data document, you will need to reestablish the data connection.

TIP

If there's a chance that you'll later need to restore a data connection, and if document storage space isn't a concern, rather than break the data connection for a document, save a copy of the document, giving it a name that lets you know that it has a data connection. Though establishing a data connection isn't all that difficult or time-consuming, you can usually save some time and guesswork by not having to reinvent that particular wheel.

10

Attaching a Data Source

To associate a Word file as the data file:

1. **Click the Mailings tab of the Ribbon, and choose Select Recipients.**

2. **As shown earlier in Figure 10.1, click Type a New List, Use an Existing List, or Choose from Outlook Contacts.** If you choose the first or third option, you can proceed as described for those data sources earlier in the chapter.

3. **In the Select Data Source dialog box (Figure 10.15), change the All Data Sources list to a particular file type if desired.**

FIGURE 10.15

Selecting a data source for a merge

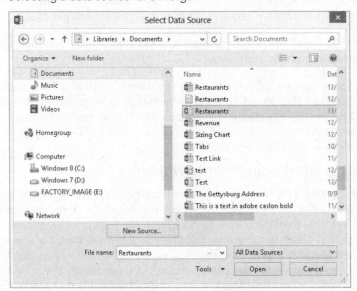

4. **Navigate to the location of the file, select it, and click Open.**

5. **Respond to any additional prompts as needed, such as selecting a delimiter or table as described earlier, and click OK.**

Note that once you've attached a data source to the document, Edit Recipient List and a number of other tools on the Mailings tab are no longer grayed out. If you plan to use the entire database, you can skip the following section.

Selecting recipients

If you don't plan to use the entire database, you can use the Mail Merge Recipients dialog box, shown in Figure 10.16, to select just the recipients you want to use. To open the dialog box, click Edit Recipient List in the Start Mail Merge group of the Mailings tab. Use the check boxes shown to include or exclude records. To quickly deselect all records, clear or select the check box at the top of the list, just to the right of Data Source.

FIGURE 10.16

Select just the target recipients using the Mail Merge Recipients dialog box.

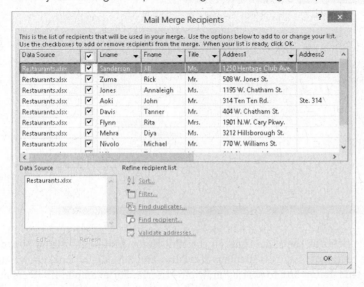

Editing a data source

Depending on your data source, you sometimes can edit the contents of the file by clicking the file in the Data Source box of the Mail Merge Recipients dialog box and then clicking Edit. Make the changes you need in the Edit Data Source dialog box, and click OK. Then click Refresh to ensure the data is updated for the merge. When your data source is Outlook contacts, note that Edit is not an option. To change your Outlook data, you must use Outlook. Once you've made your change in Outlook, you can then refresh the records you see in the Mail Merge Recipients list by highlighting the data source and clicking Refresh.

Sorting records

When editing non-Outlook data, you can sort using Word controls. Click the arrow next to a field to drop down a list of sort options, shown in Figure 10.17. For example, if you want to filter out records for which the contents are blank, click the drop-down list arrow for that field and choose Blanks. To select only records for which the e-mail address is *not* blank, click Nonblanks. To restore the list to show all records, choose the All option.

FIGURE 10.17

Quickly select records for which the current field is blank or nonblank by choosing Blanks or Nonblanks.

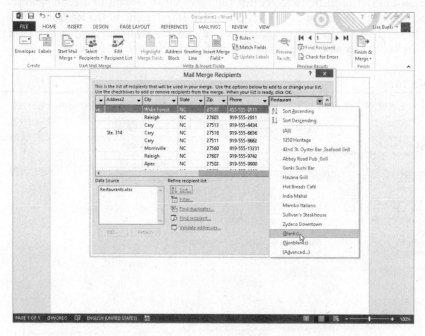

To sort by multiple fields at the same time, in the Mail Merge Recipients dialog box, choose Sort under Refine recipient list. This displays the Filter and Sort dialog box, shown in Figure 10.18. Use this dialog box to sort by multiple criteria. For example, if letters are being hand-delivered within a company, it might be useful to sort by floor and then by room number, assuming those are separate fields. (Often, sorting just by room number accomplishes both at the same time.)

FIGURE 10.18

You can sort by up to three fields.

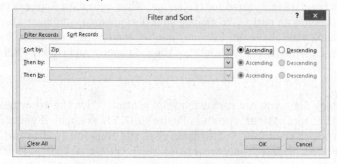

Filtering records

Word also enables you to filter records to either include or exclude records with data fields matching specific criteria. To filter records, click Filter under Refine recipient list. The Filter and Sort dialog box appears with its Filter Records tab selected, as shown in Figure 10.19. Use the options shown to filter by specific values. As shown here, you can use it to include specific Zip codes. Although the dialog box initially shows just six filter fields, you are not limited to that many. Just keep applying filters, and new rows will appear as needed.

FIGURE 10.19

You can specify multiple filter criteria.

The dialog box shown in Figure 10.19 shows the Equal to comparison. Additional operators include Not equal to, Less than, Greater than, Less than or equal, Greater than or equal, Is blank, Is not blank, Contains, and Does not contain. The latter entries help you filter by text entries in the field. Also note that you can filter a list using the field's column heading, as shown in Figure 10.17. Click the column heading drop-down list entry, and then click the column contents to filter for. To remove the filter, reopen the drop-down and click (All).

10

Understanding And and Or

When setting up filters, you can make two kinds of comparisons: *And* and *Or*. If all we had were one or the other, there would be no problem, but we have both, and we don't have parentheses to help clarify the comparisons.

It helps to understand that *And* and *Or* apply to each pair of rules. You also need to understand that the *And* rule is harder to satisfy in that it requires that two conditions be met. Depending on what comes before or follows, each and/or effectively divides the list of filters into sets of filters that are being evaluated. However, by being careful with filters, you can avoid combinations that are impossibly difficult to understand.

Suppose the filters contained the comparisons shown in Table 10.1. The first *And* applies to the Alexandria and VA filters. The second *And* applies to the Hampton and VA filters. This set of filters requires that records must be in Alexandria, VA, *or* in Hampton, VA.

TABLE 10.1   Understanding Or and And Operators

Operator	Field	Comparison	Compare to
	City	Equal to	Alexandria
And	State	Equal to	VA
Or	City	Equal to	Hampton
And	State	Equal to	VA

Finally, understand that it's perfectly possible to set up filters that make no logical sense. Hence, Table 10.1 could have been set up with all of the Operators set to *And*. There would be no matching records, of course. It's up to you to examine the collection of resulting data records to make sure that your logic is being applied as you think it should be.

Duplicates

Databases often contain duplicate records. When mailing or e-mailing, especially, you want to avoid sending the same person duplicate messages. When sending invoices to large companies, this can cause problems, especially if they are received and processed by different people, resulting in double payment, and further paperwork downstream.

To find duplicates, click the Find duplicates link in the lower section of the Mail Merge Recipients dialog box. Word displays the Find Duplicates dialog box, shown in Figure 10.20. Remove the checks beside a valid duplicate to exclude it from the data merge. Look carefully, however, because Word's criteria for what constitutes a duplicate might be different from your own.

FIGURE 10.20

Uncheck duplicate records to exclude them from the merge.

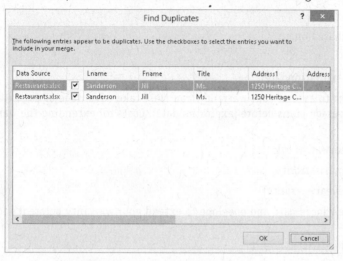

Validating addresses

The Validate addresses choice in the Mail Merge Recipients dialog box works with third-party software, such as that provided with stamps.com and other electronic postage services. If you don't have such software installed, you'll see an error message if you click the link. These services vary, but basically they check against a huge database of valid street addresses to determine whether the selected address and Zip code combination really exists. This can save considerably on costs, because it can prevent you from mailing to addresses that don't exist or are missing information such as suite number.

Assembling a Merge Document

Regardless of which merge document type you choose (letter, e-mail, envelopes, labels, or directory), the process for building it is similar. There are some additional considerations for multi-record-per-page documents, however, so we will look at those separately after discussing the common elements.

When designing a letter or e-mail you plan to send to multiple recipients using the merge feature, it's often a good idea to draft the document as you want it to appear, using placeholders in square brackets for information pertaining to the intended recipient, as shown in the following example:

10

Dear [name]:

We are writing to inform you that the warranty for:

[product]

which you purchased on:

[purchasedate]

will expire on [expirationdate].

If you would like to extend your warranty, you must take advantage of our extended warranty coverage plans before [expirationdate]. Costs for extending the warranty are:

1 Year: [oneyearwarranty]

2 Years: [twoyearwarranty]

3 Years: [threeyearwarranty]

Please use the enclosed card and envelope to extend your warranty before it's too late!

Yours truly,

[salesagent]

When you're done, edit your document and substitute merge fields for the placeholders.

Adding merge fields

After setting the data document type (using Start Mail Merge), associating a database with it (using Select Recipients), narrowing the list of recipients or records just to those records you plan to use, and drafting the data document, the next step is to insert merge fields into your document where you want the corresponding data fields to appear.

> **NOTE**
>
> *Merge fields* are special Word fields that correspond to the data fields in the attached data source file. For example, if you have a data field called Company, then you would insert the company name into your data document by using a MergeField field code with the name Company in it: { MERGEFIELD Company }. In your data document, that field displays either as <<Company>> or as the name of the company associated with the current record in the data set. Use the Mailings tab's Preview Results in the Preview results group button to toggle between the merge field name and actual data.

To insert a merge field, position the insertion point where you want the field to appear (or select the placeholder if you're replacing a placeholder with a merge field). From the Mailings tab, choose Insert Merge Field, as shown in Figure 10.21. Click the field you want to insert. Using a combination of text and merge fields that you insert, complete the assembly and wording of your document. Note that in addition to individual merge fields that you can insert using the Insert Merge Field tool, you can use special sets of merge fields to save time: Address Block and Greeting Line.

FIGURE 10.21

Merge fields are data tokens that you use where you want actual data fields to appear in the data document.

Address Block

You can insert an Address Block field, which can contain a number of elements that you can select from the Insert Address Block dialog box. To determine the contents of the Address Block, position the insertion point where you want to insert the field and click Address Block in the Write & Insert Fields group of the Mailings tab. The Insert Address Block dialog box shown in Figure 10.22 appears.

10

FIGURE 10.22

Use the Address Block tool in the Write & Insert Group of the Mailings tab to launch the Insert Address Block dialog box.

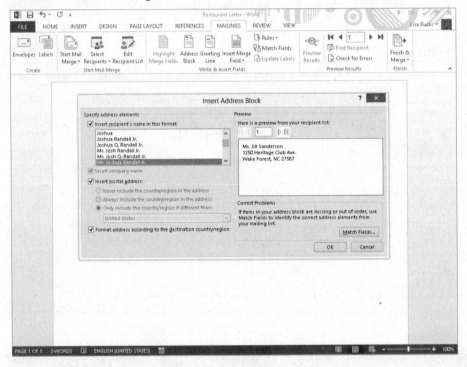

Notice that it contains three sections for selecting, previewing, and correcting your address block information (if there are problems). Make your selections as indicated, and then click OK.

- **Specify address elements:** Use this section to tell Word how to define the address block. You can include the recipient's name (click one of the listed formats to select it), the company name, the postal address, as well as the country or region. If desired, you can suppress the country or region, always include it, or include it only if it's different from the country selected. You can also tell Word to format the address according to the destination country or region.

- **Preview:** Use the First, Previous, Next, and Last buttons to preview different addresses as they will appear with the selected options. It's a good idea to preview a good sampling in case some parts of the address are treated differently from how you expect, or if there are problems with missing data that will leave "holes" in the address block. (Click Preview Results if you see merge field names instead of data.)

- **Correct Problems:** If the preview isn't what you expect, click Match Fields. Use the drop-down lists in the Match Fields dialog box to change the different data elements with which each of the fields listed is associated, as shown in Figure 10.23. If you plan to reuse the address block data either for the same database or for other databases that contain the same field names, click to enable the Remember this matching... check box. Then click OK.

FIGURE 10.23

Use the Match Fields dialog box to associate each of 11 items with data fields from your database for the Address Block.

After you finish choosing Address Block settings, click OK to insert the field in the document.

Match Fields

If you preview your recipients and the merged data still looks off, click Match Fields in the Write & Insert Fields group of the mailing tab to display the Match Fields dialog box shown in Figure 10.23. Change the specified fields from your data source as needed to match up with the field names that Word uses for merge elements, and click OK.

Greeting Line

The Greeting Line merge field, like the Address Block field, is a collection of different data elements and plain text designed to save you entry time when composing data documents. Click Greeting Line in the Write & Insert Fields group of the Mailings tab. This displays the Insert Greeting Line dialog box shown in Figure 10.24. Use the Greeting line format choices to set up the greeting line, and choose a greeting line for invalid recipient names. Use the Preview buttons to test your selected greeting line options against your actual data. If something doesn't look quite right, click Match Fields, use the previously shown controls to associate the Greeting Line components with the correct merge data fields, and click OK. Back in the Insert Greeting Line dialog box, click OK to insert the Greeting Line field code at the insertion point.

FIGURE 10.24

Set and preview greeting line components.

Rules

In assembling a data document, you sometimes need to control or modify how data and records are processed. Word provides nine commands to help you do that, as shown in Figure 10.25. The entries shown in the Rules drop-down box show how those rule keywords are displayed in the data document.

FIGURE 10.25

Use the Rules drop-down list of Word fields to control how data is merged with the data document.

These rules, which are tied to specific Word field codes, are explained in Table 10.2. Note that many of these are supported by dialog boxes that guide you through proper syntax, making them easy to use and understand.

TABLE 10.2 Merge Rules

Field	Usage/Purpose
ASK	This field prompts you to provide information and assigns a bookmark to the answer you provide; the information is stored internally. A reference to the bookmark can then be used in the mail merge document to reproduce the information you type. A default response to the prompt can also be included in the field. The ASK field displays as an empty bookmark in the mail merge document. You might use this field in conjunction with an IF field to prompt for missing information during a merge.
FILLIN	This field prompts you to enter text, and then uses your response in place of the field in the mail merge document. This is similar to the ASK field, except that the information can be used only in one place.
IF	This is used in mail merge documents to control the flow and to create a conditional statement that controls whether specific mail merge fields are printed or included in the merged document.
MERGESEQ	This field provides a counter of mail merge documents that actually result from a merge. If you merge the entire database and do not change the base sorting, and if no records are skipped, then MERGESEQ and MERGEREC will be identical.
MERGEREC	When doing a mail merge, the MERGEREC field serves as a counter of records in the data file and doesn't count the number of documents actually printed. This field is incremented by the presence of NEXT and NEXTIF fields. If you skip records using SKIPIF, MERGEREC is incremented nonetheless.
NEXT	The NEXT field is used to include more than one record in a given document. Ordinarily, when doing a mail merge, one document is printed for each record. With the NEXT field, however, you can include multiple records in a single document. This can be useful when you need to refer to several addresses from a data file. When doing a label merge, the NEXT field is provided automatically, and appears as <<Next Record>>.
NEXTIF	The NEXTIF statement works like the NEXT field except that it advances to the next record only if an expression being evaluated is true. A typical use is to skip a given record if a particular key field is blank. For example, in an e-mail merge, if you haven't otherwise excluded records with blank e-mail addresses, you can use NEXTIF to do it.
SET	The SET field is used to change the text referred to by a bookmark. SET often is used in conjunction with IF to conditionally change how particular text is defined based on external factors, such as the current date, or internal factors, such as the value(s) of particular fields.
SKIPIF	The SKIPIF field is used to cancel processing of the current database record during a mail merge. For example, you might use it to screen out a particular ZIP code.

10

Update Labels

When the data document type is Labels, the process for properly populating the fields into the document differs a bit. After selecting Labels from the Start Mail Merge drop-down list, the Label Options dialog box appears so you can select a label type and other options. After you do so and click OK, use these steps to set up the label merge document:

1. **Click View gridlines in the Table group of the Table Tools⇨Layout tab.** It's easier to work with the label layout when you can see the label boundaries.

2. **Return to the Mailings tab, and use Select Recipients in the Start Mail Merge group to select the data source as described earlier in the chapter.**

3. **Insert field codes for the address in the upper-left table cell.**

4. **Format the field codes in the upper-left cell as desired.** For example, you may want to remove the extra spacing between lines and make the font size a bit larger.

5. **Click Update Labels in the Write & Insert Fields group of the Mailings tab.** Word copies all text, merge fields, and formatting from the first cell into each of the other cells, after the Next Record control, as shown in Figure 10.26. The result is that each sheet of labels will contain data from the same number of label cells. A sheet containing nine labels will use data from nine database records.

FIGURE 10.26

When you insert a merge field into the first label cell, Word automatically puts the Next Record control into each of the other cells.

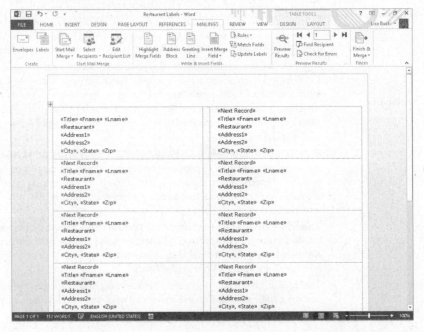

Preview Results

At any time as you go along, if you want to see what actual data will look like in your document, click the Preview Results button in the Preview Results group of the Mailings tab to toggle between the merge field codes in double angle brackets and actual data. Figure 10.27 shows field codes, while Figure 10.28 shows the preview data. Use the First, Previous, Next, Last, and Go To Record tools in the Preview Results group to move between the data records, and click Preview Results again to return to viewing field codes.

FIGURE 10.27

Data merge fields appear in double angle brackets.

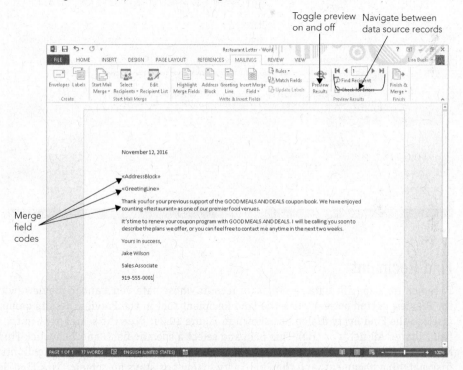

In Figure 10.28, you can see that the restaurant's address appears in the body of the document, where you clearly want the restaurant's name to appear. This can happen due to an error in either the field or the data record. You can check both and correct whichever is necessary. This shows how valuable Preview Results can be. To more easily catch errors, you can also use Highlight Merge Fields and Check for Errors, which will be discussed in the next few sections.

10

FIGURE 10.28

Use the Preview Results tools to ensure that the merge will produce the results you want.

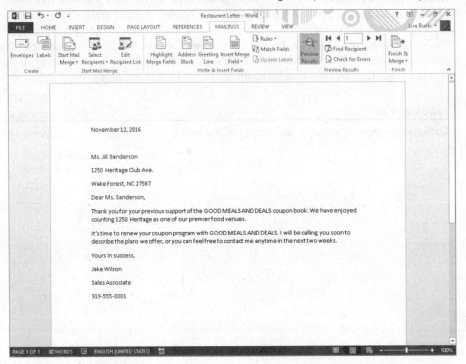

Find Recipient

To search for a specific data record or for records whose data you want to preview (with the Preview button active), click the Find Recipient tool in the Preview Results group. This displays the Find Entry dialog box shown in Figure 10.29. Type the search text in the Find field, choose All fields or click This field and select a specific field, and then click Find Next. Note that the search is not case sensitive. If there are matches, Word highlights the first matching document, and the Find Entry dialog box stays on-screen. Click Find Next to move to successive matches in the merged information, and then click Cancel when finished.

FIGURE 10.29

Use Find Entry to search for a matching record in the merged data.

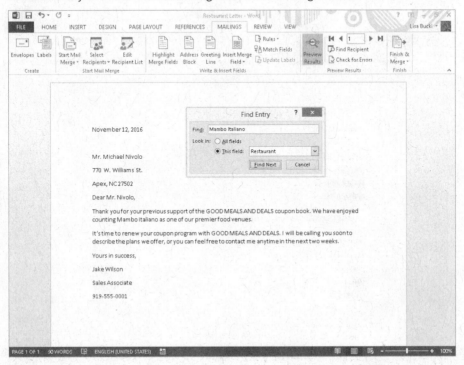

Return to this tool later, after your data document has been constructed, to preview specific data records. It's better to iron out problems before committing your merge to paper or e-mail.

Highlight Merge Fields

Use the Highlight Merge Fields tool in the Write & Insert Fields group of the Mailings tab to highlight all of the merge fields when previewing data, as shown in Figure 10.30. This can be useful if you're working on a complex document and need to recheck the logic and placement of merge fields. If, for example, you expect a given merge field result to appear in two places in the document, this tool enables you to find those locations more easily so you can verify that the correct text appears. If you're using conditional rules, such as Skip Record If, Next Record If, and If, this also helps you focus on the results so you can verify that the rules are working as expected.

FIGURE 10.30

When previewing, you can turn on highlighting to see which data is merged.

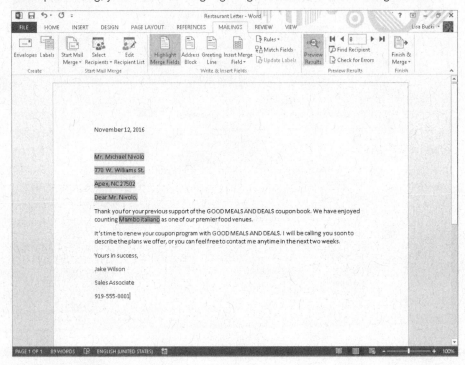

Check for Errors

To avoid wasting paper and other resources, when you think you're done, click Check for Errors in the Preview Results group of the Mailings tab to display the options shown in Figure 10.31.

FIGURE 10.31

Rather than waste paper or send out errant e-mails, use the error checking tool to avoid logical errors or other unwanted surprises.

The options in the Checking and Reporting Errors dialog box work as follows:

- **Simulate the merge and report errors in a new document:** Use this option to examine any and all errors in a new document.
- **Complete the merge, pausing to report each error as it occurs:** Use this option once you've determined that there are errors, so you can observe the error in action.
- **Complete the merge without pausing. Report errors in a new document:** Use this option to go ahead and complete the merge without stopping at each error, sending the error report to a new document.

Finishing the merge

Once the data document is ready and has been thoroughly debugged and certified as error free, it's time to go through the final motions. The Finish & Merge drop-down list in the Finish group of the Mailings tab provides three options, shown in Figure 10.32, *regardless of the type of data document chosen.*

> **WARNING**
>
> Be careful about clicking Send E-Mail Messages. You don't want to accidentally send sensitive information like a list of preferred clients to the wrong recipients. You also don't want to e-mail information that would be otherwise confusing or embarrassing, such as a set of labels.

FIGURE 10.32

Choose how you want to finish the merge.

> **NOTE**
>
> Don't forget to save and name your original merge document in addition to any documents based on it.

Editing individual documents

From the Finish & Merge drop-down list in the Finish group of the Mailings tab, choose the Edit Individual Documents option if you want to save your merged results for future use. For example, suppose you have a set of labels that seldom changes and which you need to print out every week. Rather than go through the mail merge exercise each week, save the merge labels in a separate Word document, and then print them each time you need them. That way, you don't need to go through the whole mail merge routine unless the underlying database has changed.

You might also choose this option if you don't trust other ways of proofing the results. Instead of printing from the Mailings tab, send the results to a new document where you can examine each of them, and then print when you're ready.

When you choose this option, Word displays the Merge to New Document dialog box shown in Figure 10.33. If you want Word to create a limited number of output documents, choose either Current record or indicate a From/To range. Click OK to create a new Word document with the merged data.

FIGURE 10.33

Select the desired records to merge and click OK.

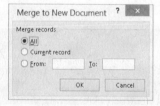

Printing documents

From the Finish & Merge drop-down list in the Finish group of the Mailings tab, choose the Print Documents option when you're certain that the merge will give you the results you want. When you click Print Documents, Word displays a dialog box with similar options to those shown earlier in Figure 10.33, this time sporting a Merge to Printer title bar. Specify which records to merge and click OK to launch the Print dialog box. Make any additional choices and decisions, including which printer to use, cross your fingers, and click OK.

TIP

If you don't trust all of the previews and error checks at this stage, and you want to be extra sure before wasting a tree, use the Name drop-down list in the Print dialog box to see whether you have an option that produces electronic images of printed pages, rather than actual printed pages. Using Office 2013 and Windows 8, you should at the very least see Microsoft XPS Document Writer, which is Microsoft's alternative to PDF files. Then you can review what actually amounts to your best possible print preview.

Sending e-mail messages

From the Finish & Merge drop-down list in the Finish group of the Mailings tab, choose the Send E-Mail Messages option if you're working on an e-mail merge. When you click Send E-mail Messages, Word displays the Merge to E-mail dialog box, shown in Figure 10.34.

FIGURE 10.34

Add a Subject line for the merged e-mail messages here.

In addition to the Send Records options (All, Current Record, and From/To), Word provides three additional options for which you should make selections before clicking OK to merge and send the messages:

- **To:** Select the data source field that holds recipient e-mail addresses.

- **Subject line:** This is very important. Studies show that 73.4 percent of all non-spam e-mail merges sent omit the subject line. Don't become a statistic! Replace that blank subject line. (This statistic was made up by the author. Nonetheless, don't send subjectless e-mails!)

- **Mail format:** Many e-mail recipients wisely have their e-mail options set up to read all e-mail as plain text (this gives them a shot at preventing any automatic naughtiness from being executed when e-mail is opened). Options provided are Attachment, Plain Text, and HTML, the latter being the default. Though Attachment seems like a good compromise for formatted e-mail, this option provides no way for you to include any message text for the body of the e-mail. When and if you use that option, make sure the subject line isn't blank.

Mail Merge Pane/Wizard

If you'd rather not use the individual tools in the Mailings tab of the Ribbon and prefer a little more assistance when performing a mail merge, Word provides the Mail Merge Wizard. Start a new blank document (or open a document you want to use as the basis for a data document). Click the Mailings tab, click the Start Mail Merge button in the Start Mail Merge group, and choose Step-by-Step Mail Merge Wizard. This opens the Mail Merge pane, shown in Figure 10.35. Just follow along its steps from there.

FIGURE 10.35

Choosing the Wizard opens the Mail Merge pane.

Step 1: Select document type

In Step 1, shown in Figure 10.35, choose the type of data document you want to create under Select document type. Click the Next: Starting document link at the bottom of the pane to move to the next wizard step.

Step 2: Starting document

The Mail Merge task pane next presents three options under Select starting document. Note that when you choose any of these options, Word explains the option in the lower part of the task pane. The options are as follows:

- **Use the current document:** Start from the current document and use the Mail Merge wizard to add recipient information (merge fields).

- **Start from a template:** Start from a template, which you can customize as needed by adding merge fields and/or other contents. If you choose this option, click Select Template to be shown a list of all of the available templates (at least the ones that Word knows about). Note that despite the option's wording, it does *not* present you with a list of "ready-to-use mail merge" templates.

- **Start from existing document:** Open an existing mail merge or other document and change it to fit the current need by changing the contents or recipients. Recent mail merge documents, if any, will be listed. If the one you want isn't listed, click Open to navigate to the one you want, select it, and then click Open.

After making your selection, choose Next: Select recipients at the bottom of the task pane.

Step 3: Select recipients

In Step 3, select from Use an existing list, Select from Outlook contacts, and Type a new list. These options, shown in Figure 10.36, correspond to the identical options described in detail earlier in the chapter. If you leave Use an existing list selected, click Browse to find the data source file, and choose a table or worksheet if prompted. In the Mail Merge Recipients dialog box that opens, use it to work with the records as described earlier. Click Next: Write your letter at the bottom of the pane to move on.

FIGURE 10.36

Select the desired recipients option and then click Next: Write your letter.

Step 4: Write your letter

In Step 4, you are greeted with four options:

- **Address block:** This enables you to insert an Address Block field as described earlier. See the discussion under "Address Block" for additional details.
- **Greeting line:** The Greeting line option enables you to insert a Greeting Line merge field. See the "Greeting Line" section for more information.
- **Electronic postage:** As indicated previously, the functioning of this option requires the installation of third-party software that enables you to apply postage to items you send.
- **More items:** This option displays the Insert Merge Field dialog box shown in Figure 10.37. Leave Database Fields selected to see the fields in your data source. Before displaying Insert Merge Field, move the insertion point to the document location where you want a merge field to appear, click More items, select the field, and click Insert. Dismiss the dialog box and repeat this series of actions for each merge field. In practice, however, if you know which fields you want to insert, select (with Shift+click or Ctrl+click) and insert them all at once, and then cut and paste them where you want them to go.

FIGURE 10.37

The associated fields in your data source are listed when you choose Database Fields.

> **TIP**
>
> Use a combination of text and merge fields to write the data document, inserting merge fields where you want database fields to appear. When you're done, click Next: Preview your letters.

Step 5: Preview your letters

In Step 5, shown in Figure 10.38, use the controls shown to move from record to record in your database. Note that the << and >> tools correspond to the Previous and Next button in the Preview Results group of the Mailings tab. When you finish previewing the merge, click Next: Complete the merge.

FIGURE 10.38

Use the final wizard steps to preview the data document and complete the merge.

Step 6: Complete the merge

The contents of the final Mail Merge pane vary depending on the document type. When the document type is a letter, the options are to send the merged results to the printer or to send them to "individual letters." Actually, that's not at all what the option does. Instead, it sends all of the merged letter results to a single new document, in which the individual letters are separated by section breaks.

Summary

In this chapter, you've learned about data considerations when preparing a data source document in Word or another application. You then learned how to use each of the mail merge tools in the Mailings tab to begin a mail merge document, attach a data source with records to a merge document, insert merge fields, and complete a data merge. You've also seen that this feature isn't just for mail merge but has many other uses as well. You should now be able to do the following:

- Create a new data source file and prepare data from various sources.
- Create a new data source list within Word.
- Use Outlook contacts as a source for mail merge data.
- Select a Word, HTML, Access, Excel, and other data file for the merge data source.
- Select just the records you want for the merge.
- Insert composite merge fields, such as the Address Block and Greeting Line, as well as control how those fields are constituted.
- Integrate the merge fields with your other document content.
- Update labels.
- Finish by merging to a document or printer.
- Use the Mail Merge Wizard.

Managing Document Security, Comments, and Tracked Changes

IN THIS CHAPTER

Understanding document protection

Using digital signatures and signature lines

Protecting a document with a password

Inserting comments

Tracking changes

Reviewing comments and changes

Comparing two documents using "legal blackline"

Combining documents that contain tracked changes

Word offers a variety of kinds of protection (although nothing is 100 percent secure). Some of the protection tools work hand in hand with other tools that facilitate collaboration and reviewing. For example, you can limit formatting or allow users only to enter tracked changes or comments.

This chapter looks at the types of document protection and review tools available to Word users and describes how to use them.

Protection Types

Word 2013's privacy settings aren't centrally located. To save you the trouble of searching to find what you can control, here's the definitive list of the different types of protection (and pseudo-protection) Word 2013 offers and where to find them:

- **Permission:** Restrict a document so it can be opened and/or changed only by specific individuals. Select File ⇨ Info ⇨ Protect Document ⇨ Restrict Access. For this to work, your system must be set up for Information Rights Management so it can connect to a Digital Rights Management server, a topic that's beyond the scope of this book.

- **Digital signature:** Sign a document with a digital signature to provide assurance that you are the source of the document. Select File ⇨ Info ⇨ Protect Document ⇨ Add a Digital Signature.

- **Inspect Document:** Inspect the document to see if it contains private or sensitive information or data. Select File ⇨ Info ⇨ Check for Issues ⇨ Inspect Document.

- **Mark as Final:** Mark a document as final to let recipients know that the document is considered the final revision. This setting makes the document read-only and makes it unavailable for additional typing, editing, proofing, or tracking changes. Note that this setting is advisory only — you can click the big Edit Anyway button — this removes the Mark as Final setting. Recipients with earlier versions of Word who have installed the Office 2010 Compatibility Pack won't even see the file as read-only. Hence, this kind of gentle protection would have to be combined with something more substantial to be meaningful. Select File ⇨ Info ⇨ Protect Document ⇨ Mark As Final.

- **Style formatting restrictions:** Limit formatting to a selection of styles as well as block Theme, Scheme, or Quick Style Set switching. Protection here is by password, and is therefore less secure and robust than when using permissions. Select File ⇨ Info ⇨ Protect Document ⇨ Restrict Editing ⇨ Limit formatting to a selection of styles.

- **Editing restrictions — Read only:** This offers password protection, which is not very secure, along with exceptions of specific areas of the document. Exceptions can be made wholesale, or you can limit them to individuals with specific Microsoft account–associated e-mail addresses. Select File ⇨ Info ⇨ Protect Document ⇨ Restrict Editing ⇨ Allow only this type of editing in the document ⇨ No changes (read only).

- **Editing restrictions — Tracked changes:** This type of protection allows only tracked changes to be made. Select File ⇨ Info ⇨ Protect Document ⇨ Restrict Editing ⇨ Allow only this type of editing in the document ⇨ Tracked changes.

- **Editing restrictions — Fill-in forms:** This type of protection allows filling in of form fields and content controls. Select File ⇨ Info ⇨ Protect Document ⇨ Restrict Editing ⇨ Allow only this type of editing in the document ⇨ Filling in forms.

- **Editing restrictions — Comments:** This type of protection allows only comments. Exceptions can be made for selected areas of the document, for everyone, or for specific individuals (using Microsoft account –associated e-mail addresses). Select File ⇨ Info ⇨ Protect Document ⇨ Restrict Editing ⇨ Allow only this type of editing in the document ⇨ Comments.

- **Password to open/modify:** This type of protection lets you specify a password to open and/or modify the document. This protection is not the same as the Editing restrictions' No Changes setting. You must choose one or the other. Select File ⇨ Save As ⇨ Computer ⇨ Browse ⇨ Tools ⇨ General Options.

11

> **NOTE**
>
> Some of these controls are also available using the Protect group on the Developer tab, which you can display via the Main Tabs list after clicking Customize Ribbon in the Word Options dialog box.

The rest of this section looks at these settings, showing how you enable protection and assessing the degree of protection provided.

Information Rights Management

A relatively strong way to protect your documents uses an Information Rights Management server to authenticate users who create or receive documents or e-mail that have restricted permissions. If your organization uses a Rights Management Services (RMS) server, your system administrator must enable Windows and Office 2013 to work with RMS. You then choose File ➪ Info ➪ Protect Document ➪ Restrict Access, and click Connect to Digital Rights Management Services and get templates to get started. From there you can use the File ➪ Info ➪ Protect Document ➪ Restrict Access commands to restrict access to the document to specified user accounts, or remove previously applied restrictions.

Using digital signatures

A *digital signature* is an electronic certificate that provides a way for recipients to verify that a document or e-mail actually came from the sender. Digital signatures do not provide 100 percent guaranteed authentication that a document is from a non-malicious sender, but generally speaking, a document signed by someone you know and trust is likely to be more trustworthy than an unsigned document from an unknown or suspicious source.

> **NOTE**
>
> Carefully check any document with a digital signature. If you receive something important and the validity of the signature is an issue, pick up the telephone and call the sender to verify the document's contents. Never share private information such as account numbers or passwords on the basis of a digital signature alone.

Before you can digitally sign a document, you must have a digital signature installed on your system. To get a signature, choose File ➪ Info ➪ Protect Document ➪ Add a Digital Signature. If this is the first time you've used this feature, Word displays the dialog box shown in Figure 11.1. Click Yes to obtain a certificate. Your system's web browser launches and displays Microsoft's Available Digital IDs page, listing partner organizations through which you can obtain a digital ID and download and install a certificate on your system.

FIGURE 11.1

If you don't already have a digital signing certificate, click Yes to learn about for-fee and for-free services.

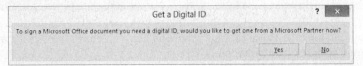

> **NOTE**
>
> You also can use the Office SelfCert utility to create your own digital certificate. SelfCert certificates are for personal use only on the computer on which they were created. To learn more about working with digital certificates on your system, see the TechNet topic "Manage Certificates" at `http://technet.microsoft.com/en-us/library/cc771377.aspx`. You can create a SelfCert signature. In Windows 8, open a File Explorer window, and navigate to `C:\Program Files (x86)\Office\Office15` (for 32-bit versions of Office), or `C:\Program Files\Office\Office15` (for 64-bit versions of Office). Locate the `SELFCERT.EXE` command in the folder and double-click it to start the process.

How to digitally sign a Word document

After you've obtained a digital signature, follow these steps to digitally sign a Word document:

1. **Choose File ➪ Info ➪ Protect Document ➪ Add a Digital Signature.** If the document has not been saved, you are prompted to save the file as a Word document. Click Yes, enter a File name, and click Save. Word then displays the Sign dialog box, shown in Figure 11.2.

FIGURE 11.2

Specify signature details here.

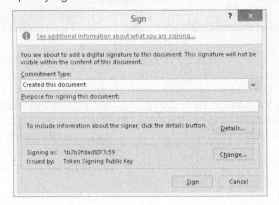

2. **Open the Commitment Type drop-down list and click the desired commitment type.**

3. **Type a Purpose for signing this document entry if desired.**

4. **To enter more information about yourself as the signer, click Details, add entries in the text boxes in the Additional Signing Information dialog box as desired, and then click OK.**

5. **If the Signing As identity/certificate isn't the one you want to use, click Change, click an alternate certificate in the Windows Security dialog box, and click OK.**

6. **Click Sign.** The Signature Confirmation message appears, as shown in Figure 11.3.

7. **Click OK to finish applying the signature.** This also marks the document as final, a feature you'll read about soon. As shown in Figure 11.4, the Backstage view indicates that the document has been signed and marked as final.

FIGURE 11.3

Don't sign a document until you're finished making changes to it.

FIGURE 11.4

The Backstage view now identifies the file as a signed document.

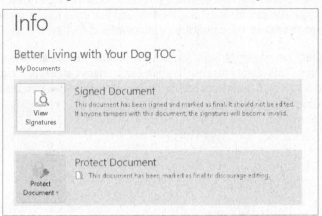

Removing a signature

Once you've signed a document, the document is locked against further changes until the signature is removed. Unlike document permissions, a digital signature can be removed from a Word document by anyone with the appropriate version of Word. Once a signature has been removed, however, it can only be signed again by the owner of the original signing certificate. Hence, if I send you a signed file and you remove my signature, you can edit the file I sent you and make any changes you want. However, you will not be able to restore my signature.

WARNING

There are ways to make a forged signature look valid, and not everyone is sufficiently skeptical. Make sure you know and trust the sender before you open a signed document.

When you open a signed document, the messages shown in Figure 11.5 appear at the top of the document. You can click Edit Anyway if you want to make changes to the document.

FIGURE 11.5

Messages tell you when a document you open has been marked as final and signed.

To view and work with signatures in the document, click the View Signatures button in the Message Bar, or choose File➪Info➪View Signatures. The Signatures pane opens at the right side of the document window. To remove a signature, move your mouse pointer over it, click the drop-down list arrow that appears, and click Remove Signature as shown in Figure 11.6. (Note that you also can view details about the signature.) At the prompt that asks whether you want to remove the signature permanently, click Yes.

Don't let the words "permanently" and "cannot be undone" in the Remove Signature message box throw you. This simply means that you can't remove someone's signature, change that $1,000 fee to $100,000, and then reaffix their signature. Once you remove someone's signature, only they can put it back.

FIGURE 11.6

View and work with digital signatures in the Signatures pane.

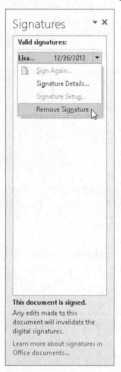

Adding a signature line

Word 2013 now includes the ability to specify a signature line to prompt for a recipient's signature. You can include a signature line on a contract, a proposal, a change order verification, or any other type of document that requires a signature to indicate agreement or approval. To add a signature line in a document:

1. **Click to position the insertion point in the location where you want the signature to appear.**

2. **Click the Insert tab, and in the Text group, click the Add a Signature Line button.** (If you click the button's down arrow, instead, click the Microsoft Office Signature Line command.) The Signature Setup dialog box shown in Figure 11.7 appears.

FIGURE 11.7

Set up the signature information here.

3. **Enter the desired information.** You can enter only a Suggested signer, or you can add other information as needed depending on what you want to include in the signature.

4. **Click OK.** Word inserts the signature line in the document.

As shown in Figure 11.8, the signature line is a special object in the document. To use it to sign the document, double-click it. The Sign dialog box appears. If you previously scanned

FIGURE 11.8

Double-click the signature line to open the Sign dialog box so you can add your signature.

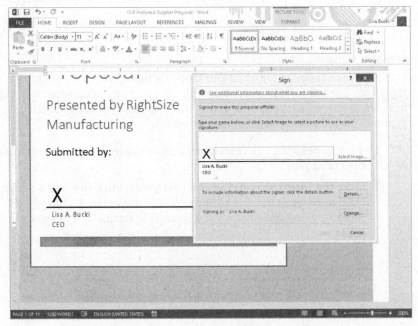

your actual signature and saved it as a graphic file, you can click Select Image and use the Browse choice in the Insert Picture window that appears to select and insert the signature file. Otherwise, just click in the text box, type your signature, and click Sign.

> **TIP**
>
> To change the information included with a signature, right-click it and then click Signature Setup to reopen the Signature Setup dialog box.

Document Inspector (removing private/personal information)

You can use the Document Inspector to see what private or personal information resides in a file and remove it. The Document Inspector checks for the kinds of information and content shown in Figure 11.9. To display the Document Inspector, choose File⇨Info⇨Check for Issues⇨Inspect Document⇨Inspect Document. By default, all eight areas are checked. Remove checks if you don't want those kinds of information removed. For example, if the purpose for sending a document to someone is to convey the XML data it contains, then remove the check next to Custom XML Data. On the other hand, if the document might contain "colorful" comments about someone's draft, you probably do want to inspect it for those. When the right checks are checked and the wrong checks are unchecked, click Inspect.

FIGURE 11.9

Use the Document Inspector to remove private/proprietary information before passing a document along to someone else.

The Document Inspector inspects the current document for each of the types of material or data indicated. If it finds any, the Document Inspector dialog box is redisplayed, with Remove All buttons next to each type of content that was found, as shown in Figure 11.10.

FIGURE 11.10

A red exclamation mark means that the Document Inspector found potentially sensitive content, and the check mark indicates that the specified type of content was not found.

> **WARNING**
>
> Make a backup copy of the document before using Remove All. Once you remove the content using the Document Inspector, you can't get it back using Undo. Particularly for comments and data, if they are content you need to preserve, make a backup copy of the document.

The Document Inspector does not provide further details about exactly what it found. You have two options: Click Remove All to remove the found items, or click Close and review the types of items found by Document Inspector. You can remove the content yourself manually or you can return to the Document Inspector and use Remove All once you're satisfied that you want something removed.

NOTE

Unlike the Selection pane, which you can use to make objects visible or hidden in a document as described in Chapter 9, "Adding Tables and Graphics to a Document," when you click Remove All in the Document Inspector, it actually does remove the hidden objects from the document — it doesn't just make toggle their visibility. So, exercise caution if you really do need those objects; it's a good idea to create a for-distribution copy of the document.

11

Formatting and editing restrictions

The Restrict Formatting and Editing settings can provide a measure of protection for your document. You can limit the type of formatting that users can apply, limit the types of changes most users can make, and apply exceptions for trusted users. Specify these settings in the Restrict Editing pane, which you can display in one of two ways:

- Choose File ⇨ Info ⇨ Protect Document ⇨ Restrict Editing.
- Click the Review tab, and click Restrict Editing in the Protect group.

Limit formatting to a selection of styles

To limit formatting to certain styles, in the Restrict Editing pane shown in Figure 11.11, click to place a check next to Limit formatting to a selection of styles. To choose which styles, click Settings. The Formatting Restrictions dialog box now appears, also shown in Figure 11.11.

FIGURE 11.11

With Limit formatting to a selection of styles checked, click Settings to choose those limits.

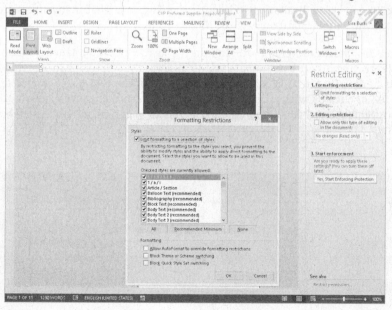

The Formatting Restrictions dialog box provides the following options:

- **Checked styles are currently allowed:** Place a check next to each style you want to allow. Remove checks for styles you want to disallow. Note that the styles listed might be limited based on settings in the Manage Styles dialog box, discussed in Chapter 7, "Using Styles to Create a Great Looking Document," so consult that earlier discussion if you need to display additional styles here. Note that Normal is not included in the list. As much as you might like to, you can't deny access to the Normal style.

- **Recommended Minimum:** If the list is too inclusive, click Recommended Minimum, and then add or remove checks as needed.

- **None:** If the style list is way too inclusive, then choose None, and place a check next to just those you want to allow.

- **All:** If the style list is way too restrictive, then click All and remove the check next to those you want to disallow.

- **Allow AutoFormat to override formatting restrictions:** If AutoFormat's rules and practices are sufficiently rigorous for your purposes, click to allow this option.

- **Block Theme or Scheme switching:** Choose this option to limit formatting to the currently applied theme or scheme.

- **Block Quick Style Set switching:** Choose this option to use style definitions from the current document and template only.

When you're ready to proceed, click OK in the Formatting Restrictions dialog box. Word next displays the message box asking whether to remove disallowed styles from the document. Click Yes to remove disallowed styles or formatting. Note that if any styles are removed, text will be reformatted using the Normal style.

Finally, click Yes, Start Enforcing Protection in the Restrict Editing pane. The Start Enforcing Protection dialog box prompts you to password-protect your formatting restrictions, if desired. Either type the password twice in the text boxes provided and then click OK, or click OK without entering passwords. Even if the level of protection isn't as strong as rights management, applying passwords to your restrictions is still better than nothing.

> **NOTE**
>
> Why would you want to impose formatting restrictions? Some publishing processes depend upon only certain styles being used. There are macros or other programs that process files so that they can be fed into other parts of the publishing process. If other styles are used, the process breaks down and requires manual intervention. Hence, it's better if only the allowed styles are used. In other cases, enterprise-wide formatting standards are strictly imposed to ensure that all documents have a consistent and professional look. Enforcing style restrictions is one way to do that.

With formatting restrictions applied, a number of formatting tools, commands, and keystrokes on the Home tab are grayed out as unavailable.

No changes (Read only)

You can protect all or part of a document against changes. You can make different exceptions for different users. Suppose, for example, that you have a document that has been written by a group of people. You want each individual to be able to edit his or her own section, but not that of others. At the same time, you don't want to have to manage different documents.

The solution is to create a document with a specific area for each individual. You make the entire document read-only, but you make an exception for each individual's section so that the individual responsible can make changes as needed.

To set a document as read-only, open the Restrict Editing pane. In the Editing restrictions section, click the check box to Allow only this type of editing in the document, and use the accompanying drop-down list to set it to No changes (Read only).

To make an exception, select the part of the document to which you want to allow changes by someone (or everyone). This selection can be any part of the document — a single letter, word, sentence, line, paragraph, and so on. If you want the exception to apply to everyone, click the check box next to Everyone. Or, if other groups are listed, you can place a check next to any of them.

To make an exception for individuals, if they are listed, click to place a check by their names. If the individuals aren't listed (or if no individuals are listed at all), click More Users. In Add Users, type the user IDs or e-mail addresses for the individuals you want to exempt from the read-only proscription, and click OK. Word attempts to verify the names/addresses you added. If they are verified, they are added to the list of individuals.

Back in the Restrict Formatting and Editing pane, you need to place a check by the name(s) and e-mail address(es) you added. As shown in Figure 11.12, Word highlights and bookmarks the text that you've indicated the checked user can edit. Add exceptions for other users as desired, and then click Yes, Start Enforcing Protection. Add and confirm a password if desired, as shown in Figure 11.13, noting that the document is not encrypted and is susceptible to hacking by malicious users. If you enable User authentication, Word will use Information Rights Management to control the permissions. Click OK to finish applying the permissions.

FIGURE 11.12

The user a1919test@hotmail.com has been granted an exception to edit the Executive Summary information.

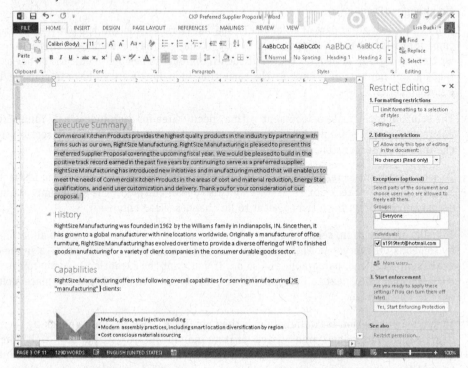

FIGURE 11.13

Applying a password to the protections

Comments

Choosing this protection option from the Editing restrictions drop-down list in the Restrict Editing pane results in protection identical to the No changes (Read only) option, except that all users can insert comments wherever they want to. Refer to the preceding discussion to see how to apply this protection, substituting Editing restrictions at the appropriate point.

Tracked changes

Another option is to allow editing but only tracked changes. That way, you can see who changed what, and when. This is an important feature in controlling the editing/revision process. To protect a document for tracked changes, open the Restrict Editing pane, click to enable Editing restrictions, and choose Tracked changes.

To turn protection on, click Yes, Start Enforcing Protection. The Start Enforcing Protection dialog box appears, where you can set and confirm a password. Note that User authentication is not available for this kind of protection. When you click OK, protection is enabled, and the document switches into Track Changes mode. To turn protection off — which is necessary for accepting/rejecting tracked changes — click Stop Protection at the bottom of the Restrict Editing pane.

Filling in forms

To protect a fill-in form that you've created in Word by adding fields and content controls or by downloading and modifying a template with fields and controls, click Restrict Editing in the Protect group of the Review tab of the Ribbon. In the Restrict Editing pane, click to enable Allow only this type of editing in the document, open the drop-down list, and click Filling in Forms. Click Yes, Start Enforcing Protection.

Applying a password to open/modify a Word document

A final kind of password protection is well hidden in Word 2013. This legacy feature offers the same weak protection already noted in that passwords aren't impossibly difficult to hack and crack. The bottom line: Rely on this kind of password protection at your own risk. It offers minimal, if any, protection. Worse, it offers the illusion of protection, and thinking a document is well protected when it's not is perhaps worse than no protection at all, because you are unlikely to be as careful with the document as you would be if you knew it was completely unprotected.

You can set two different passwords: one that enables a user to open the document, and another that enables the user to make changes. To enable this kind of password protection, choose File ➪ Save As ➪ Computer ➪ Browse. In the lower-right corner of the Save As dialog box, choose Tools ➪ General Options, to display the General Options dialog box shown in Figure 11.14. Type a password in Password to open, and/or in Password to modify. Both are optional.

FIGURE 11.14

Applying Open and Modify passwords to a Word document

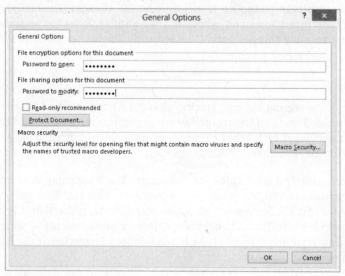

The Read-only recommended option applies only if there is no password for modifying the document. If this option is enabled, the user is provided with a read-only recommendation when the file is opened and an easy way to select read-only.

When you click OK, you are prompted to confirm any passwords and are returned to the Save As dialog box. Click Save to save the document with the password settings.

> **NOTE**
>
> The Protect Document button is irrelevant to this dialog box and serves mostly to let the user know that there are other and better protection options. If you click this button and the Restrict Editing pane is not already showing, it is displayed behind the Save As dialog box, and the General Options dialog box goes away. If the Restrict Editing pane is not already showing, clicking the Protect Document button simply causes the General Options dialog box to close.

When you try to open a password-protected file, Word prompts you to enter the relevant passwords. If you know the password to open but not the password to modify, you can click Read Only to open the document in "read only" mode. Why the quotes? Because it's only the file itself that is read only. The document window can be edited willy-nilly, unlike when using other kinds of protection discussed earlier. If you save the file under a new name, the new file will inherit the password settings, but if you copy the file to the Clipboard and save under a new name, the protection is history.

> **TIP**
> You also can use File ⇨ Info ⇨ Protect Document ⇨ Encrypt with Password to apply a password to the document.

Comments and Tracked Changes

Comments and tracked changes are two ways Word provides for reviewing others' Word documents. Comments themselves are easy to explain: They are notes, questions, suggestions, and other details that a reader offers to the author of the Word document. Although a commenter might suggest a particular edit within a comment, the Comments feature does not integrate any edits or changes into the text. It's not unusual to copy the text of a suggestion from inside a comment and paste it into the text, but comments themselves aren't part of the flow.

Tracked changes, however, are part of the flow. Tracked changes are insertions and deletions made to a Word document. You can see what was inserted or deleted, by whom, and when. That way, if you have multiple reviewers making changes in a document, you can see who made which changes, which helps in deciding how to integrate inconsistent edits.

Viewing comments and tracked changes

Because comments are not part of the main text, Word has a lot of flexibility in how it can display them. This section looks at your display options, as well as how to add and work with comments as needed. Use the choices in the Tracking and Comments groups of the Review tab to work with comments.

Word includes two views for working with comments and tracked changes: Simple Markup (the new default view) and All Markup. Choose the overall view using the Display for Review drop-down menu in the Tracking group of the Review tab.

In the default Simple Markup view, shown in Figure 11.15, a comment balloon in the right margin shows you that there's a comment. A red line appears in the left margin beside any line(s) with tracked changes. To see the comment text and author, click the comment balloon. Click the balloon again to hide the comment information.

In All Markup view, shown in Figure 11.16, a comment area appears at the right side of the screen, and comment text appears there with a dashed line and highlight showing you the selected text that the comment refers to. These are also considered comment "balloons," although they don't look as much like balloons as they do in Simple Markup view. Tracked changes are marked up using a highlight color, strikethrough for deleted information, and underlining for inserted information. If you move your mouse pointer over a tracked change, a tooltip appears to show you who made the change and when.

FIGURE 11.15

The Simple Markup view initially hides comment text and tracked changes.

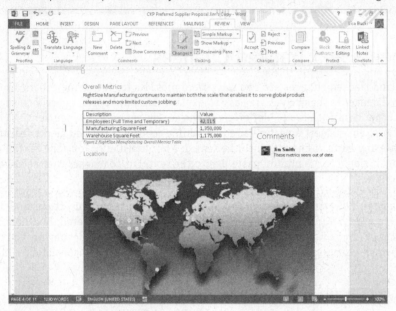

FIGURE 11.16

Hover the mouse over a tracked change to find out who made the change.

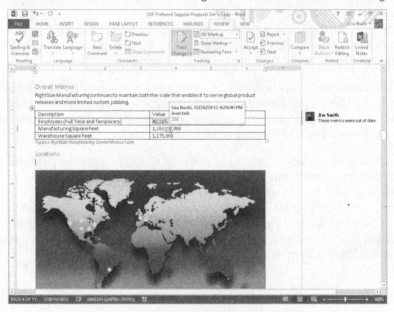

If you also want tracked changes to display as balloons in the right margin, in the Review tab's Tracking group, choose Show Markup ⇨ Balloons ⇨ Show Revisions in Balloons. To set comments to display inline (which isn't really correct, because comments themselves do not display inline), choose Show Markup ⇨ Balloons ⇨ Show All Revisions Inline. When you make this choice, no comment balloon of any type appears. Instead, the commented text is high-lighted and the reviewer's initials appear in brackets beside the comment. You can right-click the initials and click Edit Comment to see the comment in the Revisions pane at left. For the sake of consistency, this chapter assumes you are not working in the Revisions pane.

11

> **NOTE**
>
> You also can use the Reviewing Pane choice in the Tracking Group of the Review tab to display comments in the Revisions pane. I prefer not to use this feature, as it's a little harder to navigate when a document has been heavily edited and commented.

Inserting, editing, replying to, and deleting comments

To insert a new comment, first select the text that you want to comment about. In some cases, you can even click on a graphic object and insert a comment about it, but that doesn't work in all instances. Click the Review tab, and then click New Comment in the Comments group. (You also can insert a comment with Insert ⇨ Comments ⇨ Comment, but this method displays the Revisions pane, which as noted above is more cumbersome to work with than comment balloons.) In Simple Markup view, type your comment inside the yellow Comments box that opens, and then click the Close (X) button on the box. In All Markup view, a balloon appears in the right comment area. Type the comment, and then click in the text to return to normal editing.

To edit a comment, click its balloon in either Simple Markup or All Markup, and make changes in the comment box, and then click the Close (X) button or click in the text to finish.

Word 2013 includes the new ability to reply to a comment. Click the comment, and then click the Reply button (page with an arrow) at the right side of the box (see Figure 11.17). Type the comment text in the reply comment that appears, as shown in Figure 11.17, and then click Close (X) or click in the text to continue.

FIGURE 11.17

Click the page with the arrow in the Comments box to reply to a comment.

If you've taken the action recommended in a comment by another reviewer and want to leave it it place but indicate that it is no longer active, you can right-click the comment in the comment balloon or box, and click Mark Comment Done. This grays out the comment text.

To delete a comment, click the comment in either view, and then in the Comments group of the Review tab, click Delete. In All Markup view, you can right-click the comment and click Delete Comment. Click the arrow on the Delete button in the Comments group and then click Delete All Comments in Document if you're ready to remove all changes.

Tracking changes by various editors

Unlike comments, tracked changes can be displayed inline. You also have a variety of options regarding which aspects of tracked changes to display.

Track Changes Options

To see the main set of tracking options, click the dialog box launcher in the Tracking group of the Review tab. In the initial Track Changes Options dialog box that appears (see the left side of Figure 11.18) you can change some overall options such as what to show or hide. If you click Advanced Options, more detailed choices appear in the Advanced Track Changes Options

FIGURE 11.18

Use Track Changes Options to change how/if changes are tracked and displayed.

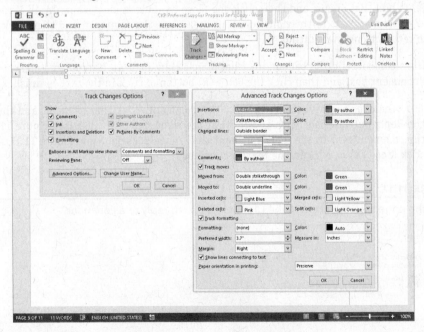

dialog box shown at the right in Figure 11.18. Make the desired changes, and then click OK to close each dialog box. Options in the Advanced Track Changes Options dialog box include:

- **Markup:** These options control the formatting and colors to use when displaying insertions, deletions, and comments, as well as how to display lines indicating where changes have been made. Default formatting is to use underlining for insertions and strikethrough for deletions. If Color is set to By author, Word automatically chooses different colors for different authors. Note, however, that whereas your comments might display as green on your computer, they might display as magenta on somebody else's. Therefore, if you're describing a change in a phone conversation, don't assume the other party is seeing exactly what you're seeing.

- **Track moves:** These options control the formatting and colors to use when displaying text that was moved from one location to another in the document. If you don't want to track moves, remove the check next to Track Moves.

- **Track formatting:** These options control how formatting changes are represented. If you don't want to track formatting changes, remove the check next to Track formatting. Note that this doesn't affect the *display* of tracked formatting. It controls whether formatting is tracked at all. When you turn this off, existing tracked formatting changes remain in the document, but subsequent formatting changes are not tracked at all. To hide tracked formatting changes, choose Show Markup in the Tracking group of the Review tab and remove the check next to Formatting.

Turning on Track Changes

To enable tracked changes, click the Track Changes button in the Tracking group of the Review tab. Notice that the upper and lower portions of that button are separate. Use the upper portion to toggle tracked changes, and use the lower portion to choose Track Changes or Lock Tracking. Lock Tracking enables you to add a password to prevent other users from turning off change tracking.

Alternatively, if Track Changes is displayed in the status bar, you can click it to toggle tracking on and off. If Track Changes is not displayed, right-click the status bar and click to place a check next to Track Changes. Then click outside the menu to close it. Once it's on the status bar, click Track Changes to turn tracking on or off. Track Changes can also be toggled using Ctrl+Shift+E.

Show Markup

If your comments don't display, it's possible that they are turned off. In the Review tab, click the drop-down arrow next to Show Markup in the Tracking group to display the options shown in Figure 11.19.

FIGURE 11.19

Click Show Markup in the Review tab to control the kinds of markup that Word displays.

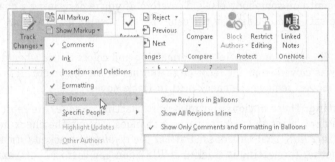

Show Markup options affect only the display of markup. They do not affect whether changes are tracked. Display options are as follows:

- **Comments:** Choose to display or not display comments.

- **Ink:** When using a tablet, touch-enabled, or other system that supports pen annotations, use this option to choose whether to display the original ink markup (in addition to the text conversion thereof).

- **Insertions and Deletions:** Use this setting to control the display of textual edits (insertions and deletions). Some users prefer to deal separately with textual and formatting edits. With this option enabled and Formatting display turned off, you can selectively focus.

- **Formatting:** Use this setting to hide or show formatting changes.

- **Balloons:** Use this setting to control the use of balloons for revisions and comments as described earlier.

- **Specific People:** Use this setting to selectively show or hide specific reviewers' edits and comments.

- **Highlight Updates:** When you are co-authoring a document on a SharePoint server or Office365, this option highlights updates by the other author(s).

- **Other Authors:** When you are co-authoring, this option lists other authors currently working on the same document.

> **TIP**
>
> You can click one of the vertical bars (lines) in the left margin of Simple Markup view to display or hide tracked changes and comments.

Display for Review

Use the Display for Review menu in the Tracking group of the Review tab to determine exactly what displays when a document contains tracked changes. As noted earlier, you use this drop-down to change between All Markup and Simple Markup views, which were discussed in the "Viewing comments and tracked changes" section earlier. Its other two options are:

- **No Markup:** All markup is hidden, and you see the document as it would appear if all changes were accepted. This view is useful when a document has been heavily edited. You can read a "clean" copy of the new version without the change tracking markup slowing you down.

- **Original:** All markup is hidden, and you see the document as it appeared before any markup occurred. This is how the document would appear if all changes were rejected.

> **TIP**
>
> It's often hard to gauge the effects of changes. It can be helpful to switch between Final and Original so you can properly assess the full impact of changes, especially when comparing paragraphs that have undergone substantial editing.

Accepting and Rejecting Changes

Use the Changes group of the Review tab, shown in Figure 11.20, to review changes to determine whether you want to accept or reject them. Use Next or Previous to navigate to the nearest comment or change. Use Accept and Reject to integrate or remove changes. You can also right-click a change and choose Accept or Reject.

Here is a brief overview of what happens when you choose Accept or Reject:

- When you accept an insertion, it is converted from a tracked change into regular text.
- When you reject an insertion, it is deleted.
- When you accept a deletion, it is removed entirely from the document.
- When you reject a deletion, the original text is restored.
- When you accept formatting changes, they are applied to the final version of the text.
- When you reject formatting changes, the formatting is removed.

Note that the Accept and Reject buttons in the Changes group of the Review tab both have upper and lower sections. The lower section of the Accept button features the options shown in Figure 11.20. Reject has similar options. Note that the third option, Accept All Changes Shown, is available only if one or more kinds of changes are hidden in the Show Markup tool.

FIGURE 11.20

Accept All Changes Shown is available only when some changes are hidden.

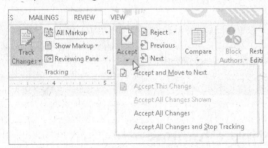

> **NOTE**
> You cannot accept or reject a comment per se. Accepting a comment leaves it alone. Rejecting a comment deletes it.

Combining Collaborative Documents

Word can compare and combine different versions of the same document. If the document was revised without tracking turned on, you learn how to compare the two different versions. If a document was revised by multiple people, whether or not Track Changes was turned on, you learn how to combine all of the different edits into a single (hopefully manageable) document.

Comparing Documents

Word enables you to compare two documents, usually different versions of the same document, using what Microsoft calls *legal blackline*. Basically, you feed Word two documents, designating one as the original document and the other as the revised document. Microsoft then creates a third document (the default setting) with markup indicating the changes. Perhaps not surprisingly, this new document contains tracked changes, and you can use Word's Review tab tools to manage the document, to decide what to keep and what to zap.

In a nutshell, suppose that you have two versions of the same document, and the second was accidentally edited without Track Changes turned on. The Compare feature enables you to correct that "oversight" by creating a new document that shows what the original document would look like if the revisions had been made with Track Changes turned on.

> **NOTE**
>
> If you have only two documents you want to compare, and neither displays tracked changes, use the Compare feature. If you have two or more documents that contain tracked changes, and you need to keep track of who changed what and when, use the Combine feature, described later in this chapter.

To initiate the comparison, in the Review tab, click Compare in the Compare group.

Word displays the Compare dialog box. Click the More button to display the full Compare Documents dialog box shown in Figure 11.21. When you first click the More button, you see the default settings for Compare. By default, all of the Comparison settings are enabled: Show changes at is set to Word level, and Show changes in is set to New document. Use the Original and Revised document drop-down arrows to choose the documents you want to compare. If the documents you seek aren't in the alphabetical list of recent files shown, choose Browse, either in the list or by clicking the Browse button to the right of the drop-down list.

Under the Revised document choice, Label changes with is set to the current default user name (from Word's Popular Options). You can change that to whatever you like — it doesn't even have to be a user's name.

Under Comparison settings, choose the elements you want included in the comparison. Under Show changes at, you can choose to compare character by character or word by word. Choose Character level if you want to see the exact edits that were performed. For example, if the original document has "word" and the revised document has "world," in which the "l" was inserted, then the Word level setting would simply show you that "word" was replaced by "world," whereas Character level would show the fact that an "l" was inserted.

FIGURE 11.21

By default, the result of the comparison is placed into a new document.

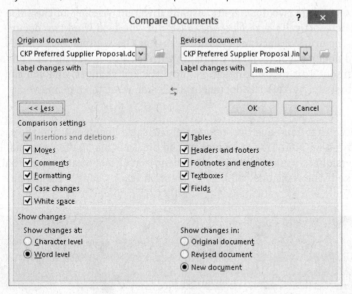

> **NOTE**
>
> The Insertions and deletions item is always grayed out and always checked. This is by design. When you use Compare or Combine, insertions and deletions will always be compared. Microsoft left this in because it might not be obvious. Hence, it displays as always checked, and it cannot be changed.

As noted, by default, Compare puts the changes into a new document. However, if it suits your purposes better, you can route the changes into the document designated as either the Original document or the Revised document under Show changes in at lower right. Note that if you've now changed your mind about which is which, you can click the Swap Documents tool.

When you're ready to make the comparison, click OK. If either of the two documents being compared contains tracked changes, for purposes of the comparison, Word displays a message telling you that it assumes that the changes are accepted. Click Yes to continue the comparison.

Word arranges the Compared Document (the Show changes in document), the Original, and the Revised into a document window, along with the Revisions pane, as shown in Figure 11.22. If you chose the Save to a new document option, note that the tentative file name is Compare Result #.

FIGURE 11.22

Word shows you exactly what editing has taken place.

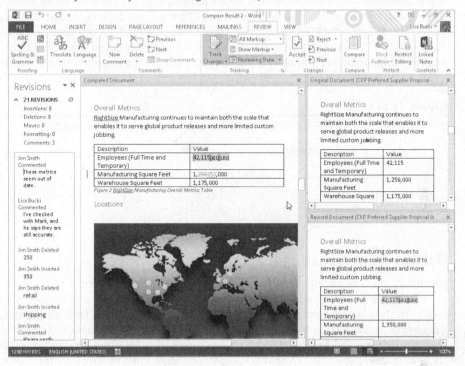

In this view, notice that the three document windows scroll at the same time. The idea is to show the original, revised, and resulting edits at the same time. Depending on screen size as well as how large the Word window is, this can be difficult. However, Word makes a valiant effort.

Use the Review tab tools, as described earlier in this chapter, to set the view as needed, and to move to the Next or Previous changes, accepting or rejecting changes as you see fit. When you're done, if you want to save the compared result, choose File ➪ Save As (or Save, but read this section's Warning first), and save as usual.

> **WARNING**
>
> Before you click Save, keep in mind that if you chose Original or Revised as the document in which to show changes, saving now will replace the corresponding document with the compared version. Once done, there's no going back. If you think you'll have a need for all three versions of the document, choose Save As, and give the compare results version a new name.

Protection

You cannot compare two documents if either of them is protected for tracked changes. When you try, Word will advise you that it can't "merge" the documents due to document protection. In fact, any kind of document protection will produce the objection shown in Figure 11.23. If you see this message, unprotect the documents you are trying to compare and try again, assuming you have the necessary permissions to unprotect the documents.

FIGURE 11.23

You can't compare two documents if either of them has protection enabled.

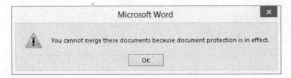

Gaining more screen real estate

If you find that the default view offered by the Compare feature doesn't give you enough room to maneuver, you can selectively display (or not) the Original and Revised documents. In the Compare group in the Review tab, click Compare, and then click Show Source Documents. You can click Hide Source Documents to close those windows. You can also close the Original and Revised documents by clicking the Xs. If you change your mind, click Compare ⇨ Show Source Documents and click Show Both to redisplay the source documents.

Combining Documents That Contain Tracked Changes

When you have multiple documents containing tracked changes and you need to keep track of who changed what (and when), use the Combine command to merge the tracked changes two at a time until all of the different reviewers' changes have been incorporated into one document. As with the Compare command, documents are combined two at a time. If any document in the paired combinations is protected, you cannot continue. Before you invest a lot of time doing comparisons, make sure that you can use the documents you're planning to compare.

Combining multiple documents containing changes

When combining or merging changes from multiple documents, it doesn't matter if the changes have been tracked. At the end of the process, changes attributable to any given reviewer will be tracked due to the way the documents are combined.

> **NOTE**
>
> The only loss for untracked changes is that you won't know exactly when the changes were made. For example, if a reviewer was making changes at 4:00 a.m., you won't know that. Depending on the reviewer, that could matter a lot, affecting how seriously you consider such sleep-deprived comments.

Suppose, for example, that document A is the original document written by Lisa Bucki, and that document B has changes that were made by Jim Smith — some of them tracked and some of them not. When you combine document A and document B, everything that is different in document B will be attributed to Jim Smith, whether tracked or not.

When you combine documents, you have the same options you have when you compare them, in terms of where the combined changes go. It works best if you always combine changes into the same document, preferably the original to which the other changes were applied. Suppose that you start with document A and give it to four reviewers. Each of them takes a whack at it at the same time, so you end up with four different revisions to document A. Let's call those revisions Bob, Jim, Ted, and Lisa. There is no temporal sequence, and it doesn't matter when each is compared with the original, A.

One way to proceed is as follows (keeping in mind that the order for combining with Bob, Jim, Ted, and Lisa doesn't matter):

- Compare A with Bob's version, putting the results in A. Save A.
- Compare A with Jim's version, putting the results in A. Save A.
- Compare A with Ted's version, putting the results in A. Save A.
- Compare A with Lisa's version, putting the results in A.

At the end of the process, A will contain tracked changes from each of the four reviewers. It won't necessarily be easy to sort out, but all of the changes *will* be in a single document.

> **NOTE**
>
> An alternative way to proceed is to insert an additional step before saving A. You could, depending on the nature of the edits, resolve each set of edits one at a time. First, examine Bob's changes and accept or reject each. Then, use the resolved version of A for the next comparison, and continue in this fashion. This might seem less cluttered and confusing, but there is a logical problem. By the time you get around to Lisa, her changes might be moot if the text she revised was deleted by Jim. Ultimately, you'll need to decide which method works best, although most users find it least confusing when they can see all of the suggestions at once. At the end of the day, however, most Word users conclude that simultaneous editing by four reviewers is a nightmare that should be avoided. Sequential edits are a lot easier to manage.

Running the Combine Documents command

To kick off the process, in the Review tab's Compare group, click the Compare button arrow, and then click Combine. The Combine Documents dialog box that appears is essentially identical to the Compare Documents dialog box in Figure 11.21. Set Original document to the earliest version you have, and set Revised document to a revised version of the original. Choose the desired options and set Show changes in to New document or Original document (but make a backup copy of the original before you combine the documents). Click OK to combine that set.

> **NOTE**
>
> Before you begin, be aware that Word cannot retain multiple formatting revisions. Therefore, after each Combine operation, if you are including formatting in the Comparison settings you enable, you should set Show Markup (in the Review tab) to just Formatting, and use Next/Previous/Accept/Reject to resolve all of the formatting changes before proceeding to the next Combine.

After the Combined Document appears, resolve any formatting changes and then repeat the process for the next revision. Continue until each of the revised versions has been combined. Finally, you'll have a version that contains all of the changes, as well as the reviewers' names. If the originals contain tracked changes, you'll also have the times the changes were made. For untracked changes in the revised versions, the revision time will be the time that the combine operation occurred for that revision and hence won't be meaningful.

Summary

In this chapter, you've learned about the many different kinds of document protection and security available in Word. You should now have a good idea about which forms of protection and security are useful, and which ones give only partial security. You've also learned about tracking changes and commenting on Word documents, as well as how to compare and combine documents. You should now be able to do the following:

- Protect a document so that only a specific kind of editing can be performed.
- Use Word's legacy password protection, while understanding its limitations.
- Add comments and enable Track Changes in a document.
- Navigate and work with comments and tracked changes.
- Set options that let you display a variety of elements when tracking changes in a document.
- Compare two documents that contain no tracked changes, automatically marking up one so you can review the changes.
- Combine an original document with independently revised versions to create a version that contains tracking.

11

Part III

Making the Numbers Work with Excel 2013

L et the number crunching begin in Part III, which covers calculating results and more in Excel 2013. You will learn how Excel organizes information on worksheets within workbooks, and how to make and format different types of cell entries, including labels and values. You'll learn to organize worksheets and how to create and use named cell ranges to save time. The part moves on to the most powerful capabilities in Excel: the ability to use formulas and functions to perform simple calculations, sophisticated math, and formulas to calculate date and time information. The part closes out with two chapters showing you how to highlight your data visually, through charts, tables, conditional formatting, sparklines, and more.

IN THIS PART

Using Excel Worksheets and Workbooks

IN THIS CHAPTER

Understanding what Excel is used for

Looking at what's new in Excel 2013

Learning the parts of an Excel window

Navigating Excel worksheets

Introducing Excel's Ribbon

Trying out Excel with a step-by-step hands-on session

This chapter is an introductory overview of Excel 2013. If you're already familiar with a previous version of Excel, reading (or at least skimming) this chapter is still a good idea.

Identifying What Excel Is Good For

Excel, as you probably know, is the world's most widely used spreadsheet software and part of the Microsoft Office suite. Other spreadsheet software is available, but Excel is by far the most popular and has been the world standard for many years.

Much of the appeal of Excel is due to the fact that it's so versatile. Excel's forte, of course, is performing numerical calculations, but Excel is also very useful for non-numeric applications. Here are just a few of the uses for Excel:

- **Number crunching:** Create budgets, tabulate expenses, analyze survey results, and perform just about any type of financial analysis you can think of.
- **Creating charts:** Create a wide variety of highly customizable charts.
- **Organizing lists:** Use the row-and-column layout to store lists efficiently.
- **Text manipulation:** Clean up and standardize text-based data.
- **Accessing other data:** Import data from a wide variety of sources.
- **Creating graphical dashboards:** Summarize a large amount of business information in a concise format.
- **Creating graphics and diagrams:** Use Shapes and SmartArt to create professional-looking diagrams.
- **Automating complex tasks:** Perform a tedious task with a single mouse click with Excel's macro capabilities.

Seeing What's New in Excel 2013

When a new version of Microsoft Office is released, sometimes Excel gets lots of new features and other times it gets very few new features. In the case of Office 2013, Excel got quite a few new features.

Here's a quick summary of what's new in Excel 2013, relative to Excel 2010:

- **Cloud storage:** Excel is tightly integrated with Microsoft's SkyDrive web-based storage.
- **Support for other devices:** Excel is available for other devices, including touch-sensitive devices such as Windows RT tablets and Windows phones.
- **New aesthetics:** Excel has a new "flat" look and displays an (optional) graphic in the title bar. The default color scheme is white, but you can choose from two other color schemes (light gray and dark gray) in the General tab of the Excel Options dialog box.
- **Single document interface:** Excel no longer supports the option to display multiple workbooks in a single window. Each workbook has its own top-level Excel window and Ribbon.
- **New types of assistance:** Excel provides recommended PivotTables and recommended charts.
- **Flash Fill:** Flash Fill is a new way to extract (by example) relevant data from text strings. You can also use this feature to combine data in multiple columns.
- **Support for Apps for Office:** You can download or purchase apps that can be embedded in a workbook file.
- **The Data Model:** Create PivotTables from multiple data tables, combined in a relational manner.

- **New Slicer option:** The Slicer feature, introduced in Excel 2010 for use with PivotTables, has been expanded and now works with tables.

- **Timeline filtering:** Similar to the Slicer, the Timeline makes it easy to filter data by dates.

- **Quick Analysis:** Quick Analysis provides single click access to various data analysis tools.

- **Enhanced chart formatting:** Modifying charts is significantly easier.

- **New worksheet functions:** Excel 2013 supports dozens of new worksheet functions.

- **Backstage:** The Backstage screen has been reorganized and is easier to use.

- **New add-ins:** Three new add-ins are included (for Office Professional Plus only): PowerPivot, Power View, and Inquire.

Understanding Workbooks and Worksheets

The work you do in Excel is performed in a workbook file. You can have as many workbooks open as you need, and each one appears in its own window. By default, Excel workbooks use an `.xlsx` file extension.

> **NOTE**
>
> In previous versions of Excel, users could work with multiple workbooks in a single window. That is no longer an option in Excel 2013. Every workbook that you open has its own window.

Each workbook contains one or more *worksheets*, and each worksheet is made up of individual cells. Each cell can contain a value, a formula, or text. A worksheet also has an invisible *draw layer,* which holds charts, images, and diagrams. Each worksheet in a workbook is accessible by clicking the tab at the bottom of the workbook window. In addition, a workbook can store chart sheets; a *chart sheet* displays a single chart and is also accessible by clicking a tab.

Newcomers to Excel are often intimidated by all the different elements that appear within Excel's window. After you become familiar with the various parts, it all starts to make sense, and you'll feel right at home.

Figure 12.1 shows you the more important bits and pieces of Excel. As you look at the figure, refer to Table 12.1 for a brief explanation of the items shown in the figure.

FIGURE 12.1

The Excel screen has many useful elements that you will use often.

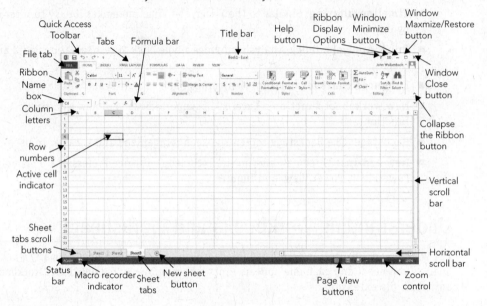

TABLE 12.1 Parts of the Excel Screen That You Need to Know

Name	Description
Active cell indicator	This dark outline indicates the currently active cell (one of the 17,179,869,184 cells on each worksheet).
Collapse the Ribbon button	Click this button to temporarily hide the Ribbon. Click it again to make the Ribbon remain visible.
Column letters	Letters range from A to XFD — one for each of the 16,384 columns in the worksheet. You can click a column heading to select an entire column of cells or drag a column border to change its width.
File tab	Click this button to open Backstage view, which contains many options for working with your document (including printing) and setting Excel options.
Formula bar	When you enter information or formulas into a cell, it appears in this bar.
Help button	Click this button to display the Excel Help system window.
Horizontal scroll bar	Use this tool to scroll the sheet horizontally.
Macro recorder indicator	Click to start recording a VBA macro. The icon changes while your actions are being recorded. Click again to stop recording.

Name box	This box displays the active cell address or the name of the selected cell, range, or object.
New sheet button	Add a new worksheet by clicking the New sheet button (which is displayed after the last sheet tab).
Page View buttons	Click these buttons to change the way the worksheet is displayed.
Quick Access Toolbar	This customizable toolbar holds commonly used commands. The Quick Access Toolbar is always visible, regardless of which tab is selected.
Ribbon	This is the main location for Excel commands. Clicking an item in the tab list changes the Ribbon that is displayed.
Ribbon Display Options	A drop-down control that offers three options related to displaying the Ribbon.
Row numbers	Numbers range from 1 to 1,048,576 — one for each row in the worksheet. You can click a row number to select an entire row of cells.
Sheet tabs	Each of these notebook-like tabs represents a different sheet in the workbook. A workbook can have any number of sheets, and each sheet has its name displayed in a sheet tab.
Sheet tab scroll buttons	Use these buttons to scroll the sheet tabs to display tabs that aren't visible. You can also right-click to get a list of sheets.
Status bar	This bar displays various messages, as well as the status of the Num Lock, Caps Lock, and Scroll Lock keys on your keyboard. It also shows summary information about the range of cells selected. Right-click the status bar to change the information displayed.
Tabs	Click these tabs to display different Ribbon commands, similar to a menu.
Title bar	This displays the name of the program and the name of the current workbook. It also by default holds the Quick Access Toolbar (on the left) and some control buttons that you can use to modify the window (on the right).
Vertical scroll bar	Use this to scroll the sheet vertically.
Window Close button	Click this button to close the active workbook window.
Window Maximize/ Restore button	Click this button to increase the workbook window's size to fill the entire screen. If the window is already maximized, clicking this button returns Excel's window to its prior size so that it no longer fills the entire screen.
Window Minimize button	Click this button to minimize the workbook window. The window displays as an icon in the Windows taskbar.
Zoom control	Use this to zoom your worksheet in and out.

12

Moving around a Worksheet

This section describes various ways to navigate the cells in a worksheet.

Every worksheet consists of rows (numbered 1 through 1,048,576) and columns (labeled A through XFD). Column labeling works like this: After column Z comes column AA, which is followed by AB, AC, and so on. After column AZ comes BA, BB, and so on. After column ZZ is AAA, AAB, and so on.

The intersection of a row and a column is a single cell, and each cell has a unique address made up of its column letter and row number. For example, the address of the upper-left cell is A1. The address of the cell at the lower right of a worksheet is XFD1048576.

At any given time, one cell is the *active cell*. The active cell is the cell that accepts keyboard input, and its contents can be edited. You can identify the active cell by its darker border, as shown in Figure 12.2. Its address appears in the Name box. Depending on the technique that you use to navigate through a workbook, you may or may not change the active cell when you navigate.

FIGURE 12.2

The active cell is the cell with the dark border — in this case, cell C8.

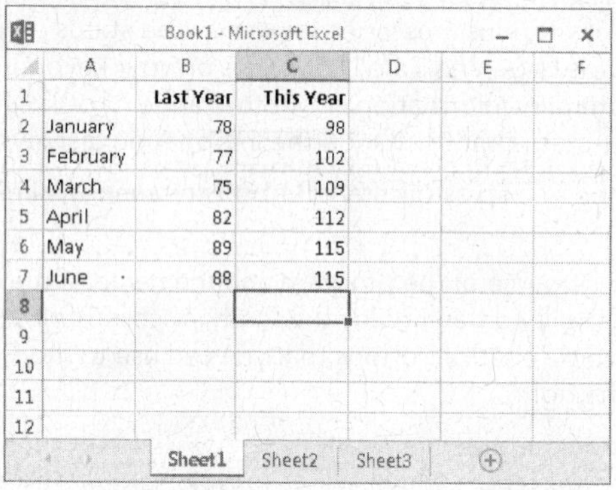

Notice that the row and column headings of the active cell appear in a different color to make it easier to identify the row and column of the active cell.

> **NOTE**
>
> Excel 2013 is also available in a version for devices such as tablets and phones. These devices use a touch interface. This book assumes the reader has a traditional keyboard and mouse in Excel — it doesn't cover the touch-related commands.

Navigating with your keyboard

Not surprisingly, you can use the standard navigational keys on your keyboard to move around a worksheet. These keys work just as you'd expect: The down arrow moves the active cell down one row, the right arrow moves it one column to the right, and so on. Page Up and Page Down move the active cell up or down one full window. (The actual number of rows moved depends on the number of rows displayed in the window.)

> **TIP**
>
> You can use the keyboard to scroll through the worksheet without changing the active cell by turning on Scroll Lock, which is useful if you need to view another area of your worksheet and then quickly return to your original location. Just press Scroll Lock and use the navigation keys to scroll through the worksheet. When you want to return to the original position (the active cell), press Ctrl+Backspace. Then, press Scroll Lock again to turn it off. When Scroll Lock is turned on, Excel displays `Scroll Lock` in the status bar at the bottom of the window.

The Num Lock key on your keyboard controls how the keys on the numeric keypad behave. When Num Lock is on, the keys on your numeric keypad generate numbers. Many keyboards have a separate set of navigation (arrow) keys located to the left of the numeric keypad. The state of the Num Lock key doesn't affect these keys.

Table 12.2 summarizes all the worksheet movement keys available in Excel.

TABLE 12.2 Excel Worksheet Movement Keys

Key	Action
Up Arrow	Moves the active cell up one row
Down Arrow	Moves the active cell down one row
Left Arrow or Shift+Tab	Moves the active cell one column to the left
Right Arrow or Tab	Moves the active cell one column to the right
Page Up	Moves the active cell up one screen
Page Down	Moves the active cell down one screen
Alt+Page Down	Moves the active cell right one screen
Alt+Page Up	Moves the active cell left one screen
Ctrl+Backspace	Scrolls the screen so that the active cell is visible
Ctrl+End	Moves the active cell to the intersection of the row with the lowermost entry (highest row number) on the worksheet and the column with the rightmost entry (highest column letter) on the worksheet

Continues

TABLE 12.2   *(continued)*

Key	Action
Up Arrow	Scrolls the screen up one row (active cell does not change)
Down Arrow	Scrolls the screen down one row (active cell does not change)
Left Arrow	Scrolls the screen left one column (active cell does not change)
Right Arrow	Scrolls the screen right one column (active cell does not change)

* With Scroll Lock on

Navigating with your mouse

To change the active cell by using the mouse, just click another cell, and it becomes the active cell. If the cell that you want to activate isn't visible in the workbook window, you can use the scroll bars to scroll the window in any direction. To scroll one cell, click either of the arrows on the scroll bar. To scroll by a complete screen, click either side of the scroll-bar's scroll box. You can also drag the scroll box for faster scrolling.

> **TIP**
>
> If your mouse has a wheel, you can use the mouse wheel to scroll vertically. Also, if you click the wheel and move the mouse in any direction, the worksheet scrolls automatically in that direction. The more you move the mouse, the faster the scrolling.

Press Ctrl while you use the mouse wheel to zoom the worksheet. If you prefer to use the mouse wheel to zoom the worksheet without pressing Ctrl, choose File ➪ Options and select the Advanced section. Under Editing options, click the Zoom on roll with IntelliMouse check box to check it.

Using the scroll bars or scrolling with your mouse doesn't change the active cell. It simply scrolls the worksheet. To change the active cell, you must click a new cell after scrolling.

Introducing Excel's Ribbon Tabs

In Office 2007, Microsoft made a dramatic change to the user interface. Traditional menus and toolbars were replaced with the Ribbon, a collection of icons at the top of the screen. The words above the icons are known as tabs: the Home tab, the Insert tab, and so on. Most users find that the Ribbon is easier to use than the old menu system; it can also be customized to make it even easier to use (see Appendix A, "Customizing Office.").

The Ribbon can either be hidden or visible (it's your choice). To toggle the Ribbon's visibility, press Ctrl+F1 (or double-click a tab at the top). If the Ribbon is hidden, it temporarily appears when you click a tab and hides itself when you click in the worksheet. The title bar has a control named Ribbon Display Options (next to the Help button). Click the control and choose one of three Ribbon options: Auto-hide Ribbon, Show Tabs, or Show Tabs and Commands.

Ribbon tabs

The commands available in the Ribbon vary, depending upon which tab is selected. The Ribbon is arranged into groups of related commands. Here's a quick overview of Excel's tabs:

- **Home:** You'll probably spend most of your time with the Home tab selected. This tab contains the basic Clipboard commands, formatting commands, style commands, commands to insert and delete rows or columns, plus an assortment of worksheet editing commands.

- **Insert:** Select this tab when you need to insert something in a worksheet — a table, a diagram, a chart, a symbol, and so on.

- **Page Layout:** This tab contains commands that affect the overall appearance of your worksheet, including some settings that deal with printing.

- **Formulas:** Use this tab to insert a formula, name a cell or a range, access the formula auditing tools, or control how Excel performs calculations.

- **Data:** Excel's data-related commands are on this tab, including data validation commands.

- **Review:** This tab contains tools to check spelling, translate words, add comments, or protect sheets.

- **View:** The View tab contains commands that control various aspects of how a sheet is viewed. Some commands on this tab are also available in the status bar.

- **Developer:** This tab isn't visible by default. It contains commands that are useful for programmers. To display the Developer tab, choose File ⇨ Options and then select Customize Ribbon. In the Customize the Ribbon section on the right, make sure Main Tabs is selected in the drop-down control, and place a check mark next to Developer.

- **Add-Ins:** This tab is visible only if you loaded an older workbook or add-in that customizes the menu or toolbars. Because menus and toolbars are no longer available in Excel 2013, these user interface customizations appear on the Add-Ins tab.

The preceding list contains the standard Ribbon tabs. Excel may display additional Ribbon tabs, resulting from add-ins or macros.

NOTE

The File tab doesn't offer a bar of commands like the other Ribbon tabs. Clicking the File tab displays a different screen (known as Backstage view), where you perform actions with your documents. This screen has commands along the left side. To exit the Backstage view, click the back arrow button in the upper-left corner.

The appearance of the commands on the Ribbon varies, depending on the width of the Excel window. When the Excel window is too narrow to display everything, the commands adapt; some of them might seem to be missing, but the commands are still available. Figure 12.3 shows the Home tab of the Ribbon with all controls fully visible. When you make the Excel window narrower or reduce your screen resolution, some groups display as a single button; however, if you click the button, all the group commands are available to you.

FIGURE 12.3

The Home tab of the Ribbon in Excel.

Contextual tabs

In addition to the standard tabs, Excel also includes *contextual tabs*. Whenever an object (such as a chart, a table, or a SmartArt diagram) is selected, specific tools for working with that object are made available in the Ribbon.

Figure 12.4 shows the contextual tabs that appear when a chart is selected. In this case, it has two contextual tabs: Chart Tools ⇨ Design and Chart Tools ⇨ Format. When contextual tabs appear, you can, of course, continue to use all the other tabs.

FIGURE 12.4

When you select an object, contextual tabs contain tools for working with that object.

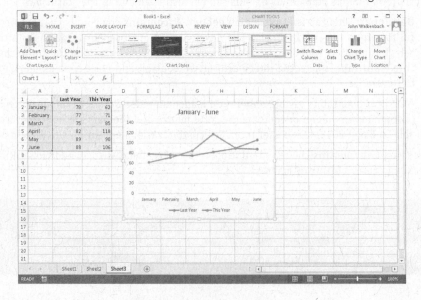

Creating Your First Excel Workbook

This section presents an introductory hands-on session with Excel. If you haven't used Excel, you may want to follow along on your computer to get a feel for how this software works.

In this example, you create a simple monthly sales projection table along with a chart.

Getting started on your worksheet

Start Excel and make sure that you have an empty workbook displayed by selecting Blank workbook from the Start screen. To create a new, blank workbook when Excel is already open, press Ctrl+N (the shortcut key for File ➪ New ➪ Blank Workbook).

The sales projection will consist of two columns of information. Column A will contain the month names, and column B will store the projected sales numbers. You start by entering some descriptive titles into the worksheet. Here's how to begin:

1. **Move the cell pointer to cell A1 (the upper-left cell in the worksheet) if needed by using the navigation (arrow) keys.** The Name box displays the cell's address.

2. **Type Month into cell A1 and press Enter.** Depending on your setup, either Excel moves the cell pointer to a different cell or the pointer remains in cell A1.

3. **Move the cell pointer to B1, type Projected Sales, and press Enter.** The text extends beyond the cell width, but don't worry about that for now.

Filling in the month names

In this step, you enter the month names in column A.

1. **Move the cell pointer to A2 and type** Jan **(an abbreviation for January).** At this point, you can enter the other month name abbreviations manually or you can let Excel do some of the work by taking advantage of the AutoFill feature.

2. **Make sure that cell A2 is selected.** Notice that the active cell is displayed with a heavy outline. At the bottom-right corner of the outline, you'll see a small square known as the *fill handle*. Move your mouse pointer over the fill handle, click, and drag down until you've highlighted from cell A2 down to cell A13.

3. **Release the mouse button, and Excel automatically fills in the month names.**

Your worksheet should resemble the one shown in Figure 12.5.

FIGURE 12.5

Your worksheet, after entering the column headings and month names

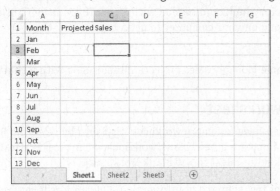

Entering the sales data

Next, you provide the sales projection numbers in column B. Assume that January's sales are projected to be $50,000, and that sales will increase by 3.5 percent in each subsequent month.

1. **Move the cell pointer to B2 and type** 50000, **the projected sales for January.** You could type a dollar sign and comma to make the number more legible, but you do the number formatting a bit later.

2. **To enter a formula to calculate the projected sales for February, move to cell B3 and type the following:** =B2*103.5%. When you press Enter, the cell displays 51750. The formula returns the contents of cell B2, multiplied by 103.5%. In other words, February sales are projected to be 103.5% of the January sales — a 3.5% increase.

3. **The projected sales for subsequent months use a similar formula, but rather than retype the formula for each cell in column B, take advantage of the Auto Fill feature.** Make sure that cell B3 is selected. Click the cell's fill handle, drag down to cell B13, and release the mouse button.

At this point, your worksheet should resemble the one shown in Figure 12.6. Keep in mind that, except for cell B2, the values in column B are calculated *with formulas*. To demonstrate, try changing the projected sales value for the initial month, January (in cell B2). You'll find that the formulas recalculate and return different values. These formulas all depend on the initial value in cell B2, though.

FIGURE 12.6

Your worksheet, after creating the formulas

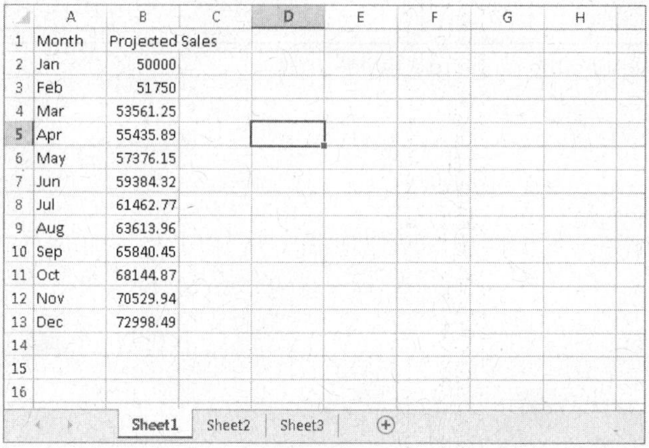

	A	B	C	D	E	F	G	H
1	Month	Projected Sales						
2	Jan	50000						
3	Feb	51750						
4	Mar	53561.25						
5	Apr	55435.89						
6	May	57376.15						
7	Jun	59384.32						
8	Jul	61462.77						
9	Aug	63613.96						
10	Sep	65840.45						
11	Oct	68144.87						
12	Nov	70529.94						
13	Dec	72998.49						
14								
15								
16								

Sheet1 | Sheet2 | Sheet3 | (+)

Formatting the numbers

The values in the worksheet are difficult to read because they aren't formatted. In this step, you apply a number format to make the numbers easier to read and more consistent in appearance:

1. **Select the numbers by dragging from cell B2 down to cell B13.** Don't drag the fill handle this time, though, because you're selecting cells, not filling a range.

2. **On the Ribbon, click Home. In the Number group, click the drop-down Number Format control (it initially displays General), and select Currency from the list.** The numbers now display with a currency symbol and two decimal places. Much better, but the decimal places aren't necessary for this type of projection.

3. **Make sure the range B2:B13 is selected, choose Home ⇨ Number, and click the Decrease Decimal button.** One of the decimal places disappears. Click that button a second time, and the values are displayed with no decimal places.

Making your worksheet look a bit fancier

At this point, you have a functional worksheet, but it could use some help in the appearance department. Converting this range to an "official" (and attractive) Excel table is a snap:

1. **Activate any cell within the range A1:B13.**

2. **Choose Insert ⇨ Tables ⇨ Table.** Excel displays the Create Table dialog box to make sure that it guessed the range properly.

3. **Click OK to close the Create Table dialog box.** Excel applies its default table formatting and displays its Table Tools ⇨ Design contextual tab.

Your worksheet should look like Figure 12.7.

FIGURE 12.7

Your worksheet, after converting the range to a table

If you don't like the default table style, just select another one from the Table Tools ➪ Design ➪ Table Styles group. Notice that you can get a preview of different table styles by moving your mouse over the Ribbon. When you find one you like, click it, and the style will be applied to your table.

Summing the values

The worksheet displays the monthly projected sales, but what about the total projected sales for the year? Because this range is a table, it's simple:

1. **Activate any cell in the table.**

2. **Choose Table Tools ➪ Design ➪ Table Style Options ➪ Total Row.** Excel automatically adds a new row to the bottom of your table, including a formula that calculates the total of the Projected Sales column.

3. **If you'd prefer to see a different summary formula (for example, average), click cell B14 and choose a different summary formula from the drop-down list.**

Creating a chart

How about a chart that shows the projected sales for each month?

1. **Activate any cell in the table.**

2. **Choose Insert ➪ Charts ➪ Recommended Charts.** Excel displays some suggested chart type options.

414

3. **In the Insert Chart dialog box, click the second recommended chart (a column chart), and click OK.** Excel inserts the chart in the center of the window. To move the chart to another location, click its border and drag it.

4. **Click the chart and choose a style using the Chart Tools⇨Design⇨Chart Styles options.**

Figure 12.8 shows the worksheet with a column chart. Your chart may look different, depending on the chart style you selected.

FIGURE 12.8

The table and chart

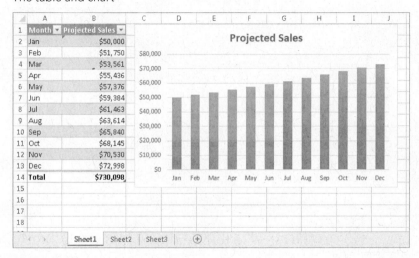

Printing your worksheet

Printing your worksheet is very easy (assuming that you have a printer attached and that it works properly).

1. **Make sure that the chart isn't selected.** If a chart is selected, the chart will print on a page by itself. To deselect the chart, just press Esc or click any cell.

2. **To make use of Excel's handy Page Layout view, click the Page Layout button on the right side of the status bar.** Excel displays the worksheet page-by-page so that you can easily see how your printed output will look. Figure 12.9 shows the worksheet zoomed out to show a complete page. In Page Layout view, you can tell immediately whether the chart is too wide to fit on one page. If the chart is too wide, drag a corner of the chart to resize it or just move the chart below the table of numbers.

FIGURE 12.9

Viewing the worksheet in Page Layout view

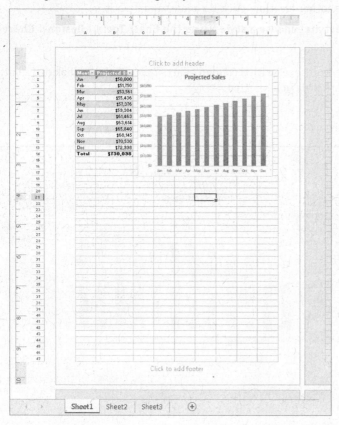

3. **When you're ready to print, choose File ⇨ Print.** At this point, you can change some print settings. For example, you can choose to print in landscape rather than portrait orientation. Make the change, and you see the result in the preview window.

4. **When you're satisfied, click the Print button in the upper-left corner.** The page is printed, and you're returned to your workbook.

Saving your workbook

Until now, everything that you've done has occurred in your computer's memory. If the power should fail, all may be lost — unless Excel's AutoRecover feature happened to kick in. It's time to save your work to a file on your hard drive.

1. **Click the Save button on the Quick Access Toolbar.** (This button looks like an old-fashioned floppy disk, popular in the previous century.) Because the workbook hasn't been saved yet and still has its default name, Excel responds with a Backstage screen that lets you choose the location for the workbook file. The Backstage screen lets you save the file to an online location or to your local computer.

2. **Select Computer, and then click Browse.** Excel displays the Save As dialog box.

3. **In the File name text box, enter a name (such as Monthly Sales Projection), and then click Save or press Enter.** Excel saves the workbook as a file. The workbook remains open so that you can work with it some more.

> **NOTE**
>
> By default, Excel saves a backup copy of your work automatically every ten minutes. To adjust the AutoRecover setting (or turn it off), choose File ➪ Options, click the Save tab, and check or clear Save AutoRecover information every *X* minutes as needed. Click OK to apply your change. However, you should never rely on Excel's AutoRecover feature. Saving your work frequently is a good idea.

12

If you've followed along, you may have realized that creating this workbook was not difficult. But, of course, you've barely scratched the surface of Excel. The remainder of this book covers these tasks (and many, many more) in much greater detail.

Summary

This chapter touched on the new features of the Excel 2013 spreadsheet program, as well as a few basics to get you started. At this point, you should be able to:

- Name a few ways to use Excel.
- Talk about some of Excel's exciting new features.
- Understand the difference between a workbook and worksheet.
- Move around a worksheet with the mouse or keyboard.
- Work with the Ribbon.
- Create and save an example workbook file.

Entering and Editing Worksheet Data

IN THIS CHAPTER

Understanding the types of data you can use

Entering text and values into your worksheets, including using the new Flash Fill feature

Entering dates and times into your worksheets

Modifying and editing information

Using built-in number formats

This chapter describes what you need to know about entering and modifying data in your worksheets. As you see, Excel doesn't treat all data equally. Therefore, you need to learn about the various types of data that you can use in an Excel worksheet.

Exploring Data Types

An Excel workbook file can hold any number of worksheets, and each worksheet is made up of more than 17 billion cells. A cell can hold any of three basic types of data:

- A numeric value
- Text
- A formula

A worksheet can also hold charts, diagrams, pictures, buttons, and other objects. These objects aren't contained in cells. Instead, they reside on the worksheet's *draw layer,* which is an invisible layer on top of each worksheet.

Understanding numeric values

Numeric values represent a quantity of some type: sales amounts, number of employees, atomic weights, test scores, and so on. Values also can be dates (such as Feb-26-2013) or times (such as 3:24 a.m.).

NOTE
Excel can display values in many different formats. In the "Applying Number Formatting" section, later in this chapter, you see how different format options can affect the display of numeric values.

Excel's Numeric Limitations

You may be curious about the types of values that Excel can handle. In other words, how large can a number be? And how accurate are large numbers?

Excel's numbers are precise up to 15 digits. For example, if you enter a large value, such as 123,456,789,123,456,789 (18 digits), Excel actually stores it with only 15 digits of precision. This 18-digit number displays as 123,456,789,123,456,000. This precision may seem quite limiting, but in practice, it rarely causes any problems.

One situation in which the 15-digit accuracy can cause a problem is when entering credit card numbers. Most credit card numbers are 16 digits, but Excel can handle only 15 digits, so it substitutes a zero for the last credit card digit. Even worse, you may not even realize that Excel made the card number invalid. The solution? Enter the credit card numbers as text. The easiest way is to preformat the cell as Text (choose Home➪Number and choose Text from the Number Format drop-down list). Or you can precede the credit card number with an apostrophe. Either method prevents Excel from interpreting the entry as a number.

Here are some of Excel's other numeric limits:

- **Largest positive number:** 9.9E+307
- **Smallest negative number:** –9.9E+307
- **Smallest positive number:** 1E–307
- **Largest negative number:** –1E–307

These numbers are expressed in scientific notation. For example, the largest positive number is "9.9 times 10 to the 307th power" — in other words, 99 followed by 306 zeros. Keep in mind, though, that this number has only 15 digits of accuracy.

Understanding text entries

Most worksheets also include text in some of the cells. Text can serve as data (for example, a list of employee names), labels for values, headings for columns, or instructions about the worksheet. Text is often used to clarify what the values in a worksheet mean or where the numbers came from.

Text that begins with a number is still considered text. For example, if you type **12 Employees** into a cell, Excel considers the entry to be text rather than a numeric value. Consequently, you can't use this cell for numeric calculations. If you need to indicate that the number 12 refers to employees, enter **12** into a cell and then type **Employees** into the cell to the right.

Understanding formulas

Formulas are what make a spreadsheet a spreadsheet. Excel enables you to enter flexible formulas that use the values (or even text) in cells to calculate a result. When you enter a formula into a cell, the formula's result appears in the cell. If you change any of the cells used by a formula, the formula recalculates and shows the new result.

Formulas can be simple mathematical expressions, or they can use some of the powerful functions that are built into Excel. Figure 13.1 shows an Excel worksheet set up to calculate a monthly loan payment. The worksheet contains values, text, and formulas. The cells in column A contain text. Column B contains four values and two formulas. The formulas are in cells B6 and B10. Column D, for reference, shows the actual contents of the cells in column B.

FIGURE 13.1

You can use values, text, and formulas to create useful Excel worksheets.

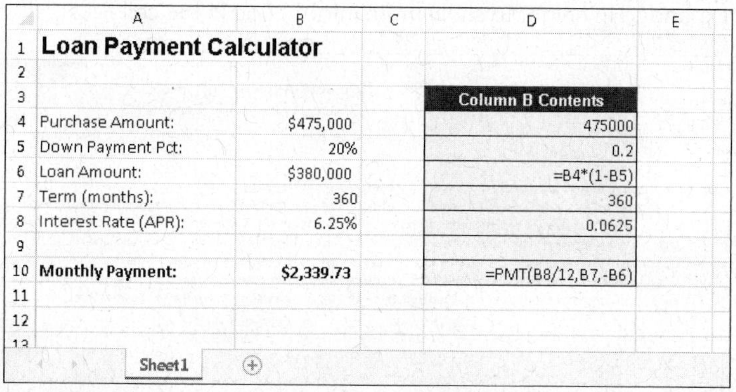

	A	B	C	D	E
1	**Loan Payment Calculator**				
2					
3				**Column B Contents**	
4	Purchase Amount:	$475,000		475000	
5	Down Payment Pct:	20%		0.2	
6	Loan Amount:	$380,000		=B4*(1-B5)	
7	Term (months):	360		360	
8	Interest Rate (APR):	6.25%		0.0625	
9					
10	**Monthly Payment:**	$2,339.73		=PMT(B8/12,B7,-B6)	
11					
12					
13					

Sheet1 ⊕

> **NOTE**
> You can find out much more about formulas in Chapter 15, "Introducing Formulas and Functions."

Entering Text and Values into Your Worksheets

To enter a numeric value into a cell, move the cell pointer to the appropriate cell, type the value, and then press Enter or one of the navigation keys. The value is displayed in the cell and also appears in the Formula bar when the cell is selected. You can include decimal

13

points and currency symbols when entering values, along with plus signs, minus signs, and commas (to separate thousands). If you precede a value with a minus sign or enclose it in parentheses, Excel considers it to be a negative number.

Entering text into a cell is just as easy as entering a value: Activate the cell, type the text, and then press Enter or a navigation key. A cell can contain a maximum of about 32,000 characters — more than enough to hold a typical chapter in this book. Even though a cell can hold a huge number of characters, you'll find that it's not possible to actually display all these characters.

TIP

If you type an exceptionally long text entry into a cell, the Formula bar may not show all the text. To display more of the text in the Formula bar, click the bottom of the Formula bar and drag down to increase the height (see Figure 13.2). Also useful is the Ctrl+Shift+U keyboard shortcut. Pressing this key combination toggles the height of the formula bar to show either one row, or the previous size.

FIGURE 13.2

The Formula bar, expanded in height to show more information in the cell

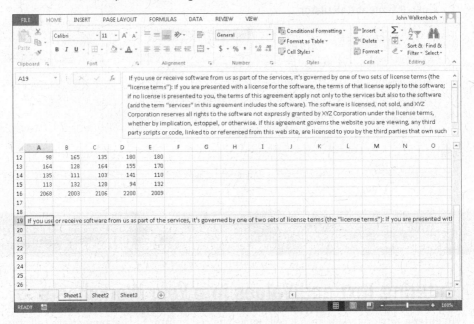

What happens when you enter text that's longer than its column's current width? If the cells to the immediate right are blank, Excel displays the text in its entirety, appearing to spill the entry into adjacent cells. If an adjacent cell isn't blank, Excel displays as much of the text as possible. (The full text is contained in the cell; it's just not displayed.) If you need to display a long text string in a cell that's adjacent to a nonblank cell, you have a few choices:

- Edit your text to make it shorter.
- Increase the width of the column (drag the border in the column letter display).
- Use a smaller font.
- Wrap the text within the cell so that it occupies more than one line. Choose Home ⇨ Alignment ⇨ Wrap Text to toggle wrapping on and off for the selected cell or range.

Entering Dates and Times into Your Worksheets

Excel treats dates and times as special types of numeric values. Dates and times are values that are formatted so that they *appear* as dates or times. If you work with dates and times, you need to understand Excel's date and time system.

Entering date values

Excel handles dates by using a serial number system. The earliest date that Excel understands is January 1, 1900. This date has a serial number of 1. January 2, 1900, has a serial number of 2, and so on. This system makes it easy to deal with dates in formulas. For example, you can enter a formula to calculate the number of days between two dates.

Most of the time, you don't have to be concerned with Excel's serial number date system. You can simply enter a date in a common date format, and Excel takes care of the details behind the scenes. For example, if you need to enter June 1, 2013, you can enter the date by typing **June 1, 2013** (or use any of several different date formats). Excel interprets your entry and stores the value 41426, which is the serial number for that date.

> **NOTE**
>
> The date examples in this book use the U.S. English system. Your Windows regional settings will affect how Excel interprets a date you've entered. For example, depending on your regional date settings, **June 1, 2013** may be interpreted as text rather than a date. In such a case, you need to enter the date in a format that corresponds to your regional date settings — for example, **1 June, 2013**.

> **NOTE**
>
> For more information about working with dates and times, see Chapter 16, "Working with Dates and Times."

Entering time values

When you work with times, you extend Excel's date serial number system to include decimals. In other words, Excel works with times by using fractional days. For example, the date serial number for June 1, 2013, is 41426. Noon on June 1, 2013 (halfway through the day), is represented internally as 41426.5 because the time fraction is added to the date serial number to get the full date/time serial number.

Again, you normally don't have to be concerned with these serial numbers or fractional serial numbers for times. Just enter the time into a cell in a recognized format. In this case, type **June 1, 2013 12:00**.

Modifying Cell Contents

After you enter a value or text into a cell, you can modify it in several ways:

- Delete the cell's contents.
- Replace the cell's contents with something else.
- Edit the cell's contents.

> **NOTE**
>
> You can also modify a cell by changing its formatting. However, formatting a cell affects only a cell's appearance. Formatting doesn't affect the cell's contents. Later sections in this chapter cover formatting.

Deleting the contents of a cell

To delete the contents of a cell, just click the cell and press the Delete key. To delete more than one cell, select all the cells that you want to delete and then press Delete. Pressing Delete removes the cell's contents but doesn't remove any formatting (such as bold, italic, or a different number format) that you may have applied to the cell.

For more control over what gets deleted, you can choose Home ⇨ Editing ⇨ Clear. This command's drop-down list has five choices:

- **Clear All:** Clears everything from the cell — its contents, its formatting, and its cell comment (if it has one)
- **Clear Formats:** Clears only the formatting and leaves the value, text, or formula
- **Clear Contents:** Clears only the cell's contents and leaves the formatting
- **Clear Comments:** Clears the comment (if one exists) attached to the cell
- **Clear Hyperlinks:** Removes hyperlinks contained in the selected cells. The text remains, but the cell no longer functions as a clickable hyperlink

> **NOTE**
>
> Clearing formats doesn't clear the background colors in a range that has been designated as a table unless you've replaced the table style background colors manually.

Replacing the contents of a cell

To replace the contents of a cell with something else, just activate the cell and type your new entry, which replaces the previous contents. Any formatting applied to the cell remains in place and is applied to the new content.

You can also replace cell contents by dragging and dropping or by pasting data from the Clipboard. In both cases, the cell formatting will be replaced by the format of the new data. To avoid pasting formatting, choose Home ⇨ Clipboard ⇨ Paste ⇨ Values (V), or Home ⇨ Clipboard ⇨ Paste ⇨ Formulas (F).

Editing the contents of a cell

If the cell contains only a few characters, replacing its contents by typing new data usually is easiest. However, if the cell contains lengthy text or a complex formula and you need to make only a slight modification, you probably want to edit the cell rather than re-enter information.

When you want to edit the contents of a cell, you can use one of the following ways to enter cell-edit mode:

- **Double-click the cell to edit the cell contents directly in the cell.**
- **Select the cell and press F2 to edit the cell contents directly in the cell.**
- **Select the cell that you want to edit and then click inside the Formula bar to edit the cell contents in the Formula bar.**

You can use whichever method you prefer. Some people find editing directly in the cell easier; others prefer to use the Formula bar to edit a cell.

> **NOTE**
>
> The Advanced tab of the Excel Options dialog box contains a section called Editing options. These settings affect how editing works. (To access this dialog box, choose File ➪ Options.) If the Allow editing directly in cells option isn't enabled, you can't edit a cell by double-clicking. In addition, pressing F2 allows you to edit the cell in the Formula bar (not directly in the cell).

All these methods cause Excel to go into *edit mode*. (The word *Edit* appears at the left side of the status bar at the bottom of the screen.) When Excel is in edit mode, the Formula bar enables two icons: Cancel (the X) and Enter (the check mark). Figure 13.3 shows these two icons. Clicking the Cancel icon cancels editing without changing the cell's contents. (Pressing Esc has the same effect.) Clicking the Enter icon completes the editing and enters the modified contents into the cell. (Pressing Enter has the same effect.)

FIGURE 13.3

While editing a cell, the Formula bar enables two new icons: Cancel (X) and Enter (check mark).

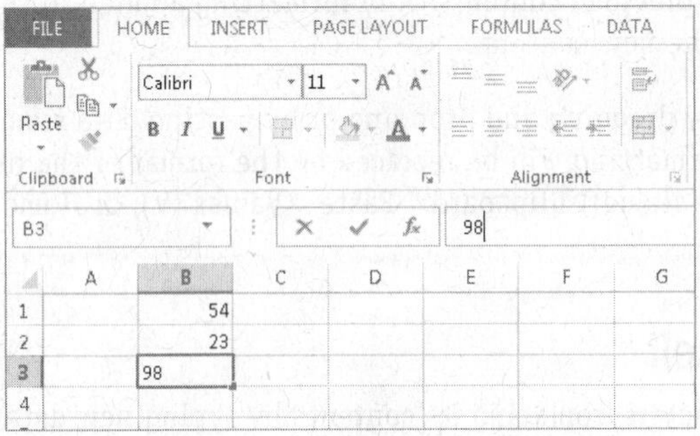

When you begin editing a cell, the insertion point appears as a vertical bar, and you can perform the following tasks:

- **Add new characters at the location of the insertion point.** Move the insertion point by:
  - Using the navigation keys to move within the cell
  - Pressing Home to move the insertion point to the beginning of the cell
  - Pressing End to move the insertion point to the end of the cell
- **Select multiple characters.** Press Shift while you use the navigation keys.
- **Select characters while you're editing a cell.** Use the mouse. Just click and drag the mouse pointer over the characters that you want to select.

Learning some handy data-entry techniques

You can simplify the process of entering information into your Excel worksheets and make your work go quite a bit faster by using a number of useful tricks, described in the following sections.

Automatically moving the cell pointer after entering data

By default, Excel automatically moves the cell pointer to the next cell down when you press the Enter key after entering data into a cell. (The exception is if you have previously used Tab to make entries across a row; when you press Enter in that case, the cell pointer moves to the next row, in the first column where you entered data in the row above.) To change this setting, choose File ⇨ Options and click the Advanced tab (see Figure 13.4). The check box that controls this behavior is labeled After pressing Enter, move selection. If you enable this option, you can choose the direction in which the cell pointer moves (down, left, up, or right).

FIGURE 13.4

You can use the Advanced tab in Excel Options to select a number of helpful input option settings.

Your choice is completely a matter of personal preference. I prefer to keep this option turned off. When entering data, I use the navigation keys rather than the Enter key (see the next section).

Using navigation keys instead of pressing Enter

Instead of pressing the Enter key when you're finished making a cell entry, you also can use any of the navigation keys to complete the entry. Not surprisingly, these navigation keys send you in the direction that you indicate. For example, if you're entering data in a row, press the right-arrow (→) key rather than Enter. The other arrow keys work as expected, and you can even use Page Up and Page Down.

Selecting a range of input cells before entering data

When a range of cells is selected, Excel automatically moves the cell pointer to the next cell in the range when you press Enter. If the selection consists of multiple rows, Excel moves down the column; when it reaches the end of the selection in the column, it moves to the first selected cell in the next column.

To skip a cell, just press Enter without entering anything. To go backward, press Shift+Enter. If you prefer to enter the data by rows rather than by columns, press Tab rather than Enter. Excel continues to cycle through the selected range until you select a cell outside of the range.

Using Ctrl+Enter to place information into multiple cells simultaneously

If you need to enter the same data into multiple cells, Excel offers a handy shortcut. Select all the cells that you want to contain the data, enter the value, text, or formula, and then press Ctrl+Enter. The same information is inserted into each cell in the selection.

Entering decimal points automatically

If you need to enter lots of numbers with a fixed number of decimal places, Excel has a useful tool that works like some old adding machines. Access the Excel Options dialog box and click the Advanced tab. Select the Automatically Insert a Decimal Point check box and make sure that the Places box is set for the correct number of decimal places for the data you need to enter.

When this option is set, Excel supplies the decimal points for you automatically. For example, if you specify two decimal places, entering **12345** into a cell is interpreted as 123.45. To restore things to normal, just clear the Automatically Insert a Decimal Point check box in the Excel Options dialog box. Changing this setting doesn't affect any values that you already entered.

> **CAUTION**
> The fixed decimal places option is a global setting and applies to all workbooks (not just the active workbook). If you forget that this option is turned on, you can easily end up entering incorrect values — or cause some major confusion if someone else uses your computer.

Using Auto Fill to enter a series of values

The Excel Auto Fill feature makes inserting a series of values or text items in a range of cells easy. It uses the Auto Fill handle (the small box at the lower right of the active cell). You can drag the Auto Fill handle to copy the cell or automatically complete a series.

Figure 13.5 shows an example. I entered **1** into cell A1 and **3** into cell A2. Then I selected both cells and dragged down the fill handle to create a linear series of odd numbers. The figure also shows an icon that, when clicked, displays some additional Auto Fill options.

FIGURE 13.5

This series was created by using Auto Fill.

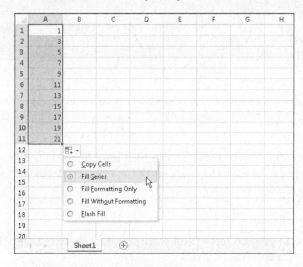

13

TIP

If you drag the Auto Fill handle while you press and hold the right mouse button, Excel displays a shortcut menu with additional fill options.

Using AutoComplete to automate data entry

The Excel AutoComplete feature makes entering the same text into multiple cells easy. With AutoComplete, you type the first few letters of a text entry into a cell, and Excel automatically completes the entry based on other entries that you already made in the column. Besides reducing typing, this feature also ensures that your entries are spelled correctly and are consistent.

Here's how it works: Suppose that you're entering product information in a column. One of your products is named Widgets. The first time that you enter **Widgets** into a cell, Excel remembers it. Later, when you start typing **Widgets** in that same column, Excel recognizes it by the first few letters and finishes typing it for you. Just press Enter, and you're done. To override the suggestion, just keep typing.

AutoComplete also changes the case of letters for you automatically. If you start entering **widgets** (with a lowercase *w*) in the second entry, Excel makes the *w* uppercase to be consistent with the previous entry in the column.

> **TIP**
> You also can access a mouse-oriented version of AutoComplete by right-clicking the cell and choosing Pick from Drop-down List from the shortcut menu. Excel then displays a drop-down box that has all the text entries in the current column, and you just click the one that you want.

Keep in mind that AutoComplete works only within a contiguous column of cells. If you have a blank row, for example, AutoComplete identifies only the cell contents below the blank row.

If you find the AutoComplete feature distracting, you can turn it off by using the Advanced tab of the Excel Options dialog box. Remove the check mark from the check box labeled Enable AutoComplete for cell values.

Forcing text to appear on a new line within a cell

If you have lengthy text in a cell, you can force Excel to display it in multiple lines within the cell: Press Alt+Enter to start a new line in a cell.

When you add a line break, Excel automatically changes the cell's format to Wrap Text. But unlike normal text wrap, your manual line break forces Excel to break the text at a specific place within the text, which gives you more precise control over the appearance of the text than if you rely on automatic text wrapping.

> **TIP**
> To remove a manual line break, edit the cell and press Delete when the insertion point is located at the end of the line that contains the manual line break. You won't see any symbol to indicate the position of the manual line break, but the text that follows it will move up when the line break is deleted.

Using AutoCorrect for shorthand data entry

You can use the AutoCorrect feature to create shortcuts for commonly used words or phrases. For example, if you work for a company named Consolidated Data Processing Corporation, you can create an AutoCorrect entry for an abbreviation, such as *cdp*. Then, whenever you type **cdp**, Excel automatically changes it to Consolidated Data Processing Corporation.

Excel includes quite a few built-in AutoCorrect terms (mostly to correct common misspellings), and you can add your own. To set up your custom AutoCorrect entries, access the Excel Options dialog box (choose File ⇨ Options) and click the Proofing tab. Then click the AutoCorrect Options button to display the AutoCorrect dialog box. In the dialog box, click the AutoCorrect tab, check the option labeled Replace Text as You Type, and then enter your custom entries. (Figure 13.6 shows an example.) You can set up as many custom entries as you like. Just be careful not to use an abbreviation that might appear normally in your text.

FIGURE 13.6

AutoCorrect allows you to create shorthand abbreviations for text you enter often.

TIP

Excel shares your AutoCorrect list with other Microsoft Office applications. For example, any AutoCorrect entries you created in Word also work in Excel.

Entering numbers with fractions

To enter a fractional value into a cell, leave a space between the whole number and the fraction. For example, to enter 6 7/8, enter 6 7/8 and then press Enter. When you select the cell, 6.875 appears in the Formula bar, and the cell entry appears as a fraction. If you have a fraction only (for example, 1/8), you must enter a zero first, like this — **0 1/8** — or Excel will likely assume that you're entering a date. When you select the cell and look at the Formula bar, you see 0.125. In the cell, you see 1/8.

Using a form for data entry

Many people use Excel to manage lists in which the information is arranged in rows. Excel offers a simple way to work with this type of data through the use of a data entry form that Excel can create automatically. This data form works with either a normal range of data, or with a range that has been designated as a table (choose Insert ⇨ Tables ⇨ Table). Figure 13.7 shows an example.

FIGURE 13.7

Excel's built-in data form can simplify many data-entry tasks.

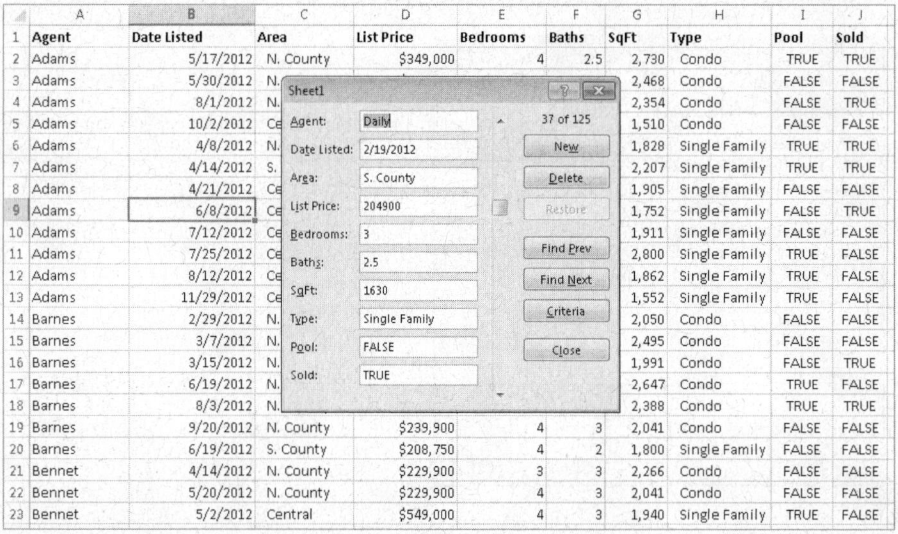

Unfortunately, the command to access the data form is not on the Ribbon. To use the data form, you must add it to your Quick Access Toolbar or add it to the Ribbon. The following instructions describe how to add this command to your Quick Access Toolbar:

1. **Right-click the Quick Access Toolbar and choose Customize Quick Access Toolbar.** The Quick Access Toolbar panel of the Excel Options dialog box appears.

2. **In the Choose commands from drop-down list, choose Commands Not in the Ribbon.**

3. **In the list box on the left, select Form.**

4. **Click the Add button to add the selected command to your Quick Access Toolbar.**

5. **Click OK to close the Excel Options dialog box.**

After performing these steps, a new icon appears on your Quick Access Toolbar.

To use a data entry form, follow these steps:

1. **Arrange your data so that Excel can recognize it as a table by entering headings for the columns in the first row of your data entry range.**

2. **Select any cell in the table and click the Form button on your Quick Access Toolbar.** Excel displays a dialog box customized to your data (refer to Figure 13.7).

3. **Fill in the information.** Press Tab to move between the text boxes. If a cell contains a formula, the formula result appears as text (not as an edit box). In other words, you can't modify formulas using the data entry form.

4. **When you complete the data form, click the New button.** Excel enters the data into a row in the worksheet and clears the dialog box for the next row of data.

You can also use the form to edit existing data.

Entering the current date or time into a cell

If you need to date-stamp or time-stamp your worksheet, Excel provides two shortcut keys that do this task for you:

- **Current date:** Ctrl+; (semicolon)
- **Current time:** Ctrl+Shift+; (semicolon)

The date and time are from the system time in your computer. If the date or time isn't correct in Excel, use the Windows Control Panel to make the adjustment.

> **NOTE**
>
> When you use either of these shortcuts to enter a date or time into your worksheet, Excel enters a static value into the worksheet. In other words, the date or time entered doesn't change when the worksheet is recalculated. In most cases, this setup is probably what you want, but you should be aware of this limitation. If you want the date or time display to update, use one of these formulas:
>
> ```
> =TODAY()
> =NOW()
> ```

Using Flash Fill

The Text to Columns Wizard works well for many types of data. But sometimes you'll encounter data that can't be parsed by that wizard. For example, the Text to Columns Wizard is useless if you have variable-width data that doesn't have delimiters. In such a case, the Flash Fill feature might save the day. But keep in mind that Flash Fill works successfully only when the data is *very* consistent.

NOTE
Flash Fill is a new feature in Excel 2013.

Flash Fill uses pattern recognition to extract data (and also concatenate data). Just enter a few examples in a column that's adjacent to the data, and choose Data⇨Data Tools⇨Flash Fill (or press Ctrl+E). Excel analyzes the examples and attempts to fill in the remaining cells. If Excel didn't recognize the pattern you had in mind, press Ctrl+Z, add another example or two, and try again.

Figure 13.8 shows a worksheet with some text in a single column. The goal is to extract the number from each cell and put it into a separate cell. The Text to Columns Wizard can't do it because the space delimiters aren't consistent. It might be possible to write an array formula, but it would be very complicated.

FIGURE 13.8

The goal is to extract the numbers in column A.

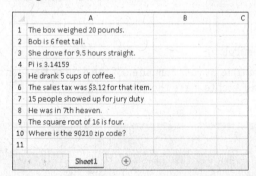

To try using Flash Fill, activate cell B1 and type the first number (**20**). Move to B2, and type the second number (**6**). Can Flash Fill identify the remaining numbers and fill them in? Choose Data⇨Data Tools⇨Flash Fill or Home⇨Editing⇨Fill⇨Flash Fill (or press Ctrl+E) and Excel fills in the remaining cells in a flash. Figure 13.9 shows the result.

FIGURE 13.9

Using manually entered examples in B1 and B2, Excel makes some incorrect guesses.

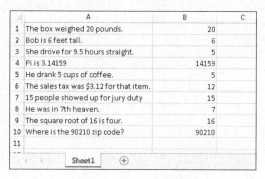

As you see, Excel identified most of the values. Accuracy increases if you provide more examples. For example, provide an example of a decimal number. Delete the suggested values, enter **3.12** in cell B6, and press Ctrl+E. This time, Excel gets them all correct (see Figure 13.10).

FIGURE 13.10

After you enter an example of a decimal number, Excel gets them all correct.

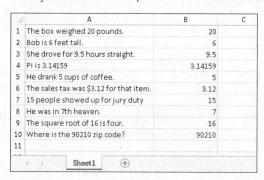

This simple example demonstrates two important points:

- **You must examine your data very carefully after using Flash Fill.** Just because the first few rows are correct, you can't assume that Flash Fill worked correctly for all rows.

- **Flash Fill increases accuracy when you provide more examples.**

Figure 13.11 shows another example, names in column A. The goal is to extract the first, last, and middle name (if it has one). In column B Excel successfully gets all the first names using only two examples (Mark and Tim). Plus, it successfully extracted all the last names (column C), using Russell and Colman. Extracting the middle names or initials (column D) eluded me until I provided examples that included a space on either side of the middle name).

FIGURE 13.11

Using Flash Fill to split names

	A	B	C	D	E
1	Mark Russell	Mark	Russell		
2	Tim Colman	Tim	Colman		
3	Sam Daniel Bains	Sam	Bains	Daniel	
4	Fred James Foster	Fred	Foster	James	
5	James J. Wehr	James	Wehr	J.	
6	Mitch Nicholls	Mitch	Nicholls		
7	Neal McCaslin	Neal	McCaslin		
8	Ned Poulakis	Ned	Poulakis		
9	Paul T. Wingfield	Paul	Wingfield	T.	
10	Peter Gans	Peter	Gans		
11	Ron E. Hoffman	Ron	Hoffman	E.	
12	Julia Hayes	Julia	Hayes		
13	Richard P Light	Richard	Light	P	
14	Ray Walker	Ray	Walker		
15	Robert F. Mahaney	Robert	Mahaney	F.	
16	Robert Fist	Robert	Fist		
17					

Sheet1   Sheet2   (+)

To summarize, Excel's new Flash Fill is an interesting idea, but it seems to work reliably only if the data is very consistent. Even when you think it worked correctly, make sure you examine the results carefully. And think twice before trusting it with important data. There's no way to document how the data was extracted. But the main limitation is that (unlike formulas) Flash Fill is not a dynamic technique. If your data changes, the flash-filled column does not update.

> **NOTE**
>
> You can also use the Flash Fill feature to create new data from multiple columns. Just provide a few examples of how you want the data combined, and Excel will figure out the pattern and fill in the column. Using Flash Fill to *create* data seems to work much better than using it to *extract* data. But then again, it's also easier to create formulas to create data from existing columns.

Applying Number Formatting

Number formatting refers to the process of changing the appearance of values contained in cells. Excel provides a wide variety of number formatting options. In the following sections, you see how to use many of Excel's formatting options to quickly improve the appearance of your worksheets.

Values that you enter into cells normally are unformatted. In other words, they simply consist of a string of numerals. Typically, you want to format the numbers so that they're easier to read or are more consistent in terms of the number of decimal places shown.

Figure 13.12 shows a worksheet that has two columns of values. The first column consists of unformatted values. The cells in the second column are formatted to make the values easier to read. The third column describes the type of formatting applied.

FIGURE 13.12

Use numeric formatting to make it easier to understand what the values in the worksheet represent.

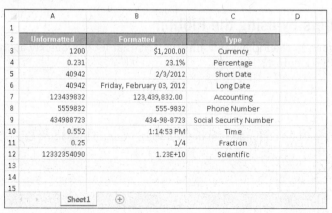

	A	B	C	D
1				
2	Unformatted	Formatted	Type	
3	1200	$1,200.00	Currency	
4	0.231	23.1%	Percentage	
5	40942	2/3/2012	Short Date	
6	40942	Friday, February 03, 2012	Long Date	
7	123439832	123,439,832.00	Accounting	
8	5559832	555-9832	Phone Number	
9	434988723	434-98-8723	Social Security Number	
10	0.552	1:14:53 PM	Time	
11	0.25	1/4	Fraction	
12	12332354090	1.23E+10	Scientific	
13				
14				
15				

Sheet1

TIP

If you move the cell pointer to a cell that has a formatted value, the Formula bar displays the value in its unformatted state because the formatting affects only how the value appears in the cell — not the actual value contained in the cell. There are a few exceptions, however. When you enter a date or a time, Excel always displays the value as a date or a time, even though it's stored internally as a value. Also, values that use the Percentage format display with a percent sign in the Formula bar.

Using automatic number formatting

Excel is smart enough to perform some formatting for you automatically. For example, if you enter **12.2%** into a cell, Excel knows that you want to use a percentage format and applies it for you automatically. If you use commas to separate thousands (such as 123,456), Excel applies comma formatting for you. And if you precede your value with a dollar sign, the cell is formatted for currency (assuming that the dollar sign is your system currency symbol).

TIP

A handy default feature in Excel makes entering percentage values into cells easier. If a cell is formatted to display as a percent, you can simply enter a normal value (for example, 12.5 for 12.5%). To enter values less than 1%, precede the value with a zero (for example, 0.52 for 0.52%). If this automatic percent entry feature isn't working (or if you prefer to enter the actual value for percents), access the Excel Options dialog box and click the Advanced tab. In the Editing Options section, locate the Enable Automatic Percent Entry check box and add or remove the check mark.

Formatting numbers by using the Ribbon

The Home ⇨ Number group in the Ribbon contains controls that let you quickly apply common number formats (see Figure 13.13).

FIGURE 13.13

You can find number formatting commands in the Number group of the Home tab.

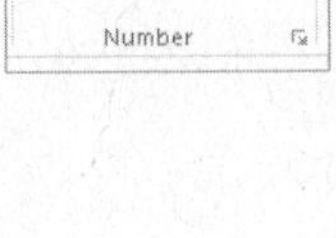

The Number Format drop-down list contains several common number formats. Additional options include an Accounting Number Format drop-down list (to select a currency format), a Percent Style button, and a Comma Style button. The group also contains a button to increase the number of decimal places, and another to decrease the number of decimal places.

When you select one of these controls, the active cell takes on the specified number format. You also can select a range of cells (or even an entire row or column) before clicking these buttons. If you select more than one cell, Excel applies the number format to all the selected cells.

Using keyboard shortcuts to format numbers

Another way to apply number formatting is to use keyboard shortcuts. Table 13.1 summarizes the keyboard shortcut combinations that you can use to apply common number formatting to the selected cells or range. Notice that these Ctrl+Shift characters are all located together, in the upper left of your keyboard.

TABLE 13.1 **Number Formatting Keyboard Shortcuts**

Key Combination	Formatting Applied
Ctrl+Shift+~	General number format (that is, unformatted values)
Ctrl+Shift+$	Currency format with two decimal places (negative numbers appear in parentheses)
Ctrl+Shift+%	Percentage format, with no decimal places
Ctrl+Shift+^	Scientific notation number format, with two decimal places
Ctrl+Shift+#	Date format with the day, month, and year
Ctrl+Shift+@	Time format with the hour, minute, and AM or PM
Ctrl+Shift+!	Two decimal places, thousands separator, and a hyphen for negative values

Formatting numbers using the Format Cells dialog box

In most cases, the number formats that are accessible from the Number group on the Home tab are just fine. Sometimes, however, you want more control over how your values appear. Excel offers a great deal of control over number formats through the use of the Format Cells dialog box, shown in Figure 13.14. For formatting numbers, you need to use the Number tab.

FIGURE 13.14

When you need more control over number formats, use the Number tab of the Format Cells dialog box.

You can bring up the Format Cells dialog box in several ways. Start by selecting the cell or cells that you want to format and then do one of the following:

- **Choose Home and click the dialog box launcher in the lower-right corner of the Number group.**
- **Choose Home ⇨ Number, click the Number Format drop-down list, and choose More Number Formats from the drop-down list.**
- **Right-click the cell and choose Format Cells from the shortcut menu.**
- **Press Ctrl+1.**

The Number tab of the Format Cells dialog box displays 12 categories of number formats. When you select a category from the list box, the right side of the tab changes to display options appropriate to that category.

The Number category has three options that you can control: the number of decimal places displayed, whether to use a thousands separator, and how you want negative numbers displayed. Notice that the Negative Numbers list box has four choices (two of which display negative values in red), and the choices change depending on the number of decimal places and whether you choose to separate thousands.

The top of the tab displays a sample of how the active cell will appear with the selected number format (visible only if a cell with a value is selected). After you make your choices, click OK to apply the number format to all the selected cells.

When Numbers Appear to Add Incorrectly

Applying a number format to a cell doesn't change the value — it only changes how the value appears in the worksheet. For example, if a cell contains 0.874543, you may format it to appear as 87%. If that cell is used in a formula, the formula uses the full value (0.874543), not the displayed value (87%).

In some situations, formatting may cause Excel to display calculation results that appear incorrect, such as when totaling numbers with decimal places. For example, if values are formatted to display two decimal places, you may not see the actual numbers used in the calculations. But because Excel uses the full precision of the values in its formula, the sum of the two values may appear to be incorrect.

Several solutions to this problem are available. You can format the cells to display more decimal places. You can use the ROUND function on individual numbers and specify the number of decimal places Excel should round to. Or you can instruct Excel to change the worksheet values to match their displayed format. To do so, access the Excel Options dialog box and click the Advanced tab. Check the Set precision as displayed check box (located in the When calculating this workbook section).

CAUTION

Selecting the Precision as displayed option changes the numbers in your worksheets to permanently match their appearance on-screen. This setting applies to all sheets in the active workbook. Most of the time, this option is *not* what you want. Make sure that you understand the consequences of using the Set Precision as displayed option.

NOTE

Chapter 15, "Introducing Formulas and Functions," discusses ROUND and other built-in functions.

The following are the number format categories, along with some general comments:

- **General:** The default format; it displays numbers as integers, as decimals, or in scientific notation if the value is too wide to fit in the cell.

- **Number:** Enables you to specify the number of decimal places, whether to use a comma to separate thousands, and how to display negative numbers (with a minus sign, in red, in parentheses, or in red and in parentheses)

- **Currency:** Enables you to specify the number of decimal places, choose a currency symbol, and how to display negative numbers (with a minus sign, in red, in parentheses, or in red and in parentheses). This format always uses a comma to separate thousands.

- **Accounting:** Differs from the Currency format in that the currency symbols always align vertically

- **Date:** Enables you to choose from several different date formats

- **Time:** Enables you to choose from several different time formats

- **Percentage:** Enables you to choose the number of decimal places and always displays a percent sign

- **Fraction:** Enables you to choose from among nine fraction formats

- **Scientific:** Displays numbers in exponential notation (with an E): 2.00E+05 = 200,000; 2.05E+05 = 205,000. You can choose the number of decimal places to display to the left of E. The second example can be read as "2.05 times 10 to the fifth."

- **Text:** When applied to a value, causes Excel to treat the value as text (even if it looks like a number). This feature is useful for such items as part numbers and credit card numbers.

- **Special:** Contains additional number formats. In the U.S. version of Excel, the additional number formats are Zip Code, Zip Code +4, Phone Number, and Social Security Number.

- **Custom:** Enables you to define custom number formats that aren't included in any other category

TIP

If a cell displays a series of hash marks (such as ########), it usually means that the column isn't wide enough to display the value in the number format that you selected. Either make the column wider or change the number format.

Summary

This chapter showed you the techniques you need to know to enter the contents for any worksheet in Excel. You learned how Excel treats different types of information—text, numbers, and formulas. You can continue on to learn to use ranges, because at this point, you should be able to do the following:

- Enter numeric, text, date, and time values.

- Erase, replace, and edit cell contents.

- Take advantage of a variety of shortcuts for entering data, including Auto Fill, AutoComplete, and Flash Fill.

- Apply number formatting to ensure your data is easy to interpret.

Essential Worksheet and Cell Range Operations

This chapter covers some basic information regarding workbooks, worksheets, and windows. You'll discover tips and techniques to help you take control of your worksheets and help you work more efficiently. Most of the work you do in Excel involves cells and ranges. Understanding how best to manipulate cells and ranges will save you time and effort, as you'll also learn in this chapter.

Learning the Fundamentals of Excel Worksheets

In Excel, each file is called a *workbook,* and each workbook can contain one or more *worksheets.* You may find it helpful to think of an Excel workbook as a notebook and worksheets as pages in the notebook. As with a notebook, you can view a particular sheet, add new sheets, remove sheets, rearrange sheets, and copy sheets. The following sections describe the operations that you can perform with worksheets.

Working with Excel windows

Each Excel workbook file that you open is displayed in a window. A workbook can hold any number of sheets, and these sheets can be either *worksheets* (sheets consisting of rows and columns) or *chart sheets* (sheets that hold a single chart). A worksheet is what people usually think of when they think of a spreadsheet. You can open as many Excel workbooks as necessary at the same time.

> **NOTE**
>
> In previous versions of Excel, you could open multiple workbooks and have them displayed in a single Excel window. With Excel 2013, you no longer have that option. An Excel 2013 window holds only one workbook. If you create or open a second workbook, it appears in a separate window.

Each Excel window has five buttons (which appear as icons) at the right side of its title bar. From left to right, they are Help, Full Screen Mode (or Exit Full Screen Mode), Minimize, Maximize (or Restore Down), and Close.

An Excel window can be in one of the following states:

- **Maximized:** Fills the entire screen. To maximize a window, click its Maximize button.
- **Minimized:** Hidden, but still open. To minimize a window, click its Minimize button.
- **Restored:** A nonmaximized size. To restore a maximized window, click its Restore Down button. To restore a minimized window, click its icon in the Windows taskbar. A window in this state can be resized and moved.

If you work with more than one workbook simultaneously (which is quite common), you need to know how to move, resize, and switch among the workbook windows.

Moving and resizing windows

To move or resize a window, make sure that it's not maximized (click the Restore Down button). Then drag its title bar with your mouse.

To resize a window, drag any of its borders until it's the size that you want it to be. When you position the mouse pointer on a window's border, the mouse pointer changes to a double-headed arrow, which lets you know that you can now drag to resize the window. To resize a window horizontally and vertically at the same time, drag any of its corners.

If you want all your workbook windows to be visible (that is, not obscured by another window), you can move and resize the windows manually, or you can let Excel do it for you. Choosing View➪ Window➪ Arrange All displays the Arrange Windows dialog box, shown in Figure 14.1. This dialog box has four window arrangement options. Just select the one that you want and click OK. Windows that are minimized aren't affected by this command.

FIGURE 14.1

Use the Arrange Windows dialog box to quickly arrange all open nonminimized workbook windows.

Switching among windows

At any given time, one (and only one) workbook window is the *active window*. The active window accepts your input and is the window on which your commands work. The active window appears at the top of the stack of windows. To work in a workbook in a different window, you need to make that window active. You can make a different window the active window in several ways:

- **Click another window, if it's visible.** The window you click moves to the top and becomes the active window. This method isn't possible if the current window is maximized.

- **Press Ctrl+F6 to cycle through all open windows until the window that you want to work with appears on top as the active window.** Pressing Shift+Ctrl+F6 cycles through the windows in the opposite direction.

- **Choose View ⇨ Window ⇨ Switch Windows and select the window that you want from the drop-down list (the active window has a check mark next to it).** This menu can display as many as nine windows. If you have more than nine workbook windows open, choose More Windows (which appears below the nine window names).

- **Click the Excel icon in the Windows taskbar.** You can then choose the window by clicking its thumbnail or clicking it in the pop-up list.

Most people prefer to do most of their work with maximized workbook windows, which enables you to see more cells and eliminates the distraction of other workbook windows getting in the way. At times, however, viewing multiple windows is preferred. For example, displaying two windows is more efficient if you need to compare information in two workbooks or if you need to copy data from one workbook to another.

> **TIP**
>
> You also can display a single workbook in more than one window. For example, if you have a workbook with two worksheets, you may want to display each worksheet in a separate window to compare the two sheets. All the window manipulation procedures described previously still apply. Choose View ⇨ Window ⇨ New Window to open an additional window for the active workbook.

14

Closing windows

If you have multiple windows open, you may want to close those windows that you no longer need. Excel offers several ways to close the active window:

- **Choose File ⇨ Close.**
- **Click the Close button (the X icon) on the workbook window's title bar.**
- **Press Alt+F4.**
- **Press Ctrl+W.**

When you close a workbook window, Excel checks whether you made any changes since the last time you saved the file. If you have made changes, Excel prompts you to save the file before it closes the window. If not, the window closes without a prompt from Excel. Oddly, Excel provides no way to tell you if a workbook has been changed since it was last saved.

Activating a worksheet

At any given time, one workbook is the active workbook, and one sheet is the active sheet in the active workbook. To activate a different sheet, just click its sheet tab, located at the bottom of the workbook window. You also can use the following shortcut keys to activate a different sheet:

- **Ctrl+PageUp:** Activates the previous sheet, if one exists
- **Ctrl+PageDown:** Activates the next sheet, if one exists

If your workbook has many sheets, all its tabs may not be visible. Use the tab scrolling controls (see Figure 14.2) to scroll the sheet tabs. The sheet tabs share space with the worksheet's horizontal scrollbar. You also can drag the tab split control (to the left of the horizontal scrollbar) to display more or fewer tabs. Dragging the tab split control simultaneously changes the number of tabs and the size of the horizontal scrollbar.

FIGURE 14.2

Use the tab scrolling controls to activate a different worksheet or to see additional worksheet tabs.

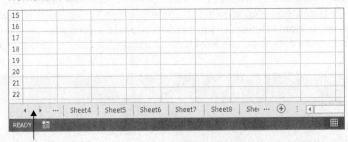

Tab scrolling controls

> **TIP**
>
> When you right-click any of the tab scrolling controls, Excel displays a list of all sheets in the workbook. You can quickly activate a sheet by selecting it from the list.

Adding a new worksheet to your workbook

Worksheets can be an excellent organizational tool. Instead of placing everything on a single worksheet, you can use additional worksheets in a workbook to separate various workbook elements logically. For example, if you have several products whose sales you track individually, you may want to assign each product to its own worksheet and then use another worksheet to consolidate your results.

Here are three ways to add a new worksheet to a workbook:

- **Click the New Sheet button, which is the plus sign icon located to the right of the last sheet tab.** A new sheet is added after the active sheet.
- **Press Shift+F11.** A new sheet is added before the active sheet.
- **Right-click a sheet tab, choose Insert from the shortcut menu, and select the General tab of the Insert dialog box that appears.** Then select the Worksheet icon and click OK. A new sheet is added before the active sheet.

Deleting a worksheet you no longer need

If you no longer need a worksheet, or if you want to get rid of an empty worksheet in a workbook, you can delete it in either of two ways:

- **Right-click its sheet tab and choose Delete from the shortcut menu.**
- **Activate the unwanted worksheet and choose Home ➪ Cells ➪ Delete ➪ Delete Sheet.**

If the worksheet contains any data, Excel asks you to confirm that you want to delete the sheet (see Figure 14.3). If you've never used the worksheet, Excel deletes it immediately without asking for confirmation.

FIGURE 14.3

Excel's gentle warning that you might be losing some data

> **TIP**
>
> You can delete multiple sheets with a single command by selecting the sheets that you want to delete. To select multiple sheets, press Ctrl while you click the sheet tabs that you want to delete. To select a group of contiguous sheets, click the first sheet tab, press Shift, and then click the last sheet tab (Excel displays the selected sheet names bold and underlined). Then use either method to delete the selected sheets.

> **CAUTION**
>
> When you delete a worksheet, it's gone for good. Deleting a worksheet is one of the few operations in Excel that can't be undone.

Changing the name of a worksheet

The default names that Excel uses for worksheets — Sheet1, Sheet2, and so on — are generic and nondescriptive. To make it easier to locate data in a multisheet workbook, you'll want to make the sheet names more descriptive.

To change a sheet's name, double-click the sheet tab. Excel highlights the name on the sheet tab so that you can edit the name or replace it with a new name.

Sheet names can contain as many as 31 characters, and spaces are allowed. However, you can't use the following characters in sheet names:

:	colon
/	slash
\	backslash
[ ]	square brackets
?	question mark
*	asterisk

Keep in mind that a longer worksheet name results in a wider tab, which takes up more space on-screen. Therefore, if you use lengthy sheet names, you won't be able to see as many sheet tabs without scrolling the tab list.

Changing a sheet tab color

Excel allows you to change the background color of your worksheet tabs. For example, you may prefer to color-code the sheet tabs to make identifying the worksheet's contents easier.

To change the color of a sheet tab, right-click the tab and choose Tab Color from the shortcut menu. Then select the color from the color gallery or palette. You can't change the text color, but Excel will choose a contrasting color to make the text visible. For example, if you make a sheet tab black, Excel will display white text.

Rearranging your worksheets

You may want to rearrange the order of worksheets in a workbook. If you have a separate worksheet for each sales region, for example, arranging the worksheets in alphabetical order might be helpful. You can also move a worksheet from one workbook to another and create copies of worksheets, either in the same workbook or in a different workbook.

You can move or copy a worksheet in the following ways:

■ **Right-click the sheet tab and choose Move or Copy to display the Move or Copy dialog box (see Figure 14.4).** Use this dialog box to specify the operation and the location for the sheet.

FIGURE 14.4

Use the Move or Copy dialog box to move or copy worksheets in the same or another workbook.

■ **To move a worksheet, drag the worksheet tab to the desired location.** When you drag, the mouse pointer changes to a small sheet, and a small arrow guides you. To move a worksheet to a different workbook, the second workbook must be open and not maximized.

■ **To copy a worksheet, click the worksheet tab, and press Ctrl while dragging the tab to its desired location.** When you drag, the mouse pointer changes to a small sheet with a plus sign on it. To copy a worksheet to a different workbook, the second workbook must be open and not maximized.

> **TIP**
>
> You can move or copy multiple sheets simultaneously. First, select the sheets by clicking their sheet tabs while holding down the Ctrl key. Then you can move or copy the set of sheets by using the preceding methods.

If you move or copy a worksheet to a workbook that already has a sheet with the same name, Excel changes the name to make it unique. For example, Sheet1 becomes Sheet1 (2).

You probably want to rename the copied sheet to give it a more meaningful name (see "Changing the name of a worksheet," earlier in this chapter).

> **NOTE**
> When you move or copy a worksheet to a different workbook, any defined names and custom formats also get copied to the new workbook.

Hiding and unhiding a worksheet

In some situations, you may want to hide one or more worksheets. Hiding a sheet may be useful if you don't want others to see it or if you just want to get it out of the way. When a sheet is hidden, its sheet tab is also hidden. You can't hide all the sheets in a workbook; at least one sheet must remain visible.

To hide a worksheet, right-click its sheet tab and choose Hide Sheet. The active worksheet (or selected worksheets) will be hidden from view.

To unhide a hidden worksheet, right-click any sheet tab and choose Unhide Sheet. Excel opens the Unhide dialog box, which lists all hidden sheets. Choose the sheet that you want to redisplay, and click OK. For reasons known only to a Microsoft programmer who is probably retired by now, you can't select multiple sheets from this dialog box, so you need to repeat the command for each sheet that you want to unhide. When you unhide a sheet, it appears in its previous position among the sheet tabs.

Preventing Sheet Actions

To prevent others from unhiding hidden sheets, inserting new sheets, renaming sheets, copying sheets, or deleting sheets, protect the workbook's structure:

1. Choose Review ⇨ Changes ⇨ Protect Workbook.

2. In the Protect Workbook dialog box, select the Structure option.

3. Provide a password (optional).

4. Click OK.

After performing these steps, several commands will no longer be available when you right-click a sheet tab: Insert, Delete Sheet, Rename Sheet, Move or Copy Sheet, Tab Color, Hide Sheet, and Unhide Sheet. Be aware, however, that this is a very weak security measure. Cracking this particular protection feature is relatively easy.

Controlling the Worksheet View

As you add more information to a worksheet, you may find that navigating and locating what you want gets more difficult. Excel includes a few options that enable you to view your sheet, and sometimes multiple sheets, more efficiently. This section discusses a few additional worksheet options at your disposal.

Zooming in or out for a better view

Normally, everything you see on-screen is displayed at 100%. You can change the *zoom percentage* from 10% (very tiny) to 400% (huge). Using a small zoom percentage can help you to get a bird's-eye view of your worksheet to see how it's laid out. Zooming in is useful if you have trouble deciphering tiny type. Zooming doesn't change the font size specified for the cells, so it has no effect on printed output.

> **TIP**
>
> Excel contains separate options for changing the size of your printed output. (Use the controls in the Page Layout ⇨ Scale to Fit group.)

Figure 14.5 shows a window zoomed to 10% and a window zoomed to 400%.

FIGURE 14.5

You can zoom in or out for a different view of your worksheets.

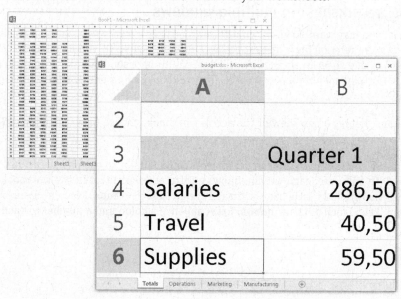

You can change the zoom factor of the active worksheet window by using any of three methods:

- **Use the Zoom slider located on the right side of the status bar.** Drag the slider, and your screen transforms instantly.
- **Press Ctrl and use the wheel button on your mouse to zoom in or out.**
- **Choose View ⇨ Zoom ⇨ Zoom, which displays a dialog box with some zoom options.**
- **Select a range of cells, and choose View ⇨ Zoom ⇨ Zoom to Selection.** The selected range will be enlarged so it fills the entire window.

> **TIP**
>
> Zooming affects only the active worksheet window, so you can use different zoom factors for different worksheets. Also, if you have a worksheet displayed in two different windows, you can set a different zoom factor for each of the windows.

> **TIP**
>
> If your worksheet uses named ranges as described later in this chapter, zooming your worksheet to 39% or less displays the name of the range overlaid on the cells. Viewing named ranges in this manner is useful for getting an overview of how a worksheet is laid out.

Viewing a worksheet in multiple windows

Sometimes, you may want to view two different parts of a worksheet simultaneously — perhaps to make referencing a distant cell in a formula easier. Or you may want to examine more than one sheet in the same workbook simultaneously. You can accomplish either of these actions by opening a new view to the workbook, using one or more additional windows.

To create and display a new view of the active workbook, choose View ⇨ Window ⇨ New Window.

Excel displays a new window for the active workbook, similar to the one shown in Figure 14.6. In this case, each window shows a different worksheet in the workbook. Notice the text in the windows' title bars: climate data.xlsx:1 and climate data.xlsx:2. To help you keep track of the windows, Excel appends a colon and a number to each window.

FIGURE 14.6

Use multiple windows to view different sections of a workbook at the same time.

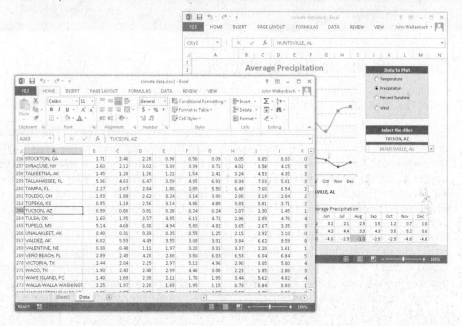

> **TIP**
>
> If the workbook is maximized when you create a new window, you may not even notice that Excel created the new window. If you look at the Excel title bar, though, you'll see that the workbook title now has : 2 appended to the name. Choose View ⇨ Window ⇨ Arrange All, and then choose one of the Arrange options in the Arrange Windows dialog box to display the open windows. If you select the Windows of active workbook check box, only the windows of the active workbook are arranged.

A single workbook can have as many views (that is, separate windows) as you want. Each window is independent. In other words, scrolling to a new location in one window doesn't cause scrolling in the other window(s). However, if you make changes to the worksheet shown in a particular window, those changes are also made in all views of that worksheet.

You can close these additional windows when you no longer need them. For example, clicking the Close button on the active window's title bar closes the active window but doesn't close the other windows for the workbook.

14

> **TIP**
>
> Multiple windows make copying or moving information from one worksheet to another easier. You can use Excel's drag-and-drop procedures to copy or move ranges.

Comparing sheets side by side

In some situations, you may want to compare two worksheets that are in different windows. The View Side by Side feature makes this task a bit easier.

First, make sure that the two sheets are displayed in separate windows. (The sheets can be in the same workbook or in different workbooks.) If you want to compare two sheets in the same workbook, choose View ➪ Window ➪ New Window to create a new window for the active workbook. Activate the first window; then choose View ➪ Window ➪ View Side by Side. If more than two windows are open, you see a dialog box that lets you select the window for the comparison. The two windows are tiled to fill the entire screen.

When using the Compare Side by Side feature, scrolling in one of the windows also scrolls the other window. If you don't want this simultaneous scrolling, choose View ➪ Window ➪ Synchronous Scrolling (which is a toggle). If you have rearranged or moved the windows, choose View ➪ Window ➪ Reset Window Position to restore the windows to the initial side-by-side arrangement. To turn off the side-by-side viewing, choose View ➪ Window ➪ View Side by Side again.

Keep in mind that this feature is for manual comparison only. Unfortunately, Excel doesn't provide a way to actually point out the differences between two sheets.

Splitting the worksheet window into panes

If you prefer not to clutter your screen with additional windows, Excel provides another option for viewing multiple parts of the same worksheet. Choosing View ➪ Window ➪ Split splits the active worksheet into two or four separate panes. The split occurs at the location of the cell pointer. If the cell pointer is in row 1 or column A, this command results in a two-pane split; otherwise, it gives you four panes. You can use the mouse to drag the individual panes to resize them.

Figure 14.7 shows a worksheet split into two panes. Notice that row numbers aren't continuous. The top pane shows rows 8 through 20, and the bottom pane shows rows 694 through 708. In other words, splitting panes enables you to display in a single window widely separated areas of a worksheet. To remove the split panes, choose View ➪ Window ➪ Split again.

FIGURE 14.7

You can split the worksheet window into two or four panes to view different areas
of the worksheet at the same time.

	A	B	C	D	E	F	G	H	I	J	K	L	M
8	ABERDEEN, SD	0.48	0.48	1.34	1.83	2.69	3.49	2.92	2.42	1.81	1.63	0.75	0.38
9	ABILENE, TX	0.97	1.13	1.41	1.67	2.83	3.06	1.69	2.63	2.91	2.90	1.30	1.27
10	AKRON, OH	2.49	2.28	3.15	3.39	3.96	3.55	4.02	3.65	3.43	2.53	3.04	2.98
11	ALAMOSA, CO	0.25	0.21	0.46	0.54	0.70	0.94	0.59	1.19	0.89	0.67	0.48	0.33
12	ALBANY, NY	2.71	2.27	3.17	3.25	3.67	3.74	3.50	3.68	3.31	3.23	3.31	2.76
13	ALBUQUERQUE, NM	0.49	0.44	0.61	0.50	0.60	0.65	1.27	1.73	1.07	1.00	0.62	0.49
14	ALLENTOWN, PA	3.50	2.75	3.56	3.49	4.47	3.99	4.27	4.35	4.37	3.33	3.70	3.39
15	ALPENA, MI	1.76	1.35	2.13	2.31	2.61	2.53	3.17	3.50	2.80	2.33	2.08	1.83
16	AMARILLO, TX	0.63	0.55	1.13	1.33	2.50	3.28	2.68	2.94	1.88	1.50	0.68	0.61
17	ANCHORAGE, AK	0.68	0.74	0.65	0.52	0.69	1.06	1.70	2.93	2.87	2.08	1.09	1.05
18	ANNETTE, AK	9.67	8.05	7.96	7.37	5.73	4.72	4.26	6.12	9.49	13.86	12.21	11.39
19	APALACHICOLA, FL	4.87	3.76	4.95	3.00	2.62	4.30	7.31	7.29	7.10	4.18	3.62	3.51
20	ASHEVILLE, NC	4.06	3.83	4.59	3.50	4.41	4.38	3.87	4.30	3.72	3.17	3.82	3.39
694	ROCKFORD, IL	19.00	24.70	36.10	47.90	59.60	68.80	72.90	70.90	62.80	51.00	37.20	24.40
695	ROSWELL, NM	40.00	45.70	52.90	60.50	69.60	78.00	80.80	78.90	72.00	61.40	48.90	40.70
696	SACRAMENTO, CA	46.30	51.20	54.50	58.90	65.50	71.50	75.40	74.80	71.70	64.40	53.30	45.80
697	SAINT CLOUD, MN	8.80	16.10	28.40	43.60	56.60	65.10	69.80	67.20	57.40	45.30	28.80	14.40
698	SALEM, OR	40.30	43.00	46.50	50.00	55.60	61.20	66.80	67.00	62.20	52.90	45.20	40.20
699	SALT LAKE CITY, UT	29.20	34.50	43.10	50.00	58.80	69.00	77.00	75.60	65.00	52.50	39.60	30.20
700	SAN ANGELO, TX	44.90	49.70	57.20	65.00	73.10	79.20	82.40	81.30	74.80	65.40	54.00	46.40
701	SAN ANTONIO, TX	50.30	54.70	62.10	68.60	75.80	81.50	84.30	84.20	79.40	70.70	60.00	52.40
702	SAN DIEGO, CA	57.80	58.90	60.00	62.60	64.60	67.40	70.90	72.50	71.60	67.60	61.80	57.60
703	SAN FRANCISCO AP, CA	49.40	52.40	54.00	56.20	58.70	61.40	62.80	63.60	63.90	61.00	54.70	49.50
704	SAN FRANCISCO C.O., CA	52.30	55.00	55.90	57.30	58.40	60.50	61.30	62.40	63.70	62.50	57.50	52.70
705	SAN JUAN, PR	76.60	76.90	77.60	79.10	80.60	82.10	82.20	82.40	82.20	81.60	79.60	77.70
706	SANTA BARBARA, CA	53.10	55.20	56.70	58.90	60.90	64.20	67.00	68.60	67.40	63.50	57.50	53.20
707	SANTA MARIA, CA	51.60	53.10	53.80	55.50	57.80	60.90	63.50	64.20	63.90	61.10	55.50	51.60
708	SAULT STE. MARIE, MI	13.20	15.60	24.90	38.40	51.30	58.60	63.90	63.30	54.80	44.40	32.40	20.20

Sheet1 | Data | +

Keeping the titles in view by freezing panes

If you set up a worksheet with column headings or descriptive text in the first column, this
identifying information won't be visible when you scroll down or to the right. Excel provides a handy solution to this problem: freezing panes. Freezing panes keeps the column or
row headings visible while you're scrolling through the worksheet.

To freeze panes, start by moving the cell pointer to the cell below the row that you want to
remain visible while you scroll vertically, and to the right of the column that you want to
remain visible while you scroll horizontally. Then choose View⇨Window⇨Freeze Panes and
select the Freeze Panes option from the drop-down list. Excel inserts dark lines to indicate
the frozen rows and columns. The frozen row and column remain visible while you scroll
throughout the worksheet. To remove the frozen panes, choose View⇨Window⇨Freeze
Panes, and select the Unfreeze Panes option from the drop-down list.

14

Figure 14.8 shows a worksheet with frozen panes. In this case, rows 1:4 and column A are frozen in place. This technique allows you to scroll down and to the right to locate some information while keeping the column titles and the column A entries visible.

FIGURE 14.8

Freeze certain columns and rows to make them remain visible while you scroll the worksheet.

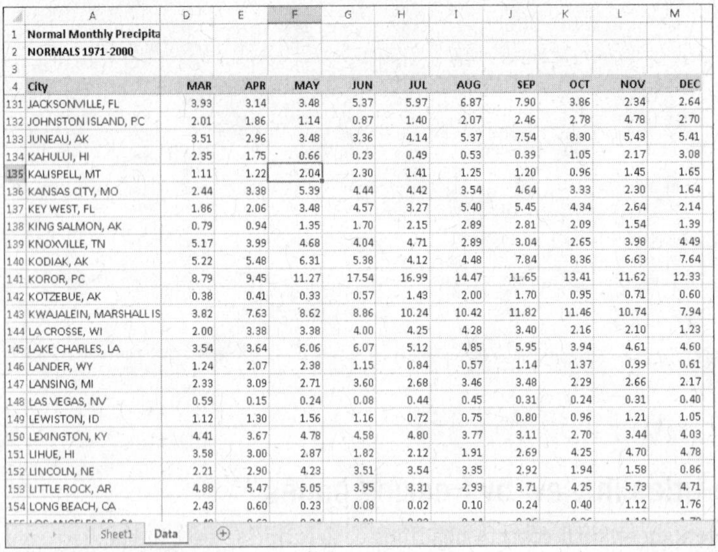

	A	D	E	F	G	H	I	J	K	L	M
1	Normal Monthly Precipita										
2	NORMALS 1971-2000										
3											
4	City	MAR	APR	MAY	JUN	JUL	AUG	SEP	OCT	NOV	DEC
131	JACKSONVILLE, FL	3.93	3.14	3.48	5.37	5.97	6.87	7.90	3.86	2.34	2.64
132	JOHNSTON ISLAND, PC	2.01	1.86	1.14	0.87	1.40	2.07	2.46	2.78	4.78	2.70
133	JUNEAU, AK	3.51	2.96	3.48	3.36	4.14	5.37	7.54	8.30	5.43	5.41
134	KAHULUI, HI	2.35	1.75	0.66	0.23	0.49	0.53	0.39	1.05	2.17	3.08
135	KALISPELL, MT	1.11	1.22	2.04	2.30	1.41	1.25	1.20	0.96	1.45	1.65
136	KANSAS CITY, MO	2.44	3.38	5.39	4.44	4.42	3.54	4.64	3.33	2.30	1.64
137	KEY WEST, FL	1.86	2.06	3.48	4.57	3.27	5.40	5.45	4.34	2.64	2.14
138	KING SALMON, AK	0.79	0.94	1.35	1.70	2.15	2.89	2.81	2.09	1.54	1.39
139	KNOXVILLE, TN	5.17	3.99	4.68	4.04	4.71	2.89	3.04	2.65	3.98	4.49
140	KODIAK, AK	5.22	5.48	6.31	5.38	4.12	4.48	7.84	8.36	6.63	7.64
141	KOROR, PC	8.79	9.45	11.27	17.54	16.99	14.47	11.65	13.41	11.62	12.33
142	KOTZEBUE, AK	0.38	0.41	0.33	0.57	1.43	2.00	1.70	0.95	0.71	0.60
143	KWAJALEIN, MARSHALL IS	3.82	7.63	8.62	8.86	10.24	10.42	11.82	11.46	10.74	7.94
144	LA CROSSE, WI	2.00	3.38	3.38	4.00	4.25	4.28	3.40	2.16	2.10	1.23
145	LAKE CHARLES, LA	3.54	3.64	6.06	6.07	5.12	4.85	5.95	3.94	4.61	4.60
146	LANDER, WY	1.24	2.07	2.38	1.15	0.84	0.57	1.14	1.37	0.99	0.61
147	LANSING, MI	2.33	3.09	2.71	3.60	2.68	3.46	3.48	2.29	2.66	2.17
148	LAS VEGAS, NV	0.59	0.15	0.24	0.08	0.44	0.45	0.31	0.24	0.31	0.40
149	LEWISTON, ID	1.12	1.30	1.56	1.16	0.72	0.75	0.80	0.96	1.21	1.05
150	LEXINGTON, KY	4.41	3.67	4.78	4.58	4.80	3.77	3.11	2.70	3.44	4.03
151	LIHUE, HI	3.58	3.00	2.87	1.82	2.12	1.91	2.69	4.25	4.70	4.78
152	LINCOLN, NE	2.21	2.90	4.23	3.51	3.54	3.35	2.92	1.94	1.58	0.86
153	LITTLE ROCK, AR	4.88	5.47	5.05	3.95	3.31	2.93	3.71	4.25	5.73	4.71
154	LONG BEACH, CA	2.43	0.60	0.23	0.08	0.02	0.10	0.24	0.40	1.12	1.76

Sheet1 Data ⊕

Most of the time, you'll want to freeze either the first row or the first column. The View ⇨ Window ⇨ Freeze Panes drop-down list has two additional options: Freeze Top Row and Freeze First Column. Using these commands eliminates the need to position the cell pointer before freezing panes.

TIP

If you designated a range to be a table (by choosing Insert ⇨ Tables ⇨ Table), you may not even need to freeze panes. When you scroll down, Excel displays the table column headings in place of the column letters. Figure 14.9 shows an example. The table headings replace the column letters only when a cell within the table is selected.

FIGURE 14.9

When using a table, scrolling down displays the table headings where the column letters normally appear.

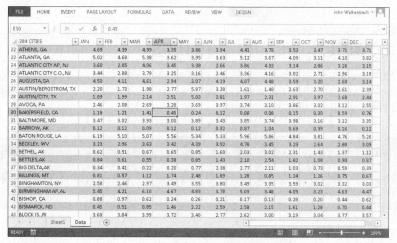

Monitoring cells with a Watch Window

In some situations, you may want to monitor the value in a particular cell as you work. As you scroll throughout the worksheet, that cell may disappear from view. A feature known as Watch Window can help. A *Watch Window* displays the value of any number of cells in a handy window that's always visible.

To display the Watch Window, choose Formulas ⇨ Formula Auditing ⇨ Watch Window. The Watch Window is actually a task pane, and you can dock it to the side of the window or drag it and make it float over the worksheet.

To add a cell to watch, click Add Watch and specify the cell that you want to watch. The Watch Window displays the value in that cell. You can add any number of cells to the Watch Window. Figure 14.10 shows the Watch Window monitoring four cells.

FIGURE 14.10

Use the Watch Window to monitor the value in one or more cells.

TIP

Double-click a cell in the Watch Window to immediately select that cell.

Working with Rows and Columns

This section discusses worksheet operations that involve complete rows and columns (rather than individual cells). Every worksheet has exactly 1,048,576 rows and 16,384 columns, and these values can't be changed.

NOTE

If you open a workbook that was created in a version of Excel prior to Excel 2007 or saved in a pre-2007 format, the workbook is opened in Compatibility Mode. These workbooks have 65,536 rows and 256 columns. If you would like to increase the number of rows and columns, save the workbook as an Excel `.xlsx` or `.xlsm` file and then reopen it.

Inserting rows and columns

Although the number of rows and columns in a worksheet is fixed, you can still insert and delete rows and columns if you need to make room for additional information. These operations don't change the number of rows or columns. Instead, inserting a new row moves down the other rows to accommodate the new row. The last row is simply removed from the worksheet if it's empty. Inserting a new column shifts the columns to the right, and the last column is removed if it's empty.

NOTE

If the last row isn't empty, you can't insert a new row. Similarly, if the last column contains information, Excel doesn't let you insert a new column. Attempting to add a row or column in such cases displays a warning dialog box shown. Click OK and then remove the contents of the non-blank cells to continue.

To insert a new row or rows, use either of these methods:

- **Select an entire row or multiple rows by clicking the row numbers in the worksheet border.** Right-click and choose Insert from the shortcut menu.
- **Move the cell pointer to the row that you want to insert, and then choose Home ⇨ Cells ⇨ Insert ⇨ Insert Sheet Rows.** If you select multiple cells in the column, Excel inserts additional rows that correspond to the number of cells selected in the column and moves the rows below the insertion down.

To insert a new column or columns, use either of these methods:

- **Select an entire column by clicking its column letter in the worksheet border, also known as the column header.** (Ctrl+click to select multiple adjacent columns.) Right-click and choose Insert from the shortcut menu.

- **Move the cell pointer to the column that you want to insert, and then choose Home ⇨ Cells ⇨ Insert ⇨ Insert Sheet Columns.** If you select multiple cells in the row, Excel inserts additional columns that correspond to the number of cells selected in the row.

You can also insert cells, rather than just rows or columns. Select the range into which you want to add new cells and then choose Home ⇨ Cells ⇨ Insert Insert Cells (or right-click the selection and choose Insert). To insert cells, the existing cells must be shifted to the right or shifted down. Therefore, Excel displays the Insert dialog box shown in Figure 14.11 so that you can specify the direction in which you want to shift the cells. Notice that this dialog box also enables you to insert entire rows or columns.

FIGURE 14.11

You can insert partial rows or columns by using the Insert dialog box.

Deleting rows and columns

You may also want to delete rows or columns in a worksheet. For example, your sheet may contain old data that is no longer needed, or you may want to remove empty rows or columns.

To delete a row or rows, use either of these methods:

- **Select an entire row or multiple rows by clicking or Ctrl+clicking the row numbers in the worksheet border (row header).** Right-click and choose Delete from the shortcut menu.

- **Move the cell pointer to the row that you want to delete, and then choose Home ⇨ Cells ⇨ Delete Sheet Rows.** If you select multiple cells in the column, Excel deletes all rows in the selection.

Deleting columns works in a similar way. If you discover that you accidentally deleted a row or column, select Undo from the Quick Access Toolbar (or press Ctrl+Z) to undo the action.

14

Hiding rows and columns

In some cases, you may want to hide particular rows or columns. Hiding rows and columns may be useful if you don't want users to see particular information, or if you need to print a report that summarizes the information in the worksheet without showing all the details.

To hide rows in your worksheet, select the row or rows that you want to hide by clicking in the row header on the left. Then right-click and choose Hide from the shortcut menu. Or you can use the commands on the Home ➪ Cells ➪ Format ➪ Hide & Unhide drop-down list.

To hide columns, use the same technique, but start by selecting columns rather than rows.

> **TIP**
>
> You can also drag the row or column's border to hide the row or column. You must drag the border in the row or column heading. Drag the bottom border of a row upward or the border of a column to the left.

A hidden row is actually a row with its height set to zero. Similarly, a hidden column has a column width of zero. When you use the navigation keys to move the cell pointer, cells in hidden rows or columns are skipped. In other words, you can't use the navigation keys to move to a cell in a hidden row or column.

Notice, however, that Excel displays a very narrow column heading for hidden columns and a very narrow row heading for hidden rows. You can drag the column heading to make the column wider — and make it visible again. For a hidden row, drag the small row heading to make the column visible.

Another way to unhide a row or column is to choose Home ➪ Editing ➪ Find & Select ➪ Go To (or its F5 equivalent) to select a cell in a hidden row or column. For example, if column A is hidden, you can press F5 and specify cell A1 (or any other cell in column A) to move the cell pointer to the hidden column. Then you can choose Home ➪ Cells ➪ Format ➪ Hide & Unhide ➪ Unhide Columns.

Changing column widths and row heights

Often, you'll want to change the width of a column or the height of a row. For example, you can make columns narrower to show more information on a printed page. Or you may want to increase row height to create a "double-spaced" effect. Excel provides several different ways to change the widths of columns and the height of rows.

Changing column widths

Column width is measured in terms of the number of characters of a *monospaced font* that will fit into the cell's width. By default, each column's width is 8.43 units, which equates to 64 pixels (px).

TIP

If hash symbols (#) fill a cell that contains a numerical value, the column isn't wide enough to accommodate the information in the cell. Widen the column to solve the problem.

Before you change the column width, you can select multiple columns so that the width will be the same for all selected columns. To select multiple columns, either drag over the column letter in the column header or Ctrl+click to select individual columns. To select all columns, click the button where the row and column headers intersect. You can change columns widths by using any of the following techniques:

- Drag the right column border with the mouse until the column is the desired width.
- Choose Home ⇨ Cells ⇨ Format ⇨ Column Width and enter a value in the Column Width dialog box.
- Choose Home ⇨ Cells ⇨ Format ⇨ AutoFit Column Width to adjust the width of the selected column so that the widest entry in the column fits. Instead of selecting an entire column, you can just select cells in the column, and the column is adjusted based on the widest entry in your selection.
- Double-click the right border of a column header to set the column width automatically to the widest entry in the column.

TIP

To change the default width of all columns, choose Home ⇨ Cells ⇨ Format ⇨ Default Width. This command displays a dialog box into which you enter the new default column width. All columns that haven't been previously adjusted take on the new column width.

CAUTION

After you manually adjust a column's width, Excel will no longer automatically adjust the column to accommodate longer numerical entries. If you enter a long number that displays as hash symbols (#), you need to change the column width manually.

14

Changing row heights

Row height is measured in points (pt; a standard unit of measurement in the printing trade — 72 pt is equal to 1 inch). The default row height using the default font is 15 pt, or 20 px.

The default row height can vary, depending on the font defined in the Normal style. In addition, Excel automatically adjusts row heights to accommodate the tallest font in the row. So, if you change the font size of a cell to 20 pt, for example, Excel makes the row taller so that the entire text is visible.

You can set the row height manually, however, by using any of the following techniques. As with columns, you can select multiple rows.

■ **Drag the lower row border with the mouse until the row is the desired height.**

■ **Choose Home ⇨ Cells ⇨ Format ⇨ Row Height and enter a value (in points) in the Row Height dialog box.**

■ **Double-click the bottom border of a row to set the row height automatically to the tallest entry in the row.** You can also choose Home ⇨ Cells ⇨ Format ⇨ Autofit Row Height for this task.

Changing the row height is useful for spacing out rows and is almost always preferable to inserting empty rows between lines of data.

Understanding Cells and Ranges

A *cell* is a single element in a worksheet that can hold a value, some text, or a formula. A cell is identified by its *address*, which consists of its column letter and row number. For example, cell D9 is the cell in the fourth column and the ninth row.

A group of cells is called a *range*. You designate a range address by specifying its upper-left cell address and its lower-right cell address, separated by a colon.

Here are some examples of range addresses:

C24	A range that consists of a single cell.
A1:B1	Two cells that occupy one row and two columns.
A1:A100	100 cells in column A.
A1:D4	16 cells (four rows by four columns).
C1:C1048576	An entire column of cells; this range also can be expressed as C:C.
A6:XFD6	An entire row of cells; this range also can be expressed as 6:6.
A1:XFD1048576	All cells in a worksheet. This range also can be expressed as either A:XFD or 1:1048576.

Selecting ranges

To perform an operation on a range of cells in a worksheet, you must first select the range. For example, if you want to make the text bold for a range of cells, you must select the range and then choose Home ⇨ Font ⇨ Bold (or press Ctrl+B).

When you select a range, the cells appear highlighted. The exception is the active cell, which remains its normal color. Figure 14.12 shows an example of a selected range (B5:C8) in a worksheet. Cell B5, the active cell, is selected but not highlighted.

FIGURE 14.12

When you select a range, it appears highlighted, but the active cell within the range is not highlighted.

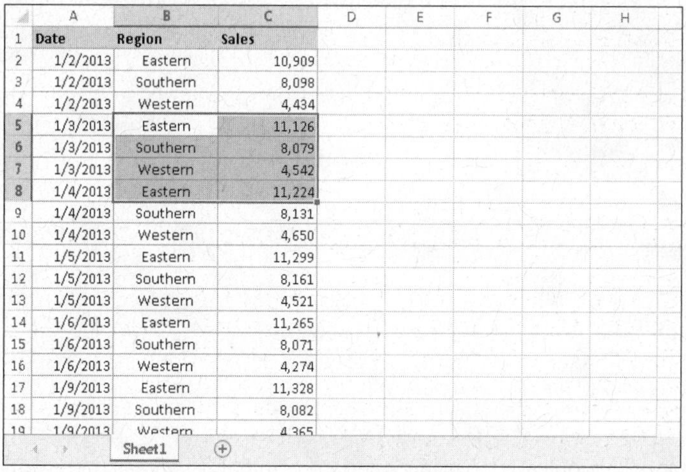

	A	B	C	D	E	F	G	H
1	Date	Region	Sales					
2	1/2/2013	Eastern	10,909					
3	1/2/2013	Southern	8,098					
4	1/2/2013	Western	4,434					
5	1/3/2013	Eastern	11,126					
6	1/3/2013	Southern	8,079					
7	1/3/2013	Western	4,542					
8	1/4/2013	Eastern	11,224					
9	1/4/2013	Southern	8,131					
10	1/4/2013	Western	4,650					
11	1/5/2013	Eastern	11,299					
12	1/5/2013	Southern	8,161					
13	1/5/2013	Western	4,521					
14	1/6/2013	Eastern	11,265					
15	1/6/2013	Southern	8,071					
16	1/6/2013	Western	4,274					
17	1/9/2013	Eastern	11,328					
18	1/9/2013	Southern	8,082					
19	1/9/2013	Western	4,365					

You can select a range in several ways:

- **Press the left mouse button and drag, highlighting the range. Then release the mouse button.** If you drag to the end of the window, the worksheet will scroll.
- **Press the Shift key while you use the arrow keys to select a range.**
- **Press F8 and then move the cell pointer with the arrow keys to highlight the range.** Press F8 again to return the navigation keys to normal movement.
- **Type the cell or range address into the Name box (located to the left of the Formula bar) and press Enter.** Excel selects the cell or range that you specified.
- **Choose Home ⇨ Editing ⇨ Find & Select ⇨ Go To (or press F5) and enter a range's address manually in the Go To dialog box.** When you click OK, Excel selects the cells in the range that you specified.

TIP

While you're selecting a range, Excel displays the number of rows and columns in your selection in the Name box. As soon as you finish the selection, the Name box reverts to showing the address of the active cell.

Quick Analysis?

When you select a range of data, Excel may display a Quick Analysis button at the lower right corner of the selection. Click the icon, and you'll see a list of analysis options that you can quickly apply to the selected data. You can add conditional formatting, create a chart, add formulas, create a pivot table, and generate Sparkline graphics. The exact options vary, depending on the data in the range.

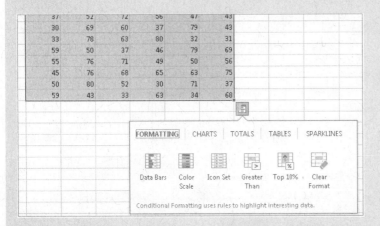

These options provide nothing that you can't do using standard commands, and all these options are discussed elsewhere in this book. If you find the Quick Analysis icon annoying, choose File⇨Options to display the Excel Options dialog box, select the General tab, and deselect Show Quick Analysis options on selection.

Selecting complete rows and columns

Often, you'll need to select an entire row or column. For example, you may want to apply the same numeric format or the same alignment options to an entire row or column. You can select entire rows and columns in much the same manner as you select ranges:

- Click the row or column header to select a single row or column.
- To select multiple adjacent rows or columns, drag over the row or column header.
- To select multiple (nonadjacent) rows or columns, press Ctrl while you click the row or column headers that you want.
- **Press Ctrl+Spacebar to select a column.** The column of the active cell (or columns of the selected cells) is highlighted.
- **Press Shift+Spacebar to select a row.** The row of the active cell (or rows of the selected cells) is highlighted.

Selecting noncontiguous ranges

Most of the time, the ranges that you select are *contiguous* — a single rectangle of cells. Excel also enables you to work with *noncontiguous ranges,* which consist of two or more ranges (or single cells) that aren't next to each other. Selecting noncontiguous ranges is also known as a *multiple selection.* If you want to apply the same formatting to cells in different areas of your worksheet, one approach is to make a multiple selection. When the appropriate cells or ranges are selected, the formatting that you select is applied to them all. Figure 14.13 shows a noncontiguous range selected in a worksheet. Three ranges are selected: A2:C3, A5:C5, and A9:C10.

FIGURE 14.13

Excel enables you to select noncontiguous ranges.

You can select a noncontiguous range in several ways:

- **Select the first range (or cell).** Then press and hold Ctrl as you drag the mouse to highlight additional cells or ranges.

- **From the keyboard, select a range as described previously (using F8 or the Shift key).** Then press Shift+F8 to select another range without canceling the previous range selections.

- **Enter the range (or cell) address in the Name box and press Enter.** Separate each range address with a comma.

- **Choose Home ⇨ Editing ⇨ Find & Select ⇨ Go To (or press F5) to display the Go To dialog box.** Enter the range (or cell) address in the Reference box, and separate each range address with a comma. Click OK, and Excel selects the ranges.

> **NOTE**
>
> Noncontiguous ranges differ from contiguous ranges in several important ways. One obvious difference is that you can't use drag-and-drop methods (described later) to move or copy noncontiguous ranges.

Selecting multisheet ranges

In addition to two-dimensional ranges on a single worksheet, ranges can extend across multiple worksheets to be three-dimensional ranges.

Suppose that you have a workbook set up to track budgets. A common approach is to use a separate worksheet for each department, making it easy to organize the data. You can click a sheet tab to view the information for a particular department.

Say you have a workbook with four sheets: Totals, Operations, Marketing, and Manufacturing. The sheets are laid out identically. The only difference is the values. The Totals sheet contains formulas that compute the sum of the corresponding items in the three departmental worksheets.

Assume that you want to apply formatting to the sheets — for example, make the column headings bold with background shading. One (albeit not-so-efficient) approach is to format the cells in each worksheet separately. A better technique is to select a multisheet range and format the cells in all the sheets simultaneously. The following is a step-by-step example of multisheet formatting, using the workbook shown in Figure 14.14.

1. **Activate the Totals worksheet by clicking its tab.**

2. **Select the range B3:F3.**

3. **Press Shift and click the Manufacturing sheet tab.** This step selects all worksheets between the active worksheet (Totals) and the sheet tab that you click — in essence, a three-dimensional range of cells (see Figure 14.14). The workbook window's title bar displays [Group] to remind you that you've selected a group of sheets and that you're in Group mode.

FIGURE 14.14

In Group mode, you can work with a three-dimensional range of cells that extend across multiple worksheets.

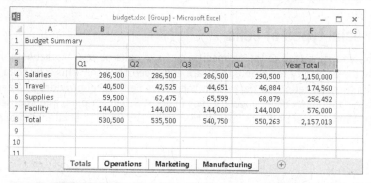

4. **Choose Home ➪ Font ➪ Bold and then choose Home ➪ Font ➪ Fill Color to apply a colored background.** Excel applies the formatting to the selected range across the selected sheets.

5. **Click one of the other sheet tabs.** This step selects the sheet and also cancels Group mode; [Group] is no longer displayed in the title bar.

When a workbook is in Group mode, any changes that you make to cells in one worksheet also apply to the corresponding cells in all the other grouped worksheets. You can use this to your advantage when you want to set up a group of identical worksheets because any labels, data, formatting, or formulas you enter are automatically added to the same cells in all the grouped worksheets.

> **NOTE**
>
> When Excel is in Group mode, some commands are disabled and can't be used. For example, in the preceding example, you can't convert all these ranges to tables by choosing Insert ➪ Tables ➪ Table.

In general, selecting a multisheet range is a simple two-step process: Select the range in one sheet, and then select the worksheets to include in the range. To select a group of contiguous worksheets, you can press Shift and click the sheet tab of the last worksheet that you want to include in the selection. To select individual worksheets, press Ctrl and click the sheet tab of each worksheet that you want to select. If all the worksheets in a workbook aren't laid out the same, you can skip the sheets that you don't want to format. When you make the selection, the sheet tabs of the selected sheets display in bold with underlined text, and Excel displays [Group] in the title bar.

TIP

To select all sheets in a workbook, right-click any sheet tab and choose Select All Sheets from the shortcut menu.

Selecting special types of cells

As you use Excel, you may need to locate specific types of cells in your worksheets. For example, wouldn't it be handy to be able to locate every cell that contains a formula — or perhaps all the formula cells that depend on the active cell? Excel provides an easy way to locate these and many other special types of cells: Select a range, and choose Home ⇨ Editing ⇨ Find & Select ⇨ Go to Special to display the Go to Special dialog box, shown in Figure 14.15.

FIGURE 14.15

Use the Go to Special dialog box to select specific types of cells.

After you make your choice in the dialog box, Excel selects the qualifying subset of cells in the current selection. Often, this subset of cells is a multiple selection. If no cells qualify, Excel lets you know with the message No cells were found.

TIP

If you bring up the Go to Special dialog box with only one cell selected, Excel bases its selection on the entire used area of the worksheet. Otherwise, the selection is based on the selected range.

Table 14.1 offers a description of the options available in the Go to Special dialog box. Some of the options are very useful.

TABLE 14.1 **Go to Special Options**

Option	What it does
Comments	Selects the cells that contain a cell comment.
Constants	Selects all nonempty cells that don't contain formulas. Use the check boxes under the Formulas option to choose which types of nonformula cells to include.
Formulas	Selects cells that contain formulas. Qualify this by selecting the type of result: numbers, text, logical values (TRUE or FALSE), or errors.
Blanks	Selects all empty cells. If a single cell is selected when the dialog box displays, this option selects the empty cells in the used area of the worksheet.
Current region	Selects a rectangular range of cells around the active cell. This range is determined by surrounding blank rows and columns. You can also press Ctrl+Shift+8 (Ctrl+*).
Current array	Selects the entire array.
Objects	Selects all embedded objects on the worksheet, including charts and graphics.
Row differences	Analyzes the selection and selects cells that are different from other cells in each row.
Column differences	Analyzes the selection and selects the cells that are different from other cells in each column.
Precedents	Selects cells that are referred to in the formulas in the active cell or selection (limited to the active sheet). You can select either direct precedents or precedents at any level.
Dependents	Selects cells with formulas that refer to the active cell or selection (limited to the active sheet). You can select either direct dependents or dependents at any level.
Last cell	Selects the bottom-right cell in the worksheet that contains data or formatting. For this option, the entire worksheet is examined, even if a range is selected when the dialog box displays.
Visible cells only	Selects only visible cells in the selection. This option is useful when dealing with a filtered list or table.
Conditional formats	Selects cells that have a conditional format applied (by choosing Home ➪ Styles ➪ Conditional Formatting). The All option selects all such cells. The Same option selects only the cells that have the same conditional formatting as the active cell.
Data validation	Selects cells that are set up for data entry validation (by choosing Data ➪ Date Tools ➪ Data Validation). The All option selects all such cells. The Same option selects only the cells that have the same validation rules as the active cell.

14

> **TIP**
>
> When you select an option in the Go to Special dialog box, be sure to note which suboptions become available. The placement of these suboptions can be misleading. For example, when you select Constants, the suboptions under Formulas become available to help you further refine the results. Likewise, the suboptions under Dependents also apply to Precedents, and those under Data validation also apply to Conditional Formats.

Selecting cells by searching

Another way to select cells is to choose Home⇨Editing⇨Find & Select⇨Find (or press Ctrl+F), which allows you to select cells by their contents. Click the Options button to display additional choices for refining the search.

Enter the text that you're looking for; then click Find All. The dialog box expands to display all the cells that match your search criteria. For example, Figure 14.16 shows the dialog box after Excel has located all cells that contain the text *Widget*. You can click an item in the list, and the screen will scroll so that you can view the cell in context. To select all the cells in the list, first select any single item in the list. Then press Ctrl+A to select them all.

FIGURE 14.16

The Find and Replace dialog box, with its results listed

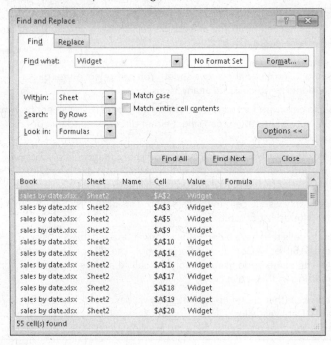

> **NOTE**
>
> The Find and Replace dialog box is nonmodal, so it allows you to return to the worksheet without dismissing the dialog box.

The Find and Replace dialog box supports two wildcard characters:

?	Matches any single character
*	Matches any number of characters

Wildcard characters also work with values when the Match Entire Cell Contents option is selected. For example, searching for 3* locates all cells that contain a value that begins with 3. Searching for 1?9 locates all three-digit entries that begin with 1 and end with 9. Searching for *00 locates values that end with two zeros.

> **TIP**
>
> To search for a question mark or an asterisk, precede the character with a tilde (~). For example, the following search string finds the text *NONE*:
>
> ~*NONE~*
>
> If you need to search for the tilde character, use two tildes.

If your searches don't seem to be working correctly, double-check these three options (which sometimes have a way of changing on their own):

- **Match case:** If this check box is selected, the case of the text must match exactly. For example, searching for smith does not locate Smith.

- **Match entire cell contents:** If this check box is selected, a match occurs if the cell contains only the search string (and nothing else). For example, searching for Excel doesn't locate a cell that contains Microsoft Excel. When using wildcard characters, an exact match is not required.

- **Look in:** This drop-down list has three options: Values, Formulas, and Comments. If, for example, Values is selected, searching for 900 doesn't find a cell that contains 900 if that value is generated by a formula (unless the formula itself contains 900).

14

Copying or Moving Ranges

As you create a worksheet, you may find it necessary to copy or move information from one location to another. Excel makes copying or moving ranges of cells easy. Here are some common things you might do:

- **Copy a cell to another location.**
- **Copy a cell to a range of cells.** The source cell is copied to every cell in the destination range.
- **Copy a range to another range.** Both ranges must be the same size.
- **Move a range of cells to another location.**

The primary difference between copying and moving a range is the effect of the operation on the source range. When you copy a range, the source range is unaffected. When you move a range, the contents are removed from the source range.

> **NOTE**
>
> Copying a cell normally copies the cell's contents, any formatting that is applied to the original cell (including conditional formatting and data validation), and the cell comment (if it has one). When you copy a cell that contains a formula, the cell references in the copied formulas are changed automatically to be relative to their new destination.

Copying or moving consists of two steps (although shortcut methods are available):

1. **Select the cell or range to copy (the source range), and copy it to the Clipboard.**
   To move the range instead of copying it, cut the range instead of copying it.

2. **Move the cell pointer to the range that will hold the copy (the destination range), and paste the Clipboard contents.**

> **CAUTION**
>
> When you paste information, Excel overwrites any cells that get in the way without warning you. If you find that pasting overwrote some essential cells, choose Undo from the Quick Access Toolbar (or press Ctrl+Z).

> **NOTE**
>
> When you copy a cell or range, Excel surrounds the copied area with an animated border. As long as that border remains animated, the copied information is available for pasting. If you press Esc to cancel the animated border, Excel removes the information from the Clipboard.

Because copying (or moving) is used so often, Excel provides many different methods. I discuss each method in the following sections. Copying and moving are similar operations, so I point out only important differences between the two.

Copying by using Ribbon commands

Choosing Home ⇨ Clipboard ⇨ Copy transfers a copy of the selected cell or range to the Windows Clipboard and the Office Clipboard. After performing the copy part of this operation, select the cell that will hold the copy and choose Home ⇨ Clipboard ⇨ Paste.

Instead of choosing Home ⇨ Clipboard ⇨ Paste, you can just activate the destination cell and press Enter. If you use this technique, Excel removes the copied information from the Clipboard so that it can't be pasted again.

NOTE

If you click the Copy button more than once before you click the Paste button, Excel may automatically display the Office Clipboard pane. To prevent this pane from appearing, click the Options button at the bottom and then remove the check mark from Show Office Clipboard Automatically.

If you're copying a range, you don't need to select an entire same-sized range before you click the Paste button. You only need to click the upper-left cell in the destination range.

TIP

The Home ⇨ Clipboard ⇨ Paste control contains a drop-down arrow that, when clicked, gives you additional paste option icons. The paste preview icons are explained later in this chapter (see "Pasting in special ways").

About the Office Clipboard

As Chapter 3 briefly introduced, Office has its own Office Clipboard. To view or hide the Office Clipboard, click the dialog box launcher in the bottom-right corner of the Home ⇨ Clipboard group.

Whenever you cut or copy information in an Office program, such as Excel or Word, the program places the information on both the Windows Clipboard and the Office Clipboard. However, the program treats information on the Office Clipboard differently from how it treats information on the Windows Clipboard. Instead of replacing information on the Office Clipboard, the program appends the information to the Office Clipboard when it's active. With multiple items stored on the Clipboard, you can then paste the items either individually or as a group. You can find out more about this feature in "Using the Office Clipboard to paste," later in this chapter.

Copying by using shortcut menu commands and keyboard shortcuts

If you prefer, you can use the following shortcut menu commands for copying and pasting:

- **Right-click the range and choose Copy (or Cut) from the shortcut menu to copy the selected cells to the Clipboard.**

14

- **Right-click and choose Paste from the shortcut menu that appears to paste the Clipboard contents to the selected cell or range.**

For more control over how the pasted information appears, use one of the buttons under Paste Options in the shortcut menu (see Figure 14.17).

FIGURE 14.17

The paste icons on the shortcut menu provide more control over how the pasted information appears.

Instead of using Paste, you can just activate the destination cell and press Enter. If you use this technique, Excel removes the copied information from the Clipboard so that it can't be pasted again.

The copy and paste operations also have keyboard shortcuts (these are the same as those available in other applications):

- **Ctrl+C copies the selected cells to both the Windows Clipboard and the Office Clipboard.**
- **Ctrl+X cuts the selected cells to both the Windows Clipboard and the Office Clipboard.**
- **Ctrl+V pastes the Windows Clipboard contents to the selected cell or range.**

Using Paste Options Buttons When Inserting and Pasting

Some cell and range operations — specifically inserting, pasting, and filling cells by dragging — result in the display of paste option buttons. For example, if you copy a range and then paste it to a different location using Home ⇨ Clipboard ⇨ Paste, a drop-down options list appears at the lower right of the pasted range. Click the list (or press Ctrl), and you see the options shown in the figure here. These options enable you to specify how the data should be pasted, such as values only or formatting only. In this case, using the paste option buttons is an alternative to using options in the Paste Special dialog box. (Read more about Paste Special in the upcoming section, "Using the Paste Special dialog box.")

Some users find these paste options buttons helpful, and others think that they're annoying. (Count me in the latter group.) To disable this feature, choose File ⇨ Options and click the Advanced tab. Remove the check mark from the two options labeled Show Paste Options button when content is pasted and Show Insert Options Buttons.

Copying or moving by using drag-and-drop

Excel also enables you to copy or move a cell or range by dragging. Unlike other methods of copying and moving, dragging and dropping does not place any information on either the Windows Clipboard or the Office Clipboard.

> **CAUTION**
>
> The drag-and-drop method of moving does offer one advantage over the cut-and-paste method: Excel warns you if a drag-and-drop move operation will overwrite existing cell contents. Oddly, you do not get a warning if a drag-and-drop copy operation will overwrite existing cell contents.

To copy using drag-and-drop, select the cell or range that you want to copy and then press Ctrl and move the mouse to one of the selection's borders (the mouse pointer is augmented with a small plus sign). Then, drag the selection to its new location while you continue to press the Ctrl key. The original selection remains behind, and Excel makes a new copy when you release the mouse button.

To move a range using drag-and-drop, don't press Ctrl while dragging the border.

> **TIP**
>
> If the mouse pointer doesn't turn into an arrow when you point to the border of a cell or range, you need to make a change to your settings. Choose File ⇨ Options to display the Excel Options dialog box, select the Advanced tab, and place a check mark on the option labeled Enable fill handle and cell drag-and-drop.

Copying to adjacent cells

Often, you need to copy a cell to an adjacent cell or range. This type of copying is quite common when working with formulas. For example, if you're working on a budget, you might create a formula to add the values in column B. You can use the same formula to add the values in the other columns. Rather than re-enter the formula, you can copy it to the adjacent cells.

Excel provides additional options for copying to adjacent cells. To use these commands, activate the cell that you're copying *and* extend the cell selection to include the cells that you're copying to. Then issue the appropriate command from the following list for one-step copying:

- **Home ⇨ Editing ⇨ Fill ⇨ Down (or Ctrl+D) copies the cell to the selected range below.**
- **Home ⇨ Editing ⇨ Fill ⇨ Right (or Ctrl+R) copies the cell to the selected range to the right.**
- **Home ⇨ Editing ⇨ Fill ⇨ Up copies the cell to the selected range above.**
- **Home ⇨ Editing ⇨ Fill ⇨ Left copies the cell to the selected range to the left.**

None of these commands places information on either the Windows Clipboard or the Office Clipboard.

> **TIP**
>
> You also can use Auto Fill to copy to adjacent cells by dragging the selection's *fill handle* (the small square in the bottom-right corner of the selected cell or range). Excel copies the original selection to the cells that you highlight while dragging. For more control over the Auto Fill operation, drag the fill handle with the right mouse button, and you'll get a shortcut menu with additional options.

Copying a range to other sheets

You can use the copy procedures described previously to copy a cell or range to another worksheet, even if the worksheet is in a different workbook. You must, of course, activate the other worksheet before you select the location to which you want to copy.

Excel offers a quicker way to copy a cell or range and paste it to other worksheets in the same workbook.

1. **Select the range to copy.**
2. **Press Ctrl and click the sheet tabs for the worksheets to which you want to copy the information.** Excel displays [Group] in the workbook's title bar.
3. **Choose Home ⇨ Editing ⇨ Fill ⇨ Across Worksheets.** A dialog box appears to ask you what you want to copy (All, Contents, or Formats).
4. **Make your choice and then click OK.** Excel copies the selected range to the selected worksheets; the new copy occupies the same cells in the selected worksheets as the original occupies in the initial worksheet.

> **CAUTION**
>
> Be careful with the Home ⇨ Editing ⇨ Fill ⇨ Across Worksheets command because Excel doesn't warn you when the destination cells contain information. You can quickly overwrite lots of cells with this command and not even realize it. So, make sure you check your work, and use Undo if the result isn't what you expected.

Using the Office Clipboard to paste

Whenever you cut or copy information in an Office program, such as Excel, you can place the data on both the Windows Clipboard and the Office Clipboard. When you copy information to the Office Clipboard, you append the information to the Office Clipboard instead of replacing what is already there. With multiple items stored on the Office Clipboard, you can then paste the items either individually or as a group.

To use the Office Clipboard, you first need to open it. Click the dialog box launcher on the bottom right of the Home ⇨ Clipboard group to toggle the Clipboard pane on and off.

> **TIP**
>
> To make the Clipboard task pane open automatically, click the Options button near the bottom of the task pane and choose the Show Office Clipboard Automatically option.

After you open the Clipboard task pane, select the first cell or range that you want to copy to the Office Clipboard and copy it by using any of the preceding techniques. Repeat this process, selecting the next cell or range that you want to copy. As soon as you copy the information, the Clipboard pane shows you the number of items that you've copied and a brief description (it will hold up to 24 items). Figure 14.18 shows the Office Clipboard with four copied items.

14

FIGURE 14.18

Use the Clipboard pane to copy and paste multiple items.

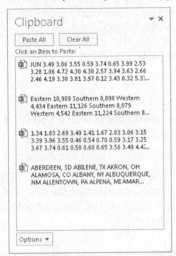

When you're ready to paste information, select the cell into which you want to paste information. To paste an individual item, click it in the Clipboard pane. To paste all the items that you've copied, click the Paste All button (which is at the top of the Clipboard pane). The items are pasted, one after the other. The Paste All button is probably more useful in Word, for situations in which you copy text from various sources and then paste it all at once.

You can clear the contents of the Office Clipboard by clicking the Clear All button.

The following items about the Office Clipboard and how it functions are worth noting:

- **Excel pastes the contents of the Windows Clipboard (the last item you copied to the Office Clipboard) when you paste by choosing Home ⇨ Clipboard ⇨ Paste, by pressing Ctrl+V, or by right-clicking and choosing Paste from the shortcut menu.**
- **The last item that you cut or copied appears on both the Office Clipboard and the Windows Clipboard.**
- **Pasting from the Office Clipboard also places that item on the Windows Clipboard.** If you choose Paste All from the Office Clipboard toolbar, you paste all items stored on the Office Clipboard onto the Windows Clipboard as a single item.
- **Clearing the Office Clipboard also clears the Windows Clipboard.**

> **CAUTION**
>
> The Office Clipboard has a serious problem that makes it virtually worthless for Excel users: If you copy a range that contains formulas, the formulas are not transferred when you paste to a different range. Only the values are pasted. Furthermore, Excel doesn't even warn you about this fact.

Pasting in special ways

You may not always want to copy everything from the source range to the destination range. For example, you may want to copy only the formula results rather than the formulas themselves. Or you may want to copy the number formats from one range to another without overwriting any existing data or formulas.

To control what is copied into the destination range, choose Home ⇨ Clipboard ⇨ Paste and use the drop-down menu shown in Figure 14.19. When you hover your mouse pointer over an icon, you'll see a preview of the pasted information in the destination range. Click the icon to use the selected paste option.

FIGURE 14.19

Excel offers several pasting options, with preview. Here, the information is copied from D2:E5 and is being pasted beginning at cell D10 using the Transpose option.

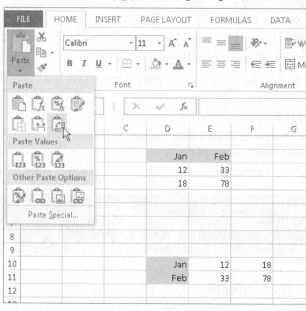

The paste options are:

- **Paste (P):** Pastes the cell's contents, formats, and data validation from the Windows Clipboard.
- **Formulas (F):** Pastes formulas but not formatting.
- **Formulas & Number Formatting (O):** Pastes formulas and number formatting only.
- **Keep Source Formatting (K):** Pastes formulas and all formatting.
- **No Borders (B):** Pastes everything except borders that appear in the source range.
- **Keep Source Column Width (W):** Pastes formulas and duplicates the column width of the copied cells.
- **Transpose (T):** Changes the orientation of the copied range. Rows become columns, and columns become rows. Any formulas in the copied range are adjusted so that they work properly when transposed.
- **Merge Conditional Formatting (G):** This icon is displayed only when the copied cells contain conditional formatting. When clicked, it merges the copied conditional formatting with any conditional formatting in the destination range.
- **Values (V):** Pastes the results of formulas. The destination for the copy can be a new range or the original range. In the latter case, Excel replaces the original formulas with their current values.
- **Values & Number Formatting (A):** Pastes the results of formulas plus the number formatting.
- **Values & Source Formatting (E):** Pastes the results of formulas plus all formatting.
- **Formatting (R):** Pastes only the formatting of the source range.
- **Paste Link (N):** Creates formulas in the destination range that refer to the cells in the copied range.
- **Picture (U):** Pastes the copied information as a picture.
- **Linked Picture (I):** Pastes the copied information as a "live" picture that is updated if the source range is changed.
- **Paste Special:** Displays the Paste Special dialog box (described in the next section).

> **NOTE**
>
> After you paste, you're offered another chance to change your mind. A Paste Options button appears at the lower right of the pasted range. Click it (or press Ctrl), and you see the paste option icons again.

Using the Paste Special dialog box

For yet another pasting method, choose Home ➪ Clipboard ➪ Paste ➪ Paste Special to display the Paste Special dialog box (see Figure 14.20). You can also right-click and choose Paste Special from the shortcut menu to display this dialog box. This dialog box has several options, explained next.

FIGURE 14.20

The Paste Special dialog box

- **All:** Pastes the cell's contents, formats, and data validation from the Windows Clipboard

- **Formulas:** Pastes values and formulas, with no formatting

- **Values:** Pastes values and the results of formulas (no formatting). The destination for the copy can be a new range or the original range. In the latter case, Excel replaces the original formulas with their current values.

- **Formats:** Copies only the formatting

- **Comments:** Copies only the cell comments from a cell or range. This option doesn't copy cell contents or formatting.

- **Validation:** Copies the validation criteria so the same data validation will apply. Data validation is applied by choosing Data ⇨ Data Tools ⇨ Data Validation.

- **All Using Source Theme:** Pastes everything, but uses the formatting from the document theme of the source. This option is relevant only if you're pasting information from a different workbook, and the workbook uses a different document theme than the active workbook.

- **All Except Borders:** Pastes everything except borders that appear in the source range
- **Column Widths:** Pastes only column width information
- **Formulas and Number Formats:** Pastes all values, formulas, and number formats (but no other formatting)
- **Values and Number Formats:** Pastes all values and numeric formats but not the formulas themselves
- **All merging conditional formats:** Merges the copied conditional formatting with any conditional formatting in the destination range. This option is enabled only when you're copying a range that contains conditional formatting.

In addition, the Paste Special dialog box enables you to perform other operations, described in the following sections.

Performing mathematical operations without formulas

The option buttons in the Operation section of the Paste Special dialog box let you perform an arithmetic operation on values and formulas in the destination range. For example, you can copy a range to another range and select the Multiply operation. Excel multiplies the corresponding values in the source range and the destination range and replaces the destination range with the new values.

This feature also works with a single copied cell, pasted to a multi-cell range. Assume that you have a range of values, and you want to increase each value by 5 percent. Enter **105%** into any blank cell and copy that cell to the Clipboard. Then select the range of values and bring up the Paste Special dialog box. Select the Multiply option, and each value in the range is multiplied by 105%.

CAUTION

If the destination range contains formulas, the formulas are also modified. In many cases, this is *not* what you want.

Skipping blanks when pasting

The Skip Blanks option in the Paste Special dialog box prevents Excel from overwriting cell contents in your paste area with blank cells from the copied range. This option is useful if you're copying a range to another area but don't want the blank cells in the copied range to overwrite existing data.

Transposing a range

The Transpose option in the Paste Special dialog box changes the orientation of the copied range. Rows become columns, and columns become rows. Any formulas in the copied range are adjusted so that they work properly when transposed. Note that you can use this check box with the other options in the Paste Special dialog box.

TIP

If you click the Paste Link button in the Paste Special dialog box, you create formulas that link to the source range. As a result, the destination range automatically reflects changes in the source range.

Using Names to Work with Ranges

Dealing with cryptic cell and range addresses can sometimes be confusing, especially when you deal with formulas, which are covered in Chapter 15. Fortunately, Excel allows you to assign descriptive names to cells and ranges. For example, you can give a cell a name such as Interest_Rate, or you can name a range JulySales. Working with these names (rather than cell or range addresses) has several advantages:

- A meaningful range name (such as Total_Income) is much easier to remember than a cell address (such as AC21).

- Entering a name is less error prone than entering a cell or range address, and if you type a name incorrectly in a formula, Excel will display a #NAME? error.

- You can quickly move to areas of your worksheet either by using the Name box, located at the left side of the Formula bar (click the arrow to drop down a list of defined names) or by choosing Home➪Editing➪Find & Select➪Go To (or pressing F5) and specifying the range name.

- Creating formulas is easier. You can paste a cell or range name into a formula by using Formula AutoComplete, another feature covered in Chapter 15.

- Names make your formulas more understandable and easier to use. A formula such as =Income—Taxes is more intuitive than =D20—D40.

Creating range names in your workbooks

Excel provides several different methods that you can use to create range names. Before you begin, however, you should be aware of a few rules:

- **Names can't contain any spaces.** You may want to use an underscore character to simulate a space (such as Annual_Total).

- **You can use any combination of letters and numbers, but the name must begin with a letter, underscore, or backslash.** A name can't begin with a number (such as 3rdQuarter) or look like a cell address (such as QTR3). If these are desirable names, though, you can precede the name with an underscore or a backslash: for example, _3rd Quarter and \QTR3.

- **Symbols — except for underscores, backslashes, and periods — aren't allowed.**

- **Names are limited to 255 characters, but it's a good practice to keep names as short as possible, but still meaningful.**

Using the Name box

The fastest way to create a name is to use the Name box (to the left of the Formula bar). Select the cell or range to name, click the Name box, and type the name. Press Enter to create the name. (You must press Enter to actually record the name; if you type a name and then click in the worksheet, Excel doesn't create the name.)

If you type an invalid name (such as May21, which is a cell address), Excel activates that address (and doesn't warn you that the name is not valid). If the name you type includes an invalid character, Excel displays an error message. If a name already exists, you can't use the Name box to change the range to which that name refers. Attempting to do so simply selects the range.

The Name box is a drop-down list and shows all names in the workbook. To choose a named cell or range, click the Name box and choose the name. The name appears in the Name box, and Excel selects the named cell or range in the worksheet.

Using the New Name dialog box

For more control over naming cells and ranges, use the New Name dialog box. Start by selecting the cell or range that you want to name. Then choose Formulas ➪ Defined Names ➪ Define Name. Excel displays the New Name dialog box, shown in Figure 14.21. Note that this is a resizable dialog box. Drag a border to change the dimensions.

FIGURE 14.21

Create names for cells or ranges by using the New Name dialog box.

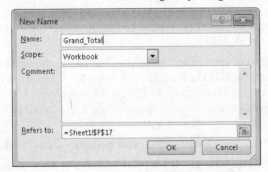

Type a name in the Name text field (or use the name that Excel proposes, if any). The selected cell or range address appears in the Refers To text field. Use the Scope drop-down list to indicate the scope for the name. The *scope* indicates where the name will be valid, and it's either the entire workbook or a particular sheet. If you like, you can add a comment that describes the named range or cell. Click OK to add the name to your workbook and close the dialog box.

Using the Create Names from Selection dialog box

You may have a worksheet that contains text that you want to use for names for adjacent cells or ranges. For example, you may want to use the text in column A to create names for the corresponding values in column B. Excel makes this task easy.

To create names by using adjacent text, start by selecting the name text and the cells that you want to name. (These items can be individual cells or ranges of cells.) The names must be adjacent to the cells that you're naming. (A multiple selection is allowed.) Then choose Formulas ⇨ Defined Names ⇨ Create from Selection. Excel displays the Create Names from Selection dialog box, shown in Figure 14.22.

The check marks in the Create Names from Selection dialog box are based on Excel's analysis of the selected range. For example, if Excel finds text in the first row of the selection, it proposes that you create names based on the top row. If Excel didn't guess correctly, you can change the check boxes. Click OK, and Excel creates the names. Using the data in Figure 14.22, Excel creates six names: January for cell B1, February for cell B2, and so on.

FIGURE 14.22

Use the Create Names from Selection dialog box to name cells using labels that appear in the worksheet.

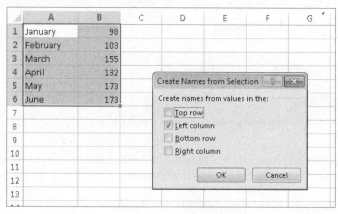

NOTE

If the text contained in a cell would result in an invalid name, Excel modifies the name to make it valid. For example, if a cell contains the text *Net Income* (which is invalid for a name because it contains a space), Excel converts the space to an underscore character. If Excel encounters a value or a numeric formula where text should be, however, it doesn't convert it to a valid name. It simply doesn't create a name — and does not inform you of that fact.

CAUTION

If the upper-left cell of the selection contains text and you choose the Top Row and Left Column options, Excel uses that text for the name of the entire range, excluding the top row and left column. So, after Excel creates the names, take a minute to make sure that they refer to the correct ranges. If Excel creates a name that is incorrect, you can delete or modify it by using the Name Manager (described next).

Managing names

A workbook can have any number of named cells and ranges. If you have many names, you should know about the Name Manager, shown in Figure 14.23.

FIGURE 14.23

Use the Name Manager to work with range names.

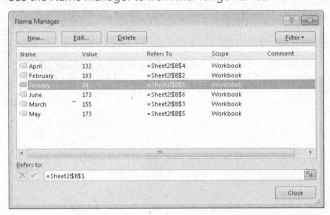

The Name Manager appears when you choose Formulas ➪ Defined Names ➪ Name Manager (or press Ctrl+F3). The Name Manager has the following features:

- **Displays information about each name in the workbook:** You can resize the Name Manager dialog box, widen the columns to show more information, and even rearrange the order of the columns. You can also click a column heading to sort the information by the column.

- **Allows you to filter the displayed names:** Clicking the Filter button lets you show only those names that meet a certain criteria. For example, you can view only the worksheet-level names.

- **Provides quick access to the New Name dialog box:** Click the New button to create a new name without closing the Name Manager.

- **Lets you edit names:** To edit a name, select it in the list and then click the Edit button. You can change the name itself, modify the Refers to range, or edit the comment.

- **Lets you quickly delete unneeded names:** To delete a name, select it in the list and click Delete.

CAUTION

Be extra careful when deleting names. If the name is used in a formula, deleting the name causes the formula to become invalid. (It displays #NAME?.) It seems logical that Excel would replace the name with its actual address — but that doesn't happen. However, deleting a name can be undone, so if you find that formulas return #NAME? after you delete a name, choose Undo from the Quick Access Toolbar (or press Ctrl+Z) to get the name back.

If you delete the rows or columns that contain named cells or ranges, the names contain an invalid reference. For example, if cell A1 on Sheet1 is named Interest and you delete row 1 or column A, the name Interest then refers to =Sheet1!#REF! (that is, to an erroneous reference). If you use Interest in a formula, the formula displays #REF.

TIP

The Name Manager is useful, but it has a shortcoming: It doesn't let you display the list of names in a worksheet range so you can view or print them. Such a feat is possible, but you need to look beyond the Name Manager.

To create a list of names in a worksheet, first move the cell pointer to an empty area of your worksheet. The list is created at the active cell position and overwrites any information at that location. Press F3 to display the Paste Name dialog box, which lists all the defined names. Then click the Paste List button. Excel creates a list of all names in the workbook and their corresponding addresses.

14

Adding Comments to Cells

Documentation that explains certain elements in the worksheet can often be helpful. One way to document your work is to add comments to cells. This feature is useful when you need to describe a particular value or explain how a formula works.

To add a comment to a cell, select the cell and use any of these actions:

- **Choose Review ➪ Comments ➪ New Comment.**
- **Right-click the cell and choose Insert Comment from the shortcut menu.**
- **Press Shift+F2.**

Excel inserts a comment that points to the active cell. Initially, the comment consists of your name, as specified in the General tab of the Excel Options dialog box (choose File⇨Options to display this dialog box). You can delete your name from the comment, if you like. Enter the text for the cell comment and then click anywhere in the worksheet to hide the comment. You can change the size of the comment by clicking and dragging any of its borders. Figure 14.24 shows a cell with a comment.

FIGURE 14.24

You can add comments to cells to help point out specific items in your worksheets.

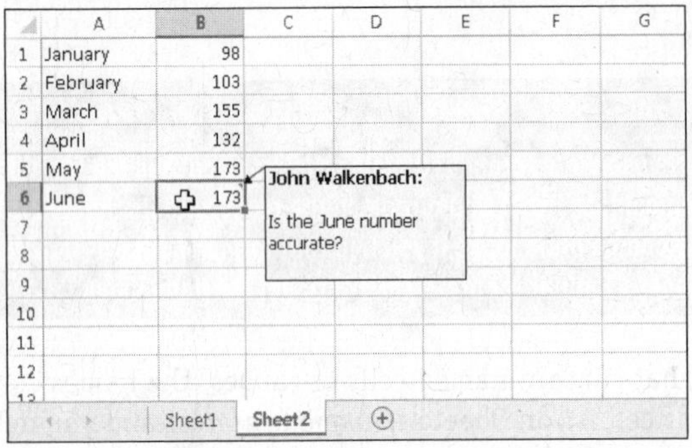

Cells that have a comment display a small red triangle in the upper-right corner. When you move the mouse pointer over a cell that contains a comment (or activate the cell), the comment becomes visible.

You can force a comment to be displayed even when its cell is not activated. Right-click the cell and choose Show/Hide Comments. Although this command refers to "comments" (plural), it affects only the comment in the active cell. To return to normal (make the comment appear only when its cell is activated or the mouse point hovers over it), right-click the cell and choose Hide Comment.

> **TIP**
>
> You can control how comments are displayed. Choose File⇨Options and then select the Advanced tab of the Excel Options dialog box. In the Display section, select the No comments or indicators option under For cells with comments, show.

Formatting comments

If you don't like the default look of cell comments, you can make some changes. Right-click the cell and choose Edit Comment. Select the text in the comment and use the commands of the Font and the Alignment groups (on the Home tab) to make changes to the comment's appearance.

For even more formatting options, right-click the comment's border and choose Format Comment from the shortcut menu. Excel responds by displaying the Format Comment dialog box, which allows you to change many aspects of its appearance, including color, border, and margins.

You can also display an image inside a comment. Right-click the cell and choose Edit Comment. Then right-click the comment's border and choose Format Comment. Select the Colors and Lines tab in the Format Comment dialog box. Click the Color drop-down list and select Fill Effects. In the Fill Effects dialog box, click the Picture tab and then click the Select Picture button to specify a graphics file. Figure 14.25 shows a comment that contains a picture.

FIGURE 14.25

This comment contains a graphics image.

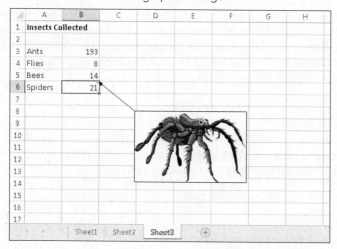

Working further with comments

Comments are there to present information, and you need to know how to read and display comments. Here are additional key actions you'll perform with comments:

- **Reading comments:** To read all comments in a workbook, choose Review ➪ Comments ➪ Next. Keep clicking Next to cycle through all the comments in a workbook. Choose Review ➪ Comments ➪ Previous to view the comments in reverse order.

> **NOTE**
> You can also access the Page Setup box from the Print panel of Backstage view.

- **Hiding and showing comments:** If you want all cell comments to be visible (regardless of the location of the cell pointer), choose Review ➪ Comments ➪ Show All Comments. This command is a toggle; select it again to hide all cell comments. To toggle the display of an individual comment, select its cell, and then choose Review ➪ Comments ➪ Show/Hide Comment.

- **Selecting comments:** To quickly select all cells in a worksheet that contain a comment, choose Home ➪ Editing ➪ Find & Select ➪ Go to Special. Then choose the Comments option and click OK.

- **Editing comments:** To edit a comment, activate the cell, right-click, and then choose Edit Comment from the shortcut menu. Or select the cell and press Shift+F2. After you make your changes, click any cell.

- **Deleting comments:** To delete a cell comment, activate the cell that contains the comment and then choose Review ➪ Comments ➪ Delete. Or right-click and then choose Delete Comment from the shortcut menu.

- **Printing comments:** Comments do not print by default. Click the dialog box launcher in the Page Layout ➪ Page Setup group. In the Page Setup dialog box, click the Sheet tab. Make your choice from the Comments drop-down control: At End of Sheet or As Displayed on Sheet. Click OK to close the Page Setup dialog box or click the Print button to print the worksheet.

Summary

This chapter taught essential skills dealing with worksheets, cells, and ranges. You should now be equipped with a wide variety of skills, including the ability to:

- Create, copy, move, and rename worksheets.
- Change worksheet zoom.
- Resize, insert, and delete rows and columns.
- Hide and redisplay rows and columns.
- Use various techniques to select cells and ranges.
- Perform standard and special copy and paste operations.
- Name ranges and work with range names.
- Add and change cell comments.

Introducing Formulas and Functions

IN THIS CHAPTER

Understanding formula basics

Entering formulas and functions into your worksheets

Understanding how to use references in formulas

Correcting common formula errors

Getting tips for working with formulas

Formulas are what make a spreadsheet program so useful. If it weren't for formulas, a spreadsheet would simply be a fancy word-processing document that has great support for tabular information. You use formulas in your Excel worksheets to calculate results from the data stored in the worksheet. When data changes, the formulas calculate updated results with no extra effort on your part. This chapter introduces formulas and functions and helps you get up to speed with this important element.

Understanding Formula Basics

A *formula* consists of special code entered into a cell. It performs a calculation of some type and returns a result, which is displayed in the cell. Formulas use a variety of operators and worksheet functions to work with values and text. The values and text used in formulas can be located in other cells, which makes changing data easy and gives worksheets their dynamic nature. For example, you can see multiple scenarios quickly by changing the data in a worksheet and letting your formulas do the work.

A formula can consist of any of these elements:

- Mathematical operators, such as + (for addition) and * (for multiplication)
- Cell references (including named cells and ranges)
- Values or text
- Worksheet functions (such as SUM or AVERAGE)

After you enter a formula, the cell displays the calculated result of the formula. The formula itself appears in the Formula bar when you select the cell, however.

Here are a few examples of formulas:

=150*.05	Multiplies 150 times 0.05. This formula uses only values, and it always returns the same result. You could just enter the value **7.5** into the cell.
=A3	Returns the value in cell A3. No calculation is performed.
=A1+A2	Adds the values in cells A1 and A2.
=Income-Expenses	Subtracts the value in the cell named Expenses from the value in the cell named Income.
=SUM(A1:A12)	Adds the values in the range A1:A12, using the SUM function.
=A1=C12	Compares cell A1 with cell C12. If the cells are identical, the formula returns TRUE; otherwise, it returns FALSE.

Note that every formula begins with an equal sign (=). The initial equal sign allows Excel to distinguish a formula from plain text.

Using operators in formulas

Excel formulas support a variety of operators. *Operators* are symbols that indicate what mathematical operation you want the formula to perform. Table 15.1 lists the operators that Excel recognizes. In addition to these, Excel has many built-in functions that enable you to perform additional calculations.

TABLE 15.1   Operators Used in Formulas

Operator	Name
+	Addition
–	Subtraction
*	Multiplication
/	Division
^	Exponentiation
&	Concatenation
=	Logical comparison (equal to)
>	Logical comparison (greater than)
<	Logical comparison (less than)
>=	Logical comparison (greater than or equal to)
<=	Logical comparison (less than or equal to)
<>	Logical comparison (not equal to)

You can, of course, use as many operators as you need to perform the desired calculation.

Here are some examples of formulas that use various operators.

Formula	What it does
=" Part-"&"23A"	Joins (concatenates) the two text strings to produce Part-23A.
=A1&A2	Concatenates the contents of cell A1 with cell A2. Concatenation works with values as well as text. If cell A1 contains 123 and cell A2 contains 456, this formula would return the text 123456.
=6^3	Raises 6 to the third power (216).
=216^(1/3)	Raises 216 to the 1/3 power. This is mathematically equivalent to calculating the cube root of 216, which is 6.
=A1<A2	Returns TRUE if the value in cell A1 is less than the value in cell A2. Otherwise, it returns FALSE. Logical comparison operators also work with text. If A1 contains Bill and A2 contains Julia, the formula would return TRUE because Bill comes before Julia in alphabetical order.
=A1<=A2	Returns TRUE if the value in cell A1 is less than or equal to the value in cell A2. Otherwise, it returns FALSE.
=A1<>A2	Returns TRUE if the value in cell A1 isn't equal to the value in cell A2. Otherwise, it returns FALSE.

Understanding operator precedence in formulas

When Excel calculates the value of a formula, it uses certain rules to determine the order in which the various parts of the formula are calculated. You need to understand these rules so your formulas produce accurate results.

Table 15.2 lists the Excel operator precedence. This table shows that exponentiation has the highest precedence (performed first) and logical comparisons have the lowest precedence (performed last).

TABLE 15.2 Operator Precedence in Excel Formulas

Symbol	Operator	Precedence
^	Exponentiation	1
*	Multiplication	2
/	Division	2
+	Addition	3
–	Subtraction	3
&	Concatenation	4

Continues

TABLE 15.2   *(continued)*

Symbol	Operator	Precedence
=	Equal to	5
<	Less than	5
>	Greater than	5

You can use parentheses to override Excel's built-in order of precedence. Expressions within parentheses are always evaluated first. For example, the following formula uses parentheses to control the order in which the calculations occur. In this case, cell B3 is subtracted from cell B2, and the result is multiplied by cell B4:

```
=(B2-B3)*B4
```

If you enter the formula without the parentheses, Excel computes a different answer. Because multiplication has a higher precedence, cell B3 is multiplied by cell B4. Then this result is subtracted from cell B2, which isn't what was intended.

The formula without parentheses looks like this:

```
=B2-B3*B4
```

It's a good idea to use parentheses even when they aren't strictly necessary. Doing so helps to clarify what the formula is intended to do. For example, the following formula makes it perfectly clear that B3 should be multiplied by B4, and the result subtracted from cell B2. Without the parentheses, you would need to remember Excel's order of precedence.

```
=B2-(B3*B4)
```

You can also *nest* parentheses within formulas — that is, put them inside other parentheses. If you do so, Excel evaluates the most deeply nested expressions first — and then works its way out. Here's an example of a formula that uses nested parentheses:

```
=((B2*C2)+(B3*C3)+(B4*C4))*B6
```

This formula has four sets of parentheses — three sets are nested inside the fourth set. Excel evaluates each nested set of parentheses and then sums the three results. This result is then multiplied by the value in cell B6.

Although the preceding formula uses four sets of parentheses, only the outer set is really necessary. If you understand operator precedence, it should be clear that you can rewrite this formula as:

```
=(B2*C2+B3*C3+B4*C4)*B6
```

But most would agree that using the extra parentheses makes the calculation much clearer.

Every left parenthesis, of course, must have a matching right parenthesis. If you have many levels of nested parentheses, keeping them straight can sometimes be difficult. If the parentheses don't match, Excel displays a message explaining the problem — and won't let you enter the formula.

In some cases, if your formula contains mismatched parentheses, Excel may propose a correction to your formula. Figure 15.1 shows an example of a proposed correction. You may be tempted simply to accept Excel's suggestion, but be careful — in many cases, the proposed formula, although syntactically correct, isn't the formula you intended and it will produce an incorrect result.

FIGURE 15.1

Excel sometimes suggests a syntactically correct formula, but not the formula you had in mind.

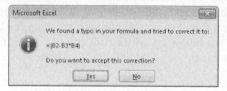

TIP

When you're editing a formula, Excel lends a hand in helping you match parentheses by displaying matching parentheses in the same color.

Using functions in your formulas

Many formulas you create use worksheet functions. These functions enable you to greatly enhance the power of your formulas and perform calculations that are difficult (or even impossible) if you use only the operators discussed previously. For example, you can use the TAN function to calculate the tangent of an angle. You can't do this complicated calculation by using the mathematical operators alone.

Examples of formulas that use functions

A worksheet function can simplify a formula significantly.

Here's an example. To calculate the average of the values in ten cells (A1:A10) without using a function, you'd have to construct a formula like this:

```
=(A1+A2+A3+A4+A5+A6+A7+A8+A9+A10)/10
```

15

Not very pretty, is it? Even worse, you would need to edit this formula if you added another cell to the range. Fortunately, you can replace this formula with a much simpler one that uses one of Excel's built-in worksheet functions, AVERAGE:

    =AVERAGE(A1:A10)

The following formula demonstrates how using a function can enable you to perform calculations that are not otherwise possible. Say you need to determine the largest value in a range. A formula can't tell you the answer without using a function. Here's a formula that uses the MAX function to return the largest value in the range A1:D100:

    =MAX(A1:D100)

Functions also can sometimes eliminate manual editing. Assume that you have a worksheet that contains 1,000 names in cells A1:A1000, and the names appear in all-capital letters. Your boss sees the listing and informs you that the names will be mail-merged with a form letter. All-uppercase letters is not acceptable; for example, JOHN F. SMITH must now appear as John F. Smith. You *could* spend the next several hours re-entering the list (ugh), or you could use a formula, such as the following, which uses the PROPER function to convert the text in cell A1 to the proper case:

    =PROPER(A1)

Enter this formula once in cell B1 and then copy it down to the next 999 rows. Then select B1:B1000 and choose Home ➪ Clipboard ➪ Copy to copy the range. Next, with B1:B1000 still selected, choose Home ➪ Clipboard ➪ Paste arrow ➪ Paste Values (V) to convert the formulas to values. Delete the original column, and you've just accomplished several hours of work in less than a minute.

One last example should convince you of the power of functions. Suppose you have a worksheet that calculates sales commissions. If the salesperson sold more than $100,000 of product, the commission rate is 7.5 percent; otherwise, the commission rate is 5.0 percent. Without using a function, you would have to create two different formulas and make sure that you use the correct formula for each sales amount. A better solution is to write a formula that uses the IF function to ensure that you calculate the correct commission, regardless of sales amount:

    =IF(A1<100000,A1*5%,A1*7.5%)

This formula performs some simple decision making. The formula checks the value of cell A1. If this value is less than 100,000, the formula returns cell A1 multiplied by 5 percent. Otherwise, it returns what's in cell A1 multiplied by 7.5 percent. This example uses three arguments, separated by commas. I discuss this in the upcoming section, "Function arguments."

New Functions in Excel 2013

Excel 2013 includes more than 50 new worksheet functions.

Nearly all the new functions are highly specialized functions that will appeal to those in engineering or math-related fields.

But there are some new functions that might appeal to a more general audience:

- ISFORMULA: Returns TRUE if the referenced cell contains a formula
- FORMULATEXT: Returns the formula in the referenced cell, as text
- SHEET: Returns the sheet number of the referenced sheet. For example, =SHEET("Sheet3") returns the sheet number for Sheet3.
- SHEETS: Returns the number of sheets in a workbook. For example, =SHEETS() returns the number of sheets in the workbook.
- IFNA: If a reference contains a #NA error, returns other text you specify

Keep in mind that these functions are not backward compatible. If you use any of these new functions, they won't work if the file is opened with an earlier version of Excel.

Function arguments

In the preceding examples, you may have noticed that all the functions used parentheses. The information inside the parentheses is the *list of arguments*.

Functions vary in how they use arguments. Depending on what it has to do, a function may use:

- No arguments
- One argument
- A fixed number of arguments
- An indeterminate number of arguments
- Optional arguments

An example of a function that doesn't use an argument is the NOW function, which returns the current date and time. Even if a function doesn't use an argument, you must still provide a set of empty parentheses, like this:

```
=NOW()
```

If a function uses more than one argument, you must separate each argument with a comma. The examples at the beginning of the chapter used cell references for arguments. Excel is quite flexible when it comes to function arguments, however. An argument can

15

consist of a cell reference, literal values, literal text strings, expressions, and even other functions. Here are some examples of functions that use various types of arguments:

- **Cell reference:** =SUM(A1:A24)
- **Literal value:** =SQRT(121)
- **Literal text string:** =PROPER("john smith")
- **Expression:** =SQRT(183+12)
- **Other functions:** =SQRT(SUM(A1:A24))

> **NOTE**
>
> A comma is the list separator character for the U.S. version of Excel. Some other versions may use a semicolon. The list separator is a Windows setting, which can be adjusted in the Windows 8 Control Panel (in the Customize Format dialog box accessed via clicking Additional settings on the Formats tab of the Region dialog box; open the dialog box by navigating to Clock, Language, and Region and clicking Region).

More about functions

All told, Excel includes more than 450 functions. And if that's not enough, you can download or purchase additional specialized functions from third-party suppliers — and even create your own custom functions (by using VBA) if you're so inclined.

Some users feel a bit overwhelmed by the sheer number of functions, but you'll probably find that you use only a dozen or so on a regular basis. And as you'll see, the Excel Insert Function dialog box (described later in this chapter) makes it easy to locate and insert a function, even if it's not one that you use frequently.

Entering Formulas into Your Worksheets

Every formula must begin with an equal sign to inform Excel that the cell contains a formula rather than text. Excel provides two ways to enter a formula into a cell: manually, or by pointing to cell references. The following sections discuss each way in detail.

Excel provides additional assistance when you create formulas by displaying a drop-down list that contains function names and range names. The items displayed in the list are determined by what you've already typed. For example, if you're entering a formula and then type the letters **SU**, you'll see the drop-down list shown in Figure 15.2. If you type an additional letter, the list is shortened to show only the matching functions. To have Excel AutoComplete an entry in that list, use the navigation keys to highlight the entry, and then press Tab. Notice that highlighting a function in the list also displays a brief description of the function. See the sidebar "Using Formula AutoComplete" for an example of how this feature works.

FIGURE 15.2

Excel displays a drop-down list when you enter a formula.

Using Formula AutoComplete

The Formula AutoComplete feature makes entering formulas easier than ever. Here's a quick walk-through that demonstrates how it works. The goal is to create a formula that uses the AGGREGATE function to calculate the average value in a range that I named TestScores. The AVERAGE function will not work in this situation because the range contains an error value.

1. **Select the cell that will hold the formula, and type an equal sign (=) to signal the start of a formula.**

2. **Type the letter** A. You get a list of functions and names that begin with A. This feature is not case sensitive, so you can use either uppercase or lowercase characters.

3. **Scroll through the list, or type** G **to narrow down the choices.**

4. **When AGGREGATE is highlighted, press Tab to select it.** Excel adds the opening parenthesis and displays another list that contains options for the first argument for AGGREGATE, as shown in Figure 15.2.

5. **Select 1 - AVERAGE and then press Tab.** Excel inserts 1, which is the code for calculating the average.

6. **Type a comma to separate the next argument.**

7. **When Excel displays a list of items for the AGGREGATE function's second argument, select 2 - Ignore Error Values and then press Tab.**

8. **Type a comma to separate the third argument (the range of test scores).**

9. **Type a** T **to get a list of functions and names that begin with** T; **you're looking for TestScores, so narrow it down a bit by typing the second character,** E.

10. **Highlight TestScores, and then press Tab.**

11. **Type a closing parenthesis and then press Enter.**

Continues

continued

The completed formula is

`=AGGREGATE(1,2,TestScores)`

Formula AutoComplete includes the following items (and each type is identified by a separate icon):

- Excel built-in functions
- User-defined functions (functions defined by the user through VBA or other methods)
- Defined names (cells or range named using the Formulas ➪ Defined Names ➪ Define Name command)
- Enumerated arguments that use a value to represent an option (only a few functions use such arguments, and AGGREGATE is one of them)
- Table structure references (used to identify portions of a table)

Entering formulas manually

Entering a formula manually involves, well, entering a formula manually. In a selected cell, you simply type an equal sign (=) followed by the formula. As you type, the characters appear in the cell and in the Formula bar. You can, of course, use all the normal editing keys when entering a formula.

Entering formulas by pointing

Even though you can enter formulas by typing in the entire formula, Excel provides another method of entering formulas that is generally easier, faster, and less error prone. This method still involves some manual typing, but you can simply *point* to the cell references instead of typing their values manually. For example, to enter the formula =A1+A2 into cell A3, follow these steps:

1. **Move the cell pointer to cell A3.**
2. **Type an equal sign (=) to begin the formula.** Notice that Excel displays Enter in the status bar (lower left of your screen).
3. **Press the up arrow twice.** As you press this key, Excel displays a moving border around cell A1, and the cell reference appears in cell A3 and in the Formula bar. In addition, Excel displays Point in the status bar.
4. **Type a plus sign (+).** A solid color border replaces the faint border, and Enter reappears in the status bar.
5. **Press the up arrow again.** The moving border encompasses cell A2 and adds that cell address to the formula.
6. **Press Enter to end the formula.**

> **TIP**
>
> Excel color-codes the range addresses and ranges when you're entering or editing a formula. This helps you quickly spot the cells that are used in a formula.

> **TIP**
>
> When creating a formula by pointing, you can also point to the data cells by using your mouse.

Pasting range names into formulas

If your formula uses named cells or ranges, you can either type the name in place of the address, or choose the name from a list and have Excel insert the name for you automatically. Two ways to insert a name into a formula are available:

- **Select the name from the drop-down list.** To use this method, you must know at least the first character of the name. When you're entering the formula, type the first character and then select the name from the drop-down list.
- **Press F3.** The Paste Name dialog box appears. Select the name from the list and then click OK (or just double-click the name). Excel enters the name into your formula. If no names are defined, pressing F3 has no effect.

Figure 15.3 shows an example. The worksheet contains two defined names: Expenses and Sales. The Paste Name dialog box is being used to insert a name (Sales) into the formula being entered in cell B9.

FIGURE 15.3

Use the Paste Name dialog box to quickly enter a defined name into a formula.

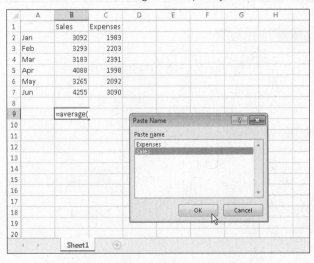

15

NOTE

See Chapter 14 for information about creating names for cells and ranges.

Inserting functions into formulas

The easiest way to enter a function into a formula is to use Formula AutoComplete (the drop-down list that Excel displays while you type a formula). To use this method, however, you must know at least the first character of the function's name.

Another way to insert a function is to use tools in the Function Library group on the Formulas tab on the Ribbon (see Figure 15.4). This method is especially useful if you can't remember which function you need. When entering a formula, click the function category (Financial, Logical, Text, and so on) to get a list of the functions in that category. Click the function you want, and Excel displays its Function Arguments dialog box. This is where you enter the function's arguments. In addition, you can click the Help on This Function link to learn more about the selected function.

FIGURE 15.4

You can insert a function by selecting it from one of the function categories.

Yet another way to insert a function into a formula is to use the Insert Function dialog box (see Figure 15.5). You can access this dialog box in several ways:

FIGURE 15.5

The Insert Function dialog box

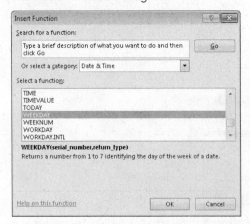

- **Choose Formulas ⇨ Function Library ⇨ Insert Function.**
- **Use the Insert Function command, which appears at the bottom of each drop-down list in the Formulas ⇨ Function Library group.**
- **Click the Insert Function button, which is directly to the left of the Formula bar.** This button displays *fx*.
- **Press Shift+F3.**

The Insert Function dialog box shows a drop-down list of function categories. Select a category and the functions in that category are displayed in the list box. To access a function that you recently used, select Most Recently Used from the drop-down list.

If you're not sure which function you need, you can search for the appropriate function by using the Search for a Function field at the top of the dialog box.

1. **Enter your search terms and click Go.** You get a list of relevant functions. When you select a function from the Select a Function list, Excel displays the function (and its argument names) in the dialog box along with a brief description of what the function does.

2. **When you locate the function you want to use, highlight it and click OK.** Excel then displays its Function Arguments dialog box, as shown in Figure 15.6.

FIGURE 15.6

The Function Arguments dialog box

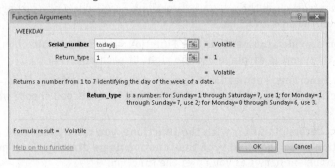

3. **Specify the arguments for the function.** The Function Arguments dialog box will vary, depending on the function you're inserting, and it will show one text box for each of the function's arguments. To use a cell or range reference as an argument, you can enter the address manually or click inside the argument box and then select (that is, point to) the cell or range in the sheet.

4. **After you specify all the function arguments, click OK.**

Tip

Yet another way to insert a function while you're entering a formula is to use the Function List to the left of the Formula bar. When you're entering or editing a formula, the space typically occupied by the Name box displays a list of the functions you've used most recently. After you select a function from this list, Excel displays the Function Arguments dialog box.

Function entry tips

Here are some additional tips to keep in mind when you use the Insert Function dialog box to enter functions:

- **You can use the Insert Function dialog box to insert a function into an existing formula.** Just edit the formula and move the insertion point to the location at which you want to insert the function. Then open the Insert Function dialog box (using any of the methods described earlier) and select the function.

- **You can also use the Function Arguments dialog box to modify the arguments for a function in an existing formula.** Click the function in the Formula bar and then click the Insert Function button (the *fx* button, to the left of the Formula bar).

- **If you change your mind about entering a function, click the Cancel button.**

- **The number of boxes you see in the Function Arguments dialog box depends on the number of arguments used in the function you selected.** If a function uses no arguments, you won't see any boxes. If the function uses a variable number of arguments (such as the AVERAGE function), Excel adds a new box every time you enter an optional argument.

- **As you provide arguments in the Function Arguments dialog box, the value of each argument is displayed to the right of each box.**

- **A few functions, such as INDEX, have more than one form.** If you choose such a function, Excel displays another dialog box that lets you choose which form you want to use.

- **As you become familiar with the functions, you can bypass the Insert Function dialog box and type the function name directly.** Excel prompts you with argument names as you enter the function.

Editing Formulas

After you enter a formula, you can (of course) edit that formula. You may need to edit a formula if you make some changes to your worksheet and then have to adjust the formula to accommodate the changes. Or the formula may return an error value, in which case you need to edit the formula to correct the error.

Here are some of the ways to get into cell edit mode:

- **Double-click the cell, which enables you to edit the cell contents directly in the cell.**
- **Press F2, which enables you to edit the cell contents directly in the cell.**
- **Select the cell that you want to edit, and then click in the Formula bar.** This enables you to edit the cell contents in the Formula bar.
- **If the cell contains a formula that returns an error, Excel will display a small triangle in the upper-left corner of the cell.** Click the cell, and you'll see an error button appear. Click the button, and you can choose one of the options for correcting the error. (The options will vary according to the type of error in the cell.)

> **TIP**
>
> You can control whether Excel displays these formula error buttons in the Formulas tab of the Excel Options dialog box. To find this setting, choose File ➪ Options ➪ Formulas. If you remove the check mark from Enable background error checking under Error Checking, Excel no longer displays these buttons.

While you're editing a formula, you can select multiple characters either by dragging over them or by pressing Shift while you use the navigation keys.

> **TIP**
>
> If you have a formula that you can't seem to edit correctly, you can convert the formula to text and tackle it again later. To convert a formula to text, just remove the initial equal sign (=). When you're ready to try again, type the initial equal sign to convert the cell contents back to a formula.

Using Cell References in Formulas

Most formulas you create include references to cells or ranges. These references enable your formulas to work dynamically with the data contained in those cells or ranges. For example, if your formula refers to cell A1 and you change the value contained in A1, the formula result changes to reflect the new value. If you didn't use references in your formulas, you would need to edit the formulas themselves in order to change the values used in the formulas.

Using relative, absolute, and mixed references

When you use a cell (or range) reference in a formula, you can use three types of references:

15

- **Relative:** The row and column references can change when you copy the formula to another cell because the references are actually offsets from the current row and column. By default, Excel creates relative cell references in formulas.

- **Absolute:** The row and column references don't change when you copy the formula because the reference is to an actual cell address. An absolute reference uses two dollar signs in its address: one for the column letter and one for the row number (for example, $A$5).

- **Mixed:** Either the row or column reference is relative, and the other is absolute. Only one of the address parts is absolute (for example, $A4 or A$4).

The type of cell reference is important only if you plan to copy the formula to other cells. The following examples illustrate this point.

Figure 15.7 shows a simple worksheet. The formula in cell D2, which multiplies the quantity by the price, is

    =B2*C2

FIGURE 15.7

Copying a formula that contains relative references

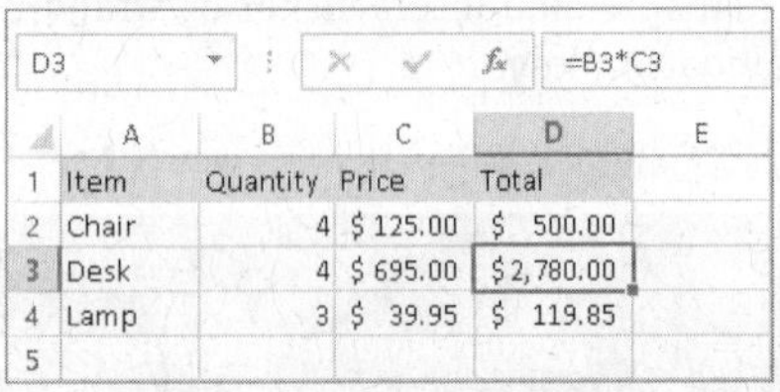

D3	▼	:	✕	✓	ƒ_x	=B3*C3	
◢	A	B	C	D	E		
1	Item	Quantity	Price	Total			
2	Chair	4	$ 125.00	$ 500.00			
3	Desk	4	$ 695.00	$ 2,780.00			
4	Lamp	3	$ 39.95	$ 119.85			
5							

This formula uses relative cell references. Therefore, when the formula is copied to the cells below it, the references adjust in a relative manner. For example, the formula in cell D3 is

    =B3*C3

But what if the cell references in D2 contained absolute references, like this?

    =$B$2*$C$2

In this case, copying the formula to the cells below would produce incorrect results. The formula in cell D3 would be exactly the same as the formula in cell D2.

Now I'll extend the example to calculate sales tax, which is stored in cell B7 (see Figure 15.8). In this situation, the formula in cell D2 is:

    = (B2*C2) *$B$7

FIGURE 15.8

Formula references to the sales tax cell should be absolute.

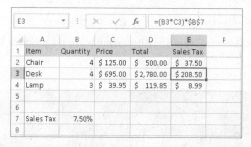

The quantity is multiplied by the price, and the result is multiplied by the sales tax rate stored in cell B7. Notice that the reference to B7 is an absolute reference. When the formula in D2 is copied to the cells below it, cell D3 will contain this formula:

    =(B3*C3)*$B$7

Here, the references to cells B2 and C2 were adjusted, but the reference to cell B7 was not — which is exactly what I want because the address of the cell that contains the sales tax never changes.

Figure 15.9 demonstrates the use of mixed references. The formulas in the C3:F7 range calculate the area for various lengths and widths. The formula in cell C3 is:

    =$B3*C$2

FIGURE 15.9

Using mixed cell references

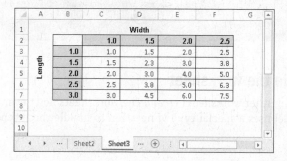

Notice that both cell references are mixed. The reference to cell B3 uses an absolute reference for the column ($B), and the reference to cell C2 uses an absolute reference for the row

15

($2). As a result, this formula can be copied down and across, and the calculations will be correct. For example, the formula in cell F7 is:

```
=$B7*F$2
```

If C3 used either absolute or relative references, copying the formula would produce incorrect results.

> **NOTE**
>
> When you cut and paste a formula (move it to another location), the cell references in the formula aren't adjusted. Again, this is usually what you want to happen. When you move a formula, you generally want it to continue to refer to the original cells.

Changing the types of your references

You can enter *nonrelative* references (that is, absolute or mixed) manually by inserting dollar signs in the appropriate positions of the cell address. Or you can use a handy shortcut: the F4 key. When you've entered a cell reference (by typing it or by pointing), you can press F4 repeatedly to have Excel cycle through all four reference types.

For example, if you enter **=A1** to start a formula, pressing F4 converts the cell reference to =$A$1. Pressing F4 again converts it to =A$1. Pressing it again displays =$A1. Pressing it one more time returns to the original =A1. Keep pressing F4 until Excel displays the type of reference that you want.

> **NOTE**
>
> When you name a cell or range, Excel (by default) uses an absolute reference for the name. For example, if you give the name `SalesForecast` to B1:B12, the Refers To box in the New Name dialog box lists the reference as `$B$1:$B$12`. This is almost always what you want. If you copy a cell that has a named reference in its formula, the copied formula contains a reference to the original name.

Referencing cells outside the worksheet

Formulas can also refer to cells in other worksheets — and the worksheets don't even have to be in the same workbook. Excel uses a special type of notation to handle these types of references.

Referencing cells in other worksheets

To use a reference to a cell in another worksheet in the same workbook, use this format:

```
SheetName!CellAddress
```

In other words, precede the cell address with the worksheet name, followed by an exclamation point. Here's an example of a formula that uses a cell on the `Sheet2` worksheet:

```
=A1*Sheet2!A1
```

This formula multiplies the value in cell A1 on the current worksheet by the value in cell A1 on `Sheet2`.

> **TIP**
>
> If the worksheet name in the reference includes one or more spaces, you must enclose it in single quotation marks. (Excel does that automatically if you use the point-and-click method when creating the formula.) For example, here's a formula that refers to a cell on a sheet named `All Depts`:
>
> `=A1*'All Depts'!A1`

Referencing cells in other workbooks

To refer to a cell in a different workbook, use this format:

```
=[WorkbookName]SheetName!CellAddress
```

In this case, the workbook name (in square brackets), the worksheet name, and an exclamation point precede the cell address. The following is an example of a formula that uses a cell reference in the `Sheet1` worksheet in a workbook named `Budget`:

```
=[Budget.xlsx]Sheet1!A1
```

If the workbook name in the reference includes one or more spaces, you must enclose it (and the sheet name) in single quotation marks. For example, here's a formula that refers to a cell on `Sheet1` in a workbook named `Budget For 2013`:

```
=A1*'[Budget For 2013.xlsx]Sheet1'!A1
```

When a formula refers to cells in a different workbook, the other workbook doesn't have to be open. If the workbook is closed, however, you must add the complete path to the reference so that Excel can find it. Here's an example:

```
=A1*'C:\Users\user name\My Documents\[Budget For 2013.xlsx]Sheet1'!A1
```

A linked file can also reside on another system that's accessible on your corporate network. The following formula refers to a cell in a workbook in the `files` folder of a computer named `DataServer`:

```
='\\DataServer\files\[budget.xlsx]Sheet1'!$D$7
```

15

TIP

To create formulas that refer to cells in a different worksheet, point to the cells rather than enter their references manually. Excel takes care of the details regarding the workbook and worksheet references. The workbook you're referencing in your formula must be open if you're going to use the pointing method.

NOTE

If you point to a different worksheet or workbook when creating a formula, you'll notice that Excel always inserts absolute cell references. Therefore, if you plan to copy the formula to other cells, make sure that you change the cell references to relative before you copy.

Using Formulas in Tables

A table is a specially designated range of cells, set up with column headers. In this section, I describe how formulas work with tables. Chapter 19 will introduce tables.

Summarizing data in a table

Figure 15.10 shows a simple table with three columns. I entered the data and then converted the range to a table by choosing Insert ⇨ Tables ⇨ Table. Note that I didn't define any names, but the table is named `Table1` by default.

FIGURE 15.10

A simple table with three columns of information

Month	Projected	Actual
Jan	4,000	3,255
Feb	4,000	4,102
Mar	4,000	3,982
Apr	5,000	4,598
May	5,000	5,873
Jun	5,000	4,783
Jul	5,000	5,109
Aug	6,000	5,982
Sep	6,000	6,201
Oct	7,000	6,833
Nov	8,000	7,983
Dec	9,000	9,821

If you'd like to calculate the total projected and total actual sales, you don't even need to write a formula. Simply click a button to add a row of summary formulas to the table:

1. **Click any cell in the table.**

2. **Place a check mark next to Table Tools⇨Design⇨Table Style Options⇨Total Row.**

3. **Click a cell in the Total Row and use the drop-down list to select the type of summary formula to use (see Figure 15.11).** For example, to calculate the sum of the Actual column, select SUM from the drop-down list in cell D15. Excel creates this formula:

```
=SUBTOTAL(109,[Actual])
```

FIGURE 15.11

A drop-down list enables you to select a summary formula for a table column.

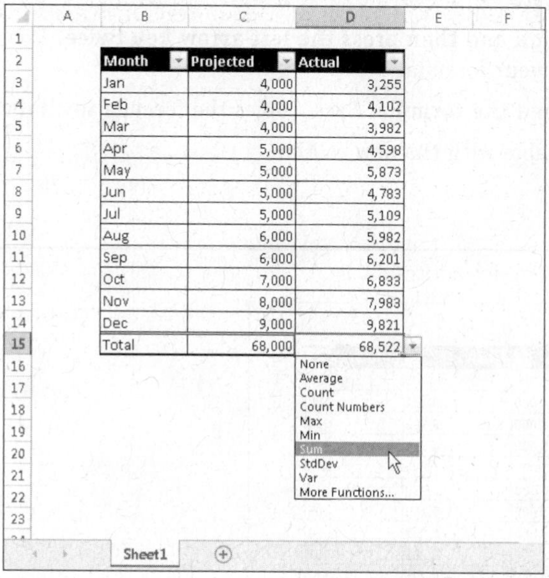

	A	B	C	D	E	F
1						
2		Month	Projected	Actual		
3		Jan	4,000	3,255		
4		Feb	4,000	4,102		
5		Mar	4,000	3,982		
6		Apr	5,000	4,598		
7		May	5,000	5,873		
8		Jun	5,000	4,783		
9		Jul	5,000	5,109		
10		Aug	6,000	5,982		
11		Sep	6,000	6,201		
12		Oct	7,000	6,833		
13		Nov	8,000	7,983		
14		Dec	9,000	9,821		
15		Total	68,000	68,522		
16				None		
17				Average		
18				Count		
				Count Numbers		
19				Max		
				Min		
20				Sum		
21				StdDev		
				Var		
22				More Functions...		
23						

Sheet1 ⊕

For the SUBTOTAL function, 109 is an enumerated argument that represents SUM. The second argument for the SUBTOTAL function is the column name, in square brackets. Using the column name within brackets creates "structured" references within a table (as discussed further in the upcoming section, "Referencing data in a table").

NOTE

You can toggle the Total Row display via Table Tools⇨Design⇨Table Style Options⇨Total Row. If you turn it off, the summary options you selected will be displayed again when you turn it back on.

15

Using formulas within a table

In many cases, you'll want to use formulas within a table to perform calculations that use other columns in the table. For example, in the table shown in Figure 15.11, you may want a column that shows the difference between the Actual and Projected amounts. To add this formula:

1. **Click cell E2 and type** Difference **for the column header.** Excel automatically expands the table for you to include the new column.

2. **Move to cell E3 and type an equal sign to signify the beginning of a formula.**

3. **Press the left arrow key.** Excel displays [@Actual], which is the column heading, in the Formula bar.

4. **Type a minus sign and then press the left arrow key twice.** Excel displays [@ Projected] in your formula.

5. **Press Enter to end the formula.** Excel copies the formula to all rows in the table.

Figure 15.12 shows the table with the new column.

FIGURE 15.12

The Difference column contains a formula.

	Month	Projected	Actual	Difference
Jan		4,000	3,255	-745
Feb		4,000	4,102	102
Mar		4,000	3,982	-18
Apr		5,000	4,598	-402
May		5,000	5,873	873
Jun		5,000	4,783	-217
Jul		5,000	5,109	109
Aug		6,000	5,982	-18
Sep		6,000	6,201	201
Oct		7,000	6,833	-167
Nov		8,000	7,983	-17
Dec		9,000	9,821	821
Total		68,000	68,522	

Examine the table, and you find this formula for all cells in the Difference column:

```
=[@Actual]-[@Projected]
```

Although the formula was entered into the first row of the table, that's not necessary. Any time a formula is entered into an empty table column, it will automatically fill all the cells in that column. And if you need to edit the formula, Excel will automatically copy the edited formula to the other cells in the column.

These steps use the pointing technique to create the formula. Alternatively, you could have
entered the formula manually using standard cell references rather than column headers.
For example, you could have entered the following formula in cell E3:

```
=D3-C3
```

If you type the cell references, Excel will still copy the formula to the other cells
automatically.

One thing should be clear, however, about formulas that use the column headers instead of
cell references: They're much easier to understand.

Referencing data in a table

Excel offers some other ways to refer to data that's contained in a table by using the table
name and column headers.

You can, of course, use standard cell references to refer to data in a table, but using the
table name and column headers has a distinct advantage: The names adjust automatically
if the table size changes by adding or deleting rows. In addition, formulas that use table
names and column headers will adjust automatically if you change the name of the table or
give a new name to a column.

15

Refer to the table shown in Figure 15.11. This table is named `Table1`. To calculate the sum of all the data in the table, enter this formula into a cell outside the table:

```
=SUM(Table1)
```

This formula will always return the sum of all the data (excluding calculated Total Row values, if any), even if rows or columns are added or deleted. And if you change the name of `Table1`, Excel will adjust formulas that refer to that table automatically. For example, if you renamed `Table1` to `AnnualData` (by using the Name Manager, or by choosing Table Tools ➪ Design ➪ Properties ➪ Table Name), the preceding formula would change to:

```
=SUM(AnnualData)
```

Most of the time, a formula will refer to a specific column in the table. The following formula returns the sum of the data in the `Actual` column:

```
=SUM(Table1[Actual])
```

Notice that the column name is enclosed in square brackets. Again, the formula adjusts automatically if you change the text in the column heading.

Even better, Excel provides some helpful assistance when you create a formula that refers to data within a table. Figure 15.13 shows the formula AutoComplete helping to create a formula by showing a list of the elements in the table. Notice that, in addition to the column headers in the table, Excel lists other table elements that you can reference: #All, #Data, #Headers, #Totals, and @ - This Row.

FIGURE 15.13

The formula AutoComplete feature is useful when creating a formula that refers to data in a table.

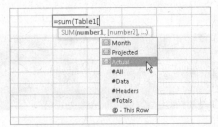

Correcting Common Formula Errors

Sometimes, when you enter a formula, Excel displays a value that begins with a hash mark or pound sign (#). This is a signal that the formula is returning an error value. You have to correct the formula (or correct a cell that the formula references) to get rid of the error display.

TIP

If the entire cell is filled with hash-mark characters, the column isn't wide enough to display the value. You can either widen the column or change the number format of the cell.

In some cases, Excel won't even let you enter an erroneous formula. For example, the following formula is missing the closing parenthesis:

```
=A1*(B1+C2
```

If you attempt to enter this formula, Excel informs you that you have unmatched parentheses, and it proposes a correction. Often, the proposed correction is accurate, but you can't count on it.

Table 15.3 lists the types of error values that may appear in a cell that has a formula. Formulas may return an error value if a cell to which they refer has an error value. This is known as the *ripple effect*—a single error value can make its way into lots of other cells that contain formulas that depend on that one cell.

TABLE 15.3   Excel Error Values

Error value	Explanation
#DIV/0!	The formula is trying to divide by zero. This also occurs when the formula attempts to divide by what's in a cell that is empty (that is, by nothing).
#NAME?	The formula uses a name that Excel doesn't recognize. This can happen if you delete a name that's used in the formula or if you have unmatched quotes when using text.
#N/A	The formula is referring (directly or indirectly) to a cell that uses the NA function to signal that data is not available. Some functions (for example, VLOOKUP) can also return #N/A.
#NULL!	The formula uses an intersection of two ranges that don't intersect.
#NUM!	A problem with a value exists; for example, you specified a negative number where a positive number is expected.
#REF!	The formula refers to a cell that isn't valid. This can happen if the cell has been deleted from the worksheet.
#VALUE!	The formula includes an argument or operand of the wrong type. (An *operand* is a value or cell reference that a formula uses to calculate a result.)

Handling circular references

When you're entering formulas, you may occasionally see a warning message like the one shown in Figure 15.14, indicating that the formula you just entered will result in a *circular*

15

reference. A circular reference occurs when a formula refers to its own value — either directly or indirectly. For example, you create a circular reference if you enter **=A1+A2+A3** into cell A3 because the formula in cell A3 refers to cell A3. Every time the formula in A3 is calculated, it must be calculated again because A3 has changed. The calculation could go on forever.

FIGURE 15.14

If you see this warning, you know that the formula you entered will result in a circular reference.

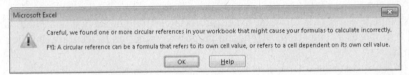

When you get the circular reference message after entering a formula, Excel gives you two options:

- **Click OK, and Excel displays a Help screen that tells you more about circular references.**
- **Click Cancel to enter the formula as is.**

Regardless of which option you choose, Excel displays a message in the left side of the status bar to remind you that a circular reference exists.

> **CAUTION**
>
> Excel won't tell you about a circular reference if the Enable iterative calculation setting is in effect. You can check this setting in the Formulas tab of the Excel Options dialog box, under Calculation options. If Enable iterative calculation is turned on, Excel performs the circular calculation exactly the number of times specified in the Maximum Iterations text box (or until the value changes by less than 0.001 or whatever value is in the Maximum Change text box). In a few situations, you may use a circular reference intentionally. In these cases, the Enable iterative calculation setting must be on. However, it's best to keep this setting turned off so that you're warned of circular references. Usually, a circular reference indicates an error that you must correct.

Often, a circular reference is quite obvious and easy to identify and correct. But when a circular reference is indirect (as when a formula refers to another formula that refers to yet another formula that refers back to the original formula), it may require a bit of detective work to get to the problem.

Specifying when formulas are calculated

You've probably noticed that Excel calculates the formulas in your worksheet immediately. If you change any cells that the formula uses, Excel displays the formula's new result with no effort on your part. All this happens when Excel's Calculation mode is set to Automatic. In Automatic Calculation mode (which is the default mode), Excel follows these rules when it calculates your worksheet:

- **When you make a change — enter or edit data or formulas, for example — Excel calculates immediately those formulas that depend on new or edited data.**

- **If Excel is in the middle of a lengthy calculation, it temporarily suspends the calculation when you need to perform other worksheet tasks; it resumes calculating when you're finished with your other worksheet tasks.**

- **Formulas are evaluated in a natural sequence.** In other words, if a formula in cell D12 depends on the result of a formula in cell D11, Excel calculates cell D11 before calculating cell D12.

Sometimes, however, you may want to control when Excel calculates formulas. For example, if you create a worksheet with thousands of complex formulas, you'll find that processing can slow to a snail's pace while Excel does its thing. In such a case, set Excel's calculation mode to Manual — which you can do by choosing Formulas ⇨ Calculation ⇨ Calculation Options ⇨ Manual (see Figure 15.15).

FIGURE 15.15

You can control when Excel calculates formulas.

15

When you're working in Manual Calculation mode, Excel displays `Calculate` in the status bar when you have any uncalculated formulas. You can use the following shortcut keys to recalculate the formulas:

- **F9:** Calculates the formulas in all open workbooks
- **Shift+F9:** Calculates only the formulas in the active worksheet. Other worksheets in the same workbook aren't calculated.
- **Ctrl+Alt+F9:** Forces a complete recalculation of all formulas

> **NOTE**
> Excel's Calculation mode isn't specific to a particular worksheet. When you change the Calculation mode, it affects all open workbooks, not just the active workbook.

Tips for Working with Formulas

In this section, I offer a few additional tips and pointers relevant to formulas.

Not hard-coding values

When you create a formula, think twice before you use any specific value in the formula. For example, if your formula calculates sales tax (which is 6.5%), you may be tempted to enter a formula, such as the following:

```
=A1*.065
```

A better approach is to insert the sales tax rate in a cell — and use the cell reference. Or you can define the tax rate as a named constant, using the technique presented earlier in this chapter. Doing so makes modifying and maintaining your worksheet easier. For example, if the sales tax rate changed to 6.75%, you would have to modify every formula that used the old value. If you store the tax rate in a cell, however, you simply change that one cell, and Excel updates all the formulas.

Using the Formula bar as a calculator

If you need to perform a quick calculation, you can use the Formula bar as a calculator. For example, enter the following formula — but don't press Enter:

```
=(145*1.05)/12
```

If you press Enter, Excel enters the formula into the cell. But because this formula always returns the same result, you may prefer to store the formula's *result* rather than the formula itself. To do so, press F9 and watch the result appear in the Formula bar. Press Enter to store the result in the active cell. (This technique also works if the formula uses cell references or worksheet functions.)

Making an exact copy of a formula

When you copy a formula, Excel adjusts its cell references when you paste the formula to a different location. Sometimes, you may want to make an exact copy of the formula. One way to do this is to convert the cell references to absolute values, but this isn't always desirable. A better approach is to select the formula in Edit mode and then copy it to the Clipboard as text. You can do this in several ways. Here's a step-by-step example of how to make an exact copy of the formula in A1 and copy it to A2:

1. **Double-click A1 (or press F2) to get into Edit mode.**
2. **Drag the mouse to select the entire formula.** You can drag from left to right or from right to left. To select the entire formula with the keyboard, press End, followed by Shift+Home.
3. **Choose Home ⇨ Clipboard ⇨ Copy (or press Ctrl+C).** This copies the selected text (which will become the copied formula) to the Clipboard.
4. **Press Esc to leave Edit mode.**
5. **Select cell A2.**
6. **Choose Home ⇨ Clipboard ⇨ Paste (or press Ctrl+V) to paste the text into cell A2.**

You can also use this technique to copy just *part* of a formula, if you want to use that part in another formula. Just select the part of the formula that you want to copy by dragging the mouse, and then use any of the available techniques to copy the selection to the Clipboard. You can then paste the text to another cell.

Formulas (or parts of formulas) copied in this manner won't have their cell references adjusted when they're pasted into a new cell. That's because the formulas are being copied as text, not as actual formulas.

> **TIP**
>
> You can also convert a formula to text by adding an apostrophe (') in front of the equal sign. Then copy the formula as usual, and paste it to its new location. Remove the apostrophe from the pasted formula, and it will be identical to the original formula. And don't forget to remove the apostrophe from the original formula as well.

Converting formulas to values

If you have a range of formulas that will always produce the same result (that is, *dead formulas*), you may want to convert them to values. For example, if you use the

15

RANDBETWEEN function to create a set of random numbers and you don't want Excel to recalculate those random numbers each time you press Enter, you can convert the formulas to values. Just follow these steps:

1. **Select A1:A20.**
2. **Choose Home ⇨ Clipboard ⇨ Copy (or press Ctrl+C).**
3. **Choose Home ⇨ Clipboard ⇨ Paste arrow ⇨ Paste Values (V).**
4. **Press Esc to cancel Copy mode.**

Summary

This chapter taught you the key details about entering formulas to perform calculations in cells. The chapter taught you how to:

- Enter formulas using operators.
- Use the order of precedence along with parentheses to ensure a formula calculates correctly.
- Include functions in formulas to perform more sophisticated calculations.
- Use various methods to include ranges and functions in formulas.
- Make changes to formulas.
- Use relative and absolute references.
- Use formulas with a table.
- See and fix formula errors.

Working with Dates and Times

IN THIS CHAPTER

Getting an overview of dates and times in Excel

Using Excel date-related functions

Working with Excel time-related functions

Many worksheets contain dates and times in cells. For example, you might track information by date or create a schedule based on time. Beginners often find that working with dates and times in Excel can be frustrating. To work with dates and times, you need a good understanding of how Excel handles time-based information. This chapter provides the information you need to create powerful formulas that manipulate dates and times.

> **NOTE**
> The dates in this chapter correspond to the U.S. English language date format: month/day/year. For example, the date 3/1/1952 refers to March 1, 1952, not January 3, 1952. This setup may not seem illogical, but that's the way Americans have been trained. Non-American readers of this book should make the adjustment, please.

How Excel Handles Dates and Times

This section presents a quick overview of how Excel deals with dates and times. It covers Excel's date and time serial number system. This section also provides some tips for entering and formatting dates and times.

Understanding date serial numbers

To Excel, a date is simply a number. More precisely, a date is a *serial number* that represents the number of days since the fictitious date of January 0, 1900. A serial number of 1 corresponds to January 1, 1900; a serial number of 2 corresponds to January 2, 1900; and so on. This system makes it possible to create formulas that perform calculations with dates. For example, you can create a formula to calculate the number of days between two dates (just subtract one from the other).

Excel supports dates from January 1, 1900, through December 31, 9999 (serial number = 2,958,465).

You may wonder about January 0, 1900. This nondate (which corresponds to date serial number 0) is actually used to represent times that aren't associated with a particular day. This concept becomes clear later in this chapter (see "Entering times").

To view a date serial number as a date, you must format the cell as a date. Choose Home⇨ Number⇨Number Format. This drop-down control provides you with two date formats. To select from additional date formats, see "Formatting dates and times," later in this chapter.

Choose Your Date System: 1900 or 1904

Excel supports two date systems: the 1900 date system and the 1904 date system. Which system you use in a workbook determines what date serves as the basis for dates. The 1900 date system uses January 1, 1900, as the day assigned to date serial number 1. The 1904 date system uses January 1, 1904, as the base date. By default, Excel for Windows uses the 1900 date system, and pre-2011 versions of Excel for Mac use the 1904 date system.

NOTE

Microsoft made a change. Excel 2011 for Mac uses the 1900 date system by default. Presumably subsequent Mac versions will as well.

Excel for Windows supports the 1904 date system for compatibility with Mac files. You can choose the date system for the active workbook in the Advanced section of the Excel Options dialog box. (It's in the When calculating this workbook subsection.) Generally, you should use the default 1900 date system. (The examples in this chapter use the default 1900 date system.) And you should exercise caution if you use two different date systems in workbooks that are linked. For example, assume that Book1 uses the 1904 date system and contains the date 1/15/1999 in cell A1. Assume that Book2 uses the 1900 date system and contains a link to cell A1 in Book1. Book2 displays the date as 1/14/1995. Both workbooks use the same date serial number (34713), but they're interpreted differently.

One advantage to using the 1904 date system is that it enables you to display negative time values. With the 1900 date system, a calculation that results in a negative time (for example, 4:00 PM–5:30 PM) cannot be displayed. When using the 1904 date system, the negative time displays as –1:30 (that is, a difference of 1 hour and 30 minutes).

Entering dates

You can enter a date directly as a serial number (if you know the serial number) and then format it as a date. More often, you enter a date by using any of several recognized date formats. Excel automatically converts your entry into the corresponding date serial number (which it uses for calculations), and it also applies the default date format to the cell so that it displays as an actual date rather than as a cryptic serial number.

For example, if you need to enter June 18, 2013 into a cell, you can enter the date by typing **June 18, 2013** (or any of several different date formats). Excel interprets your entry and stores the value 41443, the date serial number for that date. It also applies the default date format, so the cell contents may not appear exactly as you typed them.

NOTE

Depending on your regional settings, entering a date in a format such as June 18, 2013, may be interpreted as a text string. In such a case, you need to enter the date in a format that corresponds to your regional settings, such as 18 June 2013.

When you activate a cell that contains a date, the Formula bar shows the cell contents formatted by using the default date format — which corresponds to your system's *short date format*. The Formula bar doesn't display the date's serial number. If you need to find out the serial number for a particular date, format the cell with a nondate number format.

TIP

To change the default date format, you need to change a systemwide setting. In Windows Control Panel, select Clock, Language, and Region. Under Region, click Change date, time, or number formats. On the Formats tab of the Region dialog box, change the Short Date Format, and click OK. (This procedure may vary if you're running Office on a supported Windows Server version rather than Windows 7 or 8.) The setting you choose determines the default date format that Excel uses to display dates in the Formula bar.

Table 16.1 shows a sampling of the date formats that Excel recognizes (using the U.S. settings). Results will vary if you use a different regional setting.

TABLE 16.1   Date Entry Formats Recognized by Excel

Entry	Excel Interpretation (U.S. Settings)
6-18-13	June 18, 2013
6-18-2013	June 18, 2013
6/18/13	June 18, 2013
6/18/2013	June 18, 2013
6-18/13	June 18, 2013
June 18, 2013	June 18, 2013
Jun 18	June 18 of the current year

Continues

TABLE 16.1 *(continued)*

Entry	Excel Interpretation (U.S. Settings)
June 18	June 18 of the current year
6/18	June 18 of the current year
6-18	June 18 of the current year
18-Jun-2013	June 18, 2013
2013/6/18	June 18, 2013

As you can see in Table 16.1, Excel is rather flexible when it comes to recognizing dates entered into a cell. It's not perfect, however. For example, Excel does not recognize any of the following entries as dates:

■ June 18 2013

■ Jun-18 2013

■ Jun-18/2013

Rather, it interprets these entries as text. If you plan to use dates in formulas, make sure that Excel can recognize the date you enter as a date; otherwise, the formulas that refer to these dates will produce incorrect results.

If you attempt to enter a date that lies outside of the supported date range, Excel interprets it as text. If you attempt to format a serial number that lies outside the supported range as a date, the value displays as a series of hash marks (########).

Searching for Dates

If your worksheet uses many dates, you may need to search for a particular date by using the Find and Replace dialog box (Home ⇨ Editing ⇨ Find & Select ⇨ Find, or Ctrl+F). Excel is rather picky when it comes to finding dates. You must enter the date as it appears in the Formula bar. For example, if a cell contains a date formatted to display as June 19, 2013, the date appears in the Formula bar using your system's short date format (for example, 6/19/2013). Therefore, if you search for the date as it appears in the cell, Excel won't find it. But it will find the cell if you search for the date in the format that appears in the Formula bar.

Understanding time serial numbers

When you need to work with time values, you extend the Excel date serial number system to include decimals. In other words, Excel works with times by using fractional days. For example, the date serial number for June 1, 2013, is 41426. Noon (halfway through the day) is represented internally as 41426.5.

The serial number equivalent of one minute is approximately 0.00069444. The following formula calculates this number by multiplying 24 hours by 60 minutes, and dividing the result into 1. The denominator consists of the number of minutes in a day (1,440):

```
=1/(24*60)
```

Similarly, the serial number equivalent of one second is approximately 0.00001157, obtained by the following formula:

```
=1/(24*60*60)
```

In this case, the denominator represents the number of seconds in a day (86,400).

In Excel, the smallest unit of time is one 1,000th of a second. The time serial number shown here represents 23:59:59.999 (one 1,000th of a second before midnight):

```
0.99999999
```

Table 16.2 shows various times of day along with each associated time serial number.

TABLE 16.2 Times of Day and Their Corresponding Serial Numbers

Time of Day	Time Serial Number
12:00:00 AM (midnight)	0.00000000
1:30:00 AM	0.06250000
7:30:00 AM	0.31250000
10:30:00 AM	0.43750000
12:00:00 PM (noon)	0.50000000
1:30:00 PM	0.56250000
4:30:00 PM	0.68750000
6:00:00 PM	0.75000000
9:00:00 PM	0.87500000
10:30:00 PM	0.93750000

Entering times

As with entering dates, you normally don't have to worry about the actual time serial numbers. Just enter the time into a cell using a recognized format. Table 16.3 shows some examples of time formats that Excel recognizes.

TABLE 16.3   Time Entry Formats Recognized by Excel

Entry	Excel Interpretation
11:30:00 am	11:30 AM
11:30:00 AM	11:30 AM
11:30 pm	11:30 PM
11:30	11:30 AM
13:30	1:30 PM

Because the preceding samples don't have a specific day associated with them, Excel uses a date serial number of 0, which corresponds to the nonday January 0, 1900. Often, you'll want to combine a date and time. Do so by using a recognized date entry format, followed by a space, and then a recognized time entry format. For example, if you enter **6/18/2013 11:30** in a cell, Excel interprets it as 11:30 a.m. on June 18, 2013. Its date/time serial number is 41443.4791666667.

When you enter a time that exceeds 24 hours, the associated date for the time increments accordingly. For example, if you enter **25:00:00** in a cell, it's interpreted as 1:00 a.m. on January 1, 1900. The day part of the entry increments because the time exceeds 24 hours. Keep in mind that a time value without a date uses January 0, 1900, as the date.

Similarly, if you enter a date *and* a time (and the time exceeds 24 hours), the date that you entered is adjusted. If you enter **9/18/2013 25:00:00**, for example, it's interpreted as 9/19/2013 1:00:00 a.m.

If you enter a time only (without an associated date) into an unformatted cell, the maximum time that you can enter into a cell is 9999:59:59 (just less than 10,000 hours). Excel adds the appropriate number of days. In this case, 9999:59:59 is interpreted as 3:59:59 p.m. on 02/19/1901. If you enter a time that exceeds 10,000 hours, the entry is interpreted as a text string rather than a time.

Formatting dates and times

You have a great deal of flexibility in formatting cells that contain dates and times. For example, you can format the cell to display the date part only, the time part only, or both the date and time parts.

You format dates and times by selecting the cells and then using the Number tab of the Format Cells dialog box, shown in Figure 16.1. To display this dialog box, click the dialog box launcher icon in the Number group of the Home tab, or click the Number Format control and choose More Number Formats from the list that appears.

FIGURE 16.1

Use the Number tab of the Format Cells dialog box to change the appearance of dates and times.

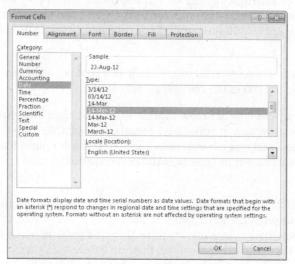

The Date category shows built-in date formats, and the Time category shows built-in time formats. Some formats include both date and time displays. Just select the desired format from the Type list, and then click OK.

> **TIP**
>
> When you create a formula that refers to a cell containing a date or a time, Excel sometimes automatically formats the formula cell as a date or a time. Often, this automation is very helpful; other times, it's completely inappropriate and downright annoying. To return the number formatting to the default General format, choose Home ⇨ Number ⇨ Number Format and choose General from the drop-down list. Or just press Ctrl+Shift+~ (tilde).

If none of the built-in formats meets your needs, you can create a custom number format. Select the Custom category and then type the custom format codes into the Type box.

Problems with dates

Excel has some problems when it comes to dates. Many of these problems stem from the fact that Excel was designed many years ago. Excel designers basically emulated the Lotus 1-2-3 program's limited date and time features, which contain a nasty bug that was duplicated intentionally in Excel (described next). If Excel were being designed from scratch today, it likely would be much more versatile in dealing with dates. Unfortunately, users are currently stuck with a product that leaves much to be desired in the area of dates.

Excel's leap year bug

A *leap year,* which occurs every four years, contains an additional day (February 29). Specifically, years that are evenly divisible by 100 are not leap years, unless they are also evenly divisible by 400. Although the year 1900 was not a leap year, Excel treats it as such. In other words, when you type **2/29/1900** into a cell, Excel interprets it as a valid date and assigns a serial number of 60.

If you type **2/29/1901**, however, Excel correctly interprets it as a mistake and doesn't convert it to a date. Instead, it simply makes the cell entry a text string.

How can a product used daily by millions of people contain such an obvious bug? The answer is historical. The original version of Lotus 1-2-3 contained a bug that caused it to treat 1900 as a leap year. When Excel was released some time later, the designers knew about this bug and chose to reproduce it in Excel to maintain compatibility with Lotus worksheet files.

Why does this bug still exist in later versions of Excel? Microsoft asserts that the disadvantages of correcting this bug outweigh the advantages. If the bug were eliminated, it would mess up millions of existing workbooks. In addition, correcting this problem would possibly affect compatibility between Excel and other programs that use dates. As it stands, this bug really causes very few problems because most users don't use dates prior to March 1, 1900.

Pre-1900 dates

The world, of course, didn't begin on January 1, 1900. People who use Excel to work with historical information often need to work with dates before January 1, 1900. Unfortunately, the only way to work with pre-1900 dates is to enter the date into a cell as text. For example, you can enter **July 4, 1776** into a cell, and Excel won't complain.

> **TIP**
>
> If you plan to sort information by old dates, you should enter your text dates with a four-digit year, followed by a two-digit month, and then a two-digit day — for example, 1776-07-04. You won't be able to work with these text strings as dates, but this format *will* enable accurate sorting.

Using text as dates works in some situations, but the main problem is that you can't perform any manipulation on a date that's entered as text. For example, you can't change its numeric formatting, you can't determine which day of the week this date occurred on, and you can't calculate the date that occurs seven days later.

Inconsistent date entries

You need to be careful when entering dates by using two digits for the year. When you do so, Excel has some rules that kick in to determine which century to use. And those rules vary, depending on the version of Excel that you use.

Two-digit years between 00 and 29 are interpreted as 21st-century dates, and two-digit years between 30 and 99 are interpreted as 20th-century dates. For example, if you enter **12/15/28**, Excel interprets your entry as December 15, 2028. But if you enter **12/15/30**, Excel sees it as December 15, 1930, because Windows uses a default boundary year of 2029. You can keep the default as is or change it via the Windows Control Panel. In the Region dialog box (or the equivalent if you're using Windows Server), click the Additional Settings button to display the Customize Format dialog box. Select the Date tab and then specify a different year.

TIP

The best way to avoid any surprises is to simply enter all years using *all* four digits for the year.

Date-Related Worksheet Functions

Excel has quite a few functions that work with dates. These functions are accessible by choosing Formulas ⇨ Function Library ⇨ Date & Time.

Table 16.4 summarizes the date-related functions available in Excel.

TABLE 16.4 Date-Related Functions

Function	Description
DATE	Returns the serial number of a particular date
DATEVALUE	Converts a date in the form of text to a serial number
DAY	Converts a serial number to a day of the month
DAYS***	Returns the number of days between two dates
DAYS360	Calculates the number of days between two dates based on a 360-day year
EDATE*	Returns the serial number of the date that represents the indicated number of months before or after the start date
EOMONTH*	Returns the serial number of the last day of the month before or after a specified number of months
ISOWEEKNUM***	Returns the ISO week number for a date
MONTH	Converts a serial number to a month
NETWORKDAYS*	Returns the number of whole work days between two dates
NETWORKDAYS.INTL**	An international version of the NETWORKDAYS function, which allows nonstandard weekend days

Continues

529

TABLE 16.4 *(continued)*

Function	Description
NOW	Returns the serial number of the current date and time
TODAY	Returns the serial number of today's date
WEEKDAY	Converts a serial number to a day of the week
WEEKNUM*	Returns the week number in the year
WORKDAY*	Returns the serial number of the date before or after a specified number of workdays
WORKDAY.INTL**	An international version of the WORKDAY function, which allows nonstandard weekend days
YEAR	Converts a serial number to a year
YEARFRAC*	Returns the year fraction representing the number of whole days between start_date and end_date

* In versions prior to Excel 2007, these functions are available only when the Analysis ToolPak add-in is installed.
** Indicates a function introduced in Excel 2010.
*** Indicates a function introduced in Excel 2013.

Displaying the current date

The following formula uses the TODAY function to display the current date in a cell:

```
=TODAY()
```

You can also display the date combined with text. The formula that follows, for example, displays text, such as Today is Tuesday, April 9, 2013:

```
="Today is "&TEXT(TODAY(),"dddd, mmmm d, yyyy")
```

It's important to understand that the TODAY function is not a date stamp. The function is updated whenever the worksheet is calculated. For example, if you enter either of the preceding formulas into a worksheet, the formulas display the current date. And when you open the workbook tomorrow, they will display the current date (not the date when you entered the formula), assuming the default Workbook Calculation option, Automatic, is selected in File ⇨ Options ⇨ Formulas, under Calculation options.

> **TIP**
>
> To enter a date stamp into a cell, press Ctrl+; (semicolon). This action enters the date directly into the cell and doesn't use a formula. Therefore, the date won't change.

Displaying any date

You can easily enter a date into a cell by simply typing it while using any of the date formats that Excel recognizes. You can also create a date by using the DATE function, which takes three arguments: the year, the month, and the day. The following formula, for example, returns a date comprising the year in cell A1, the month in cell B1, and the day in cell C1:

```
=DATE(A1,B1,C1)
```

> **NOTE**
>
> The DATE function accepts invalid arguments and adjusts the result accordingly. For example, the following formula uses 13 as the month argument and returns January 1, 2013. The month argument is automatically translated as month 1 of the following year:
>
> ```
> =DATE(2012,13,1)
> ```

Often, you'll use the DATE function with other functions as arguments. For example, the following formula uses the YEAR and TODAY functions to return the date for July 4 of the current year:

```
=DATE(YEAR(TODAY()),7,4)
```

The DATEVALUE function converts a text string that looks like a date into a date serial number. The following formula returns 40508, which is the date serial number for August 22, 2013:

```
=DATEVALUE("8/22/2013")
```

To view the result of this formula as a date, you need to apply a date number format to the cell.

> **CAUTION**
>
> Be careful when using the DATEVALUE function. A text string that looks like a date in your country may not look like a date in another country. The preceding example works fine if your system is set for U.S. date formats, but it returns an error for other regional date formats because Excel is looking for the 8th day of the 22nd month!

Generating a series of dates

Often, you want to insert a series of dates into a worksheet. For example, in tracking weekly sales, you may want to enter a series of dates, each separated by seven days. These dates will serve to identify the sales figures.

In some cases, you can use the Excel Auto Fill feature to insert a series of dates. Enter the first date and drag the cell's fill handle while holding down the right mouse button. Release the mouse button and select an option from the shortcut menu (see Figure 16.2) — Fill Days, Fill Weekdays, Fill Months, or Fill Years. Notice that Excel does not provide a Fill Weeks option.

FIGURE 16.2

Using Auto Fill to create a series of dates

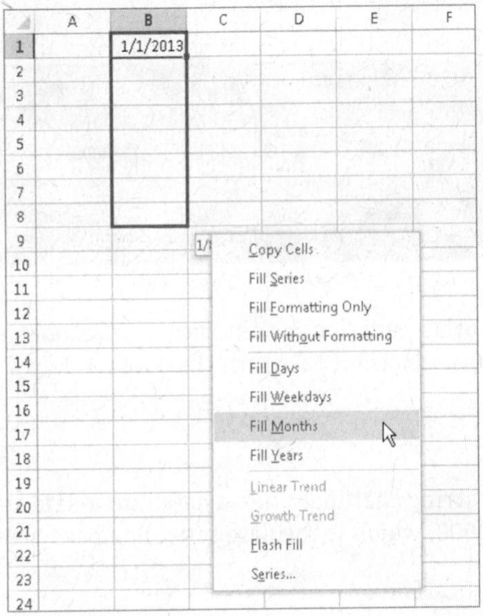

For more flexibility enter the first *two* dates in the series — for example, the starting day for week 1 and the starting day for week 2. Then select both cells and drag the fill handle down the column. Excel will complete the date series, with each date separated by the interval represented by the first two dates.

The advantage of using formulas (instead of Auto Fill) to create a series of dates is that when you change the first date, the others update automatically. You need to enter the starting date in a cell and then use formulas (copied down the column) to generate the additional dates.

The following examples assume that you enter the first date of the series into cell A1 and the formula into cell A2. You can then copy this formula down the column as many times as needed.

To generate a series of dates separated by seven days, use this formula:

```
=A1+7
```

To generate a series of dates separated by one month, you need to use a more complicated formula because months don't all have the same number of days. This formula creates a series of dates, separated by one month:

```
=DATE(YEAR(A1),MONTH(A1)+1,DAY(A1))
```

To generate a series of dates separated by one year, use this formula:

```
=DATE(YEAR(A1)+1,MONTH(A1),DAY(A1))
```

To generate a series of weekdays only (no Saturdays or Sundays), use the following formula. This formula assumes that the date in cell A1 is not a weekend day:

```
=IF(WEEKDAY(A1)=6,A1+3,A1+1)
```

Converting a nondate string to a date

You may import data that contains dates coded as text strings. For example, the following text represents August 21, 2013 (a four-digit year followed by a two-digit month, followed by a two-digit day):

```
20130821
```

To convert this string to an actual date, you can use a formula, such as the following. (This formula assumes that the coded data is in cell A1.)

```
=DATE(LEFT(A1,4),MID(A1,5,2),RIGHT(A1,2))
```

This formula uses text functions (LEFT, MID, and RIGHT) to extract the digits, and then it uses these extracted digits as arguments for the DATE function.

Calculating the number of days between two dates

A common type of date calculation determines the number of days between two dates. For example, say you have a financial worksheet that calculates interest earned on a deposit account. The interest earned depends on the number of days the account is open. If your sheet contains the open date and the close date for the account, you can calculate the number of days the account was open.

Because dates are stored as consecutive serial numbers, you can use simple subtraction to calculate the number of days between two dates. For example, if cells A1 and B1 both contain a date, the following formula returns the number of days between these dates:

```
=A1-B1
```

If cell B1 contains a more recent date than the date in cell A1, the result will be negative. If you don't care about which date is earlier and want to avoid displaying a negative value, use this formula:

```
=ABS(A1-B1)
```

Sometimes, calculating the difference between two days is more difficult. To demonstrate, consider the common fence-post analogy. If somebody asks you how many units make up a fence, you can respond with either of two answers: the number of fence posts or the number of gaps between the fence posts. The number of fence posts is always one more than the number of gaps between the posts.

To bring this analogy into the realm of dates, suppose that you start a sales promotion on February 1 and end the promotion on February 9. How many days was the promotion in effect? Subtracting February 1 from February 9 produces an answer of eight days. Actually, though, the promotion lasted nine days. In this case, the correct answer involves counting the fence posts, not the gaps. The formula to calculate the length of the promotion (assuming that you have appropriately named cells) appears like this:

`=EndDay-StartDay+1`

Calculating the number of workdays between two dates

When calculating the difference between two dates, you may want to exclude weekends and holidays. For example, you may need to know how many business days fall in the month of November. This calculation should exclude Saturdays, Sundays, and holidays. The NETWORKDAYS function can help out.

The NETWORKDAYS function calculates the difference between two dates, excluding weekend days (Saturdays and Sundays). As an option, you can specify a range of cells that contain the dates of holidays, which are also excluded. Excel has no way of determining which days are holidays, so you must provide this information in a range.

Figure 16.3 shows a worksheet that calculates the workdays between two dates. The range A2:A11 contains a list of holiday dates. The two formulas in column C calculate the workdays between the dates in column A and column B. For example, the formula in cell C15 is:

`=NETWORKDAYS(A15,B15,A2:A11)`

FIGURE 16.3

Using the NETWORKDAYS function to calculate the number of workdays between two dates

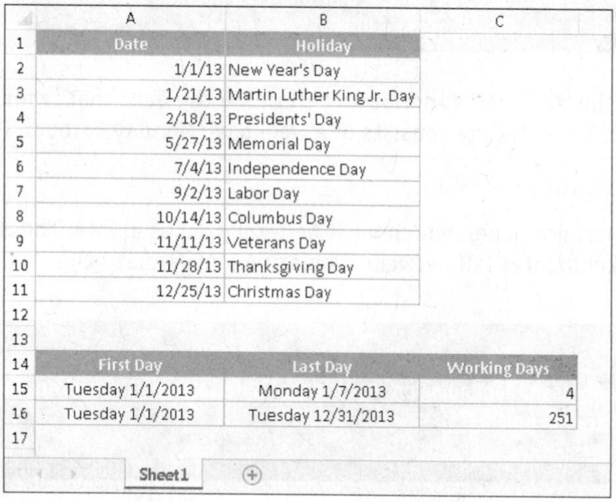

	A	B	C
1	**Date**	**Holiday**	
2	1/1/13	New Year's Day	
3	1/21/13	Martin Luther King Jr. Day	
4	2/18/13	Presidents' Day	
5	5/27/13	Memorial Day	
6	7/4/13	Independence Day	
7	9/2/13	Labor Day	
8	10/14/13	Columbus Day	
9	11/11/13	Veterans Day	
10	11/28/13	Thanksgiving Day	
11	12/25/13	Christmas Day	
12			
13			
14	**First Day**	**Last Day**	**Working Days**
15	Tuesday 1/1/2013	Monday 1/7/2013	4
16	Tuesday 1/1/2013	Tuesday 12/31/2013	251
17			

Sheet1 ⊕

This formula returns 4, which means that the seven-day period beginning with January 1 and ending on January 7 contains four workdays in the example year. In other words, the calculation excludes one holiday, one Saturday, and one Sunday. The formula in cell C16 calculates the total number of workdays in the year.

> **NOTE**
>
> Excel 2010 introduced an updated version of the NETWORKDAYS function, named NETWORKDAYS.INTL. This newer version of the function is useful if you consider weekend days to be days other than Saturday and Sunday. For example, many Muslim countries consider Thursday and Friday or Friday and Saturday as the weekend. Similarly, in Israel the workweek starts on Sunday, with the weekend spanning Thursday or Friday through Saturday. And of course, there are companies worldwide that follow a six-day work week or rotate workers in six-day shifts, meaning those instances result in single-day holidays. This function enables you to count how many workdays fall within a given timeframe, with an argument for you to specify which day(s) of the week are indeed the weekend days so that they are not included in the resulting count.

Offsetting a date using only workdays

The WORKDAY function is the opposite of the NETWORKDAYS function. For example, if you start a project on January 4 and the project requires ten working days to complete, the WORKDAY function can calculate the date you will finish the project.

The following formula uses the WORKDAY function to determine the date that is ten working days from January 4, 2013. A workday consists of a weekday (Monday through Friday).

```
=WORKDAY("1/4/2013",10)
```

The formula returns a date serial number, which must be formatted as a date. The result is January 18, 2013 (four weekend dates fall between January 4 and January 18).

The second argument for the WORKDAY function can be negative. And, as with the NETWORKDAYS function, the WORKDAY function accepts an optional third argument (a reference to a range that contains a list of holiday dates).

Calculating the number of years between two dates

The following formula calculates the number of years between two dates. This formula assumes that cells A1 and B1 both contain dates:

```
=YEAR(A1)-YEAR(B1)
```

This formula uses the YEAR function to extract the year from each date and then subtracts one year from the other. If cell B1 contains a more recent date than the date in cell A1, the result is negative.

Note that this function doesn't calculate full years. For example, if cell A1 contains 12/31/2012 and cell B1 contains 01/01/2013, the formula returns a difference of one year even though the dates differ by only one day. (See the next section for another way to calculate the number of full years.)

Calculating a person's age

A person's age indicates the number of full years that the person has been alive. The formula in the previous section (for calculating the number of years between two dates) won't calculate this value correctly. You can use two other formulas, however, to calculate a person's age.

The following formula returns the age of the person whose date of birth you enter into cell A1. This formula uses the YEARFRAC function.

```
=INT(YEARFRAC(TODAY(),A1,1))
```

> **NOTE**
>
> In versions prior to Excel 2007, the YEARFRAC function was available only when the Analysis ToolPak add-in was installed. The function is now part of Excel and does not require an add-in.

The following formula uses the DATEDIF function to calculate an age. (See the sidebar, "Where's the DATEDIF Function?")

```
=DATEDIF(A1,TODAY(),"Y")
```

Where's the DATEDIF Function?

One of Excel's mysteries is the DATEDIF function. You may notice that this function doesn't appear in the drop-down function list for the Date & Time category, nor does it appear in the Insert Function dialog box. Therefore, when you use this function, you must always enter it manually.

The DATEDIF function has its origins in Lotus 1-2-3, and apparently Excel provides it for compatibility purposes. The function has been available since Excel 5, but Excel 2000 is the only version that ever documented it in its Help system.

DATEDIF is a handy function that calculates the number of days, months, or years between two dates. The function takes three arguments: start_date, end_date, and a code that represents the time unit of interest. Here's an example of a formula that uses the DATEDIF function (it assumes cells A1 and A2 contain a date). The formula returns the number of complete years between those two dates:

=DATEDIF(A1,A2,"y")

The following table displays valid codes for the third argument. (You must enclose the codes in quotation marks.)

Continues

---

continued

Unit Code	Returns
"y"	The number of complete years in the period
"m"	The number of complete months in the period
"d"	The number of days in the period
"md"	The difference between the days in `start_date` and `end_date`. The months and years of the dates are ignored.
"ym"	The difference between the months in `start_date` and `end_date`. The days and years of the dates are ignored.
"yd"	The difference between the days of `start_date` and `end_date`. The years of the dates are ignored.

The `start_date` argument must be earlier than the `end_date` argument or else the function returns an error.

Determining the day of the year

January 1 is the first day of the year, and December 31 is the last day. But what about all those days in between? The following formula returns the day of the year for a date stored in cell A1:

```
=A1-DATE(YEAR(A1),1,0)
```

Here's a similar formula that returns the day of the year for the current date:

```
=TODAY()-DATE(YEAR(TODAY()),1,0)
```

The following formula returns the number of days remaining in the year after a particular date (assumed to be in cell A1):

```
=DATE(YEAR(A1),12,31)-A1
```

Here's the formula modified to use the current date:

```
=DATE(YEAR(TODAY()),12,31)-TODAY()
```

When you enter either formula, Excel applies date formatting to the cell. You need to apply a nondate number format to view the result as a number.

To convert a particular day of the year (for example, the 90th day of the year) to an actual date in a specified year, use the following formula, which assumes that the year is stored in cell A1 and that the day of the year is stored in cell B1:

```
=DATE(A1,1,B1)
```

This formula takes advantage of the fact that the DATE function accepts invalid dates (such as the 90th day of January) and adjusts automatically. The 90th day of January is actually the 90th day of the year.

Determining the day of the week

The WEEKDAY function accepts a date argument and returns an integer between 1 and 7 that corresponds to the day of the week. The following formula, for example, returns 3 because the first day of the year 2013 falls on a Tuesday:

```
=WEEKDAY(DATE(2013,1,1))
```

The WEEKDAY function uses an optional second argument that specifies the day numbering system for the result. If you specify 2 as the second argument, the function returns 1 for Monday, 2 for Tuesday, and so on. If you specify 3 as the second argument, the function returns 0 for Monday, 1 for Tuesday, and so on.

> **TIP**
>
> You can also determine the day of the week for a cell that contains a date by applying a custom number format. A cell that uses the following custom number format displays the day of the week, spelled out:
>
> dddd

Determining the week of the year

To determine the week of the year for a date, use the WEEKNUM function. The following function returns the week number for the data in cell A1:

```
=WEEKNUM(A1)
```

When you use the WEEKNUM function, you can specify a second optional argument to indicate the type of week numbering system you prefer. The second argument can be one of ten values, which are described in the Help system.

> **NOTE**
>
> Excel includes a new function, ISOWEEKNUM. This function returns the same result as WEEKNUM with a second argument of 21. Use this function if your organization uses the ISO week date system for numbering weeks (for fiscal or other tracking purposes), including weeks with leap years.

Determining the date of the most recent Sunday

You can use the following formula to return the date for the previous Sunday. If the current day is a Sunday, the formula returns the current date:

```
=TODAY()-MOD(TODAY()-1,7)
```

To modify this formula to find the date of a day other than Sunday, change the 1 to a different number between 2 (for Monday) and 7 (for Saturday).

Determining the first day of the week after a date

This formula returns the specified day of the week that occurs after a particular date. For example, use this formula to determine the date of the first Monday after a particular date. The formula assumes that cell A1 contains a date and cell A2 contains a number between 1 and 7 (1 for Sunday, 2 for Monday, and so on):

```
=A1+A2-WEEKDAY(A1)+(A2<WEEKDAY(A1))*7
```

If cell A1 contains June 1, 2013 (a Saturday), and cell A2 contains 2 (for Monday), the formula returns June 3, 2013. This is the first Monday following June 1, 2013.

Determining the *n*th occurrence of a day of the week in a month

You may need a formula to determine the date for a particular occurrence of a weekday. For example, suppose that your company payday falls on the second Friday of each month and you need to determine the paydays for each month of the year. The following formula makes this type of calculation:

```
=DATE(A1,A2,1)+A3-WEEKDAY(DATE(A1,A2,1))+
(A4-(A3>=WEEKDAY(DATE(A1,A2,1))))*7
```

The formula in this section assumes that

- Cell A1 contains a year.
- Cell A2 contains a month.
- Cell A3 contains a day number (1 for Sunday, 2 for Monday, and so on).
- Cell A4 contains the occurrence number (for example, 2 to select the second occurrence of the weekday specified in cell A3).

If you use this formula to determine the date of the second Friday in November 2013, it returns November 8, 2013.

> **NOTE**
>
> If the value in cell A4 exceeds the number of the specified day in the month, the formula returns a date from a subsequent month. For example, if you attempt to determine the date of the fifth Friday in October 2013 (there is no such date), the formula returns the first Friday in November.

Calculating dates of holidays

Determining the date for a particular holiday can be tricky. Some, such as New Year's Day and Independence Day in the United States always occur on the same date. For these kinds of holidays, you can simply use the DATE function. To enter New Year's Day (which always falls on January 1) for a specific year in cell A1, you can enter this function:

```
=DATE(A1,1,1)
```

Other holidays are defined in terms of a particular occurrence of a particular weekday in a particular month. For example, Labor Day falls on the first Monday in September.

Figure 16.4 shows a workbook with formulas that calculate the date for 11 U.S. holidays. The formulas, which reference the year in cell A1, are listed in the sections that follow.

FIGURE 16.4

Using formulas to determine the date for various holidays

	A	B	C	D	E
1	2013	← Enter the year			
2					
3			U.S. Holiday Calculations		
4					
5		Holiday	Description	Date	Weekday
6		New Year's Day	1st Day in January	January 1, 2013	Tuesday
7		Martin Luther King Jr. Day	3rd Monday in January	January 21, 2013	Monday
8		Presidents' Day	3rd Monday in February	February 18, 2013	Monday
9		Easter	Complicated	March 31, 2013	Sunday
10		Memorial Day	Last Monday in May	May 27, 2013	Monday
11		Independence Day	4th Day of July	July 4, 2013	Thursday
12		Labor Day	1st Monday in September	September 2, 2013	Monday
13		Columbus Day	2nd Monday in October	October 14, 2013	Monday
14		Veterans Day	11th Day of November	November 11, 2013	Monday
15		Thanksgiving Day	4th Thursday in November	November 28, 2013	Thursday
16		Christmas Day	25th Day of December	December 25, 2013	Wednesday
17					

Sheet1

New Year's Day

This holiday always falls on January 1:

```
=DATE(A1,1,1)
```

Martin Luther King, Jr., Day

This formula calculates Martin Luther King, Jr., Day for the year in cell A1:

```
=DATE(A1,1,1)+IF(2<WEEKDAY(DATE(A1,1,1)),7-WEEKDAY(DATE(A1,1,1))+2,
2-WEEKDAY(DATE(A1,1,1)))+((3-1)*7)
```

Presidents' Day

Presidents' Day occurs on the third Monday in February. This formula calculates Presidents' Day for the year in cell A1:

```
=DATE(A1,2,1)+IF(2<WEEKDAY(DATE(A1,2,1)),7-WEEKDAY(DATE(A1,2,1))+2,
2-WEEKDAY(DATE(A1,2,1)))+((3-1)*7)
```

Easter

Calculating the date for Easter is difficult because of the complicated manner in which Easter is determined. Easter Day is the first Sunday after the next full moon occurs after the vernal equinox. I found these formulas to calculate Easter on the web. I have no idea how they work. And they don't work if your workbook uses the 1904 date system. (Read about the difference between the 1900 and the 1904 date system earlier in this chapter.)

```
=DOLLAR(("4/"&A1)/7+MOD(19*MOD(A1,19)-7,30)*14%,)*7-6
```

This one is slightly shorter, but equally obtuse:

```
=FLOOR("5/"&DAY(MINUTE(A1/38)/2+56)&"/"&A1,7)-34
```

Memorial Day

The last Monday in May is Memorial Day. This formula calculates Memorial Day for the year in cell A1:

```
=DATE(A1,6,1)+IF(2<WEEKDAY(DATE(A1,6,1)),7-WEEKDAY(DATE(A1,6,1))+2,
2-WEEKDAY(DATE(A1,6,1)))+((1-1)*7)-7
```

Notice that this formula actually calculates the first Monday in June and then subtracts 7 from the result to return the last Monday in May.

Independence Day

This holiday always falls on July 4:

```
=DATE(A1,7,4)
```

Labor Day

Labor Day occurs on the first Monday in September. This formula calculates Labor Day for the year in cell A1:

```
=DATE(A1,9,1)+IF(2<WEEKDAY(DATE(A1,9,1)),7-WEEKDAY(DATE(A1,9,1))+2,
2-WEEKDAY(DATE(A1,9,1)))+((1-1)*7)
```

Columbus Day

This holiday occurs on the second Monday in October. This formula calculates Columbus Day for the year in cell A1:

```
=DATE(A1,10,1)+IF(2<WEEKDAY(DATE(A1,10,1)),
7-WEEKDAY(DATE(A1,10,1))+2,2-WEEKDAY(DATE(A1,10,1)))+((2-1)*7)
```

Veterans Day

This holiday always falls on November 11:

```
=DATE(A1,11,11)
```

Thanksgiving Day

Thanksgiving Day is celebrated on the fourth Thursday in November. This formula calculates Thanksgiving Day for the year in cell A1:

```
=DATE(A1,11,1)+IF(5<WEEKDAY(DATE(A1,11,1)),
7-WEEKDAY(DATE(A1,11,1))+5,5-WEEKDAY(DATE(A1,11,1)))+((4-1)*7)
```

Christmas Day

This holiday always falls on December 25:

```
=DATE(A1,12,25)
```

Determining the last day of a month

To determine the date that corresponds to the last day of a month, you can use the DATE function. However, you need to increment the month by 1 and use a day value of 0. In other words, the "0th" day of the next month is the last day of the current month.

The following formula assumes that a date is stored in cell A1. The formula returns the date that corresponds to the last day of the month:

```
=DATE(YEAR(A1),MONTH(A1)+1,0)
```

You can use a variation of this formula to determine how many days are in a specified month. The following formula returns an integer that corresponds to the number of days in the month for the date in cell A1:

```
=DAY(DATE(YEAR(A1),MONTH(A1)+1,0))
```

Determining whether a year is a leap year

To determine whether a particular year is a leap year, you can write a formula that determines whether the 29th day of February occurs in February or March. You can take advantage of the fact that the Excel DATE function adjusts the result when you supply an invalid argument — for example, a day of 29 when February contains only 28 days.

The following formula returns TRUE if the year in cell A1 is a leap year. Otherwise, it returns FALSE:

```
=IF(MONTH(DATE(A1,2,29))=2,TRUE,FALSE)
```

> **CAUTION**
> This function returns the wrong result (TRUE) if the year is 1900 (see "Excel's leap year bug," earlier in this chapter).

The following formula is a bit more complicated, but it correctly identifies 1900 as a non-leap year. This formula assumes that cell A1 contains a year:

```
=IF(OR(MOD(A1,400)=0,AND(MOD(A1,4)=0,MOD(A1,100)<>0)),TRUE, FALSE)
```

Determining a date's quarter

For financial reports, you may find it useful to present information in terms of quarters. The following formula returns an integer between 1 and 4 that corresponds to the calendar quarter for the date in cell A1:

```
=ROUNDUP(MONTH(A1)/3,0)
```

This formula divides the month number by 3 and then rounds up the result.

Time-Related Functions

Excel also includes a number of functions that enable you to work with time values in your formulas. This section contains examples that demonstrate the use of these functions.

Table 16.5 summarizes the time-related functions available in Excel. These functions work with date serial numbers. When you use the Insert Function dialog box, these functions appear in the Date & Time function category.

TABLE 16.5   Time-Related Functions

Function	Description
HOUR	Returns the hour part of a serial number
MINUTE	Returns the minute part of a serial number
NOW	Returns the serial number of the current date and time
SECOND	Returns the second part of a serial number
TIME	Returns the serial number of a specified time
TIMEVALUE	Converts a time in the form of text to a serial number

Displaying the current time

This formula displays the current time as a time serial number (or as a serial number without an associated date):

```
=NOW()-TODAY()
```

You need to format the cell with a time format to view the result as a recognizable time. The quickest way is to choose Home ➪ Number ➪ Format Number and select Time from the drop-down list.

Or just use the following formula, which returns the current date and time. You can apply a number format that shows the time only:

```
=NOW()
```

NOTE

Formulas that use the NOW function are updated only when the worksheet is recalculated, such as when you open the file or press F9. The time comes from your computer's clock, so if the clock is wrong, the formula will return an incorrect time.

TIP

To enter a time stamp (that doesn't change) into a cell, press Ctrl+Shift+: (colon).

Displaying any time

One way to enter a time value into a cell is to just type it, making sure that you include at least one colon (:). You can also create a time by using the TIME function. For example, the following formula returns a time comprising the hour in cell A1, the minute in cell B1, and the second in cell C1:

```
=TIME(A1,B1,C1)
```

Like the DATE function, the TIME function accepts invalid arguments and adjusts the result accordingly. For example, the following formula uses 80 as the minute argument and returns 10:20:15 AM. The 80 minutes are simply added to the hour, with 20 minutes remaining:

```
=TIME(9,80,15)
```

CAUTION

If you enter a value greater than 24 as the first argument for the TIME function, the result may not be what you expect. Logically, a formula such as the one that follows should produce a date/time serial number of 1.041667 (that is, one day and one hour).

```
=TIME(25,0,0)
```

In fact, this formula is equivalent to the following:

```
=TIME(1,0,0)
```

You can also use the DATE function along with the TIME function in a single cell. The formula that follows generates a date and time with a serial number of 41612.7708333333 — which represents 6:30 p.m. on December 4, 2013:

```
=DATE(2013,12,4)+TIME(18,30,0)
```

The TIMEVALUE function converts a text string that looks like a time into a time serial number. This formula returns 0.2395833333, the time serial number for 5:45 a.m.:

```
=TIMEVALUE("5:45 am")
```

To view the result of this formula as a time, you need to apply number formatting to the cell. The TIMEVALUE function doesn't recognize all common time formats. For example, the following formula returns an error because Excel doesn't like the periods in "a.m."

```
=TIMEVALUE("5:45 a.m.")
```

Calculating the difference between two times

Because times are represented as serial numbers, you can subtract the earlier time from the later time to get the difference. For example, if cell A2 contains 5:30:00 and cell B2 contains 14:00:00, the following formula returns 08:30:00 (a difference of 8 hours and 30 minutes):

```
=B2-A2
```

If the subtraction results in a negative value, however, it becomes an invalid time; Excel displays a series of hash marks (######) because a time without a date has a date serial number of 0. A negative time results in a negative serial number, which cannot be displayed — although you can still use the calculated value in other formulas.

If the direction of the time difference doesn't matter, you can use the ABS function to return the absolute value of the difference:

```
=ABS(B2-A2)
```

This "negative time" problem often occurs when calculating an elapsed time — for example, calculating the number of hours worked given a start time and an end time. This presents no problem if the two times fall in the same day. But if the work shift spans midnight, the result is an invalid negative time. For example, you may start work at 10:00 p.m. and end work at 6:00 a.m. the next day. Figure 16.5 shows a worksheet that calculates the hours worked. As you can see, the shift that spans midnight presents a problem (cell C3).

FIGURE 16.5

Calculating the number of hours worked returns an error if the shift spans midnight.

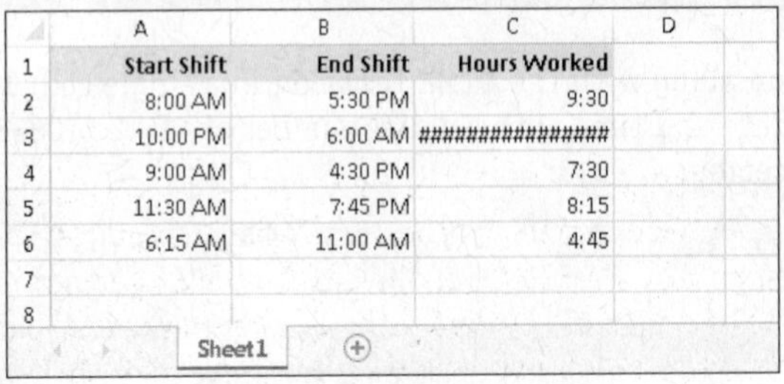

	A	B	C	D
1	**Start Shift**	**End Shift**	**Hours Worked**	
2	8:00 AM	5:30 PM	9:30	
3	10:00 PM	6:00 AM	###############	
4	9:00 AM	4:30 PM	7:30	
5	11:30 AM	7:45 PM	8:15	
6	6:15 AM	11:00 AM	4:45	
7				
8				

Sheet1 ⊕

Using the ABS function (to calculate the absolute value) isn't an option in this case because it returns the wrong result (16). The following formula, however, *does* work:

```
=IF(B2<A2,B2+1,B2)-A2
```

> **TIP**
>
> Negative times are permitted if the workbook uses the 1904 date system. To switch to the 1904 date system, use the Advanced section of the Excel Options dialog box. Select the Use 1904 Date System option. But beware! When changing the workbook's date system, if the workbook uses dates, the dates will be off by four years. (For more information about the 1904 date system, see the sidebar "Choose Your Date System: 1900 or 1904," earlier in this chapter.)

Summing times that exceed 24 hours

Many people are surprised to discover that when you sum a series of times that exceed 24 hours, Excel doesn't display the correct total. Figure 16.6 shows an example. The range B2:B8 contains times that represent the hours and minutes worked each day. The formula in cell B9 is:

```
=SUM(B2:B8)
```

FIGURE 16.6

Incorrect cell formatting makes the total appear incorrectly.

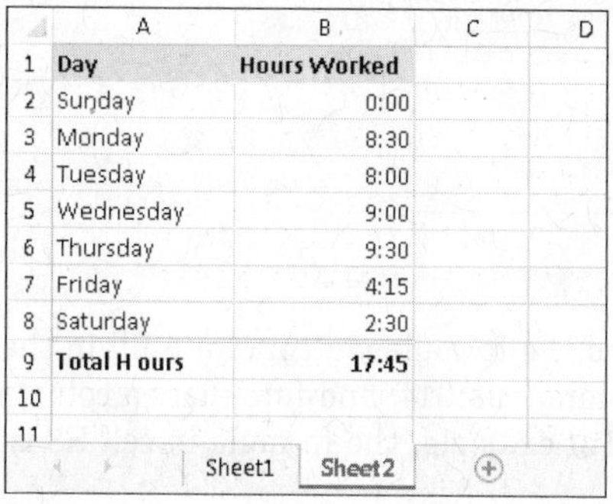

	A	B	C	D
1	**Day**	**Hours Worked**		
2	Sunday	0:00		
3	Monday	8:30		
4	Tuesday	8:00		
5	Wednesday	9:00		
6	Thursday	9:30		
7	Friday	4:15		
8	Saturday	2:30		
9	**Total H ours**	**17:45**		
10				
11				

Sheet1 | Sheet2 | (+)

As you can see, the formula returns a seemingly incorrect total (17 hours, 45 minutes). The total should read 41 hours, 45 minutes. The problem is that the formula is displaying the total as a date/time serial number of 1.7395833, but the cell formatting is not displaying the *date* part of the date/time. In other words, the answer is correct, but it appears incorrect because cell B9 has the wrong number format.

To view a time that exceeds 24 hours, you need to apply a custom number format for the cell so that square brackets surround the *hour* part of the format string. Applying the number format here to cell B9 displays the sum correctly:

    [h]:mm

Figure 16.7 shows another example of a worksheet that manipulates times. This worksheet keeps track of hours worked during a week (regular hours and overtime hours).

FIGURE 16.7

An employee timesheet workbook

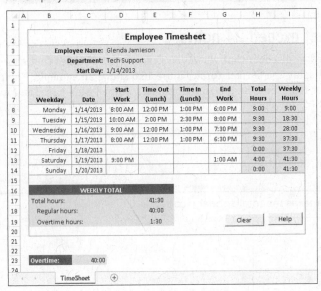

The week's starting date appears in cell D5, and the formulas in column B fill in the dates for the days of the week. Times appear in the range D8:G14, and formulas in column H calculate the number of hours worked each day. For example, the formula in cell H8 is:

    =IF(E8<D8,E8+1-D8,E8-D8)+IF(G8<F8,G8+1-G8,G8-F8)

The first part of this formula subtracts the time in column D from the time in column E to get the total hours worked before lunch. The second part subtracts the time in column F from the time in column G to get the total hours worked after lunch. I use IF functions to accommodate graveyard shift cases that span midnight — for example, an employee may start work at 10:00 p.m. and begin lunch at 2:00 a.m. Without the IF function, the formula returns a negative result.

The following formula in cell H17 calculates the weekly total by summing the daily totals in column H:

```
=SUM(H8:H14)
```

This worksheet assumes that hours in excess of 40 hours in a week are considered overtime hours. The worksheet contains a cell named Overtime, in cell C23. This cell contains a formula that returns 40:00. If your standard workweek consists of something other than 40 hours, you can change this cell.

The following formula (in cell H18) calculates regular (nonovertime) hours. This formula returns the smaller of two values: the total hours or the overtime hours:

```
=MIN(E17,Overtime)
```

The final formula, in cell H19, simply subtracts the regular hours from the total hours to yield the overtime hours:

```
=E17-E18
```

The times in the range H17:H19 and cell C23 may display time values that exceed 24 hours, so these cells use a custom number format:

```
[h]:mm
```

Converting from military time

Military time is expressed as a four-digit number from 0000 to 2359. For example, 1:00 a.m. is expressed as 0100 hours, and 3:30 p.m. is expressed as 1530 hours. The following formula converts such a number (assumed to be in cell A1) to a standard time:

```
=TIMEVALUE(LEFT(A1,2)&":"&RIGHT(A1,2))
```

The formula returns an incorrect result if the contents of cell A1 do not contain four digits. The following formula corrects the problem, and it returns a valid time for any military time value from 0 to 2359:

```
=TIMEVALUE(LEFT(TEXT(A1,"0000"),2)&":"&RIGHT(A1,2))
```

Following is a simpler formula that uses the TEXT function to return a formatted string and then the TIMEVALUE function to express the result in terms of a time:

```
=TIMEVALUE(TEXT(A1,"00\:00"))
```

Converting decimal hours, minutes, or seconds to a time

To convert decimal hours to a time, divide the decimal hours by 24. For example, if cell A1 contains 9.25 (representing hours), this formula returns 09:15:00 (9 hours, 15 minutes):

    =A1/24

To convert decimal minutes to a time, divide the decimal hours by 1,440 (the number of minutes in a day). For example, if cell A1 contains 500 (representing minutes), the following formula returns 08:20:00 (8 hours, 20 minutes):

    =A1/1440

To convert decimal seconds to a time, divide the decimal hours by 86,400 (the number of seconds in a day). For example, if cell A1 contains 65,000 (representing seconds), the following formula returns 18:03:20 (18 hours, 3 minutes, and 20 seconds):

    =A1/86400

Adding hours, minutes, or seconds to a time

You can use the TIME function to add any number of hours, minutes, or seconds to a time. For example, assume that cell A1 contains a time. The following formula adds 2 hours and 30 minutes to that time and displays the result:

    =A1+TIME(2,30,0)

You can use the TIME function to fill a range of cells with incremental times. Figure 16.8 shows a worksheet with a series of times in ten-minute increments. Cell A1 contains a time that was entered directly. Cell A2 contains the following formula, which was copied down the column:

    =A1+TIME(0,10,0)

FIGURE 16.8

Using a formula to create a series of incremental times

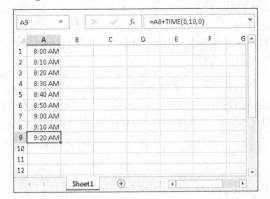

Rounding time values

You may need to create a formula that rounds a time to a particular value. For example, you may need to enter your company's time records rounded to the nearest 15 minutes. This section presents examples of various ways to round a time value.

The following formula rounds the time in cell A1 to the nearest minute:

```
=ROUND(A1*1440,0)/1440
```

The formula works by multiplying the time by 1,440 (to get total minutes). This value is passed to the ROUND function, and the result is divided by 1,440. For example, if cell A1 contains 11:52:34, the formula returns 11:53:00.

The following formula resembles this example, except that it rounds the time in cell A1 to the nearest hour:

```
=ROUND(A1*24,0)/24
```

If cell A1 contains 5:21:31, the formula returns 5:00:00.

The following formula rounds the time in cell A1 to the nearest 15 minutes (a quarter of an hour):

```
=ROUND(A1*24/0.25,0)*(0.25/24)
```

In this formula, 0.25 represents the fractional hour. To round a time to the nearest 30 minutes, change 0.25 to 0.5, as in the following formula:

```
=ROUND(A1*24/0.5,0)*(0.5/24)
```

Working with non-time-of-day values

Sometimes, you may want to work with time values that don't represent an actual time of day. For example, you may want to create a list of the finish times for a race or record the amount of time you spend in meetings each day. Such times don't represent a time of day. Instead, a value represents the time for an event (in hours, minutes, and seconds). The time to complete a test, for example, may be 35 minutes and 45 seconds. You can enter that value into a cell as:

```
00:35:45
```

Excel interprets such an entry as 12:35:45 a.m., which works fine. (Just make sure that you format the cell so that it appears as you like.) When you enter such times, which don't have an hour component, you must include at least one zero for the hour. If you omit a leading zero for a missing hour, Excel interprets your entry as 35 hours and 45 minutes.

Figure 16.9 shows an example of a worksheet set up to keep track of a person's jogging activity. Column A contains simple dates. Column B contains the distance in miles. Column C contains the time it took to run the distance. Column D contains formulas to calculate the speed in miles per hour. For example, the formula in cell D2 is:

```
=B2/(C2*24)
```

FIGURE 16.9

This worksheet uses times not associated with a time of day.

	Date	Distance	Time	Speed (mph)	Pace (min/mile)	YTD Distance	Cumulative Time
1							
2	1/1/2013	1.50	00:18:45	4.80	12.50	1.50	00:18:45
3	1/2/2013	1.50	00:17:40	5.09	11.78	3.00	00:36:25
4	1/3/2013	2.00	00:21:30	5.58	10.75	5.00	00:57:55
5	1/4/2013	1.50	00:15:20	5.87	10.22	6.50	01:13:15
6	1/5/2013	2.40	00:25:05	5.74	10.45	8.90	01:38:20
7	1/6/2013	3.00	00:31:06	5.79	10.37	11.90	02:09:26
8	1/7/2013	3.80	00:41:06	5.55	10.82	15.70	02:50:32
9	1/8/2013	5.00	01:09:00	4.35	13.80	20.70	03:59:32
10	1/9/2013	4.00	00:45:10	5.31	11.29	24.70	04:44:42
11	1/10/2013	3.00	00:29:06	6.19	9.70	27.70	05:13:48
12	1/11/2013	5.50	01:08:30	4.82	12.45	33.20	06:22:18
13							
14							

Sheet1

Column E contains formulas to calculate the pace, in minutes per mile. For example, the formula in cell E2 is:

```
=(C2*60*24)/B2
```

Columns F and G contain formulas that calculate the year-to-date distance (using column B) and the cumulative time (using column C). The cells in column G are formatted using the following number format (which permits time displays that exceed 24 hours):

```
[hh]:mm:ss
```

Summary

In this chapter, you learn how Excel treats dates and times as serial numbers. You can use dates and times in formulas, as long as you understand how serial numbers work. This chapter also introduced you to some Excel functions that work with dates and times, and showed you specific, handy examples of formulas you can build to tackle certain date and time calculation tasks. At this point, you should know how to:

- Type dates and times so that Excel recognizes them correctly.
- Use date functions to perform calculations such as determining a person's age, determining the day of the year, determining the day of the week, or calculating holiday dates.
- Use time functions to perform calculations such as determining the difference between two times or converting from military time.

16

Creating Formulas That Count and Sum

IN THIS CHAPTER

Introducing various ways to count and sum cells

Creating basic counting and summing formulas

Working with advanced counting and summing formulas

Developing conditional summing formulas

Many of the most common spreadsheet questions involve counting and summing values and other worksheet elements. It seems that people are always looking for formulas to count or to sum various items in a worksheet. If I've done my job, this chapter answers the vast majority of such questions. It contains many examples that you can easily adapt to your own situation.

Counting and Summing Worksheet Cells

Generally, a *counting formula* returns the number of cells in a specified range that meet certain criteria. A *summing formula* returns the sum of the values of the cells in a range that meet certain criteria.

Table 17.1 lists the Excel worksheet functions that come into play when creating counting and summing formulas. Not all these functions are covered in this chapter. If none of the functions in Table 17.1 can solve your problem, it's likely that an array formula can come to the rescue; refer to Excel's Help to learn more about array formulas.

> **NOTE**
>
> If your data is in the form of a table, you can use filtering to accomplish many counting and summing operations. Just set the filter criteria, and the table displays only the rows that match your criteria (the nonqualifying rows in the table are hidden). Then you can select formulas to display counts or sums in the table's total row. Chapter 19 introduces tables.

TABLE 17.1 **Excel Counting and Summing Functions**

Function	Description
COUNT	Returns the number of cells that contain a numeric value.
COUNTA	Returns the number of nonblank cells.
COUNTBLANK	Returns the number of blank cells.
COUNTIF	Returns the number of cells that meet a specified criterion.
COUNTIFS*	Returns the number of cells that meet multiple criteria.
DCOUNT	Counts the number of records that meet specified criteria; used with a worksheet database.
DCOUNTA	Counts the number of nonblank records that meet specified criteria; used with a worksheet database.
DSUM	Returns the sum of a column of values that meet specified criteria; used with a worksheet database.
FREQUENCY	Calculates how often values occur within a range of values and returns a vertical array of numbers. Used only in a multicell array formula.
SUBTOTAL	When used with a first argument of 2, 3, 102, or 103, returns a *count* of cells that comprise a subtotal; when used with a first argument of 9 or 109, returns the *sum* of cells that comprise a subtotal.
SUM	Returns the sum of its arguments.
SUMIF	Returns the sum of cells that meet a specified criterion.
SUMIFS*	Returns the sum of cells that meet multiple criteria.
SUMPRODUCT	Multiplies corresponding cells in two or more ranges and returns the sum of those products.

* These functions were introduced in Excel 2007.

Getting a Quick Count or Sum

The Excel status bar can display useful information about the currently selected cells — no formulas required. Normally, the status bar displays the sum and count of the values in the selected range. You can, however, right-click the status bar to bring up a menu with other options. You can choose any or all of the following: Average, Count, Numerical Count, Minimum, Maximum, and Sum.

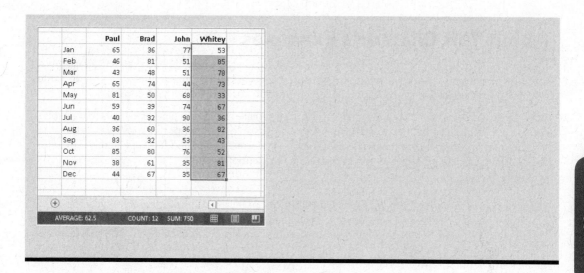

Basic Counting Formulas

The basic counting formulas presented in this section are all straightforward and relatively simple. They demonstrate the capability of the Excel counting functions to count the number of cells in a range that meet specific criteria.

Figure 17.1 shows a worksheet that uses formulas (in column E) to summarize the contents of range A1:B10 — a 20-cell range named Data. This range contains a variety of information, including values, text, logical values, errors, and empty cells.

FIGURE 17.1

Formulas in column E display various counts of the data in A1:B10.

	A	B	C	D	E	F
1	Jan	Feb		Total cells:	20	
2	525	718		Blank cells:	6	
3				Nonblank cells:	14	
4	3			Numeric values:	7	
5	552	911		Non-text cells:	17	
6	250	98		Text cells:	3	
7				Logical values:	2	
8	TRUE	FALSE		Error values:	2	
9		#DIV/0!		#N/A errors:	0	
10	Total	#NAME?		#NULL! errors:	0	
11				#DIV/0! errors:	1	
12				#VALUE! errors:	0	
13				#REF! errors:	0	
14				#NAME? errors:	1	
15				#NUM! errors:	0	
16						

Sheet1

About This Chapter's Examples

Most of the examples in this chapter use named ranges for function arguments. When you adapt these formulas for your own use, you'll need to substitute either the actual range address or a range name defined in your workbook. (See Chapter 14 for information about using named ranges.)

Also, some examples consist of array formulas. An *array formula* is a special type of formula that enables you to perform calculations that would not otherwise be possible. You can spot an array formula because it's enclosed in curly brackets when it's displayed in the Formula bar. In addition, I use this syntax for the array formula examples presented in this book. For example:

```
{=Data*2}
```

When you enter an array formula, press Ctrl+Shift+Enter (not just Enter), but *don't* type the curly brackets (Excel inserts the brackets for you). If you need to edit an array formula, don't forget to press Ctrl+Shift+Enter when you finish editing; otherwise, the array formula will revert to a normal formula, and it will return an incorrect result. (See the Help topic "Guidelines and examples of array formulas" for an introduction to array formulas.)

Counting the total number of cells

Oddly, Excel doesn't have a function that simply counts the number of cells in a range reference. To get a count of the total number of cells in a range (empty and nonempty cells), use the following formula. This formula returns the number of cells in a range named Data. It simply multiplies the number of rows (returned by the ROWS function) by the number of columns (returned by the COLUMNS function).

```
=ROWS(Data)*COLUMNS(Data)
```

This formula will not work if the Data range consists of noncontiguous cells. In other words, Data must be a rectangular range of cells.

Counting blank cells

The following formula returns the number of blank (empty) cells in a range named Data:

```
=COUNTBLANK(Data)
```

This function works only with a contiguous range of cells. If Data is defined as a noncontiguous range, the function returns a #VALUE! error.

The COUNTBLANK function also counts cells containing a formula that returns an empty string. For example, the formula that follows returns an empty string if the value in cell A1 is greater than 5. If the cell meets this condition, the COUNTBLANK function counts that cell.

```
=IF(A1>5,"",A1)
```

You can use the COUNTBLANK function with an argument that consists of entire rows or columns. For example, the following formula returns the number of blank cells in column A:

```
=COUNTBLANK(A:A)
```

The following formula returns the number of empty cells on the entire worksheet named Sheet1. You must enter this formula on a sheet other than Sheet1, or it will create a circular reference.

```
=COUNTBLANK(Sheet1!1:1048576)
```

Counting nonblank cells

To count nonblank cells, use the COUNTA function. The following formula uses the COUNTA function to return the number of nonblank cells in a range named Data:

```
=COUNTA(Data)
```

The COUNTA function counts cells that contain values, text, or logical values (TRUE or FALSE).

> **NOTE**
>
> If a cell contains a formula that returns an empty string, that cell is included in the count returned by COUNTA, even though the cell appears to be blank.

Counting numeric cells

To count only the numeric cells in a range, use the following formula (which assumes the range is named Data):

```
=COUNT(Data)
```

Cells that contain a date or a time are considered to be numeric cells. Cells that contain a logical value (TRUE or FALSE) aren't considered to be numeric cells.

Counting text cells

To count the number of text cells in a range, you need to use an array formula. The array formula that follows returns the number of text cells in a range named Data:

```
{=SUM(IF(ISTEXT(Data),1))}
```

17

Counting nontext cells

The following array formula uses the Excel `ISNONTEXT` function, which returns `TRUE` if its argument refers to any nontext cell (including a blank cell). This formula returns the count of the number of cells not containing text (including blank cells):

```
{=SUM(IF(ISNONTEXT(Data),1))}
```

Counting logical values

The following array formula returns the number of logical values (`TRUE` or `FALSE`) in a range named Data:

```
{=SUM(IF(ISLOGICAL(Data),1))}
```

Counting error values in a range

Excel has three functions that help you determine whether a cell contains an error value:

- **`ISERROR`**: Returns `TRUE` if the cell contains any error value (`#N/A`, `#VALUE!`, `#REF!`, `#DIV/0!`, `#NUM!`, `#NAME?`, or `#NULL!`)
- **`ISERR`**: Returns `TRUE` if the cell contains any error value except `#N/A`
- **`ISNA`**: Returns `TRUE` if the cell contains the `#N/A` error value

You can use these functions in an array formula to count the number of error values in a range. The following array formula, for example, returns the total number of error values in a range named Data:

```
{=SUM(IF(ISERROR(data),1))}
```

Depending on your needs, you can use the `ISERR` or `ISNA` function in place of `ISERROR`.

If you want to count specific types of errors, you can use the `COUNTIF` function. The following formula, for example, returns the number of `#DIV/0!` error values in the range named Data:

```
=COUNTIF(Data,"#DIV/0!")
```

Note that the `COUNTIF` functions works only with a contiguous range argument. If Data is a noncontiguous range, the formula returns a `#VALUE!` error.

Advanced Counting Formulas

Most of the basic examples presented earlier in this chapter use functions or formulas that perform conditional counting. The advanced counting formulas that I present in this section represent more complex examples for counting worksheet cells, based on various types of criteria.

Counting cells by using the COUNTIF function

The COUNTIF function, which is useful for single-criterion counting formulas, takes two arguments:

- **range:** The range that contains the values that determine whether to include a particular cell in the count
- **criteria:** The logical criteria that determine whether to include a particular cell in the count

Table 17.2 lists several examples of formulas that use the COUNTIF function. These formulas all work with a range named Data. As you can see, the criteria argument proves quite flexible. You can use constants, expressions, functions, cell references, and even wildcard characters (* and ?).

Note that the COUNTIF functions works only with a contiguous range argument. If *Data* is defined as a noncontiguous range, the formula returns a #VALUE! error.

TABLE 17.2 Examples of Formulas Using the COUNTIF Function

=COUNTIF(Data,12)	Returns the number of cells containing the value 12
=COUNTIF(Data,"<0")	Returns the number of cells containing a negative value
=COUNTIF(Data,"<>0")	Returns the number of cells not equal to 0
=COUNTIF(Data,">5")	Returns the number of cells greater than 5
=COUNTIF(Data,A1)	Returns the number of cells equal to the contents of cell A1
=COUNTIF(Data,">"&A1)	Returns the number of cells greater than the value in cell A1
=COUNTIF(Data,"*")	Returns the number of cells containing text
=COUNTIF(Data,"???")	Returns the number of text cells containing exactly three characters
=COUNTIF(Data,"budget")	Returns the number of cells containing the single word *budget* (not case sensitive)
=COUNTIF(Data,"*budget*")	Returns the number of cells containing the text *budget* anywhere within the text
=COUNTIF(Data,"A*")	Returns the number of cells containing text that begins with the letter *A* (not case sensitive)
=COUNTIF(Data,TODAY())	Returns the number of cells containing the current date
=COUNTIF(Data,">"&AVERAGE (Data))	Returns the number of cells with a value greater than the average of the values
=COUNTIF(Data,">"&AVERAGE (Data)+STDEV(Data)*3)	Returns the number of values exceeding three standard deviations above the mean

Continues

TABLE 17.2 *(continued)*

=COUNTIF(Data,3)+COUNTIF(Data,-3)	Returns the number of cells containing the value 3 or –3
=COUNTIF(Data,TRUE)	Returns the number of cells containing the logical value TRUE
=COUNTIF(Data,TRUE)+COUNTIF(Data,FALSE)	Returns the number of cells containing a logical value (TRUE or FALSE)
=COUNTIF(Data,"#N/A")	Returns the number of cells containing the #N/A error value

Counting cells based on multiple criteria

In many cases, your counting formula will need to count cells only if two or more criteria are met. These criteria can be based on the cells that are being counted or on a range of corresponding cells.

Figure 17.2 shows a simple worksheet used for the examples in this section. This sheet shows sales data categorized by Month, Sales Rep, and Type. The worksheet contains four named ranges that correspond to the labels in row 1.

FIGURE 17.2

This worksheet demonstrates various counting techniques that use multiple criteria.

	A	B	C	D
1	Month	SalesRep	Type	Amount
2	January	Albert	New	85
3	January	Albert	New	675
4	January	Brooks	New	130
5	January	Cook	New	1350
6	January	Cook	Existing	685
7	January	Brooks	New	1350
8	January	Cook	New	475
9	January	Brooks	New	1205
10	February	Brooks	Existing	450
11	February	Albert	New	495
12	February	Cook	New	210
13	February	Cook	Existing	1050
14	February	Albert	New	140
15	February	Brooks	New	900
16	February	Brooks	New	900
17	February	Cook	New	95
18	February	Cook	New	780
19	March	Brooks	New	900
20	March	Albert	Existing	875
21	March	Brooks	New	50
22	March	Brooks	New	875
23	March	Cook	Existing	225
24	March	Cook	New	175
25	March	Brooks	Existing	400
26	March	Albert	New	840
27	March	Cook	New	132
28				

Sheet1

> **NOTE**
>
> Several of the examples in this section use the COUNTIFS function, which was introduced in Excel 2007. The text also presents alternative versions of the formulas, which you should use if you plan to share your workbook with others who use an earlier version of Excel.

Using And criteria

An And criterion counts cells if all specified conditions are met. A common example is a formula that counts the number of values that fall within a numerical range. For example, you may want to count cells that contain a value that's greater than 100 *and* less than or equal to 200. For this example, the COUNTIFS function will do the job:

```
=COUNTIFS(Amount,">100",Amount,"<=200")
```

> **NOTE**
>
> If the data is contained in a table, you can use table referencing in your formulas. For example, if the table is named Table1, you can rewrite the preceding formula as:
>
> `=COUNTIFS(Table1[Amount],">100",Table1[Amount],"<=200")`
>
> This method of writing formulas does not require named ranges. Excel automatically creates names for the table and each column in the table.

The COUNTIFS function accepts any number of paired arguments. The first member of the pair is the range to be counted (in this case, the range named Amount); the second member of the pair is the criterion. The preceding example contains two sets of paired arguments and returns the number of cells in which Amount is greater than 100 and less than or equal to 200.

Prior to Excel 2007, you would need to use a formula like this:

```
=COUNTIF(Amount,">100")-COUNTIF(Amount,">200")
```

This formula counts the number of values that are greater than 100 and then subtracts the number of values that are greater than or equal to 200. The result is the number of cells that contain a value greater than 100 and less than or equal to 200. This formula can be confusing because the formula refers to a condition ">200" even though the goal is to count values that are less than or equal to 200.

Yet another alternate technique is to use an array formula, like the one that follows. You may find it easier to create this type of formula:

```
{=SUM((Amount>100)*(Amount<=200))}
```

Sometimes, the counting criteria will be based on cells other than the cells being counted. You may, for example, want to count the number of sales that meet all the following criteria:

- Month is January *and*
- SalesRep is Brooks *and*
- Amount is greater than 1,000.

The following formula (for Excel 2007 and later) returns the number of items that meet all three criteria. Note that the COUNTIFS function uses three sets of paired arguments.

```
=COUNTIFS(Month,"January",SalesRep,"Brooks",Amount,">1000")
```

An alternative formula, which works with all versions of Excel, uses the SUMPRODUCT function. The following formula returns the same result as the previous formula:

```
=SUMPRODUCT((Month="January")*(SalesRep="Brooks")*(Amount>1000))
```

Yet another way to perform this count is to use an array formula:

```
{=SUM((Month="January")*(SalesRep="Brooks")*(Amount>1000))}
```

Using Or criteria

An Or criterion counts cells if any of the multiple conditions is met. To count cells by using an Or criterion, you can sometimes use multiple COUNTIF functions. The following formula, for example, counts the number of sales made in January *or* February:

```
=COUNTIF(Month,"January")+COUNTIF(Month,"February")
```

You can also use the COUNTIF function in an array formula. The following array formula, for example, returns the same result as the previous formula:

```
{=SUM(COUNTIF(Month,{"January","February"}))}
```

But if you base your Or criteria on cells other than the cells being counted, the COUNTIF function won't work (refer to Figure 17.2). Suppose that you want to count the number of sales that meet at least one of the following criteria:

- Month is January *or*
- SalesRep is Brooks *or*
- Amount is greater than 1,000.

If you attempt to create a formula that uses COUNTIF, some double counting will occur. The solution is to use an array formula like this:

> {=SUM(IF((Month="January")+(SalesRep="Brooks")+(Amount>1000),1))}

Combining And and Or criteria

In some cases, you may need to combine And criteria and Or criteria when counting. For example, perhaps you want to count sales that meet both of the following criteria:

- Month is January.
- SalesRep is Brooks *or* SalesRep is Cook.

This array formula returns the number of sales that meet the criteria:

> {=SUM((Month="January")*IF((SalesRep="Brooks")+(SalesRep="Cook"),1))}

Counting the most frequently occurring entry

The MODE function returns the most frequently occurring value in a range. Figure 17.3 shows a worksheet with values in range A1:A10 (named Data). The formula that follows returns 10 because that value appears most frequently in the Data range:

> =MODE(Data)

FIGURE 17.3

The MODE function returns the most frequently occurring value in a range.

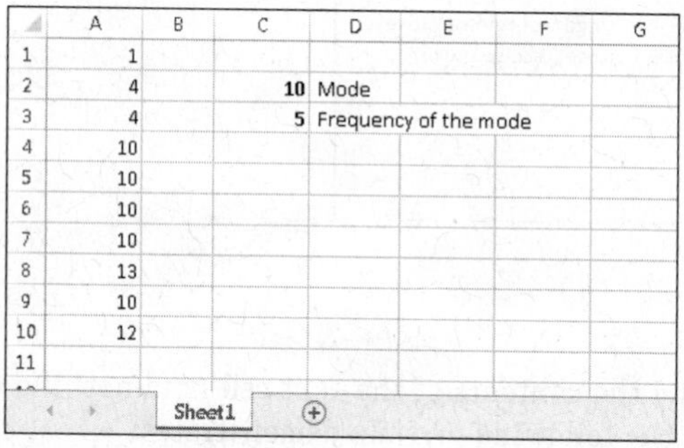

To count the number of times the most frequently occurring value appears in the range (in other words, the frequency of the mode), use the following formula:

> =COUNTIF(Data,MODE(Data))

This formula returns 5 because the modal value (10) appears five times in the Data range.

The MODE function works only for numeric values. It simply ignores cells that contain text. To find the most frequently occurring text entry in a range, you need to use an array formula.

To count the number of times the most frequently occurring item (text or values) appears in a range named Data, use the following array formula:

{=MAX(COUNTIF(Data,Data))}

This next array formula operates like the MODE function except that it works with both text and values:

{=INDEX(Data,MATCH(MAX(COUNTIF(Data,Data)),COUNTIF(Data,Data),0))}

Counting the occurrences of specific text

The examples in this section demonstrate various ways to count the occurrences of a character or text string in a range of cells. Figure 17.4 shows a worksheet used for these examples. Various text strings appear in the range A1:A10 (named Data); cell B1 is named Text.

FIGURE 17.4

This worksheet demonstrates various ways to count character strings in a range.

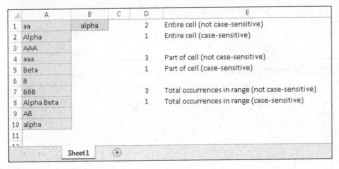

Entire cell contents

To count the number of cells containing the contents of the Text cell (and nothing else), you can use the COUNTIF function as the following formula demonstrates:

=COUNTIF(Data,Text)

For example, if the Text cell contains the string Alpha, the formula returns 2 because two cells in the Data range contain this text. This formula is not case sensitive, so it counts both Alpha (cell A2) and alpha (cell A10). Note, however, that it does not count the cell that contains Alpha Beta (cell A8).

The following array formula is similar to the preceding formula, but this one is case sensitive:

```
{=SUM(IF(EXACT(Data,Text),1))}
```

Partial cell contents

To count the number of cells that contain a string that includes the contents of the Text cell, use this formula:

```
=COUNTIF(Data,"*"&Text&"*")
```

For example, if the *Text* cell contains the text Alpha, the formula returns 3 because three cells in the Data range contain the text alpha (cells A2, A8, and A10). Note that the comparison is not case sensitive.

If you need a case-sensitive count, you can use the following array formula:

```
{=SUM(IF(LEN(Data)-LEN(SUBSTITUTE(Data,Text,""))>0,1))}
```

If the Text cells contain the text Alpha, the preceding formula returns 2 because the string appears in two cells (A2 and A8).

Total occurrences in a range

To count the total number of occurrences of a string within a range of cells, use the following array formula:

```
{=(SUM(LEN(Data))-SUM(LEN(SUBSTITUTE(Data,Text,""))))/LEN(Text)}
```

If the Text cell contains the character B, the formula returns 7 because the range contains seven instances of the string. This formula is case sensitive.

The following array formula is a modified version that is not case sensitive:

```
{=(SUM(LEN(Data))-SUM(LEN(SUBSTITUTE(UPPER(Data),UPPER(Text),""))))/
LEN(Text)}
```

Counting the number of unique values

The following array formula returns the number of unique values in a range named Data:

```
{=SUM(1/COUNTIF(Data,Data))}
```

Useful as it is, this formula does have a serious limitation: If the range contains any blank cells, it returns an error. The following array formula solves this problem:

```
{=SUM(IF(COUNTIF(Data,Data)=0,"",1/COUNTIF(Data,Data)))}
```

Creating a frequency distribution

A *frequency distribution* is a summary table that shows the frequency of each value in a range. For example, an instructor may create a frequency distribution of grades. The table would show the count of *As*, *Bs*, *Cs*, and so on. Excel provides a number of ways to create frequency distributions. You can:

- Use the FREQUENCY function.
- Create your own formulas.
- Use the Analysis ToolPak add-in.
- Use a PivotTable.

The FREQUENCY function

Using the FREQUENCY function to create a frequency distribution can be a bit tricky, and this is probably the most difficult way to create a frequency distribution. The FREQUENCY function always returns an array, so you must use it in an array formula that's entered into a multicell range.

Figure 17.5 shows some data in range A1:E25 (named Data). These values range from 1 to 500. The range G2:G11 contains the bins used for the frequency distribution. Each cell in this bin range contains the upper limit for the bin. In this case, the bins consist of <=50, 51–100, 101–150, and so on. The goal is to count the number of values that fall into each bin.

FIGURE 17.5

Creating a frequency distribution for the data in A1:E25

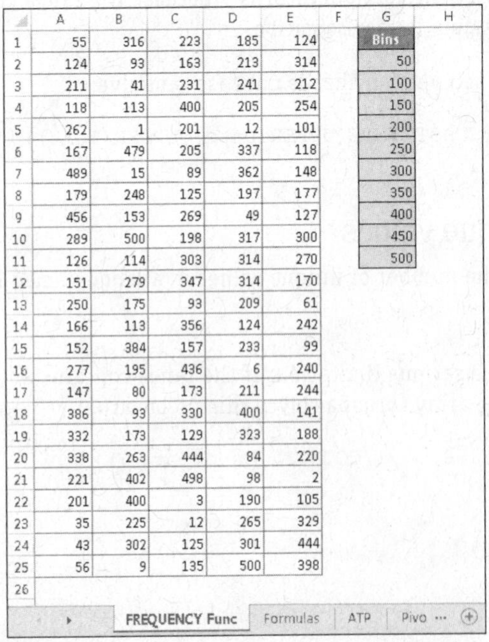

	A	B	C	D	E	F	G	H
1	55	316	223	185	124		Bins	
2	124	93	163	213	314		50	
3	211	41	231	241	212		100	
4	118	113	400	205	254		150	
5	262	1	201	12	101		200	
6	167	479	205	337	118		250	
7	489	15	89	362	148		300	
8	179	248	125	197	177		350	
9	456	153	269	49	127		400	
10	289	500	198	317	300		450	
11	126	114	303	314	270		500	
12	151	279	347	314	170			
13	250	175	93	209	61			
14	166	113	356	124	242			
15	152	384	157	233	99			
16	277	195	436	6	240			
17	147	80	173	211	244			
18	386	93	330	400	141			
19	332	173	129	323	188			
20	338	263	444	84	220			
21	221	402	498	98	2			
22	201	400	3	190	105			
23	35	225	12	265	329			
24	43	302	125	301	444			
25	56	9	135	500	398			
26								

FREQUENCY Func | Formulas | ATP | Pivo ...

To create the frequency distribution, select a range of cells that corresponds to the number of cells in the bin range (in this example, select H2:H11 because the bins are in G2:G11). Then enter the following array formula into the selected range (press Ctrl+Shift+Enter it):

```
{=FREQUENCY(Data,G2:G11)}
```

The array formula returns the count of values in the Data range that fall into each bin. To create a frequency distribution that consists of percentages, use the following array formula:

```
{=FREQUENCY(Data,G2:G11)/COUNT(Data)}
```

Figure 17.6 shows two frequency distributions — one in terms of counts and one in terms of percentages. The figure also shows a chart (histogram) created from the frequency distribution.

FIGURE 17.6

Frequency distributions created by using the FREQUENCY function

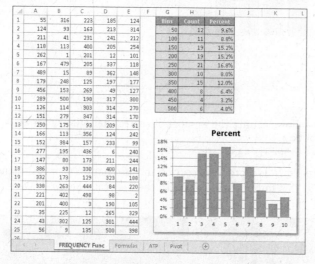

Using formulas to create a frequency distribution

Figure 17.7 shows a worksheet that contains test scores for 50 students in column B (the range is named Grades). Formulas in columns G and H calculate a frequency distribution for letter grades. The minimum and maximum values for each letter grade appear in columns D and E. For example, a test score between 80 and 89 (inclusive) earns a B. In addition, a chart displays the distribution of the test scores.

FIGURE 17.7

Creating a frequency distribution of test scores

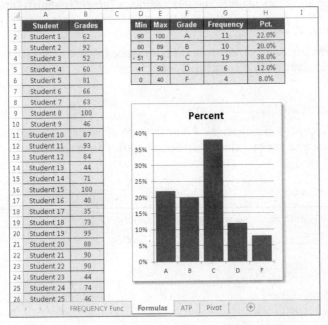

The formula in cell G2 that follows counts the number of scores that qualify for an A:

```
=COUNTIFS(Grades,">="&D2,Grades,"<="&E2)
```

You may recognize this formula from a previous section in this chapter (see "Counting cells based on multiple criteria"). This formula was copied to the four cells below G2.

> **NOTE**
>
> The preceding formula uses the COUNTIFS function, which first appeared in Excel 2007. For compatibility with previous Excel versions, use this array formula:
>
> `{=SUM((Grades>=D2)*(Grades<=E2))}`

The formulas in column H calculate the percentage of scores for each letter grade. The formula in H2, which was copied to the four cells below H2, is:

```
=G2/SUM($G$2:$G$6)
```

Using the Analysis ToolPak to create a frequency distribution

The Analysis ToolPak add-in, distributed with Excel, provides another way to calculate a frequency distribution:

1. **Enter your bin values in a range.**

2. **Choose Data ⇨ Analysis ⇨ Data Analysis.** The Data Analysis dialog box appears. If this command is not available, see the sidebar, "Is the Analysis ToolPak Available?"

3. **In the Data Analysis dialog box, select Histogram, and then click OK.** The Histogram dialog box, shown in Figure 17.8, appears.

FIGURE 17.8

The Analysis ToolPak's Histogram dialog box

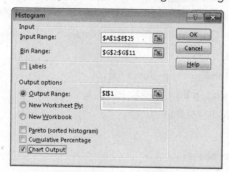

4. **Specify the ranges for your data (Input Range), bins (Bin Range), and results (Output Range), and then select any options and click OK.** Figure 17.9 shows a frequency distribution (and chart) created with the Histogram option.

FIGURE 17.9

A frequency distribution and chart generated by the Analysis ToolPak's Histogram option

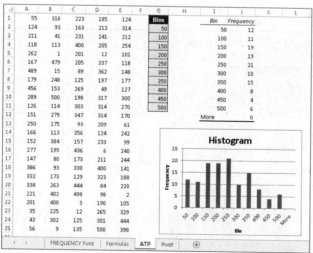

> **CAUTION**
>
> Note that the frequency distribution consists of values, not formulas. Therefore, if you make any changes to your input data, you need to rerun the Histogram procedure to update the results.

Is the Analysis ToolPak Available?

To make sure that the Analysis ToolPak add-in is available for use, click the Data tab. If the Ribbon displays the Data Analysis command in the Analysis group, you're all set. If not, you'll need to install the add-in:

1. **Choose File ⇨ Options.** The Excel Options dialog box appears.
2. **Click the Add-Ins tab on the left.**
3. **Select Excel Add-Ins from the Manage drop-down list.**
4. **Click Go to display the Add-Ins dialog box.**
5. **Place a check mark next to Analysis ToolPak.**
6. **Click OK.**

If you've enabled the Developer tab, you can display the Add-Ins dialog box by choosing Developer ⇨ Add-Ins ⇨ Add-Ins.

Note: In the Add-Ins dialog box, you see an additional add-in, Analysis ToolPak – VBA. This add-in is for programmers, and you don't need to install it.

Using a PivotTable to create a frequency distribution

If your data is in the form of a table, you may prefer to use a PivotTable and a PivotChart to create a histogram. Figure 17.10 shows the student grade data summarized in a PivotTable and a PivotChart. The counts were created by grouping.

FIGURE 17.10

Using a PivotChart to display a histogram

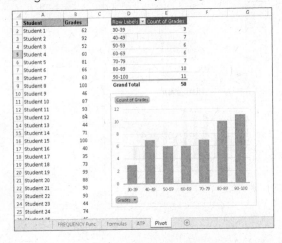

Summing Formulas

The examples in this section demonstrate how to perform common summing tasks by using formulas. The formulas range from very simple to relatively complex array formulas that compute sums by using multiple criteria.

Summing all cells in a range

It doesn't get much simpler than this. The following formula returns the sum of all values in a range named Data:

```
=SUM(Data)
```

The SUM function can take up to 255 arguments. The following formula, for example, returns the sum of the values in five noncontiguous ranges:

```
=SUM(A1:A9,C1:C9,E1:E9,G1:G9,I1:I9)
```

You can use complete rows or columns as an argument for the SUM function. The formula that follows, for example, returns the sum of all values in column A. If this formula appears in a cell in column A, it generates a circular reference error.

```
=SUM(A:A)
```

The following formula returns the sum of all values on Sheet1 by using a range reference that consists of all rows. To avoid a circular reference error, this formula must appear on a sheet other than Sheet1.

```
=SUM(Sheet1!1:1048576)
```

The SUM function is very versatile. The arguments can be numerical values, cells, ranges, text representations of numbers (which are interpreted as values), logical values, and even embedded functions. For example, consider the following formula:

```
=SUM(B1,5,"6",,SQRT(4),A1:A5,TRUE)
```

This odd formula, which is perfectly valid, contains all the following types of arguments, listed here in the order of their presentation:

- A single cell reference: B1
- A literal value: 5
- A string that looks like a value: "6"
- A missing argument: , ,
- An expression that uses another function: SQRT(4)
- A range reference: A1:A5
- A logical value: TRUE

> **CAUTION**
>
> The SUM function is versatile, but it's also inconsistent when you use logical values (TRUE or FALSE). Logical values stored in cells are always treated as 0. However, logical TRUE, when used as an argument in the SUM function, is treated as 1.

Computing a cumulative sum

You may want to display a cumulative sum of values in a range — sometimes known as a "running total." Figure 17.11 illustrates a cumulative sum. Column B shows the monthly amounts, and column C displays the cumulative (year-to-date) totals.

FIGURE 17.11

Simple formulas in column C display a cumulative sum of the values in column B.

	A	B	C	D	E
1	**Month**	**Amount**	**Year-to-Date**		
2	January	850	850		
3	February	900	1,750		
4	March	750	2,500		
5	April	1,100	3,600		
6	May	600	4,200		
7	June	500	4,700		
8	July	1,200	5,900		
9	August		5,900		
10	September		5,900		
11	October		5,900		
12	November		5,900		
13	December		5,900		
14	**TOTAL**	**5,900**			
15					
16					

The formula in cell C2 is:

```
=SUM(B$2:B2)
```

Notice that this formula uses a *mixed reference* — that is, the first cell in the range reference always refers to the same row (in this case, row 2). When this formula is copied down the column, the range argument adjusts such that the sum always starts with row 2 and ends with the current row. For example, after copying this formula down column C, the formula in cell C8 is:

```
=SUM(B$2:B8)
```

You can use an IF function to hide the cumulative sums for rows in which data hasn't been entered. The following formula, entered in cell C2 and copied down the column, is:

```
=IF(B2<>"",SUM(B$2:B2),"")
```

Figure 17.12 shows this formula at work.

FIGURE 17.12

Using an IF function to hide cumulative sums for missing data

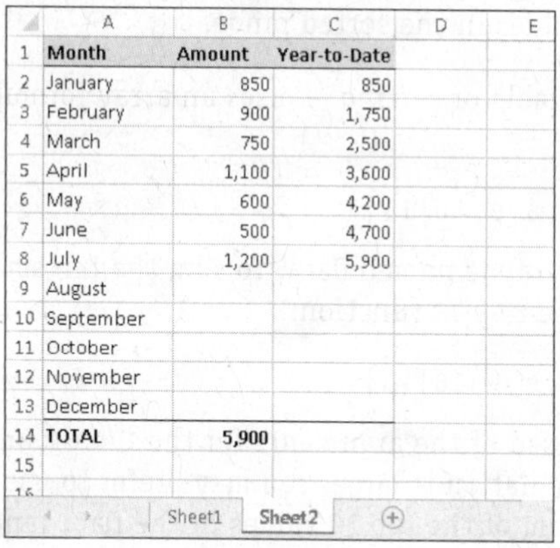

	A	B	C	D	E
1	**Month**	**Amount**	**Year-to-Date**		
2	January	850	850		
3	February	900	1,750		
4	March	750	2,500		
5	April	1,100	3,600		
6	May	600	4,200		
7	June	500	4,700		
8	July	1,200	5,900		
9	August				
10	September				
11	October				
12	November				
13	December				
14	TOTAL	5,900			
15					
16					

Sheet1 Sheet2 ⊕

Ignoring errors when summing

The SUM function does not work if the range to be summed includes any errors. For example, if one of the cells to be summed displays #N/A, the SUM function will also return #N/A.

To add the values in a range and ignore the error cells, use the AGGREGATE function. For example, to sum a range named Data (which may have error values), use this formula:

```
=AGGREGATE(9,6,Data)
```

The AGGREGATE function is very versatile, and can do a lot more than just add values. In this example, the first argument (9) specifies SUM. The second argument (6), means ignore error values.

The arguments are described in the Excel Help. Excel also provides good autocomplete assistance when you enter a formula that uses this function.

CAUTION

The AGGREGATE function was introduced in Excel 2010. For compatibility with earlier versions use this array formula:

```
{=SUM(IF(ISERROR(Data),"",Data))}
```

Summing the "top *n*" values

In some situations, you may need to sum the *n* largest values in a range — for example, the top ten values. If your data resides in a table, you can use autofiltering to hide all but the top *n* rows and then display the sum of the visible data in the table's total row.

Another approach is to sort the range in descending order and then use the SUM function with an argument consisting of the first *n* values in the sorted range.

A better solution — which doesn't require a table or sorting — uses an array formula like this one:

$$\{=\text{SUM}(\text{LARGE}(\text{Data},\{1,2,3,4,5,6,7,8,9,10\})))\}$$

This formula sums the ten largest values in a range named Data. To sum the ten smallest values, use the SMALL function instead of the LARGE function:

$$\{=\text{SUM}(\text{SMALL}(\text{Data},\{1,2,3,4,5,6,7,8,9,10\})))\}$$

These formulas use an array constant comprised of the arguments for the LARGE or SMALL function. If the value of *n* for your top-*n* calculation is large, you may prefer to use the following variation. This formula returns the sum of the top 30 values in the Data range. You can, of course, substitute a different value for 30. Figure 17.13 shows this array formula in use.

$$\{=\text{SUM}(\text{LARGE}(\text{Data},\text{ROW}(\text{INDIRECT}("1:30"))))\}$$

FIGURE 17.13

Using an array formula to calculate the sum of the 30 largest values in a range

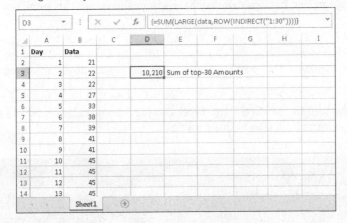

Conditional Sums Using a Single Criterion

Often, you need to calculate a *conditional sum*. With a conditional sum, values in a range that meet one or more conditions are included in the sum. This section presents examples of conditional summing by using a single criterion.

The SUMIF function is very useful for single-criterion sum formulas. The SUMIF function takes three arguments:

- **range:** The range containing the values that determine whether to include a particular cell in the sum

- **criteria:** An expression that determines whether to include a particular cell in the sum

- **sum_range:** Optional. The range that contains the cells you want to sum. If you omit this argument, the function uses the range specified in the first argument.

The examples that follow demonstrate the use of the SUMIF function. These formulas are based on the worksheet shown in Figure 17.14, set up to track invoices. Column F contains a formula that subtracts the date in column E from the date in column D. A negative number in column F indicates a past-due payment. The worksheet uses named ranges that correspond to the labels in row 1.

FIGURE 17.14

A negative value in column F indicates a past-due payment.

	A	B	C	D	E	F	G
1	InvoiceNum	Office	Amount	DateDue	Today	Difference	
2	AG-0145	Oregon	$5,000.00	4/1/2013	5/5/2013	-34	
3	AG-0189	California	$450.00	4/19/2013	5/5/2013	-16	
4	AG-0220	Washington	$3,211.56	4/28/2013	5/5/2013	-7	
5	AG-0310	Oregon	$250.00	4/30/2013	5/5/2013	-5	
6	AG-0355	Washington	$125.50	5/4/2013	5/5/2013	-1	
7	AG-0409	Washington	$3,000.00	5/10/2013	5/5/2013	5	
8	AG-0581	Oregon	$2,100.00	5/24/2013	5/5/2013	19	
9	AG-0600	Oregon	$335.39	5/24/2013	5/5/2013	19	
10	AG-0602	Washington	$65.00	5/28/2013	5/5/2013	23	
11	AG-0633	California	$250.00	5/31/2013	5/5/2013	26	
12	TOTAL		$14,787.45			29	

Sheet1 ⊕

Summing only negative values

The following formula returns the sum of the negative values in column F. In other words, it returns the total number of past-due days for all invoices. For this worksheet, the formula returns –63.

```
=SUMIF(Difference,"<0")
```

Because you omit the third argument, the second argument (`"<0"`) applies to the values in the Difference range.

You don't need to hard-code the arguments for the SUMIF function into your formula. For example, you can create a formula, such as the following, which gets the criteria argument from the contents of cell G2:

```
=SUMIF(Difference,G2)
```

This formula returns a new result if you change the criteria in cell G2.

Summing values based on a different range

The following formula returns the sum of the past-due invoice amounts (in column C):

```
=SUMIF(Difference,"<0",Amount)
```

This formula uses the values in the Difference range to determine whether the corresponding values in the Amount range contribute to the sum.

Summing values based on a text comparison

The following formula returns the total invoice amounts for the Oregon office:

```
=SUMIF(Office,"=Oregon",Amount)
```

Using the equal sign in the argument is optional. The following formula has the same result:

```
=SUMIF(Office,"Oregon",Amount)
```

To sum the invoice amounts for all offices *except* Oregon, use this formula:

```
=SUMIF(Office,"<>Oregon",Amount)
```

Summing values based on a date comparison

The following formula returns the total invoice amounts that have a due date after May 1, 2013:

```
=SUMIF(DateDue,">="&DATE(2013,5,1),Amount)
```

Notice that the second argument for the SUMIF function is an expression. The expression uses the DATE function, which returns a date. Also, the comparison operator, enclosed in quotes, is concatenated (using the & operator) with the result of the DATE function.

The formula that follows returns the total invoice amounts that have a future due date (including today):

```
=SUMIF(DateDue,">="&TODAY(),Amount)
```

Conditional Sums Using Multiple Criteria

The examples in the preceding section all used a single comparison criterion. The examples in this section involve summing cells based on multiple criteria.

Figure 17.15 shows the sample worksheet again, for your reference. The worksheet also shows the result of several formulas that demonstrate summing by using multiple criteria.

FIGURE 17.15

This worksheet demonstrates summing based on multiple criteria.

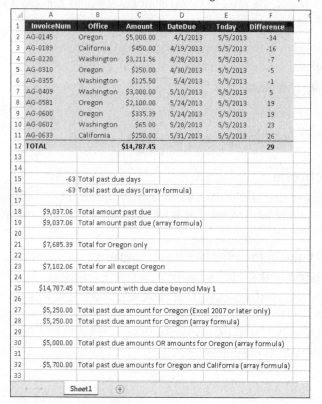

	A	B	C	D	E	F
1	**InvoiceNum**	**Office**	**Amount**	**DateDue**	**Today**	**Difference**
2	AG-0145	Oregon	$5,000.00	4/1/2013	5/5/2013	-34
3	AG-0189	California	$450.00	4/19/2013	5/5/2013	-16
4	AG-0220	Washington	$3,211.56	4/28/2013	5/5/2013	-7
5	AG-0310	Oregon	$250.00	4/30/2013	5/5/2013	-5
6	AG-0355	Washington	$125.50	5/4/2013	5/5/2013	-1
7	AG-0409	Washington	$3,000.00	5/10/2013	5/5/2013	5
8	AG-0581	Oregon	$2,100.00	5/24/2013	5/5/2013	19
9	AG-0600	Oregon	$335.39	5/24/2013	5/5/2013	19
10	AG-0602	Washington	$65.00	5/28/2013	5/5/2013	23
11	AG-0633	California	$250.00	5/31/2013	5/5/2013	26
12	**TOTAL**		**$14,787.45**			29
13						
14						
15		-63	Total past due days			
16		-63	Total past due days (array formula)			
17						
18	$9,037.06		Total amount past due			
19	$9,037.06		Total amount past due (array formula)			
20						
21	$7,685.39		Total for Oregon only			
22						
23	$7,102.06		Total for all except Oregon			
24						
25	$14,787.45		Total amount with due date beyond May 1			
26						
27	$5,250.00		Total past due amount for Oregon (Excel 2007 or later only)			
28	$5,250.00		Total past due amount for Oregon (array formula)			
29						
30	$5,000.00		Total past due amounts OR amounts for Oregon (array formula)			
31						
32	$5,700.00		Total past due amounts for Oregon and California (array formula)			
33						

Sheet1 ⊕

Using And criteria

Suppose that you want to get a sum of the invoice amounts that are past due *and* associated with the Oregon office. In other words, the value in the Amount range will be summed only if both of the following criteria are met:

- The corresponding value in the Difference range is negative, *and*
- The corresponding text in the Office range is Oregon.

If the worksheet won't be used by anyone running a version prior to Excel 2007, the following formula does the job:

```
=SUMIFS(Amount,Difference,"<0",Office,"Oregon")
```

The following array formula returns the same result and will work in all versions of Excel:

```
{=SUM((Difference<0)*(Office="Oregon")*Amount)}
```

Using Or criteria

Suppose that you want to get a sum of past-due invoice amounts *or* ones associated with the Oregon office. In other words, the value in the Amount range will be summed if either of the following criteria is met:

- The corresponding value in the Difference range is negative, *or*
- The corresponding text in the Office range is Oregon.

This example requires an array formula:

```
{=SUM(IF((Office="Oregon")+(Difference<0),1,0)*Amount)}
```

A plus sign (+) joins the conditions; you can include more than two conditions.

Using And and Or criteria

As you may expect, things get a bit tricky when your criteria consists of both And and Or operations. For example, you may want to sum the values in the Amount range when both of the following conditions are met:

- The corresponding value in the Difference range is negative.
- The corresponding text in the Office range is Oregon or California.

Notice that the second condition actually consists of two conditions joined with Or. The following array formula does the trick:

```
{=SUM((Difference<0)*IF((Office="Oregon")+
(Office="California"),1)*Amount)}
```

Summary

This chapter provided valuable tips and tricks that will assist in creating formulas that handle particular counting and summing operations in a worksheet. Applying any of the examples covered in this chapter will save you significant time while making your worksheets into more powerful business tools. At this point, you should understand how to:

- Create a formula that counts the number of different types of cells — such as blanks, nonblanks, text, and numeric — in a range.
- Use COUNTIF and other advanced counting techniques in formulas.
- Count unique values and create frequency distribution formulas.
- Create formulas that sum a range or find cumulative sums.
- Calculate conditional sums using one or more criteria.

17

Getting Started Making Charts

When most people think of Excel, they think of crunching rows and columns of numbers. But as you probably know already, Excel is no slouch when it comes to presenting data visually in the form of charts. In fact, Excel is probably the most commonly used software in the world for creating charts. This chapter presents an introductory overview of Excel's charting ability.

What Is a Chart?

A *chart* is a visual representation of numeric values. Charts (also known as *graphs*) have been an integral part of spreadsheets since the early days of Lotus 1-2-3. Charts generated by early spreadsheet products were quite crude, but they've improved significantly over the years. Excel provides you with the tools to create a wide variety of highly customizable professional-quality charts.

Displaying data in a well-conceived chart can make your numbers more understandable. Because a chart presents a picture, charts are particularly useful for summarizing a series of numbers and their interrelationships. Making a chart can often help you spot trends and patterns that may otherwise go unnoticed. If you're unfamiliar with the elements of a chart, see the sidebar later in this chapter, "Parts of a Chart."

Figure 18.1 shows a worksheet that contains a simple column chart that depicts a company's sales volume by month. Viewing the chart makes it very apparent that sales were down in the summer months (June through August), but they increased steadily during the final four months of the year. You could, of course, arrive at this same conclusion simply by studying the numbers. But viewing the chart makes the point much more quickly.

FIGURE 18.1

A simple column chart depicts the monthly sales volume.

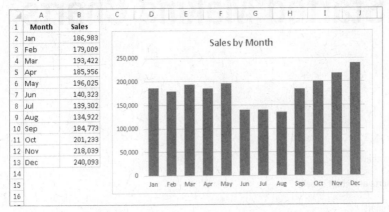

A column chart is just one of many different types of charts that you can create with Excel. Later in this chapter, I discuss all chart types so you can make the right choice for your data.

Understanding How Excel Handles Charts

Before you can create a chart, you must have some numbers — sometimes known as *data*. The data, of course, is stored in the cells in a worksheet. Normally, the data that a chart uses resides in a single worksheet, but that's not a strict requirement. A chart can use data that's stored in a different worksheet or even in a different workbook.

A chart is essentially an object that Excel creates upon request. This object consists of one or more data series, displayed graphically. The appearance of the data series depends on the selected chart type. For example, if you create a line chart that uses two data series, the chart contains two lines, each representing one data series. The data for each series is stored in a separate row or column. Each point on the line is determined by the value in a single cell and is represented by a marker. You can distinguish each of the lines by its thickness, line style, color, or data markers (squares, circles, and so on).

Figure 18.2 shows a line chart that plots two data series across a 12-month period. I used different data markers (squares versus circles) to identify the two series, as shown in the legend at the bottom of the chart. The chart clearly shows the sales in the Western Region are declining steadily, while Eastern Region sales are increasing a bit after remaining level for several months.

FIGURE 18.2

This line chart displays two data series.

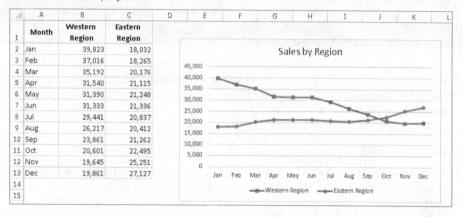

A key point to keep in mind is that charts are *dynamic*. In other words, a chart series is linked to the data in your worksheet. If the data changes, the chart is updated automatically to reflect those changes.

After you create a chart, you can always change its type, change the formatting, add or remove specific elements (such as the title or legend), add new data series to it, or change an existing data series so that it uses data in a different range.

A chart is either embedded in a worksheet or displayed on a separate chart sheet. It's very easy to move an embedded chart to a chart sheet (and vice versa).

Embedded charts

An *embedded chart* basically floats on top of a worksheet, on the worksheet's drawing layer. The charts shown previously in this chapter are both embedded charts.

As with other drawing objects (such as Shapes or SmartArt), you can move an embedded chart, resize it, change its proportions, adjust its borders, and perform other operations. Using embedded charts enables you to print the chart next to the data that it uses.

To make any changes to the actual chart in an embedded chart object, you must click it to *activate* the chart. When a chart is activated, Excel displays the Chart Tools contextual tabs. The Ribbon provides many tools for working with charts, and even more tools are available in the Format task pane.

NOTE

Excel 2013 incorporates some additional features that make it even easier to make your chart look exactly how you want it. When you select a chart, you see three icons to the right of the chart that adjust various aspects of the chart. I describe these new tools later in this chapter.

With one exception, every chart starts out as an embedded chart. The exception is when you create a default chart by selecting the data and pressing F11. In that case, the chart is created on a chart sheet.

Chart sheets

When a chart is on a chart sheet, you view it by clicking its sheet tab. A chart sheet contains a single chart. Chart sheets and worksheets can be interspersed in a workbook.

To move an embedded chart to a chart sheet, click the chart to select it and then choose Chart Tools ➪ Design ➪ Location ➪ Move Chart. The Move Chart dialog box, shown in Figure 18.3, appears. Select the New Sheet option and provide a name for the chart sheet (or accept Excel's default name). Click OK, the chart is moved, and the new chart sheet is displayed.

FIGURE 18.3

The Move Chart dialog box lets you move a chart to a chart sheet.

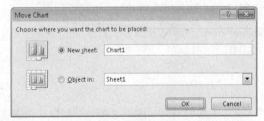

TIP

This operation also works in the opposite direction: You can select a chart on a chart sheet and relocate it to a worksheet as an embedded chart. In the Move Chart dialog box, choose Object In, and then select the worksheet from the drop-down list.

When you place a chart on a chart sheet, the chart occupies the entire sheet. If you plan to print a chart on a page by itself, using a chart sheet is often your better choice. If you have many charts, you may want to put each one on a separate chart sheet to avoid cluttering your worksheet. This technique also makes locating a particular chart easier because you can change the names of the chart sheets' tabs to provide a description of the chart that it contains.

The Excel Ribbon changes when a chart sheet is active, similar to the way it changes when you select an embedded chart. You have access to the same editing tools for embedded charts and charts on chart sheets.

If the chart isn't fully visible in the window, you can use the scroll bars to scroll it, or adjust the zoom factor to make it smaller. You can also change its orientation (tall or wide) by choosing Page Layout ⇨ Page Setup ⇨ Orientation.

Parts of a Chart

Refer to the accompanying chart as you read the following description of the chart's elements.

The particular chart is a *combination chart* that displays two *data series*: Sales Calls and Units Sold. Sales Calls are plotted as vertical columns, and the Units Sold are plotted as a line with circular markers. Each column (or marker on the line) represents a single *data point* (the value in a cell). The chart data is stored in the range A1:C7.

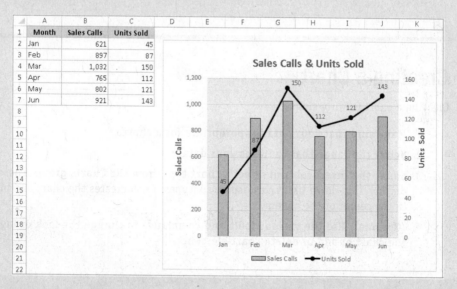

It has a horizontal axis, known as the *category axis*. This axis represents the category for each data point (January, February, and so on).

It has two vertical axes, known as *value axes*, and each one has a different scale. The axis on the left is for the columns (Sales Calls), and the axis on the right is for the line (Units Sold).

Continues

continued

The value axes also display scale values. The axis on the left displays scale values from 0 to 1,200, in major unit increments of 200. The value axis on the right uses a different scale: 0 to 160, in increments of 20.

Why two value axes? A chart with two value axes is appropriate because the two data series vary dramatically in scale. If the Sales data were plotted using the left axis, the line would barely be visible.

Most charts provide some method of identifying the data series or data points. A legend, for example, is often used to identify the various series in a chart. In this example, the legend appears on the bottom of the chart. Some charts also display data labels to identify specific data points. This chart displays data labels for the Units Sold series, but not for the Sales Calls series. In addition, most charts (including the example chart) contain a chart title and additional labels to identify the axes or categories.

It also contains horizontal gridlines (which correspond to the left value axis). Gridlines are basically extensions of the value axis scale, which makes it easier for the viewer to determine the magnitude of the data points.

All charts have a chart area (the entire background area of the chart) and a plot area. The plot area shows the actual chart, and in this example, the plot area has a different background color.

Charts can have additional parts or fewer parts, depending on the chart type. For example, a pie chart has slices and no axes. A 3-D chart may have walls and a floor. You can also add many other types of items to a chart. For example, you can add a trend line or display error bars. In other words, after you create a chart, you have a great deal of flexibility in customizing it.

Creating a Chart

Creating a chart is fairly simple:

1. **Make sure that your data is appropriate for a chart.**

2. **Select the range that contains your data.**

3. **Select the Insert tab and select a chart type from the Charts group.** These icons display drop-down lists that display subtypes. Excel creates the chart and places it in the center of the window.

4. **(Optional) Use the various tools and commands to change the look or layout of the chart or add or delete chart elements.**

> **NOTE**
>
> Excel 2013 includes a new option in the Insert ⇨ Charts groups: Recommended Charts. If you choose this option, the Insert Chart dialog box appears with two tabs. The Recommended Charts tab contains a list of suggested chart types appropriate for your data; sometimes this feature can be useful, but you can't always assume that all the recommended charts are suitable. The second tab, All Charts, gives you access to all of Excel's chart types. The charts displayed in the Insert Chart dialog box are not generic thumbnails; the charts depict your actual data.

Hands On: Creating and Customizing a Chart

This section contains a step-by-step example of creating a chart and applying some customizations. If you've never created a chart, this is a good opportunity to get a feel for how the process works.

Figure 18.4 shows a worksheet with a range of data. This data shows customer survey results by month, broken down by customers in three age groups. In this case, the data resides in a table (created by choosing Insert ➪ Tables ➪ Table), but that's not a requirement to create a chart.

FIGURE 18.4

The source data for the hands-on chart example

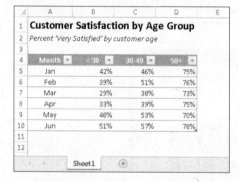

Selecting the data

The first step is to select the data for the chart. Your selection should include such items as labels and series identifiers (row and column headings). For this example, select the entire table (range A4:D10). This range includes the category labels but not the title (which is in A1).

Choosing a chart type

After you select the data, select a chart type from the Insert ⇨ Charts group. Each control in this group is a drop-down list, which lets you further refine your choice by selecting a subtype.

For this example, let Excel recommend a chart type. Choose Insert ⇨ Charts ⇨ Recommended Charts. Excel displays the dialog box shown in Figure 18.5. This dialog box shows several recommended charts, using your actual data. Select the first choice, Clustered Column, and click OK. Excel inserts the chart in the middle of the workbook window. You can move the chart by dragging any of its borders. You can also resize it by dragging in one of its corners. Figure 18.6 shows the chart positioned next to the source data range.

FIGURE 18.5

Letting Excel recommend a chart type

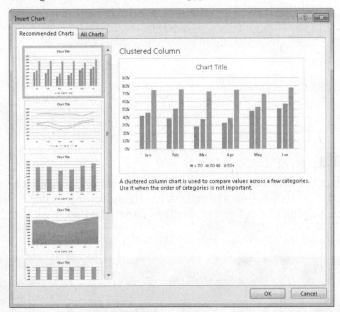

FIGURE 18.6

A clustered column chart created from the data in the table

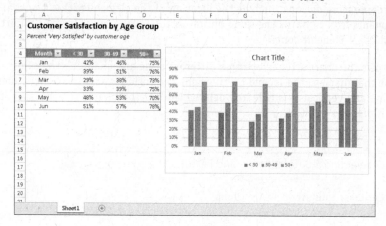

Experimenting with different styles

The chart looks pretty good, but it's just one of several predefined styles for a clustered column chart.

To see some other looks for the chart, select the chart (click it) and check out a few other predefined styles in the Chart Tools ⇨ Design ⇨ Chart Styles group. Just hover your mouse over a thumbnail in the gallery, and your chart shows a Live Preview of the new style. If you find a style you like, click the thumbnail to apply the style. Notice that this Ribbon group also includes a Change Colors tool, which lets you quickly modify the colors used in the chart.

You can also access the chart styles and colors by using the Chart Styles button, which appears to the right of the chart when you select it (the button displays a paintbrush). The choices are presented in a scrollable list. The choices are exactly the same as those displayed in the Chart Tools ⇨ Design ⇨ Chart Styles group.

Experimenting with different layouts

Every chart type has a set of layouts that you can choose from. A layout contains additional chart elements, such as a title, data labels, axes, and so on. You can add your own elements to your chart, but often, using a predefined layout saves time. Even if the layout isn't exactly what you want, it may be close enough that you need to make only a few adjustments.

To try a different predefined layout, select the chart and choose Chart Tools ⇨ Design ⇨ Chart Layouts ⇨ Quick Layout.

To manually add or remove elements from the chart, click the Chart Elements button, which appears to the right of the chart and has an image of a plus sign. Note that each item expands to provide more options, such as the location of the element within the chart. The Chart Elements icon contains the same option as the Chart Tools⇨Design⇨Chart Layouts⇨Add Chart Element control.

Figure 18.7 shows the chart after selecting a different style and changing the colors. I chose a layout that displays the legend on the right and includes axis titles. I customized the generic title and vertical axis title and deleted the horizontal axis title because it's obvious that it displays months.

FIGURE 18.7

The chart, after selecting a different style and layout

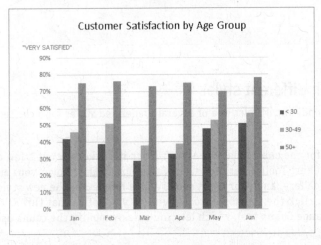

TIP

You can link the chart title to a cell so the title always displays the contents of a particular cell. To create a link to a cell, click the chart title, type an equal sign (=), click the cell, and press Enter. Excel displays the link in the Formula bar.

Experiment with the Chart Tools⇨Design tab to make other changes to the chart. Also try the tools that appear to the right of the chart when you click it. For example, you can remove the gridlines add axis titles, relocate the legend, and so on. Making these changes is easy and fairly intuitive.

Up until now, the changes made to the chart have been strictly cosmetic. The following sections describe how to make more substantial changes to a chart.

Trying another view of the data

The chart, at this point, shows six clusters (months) of three data points in each (age groups). Would the data be easier to understand if you plotted the information in the opposite way?

Try it. Select the chart and then choose Chart Tools ⇨ Design ⇨ Data ⇨ Switch Row/Column. Figure 18.8 shows the result of this change.

FIGURE 18.8

The chart, after changing the row and column orientation

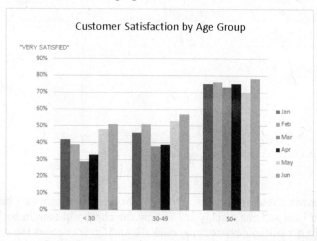

> **NOTE**
>
> The orientation of the data has a drastic effect on the look of your chart. Excel has its own rules that it uses to determine the initial data orientation when you create a chart. If Excel's orientation doesn't match your expectation, it's easy enough to change.

The chart, with this new orientation, reveals information that wasn't so apparent in the original version. The <30 and 30–49 age groups both show a decline in satisfaction for March and April. The 50+ age group didn't have this problem, however.

Trying other chart types

Although a clustered column chart seems to work well for this data, there's no harm in checking out some other chart types. Choose Design ⇨ Type ⇨ Change Chart Type to experiment with other chart types. This command displays the Change Chart Type dialog box, shown in Figure 18.9. The figure shows how the data would look as a line chart.

FIGURE 18.9

Use this dialog box to change the chart type.

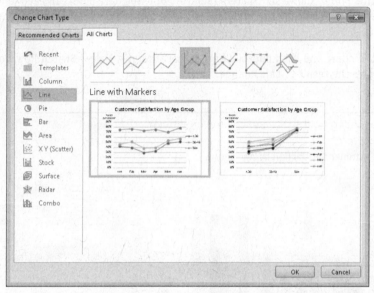

The main chart categories are listed on the left, and the subtypes are shown as a horizontal row of icons. Select an icon and the display shows how the chart will look in both data orientations. When you find a suitable chart type, click OK and Excel changes the chart. Notice that this dialog box has a tab at the top that lets you access Excel's recommended chart types for the data.

If you don't like the result after clicking OK, select Undo from the Quick Access Toolbar.

TIP

You can also change the chart type by selecting the chart and using the controls in the Insert ⇨ Charts group.

Figure 18.10 shows a few different chart type options using the customer satisfaction data.

FIGURE 18.10

The customer satisfaction data, displayed using four different chart types

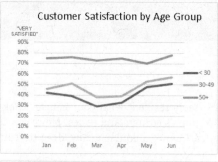 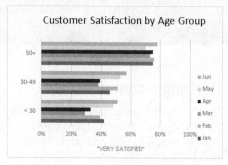

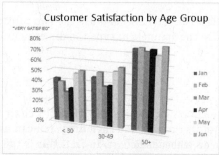 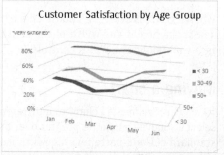

> **TIP**
>
> The styles displayed in the gallery depend on the workbook's theme. When you choose Page Layout ⇨ Themes ⇨ Themes to apply a different theme, you'll have a new selection of chart styles and colors designed for the selected theme.

Working with Charts

This section covers some common chart modifications:

- Resizing and moving charts
- Copying a chart
- Deleting a chart
- Adding chart elements
- Moving and deleting chart elements
- Formatting chart elements
- Printing charts

Resizing a chart

If your chart is an embedded chart, you can freely resize it with your mouse. Click the chart's border. Square handles appear on the chart's corners and edges. Move the mouse pointer over a handle and when the pointer turns into a double arrow, drag to resize the chart.

When a chart is selected, choose Chart Tools➪Format➪Size and use the two controls to adjust the height and width of the chart. Use the spinners or type the dimensions directly into the Height and Width controls.

Moving a chart

To move an embedded chart to a different location on a worksheet, click the chart to select it, move the mouse pointer over one of its borders, and then drag. You can use standard cut-and-paste techniques to move an embedded chart. In fact, this is the only way to move a chart from one worksheet to another. Select the chart and choose Home➪Clipboard➪Cut (or press Ctrl+X). Then activate a cell near the desired location and choose Home➪Clipboard➪Paste (or press Ctrl+V). The new location can be in a different worksheet or even in a different workbook. If you paste the chart to a different workbook, the chart will be linked to the data in the original workbook.

To move an embedded chart to a chart sheet (or vice versa), select the chart and choose Chart Tools➪Design➪Location➪Move Chart; the Move Chart dialog box appears. Choose New Sheet and provide a name for the chart sheet (or use the Excel proposed name).

Copying a chart

To make an exact copy of an embedded chart on the same worksheet, click the chart's border, press and hold the Ctrl key, and drag. Release the mouse button, and a new copy of the chart is created.

To make a copy of a chart sheet, use the same procedure, but drag the chart sheet's tab.

You also can use standard copy-and-paste techniques to copy a chart. Select the chart (an embedded chart or a chart sheet) and choose Home➪Clipboard➪Copy (or press Ctrl+C). Then activate a cell near the desired location and choose Home➪Clipboard➪Paste (or press Ctrl+V). The new location can be in a different worksheet or even in a different workbook.

If you paste the chart to a different workbook, it will be linked to the data in the original workbook.

Deleting a chart

To delete an embedded chart, press Ctrl and click the chart (to select the chart as an object). Then press Delete. When the Ctrl key is pressed, you can select multiple charts, and then delete them all with a single press of the Delete key.

To delete a chart sheet, right-click its sheet tab and choose Delete from the shortcut menu. To delete multiple chart sheets, select them by pressing Ctrl while you click the sheet tabs.

Adding chart elements

To add new elements to a chart (such as a title, legend, data labels, or gridlines), activate the chart and click the Chart Elements button, which appears to the right of the chart. Click the check box beside one of the listed chart elements to display or hide it. Note that each item expands to display additional options.

You can also use the Add Chart Element control on the Chart Tools ⇨ Design ⇨ Chart Layouts group.

Moving and deleting chart elements

Some elements within a chart can be moved: titles, legend, and data labels. To move a chart element, simply click it to select it and then drag it by its border.

The easiest way to delete a chart element is to select it and then press Delete. You can also use the controls on the Chart Elements icon, which appears to the right of the chart.

> **NOTE**
>
> A few chart elements consist of multiple objects. For example, the data labels element consists of one label for each data point. To move or delete one data label, click once to select the entire element and then click a second time to select the specific data label. You can then move or delete the single data label.

Formatting chart elements

Many users are content to stick with the predefined chart styles and layouts. For more precise customizations, Excel allows you to work with individual chart elements and apply additional formatting. You can use the Ribbon commands for some modifications, but the easiest way to format chart elements is to right-click the element and choose Format *<Element>* from the shortcut menu. The exact command depends on the element you select. For example, if you right-click the chart's title, the shortcut menu command is Format Chart Title.

The Format command displays a pane with options for the selected element. Changes that you make appear immediately. When you select a new chart element, the dialog box changes to display the properties for the newly selected element. You can keep this task pane displayed while you work on the chart. It can be docked along the left or right part of the window or made free floating and sizable.

TIP

If the Format pane doesn't appear, you can double-click a chart element to display it.

Refer to the "Exploring the Format Pane" sidebar for an explanation of how the Format task panes work.

TIP

If you apply formatting to a chart element and decide that it wasn't such a good idea, you can revert to the original formatting for the particular chart style. Right-click the chart element and choose Reset to Match Style from the shortcut menu. To reset the entire chart, select the chart area when you issue the command.

Exploring the Format Pane

The Format pane can require some exploration. It contains many options that aren't visible, and you sometimes have to do quite a bit of clicking to find the formatting option you're looking for. The accompanying figure shows the task pane for the chart title. The name of the task pane depends on which chart element is selected. The task pane varies quite a bit, depending on which chart element is selected.

Notice that the task pane displays two choices along the top: Title Options and Text Options. Click Title Options, and you see three icons: Fill & Line, Effects, and Size & Properties. Each of these icons has its own set of controls, which can be expanded or contracted by clicking the triangle icon to the left of the category name.

Similarly, the Text Options choice displays three icons: Text Fill & Outline, Text Effects, and Textbox. Again, each of these icons has its own set of options that you can expand or collapse using the triangle icons.

So, if you want to change the color of the text in a chart's title by using the Format Chart Title pane, you would follow these steps:

1. **If the Format pane is displayed, click the chart's title; if the pane is not displayed, double-click the chart's title.**
2. **In the Format Chart Title pane, click Text Options at the top.**
3. **Click the Text Fill & Outline icon.**
4. **Expand the Text Fill section.**
5. **Choose a color from the Color control.**

At first, the Format pane will seem complicated and confusing. But as you get acquainted with it, it gets much easier to use.

Also, keep in mind that many formatting choices are available on the Ribbon. For example, a quicker way to change the text color in a chart title is to select the title, click the Home tab on the Ribbon, and use the Font Color control.

Printing charts

Printing embedded charts is nothing special; you print them the same way that you print a worksheet. As long as you include the embedded chart in the range that you want to print, Excel prints the chart as it appears on-screen. When printing a sheet that contains embedded charts, it's a good idea to preview first (or use Page Layout view) to ensure that your charts don't span multiple pages. If you created the chart on a chart sheet, Excel always prints the chart on a page by itself.

TIP

If you select an embedded chart and choose File ⇨ Print, Excel prints the chart on a page by itself and does *not* print the worksheet.

If you don't want a particular embedded chart to appear on your printout, access the Format Chart Area pane and select the Size & Properties icon. Then Expand the Properties section and clear the Print Object check box.

18

Understanding Chart Types

People who create charts usually do so to make a point or to communicate a specific message. Often, the message is explicitly stated in the chart's title or in a text box within the chart. The chart itself provides visual support.

Choosing the correct chart type is often a key factor in the effectiveness of the message. Therefore, it's often well worth your time to experiment with various chart types to determine which one conveys your message best.

In almost every case, the underlying message in a chart is some type of comparison. Examples of some general types of comparisons include:

- **Comparing an item to other items:** A chart may compare sales in each of a company's sales regions.
- **Comparing data over time:** A chart may display sales by month and indicate trends over time.
- **Making relative comparisons:** A common pie chart can depict relative proportions in terms of pie "slices."
- **Comparing data relationships:** An XY chart is ideal for this comparison. For example, you might show the relationship between monthly marketing expenditures and sales.
- **Comparing frequency:** You can use a common histogram, for example, to display the number (or percentage) of students who scored within a particular grade range.
- **Identifying outliers or unusual situations:** If you have thousands of data points, creating a chart may help identify data that isn't representative.

Choosing a chart type

A common question among Excel users is "How do I know which chart type to use for my data?" Unfortunately, this question has no cut-and-dried answer. Perhaps the best answer is a vague one: Use the chart type that gets your message across in the simplest way. A good starting point is Excel's recommended charts. Select your data and choose Insert ⇨ Charts ⇨ Recommended Charts to see the chart types that Excel suggests. Remember that these suggestions are not always the best choices.

> **NOTE**
>
> In the Ribbon, the Charts group of the Insert tab shows the Recommended Charts button, plus eight other drop-down buttons. Some of these drop-down buttons display multiple chart types. For example, stock, surface, and radar charts are all available from a single drop-down button. Similarly, scatter charts and bubble charts share a single button. Probably the easiest way to choose a particular chart type is to select Insert ⇨ Charts ⇨ Recommended Charts, which displays the Insert Chart dialog box. Select the All Charts tab and you'll have a concise list of all chart types and subchart types.

Figure 18.11 shows the same set of data plotted by using six different chart types. Although all six charts represent the same information (monthly website visitors), they look quite different from one another.

FIGURE 18.11

The same data, plotted by using six chart types

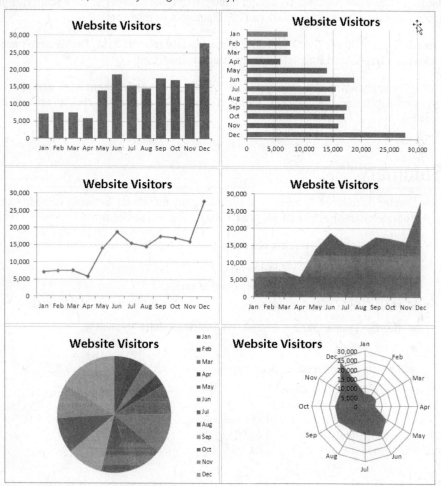

The column chart (upper left) is probably the best choice for this particular set of data because it clearly shows the information for each month in discrete units. The bar chart (upper right) is similar to a column chart, but the axes are swapped. Most people are more accustomed to seeing time-based information extend from left to right rather than from top to bottom, so this isn't the optimal choice.

The line chart (middle left) may not be the best choice because it can imply that the data is continuous — that points exist in between the 12 actual data points. This same argument may be made against using an area chart (middle right).

The pie chart (lower left) is simply too confusing and does nothing to convey the time-based nature of the data. Pie charts are most appropriate for a data series in which you want to emphasize proportions among a relatively small number of data points. If you have too many data points, a pie chart can be impossible to interpret.

The radar chart (lower right) is clearly inappropriate for this data. People aren't accustomed to viewing time-based information in a circular direction!

Fortunately, changing a chart's type is easy, so you can experiment with various chart types until you find the one that represents your data accurately, clearly, and as simply as possible.

Summary

This chapter introduced Excel charts, including the difference between embedded charts and separate chart sheets, and parts of a chart. You learned how to:

- Create a chart, including choosing a recommended or other chart type.
- Change the chart style or layout.
- Display and work with various chart elements.
- Move, resize, and copy a chart.
- Use the Format pane for formatting various chart elements.
- Print a chart.
- Experiment with more chart types.

Communicating Data Visually

IN THIS CHAPTER

This chapter explores some versatile formatting features for summarizing, highlighting, and presenting data. The chapter starts by introducing Excel's table feature, which you can use to not only apply colorful formatting to a list of data, but also to filter and total the data, among other benefits.

You can apply conditional formatting to a cell so that the cell looks different, depending on its contents. Conditional formatting is a useful tool for visualizing numeric data. In some cases, conditional formatting may be a viable alternative to creating a chart.

Finally, you can create sparklines to illustrate data values within a cell. Sparklines appear like mini charts and offer a surprising amount of formatting flexibility.

Creating a Table

A *table* is a rectangular range of structured data. Each row in the table corresponds to a single entity. For example, a row can contain information about a customer, a bank transaction, an employee, a product, and so on. Each column contains a specific piece of information. For example, if each row contains information about an employee, the columns can contain data such as name, employee number, hire date, salary, department, and so on. Tables typically have a header row at the top that describes the information contained in each column.

You must tell Excel to convert a range of data into an "official" table. You do this by selecting any cell within the range and then choosing Insert ➪ Tables ➪ Table. When you explicitly identify a range as a table, Excel can respond more intelligently to the actions you perform with that range. For example, if you create a chart from a table, the chart will expand automatically as you add new rows to the table. And if you enter a formula into a cell, Excel will propagate the formula to other rows in the table. Figure 19.1 shows a range converted to a table by choosing Insert ➪ Tables ➪ Table. Notice the drop-down list arrows at the top.

FIGURE 19.1

An Excel table

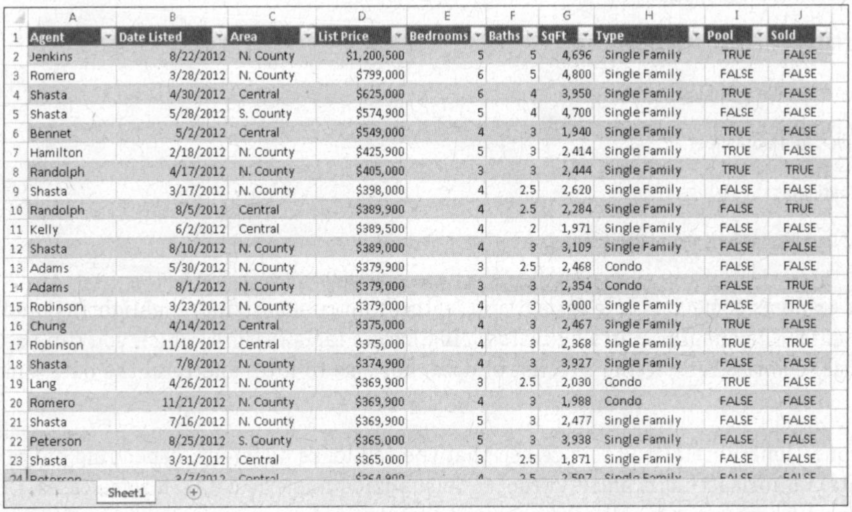

	A	B	C	D	E	F	G	H	I	J
1	Agent	Date Listed	Area	List Price	Bedrooms	Baths	SqFt	Type	Pool	Sold
2	Jenkins	8/22/2012	N. County	$1,200,500	5	5	4,696	Single Family	TRUE	FALSE
3	Romero	3/28/2012	N. County	$799,000	6	5	4,800	Single Family	FALSE	FALSE
4	Shasta	4/30/2012	Central	$625,000	6	4	3,950	Single Family	TRUE	FALSE
5	Shasta	5/28/2012	S. County	$574,900	5	4	4,700	Single Family	FALSE	FALSE
6	Bennet	5/2/2012	Central	$549,000	4	3	1,940	Single Family	TRUE	FALSE
7	Hamilton	2/18/2012	N. County	$425,900	5	3	2,414	Single Family	TRUE	FALSE
8	Randolph	4/17/2012	N. County	$405,000	3	3	2,444	Single Family	TRUE	TRUE
9	Shasta	3/17/2012	N. County	$398,000	4	2.5	2,620	Single Family	FALSE	FALSE
10	Randolph	8/5/2012	Central	$389,900	4	2.5	2,284	Single Family	FALSE	TRUE
11	Kelly	6/2/2012	Central	$389,500	4	2	1,971	Single Family	FALSE	FALSE
12	Shasta	8/10/2012	N. County	$389,000	4	3	3,109	Single Family	FALSE	FALSE
13	Adams	5/30/2012	N. County	$379,900	3	2.5	2,468	Condo	FALSE	FALSE
14	Adams	8/1/2012	N. County	$379,000	3	3	2,354	Condo	FALSE	TRUE
15	Robinson	3/23/2012	N. County	$379,000	4	3	3,000	Single Family	FALSE	TRUE
16	Chung	4/14/2012	Central	$375,000	4	3	2,467	Single Family	TRUE	FALSE
17	Robinson	11/18/2012	Central	$375,000	4	3	2,368	Single Family	TRUE	TRUE
18	Shasta	7/8/2012	N. County	$374,900	4	3	3,927	Single Family	FALSE	FALSE
19	Lang	4/26/2012	N. County	$369,900	3	2.5	2,030	Condo	TRUE	FALSE
20	Romero	11/21/2012	N. County	$369,900	4	3	1,988	Condo	FALSE	FALSE
21	Shasta	7/16/2012	N. County	$369,900	5	3	2,477	Single Family	FALSE	FALSE
22	Peterson	8/25/2012	S. County	$365,000	5	3	3,938	Single Family	FALSE	FALSE
23	Shasta	3/31/2012	Central	$365,000	3	2.5	1,871	Single Family	FALSE	FALSE
24	Peterson	3/7/2012	Central	$364,900	4	2.5	2,507	Single Family	FALSE	FALSE

Sheet1

What's the difference between a standard range and a table? With a table:

- Activating any cell in the table gives you access to the Table Tools ➪ Design contextual tab on the Ribbon (see Figure 19.2).

FIGURE 19.2

When you select a cell in a table, you can use the commands located on the Table Tools ⇨ Design tab.

- **The cells contain background color and text color formatting.** This formatting is optional.

- **Each column header contains a Filter Button — a drop-down list that you can use to sort the data or filter the table to display only rows that meet certain criteria.** Displaying the Filter Button is optional.

- **You can create easy-to-use Slicers to simplify filtering data.**

- **If the active cell is within the table, when you scroll down the sheet so that the header row disappears, the table headers replace the column letters in the worksheet header.**

- **Tables support calculated columns.** A single formula in a column is automatically propagated to all cells in the column.

- **Tables support structured references.** Instead of using cell references, formulas can use table names and column headers.

- **The lower-right corner of the lower-right cell contains a small control that you can click and drag to extend the table's size, either horizontally (add more columns) or vertically (add more rows).**

- **Selecting rows and columns within the table is simplified.**

Most of the time, you'll create a table from an existing range of data. However, Excel also enables you to create a table from an empty range so that you can fill in the details later. The following instructions assume that you already have a range of data that's suitable for a table.

1. **Make sure that the range doesn't contain any completely blank rows or columns; otherwise, Excel will not guess the table range correctly.**

2. **Select any cell within the range.**

3. **Choose Insert ⇨ Tables ⇨ Table (or press Ctrl+T).** Excel responds with its Create Table dialog box, shown in Figure 19.3. Excel tries to guess the range, as well as whether the table has a header row. Most of the time, it guesses correctly. If not, correct the range in the Where is the data for your table? Text box.

4. **Click OK.** The range is converted to a table (using the default table style), and the Table Tools ⇨ Design tab of the Ribbon appears.

19

FIGURE 19.3

Use the Create Table dialog box to verify that Excel selected the table dimensions correctly.

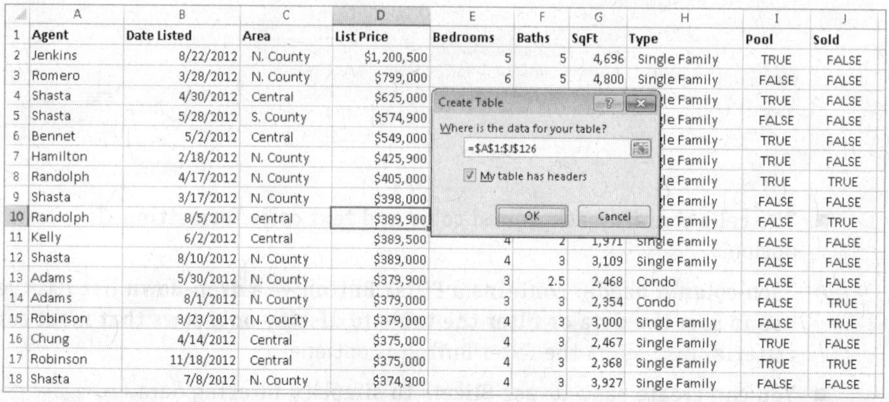

	A	B	C	D	E	F	G	H	I	J
1	Agent	Date Listed	Area	List Price	Bedrooms	Baths	SqFt	Type	Pool	Sold
2	Jenkins	8/22/2012	N. County	$1,200,500	5	5	4,696	Single Family	TRUE	FALSE
3	Romero	3/28/2012	N. County	$799,000	6	5	4,800	Single Family	FALSE	FALSE
4	Shasta	4/30/2012	Central	$625,000				le Family	TRUE	FALSE
5	Shasta	5/28/2012	S. County	$574,900				le Family	FALSE	FALSE
6	Bennet	5/2/2012	Central	$549,000				le Family	TRUE	FALSE
7	Hamilton	2/18/2012	N. County	$425,900				le Family	TRUE	FALSE
8	Randolph	4/17/2012	N. County	$405,000				le Family	TRUE	TRUE
9	Shasta	3/17/2012	N. County	$398,000				le Family	FALSE	FALSE
10	Randolph	8/5/2012	Central	$389,900				le Family	FALSE	TRUE
11	Kelly	6/2/2012	Central	$389,500	4	2	1,971	Single Family	FALSE	FALSE
12	Shasta	8/10/2012	N. County	$389,000	4	3	3,109	Single Family	FALSE	FALSE
13	Adams	5/30/2012	N. County	$379,900	3	2.5	2,468	Condo	FALSE	FALSE
14	Adams	8/1/2012	N. County	$379,000	3	3	2,354	Condo	FALSE	TRUE
15	Robinson	3/23/2012	N. County	$379,000	4	3	3,000	Single Family	FALSE	TRUE
16	Chung	4/14/2012	Central	$375,000	4	3	2,467	Single Family	TRUE	FALSE
17	Robinson	11/18/2012	Central	$375,000	4	3	2,368	Single Family	TRUE	TRUE
18	Shasta	7/8/2012	N. County	$374,900	4	3	3,927	Single Family	FALSE	FALSE

Create Table dialog box:
Where is the data for your table?
=$A$1:$J$126
☑ My table has headers
OK   Cancel

> **NOTE**
>
> Excel may not specify the table's dimensions correctly if the table isn't separated from other information by at least one empty row or column. If Excel doesn't choose the range correctly, just specify the exact range for the table in the Create Table dialog box. Better yet, click Cancel and rearrange your worksheet such that the table is separated from your other data by at least one blank row or column.

To create a table from an empty range, just select the range and choose Insert ⇨ Tables ⇨ Table. Excel creates the table, adds generic column headers (such as Column1 and Column2), and applies table formatting to the range. Almost always, you'll want to replace the generic column headers with more meaningful text.

Changing the Look of a Table

When you create a table, Excel applies the default table style. The actual appearance depends on which document theme is used in the workbook (Page Layout ⇨ Themes ⇨ Themes). If you prefer a different look, you can easily change the entire look of the table.

Select any cell in the table and choose Table Tools ⇨ Design ⇨ Table Styles. (At a lower screen resolution, you will need to click the Quick Styles button in the Table Styles group of the Design tab.) The Ribbon shows one row of styles, but if you click the More button at the bottom of the scroll bar to the right, the Table Styles group expands, as shown in Figure 19.4. The styles are grouped into three categories: Light, Medium, and Dark. Notice that you get a Live Preview on the table as you move your mouse among the styles. When you see one you like, just click to apply it. For a different set of table style choices, choose Page Layout ⇨ Themes ⇨ Themes to select a different document theme.

FIGURE 19.4

Excel offers many different table styles.

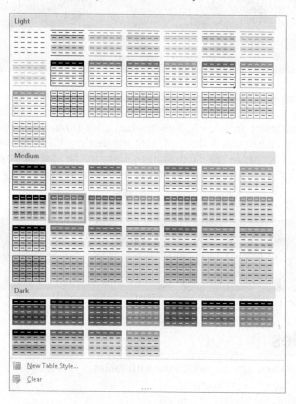

You can change some elements of the style by using the check box controls in the Table Tools ⇨ Design ⇨ Table Style Options group. These controls determine whether various elements of the table are displayed, and whether some formatting options are in effect:

- **Header Row:** Toggles the display of the Header Row
- **Total Row:** Toggles the display of the Total Row
- **First Column:** Toggles special formatting for the first column. Depending on the table style used, this command might have no effect.
- **Last Column:** Toggles special formatting for the last column. Depending on the table style used, this command might have no effect.
- **Banded Rows:** Toggles the display of *banded* (alternating color) rows
- **Banded Columns:** Toggles the display of banded columns
- **Filter Button:** Toggles the display of the drop-down buttons in the table's header row

19

> **TIP**
>
> If applying table styles isn't working, it's probably because the range was already formatted before you converted it to a table. Table formatting doesn't override normal formatting. To clear existing background fill colors, select the entire table and choose Home ➪ Font ➪ Fill Color ➪ No Fill. To clear existing font colors, choose Home ➪ Font ➪ Font Color ➪ Automatic. To clear existing borders, choose Home ➪ Font ➪ Borders ➪ No Borders. After you issue these commands, the table styles should work as expected.

If you'd like to create a custom table style, choose Table Tools ➪ Design ➪ Table Styles ➪ New Table Style to display the New Table Style dialog box. You can customize any or all of the 12 items in the Table Element list. Select an element from the list, click Format, and specify the formatting for that element. When you're finished, give the new style a name and click OK. Your custom table style will appear in the Table Styles gallery in the Custom category. Unfortunately, custom table styles are available only in the workbook in which they were created.

> **TIP**
>
> If you want to make changes to an existing table style, locate it in the Ribbon and right-click. Choose Duplicate from the shortcut menu. Excel displays the Modify Table Style dialog box with all the settings from the specified table style. Make your changes, give the style a new name, and click OK to save it as a custom table style.

Working with Tables

This section describes some common actions you'll take with tables.

Navigating in a table

Selecting cells in a table works just like selecting cells in a normal range. One difference is when you use the Tab key. Pressing Tab moves to the cell to the right, but when you reach the last column, pressing Tab again moves to the first cell in the next row.

Selecting parts of a table

When you move your mouse around in a table, you may notice that the pointer changes shapes. These shapes help you select various parts of the table.

- **To select an entire column:** Move the mouse to the top of a cell in the header row, and the mouse pointer changes to a down-pointing arrow. Click to select the data in the column. Click a second time to select the entire table column (including the Header Row and the Total Row, if it has one). You can also press Ctrl+Spacebar (once or twice) to select a column.

- **To select an entire row:** Move the mouse to the left of a cell in the first column, and the mouse pointer changes to a right-pointing arrow. Click to select the entire table row. You can also press Shift+Spacebar to select a table row.
- **To select the entire table:** Move the mouse to the upper-left part of the upper-left cell. When the mouse pointer turns into a diagonal arrow, click to select the data area of the table. Click a second time to select the entire table (including the Header Row and the Total Row). You can also press Ctrl+A (once or twice) to select the entire table.

> **TIP**
> Right-clicking a cell in a table displays several selection options in the shortcut menu.

Adding new rows or columns

To add a new column to the end of a table, select a cell in the column to the right of the table and start entering the data. Excel automatically extends the table horizontally and adds a generic column name for the new column. Similarly, if you enter data in the row below a table, Excel extends the table vertically to include the new row.

> **NOTE**
> An exception to automatically extending tables is when the table is displaying a Total Row. If you enter data below the Total Row, the table won't be extended and the data won't be part of the table.

To add rows or columns within the table, right-click and choose Insert from the shortcut menu. The Insert shortcut menu command displays additional menu items:

- Table Columns to the Left
- Table Columns to the Right
- Table Rows Above
- Table Rows Below

> **TIP**
> When the cell pointer is in the bottom-right cell of a table, pressing Tab inserts a new row at the bottom of the table, above the Total Row (if the table has one).

When you move your mouse to the resize handle at the bottom-right cell of a table, the mouse pointer turns into a diagonal line with two arrowheads. Drag down to add more rows to the table. Drag to the right to add more columns.

19

When you insert a new column, the Header Row displays a generic description, such as Column1, Column2, and so on. Typically, you'll want to change these names to more descriptive labels. Just select the cell, type new text, and press Enter.

Deleting rows or columns

To delete a row (or column) in a table, select any cell in the row (or column) to be deleted. To delete multiple rows or columns, select a range of cells. Then right-click and choose Delete ⇨ Table Rows (or Delete ⇨ Table Columns).

> **NOTE**
>
> To move a table to a new location in the same worksheet, move the mouse pointer to any of its borders. When the mouse pointer turns into a cross with four arrows, Drag the table to its new location on the current sheet or another visible worksheet. It may be easier to cut and paste to move a table to another worksheet or workbook. Press Ctrl+A *twice* to select the entire table, then press Ctrl+X to cut it. Display the destination worksheet, click in the upper-left corner of the range where you want to paste the table, and press Ctrl+V.

Excel Remembers

When you do something with a complete column in a table, Excel remembers that and extends that "something" to all new entries added to that column. For example, if you apply currency formatting to a column and then add a new row, Excel applies currency formatting to the new value in that column. The same thing applies to other operations, such as conditional formatting, cell protection, data validation, and so on. And if you create a chart using the data in a table, the chart will be extended automatically if you add new data to the table.

Working with the Total Row

The Total Row in a table contains formulas that summarize the information in the columns. When you create a table, the Total Row isn't turned on. To display the Total Row, choose Table Tools ⇨ Design ⇨ Table Style Options and put a check mark next to Total Row.

By default, a Total Row displays the sum of the values in a column of numbers. In some cases, you'll want a different type of summary formula. (For more information about formulas, including the use of formulas in a table column, see Chapter 15.) When you select a cell in the Total Row, a drop-down arrow appears in the cell. Click the arrow, and you can select from a number of other summary formulas (see Figure 19.5):

FIGURE 19.5

Several types of summary formulas are available for the Total Row.

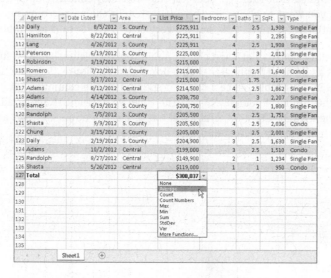

- **None:** No formula
- **Average:** Displays the average of the numbers in the column
- **Count:** Displays the number of entries in the column (Blank cells are not counted.)
- **Count Numbers:** Displays the number of numeric values in the column (Blank cells, text cells, and error cells are not counted.)
- **Max:** Displays the maximum value in the column
- **Min:** Displays the minimum value in the column
- **Sum:** Displays the sum of the values in the column
- **StdDev:** Displays the standard deviation of the values in the column (*Standard deviation* is a statistical measure of how "spread out" the values are.)
- **Var:** Displays the variance of the values in the column (*Variance* is another statistical measure of how "spread out" the values are.)
- **More Functions:** Displays the Insert Function dialog box so that you can select a function that isn't in the list

> **CAUTION**
>
> If you have a formula that refers to a value in the Total Row of a table, the formula returns an error if you hide the Total Row. But if you make the Total Row visible again, the formula works as it should.

Removing duplicate rows from a table

If data in a table was compiled from multiple sources, the table may contain duplicate items. Most of the time, you want to eliminate the duplicates. In the past, removing duplicate data was essentially a manual task, but it's very easy if the data is in a table.

Start by selecting any cell in your table. Then choose Table Tools ➪ Design ➪ Tools ➪ Remove Duplicates. Excel opens the Remove Duplicates dialog box shown in Figure 19.6. The dialog box lists all the columns in your table. Place a check mark next to the columns that you want to be included in the duplicate search. Most of the time, you'll want to select all the columns, which is the default. Click OK, and Excel weeds out the duplicate rows and displays a message that tells you how many duplicates it removed.

FIGURE 19.6

Removing duplicate rows from a table is easy.

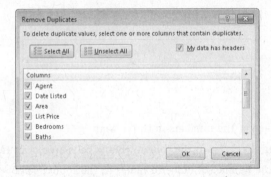

When you select all columns in the Remove Duplicates dialog box, Excel will delete a row only if the content of every column is duplicated. In some situations, you may not care about matching some columns, so you would deselect those columns in the Remove Duplicates dialog box. When duplicate rows are found, the first row is kept and subsequent duplicate rows are deleted.

> **TIP**
>
> Data does not have to be in the form of a designated table to remove duplicates. To remove duplicate rows from a normal range, choose Data ➪ Data Tools ➪ Remove Duplicates.

> **CAUTION**
>
> It's important to understand that duplicate values are determined by the value *displayed* in the cell — not necessarily the value *stored* in the cell. For example, assume that two cells contain the same date. One of the dates is formatted to display as 5/15/2012, and the other is formatted to display as May 15, 2012. When removing duplicates, Excel considers these dates to be different.

Sorting and filtering a table

Each item in the Header Row of a table contains a drop-down arrow known as a Filter Button. When clicked, the Filter Button displays sorting and filtering options (see Figure 19.7).

FIGURE 19.7

Each column in a table has sorting and filtering options.

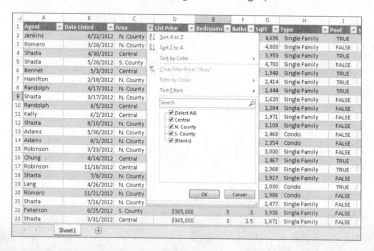

Sorting a table

Sorting a table rearranges the rows based on the contents of a particular column. You may want to sort a table to put names in alphabetical order. Or, maybe you want to sort your sales staff by the totals sales made.

To sort a table by a particular column, click the Filter Button in the column header and choose one of the sort commands. The exact command varies, depending on the type of data in the column. You can also select Sort by Color to sort the rows based on the background or text color of the data. This option is relevant only if you've overridden the table style colors with custom formatting.

You can sort on any number of columns. The trick is to sort the least significant column first and then proceed until the most significant column is sorted last. For example, in a real estate table, you may want to sort the list by agent. And within each agent's group, sort the rows by area. And within each area, sort the rows by list price. For this type of

19

sort, first sort by the List Price column, then sort by the Area column, and then sort by the Agent column. Figure 19.8 shows the table sorted in this manner.

FIGURE 19.8

A table, after performing a three-column sort

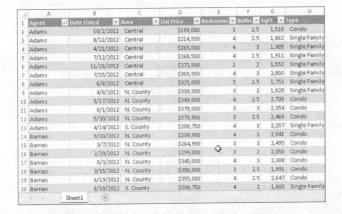

> **NOTE**
> When a column is sorted, the Filter button in the header row displays a different graphic to remind you that the table is sorted by that column.

Another way of performing a multiple-column sort is to use the Sort dialog box (choose Home ➪ Editing ➪ Sort & Filter ➪ Custom Sort). Or right-click any cell in the table and choose Sort ➪ Custom Sort from the shortcut menu.

In the Sort dialog box, use the drop-down lists to specify the sort specifications. In this example, you start with Agent. Then click the Add Level button to insert another set of search controls. In this new set of controls, specify the sort specifications for the Area column. Then add another level and enter the specifications for the List Price column. Click OK to apply the sort. This technique produces exactly the same sort as described in the previous paragraph.

Filtering a table

Filtering a table refers to displaying only the rows that meet certain conditions. The other rows are hidden. Note that the *entire* rows are hidden. Therefore, if you have other data to the left or right of your table, that information will also be hidden. If you plan to filter your list, don't include any other data to the left or right of your table.

Using the example real estate table we've been discussing, assume that you're only interested in the data for the N. County area. Click the Filter Button in the Area Row

Header and remove the check mark from Select All, which unselects everything. Then, place a check mark next to N. County and click OK. The table, shown in Figure 19.9, is now filtered to display only the listings in the N. County area. Notice that some of the row numbers are missing. These rows are hidden and contain data that does not meet the specified criteria.

FIGURE 19.9

This table is filtered to show only the information for N. County.

	Agent	Date Listed	Area	List Price	Bedrooms	Baths	SqFt	Type	Pool	Sold
9	Adams	4/8/2012	N. County	$339,900	3	2	1,828	Single Family	TRUE	TRUE
10	Adams	5/17/2012	N. County	$349,000	4	2.5	2,730	Condo	TRUE	TRUE
11	Adams	8/1/2012	N. County	$379,000	3	3	2,354	Condo	FALSE	TRUE
12	Adams	5/30/2012	N. County	$379,900	3	2.5	2,468	Condo	FALSE	FALSE
14	Barnes	9/20/2012	N. County	$239,900	4	3	2,041	Condo	FALSE	FALSE
15	Barnes	3/7/2012	N. County	$264,900	3	3	2,495	Condo	FALSE	FALSE
16	Barnes	2/29/2012	N. County	$299,000	3	2	2,050	Condo	FALSE	FALSE
17	Barnes	8/3/2012	N. County	$345,000	4	3	2,388	Condo	TRUE	TRUE
18	Barnes	3/15/2012	N. County	$350,000	3	2.5	1,991	Condo	FALSE	TRUE
19	Barnes	6/19/2012	N. County	$355,000	4	2.5	2,647	Condo	TRUE	FALSE
23	Bennet	6/24/2012	N. County	$229,500	6	3	2,700	Single Family	TRUE	FALSE
24	Bennet	4/14/2012	N. County	$229,900	3	3	2,266	Condo	FALSE	FALSE
25	Bennet	5/20/2012	N. County	$229,900	4	3	2,041	Condo	FALSE	FALSE
44	Hamilton	2/18/2012	N. County	$425,900	5	3	2,414	Single Family	TRUE	FALSE
47	Jenkins	4/15/2012	N. County	$238,000	4	2.5	1,590	Condo	FALSE	TRUE
48	Jenkins	4/2/2012	N. County	$248,500	4	2.5	2,101	Single Family	TRUE	TRUE
49	Jenkins	4/24/2012	N. County	$349,900	4	3	2,290	Single Family	TRUE	TRUE
50	Jenkins	8/22/2012	N. County	$1,200,500	5	5	4,696	Single Family	TRUE	FALSE
62	Lang	8/16/2012	N. County	$264,900	3	2.5	2,062	Condo	FALSE	FALSE
63	Lang	7/15/2012	N. County	$349,000	4	3	3,930	Single Family	TRUE	FALSE
64	Lang	6/16/2012	N. County	$359,000	3	2.5	2,210	Single Family	FALSE	FALSE
65	Lang	4/26/2012	N. County	$369,900	3	2.5	2,030	Condo	TRUE	FALSE
74	Peterson	6/11/2012	N. County	$235,990	4	2	1,656	Condo	TRUE	FALSE
75	Peterson	4/8/2012	N. County	$259,900	4	3	1,734	Condo	FALSE	TRUE
76	Peterson	3/31/2012	N. County	$309,900	5	3	2,447	Condo	TRUE	FALSE
89	Randolph	4/14/2012	N. County	$259,900	3	2.5	2,122	Condo	FALSE	TRUE

Sheet1

Also notice that the Filter Button in the Area column now shows a different graphic — an icon that indicates the column is filtered.

You can filter by multiple values in a column using multiple check marks. For example, to filter the table to show only N. County and Central, place a check mark next to both values in the drop-down list in the Area Row Header.

You can filter a table using any number of columns. For example, you may want to see only the N. County listings in which the Type is Single Family. Just repeat the operation using the Type column. All tables then display only the rows in which the Area is N. County and the Type is Single Family.

For additional filtering options, select Text Filters (or Number Filters, if the column contains values). The options are fairly self-explanatory, and you have a great deal of flexibility in displaying only the rows that you're interested in. For example, you can display rows in which the List Price is greater than or equal to $200,000, but less than $300,000 (see Figure 19.10). Click OK to apply the filter and close the Custom AutoFilter dialog box.

19

FIGURE 19.10

Specifying a more complex numeric filter

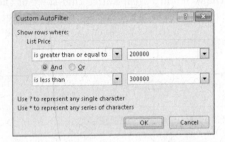

In addition, you can right-click a cell and use the Filter command on the shortcut menu. This menu item leads to several additional filtering options.

> **NOTE**
>
> As you may expect, when you use filtering, the Total Row is updated to show the total only for the visible rows.

When you copy data from a filtered table, only the visible data is copied. In other words, rows that are hidden by filtering don't get copied. This filtering makes it very easy to copy a subset of a larger table and paste it to another area of your worksheet. Keep in mind, though, that the pasted data is not a table — it's just a normal range. You can, however, convert the copied range to a table.

To remove filtering for a column, click the drop-down in the Row Header and select Clear Filter. If you've filtered using multiple columns, it may be faster to remove all filters by choosing Home ➪ Editing ➪ Sort & Filter ➪ Clear.

Converting a table back to a range

If you need to convert a table back to a normal range, just select a cell in the table and choose Table Tools ➪ Design ➪ Tools ➪ Convert to Range. The table style formatting remains intact, but the range no longer functions as a table.

About Conditional Formatting

Conditional formatting enables you to apply cell formatting selectively and automatically, based on the contents of the cells. For example, you can apply conditional formatting in such a way that all negative values in a range have a light-yellow background color. When you enter or change a value in the range, Excel examines the value and checks the conditional formatting rules for the cell. If the value is negative, the background is shaded; otherwise, no formatting is applied.

Conditional formatting is an easy way to quickly identify erroneous cell entries or cells of a particular type. You can use a format (such as bright-red cell shading) to make particular cells easy to identify.

Figure 19.11 shows a worksheet with nine ranges, each with a different type of conditional formatting rule applied. Here's a brief explanation of each:

- **Greater than ten:** Values greater than ten are highlighted with a different background color. This rule is just one of many numeric-value-related rules that you can apply.
- **Above average:** Values that are higher than the average value are highlighted.
- **Duplicate values:** Values that appear in the range more than once are highlighted.
- **Words that contain X:** If the cell contains X (upper- or lowercase), the cell is highlighted.
- **Data bars:** Each cell displays a horizontal bar, the length of which is proportional to its value.

FIGURE 19.11

This worksheet demonstrates a few conditional formatting rules.

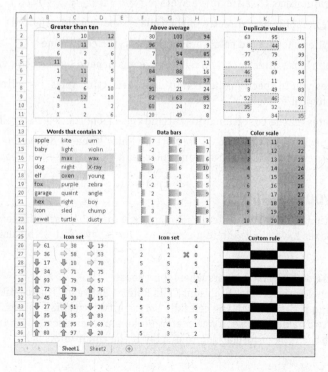

- **Color scale:** The background color varies, depending on the value of the cells. You can choose from several different color scales or create your own.

- **Icon set:** One of several icon sets. It displays a small graphic in the cell. The graphic varies, depending on the cell value.

- **Icon set:** Another icon set, with all but one icon in the set hidden

- **Custom rule:** The rule for this checkerboard pattern is based on a formula:

```
=MOD(ROW(),2)=MOD(COLUMN(),2)
```

Specifying Conditional Formatting

To apply a conditional formatting rule to a cell or range, select the cells and then use one of the commands from the Home ➪ Styles ➪ Conditional Formatting drop-down list to specify a rule. The choices are:

- **Highlight Cell Rules:** Examples include highlighting cells that are greater than a particular value, between two values, contain specific text string, contain a date, or are duplicated.

- **Top Bottom Rules:** Examples include highlighting the top ten items, the items in the bottom 20%, and items that are above average.

- **Data Bars:** Applies graphic bars directly in the cells, proportional to the cell's value

- **Color Scales:** Applies background color, proportional to the cell's value

- **Icon Sets:** Displays icons directly in the cells. The icons depend on the cell's value.

- **New Rule:** Enables you to specify other conditional formatting rules, including rules based on a logical formula

- **Clear Rules:** Deletes all the conditional formatting rules from the selected cells

- **Manage Rules:** Displays the Conditional Formatting Rules Manager dialog box, in which you create new conditional formatting rules, edit rules, or delete rules

Formatting types you can apply

When you select a conditional formatting rule, Excel displays a dialog box specific to that rule. These dialog boxes have one thing in a common: a drop-down list with common formatting suggestions.

Figure 19.12 shows the dialog box that appears when you choose Home ➪ Styles ➪ Conditional Formatting ➪ Highlight Cells Rules ➪ Between. This particular rule applies the formatting if the value in the cell falls between two specified values. In this case, you enter the two values (or specify cell references), and then use choices from the drop-down list to set the type of formatting to display if the condition is met.

FIGURE 19.12

One of several different conditional formatting dialog boxes

The formatting suggestions in the drop-down list are just a few of thousands of different formatting combinations. If none of Excel's suggestions are what you want, choose the Custom Format option to display the Format Cells dialog box. You can specify the format in any or all of the four tabs: Number, Font, Border, and Fill.

> **NOTE**
>
> The Format Cells dialog box used for conditional formatting is a modified version of the standard Format Cells dialog box. It doesn't have the Alignment and Protection tabs, and some of the Font formatting options are disabled. The dialog box also includes a Clear button that clears any formatting already selected.

Making your own rules

For maximum control, Excel provides the New Formatting Rule dialog box, shown in Figure 19.13. Access this dialog box by choosing Home ⇨ Styles ⇨ Conditional Formatting ⇨ New Rules.

FIGURE 19.13

Use the New Formatting Rule dialog box to create your own conditional formatting rules.

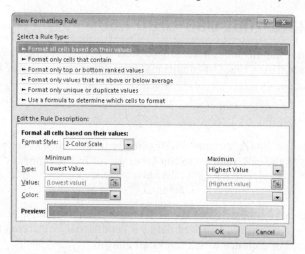

19

Use the New Formatting Rule dialog box to adjust any of the conditional format rules available via the Ribbon, as well as creating unique new rules. First, select a general rule type from the list at the top of the dialog box. The bottom part of the dialog box varies, depending on your selection at the top. After you specify the rule, click the Format button to specify the type of formatting to apply if the condition is met. An exception is the first rule type (Format All Cells Based on Their Values), which doesn't have a Format button (it uses graphics rather than cell formatting).

Here is a summary of the rule types:

- **Format all cells based on their values:** Use this rule type to create rules that display data bars, color scales, or icon sets.
- **Format only cells that contain:** Use this rule type to create rules that format cells based on mathematical comparisons (greater than, less than, greater than or equal to, less than or equal to, equal to, not equal to, between, not between). You can also create rules based on text, dates, blanks, nonblanks, and errors.
- **Format only top- or bottom-ranked values:** Use this rule type to create rules that involve identifying cells in the top n, top $n\%$, bottom n, and bottom $n\%$.
- **Format only values that are above or below average:** Use this rule type to create rules that identify cells that are above average, below average, or within a specified standard deviation from the average.
- **Format only unique or duplicate values:** Use this rule type to create rules that format unique or duplicate values in a range.
- **Use a formula to determine which cells to format:** Use this rule type to create rules based on a logical formula (see "Creating Formula-Based Rules," later in this chapter).

Conditional Formats That Use Graphics

This section describes the three conditional formatting options that display graphics: data bars, color scales, and icon sets. These types of conditional formatting can be useful for visualizing the values in a range.

Using data bars

The *data bars conditional format* displays horizontal bars directly in the cell. The length of the bar is based on the value of the cell, relative to the other values in the range.

A simple data bar

Figure 19.14 shows an example of data bars. It's a list of tracks on 37 Bob Dylan albums, with the length of each track in column D. I applied data bar conditional formatting to the values in column D. You can tell at a glance which tracks are longer.

FIGURE 19.14

The length of the data bars is proportional to the track length in the cell in column D.

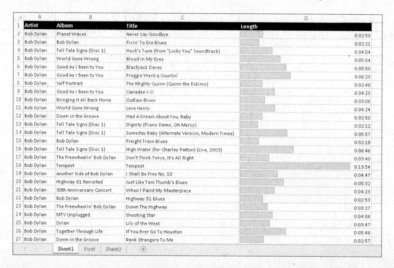

	A	B	C	D
1	Artist	Album	Title	Length
2	Bob Dylan	Planet Waves	Never Say Goodbye	0:02:53
3	Bob Dylan	Bob Dylan	Fixin' To Die Blues	0:02:21
4	Bob Dylan	Tell Tale Signs (Disc 1)	Huck's Tune (from "Lucky You" Soundtrack)	0:04:04
5	Bob Dylan	World Gone Wrong	Blood in My Eyes	0:05:04
6	Bob Dylan	Good As I Been to You	Blackjack Davey	0:05:50
7	Bob Dylan	Good As I Been to You	Froggie Went a Courtin'	0:06:23
8	Bob Dylan	Self Portrait	The Mighty Quinn (Quinn the Eskimo)	0:02:48
9	Bob Dylan	Good As I Been to You	Canadee-I-O	0:04:23
10	Bob Dylan	Bringing It All Back Home	Outlaw Blues	0:03:06
11	Bob Dylan	World Gone Wrong	Love Henry	0:04:24
12	Bob Dylan	Down in the Groove	Had A Dream About You, Baby	0:02:50
13	Bob Dylan	Tell Tale Signs (Disc 1)	Dignity (Piano Demo, Oh Mercy)	0:02:12
14	Bob Dylan	Tell Tale Signs (Disc 1)	Someday Baby (Alternate Version, Modern Times)	0:05:57
15	Bob Dylan	Bob Dylan	Freight Train Blues	0:02:19
16	Bob Dylan	Tell Tale Signs (Disc 1)	High Water (for Charley Patton) (Live, 2003)	0:06:46
17	Bob Dylan	The Freewheelin' Bob Dylan	Don't Think Twice, It's All Right	0:03:40
18	Bob Dylan	Tempest	Tempest	0:13:54
19	Bob Dylan	Another Side of Bob Dylan	I Shall Be Free No. 10	0:04:47
20	Bob Dylan	Highway 61 Revisited	Just Like Tom Thumb's Blues	0:05:32
21	Bob Dylan	30th Anniversary Concert	When I Paint My Masterpiece	0:04:23
22	Bob Dylan	Bob Dylan	Highway 51 blues	0:02:53
23	Bob Dylan	The Freewheelin' Bob Dylan	Down The Highway	0:03:27
24	Bob Dylan	MTV Unplugged	Shooting Star	0:04:06
25	Bob Dylan	Dylan	Lily of the West	0:03:47
26	Bob Dylan	Together Through Life	If You Ever Go To Houston	0:05:48
27	Bob Dylan	Down in the Groove	Rank Strangers To Me	0:02:57

Sheet1   Pivot   Sheet2   +

TIP

When you adjust the column width, the bar lengths adjust accordingly. The differences among the bar lengths are more prominent when the column is wider.

Excel provides quick access to 12 data bar styles via Home ⇨ Styles ⇨ Conditional Formatting ⇨ Data Bars. For additional choices, click the More Rules option, which displays the New Formatting Rule dialog box. Use this dialog box to:

- Show the bar only (hide the numbers).
- Specify Minimum and Maximum values for the scaling.
- Change the appearance of the bars.
- Specify how negative values and the axis are handled.
- Specify the direction of the bars.

NOTE

Oddly, if you add data bars using one of the 12 data bar styles, the colors used for data bars are *not* theme colors. If you apply a new document theme, the data bar colors do not change. However, if you add the data bars by using the New Formatting Rule dialog box, the colors you choose *are* theme colors.

Using data bars in lieu of a chart

Using the data bars conditional formatting can sometimes serve as a quick alternative to creating a chart. Figure 19.15 shows a three-column range (in B3:D14) with data bars conditional formatting in column D (column D contains references to the values in column C). The conditional formatting in column D uses the Show Bars Only option, so the values are not displayed.

FIGURE 19.15

Comparing data bars conditional formatting (top) with a bar chart.

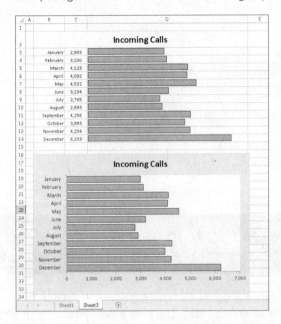

Figure 19.15 also shows an actual bar chart created from the same data. The bar chart takes about the same amount of time to create and is a lot more flexible. But for a quick-and-dirty chart, data bars may be a good option — especially when you need to create several such charts.

Using color scales

The *color scale conditional formatting option* varies the background color of a cell based on the cell's value, relative to other cells in the range.

A color scale example

Figure 19.16 shows examples of color scale conditional formatting. The example on the left depicts monthly sales for three regions. Conditional formatting was applied to the range B4:D15. The conditional formatting uses a three-color scale, with red for the lowest value, yellow for the midpoint, and green for the highest value. Values in between are displayed using a color within the gradient. It's clear that the Central region consistently has lower sales volumes, but the conditional formatting doesn't help identify monthly difference for a particular region.

FIGURE 19.16

Two examples of color scale conditional formatting

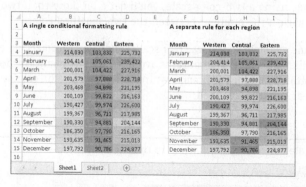

The example on the right shows the same data, but conditional formatting was applied to each region separately. This approach facilitates comparisons within a region and can also help identify high or low sales months. Neither one of these approaches is necessarily better. The way you set up conditional formatting depends entirely on what you're trying to visualize.

Excel provides four two-color scale presets and four three-color scale presets, which you can apply to the selected range by choosing Home ⇨ Styles ⇨ Conditional Formatting ⇨ Color Scales. To customize the colors and other options, choose Home ⇨ Styles ⇨ Conditional Formatting ⇨ Color Scales ⇨ More Rules. The New Formatting Rule dialog box, shown in Figure 19.17, appears. Adjust the settings, and watch the Preview box to see the effects of your changes.

FIGURE 19.17

Use the New Formatting Rule dialog box to customize a color scale.

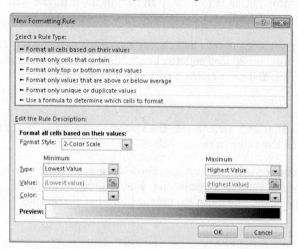

19

An extreme color scale example

It's important to understand that color scale conditional formatting uses a gradient. For example, if you format a range using a two-color scale, you'll get a lot more than two colors. You'll also get colors within the gradient between the two specified colors.

Figure 19.18 shows an extreme example that uses color scale conditional formatting on a range of more than 6,000 cells. The worksheet contains average daily temperatures for an 18-year period. Each row contains 365 (or 366) temperatures for the year. The columns are very narrow so the entire year can be visualized.

FIGURE 19.18

This worksheet uses color scale conditional formatting to display daily temperatures.

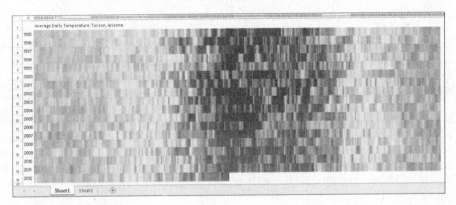

Using icon sets

Yet another conditional formatting option is to display an icon in the cell. The icon displayed depends on the value of the cell.

To assign an icon set to a range, select the cells and choose Home ⇨ Styles ⇨ Conditional Formatting ⇨ Icon Sets. Excel provides 20 icon sets to choose from. The number of icons in the sets ranges from three to five. You can't create a custom icon set.

An icon set example

Figure 19.19 shows an example that uses an icon set. The symbols graphically depict the status of each project, based on the value in column C.

By default, the symbols are assigned using percentiles. For a three-symbol set, the items are grouped into three percentiles. For a four-symbol set, they're grouped into four percentiles. And for a five-symbol set, the items are grouped into five percentiles.

FIGURE 19.19

Using an icon set to indicate the status of projects

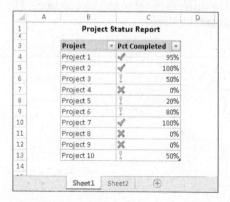

If you would like more control over how the icons are assigned, choose
Home ⇨ Styles ⇨ Conditional Formatting ⇨ Icon Sets ⇨ More Rules to display the New
Formatting Rule dialog box. To modify an existing rule, choose Home ⇨ Styles ⇨ Conditional
Formatting ⇨ Manage Rules. Then select the rule to modify and click the Edit Rule button.

Figure 19.20 shows how to modify the icon set rules such that only projects that are
100 percent completed get the check mark icons. Projects that are 0 percent completed get
the X icon. All other projects get no icon. Click OK to apply the change.

FIGURE 19.20

Changing the icon assignment rule

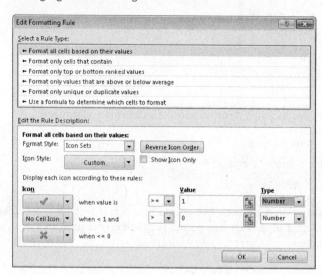

Another icon set example

Figure 19.21 shows a table that contains two test scores for each student. The Change column contains a formula that calculates the difference between the two tests. The Trend column uses an icon set to display the trend graphically.

FIGURE 19.21

The arrows depict the trend from Test 1 to Test 2.

	A	B	C	D	E
1					
2	Student	Test 1	Test 2	Change	Trend
3	Amy	59	65	6	⬆
4	Bob	82	78	-4	➡
5	Calvind	98	92	-6	⬇
6	Doug	56	69	13	⬆
7	Ephraim	98	89	-9	⬇
8	Frank	67	75	8	⬆
9	Gretta	78	87	9	⬆
10	Harold	87	92	5	⬆
11	Inez	56	85	29	⬆
12	June	87	72	-15	⬇
13	Kenny	87	88	1	➡
14	Lance	92	92	0	➡
15	Marvin	82	73	-9	⬇
16	Noel	98	100	2	➡
17	Opie	84	73	-11	⬇
18	Paul	94	93	-1	➡
19	Quinton	68	92	24	⬆
20	Rasmus	91	90	-1	➡
21	Sam	85	86	1	➡
22	Ted	72	92	20	⬆
23	Ursie	80	75	-5	⬇
24	Valerie	77	65	-12	⬇
25	Wally	64	45	-19	⬇
26	Xerxes	59	63	4	➡
27	Yolanda	89	99	10	⬆
28	Zippy	85	82	-3	➡
29					

Sheet1 Sheet2 ⊕

This example uses the icon set named 3 Arrows, and with the rule customized:

- **Up Arrow:** When value is >= 5
- **Level Arrow:** When value < 5 and > −5
- **Down Arrow:** When value is <= −5

In other words, a difference of no more than five points in either direction is considered an even trend. An improvement of at least five points is considered a positive trend, and a decline of five points or more is considered a negative trend.

In some cases, using icon sets can cause your worksheet to look a bit cluttered. Displaying an icon for every cell in a range might result in visual overload. For the example of the test results table, you could hide the level (right pointing) arrows by clicking the down arrow beside that cell in the Edit Formatting Rule dialog box and clicking No Cell Icon in the palette that appears.

Creating Formula-Based Rules

Excel's conditional formatting feature is versatile, but sometimes it's just not quite versatile enough. Fortunately, you can extend its versatility by writing conditional formatting formulas.

The examples later in this section describe how to create conditional formatting formulas to:

- Identify text entries.
- Identify dates that fall on a weekend.
- Format cells that are in odd-numbered rows or columns (for dynamic alternate row or columns shading).
- Format groups of rows (for example, shade every two groups of rows).
- Display a sum only when all precedent cells contain values.

Some of these formulas may be useful to you. If not, they may inspire you to create other conditional formatting formulas.

To specify conditional formatting based on a formula, select the cells and then choose Home ➪ Styles ➪ Conditional Formatting ➪ New Rule. The New Formatting Rule dialog box appears. Click the rule type Use a formula to determine which cells to format, and then specify the formula. You can type the formula directly into the box or enter a reference to a cell that contains a logical formula. As with normal Excel formulas, the formula you enter here must begin with an equal sign (=). Click OK to finish creating the rule.

19

Understanding relative and absolute references

If the formula that you enter into the New Formatting Rule dialog box contains a cell reference, that reference is considered a *relative reference*, based on the upper-left cell in the selected range.

For example, suppose that you want to set up a conditional formatting condition that applies shading to cells in range A1:B10 only if the cell contains text. None of Excel's conditional formatting options can do this task, so you need to create a formula that will return TRUE if the cell contains text and FALSE otherwise. Follow these steps:

1. **Select the range A1:B10 and ensure that cell A1 is the active cell.**
2. **Choose Home ⇨ Styles ⇨ Conditional Formatting ⇨ New Rule.** The New Formatting Rule dialog box appears.
3. **Click the Use a formula to determine which cells to format rule type.**
4. **Enter the following formula in the Formula box:**

   ```
   =ISTEXT(A1)
   ```

5. **Click the Format button.** The Format Cells dialog box appears.
6. **From the Fill tab, specify the cell shading that will be applied if the formula returns TRUE.**
7. **Click OK to return to the New Formatting Rule dialog box (see Figure 19.22).**

FIGURE 19.22

Creating a conditional formatting rule based on a formula

8. **Click OK to close the New Formatting Rule dialog box.**

Notice that the formula entered in Step 4 contains a relative reference to the upper-left cell in the selected range.

Generally, when entering a conditional formatting formula for a range of cells, you'll use a reference to the active cell, which is typically the upper-left cell in the selected range. One exception is when you need to refer to a specific cell. For example, suppose that you select range A1:B10, and you want to apply formatting to all cells in the range that exceed the value in cell C1. Enter this conditional formatting formula:

```
=A1>$C$1
```

In this case, the reference to cell C1 is an *absolute reference;* it will not be adjusted for the cells in the selected range. In other words, the conditional formatting formula for cell A2 looks like this:

```
=A2>$C$1
```

The relative cell reference is adjusted, but the absolute cell reference is not.

Conditional formatting formula examples

Each of these examples uses a formula entered directly into the New Formatting Rule dialog box, after selecting the Use a Formula to Determine Which Cells to Format rule type. You decide the type of formatting that you apply conditionally.

Identifying weekend days

Excel provides a number of conditional formatting rules that deal with dates, but it doesn't let you identify dates that fall on a weekend. Use this formula to identify weekend dates:

```
=OR(WEEKDAY(A1)=7,WEEKDAY(A1)=1)
```

This formula assumes that a range is selected and that cell A1 is the active cell.

Highlighting a row based on a value

Figure 19.23 shows a worksheet that contains a conditional formula in the range A3:G28. If a name entered in cell B1 is found in the first column, the entire row for that name is highlighted.

19

FIGURE 19.23

Highlighting a row, based on a matching name

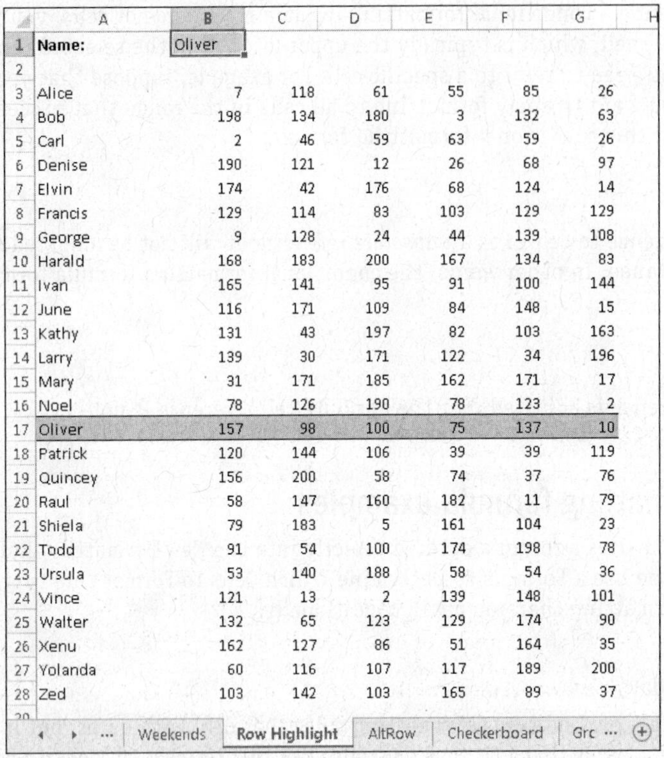

	A	B	C	D	E	F	G	H
1	Name:	Oliver						
2								
3	Alice	7	118	61	55	85	26	
4	Bob	198	134	180	3	132	63	
5	Carl	2	46	59	63	59	26	
6	Denise	190	121	12	26	68	97	
7	Elvin	174	42	176	68	124	14	
8	Francis	129	114	83	103	129	129	
9	George	9	128	24	44	139	108	
10	Harald	168	183	200	167	134	83	
11	Ivan	165	141	95	91	100	144	
12	June	116	171	109	84	148	15	
13	Kathy	131	43	197	82	103	163	
14	Larry	139	30	171	122	34	196	
15	Mary	31	171	185	162	171	17	
16	Noel	78	126	190	78	123	2	
17	Oliver	157	98	100	75	137	10	
18	Patrick	120	144	106	39	39	119	
19	Quincey	156	200	58	74	37	76	
20	Raul	58	147	160	182	11	79	
21	Shiela	79	183	5	161	104	23	
22	Todd	91	54	100	174	198	78	
23	Ursula	53	140	188	58	54	36	
24	Vince	121	13	2	139	148	101	
25	Walter	132	65	123	129	174	90	
26	Xenu	162	127	86	51	164	35	
27	Yolanda	60	116	107	117	189	200	
28	Zed	103	142	103	165	89	37	

◄ ► ⋯ | Weekends | **Row Highlight** | AltRow | Checkerboard | Grc ⋯ ⊕

The conditional formatting formula is:

```
=$A3=$B$1
```

Notice that a mixed reference is used for cell A3. Because the column part of the reference is absolute, the comparison is always done using the contents of column A.

Displaying alternate-row shading

The conditional formatting formula that follows was applied to the range A1:D18, as shown in Figure 19.24, to apply shading to alternate rows.

```
=MOD(ROW(),2)=0
```

FIGURE 19.24

Using conditional formatting to apply formatting to alternate rows

	A	B	C	D	E
1	945	32	76	956	
2	176	795	573	874	
3	790	689	904	439	
4	653	873	379	656	
5	762	795	783	347	
6	670	514	706	321	
7	594	304	64	608	
8	321	722	510	275	
9	743	628	174	158	
10	494	462	979	616	
11	933	25	871	737	
12	821	49	209	156	
13	474	755	451	96	
14	146	175	813	297	
15	939	981	669	512	
16	824	769	16	668	
17	767	650	302	111	
18	375	998	438	59	
19					
20					

AltRow | Checkerboard | Grc ...

Alternate row shading can make your spreadsheets easier to read. If you add or delete rows within the conditional formatting area, the shading is updated automatically.

This formula uses the ROW function (which returns the row number) and the MOD function (which returns the remainder of its first argument divided by its second argument). For cells in even-numbered rows, the MOD function returns 0, and cells in that row are formatted.

For alternate shading of columns, use the COLUMN function instead of the ROW function.

Creating checkerboard shading

The following formula is a variation on the example in the preceding section. It applies formatting to alternate rows and columns, creating a checkerboard effect.

```
=MOD(ROW(),2)=MOD(COLUMN(),2)
```

Shading groups of rows

Here's another row shading variation. The following formula shades alternate groups of rows. It produces four shaded rows, followed by four unshaded rows, followed by four more shaded rows, and so on.

```
=MOD(INT((ROW()-1)/4)+1,2)=1
```

For different sized groups, change the 4 to some other value. For example, use this formula to shade alternate groups of two rows:

```
=MOD(INT((ROW()-1)/2)+1,2)=1
```

Displaying a total only when all values are entered

Supppose a range has a formula that uses the SUM function in cell C6. Conditional formatting is used to display the sum only when all of the four cells above aren't blank. The conditional formatting formula you would apply to cell C6 (and cell B6, which contains the label for the row) is:

```
=COUNT($C$2:$C$5)=4
```

This formula returns TRUE only if C2:C5 contains no empty cells. The conditional formatting applied to B6:C6 is a dark background color. The text color in those cells is white, so it's legible only when the conditional formatting rule is satisfied. Figure 19.25 shows the worksheet when one of the values is missing.

FIGURE 19.25

A missing value causes the sum to be hidden.

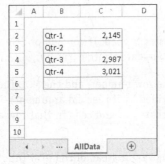

Working with Conditional Formats

This section describes some additional information about conditional formatting that you may find useful.

Managing rules

The Conditional Formatting Rules Manager dialog box is useful for checking, editing, deleting, and adding conditional formats. First select any cell in the range that contains conditional formatting. Then choose Home ⇨ Styles ⇨ Conditional Formatting ⇨ Manage Rules.

You can specify as many rules as you like by clicking the New Rule button. As you can see in Figure 19.26, cells can even use data bars, color scales, and icon sets all at the same time — if you can think of a good reason to apply all those types of formatting to one set of data.

FIGURE 19.26

This range uses data bars, color scales, and icon sets.

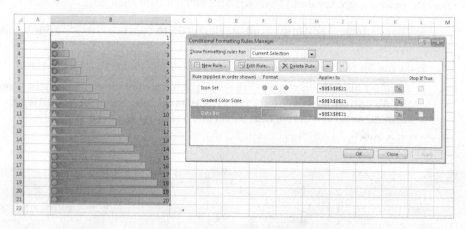

Copying cells that contain conditional formatting

Conditional formatting information is stored with a cell much like standard formatting information is stored with a cell. As a result, when you copy a cell that contains conditional formatting, you also copy the conditional formatting.

> **TIP**
>
> To copy only the formatting (including conditional formatting), copy the cells and then use the Paste Special dialog box and select the Formats option. Or choose Home ⇨ Clipboard ⇨ Paste ⇨ Formatting (R).

If you insert rows or columns within a range that contains conditional formatting, the new cells have the same conditional formatting.

Deleting conditional formatting

When you press Delete to delete the contents of a cell, you don't delete the conditional formatting for the cell (if any). To remove all conditional formats (as well as all other cell formatting), select the cell and then choose Home ⇨ Editing ⇨ Clear ⇨ Clear Formats. Or choose Home ⇨ Editing ⇨ Clear ⇨ Clear All to delete the cell contents and the conditional formatting.

To remove only conditional formatting (and leave the other formatting intact), choose Home ➪ Styles ➪ Conditional Formatting ➪ Clear Rules.

Locating cells that contain conditional formatting

You can't always tell, just by looking at a cell, whether it contains conditional formatting. You can, however, use the Go to Special dialog box to select such cells.

1. **Choose Home ➪ Editing ➪ Find & Select ➪ Go to Special.** The Go to Special dialog box appears.

2. **In the Go to Special dialog box, select the Conditional Formats option.**

3. **To select all cells on the worksheet containing conditional formatting, select the All option; to select only the cells that contain the same conditional formatting as the active cell, select the Same option.**

4. **Click OK.** Excel selects the cells for you.

> **NOTE**
>
> The Excel Find and Replace dialog box includes a feature that allows you to search your worksheet to locate cells that contain specific formatting. This feature does *not* locate cells that contain formatting resulting from conditional formatting.

Introducing Sparklines

A *sparkline is* a small chart that's displayed in a single cell. A sparkline allows you to quickly spot time-based trends or variations in data. Because they're so compact, sparklines are almost always used in a group.

Although sparklines look like miniature charts (and can sometimes take the place of a chart), this feature is completely separate from the charting feature covered in Chapter 18. For example, charts are placed on a worksheet's draw layer, and a single chart can display several series of data. A sparkline is displayed inside a cell and displays only one series of data.

This chapter introduces sparklines and presents examples that demonstrate how they can be used in your worksheets.

> **NOTE**
>
> Sparklines were introduced in Excel 2010. If you create a workbook that uses sparklines, and that workbook is opened using a previous version of Excel, the cells holding sparklines will be empty.

Sparkline Types

Excel supports three types of sparklines. Figure 19.27 shows examples of each, displayed in column H. Each sparkline depicts the six data points to the left.

FIGURE 19.27

Three groups of sparklines

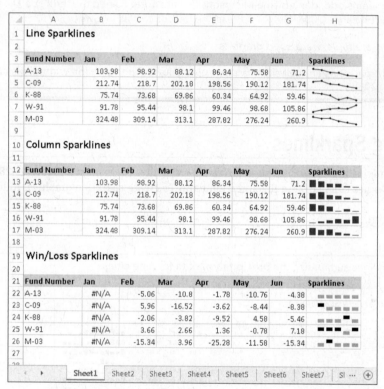

- **Line:** Similar to a line chart. As an option, the line can display with a marker for each data point. The first group in Figure 19.27 shows line sparklines, with markers. A quick glance reveals that, with the exception of Fund Number W-91, the funds have been losing value over the six-month period.

- **Column:** Similar to a column chart. The second group in Figure 19.27 shows the same data displayed with column sparklines.

- **Win/Loss:** A "binary"-type chart that displays each data point as a high block or a low block. The third group shows win/loss sparklines. Notice that the data is different. Each cell displays the *change* from the previous month. In the sparkline, each data point is depicted as a high block (win) or a low block (loss). In this example, a positive change from the previous month is a win, and a negative change from the previous month is a loss.

Why Sparklines?

If the term *sparkline* seems odd, don't blame Microsoft. Edward Tufte coined the term *sparkline*, and in his book, *Beautiful Evidence* (2006, Graphics Press), he describes it as follows:

> *Sparklines: Intense, simple, word-sized graphics*

In the case of Excel, sparklines are cell-sized graphics. As you see in this chapter, sparklines aren't limited to lines.

Creating Sparklines

Sparklines provide a great way to summarize data visually. For example, Figure 19.28 shows column sparklines summarizing precipitation data. To create sparkline graphics, follow these steps:

FIGURE 19.28

Column sparklines summarize the precipitation data for nine cities.

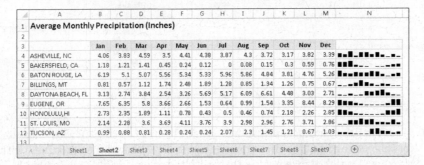

1. **Select the data that will be depicted (data only, not column headings); if you're creating multiple sparklines, select all the data.** In the example in Figure 19.28, you would start by selecting B4:M12.

2. **With the data selected, click the Insert tab, and in the Sparklines group, click one of the three sparkline types: Line, Column, or Win/Loss.** The Create Sparklines dialog box, shown in Figure 19.29, appears.

FIGURE 19.29

Use the Create Sparklines dialog box to specify the data range and the location for the Sparkline graphics.

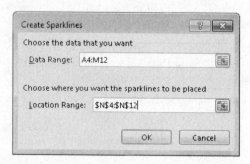

3. **Specify the location for the sparklines in the Location Range box.** Typically, you'll put the sparklines next to the data, but that's not a requirement. Most of the time, you'll use an empty range to hold the sparklines. However, Excel doesn't prevent your from inserting sparklines into cells that already contain data. The sparkline location that you specify must match the source data in terms of number of rows or number of columns. For this example, you would specify N4:N12 as the Location Range.

4. **Click OK.** Excel creates the sparklines graphics of the type you specified.

The sparklines are linked to the data, so if you change any of the values in the data range, the sparkline graphic will update. Often, you'll want to increase the column width or row height to improve the readability of the sparklines.

> **TIP**
>
> Most of the time, you'll create sparklines on the same sheet that contains the data. If you want to create sparklines on a different sheet, start by activating the sheet where the sparklines will be displayed. Then, in the Create Sparklines dialog box, specify the source data either by pointing or by typing the complete sheet reference (for example, **Sheet1A1:C12**). The Create Sparklines dialog box lets you specify a different sheet for the Data Range, but not for the Location Range. Or, you can just create the sparklines on the same sheet as the data, and then cut and paste the cells to a different worksheet.

Understanding Sparkline Groups

In most situations, you'll probably create a *group* of sparklines — one for each row or column of data. A worksheet can hold any number of sparkline groups. Excel remembers each group, and you can work with the group as a single unit. For example, you can select one sparkline in a group, and then modify the formatting of all sparklines in the group. When you select one sparkline cell, Excel displays an outline of all the other sparklines in the group.

You can, however, perform some operations on an individual sparkline in a group:

■ **Change the sparkline's data source.** Select the sparkline cell and choose Sparkline Tools ➪ Design ➪ Sparkline ➪ Edit Data ➪ Edit Single Sparkline's Data. Excel displays a dialog box that lets you change the data source for the selected sparkline.

■ **Delete the sparkline.** Select the sparkline cell and choose Sparkline Tools ➪ Design ➪ Group ➪ Clear ➪ Clear Selected Sparklines.

Both operations are available from the shortcut menu that appears when you right-click a sparkline cell.

You can also ungroup a set of sparklines by selecting any sparkline in the group and choosing Sparkline Tools ➪ Design ➪ Group ➪ Ungroup. After you ungroup a set of sparklines, you can work with each sparkline individually.

Customizing Sparklines

When you select a cell that contains a sparkline, Excel displays an outline around all the sparklines in its group. You can then use the commands on the Sparkline Tools ➪ Design tab to customize the group of sparklines.

Sizing sparkline cells

When you change the width or height of a cell that contains a sparkline, the sparkline adjusts accordingly. In addition, you can insert a sparkline into merged cells. Figure 19.30 shows the same sparkline, displayed at four sizes resulting from column width, row height, and merged cells. As you can see, the size and proportions of the cell (or merged cells) make a big difference in the appearance.

FIGURE 19.30

A sparkline at various sizes

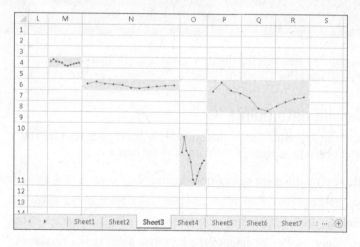

Handling hidden or missing data

By default, if you hide rows or columns that are used in a sparkline graphic, the hidden data does not appear in the sparkline. Also, missing data (an empty cell) is displayed as a gap in the graphic. To change these settings, choose Sparkline Tools ⇨ Design ⇨ Sparkline ⇨ Edit Data ⇨ Hidden and Empty Cells. In the Hidden and Empty Cell Settings dialog box that appears, choose Gaps, Zero, or Connect data points with line under Show empty cells as. Click to place a check beside Show data in hidden rows and columns if desired, and then click OK.

As mentioned earlier, Excel supports three sparkline types: Line, Column, and Win/Loss. After you create a sparkline or group of sparklines, you can easily change the type by selecting the sparkline and clicking one of the three icons in the Sparkline Tools ⇨ Design ⇨ Type group. If the selected sparkline is part of a group, all sparklines in the group are changed to the new type.

> **TIP**
>
> If you've customized the appearance, Excel remembers your customization settings for each type if you switch among sparkline types.

Changing sparkline colors and line width

After you've created a sparkline, changing the color is easy. Use the controls in the Sparkline Tools ⇨ Design ⇨ Style group.

19

> **NOTE**
>
> Colors used in sparkline graphics are tied to the document theme. Therefore, if you change the theme (by choosing Page Layout ⇨ Themes ⇨ Themes), the sparkline colors will change to the new theme colors.

For Line sparklines, you can also specify the line width. Choose Sparkline Tools ⇨ Design ⇨ Style ⇨ Sparkline Color ⇨ Weight.

Highlighting certain data points

Use the commands in the Sparkline Tools ⇨ Design ⇨ Show group to customize the sparklines to highlight certain aspects of the data. The options are:

- **High Point:** Apply a different color to the highest data point in the sparkline.
- **Low Point:** Apply a different color to the lowest data point in the sparkline.
- **Negative Points:** Apply a different color to negative values in the sparkline.
- **First Point:** Apply a different color to the first data point in the sparkline.
- **Last Point:** Apply a different color to the last data point in the sparkline.
- **Markers:** Show data markers in the sparkline. This option is available only for Line sparklines.

You control the color of the highlighting by using the Marker Color control in the Sparkline Tools ⇨ Design ⇨ Style group. Unfortunately, you can't change the size of the markers in Line sparklines. Figure 19.31 shows some Line sparklines with various types of highlighting applied.

FIGURE 19.31

Highlighting options for Line Sparklines

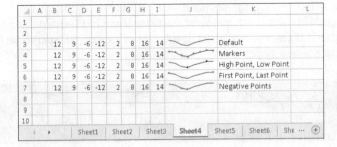

Adjusting sparkline axis scaling

When you create one or more sparklines, they all use (by default) automatic axis scaling. In other words, the minimum and maximum vertical axis values are determined automatically for each sparkline in the group, based on the numeric range of the data used by the sparkline.

The Sparkline Tools ⇨ Design ⇨ Group ⇨ Axis command lets you override this automatic behavior and control the minimum and maximum value for each sparkline or for a group of sparklines. For even more control, you can use the Custom Value option and specify the minimum and maximum for the sparkline group.

> **NOTE**
>
> Sparklines don't actually display a vertical axis, so you're essentially adjusting an invisible axis.

Figure 19.32 shows two groups of sparklines. The group at the top uses the default axis settings (Automatic for Each Sparkline). Each sparkline shows the six-month trend for the product, but there is no indication of the magnitude of the values.

FIGURE 19.32

The bottom group of sparklines shows the effect of using the same axis minimum and maximum values for all sparklines in a group.

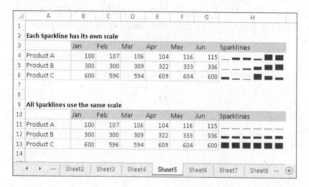

For the sparkline group at the bottom (which uses the same data), the vertical axis minimum and maximum was changed to use the Same for All Sparklines setting. With these settings in effect, the magnitude of the values *across* the products is apparent — but the trend across the months within a product is not apparent.

The axis scaling option you choose depends upon what aspect of the data you want to emphasize.

Specifying a Date Axis

Normally, data displayed in a sparkline is assumed to be at equal intervals. For example, a sparkline might display a daily account balance, sales by month, or profits by year. But what if the data isn't at equal intervals?

Figure 19.33 shows data, by date, along with a sparklines graphic created from column B. Notice that some dates are missing, but the sparkline shows the columns as if the values were spaced at equal intervals.

FIGURE 19.33

The sparkline displays the values as if they are at equal time intervals.

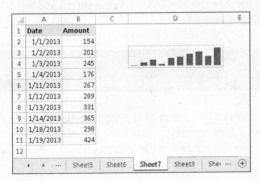

To better depict the data, the solution is to specify a date axis. Select the sparkline and choose Sparkline Tools ⇨ Design ⇨ Group ⇨ Axis ⇨ Date Axis Type. Excel displays a dialog box, asking for the range that contains the dates. In this example, specify range A2:A11. Click OK, and the sparkline displays gaps for the missing dates (see Figure 19.34).

FIGURE 19.34

After specifying a date axis, the sparkline shows the values accurately.

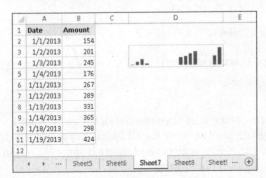

Auto-Updating Sparklines

If a sparkline uses data in a normal range of cells, adding new data to the beginning or end of the range does *not* force the sparkline to use the new data. You need to use the Edit Sparklines dialog box to update the data range (choose Sparkline Tools ⇨ Design ⇨ Sparkline ⇨ Edit Data). But, if the sparkline data is in a column within a table (created by choosing Insert ⇨ Tables ⇨ Table), then the sparkline will use new data that's added to the end of the table.

Figure 19.35 shows an example. The sparkline was created using the data in the Rate column of the table. When you add the new rate for September, the sparkline will automatically update its Data Range.

FIGURE 19.35

Creating a sparkline from data in a table

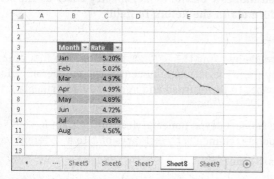

Displaying a Sparkline for a Dynamic Range

The example in this section describes how to create a sparkline that displays only the most recent data points in a range. Figure 19.36 shows a worksheet that tracks daily sales. The sparkline, in merged cells E4:E5, displays only the seven most recent data points in column B. When new data is added to column B, the sparkline will adjust to show only the most recent seven days of sales.

FIGURE 19.36

Using a dynamic range name to display only the last seven data points in a sparkline

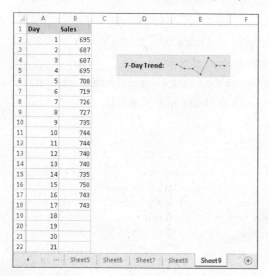

Start this process by creating a dynamic range name. Here's how:

1. **Choose Formulas ➪ Defined Names ➪ Define Name, specify Last7 as the Name, and enter the following formula in the Refers To field:**

   `=OFFSET($B$2,COUNTA($B:$B)-7-1,0,7,1)`

   This formula calculates a range by using the OFFSET function. The first argument is the first cell in the range (B2). The second argument is the number of cells in the column (minus the number to be returned and minus 1 to accommodate the label in B1).

   This name always refers to the last seven nonempty cells in column B. To display a different number of data points, change both instances of 7 to a different value.

2. **Chose Insert ➪ Sparklines ➪ Line.**

3. **In the Data Range field, type** Last7 **(the dynamic range name); specify** cell E4 **as the Location Range.** The sparkline shows the data in range B11:B17.

4. **Add new data to column B.** The sparkline adjusts to display only the last seven data points.

Summary

In this chapter, you learned about features you can use to organize and communicate the meaning of data in a visual way. The chapter introduced tables, conditional formatting, and sparklines in Excel. Your Excel skill set now includes the ability to:

- Convert a range to a table and apply a table style.
- Navigate in and edit a table.
- Sort and filter a table, and display and use a total row.
- Convert a table back to a regular range of cells.
- Apply conditional formatting using data bars, color scales, and icon sets.
- Edit a conditional formatting rule or create your own rule.
- Create and adjust sparklines.

Part IV

Persuading and Informing with PowerPoint 2013

Summarizing and presenting your ideas in their best light can be make or break in situations such as when you want to win a contract, persuade colleagues to handle a project in a certain way, demonstrate the progress your team has made, find new donors or volunteers, and many others. PowerPoint 2013 provides the tools you need to create a presentation that will win over your audience. Part IV shows you what PowerPoint offers, including how to create presentation files, how to add slides and content, and how to choose the best design elements for the slides delivering your message. The part also shows you how to organize and illustrate data and your message with tables, charts, SmartArt, and pictures. From there, you'll see how to (literally) animate the presentation and prepare materials for your audience. Finally, this part teaches you the best practices for delivering a polished performance before your audience.

IN THIS PART

A First Look at PowerPoint 2013

A presentation is any kind of interaction between a speaker and audience, but it usually involves one or more of the following: computer-displayed slides, noncomputerized visual aids (such as transparencies or 35mm slides), hard-copy handouts, and/or speaker's notes. PowerPoint enables you to create all of these types of visual aids, plus many other types that you'll learn about as you go along.

In this chapter you'll get a big-picture introduction to PowerPoint 2013, and then we'll fire up the program and poke around a bit to help you get familiar with the interface. You'll find out how to use the tabs and panes, learn about some of the new features, and see how to work with the various views and key screen settings.

Who Uses PowerPoint and Why?

PowerPoint is a popular tool for people who give presentations as part of their jobs and also for their support staff. With PowerPoint, you can create visual aids that help get the message across to an audience. Although the traditional kind of presentation is a live speech presented at a podium, advances in technology have made it possible to give presentations in numerous other ways, and PowerPoint has kept pace. With PowerPoint, you can present in these formats:

- **Podium:** For live presentations, PowerPoint helps the lecturer emphasize key points through the use of computer-based shows (from a notebook or tablet PC, for example) or overhead transparencies.

- **Kiosk shows:** These are self-running presentations that provide information in an unattended location. You have probably seen such presentations listing meeting times and rooms in hotel lobbies and as sales presentations at trade show booths.

- **CDs and DVDs:** You can package a PowerPoint presentation on a CD or DVD and distribute it with a press release, a marketing push, or a direct mail campaign. The presentation can be in PowerPoint format, or it can be converted to some other format, such as PDF or a video.

- **Internet formats:** You can use PowerPoint to create a show that you can present live over a network or the Internet, while each participant watches from their own computer. You can even store a self-running or interactive presentation on a website in a variety of formats and make it available for the public to download and run on a PC.

When you start your first PowerPoint presentation, you may not be sure which delivery method you will use. However, it's best to decide the presentation format before you invest too much work in your materials because the audience's needs are different for each medium.

> **NOTE**
>
> Because PowerPoint is so tightly integrated with the other Microsoft Office 2013 components, you can easily share information between them. For example, if you have created a graph in Excel, you can use it on a PowerPoint slide. Or, you can export your PowerPoint presentation into Word as handouts. Chapter 40, "Integrating Office Application Information," shows you a number of ways that you can share information between Office applications.

Most people associate PowerPoint with sales presentations, but PowerPoint is useful for people in many other lines of work as well. Here's a sampling of how real people use PowerPoint in their daily jobs:

- **Sales:** More people use PowerPoint for selling goods and services than for any other reason. Armed with a laptop computer and a PowerPoint presentation, a salesperson can make a good impression on a client anywhere in the world. Figure 20.1 shows a slide from a sample sales presentation. With PowerPoint, you can create a number of sales tools: live presentations in front of clients with the salesperson present and running the show, self-running presentations that flip through the slides at specified intervals so that passersby can read them or ignore them as they wish, and user-interactive product information demos distributed on CD/DVD that potential customers can view at their leisure on their own PCs.

- **Marketing:** The distinction between sales and marketing can be rather blurred at times, but marketing generally refers to the positioning of a product in the media rather than its presentation to a particular company or individual. Marketing representatives are often called upon to write advertising copy, generate camera-ready layouts for print advertisements, design marketing flyers and shelf displays, and produce other creative selling materials. By combining the Office 2013 online clip art collection and drawing tools with some well-chosen fonts and borders, a marketing person can come up with some very usable designs in PowerPoint.

- **Human Resources:** Human resources personnel often deliver presentations to new employees to explain the policies and benefits of the company. A well-designed, attractive presentation gives a positive impression of the company, starting the new hires off on the right foot. One of the most helpful features in PowerPoint for the human resources professional is the SmartArt tool. With it, you can easily diagram the reporting structure of the company and make changes whenever necessary with a few mouse clicks.

- **Education and Training:** Most courses include a lecture section in which the instructor outlines the content, and PowerPoint can help make the lecture portion of the class go smoothly. PowerPoint's interactive controls even let you create quizzes that each student can take on-screen to gauge their progress. Depending on the button the student clicks, you can set up the quiz to display a "Yes, you are correct!" or "Sorry, try again" slide.

FIGURE 20.1

PowerPoint offers unparalleled flexibility for presenting information to potential customers.

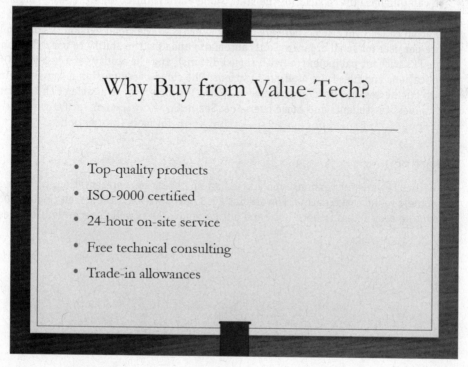

649

- **Hotel and Restaurant Management:** Service organizations such as hotels and restaurants often need to inform their customers of various facts but need to do so unobtrusively so that the information will not be obvious except to those looking for it. For example, a convention center hotel might provide a printed list of the meetings taking place in its meeting rooms, or a restaurant might show pictures of the day's specials on a video screen in the waiting area. You can use PowerPoint to do either.

What's New in PowerPoint 2013?

PowerPoint 2013 is very much like PowerPoint 2010 in its basic functionality. It uses a tabbed Ribbon across the top, rather than a traditional menu system, and employs dialog boxes and a Quick Access Toolbar in the same ways that 2010 did.

This doesn't mean that there aren't changes and improvements though! The following sections outline the major differences you will see when you upgrade from PowerPoint 2010 to PowerPoint 2013.

Cloud integration

You can purchase Office 2013 (or the standalone PowerPoint 2013) either as a traditional boxed application, as a download (with an optional backup DVD) or as a cloud-based subscription called Office 365. There are several benefits to the cloud version, including lower price per user for small organizations, automatic updates, the ability to use Office on multiple PCs without paying extra (with some editions), and the ability to access your Office applications and files from multiple locations. The cloud-based version is marked primarily to businesses, but versions are also available (or soon to be available at this writing) for university students and home users too. See `http://www.microsoft.com/en-us/office365/office-professional-plus.aspx` for more information.

Start screen

In earlier PowerPoint versions, you started up in a blank new presentation, which some beginners found intimidating. PowerPoint 2013 opens with a Start screen (Figure 20.2), providing easy access to both local and online templates as well as recently used files.

FIGURE 20.2

PowerPoint 2013 opens with a Start screen that offers links to templates and recent files.

Improved shape merging

If you have ever tried to create anything with the drawing tools in an Office app, you know that it can be frustrating because the shapes provided don't always match the shapes you want. Office 2013's drawing tools contain several new commands and capabilities that make the process of creating just the right shapes much easier. You can find the Merge Shapes button on the Insert Shapes group of the Drawing Tools ⇨ Format tab when two or more shapes are selected. Clicking Merge Shapes opens a menu of merge types.

These new commands are all focused around merging two or more shapes into a single shape, using actions like Union, Combine, Intersect, Fragment, and Subtract. For example, suppose you want a shape that consists of a rounded rectangle with two arrows emerging from it. You could start with the three separate shapes shown at the left in Figure 20.3 and then use the Union command to join them into a single shape, as shown on the right.

20

FIGURE 20.3

Drawn shapes, before and after merging

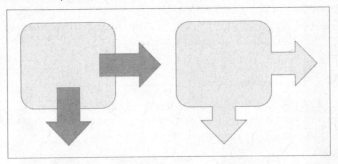

Improved Smart Guides

PowerPoint 2013 makes it easier than ever to precisely align and evenly space objects with one another. When you drag an object to position it, dotted guidelines called Smart Guides (or alignment guides) appear, showing its relationship to other objects on the slide and allowing you to easily snap the object into precise alignment and spacing. Earlier versions of PowerPoint had alignment commands, but you had to specifically issue them; Smart Guides present themselves automatically whenever they might be needed. Figure 20.4 shows an example. Smart Guides are covered in Chapter 24, "Using SmartArt Diagrams, Clip Art, and Pictures."

FIGURE 20.4

Alignment guides make it easier to align objects and text on slides.

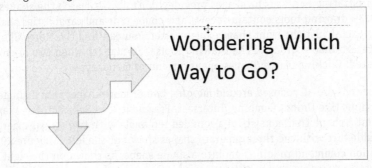

You can also create permanent drawing guides on the slide masters, making it easier to position content on slide masters and layout masters. Chapter 22, "Working with Layouts, Themes, and Masters," covers modifying slide masters.

Improved comments

PowerPoint has included a Comments feature in the past, but it hasn't been very robust. In PowerPoint 2013, there is a Comments pane that you can use in Normal view to display and manage comments. See Figure 20.5. Comments in PowerPoint work much like comments in Word, as described in Chapter 11, "Managing Document Security, Comments, and Tracked Changes."

FIGURE 20.5

The Comments pane helps you display and respond to comments.

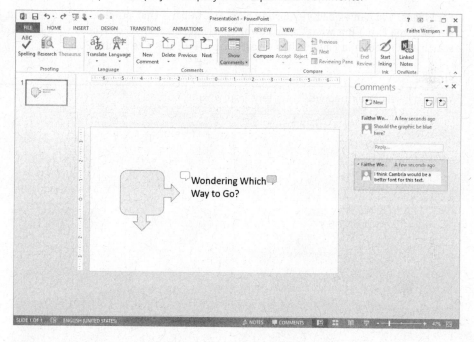

SkyDrive integration

SkyDrive is Microsoft's online file storage service. Each user gets a certain amount of free space there, and you can purchase additional space.

In Office 2013 apps, you can save directly to the logged-in user's SkyDrive, making it as easy to save files to your SkyDrive as it is to save to any local folder on your hard disk. Files saved to SkyDrive are private and secure, and you can access them from any Internet-connected computing device, no matter where you are. For more information about SkyDrive, see Chapter 39.

20

Online pictures and videos

PowerPoint 2013, like other Office 2013 applications, includes integration with online picture and video sharing services such as YouTube and Flickr, enabling you to easily access your own and other people's online content for use in your presentations.

Microsoft's clip art collection is now accessed entirely online from Office.com and is licensed for you to use for most purposes. You can also easily import pictures from your own SkyDrive and from a Bing image search. To help you avoid copyright problems, by default, the Bing image search returns only results licensed under Creative Commons (a public user license; you will need to check the terms of use for specific images you want to use).

For videos, you can embed video code from any website that provides it. (PowerPoint 2010 also allowed this.) But what's new now is that you can search for videos with Bing video search and select and embed clips directly from YouTube. See Figure 20.6.

FIGURE 20.6

You can insert or embed video content from online sources.

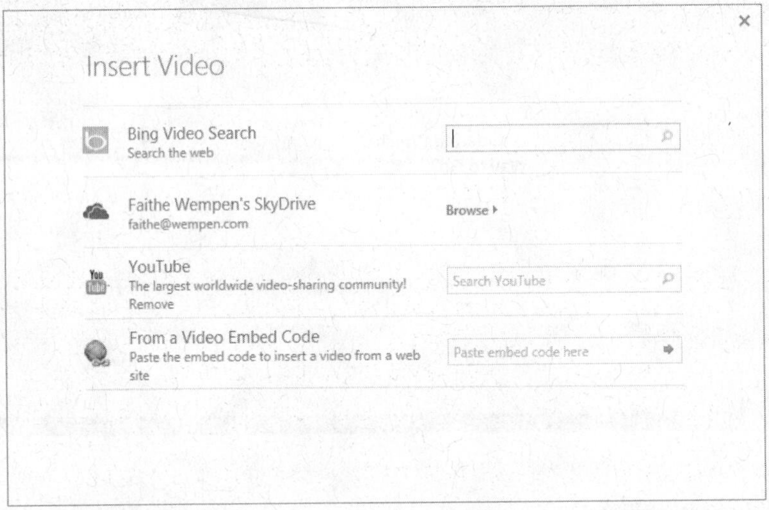

Improved presenter tools

PowerPoint 2013 improves on-screen presentation capabilities in several ways. First, the tools available to you in Slide Show view are now more robust, including the ability to zoom in on a particular area of a slide and to select a slide to jump to from an array of thumbnail images.

Presenter view can now be viewed on one monitor, allowing you to rehearse without connecting anything else. Presenter view has also been enhanced, with extra display settings and easier-to-use slide controls. See Figure 20.7.

FIGURE 20.7

Presenter view is now easier to use.

. . . And other new features

Besides the features I've just outlined, there are plenty more nice surprises awaiting upgraders:

- **Theme variants:** For many years now, PowerPoint users have complained that the templates PowerPoint provides are not customizable enough. For example, what if a certain template has a perfect background graphic but the colors are all wrong? PowerPoint 2013 solves this by providing color variants for many of the built-in themes.

- **Touch controls:** All of the Office 2013 apps, including PowerPoint, are more easily controlled with touch screens than their predecessors. You can use PowerPoint 2013 in the traditional way, with a mouse, or by pointing, tapping, swiping, and dragging on a touch screen.

- **Eyedropper tool:** Some graphics programs enable you to use an Eyedropper tool to pick up a color from one object and copy that color to another object. Now you can do that in Office applications too. For example, you could pick up a color from a photograph on a slide and apply it to the text on the slide so that everything matches. This is great for matching colors for themes. You'll find the Eyedropper tool on the Shape Fill and Shape Outline buttons' menus on the Drawing Tools Format tab when working with shapes.

- **MP4 support:** PowerPoint 2010 was revolutionary in that it allowed users to create their own video versions of their presentations. However, only one video format

20

was supported. PowerPoint 2013 adds MP4 support, making the resulting videos much more widely shareable because MP4 is one of the most common video formats for online use. You can still save your presentation to the Windows Media Video (.wmv) format, too.

■ **Welcome Back:** When you reopen a presentation that you were previously working on, the last slide you were editing automatically reappears. This is essentially the same as the Resume Reading feature in Word 2013.

Starting and Exiting PowerPoint

Now that you have seen some of the potential uses for PowerPoint and toured the new features, let's get started using the program.

You can start PowerPoint just as you would any other program in Windows: from the Start screen (in Windows 8) or the Start menu (in Windows 7). Office 2013 runs only under those two desktop operating systems (as well as a couple of the server versions, which are not being covered in this book).

In Windows 8:

1. **Press the Windows logo key, ⊞, on the keyboard to display the Start screen; or on a touch screen, swipe in from the right and tap Start.** The Windows Start screen appears.

2. **Scroll to the right if needed to find the PowerPoint 2013 tile, and click or tap it.** The program starts.

In Windows 7:

1. **Click the Start button.** The Start menu opens.

2. **Click All Programs.**

3. **Click Microsoft Office.**

4. **Click PowerPoint 2013.** The program starts.

When PowerPoint 2013 opens, its own Start screen appears, as you saw back in Figure 20.2, offering help for opening existing files or starting new ones. If you want to bypass the Start screen and jump immediately to a new blank presentation (as in earlier versions of PowerPoint), just press the Esc key.

> **TIP**
>
> If you want quick access to PowerPoint from the Windows 8 Desktop, add a shortcut to PowerPoint to the taskbar. To do so, right-click the PowerPoint 2013 tile on the Start screen and click Pin to taskbar. From then on, you can start PowerPoint by clicking the PowerPoint 2013 icon on the taskbar.

When you are ready to leave PowerPoint, click the Close (X) button in the top-right corner of the PowerPoint window. If you have any unsaved work, PowerPoint asks if you want to save your changes. Because you have just been playing around in this chapter, you probably do not have anything to save yet. (If you do have something to save, see "Saving Your Work" in Chapter 21 and Chapter 3, "Mastering Fundamental Operations," to learn more about saving.) Click No to decline to save your changes, and you're outta there.

> **NOTE**
> Chapter 2, "Navigating in Office," explains how to use the various screen elements in PowerPoint and other Office applications.

Changing the View

A *view* is a way of displaying your presentation on-screen. PowerPoint comes with several views because at different times during the creation process, it is helpful to look at the presentation in different ways. For example, when you add a graphic to a slide, you need to work closely with that slide, but when you rearrange the slide order, you need to see the presentation as a whole.

PowerPoint offers the following presentation views:

- **Normal:** A combination of several resizable panes so you can see the presentation in multiple ways at once. Normal is the default view.

- **Outline:** A variant of Normal view in which slide content appears as a text outline in the left pane rather than as graphical slide thumbnails. This view is available only from the View tab.

- **Slide Sorter:** A light-table-type overhead view of all the slides in your presentation, laid out in sections and rows, suitable for big-picture rearranging.

- **Slide Show:** The view you use to show the presentation on-screen. Each slide fills the entire screen in its turn. This view is not available from the View tab, but it is available in several other places, including in the status bar and in the Quick Access Toolbar.

- **Reading:** Similar to Slide Show view, except it's windowed and the status bar remains in view. You can use Reading view to check your work as if you were showing the slide show but still retain access to certain commands.

- **Notes Page:** A view with the slide at the top of the page and a text box below it for typed notes. (You can print these notes pages to use during your speech.) This view is available only from the View tab.

20

> **NOTE**
>
> This chapter covers only the presentation views (that is, regular views in which you can see the individual content of each slide). The master views are discussed in Chapter 22; master views enable you to make global changes to many slides at once.

There are two ways to change a view: Click a button in the Presentation Views group of the View tab, or click one of the view buttons at the right end of the status bar at the bottom of the screen, shown in Figure 20.8. Not every view is available in both places.

FIGURE 20.8

Select a view from the View tab or from the viewing controls in the bottom-right corner of the screen.

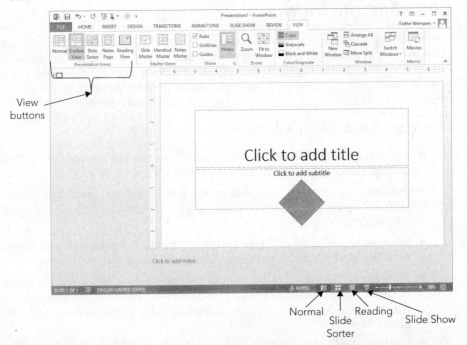

> **TIP**
>
> When you save, close, and reopen a file, PowerPoint opens it in the view in which you left the file. To have the files always open in a particular view, choose File ➪ Options ➪ Advanced, and in the Display section, click the drop-down arrow on the Open All Documents Using This View list and select the desired view. The options on this list include some custom versions of Normal view that have certain panes turned off. For example, you can open all documents in Normal — Slide Only to always start in Normal view with just the main editing pane open.

Normal and Outline views

Normal view, shown in Figure 20.9, is a very flexible view that contains a little bit of everything. In the center is the Slide pane, where the active slide appears; and to its left is the Thumbnails pane, containing a set of thumbnail images that represent the presentation's slides.

FIGURE 20.9

Normal view, the default, shows slide thumbnails at the left and an editing window at the right.

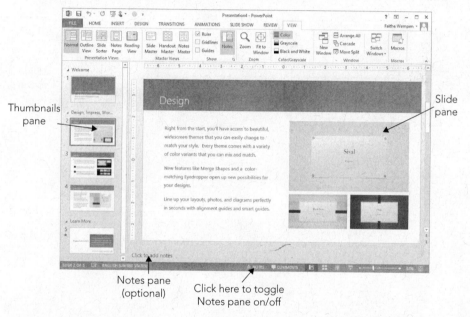

Outline view (shown in Figure 20.10) is identical to Normal view except instead of the slide thumbnails on the left, you see a text outline. (Note that the outline omits any sections created in the presentation.)

An optional Notes pane is available at the bottom of the window; click Notes on the status bar to display or hide it. An optional Comments pane appears and disappears on the right when you click Comments on the status bar.

Each of the panes in Normal view has its own scroll bar, so you can move in it independently of the other panes. You can resize the panes by dragging the dividers between the panes. For example, to give the notes area more room, point the mouse pointer at the

20

divider line between it and the slide area so that the mouse pointer becomes a double-headed arrow, and then hold down the left mouse button as you drag the line up to a new spot. To get the Thumbnails (or Outline) pane out of the way, drag the divider between it and the slide editing pane as far as possible to the left.

The left pane is useful because it lets you jump quickly to a specific slide by clicking its thumbnail (Normal view) or some of its text content (Outline view).

FIGURE 20.10

Outline view shows a text outline at the left and an editing window at the right.

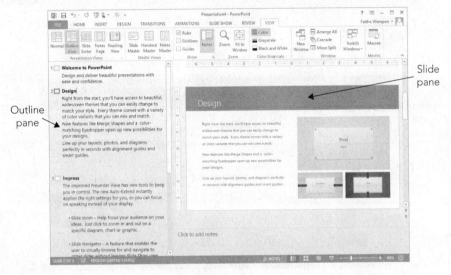

Slide Sorter view

If you have ever worked with hard copies of slides, such as 35mm slides, you know that it can be helpful to lay the slides out on a big table and plan the order in which to show them. You rearrange them, moving this one here, that one there, until the order is perfect. You might even start a pile of backups that you will not show in the main presentation but will hold back in case someone asks a pertinent question. That's exactly what you can do with Slide Sorter view, as shown in Figure 20.11. It lays out the slides in miniature, so you can see the big picture. You can drag the slides around and place them in the perfect order. You can also return to Normal view to work on a slide by double-clicking the slide.

FIGURE 20.11

Use the Slide Sorter view for a bird's-eye view of the presentation.

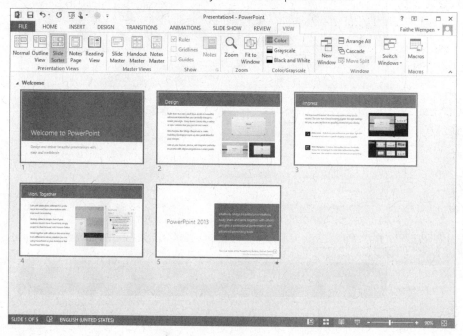

Slide Show view and Reading views

When it's time to rehearse the presentation, nothing shows you the finished product quite as clearly as Slide Show view does. In Slide Show view, the slide fills the entire screen. You can move from slide to slide by pressing the Page Up and Page Down keys or by using one of the other movement methods available (covered in Chapter 26).

Notice in Figure 20.12 the black bars above and below the slide. The default slide dimensions in PowerPoint 2013 are set for a wide-screen monitor (16:9 aspect ratio). If you are using a regular monitor (4:3) but showing wide-screen slides, black bars fill in the extra space at the top and bottom. You can correct this problem by changing the slide size on the Design tab. When you change the slide size, PowerPoint prompts you to specify how to adjust the existing content to fit the new format.

20

FIGURE 20.12

Slide Show view lets you practice the presentation in real life.

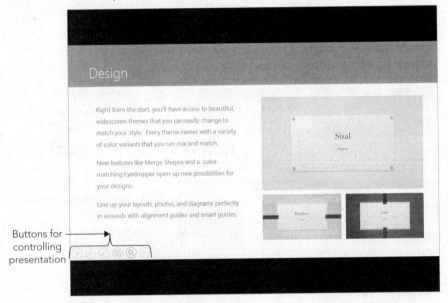

When you move your mouse in Slide Show view, buttons appear in the bottom-left corner for controlling the show without leaving it. To leave the slide show, choose End Show from the menu or just press the Esc key.

> **TIP**
>
> When entering Slide Show view, the method you use determines which slide you start on. If you use the Slide Show View button in the bottom-right corner of the screen, the presentation will start with whatever slide you have selected. (You can also press Shift+F5 to do this or choose Slide Show ⇨ From Current Slide.) If you use the Slide Show ⇨ Start Slide Show ⇨ From Beginning command, or press F5, the presentation will start at the beginning.

Reading view is like Slide Show view except it runs within the PowerPoint app window rather than full screen and it doesn't have the powerful slide show tools that you get with Slide Show view (covered in Chapter 18), such as the ability to draw on a slide or skip to a certain slide. You still see the PowerPoint application's title bar, and you still see the status bar at the bottom. You can move between slides by clicking with the mouse or by using the arrow keys on the keyboard. As with Slide Show view, you can exit from Reading view by pressing Esc to return to the previously accessed view.

Notes Page view

When you give a presentation, your props usually include more than just your brain and your slides. You typically have all kinds of notes and backup material for each slide — figures on last quarter's sales, sources to cite if someone questions your data, and so on. In the old days of framed overhead transparencies, people used to attach sticky notes to the slide frames for this purpose and hope that nobody asked any questions that required diving into the four-inch-thick stack of statistics they brought.

Today, you can type your notes and supporting facts directly in PowerPoint. As you saw earlier, you can type them directly into the Notes pane below the slide in Normal or Outline view. Just click the Notes button in the status bar to display the Notes pane, and start typing away. However, if you have a lot of notes to type, you might find it easier to work with Notes Page view instead.

Notes Page view is accessible only from the View tab. In this view, you see a single slide (uneditable) with an editable text area below it called the *notes placeholder*, which you can use to type your notes. See Figure 20.13. You can refer to these notes as you give an on-screen presentation, or you can print notes pages to stack neatly on the lectern next to you during the big event. If your notes pages run off the end of the page, PowerPoint even prints them as a separate page. If you have trouble seeing the text you're typing, zoom in on it, as described in the next section.

FIGURE 20.13

Notes Page view offers a special text area for your notes, separate from the slides.

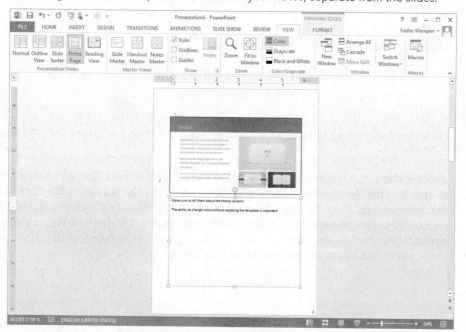

Zooming In and Out

If you need a closer look at your presentation, you can zoom the view in or out to accommodate almost any situation. For example, if you have trouble placing a graphic exactly at the same vertical level as some text in a box next to it, you can zoom in for more precision. (The new Smart Guides feature in PowerPoint 2013 helps with that situation too.) You can view your work at various magnifications on-screen without changing the size of the surrounding tools or the size of the print on the printout.

In Normal view, each of the panes has its own individual zoom. To set the zoom for the Thumbnails pane only, for example, select it first; then choose a zoom level. Or to zoom only in the Slide pane (the main editing pane), click it first. In a single-pane view, such as Notes Page or Slide Sorter, a single zoom setting affects the entire work area.

The larger the zoom number, the larger the details on the display. A zoom of 10% would make a slide so tiny that you couldn't read it. A zoom of 400% would make a few letters on a slide so big they would fill the entire pane.

An easy way to set the zoom level is to drag the Zoom slider in the status bar, or click its plus or minus buttons to change the zoom level in increments, as shown in Figure 20.14. You can also hold down the Ctrl key and roll the scroll wheel on your mouse, if it has one.

FIGURE 20.14

Zoom in or out to see more or less of the slide(s) at once.

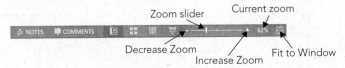

To resize the current slide so that it is as large as possible while still fitting completely in the Slides pane, click the Fit Slide to Current Window button, or Choose View➪Zoom➪Fit to Window.

Another way to control the zoom is with the Zoom dialog box. Choose View➪Zoom➪Zoom to open it. (You can also open that dialog box by clicking the % next to the Zoom slider in the lower-right corner of the screen.) Make your selection, as shown in Figure 20.15, by clicking the appropriate button, and then click OK. Notice that you can type a precise zoom percentage in the Percent text box. You can specify any percentage you like, up to 400%. (Some panes and views will not go higher than 100%.)

FIGURE 20.15

You can zoom with this Zoom dialog box rather than the slider if you prefer.

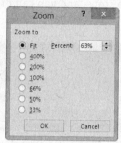

Enabling Optional Display Elements

PowerPoint has a lot of optional screen elements that you may (or may not) find useful, depending on what you're up to at the moment. The following sections describe them.

Ruler

Vertical and horizontal rulers around the Slide pane can help you place objects more precisely. To toggle them on or off, select or deselect the Ruler check box in the show group of the View tab, as shown in Figure 20.16. Rulers are available only in Normal, Outline, and Notes Page views.

FIGURE 20.16

Rulers and gridlines help position objects on a slide.

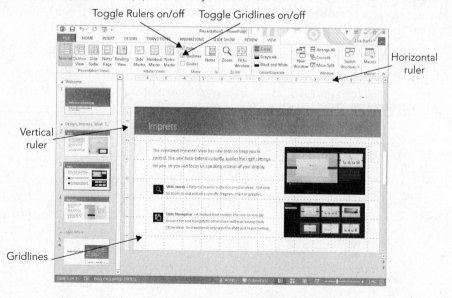

The rulers help with positioning no matter what content type you are working with, but when you are editing text in a text frame they have an additional purpose. The horizontal ruler shows the frame's paragraph indents and any custom tab stops, and you can drag the indent markers on the ruler just as you can in Word.

NOTE

The ruler's unit of measure is controlled from Regional Settings in Control Panel in Windows. Choose Clock, Language, and Region, and then click the Region heading (or Region and Language in Windows 7) to open the Region (or Region and Language) dialog box. On the Formats tab, click Additional settings and choose U.S. or Metric from the Measurement system drop-down list.

TIP

The display of the vertical ruler is optional. To disable it while retaining the horizontal ruler, choose File ⇨ Options, click Advanced, and in the Display section, clear the Show vertical ruler check box.

Gridlines

Gridlines are nonprinting dotted lines at regularly spaced intervals that can help you line up objects on a slide. Figure 20.16 shows gridlines (and the ruler) enabled.

To turn gridlines on or off, use either of these methods:

- Press Shift+F9.
- On the View tab, in the Show group, select or deselect the Gridlines check box.

There are many options you can set for the gridlines, including whether objects snap to it, whether the grid is visible, and what the spacing should be between the gridlines. To set grid options, follow these steps:

1. **On the View tab, click the dialog box launcher in the Show group.** The Grid and Guides dialog box opens (see Figure 20.17).

FIGURE 20.17

Set grid options and spacing.

2. **In the Snap to section, select or deselect the Snap objects to grid check box.** This setting specifies whether or not objects will automatically align with the grid.

3. **In the Grid settings section, enter the amount of space you want between gridlines.**

4. **Select or deselect the Display grid on screen check box to display or hide the grid.** (Note that you can make objects snap to the grid without the grid being displayed.)

5. **Click OK.**

Guides

Guides are like gridlines except they are individual lines, rather than a grid of lines, and you can drag them to different positions on the slide. As you drag a guide, a numeric indicator appears to let you know the ruler position, as shown in Figure 20.18. Use the Grid and Guides dialog box shown in Figure 20.17 to turn guides on/off, or press Alt+F9.

FIGURE 20.18

Guides are movable, nonprinting lines that help with alignment.

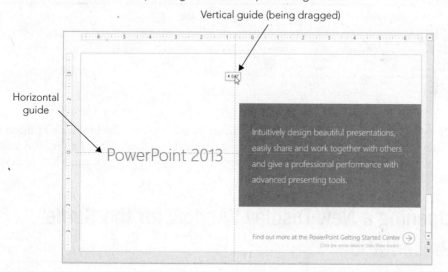

You can create additional sets of guide lines by holding down the Ctrl key while dragging a guide (to copy it). You can have as many horizontal and vertical guides as you like, all at positions you specify. You can also save your custom guides (new in PowerPoint 2013).

Color/Grayscale/Pure Black and White views

Most of the time you will work with your presentation in color. However, if you plan to print the presentation in black and white or grayscale (for example, on black-and-white handouts), you should check to see what it will look like without color.

> **TIP**
>
> This Color/Grayscale/Pure Black and White option is especially useful when you are preparing slides that will eventually be faxed because a fax is pure black and white in most cases. Something that looks great on a color screen could look like a shapeless blob on a black-and-white fax. It doesn't hurt to check.

Click the Grayscale or the Black and White button in the Color/Grayscale group of the View tab to switch to one of those views. When you do so, a Grayscale or Black and White tab becomes available. The Grayscale tab is shown in Figure 20.19. From its Change Selected Object group, you can fine-tune the grayscale or black-and-white preview. Choose one that shows the object to best advantage; PowerPoint will remember that setting when printing or outputting the presentation to a grayscale or black-and-white source.

FIGURE 20.19

Select a grayscale or a black-and-white preview type.

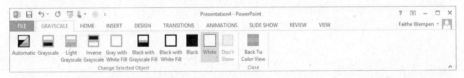

When you are finished, click the Back to Color View button on the Grayscale or Black and White tab. Changing the Black and White or Grayscale settings doesn't affect the colors on the slides; it only affects how the slides will look and print in black and white or grayscale.

Opening a New Display Window for the Same Presentation

Have you ever wished you could be in two places at once? Well, in PowerPoint, you actually can. PowerPoint provides a way to view two spots in the presentation at the same time by opening a new window.

To display a new window, display the View tab and click New Window in the Window group. Then use Arrange All or Cascade to view both windows at once.

You can use any view with any window, so you can have two slides in Normal view at once, or Slide Sorter and Notes Pages view, or any other combination. Both windows contain the same presentation, so any changes you make in one window are reflected in the other window.

Arranging windows

When you have two or more windows open, whether they are for the same presentation or different ones, you need to arrange them for optimal viewing. You saw earlier in this chapter how to resize a window, but did you know that PowerPoint can do some of the arranging for you?

When you want to arrange the open windows, do one of the following:

- **Tile the windows.** On the View tab in the Window group, click Arrange All to tile the open windows so there is no overlap.
- **Cascade the windows.** On the View tab in the Window group, click Cascade to arrange the open windows so that the title bars cascade from upper left to lower right on the screen. Click a title bar to activate a window.

These commands do not apply to minimized windows. If you want to include a window in the arrangement, make sure you restore it from its minimized state first.

Switching among windows

If you have more than one window open and can see at least a corner of the window you want, click it to bring it to the front. If you have one of the windows maximized, on the other hand, or if another window is obscuring the one you want, click Switch Windows (in the Window group of the View tab) and select the window you want to view.

Summary

This chapter provided an introduction to PowerPoint. You learned about PowerPoint 2013's new features, and now know how to:

- Start and exit PowerPoint.
- Navigate the user interface.
- Choose the best view for the type of work you need to do on the presentation.
- Work with other display features, such as zooming and rulers.
- Work with multiple open presentation windows.

20

Creating a Presentation, Slides, and Text

IN THIS CHAPTER

Starting a new presentation

Saving your work

Setting passwords for file access

Closing and reopening presentations

Creating new slides

Inserting content from external sources

Managing slides

Using content placeholders

Creating text boxes manually

Working with text boxes

I f you're an experienced Windows and PowerPoint user, starting new presentations and saving files may be second nature to you. If so — great! You may not need this chapter. On the other hand, if you aren't entirely certain about some of the finer points, such as saving in different formats or locations, stick around.

Even people who consider themselves "advanced" users may benefit from this chapter because it looks at some of the unique advanced saving features of Office applications and explains how to secure files with passwords.

In this chapter, you'll learn how to build a simple text-based presentation by creating new slides and entering text on them. You'll learn how to import content from other programs, and how to create, size, and position text boxes to hold the text for your presentation.

Starting a New Presentation

You can start a blank presentation, or you can base the new presentation on a template or on another presentation. Using a template or existing presentation can save you some time. However, if you have a specific vision you're going for, starting a presentation from scratch gives you a clean canvas to work from.

Starting a blank presentation

When you open PowerPoint, a Start screen appears. From here you can click Blank Presentation, as shown in Figure 21.1, or you can just press Esc at the Start screen to access a blank presentation.

FIGURE 21.1

Use the Blank Presentation tile on the Start screen to start a new presentation.

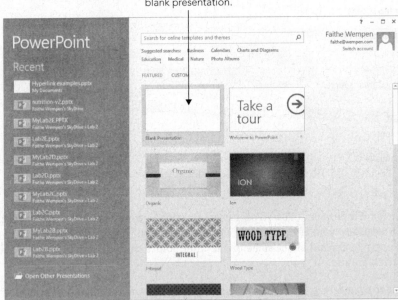

If you want to start a blank presentation at some time other than when you start up PowerPoint, you can do the following:

1. **Choose File ⇨ New.** The same selection of templates and themes appears as in Figure 21.1.

2. **Click Blank Presentation.**

TIP

Press the Ctrl+N shortcut key to start a new blank presentation.

A new blank presentation begins automatically with one slide. Just add your content to it, add more slides if needed, change the formatting (as you'll learn in upcoming chapters), and go for it.

Starting a presentation from a template

A *template* is a file that contains starter settings — and sometimes starter content — on which you can base new presentations. Templates vary in their exact offerings but can include sample slides, a background graphic, custom color and font themes, and custom positioning for object placeholders.

The sample templates stored on your computer (such as the Welcome to PowerPoint template shown in Figure 21.1) appear as tiles on the Start screen along with tiles for the themes and on the New screen when you choose File ➪ New, as in the preceding section. You can click whichever one you want to use.

Only a few sample templates are stored on your hard disk because Microsoft assumes that most people have an always-on Internet connection these days. When you are connected to the Internet, you can access the complete Office.com library of template files. Use the Search for online templates and themes box to search for templates in a particular category or with certain keywords associated with them.

Follow these steps to locate a template and use it to start a new presentation:

1. **Choose File ➪ New.**
2. **In the Search for online templates and themes box, type a keyword or phrase to search for and press Enter, or click one of the category links on the Suggested searches line below the Search box.** See Figure 21.2. A list of templates appears that match your criteria.

FIGURE 21.2

Search for templates by keyword or click a category.

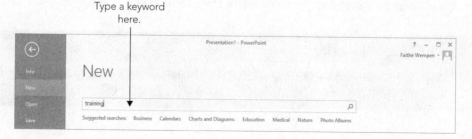

673

3. **Click a template to see a preview of it, as shown in Figure 21.3.**

FIGURE 21.3

Preview a template before selecting it.

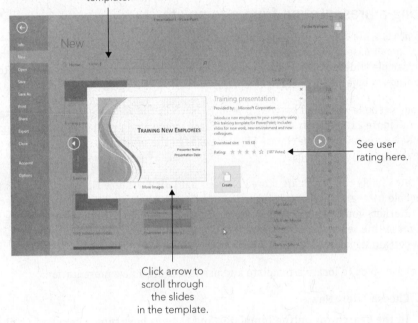

Click away from the pop-up window to close it without selecting this template.

See user rating here.

Click arrow to scroll through the slides in the template.

4. **Click Create.** A new presentation is created based on that template.

Using a personal template

In the section, "Saving in a different format," later in this chapter, you will learn how to save a presentation file in template format so you can use it as a basis for new presentations. These are called *personal templates* in PowerPoint 2013.

> **NOTE**
>
> For PowerPoint to find your personal templates, you must tell it where they are stored. To do so, choose File ⇨ Options, click the Save tab, and then enter the path to that location in the Default personal templates location text box. Then click OK.

When you specify a default location for personal templates or download or create and save a template, the New screen has two categories below the suggested searches: Featured and Personal (or Custom). Personal appears if you have not specified a Workgroup Templates location (covered later in this chapter), and Custom appears instead if you have done so.

You can click Personal or Custom to see the locations that hold your own personal templates and themes. The Document Themes folder appears here (you'll learn more about it in Chapter 22, "Working with Layouts, Themes, and Masters") and also whatever folder you specified as the default personal templates location (see the preceding note). In addition, if you have specified a Workgroup Templates location, that folder appears here too.

To access your personal templates, follow these steps:

1. **Choose File ⇨ New.**
2. **Click Personal or click Custom.** An icon appears for the location you have defined as your personal template folder as well as an icon for Document Themes. There may also be a Workgroup Templates folder shown. See Figure 21.4.

FIGURE 21.4

Choose Personal or Custom to see your personal template location.

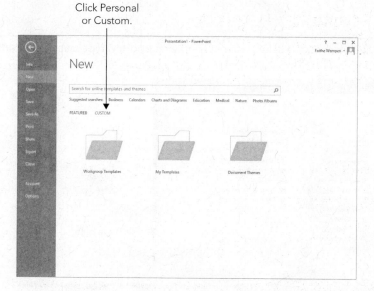

3. **Click the icon for your personal template folder (My Templates).** Thumbnails appear for your personal templates.
4. **Click the desired personal template.** A new presentation opens based on that template.

Basing a new presentation on existing content

If you already have a presentation that's similar to the new one you need to create, you can base the new presentation on the existing one. To do so, open the existing presentation and then use Save As (covered in the next section, "Saving Your Work") to save it under a new name.

PowerPoint can open files in several formats other than its own, so you can start a new presentation based on some work you have done elsewhere. For example, you can open a Word outline in PowerPoint. The results might not be very attractive, but you can fix that later with some text editing, slide layouts, and design changes.

To open a file from another application, do the following:

1. **Choose File ⇨ Open.** The Open screen appears.
2. **Click Computer.**
3. **Click Browse.** The Open dialog box appears.
4. **Click the File Type button (currently set to All PowerPoint Presentations) and choose the file type.** For example, to open a text file, choose All Outlines, as shown in Figure 21.5.

FIGURE 21.5

By changing the file type you can select a file of another supported type, such as an outline document.

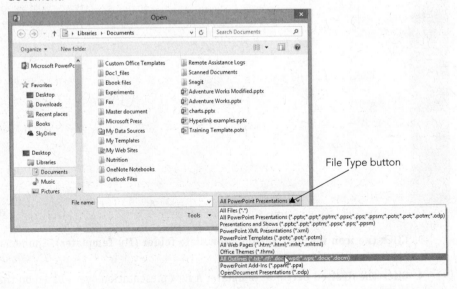

5. **Navigate to the location containing the file you want to open.**

6. **Select the desired file, and then click Open.**

7. **Save your work as a PowerPoint file by choosing File ⇨ Save As.**

See the next section for more information about saving.

Saving Your Work

PowerPoint is typical of most Windows programs in the way that it saves and opens files. The entire PowerPoint presentation is saved in a single file incorporating any graphics, charts, or other elements. The first time you save a presentation, PowerPoint prompts you for a name and location. Thereafter, when you save that presentation, PowerPoint uses the same settings and does not prompt you for them again.

Understanding save locations

Where can you save your files? You can save files in any location on your local hard disk, on a removable drive such as a USB flash drive, to a network location, to your SkyDrive, or to a SharePoint server, just to name a few. A more pertinent question is, where *should* you save your files? That depends on your situation.

In most Office 2013 apps, the default save location is your SkyDrive. Your SkyDrive is a free online storage location that Microsoft provides to anyone who wants it. (You don't even have to be a Windows or Office user.) Your SkyDrive is available no matter what computer you are logged into, as long as you have an Internet connection, so it's a good choice for people who have multiple PCs that they alternate between. See Chapter 39 for more information about saving to your SkyDrive.

The main drawback to using your SkyDrive is that if your Internet connection isn't available, neither are your files. People with intermittent or inconsistent Internet service may want to store files on the local hard drive, where they are always available. Saving to your Documents library is a safe bet, but you can also create your own folders on your hard drive and save there.

If you have a local network in your home or office, you might have a central file storage location on that network. For example, all the people in your department might save their files to the same network share so that the files are available to everyone at all times. Some companies maintain SharePoint servers for file sharing; others just make network drives and folders available to all the users who need them.

If you want local portability, consider saving to a removable drive such as a USB flash drive or an external hard drive. You can then plug the storage device into some other computer whenever you need file transport, and you don't have to worry about a network or Internet connection being available.

Saving for the first time

If you haven't previously saved the presentation you are working on, Save and Save As do the same thing: They open the Save As screen. From there, you can specify a name, file type, and file location. Follow these steps:

1. **Choose File ⇨ Save.** The Save As screen appears. Your SkyDrive is selected by default, as shown in Figure 21.6.

FIGURE 21.6

The Save As screen

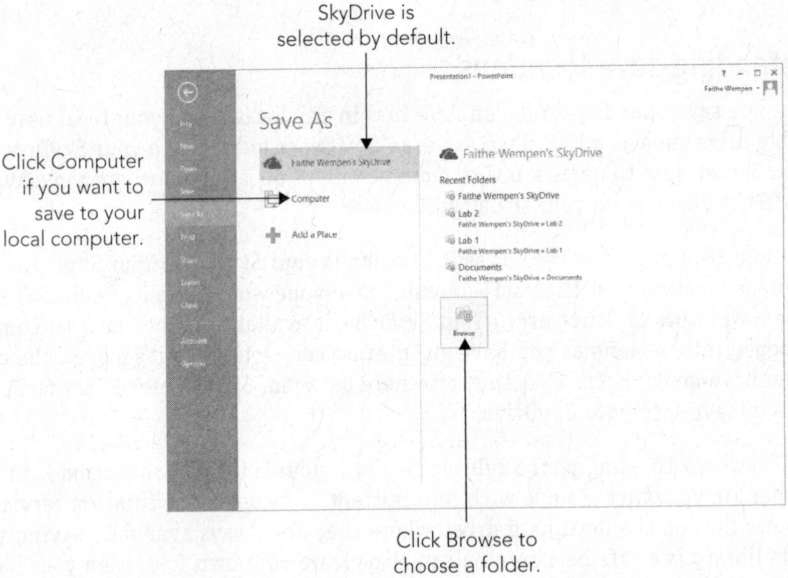

SkyDrive is
selected by default.

Click Computer
if you want to
save to your
local computer.

Click Browse to
choose a folder.

2. **(Optional) If you want to save to your Documents library, click Computer.**

TIP

Each user has a Documents library, which is a composite location that represents multiple actual folders. If you save to the Documents library, the file is actually saved in the default storage location for the library, which is `C:\Users\user name\My Documents`.

3. **Click the Browse button. The Save As dialog box opens.**

21

> **NOTE**
>
> To save in a different location than your SkyDrive or computer, see the section "Changing drives and folders" later in this chapter. To save in a different format, see the section "Saving in a different format."

4. **In the File name box, type the name you want to use for the presentation, replacing the placeholder name that appears there.** See Figure 21.7.

FIGURE 21.7

The Save As dialog box

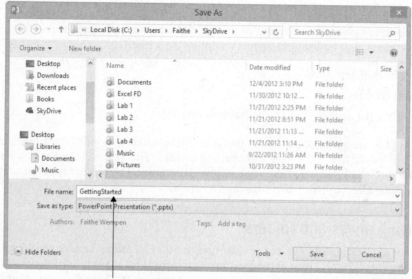

Type the desired
file name here.

5. **Click Save.** The file is saved.

File names can be up to 255 characters. For practical purposes, however, keep the names short. You can include spaces in the file names and most symbols except <, >, ?, *, /, and \. However, if you plan to post the file on a network or the Internet at some point, you should avoid using spaces; use the underscore character instead to simulate a space, if necessary. File names that include exclamation points also cause problems, so beware of that. Generally, it is best to avoid punctuation marks in file names.

TIP

If you want to transfer your presentation file to a different computer and show it from there, and that other computer does not have the same fonts as yours, you should embed the fonts in your presentation so that the desired fonts are available on the other PC. To embed fonts from the Save As dialog box, click the Tools button, choose Save Options, and under Preserve fidelity when sharing this presentation click Embed fonts in the file check box to check it, and click OK. This option makes the saved file larger than normal, so choose it only when necessary. For more information on advanced saving features, see the section "Specifying save options."

Saving subsequent times

After you have saved a presentation once, you can resave it with the same settings (same file type, name, and location) in any of the following ways:

- Choose File ⇨ Save.
- Press Ctrl+S.
- Click the Save button on the Quick Access Toolbar.

If you need to save your presentation under a different name, as a different file type, or in a different location, use the Save As command instead. This reopens the Save As screen, as in the preceding steps, so that you can save differently. The originally saved copy will remain under the original name, type, and location.

Changing drives and folders

The Office applications enable you to save files to other locations besides your SkyDrive or the Documents library. These other locations can include local hard disk folders, USB flash drives and other flash media, other hard disks in the same PC, hard disks on other PCs in a network, hard disks on web servers on the Internet, or writeable CDs or DVDs.

The Navigation pane on the left side of the Save As dialog box is home to several collapsible/expandable categories. Double-click a category to open it and then make selections from within it (see Figure 21.8). You can choose from the following categories:

- **Favorites:** Shortcuts for popular locations such as Downloads and Desktop appear in the Favorites list, and you can also add your own shortcuts here.
- **Libraries:** Libraries are virtual folders that organize locations by the types of files they contain. Double-click Libraries and then click through a category such as Documents or Pictures.

FIGURE 21.8

The Save As dialog box contains a number of shortcuts for navigation in the left pane.

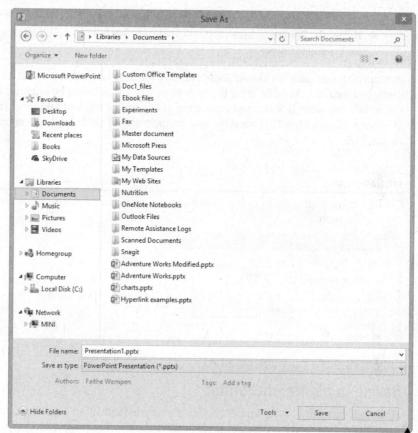

Drag corner
of dialog box
to resize it
if desired.

- **Homegroup:** Windows 7 and 8 have a home networking feature called Homegroup; if you use it to set up your network, you can browse other network computers by clicking here.

- **Computer:** Browse the complete drive and folder listing for your local PC here.

- **Network:** Browse to local network locations such as the folders on a networked external hard disk.

You can also navigate via the Address bar. The Address bar shows the path to the currently displayed location. You can jump directly to any of those levels by clicking the name there. You can also click the right-pointing arrow to the right of any level to see a menu of other folders within that location and jump to any of them from the menu, as shown in Figure 21.9.

FIGURE 21.9

Click an arrow on the Address bar to see a menu of locations at the chosen level within the current path.

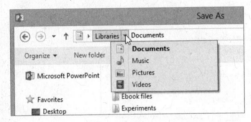

Saving in a different format

All PowerPoint 2007, 2010, and 2013 files save by default in an XML-based file format called PowerPoint Presentation (*.pptx). eXtensible Markup Language (XML) is a text-based coding system similar to HTML that describes formatting by using inline bracketed codes and style sheets. XML-based data files are smaller than the data files from earlier PowerPoint versions, and they support all of the latest PowerPoint features. For best results, use this format whenever you don't have a reason to use some other format.

There are also several variants of this format for specialty uses. For example, there's a macro-enabled version with a .pptm filename extension. There are also "show" variants (.ppsx and .ppsm) that open in Slide Show view by default and template variants (.potx and .potm) that function as templates.

Not everyone has PowerPoint 2007 or higher; you might sometimes need to share files with people who have some earlier version of PowerPoint. Users of PowerPoint 2003 can download a compatibility pack that will allow them to accept the new files, but you can't assume that everyone who has an earlier version of PowerPoint will download it. Therefore, you might need to save presentations in other file formats to share files with other people.

The available formats are shown in Table 21.1. In the Save As dialog box, open the Save as type drop-down list and select the desired format, as shown in Figure 21.10.

FIGURE 21.10

Choose a different format, if necessary, from the Save As Type drop-down list.

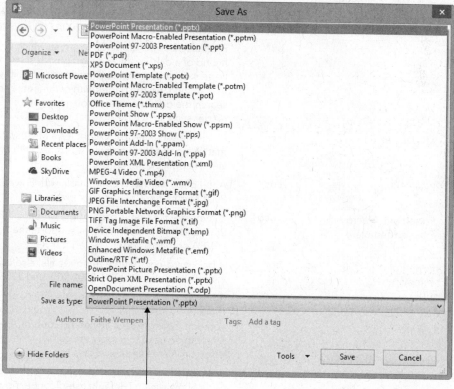

Click here to open
list of file types.

TABLE 21.1   PowerPoint Save As Formats

Presentations		
Format	**File name extension**	**Usage notes**
PowerPoint Presentation	.pptx	The default; use in most cases. Can open only in PowerPoint 2007 and higher (or on an earlier version with compatibility pack installed).
PowerPoint Macro-Enabled Presentation	.pptm	Same as .pptx, except it supports the storage of VBA or macro code.
PowerPoint 97–2003 Presentation	.ppt	A backward-compatible format for sharing files with users of PowerPoint 97, 2000, 2002 (XP), and 2003.
PDF	.pdf	Produces files in Adobe PDF format, which is a hybrid of a document and a graphic. It shows each page exactly as it will be printed and yet allows the user to mark up the pages with comments and to search the document text. You must have a PDF reader such as Adobe Acrobat to view PDF files.
XPS Document	.xps	Much the same as PDF except it's a Microsoft format. Windows Vista and higher comes with an XPS viewer application.
PowerPoint Template	.potx	A template file that is compatible with PowerPoint 2007 and higher.
PowerPoint Macro-Enabled Template	.potm	A template file that is compatible with PowerPoint 2007 and higher and that that supports the storage of VBA or macro code.
PowerPoint 97–2003 Template	.pot	A backward-compatible template file, also usable with PowerPoint 97, 2000, 2002 (XP), and 2003.
Office Theme	.thmx	Somewhat like a template, but it contains only theme settings (fonts, colors, and effects). Use this if you don't want to save any of the content. Theme files can be used to supply the colors, fonts, and effects to Word and Excel files too.
PowerPoint Show	.ppsx	Just like a regular PowerPoint file, except it opens in Slide Show view by default; useful for distributing presentations to the audience on disk.
PowerPoint Macro-Enabled Show	.ppsm	Same as PowerPoint Show (.ppsx), except it supports the storage of VBA or macro code.
PowerPoint 97–2003 Show	.pps	Same as a regular backward-compatible presentation file, except it opens in Slide Show view by default.

PowerPoint Add-In	.ppam	A file that contains executable code (usually VBA) that extends PowerPoint's capabilities.
PowerPoint 97–2003 Add-In	.ppa	Same as PowerPoint Add-In (.ppam), except the add-in is backward compatible.
PowerPoint XML Presentation	.xml	A presentation in XML format, suitable for integrating into an XML information storage system.
Graphics/other		
MPEG-4 Video	.mp4	A video version of the presentation using MPEG-4 format.
Windows Media Video	.wmv	A video version of the presentation using WMV format.
GIF Graphics Interchange Format	.gif	Static graphic. GIFs are limited to 256 colors.
JPEG File Interchange Format	.jpg	Static graphic. JPG files can be very small, making them good for web use. A lossy compression format, so picture quality may not be as good as with a lossless format.
PNG Portable Network Graphics Format	.png	Static graphic. Similar to GIF except without the color depth limitation. Uses lossless compression; takes advantage of the best features of both GIF and JPG.
TIFF Tagged Image File Format	.tif	Static graphic. TIF is a high-quality file format suitable for slides with high-resolution photos. A lossless compression format.
Device Independent Bitmap	.bmp	Static graphic. BMP is the native format for Windows graphics, including Windows background wallpaper.
Windows Metafile	.wmf	Static graphic. A vector-based format, so it can later be resized without distortion. Not Mac compatible.
Enhanced Windows Metafile	.emf	Enhanced version of WMF; not compatible with 16-bit applications. Also vector-based and not Mac compatible.
Outline/RTF	.rtf	Text and text formatting only; excludes all non-text elements. Only text in slide placeholders will be converted to the outline. Text in the Notes area is not included.
PowerPoint Picture Presentation	.pptx	Saves all the slides as pictures and puts them into a new blank presentation.
Strict Open XML Presentation	.pptx	A variant of XML that fully supports the Open XML standard.
OpenDocument Presentation	.odp	A presentation that conforms to the new OpenDocument standard for exchanging data between applications.

> **TIP**
>
> If you consistently want to save in a different format, choose File ⇨ Options ⇨ Save. Then, choose a different format from the Save files in this format drop-down list under Save presentations. This makes your choice the default in the Save as type drop-down list in the Save As dialog box. Not all of the formats are available here; your choices are PowerPoint Presentation (the default), PowerPoint Macro-Enabled Presentation, PowerPoint Presentation 97–2003, Strict Open XML Presentation, and OpenDocument Presentation.

Table 21.1 lists a lot of choices, but don't let that overwhelm you. You have three main decisions to make:

- **PowerPoint 2007–2013 format or backward compatible with PowerPoint 97–2003:** Unless compatibility is essential, go with the newer format because you get access to all of the new features. (See Table 21.2 to learn what you'll lose with backward compatibility.) If you use a backward-compatible format, some of the features described in this book work differently or aren't available at all.

- **Macro enabled or not:** If you plan to create and store macros, use a macro-enabled format; if not, use a file format that does not include macro support, for a slightly safer file (because a file cannot carry viruses if it can't carry macro code).

- **Regular presentation or PowerPoint Show:** The "show" variant starts the presentation in Slide Show view when it is loaded in PowerPoint; that's the only difference between it and a regular presentation. You can build your presentation in a regular format and then save in show format right before distribution. PowerPoint shows can be opened and edited in PowerPoint the same as any other file.

Most of the other choices from Table 21.1 are special-purpose formats and not suitable for everyday use. The following sections explain some of those special file types.

TABLE 21.2 PowerPoint 2013 Features Not Supported in the PowerPoint 97–2003 File Format

Feature	Issues
SmartArt graphics	Converted to uneditable pictures
Charts (except Microsoft Graph charts)	Converted to editable OLE objects, but the chart might appear different
Custom slide layouts	Converted to multiple masters
Drop shadows	Soft shadows converted to hard shadows
Equations	Converted to uneditable pictures
Heading and body fonts	Converted to non-theme formatting

Effects:	Converted to uneditable pictures
■ 2-D or 3-D WordArt text	
■ Gradient outlines for shapes or text	
■ Strikethrough and double-strikethrough	
■ Gradient, picture, and texture fills on text	
■ Soft edges, reflections, some types of shadows	
■ Most 3-D effects	
Themes	Converted to non-theme formatting
Theme colors	Converted to non-theme colors
Theme effects	Converted to non-theme effects
Theme fonts	Converted to non-theme fonts

Saving slides as graphics

If you save your presentation in one of the graphic formats shown in the Graphics/other section of Table 21.1, the result is a series of individually named graphic files, one per slide. (The original presentation continues to exist as a separate file.) If you choose one of these formats, you're asked whether you want to export the current slide only or all slides. If you choose to export all slides, PowerPoint creates a new folder in the selected folder with the same name as the original presentation file and places the graphics files in it.

> **TIP**
>
> The Picture Presentation format does something unique: It converts each slide to an image and then places the images in a new presentation file. This is one way to make sure your slides are not edited by anyone who uses the presentation.

Saving slide text only

If you want to export the text of the slides to some other application, consider the Outline/ RTF format, which creates an outline similar to what you see in the Outline pane in PowerPoint. This file can then be opened in Word or any other application that supports Rich Text format (RTF) text files. Only text in placeholders is exported, though, not text in manually inserted text boxes. If you aren't sure which text will be included, view the presentation in the Outline pane; any text that doesn't appear there will not be exported.

Specifying save options

The save options enable you to fine-tune the saving process for special needs. For example, you can employ save options to embed fonts, to change the interval at which PowerPoint saves AutoRecover information, and more.

There are two ways to access the Save options:

- Choose File ⇨ Options ⇨ Save.
- From the Save As dialog box, click Tools ⇨ Save Options.

The PowerPoint Options dialog box appears (Figure 21.11). Set any of the options you want to set and click OK when you are finished.

FIGURE 21.11

Set save options to match the way you want PowerPoint to save your work.

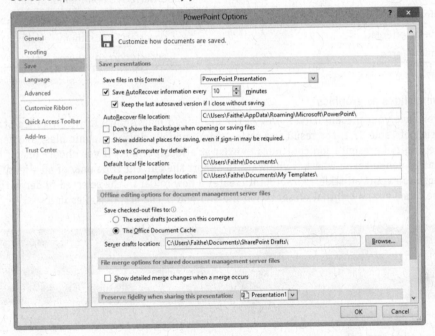

Table 21.3 summarizes the save options. One of the most important features described in Table 21.3 is AutoRecover, which is turned on by default. This means if a system error or a power outage causes PowerPoint to terminate unexpectedly, you do not lose all of your work. The next time you start PowerPoint, it opens the recovered file and asks if you want to save it.

CAUTION

AutoRecover is *not* a substitute for saving your work the regular way. It does not save in the same sense that the Save command does; it only saves a backup version as PowerPoint is running. If you quit PowerPoint normally, that backup version is erased. The backup version is available for recovery only if PowerPoint terminates abnormally (because of a system lockup or a power outage, for example).

TABLE 21.3 Save Options

Feature	Purpose
Save files in this format	Sets the default file format to appear in the Save As dialog box. Your choices are a regular presentation, a macro-enabled presentation, or a 97–2003 backward-compatible presentation.
Save AutoRecover information every *x* minutes	PowerPoint saves your work every few minutes so that if the computer has problems and causes PowerPoint to terminate abnormally, you do not lose much work. Lower this number to save more often (for less potential data loss) or raise it to save less often (for less slowdown/delay related to repeated saving).
AutoRecover file location	Specify the location in which AutoRecover drafts should be saved. By default, it is `C:\Users\user name\AppData\Roaming\Microsoft\PowerPoint`.
Don't show the Backstage when opening or saving files	When enabled, bypasses Backstage view (that is, the default File menu choices for opening and saving) and goes directly to the Open or Save dialog boxes, respectively.
Show additional places for saving, even if sign-in may be required	When disabled, hides the SkyDrive sign-in option; disable this if you don't intend to use SkyDrive to save your work.
Save to Computer by default	When enabled, saves to your default local file location (see the next option) by default.
Default local file location	Specify the location that you want to start from when saving with the Save As dialog box. By default, it is your Documents library.
Default personal templates location	Specify the location containing any templates you have created or acquired separately from the ones PowerPoint itself provides.
Save checked-out files to	Sets the location in which any drafts will be saved that you have checked out of a web server library such as SharePoint. If you choose "The server drafts location on this computer," then you must specify what that location will be in the Server drafts location box. If you choose to save to the Office document cache, it's not an issue because every save goes immediately back to the server.
Show detailed merge changes when a merge occurs	Shows full information about what was changed when you merge two PowerPoint files that are stored on a shared document management server.
Embed fonts in the file	Turn this on if you are saving a presentation for use on a different PC that might not have the fonts installed that the presentation requires. You can choose to embed the characters in use only (which minimizes the file size, but if someone tries to edit the presentation, they might not have all of the characters they need) or to embed all characters in the font set. Unlike the others, this setting applies only to the current presentation file.

Setting Passwords for File Access

If a presentation contains sensitive or confidential data, you can encrypt the file and protect it with a password. Encryption is a type of "scrambling" done to the file so that nobody can see it, either from within PowerPoint or with any other type of file-browsing utility.

You can enter two separate passwords for a file: the Open password and the Modify password. Use an Open password to prevent unauthorized people from viewing the file at all. Use a Modify password to prevent people from making changes to the file.

You can use one, both, or neither of the password types. For example, suppose you have a personnel presentation that contains salary information. You might use an Open password and distribute that password to a few key people in the human resources department who need access to it. But then you might use a Modify password to ensure that none of those people make any changes to the presentation as they are viewing it.

For the Open password, you can specify an encryption method and strength. Many encryption codes are available, and the differences between them are significant mostly to high-end technical users. However, if you do have a preference, you can choose it when you choose the Open password.

To manage a file's passwords and other security settings, follow these steps:

1. **Begin to save the file as you normally would from the Save As dialog box.**

2. **In the Save As dialog box, click Tools, and choose General Options.** The General Options dialog box opens (Figure 21.12).

FIGURE 21.12

Set a password to prevent unauthorized access.

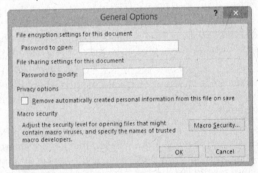

3. **If you want an Open password, enter it in the Password to open box.**

4. **If you want a Modify password, enter it in the Password to modify box.** (You don't have to use both an Open and a Modify password; you can use just one or the other if you like.)

5. **(Optional) If you want your personal information stripped from the file, such as your name removed from the Author field of the Properties box, select the Remove automatically created personal information from this file on save check box.**

6. **(Optional) If desired, adjust the macro security level for PowerPoint (all files, not just this one) by clicking the Macro Security button and making changes to the settings in the Trust Center; then click OK to return to the General Options dialog box.**

7. **Click OK.** If you specified a password in step 3, a confirmation box appears for it.

8. **If the confirmation box appears, retype the same password and click OK.** If you specified a password in step 4, a confirmation box appears for it.

9. **If the confirmation box appears, retype the same password and click OK.**

10. **Continue saving as you normally would.**

When you (or someone else) open the file, a Password prompt appears. The Open password must be entered to open the presentation file. The Modify password will *not* work. After that hurdle, if you have set a separate Modify password, a prompt for that appears. Your choices are to enter the Modify password, to cancel, or to click the Read-Only option to open the presentation in Read-Only mode.

> **CAUTION**
>
> Here's a security hole to be aware of: If you add a Modify password to a PPTX file and then save it as a `.pptx` file, it can be opened *and* edited in PowerPoint 2003 or earlier if you installed the Compatibility Pack that allows opening of `.pptx` files, even if the user does not know the password. However, if you save the file in PowerPoint 2013 as a PowerPoint 97–2003 file (PPT file), it cannot be edited in earlier versions without the password.

Closing and Reopening Presentations

You can have several presentation files open at once and switch freely between them, but this can bog down your computer's performance somewhat. Unless you are doing some cut-and-paste work, it's best to have only one presentation file open — the one you are actively working on. It's easy to close and open presentations as needed.

Closing a presentation

When you exit PowerPoint, the open presentation file automatically closes and you're prompted to save your changes if you have made any. If you want to close a presentation file without exiting PowerPoint, follow these steps:

1. **Choose File ⇨ Close.** If you have not made any changes to the presentation since the last time you saved, you're done. If you have made any changes to the presentation, you're prompted to save them.

2. **If you don't want to save your changes, click Don't Save, and you're done.**

3. **If you want to save your changes, click Save.** If the presentation has already been saved once, you're done. If the presentation has not been saved before, the Save As dialog box appears.

4. **Type a name in the File name text box and click Save.**

Opening a presentation

To open a recently used presentation, choose File➪Open and click one of the presentations on the Recent Presentations list on the right. Up to 25 can appear by default (see Figure 21.13).

FIGURE 21.13

Recently opened presentations appear when you select Open from the File menu.

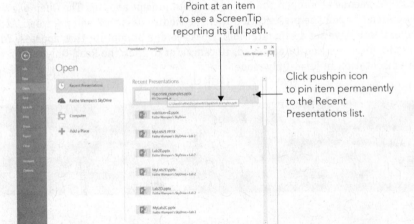

Point at an item
to see a ScreenTip
reporting its full path.

Click pushpin icon
to pin item permanently
to the Recent
Presentations list.

> **TIP**
>
> To pin a certain file to the File menu's list so that it never scrolls off, click the pushpin icon to the right of the file's name on the menu.

> **TIP**
>
> You can increase or decrease the number of recently used files that appear on the Recent Presentations list. Choose File➪Options➪Advanced, and in the Display section, set the Show this number of Recent Presentations box.

> **TIP**
>
> You can right-click an entry on the Recent Presentations list for additional options, such as Open a Copy, Copy Path to Clipboard, and Remove from List.

If the presentation you want to open does not appear on the Recent Presentations list, follow these steps to find and open it:

1. **If the Open screen does not already appear, choose File⇨Open.**
2. **Click the location from which you want to open a presentation, which may be your SkyDrive or Computer (for locally stored files).**
3. **If a shortcut appears to the folder that contains the file you want, click it.** Otherwise, click Browse to browse for the location. The Open dialog box appears.
4. **Choose the file you want to open.** If necessary, change the location to find the file.

NOTE

See the section "Changing Drives and Folders" earlier in this chapter if you need help.

5. **Click Open.** The presentation opens.

To open more than one presentation at once, hold down the Ctrl key as you click each file you want to open. When you click the Open button, they all open in their own windows. For more information, see the sidebar "Working with Multiple Presentations" later in this chapter.

The Open button in the Open dialog box has its own drop-down list from which you can select commands that open the file in different ways. See Figure 21.14, and refer to Table 21.4 for an explanation of the available options.

FIGURE 21.14

The Open button's menu contains several special options for opening a file.

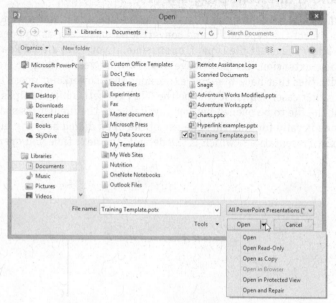

TABLE 21.4 **Open Options**

Open button setting	Purpose
Open	The default; simply opens the file for editing.
Open Read-Only	Allows changes but prevents those changes from being saved under the same name.
Open as Copy	Opens a copy of the file, leaving the original untouched.
Open in Browser	Applicable only for web-based presentations; opens it for viewing in a web browser. PowerPoint 2013 does not save in web format, so it applies only to web-based presentations created in earlier versions of PowerPoint that supported that feature.
Open in Protected View	Opens the file in an uneditable view. This option not only prevents you from saving any changes to the file, it also prevents you from *making* changes.
Open and Repair	Opens the file, and identifies and repairs any errors it finds in it.
Show Previous Versions	Applicable only if the presentation file is stored on an NTFS volume under Windows 7, this feature enables you to access the Versions feature in Windows 7 that stores previous versions of files. It is not applicable to Windows 8, which does not store previous versions in the same way.

Opening a file from a different program

Just as you can save files in various program formats, you can open files from various programs. PowerPoint can detect the type of file and convert it automatically as you open it, so you do not have to know the exact file type. (For example, if you have an old PowerPoint file with a .ppt filename extension, you don't have to know what version it came from.) The only problem is with files that have filename extensions that PowerPoint doesn't automatically recognize. In that case, you must change the File Type setting in the Open dialog box to All Files so that the file to be opened becomes available on the file list, as shown in Figure 21.15. The change is valid for only this one use of the Open dialog box; the file type reverts to All PowerPoint Presentations, which is the default, the next time you open the dialog box.

FIGURE 21.15

To open files from different programs, change the File Type setting to All Files.

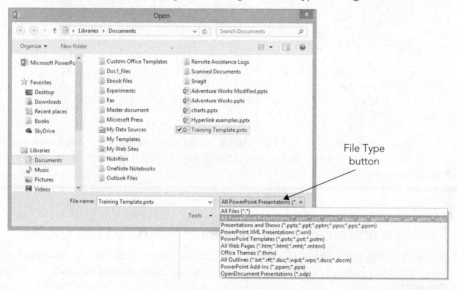

File Type
button

> **CAUTION**
>
> PowerPoint opens only presentation files and text-based files such as Word outlines. If you want to include graphics from another program in a PowerPoint presentation, insert them using the Picture command on the Insert tab. Do not attempt to open them with the Open dialog box.

Working with Multiple Presentations

You will usually work with only one presentation at a time. But occasionally you may need to have two or more presentations open at once — for example, to make it easier to copy text or slides from one presentation to another.

To open another presentation, choose File ➪ Open and select the one you want, the same as usual.

When more than one presentation is open, you can switch among them by selecting the one you want to see from the taskbar in Windows. Alternatively, you can click the Switch Windows button in the Window group on the View tab and select any open presentation from there, as shown in the following screen shot.

Continues

continued

Switch between open windows of all applications — not just PowerPoint — by pressing Alt+Esc repeatedly to cycle through them or by holding down the Alt key and pressing Tab to browse through thumbnails of open windows.

Finding a presentation file to open

If you have forgotten where you saved a particular presentation file, you're not out of luck. The Open dialog box includes a Search box that can help you locate it, as shown in Figure 21.16.

FIGURE 21.16

Use the Search box in the Open dialog box to look for a file.

Type word(s) to
search for here.

Search results
appear
immediately.

To search for a file, follow these steps:

1. **Choose File ⇨ Open, click the location in which to search (SkyDrive or Computer), and then click Browse to display the Open dialog box.**

2. **Navigate to the general location of the file.** For example, if you know it is on the C: drive, display the top-level listing for the C: drive.

3. **Click in the Search box and type part of the file name (if you know it) or a word or phrase used in the file.**

4. **Press Enter.** A list of files that match that specification appears.

5. **Open the file as you normally would.**

Setting File Properties

File properties are facts about each file that can help you organize them. If you have a lot of PowerPoint files, using file properties can help you search intelligently for them using the Search feature you learned about in the preceding section. For example, you can specify an author, a manager, and a company for each file and then search based on those values.

You can set a file's properties by doing the following:

1. **Choose File ⇨ Info.**

2. **Click the Properties heading (on the right side of the Info screen), and on the menu that appears, click Show Document Panel.** The Document Panel appears above the presentation window.

3. **Fill in any information you want to store about the presentation, as shown in Figure 21.17.**

FIGURE 21.17

Enter information to store in the file's properties.

4. **Click the down arrow to the right of Document Properties in the Document Panel, and choose Advanced Properties.** The Properties dialog box for the file appears.

5. **Click the Summary tab, and confirm or change any information there.** This is the same information that you entered in the Properties Ribbon, with the addition of a couple of other fields, as shown in Figure 21.18.

FIGURE 21.18

The Summary tab has many of the same fields as the Ribbon.

6. **Click the Custom tab, choose any additional fields you need, and set values for** them. For example, click the Client field on the Name list, and type a value for it in the Value text box. Repeat this for any of the other custom fields.

7. **Review the information on the Statistics and Contents tab if desired.** (You can't change that information.)

8. **Click OK.**

Now you can use the contents of the properties fields when performing a search.

Creating New Slides

Different templates start a presentation with different numbers and types of slides. A blank presentation has only a single slide, and you must create any others that you want.

There are several ways to create new slides. For example, you can type new text in the outline and then promote it to slide status, or you can add slides with the New Slide button that is on the Home tab. You can also copy existing slides, either within the same presentation or from other sources. The following sections outline these procedures in more detail.

Creating new slides from Outline view

As discussed in Chapter 20, Outline view shows the text from the presentation's slides in a hierarchical tree, with the slide titles at the top level (the slide level) and the various levels of bulleted lists on the slides displaying as subordinate levels. Text that you type in the Outline pane appears on the slide, and vice versa, as shown in Figure 21.19.

FIGURE 21.19

When you type text into the Outline pane, it automatically appears on the current slide.

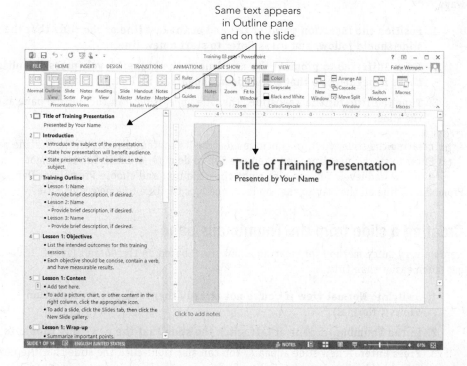

NOTE

Outline view doesn't show all of the text in all cases; see "Creating Text Boxes Manually" later in this chapter to find out why text in some text boxes does not appear in the outline.

Follow these steps to create a new slide from Outline view:

1. **Switch to Outline view (View ⇨ Presentation Views ⇨ Outline View).**

   As you learned in Chapter 20, Outline view is like Normal view except the left pane is an Outline pane, containing a text outline instead of slide thumbnail images.

2. **Click at the end of the existing line on the Outline pane that the new slide should follow.**

3. **Click Home ⇨ Slides ⇨ New Slide.** A new line appears in the Outline pane, with a slide symbol to its left.

4. **Type the title for the new slide.** The title appears both in the Outline pane and on the slide.

You can also create a new slide by starting a new line in the Outline pane and then promoting it to slide level by pressing Shift+Tab. Follow these steps to insert a new slide in this way:

1. **Position the insertion point at the end of the last line of the slide that the new slide should follow, and press Enter to start a new line.**

2. **Press Shift+Tab to promote the new line to the highest level (press it multiple times if needed), so that a slide icon appears to its left.**

3. **Type the title for the new slide.** The title appears both in the Outline pane and on the slide.

After creating the slide, you can continue creating its content directly in the Outline pane. Press Enter to start a new line, and then use Tab to demote, or Shift+Tab to promote, the line to the desired level. You can also right-click the text and choose Promote or Demote. Promoting a line all the way to the top level changes the line to a new slide title.

Creating a slide from the Thumbnails pane

Here's a very quick method for creating a new slide, based on the default layout. It doesn't get much easier than this:

1. **Switch to Normal view if you're not already there (View ⇨ Presentation Views ⇨ Normal).**

2. **In the Thumbnails pane at left, click the slide that the new slide should follow.**

3. **Press Enter.** A new slide appears. You can also right-click the slide that the new one should follow and choose New Slide.

The drawback to creating a slide in any of the ways you have learned about so far in this chapter is that you cannot specify the layout. You have to change the layout afterwards if you don't get the kind you want. To choose a layout other than the default one, see the next section.

> **NOTE**
>
> The layout you get when you create a new slide from the Thumbnails pane depends on what layout the preceding slide has. If the preceding slide is Title Slide or Title and Content, you get a Title and Content slide. With any other type, you get the same type as the previous one. For example, if the previous slide was Title Only, that's what you get.

21

Creating a slide from a layout

A *slide layout* is a layout guide that tells PowerPoint what placeholder boxes to use on a particular slide and where to position them. Although slide layouts can contain placeholders for text, they also contain graphics, charts, tables, and other useful elements. After you create a new slide with placeholders, you can click a placeholder to open whatever controls you need to insert that type of object.

> **TIP**
>
> See the section, "Using Content Placeholders" for more information on inserting objects.

When you create new slides using one of the methods described in the preceding sections, the new slides use the Title and Content layout, which consists of a slide title and a single, large placeholder box for content. If you want to use another layout, such as a slide with two adjacent but separate frames of content, you must either switch the slide to a different layout after its creation (using the Layout button's menu on the Home tab), or you must specify a different layout when you initially create the slide.

To specify a certain layout as you are creating a slide, follow these steps:

1. **In Normal or Slide Sorter view, select or display the slide that the new one should follow.**

   You can select a slide by clicking its thumbnail image in Slide Sorter view or on the Thumbnails pane in Normal view. You can also move the insertion point to the slide's text in the Outline pane.

2. **On the Home tab, do one of the following:**

   - To add a new slide using the same layout as the selected slide, click the top (graphical) portion of the New Slide button in the Slides group.

   - To add a new slide using another layout, click the bottom (text) portion of the New Slide button and then select the desired layout from the menu, as shown in Figure 21.20.

FIGURE 21.20

Create a new slide, based on the layout of your choice.

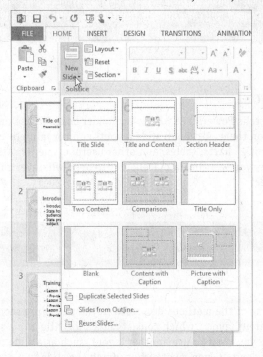

> **TIP**
>
> The layouts that appear on the menu come from the slide master. To customize these layouts, click View ⇨ Master Views ⇨ Slide Master. You will learn more about the slide master and about changing layouts in Chapter 22.

Copying slides

Another way to create a new slide is to copy an existing one in the same presentation. This is especially useful when you are using multiple slides to create a progression because one slide is typically identical to the next slide in a sequence, except for a small change.

There are several ways to copy one or more slides. One way is to use the Windows Clipboard, as in the following steps:

1. **Select the slide or slides that you want to copy.** See "Selecting Slides" later in this chapter for more information about selecting slides.

> **CAUTION**
>
> If you select from the Outline pane in Outline view, make sure that you click the icon to the left of the slide's title so that the entire slide is selected; if you select only part of the text on the slide, then only the selected part is copied.

2. **Press Ctrl+C.** You can also click Home ⇨ Clipboard ⇨ Copy, or right-click the selection and click Copy.

3. **Select the slide that the pasted slide or slides should follow.** Or, if working in Outline view, click in the Outline pane to place the insertion point where you want the insertion.

4. **Press Ctrl+V.** You can also click Home ⇨ Clipboard ⇨ Paste, or right-click the destination and click Paste.

PowerPoint also has a Duplicate Selected Slides command that does the same thing as a copy and paste. Although it may be a little faster, it gives you less control as to where the pasted copies will appear. PowerPoint pastes the slides immediately after the last slide in the selection. For example, if you selected slides 1, 3, and 6 and issued the Duplicate Selected Slides command, then the copies are placed after slide 6.

Follow these steps to try out the Duplicate Selected Slides command.

1. **Select the slide or slides to be duplicated.**

2. **On the Home tab in the Slides group, click the bottom part of the New Slide button to open its menu.**

3. **Click Duplicate Selected Slides.** As an alternative, you can right-click a slide (or a group of selected slides) in the Thumbnails pane and choose Duplicate Slide.

> **TIP**
>
> To make duplication even faster, you can place the Duplicate Selected Slides command on the Quick Access Toolbar. To do that, right-click the command on the menu and choose Add to Quick Access Toolbar.

Inserting Content from External Sources

Many people find that they can save a lot of time by copying text or slides from other programs or from other PowerPoint presentations to form the basis of a new presentation. There's no need to reinvent the wheel each time! The following sections look at various ways to bring in content from external sources.

Copying slides from other presentations

There are several ways to copy slides from other presentations. You can:

- Open the presentation, save it under a different name, and then delete the slides that you *don't* want, leaving a new presentation with the desired slides ready for customization.
- Open two PowerPoint windows side-by-side and drag-and-drop slides between them.
- Open two PowerPoint presentations, copy slides from one of them to the Clipboard (Ctrl+C), and then paste them into the other presentation (Ctrl+V).
- Use the Reuse Slides feature in PowerPoint, as described next.

To reuse slides from other presentations with the Reuse Slides feature, follow these steps:

1. **On the Home tab in the Slides group, click the lower portion of the New Slide button to open its menu.**
2. **Click Reuse Slides.** The Reuse Slides pane appears at the right.
3. **Click the Open a PowerPoint File hyperlink.** Or, click the Browse button and then click Browse File.
4. **In the Browse dialog box, select the presentation from which you want to copy slides, and click Open.** Thumbnail images of the slides in the presentation appear in the Reuse Slides pane, as shown in Figure 21.21.

FIGURE 21.21

Choose individual slides to copy to the current presentation.

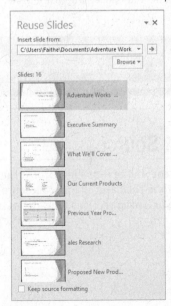

5. **(Optional) If you want to keep the source formatting when copying slides, select the Keep source formatting check box at the bottom of the task pane.**

6. **(Optional) To see an enlarged image of one of the slides, move the mouse pointer over it.**

7. **Do any of the following:**

   ■ To insert a single slide, click it.

   ■ To insert all slides at once, right-click any slide and choose Insert All Slides.

   ■ To copy only the theme (not the content), right-click any slide in the Reuse Slides pane and choose Apply Theme to All Slides, or Apply Theme to Selected Slides.

Inserting new slides from an outline

All of the Microsoft Office applications work well together, so it's easy to move content between them. For example, you can create an outline for a presentation in Microsoft Word and then import it into PowerPoint. PowerPoint uses the heading styles that you assigned in Word to decide which items are slide titles and which items are slide content. The top-level headings (Heading 1) form the slide titles.

To try this out, open Word, switch to Outline view (View ➪ Views ➪ Outline), and then type a short outline of a presentation. Press Tab to demote, or Shift+Tab to promote, a selected line. Then save your work, go back to PowerPoint, and follow these steps to import it:

1. **On the Home tab in the Slides group, click the lower portion of the New Slide button to open its menu.**

2. **Click Slides from Outline.** The Insert Outline dialog box opens.

3. **Select the file containing the outline text that you want to import.**

4. **Click Insert.** PowerPoint imports the outline.

If there were already existing slides in the presentation, they remain untouched. (This includes any blank slides, and so you might need to delete the blank slide at the beginning of the presentation after importing.) All of the Heading 1 lines from the outline become separate slide titles, and all of the subordinate headings become bullet points in the slides.

Tips for better outline importing

Although PowerPoint can import any text from any Word document, you may not always get the results that you want or expect. For example, you may have a document that consists of a series of paragraphs with no heading styles applied. When you import this document into PowerPoint, it might look something like Figure 21.22.

FIGURE 21.22

A Word document consisting mainly of plain paragraphs makes for an unattractive presentation.

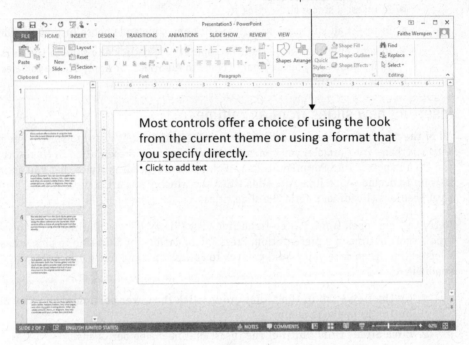

Figure 21.22 is a prime example of what happens if you don't prepare a document before you import it into PowerPoint. PowerPoint makes each paragraph its own slide and puts all of the text for each one in the title placeholder. It can't tell which ones are actual headings and which ones aren't because there are no heading styles in use. The paragraphs are too long to fit on slides, and so they overrun their placeholders. Extra blank lines are interpreted as blank slides. Quite a train wreck, isn't it? Figure 21.22 also illustrates an important point to remember: Regular paragraph text does not work very well in PowerPoint. PowerPoint text is all about short, snappy bulleted lists and headings. The better that you prepare the outline before importing it, the less cleanup you will need to do after importing. Here are some tips:

- **Apply heading styles to the text that you want to import.** Paragraphs formatted using non-heading styles in Word do not import into PowerPoint unless you use no heading styles at all in the document (as in Figure 21.22).

- **Stick with basic styles only in the outline: for example, just Heading 1, Heading 2, and so on.**

- **Delete all blank lines above the first heading.** If you don't, you will have blank slides at the beginning of your presentation.

- **Strip off as much manual formatting as possible from the Word text, so that the text picks up its formatting from PowerPoint.** To strip off formatting in Word, select the text and press Ctrl+spacebar.

- **Do not leave blank lines between paragraphs.** These will translate into blank slides or blank bulleted items in PowerPoint.

- **Delete any graphic elements, such as clip art, pictures, charts, and so on.** They will not transfer to PowerPoint anyway and may confuse the import utility.

Importing from other text-based formats

In addition to Word, PowerPoint also imports from plain text files, from WordPerfect (5.x or 6.x), from Microsoft Works, from Rich Text Format, and from web pages. The procedure is the same as in the preceding steps. By default, the file type in the Insert Outline dialog box is set to All Files, so you should see all usable files automatically, provided they have the correct extensions.

If you are setting up a plain text file for import, you obviously won't have the outlining tools from Word at your disposal. Instead, you must rely on tabs. Each line that should be a title slide should start at the left margin; first-level bullet paragraphs should be preceded by a single Tab; second-level bullets should be preceded by two Tabs, and so on.

Post-import cleanup

After importing text from an outline, there will probably be a few minor corrections that you need to make. Run through this checklist:

- **The first slide in the presentation might be blank.** If it is, then delete it.

- **The Title Slide layout may not be applied to the first slide; apply that layout, if necessary.** You can use the Layout list in the Slides group of the Home tab.

- **A theme may now be applied; choose one from the Design tab, if necessary, or format your slide masters and layouts as desired.** See Chapter 22 for more information about working with themes.

- **Some of the text might contain manual formatting that interferes with the theme formatting and creates inconsistency.** Remove any manual formatting that you notice. One way to do this is to switch to Outline view, select all of the text in the Outline pane by pressing Ctrl+A, and then strip off the manual formatting by pressing Ctrl+Spacebar or by clicking the Reset button in the Slides group on the Home tab.

- **If some of the text is too long to fit comfortably on a slide, change to a different slide layout, such as a two-column list, if necessary.** You might also need to split the content into two or more slides.

- **There might be some blank bullet points on some slides (if you missed deleting all of the extra paragraph breaks before importing).** Delete these bullet points.

Opening a Word document as a new presentation

Instead of importing slides from a Word document or other text-based document, as described in the preceding section, you can simply open the Word document in PowerPoint. PowerPoint starts a new presentation file to hold the imported text. This saves some time if you are starting a new presentation anyway, and you don't have any existing slides to merge with the incoming content.

To open a Word document in PowerPoint, follow these steps:

1. **Choose File ➪ Open.** The Open screen appears.
2. **Select the location where the Word document is stored, such as your SkyDrive or Computer.**
3. **Click Browse, and then navigate to the folder containing the Word document.**
4. **Change the file type to All Outlines.**
5. **Select the document.**
6. **Click Open.** The document outline becomes a PowerPoint presentation, with all Heading 1 paragraphs becoming slide titles.

> **CAUTION**
>
> You may find that you can't open or insert a Word outline in PowerPoint if it is currently open in Word. This limitation is an issue only for Word files, not plain text or other formats.

Importing text from web pages

PowerPoint accepts imported text from several web-page formats, including HTML and MHTML (Single File Web Page). It is helpful if the data is in an orderly outline format, or if it was originally created from a PowerPoint file, because there will be less cleanup needed.

There are several ways to import from a web page:

- Open a web-page file as you would an outline (see the preceding section), but set the file type to All Web Pages.
- Insert the text from the web page as you would a Word outline (in the Home tab, click Slides ➪ New Slide ➪ Slides from Outline).
- Reuse slides from a web presentation as you would from any other presentation (in the Home tab, click Slides ➪ New Slide ➪ Reuse Slides).

CAUTION

You should use one of the above methods rather than pasting HTML text directly into PowerPoint. This is because when you paste HTML text, you might get additional HTML tags that you don't want, including cross-references that might cause your presentation to try to log onto a web server every time you open it.

When importing from a web page, don't expect the content to appear formatted the same way that it was on the web page. We're talking strictly about text import here. The formatting on the web page comes from HTML tags or from a style sheet, neither of which you can import. If you want an exact duplicate of the web page's appearance, take a picture of the page with the Shift+PrintScreen command, and then paste it into PowerPoint (Ctrl+V) as a graphic.

If you are importing an outline from an MHTML-format web page that contains pictures, the pictures are also imported into PowerPoint. If importing from a regular HTML file, you cannot import the pictures.

TIP

If you need to show a live web page from within PowerPoint, try Shyam Pillai's free LiveWeb add-in, found at `www.mvps.org/skp/liveweb.htm`.

Managing Slides

After inserting a few slides into a presentation, and perhaps building some content on them, you might decide to make some changes, such as rearranging, deleting, and so on. The following sections explain how to manage and manipulate the slides in a presentation.

Selecting slides

Before you can issue a command that acts upon a slide or a group of slides, you must select the slides that you want to affect. You can do this from either Normal or Slide Sorter view, but Slide Sorter view makes it easier because you can see more slides at once. From Slide Sorter view, or from the Thumbnails pane in Normal view, you can use any of these techniques to select slides:

- **To select a single slide, click it.**
- **To select multiple slides, hold down the Ctrl key as you click each one.**
  Figure 21.23 shows slides 1, 3, and 6 selected, as indicated by the shaded border around the slides.

FIGURE 21.23

Select slides in Slide Sorter view by holding down the Ctrl key and clicking each slide.

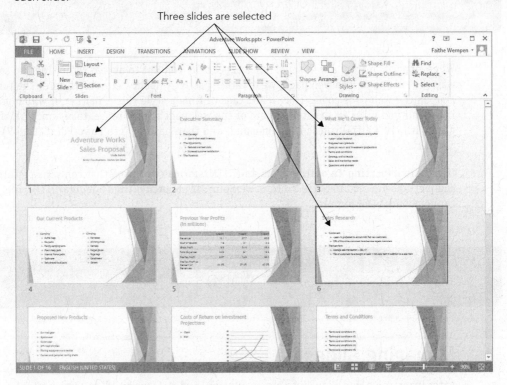

- **To select a contiguous group of slides (for example, slides 1, 2, and 3), click the first slide, and then hold down the Shift key as you click the last one.** All of the slides in between are selected as well.

To cancel the selection of multiple slides, click anywhere outside of the selected slides.

To select slides from Outline view, click the slide icon to the left of the slide's title; this selects the entire slide, as shown in Figure 21.24. It's important to select the entire slide and not just part of its content before issuing a command such as Delete, because otherwise, the command only affects the portion that you selected.

FIGURE 21.24

Select slides in the Outline pane by clicking the slide icon to the left of the slide title.

Click here to select all the text on the slide

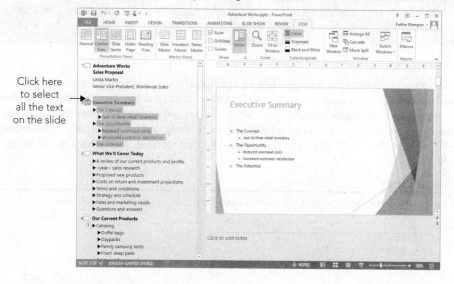

Deleting slides

You may want to get rid of some of the slides, especially if you created your presentation using a template that contained a lot of sample content. For example, the sample presentation may be longer than you need, or you may have inserted your own slides instead.

Select the slide or slides that you want to delete, and then do either of the following:

- Right-click the selection and choose Delete Slide.
- Press the Delete key on the keyboard.

Undoing mistakes

Here's a command that can help you in almost all of the other chapters in this book: undoing. The Undo command allows you to reverse past actions. For example, you can use it to reverse all of the deletions that you made to your presentation in the preceding section. The easiest way to undo a single action is to click the Undo button on the Quick Access Toolbar or press Ctrl+Z. You can click it as many times as you like; each time you click it, you undo one action.

You can undo multiple actions at once by opening the Undo button's drop-down list, as shown in Figure 21.25. Just drag the mouse across the actions that you want to undo (you don't need to hold down the mouse button). Click when the desired actions are selected, and presto, they are all reversed. You can select multiple actions to undo, but you can't skip around. For example, to undo the fourth item, you must undo the first, second, and third ones, as well.

FIGURE 21.25

Use the Undo button to undo your mistakes and the Redo button to reverse an Undo operation.

The Redo command is the opposite of Undo. If you make a mistake with the Undo button, you can fix the problem by clicking the Redo button. Like the Undo button, it has a drop-down list, and so you can redo multiple actions at once.

The Redo command is available only immediately after you use the Undo command. If Redo isn't available, a Repeat button appears in its place. The Repeat command enables you to repeat the last action that you performed (and it doesn't have to be an Undo operation). For example, you can repeat some typing, or some formatting. Figure 21.26 shows the Repeat button.

FIGURE 21.26

The Repeat button appears when Redo is not available, and enables you to repeat actions.

Repeat
button

Rearranging slides

The best way to rearrange slides is to do so in Slide Sorter view. In this view, the slides in your presentation appear in thumbnail view, and you can move them around on the screen to different positions, just as you would manually rearrange pasted-up artwork on a table. Although you can also do this from the Thumbnails pane in Normal view, you are able to see fewer slides at once. As a result, it can be more challenging to move slides around, for example, from one end of the presentation to another. To rearrange slides, use the following steps:

1. **Switch to Slide Sorter view or Normal view.**

2. **Select the slide that you want to move.** You can move multiple slides at once if you like (which is a lot easier in Slide Sorter view than in Normal view).

3. **Drag the selected slide to the new location.** The slide moves as you drag, as shown in Figure 21.27.

FIGURE 21.27

As you drag a slide, its new position is indicated by slides shifting in the view.

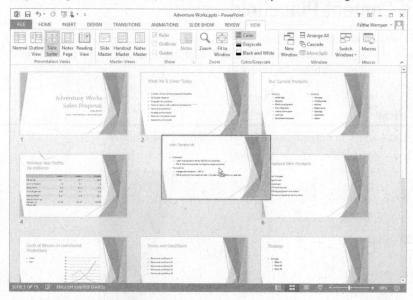

4. **Release the mouse button.** The slide moves to the new location.

You can also rearrange slides in Outline view. This is not quite as easy as using Slide Sorter view, but it's more versatile. Not only can you drag entire slides from place to place, but you can also move individual bullets from one slide to another.

Follow these steps to move content in Outline view:

1. **Switch to Outline view.**
2. **Position the mouse pointer over the slide's icon in the Outline pane.** The mouse pointer changes to a four-headed arrow.
3. **Click on the icon.** PowerPoint selects all of the text in that slide.
4. **Drag the slide's icon up or down to a new position in the outline and then release the mouse button.** All of the slide's text moves with it to the new location.

There are also keyboard shortcuts for moving a slide up or down in the Outline pane that may be faster than clicking the toolbar buttons. You can press the Alt+Shift+Up Arrow keys to move a slide up, and the Alt+Shift+Down Arrow keys to move a slide down.

These shortcuts work equally well with single bullets from a slide. Just click to the left of a single line to select it, instead of clicking the Slide icon in step 3.

Using Content Placeholders

Now that you know something about inserting and managing entire slides, let's take a closer look at the content within a slide. The default placeholder type is a multipurpose content placeholder, as shown in Figure 21.28.

FIGURE 21.28

A content placeholder can contain a variety of different elements.

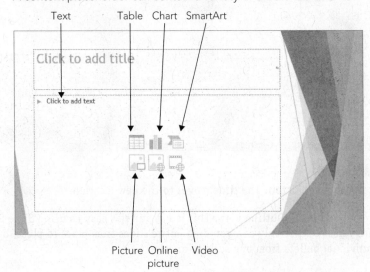

Inserting content into a placeholder

To type text into a content placeholder, click inside the placeholder box and start typing. You can enter and edit text as you would in any word-processing program. To insert any other type of content into a placeholder, click one of the icons shown in Figure 21.28. A dialog box opens to help you select and insert that content type.

A content placeholder can hold only one type of content at a time. If you click in the placeholder and type some text, the icons for the other content types disappear. To access them again, you must delete all of the text from the placeholder.

Placeholders versus manually inserted objects

You can insert content on a slide independently of a placeholder by using the Insert tab's buttons and menus. This technique allows you to insert an item in its own separate frame on any slide, to coexist with any placeholder content. You can learn how to insert each content type in the chapters in which they are covered.

Creating Text Boxes Manually

The difference between a placeholder-inserted object and a manually inserted one is most significant with text boxes. Although you might think that text boxes are all alike, there are actually some significant differences between placeholder text boxes and manually inserted ones.

Here are some of the characteristics of a text placeholder:

- You cannot create new text placeholder boxes on your own, except in Slide Master view.

> **NOTE**
> You learn how to use Slide Master view to create your own layouts that contain custom text placeholders in Chapter 22. If you move or resize any type of placeholder on a slide in Normal view, that may disconnect it from future formatting changes you make in the slide master. The best practice is to make design and layout changes in the slide master rather than on individual slides.

- If you delete all of the text from a text placeholder, the placeholder instructions return (in Normal or Outline view).
- A text placeholder box has a fixed size on the slide, regardless of the amount or size of text that it contains. You can resize it manually, but if you reapply the layout, the placeholder box snaps back to the original size.

- AutoFit is turned on by default in a text placeholder, so that if you type more text than will fit, or resize the frame so that the existing text no longer fits, the text shrinks in size.

- The text that you type in a text placeholder box appears in the Outline pane in Outline view.

A manual text box, on the other hand, is one that you create yourself using the Text Box tool in the Text group of the Insert tab. Here are some characteristics of a manual text box:

- You can create a manual text box anywhere, and you can create as many as you like, regardless of the layout.

- If you delete all of the text from a manual text box, the text box remains empty or disappears completely. No placeholder instructions appear.

- A manual text box starts out small vertically, and expands as you type more text into it.

- A manual text box does not use AutoFit by default; the text box simply becomes larger to make room for more text.

- You cannot resize a manual text box so that the text that it contains no longer fits; PowerPoint refuses to make the text box shorter vertically until you delete some text from it. (However, you can decrease its horizontal width.)

- Text typed in a manual text box does not appear in the Outline pane in Outline view.

Figure 21.29 shows two text placeholders (one empty) and a text box in Outline view. Notice that the empty placeholder contains filler text to help you remember that it is there. Notice also that only the text from the placeholder appears in the Outline pane; the text-box text does not. Empty text boxes and placeholders do not show up in Slide Show view, so you do not have to worry about deleting any unneeded ones.

FIGURE 21.29

Two text placeholders and a text box

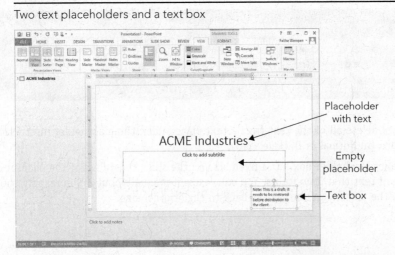

When should you use a manual text box?

Graphical content such as photos and charts can work well either in placeholders or as manually inserted objects. However, when it comes to text, you should stick with placeholders as often as possible. Placeholder text appears in the Outline pane in Outline view, whereas text in a manually inserted text box does not. When the bulk of a presentation's text is in manually created text boxes, Outline view becomes less useful because it doesn't contain the complete presentation text. In addition, when you change to a different formatting theme that includes different positioning for placeholders — for example, to accommodate a graphic on one side — the manual text boxes do not shift. As a result, they might end up overlapping the new background graphic with unattractive results. In a case such as this, you would need to manually go through each slide and adjust the positioning of each text box.

However, there are times when a manually created text box is preferable or even necessary. For example, suppose that you have a schematic diagram of a machine and you need to label some of the parts. Manually placed text boxes are perfect for these little snippets of text that are scattered over the surface of the picture. Manual text boxes are also useful for warnings, tips, and any other information that is tangential to the main discussion. Finally, if you want to vary the placement of the text on each slide (consciously circumventing the consistency provided by layouts), and you want to precisely position each box, then manual text boxes work well because they do not shift their position when you apply different themes or templates to the presentation.

> **TIP**
>
> If you insert text in a placeholder and then change the slide's layout so that the slide no longer contains that placeholder (for example, if you switch to Title Only or Blank layout), the text remains on the slide, but it becomes an *orphan*. If you delete the text box, then it simply disappears; a placeholder does not reappear. However, it does not become a manual text box, because its content still appears in the Outline pane, while a manual text box's content does not.

Creating a manual text box

To manually place a text box on a slide, follow these steps:

1. **Click Insert ➪ Text ➪ Text Box.** The mouse pointer turns into a vertical line. You can alternately use the Text Box icon in any of the Shapes galleries, such as the one on the Insert tab in the Illustrations group.

2. **Do either of the following:**

   ■ To create a text box that automatically enlarges itself horizontally as you type more text, but does not automatically wrap text to the next line, click once where you want the text to start, and begin typing.

- To create a text box with a width that you specify, and that automatically wraps text to the next line and grows in height as needed, click and drag to draw a box where you want the text box to be. Its height will initially snap back to a single line's height, regardless of the height that you initially draw; however, it will grow in height as you type text into it.

3. **Type the text that you want to appear in the text box.**

Working with Text Boxes

Text boxes (either placeholder or manual) form the basis of most presentations. Now that you know how to create them, and how to place text in them, let's take a look at how to manipulate the boxes themselves.

> **NOTE**
>
> Are you looking for information about formatting text boxes — perhaps to apply a background color or a border to one? See "Formatting a picture or shape" in Chapter 9.

Selecting text boxes

On the surface, this topic might seem like a no-brainer. Just click it, right? Well, almost. A text box has two possible "selected" states. One state is that the box itself is selected, and the other is that the insertion point is within the box. The difference is subtle, but it becomes clearer when you issue certain commands. For example, if the insertion point is in the text box and you press Delete, PowerPoint deletes the single character to the right of the insertion point. However, if you select the entire text box and press Delete, PowerPoint deletes the entire text box and everything in it.

To select the entire text box, click its border. You can tell that it is selected because the border appears as a solid line. To move the insertion point within the text box, click inside the text box. You can tell that the insertion point is there because you can see it flashing inside.

In the rest of this book, when you see the phrase "select the text box," it means the box itself should be selected, and the insertion point should *not* appear in it. For most of the upcoming sections it does not make any difference, although in a few cases it does.

> **TIP**
>
> When the insertion point is flashing in a text box, you can press Esc to select the text box itself.

You can select more than one text box at once by holding down the Shift key as you click additional text boxes. This technique is useful when you want to select more than one text box, for example, so that you can format them in the same way, or so that you can resize them by the same amount.

Sizing a text box

The basic techniques for sizing text boxes in PowerPoint are the same for every object type (for that matter, they are also the same as in other Office applications). To resize a text box, or any object, follow these steps:

1. **Position the mouse pointer over a selection handle for the object until the mouse pointer changes to a double-headed arrow.** If you want to resize proportionally, make sure that you use a corner selection handle, and hold down the Shift key as you drag.

2. **Drag the selection handle to resize the object's border.**

> **CAUTION**
>
> Allowing PowerPoint to manage placeholder size and position through layouts in the slide master ensures consistency among your slides (even when you use custom text boxes to emphasize other information). When you start changing the sizes and positions of placeholders on individual slides, you can end up creating consistency problems, such as headings that aren't in the same spot from slide to slide, or company logos that shift between slides. As noted earlier, resizing and moving placeholders can prevent formatting changes made in the slide master from applying.

You can also set a text box's size from the Size group on the Drawing Tools ⇨ Format tab. When the text box is selected, its current dimensions appear in the Height and Width boxes, as shown in Figure 21.30. You can change the dimensions within these boxes.

FIGURE 21.30

You can set an exact size for a text box from the Format tab's Size group.

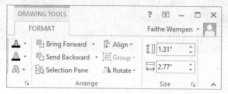

You can also set the size of a text box from the Size and Position task pane:

1. **Click the dialog box launcher in the Size group on the Drawing Tools ⇨ Format tab, as shown in Figure 21.30.** The Format Shape pane opens with the Size options displayed. See Figure 21.31.

FIGURE 21.31

You can adjust the size of the text box from the Size controls in the Format Shape pane.

2. **Set the height and width for the text box in the Height and Width boxes, respectively.** To keep the size proportional, select the Lock Aspect Ratio check box in the Scale section before you start adjusting the height or width.

3. **(Optional) Click the Close (X) button in the upper right corner of the task pane to close it.**

> **TIP**
>
> Task panes are *non-modal*. This means that you can leave them open and continue to work on your presentation. It also means that any changes that you make are applied immediately; there is no OK button to accept your changes or Cancel button to reverse them. To reverse a change, you can use the Undo command (Ctrl+Z).

Positioning a text box

To move an object, drag it by any part of its border other than a selection handle. Select the object, and then position the mouse pointer over a border so that the pointer turns into a four-headed arrow. Then drag the object to a new position. With a text box, you must position the mouse pointer over a border and not over the inside of the frame; with all other object types, you don't have to be that precise; you can move an object by dragging anywhere within it.

You can also set an exact position by using the Format Shape task pane:

1. **Click the dialog box launcher in the Size group on the Drawing Tools⇨Format tab, as shown in Figure 21.30.** The Format Shape dialog box opens with the Size controls displayed, as in Figure 21.31.

2. **Click the Size heading to collapse the Size section, and then click the Position heading to expand the Position section.** The Position controls appear, as shown in Figure 21.32.

3. **Set the horizontal and vertical position, and the point from which it is measured.** By default, measurements are from the top-left corner of the slide.

FIGURE 21.32

You can adjust the position with the Position controls.

4. **(Optional) Click the Close (X) button in the upper right corner of the task pane to close it.**

Changing a text box's AutoFit behavior

When there is too much text to fit in a text box, there are three things that may happen:

- **Do not AutoFit.** The text and the box can continue at their default sizes, and the text can overflow out of the box or be truncated.

- **Shrink text on overflow.** The text can shrink its font size to fit in the text box. This is the default setting for placeholder text boxes.

- **Resize shape to fit text.** The text box can enlarge to the size needed to contain the text. This is the default setting for manual text boxes.

Whenever there is too much text in a placeholder box, the AutoFit icon appears in the bottom-left corner. Click that icon to display a menu, as shown in Figure 21.33. From that menu, you can turn AutoFit on or off. Depending on the text-box type, you might not have all the menu items shown in Figure 21.33.

FIGURE 21.33

You can use the AutoFit icon's menu to change the AutoFit setting for a text box.

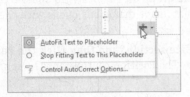

With a manual text box, the AutoFit icon does not appear, and so you must adjust the AutoFit behavior in the text box's properties. The following method works for both manual and placeholder boxes:

1. **Right-click the border of the text box and choose Format Shape.** The Format Shape task pane opens.

2. **Click Text Options.** Three icons appear: Text Fill & Outline, Text Effects, and Text Box.

   You can point at an icon to see a ScreenTip containing its name.

3. **Click the Text Box icon.** Controls appear that pertain to the text box itself. See Figure 21.34.

FIGURE 21.34

Click the Text Box icon to change text box options, including AutoFit behavior.

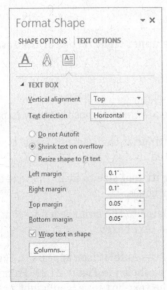

4. **Click one of the AutoFit options, as shown in Figure 21.34.**

5. **(Optional) Click the Close (X) button in the upper right corner of the task pane to close it.**

One other setting that also affects AutoFit behavior is the Wrap Text in Shape option. This on/off toggle, which appears as a check box in Figure 21.34, enables text to automatically wrap to the next line when it reaches the right edge of the text box. By default, this setting is On for placeholder text boxes and for manual text boxes that you create by dragging. However, it is Off by default for manual text boxes that you create by clicking.

Table 21.5 summarizes the various AutoFit behaviors and how they interact with one another.

TABLE 21.5   AutoFit and Resize Shape to Fit Text Behaviors

Setting	Default for	When wrap text in shape is on	When wrap text in shape is off
Do Not Autofit	n/a	Text overflows at bottom of text box	Text overflows at right and text box only
Shrink Text on Overflow	Placeholders	Text shrinks to fit	Text shrinks to fit
Resize Shape to Fit Text	Manual text boxes	Text box expands vertically only (default for manual text that you create by dragging)	Text box expands vertically and horizontally (default for manual box that you create by text box clicking). However, if you clicked to create the text box initially, the width keeps expanding until you press Enter.

Summary

In this chapter, you mastered core skills such as how to create presentations and add textual content to slides. You can now confidently:

- Create new presentations from scratch and from templates.
- Save, open, close, and delete PowerPoint presentation files.
- Save files in different formats and search for missing presentations.

- Create a new slide with the desired layout.
- Select, rearrange, and delete slides.
- Add text content on a slide and use content from outside sources.
- Understand the difference between a content placeholder and a manually inserted object such as a text box.
- Create and work with your own text boxes.

Working with Layouts, Themes, and Masters

Most presentations consist of multiple slides, so you'll need a way of ensuring consistency among them. Not only will you want each slide (in most cases) to have the same background, fonts, and text positioning, but you will also want a way of ensuring that any changes you make to those settings later automatically populate across all your slides.

To accomplish these goals, PowerPoint offers layouts, themes, and masters. Layouts determine the positioning of placeholders; themes assign color, font, and background choices; and masters transfer theme settings to the slides and provide an opportunity for repeated content, such as a logo, on each slide. In this chapter you learn how to use layouts, themes, and masters to create a presentation that is attractive, consistent, and easy to manage.

Understanding Layouts and Themes

As you learned in Chapter 21, a *layout* is a positioning template. The layout used for a slide determines what content placeholders will appear and how they will be arranged. For example, the layout shown in Figure 22.1 is called Title Slide, and it contains a Title placeholder and a Subtitle placeholder.

FIGURE 22.1

This slide uses the Title Slide layout and the Facet theme.

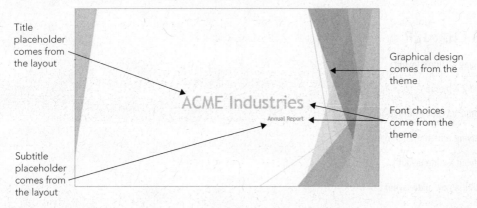

A *theme* is a group of design settings. It includes color settings, font choices, object effect settings, and in some cases also a background graphic. In Figure 22.1, the theme applied is called Facet, and it is responsible for the colored shapes and lines on the edges, the colors of those graphics, and the fonts used on the slide.

A theme is applied to a *slide master*, which is a sample slide and not part of the regular presentation, existing only behind-the-scenes to provide its settings to the real slides. It holds the formatting that you want to be consistent among all the slides in the presentation (or at least a group of them, because a presentation can have multiple slide masters). Technically, you do not apply a theme to a slide; you apply a theme to a slide master, and then you apply a slide master to a slide. That's because a slide master can actually contain some additional elements besides the formatting of the theme such as extra graphics, dates, footer text, and so on.

Themes versus templates

As you learned in Chapter 20, a template is a file on which you can base new presentations. Templates typically have a .potx extension (or a .potm extension if macro-enabled). A template may contain one or more themes (that is, sets of design choices, like backgrounds, layouts, and font choices), plus one or more slides containing sample text.

A *theme* is both simpler than and more complex than a template. A theme can exist either inside of a template or as a separate file with a `.thmx` extension. A theme is simpler because it cannot hold some of the things a template can hold, such as sample content. A theme can provide only font, color, effect, and background settings to the presentation. (It can also provide slide layouts, discussed a bit later.) On the other hand, a theme can also do more than a PowerPoint template, in that you can apply a theme saved as a separate file to other Office applications, so you can share its color, font, and effect settings with Word or Excel, for example.

Where themes are stored

A theme is an XML file (or a snippet of XML code embedded in a presentation or template file). A theme can come from any of these sources:

- **Built-in:** Some themes are embedded in PowerPoint itself and are available from the Themes gallery on the Design tab regardless of the template in use.
- **Custom (automatically loaded):** The default storage location for user-created theme files in Windows 7 and 8 is `C:\Users\user name\AppData\Roaming\Microsoft\Templates\Document Themes`. All themes (and templates containing themes) stored here are automatically displayed among the gallery of theme choices on the Design tab, in a Custom category.

> **TIP**
>
> If you don't want to delete a custom theme file, but you also don't want it showing up in the gallery all the time, move the file to a folder outside of the Document Themes folder hierarchy. For example, create an Unused Themes folder on your hard disk and move it there until you need it. When you want to use the custom color theme again, move the file back to its original location.

- **Inherited from starting template:** If you start a presentation using a template other than the default blank one, that template might have one or more themes included in it.
- **Stored in current presentation:** If you modify a theme in Slide Master view while you are working on a presentation, the modified code for the theme is embedded in that presentation file.
- **Stored in a separate file:** If you save a theme (using any of a variety of methods you'll learn later in this chapter), you create a separate theme file with a `.thmx` extension. These files can be shared among other Office applications, so you can standardize settings such as font and color choices across applications. (Some of the unique PowerPoint portions of the theme are ignored when you use the theme in other applications.)

Themes, layouts, and Slide Master view

In PowerPoint 2013, the slide master has separate layout masters for each layout, and you can customize and create new layouts. Look at Figure 22.2, which shows Slide Master view. Notice along the left side that there is a different, separately customizable layout master for each available layout, all grouped beneath the slide master. Any changes you make to the slide master trickle down to the individual layout masters, but you can also customize each of the individual layout masters to override a trickle-down setting. For example, on a particular layout you can choose to omit the background graphic to free up its space on the slide for extra content.

FIGURE 22.2

Slide Master view enables you to make design changes that affect the entire presentation.

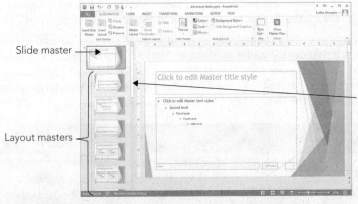

Slide master

Click to edit Master title style

Drag divider between the panes to the right to make slide master and layout masters easier to see.

Layout masters

> **TIP**
>
> Figure 22.2 shows the left pane slightly enlarged so that the slide master and layout masters appear larger than the default. If you would like your screen to look like that, drag the divider between the panes to the right until the thumbnails in the left pane are a readable size.

A *master* is a set of specifications that govern overall formatting and appearance. PowerPoint actually has three masters: the slide master (for slides), the handout master (for handouts), and the notes master (for speaker notes). This chapter deals only with the slide master. For more on the handout and notes masters, see Chapter 25.

The *slide master* holds the settings from a theme and applies them to one or more slides in your presentation. A slide master is not exactly the same thing as a theme because the theme can also be external to PowerPoint and used in other programs, but there's a rough equivalency there. A slide master is the representation of a particular theme applied to a particular presentation.

NOTE

Which themes appear in Slide Master view? The ones you have applied to at least one slide in the presentation, plus any custom themes copied from another presentation (see the section "Copying a theme from another presentation" for more details) and any themes inherited from the template used to create the presentation. The built-in themes do not show up here unless they are in use.

When you make changes to a slide master, those changes trickle down to the individual layout masters associated with it. When you make changes to an individual layout master, those changes are confined to that layout in that master only.

To enter Slide Master view, choose View ➪ Master Views ➪ Slide Master. A Slide Master tab appears. To exit from Slide Master view, choose Slide Master ➪ Close ➪ Close Master View or select a different view from the View tab.

Changing a Slide's Layout

As you construct your presentation, you may find it useful to change a slide's layout. For example, you might want to switch from a slide that contains one big content placeholder to one that has two side-by-side content placeholders, to compare/contrast two lists, drawings, or diagrams.

Many of the layouts PowerPoint provides contain multipurpose placeholders that accept various types of content. For example, the default layout, called Title and Content, has placeholders for a slide title plus a placeholder where you can choose a single type of content to insert — text, a table, a chart, a picture, a piece of clip art, a SmartArt diagram, or a video. You choose the layout you want based on the number and arrangement of the placeholders, and not the type of content that will go into them.

When you change to a different layout, PowerPoint changes the type and/or positioning of the placeholders on it according to the associated layout in the slide master. If the previous placeholders had content in them, that content shifts to a new location on the slide to reflect the different positioning for that placeholder type. If the new layout does not contain a placeholder appropriate for that content, the content remains on the slide but becomes *orphaned*. This means it is a free-floating object, outside of the layout. You need to manually position an orphaned object if it's not in the right spot. However, if you later apply a different layout that does contain a placeholder for the orphaned object, it snaps back into that placeholder.

22

To switch a slide to a different layout, follow these steps:

1. **Select the slide or slides to affect.**
2. **Click Home ⇨ Slides ⇨ Layout.** A menu of layouts appears, as shown in Figure 22.3.

FIGURE 22.3

Switch to a different layout for the selected slide(s).

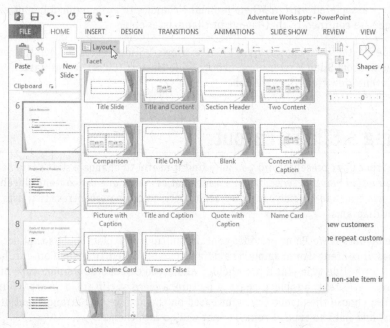

3. **Click the desired layout.**

> **NOTE**
> If you want to modify a built-in layout, or create your own layouts, see "Customizing and Creating Layouts" later in this chapter.

When a presentation has more than one slide master defined, separate layouts appear for each of the slide masters. Figure 22.4 shows the Layout menu for a presentation that has two slide masters.

FIGURE 22.4

When there are multiple slide masters, each one's layouts are separate.

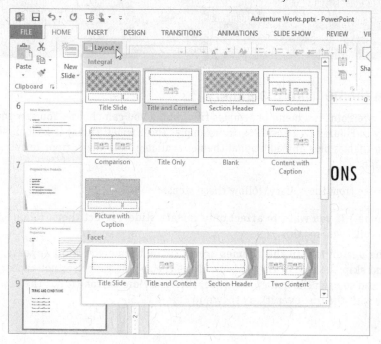

Applying a Theme

As you learned in "Understanding Layouts and Themes" at the beginning of this chapter, themes enable you to apply different designs to the presentation. A theme includes a background graphic (usually), color and font choices, and graphic effect settings. A theme can also include custom layouts.

The method for applying a theme depends on whether that theme is already available in the current presentation or not. Some themes are built into PowerPoint so that they are always available; other themes are available only when you use certain templates, or when you specifically apply them from an external file. The following sections explain each of those possibilities.

Applying a theme from the gallery

A gallery in PowerPoint is a menu of samples from which you can choose. You saw the Layout gallery in Figures 22.2 and 22.3, for example. The Themes gallery is a menu of all of the built-in themes plus any additional themes available from the current template or presentation file.

To select a theme from the gallery, follow these steps:

1. **(Optional) If you want to affect only certain slides, select them.** (Slide Sorter view works well for this.)

2. **On the Design tab, in the Themes group, if the theme you want appears, click it, and skip the rest of these steps.** If the theme you want does not appear, you will need to open the gallery. To do so, click the More button (it has the down arrow with the line over it), as shown in Figure 22.5.

FIGURE 22.5

Open the Themes gallery by clicking the More button.

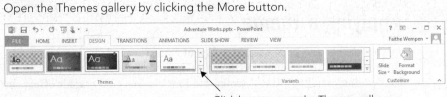

Click here to open the Themes gallery.

The Themes gallery opens, as shown in Figure 22.6. The gallery is divided into sections based upon the source of the theme. Themes stored in the current presentation appear at the top, under the This Presentation heading; custom themes you have added (if any) appear next, under a Custom heading. Figure 22.6 does not show any custom themes. Built-in themes appear at the bottom, under the Office heading.

FIGURE 22.6

Select the desired theme from the gallery.

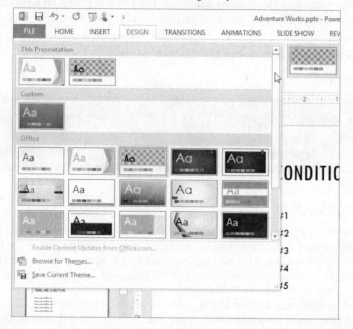

> **TIP**
> You can drag the gallery's bottom-right corner to resize it.

3. **Click the theme you want to apply.**
   - If you selected multiple slides in step 1, the theme is applied only to them.
   - If you selected a single slide in step 1, the theme is applied to the entire presentation.

To override the default behavior in step 3, so that you can apply a different theme to a single slide, right-click instead of clicking in step 3 and choose Apply to Selected Slide(s) from the shortcut menu.

Applying a theme from a theme or template file

You can open and use externally saved theme files in any Office application. This makes it possible to share color, font, and other settings between applications to create consistency between documents of various types. You can also save and load themes from templates. (To create your own theme files, see "Creating a new theme" later in this chapter.)

To apply a theme to the presentation from a theme or template file, follow these steps:

1. **On the Design tab, open the Themes gallery in the Themes group (see Figure 22.6) and click Browse for Themes.** The Choose Theme or Themed Document dialog box opens.

2. **Navigate to the folder containing the file and select it.**

3. **Click Apply.**

> **NOTE**
>
> Any custom themes you might have previously saved are located by default in `C:\Users\`*`user name`*`\ AppData\Roaming\Microsoft\Templates\Document Themes`. However, you don't need to navigate to that location to open a theme file because all themes stored here are automatically included in the gallery already.

Applying a theme variant

Some themes come in several versions, called *variants*. These variants have the same basic slide layouts and background graphics as the original, but may have different color, font, and/or effect choices. For example, a theme that has a white background and black text might have a black-background variant with white text. Variants are new in PowerPoint 2013.

To apply a variant, first apply the desired theme, using any of the methods you learned about earlier in this chapter. Then, on the Design tab, click one of the variants in the Variants group. See Figure 22.7.

FIGURE 22.7

Select a variant for the chosen theme from the Design tab.

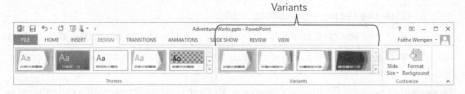

The Variants group, like the Themes group, has a More button (down-pointing arrow button with a line over it) that you can click to open up a full gallery of choices. However, most themes have only a few variants to choose from, so all the variants may already be visible without opening the gallery.

Managing Themes

Themes are applied to slide masters to specify the background, color, font, and effect formatting for all the slides that have that slide master assigned to them. (A single presentation file can have multiple slide masters, and therefore multiple themes.)

Some themes are built into PowerPoint, and you can also create and save your own themes as separate files and apply them to other presentations or even to other Office documents, such as in Word and Excel. In this section you learn how to create new themes, manage theme files, and apply themes across multiple presentations.

Creating a new theme

To create a new theme, first format a slide master exactly the way you want, including any custom layouts, backgrounds, colors, and font themes. (You will learn how to make those changes later in this chapter.) Then save the slide master's formatting as a new theme by following these steps:

1. **Open Slide Master view if it is not already open (View ⇨ Master Views ⇨ Slide Master), and select the desired slide master in the left pane.**

   You should have already formatted this slide master the way you want the new theme to be. If you haven't yet, see the sections "Changing Colors, Fonts, and Effects" and "Changing the Background" later in this chapter to make the needed changes.

> **NOTE**
>
> As you learned in "Themes, layouts, and Slide Master view" earlier in this chapter, the default slide master is the larger thumbnail at the top of the tree in the left pane. Notice that there are slightly smaller thumbnail images under it; those are its individual layout masters. There may be more than one slide master; scroll the left pane down to see if there's another Slide Master below the default one.

2. **Click Slide Master ⇨ Edit Theme ⇨ Themes ⇨ Save Current Theme.** The Save Current Theme dialog box opens.

   The default location shown in the Save Current Theme dialog box is `C:\Users\ user name\AppData\Roaming\Microsoft\Templates\Document Themes` where user name is the current Windows user.

3. **Type a name for the theme file in the File name text box.** See Figure 22.8.

FIGURE 22.8

Save the current slide master's settings as a new theme.

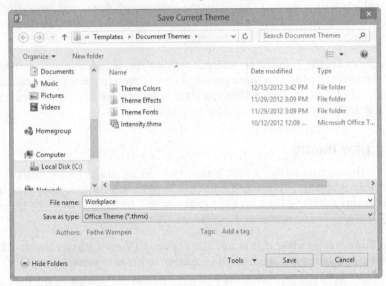

4. **Click Save.** The new theme is saved to your hard disk.

The new theme is now available from the Themes gallery in all presentations you create, as long as you are signed into Windows as the same user on the same PC. All of the theme's formatting is available, including any custom color or font themes it includes. You can use the saved theme in other programs too; in Word or Excel, choose Page Layout ⇨ Themes in one of those programs.

Renaming a theme

You can rename a theme file by renaming the .thmx file from File Explorer (Windows Explorer in Windows 7), from outside of PowerPoint. By default, theme files are stored in: C:\Users\user name\AppData\Roaming\Microsoft\Templates\Document Themes.

Don't want to leave PowerPoint to do this? You can also rename a theme file from inside PowerPoint by using any dialog box that saves or opens files. For example, to use the Choose Theme or Themed Document dialog box to rename a theme, follow these steps:

1. **From the Design or Slide Master tab, click Themes, and choose Save Current Theme.** The Choose Theme or Themed Document dialog box opens.

2. **If needed, navigate to**

   `C:\Users\`*user name*`\AppData\Roaming\Microsoft\Templates\Document Themes.` (That location may appear automatically.)

3. **Right-click the theme file and choose Rename.** See Figure 22.9.

FIGURE 22.9

Right-click the theme file and choose Rename.

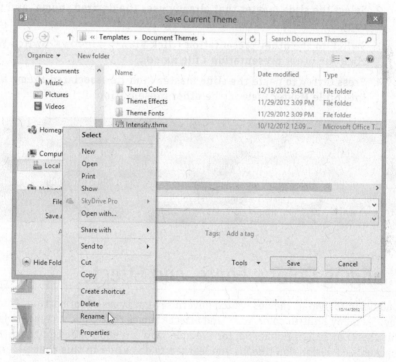

4. **Type the new name for the theme and press Enter.**
5. **Click Cancel to close the dialog box.**

Deleting a theme

A custom theme file continues appearing on the Themes gallery indefinitely. If you want to remove it from there, you must delete it. The easiest way to delete a theme is to right-click it in the Themes gallery and choose Delete.

You can also browse to the folder containing your saved custom themes and delete from there. See the previous section, "Renaming a theme," to learn an easy way to get access to that folder without leaving PowerPoint.

Copying a theme from another presentation

One easy way to copy a theme from one presentation to another is copy a slide master that has that theme applied to it. Follow these steps to learn how to do that:

1. **Open both presentations, and switch to Slide Master view in both presentations (View ➪ Master Views ➪ Slide Master).**
2. **Select the slide master that already uses the desired theme, and press Ctrl+C to copy it.**
3. **Switch to the other presentation (click View ➪ Window ➪ Switch Windows and click the other presentation's file name).**
4. **Press Ctrl+V to paste the slide master (and its associated theme and layouts) into Slide Master view in the other presentation.**

> **TIP**
>
> As you will learn in "Preserving a slide master" later in this chapter, you can preserve a slide master in Slide Master view so that it doesn't get deleted automatically when there are no slides based on it. By creating new slide masters, applying themes to them, and then preserving them, you can create a whole library of themes in a single presentation or template file. Then to make this library of themes available in another presentation, you simply base the new presentation on that existing presentation (or template).

Changing Colors, Fonts, and Effects

In addition to overall themes, which govern several types of formatting, PowerPoint also provides many built-in color, font, and effect themes that you can apply separately from your choice of design theme. So, for example, you can apply a design theme that contains a background design you like, as you learned to do earlier in this chapter, and then change the colors, fonts, and effects for it.

In the following sections, you'll learn how to apply some of these built-in color, font, and effect settings to a presentation without changing the theme. For example, you might choose to make changes in the colors, fonts, and/or effects to customize a theme, and then save it as a custom theme, as you learned in "Creating a new theme" earlier in this chapter.

Understanding color placeholders

To understand how PowerPoint changes colors when you choose a different theme or variant, you must know something about how PowerPoint handles colors in general.

PowerPoint uses a set of color placeholders for the bulk of its color formatting. Because each item's color is defined by a placeholder, and not as a fixed color, you can easily change the colors by switching to a different color theme. This way if you decide, for example, that you want all the slide titles to be blue rather than green, you make the change once and it is applied to all slides automatically.

A group of colors assigned to preset placeholders is a *color theme*. PowerPoint contains 20+ built-in color themes that are available regardless of the overall theme applied to the presentation. Because design themes use placeholders to define their colors, you can apply the desired design theme to the presentation and then fine-tune the colors afterward by experimenting with the built-in color themes.

How many color placeholders are there in a color theme? There are actually 12, but sometimes not all of them are available to be applied to individual objects. When you choose a color theme, the gallery of themes from which you choose shows only the first eight colors of each color theme. It doesn't matter so much here because you can't apply individual colors from there anyway. When selecting colors from a color picker (used for applying fill and border color to specific objects), as in Figure 22.10, there are 10 theme swatches. And when you define a new custom color theme, there are 12 placeholders to set up. The final two are for visited and unvisited hyperlinks; these colors aren't included in a color picker.

FIGURE 22.10

PowerPoint uses color pickers such as this one to enable you to easily apply color placeholders to objects.

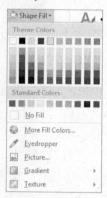

Changing the color theme

After applying the overall theme you want, you might want to apply different colors. One way to get different colors, as you saw earlier in this chapter, is to apply a variant. The variants are just the tip of the iceberg, though; many more color themes are available.

To switch to a different color theme from Normal, Outline, or Slide Sorter views, choose Design ➪ Variants ➪ More button ➪ Colors, and then click the desired color theme in the gallery.

TIP

If you want to apply a different color theme, font theme, or effects theme to the current slide only from the Design tab, right click the desired item after you've displayed its gallery, and then click Apply to Selected Slides.

Or, if you prefer to work in Slide Master view follow these steps:

1. **Open Slide Master view (View ➪ Master Views ➪ Slide Master) and click the desired slide master.**
2. **Click Slide Master ➪ Background ➪ Colors.** A gallery of color themes opens. See Figure 22.11.

FIGURE 22.11

Choose the desired color theme.

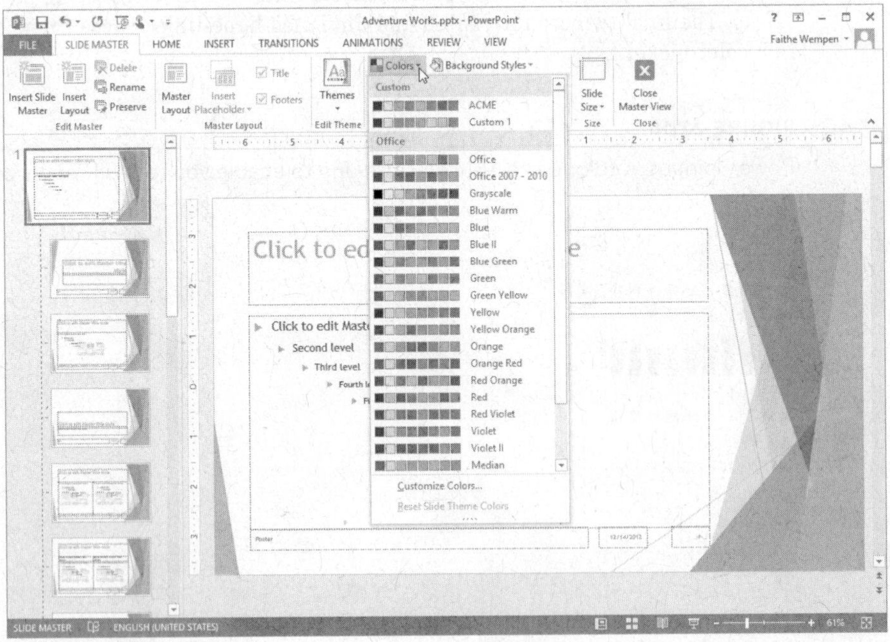

3. **(Optional) Point to a color theme and observe the preview on the slide behind the list.**
4. **Click the desired color theme.**

Understanding font placeholders

By default in most themes and templates, text box fonts are not set to a specific font, but to one of two designations: Heading or Body. Then a *font theme* defines what specific fonts to use as Heading and Body. To change the fonts across the entire presentation, all you have to do is apply a different font theme.

A *font theme* is an XML-based specification that defines a pair of fonts: one for headings and one for body text. Then that font is applied to the text boxes in the presentation based on their statuses of Heading or Body. For example, all of the slide titles are usually set to Heading, and all of the content placeholders and manual text boxes are usually set to Body.

In a blank presentation (default blank template), when you click inside a slide title placeholder box, you see Calibri Light (Headings) in the Font group on the Home tab. Figure 22.12 shows that the current font is Calibri Light, but that it is being used only because the font theme specifies it. You could change the font theme to Verdana/ Verdana, for example, and then the font designation for that box would appear as Verdana (Headings). The word (Headings) might be truncated, as it is in Figure 22.12, if your PowerPoint window is not wide enough to allow it to display in full.

FIGURE 22.12

When some text is using a font placeholder rather than a fixed font, (Headings) or (Body) appears after its name in the Font group on the Home tab.

In some font themes, the same font is used for both headings and body. In many other font themes, though, the heading and body fonts are different. The default font theme for blank presentations is Calibri Light/Calibri — the same basic font, but with a thinner version for the headings.

Changing the font theme

After applying a design theme, you might decide you want to use different fonts in the presentation. To switch to a different font theme from Normal, Outline, or Slide Sorter views, choose Design ➪ Variants ➪ More button ➪ Fonts, and then click the desired font theme in the gallery.

Alternately, in Slide Master view follow these steps:

1. **Open Slide Master view (View ➪ Master Views ➪ Slide Master) and click the desired slide master.** See the note in the previous section about selecting slide masters vs. layout masters.

2. **Click Slide Master ⇨ Background ⇨ Fonts.** A gallery of font themes opens. See Figure 22.13.

FIGURE 22.13

Select the font theme you want for your slide.

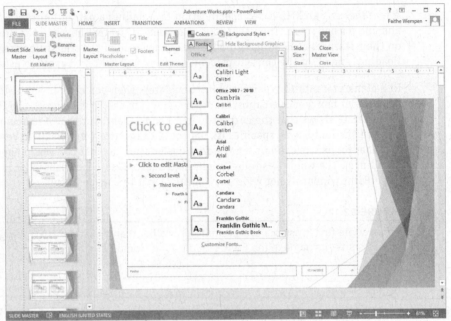

3. **(Optional) Point to a font theme and observe the change on the slide behind the list.**

4. **Click the desired font theme.**

Changing the effect theme

Effect themes apply to several types of drawings that PowerPoint can construct, including SmartArt, charts, and drawn lines and shapes. They make the surfaces of objects formatted with 3-D attributes look like different textures (more or less shiny-looking, colors more or less deep, and so on).

To change the effect theme from Normal, Outline, or Slide Sorter views, choose Design ⇨ Variants ⇨ More button ⇨ Effects, and then click the desired effect theme in the gallery.

Or, if you prefer to work in Slide Master view, follow these steps:

1. **Open Slide Master view (View ⇨ Master Views ⇨ Slide Master) and click the desired slide master.** See the note in the previous section about selecting slide masters vs. layout masters.

2. **Click Slide Master ⇨ Background ⇨ Effects.** A menu of effect options appears. See Figure 22.14.

FIGURE 22.14

Select the desired effect theme.

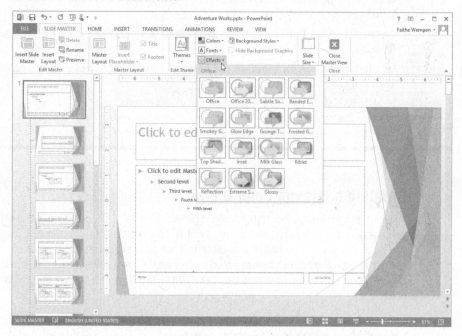

3. **(Optional) Point to a theme and observe the change on the slide master behind the list.** (This works only if you have an object on that slide that is affected by the effect theme; see the sidebar "Setting Up a Graphic on Which to Test Effect Themes" to set up such an object.)

4. **Click the desired effect theme.**

Setting Up a Graphic on Which to Test Effect Themes

Effect themes are most evident when you use colorful 3-D graphics, so do the following to construct a dummy diagram that you can use to try out effect themes:

1. **Switch to Slide Master view.** (Or, if you're working in Normal view, insert a slide using the Title and Content slide layout, click the Insert a SmartArt Graphic button in the content placeholder, and skip to step 3.)

2. **Ctlick Insert ⇨ Illustrations ⇨ SmartArt.** The Choose a SmartArt Graphic dialog box opens.

3. **Click Cycle, click the top left diagram, and click OK.** A SmartArt diagram appears on the slide master.

4. **On the SmartArt Tools Design tab, click Change Colors, and click the first sample under Colorful.**

5. **On the SmartArt Tools ⇨ Design tab, open the SmartArt Styles gallery and click the first sample under 3-D.**

Now you have a diagram on which you can see the effect themes applied. After using this diagram to help you choose the desired effect theme, delete the diagram from the slide master. To delete the diagram, select the diagram's outer frame and press the Delete key on the keyboard.

Creating a custom color theme

You can define your own custom color themes, and save them for reuse in other presentations. By default, these are saved in the personal folders for the logged-in user on the local PC, and they remain available to that user regardless of the theme or template in use. These custom color themes are also included if you save the design theme as a separate theme file (.thmx), so that you can take those settings to another PC or send them to some other user.

A custom color theme defines specific colors for each of the 12 color placeholders (including the two that you can't directly use — the ones for hyperlinks). To create a custom color theme, first apply a color theme to the current presentation that is as close as possible to the color theme you want. This makes it easier because you have to redefine fewer placeholders. Then follow these steps:

1. **Open Slide Master view if it is not already open (View ⇨ Master Views ⇨ Slide Master).**

2. **Click Slide Master ⇨ Background ⇨ Colors and choose Customize Colors.** The Create New Theme Colors dialog box opens.

TIP

If working in Normal, Outline, or Slide Sorter view, you also can choose Design ⇨ Variants ⇨ More button ⇨ Colors ⇨ Customize Colors in place of Steps 1 and 2.

3. **Type a name for the new color theme in the Name box, replacing the default name** (Custom 1, or other number if there is already a Custom 1).

4. **Click a color placeholder and open its menu.** See Figure 22.15.

FIGURE 22.15

Select the color for the chosen placeholder.

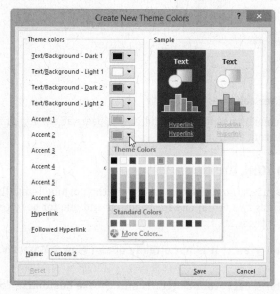

5. **Click a color in the Standard Colors section.** Or, if none of the colors there fit your needs, click More Colors, select a color from the Colors dialog box (see Figure 22.16), and click OK. The Colors dialog box has two tabs: The Standard tab has color swatches, and the Custom tab enables you to define a color numerically by its RGB (Red Green Blue) or HSL (Hue Saturation Lightness).

FIGURE 22.16

Choose a custom color if none of the standard colors is appropriate.

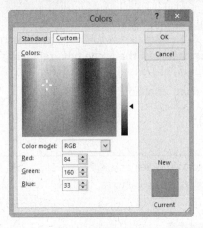

6. **Redefine any other colors as needed.**
7. **Click Save.** The color theme is saved, and now appears at the top of the Colors gallery, in the Custom area.

Creating a custom font theme

You can create your own custom font themes, which are then available in all presentations. A custom font theme defines two fonts: one for headings and one for body text. To create a custom font theme, follow these steps:

1. **Open Slide Master view if it is not already open (View ⇨ Master Views ⇨ Slide Master).**
2. **Click Slide Master ⇨ Background ⇨ Fonts and choose Customize Fonts.** The Create New Theme Fonts dialog box opens. See Figure 22.17.

TIP

If working in Normal, Outline, or Slide Sorter view, you also can choose Design ⇨ Variants ⇨ More button ⇨ Fonts ⇨ Customize Fonts in place of Steps 1 and 2.

FIGURE 22.17

Create a new custom font theme by specifying the fonts to use.

3. **Type a name for the new font theme in the Name box, replacing the default text there.**

4. **Open the Heading font drop-down list and select the desired font for headings.**

5. **Open the Body font drop-down list and select the desired font for body text.**

6. **Click Save.** The font theme is saved, and now appears at the top of the Fonts list, in the Custom area.

> **NOTE**
> You cannot create custom effect themes.

Sharing a custom color or font theme with others

A custom color theme or font theme is available only to the currently logged-in user on the PC on which it is created. If you want to share it with another user on the same PC, you can copy it into his or her user folder. In File Explorer (Windows Explorer), start out at `C:\Users\user name\AppData\Roaming\Microsoft\Templates\Document Themes` where *user name* is that user's login name and then navigate to the appropriate subfolder there: Theme Colors or Theme Fonts.

The default color and font themes are located in `C:\Program Files\Microsoft Office\Document Theme`, in the Theme Colors or Theme Fonts folder, respectively.

Another way to share a custom color or font theme is to save the (design) theme to a theme file (.thmx). See "Creating a new theme" earlier in this chapter. The resulting theme file will contain the custom colors and fonts.

Deleting a custom color or font theme

A custom color or font theme remains until you delete it. The easiest way to do so is to click the button for the appropriate type (Color or Font) on the Slide Master tab in Slide

Master view, and then right-click the theme in the gallery and click Delete. Or in other views, you can click the More button in the Variants group of the design tab, point to Color or Font, and then right-click the theme in the gallery and click Delete.

You can also delete the color or font theme from outside of PowerPoint. To delete a theme color, use File Explorer (Windows Explorer) to navigate to this folder: `C:\Users\` `user name\AppData\Roaming\Microsoft\Templates\Document Themes\Theme` `Colors` where *user name* is your Windows sign-in name, and you'll find an `.xml` file for each of your custom color themes. (You'll find the font themes in `.xml` files in the Theme Fonts folder.) Delete the files for the color or font themes that you want to delete.

Changing the Background

The *background* is the color, texture, pattern, or image that is applied to the entire slide (or slide master), on which everything else sits. By its very definition, it applies to the entire surface of the slide; you cannot have a partial background. However, you can have a *background graphic* overlaid on top of the background. A background graphic is a graphic image placed on the slide master that complements and works with the background.

It's important to understand the distinction between a background and a background graphic because even though most themes contain both, they are set up differently. Making the change you want to the overall appearance of your slides often involves changing both. For example, Figure 22.18 shows the Facet theme applied to a slide. The slide background is pure white, and a green background graphic is overlaid on it. This background graphic is composed of several different shapes, colors with different shades of green, plus a few gray straight lines. Each of those graphic objects can be individually edited, moved, or even deleted from the slide master. The white background itself can be changed via the Format Background command.

FIGURE 22.18

A slide's background is separate from its background graphic(s) if any are present.

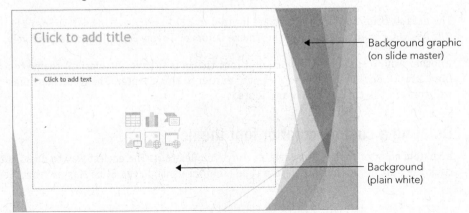

Background graphic (on slide master)

Background (plain white)

Most themes consist of both background formatting (even if it is just a solid color) and a background graphic. The background graphics included in the built-in themes in PowerPoint are unique to those themes, and not available as separate graphics outside of them. So, for example, if you want the colored shapes shown in Figure 22.18, the only way to get them is to apply the Facet theme. Because the decorative background graphics are unique to each theme, many people choose a theme based on the desired background graphics, and then customize the slide master's appearance to modify the theme as needed.

> **TIP**
>
> To use a background graphic from one template with the look and feel of another, apply the first theme to a slide, and then in Slide Master view copy the background graphic to the Clipboard. Then apply the second theme, and paste the graphic from the Clipboard onto the second Slide Master.

Applying a background style

Background styles are preset background formats that come with the built-in themes in PowerPoint. Depending on the theme you apply, different background styles are available. These background styles use the color placeholders from the theme, so their color offerings change depending on the color theme applied.

To apply a background style, follow these steps:

1. **Switch to Slide Master view.**
2. **(Optional) To affect certain layouts, select the layout(s) to affect from the left pane.** To select more than one layout at once, hold down the Ctrl key as you click the layouts you want. Or, to affect all layouts, select the Slide Master itself.
3. **Click Slide Master ➪ Background ➪ Background Styles.** A gallery of styles appears, as shown in Figure 4.19.

FIGURE 22.19

Apply a preset background style.

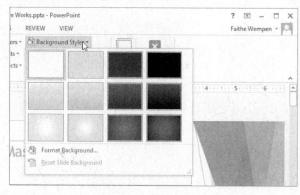

4. **Click the desired style to apply it to the selected layouts only (or to all layouts if you selected the Slide Master in step 2).** Alternatively, you can right-click the desired style and choose Apply to All Layouts to apply the change to all layouts even if you did not select the Slide Master in step 2.

You cannot customize background styles or add your own custom background styles; there are always 12 of them, and they are always determined by the theme. If you need a different background, you can apply a custom background fill, as described in the following sections, which lets you modify the background in a variety of ways.

Applying a custom background fill

A custom background fill can include solid colors, gradients, textures, or graphics. Here's how to specify your own background fill, which involves the following steps:

1. **(Optional) To affect only certain slides, select them.** You can do this in Normal, Outline, or Slide Sorter view. (Or, to affect certain layouts, go into Slide Master view and choose the layouts you want to customize, or select the slide master to customize all layouts at once.)

2. **Click Design ⇨ Customize ⇨ Format Background.** Or, if you are in Slide Master view, click Slide Master ⇨ Background ⇨ Background Styles ⇨ Format Background. The Format Background pane opens.

   The Fill settings are expanded by default, as shown in Figure 22.20. Each of the listed options buttons displays a separate group of settings when clicked.

FIGURE 22.20

Click the option button for the fill type that best fits your needs.

3. **Choose the option button that best describes the type of fill you want.** The controls change for the type you chose. Figure 22.20 shows the controls for a solid fill.

4. **Set the options for the fill type that you chose.** For example, in Figure 22.20 where Solid fill is selected, click the Color button and choose a color. The changes you make apply immediately. (Chapter 23 covers how to specify some of the other fill types.)

5. **(Optional) To apply the change to all slides, click Apply to All.** Otherwise the change will apply only to the slides (or layouts) you selected in step 1.

6. **(Optional) To apply a different background to some other slides, select them and repeat steps 3 and 4.** The Format Background task pane can stay open as long as you need it. Its changes are applied immediately.

7. **When you are finished with the Format Background pane, click its Close (X) button in its upper right corner to close it.**

Working with background graphics

In Figure 22.20, one of the fill types you saw on the list was Picture or texture fill. This type of fill covers the entire background with the picture or texture that you specify.

That's not what we mean by a background graphic in this section, however. A *background graphic* in the context of the following discussion is an object or a picture overlaid on top of the background on the slide master, like those shapes I pointed out in Figure 22.18. The background graphics complement the background, and might or might not cover the entire background.

> **NOTE**
>
> Many of the theme-provided background graphics actually consist of multiple shapes, and in some cases they are grouped together. You can ungroup them so that you can modify or remove only a portion of the background graphic.

Displaying and hiding background graphics

Sometimes a background graphic can get in the way of the slide's content. For example, on a slide that contains a large chart or diagram, a background graphic around the border of the slide can overlap the content. You don't have to delete the background graphic entirely to solve this problem; you can turn it off for individual slides. To hide the background graphics on one or more slides, follow these steps:

1. **Select the slide or slides to affect.**
2. **Click Design ⇨ Customize ⇨ Format Background.** The Format Background pane opens.
3. **Select the Hide background graphics check box.** The background graphic disappears from the slide. See Figure 22.21.

FIGURE 22.21

Mark the Hide background graphics check box to suppress the background graphics on the selected slide.

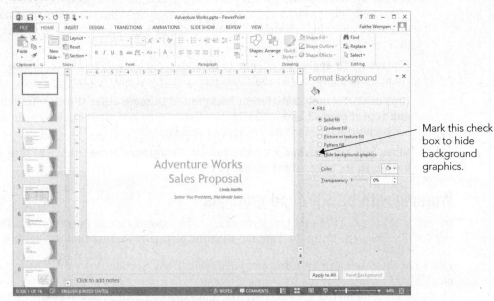

Deselect the check box to redisplay the background graphics later as needed.

If you want to hide the background graphics on all the slides that use a particular layout master or slide master, do the following:

1. **Click View ⇨ Master Views ⇨ Slide Master to enter Slide Master view.**
2. **In the left pane, select the slide master or layout master(s) to affect.**
3. **On the Slide Master tab, mark the Hide Background Graphics check box.**

Deleting background graphics

The background graphics reside on the slide master, so to remove one, you must use Slide Master view. Follow these steps:

1. **Click View ⇨ Master Views ⇨ Slide Master.** Slide Master view opens.
2. **Select the slide master or layout master that contains the graphic to delete.**
3. **Click the background graphic to select it.**
4. **Press the Delete key on the keyboard.**

Adding your own background graphics

You can add your own background graphics, either to the slide master or to individual layout masters. This works just like adding any other graphic to a slide, except you add it to the master instead of to an individual slide.

Inserting pictures is covered in greater detail in Chapters 9 and 24, but here are the basic steps for adding a background graphic:

1. **Display the slide master or layout master on which you want to place the background graphic.**

2. **Do any of the following:**

   - Click Insert ➪ Images ➪ Pictures. Select a picture to insert and click Insert.
   - Click Insert ➪ Images ➪ Online Pictures. Search for a piece of clip art to use, or an image from another online source, and insert it on the master.
   - In any application (including PowerPoint), copy any graphic to the Clipboard by pressing Ctrl+C; then display the master and paste the graphic by pressing Ctrl+V.

Working with Placeholders

Recall from earlier in this chapter that when you enter Slide Master view, one or more slide masters appear in the left pane, with its own subordinate layout masters. The slide master and each layout master has five preset placeholders that you can individually remove or move around. Figure 22.22 points them out on a slide master with the Facet theme applied, but they might be in different locations in other themes:

- **Title:** The placeholder for the title on each slide
- **Text:** The main content placeholder on each slide
- **Date:** The box that displays the current date on each slide
- **Slide number:** The box that displays the slide number on each slide
- **Footer:** A box that displays repeated text at the bottom of each slide

FIGURE 22.22

Each slide master contains these placeholders (or can contain them).

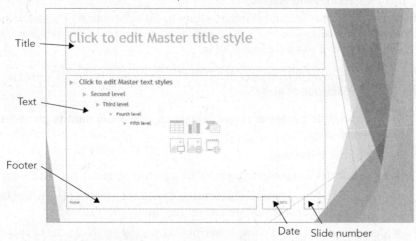

Each of these elements on the slide master trickles down to the layout masters beneath it, so formatting, moving, or deleting one of these elements from the slide master also changes it on each of the layouts.

> **NOTE**
> Even though the placeholders are there on the slide master and/or layout master, the Date, Slide number, and Footer placeholders do not display on the slides unless you enable them. See "Displaying the date, number, and footer on slides" later in this chapter to learn how.

Formatting a placeholder

You can format the text in each of the placeholders on the slide master just like any regular text, and that formatting carries over to all slides and layouts based on it. For example, if you format the code in the Slide Number box with a certain font and size, it will appear that way on every slide that uses that slide master. You can also format the placeholder boxes just like any other text boxes. For example, you can add a border around the page number's box, and/or fill its background with color.

22

TIP

If you want to make all of the text in a heading all-caps or small-caps, use the Font dialog box. To do so, from the Home tab, click the dialog box launcher in the Font group and select the Small Caps or All Caps check box.

Moving, deleting, or restoring placeholders

You can move each of the placeholders on the slide master or an individual layout master. For example, you might decide you want the Footer box at the top of the slide rather than the bottom, or that you want to center the slide number at the bottom of the slide:

- To move a placeholder, click it to select it and then drag its border, just as you did with text boxes in Chapter 21.

- To delete one of the placeholders on the slide master, select its box and press the Delete key on the keyboard. Deleting it from the slide master deletes it from all of the associated layouts as well. It also deletes any special formatting they had, so if you add them back later, you have to reformat them.

- On an individual layout master, you can quickly delete and restore the Title and Footer placeholders by selecting or deselecting the Title and Footers check boxes on the Slide Master tab. The "footer" that this check box refers to is actually all three of the bottom-of-the-slide elements: the actual footer, the date box, and the slide number box.

- You can also individually delete the placeholders from a layout master, the same as you can on a slide master. Just select a placeholder box and press the Delete key.

- To restore deleted Date, Footer, or Slide Number placeholders on an individual layout master, display the Slide Master tab and select the Footers check box. If any of the footer placeholders (Date, Footer, or Slide Number) were previously deleted, they reappear.

- To control the status for each of the placeholders on the slide master, select the slide master in the left pane and then click Slide Master ➪ Master Layout ➪ Master Layout to open the Master Layout dialog box. From there, mark the check boxes for the placeholders you want to display or hide and click OK. See Figure 22.23. This action is available only for the slide master, not for individual layout masters.

FIGURE 22.23

Set each placeholder's on/off status in the Master Layout dialog box.

> **CAUTION**
>
> Restored placeholders might not appear in the same spots as they did originally; you might need to move them. To put the placeholders back to their original locations, reapply the theme from the Themes button on the Slide Master tab.

Displaying the date, number, and footer on slides

Even though the placeholders for Date, Number, and Footer might appear on the slide master, they do not appear on the actual slides in the presentation unless you enable them. This might seem counterintuitive at first, but it's actually a benefit. PowerPoint enables you to turn the date, number, and footer on and off without having to delete, re-create, or reformat their placeholders. You can decide at the last minute whether you want them to display or not, and you can choose differently for different audiences and situations.

You can control all three areas from the Header and Footer dialog box. To open it, click Insert ⇨ Text ⇨ Header and Footer. Then on the Slide tab, select the check boxes for each of the three elements that you want to use, as shown in Figure 22.24.

FIGURE 22.24

Choose which footer elements should appear on slides.

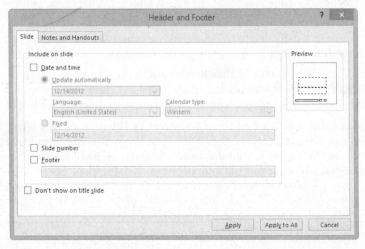

Date and time

You can set Date and Time either to Update Automatically or to Fixed:

- **Update automatically:** Pulls the current date from the computer's clock and formats it in whatever format you choose from the drop-down list. You can also select a language and a Calendar Type (although this is probably not an issue unless you are presenting in some other country than the one for which your version of PowerPoint was developed).

■ **Fixed:** Prints whatever you enter in the Fixed text box. When Fixed is enabled, it defaults to today's date in the m/dd/yyyy format.

> **TIP**
>
> In addition to (or instead of) placing the date on each slide, you can insert an individual instance of the current date or time on a slide, perhaps as part of a sentence. To do so, position the insertion point inside a text box or placeholder and then click Insert ⇨ Text ⇨ Date and Time. Select the format you want from the dialog box that appears and click OK. If the insertion point is not in an editable text area when you click Date and Time, the Header and Footer dialog box opens instead; click Cancel, reposition the insertion point, and try again.

Slide number

This option shows the slide number on each slide, wherever the Number placeholder is positioned. You can format the Number placeholder on the slide master with the desired font, size, and other text attributes

By default, slide numbering starts with 1. You can start with some other number if you like by following these steps:

1. **Close Slide Master view if it is open.** To do so, click Slide Master ⇨ Close ⇨ Close Master View.
2. **Click Design ⇨ Customize ⇨ Slide Size ⇨ Custom Slide Size.** The Slide Size dialog box opens.
3. **In the Number slides from box, increase the number to the desired starting number.**
4. **Click OK.**

> **TIP**
>
> You can insert the slide number on an individual slide, either instead of or in addition to the numbering on the slide master. Position the insertion point, and then click Insert ⇨ Text ⇨ Insert Slide Number. If you are in Slide master view, this places a code on the slide master for the slide number that looks like this: <#>. If you are on an individual slide, it inserts the same code, but the code itself is hidden and the actual number appears. If the insertion point is not in an editable text area when you click Insert Slide Number, the Header and Footer dialog box opens instead; click Cancel, reposition the insertion point, and try again.

Footer

The footer is blank by default. Select the Footer check box, and then enter the desired text in the Footer box. You can then format the footer text from the slide master as you would any other text. You can also enter the footer text in the Header and Footer dialog box's Footer text box.

Don't show on title slide

This check box in the Header and Footer dialog box suppresses the date/time, page number, and footer on slides that use the Title Slide layout. Many people like to hide those elements on title slides for a cleaner look and to avoid repeated information (for example, if the current date appears in the subtitle box on the title slide).

Customizing and Creating Layouts

In addition to customizing the slide master (including working with its preset placeholder boxes, as you just learned), you can fully customize the individual layout masters.

A layout master takes some of its settings from the slide master with which it is associated. For example, by default it takes its background, fonts, theme colors, and preset placeholder positioning from the slide master. But the layout master also can be individually customized; you can override the slide master's choices for background, colors, and fonts; and you can create, modify, and delete various types of content placeholders.

Understanding content placeholders

You can insert seven basic types of content on a PowerPoint slide: Text, Picture, Chart, Table, Diagram, Media (video or sound), and Clip Art. A placeholder on a slide master or layout master can specify one of these types of content that it will accept, or you can designate it as a Content placeholder, such that it will accept any of the seven types. Most of the layouts that PowerPoint generates automatically for its themes use the Content placeholder type because it offers the most flexibility. By making all placeholders Content placeholders rather than a specific type, PowerPoint can get by with fewer separate layout masters because users will choose the desired layout based on the positioning of the placeholders, not their types.

A Content placeholder appears as a text placeholder with a small palette of buttons in the center, one for each of the content types. Each content placeholder can hold only one type of content at a time, so as soon as the user types some text into the content placeholder or clicks one of the buttons in the palette and inserts some content, the placeholder becomes locked into that one type of content until the content is deleted from it.

> **NOTE**
>
> If a slide has a placeholder that contains some content (any type), selecting the placeholder and pressing Delete removes the content. To remove the placeholder itself from the layout, select the empty placeholder and press Delete. If you then want to restore the placeholder, reapply the slide layout to the slide.

You can move and resize a placeholder on a layout master as you would any other object. Drag a selection handle on the frame to resize it, or drag the border of the frame (not on a selection handle) to move it.

> **NOTE**
>
> The Content placeholder icons are shown in Chapter 21 in Figure 21.28.

Adding a custom placeholder

You can add a custom placeholder to an individual layout master. This makes it easy to build your own custom layouts.

To add a custom placeholder, follow these steps:

1. **In Slide Master view, select the layout master to affect.**
2. **On the Slide Master tab in the Master Layout group, click the bottom part of the Insert Placeholder button to open its menu.**
3. **Click Content to insert a generic placeholder, or click one of the specific content types.** See Figure 22.25. The mouse pointer becomes a cross-hair.

FIGURE 22.25

Create a new placeholder on a slide.

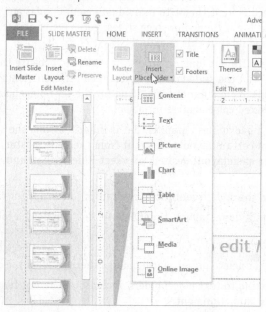

759

4. **Drag on the slide to draw the placeholder box of the size and position desired.**

   A rectangle appears showing where the placeholder box will go. When you release the mouse button, the new placeholder appears on the slide.

Deleting and restoring a custom placeholder

To delete a custom placeholder, select it and press the Delete key, just as you learned to do earlier with the preset placeholders.

The difference between custom and preset placeholders is not in the deleting, but rather in the restoring. You can immediately undo a deletion with Ctrl+Z, but you cannot otherwise restore a deleted custom placeholder from a layout master. PowerPoint retains no memory of the content placeholders on individual layouts. Therefore, you must re-create any content placeholders that you have accidentally deleted.

> **TIP**
>
> To restore one of the built-in layouts, copy it from another slide master. See the sections "Duplicating and deleting layouts" and "Copying layouts between slide masters" later in this chapter.

Overriding the slide master formatting for a layout

You can apply formatting to a layout in almost exactly the same ways as you apply formatting to a regular slide or to a slide master. Only a few things are off-limits:

- You cannot apply a different theme to individual layouts under a common slide master. To use a different theme for some slides, you have to create a whole new slide master (covered later in this chapter).

- You cannot apply a different font, color, or effect theme, because these are related to the main theme and the slide master. If you need different fonts or colors on a certain layout, specify fixed font formatting for the text placeholders in that layout, or specify fixed color choices for objects.

- You cannot delete a background graphic that is inherited from the slide master; if you want it only on certain layouts, delete it from the slide master, and then paste it individually onto each layout desired, or select Hide Background Graphics from certain layouts.

- You cannot change the slide orientation (portrait or landscape) or the slide size.

So what *can* you do to an individual layout, then? Plenty. You can do the following:

- Apply a different background.

- Reposition, resize, or delete preset placeholders inherited from the slide master.

- Apply fixed formatting to text placeholders, including different fonts, sizes, colors, attributes, indents, and alignment.

- Apply formatting using theme colors and theme fonts.

- Apply fixed formatting to any placeholder box, including different fill and border styles and colors.

- Create manual text boxes and type any text you like into them. You might do this to include copyright notice on certain slide layouts, for example. However, keep in mind that such text boxes can't be edited on the individual slides.

- Insert pictures or clip art that should repeat on each slide that uses a certain layout.

Creating a new layout

In addition to modifying the existing layouts, you can create your own brand-new layouts, defining the exact placeholders you want. To create a new layout, follow these steps:

1. **From Slide Master view, click the slide master with which to associate the new layout.**

2. **Click Slide Master ➪ Edit Master ➪ Insert Layout.** A new layout appears. Each new layout you create starts with preset placeholders inherited from the slide master for Title, Footer, Date, and Slide Number.

3. **(Optional) Hide or delete any of the preset placeholders that you don't want.**

4. **Insert new placeholders as needed.** To insert a placeholder, see the section "Adding a custom placeholder" earlier in the chapter.

5. **(Optional) Name the layout.** See "Renaming a layout" later in this chapter to do so.

> **NOTE**
>
> The new layout is part of the slide master, but not part of the theme. The theme is applied to the slide master, but at this point their relationship ends; and changes that you make to the slide master do not affect the existing theme. To save your custom layout(s), you have two choices: You can save the presentation as a template, or you can save the theme as a separate file. You learn more about saving themes in "Managing Themes" earlier in this chapter.

Renaming a layout

Layout names can help you determine the purpose of a layout if it is not obvious from viewing its thumbnail image.

To change the name of a layout, or to assign a name to a new layout you've created, follow these steps:

1. **In Slide Master view, right-click the layout and choose Rename Layout.** The Rename Layout dialog box opens.

2. **Type a new name for the layout, replacing the existing name.**

3. **Click Rename.**

Duplicating and deleting layouts

You might want to copy a layout to get a head start on creating a new one. To copy a layout, right-click the layout in Slide Master view and choose Duplicate Layout. A copy of the layout appears below the original.

If you are never going to use a certain layout, you might as well delete it; every layout you can delete makes the file a little bit smaller. To delete a layout, right-click the layout in Slide Master view and choose Delete Layout.

> **CAUTION**
>
> You might have a couple of layouts at the bottom of the list that employ vertical text. These are for users of Asian languages. They show up in the New Slide and Layout galleries on the home tab if you have certain Asian languages enabled on your system. Don't delete them if you will sometimes need to create Asian-language slides.

Copying layouts between slide masters

When you create additional slide masters in the presentation, any custom layouts you've created for the existing slide masters do not carry over. You must manually copy them to the new slide master.

To copy a layout from one slide master to another, follow these steps:

1. **In Slide Master view, select the layout to be copied.**
2. **Press Ctrl+C.**
3. **Select the slide master under which you want to place the copy.**
4. **Press Ctrl+V.**

You can also copy layouts between slide masters in different presentations. To do so, open both presentation files, and then perform the previous steps. The only difference is that after step 2, you must switch to the other presentation's Slide Master view.

Managing Slide Masters

Let's review the relationship one more time between slide masters and themes. A theme is a set of formatting specs (colors, fonts, and effects) that can be used in PowerPoint, Word, or Excel. Themes are not applied directly to slides — they are applied to slide masters, which govern the formatting of slides. The slide masters exist within the presentation file itself. You can change them by applying different themes, but they are essentially "built in" to the presentation file.

When you change to a different theme for all of the slides in the presentation, your slide master changes its appearance. You can tweak that appearance in Slide Master view. As long as all of the slides in the presentation use the same theme, you need only one slide master. However, if you apply a different theme to some of your slides, you need another slide master, because a slide master can have only one theme applied to it at a time. PowerPoint automatically creates the additional slide master(s) for you when you apply a different design to some slides but not to others.

If you later reapply a single theme to all of the slides in the presentation, you do not need multiple slide masters anymore, so the unused one is automatically deleted. In addition to all this automatic creation and deletion of slide masters, you can also manually create and delete slide masters on your own. Any slide masters that you create manually are automatically preserved, even if they aren't always in use. You must manually delete them if you don't want them anymore.

In the following sections, you learn how to create and delete slide masters manually, and how to rename them. You also learn how to lock one of the automatically created slide masters so that PowerPoint does not delete it if it falls out of use.

Creating and deleting slide masters

To create another slide master, start out in Slide Master view (of course), and then click Slide Master➪Edit Master➪Insert Slide Master. The new slide master appears below the existing slide master(s) and all its individual layout masters in the left pane of Slide Master view. From there, just start customizing it. You can apply a theme to it, modify its layouts and placeholders, and all the usual things you can do to a slide master. Another way to create a new slide master is to duplicate an existing one. To do this, right-click the existing slide master and choose Duplicate Master.

To delete a slide master, select it in Slide Master view (make sure you select the slide master itself, not just one of its layouts) and press the Delete key. If any of that slide master's layouts were applied to any slides in the presentation, those slides automatically convert to the default slide master's equivalent layout. If no exact layout match is found, PowerPoint does its best: It uses its default Title and Content layout and includes any extra content as orphaned items.

Renaming a slide master

Slide master names appear as category headings on the Layout list as you are selecting layouts. For example, in Figure 22.26, the slide master names are Facet and Intensity.

FIGURE 22.26

Slide master names form the category titles on the Layout list.

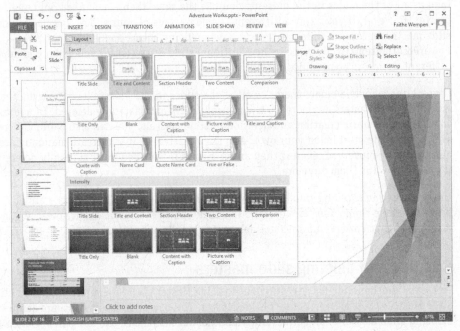

To rename a slide master, follow these steps:

1. **In Slide Master view, right-click the slide master and choose Rename Master.**
   The Rename Master dialog box opens.

2. **Type a new name for the master, replacing the existing name.**

3. **Click Rename.**

Preserving a slide master

Unless you have created the slide master yourself, it is temporary. Slide masters come and go as needed, as you format slides with various themes. To lock a slide master so that it doesn't disappear when no slides are using it, right-click the slide master and choose Preserve Master, or click Slide Master ⇨ Edit Master ⇨ Preserve. The Preserve button on the Slide Master tab appears selected, indicating the slide master is preserved. To unpreserve it, click the Preserve button again, or right-click the slide master again and choose Preserve Master. See Figure 22.27.

FIGURE 22.27

The Preserve Master command saves a slide master so that PowerPoint cannot automatically delete it.

Summary

In this chapter you learned how themes and slide masters make it easy to apply consistent formatting in a presentation, and how layout masters are associated with slide masters and provide consistent layouts for the slides based on them. You learned:

- The difference between themes and templates.

- How to apply a theme and customize it with color themes, font themes, and effect themes.

- How to save, rename, and delete themes.

- How to use masters and layouts to control the presentation and slide content.

- How to work in Slide Master view to make various changes to the master and layouts.

Working with Tables and Charts

IN THIS CHAPTER

Creating a new table

Moving around in a table

Selecting rows, columns, and cells

Editing a table's structure

Applying table styles

Formatting table cells

Understanding charts

Starting a new chart

Working with chart data

Chart types and chart layout presets

Working with labels

Controlling the axes

Formatting a chart

Y ou can type tabular data — in other words, data in a grid of rows and columns — directly into a table or import it from other applications. You can also apply formatting that makes tabular data easier to read and more attractive. When you need to create a quick chart without data from another source, PowerPoint's charting tools work perfectly. The PowerPoint 2013 charting interface is based on the one in Excel, so you can also use PowerPoint to create equally effective and professional charts.

In this chapter, you'll learn how to create and manage PowerPoint tables and how to create charts that present numeric data in a visual format.

Creating a New Table

A table is a great way to organize little bits of data into a meaningful picture. For example, you might use a table to show sales results for several salespeople or to contain a multicolumn list of team member names. There are several ways to insert a table, and each method has its purpose. The following sections explain each of the table creation methods.

NOTE

Text from a table does not appear in the presentation's outline.

A table can be part of a content placeholder, or it can be a separate, free-floating item. If the active slide has an available placeholder that can accommodate a table, and there is not already content in that placeholder, the table is placed in it. Otherwise the table is placed as an independent object on the slide and is not part of the layout.

TIP

Depending on what you want to do with the table, it could be advantageous in some cases to *not* have the table be part of the layout. For example, perhaps you want the table to be a certain size and to not change when you apply a different theme. To ensure that the table is not part of the layout, start with a slide that uses a layout that contains no table-compatible placeholder, such as Title Only.

Creating a table with the Insert Table dialog box

To create a basic table with a specified number of rows and columns, you can use the Insert Table dialog box. You can open it in either of two ways (see Figure 23.1):

FIGURE 23.1

Open the Insert Table dialog box from either the Table menu or a content placeholder.

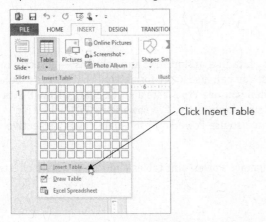

Click Insert Table

- In a content placeholder, click the Insert Table button.
- On the Insert tab, click Tables ➪ Table ➪ Insert Table.

In the Insert Table dialog box, shown in Figure 23.2, specify a number for rows and columns and click OK. The table then appears on the slide.

FIGURE 23.2

Enter the number of rows and columns to specify the size of the table that you want to create.

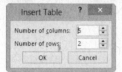

Creating a Table from the Table button

When you opened the Table button's menu (see Figure 23.1) in the preceding section, you probably couldn't help but notice the grid of white squares. Another way to create a table is to drag across this grid until you select the desired number of rows and columns. The table appears immediately on the slide as you drag, so you can see how it will look, as shown in Figure 23.3.

23

FIGURE 23.3

Drag across the grid in the Table button's menu to specify the size of the table that you want to create.

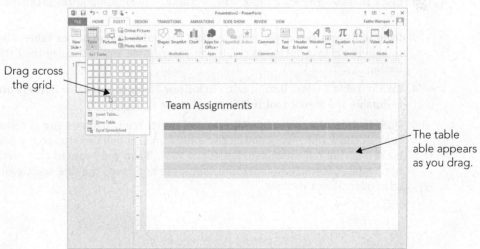

Drag across the grid.

Team Assignments

The table able appears as you drag.

Other than the method of specifying rows and columns, this process is identical to creating a table via the Insert Table dialog box because the same issues apply regarding placeholders versus free-floating tables. If a placeholder is available, PowerPoint uses it.

> **NOTE**
>
> When you create a table from the Insert Table dialog box or the Table button, the table is automatically formatted with one of the preset table styles. You learn how to change this later in the chapter.

Drawing a table

Drawing a table enables you to use your mouse pointer like a pencil to create every row and column in the table in exactly the positions you want. You can even create unequal numbers of rows and columns. This method is a good one to use whenever you want a table that is nonstandard in some way — different row heights, different column widths, different numbers of columns in some rows, and so on. To draw a table, follow these steps:

1. **Start on a new slide, and click Home ⇨ Slides ⇨ Layout ⇨ Title Only to switch to a layout that contains no content placeholders.** Add a title in the Title placeholder if you want one.

   Opening a new slide with a Title Only layout isn't a requirement for drawing a table, but it will make it easier your first time because it gives you a blank area in which to draw the table, without any placeholders in the way.

2. **Click Insert ⇨ Tables ⇨ Table ⇨ Draw Table.** The mouse pointer turns into a pencil.

3. **Drag to draw a rectangle representing the outer frame of the table.** Then release the mouse button to create the outer frame and to display the Table Tools Design tab.

4. **On the Table Tools ⇨ Design tab, click Draw Table in the Draw Borders group to re-enable the Pencil tool if it is not already enabled.**

5. **Drag to draw the rows and columns you want.** You can draw a row or column that runs all the way across or down the table's frame, or you can stop at any point to make a partial row or column. See Figure 23.4. When you begin to drag vertically or horizontally, PowerPoint locks into that mode and keeps the line exactly vertical or horizontal and straight.

FIGURE 23.4

You can create a unique table with the Draw Table tool.

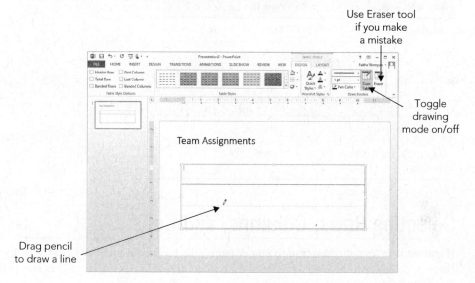

6. **(Optional) To erase a line, click the Eraser button in the Draw Borders group of the Table Tools ⇨ Design tab, and then click the line to erase.** Then click the Draw Table button on the Table Tools Design tab to return the mouse pointer to its drawing (pencil) mode.

7. **When you finish drawing the table, press Esc or click Draw Table again to toggle the drawing mode off.**

TIP

If you need a table that is mostly uniform but has a few anomalies, such as a few combined cells or a few extra divisions, create the table using the Insert Table dialog box or the grid on the Table button, and then use the Draw Table and/or Eraser buttons on the Table Tools ⇨ Design tab to modify it.

Moving around in a Table

Each cell is like a little text box. To type in a cell, click in it and type. It's pretty simple! You can also move between cells with the keyboard. Table 23.1 lists the keyboard shortcuts for moving the insertion point in a table.

TABLE 23.1   Moving the Insertion Point in a Table

To Move To:	Press This:
Next cell	Tab
Previous cell	Shift+Tab
Next row	Down Arrow
Previous row	Up Arrow
Tab stop within a cell	Ctrl+Tab
New paragraph within the same cell	Enter

Selecting Rows, Columns, and Cells

If you want to apply formatting to one or more cells or issue a command that acts upon them, such as Copy or Delete, you must first select the cells to be affected, as shown in Figure 23.5:

- **A single cell:** Move the insertion point by clicking inside the desired cell. At this point, any command acts on that individual cell and its contents, not the whole table, row, or column. Drag across multiple cells to select them.

- **An entire row or column:** Click any cell in that row or column and then click Table Tools ⇨ Layout ⇨ Table ⇨ Select and choose Select Column (see Figure 23.5) or Select Row. Alternatively, position the mouse pointer above the column or to the left of the row, so that the mouse pointer turns into a black arrow, and then click to select the column or row. (You can drag to extend the selection to additional columns or rows when you see the black arrow.)

There are two ways to select the entire table — or rather, two senses in which the entire table can be "selected":

- **Select all table cells:** When you select all of the cells, they all appear with shaded backgrounds, and any text formatting command that you apply at that point affects all of the text in the table. To select all cells, do any of the following:
  - Drag across all of the cells in the entire table.
  - Click inside the table, and then press Ctrl+A.
- **Select the entire table:** When you do this, the table's frame is selected, but the insertion point is not anywhere within the table and cells do not appear with a

shaded background. You do this kind of selection before moving or resizing the table, for example. To select the entire table, do any of the following:

- Click Table Tools ➪ Layout ➪ Table ➪ Select ➪ Select Table. (Refer to Figure 23.5.)
- Click the frame of the table.
- Click inside the table, and then press Esc once.
- Right-click the table and choose Select Table.

FIGURE 23.5

Select a row or column with the Select button's menu, or click above or to the left of the column or row.

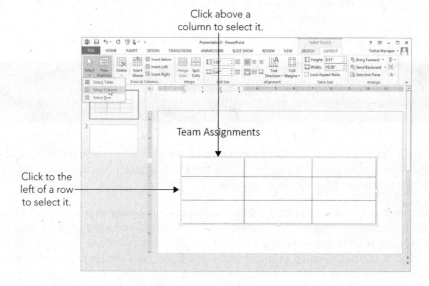

Editing a Table's Structure

Now that you've created a table, let's look at some ways to modify the table's structure, including resizing the entire table, adding and deleting rows and columns, and merging and splitting cells.

Resizing the overall table

As with any other framed object in PowerPoint, dragging the table's outer frame resizes it. Position the mouse pointer over one of the selection handles (the white squares on the sides and corners) so that the mouse pointer becomes a double-headed arrow, and drag to resize the table. See Figure 23.6.

FIGURE 23.6

To resize a table, drag a selection handle on its frame.

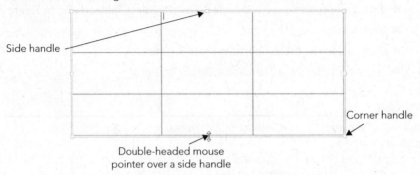

Side handle

Corner handle

Double-headed mouse
pointer over a side handle

> **NOTE**
>
> If you drag when the mouse pointer is over any other part of the frame, so that the mouse pointer becomes a four-headed arrow, you move the table rather than resize it.

To maintain the aspect ratio (height to width ratio) for the table as you resize it, hold down the Shift key as you drag a corner of the frame. If maintaining the aspect ratio is not critical, you can drag either a corner or a side.

All of the rows and columns maintain their spacing proportionally to one another as you resize them. However, when a table contains text that would no longer fit if its row and column were shrunken proportionally with the rest of the table, the row height does not shrink fully; it shrinks as much as it can while still displaying the text. The column width does shrink proportionally, regardless of cell content.

You can also specify an exact size for the overall table frame by using the Table Size group on the Table Tools ⇨ Layout tab, as shown in Figure 23.7. From there you can enter Height and Width values. To maintain the aspect ratio, select the Lock Aspect Ratio check box *before* you change either the Height or Width setting.

FIGURE 23.7

Set a precise height and width for the table from the Table Size group.

Inserting or deleting rows and columns

Here's an easy way to create a new row at the bottom of the table: Position the insertion point in the bottom-right cell and press Tab. Need something more complicated than that? The Table Tools⇨Layout tab contains buttons in the Rows & Columns group for inserting rows or columns above, below, to the left, or to the right of the selected cell(s), as shown in Figure 23.8. By default, each button inserts a single row or column at a time, but if you select multiple existing ones beforehand, these commands insert as many as you've selected. For example, to insert three new rows, select three existing rows and then click Insert Above or Insert Below.

FIGURE 23.8

Insert rows or columns by using these buttons on the Layout tab.

Alternatively, you can right-click any existing row or column, point to Insert, and choose one of the commands on the submenu. These commands are the same as the names of the buttons in Figure 23.8.

CAUTION

Adding new rows increases the overall vertical size of the table frame, even to the point where it runs off the bottom of the slide. You might need to adjust the overall frame size after adding rows. On the other hand, inserting columns does not change the overall frame size; it simply resizes the existing columns so that they all fit and are all a uniform size (unless you have manually adjusted any of them to be a custom size).

To delete a row or column (or more than one of each), select the row(s) or column(s) that you want to delete, and then open the Delete button's menu on the Table Tools⇨Layout tab and choose Delete Rows or Delete Columns in the Delete group. At a lower screen resolution, you may need to click the Delete button first to see the choices for this group.

NOTE

You cannot insert or delete individual cells in a PowerPoint table. (This is unlike in Excel, where you can remove individual cells and then shift the remaining ones up or to the left.)

Merging and splitting cells

If you need more rows or columns in some spots than others, you can use the Merge Cells and Split Cells commands. Here are some ways to merge cells:

- Click Table Tools ⇨ Design ⇨ Draw Borders ⇨ Eraser, and then click the line you want to erase. The cells on either side of the deleted line are merged.
- Select the cells that you want to merge and click Table Tools ⇨ Layout ⇨ Merge ⇨ Merge Cells.
- Select the cells to merge, right-click them, and choose Merge Cells.

Here are some ways to split cells:

- Click Table Tools ⇨ Design ⇨ Draw Borders ⇨ Draw Table, and then drag to draw a line in the middle of a cell to split it.
- Select the cell that you want to split, right-click it, and choose Split Cells. In the Split Cells dialog box (see Figure 23.9), select the number of pieces in which to split in each direction, and click OK.
- Select the cell to split, and then click Table Tools ⇨ Layout ⇨ Merge ⇨ Split Cells. In the Split Cells dialog box (see Figure 23.9), select the number of pieces in which to split in each direction, and click OK.

FIGURE 23.9

Specify how the split should occur.

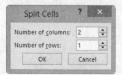

Applying Table Styles

The quickest way to format a table attractively is to apply a table style to it. When you insert a table using any method except drawing it, a table style is applied to it by default; you can change to some other style if desired, or you can remove all styles from the table, leaving it plain black and white.

When you hover the mouse pointer over a table style, a Live Preview of it appears in the active table. The style is not actually applied to the table until you click the style to select it, however.

If the style you want appears in the Table Tools ⇨ Design tab's Table Styles group, you can click it from there without opening the gallery. If not, you can scroll row by row through the gallery by clicking the up/down arrow buttons, or you can open the gallery's full menu, as shown in Figure 23.10.

FIGURE 23.10

Apply a table style from the gallery.

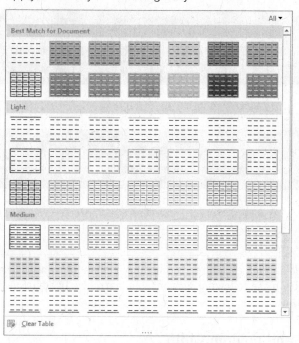

To remove all styles from the table, choose Clear Table from the bottom of the gallery. This reverts the table to default settings: no fill, and plain black 1-point borders on all sides of all cells.

The table styles use theme-based colors, so if you change to a different presentation theme or color theme, the table formatting might change. (Colors, in particular, are prone to shift.)

By default, the first row of the table (a.k.a. the *header row*) is formatted differently from the others, and every other row is shaded differently. (This is called *banding*.) You can control how different rows are treated differently (or not) from the Table Style Options group on the Table Tools Design tab. There is a check box for each of six settings:

- **Header Row:** The first row
- **Total Row:** The last row

- **First Column:** The leftmost column
- **Last Column:** The rightmost column
- **Banded Rows:** Even and odd rows each have specific formatting
- **Banded Columns:** Even and odd columns each have specific formatting

CAUTION

With some of the styles, there is not a whole lot of difference between some of the settings. For example, you might have to look very closely to see the difference between First Column being turned on or off; ditto with Last Column and Total Row.

TIP

You can right-click one of the thumbnails in the Table Style gallery and choose Set as Default to change the default table style.

Formatting Table Cells

Although table styles provide a rough cut on the formatting, you might want to fine-tune your table formatting as well. In the following sections you learn how to adjust various aspects of the table's appearance.

Changing row height and column width

You might want a row to be a different height or a column a different width than others in the table. To resize a row or column, follow these steps:

1. **Position the mouse pointer on the border below the row or to the right of the column that you want to resize.** The mouse pointer turns into a double line with arrows on each side of it.
2. **Hold down the mouse button as you drag the row or column to a new height or width.** A dotted line appears showing where it will go.
3. **Release the mouse button.**

You can also specify an exact height or width measurement using the Height and Width boxes in the Cell Size group on the Table Tools ⇨ Layout tab. Select the row(s) or column(s) to affect, and then enter sizes in inches or use the spin buttons, as shown in Figure 23.11.

FIGURE 23.11

Set a precise size for a row or column.

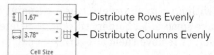

The Distribute Rows Evenly and Distribute Columns Evenly buttons in the Cell Size group (see Figure 23.11) adjust each row or column in the selected range so that the available space is occupied evenly among them. This is handy especially if you have drawn the table yourself rather than allowed PowerPoint to create it initially. If PowerPoint creates the table, the rows and columns are already of equal height and width by default.

You can also double-click the border between two columns to size the column to the left so that the text fits exactly within the width.

Table margins and alignment

Remember, PowerPoint slides do not have any margins per se; everything is in a frame. An individual cell does have internal margins, however.

You can specify the internal margins for cells using the Cell Margins button on the Table Tools ⇨ Layout tab, as follows:

1. **Select the cells to which the setting should apply.** To apply settings to the entire table, select the entire table.

2. **Click Table Tools ⇨ Layout ⇨ Alignment ⇨ Cell Margins.** A menu of margin presets opens.

3. **Click one of the presets or choose Custom Margins, and then follow these steps:**

   a. In the Cell Text Layout dialog box, set the Left, Right, Top, and Bottom margin settings, as shown in Figure 23.12.

   b. Click OK.

FIGURE 23.12

You can set the internal margins on an individual cell basis for each side of the cell.

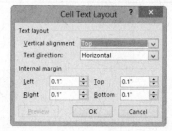

Applying borders

The border lines around the cells are very important because they separate the data in each cell from the data in other cells. By default (without a table style), there's a 1-point border around each side of each cell, but you can make some or all borders thicker, a different line style (dashed, for example), or a different color, or remove them altogether to create your own effects. Here are some ideas:

- To make items appear to "float" in multiple columns on the slide (that is, to make it look as if they are not really in a table at all — just lined up extremely well), remove all table borders.

- To create a header row at the top without using the settings in the Table Style Options group, make the border beneath the first row of cells darker or thicker than the others.

- To make certain rows or columns appear as if they are outside of the table, turn off their borders on all sides except the side that faces the other cells.

- To make certain items appear as if they have been crossed off a list, format the cells they are in with diagonal borders. This creates the effect of an *X* running through each cell. These diagonal lines are not really borders in the sense that they don't go around the edge of the cell, but they're treated as borders in PowerPoint.

When you apply a top, bottom, left, or right border, those positions refer to the entire selected block of cells if you have more than one cell selected. For example, suppose you select two adjacent cells in a row and apply a left border. The border applies only to the leftmost of the two cells. If you want the same border applied to the line between the cells too, you must apply an inside vertical border.

To apply a border, follow these steps:

1. **Select the cell(s) that you want to affect.**

2. **In the Draw Borders group on the Table Tools ⇨ Design tab, select a line style, width, and color from the Pen Style, Pen Weight, and Pen Color drop-down lists, shown in Figure 23.13.**

FIGURE 23.13

Use the Draw Borders group's lists to set the border's style, thickness, and color.

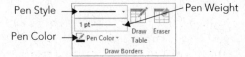

> **TIP**
> Try to use theme colors rather than fixed colors whenever possible so that if you change to a different color theme later, the colors you originally chose won't clash.

3. **Open the Borders button's menu in the Table Styles group of the Design tab and choose the sides of the selected area to which the new settings should apply.** See Figure 23.14. For example, to apply the border to the bottom of the selected area, click Bottom Border.

FIGURE 23.14

Select the side(s) to apply borders to for the chosen cells.

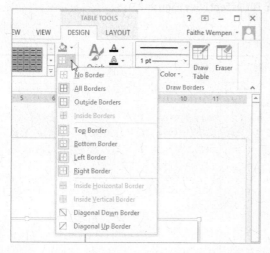

If you want to remove all borders from all sides, choose No Border from the menu.

4. **If necessary, repeat step 3 to apply the border to other sides of the selection.** Some of the choices on the Borders button's menu apply to only one side; others apply to two or more at once.

Applying fills

By default, table cells have a transparent background so that the color of the slide beneath shows through. When you apply a table style, as you learned earlier in the chapter, the style specifies a background color — or in some cases, multiple background colors depending on the options you choose for special treatment of certain rows or columns.

You can also manually change the fill for a table to make it either a solid color or a special fill effect. You can apply this fill to individual cells, or you can apply a background fill for the entire table.

Filling individual cells

Each individual cell has its own fill setting; in this way a table is like a collection of individual object frames, rather than a single object. To set the fill color for one or more cells, follow these steps:

1. **Select the cell(s) to affect, or to apply the same fill color to all cells, select the table's outer frame.**

2. **On the Table Tools ⇨ Design tab, click the down arrow next to the Shading button in the Table Styles group to open its palette.**

3. **Select the desired color or fill effect.** See Figure 23.15.

FIGURE 23.15

Apply a fill effect to the selected cell(s).

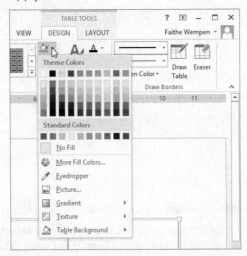

TIP

For a semitransparent, solid-color fill, first apply the fill and then right-click the cell and choose Format Shape. In the Format Shape pane, click Fill to display its settings, and then drag the Transparency slider. For some types of fills, you can also set the transparency when you initially apply the fill.

Applying an overall table fill

You can apply a solid color fill to the entire table that is different from the fill applied to the individual cells. The table's fill color is visible only in cells in which the individual fill is set to No Fill (or a semitransparent fill, in which case it blends).

To apply a fill to the entire table, open the Shading button's menu and point to Table Background, as shown in Figure 23.16, and then choose a color.

FIGURE 23.16

Apply a fill to the table's background.

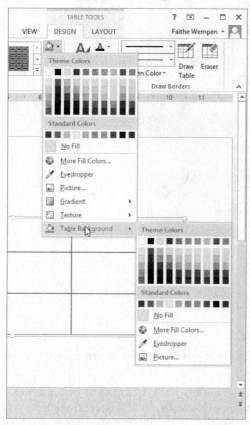

To test the new background, select some cells and choose No Fill for their fill color. The background color appears in those cells. If you want to experiment further, try applying a semitransparent fill to some cells, and see how the color of the background blends with the color of the cell's fill.

Filling a table with a picture

When you fill one or more cells with a picture, each cell gets its own individual copy of it. For example, if you fill a table with a picture of a koala and the table has six cells, you get six koalas, as shown in Figure 23.17.

FIGURE 23.17

When you apply a picture fill to a table, each cell gets its own copy.

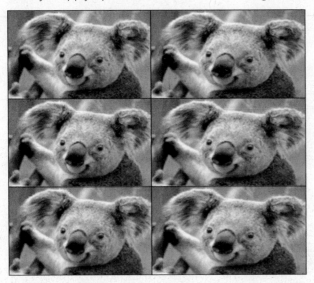

If you want a single copy of the picture to fill the entire area behind the table, do the following:

1. **Select the table's outer frame.**

2. **Click Table Tools ⇨ Design ⇨ Table Styles ⇨ Shading (down arrow) ⇨ Table Background ⇨ Picture.**

3. **In the Insert Pictures window (Figure 23.18), to use your own picture, click Browse and locate and select the picture.** Or, to find a picture online, type a keyword for the picture in the Office.com Clip Art box and press Enter, and then click the desired picture.

FIGURE 23.18

Select a picture to use as the background of the table.

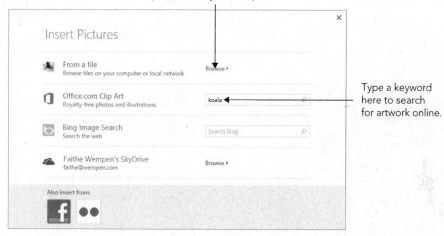

Applying a shadow to a table

You can apply a shadow effect to a table so that it appears "raised" off the slide background. You can make it any color you like, and adjust a variety of settings for it.

> **NOTE**
>
> If the cells have no fill, the shadow will apply to the gridlines, not to the table as a whole object.

Here's a very simple way to apply a shadow to a table:

1. **Select the table's outer frame.**
2. **Choose Table Tools ➪ Design ➪ Table Styles ➪ Effects ➪ Shadow.**
3. **Click the shadow type you want.**

Here's an alternative method that gives you a bit more control:

1. **Select the table's outer frame, and then right-click the frame and choose Format Shape.** The Format Shape task pane appears.
2. **Click Shape Options, and then click the Effects icon.**
3. **Click Shadow to expand that category, as shown in Figure 23.19.**

FIGURE 23.19

Apply a shadow to a table.

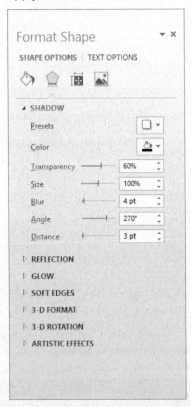

4. **Click the Presets button, and click the desired preset.**

5. **Click the Color button, and click the desired color.**

6. **(Optional) If desired, drag any of the sliders to fine-tune the shadow.** These are covered in greater detail in Chapter 9.

7. **Click Close to close the Format Shape pane when you are finished.**

Applying a 3-D effect to a table

PowerPoint does not enable you to apply 3-D effects to tables, so you have to fudge that by creating the 3-D effect with rectangles and then overlaying a transparent table on top of the shapes. As you can see in Figure 23.20, it's a pretty convincing facsimile.

FIGURE 23.20

This 3-D table is actually a plain table with a 3-D rectangle behind it.

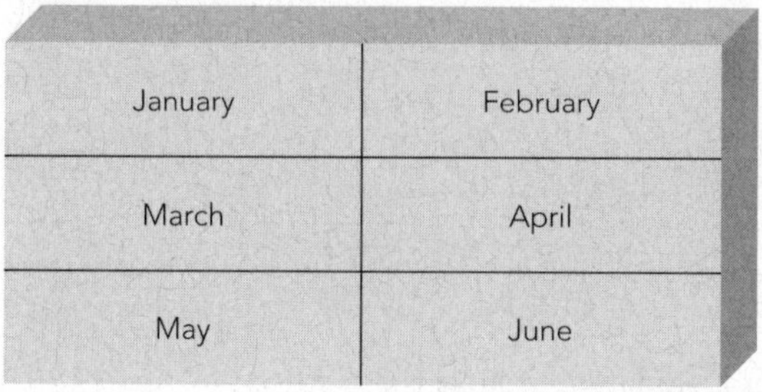

You might need to read Chapter 9 first to do some of these steps, but here's the basic procedure:

1. **Create a rectangle from the Shapes group on the Insert tab, and apply a 3-D effect to it (from Drawing Tools ⇨ Format ⇨ Shape Styles ⇨ Shape Effects ⇨ 3-D Rotation).** Use any effect you like. To create the traditional "box" appearance as in Figure 23.20, apply the second Oblique preset, and then in the 3-D Format options, increase the Depth setting to about 100 points.

2. **Size the rectangle so that its face is the same size as the table.**

3. **Click Drawing Tools ⇨ Format ⇨ Arrange ⇨ Send Backward ⇨ Send to Back to send the rectangle behind the table.**

4. **Set the table's fill to No Fill if it is not already transparent.**

5. **(Optional) Set the table's outer frame border to None to make its edges appear to blend with the edges of the rectangle.** To do that, open the Borders button's menu on the Table Tools Design tab and select Outside Borders to toggle that off.

Changing text alignment

If you followed the preceding steps to create the effect shown in Figure 23.20, you probably ran into a problem: Your text probably didn't center itself in the cells. That's because, by default, each cell's vertical alignment is set to Top, and its horizontal alignment is set to Left.

Although the vertical and horizontal alignments are both controlled from the Alignment group on the Table Tools Layout tab, they actually have two different scopes. Vertical alignment applies to the entire cell as a whole, whereas horizontal alignment can apply differently to individual paragraphs within the cell. To set vertical alignment for a cell, follow these steps:

1. **Select one or more cells to affect.** To affect only one cell, you do not have to select it; just click inside it.

2. **On the Table Tools ⇨ Layout tab, in the Alignment group, click one of the vertical alignment buttons: Align Top, Center Vertically, or Align Bottom.** See Figure 23.21.

23

FIGURE 23.21

Set the vertical and horizontal alignment of text from the Alignment group.

Horizontal alignment

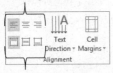

Vertical alignment

To set the horizontal alignment for a paragraph, follow these steps:

1. **Select one or more paragraphs to affect.** If you select multiple cells, all paragraphs within those cells are affected. If you click in a cell without selecting anything, the change affects only the paragraph in which you clicked.

2. **On the Table Tools ⇨ Layout tab, in the Alignment group, click one of the horizontal alignment buttons: Align Left, Center, or Align Right.** See Figure 23.21. You can also use the paragraph alignment buttons on the Home tab for horizontal alignment or the buttons on the mini toolbar.

> **TIP**
>
> The horizontal alignments all have keyboard shortcuts: Ctrl+L for left, Ctrl+E for center, and Ctrl+R for right.

Changing text direction

The default text direction for table cells is Horizontal, which reads from left to right (at least in countries where that's how text is read). Figure 23.22 shows the alternatives.

FIGURE 23.22

You can set types of text direction.

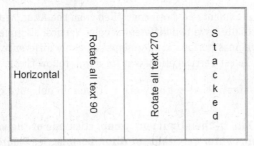

To change the text direction for a cell, follow these steps:

1. **Select the cell(s) to affect.** To affect only a single cell, move the insertion point into it.

2. **On the Table Tools Layout tab, click Text Direction.**

3. **Select a text direction from the menu that appears.**

NOTE

You cannot set text direction for individual paragraphs; the setting applies to the entire cell.

Understanding Charts

PowerPoint's charting feature is based upon the same Escher 2.0 graphics engine that is used for drawn objects. Consequently, most of what you have learned about formatting objects in earlier chapters (for example Chapter 9 in the part about Word) also applies to charts. For example, you can apply shape styles to the individual elements of a chart and apply WordArt styles to chart text. However, there are also many chart-specific formatting and layout options, as you will see throughout this chapter.

The sample chart shown in Figure 23.23 contains these elements:

- **Data series:** Each different bar color represents a different series: Morning, Afternoon, and Evening.
- **Legend:** Colored squares in the Legend box describe the correlation of each color to a data series.
- **Categories:** The North, South, East, and West labels along the bottom of the chart are the categories.
- **Category axis:** The horizontal line running across the bottom of the chart is the category axis, also called the horizontal axis.
- **Value axis:** The vertical line running up the left side of the chart, with the numbers on it, is the value axis, also called the vertical axis.
- **Data points:** Each individual bar is a data point. The numeric value for that data point corresponds to the height of the bar, measured against the value axis.
- **Walls:** The walls are the areas behind the data points. On a 3-D chart, as shown in Figure 23.23, there are both back and side walls. On a 2-D chart, there is only the plot area behind the chart.
- **Floor:** The floor is the area on which the data points sit. A floor appears only in a 3-D chart.

FIGURE 23.23

Parts of a chart

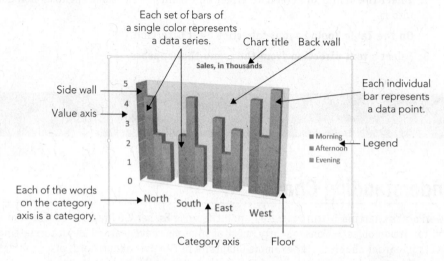

Starting a New Chart

The main difficulty with creating a chart in a non-spreadsheet application such as PowerPoint is that there is no data table from which to pull the numbers. Therefore, PowerPoint creates charts using data that you have entered in an Excel window. By default, it contains sample data, which you can replace with your own data.

You can place a new chart on a slide in two ways: You can either use a chart placeholder from a layout or place one manually. Follow these steps to place a chart:

1. **On the Insert tab, click Chart. Or, click the Insert Chart button on the content placeholder.** The Insert Chart dialog box opens (Figure 23.24).

FIGURE 23.24

Select the desired chart type.

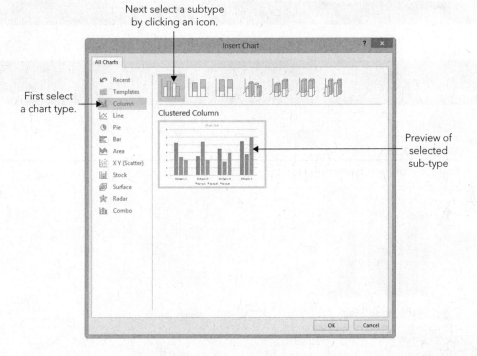

2. **In the list at the left, select the desired chart type.** Column is selected by default (and in Figure 23.24), but you can pick any type you like.

3. **From the icons along the top of the dialog box, click the icon that best represents the subtype of chart you want.** In Figure 23.24, the Clustered Column type is selected. A sample of the selected chart subtype appears below the icons.

   See Table 23.2 for an explanation of the chart types. Figure 23.25 and Figure 23.26 show examples of some of the chart types.

4. **Click OK.** The chart appears on the slide, and an Excel datasheet opens with sample data.

5. **Modify the sample data as needed.** To change the range of cells that appear in the chart, see the section "Redefining the Data Range" later in this chapter. If you want, you can then close the Excel window to move it out of the way.

NOTE

A chart inserted into PowerPoint is an embedded object; it exists only within PowerPoint, even though it is an Excel chart.

NOTE

After you have closed the Excel window, you can open it again by clicking Edit Data on the Chart Tools Design tab.

FIGURE 23.25

Examples of chart types, from top left, clockwise: column, line, bar, and pie

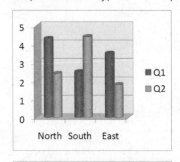
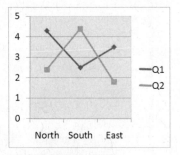
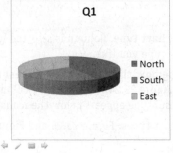
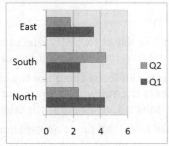

FIGURE 23.26

Examples of chart types, from top left, clockwise: area, scatter, donut, and surface

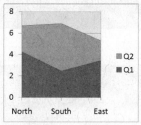
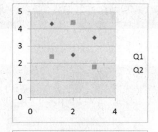
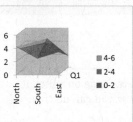
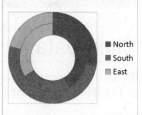

TABLE 23.2   Chart Types in PowerPoint's Charting Tool

Type	Description
Column	Vertical bars, optionally with multiple data series. Bars can be clustered, stacked, or based on a percentage and either 2-D or 3-D.
Line	Shows values as points, and connects the points with a line. Different series use different colors and/or line styles.
Pie	A circle broken into wedges to show how parts contribute to a whole. This de-emphasizes the actual numeric values. In most cases, this type is a single-series only. The donut variant is similar to a pie but with multiple concentric rings so that multiple series can be illustrated.
Bar	Just like a column chart, but horizontal.
Area	Just like a column chart, but with the spaces filled in between the bars.
XY (Scatter)	Shows values as points on both axes, but does not connect them with a line. However, you can add trend lines. The bubble variant uses bubbles of varying sizes to represent a third data variable rather than each data point being a fixed size.
Stock	A special type of chart that is used to show stock prices.
Surface	A 3-D sheet that is used to illustrate the highest and lowest points of the data set.
Radar	Shows changes of data frequency in relation to a center point.

23

> **NOTE**
>
> At any point, you can return to your PowerPoint presentation by clicking anywhere outside of the chart on the slide. To edit the chart again, you can click the chart to redisplay the chart-specific tabs.

> **TIP**
>
> If you delete a column or row by selecting individual cells and pressing Delete to clear them, the empty space that these cells occupied remains in the chart. To completely remove a row or column from the data range, select the row or column by clicking its header (letter for column; number for row) and click Delete on the Home tab in Excel.

Working with Chart Data

After you create a chart, you might want to change the data range on which it is based or how this data is plotted. The following sections explain how you can do this.

Plotting by rows versus by columns

By default, the columns of the datasheet form the data series. However, if you want, you can switch the data around so that the rows form the series. Figure 23.27 and Figure 23.28 show the same chart plotted both ways so that you can see the difference. (The data for this chart appears in the next section of the chapter, in Figure 23.29, in case you want to reference it.)

What does the term *data series* mean? Take a look at Figure 23.27 and Figure 23.28. Notice that there is a legend beneath to each chart that shows what each color (or shade of gray) represents. Each of these colors, and the label associated with it, is a series. The other variable (the one that is not the series) is plotted on the chart's horizontal axis.

FIGURE 23.27

A chart with quarters as the series

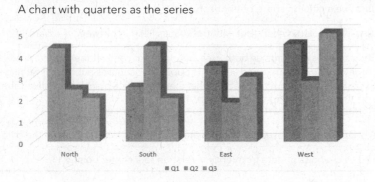

FIGURE 23.28

A chart with regions as the series

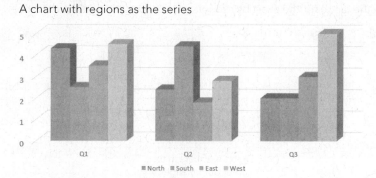

To switch back and forth between plotting by rows and by columns in the data sheet, click the Switch Row/Column button on the Chart Tools⇨Design tab. If the button is not available, open the data sheet by choosing Chart Tools⇨Design⇨Data⇨Edit Data, and then the button will become available.

A chart can carry a very different message when you arrange it by rows versus by columns. For example, in Figure 23.27, the chart compares the quarters. The message here is about improvement — or lack thereof — over time. Contrast this to Figure 23.28, where the series data is the regions. Here, you can compare one region to another. The overriding message here is about competition — which division performed the best in each quarter? It's easy to see how the same data can convey very different messages; make sure that you pick the arrangement that tells the story that you want to tell in your presentation.

Redefining the data range

After you have created your chart, you may decide that you need to use more or less data. Perhaps you want to exclude a month or quarter of data or to add another region or salesperson. To add or remove a data series, you can simply edit the datasheet. To do so, follow these steps:

1. **On the Chart Tools⇨Design tab in the Data group, click Edit Data.** The Excel datasheet appears. A blue outline appears around the range that is to be plotted, and other colors of outlines appear around the ranges containing the labels. The colors of those ranges vary depending on the chart type.

2. **(Optional) To change the data range to be plotted, drag the bottom-right corner of the blue outline.** For example, in Figure 23.29, the West division is being excluded.

   You can also enlarge the data range by expanding the blue outline. For example, you could enter another series in column E in Figure 23.29 and then extend the outline to encompass column E.

FIGURE 23.29

You can redefine the range for the chart by dragging the blue outline on the datasheet.

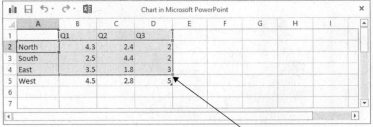

Drag the square in the
corner of the range to
change the range.

The preceding steps work well if the range that you want to include is contiguous, but what if you wanted to exclude a row or column that is in the middle of the range? To define the range more precisely, follow these steps:

1. **On the Chart Tools ⇨ Design tab in the Data group, click Select Data.** The Select Data Source dialog box opens, shown in Figure 23.30, along with the Excel datasheet if it was not already displayed.

FIGURE 23.30

To fine-tune the data ranges, you can use the Select Data Source dialog box.

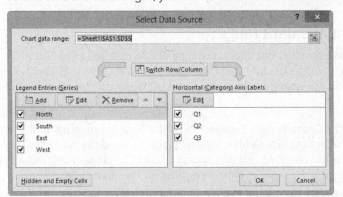

2. **Do any of the following:**

   ■ To remove a series, select it from the Legend Entries (Series) list and click Remove.

- To add a series, click Add, and then drag across the range on the datasheet to enter it into the Edit Series dialog box; then click OK to accept it.

- To edit a series, select it in the Legend Entries (Series) list and click Edit. Then drag across the range or make a change in the Edit Series dialog box, and click OK.

3. **(Optional) To redefine the range from which to pull the horizontal axis labels, click the Edit button in the Horizontal (Category) Axis Labels section.** A dotted outline appears around the current range; drag to redefine that range and click OK.

4. **(Optional) To redefine how empty or hidden cells should be treated, click the Hidden and Empty Cells button.** In the Hidden and Empty Cell Settings dialog box that appears, choose whether to show data in hidden rows and columns and whether to define empty cells as gaps in the chart or as zero values. Then click OK. The Hidden and Empty Cell Settings dialog box is shown in Figure 23.31.

FIGURE 23.31

Specify what should happen when the data range contains blank or hidden cells.

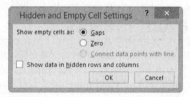

5. **When you are finished editing the settings for the data ranges, click OK to close the Select Data Source dialog box.**

6. **(Optional) Close the Excel datasheet window, or leave it open for later reference.**

Filtering the chart data

New in PowerPoint 2013, you can use the Chart Filters feature to quickly exclude certain rows or columns from the chart. When the chart is selected on the slide, a set of three icons appears to its right: Chart Elements, Chart Styles, and Chart Filters. If you click Chart Filters, a flyout appears with check boxes for each of the series and categories, as shown in Figure 23.32. Clear the check box for anything you don't want to see on the chart, and then click Apply. The Select Data hyperlink at the bottom of the panel opens the Select Data Source dialog box, the same as in the previous section.

Turn off certain series or categories from this panel if desired.

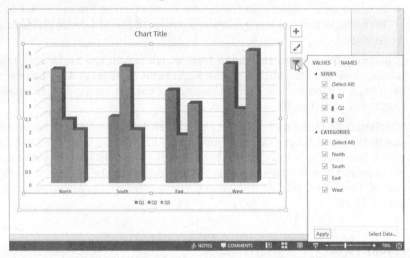

Chart Types and Chart Layout Presets

The default chart is a 2-D clustered column chart. However, there are a lot of alternative chart types to choose from. Not all of them will be appropriate for your data, of course, but you may be surprised at the different spin on the message that a different chart type presents.

> **CAUTION**
>
> Many chart types come in both 2-D and 3-D models, and you can choose which chart type looks most appropriate for your presentation. However, try to be consistent. For example, it looks nicer to stay with all 2-D or all 3-D charts rather than mixing the types in a presentation.

You can revisit your choice of chart type at any time by following these steps:

1. **Select the chart, if needed, so that the Chart Tools ⇨ Design tab becomes available.**

2. **Click Chart Tools ⇨ Design ⇨ Type ⇨ Change Chart Type.** The Change Chart Type dialog box opens. It looks just like the Insert Chart dialog box you saw in Figure 23.24.

3. **Select the desired type, just as you did when you originally created the chart.**

4. **Click OK.**

This is the basic procedure for the overall chart type selection, but there are also many options for fine-tuning the layout. The following sections explain these options.

PowerPoint provides a limited number of preset Quick Layouts for each chart type. A layout is a combination of optional chart elements (such as legend, data table, data labels, and so on) in a particular arrangement. Quick Layouts are good starting points for creating your own layouts, which you will learn about in this chapter. To choose a Quick Layout, click Chart Tools⇨Design⇨Chart Layouts⇨Quick Layouts and select a layout from the gallery, as shown in Figure 23.33.

FIGURE 23.33

You can choose one of the preset Quick Layouts that fits your needs.

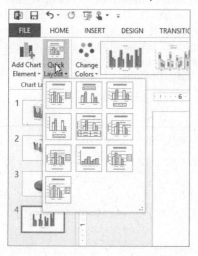

Working with Chart Elements

Charts are effective only if the audience understands what the data points represent. Labels and other descriptive elements on a chart can make all the difference in its usability. Figure 23.34 points out some of the various *chart elements* that you can use.

FIGURE 23.34

Chart elements such as labels help to make it clear to the audience what the chart represents.

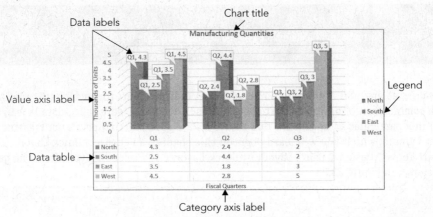

To change the setting for a particular element, choose Chart Tools ➪ Design ➪ Chart Layouts ➪ Add Chart Element to open a menu of elements. Then point at a particular element to see a submenu with additional options on it. If none of the choices on the submenu meet your needs, click More Options to open a task pane with a more extensive set of options. The exact name of the More Options command varies depending on the chart element; for example, for Chart Title, it is More Title Options. Figure 23.35 shows the submenu for Chart Title.

FIGURE 23.35

Control individual chart elements from the Add Chart Element button's menu.

CAUTION

When working with a chart element such as data labels that could potentially affect the whole chart, a single data series, or a single data point, make sure you select the part of the chart you want to affect before issuing the command. For example, to apply data labels to all data points on the whole chart, select the outer frame of the chart first, or to add them only to a specific data series, select that data series first.

You can also quickly control chart elements by clicking the Chart Elements button that appears to the right of the chart when the chart is selected. Mark or clear the check boxes in the Chart Elements flyout to toggle a particular element on or off. For some elements, if you hover the mouse pointer over the option in the panel, a right-pointing triangle appears to its right. You can click that triangle for a submenu, as shown in Figure 23.36.

FIGURE 23.36

Click the Chart Elements icon to the right of a chart for quick access to chart elements.

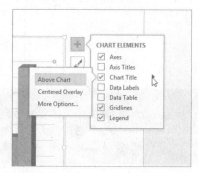

You can format the text in any of the chart elements just as you format any other text. To do this, select the text and then use the controls in the Font group on the Home tab. This allows you to choose a font, size, color, alignment, and so on. To format more than one chart element at a time, select one, and then hold down Ctrl as you click on other chart elements to select them also.

TIP

To quickly increase the size of all text in the chart, select the chart's outer frame, and then on the Home tab, in the Font group, click the Increase Font Size button repeatedly until all text is the desired size.

You can also format a chart element by right-clicking it and choosing Format *Name*, where *Name* is the type of element. For example, you could right-click the vertical axis title on the chart and then choose Format Axis Title. This opens a task pane with controls appropriate for the selected chart element. As with other panes, there are section names in all caps at the top, and under the chosen selection name are icons that represent pages of options.

Within a page of options are smaller uppercase headings indicating collapsible/expandable sections. Figure 23.37 shows an example.

FIGURE 23.37

Pane options are organized as shown here.

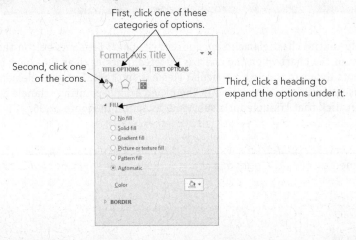

In some cases, the task pane contains only standard formatting controls that you would find for any object, such as Border, Fill, Shadow, Glow, Alignment, and so on. In other cases, in addition to the standard formatting types, there is also a unique section that contains extra options that are specific to the content type. For example, there is a Legend Options section in which you can set the position of a legend.

The following sections look at each of the chart elements more closely. These sections will not dwell on the basic formatting that you can apply to them (fonts, sizes, borders, fills, and so on) because this formatting is the same for all of them, as it is with any other object. Instead, they concentrate on the options that make each chart element different.

Working with chart titles

A *chart title* is text that typically appears above the chart — and sometimes overlapping it — and indicates what the chart represents. Although you would usually want either

> **NOTE**
>
> PowerPoint uses Format panes that are related to the various parts of the chart. These task panes are *nonmodal*, which means that they can stay open indefinitely, that their changes are applied immediately, and that you don't have to close the task pane to continue working on the presentation.

a chart title *or* a slide title, but not both, this could vary if you have multiple charts or different content on the same slide.

You can select a basic chart title, either above the chart or overlapping it, from the Chart Title submenu from the Add Chart Element button's menu, as shown in Figure 23.35. You can also drag the chart title around after placing it. For more options, you can choose More Title Options from the bottom of the submenu to open the Format Chart Title pane. However, in this dialog box there is nothing that specifically relates to chart titles; the available options are for formatting (Fill, Border, and so on), as for any text box.

Working with axis titles

An *axis title* is text that defines the category or the unit of measurement on an axis. For example, in Figure 23.34, the vertical axis title is Thousands of Units.

Axis titles are defined separately for the vertical and the horizontal axes. Click Chart Tools⇨Design⇨Chart Layouts⇨Add Chart Element⇨Axis Titles and then select either Primary Horizontal or Primary Vertical to toggle one or the other on or off. Alternatively, you can click the Chart Elements button to the right of the chart frame and mark the Axis Titles check box to turn both of them on at once or point to the right-pointing arrow and then mark or clear the Primary Horizontal and Primary Vertical check boxes individually, as shown in Figure 23.38. When you turn on an axis title, a text box appears containing default place-holder text, "Axis Title." Click in this text box and type your own label to replace it.

> **CAUTION**
>
> If you turn off an axis title and then turn it back on again, you will need to retype the axis title; it returns to the generic placeholder text.

If you've plotted any data on a secondary axis, you'll see Secondary Horizontal and Secondary Vertical Axis Title options as well on the submenu.

FIGURE 23.38

Turn axis titles on or off from the Axis Titles submenu.

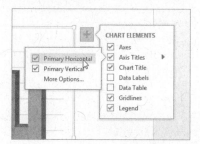

For more control, choose More Options from the submenu, or right-click the axis title and choose Format Axis Title, to open the Format Axis Title task pane.

Look back at Figure 23.34 and notice that the vertical axis title runs sideways from top to bottom. You can change the text's orientation for an axis by doing the following:

1. **Right-click the vertical axis title and choose Format Axis Title.** The Format Axis Title pane opens.
2. **Click Title Options, and then click the Size & Properties icon.** The Alignment controls appear. See Figure 23.39.

FIGURE 23.39

Select a text direction from the Format Axis Title pane.

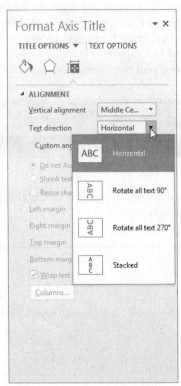

3. **Open the Text Direction drop-down list and choose the desired text direction, such as Horizontal.** The title appears horizontally, like regular text, to the left of the vertical axis.

- **Rotate All Text 90°:** The title appears vertically along the vertical axis, with the letters rotated 90 degrees (so that their bases run along the axis from top to bottom).

- **Rotate All Text 270°:** The title appears vertically along the vertical axis, with the letters rotated 270 degrees (so that their bases run along the axis from bottom to top).

- **Stacked:** The title appears vertically along the vertical axis, but each letter remains unrotated, so that the letters are stacked one on top of the other.

Figure 23.40 shows some examples.

FIGURE 23.40

Text direction examples. From left to right: Rotate All Text 270°, Stacked, and Horizontal.

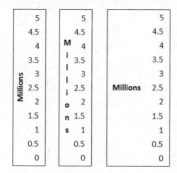

Each type of vertical axis shrinks the chart somewhat when you activate it, but the Horizontal option shrinks the chart more than the others because it requires more space to the left of the chart.

Working with legends

The *legend* is the little box that appears next to the chart (or sometimes above or below it). It provides the key that describes what the different colors or patterns mean. For some chart types and labels, you may not find the legend to be useful. If it is not useful for the chart that you are working on, you can turn it off. To turn off the legend, you can do any of the following:

- Click the legend box to select it and press the Delete key on the keyboard.

- Click Chart Tools ➪ Design ➪ Chart Layouts ➪ Add Chart Element ➪ Legend ➪ None.

- Click the Chart Elements button to the right of the chart, and in the Chart Elements flyout, clear the Legend check box.

To turn the legend back on, click the Chart Elements button again and mark the Legend check box; this places the legend in the default position for that chart type. If you want to choose a different legend location, click Chart Tools⇨Design⇨Chart Layouts⇨Add Chart Element⇨Legend and select the position that you want for it, as shown in Figure 23.41.

FIGURE 23.41

You can select a legend position, or turn the legend off altogether, from the Legend sub-menu.

To resize a legend box, you can drag one of its selection handles. The text and keys inside the box do not change in size, although they may shift in position.

When you right-click the legend and choose Format Legend, or when you choose More Legend Options from the Legend submenu (see Figure 23.41), the Format Legend pane opens with the Legend Options controls displayed, as shown in Figure 23.42. From here, you can choose the legend's position in relation to the chart and whether or not it should overlap the chart. If it does not overlap the chart, the plot area will be automatically reduced to accommodate the legend.

FIGURE 23.42

You can set legend options in the Format Legend pane.

NOTE

The controls in the Legend Options section refer to the legend's position in relation to the chart, not to the orientation or alignment of the legend text within the legend box.

Adding data labels

Data labels show the numeric values (or other information) that are represented by each bar or other shape on the chart. These labels are useful when the exact numbers are important or where the chart is so small that it is not clear from the axes what the data points represent.

To turn on data labels for the chart, do one of the following:

- Click the Chart Elements icon to the right of the chart, and in the flyout that appears, mark the Data Labels check box. This method places plain black numeric labels on each data point, with a transparent background on the data label box and no border.

- Click Chart Tools ⇨ Design ⇨ Chart Layouts ⇨ Add Chart Element ⇨ Data Labels ⇨ Data Callout. This method places white callout boxes for each data point, showing both the numeric value and the category name.

If you want additional options besides those two data label types, follow these steps:

1. **Select the data series or data point you want to affect.** To select a data series, click one of the bars (or other shapes) in the desired data series. To select a single data point, click again on the same bar (or shape).

2. **Choose Chart Tools ⇨ Design ⇨ Chart Layouts ⇨ Add Chart Element ⇨ Data Labels ⇨ More Data Label Options to open the Format Data Labels pane.**

   Make sure the Label Options heading is selected, and make sure the Label Options icon is selected. If needed, expand the Label Options controls under the icon, as shown in Figure 23.43. The options available depend on whether it's a 2-D or 3-D chart and on what type of chart it is. Figure 23.43 shows the options for a 3-D column chart.

FIGURE 23.43

Control data label options from the Format Data Labels pane.

3. **Mark or clear the check boxes for the types of label content under the Label Contains heading.** For example, you can show the series and/or category name, the value, and the legend key (the colored square that represents the series name).

4. **If you are working with a 2-D chart, choose a label position from the Label Options controls in the task pane.** A label can be on the center of the bar (or other shape), inside it, or outside it. This option does not appear when you're working with a 3-D chart.

5. **To change the shape of the data label text box, right-click any of the data labels in the series and choose Change Data Label Shapes, and then click the desired shape.** See Figure 23.44.

FIGURE 23.44

Change the shape of the data label box if desired.

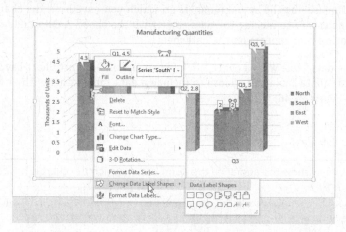

FIGURE 23.45

Change the background fill for the data label box if desired.

6. **To change the fill of the data label text box, in the Format Data Labels pane, click Label Options, and then click the Fill & Line icon and expand the Fill category to display the fill options.** To make the data label text boxes transparent, choose No Fill, or to apply some other fill color, select it as you would for any text box or drawn shape. See Figure 23.45.

Adding a data table

Sometimes the chart tells the full story that you want to tell, but other times the audience may benefit from seeing the actual numbers on which you have built the chart. In these cases, it is a good idea to include the data table with the chart. A data table contains the same information that appears on the datasheet.

To display the data table with a chart, click Chart Tools ⇨ Design ⇨ Chart Layouts ⇨ Add Chart Element ⇨ Data Table and choose to include a data table either with or without a legend key. See Figure 23.46.

FIGURE 23.46

Use a data table to show the audience the numbers on which the chart is based.

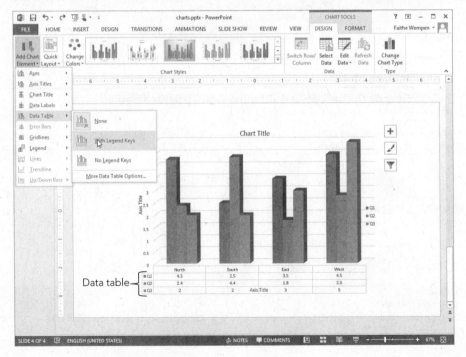

To format the data table, choose More Data Table Options from the Data Table submenu in Figure 23.46. In the Format Data Table pane that appears, you can set data table border options, as shown in Figure 23.47. For example, you can display or hide the horizontal, vertical, and outline borders for the table from here.

FIGURE 23.47

Use the Data Table Options controls to specify which borders should appear in the data table.

Controlling the Axes

No, axes are not the tools that chop down trees. *Axes* is the plural of *axis*, and an axis is the side of the chart containing the measurements against which your data is plotted.

You can change the various axes in a chart in several ways. For example, you can make an axis run in a different direction (such as from top to bottom instead of bottom to top for a vertical axis), and you can turn the text on or off for the axis and change the axis scale.

Displaying or hiding an axis

Most of the time you will want to display all axes for a chart. However, in some special cases it may be appropriate to turn off an axis. To do so, click Chart Tools ⇨ Design ⇨ Chart Layouts ⇨ Add Chart Element ⇨ Axes and then click Primary Horizontal or Primary Vertical to toggle either of those off (or back on again). See Figure 23.48.

FIGURE 23.48

Turn axes off or on here.

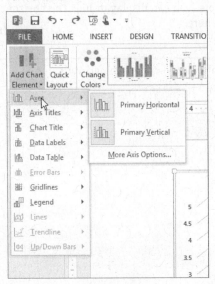

To control how an axis appears (other than just whether or not it appears at all), choose More Axis Options from the submenu. The options for axes are covered in the following sections.

Setting axis scale options

The *scale* determines which numbers will form the start point and endpoint of the axis line. PowerPoint 2013 calls the scale the *bounds* of the axis because the minimum and maximum values on the scale define lower and upper boundaries for the axis.

Changing the axis scale can make a big difference in how an audience perceives the same data. For example, take a look at the chart in Figure 23.49. The bars are so close to one another in value that it is difficult to see the difference between them. Compare this chart to one showing the same data in Figure 23.50, but with an adjusted scale. Because the scale is smaller, the differences now appear more dramatic.

FIGURE 23.49

This chart does not show the differences between the values very well.

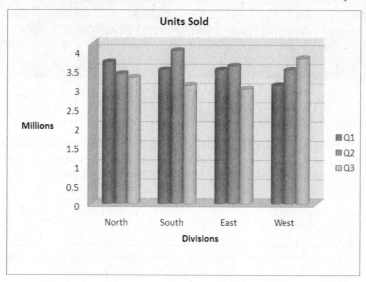

FIGURE 23.50

A change to the values of the axis scale makes it easier to see the differences between values.

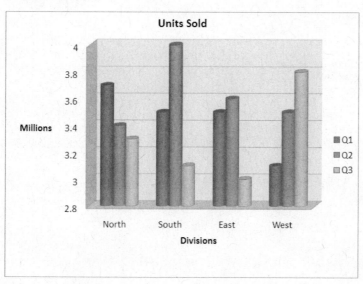

> **TIP**
>
> PowerPoint's charting feature has an automatic setting for the scale that is turned on by default. However, you may sometimes want to override this setting for a different effect, such as to minimize or enhance the difference between data series. This is a good example of "making the data say what you want." For example, if you wanted to make the point that the differences between three months were insignificant, then you would use a larger scale. If you wanted to highlight the importance of the differences, then you would use a smaller scale.

To set the scale (bounds) for an axis, follow these steps:

1. **Right-click the axis on the chart that contains the values you are plotting, and click Format Axis.** (This is typically the vertical axis on a column chart.) The Format Axis pane appears, displaying the Axis Options, as shown in Figure 23.51.

FIGURE 23.51

You can set axis options in the Format Axis pane, including the axis scale (bounds).

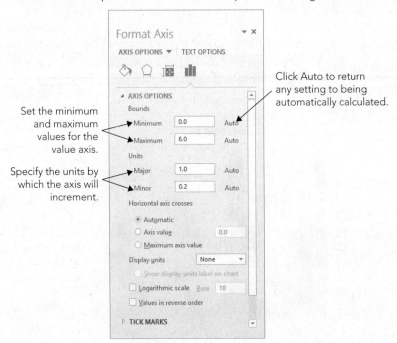

814

2. **If you do not want the automatic value for one of the measurements, enter a different number in its text box under Bounds.** To change your mind and go back to automatic settings for these, click Auto next to the text box.

   - **Minimum:** is the starting number. The usual setting is 0, as shown in Figure 23.49, although in Figure 23.50, it is set to 2.8.

   - **Maximum:** is the top number. This number is 4 in both Figure 23.49 and Figure 23.50.

3. **If you want the units on the axis to display differently, change the values in their boxes under Units.** To change your mind and go back to automatic settings for these, click Auto next to the box.

   - **Major** determines the axis text. It is also the unit by which gridlines stretch out across the back wall of the chart. In Figure 23.49, gridlines appear at increments of 0.5 million units; in Figure 23.50, they appear by 0.2 million units.

   - **Minor** is the interval of smaller gridlines between the major ones. Most charts look better without minor units because they can make a chart look cluttered. In most cases, you should leave this setting at Auto. You can also use this feature to place tick marks on the axes between the labels of the major units.

4. **(Optional) If you want to change where the axes cross, select Axis value in the Horizontal axis crosses section, and then enter a numeric value in its box.** Changing this value recalculates the numbers in the Bounds and Units sections that are set to Auto.

5. **(Optional) If you want to activate any of these special features, select their check boxes.**

   - **Logarithmic scale.** Rarely used by ordinary folks, this check box recalculates the Minimum, Maximum, Major, and Minor values according to a power of 10 for the value axis, based on the range of data. (If this explanation doesn't make any sense to you, then you're not the target audience for this feature.)

   - **Values in reverse order.** This check box turns the scale backward so that the greater values appear at the bottom or left.

6. **(Optional) Choose a display unit from the Display units drop-down list.** This option can help simplify large numbers. For example, if you set display units to Thousands, then the number 1000 appears as 1 on the chart. If you then select the Show Display Units Label on Chart check box, an axis label will appear as Thousands.

7. **(Optional) Expand the Tick Marks section below the axis options, and set tick-mark types for major and minor marks (see Figure 23.52).** These marks appear as little lines on the axis to indicate the units. You can use tick marks either with or without gridlines.

23

FIGURE 23.52

You can choose what tick marks to use, if any.

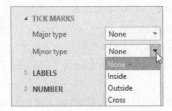

8. **Close the task pane when finished.**

Setting a number format

You can apply a number format to axes and data labels that show numeric data. This is similar to the number format that is used for Excel cells; you can choose a category, such as Currency or Percentage, and then fine-tune this format by choosing a number of decimal places, a method of handling negative numbers, and so on.

To set a number format, follow these steps:

1. **Right-click the axis containing the numbers you want to format, and choose Format Axis.**

2. **In the Format Axis pane that appears, click the Axis Options text at the top, and then click the Axis Options icon.**

3. **Expand the Number section if it is not already expanded.** (Collapse any previously open sections for easier reading.)

4. **Choose a number format.** You can select the number format in either of two ways:

   - Select the Linked to source check box if you want the number format to be taken from the number format that is applied to the datasheet in Excel. If you use this method, you don't have to complete the rest of the steps here.

   - Click the desired number format in the Category list. Options appear that are specific to the format that you selected. For example, Figure 23.53 shows the options for the Number type of format, which is a generic format.

5. **(Optional) Fine-tune the numbering format by changing the code in the Format Code text box.** The number signs (#) represent optional digits, while the zeroes represent required digits.

6. **Close the task pane.**

FIGURE 23.53

Select a number format in the Format Axis pane.

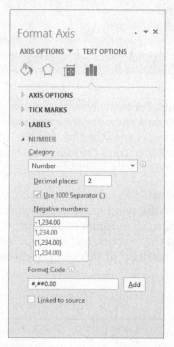

Formatting a Chart

In the following sections, you learn about chart formatting. There is so much that you can do to a chart that this subject could easily take up its own chapter! For example, just as with any other object, you can resize a chart. You can also change the fonts; change the colors and shading of bars, lines, or pie slices; use different background colors; change the 3-D angle; and much more.

> **NOTE**
>
> To clear the formatting that is applied to a chart element, select it and then click Chart Tools ⇨ Format ⇨ Current Selection ⇨ Reset to Match Style. This strips off the manually applied formatting from that element, returning it to whatever appearance is specified by the chart style that you have applied. (See "Applying Chart Styles" later in this chapter for details about styles.)

There are several ways of formatting a chart's elements. For text elements, you can use the Font group's tools on the Home tab. The text elements on a chart use the exact same text formatting controls as any other text on a slide. You can change the font, the size, the text attributes (like bold and italic), and so on. PowerPoint treats the individual text boxes within the chart as it would treat any other text boxes.

For simple formatting of a graphical element, like changing its outline or fill color, your best bet is the Chart Tools ⇨ Format tab's controls. You can select any chart element and then choose its border and fill color from here. For example, in Figure 23.54, Vertical (Value) Axis Major Gridlines is selected, which you can see in the selection box at the far left end of the Ribbon. You could use the Shape Outline drop-down list at this point to choose a different color or thickness for the gridlines.

FIGURE 23.54

Format a chart element's outline and fill quickly and easily from the Chart Tools ⇨ Format tab.

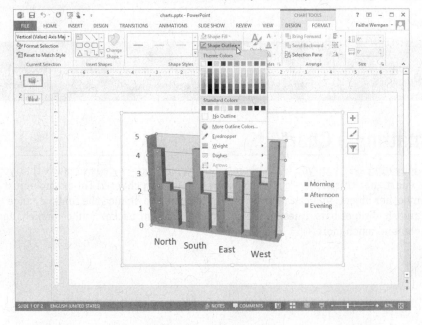

For more extensive or uncommon formatting, use the task pane instead. You can open the task pane for the selected chart element by right-clicking it and choosing Format *Element Name* from the submenu, or by choosing Chart Tools ⇨ Format ⇨ Current Selection ⇨ Format Selection.

The sections in the pane vary, depending on the type of chart element you are formatting. There are generally two main sections, indicated by words at the top of the pane. For example, in the Format Chart Title pane, the two main sections are Title Options and Text Options. Beneath these main section headings are a series of icons. The icons are different depending on the main section that's active. For example, in Figure 23.55, with Title Options selected, the three icons that appear are Fill & Line, Effects, and Size & Properties. In Figure 23.56, with Text Options selected, the icons that appear are Text Fill & Outline, Text Effects, and Textbox. This is an example of just one pane; each chart element type has its own unique combination of options in its pane.

FIGURE 23.55

When Title Options is selected for a chart title, these are the icons available.

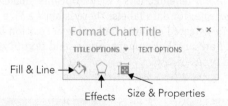

FIGURE 23.56

When Text Options is selected for a chart title, these are the icons available.

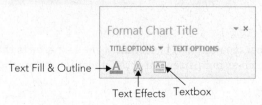

For most chart elements, the following sections are available from the Fill & Line icon:

- **Fill:** You can choose No Fill, Solid Fill, Gradient Fill, Picture or Texture Fill, Pattern Fill, or Automatic. When you select Automatic, the color changes to contrast with the background color specified by the theme.

- **Border:** You can choose No Line, Solid Line, Gradient Line, or Automatic. When you select Automatic, the color changes to contrast with the background color specified by the theme. You can also set a width, a compound type (that is, a line made up of multiple lines), and a dash type.

Most chart elements include these choices with the Effects icon:

- **Shadow:** You can apply a preset shadow in any color you want, or you can fine-tune the shadow in terms of transparency, size, angle, and so on. You might need to apply a fill to the box in order for the shadow to appear. This shadow is for the text box, not for the text within it; use the Font group on the Home tab to apply the text shadow, or use the shadows available for WordArt.

- **Glow:** These options add a colored halo effect around the element. You can choose a preset or select a color, size, and amount of transparency yourself.

- **Soft Edges:** These options blur the edges of the element. You can choose a preset or specify a precise size of the soft edge.

- **3-D Format:** You can define 3-D settings for the text box, such as Bevel, Depth, Contour, and Surface.

Depending on the chart element selected, the third icon may be Size & Properties, as in Figure 23.55, or something else. For example, for legends, it is Legend Options. Some elements may even have a fourth icon. For example, for data labels, there is both a Size & Position icon and a Label Options icon. If the selected element has a Size & Position icon, you can use its controls to set vertical and horizontal alignment, angle, and text direction as well as control AutoFit settings for some types of text.

> **NOTE**
>
> Alignment is usually not relevant in a short label or title text box. The text box is usually exactly the right size to hold the text, and so there is no other way for the text to be aligned. Therefore, no matter what alignment you choose, the text looks very much the same.

From the Home tab or the Mini Toolbar, you can also choose all of the text effects that you learned about earlier in this book, such as font, size, font style, underline, color, alignment, and so on.

Applying chart styles

Chart styles are presets that you can apply to charts in order to add colors, backgrounds, and fill styles. The Chart Styles gallery, shown in Figure 23.57, is located on the Chart Tools⇨Design tab, which appears when you select a chart. Point to a sample in the gallery to see its style previewed on the chart.

FIGURE 23.57

You can apply a chart style using the Chart Styles gallery.

Click here to choose color variants.

Chart Styles

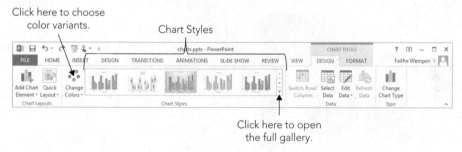

Click here to open the full gallery.

If you used PowerPoint 2010, it might seem at first glance that there are fewer chart styles in PowerPoint 2013. However, this is an illusion because in PowerPoint 2010, the different color variations were included in the Chart Style gallery as separate entities. By separating the color choices from the style choices, PowerPoint 2013 actually provides more choices and more flexibility.

Each of the chart styles uses whatever colors are assigned to the placeholders in your current color theme for the presentation. You can change the colors for the chart only, without having to change the colors for the whole presentation, by clicking the Change Colors button to the left of the Chart Styles gallery. However, the colors on the Change Colors button's menu are indirectly related to the color theme in use for the whole presentation; they are various tints and shades of the theme colors, in various combinations. To change colors completely, you must change the whole presentation's colors, as you learned to do in Chapter 22 "Working with Layouts, Themes, and Masters."

> **NOTE**
>
> You cannot add to the presets in the Chart Styles gallery, but you can save a group of settings as a template. To do this, right-click the chart's outer frame and choose Save as Template.

New in PowerPoint 2013, you can also apply chart styles via the Chart Styles icon that appears to the right of the chart when it is selected on the slide. Click the Chart Styles button, as shown in Figure 23.58, and then click the desired style. You can click Color at the top of the panel to select colors from there also, as you would from the Change Colors button on the Chart Tools Design tab.

FIGURE 23.58

Click the Chart Styles button to the right of the chart to quickly apply a different style or color.

Chart Styles button

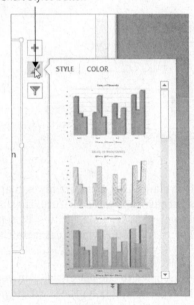

Formatting the chart area and plot area

The *chart area* is the entire chart, everything within the big frame that contains the plotted data and all the associated elements: the legend, the data series, the data table, the titles, and so on. Right-click anywhere within the chart area (not on any specific element) and choose Format Chart Area to open the Format Chart Area pane.

The Format Chart Area pane has many of the same sections the pane for text boxes has. Under Chart Options you'll find Fill & Line, Effects, and Size & Properties. Under Text Options are Text Fill & Outline, Text Effects, and Textbox. Any settings you apply to the chart area will apply to all the text and objects within the chart area unless a specific chart element is formatted differently to override that.

The *plot area* is the part of the chart where the data is plotted. It includes the data series and axes as well as any data labels, but it excludes the axis titles, the chart title, and the legend. You can choose to format the plot area differently from the chart area if you like, although it's not common to do so. For example, you could apply a different background fill color to the plot area, as in Figure 23.59. By default the plot area's background is transparent, so the background of the chart area shows through. If, in turn, the chart area is also transparent, then the background of the slide behind them both shows through.

FIGURE 23.59

The plot area has a different fill color than the chart area in this example.

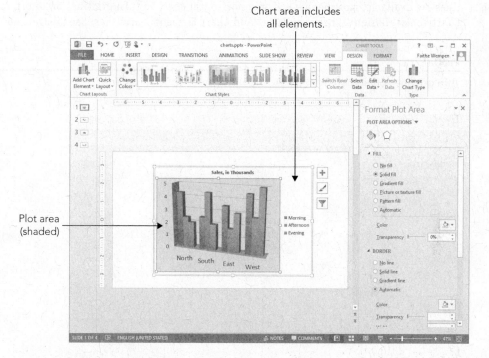

Formatting the legend

When you use a multiseries chart, the value of the legend is obvious — it tells you which colors represent which series. Without the legend, your audience will not know what the various bars or lines mean. You can do all of the same formatting for a legend that you can for other chart elements. Just right-click the legend, choose Format Legend from the shortcut menu, and then use the Format Legend task pane to make your modifications. For example, you could apply a background fill to the legend box, place a border around it, and so on. You could also change the font and size used for the legend text from the Fonts group on the Home tab.

Formatting gridlines and walls

Gridlines help the reader's eyes move across the chart. Gridlines are related to the axes, which you learned about earlier in this chapter. Although both vertical and horizontal gridlines are available, most people use only horizontal ones. To turn gridlines on or off, click Chart Tools ⇨ Design ⇨ Chart Layouts ⇨ Add Chart Element ⇨ Gridlines. See Figure 23.60.

FIGURE 23.60

Turn gridlines on and off from the Add Chart Element button's menu.

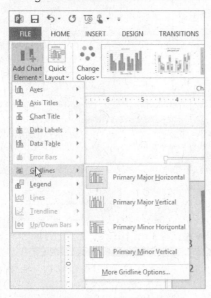

In most cases, the default gridlines that PowerPoint adds work well. However, you may want to make the lines thicker or a different color. Apply those changes by selecting the gridlines and then using the Chart Tools ⇨ Format tab's commands. You can select one of the Shape Styles from there, or use the Shape Outline and/or Shape Effects drop-down lists to apply formatting.

NOTE

Gridline spacing is based on the major and minor units that you have set in the Format Axis dialog box (vertical or horizontal). To set this spacing, see "Setting axis scale options" earlier in this chapter.

Walls are nothing more than the space between the gridlines, formatted in a different color than the plot area. You can set the walls' fill to None to hide them. To set the wall color, right-click the wall and choose Format Wall, and then choose a fill color in the Format Wall pane.

NOTE

You can format walls only on 3-D charts; 2-D charts do not have them. To change the background behind a 2-D chart, you must format the plot area.

Formatting the data series

To format a data series, just right-click the bar, slice, or chart element, and choose Format Data Series from the shortcut menu. Then, depending on your chart type, different series options appear that you can use to modify the series appearance. Here are the icons available for bar and column charts, for example:

- **Fill & Line:** These options enable you to choose a fill and a border for the series, with choices for fill including solid, gradient, or picture/texture. Under Border you can choose a border color, style, and thickness. This is just like filling drawn shapes, as you learned in Chapter 9.

- **Effects:** These options include the same standard options available for any drawn object, including Shadow, Glow, Soft Edges, and 3-D Format.

- **Series Options:** This section contains options that are specific to the selected chart type. For example, when you're working with a 3-D bar or column chart, the series options include Gap Depth and Gap Width, which determine the thickness and depth of the bars. For a pie chart, you can set the rotation angle for the first slice as well as whether a slice is "exploded" or not. For charts involving bars and columns, you can choose a shape option such as Box, Full Pyramid, Partial Pyramid, Cylinder, Full Cone, or Partial Cone. The partial options truncate the top part of the shape when it is less than the largest value in the chart.

Other chart types have very different series options available. For example, a line chart has Line and Marker Options, including marker Fill, line Color, line Style, marker outline Color, and marker type.

Rotating a 3-D Chart

3-D charts can be rotated in one or more directions: X (side to side), Y (top to bottom), and Perspective (the angle from which you view it). There is also a Z rotation (pivoting around a center point), but it is inactive for most chart types.

The Right Angle Axes check box (in the Format Plot Area task pane) is very important when setting chart rotation for most chart types. If the Right Angle Axes option is enabled, the chart axes do not rotate — only the data bars (or other shapes) rotate. If Right Angle Axes is disabled, the entire content of the plot area rotates together as a whole, including the axes. Figure 23.61 shows a rotated chart where Right Angle Axes is turned off.

FIGURE 23.61

Right Angle Axes is disabled, and both X Rotation and Y Rotation are set to 30°.

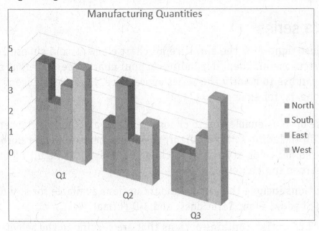

To set a chart's rotation, follow these steps:

1. **Select the chart's plot area.** You can do this by clicking it, or by displaying the Chart Tools⇨Format tab and selecting Plot Area from the drop-down list in the Current Selection group.

2. **Display the Format Plot Area pane.** You can do this by right-clicking the plot area and choosing Format Plot Area, or by clicking Chart Tools⇨Format⇨Current Selection⇨Format Selection.

3. **In the Format Plot Area pane, click the Effects icon, and then expand the 3-D Rotation controls.**

4. **Mark or clear the Right Angle Axes check box as desired, depending on how you want the chart to appear.** If the feature is off, the whole plot area rotates, including the axes; if the feature is on, only the data series rotate.

5. **Click the increment buttons to increase or decrease the X Rotation, Y Rotation, and/or Perspective settings as desired.** You may need to experiment with these to find the settings that show your chart the way you want it. See Figure 23.62.

FIGURE 23.62

Set the 3-D Rotation options for the chart in its Format Plot Area pane.

6. **Close the pane when you are finished working with the chart's rotation.**

Summary

In this chapter, you learned the ins and outs of creating and formatting tables and charts in PowerPoint, including how to:

- Insert tables using multiple methods.
- Add text in a table, navigate, and select rows and columns.
- Work with the table structure, such as adding and removing rows and columns and changing table size.
- Use table styles and other formatting to enhance a table.
- Create a chart and specify how it plots data.
- Change chart type and data range.
- Use optional text elements on them such as titles, data labels, and so on to clarify the chart.
- Format the various parts of the chart.

Using SmartArt Diagrams, Clip Art, and Pictures

IN THIS CHAPTER

Understanding SmartArt types and their uses

Inserting, editing, and modifying a SmartArt graphic

Modifying an organization chart structure

Resizing, restructuring, and formatting a SmartArt graphic

Choosing and inserting appropriate clip art

Modifying clip art

Inserting, sizing, and cropping photos

Adjusting and correcting photos

Compressing images

Just as charts and graphs can enliven a boring table of numbers, a SmartArt graphic can enliven a conceptual discussion. SmartArt helps the audience understand the interdependencies of objects or processes in a visual way, so they don't have to juggle that information mentally as you speak. Some potential uses include organizational charts, hierarchy diagrams, and flow charts. Similarly, the right clip, image, or photo can highlight a concept or present a product with clarity that words cannot deliver.

In this chapter you will learn how to create and fine-tune SmartArt diagrams, and how to select and insert clip art into your presentations. You'll also learn how to integrate and work with photos in a PowerPoint presentation.

Understanding SmartArt Types and Their Uses

SmartArt is a special class of vector graphic object that combines shapes, lines, and text placeholders. SmartArt is most often used to illustrate relationships between bits of text.

The SmartArt interface is similar regardless of the type of graphic you are creating. You can type directly into the placeholders on the SmartArt graphic, or you can display a Text pane to the side of the graphic and type into that, much as you would type into an Outline pane, to have text appear in a slide's text placeholder boxes. See Figure 24.1. You can also select some text, right-click it, and choose Convert to SmartArt.

FIGURE 24.1

A typical SmartArt graphic being constructed

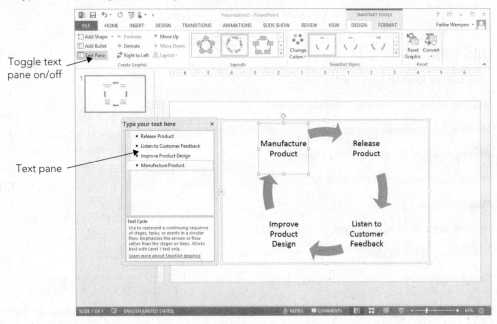

There are eight types of SmartArt graphics in PowerPoint 2013, and each is uniquely suited for a certain type of data delivery.

List

A List graphic presents information in a fairly straightforward, text-based way, somewhat like a fancy outline. List graphics are useful when information is not in any particular order or when the process or progression between items is not important. The list can have multiple levels, and you can enclose each level in a shape or not. Figure 24.2 shows an example.

FIGURE 24.2

FIGURE 24.2

A List graphic de-emphasizes any progression between items.

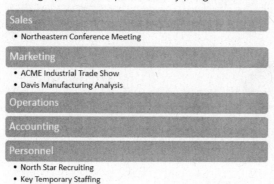

Process

A Process graphic is similar to a list, but it has directional arrows or other connectors that represent the flow of one item to another. This adds an extra aspect of meaning to the graphic. For example, in Figure 24.3, the way the boxes are staggered and connected with arrows implies that the next step begins before the previous one ends.

FIGURE 24.3

A Process graphic shows a flow from point A to point B.

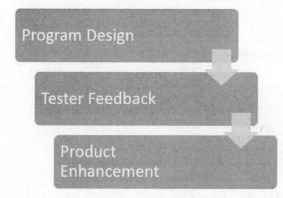

Cycle

A Cycle graphic also illustrates a process, but a repeating or recursive one — usually a process in which there is no fixed beginning point or endpoint. You can jump into the cycle at any point. In Figure 24.4, for example, the ongoing process of product development and improvement is illustrated.

FIGURE 24.4

A Cycle graphic traces the steps of a repeating process.

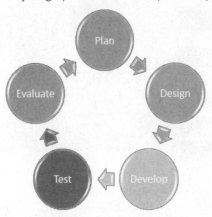

Hierarchy

A Hierarchy chart is an organization chart. It shows structure and relationships between people or things in standardized levels. For example, it can show who reports to whom in a company's employment system. It is useful when describing how the organization functions and who is responsible for what. In Figure 24.5, for example, three organization levels are represented, with lines of reporting drawn between each level. Hierarchy graphics can also run horizontally, for use in tournament rosters.

FIGURE 24.5

A Hierarchy graphic, also called an organization chart, explains the structure of an organization.

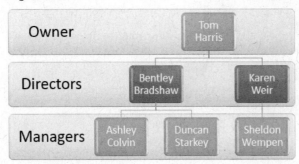

Wondering Whether to Include an Organization Chart?

Should you include your company's organization chart in your presentation? That's a question that depends on your main message. If your speech is about the organization, you should. If not, show the organization structure only if it serves a purpose to advance your speech. Many presenters have found that an organization chart makes an excellent backup slide. You can prepare it and have it ready in case a question arises about the organization. Another useful strategy is to include a printed organization chart as part of the handouts you distribute to the audience, without including the slide in your main presentation.

Relationship

Relationship graphics graphically illustrate how parts relate to a whole. One common type of Relationship graphic is a Venn diagram, as in Figure 24.6, showing how categories of people or things overlap. Relationship graphics can also break things into categories or show how parts contribute to a whole, as with a pie chart.

FIGURE 24.6

A Relationship graphic shows how parts relate to a whole.

Matrix

A Matrix also shows the relationship of parts to a whole, but it does so with the parts in orderly looking quadrants. You can use Matrix graphics when you do not need to show any particular relationship between items but you want to make it clear that they make up a single unit. See Figure 24.7.

FIGURE 24.7

A Matrix graphic uses a grid to represent the contributions of parts to a whole.

Pyramid

A Pyramid graphic is just what the name sounds like — it's a striated triangle with text at various levels, representing not only the relationship between the items but also that the items at the smaller part of the triangle are less numerous or more important. For example, the graphic in Figure 24.8 shows that there are many more workers than there are executives.

FIGURE 24.8

A Pyramid graphic represents the progression between less and more of something.

> **TIP**
>
> In Pyramid graphics and some other cases, labels do not confine themselves to within the associated shape. If this is a problem, you might be able to make the labels fit with a combination of line breaks (Shift+Enter) and font changes.

Picture

The Picture category is a collection of SmartArt graphic types from the other categories that include picture placeholders in them. You'll find List, Process, and other types of graphics here; the Picture category simply summarizes them.

Inserting a SmartArt Graphic

All SmartArt graphics start out the same way — you insert them on the slide as you can any other slide object. That means you can either use a SmartArt placeholder on a slide layout or insert the SmartArt graphic manually.

To use a placeholder, start with a slide that contains a layout with a SmartArt placeholder in it, or change the current slide's layout to one that does. Then click the Insert a SmartArt Graphic button in the placeholder, as shown in Figure 24.9. To insert from scratch, click the SmartArt button in the Illustrations group of the Insert tab.

FIGURE 24.9

Click the Insert a SmartArt Graphic button in the placeholder on a slide.

Insert SmartArt Graphic

Another way to start a new SmartArt graphic is to select some text and then right-click the selection and choose Convert to SmartArt.

Any way you start it, the Choose a SmartArt Graphic dialog box opens (Figure 24.10). Select one of the SmartArt categories, click the desired SmartArt object, and click OK, and the graphic appears. From there it's just a matter of customizing.

24

FIGURE 24.10

Select the graphic type you want to insert.

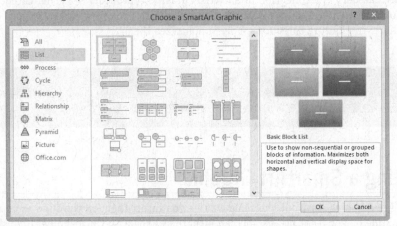

When you select a graphic, SmartArt Tools contextual tabs become available (Design and Format). You will learn what each of the buttons on them does as this chapter progresses. The buttons change depending on the type of graphic.

Editing SmartArt Text

All SmartArt has text placeholders, which are basically text boxes. You simply click in one of them and type. Then use the normal text-formatting controls (Font, Font Size, Bold, Italic, and so on) on the Home tab to change the appearance of the text, or use the WordArt Styles group on the Format tab to apply WordArt formatting.

You can also display a Text pane, as shown in Figure 24.1, and type or edit the graphic's text there. The Text pane serves the same purpose for a graphic that the Outline pane in Outline view serves for the slide as a whole.

Here are some tips for working with SmartArt text:

- To leave a text box empty, just don't type anything in it. The *[Text]* placeholders do not show up in a printout or in Slide Show view.

- To promote a line of text, press Shift+Tab; to demote it, press Tab in the Text pane.

- Text wraps automatically, but you can press Shift+Enter to insert a line break if necessary.

- In most cases, the text size shrinks to fit the graphic in which it is located. There are some exceptions to that, though; for example, at the top of a pyramid, the text can overflow the tip of the pyramid.

- All of the text is the same size, so if you enter a really long string of text in one box, the text size in all of the related boxes shrinks too. You can manually format parts of the SmartArt graphic to change this behavior, as you will learn later in the chapter.

- If you resize the SmartArt graphic, its text resizes automatically.

Modifying SmartArt Structure

The structure of the SmartArt graphic includes how many boxes it has and where they are placed. Even though the graphic types are all very different, the way you add, remove, and reposition shapes in them is surprisingly similar across all types.

> **NOTE**
>
> When you add a shape, you add both a graphical element (a circle, a bar, or other) and an associated text placeholder. The same applies to deletion; removing a shape also removes its associated text placeholder from the SmartArt graphic.

24

Inserting and deleting shapes

To insert a shape in a SmartArt graphic, follow these steps:

1. **Click a shape that is adjacent to where you want the new shape to appear.**
2. **Click SmartArt Tools ⇨ Design ⇨ Create Graphic ⇨ Add Shape.**

You can click the top part of the Add Shape button to add a shape of the same level and type as the selected one, or you can click the bottom part of the button to open a menu from which you can choose other variants. The choices on the menu depend on the graphic type and the type of shape selected. For example, in Figure 24.11, you can insert a shape into a SmartArt graphic either before or after the current one (same outline level), or you can insert a shape that is subordinate (below) or superior to (above) the current one.

FIGURE 24.11

Add a shape to the SmartArt graphic.

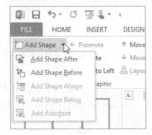

To delete a shape, click it to select it in the SmartArt graphic, and then press the Delete key on the keyboard. You might need to delete subordinate shapes before you can delete the main shape.

> **NOTE**
>
> Not all SmartArt graphic types can accept different numbers of shapes. For example, the four-square matrix graphic is fixed at four squares.

Adding bullets

In addition to adding shapes to the SmartArt graphic, you can add bullets — that is, subordinate text to a shape. To do so, click the Add Bullet button. Bullets appear indented under the shape's text in the Text pane, as shown in Figure 24.12.

FIGURE 24.12

Create subordinate bullet points under a shape.

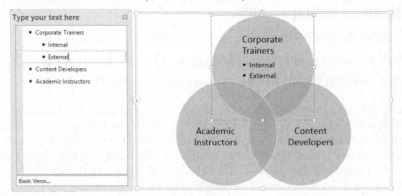

Promoting and demoting text

The difference between a shape and a bullet is primarily a matter of promotion and demotion in the Text pane's outline. The Text pane works just as the regular Outline pane does in this regard; you can promote with Shift+Tab or demote with Tab. You can also use the Promote and Demote buttons on the SmartArt Tools ⇨ Design tab.

Changing the flow direction

Each SmartArt graphic flows in a certain direction. A cycle graphic flows either clockwise or counterclockwise. A pyramid flows either up or down.

If you realize after typing all of the text that you should have made the SmartArt graphic flow in the other direction, you can change it by clicking the Right to Left button on the SmartArt Tools ⇨ Design tab. It is a toggle; you can switch back and forth freely.

Reordering shapes

Not only can you reverse the overall flow of the SmartArt graphic, you can also move around individual shapes. For example, suppose you have a graphic that illustrates five steps in a process and you realize that steps 3 and 4 are out of order. You can move one of them without having to retype all of the labels.

The easiest way to reorder the shapes is to select one and then click the Reorder Down or Reorder Up button on the SmartArt Tools ⇨ Design tab.

If you have more complex reordering to do, you might prefer to work in the Text pane instead, cutting and pasting text like this:

1. **Display the Text pane if it does not already appear.** You can either click the arrow button to the left of the graphic or click the Text Pane button in the Create Graphic group of the SmartArt Tools ⇨ Design tab.
2. **Select some text to be moved in the Text pane.**
3. **Press Ctrl+X to cut it to the Clipboard.**
4. **Click in the Text pane at the beginning of the line above which it should appear.**
5. **Press Ctrl+V to paste.**

Repositioning shapes

You can individually select and drag each shape to reposition it on the SmartArt graphic. Any connectors between it and the other shapes are automatically resized and extended as needed. For example, in Figure 24.13, notice how the arrows that connect the circles in the cycle graphic have elongated as one of the circles has moved out.

FIGURE 24.13

When you move pieces of a SmartArt graphic, connectors move and stretch as needed.

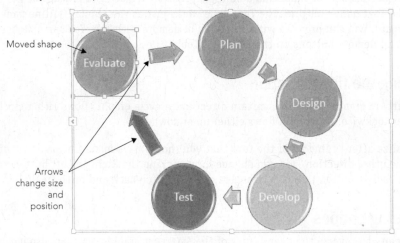

Resetting a SmartArt graphic

After making changes to a SmartArt graphic, you can return it to its default settings with the Reset Graphic button on the SmartArt Tools ⇨ Design tab. This strips off everything, including any SmartArt styles and manual positioning, and makes it exactly as it was when you inserted it except it keeps the text that you've typed.

Changing to a different SmartArt layout

The layouts are the graphic types. When you insert a SmartArt graphic you choose a type, and you can change that type at any time later.

To change the layout type, use the Layouts gallery on the Design tab, as shown in Figure 24.14. You can open the gallery and click the desired type, or click More Layouts at the bottom of its menu to redisplay the same dialog box as in Figure 24.10, the Choose a SmartArt Graphic dialog box, from which you can choose any layout.

FIGURE 24.14

Switch to a different graphic layout.

Click here to open gallery to choose layouts.

Modifying a Hierarchy Graphic Structure

Hierarchy graphics (organization charts) show the structure of an organization. They have some different controls for changing their structure compared to other graphics, so the following sections look at them separately.

Inserting and deleting shapes

The main difference when inserting an organization chart shape (that is, a box into which you will type a name) is that you must specify which existing box the new one is related to and how it is related.

For example, suppose you have a supervisor already in the chart and you want to add some people to the chart who report to him. You would first select his box on the chart and then insert the new shapes with the Add Shape button. For a box of the same level, or of the previously inserted level, click the top part of the button; for a subordinate or other relationship, open the button's menu. See Figure 24.15. The chart can have only one box at the top level, however, just as a company can have only one CEO.

FIGURE 24.15

Add more shapes to a hierarchy graphic.

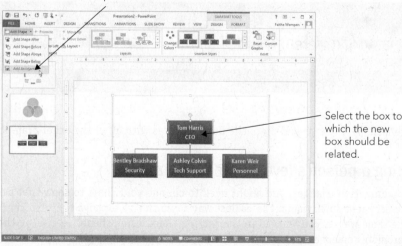

Choose the type of
relationship to the selection.

Select the box to
which the new
box should be
related.

When you insert a new shape in a hierarchy graphic, four of the options are the same as with any other SmartArt graphic, and one is new: Add Shape After and Add Shape Before insert shapes of the same level as the selected one, and Add Shape Above and Add Shape Below insert a superior and subordinate level, respectively. The new option, Add Assistant, adds a box that is neither subordinate nor superior but a separate line of reporting, as shown in Figure 24.16.

FIGURE 24.16

An Assistant box in a hierarchy chart.

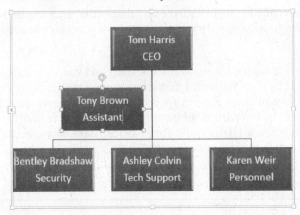

> **NOTE**
>
> An *assistant* is a person whose job is to provide support to a certain person or office. An executive secretary is one example. In contrast, a *subordinate* is an employee who may report to a manager but whose job does not consist entirely of supporting that manager. Confused? Don't worry about it. You don't have to make a distinction in your organization chart.

To delete a shape, select it and press the Delete key, as with all of the other graphic types.

Changing a person's level in the organization

As the organization changes, you might need to change your chart to show that people report to different supervisors. The easiest way to do that is to move the text in the Text pane, the same way as you learned in the section "Reordering shapes" earlier in this chapter. To promote someone, select their box and press Shift+Tab.

To change who someone reports to, select their box and press Ctrl+X to cut it to the Clipboard. Then select the box of the person they now report to, and press Ctrl+V to paste.

Controlling subordinate layout options

When subordinates report to a supervisor, you can list the subordinates beneath that supervisor in a variety of ways. In Standard layout, each subordinate appears horizontally beneath the supervisor, as shown in Figure 24.17.

FIGURE 24.17

This is the standard layout for a branch of an organization chart.

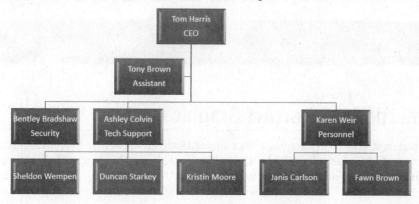

However, in a large or complex organization chart, the graphic can quickly become too wide with the Standard layout. Therefore, there are "hanging" alternatives that make the chart more vertically oriented. The alternatives are Both, Left Hanging, and Right Hanging. They are just what their names sound like. Figure 24.18 shows examples of Right.

FIGURE 24.18

Hanging layouts make the chart more vertically oriented.

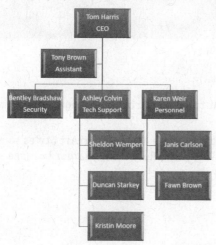

The layout is chosen for individual branches of the organization chart, so before selecting an alternative layout, you must click on the supervisor box whose subordinates you want to change. To change a layout, follow these steps:

1. **Click the box for the supervisor whose layout you want to change.**
2. **Choose SmartArt Tools ⇨ Design ⇨ Create Graphic ⇨ Layout.** A menu of layout options appears.
3. **Choose one of the layouts (Standard, Both, Left Hanging, or Right Hanging).**

> **NOTE**
> If the Layouts button's menu is grayed out, you do not have a box selected in a hierarchy graphic.

Formatting a SmartArt Graphic

You can format a SmartArt graphic either automatically or manually. Automatic formatting is the default, and many PowerPoint users don't even realize that manual formatting is a possibility. The following sections cover both.

Applying a SmartArt style

SmartArt Styles are preset formatting specs (border, fill, effects, shadows, and so on) that you can apply to an entire SmartArt graphic. They make it easy to apply surface texture effects that make the shapes look reflective or appear to have 3-D depth or perspective.

> **NOTE**
> SmartArt Styles do not include color changes. Those are separately controlled with the Change Colors button on the SmartArt Tools ⇨ Design tab.

To apply a SmartArt style, follow these steps:

1. **Select the SmartArt graphic so that the SmartArt Tools Design tab becomes available.**
2. **On the SmartArt Tools ⇨ Design tab, click one of the SmartArt Styles samples (see Figure 24.19), or open the gallery and select from a larger list (see Figure 24.20).**

FIGURE 24.19

Select a SmartArt Style.

Click here to open
the gallery to select
styles.

FIGURE 24.20

Open the SmartArt Style gallery for more choices.

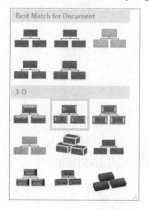

Changing SmartArt colors

After you apply a SmartArt style, as in the preceding section, you might want to change the colors used in the graphic.

The easiest way to apply colors is to use the Change Colors button's menu in the SmartArt Styles group of the Design tab. You can select from a gallery of color schemes. As shown in Figure 24.21, you can choose a Colorful scheme (one in which each shape has its own color, or the shapes at each level have their own colors), or you can choose a monochrome color scheme based on any of the current presentation color theme's color swatches.

Notice the command at the bottom of the menu in Figure 24.21: Recolor Pictures in SmartArt Graphic. You can toggle this button on or off. When the button is toggled on, it applies a color tint to any pictures that are part of the graphic.

FIGURE 24.21

Select a color scheme from the Change Colors button's menu.

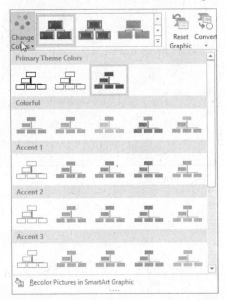

Manually applying colors and effects to individual shapes

In addition to formatting the entire graphic with a SmartArt Style, you can format individual shapes using Shape Styles, just as you did in Chapter 9 objects in Word. Here's a quick review:

1. **Select a shape in a SmartArt graphic.**
2. **On the SmartArt Tools ⇨ Format tab, select a shape style from the Shape Styles gallery.**
3. **(Optional) Fine-tune the style by using the Shape Fill, Shape Outline, and/or Shape Effects buttons and their associated menus.**

Manually formatting SmartArt text

WordArt formatting works the same in a SmartArt graphic as it does everywhere else in PowerPoint. Use the WordArt Styles gallery and controls on the SmartArt Tools ⇨ Format tab to apply text formatting to individual shapes, or select the entire graphic to apply the changes to all shapes at once.

Making a shape larger or smaller

In some SmartArt types, it is advantageous to make certain shapes larger or smaller than the others. For example, if you want to emphasize a certain step in a process, you can create a SmartArt graphic where that step's shape is larger. Then you can repeat that same graphic on a series of slides, but with a different step in the process enlarged on each copy, to step through the process. There are several options for this:

- You can manually resize a shape by dragging its selection handles, the same as with any other object. However, this is imprecise, and can be a problem if you want multiple shapes to be enlarged because they won't be consistently so.

- You can set a precise size for the entire SmartArt graphic by adjusting the height and width measurements in the Size group on the SmartArt Tools ⇨ Format tab, as shown in Figure 24.22. However, if different shapes are already different sizes and you want to resize them in proportion, this won't help.

FIGURE 24.22

Change the size of the entire SmartArt graphic or an individual shape.

Change the size of an
individual shape or
a group of shapes here.

Change the overall
size of the SmartArt
graphic here.

- You can use the Larger or Smaller buttons in the Shapes group of the Format tab to bump up or down the sizes of one or more shapes slightly with each successive click.

Resizing the entire SmartArt graphic object

When you resize the entire SmartArt object as a whole, everything within its frame changes size proportionally. There are several ways to do this:

- Drag a corner selection handle on the SmartArt graphic's outer frame.

- Use the Size controls on the SmartArt Tools ⇨ Format tab to enter a precise height and width.

- Right-click the outer frame of the SmartArt object and choose Size and Position. The Format Shape pane opens (Figure 24.23). Under the Size heading, enter a height and width in inches, or scale it by a percentage in the Scale Height and Scale Width boxes. Select the Lock Aspect Ratio check box if you want to maintain the proportions.

24

FIGURE 24.23

Right-click the graphic and choose Size and Position to open this task pane.

Editing in 2-D

If you choose one of the 3-D selections from the SmartArt Style gallery, the text might become a bit hard to read and edit when you are working with the graphic at a small zoom percentage. There are a couple of ways around this:

- Right-click a shape and choose Edit Text. The face of the shape appears in 2-D temporarily, making it easier to edit the text.
- Click the Edit in 2-D button in the Shapes group of the SmartArt Tools ⇨ Format tab. The entire graphic appears in 2-D temporarily.

TIP

Even though the face of the shape appears in 2-D, which you think would make it easier to read, in some SmartArt types and styles the text might still be fuzzy and hard to read. You might be better off editing it in the Text pane.

Changing the shapes used

Each SmartArt layout has its own defaults that it uses for the shapes, but you can change these manually. On the SmartArt Tools⇨Format tab, click Change Shape to open a palette of shapes. Then click the desired shape to apply to the selected shape. You can also access this from the right-click menu.

Each shape is individually configurable. If you simply select the entire graphic, the Change Shape button is not available; you must select each shape you want to change. Hold down the Shift key as you click on each one to be selected. Figure 24.24 shows a SmartArt graphic that uses some different shapes.

FIGURE 24.24

You can apply different shapes within a SmartArt graphic.

Saving a SmartArt Graphic as a Picture

SmartArt graphics work only within Office applications, but you can easily export one for use in any other application. It is exported as a picture (by default a PNG file), which you can then import into any application that accepts pictures. To save a SmartArt graphic as a picture, follow these steps:

1. **Select the outer frame of the SmartArt object.**
2. **Right-click the frame and choose Save as Picture.** The Save As Picture dialog box opens.
3. **(Optional) Open the Save as type list and select a different file type if desired.**
4. **Click the Save button to complete the save.**

24

> **TIP**
>
> PowerPoint can save pictures in GIF, JPEG, TIFF, PNG, BMP, WMF, and EMF formats. Different formats have different qualities and advantages. EMF and WMF can be ungrouped, but not the other formats. EMF does not result in a quality loss when resized, but most of the others do. JPG doesn't use a transparent background, but PNG does.

Choosing Appropriate Artwork

Before we get started with the "how" of images in PowerPoint, take a moment to think about the "why." Don't just use any old image! You must never use artwork simply because you can; it must be a well-thought-out decision. Here are some tips for using artwork appropriately:

- **Use for fun:** Use cartoonish images only if you specifically want to impart a light-hearted, fun feel to your presentation.

- **Use one style:** The clip art available from Office.com includes many styles of drawings, ranging from simple black-and-white shapes to very complex, shaded color drawings and photographs. Try to stick with one type of image rather than bouncing among several drawing styles.

- **Use only one piece per slide:** Also, do not use artwork on every slide, or it becomes overpowering.

- **Avoid repetition:** Don't repeat the same artwork on more than one slide in the presentation unless you have a specific reason to do so.

- **Avoid with bad news:** If your message is very serious, or you are conveying bad news, don't use artwork . It looks frivolous in these situations.

- **Better none than bad:** If you can't find artwork that is exactly right for the slide, then don't use any. It is better to have none than to have an inappropriate image.

- **Buy appropriate art:** If artwork is important, and Office.com doesn't have what you want, you can buy more. Don't try to struggle along with the clips and images that come with Office if they aren't meeting your needs; impressive artwork collections are available at reasonable prices at your local computer store as well as online.

Inserting Clip Art

Clip art is pre-drawn art available online for use with the Office applications. There are thousands of images that you can use royalty free in your work, without having to draw your own. For example, suppose you are creating a presentation about snow skiing equipment. Rather than hiring an artist to draw a picture of a skier, you can use one of PowerPoint's stock drawings of skiers and save yourself a bundle.

Being an owner of a Microsoft Office product entitles you to use the huge royalty free clip-art collection that Microsoft maintains at Office.com, and if you are connected to the Internet while you are using PowerPoint, PowerPoint can automatically pull clips from that collection as easily as it can from your own hard drive.

Earlier versions of PowerPoint included robust search and management capabilities for clip art and an application called the Clip Organizer. In contrast, PowerPoint 2013 provides only a very basic search box for searching for clip art by keyword at Office.com.

You can insert clip art on a slide either with or without a content placeholder. If you use a content placeholder, PowerPoint inserts the clip art wherever the placeholder is; if you don't, PowerPoint inserts the clip art at the center of the slide. (You can move it afterward, of course.) To insert clip art into a content placeholder, click the Online Pictures button on the placeholder (see Figure 24.25). To insert clip art without a content placeholder, choose Insert ⇨ Images ⇨ Online Pictures.

FIGURE 24.25

Click the Online Pictures icon in a content placeholder to insert clip art into the placeholder.

 —— Online Pictures

Whichever method you use, the Insert Pictures dialog box opens (see Figure 24.26). In it are three options:

- **Office.com Clip Art:** You can use the Search box on this line to search Microsoft's clip art collection by keyword.

- **Bing Image Search:** You can use the Search box on this line to use the Bing search engine to look for pictures on the Internet by keyword. These are mostly photographic images, which you'll learn more about later in this chapter.

- **(Your Name) SkyDrive:** You can click Browse to browse the content of your own SkyDrive and insert pictures from there. (See Chapter 39 for more information about using your SkyDrive.)

FIGURE 24.26

Type a keyword in the Office.com Clip Art search box.

Search for clip art.

Type a keyword into the Search box next to Office.com Clip Art and then press Enter to perform the search. Search results appear in that same dialog box, as shown in Figure 24.27.

FIGURE 24.27

Search results appear showing thumbnails of available images.

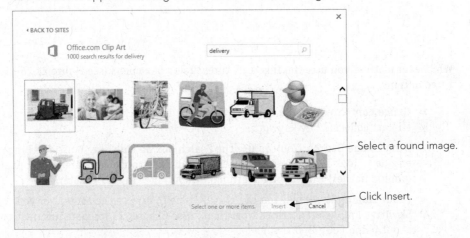

Select a found image.

Click Insert.

Click the image you want to insert (or click multiple images to insert several at once) and then click the Insert button. If the Insert button doesn't appear, make sure an image is selected; Insert doesn't appear until you do that.

Browsing clips at Office.com

When you search for clip art while connected to the Internet, as you learned to do in the preceding section, the Office.com clip art automatically appears. However, you can also visit the Office.com website to browse the clip art directly. There are some advantages to browsing clip art this way. For example, you can narrow down your search to only certain media types (such as only line-art illustrations or only photos), and you can filter the search results by image size.

To browse the Office.com clip art on the web, open a web browser window, navigate to http://office.microsoft.com and click the Images link. From there, type a keyword in the Search All Images box at the top of the page and press Enter to initiate a search. See Figure 24.28. This page is constantly changing, so it may look different when you visit it.

FIGURE 24.28

Visit the Office.com clip art web page for more information and more clip art.

24

In the search results window, a bar appears along the left side with filters for media types and image size. To limit the results to a certain category, click one of these filters. For example, in Figure 24.29, the list has been filtered to show only illustrations.

FIGURE 24.29

Search results from Office.com are filtered to show only illustrations.

NOTE

What's the difference between an illustration and a photo? An illustration is a line art drawing, which some would call "true clip art." It is a drawing, rather than a photo. Clip art images are vector graphics, which means they are created with mathematical formulas that draw each line and fill each shape with color. Vector graphics take up less disk space than photos, and they look good at any size. In contrast, photos are raster graphics; they are composed of a grid of tiny colored dots. See "Understanding Raster Graphics" later in this chapter for more details.

Another advantage of using the web interface for clip art is that you can copy the clip art to your hard disk for later use.

In the list of clips that the site finds, point to a clip that you want. A pop-up for it appears, as shown in Figure 24.30.

FIGURE 24.30

Point at a found clip to display a pop-up.

> **NOTE**
>
> The first time you attempt to select one of the options from a clip's pop-up, you may be prompted to download the Office.com control. You must do so in order to access clip art via the Office.com website. If a User Account Control window appears asking if you want the program to make changes to this computer, click Yes. You may need to restart your computer and come back to the Office.com web page after the restart.

The following options are available in the pop-up:

- **View Details:** Opens a web page specifically for this clip, where you can see information about the clip including its dimensions, resolution, and file size.

- **Copy:** Copies the clip to your Windows Clipboard, from which you can paste it into PowerPoint or any other application that accepts input from the Clipboard. After clicking Copy, switch to PowerPoint or whatever program you like, position the insertion point or select the placeholder, and press Ctrl+V or choose Home ⇨ Clipboard ⇨ Paste.

- **Download:** Downloads the clip-art image's file to your hard drive so you can use it later when you don't have an Internet connection. A Message Bar appears at the bottom of the browser window asking whether you want to save or open the file. See Figure 24.31. Click Save, and the file is saved to the Downloads folder for your user account (C:\Users*user name*\Downloads). You can then insert it in PowerPoint using the procedure outlined in "Inserting Photos" later in this chapter. If you instead choose Open, the file is opened in Paint (or your default editor for the file type), where you can modify it if you like before inserting it into PowerPoint. However, the next section of this chapter covers modifying clip art from within PowerPoint, so you may want to investigate that method instead if you want to make some changes to the clip.

FIGURE 24.31

Respond to the information bar message by choosing to open or save the file.

Modifying clip art

Most of the modifications that you will learn about later in this chapter apply to both photographs and clip art. For example, you can increase or decrease brightness and contrast, apply color washes, crop, rotate, and so on. However, there are also some special modifications that apply only to clip art and other vector images. They are covered in the following sections.

Recoloring a clip

One of the top complaints about clip art is that the colors are wrong. For example, you may have the perfect drawing, but its colors clash with your presentation design. You can recolor individual parts of a clip by changing it to a Microsoft drawing object and then selecting and coloring individual lines or shapes. For more information, see the section "Deconstructing and editing a clip" later in this chapter.

On a more basic level, PowerPoint 2013 provides a Recolor option that enables you to apply a single-color wash to an image based on any of the theme's colors or any fixed color. To apply a color wash to a clip, follow these steps:

1. **Insert the clip on a slide in PowerPoint, and then select the clip.** The Picture Tools ⇨ Format tab becomes available.

2. **On the Picture Tools ⇨ Format tab, click Color in the Adjust group to open the menu shown in Figure 24.32.**

FIGURE 24.32

Select a color wash to apply to the clip.

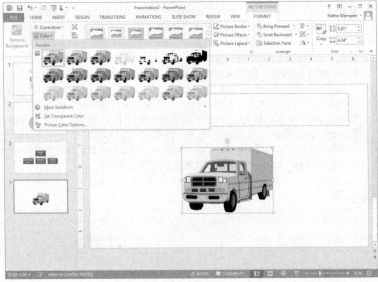

3. **Click the color wash that you want to apply, or click More Variations to choose another color.**

Setting a transparent color

Some clips enable you to redefine one of the colors as see-through so that anything behind it shows through. This doesn't work on all clips because most clips already have a color defined as transparent: the background. This is why a clip art image appears to float directly on a colored background rather than being locked into a rectangle. However, for clips that do not have a transparent color already defined, you can define one.

To set a transparent color, open the Color menu, as in the preceding section (Figure 24.32). Then choose Set Transparent Color, and click a color in the image.

Deconstructing and editing a clip

Have you ever wished that you could open a clip-art image in an image-editing program and make some small change to it? Well, you can. And what's more, you can do it without leaving PowerPoint.

Because clip art is composed of vector-graphic lines and fills, you can literally take it apart piece by piece. Not only can you apply certain colors (as in the preceding section), but you can also choose individual lines and shapes from it to recolor, move, and otherwise modify.

1. **After placing the clip on a slide, right-click the clip and choose Edit Picture.** A message appears telling you that it is an imported picture and asking whether you want to convert it to a Microsoft Office drawing object.

24

2. **Click Yes.** Each individual shape and line in the clip is now a separate object that you can select individually.

To recolor an individual line or shape, follow these steps:

1. **Select the line or shape to be modified within the image.** Selection handles appear around it.
2. **Click Drawing Tools ⇨ Format ⇨ Shape Styles ⇨ Shape Fill and select a fill color.** See Figure 24.33.

FIGURE 24.33

Change the fill color of an individual shape within the clip.

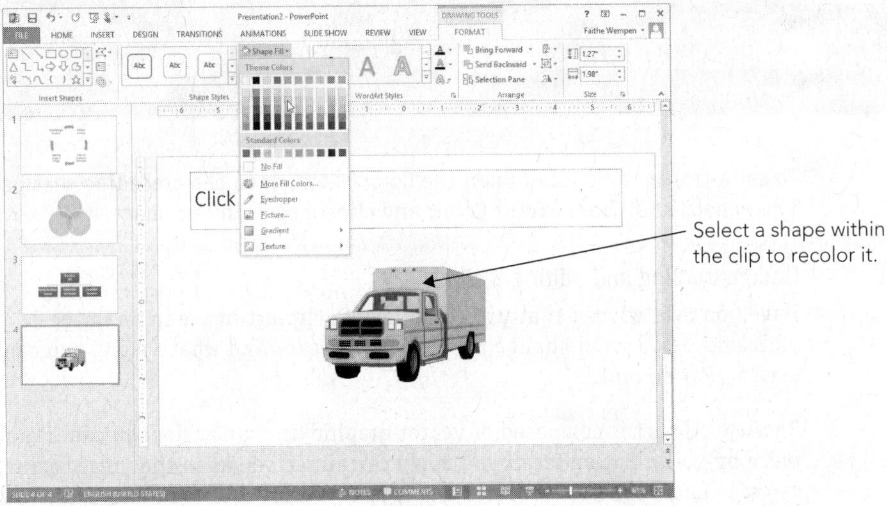

Select a shape within the clip to recolor it.

3. **Click Drawing Tools ⇨ Format ⇨ Shape Styles ⇨ Shape Outline and select an outline color.**

To move the pieces of the clip around, just drag the selected piece where you want it. If a particular piece doesn't move separately from the rest, right-click the image and choose Group ⇨ Ungroup to break up the image into individual shapes, and then the shape you want to move will be individually movable.

Understanding Raster Graphics

As explained earlier in this chapter, there are two kinds of graphics in the computer world: *vector* and *raster*. Vector graphics (clip art, drawn lines and shapes, and so on) are created with mathematical formulas. Some of the advantages of vector graphics are their small file size and the fact that they can be resized without losing any quality. The main disadvantage of a vector graphic is that it doesn't look "real." Even when an expert artist draws a vector graphic, you can still tell that it's a drawing, not a photograph. For example, perhaps you've seen the game *The Sims*. Those characters and objects are 3-D vector graphics. They look pretty good but there's no way you would mistake them for real people and objects.

In the rest of this chapter, we'll be working mostly with raster graphics — in other words, digital photos, like the ones you might take with your own digital camera or phone. A raster graphic is made up of a very fine grid of individual colored *pixels* (dots). The grid is sometimes called a *bitmap*. Each pixel has a unique numeric value representing its color. Figure 24.34 shows a close-up of a raster image. You can create raster graphics from scratch with a "paint" program on a computer, but a more common way to acquire a raster graphic is by using a scanner or digital camera as an input device.

FIGURE 24.34

A raster graphic, normal size (right) and zoomed in to show individual pixels (left)

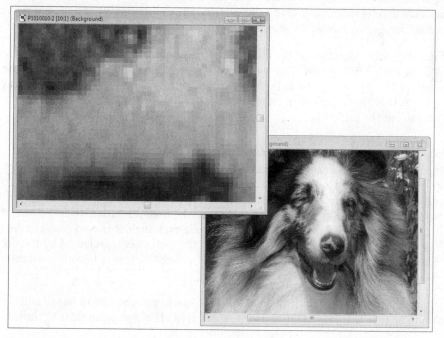

> **NOTE**
>
> The term *bitmap* is sometimes used to refer generically to any raster graphic, but it is also a specific file format for raster graphics, with a `.bmp` file name extension.

Because there are so many individual pixels and each one must be represented numerically, raster graphics are much larger than vector graphics. They take longer to load into the PC's memory, take up more space when you store them as separate files on disk, and make your PowerPoint presentation file much larger. You can compress a raster graphic so that it takes up less space on disk, but the quality may suffer. Therefore, it's best to use vector graphics when you want simple lines, shapes, or cartoons and reserve raster graphics for situations where you need photographic quality.

The following sections explain some of the technical specifications behind raster graphics; you'll need this information to make the right decisions about the way you capture the images with your scanner or digital camera and the way you use them in PowerPoint.

Resolution

The term *resolution* has two subtly different meanings. One is the size of an image, expressed in the number of pixels of width and height, such as 800 × 600. The other meaning is the number of pixels per inch when the image is printed, such as 100 dots per inch (dpi). The former meaning is used mostly when referring to images of fixed physical size, such as the display resolution of a monitor. In this book, the latter meaning is mostly used.

If you know the resolution of the picture (that is, the number of pixels in it) and the resolution of the printer on which you will print it (for example, 300 dpi), you can figure out how large the picture will be in inches when you print it at its native size. Suppose you have a picture that is 900 pixels square and you print it on a 300 dpi printer. This makes it 3" square on the printout.

Resolution on preexisting graphics files

When you acquire an image file from an outside source, such as downloading it from a website or getting it from a CD of artwork, its resolution has already been determined. Whoever created the file originally made that decision. For example, if the image was originally scanned on a scanner, whoever scanned it chose the scan resolution — that is, the dpi setting. That determined how many individual pixels each inch of the original picture would be divided into. At a 100 dpi scan, each inch of the picture is represented by 100 pixels vertically and horizontally. At 300 dpi, each inch of the picture is broken down into three times that many.

If you want to make a graphic take up less disk space, you can use an image-editing program to change the image size, and/or you can crop off one or more sides of the image.

CAUTION

If you crop or decrease the size of an image in an image-editing program, save the changes under a different file name. Maintain the original image in case you ever need it for some other purpose. Decreasing the image resolution decreases its dpi setting, which decreases its quality. You might not notice any quality degradation on-screen, but you will probably notice a difference when you are printing the image at a large size. That's because the average monitor displays only 96 dpi, but the average printer prints at 600 dpi or higher.

PowerPoint slides do not usually need to be printed at a professional-quality resolution, so image quality on a PowerPoint printout is not usually an issue. However, if you use the picture for something else later, such as printing it as a full-page color image on photo paper, then a high dpi file can make a difference.

Resolution on graphics you scan yourself

When you create an image file yourself by using a scanner, you choose the resolution, expressed in dpi, through the scanner software. For example, suppose you scan a 4″ × 6″ photo at 100 dpi. The scanner will break down each 1″ section of the photo horizontally and vertically into 100 separate pieces and decide on a numeric value that best represents the color of each piece. The result is a total number of pixels of 4 × 100 × 6 × 100, or 240,000 pixels. Assuming each pixel requires 3 bytes of storage, the fill becomes approximately 720KB in size. The actual size varies slightly depending on the file format.

Now, suppose you scan the same photo at 200 dpi. The scanner breaks down each 1″ section of the photo into 200 pieces so that the result is 4 × 200 × 6 × 200, or 960,000 pixels. Assuming again that 1 pixel required 3 bytes for storage (24 bits), the file will be approximately 2.9MB in size. That's a big difference.

The higher the resolution in which you scan, the larger the file becomes, but the details of the scan also become finer. However, unless you are zooming in on the photo, you cannot tell a difference between subtle dpi and resolution differences. That's because most computer monitors display at 96 dpi, so any resolution higher than that does not improve the output.

Let's look at an example. In Figure 24.35 you can see two copies of an image open in a graphics program. The same photo was scanned at 75 dpi (left) and 150 dpi (right). However, the difference between them is not significant when the two images are placed on a PowerPoint slide, as shown in Figure 24.36. The lower-resolution image is at the top left, but there is no observable difference in the size at which they are being used.

24

FIGURE 24.35

At high magnification, the difference in dpi for a scan is apparent.

75 dpi   150 dpi

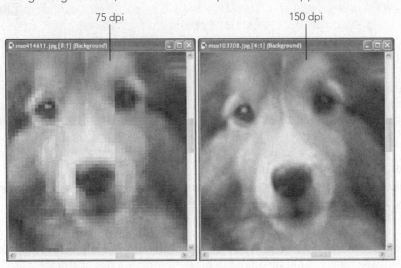

FIGURE 24.36

When the image is used at a normal size, there is virtually no difference between a high-dpi and low-dpi scan.

75 dpi

150 dpi

Scanners and Color Depth

If you are shopping for a scanner, you will probably notice that they're advertised with higher numbers of bits than the graphics formats support. This is for error correction. If there are extra bits, it can throw out the bad bits to account for "noise" and still end up with a full set of good bits. Error correction in a scan is a rather complicated process, but fortunately your scanner driver software takes care of it for you.

Resolution on digital camera photos

Top-quality digital cameras today take very high-resolution pictures, much higher than you will need for an on-screen PowerPoint presentation. At a typical size and magnification, a high-resolution graphic file is overkill; it wastes disk space needlessly. Therefore, you may want to adjust the camera's image size so that it takes lower-resolution pictures for your PowerPoint show.

However, if you think you might want to use those same pictures for some other purpose in the future, such as printing them in a magazine or newsletter, then go ahead and take them with the camera's highest setting, but then compress them in PowerPoint or resize copies of them in a third-party image-editing program. See the section "Compressing Images" later in this chapter to learn how.

Color depth

Color depth is the number of bits required to describe the color of a single pixel in the image. For example, in 1-bit color, a single binary digit represents each pixel. Each pixel is either black (1) or white (0). In 4-bit color, there are 16 possible colors because there are 16 combinations of 1s and 0s in a four-digit binary number. In 8-bit color there are 256 combinations.

For most file formats, the highest number of colors you can have in an image is 16.7 million colors, which is 24-bit color (also called *true color*). It uses 8 bits each for red, green, and blue.

There is also 32-bit color, which has the same number of colors as 24-bit but adds 8 more bits for an alpha channel. The alpha channel describes the amount of transparency for each pixel. This is not so much an issue for single-layer graphics, but in multilayer graphics, such as the ones you can create in high-end graphics programs like Photoshop, the extent to which a lower layer shows through an upper one is important.

> **TIP**
>
> For a great article on alpha channel usage in PowerPoint by Geetesh Bajaj, go to www.indezine.com/products/powerpoint/ppalpha.html.

24

A color depth of 48-bit is fairly new, and it's just like 24-bit color except it uses 16 rather than 8 bits to define each of the three channels: red, green, and blue. It does not have an alpha channel bit. Because the human eye cannot detect the small differences it introduces, 48-bit color depth is not really necessary. Of the graphics formats that PowerPoint supports, only PNG and TIFF support 48-bit color depth.

Normally, you should not decrease the color depth of a photo to less than 24-bit unless there is a major issue with lack of disk space that you cannot resolve any other way. To decrease the color depth, you would need to open the graphic file in a third-party image-editing program and use the command in that program for decreasing the number of colors. Before going through that, try compressing the images in the presentation (see the section "Compressing Images" later in the chapter) to see if that solves the problem.

File format

Many scanners scan in JPEG format by default, but most also support TIF, and some also support other formats. Images you acquire from a digital camera are almost always JPEG. Images from other sources may be any of dozens of graphics formats, including PCX, BMP, GIF, or PNG.

Different graphic formats can vary tremendously in the size and quality of the image they produce. The main differentiators between formats are the color depth they support and the type of compression they use (which determines the file size).

Remember that each pixel in a 24-bit image requires 3 bytes. (That's derived by dividing 24 by 8 because there are 8 bits in a byte.) Then you multiply that by the height and then by the width to determine the image size. Well, that formula was not completely accurate because it does not include compression. *Compression* is an algorithm (basically a math formula) that decreases the amount of space that the file takes up on the disk by storing the data about the pixels more compactly. A file format will have one of these three states in regard to compression:

- **No compression:** The image is not compressed.
- **Lossless compression:** The image is compressed, but the algorithm for doing so does not throw out any pixels so there is no loss of image quality when you resize the image.
- **Lossy compression:** The image is compressed by recording less data about the pixels, so when you resize the image, there may be a loss of image quality.

Table 24.1 provides a brief guide to some of the key features for the most common graphic formats. Generally speaking, for most on-screen presentations JPEG should be your preferred choice for graphics because it is compact and web accessible (although PNG is also a good choice and uses lossless compression and allows for transparency where needed).

TABLE 24.1 **Popular Graphics Formats**

Extension	Pronunciation	Compression	Maintains transparency	Notes
JPEG or JPG	"Jay-peg"	Yes	No	Stands for Joint Photographic Experts Group. Very small image size. Uses lossy compression. Common on the web. Up to 24-bit.
GIF	"gif" or "jif"	Yes	No	Stands for Graphic Interchange Format. Limited to 8-bit (256 color). Uses proprietary compression algorithm. Allows animated graphics, which are useful on the web. Color depth limitation makes this format unsuitable for photos.
PNG	"ping"	Yes	Yes	Stands for Portable Network Graphic. An improvement on GIF. Up to 48-bit color depth. Lossless compression, but smaller file sizes than TIF. Public domain format.
BMP	"B-M-P" or "bump" or "bitmap"	No	No	Default image type for Windows XP. Up to 24-bit color. Used for some Windows wallpaper and other Windows graphics.
PCX	"P-C-X"	Yes	No	There are three versions: 0, 2, and 5. Use version 5 for 24-bit support. Originally introduced by a company called ZSoft; sometimes called ZSoft Paintbrush format.
TIF or TIFF	"tiff"	Optional	Yes	Stands for Tagged Image File Format. Supported by most scanners and some digital cameras. Up to 48-bit color. Uses lossless compression. Large file size but high quality.

24

TIP

If you are not sure what format you will eventually use for an image, scan it in TIF format and keep the TIF copy on your hard disk. You can always save a copy in JPEG or other formats when you need them for specific projects. The TIF format's compression is lossless, so it results in a high-quality image.

Inserting Photos

Now that you know all about the factors that go into creating and selecting raster images, it's time to get down to the business of inserting the images on your PowerPoint slides. In the following sections you will learn to do just that. You'll find out how to acquire photos via a Bing search for situations in which you don't already have what you need and how to insert images from your own computer that you have already acquired. (An Office.com clip art search also might return photos in addition to clip art illustrations.)

Searching for photos with Bing

Bing is Microsoft's search engine on the web, and PowerPoint has a built-in interface for using Bing's image search capabilities to find photos you can use in your presentations. It's something like the clip art search you learned about earlier in this chapter, but the search results are not confined to just Microsoft's own servers, and only photos (raster based images) are shown.

To search for a photo with Bing and place it in your presentation, follow these steps:

1. **Display the slide on which you want to place the image.**

2. **Click the Online Pictures icon in the content placeholder, or choose Insert ⇨ Images ⇨ Online Pictures.** The Insert Pictures dialog box opens. It's the same dialog box as in Figure 24.26 earlier in the chapter.

3. **Click in the Search Bing text box and type the keyword to search for.** Then press Enter to perform the search. Search results appear in that same dialog box, as shown in Figure 24.37.

FIGURE 24.37

Search results appear showing thumbnails of available images.

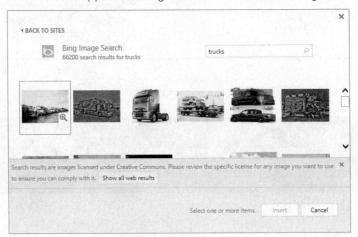

4. **Click the image you want to insert, and click the Insert button.** The image is downloaded to your PC and inserted on the slide. From here you can work with it just as if it was any other photo.

Inserting pictures from files

If you already have the picture(s) you want to use, you can insert them from your own computer's drive using the Pictures button on the Insert tab. Assuming you have already acquired the images you need, use the following steps to insert one into PowerPoint:

1. **Display the slide on which you want to place the image.**

2. **If the slide has a content placeholder for pictures, as in Figure 24.38, click the button for inserting pictures.** Otherwise, choose Insert ➪ Images ➪ Pictures. The Insert Picture dialog box opens. The default location shown is the Pictures library on your local hard disk.

FIGURE 24.38

You can insert a picture by using the Pictures content placeholder button.

Pictures

3. **Select the picture to import.** See Figure 24.39. You can switch the view by using the View (or Views) button in the dialog box to see thumbnails or details if either is effective in helping you determine which file is which.

FIGURE 24.39

Select the picture to be inserted.

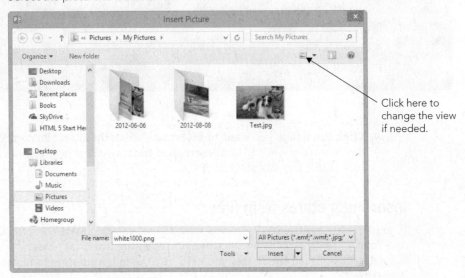

Click here to change the view if needed.

4. **Click Insert.** The picture is inserted.

> **TIP**
>
> If you have a lot of graphics in different formats, consider narrowing down the list that appears by selecting a specific file type from the file type list. By default it is set to All Pictures.

Linking to a graphic file

If you have a sharp eye, you may have noticed that the Insert button in Figure 24.39 has a drop-down list associated with it. That list has these choices:

- **Insert:** The default, inserts the graphic but maintains no connection.
- **Link to File:** Creates a link to the file, but does not maintain a local copy of it in PowerPoint
- **Insert and Link:** Creates a link to the file, and also inserts a local copy of its current state, so if the linked copy is not available in the future, the local copy will still appear

Use Link to File whenever you want to insert a pointer rather than the original. When the presentation opens, it pulls in the graphic from the disk. If the graphic is not available, it displays an empty frame with a red X in the corner in the graphic's place. Using Link to File keeps the size of the original PowerPoint file very small because it doesn't actually contain the graphic — it only links to it. However, if you move or delete the graphic, PowerPoint won't be able to find it anymore.

The important thing to know about this link in the Link to File feature is that it is not the same thing as an OLE link. This is not a dynamic link that you can manage. It is a much simpler link and much less flexible. You can't change the file location to which it is linked, for example; if the location of the graphic changes, you must delete it from PowerPoint and reinsert it.

> **TIP**
>
> If you are building a graphic-heavy presentation on an older computer, you might find that it takes a long time to move between slides and for each graphic to appear. You can take some of the hassle away by using Link to File instead of inserting the graphics. Then temporarily move the graphic files to a subfolder so PowerPoint can't find them. It displays the placeholders for the graphics on the appropriate slides, and the presentation file is much faster to page through and edit. Then when you are ready to finish up, close PowerPoint and move the graphic files back to their original locations so PowerPoint can find them again when you reopen the presentation file.

Capturing and inserting screenshots

A *screenshot* is a picture that you take of your computer screen using Windows itself (or a screen capture utility). Most of the images in this book are screenshots. You might want to take screenshots to illustrate the steps in a computer-based procedure and then create a PowerPoint presentation that teaches others to perform that procedure. You can also take screen shots on some mobile devices.

Windows has always had a basic screenshot capability built into it: the Print Screen key. You can press Print Screen at any time to copy an image of the screen to the Clipboard. Then you can paste directly onto your slide, or you can open a graphics-editing program such as Paint and paste from the Clipboard to save the file.

In PowerPoint 2013, you can also capture and insert screenshots directly, bypassing the Clipboard and an outside graphics program. The Screenshot command in PowerPoint also enables you to capture individual windows rather than the entire screen.

To capture a screenshot of an open window, follow these steps:

1. **Open the window for which you want to capture the screenshot.** Do not minimize it.

2. **Switch to PowerPoint, and display the slide on which you want to place the screenshot.**

3. **Choose Insert ⇨ Images ⇨ Screenshot.** A menu appears showing thumbnails of the available windows. See Figure 24.40.

FIGURE 24.40

Capture a window using the Screenshot command.

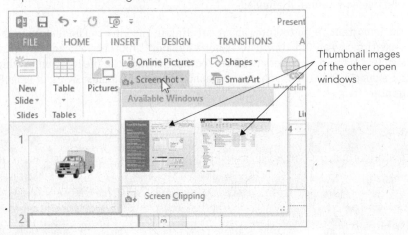

4. **Click the thumbnail image of the window you want to capture.** The image is immediately inserted as a new picture on the active slide.

> **NOTE**
>
> The Screenshot command does not show every open window as a thumbnail; it shows each tab of Internet Explorer and each open Office application window except for PowerPoint itself. If you want to capture a window other than the ones shown in the thumbnails, you must use the Screen Clipping command.

If the window you want does not appear on the thumbnails list, or if you want different cropping, use the Screen Clipping command instead. Follow these steps:

1. **Display the window that you want to capture.**

2. **Using the taskbar, switch to PowerPoint.**

3. **Choose Insert ⇨ Images ⇨ Screenshot ⇨ Screen Clipping.** The PowerPoint window is minimized, and the window immediately beneath it appears, with a whitewash overlay on it.

4. **Drag to define the rectangular area you want to crop.** When you release the mouse button, the defined area appears in PowerPoint as a new image.

> **TIP**
>
> If you need better cropping than you can get with the Screenshot command, use the cropping techniques in the following section to fine-tune the crop after insertion into PowerPoint. If you need more robust screen capture capabilities, consider an application that is specifically designed for screen captures such as SnagIt (`snagit.com`).

Sizing and Cropping Photos

After placing a picture on a slide, you will probably need to adjust its size, and/or crop it, to make it fit in the allotted space the way you want it. The following sections explain these techniques.

Sizing a photo

Sizing a photo is just like sizing any other object. Drag its selection handles. Drag a corner to maintain the aspect ratio, or drag a side to distort it. (Distorting a photo is seldom a good idea, though, unless you're after some weird funhouse effect.)

You can also specify an exact size for a photo the same as for drawn objects. Right-click the photo and choose Size and Position to set a size in the Format Picture task pane (see Figure 24.41). Alternatively, you can display the Picture Tools⇨Format tab and then use the Height and Width boxes in the Size group, also shown in Figure 24.41.

FIGURE 24.41

Size a photo via either the dialog box or the Format tab.

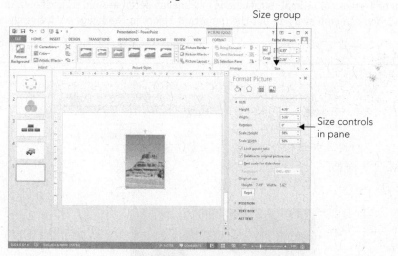

The most straightforward way to specify the size is in inches in the Height and Width boxes, either in the dialog box or on the tab. These measurements correspond to the markers on the on-screen ruler in Normal view. The size of a slide varies depending on how you have it set up (by using the Page Setup tab), but an average slide size is 10 inches wide by 7.5 inches tall. You can also size the photo using the Scale controls in the Format Picture pane, in which you adjust the size based on a percentage of the original size.

Note that the scale is based on the original size, not the current size. So, for example, if you set Height and Width to 50%, close the dialog box, and then reopen it and set them each to

75%; the net result will be 75% of the original, not 75% of the 50%. However, you can override this by deselecting the Relative to original picture size check box (see Figure 24.41).

If you are setting up a presentation for the primary purpose of showing full-screen graphics, you can use the Best scale for slide show check box (see Figure 24.41). This enables you to choose a screen resolution, such as 640 × 480 or 800 × 600, and size the pictures so that they will show to the best advantage in that resolution. Choose the resolution that corresponds to the display setting on the PC on which you will show the presentation. To determine what the resolution is on the PC, right-click the Windows Desktop and choose Screen Resolution.

> **TIP**
> When possible, develop your presentation at the same Windows screen resolution as the PC on which you present the show.

Cropping a photo

Cropping is for those times you want only a part of the image. For example, you might have a great photo of a person or animal, but there is extraneous detail around it, as shown in Figure 24.42. You can crop away all but the important object in the image with a cropping tool.

FIGURE 24.42

This picture can benefit from cropping.

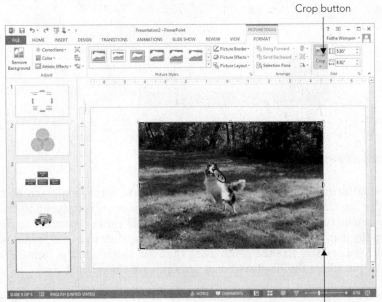

Crop button

Crop handles appear
in the corners and on the
sides of the image.

TIP

Here's something important to know: Cropping and sizing a picture in PowerPoint does not reduce the overall size of the PowerPoint presentation file. When you insert a picture, PowerPoint stores the whole thing at its original size and continues to store it that way regardless of any manipulations you perform on it within PowerPoint. That's why it's recommended throughout this chapter that you do any editing of the photo in a third-party image-editing program before you import it into PowerPoint. However, there's a workaround. If you use the Compress Pictures option (covered later in this chapter), it discards any cropped portions of the images. That means the file size decreases with the cropping, and that you can't reverse the cropping later.

You can crop two sides at once by cropping at the corner of the image, or you can crop each side individually by cropping at the sides. To crop an image, do the following:

1. **Select the image so the Picture Tools ⇨ Format tab becomes available.**
2. **Click Picture Tools ⇨ Format ⇨ Size ⇨ Crop.**
3. **Position the pointer over one of the crop handles on the image frame, and drag toward the center until the image is cropped the way you want.** When the mouse pointer is over one of the crop handles, it changes to a cropping tool (see Figure 24.42).
4. **Repeat step 3 for each side.** Then click the Crop button again, or press Esc, to turn cropping off.
5. **Resize the cropped image if needed.**

Figure 24.43 shows the result of cropping and resizing the image from Figure 24.42.

FIGURE 24.43

The picture has been improved by cropping and resizing it.

24

To undo a crop, reenter cropping mode by clicking the Crop button again, and then drag the side(s) back outward again. Or you can simply reset the photo, as described in the following section.

You can also crop to a shape or crop to a particular aspect ratio (that is, ratio of height to width).

Cropping to a shape crops the picture so that it fits inside one of the drawing shapes that PowerPoint provides, such as a star, triangle, or arrow.

To crop to a shape, follow these steps:

1. **Select the picture.**

2. **On the Picture Tools ⇨ Format tab, click the down arrow under the Crop button in the Size group, and point to Crop to Shape.** A palette of shapes appears, as shown in Figure 24.44.

FIGURE 24.44

You can crop a picture to a shape.

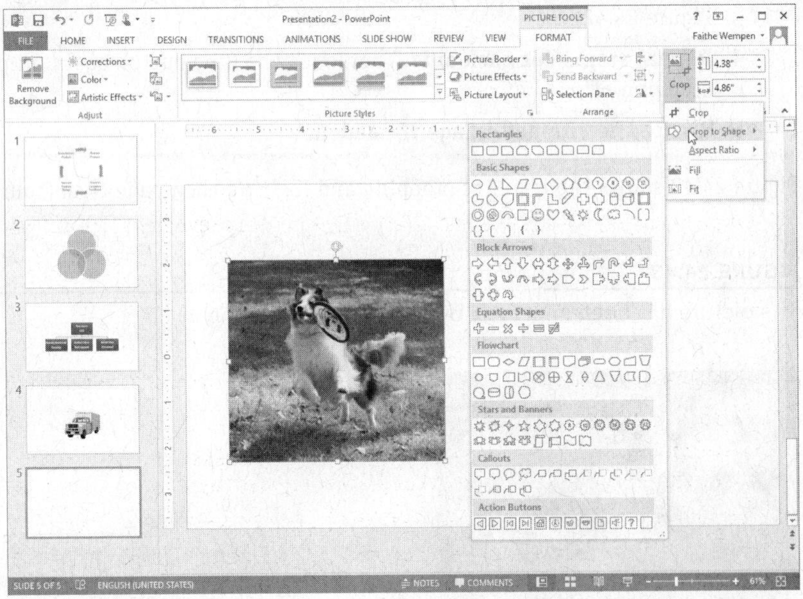

3. **Click the shape to which you want the picture cropped.**

After cropping to a shape, you'll notice the central part of the image might not be exactly centered within the shape. To adjust the centering of the picture within the crop area, right-click the picture and choose Format Picture to open the Format Picture pane. Click the Picture icon (rightmost icon), and then adjust the values in the Crop section, as shown in Figure 24.45.

FIGURE 24.45

Set a precise amount of cropping in the Format Picture pane.

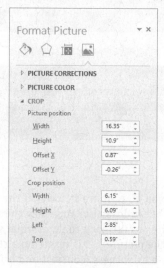

You can also crop to an aspect ratio. PowerPoint offers several preset ratios to choose from that correspond to common picture sizes, such as 2:3, 3:4, and 3:5. Here's how to apply an aspect ratio crop:

1. **Select the picture.**
2. **On the Picture Tools ⇨ Format tab, click the down arrow under the Crop button in the Size group, and point to Aspect Ratio.** A list of ratios appears.
3. **Click the ratio you want to use.** Crop marks appear on the image, and the portion of the image that will be excluded appears in gray.
4. **Drag the crop markers to adjust the crop as desired, and then click the Crop button or press Esc on your keyboard to finalize the cropping operation.**

You can also crop "by the numbers" with the Crop settings in the Format Picture dialog box. Here's how to do that:

1. **Select the picture.**
2. **Right-click the picture and choose Format Picture to display the Format Picture pane.**

3. **Click the Picture icon (rightmost icon) and then click Crop if needed to expand the Crop section.**

4. **Use the controls under Picture Position (see Figure 24.45) to manually enter cropping amounts for each side.**

> **NOTE**
>
> To crop from the bottom, decrease the Height setting; to crop from the right, decrease the Width setting. The Left and Top settings crop from those sides, respectively.

> **CAUTION**
>
> You cannot uncrop after compressing the picture (assuming you use the default compression options that include deleting cropped areas of pictures). By default, saving compresses and makes crops permanent, so be sure to undo any unwanted cropping before you save.

Resetting a photo

Once the picture is in PowerPoint, any manipulations you do to it are strictly on the surface. It changes how the picture appears on the slide, but it doesn't change how the picture is stored in PowerPoint. Consequently, you can reset the picture back to its original settings at any time (provided you have not compressed the picture). This resetting also clears any changes you make to the image's size, contrast, and brightness (contrast and brightness changes are discussed in the next section).

To reset the picture, right-click it and choose Format Picture to display the Format Picture pane. Click the Size & Properties icon (third from left), and in the Size section, click the Reset button.

Adjusting and Correcting Photos

PowerPoint has some powerful features for adjusting, correcting, and applying artistic effects to photos. Not only can you adjust the brightness and contrast, but you can sharpen or soften an image, tint it, make it black and white, and apply several types of artistic effects to it that make it look like it was created in some other medium, such as charcoal pencil or collage.

Applying brightness and contrast corrections

You can adjust the brightness and contrast for any photo in PowerPoint, and you can adjust the sharpness or softness of the image.

Brightness refers to the overall level of light in a picture. The brighter the setting, the lighter each pixel of the image is. Brightness does not affect the color hues. You might increase the brightness on a photo that was taken in a dimly lit room, for example.

Contrast refers to the difference between the lighter areas and the darker areas of the photo. Adjusting contrast makes the lights lighter and the darks darker. Increasing the contrast of a picture makes its image more distinct; this can be good for an older, washed-out picture, for example.

Sharpness/softness is controlled with a slider, with the default being right in the middle between them. When you sharpen an image, the edges of the objects in the picture appear more distinct; when you soften an image, the edges are blurred. PowerPoint finds the edges of objects by looking for areas where the color changes dramatically from one spot to the adjacent one.

The easiest way to access those controls is through the Corrections button in the Adjust group of the Picture Tools⇨Format tab. Click the button and then click one of the preset thumbnails, as shown in Figure 24.46. Brightness and contrast are two separately adjustable settings, but the presets on the menu shown in Figure 24.46 combine them. In the Brightness/Contrast section, the sample in the upper-left corner decreases both, and the sample in the lower right increases both. In between, the samples combine settings in various ways. Point at a sample to see a pop-up ScreenTip listing its specifics.

FIGURE 24.46

Choose sharpen/soften, brightness, and contrast presets.

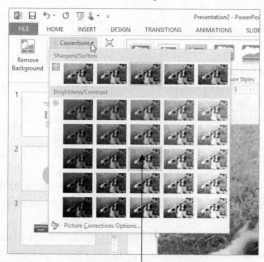

Center value in each section
represents the default
(unaltered) image.

To choose a value other than the ones listed, click Picture Corrections Options to open the Format Picture pane to the Picture Corrections controls. From here you can choose presets, or you can drag sliders or enter exact percentages for each setting individually. See Figure 24.47.

FIGURE 24.47

Drag sliders to adjust brightness, contrast, and sharpen or soften settings individually.

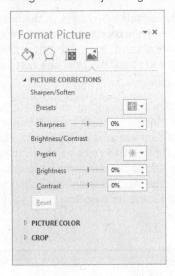

Recoloring a picture

Several color options are available from the Color button's drop-down list in the Adjust group of the Picture Tools ⇨ Format tab. You can apply color washes to the image, make it black and white or grayscale, make it look washed out, and more. You can point at a sample to see a preview of it on the selected image.

The Color menu has three sections (see Figure 24.48):

- **Color Saturation:** This refers to the vibrancy of the colors. At the low end is grayscale — no colors at all, or 0% saturation. The center point is 100% saturation, the default. At the high end is a very vividly colored version of the image at 400% saturation.

- **Color Tone:** The presets in this section enable you to adjust the "temperature" of the image, from very cool (increased blue and green) to very warm (increased red and yellow). Color tones are measured numerically; the higher the number, the warmer the tone. 4700 K is very cool; 11200 kelvin (K) is very warm.

> **NOTE**
>
> Color temperature is measured by something called the Kruithof curve. It is named after Dutch physicist Arie Andries Kruithof, and it describes and assigns numeric values to colors like blue and green as cooler than colors like red and yellow. The temperatures are expressed on the Kelvin temperature scale (K).

- **Recolor:** These presets enable you to radically adjust the colors of the image by choosing a grayscale, sepia, black-and-white, washout, or other preset or by applying a colored wash over the picture. Here's where you'll find the equivalent settings to the Recolor presets from earlier versions of PowerPoint, but also many more options. For more colors to choose from, point to More Variations and choose from the fly-out palette of colors. The last two rows of colors (darks and lights) are based on the theme colors.

FIGURE 24.48

Choose color presets to apply to the image.

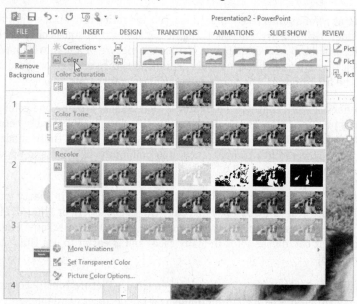

You can also choose Picture Color Options from the menu in Figure 24.48 to open the Format Picture pane and display the Picture Color settings. Here you'll find buttons that open menus with the same presets as on the menu and also sliders for fine-tuning the Saturation and Temperature.

Setting a transparent color and removing a background

The Transparent Color feature, which you also learned about earlier in this chapter, can be used to remove one of the colors from the photo, making the areas transparent that were previously occupied by that color. For example, suppose you have a scanned photo of your CEO and you want to make the background transparent so it looks like his head is sitting right on the slide. This feature could help you out with that.

To set a transparent color, select the image and then choose Picture Tools ⇨ Format ⇨ Adjust ⇨ Color ⇨ Set Transparent Color. Then, on the image, click an area that contains the color you want to make transparent.

Setting a transparent color sounds like a great idea, but in reality it does not work as well with photos as it does with clip art. For one thing, it replaces all instances of that color, not just in the background. So, for example, if you have a picture of a man with a white shirt on a white background and choose to make white the transparent color (because you want to drop out the background), the man's shirt becomes transparent too.

Another reason it doesn't work that well on photos is that what looks like one color in a photo is not usually just one color. Think of a blue sky, for example. It probably consists of at least two dozen different shades of blue. If you try to make one of those shades of blue transparent using PowerPoint's transparency tool, you'll probably just end up with splotches of transparent areas.

So what's the solution? One workaround is to use alpha channels in a third-party image-editing program to create true transparency and save the image as TIF or PNG. (JPEG format does not support alpha channels.) An easier way, however, is to use PowerPoint's Remove Background command. It can do the trick in many cases and is easier to use than most photo-editing programs.

To remove the background, select the picture and then choose Picture Tools ⇨ Format ⇨ Adjust ⇨ Remove Background. The Background Removal tab becomes available, and the areas of the image that PowerPoint plans to remove appear with a purple wash over them (shown in Figure 24.49).

FIGURE 24.49

The Background Removal tab provides tools for helping you separate a picture's subject from its background.

Use these tools to mark areas to include or exclude.

Drag selection handles to change area.

If PowerPoint has correctly guessed at the edges of the image subject, click Keep Changes to accept the background removal as is.

If it has not gotten it quite right, do any of the following to make corrections:

■ **PowerPoint-generated border:** A dotted border appears around what PowerPoint thinks is the central part of the image. Drag the selection handles along this border to expand it to allow additional parts of the image to be preserved if needed.

■ **To include more image sections:** Click Mark Areas to Keep in the Refine group and then drag on the image, in the purple shaded areas, to delineate additional parts of the image that should not be removed.

■ **To exclude image sections:** Click Mark Areas to Remove in the Refine group and then drag on the image, in the areas that are *not* purple shaded, to mark additional parts of the image that *should* be removed.

■ **For mistakes:** If you make a mistake and mark an area you shouldn't have, click Delete Mark in the Refine group and then click on that mark.

Applying artistic effects

Artistic effects are special types of transformations you can apply to images to make them appear as if they were created in some medium other than photography. For example, you can make a photo look like a pencil sketch or a painting.

To apply artistic effects, select the picture and then choose Picture Tools⇨Format⇨Adjust ⇨Artistic Effects and choose from the menu that appears, as shown in Figure 24.50. Each effect is mutually exclusive with the others; when you select a different effect, the previously applied effect is removed.

FIGURE 24.50

Apply artistic effects from the Format tab.

The Pencil sketch effect has been applied.

For more control over the artistic effects, choose Artistic Effects Options. This opens the Format Picture pane with the Artistic Effects settings displayed. From here, after selecting one of the effects, you can make fine adjustments with the sliders and other controls that appear. There are different controls for different effects; Figure 24.51 shows the ones for the Pencil Sketch effect.

FIGURE 24.51

Fine-tune the chosen effect in the Format Picture pane.

Applying picture styles and effects

You can format pictures using the same effects you learned about in Chapter 9. Click the Picture Effects button on the Format tab, and then choose one of the categories there, such as Shadow, Reflection, Glow, or Bevel.

You can also choose a preset Picture Style from the Picture Styles group on the Picture Tools ⇨ Format tab. Click one of the samples displayed in that group, or open the gallery of picture styles for even more choices. See Figure 24.52.

24

FIGURE 24.52

Choose a picture style as a shortcut to applying combinations of effects.

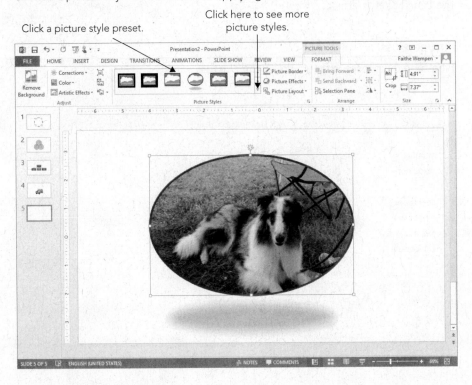

Compressing Images

Having an image that is too large (that is, too high a dpi) is not a problem quality wise. You can resize it in PowerPoint to make it as small as you like; just drag its selection handles. There will be no loss of quality as it gets smaller.

However, as mentioned earlier in the chapter, inserting a picture file that is much larger than necessary can increase the overall size of the PowerPoint file, which can become problematic if you plan to distribute the presentation in a form where space or bandwidth is an issue.

To avoid problems with overly large graphic files, you can compress the images to reduce their resolution and remove any cropped portions. You can do this from within PowerPoint or with a third-party utility.

Reducing resolution and compressing images in PowerPoint

PowerPoint offers an image compression utility that compresses all of the pictures in the presentation in a single step and reduces their resolution to the amount needed for the type of output you specify (e-mail, Screen, or Print).

Picture resolution is measured in PowerPoint in pixels per inch, or ppi. This roughly translates to dots per inch (dpi) on a printout. A computer screen shows 96 pixels per inch, so you do not need higher resolution than that if you are only showing your presentation on-screen. However, if you are distributing the presentation in other forms, a higher resolution might be appropriate.

To reduce resolution and compress images, do the following:

1. **Click a picture so that the Picture Tools Format tab appears.**
2. **Choose Picture Tools ⇨ Format ⇨ Adjust ⇨ Compress Pictures.** The Compress Pictures dialog box appears, as shown in Figure 24.53.

FIGURE 24.53

Click OK to compress with the default settings.

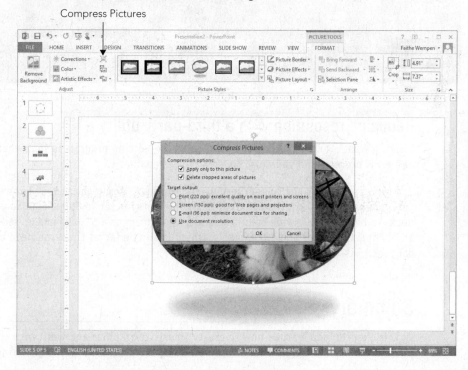

3. **(Optional) If you do not want to compress all of the pictures, make sure the Apply only to this picture check box is marked.**

4. **(Optional) If you wish to save additional space by deleting the cropped-out areas of pictures, select the Delete Cropped areas of pictures check box.**

5. **Select the desired amount of compression:**

   - **Print (220 ppi):** Choose this if you are printing the presentation on paper; it keeps the photos at a resolution where they will look crisp on a printout.

   - **Screen (150 ppi):** Choose this if you are displaying the presentation using a projector or distributing via the Internet. Some projectors have a higher resolution than a monitor.

   - **E-mail (96 ppi):** Choose this if you are e-mailing the presentation to others because this lower setting results in a smaller file that will transmit more easily via e-mail.

   - **Use Document Resolution:** Use this to match the resolution of the pictures to the resolution defined in PowerPoint Options (File ⇨ Options ⇨ Advanced).

6. **Click OK to perform the compression.**

> **CAUTION**
>
> Some e-mail servers have limits on the file sizes they will accept, so keeping the PowerPoint file as small as possible when distributing via e-mail is a good idea. If you send someone an e-mail with a large file attached to it, the server may reject the message, but you might not get an error message back from the server at all, or you might not get one for several days.

Reducing resolution with a third-party utility

Working with resolution reduction from an image-editing program is somewhat of a trial-and-error process, and you must do each image separately.

You can approximate the correct resolution by simply "doing the math." For example, suppose you have a 10″ × 7.5″ slide. Your desktop display is set to 800 × 600. So your image needs to be 800 pixels wide to fill the slide. Your image is a 5″ × 3″ image, so if you set it to 200 dpi, that gives you 1,000 pixels, which is a little larger than you need but in the ballpark.

Summary

In this chapter, you learned how to create SmartArt graphics and work with clip art and pictures in a presentation. You should now be comfortable with tasks including:

- Selecting a SmartArt graphic type and creating the graphic.
- Adding and working with the graphic text.
- Rearranging and formatting shapes.
- Inserting online clip art or pictures on a slide.
- Recoloring or working with parts of clip art.
- Formatting a photo, including changing color, cropping, and special effects.

24

Building Animation Effects, Transitions, and Support Materials

IN THIS CHAPTER

Assigning transitions to slides

Animating slide content

Creating audience handouts

Creating speaker notes

Printing your hard-copy materials

You invest hard work in creating presentation content so that you can deliver your important message to an audience. When you are delivering a live presentation — also called a slide show — you need to make sure that your speaking manner and the presentation have enough zip to hold the audience members' interest. This chapter teaches you how to add that zip with transitions and animation effects, and how to print the support materials you'll need to ensure that the audience can follow along.

Understanding Animation and Transitions

In PowerPoint, *animation* is the way that individual objects enter or exit a slide. All of the objects on a slide with no animation simply appear at the same time when you display it. If you'd prefer for the on-screen show to be more lively and engaging, you can apply animation to a slide so that the bullet points fly in from the left, one at a time, and the graphic drops down from the top afterward.

A *transition* is another kind of animation. A transition refers to the entry or exit of the entire slide rather than of an individual object on the slide.

Here are some ideas for using animation effectively in your presentations:

- Animate parts of a chart so that the data appears one series at a time. This technique works well if you want to talk about each series separately.

- Set up questions and answers on a slide so that the question appears first, and then, when you click the question, the answer appears.

- Dim each bullet point when the next one comes into view so that you are, in effect, highlighting the current one.

- Make an object appear and then disappear. For example, you might have an image of a lightning bolt that flashes on the slide for one second and then disappears, or a picture of a race car that drives onto the slide from the left and then immediately drives out of sight to the right.

- Rearrange the order in which objects appear on the slide. For example, you could make numbered points appear from the bottom up for a top ten list.

Assigning Transitions to Slides

Transitions determine how you get from slide A to slide B. Back in the old slide projector days, there was only one transition: The old slide was pushed out, and the new slide dropped into place. However, with a computerized presentation, you can choose from all kinds of fun transitions, including wipes, blinds, fly-ins, and much more. These transitions are almost exactly like the animations, except that they apply to the whole slide (or at least the background — the base part of the slide — if the slide's objects are separately animated).

> **NOTE**
>
> The transition effect for a slide refers to how the slide enters and not how it exits. As a result, if you want to assign a particular transition while moving from slide 1 to slide 2, you would assign the transition effect to slide 2.

The individual transitions are hard to describe in words; it is best if you just view them on-screen to understand what each one does. You should try out several transitions before making your final selection.

Setting transition effects and timings

The default transition effect is None. One slide replaces another with no special effect. If you want something flashier than that, you must choose it from the Transitions tab.

As you are setting up the transition effect, you have a choice of allowing it to occur manually (that is, On Mouse Click) or automatically. Generally speaking, if there is a live person controlling and presenting the show, transitions should be manual. With manual transitions, the presenter must click the mouse to move to the next slide. This might sound like a lot of work, but it helps the speaker to maintain control of the show. If someone in the audience asks a question or wants to make a comment, the show does not continue on blindly but pauses to accommodate the delay. However, if you are preparing a self-running presentation, such as for a kiosk, automatic transitions are a virtual necessity. Later you will learn how to set the timing between slides. Timings also are in effect when you record timings or narration, as described later under, "Rehearsing and recording transition timings."

To assign a transition effect and control its timing, follow these steps:

1. **View or select the slide in Normal or Slide Sorter view.** If you use Slide Sorter view, you can more easily select multiple slides to which you can apply the transition.

2. **(Optional) On the Transitions tab, in the Transition to This Slide group, click the transition you want to use.** Open the gallery to see additional transitions if needed.

   If you do not want a transition effect, do not choose a transition; instead leave the default transition (None) selected.

3. **Click Effect Options and select any options for the chosen effect transition as desired.** The effects listed will be different depending on the transition you chose. Figure 25.1 shows the options available for the Push transition.

FIGURE 25.1

Select a transition.

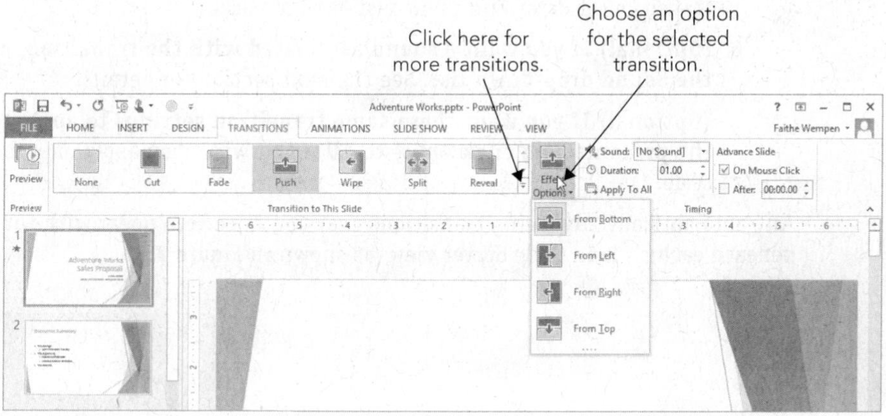

891

4. **In the Timing group, mark or clear the following check boxes:**

   - **On Mouse Click:** Transitions when you click the mouse.
   - **After:** Transitions after a specified amount of time has passed. (Enter the time, in seconds, in the associated text box.)

> **NOTE**
>
> It is perfectly okay to leave the On Mouse Click check box selected, even if you choose automatic transitions — in fact, this is a good idea. There may be times when you want to manually advance to the next slide before the automatic transition time has elapsed, and leaving this option selected allows you to do so.

> **CAUTION**
>
> You will probably want to assign automatic transitions to either all or none of the slides in the presentation, but not a mixture of the two. This is because mixed transition times can cause confusion when some of the slides automatically advance and others do not. However, there may be situations in which you need to assign different timings and effects to the various slides' transitions.

5. **(Optional) Adjust the Duration setting to specify how quickly the transition effect will occur.** This is not the timing between slides but rather the timing from the beginning to the end of the transition effect itself. For example, for a Fade transition, it determines how fast the fade occurs.

6. **(Optional) If you want a sound associated with the transition, select it from the Sound drop-down list.** See the next section for details.

7. **(Optional) If you want these same transition settings to apply to all slides in the presentation, click Apply to All.** Otherwise they apply only to the current slide.

Any automatically advancing transitions that you have set appear with the timings beneath each slide in Slide Sorter view, as shown in Figure 25.2.

FIGURE 25.2

You can view slide timings in Slide Sorter view.

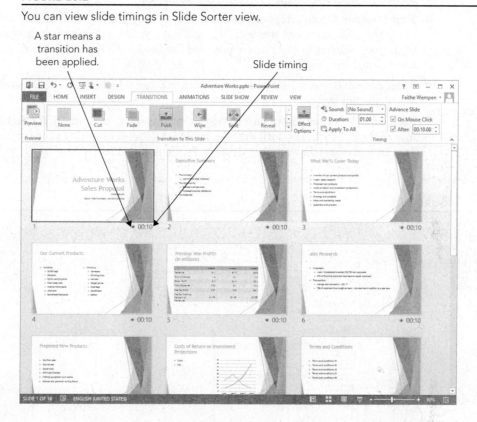

More about transition sounds

In the Transitions tab's Sound menu, shown in Figure 25.3, you can choose from among PowerPoint's default sound collection, or you can choose any of the following:

- **No Sound:** Does not assign a sound to the transition.

- **Stop Previous Sound:** Stops any sound that is already playing. This usually applies where the previous sound was very long and was not finished when you moved on to the next slide or in cases where you used the Loop Until Next Sound transition (see the last item on this list).

- **Other Sound:** Opens a dialog box from which you can select another WAV sound file stored on your system.

- **Loop Until Next Sound:** An on/off toggle that sets whatever sound you select to loop continuously either until another sound is triggered or until a slide transition or animated object appears that has Stop Previous Sound set.

FIGURE 25.3

Select a transition sound.

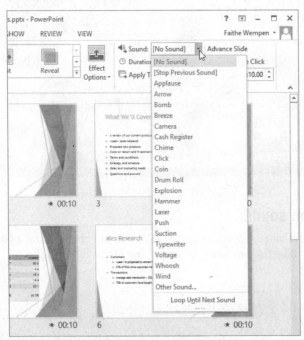

> **NOTE**
> Sounds associated with transitions can get annoying to your audience very quickly. Don't use them gratuitously.

Rehearsing and recording transition timings

The trouble with setting the same automatic timings for all slides is that not all slides deserve or need equal time on-screen. For example, some slides may have more text than others or more complex concepts to grasp. To allow for the differences, you can manually set the timings for each slide, as described in the preceding section. However, another way is to use the Rehearse Timings feature to run through your presentation in real time and allow PowerPoint to set the timings for you, based on that rehearsal. This is especially important if you have complex animations on the slide, because the transition timing will force all animations to run within that timeframe despite the timing set on the individual animations. Therefore you want to make sure that the transition timing is adequate to incorporate all animations.

> **NOTE**
>
> When you set timings with the Rehearse Timings feature, PowerPoint ignores any hidden slides. If you later unhide these slides, they are set to advance automatically. You need to individually assign them an After transition time, as described earlier in the chapter.

To set transition timings with the Rehearse Timings feature, follow these steps:

1. **On the Slide Show tab in the Set Up group, click Rehearse Timings.** The slide show starts with the Recording toolbar, shown in Figure 25.4, in the upper-left corner.

FIGURE 25.4

Use the Recording toolbar to set timings for automatic transitions.

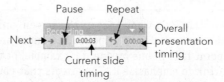

Pause   Repeat

Next   Overall presentation timing

Current slide timing

> **NOTE**
>
> If you want to record voiceover narration as you rehearse and record the timings, click Record Slide Show in step 1 instead of Rehearse Timings. (Have your microphone ready to go before you do that.)

2. **Click through the presentation, displaying each slide for as long as you want it to appear in the actual show.** To move to the next slide, you can click the slide, click the Next button in the Recording toolbar (right-pointing arrow), or press Page Down.

25

When setting timings, it may help to read the text on the slide, slowly and out loud, to simulate how an audience member who reads slowly would proceed. When you have read all of the text on the slide, pause for one or two more seconds and then advance. If you need to pause the rehearsal at any time, click the Pause button. When you are ready to resume, click the Pause button again.

If you make a mistake on the timing for a slide, click the Repeat button to begin timing this slide again from 00:00.

When you reach the final slide, a dialog box appears, asking whether you want to keep the new slide timings.

> ### TIP
>
> If you want a slide to display for a fairly long time, such as 30 seconds or more, you might find it faster to enter the desired time in the Current Slide Timing text box on the Recording toolbar rather than waiting the full amount of time before advancing. To do this, click in the text box, type the desired time, and press Tab. You must press the Tab key after entering the time (do not click the Next button) or PowerPoint will not apply your change.

3. **Click Yes to accept the new slide timings.**

> ### TIP
>
> If you want to temporarily discard the rehearsed timings, deselect the Use Timings check box in the Set Up group of the Slide Show tab. This turns off all automatic timings and allows the show to advance through mouse-clicks only. To clear timings altogether, choose Slide Show ➪ Set Up ➪ Record Slide Show ➪ Clear ➪ Clear Timings on All Slides.

Animating Slide Content

Whereas transitions determine how a slide (as a whole) enters the screen, animations determine what happens to the slide's content after that point. You might animate a bulleted list by having each bullet point fade in one by one, for example, or you might make a picture gradually grow or shrink to emphasize it. The effects that you can create are limited only by your imagination.

Animation gives you full control over how the objects on your slides appear, move, and disappear. You can not only choose from the full range of animation effects for each object, but you can also specify in what order the objects appear and what sound is associated with their appearance.

Understanding animations

The Animations tab provides many settings and shortcuts for creating animation events. An *event* is an animation occurrence, such as an object entering or exiting the slide.

An event can also consist of an object on the slide moving around in some way (spinning, growing, changing color, and so on).

Each animation event appears as a separate entry in the Animation pane. You can display or hide the Animation pane by choosing Animations ⇨ Advanced Animation ⇨ Animation Pane at any time.

When you animate bulleted lists and certain other types of text groupings, the associated events may be collapsed or expanded in the Animation pane. For example, in Figure 25.5, an animated bulleted list's events are collapsed.

Notice the following in Figure 25.5:

- The text box containing the bulleted list is named Rectangle 3. PowerPoint considers a text box a shape, and by default text boxes are rectangular.

- It has a green star on it. Green means entrance; this is an entrance effect. (Yellow means emphasis, and red means an exit effect.) A line instead of a star means it is a motion path.

- It has a double down-pointing arrow below it. That indicates that there are collapsed animation events beneath it.

FIGURE 25.5

The animation events for a bulleted list are collapsed.

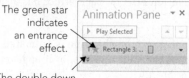

The green star indicates an entrance effect.

The double down arrow indicates more events are collapsed.

> **TIP**
> To assign meaningful names to slide objects so it's easier to tell what you are working with when animating, choose Home ⇨ Editing ⇨ Select ⇨ Selection Pane. Then in that pane, you can edit each object's name.

In Figure 25.6, the events are expanded. To expand or collapse a group of events, click the double up-pointing or down-pointing arrow. Notice that each bulleted list item on the slide has a number next to it that corresponds to one of the numbered animation events in the Animation pane. This is because by default, when you select a bulleted list placeholder and apply animation, it sets up the bullets to animate one at a time, from the top of the list down. If you apply an Entrance animation (see the next section), that means the bullets will enter the slide one at a time.

25

FIGURE 25.6

The events are expanded.

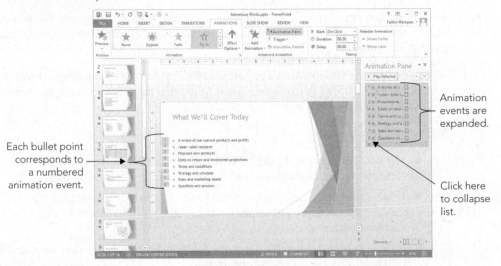

Each bullet point corresponds to a numbered animation event.

Animation events are expanded.

Click here to collapse list.

Choosing an animation effect

There are four categories of custom animation effects. Each effect has a specific purpose as well as a different icon color:

- **Entrance (green):** The item's appearance on the slide is animated. It does not appear right away when the rest of the slide appears, or it appears in some unusual way (such as flying or fading), or both.

- **Emphasis (yellow):** The item is already on the slide and is modified in some way. For example, it may shrink, grow, wiggle, or change color.

- **Exit (red):** The item disappears from the slide before the slide itself disappears, and you can specify that it does so in some unusual way.

- **Motion Paths (gray):** The item moves on the slide according to a preset path.

Within each of these broad categories are a multitude of animations. Although the appearance of the icons may vary, the colors (on the menus from which you choose them and on the effects listed in the Animation pane) always match the category.

Different effect categories have different choices. For example, the Emphasis category, in addition to providing movement-based effects, also has effects that change the color, background, or other attributes of the object.

You can choose animation effects in any of these ways (all from the Animations tab) after selecting the object to be animated:

- Click one of the animation samples in the Animations group.
- Click the Add Animation button in the Advanced Animation group, and choose an effect from the menu that appears. See Figure 25.7.
- Click the More down arrow to open the gallery in the Animation group, and choose an effect from the gallery that appears. (This gallery is identical to the one provided by the Add Animation button.)

FIGURE 25.7

Choose an animation effect to apply.

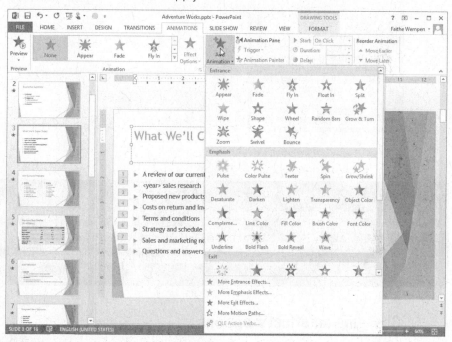

- Click the Add Animation button and then choose one of the "More" commands at the bottom, depending on the type of animation you want. For example, you might want to choose More Entrance Effects. This opens a dialog box with a full listing of the effects of that type, shown in Figure 25.8.

25

FIGURE 25.8

The More command opens a dialog box of effects for the chosen type.

> **NOTE**
>
> Why are there two seemingly identical menus on the Animations tab — one in the Animation gallery and one from the Add Animation button? If an object does not currently have any animation assigned to it, there is no difference; either one will work equally well. However, if the object already has an animation, you can use the Animation gallery to change an existing animation. Add Animation can be used to add additional animation to an object that is already animated.

Changing an effect's options

After applying an animation, you can control its options with the Effect Options button in the Animation group on the Animations tab. The options that appear there depend on the effect you have chosen. Some effects have a direction for entrance or exit, for example.

For access to a full range of effect options, do the following:

1. **In the Animation pane, right-click the desired animation event and choose Effect Options.** An Effect Options dialog box opens for the chosen event. The controls that appear may be different depending on the event.

2. **On the Effect tab, use the controls provided to fine-tune the effect.** For example, as Figure 25.9 shows, you can smooth out the start and end of the animation by a certain amount, set a bounce for the end, and dim the object after animation.

3. **Use the settings on the Timing and Text Animation tabs to further customize the effect.** The timing controls are also found in the Timing group of the Animations tab. Text animation settings may include choices such as setting the grouping: determining whether text should appear As One Object, All At Once, or By Paragraph; additionally you often can specify a timing for individual text items and specify whether they appear in regular or reverse order.

4. **Click OK to apply the effect settings.**

FIGURE 25.9

Fine-tune an effect's options from the Effect tab of the Effect Options dialog box.

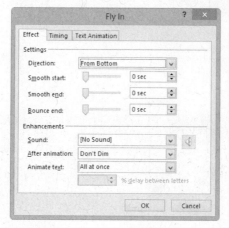

Animating parts of a chart

If you create a chart using PowerPoint's charting tool, then you can display the chart all at once or apply a custom animation effect to it. For example, you can make the chart appear by series (divided by legend entries), by category (divided by X-axis points), or by individual element in a series or category. Figure 25.10 and Figure 25.11 show progressions based on series and category.

FIGURE 25.10

In this progression, the chart is appearing by series.

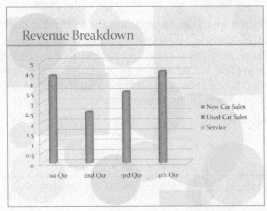

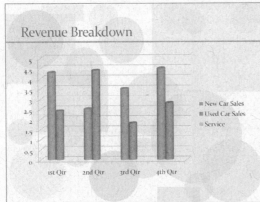

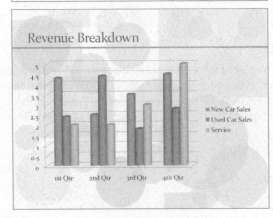

FIGURE 25.11

Here, the chart is appearing by category.

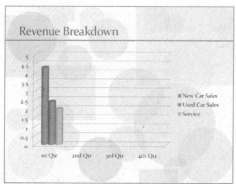
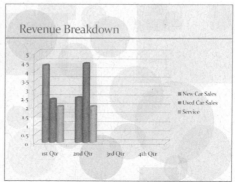
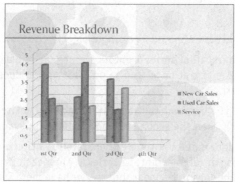
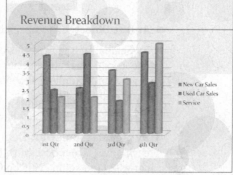

Along with making various parts of the chart appear at different times, you can also make them appear using any of the animated techniques that you have already learned, such as flying in, dropping in, fading in, and so on. You can also associate sounds with the parts and dim them or change them to various colors when the animation is finished.

To animate a chart, you must first set up the entire chart to be animated, just as you would any other object on a slide.

Then, to set up the chart so that different parts of it are animated separately, do the following:

1. **Choose Animations ⇨ Animation ⇨ Effect Options.**
2. **Choose any of the following options from the Sequence section of the menu (see Figure 25.12):**

FIGURE 25.12

You can animate the chart by series, by category, or by individual data points.

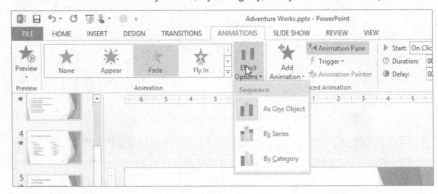

- **As One Object:** The entire chart is animated as a single object.

- **By Series:** In a multiseries chart, all of series 1 enters at once (all the bars of one color), then all of series 2 enters at once, and so on. This option doesn't appear for a single-series chart.

- **By Category:** All the bars for the first category appear at once (an entire grouping of multicolored bars), then the second category's bars, and so on.

- **By Element in Series:** Each data point is animated separately, in this order: each point (from bottom to top or left to right) in series 1, then each point in series 2, and so on. This option does not appear unless you have more than one category and series.

- **By Element in Category:** Each data point is animated separately, in this order: each point (from bottom to top or left to right) in category 1, then each point in category 2, and so on. This option does not appear unless you have more than one category and series.

You can also set up chart animation from the Effect Options dialog box. Collapse the chart's animation in the Animation pane (if needed), and then right-click it and choose Effect Options. In the dialog box that appears, click the Chart Animation tab, and make your selection there. The choices are exactly the same as on the menu (Figure 25.12), plus there is one additional check box: Start Animation by Drawing the Chart Background, which is on by default. It animates the grid and legend. If you deselect this option, these items appear immediately on the slide, and the data bars, slices, or other chart elements appear separately from them.

You do not have to use the same animation effect for each category or each series of the chart. After you set up the chart to animate each piece individually, individual entries appear for each piece on the list in the Animation pane. You can expand this list and then apply individual settings to each piece. For example, you could have some data bars on a chart fly in from one direction, and other data bars fly in from another direction. You can also reorder the pieces so that the data points build in a different order from the default order.

> **TIP**
>
> Not all animation effects are available for every type of chart and every series or category animation. If a particular animation is not working, try a simpler one, such as Fade or Wipe.

The When and How of Handouts

Presentation professionals are divided about how and when to use handouts most effectively. Here are some of the many conflicting viewpoints. I can't say who is right or wrong, but each of these statements brings up issues that you should consider. The bottom line is that each of them is an opinion on how much power and credit to give to the audience; your answer may vary depending on the audience you are addressing.

- **You should give handouts at the beginning of the presentation. The audience can absorb the information better if they can follow along on paper.**

  This approach makes a lot of sense. Research has proven that people absorb more facts if presented with them in more than one medium. This approach also gives your audience free will; they can listen to you or not, and they still have the information. It's their choice, and this can be extremely scary for less-confident speakers. It's not just a speaker confidence issue in some cases, however. If you plan to give a lot of extra information in your speech that's not on the handouts, people might miss it if you distribute the handouts at the beginning because they're reading ahead.

- **You shouldn't give the audience handouts because they won't pay as close attention to your speech if they know that the information is already written down for them.**

  This philosophy falls at the other end of the spectrum. It gives the audience the least power and shows the least confidence in their ability to pay attention to you in the presence of a distraction (handouts). If you truly don't trust your audience to be professional and listen, this approach may be your best option. However, don't let insecurity as a speaker drive you prematurely to this conclusion. The fact is that people won't take away as much knowledge about the topic without handouts as they would if you provide handouts. So, ask yourself if your ultimate goal is to fill the audience with knowledge or to make them pay attention to you.

- **You should give handouts at the end of the presentation so that people will have the information to take home but not be distracted during the speech.**

25

This approach attempts to solve the dilemma with compromise. The trouble with it, as with all compromises, is that it does an incomplete job from both angles. Because audience members can't follow along on the handouts during the presentation, they miss the opportunity to jot notes on the handouts. And because the audience knows that handouts are coming, they might nod off and miss something important. The other problem is that if you don't clearly tell people that handouts are coming later, some people spend the entire presentation frantically copying down each slide on their own notepaper.

Creating Handouts

To create handouts, you simply decide on a layout (a number of slides per page) and then choose that layout from the Print settings as you print. No muss, no fuss! If you want to get more involved, you can edit the layout in Handout Master view before printing.

Choosing a layout

Assuming you have decided that handouts are appropriate for your speech, you must decide on the format for them. You have a choice of one, two, three, four, six, or nine slides per page.

- **1 Slide:** Places a single slide vertically and horizontally "centered" on the page.

- **2 Slides:** Prints two big slides on each page. This layout is good for slides that have a lot of fine print and small details or for situations in which you are not confident that the reproduction quality will be good. There is nothing more frustrating for an audience than not being able to read the handouts!

- **3 Slides:** Makes the slides much smaller — less than one-half the size of the ones in the two-slide layout. But you get a nice bonus with this layout: lines to the side of each slide for note-taking. This layout works well for presentations with slides that are big and simple and the speaker is providing a lot of extra information that isn't on the slides. The audience members can write the extra information in the note-taking space provided.

- **4 Slides:** Uses the same size slides as the three-slide layout, but they are spaced out two-by-two without note-taking lines. However, there is still plenty of room above and below each slide, so the audience members still have lots of room to take notes.

> **NOTE**
>
> The four-, six-, and nine-slide handout layouts come in two varieties: vertical and horizontal. This does not refer to the orientation of the slides or the paper but rather to the order in which the slides appear. A vertical layout runs the first slide in the top-left corner, the second slide below that, and so on so that slides are ordered in vertical columns. A horizontal layout, in contrast, places the first slide in the top-left corner and the second slide to its right, running the slides in horizontal rows. Horizontal ordering is more common in the United States and Europe; vertical ordering is more common in Asia.

- **6 Slides:** Uses slides the same size as the three-slide and four-slide layouts, but crams more slides on the page at the expense of note-taking space. This layout is good for presentations with big, simple slides where the audience does not need to take notes. If you are not sure if the audience will benefit at all from handouts being distributed, consider whether this layout would be a good compromise. This format also saves paper, which might be an issue if you need to make hundreds of copies.

- **9 Slides:** Makes the slides very tiny, almost like a Slide Sorter view, so that you can see nine at a time. This layout makes them very hard to read unless the slide text is extremely simple. I don't recommend this layout in most cases because the audience really won't get much out of such handouts.

> **TIP**
>
> One good use for the nine-slide model is as an index or table of contents for a large presentation. You can include a nine-slides-per-page version of the handouts at the beginning of the packet that you give to the audience members and then follow it up with a two-slides-per-page version that they can refer to if they want a closer look at one of the slides.

Finally, there is an Outline handout layout, which prints an outline of all of the text in your presentation — that is, all of the text that is part of placeholders in slide layouts; any text in extra text boxes you have added manually is excluded. It is not considered a handout when you are printing, but it is included with the handout layouts in the handout master. More on this type of handout later in the chapter.

Printing handouts

When you have decided which layout is appropriate for your needs, print your handouts as follows:

1. **(Optional) If you want to print only one particular slide or a group of slides, select the slide or slides you want in either Slide Sorter view or in the slide thumbnails task pane on the left.**

2. **Select File ➪ Print.** The Print options appear.

3. **Enter a number of copies in the Copies text box.** The default is 1. If you want the copies collated (applicable to multipage printouts only), make sure you mark the Collate check box.

4. **Set options for your printer or choose a different printer.** See the section "Setting printer-specific options" later in this chapter for help with this.

5. **If you do not want to print all the slides, type the slide numbers that you want into the Slides box.** Indicate a contiguous range with a dash. For example, to print slides 1 through 9, type **1-9**. Indicate noncontiguous slides with commas. For example, to print slides 2, 4, and 6, type **2, 4, 6**. Or to print slides 2 plus 6 through 10, type **2, 6-10**. To print them in reverse order, type them in reverse order, such as **10-6, 2**.

25

Alternatively, you can click Print All Slides to open a menu of range choices and choose one of these from its list:

- **Print Selection:** To print multiple slides you selected before you issued the Print command. It is not available if you did not select any slides beforehand.

- **Print Current Slide:** To print whatever slide you selected before you issued the Print command.

- **Custom Range:** To print the slides whose numbers you type in the Slides text box. When you enter slide numbers in the Slides text box, this option gets selected automatically, so usually you don't have to select this option manually.

- **Custom Show:** To print a certain custom show you have set up. Each custom show you have created appears on the list. You won't see this option if you haven't created any.

6. **(Optional) Hidden slides are printed by default.** If you don't want to print hidden slides, click the same button again to reopen the menu and click Print Hidden Slides to toggle the check mark off next to that command.

7. **Click Full Page Slides to open a menu of views you can print.**

8. **On the menu that appears, click the number and layout of handouts you want.** See Figure 25.13.

FIGURE 25.13

Choose which handout layout you want.

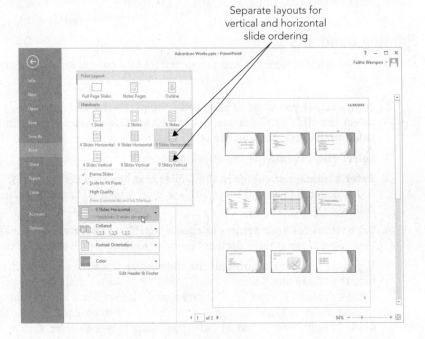

Separate layouts for
vertical and horizontal
slide ordering

9. **(Optional) Click the Color button and select the color setting for the printouts:**

   - **Color:** This is the default. It sends the data to the printer assuming that color will be used. When you use this setting with a black-and-white printer, it results in slides with grayscale or black backgrounds. Use this setting if you want the handouts to look as much as possible like the on-screen slides.

   - **Grayscale:** Sends the data to the printer assuming that color will not be used. Colored backgrounds are removed, and if text is normally a light color on a dark background, that is reversed. Use this setting if you want PowerPoint to optimize the printout for viewing on white paper.

   - **Pure Black and White:** This format hides most shadows and patterns, as described in Table 25.1. It's good for faxes and overhead transparencies.

TABLE 25.1   Differences between Grayscale and Pure Black and White

Object	Grayscale	Pure Black and White
Text	Black	Black
Text shadows	Grayscale	Black
Fill	Grayscale	Grayscale
Lines	Black	Black
Object shadows	Grayscale	Black
Bitmaps	Grayscale	Grayscale
Clip Art	Grayscale	Grayscale
Slide backgrounds	White	White
Charts	Grayscale	White

10. **(Optional) If desired, open the drop-down list from which you chose the handout layout and select any of these additional options:**

25

- **Frame Slides:** Draws a black border around each slide image. Useful for slides being printed with white backgrounds.
- **Scale to Fit Paper:** Enlarges the slides to the maximum size they can be and still fit on the layout (as defined in the handout master, covered later in this chapter).
- **High Quality:** Optimizes the appearance of the printout in small ways, such as allowing text shadows to print.
- **Print Comments and Ink Markup:** Prints any comments that you have inserted with the Comments feature in PowerPoint.

11. **Check the preview of your handouts, which appears at the right.** Make any necessary changes.
12. **Click Print.** The handouts print, and you're ready to roll!

CAUTION

Beware of the cost of printer supplies. If you are planning to distribute copies of the presentation to a lot of people, it may be tempting to print all of the copies on your printer. But the cost per page of printing is fairly high, especially if you have an inkjet printer. You will quickly run out of ink in your ink cartridge and have to spend $20 or more for a replacement. Consider whether it might be cheaper to print one original and take it to a copy shop or have the handouts printed at a local or chain office supply store.

Setting printer-specific options

In addition to the Print settings in PowerPoint that you learned about in the preceding section, there are controls you can set that affect the printer you have chosen.

A printer's name appears under the Printer heading on the Print screen in Backstage view. Click that printer's name to open a menu of additional printers you can select instead. These are the printers installed on your PC (either local or network).

NOTE

Some of the "printers" listed are not really physical printers but drivers that create other types of files. For example, Fax saves a copy of the file in a format that is compatible with the fax driver included in Windows. It doesn't produce a hard copy printout.

After selecting the desired printer, click the Printer Properties hyperlink beneath the name. A Properties dialog box opens that is specific to that printer. Figure 25.14 shows the box for a Brother MFC-9320CW printer, an all-in-one laser. Notice that there are two tabs: Layout and Paper/Quality. The tabs may be different for your printer. For some printers, more settings are available if you click an Advanced button; when you click the Advanced button shown in Figure 25.14, for example, the Advanced Options dialog box in Figure 25.15 appears.

FIGURE 25.14

Each printer's options are slightly different, but the same types of settings are available for most printers.

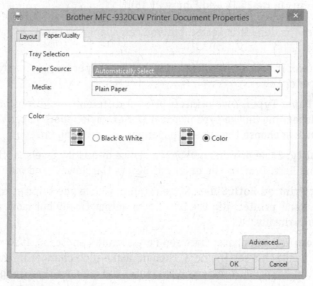

FIGURE 25.15

Some printers show more options in an Advanced Options dialog box (or similar).

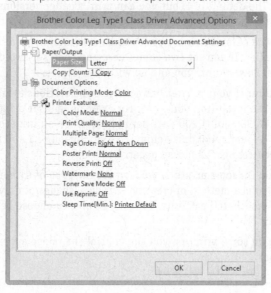

These settings affect how the printer behaves in all Windows-based programs, not just in PowerPoint, so you need to be careful not to change anything that you don't want globally changed. Here are some of the settings you may be able to change on your printer (not all of these are shown in Figure 25.14 and Figure 25.15):

- **Paper Size:** The default is Letter, but you can change to Legal, A4, or any of several other sizes.

- **Paper Source:** If your printer has more than one paper tray, you may be able to select Upper or Lower.

- **Media or Paper Type:** Some printers print at different resolutions or with different settings depending on the type of paper (for example, photo paper versus regular paper). You can choose the type of paper you are printing on.

- **Print Quality:** Some printers give you a choice of quality levels, such as Draft, Normal, and Best. Draft is the quickest; Best is the slowest and may use more ink.

- **Duplex or Print on Both Sides:** Some printers enable you to print on both sides of the paper. Some printers flip the paper over automatically but most prompt you to flip it over manually.

- **Orientation:** You can choose between Portrait and Landscape. It's not recommended that you change this setting here, though; make such changes in the Page Setup dialog box in PowerPoint instead. Otherwise, you may get the wrong orientation on a printout in other programs.

- **Page Order:** You can choose Front to Back or Back to Front. This determines the order in which the pages print.

- **Pages per Sheet:** The default is 1, but you can print smaller versions of several pages on a single sheet. This option is usually only available on PostScript printers.

- **Copies:** This sets the default number of copies that should print. Be careful; this number is a multiplier. If you set two copies here and then set two copies in the Print dialog box in PowerPoint, you end up with four copies.

- **Graphics Resolution:** If your printer has a range of resolutions available, you may be able to choose the resolution you want. For example, a laser printer might have you choose between 300 and 1,200 dots per inch (dpi); on an inkjet printer, choices are usually 360, 720, and 1,440 dpi. Achieving a resolution of 1,440 on an inkjet printer usually requires special glossy paper.

- **Graphic Dithering:** On some printers, you can set the type of dithering that makes up images. *Dithering* is a method of creating shadows (shades of gray) from black ink by using tiny crosshatch patterns. You may be able to choose between Coarse, Fine, and None.

- **Image Intensity:** On some printers, you can control the image appearance with a light/dark slide bar.

Some printers, notably inkjets, come with their own print-management software. If that's the case, you may have to run that print-management software separately from outside of PowerPoint for full control over the printer's settings. You can usually access such software from the Windows Start menu.

Using the Handout Master

Just as the slide master controls your slide layout, the handout master controls your handout layout. To view the handout master, as shown in Figure 25.16, click Handout Master in the Master Views group of the View tab. Unlike the slide master and title master, you can have only one handout master layout per presentation.

FIGURE 25.16

The handout master lets you define the handout layout to be printed.

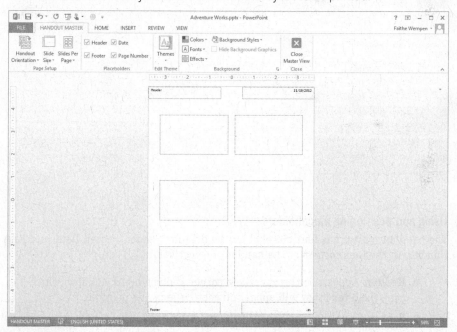

You can do almost exactly the same things with the handout master that you can with the slide master. The following sections describe some of the common activities.

25

Setting the number of slides per page

You can view the handout master with various numbers of slides per page to help you see how the layout will look when you print it. The settings you can change apply to all the layouts for each number of slides per page. For example, if you apply a header or footer or a page background for a three-slides-per-page layout, it also applies to the four-slides-per-page layout as well as all the others. To choose the number of slides per page to display as you work with the handout master, click the Slides per Page button in the Page Setup group of the Handout Master tab, and then make your selection from its menu. See Figure 25.17.

FIGURE 25.17

Choose a number of slides per page.

Using and positioning placeholders

The handout master has four placeholders by default: Header, Footer, Date, and Page Number, in the four corners of the handout respectively:

- **Header:** Appears in the upper-left corner and is a blank box into which you can type fixed text that will appear on each page of the printout.
- **Footer:** Same thing as Header but appears in the lower-left corner.
- **Date:** Appears in the upper-right corner and shows today's date by default.
- **Page Number:** Appears in the lower-right corner and shows a code for a page number, <#>. This will be replaced by an actual page number when you print.

In each placeholder box, you can type text (replacing, if desired, the Date and Page codes already there). You can also drag the placeholder boxes around on the layout.

There are two ways to remove the default placeholders from the layout. You select the placeholder box and press Delete, or you can clear the check box for that element in the Placeholders group of the Handout Master tab, as shown in Figure 25.18.

FIGURE 25.18

Turn on/off placeholder elements from the Handout Master tab.

Mark or clear check boxes for placeholders.

> **NOTE**
>
> Because the header and footer are blank by default, there is no advantage to deleting these placeholders unless they have something in them you want to dispose of; having a blank box and having no box at all have the same result.

> **TIP**
>
> You can't move or resize the slide placeholder boxes on the handout master, nor can you change the handout master's margins. If you want to change the size of the slide boxes on the handout or change the margins of the page, consider exporting the handouts to Word (File ⇨ Export ⇨ Create Handouts ⇨ Create Handouts) and working on them there.

Setting handout and slide orientation

Orientation refers to the direction on the page the material runs. If the top of the paper is one of the narrow edges, it's called Portrait; if the top of the paper is a wide edge, it's Landscape. Figure 25.19 shows the difference in handout orientation. To change this setting, on the Handout Master tab, click Handout Orientation.

25

FIGURE 25.19

Portrait (left) and Landscape (right) handout orientation

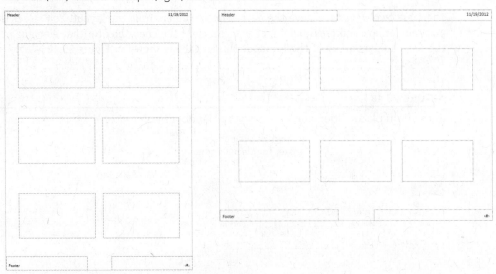

You can also set the slide size, either the Widescreen setting (16:9) or the Standard setting (4:3). PowerPoint 2013 defaults to Widescreen, both for the slides themselves and for the slide images on the handouts. To adjust this setting, on the Handout Master tab, click Slide Size and make your selection of Standard or Widescreen, or click Custom Slide Size to open the Slide Size dialog box and set a custom height and width. See Figure 25.20.

FIGURE 25.20

You can set any slide size and orientation combination in the Slide Size dialog box.

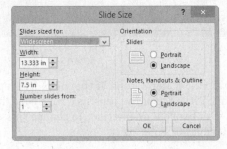

In the Slide Size dialog box, shown in Figure 25.20, you can also set a slide orientation. This is different from the orientation of the handout as a whole. The default slide orientation is landscape; setting the slide orientation to Portrait results in a layout like the one on the right in Figure 25.21. If you choose such a slide layout, PowerPoint prompts you to specify whether slide content should be sized to fit the new layout on the handouts or cropped.

FIGURE 25.21

Landscape (left) and Portrait (right) slide orientation

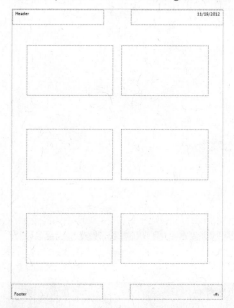 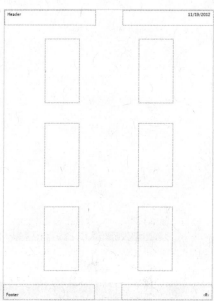

Formatting handouts

You can manually format any text on a handout layout using the formatting controls on the Home tab, the same as with any other text. Such formatting affects only the text you select and only on the layout you're working with. You can also select the entire placeholder box and apply formatting.

You can also apply Colors, Fonts, and/or Effects schemes from the Edit Theme group, as shown in Figure 25.22, much as you can do for the presentation as a whole. The main difference is that you cannot select an overall theme from the Themes button; all the themes are unavailable from the list while in Handout Master view. The settings you apply here affect only the handouts, not the presentation as a whole.

25

FIGURE 25.22

Apply color, font, and/or effect schemes from the Edit Theme group.

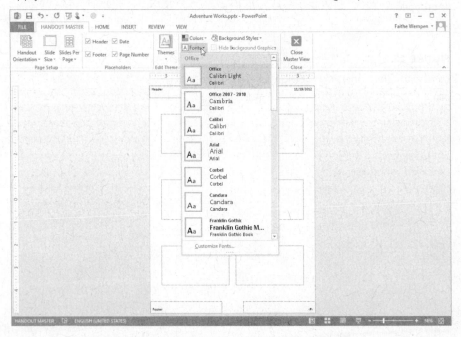

> **NOTE**
>
> You probably won't have much occasion to apply an Effects scheme to a handout layout because handouts do not usually have objects that use effects (that is, drawn shapes, charts, or SmartArt diagrams).

Creating Speaker Notes

Speaker notes are like handouts, but for you. Only one printout format is available for them: the Notes Pages layout. It consists of the slide on the top half (the same size as in the two-slides-per-page handout) with the blank space below it for your notes to yourself.

Speaker notes printed in PowerPoint are better than traditional note cards for several reasons. For one thing, you can type your notes right into the computer and print them out on regular paper. There's no need to jam a note card into a typewriter and use messy correction fluid or erasers to make changes. The other benefit is that each note page contains a picture of the slide, so it's not as easy to lose your place while speaking when compared to using traditional note cards.

Typing speaker notes

You can type your notes for a slide in Normal view (in the Notes pane) or in Notes Page view. The latter shows the page more or less as it will look when you print your notes pages; this can help if you need to gauge how much text will fit on the printed page.

To switch to Notes Page view, on the View tab click Notes Page in the Presentation Views group as shown in Figure 25.23. Unlike with some of the other views, there is no shortcut button for this view in the bottom-right corner of the PowerPoint window. Once you're in Notes Page view, you can zoom and scroll just like in any other view to see more or less of the page at once. You can scroll further to move from slide to slide, or you can move from slide to slide in the traditional ways (the Page Up and Page Down keys on the keyboard or the Next Slide or Previous Slide buttons on-screen).

FIGURE 25.23

Notes Page view is one of the best ways to work with your speaker notes.

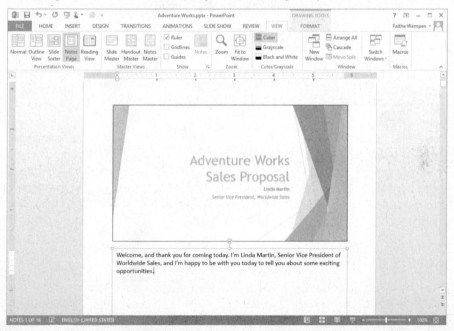

> **NOTE**
> Use the Zoom control to zoom in or out until you find the optimal view so that the text you type is large enough to be clear, but small enough so that you can see across the entire width of the note area. I find that 100 percent works well on my screen, but yours may vary.

25

Just type your notes in the Notes area, the same as you would type in any text box in PowerPoint. The lines in the paragraph wrap automatically. Press Enter to start a new paragraph. When you're done, move to the next slide.

Changing the notes page layout

Just as you can edit your handout layouts, you can also edit your notes page layout. Just switch to its master and make your changes. Follow these steps:

1. **On the View tab in the Master Views group, click Notes Master.**

2. **Edit the layout, as you have learned to edit other masters.** See Figure 25.24. This can include the following actions:

   - Moving placeholders for the slide, the notes, or any of the header or footer elements

   - Changing the font used for the text in any of those areas

   - Resizing the placeholder for the slide graphic

FIGURE 25.24

You can edit the layout of the notes pages in Notes Master view.

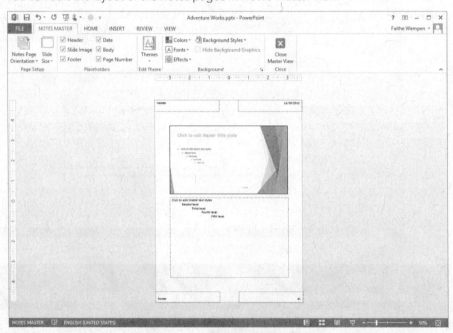

- Resizing the Notes pane
- Adding clip art or other graphics to the background
- Adding a colored, textured, or patterned background to the notes page

3. **When you are finished, click the Close Master View button to return to Normal view.**

Printing notes pages

When you're ready to print your notes pages, follow these steps:

1. **Choose File ⇨ Print.** The Print controls appear.
2. **Click the button immediately below the Slides box, and choose Notes Pages as the type of layout to print.**
3. **Set any other options, just as you did when printing handouts earlier in the chapter.** (If you need to choose which printer to use or to set the options for that printer, see the section "Setting printer-specific options" earlier in this chapter.) There are no special options for notes pages.
4. **Click Print.** The notes pages print.

> **CAUTION**
>
> If you print notes pages for hidden slides, you may want to arrange your stack after they're printed so that the hidden slides are at the bottom. That way you won't get confused when giving the presentation.

Printing an Outline

If text is the main part of your presentation, you might prefer to print an outline instead of mini-slides. You can use the outline for speaker notes, audience handouts, or both. To print the text from Outline view, follow these steps:

1. **View the outline in Normal or Outline view.**
2. **Choose File ⇨ Print.** The Print controls appear.
3. **Click the button immediately below the Slides text box, and choose Outline as the type of layout to print.**
4. **Set any other print options, as you learned in the section "Printing handouts" earlier in the chapter.**
5. **Click Print.**

Be aware, however, that the outline will not contain text that you've typed in manually placed text boxes or any other non-text information, such as tables, charts, and so on.

25

Printing Slides

Of course, you can print your slides one per page rather than printing handouts or notes pages. You may print slides, for example, when you need to send a presentation to a client rather than presenting it in person. Printing presentation slides works just like printing a document from any other applcation:

1. **Choose File ⇨ Print.** The Print controls appear.
2. **Select the printer to use from the Printer drop-down list.** The printer becomes the current or active printer.
3. **On the button immediately below the Slides text box, make sure that Full Page Slides is selected.**
4. **Set any other print options, as you learned in the section "Printing handouts" earlier in the chapter.**
5. **Click Print.**

Be aware, however, that the outline will not contain text that you've typed in manually placed text boxes or any other non-text information, such as tables, charts, and so on.

Summary

In this chapter, you learned how to add transitions and animate the objects on your slides to create some great special effects. You also learned how to create a hard copy to support your presentation. You can now:

- Add a transition to one slide or all the slides.
- Determine whether slides advance when you click or automatically.
- Add sounds and set transition timings.
- Add an animation effect to an object, list, or chart.
- Change animation effect settings, including timing and order.
- Create a variety of handouts for your audience.
- Enter and print out speaker notes for yourself.

Delivering a Live Presentation

IN THIS CHAPTER

Starting and ending a show

Using the on-screen show controls

Using the on-screen pen

Hiding slides for backup use

Using custom shows

Creating and using sections

Giving a presentation on a different computer

Delivering an online presentation

Working with audio-visual equipment

It's show time! Well, actually I hope for your sake that it is *not* time for the show this very instant because things will go much more smoothly if you can practice using PowerPoint's slide-show controls before you have to go live.

Presenting the show can be as simple or as complex as you make it. At the most basic level, you can start the show, move through it slide by slide with simple mouse clicks or key presses, and then end the show. However, to take advantage of PowerPoint's extra slide-show features, you should spend a little time studying the following sections.

> **NOTE**
> The first part of this chapter assumes that you are showing your presentation on a PC that has PowerPoint 2013 installed; sections later in this chapter discuss other situations.

Starting and Ending a Show

To start a show, do any of the following:

- On the Slide Show tab in the Start Slide Show group, click either From Beginning or From Current Slide.
- Click the Slide Show View button in the bottom-right corner of the screen (to begin from the current slide).
- Press F5 (to begin from the beginning).
- Press Shift+F5 (to begin from the current slide).

Once the show is underway, you can control the movement from slide to slide as described in the section "Moving from Slide to Slide."

To end the show, do any of the following:

- Right-click and choose End Show.
- Press Esc, – (minus), or Ctrl+Break.

If you want to temporarily pause the show while you have a discussion, you can blank the screen by pressing W or , (comma) for a white screen or B or . (period) for a black screen. To resume the show, press any key.

Using the On-Screen Show Controls

When you display a slide show, the mouse pointer and show controls are hidden. To make them appear, you can move the mouse. When you do this, very faint buttons, shown in Figure 26.1, appear in the bottom-left corner of the slide show and the mouse pointer also appears. PowerPoint calls this row of buttons the *popup toolbar*. The buttons on this toolbar are different from the ones in earlier versions of PowerPoint, and they offer many additional capabilities. From left to right, the buttons are as follows:

- **Back:** The leftmost button, takes you back to the previous slide or to the previous animation event if the present slide contains animation.
- **Forward:** Moves you to the next slide. Normally, you can just click to go to the next slide, but if you are using the pen (covered later in this chapter), then clicking it causes it to draw rather than advance the presentation. In this situation, you can use the Forward button.
- **Pointers:** Opens a menu for controlling the appearance of the pen or pointer. (I discuss this feature later in this chapter.)

- **See All Slides:** Opens a slide-sorter-like view within Slide Show view, from which you can quickly select the slide you want to jump to by looking at thumbnails.

- **Zoom:** Enables you to zoom in on a portion of a slide and then zoom back out again.

- **Options:** Opens the menu shown in Figure 26.2. It contains a variety of commands for controlling the presentation, including setting arrow options and controlling display settings and Presenter view. You can also open this menu by right-clicking anywhere on the slide.

FIGURE 26.1

These buttons appear in the bottom-left corner of a slide in Slide Show view.

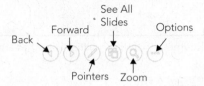

FIGURE 26.2

Click the Options button or right-click on the slide to open this menu.

There are a lot of shortcut keys to remember when working in Slide Show view, and so PowerPoint provides a handy summary of these keys. To see them, right-click and choose Help, or press F1. The Slide Show Help dialog box appears (Figure 26.3). The dialog box has several tabbed pages; click a tab to browse for the shortcuts of interest to you. Click OK to close this dialog box when you are done.

FIGURE 26.3

The Slide Show Help dialog box provides a quick summary of the shortcut keys that are available during a presentation.

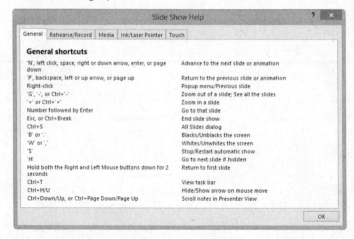

Moving from slide to slide

The simplest way to move through a presentation is to move to the next slide. To do so, you can use any of these methods:

- Press any of these keys: N, Spacebar, Right Arrow, Down Arrow, Enter, or Page Down.
- Click the left mouse button.
- Right-click and choose Next.
- Click the right-pointing arrow button in the bottom-left corner of the slide.

If you have animated any elements on a slide, these methods advance the animation and do not necessarily move to the next slide. For example, if you have animated your bulleted list so that the bullets appear one at a time, then any of the actions in this list make the next bullet appear rather than making the next slide appear. Only after all of the objects on the current slide have displayed does PowerPoint advance to the next slide. If you need to immediately advance to the next slide, you can use the instructions in the next section, "Jumping to specific slides."

To back up to the previous slide, use any of these methods:

- Press any of these keys: P, Backspace, left arrow, up arrow, or Page Up.
- Click the left-pointing arrow button on the bottom-left corner of the slide.
- Right-click and choose Previous.

You can also go back to the last slide that you viewed. To do this, right-click and choose Last Viewed. Although you would think that the last slide viewed would be the same as the previous slide, this is not always the case. For example, if you jump around in the slide show — such as to a hidden slide — then the last slide viewed is not the previous slide in the show but the hidden slide that you have just viewed.

Jumping to specific slides

There are several ways to jump to a particular slide. One of the easiest ways is to use See All Slides to locate the slide from its thumbnail image. To do so, follow these steps:

1. **During the slide show, right-click to display the shortcut menu.**
2. **Select See All Slides.** Thumbnail images of the slides appear, as shown in Figure 26.4.

FIGURE 26.4

You can go to a specific slide using the See All Slides command on the menu.

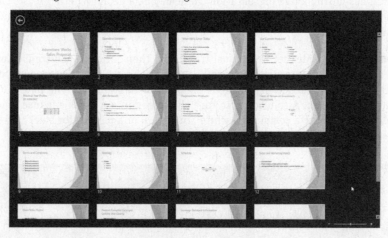

3. **Click the slide to which you want to jump.**

You can also jump to a certain slide by typing its number and pressing Enter. For example, to go to the third slide, you would type **3** and then press Enter. Another way is to press Ctrl+S to open an All Slides dialog box listing the titles of all of the slides in the presentation. You can click a slide to select it and then click Go To, as shown in Figure 26.5.

FIGURE 26.5

The All Slides dialog box lists the titles of all of the slides so that you can select the one you want to go to.

To jump back to the first slide in the presentation, hold down both the left and right mouse buttons for two seconds (or type **1** and press Enter).

Blanking the screen

Sometimes during a live presentation there may be a delay. Whether it is a chatty audience member with a complicated question, a fire drill, or just an intermission, you will want to pause the show.

If you have the slides set for manual transition, then the slide you stopped on remains on the screen until you resume. However, you may not want this. For example, it may be distracting to the audience, especially if the pause is to allow someone to get up and speak in front of the screen. A solution is to turn the screen into a blank expanse of black or white. To do so, type **W** or a comma (for white), or type **B** or a period (for black). To return to the presentation, you can press the same key or press any key on the keyboard.

> **TIP**
>
> While the screen is completely black or white, you can draw on it with the pen tool so that it becomes a convenient "scratch pad." Annotations you make with the pen on the blank screen are not saved; when you resume the presentation, they are gone forever. (In contrast, you do have the opportunity to save any annotations you make on the slides themselves, as you will learn in the next section.)

Using the On-Screen Pen

Have you ever seen a coach in a locker room drawing out football plays on a chalkboard? Well, you can do the same thing in PowerPoint. You can have an impromptu discussion of concepts that are illustrated on slides and punctuate the discussion with your own circles, arrows, and lines. Perhaps during the discussion portion of your presentation, you may decide that one point on the slide is not important. In this case, you can use the pen to cross it out. Conversely, a certain point may become really important during a discussion and you want to emphasize it. In this case, you can circle it or underline it with the pen cursor.

You can choose your pen color as follows:

1. **Move the mouse to make the buttons appear.**

2. **Click the Pointers button (the one that looks like a pen).** A menu appears. Alternatively, you can right-click and then choose Pointer Options to see a similar menu. (The main difference is that on the right-click version, you have to select the Ink Color command for access to the ink color swatches.)

3. **Click the color you want, as shown in Figure 26.6.** (If you're using the right-click version of the menu, point to Ink Color first.)

FIGURE 26.6

You can select a pen type and an ink color for it.

You can turn on the type of pen that you want, as follows:

1. **Click the Pointers button again.**
2. **Click the type of pen that you want:**
   - **Pen:** A thin solid line
   - **Highlighter:** A thick, semitransparent line

> **NOTE**
> The on-screen buttons in the slide show continue to work while you have a pen enabled, but you have to click them twice to activate them — once to tell PowerPoint to temporarily switch out of the Pen mode and then again to open the menu.

You can also turn on the default pen by pressing Ctrl+P and then return to the arrow again by pressing Ctrl+A or Esc.

After enabling a pen, just drag and draw on the slide to make your mark. You should practice drawing lines, arrows, and other shapes because it takes a while to master. Figure 26.7 shows an example of using the pen.

FIGURE 26.7

You can draw on the slide with the pen tools.

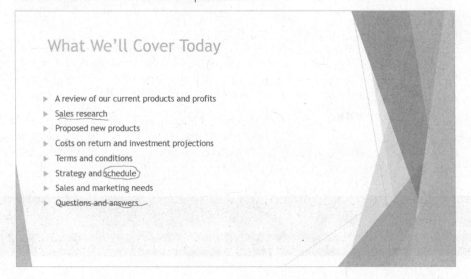

To erase your lines and try again, press E (for Erase), or open the Pointer menu (or right-click and choose Pointer Options) and choose Erase All Ink on Slide. To erase just a part of the ink, open the Pointer menu, choose Eraser, and then use the mouse pointer to erase individual lines.

When you exit Slide Show view after drawing on slides, a dialog box appears, asking whether you want to keep or discard your annotations. If you choose Keep, the annotations become drawn objects on the slides, which you can then move or delete, similar to a line drawn with the drawing tools.

The pen remains a pen when you advance from slide to slide. To change the pen back to a pointer again, open the Pointer menu and choose Arrow, press Ctrl+A, or press Esc.

Hiding Slides for Backup Use

You may not always want to show every slide that you have prepared. Sometimes it pays to prepare extra data in anticipation of a question that you think someone might ask or to hold back certain data unless someone specifically requests it.

By hiding a slide, you keep it filed in reserve, without making it a part of the main slide show. Then, at any time during the presentation when (or if) it becomes appropriate, you can display that slide. Hiding refers only to whether the slide is a part of the main presentation's flow; it has no effect in any other view.

Hiding and unhiding slides

Slide Sorter view is a good view from which to hide and unhide slides because an indicator appears below each slide to show whether it is hidden. This way, you can easily determine which slides are a part of the main presentation. In the slide thumbnail pane in Normal view, hidden slides appear ghosted out.

Follow these steps to hide a slide:

1. **Switch to Slide Sorter view.**

2. **Select the slide or slides that you want to hide.** Remember, to select more than one slide, hold down the Ctrl key as you click the ones that you want.

3. **Click the Hide Slide button in the Set Up group of the Slide Show tab of the ribbon, or right-click one of the selected slides and choose Hide Slide from the shortcut menu.** A diagonal line crosses through the slide indicating that it is hidden. The slide's content also appears dimmed.

To unhide a slide, select the slide and click Hide Slide again. The slide's number returns to normal. You can also right-click a slide and choose Hide Slide again to toggle the hidden attribute off.

> **TIP**
>
> To quickly unhide all slides, select all of the slides (press Ctrl+A) and then click the Hide Slides button twice. The first click hides all of the remaining slides that were not already hidden, and the second click unhides them all.

Showing a hidden slide during a presentation

When you advance from one slide to the next during a show, hidden slides do not appear. (This is what being hidden is about, after all.) If you need to display one of the hidden slides, follow these steps:

1. **In Slide Show view, click the See All Slides button in the bottom-left corner of the screen, or right-click and choose See All Slides.**

   Thumbnails of the slides appear, and hidden slides appear dimmed and with a diagonal line drawn through their numbers, as in Figure 26.8.

FIGURE 26.8

Hidden slides appear dimmed.

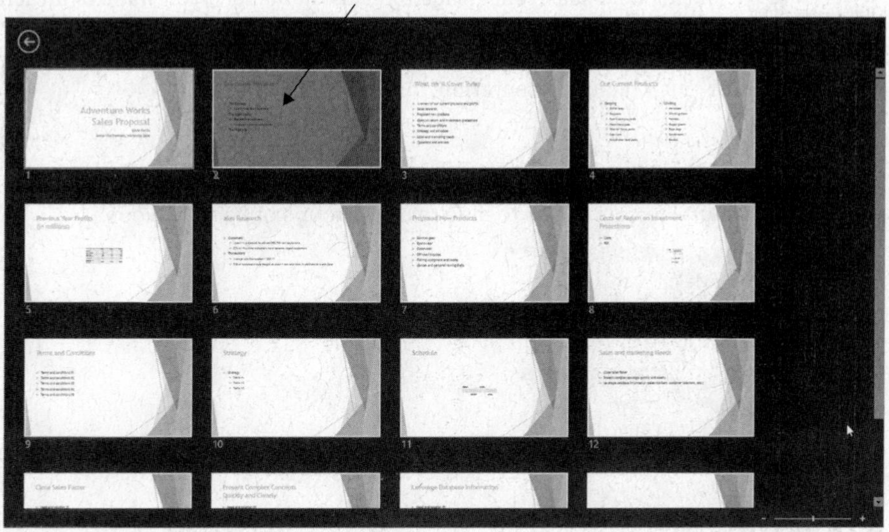

Hidden slide

2. **Click the hidden slide to which you want to jump.**

Once you display a hidden slide, you can easily return to it later. When you move backward through the presentation (using the Backspace key, the Left or Up Arrow key, or the on-screen Back button), any hidden slides that you displayed previously are included in the slides that PowerPoint scrolls back through. However, when you move forward through the presentation, the hidden slide does not reappear, regardless of when you viewed it previously. You can always jump back to it again using the preceding steps. You can also set up hyperlinks to go to, and leave, hidden slides.

Using Custom Shows

Many slide shows have a linear flow: First you show slide one, and then slide two, and so on, until you have completed the entire presentation. This format is suitable for situations where you are presenting clear-cut information with few variables, such as a presentation about a new insurance plan for a group of employees. However, when the situation becomes more complex, a single-path slide show may not suffice. This is especially true when you are presenting a persuasive message to decision makers; you want to anticipate their questions and their need for more information and have many backup slides, or even entire backup slide shows, that are prepared in case questions arise. Figure 26.9 shows a flow chart for this kind of presentation.

FIGURE 26.9

You can use custom shows to hide related groups of backup slides.

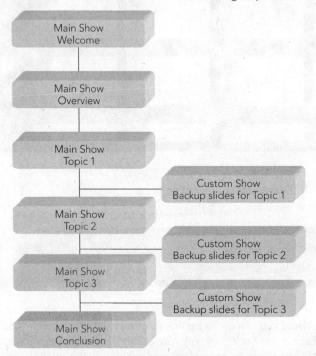

Another great use for custom shows is to set aside a group of slides for a specific audience. For example, you might need to present essentially the same information to employees at two different sites. In this case, you could create two custom shows within the main show and include in each show slides that they both have in common as well as slides that are appropriate for only one audience or the other. Figure 26.10 shows a flow chart for this kind of presentation.

FIGURE 26.10

You can create custom shows that allow you to use the same presentation for multiple audiences.

Notice in Figure 26.10 that although some of the slides in the two custom shows are the same, they repeat in each custom show rather than jumping back to the main presentation. This is because it is much easier to jump to the custom show once and stay there than it is to keep jumping into and out of the show.

Slides in a custom show remain a part of the main presentation. Placing a slide in a custom show does not exclude it from the regular presentation flow. However, you may decide that you no longer want to show the main presentation in its present form; you may just want to use it as a resource pool from which you can select slides for other custom shows. To learn how to set up PowerPoint so that a custom show rather than the main presentation starts when you enter Slide Show view, see the section "Using a custom show as the main presentation" later in this chapter.

Ideas for using custom shows

Here are some ideas to start you thinking about how and why you might want to include some custom shows in your presentation files:

- **Avoiding duplication:** If you have several shows that use about 50 percent of the same slides and the other 50 percent are different ones, you can create all of the shows as custom shows within a single presentation file. This way, the presentations can share the 50 percent of the slides that they have in common.

- **Managing change:** By creating a single presentation file with custom shows, you make it easy to manage changes. If any changes occur in your company that affect any of the common slides, making the change once in your presentation file makes the change to each of the custom shows immediately.

- **Overcoming objections:** You can anticipate client objections to your sales pitch and prepare several custom shows, each of which addresses a particular objection. Then, whatever reason your potential customer gives for not buying your product, you have a counteractive argument at hand.

- **Covering your backside:** If you think that you may be asked for specific figures or other information during a speech, you can have this information ready in a custom show (or on a few simple hidden slides, if there is not a lot of information) to display if needed. No more going through the embarrassment of having to say, "I'm not sure, but let me get back to you on that."

Creating custom shows

To create a custom show, first create all of the slides that should go into it. Start with all of the slides in the main presentation. Then follow these steps:

1. **On the Slide Show tab, click Custom Slide Show in the Start Slide Show group, and then click Custom Shows.** The Custom Shows dialog box opens.

> **NOTE**
>
> If no custom shows are defined yet, the Custom Shows command is the only item that appears on this menu. Otherwise, your existing custom shows appear on and can be run from the menu.

2. **Click New.** The Define Custom Show dialog box opens.

3. **Type a name for your custom show in the Slide show name text box, replacing the default name.**

4. **In the Slides in presentation list, click the check box for the first slide that you want to appear in the custom show.**

   You can select multiple slides before clicking Add in Step 5. However, be aware that if you do this, the slides move to the Slides in Custom Show pane in the order that they originally appeared. If you want them in a different order, copy each slide over separately, in the order that you want, or rearrange the order as described in step 7.

5. **Click Add to copy the slide to the Slides in custom show list. See Figure 26.11.**

FIGURE 26.11

Use the Add button to copy slides from the main presentation into the custom show.

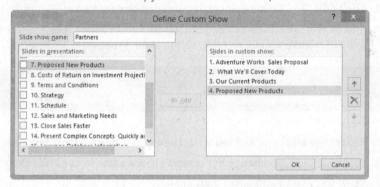

6. **If you need to select more slides, repeat steps 4 and 5 for each slide that you want to include in the custom show.**

7. **If you need to rearrange the slides in the custom show, click the slide that you want to move in the Slides in custom show list and then click the up or down arrow button to change its position.**

8. **When you are finished building your custom show, click OK.** The new show appears in the Custom Shows dialog box.

9. **(Optional) To test your custom show, click the Show button.** Otherwise, click Close to close the Custom Shows dialog box.

Editing custom shows

You can manage your custom shows from the Custom Shows dialog box, the same place in which you created them. This includes editing, deleting, or making a copy of a show. To change which slides appear in a custom show, and in what order, follow these steps:

1. **On the Slide Show tab, click Custom Slide Show in the Start Slide Show group, and then click Custom Shows.** The Custom Shows dialog box appears (Figure 26.12).

FIGURE 26.12

Select a custom show and then click the appropriate button to edit, copy, or delete it.

2. **If you have more than one custom show, click the one that you want to edit.**

3. **Click Edit.** The Define Custom Show dialog box reappears (Figure 26.11).

4. **Add or remove slides as needed.** To add a slide, select it in the left pane and click Add. To remove a slide, select it in the right pane and click Remove.

> **NOTE**
> Removing a slide from a custom show does not remove it from the overall presentation.

5. **Rearrange slides as needed with the up and down arrow buttons.**

6. **(Optional) You can change the custom show's name in the Slide show name text box.**

7. **Click OK.** PowerPoint saves your changes.

8. **Click Close to close the Custom Shows dialog box.**

Copying custom shows

A good way to create several similar custom shows is to create the first one and then copy it. You can then make small changes to the copies as necessary. To copy a custom show, follow these steps:

1. **On the Slide Show tab, click Custom Slide Show in the Start Slide Show group and then click Custom Shows.** The Custom Shows dialog box appears (Figure 26.12).

2. **If you have more than one custom show, select the show that you want to copy.**

3. **Click Copy.** A copy of the show appears in the dialog box. The file name includes the words *Copy of* so that you can distinguish it from the original.

4. **Edit the copy, as explained in the preceding section, to change its name and content.**

5. **When you are finished, click Close to close the Custom Shows dialog box.**

Deleting custom shows

It is not necessary to delete a custom show when you do not want it anymore; it does not do any harm remaining in your presentation. Because custom shows do not display unless you call for them, you can simply choose not to display it. However, if you want to make your presentation more orderly, you can delete a custom show that you no longer want. Follow these steps:

1. **On the Slide Show tab, click Custom Slide Show in the Start Slide Show group and then click Custom Shows.** The Custom Shows dialog box appears (Figure 26.12).
2. **Select the show that you want to delete.**
3. **Click Remove.** The show disappears from the list.
4. **Click Close to close the Custom Shows dialog box.**

Displaying a custom show

To start your presentation with a custom show, on the Slide Show tab, click Custom Slide Show in the Start Slide Show group and then click the name of the custom show on the drop-down menu. The custom show runs.

You can also call up the custom show at any time during your main presentation. There are two ways to do this: You can navigate to the custom show with PowerPoint's regular presentation controls, or you can create a hyperlink to the custom show on your slide.

Navigating to a custom show

During a presentation, you can jump to any of your custom shows by following these steps from Slide Show view:

1. **Click the Options button, or right-click to open the menu.**
2. **Choose Custom Show and then select the custom show that you want, as shown in Figure 26.13.** The custom show starts.

FIGURE 26.13

Choose the custom show that you want to jump to.

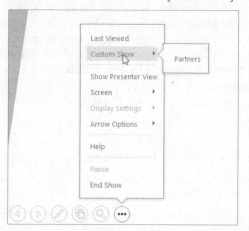

When you start a custom show, you are no longer in the main presentation. To verify this, open the shortcut menu again, choose Go to Slide, and check out the list of slides. This list shows only the slides that belong to the custom show.

Navigating back to the main show

To return to the main show, follow these steps:

1. **Press Ctrl+S to open the All Slides dialog box.**
2. **Open the Show drop-down list and choose All Slides.**
3. **Select the slide that you want to go to.** You can choose from all of the slides in the entire presentation.
4. **Click Go To.**

> **TIP**
>
> To avoid having to press Ctrl+S to return to the main show, you can create a hyperlink or action button for a specific slide in your main show.

Creating a hyperlink to a custom show

Although you learn a lot about hyperlinks in upcoming chapters, here is a preview. Hyperlinks are hot links that you place on your slides. When you click a hyperlink, you jump the display to some other location. This is why they are called *hot*. A hyperlink can jump to an Internet location, a different spot in your presentation, an external file (such as a Word document), or just about anywhere else.

One way to gain quick access to your custom shows in a presentation is to create hyperlinks for them on certain key slides that act as jumping points. You can insert a text hyperlink into any text box, and its text becomes the marker that you click. For example, if you insert a hyperlink for a custom show called Radio Spots, then the hyperlink text could read Radio Spots. If you want to get fancier, you can select some existing text or an existing graphic object and then attach the hyperlink to it. For example, as shown in Figure 26.14, I have inserted a clip-art image of a radio and set it up to be a hyperlink to the custom show that provides details about the radio spots.

FIGURE 26.14

You can create hyperlinks on slides that display custom shows.

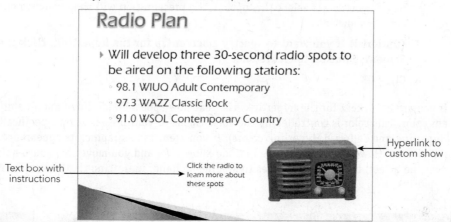

Follow these steps:

1. **If you are attaching the hyperlink to another object (such as the radio in Figure 26.14) or some text, then select the object or text.**

2. **On the Insert tab, click Hyperlink in the Links group.** The Insert Hyperlink dialog box appears.

3. **Click the Place in This Document icon along the left side of the dialog box.**

4. **In the Select a Place in This Document pane, scroll down to the Custom Shows list.**

5. **Click the custom show that you want to jump to with this hyperlink, as shown in Figure 26.15.**

FIGURE 26.15

Choose one of your custom shows as the place to jump to when the user clicks the hyperlink.

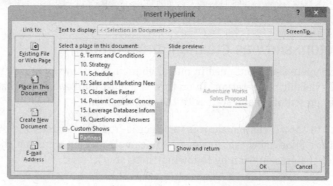

6. **(Optional) If you want to return to the same spot that you left in the main presentation after viewing this custom show, select the Show and Return check box.** If you do not select this option, the presentation will simply end when the custom show ends.

7. **(Optional) If you want to specify a ScreenTip for the hyperlink, click the ScreenTip button to create one.**

8. **Click OK.**

If you are using text for the hyperlink, the text now appears underlined and in a different color. This color is controlled by the color theme of your presentation (specifically the Hyperlink and Followed Hyperlink colors). If you are using a graphic, its appearance does not change. However, when you are in Slide Show view and you move the mouse pointer over the object, the pointer changes to a pointing hand, indicating that the object is a hyperlink.

> **TIP**
>
> If you do not want your linked text to be underlined or to change colors upon return, you can draw a rectangle with no border and 99 percent white fill over the top of the text and link to the rectangle instead. Because this shape is on top of the text, you click it instead of the text. Keep in mind that you should create your link before changing the border and fill of the shape to almost no color.

Another way to use hyperlinks for custom shows is to set up the first few slides generically for all audiences and then to branch off into one custom show or another, based on user input. The diagram in Figure 26.9 is an example of this type of presentation. After the first two slides, you could set up a "decision" slide that contains two hyperlinks — for example, one for digital products and one for audio products. The user would then click the hyperlink they want.

> **TIP**
>
> You can also create hyperlinks to custom shows by using action buttons. Action buttons are a special type of drawn shape that is designed specifically for creating hyperlinks within a presentation.

Using a custom show as the main presentation

If you have a complete show contained in one of your custom shows, you may sometimes want to show it as the default presentation. To do this, you must tell PowerPoint that you want to bypass the main presentation and start with the custom show.

The easiest way to show a custom show is to select it from the Custom Slide Show drop-down menu on the Slide Show tab. However, you can also set up a custom show to be the default show for the presentation by following these steps:

1. **On the Slide Show tab, click Set Up Slide Show in the Set Up group.** The Set Up Show dialog box appears.

2. **Click Custom Show, and then open the Custom show drop-down list and choose the show that you want to use, as shown in Figure 26.16.**

FIGURE 26.16

Use the Set Up Show dialog box to control which of your custom shows runs when you start the show.

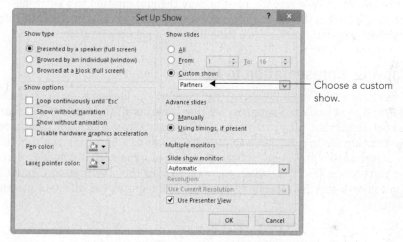

Choose a custom show.

3. **Click OK.** Now, when you start the show, the custom show runs.

> **TIP**
>
> You do not have to set up a custom show to narrow down the list of slides that appear when you run your presentation. You can choose which slides you want to show by using the From and To boxes in the Show slides section, shown in Figure 26.16. For example, to show slides 5 to 10, you would type **5** in the From box and **10** in the To box.

Giving a Presentation on a Different Computer

The computer on which you create a presentation is usually not the same computer that you will use to show it. For example, you may be doing the bulk of your work on your desktop computer in your office in Los Angeles but you need to use your laptop computer to give the presentation in Phoenix.

One way to transfer a presentation to another computer is simply to copy the PowerPoint file (the file with the .pptx file name extension) using a USB flash drive or other removable media. However, this method is imperfect because it assumes that the other computer has all of the fonts, sounds, and other elements that you need for every part of the show. This can be a dangerous assumption. For example, suppose your presentation contains a link to some Excel data. If you do not also copy the Excel file, then you cannot update the data when you are on the road.

A better way to ensure that you are taking everything you need while traveling is to use the Package Presentation for CD feature in PowerPoint. This feature reads all of the linked files and associated objects and ensures that they are transferred along with the main presentation. You do not actually need to copy the presentation to a writeable CD, and you do not need a CD-R or CD-RW drive to use this feature. You can copy the presentation package anywhere you want, such as to a flash drive or a network location.

Copying a presentation to CD

If you have a CD-R or CD-RW drive, then copying the presentation to CD is an attractive choice. It produces a self-running disc that contains all the presentation files and their needed linked files, plus a web page (HTML format) from which you can choose which presentation file to run. That web page also contains a hyperlink you can use to download the PowerPoint Viewer application if needed. (You need it only if PowerPoint itself is not installed on the PC on which you want to view the presentation.) Figure 26.17 shows a sample web page for accessing a package that contains two different presentations, for example.

FIGURE 26.17

The Package for CD command generates a CD containing all data files needed to show the presentation plus a browser-based interface like the one shown here.

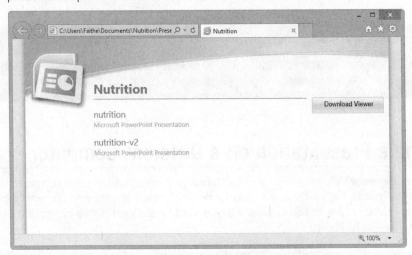

Here is the basic procedure, which is elaborated on in the following sections:

1. **Place a blank CD-R or CD-RW disc in your writeable CD or DVD drive.**

2. **Make sure the presentation is exactly the way you want it.** If you are using a CD-R disc, keep in mind that this disc type is not rewriteable, and so you should ensure that the presentation is exactly as you want it.

3. **Choose File ⇨ Export ⇨ Package Presentation for CD ⇨ Package for CD.** The Package for CD dialog box opens (Figure 26.18).

FIGURE 26.18

Use the Package for CD feature to place all of the necessary files for the presentation on a CD.

4. **Type a name for the CD; this is similar to adding a volume label for the disc.**

5. **(Optional) Add more files to the CD if you want.** See the next section, "Creating a CD containing multiple presentation files," for more details.

6. **(Optional) Set any options that you want.** See the section "Setting copy options" later in this chapter, for more details.

7. **Click Copy to CD.**

8. **If a warning appears asking if you want to include linked files in your package, click Yes.**

The CD-writing process may take several minutes, depending on the writing speed of your CD drive and the size of the presentation files that you are placing on it.

If a message appears that the package will not include comments, revisions, or ink annotations, click Continue. This message appears only if your presentation contains any of those things.

A message appears when the files are successfully copied to the CD asking whether you want to copy the same files to another CD.

9. **Click Yes or No.** If you choose No, then you must also click Close to close the Package for CD dialog box.

The resulting CD automatically plays the presentations when you insert it in any computer. You can also browse the CD's contents to open the PowerPoint Viewer separately and use it to play specific presentations.

> **CAUTION**
>
> File corruption can occur on a CD drive during the writing process. After burning a CD, test it thoroughly by running the complete presentation from CD before you rely on the CD copy as the version that you take with you while traveling.

Creating a CD containing multiple presentation files

By default, the active presentation is included on the CD, but you can also add others, up to the capacity of your disc. For example, if you have several versions of the same presentation for different audiences, a single CD can contain all of them. As you are preparing to copy the files using the Package for CD dialog box, shown in Figure 26.18, follow these steps to add more files:

1. **Click Add.** An Add dialog box opens, similar to the Open dialog box that you use to open PowerPoint files.

2. **Select the additional files that you want to include, and click Add to return to the Package for CD dialog box.** The list of files now appears as shown in Figure 26.19.

FIGURE 26.19

When you specify multiple files for a CD, you can specify the order in which they should play.

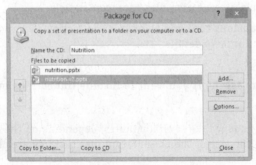

You can select multiple files from the same location by holding down the Ctrl key as you click the ones you want. To include multiple files from different locations, repeat steps 1 and 2 for each location.

3. **(Optional) Rearrange the list by clicking a presentation and then clicking the up or down arrow buttons to the left of the list.**

4. **If you need to remove a presentation from the list, click it and then click Remove.**

5. **Continue making the CD as you normally would.**

Setting copy options

The default copy options are suitable in most situations. However, you may sometimes want to modify them. To do this, open the Package Presentation for CD dialog box, and follow these steps:

1. **Click Options.** The Options dialog box opens (Figure 26.20).

FIGURE 26.20

You can set options for copying the presentations to a CD.

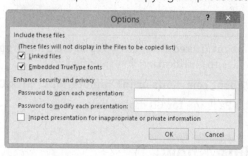

The Linked files check box is selected by default; this option tells PowerPoint to include the full copies of all linked files. You can deselect this option if you want; a static copy of the linked data will remain in the presentation, but the link will not work. You should leave this option selected if you have sounds or multimedia files in your presentation that are linked rather than embedded.

The Embedded TrueType fonts check box is also selected by default. If you are sure that the destination computer contains all of the fonts that are used in the presentation, then deselect this option. This makes the presentation file slightly smaller. Remember, not all fonts can be embedded; this depends on the level of embedding allowed by the font's manufacturer.

2. **If you want to add passwords for the presentations, do so in the Enhance Security and Privacy section.** There are separate text boxes for the password needed to open and the password needed to modify the presentation.

3. **Select the Inspect presentations for inappropriate or private information check box if you want to check the presentation for private information, such as your name or any comments.** The Document Inspector window opens. Select the types of content you want to check for and click Inspect.

4. **Click OK, and then write the CD as you normally would.**

Copying a presentation to other locations

Although it is not well known, you can also use the Package Presentation for CD feature to copy presentation files and their associated support files to any location you want. For example, you can transfer files to another computer on a network or place them on a USB flash drive or other removable media. To do so, follow these steps:

1. **In the Package for CD dialog box, set up the package exactly the way you want it, including all of the presentation files and options.** See the preceding sections for more information.

2. **Click Copy to Folder.** A Copy to Folder dialog box appears.

3. **Type a name for the new folder in the Folder name text box.**

4. **Type a path for the folder in the Location text box.** You also can use the Browse button to select the folder.

5. **Click OK.**

6. **If a warning appears about linked files, click Yes or No as appropriate.** PowerPoint copies the files to the location you specified.

7. **If a warning appears about comments or ink annotations, click Continue.**

8. **Click Close to close the Package for CD dialog box.**

Presenting an Online Show

Presenting online (which was called presentation broadcasting in earlier PowerPoint versions) enables you to show your presentation in real time via a network. This makes it possible for people to attend a live show when they cannot be there in person. It uses the Office Presentation Service, a free service that Microsoft makes available to PowerPoint users. You need a Microsoft account, which is also free, to use the service.

Before it's time to broadcast your presentation "for real," you will probably want to do a practice run to make sure you understand the broadcasting feature.

Follow these steps:

1. **Choose Slide Show ⇨ Start Slide Show ⇨ Present Online ⇨ Office Presentation Service.** The Present Online dialog box opens. See Figure 26.21.

FIGURE 26.21

Choose whether remote viewers can download the presentation, and then connect to a server.

2. **If desired, mark the Enable remote viewers to download the presentation check box.**

3. **If there are any warnings in the dialog box, as in Figure 26.21, click their hyperlinks to resolve the issues.** For example, in Figure 26.21, you could click Optimize Media. If you follow one of these hyperlinks, repeat steps 1 and 2 to return to this spot after you are finished.

4. **Click Connect.** You are connected to the broadcast server. (You may be prompted for your sign-in information; sign in if prompted.) A link appears for participants to use to see the broadcast.

5. **Copy this link to the Clipboard (click Copy Link, or select it and press Ctrl+C) and then paste it into an e-mail, instant message, or other medium through which you want to share it with others.** You can click Send in E-Mail to automatically start a new e-mail containing the link.

6. **Click Start Presentation.** The show begins in Slide Show view on your PC.

7. **Show the presentation as you would normally.** When you are finished, Normal view reappears.

8. **On the Present Online tab on the Ribbon, click End Online Presentation.**

9. **At the confirmation box, click End Online Presentation.**

As you are broadcasting, a Present Online tab appears in Normal view. (You can return to Normal view at any time to work with it.) There you'll find the following options, as shown in Figure 26.22:

- **Use Presenter View:** If you have more than one monitor, you can choose to use Presenter view on one of them by marking this check box.

- **Share Meeting Notes:** When you click Share Meeting Notes, a Choose Notes to Share with Meeting dialog box opens. Click the New Notebook button, and OneNote appears. Use it to create a new notebook, and then close OneNote and return to PowerPoint. In the Choose Notes to Share with Meeting dialog box, click the plus sign next to the new notebook to view its sections; click New Section 1 to select it. Then click the OK button to close the dialog box. The notebook opens in OneNote; you can switch back and forth between this notebook and PowerPoint as the presentation progresses.

- **Send Invitations:** Use this command to reopen the dialog box containing the link to the presentation URL, in case you need to send it to anyone else.

FIGURE 26.22

Use the Present Online tab to set options for your broadcast.

Working with Audio-Visual Equipment

The first part of this chapter assumed that you were using a computer with a single monitor to show your presentation, but this may not always be the case. This part of the chapter looks at the entire range of audio-visual options from which you can choose. There are many models of projection equipment in conference rooms all across the world, but most of them fall into one of these categories:

- **Noncomputerized equipment:** This can include an overhead transparency viewer, a 35mm slide projector, or other older technology. You face two challenges if you need to work with this category of equipment: One challenge is figuring out how the equipment works because every model is different, and the other challenge is producing attractive versions of your slides to work with the older technology. There are companies that can produce 35mm slides from your PowerPoint files, or you can invest in a slide-making machine yourself. For transparencies, you simply print your slides on transparency film that is designed for your type of printer.

- **Single computer with a single monitor:** If there is a computer with a monitor in the meeting room, then you can run your presentation on that computer. You can do this with the Package Presentation for CD feature that is discussed in the preceding sections and then run the presentation directly from the CD, provided that PC has PowerPoint or the PowerPoint Viewer on it.

- **Single computer with a dual-monitor system:** On systems with dual monitors, one monitor is shown to the audience and the other is for your own use, via Presenter View. This is useful when you want to display your speaker notes on the monitor that the audience does not see. However, you might need to set up multi-monitor support in Windows so that you can view different displays on each monitor.

- **Projection system (LCD) or large monitor without a computer:** If the meeting room has a large monitor but no computer, you will need to bring your own laptop computer and connect it to the monitor. Most of these systems use a standard VGA plug and cable.

The following sections look at some of these options in more detail.

Presenting with two screens

If you have two monitors — either your laptop computer screen and an external monitor or two external monitors hooked up to the same computer — you can display the presentation on one of them and your own notes on the other one. This is a very handy setup! The details are covered in the next sections.

> **CAUTION**
>
> To use two screens, you need the full version of PowerPoint on your laptop, not just the PowerPoint Viewer. You also need compatible hardware. For example, your laptop must have an external VGA port and a built-in video card that supports DualView (a Windows feature) in your version of Windows. If you have a desktop computer, you must have two separate video cards or a video card with two separate video ports.

Configuring display hardware for multi-screen viewing

First, you need to prepare your hardware. On a laptop computer, this means enabling both the built-in and the external monitor ports and connecting an external monitor. Some laptops toggle between internal, external, and dual monitors with an Fn key combination; refer to your laptop's documentation.

On a desktop computer, install a second video card and monitor, and then do the following to set them up in Windows:

1. **When Windows restarts after you install the second video card, right-click the Desktop and choose Screen Resolution.**

   A sample area displays two monitors. Figure 26.23 shows the Screen Resolution dialog box for Windows 7; the dialog boxes for other Windows versions are similar.

FIGURE 26.23

You must set up the second monitor in Windows before setting it up in PowerPoint.

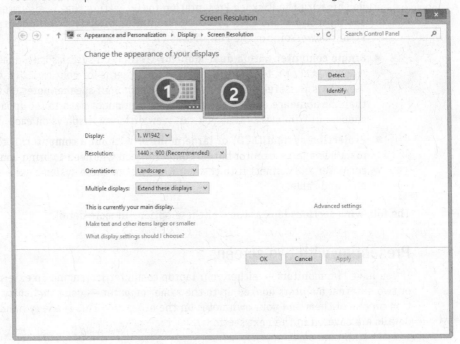

The monitor that you use most of the time should be monitor 1, and the other one should be monitor 2. To determine which is which, click Identify; large numbers appear briefly on each screen.

2. **If you need to swap the numbering of the monitors, click the one that should be the primary monitor and then select Make this my main display.** This option will be unavailable if the currently selected monitor is already set to be the primary one.

3. **Select the secondary monitor, and then select Extend these displays from the Multiple displays drop-down list.**

4. **(Optional) If the monitors are not arranged in the sample area in the way that they are physically positioned on your desk, drag the icons for the monitors to where you want them.**

5. **(Optional) Click a monitor in the sample area to adjust its display settings.**

6. **Click OK.** You are now ready to work with the two monitors in PowerPoint.

You can now drag items from your primary monitor to your secondary one! This can also be useful outside of PowerPoint. For example, you can have two applications open at once, each in its own monitor window.

TIP

In Windows 8, after you attach the second monitor, you can press the Windows key+P to open the Second screen pane at right and choose what appears on the second screen.

Setting up a presentation for two screens

If you have two monitors available, and configured as described in the preceding section, you can use the following steps to help PowerPoint recognize and take advantage of these monitors:

1. **Open the presentation in PowerPoint.**

2. **On the Slide Show tab, click Set Up Slide Show in the Set Up group.** The Set Up Show dialog box opens (Figure 26.24).

FIGURE 26.24

You can set up the show for multiple monitors in the Set Up Show dialog box.

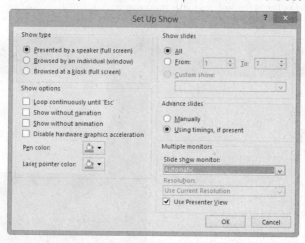

3. **In the Multiple monitors section, open the Slide show monitor drop-down list and choose the monitor that the audience will see.** This list shows only Automatic and Primary Monitor if you do not have multiple monitors enabled (see the preceding section).

4. **Select the Use Presenter View check box.** This will give you a separate, very useful control panel on the other monitor during the show, as described in the next section.

5. **Click OK.** You are now ready to show the presentation using two separate displays — one for you and one for the audience.

Presenting with two screens using Presenter View

Presenter View is a special view of the presentation that is available on systems with more than one monitor if you have enabled Presenter View, as described in the preceding section. This view provides many useful tools for managing the show behind the scenes, as shown in Figure 26.25. It appears automatically on the non-audience monitor when you enter Slide Show view.

TIP

New in PowerPoint 2013, you can experiment with Presenter View even if you don't have multiple monitors. While in Slide Show view, right-click anywhere and then choose Show Presenter View.

FIGURE 26.25

Presenter View provides tools for helping you manage your slide show from a second monitor.

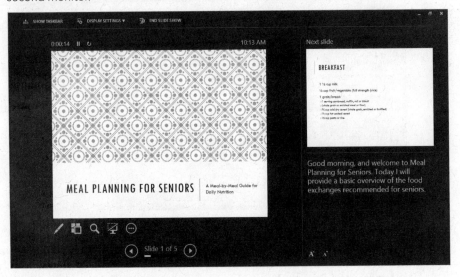

Here are some of the key features of Presenter View:

- The current slide (the one the audience is viewing) appears at the left. The next slide appears at the upper right.

- The speaker notes for each slide appear in the lower-right pane. You cannot edit them from here, however. Buttons for making the text larger or smaller appear below the speaker notes pane so you can adjust the font size.

- A time and duration display appears above the current slide. It tells you the current time and how long this slide has been displayed.

- Below the current slide are a series of icons that roughly correspond to the icons you see in Slide Show view in the lower-left corner. From left to right, they are as follows:

  - **Pen and Laser Pointer Tools:** Opens a menu from which you can choose a pen, laser pointer, highlighter, or arrow and choose the ink color. You can also erase any annotations you have made with the Eraser tool here.

  - **See All Slides:** Opens a page of thumbnail images of all the slides in the presentation so you can quickly jump to the one you want

  - **Zoom:** Zooms in on a part of the slide

  - **Black or Unblack Slide Show:** Toggles between showing the slide and showing a black screen

  - **More Slide Show Options:** Opens a menu of additional control options. For example, you can hide Presenter view from here, show a black or white screen, show or hide ink markup, get help, or end the show.

- Forward and back arrows appear at the bottom of the screen; you can use these to move through the presentation.

- At the top of the screen are three buttons:

  - **Show Taskbar:** Shows or hides the Windows taskbar so you can switch out of Slide Show view to take care of some other task

  - **Display Settings:** Opens a menu from which you can see which monitor is displaying Presenter View and which is displaying the full-screen show to the audience and switch them if you like

  - **End Slide Show.** Exits from Slide Show view

- The panes are adjustable by dragging the dividers between them, so you can have larger thumbnails, a smaller slide display, more or less room for notes, and so on.

Summary

In this chapter, you learned how to prepare for a big presentation. You now know how to:

- Control a presentation on-screen using your computer.
- Jump to different slides and take notes on-screen during a meeting.
- Create and run a custom show.
- Package a presentation and move it to another computer.
- Set up single and multi-screen audio-visual equipment to work with your laptop.

Part V

Organizing Messages, Contacts, and Time with Outlook

Most versions of Office 2013 include Outlook 2013. While often primarily thought of as an e-mail program, Outlook also enables you to organize messages, maintain detailed contact information, stay on top of your schedule, and manage your list of tasks. You can use Outlook for any of these features by itself, or all of them, as required for your personal time management. This part of the book introduces you to each of the core functions in Outlook.

Fundamentals of E-mail

IN THIS CHAPTER

Before you can send and receive e-mail using Outlook 2013, you must set up at least one e-mail account, providing Outlook with the information it needs to connect to your online e-mail account. From there, you can compose, send, and receive messages. Outlook provides great tools for creating and organizing your messages, as well as options for customizing how it works with your messages. This chapter helps you learn the basics for all of those actions in Outlook.

Setting Up Your E-mail Accounts

Before you can use Outlook to send and receive e-mail, you must set up your e-mail account. You can have more than one account — you'll follow the same steps for each one. There are two parts to this.

First, your account must be set up on the server or at your ISP. This is not done in Outlook. If your account is at your workplace, it will likely have been set up by an IT person, and he or she will have provided you with the required information such as your e-mail address and login and password information. If you are setting up a home or small-business account, you may be doing this yourself. The details depend on your ISP, and as part of the process you will need to specify your credentials to gain access.

Second, you must set up your account in Outlook. This process provides Outlook with the information, such as your e-mail address or login/user name and password, that are needed to connect to your e-mail server and send and receive messages. If you are at work, you may be lucky enough to have an IT administrator set up Outlook for you, in which case you can skip this section. If you must do it yourself, the minimum information you need is your login and password. You may also need to know the addresses for your organization's or ISP's e-mail server. The URL looks much like a web page address and will be something like mail.hosting.com. Some mail accounts require two addresses, one for incoming mail and another for outgoing mail.

Outlook supports several different kinds of e-mail accounts including a Microsoft Exchange Server account. The account setup process differs depending on whether you have an Exchange account, a web-based account such as Outlook.com or Gmail, or one of the other supported account types (POP and IMAP). All of these procedures are covered in the following sections.

E-mail Terminology

E-mail acronyms can be confusing! *POP* stands for Post Office Protocol, a technology for receiving e-mail. You'll also see *POP3* used; they mean the same thing. *IMAP* stands for Internet Mail Access Protocol, another incoming mail technology. *SMTP* is Simple Mail Transfer Protocol, the almost universally used technology for sending e-mail.

Automatic e-mail account setup

Outlook can automatically configure some e-mail accounts, a feature called Auto Account Setup. This works for some but not all POP, IMAP, Exchange Server, or web-based accounts.

To use the automated e-mail account setup feature in many cases, you need to have your e-mail address and your password. (You may not even need that much information if your company server is set up to automate account setup.) Then, here are the steps to follow:

1. **Choose File ⇨ Info, and then click the Add Account button to display the Add Account dialog box.** The dialog box, shown in Figure 27.1, asks for three pieces of information:

   - Your name
   - Your e-mail address
   - Your password

FIGURE 27.1

The Add Account dialog box

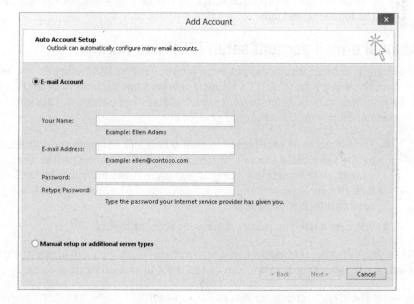

2. **After you enter the information, click Next.** Outlook will try to connect to your e-mail server and set up the account.

If you are continuing with automatic account setup, Outlook will attempt to connect to your e-mail server and set up the account. In most cases, this will work just as it is supposed to, and you will just click the Finish button in the Add Account dialog box. The new account will be listed in the accounts drop-down list on the Info page in Backstage, and you'll be able to start sending and receiving messages. However, this automated process does not always work. You may encounter one of the following situations:

- Outlook tells you that it cannot establish an encrypted connection to the server and offers to try again using an unencrypted connection. Click Next to proceed. The process will either complete properly or you'll encounter one of the other conditions in this list.

- Outlook cannot establish a connection to your account and asks you to verify the spelling of your e-mail address. Make any needed corrections and click Next to try again. The process will either complete properly or you'll encounter the final condition in this list.

- If the preceding steps fail, Outlook will require that you manually configure the server settings. The Manual setup or additional server types option will be automatically selected in the Add Account dialog box. Click Next to continue. The manual account setup steps differ for the various account types and are covered in the following sections.

Manual e-mail account setup (POP and IMAP)

If automatic account setup does not work for your POP or IMAP account, you will have to perform the setup manually. It's a bit more involved but nothing to be afraid of. You need some information in addition to your e-mail address and password. This information should be available from your ISP or your IT person:

- The addresses of your incoming mail server and outgoing mail server. These may be the same but are usually different. For POP incoming mail servers, the address usually looks something like `pop.example.com`. For outgoing mail servers, it may look like `mail.example.com` or `smtp.example.com`. Your ISP will provide the correct information to enter.

- The user name and password for your account login.

When you have this information, you are ready to begin. You will arrive at this dialog box if automatic setup failed, so you can go to Step 4 in the following process.

Here are the steps to follow for manual account setup:

1. **Choose File ➪ Info, and then click the Add Account button to display the Add Account dialog box.**

2. **Select the Manual setup or additional server types option.**

3. **Click Next to display the dialog box shown in Figure 27.2.** This is where you select the type of account to set up.

FIGURE 27.2

Select the type of account to set up.

4. **Select the POP or IMAP option, and then click Next.** In the dialog box shown in Figure 27.3, enter all the requested information in the corresponding boxes, and be sure to select the type of e-mail server from the Account Type list. The Remember password and Require logon using secure password authentication (SPA) options are explained later in this chapter. Most people should leave these at their default settings. The More Settings button is also explained later in this chapter.

5. **After you have entered all the information, click the Test Account Settings button.** If the test works, click Next and then Finish to complete the account setup. If the test does not work, please refer to the next section ("If your account settings don't work") for steps to resolve the problem.

Two other options of note are available in the Add Account dialog box. If you select the Remember password option, Outlook will be able to log on automatically to your e-mail account as needed. Otherwise, you will be prompted for the password each time you send and receive e-mail.

Secure Password Authentication (SPA) is an additional level of security that some mail servers have implemented. If your server requires this, you should have been told and given any additional credentials required for login. You would need to check the Require logon using Secure Password Authentication (SPA) option shown in Figure 27.3.

FIGURE 27.3

Entering required information for manual POP or IMAP e-mail account setup

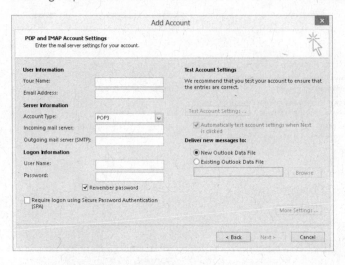

If your account settings don't work

It's not uncommon for e-mail account settings to not work at first. When you click the Test Account Settings button, Outlook tries to log on to your incoming mail server and send a test message via your outgoing mail server. One or both of these tests may fail, and the results shown in the Test Account Settings dialog box (shown in Figure 27.4, which depicts a failed test) will tell you the results. Note also that this dialog box has an Errors tab, shown in Figure 27.5. The information on this tab may give you a clue as to where the problem lies. For example, if the problem is reported as "Your e-mail server rejected your login," the problem almost surely lies with the user name or password that you entered.

The most common cause of problems is simply mistyping some of the information required in the account setup dialog box. Everything must be 100 percent correct!

FIGURE 27.4

This dialog box displays the results of testing your e-mail account settings.

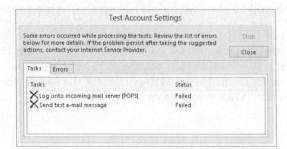

If the test failed in the outgoing mail server part, it most likely means that your outgoing mail server requires authentication. Setting this option is examined in the following section.

FIGURE 27.5

The Errors tab provides details on why the Account Settings Test failed.

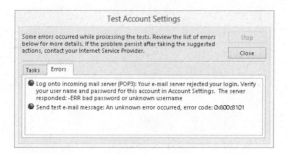

More account settings

The Add Account dialog box, shown in Figure 27.3, has a button labeled More Settings. You may not need to make any changes here, but if you do, you can refer to this section for the details.

Clicking the More Settings button brings up the Internet E-mail Settings dialog box. This dialog box has four tabs for POP and IMAP accounts and a fifth for IMAP accounts only. The next sections look at these in turn.

General

The General tab, shown in Figure 27.6, has these three entries:

- **Mail Account:** This is the name Outlook uses to refer to the account, for example, in the Account list. The default is your e-mail address, but you can change it to anything you like, such as *Work E-mail* or *Windows Live Account*.

- **Organization:** If you enter your organization name here, it will be included in the headers of all e-mail messages you send. Recipients normally do not see these headers, and Outlook does not make use of this information in any way. Other e-mail programs may, however.

- **Reply E-mail:** When recipients receive an e-mail from you and reply by clicking the Reply button in their e-mail program, their reply message is sent to this address. By default, it is the e-mail address associated with the current e-mail account, but if you have more than one e-mail account, you can enter another address here.

FIGURE 27.6

The General tab in the Internet E-mail Settings dialog box

Outgoing Server

The Outgoing Server tab, shown in Figure 27.7, lets you specify authentication — that is, login — settings for your outgoing mail server. By default, this option is turned off because many outgoing mail servers do not require authentication. If yours does, select the My Outgoing Server (SMTP) Requires Authentication box, and then select other options and enter information as follows:

- **Use same settings as my incoming mail server:** Outlook will log on to your outgoing mail server using the same user name and password that you specified for your incoming mail server. This is the most commonly used setting.

- **Log on using:** Select this option if your outgoing server requires different credentials than for retrieving your mail. Then enter your User Name and Password in the corresponding fields. The Remember Password and Require Secure Password Authentication (SPA) options work the same as was described for them in the previous section, "Manual e-mail account setup (POP and IMAP)."

- **Log on to incoming mail server before sending mail:** Select this option only if your incoming mail server is the same as your outgoing mail server. You will know that this is the case when you are given the same address for both servers and enter this address for both during account setup.

Advanced

The Advanced tab contains options that most people will never need to change. You may not be "most people," however, so I explain these settings here. Note that the options available on this tab differ slightly for POP and IMAP accounts. Figure 27.8 shows the tab for POP accounts.

FIGURE 27.7

The Outgoing Server tab in the Internet E-mail Settings dialog box

FIGURE 27.8

The Advanced tab for POP accounts in the Internet E-mail Settings dialog box

The advanced settings that are common to both POP and IMAP accounts are the following:

- **Server Port Numbers, Incoming server:** The default values are 110 for POP servers and 143 for IMAP servers. For security reasons, many corporate servers are set up on different ports, so if yours is, you can enter the correct port numbers here.

- **Server Port Numbers, Outgoing server:** Regardless of whether your incoming server is POP or IMAP, your outgoing server will use SMTP, and the default port number is 25. Do not change this unless you know that your outgoing mail server uses a different port.

- **Server Timeouts.** This is the amount of time that Outlook will wait for the mail server to respond when retrieving or sending e-mail. The default setting of 1 minute works fine in most cases. If you find Outlook timing out, it probably means that you are working over a slow connection or that your server is often busy. Try a longer time-out setting to resolve this problem.

POP accounts also include the This server requires an encrypted connection (SSL) setting. Turn this option on for the incoming or outgoing mail server, or both, if required.

If you are working with an IMAP account, there is one unique option, Root Folder Path, which specifies the root folder of the mailbox. Normally, you can leave this blank and Outlook will use the default root folder on the server. If you need to specify a different root folder, enter it here.

If you are working with a POP account, you have several settings available that control how Outlook handles messages on the server:

- **Leave a copy of messages on the server:** By default, messages that you have received are removed from the server as soon as they are downloaded to Outlook. Turn this option on if you want Outlook to leave the messages on the server after download. This can be useful if you want to retrieve your messages later from another computer.

- **Remove from server after x days:** Specifies how long messages are to be retained on the server after they have been downloaded.

- **Remove from server when deleted from 'Deleted Items':** A message is retained on the server until you permanently delete it in Outlook.

To work with message handling settings for an IMAP account, use the Sent Items and Deleted Items sections on the Advanced tab in the Internet E-mail Settings dialog box.

Manual e-mail account setup (Exchange Server)

If automatic account setup does not work for your Exchange account, you must exit Outlook and set up the account through the Windows Control Panel. Although some of the dialog boxes look the same, you cannot set up an Exchange account manually while Outlook is running. To complete this setup, you need to know the DNS address of your Exchange server (typically), the user name that has been set up for you, and your password.

Downloading an Exchange Profile

Some Exchange account providers give you the option of downloading an Exchange profile file to your computer. When you run this file, it sets up the Exchange profile for you. If available, this is an easy and error-free way to set up an Exchange profile.

These are the steps to set up an Exchange account:

1. **Make sure that Outlook is not running.**

2. **Start Control Panel.** In Windows 8 from the desktop, select the Settings charm, and then click Control Panel under Settings. In Windows 7, select the Control Panel from the Windows Start menu.

3. **Type** Mail **in the search box in the upper-right corner of the Control Panel window.**

4. **Click the Mail choice in the list of results to display the Mail Setup - Outlook dialog box.**

5. **Click the E-mail Accounts button to open the Account Settings dialog box.** This is the same dialog box that you can use when editing accounts from within Outlook, a topic you'll learn about shortly.

6. **On the E-mail tab, click the New button to display the Add Account dialog box.**

7. **Select the Manual setup or additional server types option, and then click Next.**

8. **In the next dialog box, select the Microsoft Exchange Server or compatible service option, and then click Next.**

9. **In the next dialog box, shown in Figure 27.9, enter your Exchange Server address and User Name, and then click Next.**

FIGURE 27.9

Entering information about your Exchange server and user name

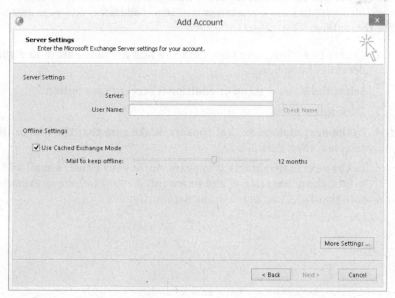

10. **If a dialog box appears asking whether you want to continue, click OK.**

11. **Click Finish.**

After setting up your account, you can start Outlook. You will be prompted for the Exchange account password. If the connection is established, Outlook displays "Connected to Microsoft Exchange" at the right end of the status bar (which is at the bottom of the Outlook window).

Manual e-mail account setup (web)

You may have a web-based e-mail account if you have signed up for Outlook.com, Gmail, or Yahoo! Mail. Or, you may have an older existing account from Windows Live or Hotmail. Other e-mail providers may also have web-based e-mail accounts that are compatible with Outlook. If so, they will have provided you with the information you need to set up the account when you signed up.

Webmail accounts are designed primarily for web use — that is, you will use a browser such as Internet Explorer to log on to your e-mail account and read and send messages. However, it can be useful to set up an Outlook account for your webmail, too, so that you can download and read mail in Outlook and use the program's various features to organize your messages. Be aware that not all web e-mail accounts are compatible with Outlook, and for some, such as Gmail, you have to enable an account option for POP e-mail. For others, such as Yahoo! Mail in the U.S., you have to sign up for a premium mail service.

To set up your web e-mail account in Outlook, you need your e-mail address and password. You will also need to know the address mail server addresses and your user name. Then, follow these steps:

1. **Choose File ⇨ Info, and then click the Add Account button to display the Add Account dialog box.**

2. **Select the Manual setup or additional server types option.**

3. **Click Next.**

4. **In the next dialog box that appears, make sure that the POP or IMAP option is selected; then click Next.**

5. **In the next dialog box that appears, enter your name, e-mail address, server information, user name, and password.** Figure 27.10 shows example entries. Make sure that POP3 is selected in the Account Type list.

FIGURE 27.10

Entering information for manual webmail account setup

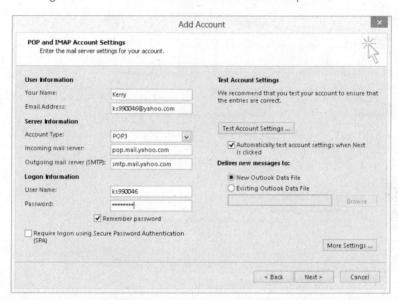

6. **Click Next to complete account setup as for other account types.**

TIP

The Microsoft Support article at `http://support.microsoft.com/kb/2758902` has listings of the ingoing and outgoing mail server addresses for leading webmail services. If you can't find the right addresses in your service provider's help information, try the addresses listed in this article.

Modifying Account Settings

If you should need to change your account settings, the procedure is similar to setting up the account in the first place. Choose File⇨Info, click the Account Settings button, and then click Account Settings to display the Account Settings dialog box. Make sure that the E-mail tab is displayed, as shown in Figure 27.11. Select the account of interest (necessary only if you have more than one) and then click the Change button. You are taken through one or more dialog boxes where you can view and change the settings for this account. The settings depend on the type of account and were explained earlier in this chapter in the section on setting up e-mail accounts.

FIGURE 27.11

Work with settings for existing accounts here.

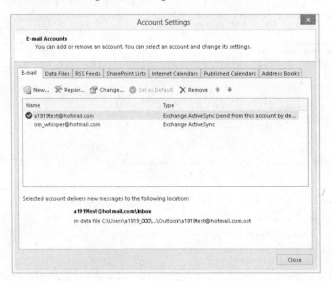

You can take several other actions with e-mail accounts in the Account Settings dialog box, as follows:

- **Repair:** Outlook tries to connect to your e-mail provider and refresh your account settings. This is the first step to try if an e-mail account has suddenly stopped working.

- **Remove:** Deletes the account

- **Set as Default:** If you have two or more e-mail accounts, this option makes the selected account the default.

What exactly is the default e-mail account? It's the account that is used to send e-mail messages that you create from scratch. When you create an e-mail message by replying to a message you have received, it is sent using the account that the message was received through. Note, however, that when you are composing an e-mail message, you can always change the account that the message is to be sent from. This feature is explained in the later section titled "Changing the send account."

Using Outlook Profiles

An *Outlook profile* stores information about a user's accounts and settings. All Outlook users have at least one profile, and for many people that is all that is needed. In some circumstances, multiple profiles can be useful. This section explains how to create and use profiles in Outlook.

Understanding profiles

In the first part of this chapter, you learned how to set up your e-mail accounts. Later chapters in this part of the book deal with configuring other aspects of Outlook such as RSS feeds and the screen appearance. All this information constitutes your profile. The vast majority of users never need more than one profile, but in some situations they can be useful, such as the following:

- If you want to completely segregate two or more types of information, such as work and personal, you can create a profile for each.

- If you want to keep your regular POP and IMAP e-mail accounts separate from an Exchange account

- If more than one person uses the same computer, each person can have his or her own profile.

The third reason is usually a moot point because Windows 7 and 8 provide for different user accounts for signing in to Windows, which automatically gives each user his or her own Outlook profile. If, however, you want more than one person to use the same Windows sign-in and have separate Outlook data, you can use profiles.

Please note that creating an Outlook profile is not the same as creating a separate personal folder file. Although a given Outlook profile can have one or more personal folder files, each profile's folders are usually kept separate from other profiles.

Creating a new profile

When you first install Outlook, a wizard walks you through the steps of creating a profile. To create a new profile, you do not use Outlook, but rather the Windows Control Panel, as follows:

1. **Open the Control Panel.** In Windows 8 from the desktop, select the Settings charm, and then click Control Panel under Settings. In Windows 7, select the Control Panel from the Windows Start menu.

2. **Type** Mail **in the search box in the upper-right corner.**

3. **Click the Mail choice in the list of results.** The Mail Setup – Outlook dialog box appears.

4. **Click the Show Profiles button to open the Mail dialog box.** This dialog box lists the existing profiles; the default profile is named *Outlook*.

5. **Click the Add button to open the New Profile dialog box.**

6. **Enter a name for the new profile and click OK.**

7. **Follow the on-screen prompts to set up your e-mail account.** This procedure is covered earlier in this chapter.

Other actions you can take in the Mail dialog box are the following:

- **Remove:** Removes the selected profile from the system.
- **Properties:** Lets you view and edit the properties of the profile including the e-mail account settings and data files.
- **Copy:** Makes a copy of the selected profile under a new name. This is useful if you want a new profile that has some of the same settings as an existing one. Create a copy, then edit it as needed.
- **Prompt for a profile to be used:** If this option is selected and you have more than one profile, Outlook will prompt you to select the profile you want to use each time the program starts.
- **Always use this profile:** Select the profile that you want Outlook to use from the list.

Switching profiles

You cannot switch from one profile to another while Outlook is running. If you selected the Prompt for a profile option (as explained in the preceding section), quit Outlook and restart it; then select the desired profile when prompted.

If you selected the Always Use This Profile option (also explained in the preceding section), you must perform the following steps:

1. **Quit Outlook.**
2. **Open the Control Panel.**
3. **In the Control Panel, open Mail.**
4. **Click the Show Profiles button.**
5. **Select the Prompt for a profile to be used option.**
6. **Close all dialog boxes.**
7. **Restart Outlook.**

Composing and Sending Messages

Outlook's e-mail features are sophisticated and comprehensive. Underneath all that power, however, are the fundamental tasks of composing, sending, and reading messages. This section explains the basics of composing and sending e-mail messages.

Quick compose and send

Outlook provides much flexibility when it comes to creating and formatting e-mail messages. Often, however, all you want to do is to quickly create and send a basic message. Here's how:

1. **Click Mail button in the Navigation Bar.** The new navigation bar
2. **On the Home tab, click the New Email button in the New group to create a new, blank e-mail message.** The new message appears, as shown in Figure 27.12.

FIGURE 27.12

A blank e-mail message ready to be composed and sent

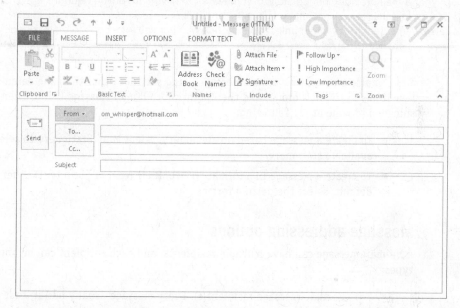

3. **Type the recipient's address in the To field; or click the To button, select a recipient from your Address Book, and click OK.**
4. **Type the message subject in the Subject text box.**
5. **Type the body of the message in the main section of the message window.**
6. **Click the Send button.**

That's all there is to it. Depending on Outlook's Send and Receive options, your message is sent immediately or placed in the Outbox to be sent the next time a Send or Receive is performed. If you want to be sure that the message is sent immediately, press F9.

Sending a Message

When you click the Send button to send an e-mail message, Outlook places the message in the Outbox. This is one of the mail folders displayed in the Folder Pane at left, which is collapsed by default. Depending on your connection status and Outlook option settings, the message may be transmitted to your e-mail provider immediately, or it may wait until you are online or until a timed Send/Receive occurs. In either case, once the message is sent, it is removed from the Outbox folder, and a copy is saved in the Sent Items folder unless your settings do not call for a copy to be retained.

You can also create a new e-mail message using settings other than the defaults by clicking New Items in the New group, and then pointing to E-mail Message Using. Then, in the submenu, do one of the following:

- To create a message based on stationery, select More Stationery to select from all available stationery.

- To create a message in a format (HTML, Rich Text, or plain text) other than the default, select the desired format.

Message addressing options

An e-mail message can have multiple recipients, and each recipient can be one of three types:

- **To:** The main message recipient(s). Every message usually has at least one recipient in the To field.

- **Cc (Carbon Copy):** Generally you use Cc when a person needs to be aware of the content of the message but is not a primary recipient — that is, does not need to respond or take action. All recipients of a message can see who is in the Cc list.

- **Bcc (Blind Carbon Copy):** This is like Cc, but the names and e-mail addresses of Bcc recipients are not visible to any other recipients of the message.

> **TIP**
>
> By default, an e-mail window does not display the Bcc field with the other addressing information; it displays just the To and Cc fields. If you want the Bcc field displayed, click the Options tab at the top of the message window and click the Bcc button in the Show Fields group.

Changing the Reply To address

By default, the Reply To address that is part of every e-mail message you send is the reply address that you specified when you set up the e-mail account or the account you select using the From button in the message window when you have multiple accounts set up. There may be situations in which you want replies to a message that you send directed to an e-mail address that's different from the address used to send the message. To do so, follow these steps:

1. **In the message window, click the Direct Replies To button in the More Options group of the Options tab on the Ribbon.** Outlook will open the Message Options dialog box.

2. **Under Delivery options, make sure that the Have replies sent to option is checked.**

3. **Enter the desired reply address in the adjacent text box, or click the Select Names button to choose from your Address Book.**

4. **Click Close.**

Entering recipients manually

You can type recipients directly into the To, Cc, and Bcc fields. To enter more than one recipient in a field, use a semicolon as a separator between addresses.

By default, Outlook's AutoComplete feature is turned on for all recipient fields. As you start entering an address or name, Outlook displays suggestions based on what you have entered in the past. The suggestions come from a list of names and e-mail addresses that you have entered previously. Outlook will narrow the list as you enter more of the name or address. If the recipient you want is displayed, select it by clicking. You can also highlight it with the up- and down-arrow keys and press Enter. Otherwise, just continue typing in the full name or address.

When Outlook is first installed, the AutoComplete list is empty, so it may seem to not be working. As you continue to use Outlook, however, it will become a useful tool. Names that you use less frequently move to the bottom of the list and eventually disappear.

Entering recipients from your contacts (Address Book)

Any recipients you have added as Contacts (see Chapter 29) are listed in your Address Book and can be added to an e-mail message with a few clicks. If you refer back to Figure 27.12, you can see that the e-mail window has To and Cc buttons next to the corresponding fields. If the Bcc field is visible, it will have an adjacent Bcc button. Click on any of these buttons to open the Select Names dialog box, shown in Figure 27.13.

27

FIGURE 27.13

Selecting e-mail recipients from your Address Book

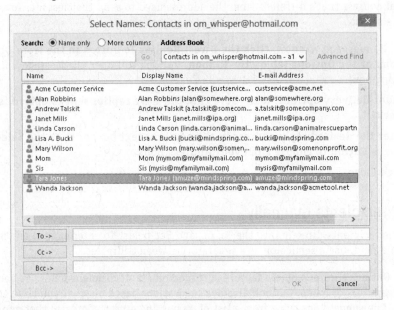

Deleting AutoComplete Items

If someone changes his or her e-mail address, you may find that old, invalid address still appearing on the AutoComplete list. When the list is displayed and you see an address that you no longer want, use the down-arrow key to highlight it; then press Delete.

If you have more than one Address Book, you should select it from the Address Book drop-down list. The default Address Book, which is adequate for many Outlook users, is called *Contacts*. The entries in the selected Address Book are displayed in an alphabetized list. Then, add recipients to your message as follows:

- Select a single recipient by clicking it. Select multiple recipients by holding down Ctrl while clicking.

- Add the selected recipient(s) to the To, Cc, or Bcc field by clicking on the corresponding button.

- Add the selected recipients to the active field by pressing Enter. The active field is the one corresponding to the button you clicked — To, Cc, or Bcc — to display the Select Names dialog box.

- Add a single recipient to the active field by double-clicking on the recipient in the list.

- To remove a recipient from the To, Cc, or Bcc field, click it — the entire name will become highlighted — and press Delete.

When you are finished adding recipients, click the OK button to return to the message.

Sending attachments

An *attachment* is a file that you send along with an e-mail message. When the recipient receives the message, he or she can save the file to disk and open it. Attachments can be a very useful way to pass documents around — whether you're sending photos of the kids to other family members or distributing a Word document to your colleagues for review.

You should be aware of some concerns with attachments. One has to do with file size. Most e-mail accounts limit the size of attachments that can accompany an e-mail message. The limit varies between different accounts, but 10 MB is a common figure. Even if your account allows you to send large attachments, the recipient's account may prohibit receiving them.

Another concern about attachments relates to security. Certain types of files can harm your computer by introducing a virus or by other means. Outlook and other e-mail client programs block potentially harmful attachments based on the file name extension, which indicates the type of file. For example, executable program files use the .exe extension and are blocked by Outlook.

One approach to dealing with both of these concerns is to use a file-archiving utility to compress your files into a ZIP or other kind of archive. Compression not only reduces the file size but also may enable you to send certain types of files that might be blocked on the receiving end based on settings in the recipient's e-mail program or settings on the ISP or company e-mail server.

What kinds of files can you send and receive as attachments (when not blocked as noted above)? Any image file is okay, including those with the .jpg, .gif, .png, and .tif extensions. So are text files (.txt extension), XML files (.xml extension), PDF files, and most Microsoft Office documents: Word (.doc and .docx extensions), Excel (.xls and .xlsx extensions), and PowerPoint (.ppt and .pptx extensions). ZIP archives (.zip extension) are OK, too.

When you are composing an e-mail message, you attach a file as follows:

1. **If necessary, click the Message tab on the Ribbon in the message window.**

2. **Click the Attach File button (with a paper clip icon) in the Include group.**
   Outlook opens the Insert File dialog box, which looks like any other dialog box for opening or saving files.

3. **If necessary, navigate to the folder containing the file.**

27

4. **Click on the name of the file to attach.** To attach multiple files from the same folder, hold down the Ctrl key while clicking.

5. **Click the Insert button.** From that point you can finish creating the message as necessary and click Send.

After you have attached one or more files, the message displays an Attached line in the header, as shown in Figure 27.14. The attached files are listed here along with the file size. If you change your mind and want to remove a file, click on its name in the Attached box and press Delete.

FIGURE 27.14

The names of attached files are displayed in the message header.

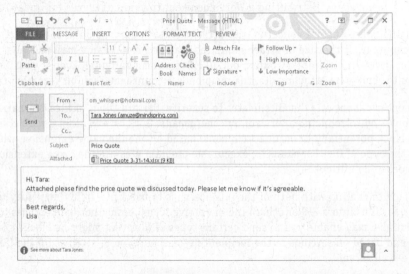

Reading and Replying to Messages

When Outlook receives an e-mail message, it places it in your Inbox folder by default, as shown in Figure 27.15. To view the Folder Pane, which is collapsed by default, click the arrow button (Expand the Folder Pane) at the top of the collapsed pane and the left side of the screen. Depending on the e-mail account type, the messages may appear in the Inbox folder under Outlook Data file; for other types of accounts, Outlook creates a separate set of local folders, and the Inbox folder under the e-mail address for that account receives the incoming messages. The number of unread messages appears in blue beside the folder name. By default, messages are sorted by the time and date they were received in the message list in the middle pane. You can see that the sender, the subject, the time and date received, and the message size are displayed. Please also note the following:

- A message that you have not yet read is displayed in bold type. A message that has been read is displayed in normal type.

- If the message includes one or more attachments, a paper clip icon is displayed.

- By default in Outlook 2013, the message list shows a one line preview of the message body. To change this, choose View⇨Arrangement⇨Message Preview, and then click another preview style.

- For security reasons, most pictures do not download by default. You can click the Click here to download pictures message to download and display the hidden pictures when you trust the message sender.

FIGURE 27.15

Messages that you receive are placed in your Inbox folder.

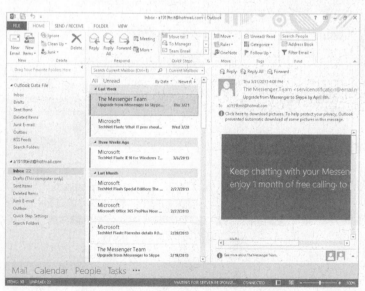

New Alerts

On Windows 8 when notifications are enabled (as they are by default), Outlook 2013 displays new alerts, such as the alert for a newly received e-mail message, as shown here.

Reading a message

To read a message, click on it in the message list. The message appears in the Reading Pane at the right (by default), as shown in Figure 27.16.

FIGURE 27.16

Reading an e-mail message

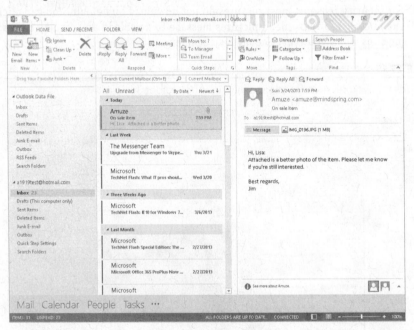

TIP

You also can open a message in its own window by double-clicking on the message.

While you have an e-mail message open, you can carry out the following actions:

- Print the message by clicking File ⇨ Print ⇨ Print.
- Close the message and delete it by clicking the Delete button in the Delete group of the Home tab on the Ribbon. Outlook moves the message to the Deleted Items folder.

Other actions that you can take with an e-mail message are covered later in this chapter.

NOTE

If you are working with a web-based e-mail account, such as a Hotmail account, you may see additional folders, including a Sync Issues folder, appear in the list of folders, after you have added content that is synched with the online account.

You can also move the message from the Inbox to another folder. Doing so is useful when you want to organize received e-mail messages. (You'll learn more about working with Outlook folders later in the chapter.) The basic steps for moving an open message are the following:

1. **Click the Move button in the Move group on the Home tab of the Ribbon.**
2. **Select Other Folder from the menu.** Outlook displays the Move Items dialog box, as shown in Figure 27.17.
3. **Click on the destination folder.** Or, to create a new folder, click the New button. Details on creating a new folder are presented later in the chapter.
4. **Click OK.** The message is closed and moved to the specified folder.

FIGURE 27.17

Moving an e-mail message to another folder

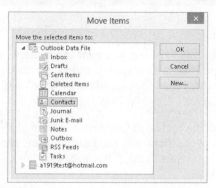

When you are moving an e-mail message to another folder, you are given the opportunity to create a new folder. When you click the New button in the Move Item dialog box, Outlook opens the Create New Folder dialog box. Then, follow these steps:

1. **Enter the name for the new folder in the Name box.**
2. **Make sure that Mail and Post Items is selected in the Folder Contains list.**
3. **Click the location for the new folder in the list.** The new folder is created as a subfolder to the item you select here.
4. **Click OK to close the dialog box and return to the Move Items dialog box.** The new folder is selected in the list.
5. **Click OK to complete moving the mail message.**

Marking messages as read or unread

The preview line(s) for messages that have not been read are displayed in bold font and have a line or bar along the left side in the message list. When you open a message, it is marked as read and displayed in normal font without the bar or line. You can control how a message is flagged. Perhaps you open a message and then are called away; you might want to mark it as unread so that you will be sure to look at it again later.

If the message is open in its own window, simply click the Mark Unread button in the Tags group on the Message tab of the Ribbon. If no message is open, you can select a message in the message list for the Inbox (or whatever mail folder you are in) and then click Unread/Read in the Tags group of the Home tab or right-click the message and click Mark as Unread. You can also move the mouse pointer over the line to the left of the message; when it becomes a wider bar, click it to toggle the message between read and unread status.

> **TIP**
> You can filter the message list using the All and Unread choices at the top. Click Unread to see only messages you haven't read in the list, or click All to see all messages.

Using the Reading Pane

You already learned that Outlook's Reading Pane lets you view the contents of a message without opening it. When the Reading Pane is displayed, it shows the contents of whatever message is selected in the message list for the Inbox (or whatever other mail folder you are working in).

The Reading Pane can be displayed at the bottom of the screen instead of the default position at the right. To control the display of the Reading Pane, choose View ⇨ Layout ⇨ Reading Pane, and then select Right, Bottom, or Off.

Other actions for received messages

When you are viewing a message that you have received, you can take several other actions besides those already described with the message. Each of these actions is available via the Home tab on the Ribbon:

- **Create Rule:** Lets you create a rule for handling similar messages. Rules are covered in Chapter 28.

- **Block Sender:** Adds the message sender to your Blocked Senders list and moves the message to the Junk e-mail folder. You'll find more details on dealing with junk e-mail in Chapter 28.

- **Categorize:** Assign the message to an Outlook category.

- **Follow Up:** Flag the message for follow-up, or create a reminder associated with the message. To toggle a message between flagged and unflagged, you can now move the mouse pointer over the message in the message list, and click the flag icon that appears in the upper-right corner of the message preview.

- **Find:** Find other messages from the same sender or that are related by subject or content.

Replying to and forwarding messages

Replying to and forwarding messages are two very useful things you can do with e-mail using Outlook. When an e-mail message is open in its own message window, you have five buttons in the Respond group of the Message tab of the Ribbon. These same buttons are also found in the Respond group of the Home tab when a message window is not open:

- **Reply:** Creates a new message addressed to the person who sent you the original message. By default, the new message contains the entire original message, and the subject of the new message is "Re:" followed by the subject of the original message.

- **Reply to All:** Same as Reply except the new message is also addressed to all people in the To and Cc lines of the original message.

- **Forward:** Creates a new, unaddressed message. The new message quotes the entire original message, includes any attachments that were sent with the original message, and the subject is "FW:" followed by the subject of the original message.

- **Reply with Meeting:** This creates a response message that is also a meeting invitation. You can specify a Start time and End time for the meeting in addition to other message information.

- **More Respond Actions:** Click this option, then click Forward As Attachment to create a new message with the original message included as a file attachment rather than shown in the body of the e-mail.

At this point, the new message is ready for editing. You can add your own text to the body of the message, add or remove recipients (you must add at least one recipient when forwarding), add attachments, and so on. When you're finished, click Send.

You also can click Reply, Reply All, or Forward at the top of the Reading Pane. Outlook 2013's new inline reply feature enables you to type your message reply right within the Reading Pane, as shown in the example in Figure 27.18. Type your message text, and click send. You can use Compose Tools ⇨ Message ⇨ Include ⇨ Attach File to add a file attachment. If you want to open the message in its own window, click Pop Out at the top of the Reading Pane, or click Discard if you want to cancel the message. Click the Send button to send the message when it's ready.

FIGURE 27.18

Responding inline in the Reading Pane

After you send the response message, an icon with an envelope and an arrow appears on the message preview in the message list to indicate that you've replied to the message. In the Reading Pane, the message header also now includes information about when you sent your reply message for record keeping purposes.

Working with received attachments

Outlook lets you save attachments to disk and also lets you view attachments without opening them in their native application. The viewing option is available for many attachment types including most image files, Word documents, and Excel workbooks.

Saving attachments

When a received message includes one or more attachments, it will have a small, paper clip icon displayed in the message preview in the message list. There are two ways to save attachments. The first method is easiest. Right-click the attachment in the Reading Pane, and click Save As. Then use the Save Attachment dialog box to finish the save.

The second method also lets you save attachments without opening the message:

1. **Select the message in the message list for the Inbox (or whatever mail folder you are working in) or open the message by double-clicking on it.**

2. **Choose File ⇨ Save Attachments.**

Outlook opens the Save All Attachments dialog box, shown in Figure 27.19.

FIGURE 27.19

Saving all message attachments simultaneously

3. **If you want to save just some of the attachments, select them by clicking and Ctrl+clicking (to select more than one individual attachment) or Shift+clicking (to select a group of adjacent attachments).**

4. **Click OK.**

5. **Navigate to the folder where you want the attachment saved.**

6. **Click Save.**

Viewing attachments

When a message that you receive includes one or more attachments, they are listed below the message details (both in the Reading Pane and when the message is open). You also see a Message button next to the attachment names. You can take the following actions:

- Click on an attachment name to view the attachment.
- Click the Message button to return to the message.

Figure 27.20 shows the Message button and an attached file name, along with an attachment that is being viewed in the Reading Pane.

FIGURE 27.20

Viewing an attachment

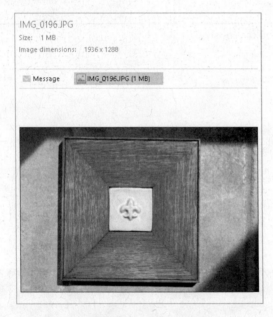

Opening attachments

You usually open an attachment in its native application by saving the attachment to disk, as described previously, and then starting the application and opening the file as usual. You can, however, open an attachment directly from Outlook by following these steps:

1. **Open the message or select it in the message list so that it appears in the Reading Pane.**
2. **Right-click on the attachment name.**
3. **Select Open from the shortcut menu.**

Depending on the file type, Outlook may display a warning dialog box asking whether you want to open or save the file. Click Open, and the attachment is opened in its native application.

The reason for the cautionary dialog box in Step 3 is security. Some kinds of files, such as Word documents and Excel workbooks, have the potential to contain malicious macro code that can harm your system. This code is harmless unless the file is opened, so you may want to save it to disk first and run a virus scan before opening it.

If you do open an attachment this way, you can work with it in the application as you normally would, including saving to disk.

27

> **NOTE**
>
> A native, or default, application is an application that is registered on your system for working with a particular kind of file. Usually, only one application can be *native*, such as Microsoft Word for Word files and Excel for Excel files. For other kinds of files, such as image files, you may select from several possibilities rather than clicking Open in Step 3 above, depending on what's installed on your system. For example, on my system, Photoshop is registered as the native application for most image files, but on your system it might be Paint Shop Pro or CorelDraw.

Understanding the Inbox Display

The message list provides you with a lot of information about the messages it contains. Some icons appear to the right of the message name in the default view. If you change to the Preview view (by using the Change View button in the Current View group of the Group tab), the list expands to include more columns, or fields, with each field identified at the top of the display. It's important for you to understand the meaning of the icons and fields in the Inbox display. They are:

- **Importance (Exclamation Point Icon):** A red exclamation point is displayed in this field if the sender marked the message as having high importance. Nothing is displayed for normal importance, and a blue down arrow indicates messages of Low Importance.

- **Reminder (Bell Icon):** A bell is displayed in this field if the message has been associated with a reminder.

- **Icon (Page Icon):** Displays an envelope icon for messages that you've replied to

- **Attachment (Paper Clip Icon):** Displays a paper clip icon if the message includes one or more attachments

- **From:** The name or e-mail address of the message sender

- **Subject:** The message subject

- **Received:** The time and date the message was received
- **Size:** The size of the message including any attachments
- **Categories:** If the message has been assigned to a category, the category name and icon are displayed here.
- **Follow-Up (Flag Icon):** Displays a flag indicating the follow-up status of the message. A clear flag indicates no follow-up status. Various colored flags indicate other follow-up statuses, such as due tomorrow or due next week. A check mark indicates complete.

In the Preview view, you can sort the messages in the Inbox by any of the fields that are displayed. Simply click on the field heading to sort by that field in ascending order; click a second time to sort in descending order. (Sorting by the Received field in the descending order is the default.) If the field heading is wide enough, it displays an upward- or downward-pointing arrow to show you that the messages are sorted by that field in ascending or descending order, respectively.

The default Compact view enables you to open the Arrange By menu in the Arrangement group of the View tab and choose a field to sort by. You also can click the name of the current sort (By Date, by default) at the top of the message list, and choose a sort field from the menu that appears. Then use the choice to the right to toggle the sort order between Newest/Oldest or another pair of choices.

Understanding Files and Folders

Most computer users are familiar with the idea of a *file*. A file is a unit of storage on a disk that contains data, such as a word processing document, a spreadsheet, or a digital photograph. Outlook uses files to store all of its information, ranging from e-mail account settings and user options to all of its e-mail messages, appointments, tasks, and other items. In fact, for a single-user setup Outlook uses a single file called an *Outlook Personal Folders file* to store just about everything.

Most computer users are also familiar with the concept of a *folder* (sometimes referred to as a *directory*). Folders are used to divide a hard disk into discrete storage areas; can you imagine the confusion if all your files were stored in the same location? Outlook uses folders, too, but they are not the same as disk folders. They serve the same purpose — to help organize the items that are stored — but they exist within the Outlook Personal Folders file and not as separate folders on your hard disk.

Outlook folders come in different types based on the kind of item they are designed to hold. For example, your Inbox is a folder, and it is intended to hold e-mail messages, but you cannot store a contact there.

Outlook Data Files

For most Outlook users who upgrade from an earlier version of Outlook, program data and items are stored in an Outlook Personal Folders file. The file has the `.pst` extension and is by default named *Outlook.pst*. The folder on your hard disk where this file is normally kept is `C:\Users\user name\My Documents\Outlook Files` in both Windows 8 and Windows 7.

Here, `user name` is the name you have used to log on to Windows. If the computer is configured for more than one user, each will have his or her own separate and independent Outlook Personal Folders file.

> **NOTE**
>
> If you open a folder window, and double-click the C: disk under Computer in the Navigation pane, you can then navigate to `C:\Users\user name\My Documents`. However, in other spots in Windows 7 and 8, this path may appear as `C:\Users\user name\Documents`, instead.

You can have more than one Personal Folders file, but only one is designated as the default, which means that Outlook uses it to store account settings, messages, and other items. Additional PST files are used for special purposes, such as archiving old items. You cannot change the storage location of the default PST file.

Offline folders file

As noted earlier, for most types of e-mail accounts, you now will have an Offline Folders file (which has the `.ost` extension) for all new items for the account. By default, your mail service provider keeps copies of your messages and other items on the server, and Outlook keeps a local copy of the items on your system, in the folders file for that e-mail account. Doing so allows you to work with your Outlook items when a connection to the mail server is not available.

Working with Outlook Folders

Outlook folders enable you to organize all the myriad items that you work with in Outlook. Outlook comes with a default set of folders that is a good starting point, but many users find these folders insufficient. This section shows you how to create new folders and work with folders and folder items.

As mentioned earlier, Outlook folders are designed to hold a specific type of item. The choices are as follows:

- **Calendar Folders:** Calendar folders hold appointments and other scheduling items.
- **Mail Folders:** Mail folders hold e-mail messages.

- **Contacts Folders:** Contacts folders hold contact information.
- **Journal Folders:** Journal folders hold journal entries.
- **Task Folders:** Task folders hold task items.
- **Notes Folders:** Notes folders hold notes.

You cannot move an item into a folder of the wrong type, such as moving an e-mail message into a Contacts folder. The one exception to this rule is the Deleted Items folder, which can hold any type of item.

> **NOTE**
>
> Note that RSS feed items are treated like e-mail messages by Outlook when it comes to folder types. Also, you will only see the Notes and Journal folders in the Folder Pane if you upgraded and have previous Note and Journal entries. These folders remain to support those legacy features.

Outlook's default folders

When installed, Outlook has a set of default folders that are located at the top level in your Personal Folders file. You cannot rename, move, or delete these default folders. (Note that only the mail related folders appear in the Folder Pane when you are working with e-mail messages.) They are as follows:

- **Calendar:** Holds calendar items (appointments, etc.)
- **Contacts:** Holds your contacts
- **Deleted Items:** Holds any and all items you have deleted before they are permanently deleted. See the section "Deleting Items and Using the Deleted Items Folder," later in this chapter.
- **Drafts:** Holds e-mail messages you have started composing but not yet sent
- **Inbox:** Holds received e-mails
- **Journal:** Holds your journal items
- **Junk E-mail:** Holds e-mail that has been flagged as junk (spam)
- **Notes:** Holds your legacy notes
- **Outbox:** Holds e-mails that you have sent but that have not yet been transferred to your e-mail server
- **RSS Feeds:** Holds content from your subscribed RSS feeds
- **Sent Items:** Holds copies of e-mail messages that you have sent

Creating a new e-mail folder

E-mail folders get their own section because Outlook treats them a bit differently from other folders. To be more specific, you cannot organize e-mail folders into groups, but rather you have to organize them hierarchically when you create them.

When you create a new e-mail folder, you can place it at the top level — the same level as the default folders for your e-mail account. You can also put it within an existing folder. You can put folders within folders to essentially any level and thereby organize your e-mail messages in the way that best suits you.

Look at the example in Figure 27.21, which shows the Outlook Data File's default e-mail folders, as well as the local default for an e-mail account. You can see that they are all at the same level.

FIGURE 27.21

The organization of Outlook's default e-mail folders

Suppose that you want to organize e-mails from your clients by creating an e-mail folder for each client. For example, say that you have three clients: Acme, Consolidated, and National. One approach is to create three new folders at the top level. The resulting structure is shown under the hotmail account in Figure 27.22. This is the only approach that's allowed for web-based accounts.

Another approach is to use the ability to create folders within other folders, resulting in a hierarchy of folders that is structured according to the folder contents. This approach can be implemented by creating a Clients folder at the top level and then creating Acme, Consolidated, and National subfolders within the Clients folder. This structure is shown in Figure 27.23. Note that a folder that contains other folders — Clients, in this case — displays an adjacent arrow icon that you can click to show or hide the subfolders.

FIGURE 27.22

New e-mail folders can be created at the top level of the folder hierarchy.

FIGURE 27.23

New e-mail folders can also be created in a hierarchical structure by placing folders within other folders.

In any event, you do not have to decide all the details of your e-mail folder structure ahead of time because you can always move the folders around if needed.

Now you can get to the details of creating a new e-mail folder. Here are the steps to follow:

1. **If necessary, click the Mail button in the Navigation Bar at the bottom of Outlook to display the mail folders.**

2. **If you want the new folder at the top level, right-click on your account name (which by default is your e-mail address, unless you've changed it to another name).** Otherwise, right-click on the folder that you want the new folder in.

3. **Select New Folder from the shortcut menu.** Outlook displays a new blank folder name line under the folder you right-clicked in Step 2.

4. **Type the name of the new folder and press Enter.**

Creating a new non–e-mail folder

Non–e-mail folders — those for tasks, calendar, contacts — are handled a bit differently than mail folders. You can only create folders for some items for the default mail account, so if you are using multiple accounts, make sure that you have set the appropriate account as the default.

> **CAUTION**
>
> You cannot create new calendar, task, or contact folders under an e-mail account that relies on Exchange ActiveSync, and will see an error message if you try to do so. In such a case, you should be able to add the new folders under the Outlook Data file, if set up.

The following steps show how to create a non–e-mail folder:

1. **Click the appropriate choice in the Navigation Bar corresponding to where you want to add a new folder — Calendar, People (contacts), or Tasks.**

2. **Click the Folder tab in the Ribbon.**

3. **For People and Tasks, click New Folder in the New group; for Calendar, click New Calendar in the New Group.** Outlook displays the Create New Folder dialog box (refer to Figure 27.24). The folder for the type of item you selected in Step 1 — Calendar, for example — is highlighted in the folder list.

FIGURE 27.24

Creating a new folder, in this case for calendar items

4. **Enter the name of the new folder in the Name box.**

5. **Make sure that the Folder contains list displays the appropriate type of item for the folder you are creating.**

6. **Click OK.**

After you create a non–e-mail folder, it is displayed in the Folder Pane along with other folders, including the default one, for that type of item. Figure 27.25 shows an example for Tasks after creating two new task folders called *Work* and *Personal*.

FIGURE 27.25

User-created folders for non–e-mail items are displayed along with the default folders in the Folder Pane.

CAUTION

You can create new Task folders if you want, but be forewarned that task items you move from the default task folder to a new folder are not updated if you have assigned the task to someone else and receive accept, decline, or progress update messages.

Changing the Default E-mail Account.

To change the default e-mail account:

1. **Choose File ⇨ Info from the main Outlook window, click the Account Settings button, and then click Account Settings to display the Account Settings dialog box.**

2. **If necessary, click the E-mail tab.** The current default account is indicated in the account list by "(send from this account by default)."

3. **Click another account in the list.**

4. **Click the Set as Default button.**

5. **Click Close.**

Organizing folders in groups

Outlook folders that are not e-mail folders can be organized into groups. This is similar in concept to organizing e-mail folders by their location in the folder hierarchy, but the procedures are a bit different.

By default, every category of non–e-mail items has a single group with a name such as *My Contacts*, *My Tasks*, and *My Calendars*. If you create new folders, they are displayed as part of this default group. For example, Figure 27.25 shows the My Tasks folders after adding two new folders to the default Tasks folder. They are all part of the default My Tasks group (which can be expanded or collapsed using the adjacent arrow).

By creating new groups, you can organize folders as desired. Consider the examples in Figure 27.26. It has both *Career* and *Personal* groups, with two folders under each group. With such a structure, you can expand and contract individual groups to find just the items you need.

FIGURE 27.26

You can organize folders into separate groups.

Creating a new group

To create a new group, right-click on an existing group (for example, My Tasks in Figure 27.26) and select New Folder Group in the shortcut menu. Then, type in the name for the group and press Enter.

A newly created group is empty, as you might expect. To move a folder to it, drag the folder to the destination group.

To create a new folder within a group, follow the procedures earlier in this chapter for creating a new folder; then move it to the desired group.

Working with groups

You can take the following actions with a group by right-clicking on it and selecting one of the following options from the shortcut menu:

- Rename Group
- Delete Group
- Arrange by Name — order the folders in the group alphabetically.
- Move Up/Down in List — change the position of the group in the list.

Additional actions you can take with groups are covered in the next section.

Working with folders, groups, and items

This section covers the everyday tasks that you need to perform with your folders, groups, and Outlook items to keep them organized.

Viewing folder contents

When you switch from one type of item to another — for example, from viewing mail items to viewing contact items — Outlook automatically displays the contents of one folder, usually the default one, in the main Outlook window. To view the contents of another folder (also called *opening the folder*), expand the Folder Pane if needed, and then:

- Click the folder to display its contents in the main window.
- Right-click on the folder and select Open in New Window to view the folder's contents in a new window.

You can open as many new windows as you want. When you close a window, Outlook continues running as long as at least one window is open.

Moving or copying items

Outlook lets you move or copy items between folders. For some types of items, only moving is allowed. To move or copy one or more items, you must first select them, as follows:

- To select a single item, click on it.
- To select multiple contiguous items, click on the first item and then hold down the Shift key and click on the last item.
- To select multiple noncontiguous items, click on the first item and then hold down the Ctrl key and click on each additional item.
- To select all items in the folder, press Ctrl+A. You can then deselect individual items with Ctrl+click.
- To deselect multiple items, release any key and click on any non-selected item.

Now you can move or copy the selected items in one of several ways:

- Drag the item or group of items to the destination folder and drop.
- Click the Move button in the Actions group of the Home tab. In the menu that appears, select the destination folder to which you want to move the item or click Copy to Folder to specify another folder to copy the item, instead.

Moving, copying, deleting, and renaming folders

As you fine-tune your Outlook organization, you may want to move folders to new locations in the Folder Pane. Depending on the type of folder, you may be able to copy a folder as well. E-mail folders can be moved to a new location in the folder hierarchy, whereas other folders can be moved from one group to another.

- To move an e-mail folder, drag it to the new location. For example, Figure 27.27 shows how you move the National folder from its location in the Clients folder to a new location in the Key Clients folder.

FIGURE 27.27

Moving an e-mail folder to a new location

- To move a non–e-mail folder, drag it from the current group to the new group.
- To delete a folder, right-click on it and select Delete Folder in the shortcut menu.
- To rename a folder, right-click on it and select Rename Folder in the shortcut menu; then type in the new name and press Enter.

Deleting Items and Using the Deleted Items Folder

When you delete a folder or an Outlook item, it does not get deleted immediately. Rather, it goes to the Deleted Items folder. This is a safety feature that allows users to recover from accidental deletions. You can "delete" items in the usual way (select them and press Delete), or you can drag them to the Deleted Items folder.

> **NOTE**
>
> If an item has not been permanently deleted — that is, if it is still in the Deleted Items folder — you can *undelete* it by moving it back to its original folder (or another folder of the same type).

When you delete an item from the Deleted Items folder, it is truly gone for most e-mail users. Most people prefer to delete items from this folder manually by selecting one or more items and pressing Delete. To delete all items from the Deleted Items folder, choose File➪Info➪Cleanup Tools➪Empty Deleted Items Folder. You can also tell Outlook to automatically empty the Deleted Items folder whenever the program exits, as follows:

1. **Choose File➪Options to open the Outlook Options dialog box.**

2. **Click Advanced in the list at the left (shown in Figure 27.28).**

FIGURE 27.28

Setting options for emptying the Deleted Items folder

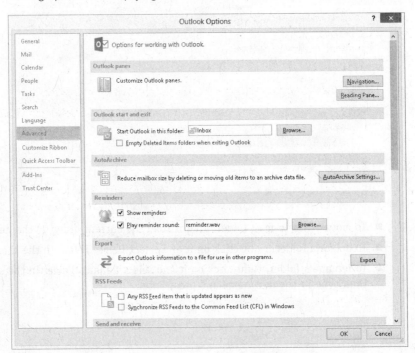

3. Click to check the Empty Deleted Items folder when exiting Outlook option under Outlook start and exit.

4. Click OK.

Setting Options for an Individual E-mail Message

Although you can create and send e-mail messages using all of Outlook's default settings, you would be missing a lot of flexibility and convenience if you did so. The various e-mail options that Outlook offers let you use e-mail in the way that is most convenient and productive for you. These options fall into two categories: those that apply to a single message and those that apply globally. This section explains a variety of options available for individual e-mail messages that you create.

Changing the send account

This topic is relevant only if you have two or more e-mail accounts. By default, messages are sent as follows:

- Messages you create from scratch are sent using the default e-mail account.
- Messages that are replies to a message you received are sent using the account through which the original message was received.
- Messages you forward are sent using the account through which the original message was received.
- To change the send account for a message:
  1. **Create the new message.** A new message window appears.
  2. **Click the From button above the To button, and then click the desired account.**

Saving sent items

By default, e-mail messages that you send are saved in the Sent Items folder. You can change this location for an individual message in its Message window as follows:

1. **Click the Save Sent Item To button in the More Options group of the Options tab of the Ribbon.**

2a. **To save the item to a folder other than the default, click Other Folder and then select the folder.**

2b. **To not save the item at all, click Do Not Save.**

Sending items with a message

You learned earlier how you can attach a file to a message. Outlook also lets you attach certain items, specifically calendars and business cards, to a message.

Sending a calendar

Sending calendar information with a message can be useful to let colleagues know when you are and are not available for a meeting. To send calendar information with an e-mail message, click the Attach Item button in the Include section of the Message tab on the Ribbon, and then click Calendar. Outlook displays the Send a Calendar via E-mail dialog box, shown in Figure 27.29. You make entries in this dialog box to specify the calendar information that will be sent, as follows:

1. **If you have more than one calendar, select the calendar to use from the Calendar list.**

2. **Select the date range from the Date Range list. Predefined ranges include Today, Tomorrow, Next 7 Days, and Whole Calendar.** Select Specify Dates from the list to enter a custom date range.

3. **From the Detail list, select the level of calendar detail that you want included in the message.** The choices are the following:

   ■ **Availability Only:** Time is shown as Free, Busy, Tentative, or Out of Office.

   ■ **Limited Details:** In addition to availability, this option includes the subjects of calendar items.

   ■ **Full Details:** In addition to availability, this option includes the full detail of calendar items.

FIGURE 27.29

Sending calendar information in an e-mail message

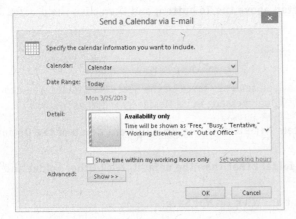

4. **Select the Show time within my working hours only check box to limit the sent calendar information to these hours.** By default, they are 8:00 a.m. to 5:00 p.m., Monday–Friday. Click the Set Working Hours link to change this setting.

5. **Click the Show button to display three additional options.** Two of them relate to what information is included in the message. These options are relevant only if you selected Limited Details or Full Details. The third option determines the format of the sent calendar: Daily Schedule or List of Events.

6. **Click OK to close the dialog box and insert the calendar information in the message.**

When calendar information is inserted into an e-mail message, at the top is a calendar of the month or months involved with the relevant days highlighted and underlined, as shown for March 25–31 in Figure 27.30. The recipient can click these days to go to the detail section for that day.

FIGURE 27.30

This part of the calendar information includes links to individual days.

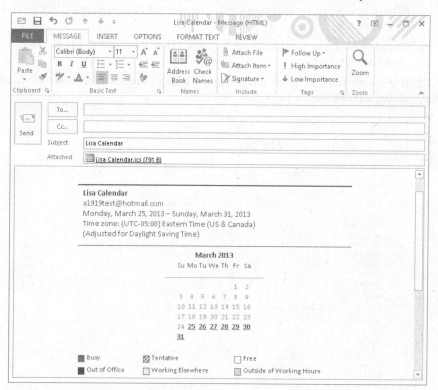

If the calendar information was sent using the Daily Schedule option, the message recipient can scroll down to see details about the schedule. You can see that blocks of time during each day are marked as Free, Busy, and so on.

If the calendar information was sent using the List of Events option, the message lists specific calendar events only — free time is not explicitly marked.

Sending a business card

A *business card* is just what it sounds like — an electronic representation of the information normally found on a paper business card. Every entry in a Contacts list automatically has a business card created for it. You can insert these cards into e-mail messages to send contact information to e-mail recipients. When you do so, a visual representation of the business card is added to the message, and a VCF file is attached to the message. The recipient can use the VCF file to quickly add the contact information to his or her own Contacts list.

To send a business card with an e-mail message from the Message window:

1. **Click the Attach Item button in the Include group of the Message tab on the Ribbon and point to Business Card.** The menu that is displayed lists recently sent business cards.

2. **Click the card you want to send, or click Other Business Cards to select from your Contacts list.**

3. **If you selected Other Business Cards, Outlook displays the Insert Business Card dialog box, as shown in Figure 27.31.**

FIGURE 27.31

Selecting a business card to include in an e-mail message

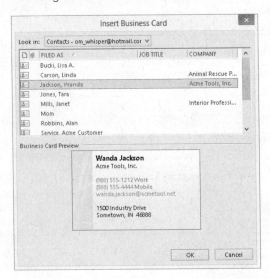

4. **If you have more than one e-mail account (and therefore more than one Address Book), select the desired one from the Look in list.**

5. **Click the contact whose business card you want to include.** The card is previewed in the lower part of the dialog box.

6. **If you want to include more than one card, hold down Ctrl while clicking.**

7. **Click OK.**

Your Own Business Card

If you create an entry for yourself in your Contacts list, you can send your own business card with e-mail messages.

Setting message importance and sensitivity

An e-mail message can be flagged as having low importance or high importance. Normal is the default. The recipient's e-mail program may indicate the importance of a message in some way. For example, Outlook displays an exclamation point next to the message in the Inbox if it is marked as having high importance. Many e-mail clients, including Outlook, also allow recipients to sort their received messages by importance.

To mark a message with high importance, click the High Importance button (a red exclamation point) in the Tags group of the Message tab on the Ribbon. To change a message to low importance, click the Low Importance button (a downward-pointing arrow).

Assigning a message to a Category

Outlook's categories are a powerful tool for organizing all kinds of information. When you create a message, you can assign it to a category. Then you can find the message — the saved copy of the sent message, that is — based on this category. To assign a category to a message in the message window:

1. **Click the Tags group dialog box launcher in the Tags group of the Message tab on the Ribbon to display the Message Options dialog box.**

2. **At the lower left of the dialog box, click the Categories button.**

3. **Select the desired category from the menu.** Or, click Clear All Categories to remove any category assignment from the message. (Use the All Categories choice to create and delete categories.)

Requesting delivery and read receipts

When you send a message, you can request delivery or read receipts (or both) by selecting the corresponding check box in the Tracking group of the Options tab of the Ribbon in the message window. A delivery receipt is generated when the message is delivered to the recipient, and a read receipt is generated when the message is opened by the recipient (assuming that the recipient also has this functionality enabled and clicks Yes to confirm sending the receipt when prompted). The receipt consists of an e-mail message back to you that contains the date and time that the original message was delivered or read.

Delivery and read receipts sound like a great idea, but their usefulness in practice is limited. The delivery receipt must be generated by the e-mail server software, and sometimes this feature is turned off by the server administrator to reduce the load on the server. Even if you do receive a delivery receipt, there is no guarantee that the recipient has read the message. Likewise, the read receipt is sent by Outlook (or whatever other e-mail program the recipient is using), and the user may have this feature turned off.

When you have sent a message and requested a receipt, Outlook automatically processes the receipt when and if it arrives (unless you have turned this feature off under Tracking Options, as explained later in this chapter). When you open the message in the Sent Items folder, the Message tab of the Ribbon displays a Show group with Message and Tracking buttons. Click the Tracking button to view the details of any receipts that have been received for this message. Click the Message button to return to the message text.

Be aware that if Outlook has not yet received and processed any receipt for a message, the Tracking button is not available on the Message tab of the Ribbon.

Delaying delivery and setting message expiration

If you do not want a message delivered right away, you can specify a "Do not deliver before" date. If you are sending a message that is relevant for only a limited period, you can set an expiration date for the message. When the recipient receives the message, that message will behave normally until the expiration date, after which it will display in the Inbox (or whatever folder it is in) with a line through it. The recipient can still open the message, but the strikethrough provides a visual indication that the message has expired. Other e-mail programs may handle message expiration differently.

Set these two options from the message window, as follows:

1. **Click the Delay Delivery button in the More Options group of the Options tab of the Ribbon in the Message window.** Outlook displays the Properties dialog box (Figure 27.32).

FIGURE 27.32

Delaying the delivery of a message

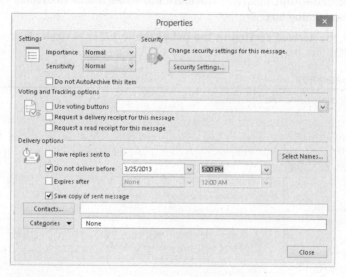

2. **In the Delivery options section, make sure that Do not deliver before is checked.**

3. **Enter the desired date and time in the adjacent text boxes.**

4. **In the Delivery options section of the dialog box, check the Expires after check box.**

5. **Enter the desired expiration date and time in the adjacent text boxes.**

6. **Click the Close button.**

If you are using a Microsoft Exchange e-mail account, the message is sent to the server and held there until the specified date and time. If you are using another kind of e-mail account, the message is held in Outlook's Outbox until the first send operation that occurs after the specified date and time.

Setting Global E-mail Options

Many of Outlook's options apply globally to all messages and to e-mail in general. You select these options using several dialog boxes that display the options in related groups. This section follows the same organization.

To view and change e-mail preferences:

1. **Choose File⇨Options from the main Outlook window to display the Outlook Options dialog box.**

2. **Click the desired section in the list at the left.** For example, Figure 27.33 shows the Mail options.

FIGURE 27.33

Setting global e-mail preferences

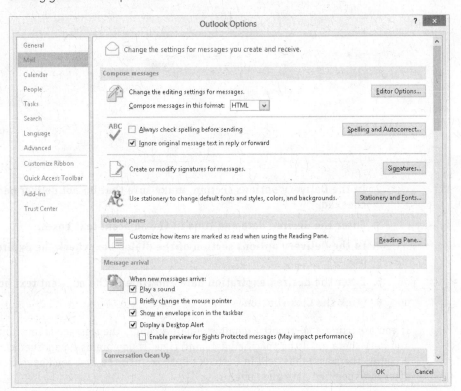

3. **Set options in this dialog box as explained in the following sections.**

4. **Click OK.**

Some key options in the Mail section of the Outlook Options dialog box include:

- **Compose messages in this format:** Select the default message format.
- **Save copies of messages in the Sent Items folder:** When you send a message, a copy is saved in the Sent Items folder.

- **Automatically save items that have not been sent after this many minutes:** Messages that you have started composing but have not sent are saved in the Drafts folder.

- **Save to this folder:** Specifies the folder when Outlook automatically saves items (for example, messages that you have started composing but have not sent yet).

- **When new messages arrive:** The settings under this section determine whether Outlook plays a sound or displays an alert when a message arrives.

- **Default Importance level and Default Sensitivity level:** Specifies the default importance and sensitivity levels for new messages that you create.

- **Tracking:** View and set tracking options in this section.

The Replies and forwards section of this tab determines what Outlook does when you reply to a message or forward a message. You set the When replying to a message and When forwarding a message settings independently, but the options are essentially the same, as follows:

- **Do not include original message:** Replies are sent without the original message. This is not applicable to forwarded messages.

- **Attach original message:** Replies and forwards are sent with the original message included as an attachment.

- **Include original message text:** Replies and forwards are sent with the original message included as part of the new message.

- **Include and indent original message text:** Replies and forwards are sent with the original message included as part of the new message, indented with respect to the other parts of the message.

- **Prefix each line of the original message:** Replies and forwards are sent with the original message included as part of the new message, with each line of the original message prefixed by what is entered in the Prefix Each Line With field (by default, this is the > sign).

Summary

This chapter explained the fundamentals of setting up your e-mail account and sending and receiving e-mail messages in Outlook. You can now:

- Compose and send a message, including adding file attachments.
- Open the collapsed Folder Pane.
- View received messages in your account Inbox.

- Use the message list to see a message preview, and use the Reading Pane to view message contents and attachments.
- Respond to messages.
- Organize your e-mail messages, tasks, calendars, and contacts in folders.
- Control message priority and timing, and add special items such as business cards.
- Work with Outlook options.

Processing and Securing E-mail

IN THIS CHAPTER

Understanding junk e-mail filtering

Setting junk e-mail options

Defining blocked and allowed lists

Understanding e-mail rules

Defining a new rule

Looking at some rule examples

Managing e-mail rules

Protecting against viruses

Understanding Outlook's attachment blocking

Implementing macro security

Using certificates and digital signatures

Encrypting and digitally signing messages

Junk e-mail, often called *spam*, is a problem for most e-mail users. It can range from a minor annoyance for a home user to a major problem for a large organization, clogging mail servers and reducing the efficiency of employees. Fortunately, Outlook provides you with tools that greatly reduce the spam problem. You also can use message rules to process incoming e-mail, cutting down on the amount of time you spend moving messages around or deleting them. Computer security has unfortunately become a very important topic. With the almost universal use of the Internet and e-mail, it's easier than ever for various kinds of malicious software such as viruses to spread. Security issues also include message privacy and verification of people's identities. Because e-mail is the favored means of spreading such malware, Outlook users have to be particularly vigilant. This chapter explains the various tools that Outlook provides to make you more efficient in dealing with spam and managing messages, and to enhance your security.

Understanding Junk E-mail Filtering

Junk e-mail filtering works based on two principles. The first is the content of the message — certain keywords and phrases are considered likely to be spam. The other is the identity of the sender. You can define a *safe list* — people whose messages are never treated as spam regardless of content. Likewise, you can define a *blocked list* — people whose messages are always treated as spam regardless of content. In either case, messages that Outlook flags as spam are placed in the Junk E-mail folder rather than the Inbox.

Why doesn't Outlook just delete spam messages? The fact is that content-based spam filtering is not perfect, and legitimate messages are sometimes caught as spam. Some people like to quickly scan their Junk E-mail folder before permanently deleting the messages just to make sure that a legitimate message has not been caught. However, if you want spam to be deleted automatically, you can tell Outlook to do this. See the next section, "Setting Junk E-mail Options," for details.

Third-Party Anti-Spam Software

Several anti-spam programs on the market work in conjunction with Outlook to catch spam. These programs may provide more sophisticated filtering options and other features. If you are using one of these programs, you may want to turn Outlook's spam filtering off. You do not have to, however; leaving it on does no harm and may, in fact, catch spam that the other program misses.

Setting Junk E-mail Options

You set Outlook's filtering and handling of junk e-mail in the Junk E-mail Options dialog box, as follows:

1. **Click the Junk button in the Delete group of the Home tab in the main Outlook window, and then click Junk E-mail Options to display the Junk E-mail Options dialog box.**
2. **If necessary, click the Options tab (shown in Figure 28.1).**

FIGURE 28.1

Setting options for junk e-mail filtering

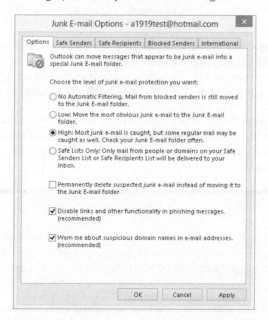

3. **Choose option settings as described in the following list.**
4. **Click OK.**

The first option in this dialog box determines the level of filtering based on message content. You have four levels to choose from:

- **No Automatic Filtering:** Messages are not filtered based on their content.

- **Low:** Only obvious spam is treated as such. Some spam will get through to your Inbox.

- **High:** More stringent spam rules are applied when message content is scanned. Some legitimate messages may be treated as spam.

- **Safe Lists Only:** Only messages from senders on your safe lists (explained later in this chapter) are allowed through; all other messages are treated as spam regardless of their content.

The other options in this dialog box are as follows:

- **Permanently delete suspected junk e-mail...:** Messages that Outlook considers to be spam are deleted rather than moved to the Junk E-mail folder. You may not want to use this option unless you are sure that legitimate messages are not mistakenly being tagged as spam.

- **Disable links and other functionality in phishing messages:** Phishing messages (see the "Phishing" sidebar) usually contain links to web pages where you are asked for confidential information such as passwords. If this option is selected, Outlook disables these links.

- **Warn me about suspicious domain names in e-mail addresses:** A spoofed domain name is one that is not what it appears to be. For example, a link might display www.microsoft.com but actually be a link to another domain. If this option is selected, Outlook warns you about possible spoofed domain names in a message.

You may want to check the Junk E-mail folder from time to time to see if it is trapping messages you need. You can select and move those messages back to the Inbox or another folder. To delete all junk e-mail, right-click the folder and click Empty Folder, clicking Yes if a confirmation message appears.

Phishing

Phishing is a particularly dangerous kind of junk e-mail. A *phishing message* pretends to be from a company you do business with, for example, PayPal or eBay. The message asks you to take some seemingly legitimate action, such as resetting your password. When you follow the link to a website, the site looks just like the real thing, but it is not — it's a fake website set up by the phisher. The result is that some unscrupulous person now has your password, and you can imagine the possible consequences.

NOTE
Is spam related to viruses? Not directly, although viruses often arrive as part of a spam message (but can come with a legitimate message too).

Blocking and Allowing Specific Addresses

A very useful tool in the fight against spam is Outlook's ability to define lists of e-mail addresses and domains that are always blocked or always allowed through.

Defining safe senders

A *safe sender* is a person, or more precisely an e-mail address, whose e-mail messages are always considered to be OK — not spam — regardless of the content. Sometimes a Safe Senders list is called a *white list*. You can create a Safe Senders list based on your contacts and by entering individual addresses. You can also specify entire domains as safe — for example, all messages from Microsoft.com would be considered to be safe. Here are the steps to follow:

1. **Click the Junk button in the Delete group of the Home tab in the main Outlook window, and then click Junk E-mail Options to display the Junk E-mail Options dialog box.**

2. **Click the Safe Senders tab (shown in Figure 28.2).**

FIGURE 28.2

Defining your Safe Senders list

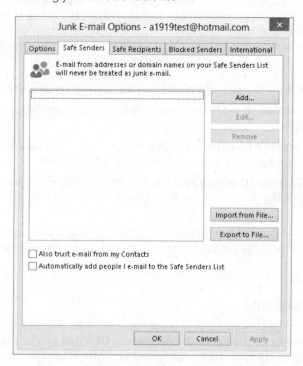

3. **To add an address or domain to the list, click the Add button.**

4. **Enter the address (for example,** someone@microsoft.com**) or the domain (for example,** microsoft.com **or** @microsoft.com**).**

5. **Click OK to add the address or domain to the safe list.**

6. **To edit or remove a safe list entry, highlight it in the list and then click the Edit or Remove button.**

7. **Click OK.**

The other two options in this dialog box are self-explanatory. Having the Also Trust e-mail from my Contacts check box selected saves you the effort of entering these addresses manually.

The Import from File and Export to File tools are useful if you want to transfer a safe list between Outlook and another e-mail program, or pass your safe list to a friend or colleague. The import/export format is a plain-text file with one address per line.

Blocking/allowing individual senders

The shortcut menu is a fast way to add addresses to your safe and blocked lists. All you have to do is right-click on the message in the message list for the Inbox or selected folder, point to Junk in the shortcut menu, and then choose the desired action from the submenu. If you have opened a message, you can use the commands in the Junk list in the Delete group of the Message tab on the Ribbon to perform the same commands:

- **Block Sender:** Adds the message sender to your Blocked Senders list.
- **Never Block Sender:** Prevents messages from the sender from being placed in the Junk E-mail folder.
- **Never Block Sender's Domain:** Prevents messages from all senders from a particular domain from being placed in the Junk E-mail folder.
- **Never Block This Group or Mailing List:** Prevents messages addressed to the same group or mailing list used in the message from being placed in the Junk E-mail folder.
- **Not Junk:** This command is available only if the message is in your Junk E-mail folder. Click to move the message to the Inbox and add the sender to your Safe Senders list.

Defining safe recipients

The Safe Recipients list, located on another tab in the Junk E-mail Options dialog box, is similar to the Safe Senders list, but it marks messages as OK based on their *recipients* rather than their sender. This is useful when you are on a distribution list or in another situation in which you receive e-mails that are sent to a list of recipients, including you. When an e-mail address is on the Safe Recipients list, any message sent to you *and* to that address will never be treated as spam, regardless of the message sender and content. The Safe Recipients tab works exactly the same as the Safe Senders tab, described in the previous section.

Defining blocked senders

A *blocked sender* is an e-mail address or domain whose messages are always treated as spam. The Blocked Senders tab in the Junk E-mail Options dialog box works exactly like the Safe Senders tab as described earlier.

International junk e-mail options

You may receive some e-mails that appear to be gibberish — random, meaningless characters. These messages occur when a sender's e-mail program uses a different character encoding than the one you are using. For example, a person in China likely uses Chinese encoding to create a message in Chinese characters. If your e-mail reader is set to use, say, English encoding, the message displays as gibberish. Outlook lets you block messages that use specified character encodings. It also lets you block e-mails from certain countries based on the top-level domain of the sender's address. Here are the steps to follow:

1. **Click the Junk button in the Delete group of the Home tab in the main Outlook window, and then click Junk E-mail Options to display the Junk E-mail Options dialog box.**

2. **Click the International tab.**

3. **To block top-level domains, click the Blocked Top-Level Domains button to display a list of domains (Figure 28.3).**

FIGURE 28.3

Specifying top-level domains to block

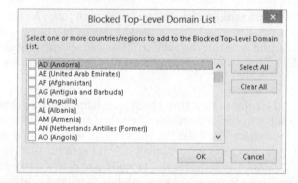

> **NOTE**
>
> The top-level domain of an e-mail address is the part after the last period. People in the United States are used to seeing top-level domains such as `.com`, `.org`, and `.edu` that indicate the type or organization. In the rest of the world, however, the top-level domain usually identifies the country of origin — for example, `.ca` for Canada, `.cn` for China, and `.fr` for France.

4. **Select the domains you want to block, and then click OK.**

5. **To block character encodings, click the Blocked Encodings List to display a list of encodings (Figure 28.4).**

Specifying character encodings to block

6. **Select the character encodings you want to block, and then click OK.**

7. **Click OK to close the Junk E-mail Options dialog box.**

Understanding E-mail Rule Basics

Outlook lets you automate the handling of e-mail messages with *rules*. A rule can perform actions such as moving messages from a specific person to a designated folder or deleting messages with certain words in the subject. Rules can also display alerts, play sounds, and move InfoPath forms and RSS feed items. Rules can help you save time and stay organized.

Outlook e-mail rules are all similar in that they specify a *condition* and an *action*. A rule can be defined to apply to e-mail messages when they arrive, which is most common, and to messages as you send them. The Rules Wizard, through which you create rules, provides a set of partially defined rules for commonly needed actions — all you need to do is fill in the details. This wizard also provides the capability to define a rule completely from scratch, a feature you'll use if one of the existing rule templates does not meet your needs.

Creating a New Rule

To create a new e-mail rule, click the Rules button in the Move group of the Home tab in the Outlook window, and then click Manage Rules & Alerts. Outlook displays the Rules and Alerts dialog box, in which you should select the E-mail Rules tab. If you have any rules already defined, they are listed here. You can work with existing rules as described later in this chapter. To create a new rule, click the New Rule button to display the Rules Wizard, as shown in Figure 28.5.

FIGURE 28.5

The first step in defining a new rule

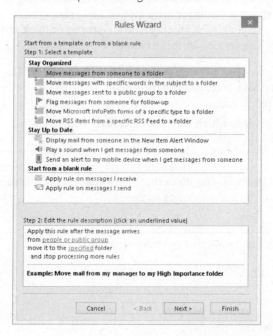

You can see that this dialog box has two parts, Step 1: Select a template at the top, and Step 2: Edit the rule description at the bottom. The following sections look at these in turn.

Selecting a rule template

The first step, selecting a template, of this dialog box is divided into three subsections, each containing two or more templates:

- **Stay Organized:** Templates that move, delete, or flag messages or other items
- **Stay Up to Date:** Templates for alerting you when messages arrive
- **Start from a blank rule:** Templates that are empty and let you define a rule from scratch

The remainder of this section deals with the first two of these categories. Starting from a blank rule is covered separately later in this chapter.

When you click on an item in the Select a Template section, the Step 2: Edit the rule description section displays the rule definition along with an example. Editing the definition is covered next.

Editing a rule description

A rule definition contains underlined elements that represent the parts of the rule that you can edit. Figure 28.5, for example, shows a definition with two editable elements: *people or public group* and *specified*. When you click such an underlined element, Outlook opens a dialog box in which you can specify the details. In this example:

- Click people or public group to open a dialog box in which you can select the people, distribution lists, or both from your Address Book. The rule will be applied to messages from the selected people.

- Click specified to select a folder to which matching messages will be moved.

After you have made selections for the editable rule items, the rule displays the selected information. An example is shown in Figure 28.6, in which the rule is defined to move messages from "Alan Robbins" to the "Clients" folder. Note that these elements of the rule are still underlined and can be clicked on to make changes as needed.

FIGURE 28.6

A completed rule definition displays the details that you have specified.

Finishing the rule

At this point, the rule is ready to use. You can click Finish in the Rules Wizard dialog box to save the rule. In some cases, you may want to fine-tune the rule; if so, click the Next button. Fine-tuning a rule is essentially the same as creating a rule from a blank template, which is covered in the next section.

Creating a rule from a blank template

If the rule templates that Outlook provides do not suit your needs, you can create a rule from a blank template. In the first step of the Rules Wizard, shown earlier in Figure 28.5, you must select one of the following from the Start from a blank rule section:

- **Apply rule on messages I receive:** Creates a rule that works with messages you receive.

- **Apply rule on messages I send:** Creates a rule that works with messages you send.

After making your selection, click the Next button. Outlook displays the next Rules Wizard step as shown in Figure 28.7. You use this dialog box to specify the conditions for the rule. You can have more than one condition for a rule. When you do, all conditions must be met for a message to be processed. The steps to follow are:

1. **Click the box next to a description to place a checkmark in the box and add the condition to the rule description.** Note that you may see a warning message alerting you to the consequences of applying some conditions.

FIGURE 28.7

Selecting conditions for a rule

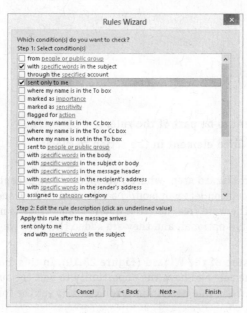

2. **If the condition requires it, click the underlined element in the description to specify the details.**

3. **Repeat Steps 1 and 2 if needed to add conditions to the rule.**

4. **Click the Next button to proceed to the next Wizard step, where you will define the rule's action.** This dialog box is shown in Figure 28.8.

FIGURE 28.8

Selecting an action for a rule

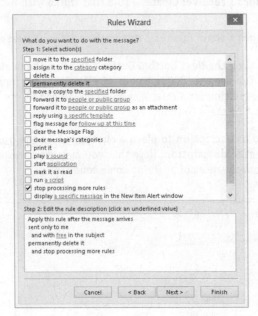

5. **Select the action that you want to be part of the rule.**

6. **If necessary, click any underlined element in the action to specify the details.**

7. **Click Next to display the next Wizard step, where you specify any exceptions to the rule (Figure 28.9).** An exception lets you modify a rule, as in this example: "If the message subject contains the word free, delete it unless the message is marked High Importance." Exceptions are optional, and they are added the same way as conditions and actions.

8. **Click Next to go to the final step of the Wizard (Figure 28.10).** In this dialog box, you specify a name for the rule and have the opportunity to edit the rule by clicking underlined elements in the rule description. You can also set the following options:

FIGURE 28.9

Specifying exceptions for a rule

FIGURE 28.10

The final step of the Rules Wizard

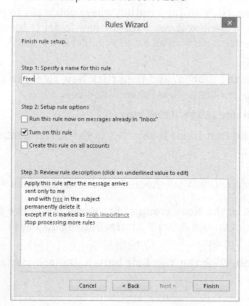

- ■ **Run this rule now on messages already in "*Inbox*":** Apply the rule to messages already in the Inbox folder for your account.

- ■ **Turn on this rule:** Enable the rule for newly received or sent messages.

- ■ **Create this rule on all accounts:** Apply the rule for all your e-mail accounts (relevant only if you have multiple accounts).

9. **Click Finish to complete the rule definition and return to the Rules and Alerts dialog box.** You can then click OK to close the Rules and Alerts dialog box if you are finished.

Some Rule Examples

Outlook e-mail rules are admittedly rather complex. It may help you to understand them if you follow the steps required to define a few different kinds of rules.

Rule example 1

This first rule example shows you how to define a rule that moves all messages from a certain domain to a specified folder. It would be useful if, for example, you are doing some contracting work for a company and are interacting with several people there. This rule moves all e-mail that you receive from anyone at that company into one folder, helping you to stay organized.

The first step is to create the folder:

1. **In the mail Folder Pane, click on the location where you want to place the new folder.** You can click on a mailbox if you want the new folder to be at the top level in that mailbox. You can also click on an existing folder to create the new folder within that folder.

2. **Click the Folder tab on the Ribbon, and then click New Folder in the New Group.** Outlook displays the Create New Folder dialog box.

3. **Enter the new folder name in the Name box.**

4. **Make sure that Mail and Post Items is selected in the Folder Contains list.**

5. **Click OK.**

Now that you have created the folder, you can proceed to defining the rule:

1. **Click the Rules button in the Move group of the Home tab in the Outlook window, and then click Manage Rules & Alerts.** Outlook displays the Rules and Alerts dialog box, with the E-mail Rules tab selected.

2. **On the E-mail Rules tab, click the New Rule button.** Outlook displays the Rules Wizard dialog box.

3. **In the Stay Organized section, click the Move messages from someone to a folder template.**

4. **In the Edit the rule description section, click the people or public Group link.** Outlook displays the Rule Address dialog box (Figure 28.11).

FIGURE 28.11

Specifying an address to be part of a new e-mail rule

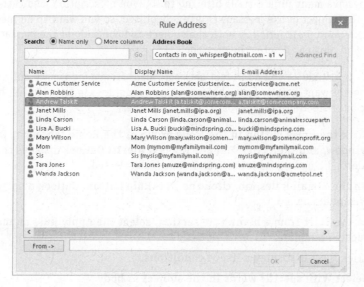

5. **If you wanted to move messages from a single individual who is in your Contacts list, you could click that person's entry in the list and then click the From button.** If you want to move all messages from a domain, enter the domain (such as **acme.com**) in the From box.

6. **Click OK.**

7. **If you see a dialog box claiming not to recognize the domain entered in Step 5 because it is not a complete e-mail address, click Cancel.** This is OK; closing this dialog box returns you to the Rules Wizard.

8. **In the Edit the rule description section, click the *specified* link.** Outlook displays the Rules and Alerts dialog box.

9. **Select the desired destination folder and then click OK.** Note that if you had not created the new folder earlier, you could do it now by clicking the New button in this dialog box.

10. **Back in the Rules Wizard dialog box, click the Finish button to close the Rules Wizard and return to the Rules and Alerts dialog box.**

After you create a rule, you will see it listed in the Rules and Alerts dialog box. It is assigned a default name based on the information in the rule. You can, if desired, change the rule name as explained later in this chapter in the section on managing rules.

Rule example 2

This rule example shows you how you can use a rule to help guard against spam. Let's say that you receive many junk e-mails offering to sell you prescription medication online. However, the subject of the message is often disguised, so you want to define a rule that looks for the word *prescription* in both the subject and the body of the message, and if the word is found, Outlook deletes the message.

But there's a wrinkle — you do in fact get some meds from a legitimate online drug store, and you do not want e-mails from that store to be caught — so the rule will have to include an exception. Here are the steps for creating this rule:

1. **Click the Rules button in the Move group of the Home tab in the Outlook window, and then click Manage Rules & Alerts.** Outlook displays the Rules and Alerts dialog box, with the E-mail Rules tab selected.

2. **On the E-mail Rules tab, click the New Rule button.** Outlook displays the Rules Wizard dialog box.

3. **In the Start from a blank rule section, select the Apply Rule on messages I receive template.**

4. **Click Next to display a list of conditions.**

5. **Select With specific words in the subject or body.**

6. **In the lower part of this dialog box, click the specific words link to open the Search Text dialog box (Figure 28.12).**

FIGURE 28.12

Use this dialog box to specify words that will be searched for in a message.

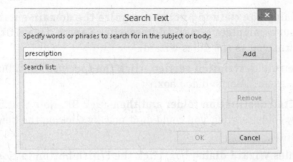

7. **Enter** prescription **in the upper box, and then click Add to add the word to the list.** If you wanted to search for more than one word, you would repeat this step as needed.

8. **Click OK to return to the Rules Wizard dialog box.**

9. **Click Next to display a list of actions.**

10. **Select the delete it action.** Doing so tells Outlook to move matching messages to the Deleted Items folder. You can also select the Permanently Delete It action, which does precisely what it says.

11. **Click Next to display a list of exceptions.**

12. **Select the except if from people or public group exception.**

13. **In the lower part of the dialog box, click the people or public group link to display the Rule Address dialog box.**

14. **If the legitimate online pharmacy's address is in your Contacts list, you can add it using the From button.** Otherwise, just type it in the From box and then click OK.

15. **Back in the Rules Wizard dialog box, click Finish to complete your rule definition.**

Rule example 3

Our final rule example shows you how to process messages that you send. Suppose that your major client is Acme Corporation and you have created an Outlook category specifically for items that are related to Acme. You want all messages you send to Acme to be placed in this category automatically. Here's how:

1. **Click the Rules button in the Move group of the Home tab in the Outlook window, and then click Manage Rules & Alerts.** Outlook displays the Rules and Alerts dialog box, with the E-mail Rules tab selected.

2. **On the E-mail Rules tab, click the New Rule button.** Outlook displays the Rules Wizard dialog box.

3. **In the Start from a blank rule section, select the Apply Rule on messages I send template.**

4. **Click Next to display a list of conditions.**

5. **Select Sent to people or public group.**

6. **In the lower part of the dialog box, click the People or public group link to open the Rule Address dialog box.**

28

7. Enter the domain (acme.com in this example) in the To box and then click OK.

8. Click Cancel in the dialog box claiming not to recognize the domain because it is not a complete e-mail address. You will return to the Rules Wizard.

9. Click Next to display a list of actions.

10. Select the Assign it to the category option.

11. In the lower part of the dialog box, click the category link to open the Color Categories dialog box (Figure 28.13).

FIGURE 28.13

Selecting a category to assign sent messages to

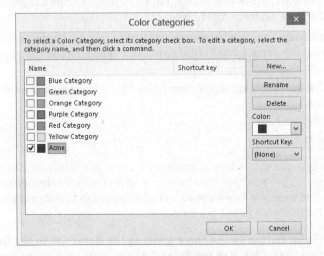

12. Select the desired category — in this case, it would be Acme — then click OK to return to the Rules Wizard dialog box.

13. Back in the Rules Wizard dialog box, click Finish to complete your rule definition.

Managing Rules

When you select Rules ➪ Manage Rules & Alerts from the Move group of the Home tab, the E-mail Rules tab in the Rules and Alerts dialog box lists all the rules that are defined

(Figure 28.14). If you have more than one rule, they are applied in top-down order. The actions you can take in this dialog box are the following:

- To edit a rule, click on it and then click the Change Rule button. Then select Edit Rule Settings or Rename Rule from the menu.

- To change a rule's position in the list, click on it and then click the up- or down-arrow button.

- To copy a rule, click on it and then click the Copy button. Outlook will make a copy of the rule, which you can then rename and modify as desired.

- To delete a rule, click on it and then click the Delete button.

- To run rules, click the Run Rules Now button. Then, in the dialog box that is displayed, select the rules to run and the folder(s) and messages to apply the rules to (Figure 28.15), and click Run Now.

- To deactivate a rule, click the adjacent check box to remove the checkmark.

- To import or export your rules from or to other versions of Outlook, or for use by a friend or colleague, click the Options button.

FIGURE 28.14

You manage your e-mail rules in the Rules and Alerts dialog box.

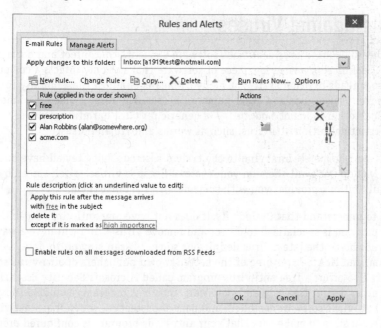

FIGURE 28.15

Running rules manually

Protecting against Viruses

Everyone has heard about *viruses*, malicious software elements that infect and harm computer systems. Technically, a *virus* is a piece of software that not only infects a computer system but also spreads to other systems usually by means of a host file, similarly to biological viruses that cause colds and other human illnesses. The term is often used more broadly to include other kinds of *malware* — a generic term for harmful software — that do not fit the strict definition of a virus, such as worms and Trojan horses.

Viruses range from the merely annoying to the truly disastrous, but they all have one thing in common — you do not want them on your system! Because viruses often spread by means of e-mail, Outlook provides you with some defenses against them.

It's important to understand that Outlook itself does not have any anti-virus capabilities. An anti-virus program is specialized to detect and remove viruses and will have a way to automatically download the latest virus definitions so that it can stay up-to-date. Symantec, Zone Alarm, and McAfee are three of the better-known publishers of anti-virus software. Microsoft also offers a free anti-virus program called Microsoft Security Essentials, and there are other decent freeware and shareware antivirus programs available. Most systems have anti-virus software installed, and part of protecting yourself against viruses that come with e-mail is to make sure that your anti-virus program is configured properly.

Specifically, you should set the anti-virus program's options so that it always scans incoming e-mail and attachments for viruses before they get to Outlook. It's also advisable to set the program to scan outgoing e-mail and attachments in order to prevent you from inadvertently spreading a virus that you have been infected with through other means (such as a floppy disk).

On-demand e-mail scan

If you have an Outlook-compatible anti-virus program installed, you may find that it has added a command or option for working with the anti-virus program. The details of how the virus scan works and how you set options depend on the specific anti-virus program that you have installed. Please refer to that program's documentation for more information. However, the possible commands fall into two categories:

- **Scan for Viruses:** Opens your anti-virus program and performs an immediate virus scan of e-mail items according to the program options. Use this command when you are not sure that the anti-virus program's automatic scanning is enough.

- **E-mail Scan Properties:** Opens your anti-virus program's Options dialog box, in which you can specify the details of how the program scans e-mail items for viruses.

People worry about getting viruses via e-mail, so it can be a good idea to reassure them that messages from you are safe. You could include a brief note at the bottom of every e-mail that you send that states, "This e-mail message and any attachments have been scanned for viruses by XXX" (where XXX is the name of the anti-virus program in use).

28

Dealing with Attachments

One of the most common ways for viruses to spread is by means of e-mail attachments. However, all attachments are not equal in their ability to spread a virus. Certain file types are potentially very dangerous, such as executable programs, batch files, and installation files. Others, such as image and music files, are generally safe.

Automatically blocked attachments

Because of the potential danger posed by some file types, Outlook blocks certain kinds of attachments that are sent to you; you receive the message with a notification that an unsafe attachment has been blocked. This blocking is built into Outlook and cannot be turned off or changed. Some of the more common blocked file types are listed in Table 28.1.

You can search Outlook Help for *blocked file types* to see the whole list, which includes many file types you may not be familiar with.

Outlook also catches these file types on the way out — that is, if you try to send them as an attachment. They aren't necessarily blocked, but Outlook reminds you that the recipient may not be able to receive them (and definitely won't if he or she uses Outlook) and asks you if you want to proceed.

TABLE 28.1   File Types Blocked by Outlook by Default

Extension	File Type
ASP	Active Server Page
BAS	BASIC source code
BAT	Batch processing
CER	Internet Security Certificate file
CHM	Compiled HTML help
CMD	DOS CP/M command file, or a command file for Windows NT
COM	Command
EXE	Executable file
GADGET	Windows Vista gadget
HLP	Windows Help file
JSE	JScript encoded script file
MSC	Microsoft Management Console Snap-in control file (Microsoft)
MSI	Windows Installer File (Microsoft)
MSP	Windows Installer Update
OPS	Office Profile settings file
PIF	Windows Program Information file (Microsoft)
PST	Exchange Address Book file, Outlook Personal Folder File (Microsoft)
TMP	Temporary file/folder
URL	Internet location
VB	VBScript file or any Visual Basic source
VBE	VBScript encoded script file
VBS	VBScript script file, Visual Basic for Applications script
WS	Windows script file
WSC	Windows script component
WSF	Windows script file
WSH	Windows Script Host settings file

> **NOTE**
>
> If you use an Exchange account for e-mail, these same file types are blocked by default. However, the Exchange administrator can modify the list if needed.

Other attachment types

Some other file types are not on the blocked list even though they have the potential to carry viruses. These file types are not blocked because they are very commonly sent as attachments. They include Microsoft Word documents (.docx), Excel workbooks (.xlsx), and PowerPoint files (.pptx). When you receive this kind of file as an attachment, it's important for you to be aware of the potential for harm. Even if you have anti-virus software, you cannot be sure that it will catch every virus, particularly because new ones are created regularly.

The general rule is to not open any such file unless you trust the source. It is also wise to have macro security set to a safe level, as described elsewhere in this chapter.

Sending blocked file types

Many people have perfectly legitimate reasons for sending blocked file types as attachments. You have two ways to get around Outlook's restrictions to do this:

1. **Change the file's extension.** For example, if you want to forward a compiled HTML Help file named *MyHelp.CHM*, change the file extension to something that Outlook won't block, such as *MyHelp.TXT*. In your message, instruct the file recipient to change the file extension back before using the file.

2. **Put the file in a** .zip **or other kind of archive.** This kind of file is permitted by Outlook. You need to instruct the recipient as to how the file can be extracted, of course.

> **NOTE**
>
> When you create a .zip file, you have the option of protecting it with a password. Although doing so can provide security against unauthorized access to the .zip file's contents, it can prevent anti-virus software from checking the .zip file's contents for viruses. Also note that .zip files and other archives are often blocked by corporate mail servers as a security measure. You can use suggestion number one above to try to bypass this issue.

Macro Security

A *macro* is a sequence of program commands that have been recorded and saved and can be executed with a single command. Outlook has its own macro capabilities. More germane to the topic of security, however, are the macros in programs such as Microsoft Word and

Excel. Such macros are part of the document file and as such are included when the file is sent as an e-mail attachment. (However, you can identify files that contain macros because the file name extension changes, from .docx to .docm for a Word document, for example.) A malicious macro can be set to execute automatically when the file is opened and can potentially wreak havoc on your system and data files. Such viruses are called *macro viruses*.

Anti-virus programs catch most macro viruses, and the precaution of not opening attachments from unknown sources is another layer of protection. The final layer of protection against macro viruses is the macro security level in your programs.

Macro security applies to all Office programs, and it is set in the Trust Center. The Trust Center is an Office component, not specifically part of Outlook or any other program. On Outlook, you access the Trust Center by clicking File, then clicking Options to open the Outlook Options dialog box. Then, in the list on the left, click Trust Center. Finally, click the Trust Center Settings button, and click Macro Settings in the list at the left to display the macro security settings shown in Figure 28.16.

FIGURE 28.16

Setting macro security in the Trust Center

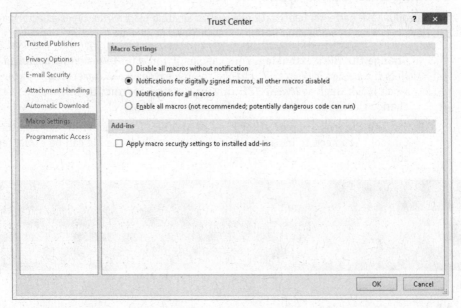

You can see that the options mention "signed macros." *Digital signing* is a way that the person who creates a macro can "sign" it so that the recipient can be assured that it comes from a trusted source. You'll learn more about digital signatures later in this chapter.

You can choose from four levels of macro security, described here from the strictest to the least strict:

- **Disable all macros without notification:** No macros, whether signed or not, are ever run.

- **Notifications for digitally signed macros, all other macros disabled:** For a signed macro, the program displays a notification message and asks you whether it should be run. Unsigned macros are never run. This is the default macro security level.

- **Notifications for all macros:** The program displays a notification message for any macro, signed or unsigned, and asks you whether it should be run.

- **Enable all macros:** All macros are run without a notification message. For reasons that are probably obvious, this level is not recommended.

The default level of macro security for all Office programs is recommended. You can always set a lower level temporarily if you want to run some unsigned macros from a trusted source.

Using Certificates and Digital Signatures

A *certificate*, also known as a *digital ID*, provides a higher level of security with Outlook. You can use a certificate to send encrypted e-mails so that only the intended recipient can view the contents. You can also use them to sign messages to prevent tampering and prove your identity. Finally, you can use a digital ID in lieu of a user name and password to access certain restricted websites, although this use is not relevant to Outlook.

Digital IDs are based on the technique of a *public/private key pair*. These are two long numbers that are related to each other. You can use either key of the pair to encrypt data, and only people who have the other key of the pair are able to un-encrypt the data. When you have a digital signature, you keep your private key secret and make your public key freely available. Here's how it works:

- To send an encrypted message to people, you use their public key to encrypt it. Only they can decrypt the message because no one else has their private key.

- To prove your identity, encrypt some data using your private key. When recipients of a message decrypt the data using your public key, if the data is intact they will know that you must have encrypted it because nobody else has your private key.

Digital certificates have expiration dates, typically one year after they are issued.

Obtaining a digital ID

If you are using Outlook at work, your employer may provide a digital ID to you that you'll import as described in the next section. Otherwise, you can get your own. Digital IDs are provided by independent companies for a small fee. A digital ID is linked to a specific e-mail address and cannot be used with other addresses.

To get your own digital ID:

1. **Click the File tab, click Options, and then click Trust Center in the list at the left.**
2. **Click the Trust Center Settings button.**
3. **Select E-mail Security from the list on the left side of the Trust Center window to display the E-mail Security page (Figure 28.17).**

FIGURE 28.17

Using the Trust Center to get a digital ID

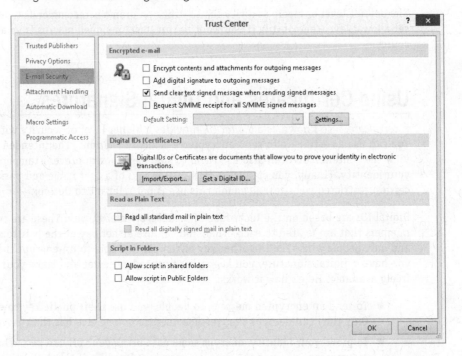

4. **Click the Get a Digital ID button.** Your web browser opens and displays a Microsoft page that lists companies that sell digital IDs.
5. **Select the company you want, and follow the prompts to register for and pay for your digital ID.**

After you complete the ordering process, the issuing company will send you an e-mail containing instructions for installing the digital ID.

Importing/exporting digital IDs

Digital IDs can be provided to you in a file as well as obtained over the web, as described in the previous section. Your employer may provide you with an ID in a file; you can also export an existing ID to a file for backup purposes or to install it on multiple computers, such as both a personal and a work computer. These files are password protected for security reasons.

To import a digital ID:

1. **Click the File tab, click Options, and then click Trust Center in the list at the left.**
2. **Click the Trust Center Settings button.**
3. **Select E-mail Security from the list on the left.**
4. **Under Digital IDs, click the Import/Export button to display the Import/Export Digital ID dialog box (Figure 28.18).**

FIGURE 28.18

The Import/Export Digital ID dialog box

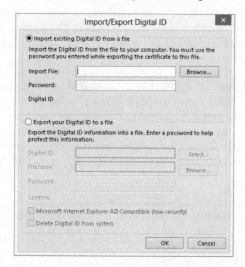

5. **Select the Import existing Digital ID from a file option.**
6. **Enter the name of the file in the Import File box, or use the Browse button to locate it.** Digital ID files have the .epf, .pfx, or .p12 extension.
7. **Enter the file password in the Password box.**
8. **If the Digital ID box is available, enter a name of your choosing for the certificate.**
9. **Click OK.** The Importing a new private exchange key dialog box appears.
10. **If necessary, use the Set Security Level button to change the security level, and then click OK and click Yes in the Security Warning dialog box.**

Exporting a digital ID uses the same dialog box as shown in Figure 28.18, except you must select the Export your Digital ID to a file option. Then, follow these steps:

1. **If you have more than one digital ID, use the Select button to choose the ID to export.**
2. **Enter the export file name in the Filename box, or use the Browse button to select an export location.**
3. **Enter and confirm the password in the boxes provided.**
4. **Select the Microsoft Internet Explorer 4.0 Compatible option only if you will use the exported ID with older versions of Internet Explorer.**
5. **Select Delete Digital ID from system if you want to completely delete the ID rather than export it.**
6. **Click OK.**

Receiving digitally signed messages

When you receive a digitally signed message, the only difference is that the message says "Signed By XXXX" (where XXXX is the sender's e-mail address) in the header, just below the subject line. You can use such a message to add the sender's public key to your Contacts list, as explained in the next section.

Just because a message is signed does not mean that the signature is legitimate. On the same line that "Signed By XXXX" is displayed, Outlook displays a red ribbon icon, as shown in Figure 28.19, to indicate that the signature is valid. If the signature is not valid, the message "There are problems with the signature" is displayed, and you can click a button to view the details. A digital signature could be invalid because it has expired, the issuing authority has revoked it, or the server that verifies the certificate is invalid.

FIGURE 28.19

The red ribbon icon indicates that the digital signature in a message is valid.

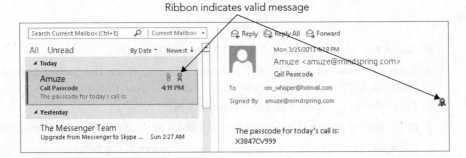

Obtaining other people's public keys

To send an encrypted message to people, you must have their public key. You can get this from a signed message that an intended recipient sent you. That recipient's certificate will be added to his or her entry in Contacts, and it will be available for you to use to send encrypted e-mail. Follow these steps to send an encrypted e-mail message:

1. **Select or open the digitally signed message.**

2. **Right-click on the sender's name or address in the From box.**

3. **Choose Add to Outlook Contacts from the shortcut menu.**

4. **If the contact already exists in your Contacts folder, Outlook notifies you.** Select Update Information of Selected Contact.

5. **Click Save to finish saving the contact.**

You can view a contact's certificates by choose Home ⇨ Find ⇨ Address book, choosing the list where you stored the contract from the Address Book drop-down list, and then double-clicking the contact. In the contact window, choose Contact ⇨ Show ⇨ Certificates (maximize the window to see the Show group). Outlook displays a list of the contact's certificates, if there are any, as shown in Figure 28.20. You can take the following actions by clicking the buttons at the right side of this window:

- **Properties:** View the certificate details, including the name of the issuing company and its expiration date.

- **Set as Default**: If the contact has more than one certificate, this command sets the one that will be used as the default for encrypting messages to the contact.

- **Import:** This option lets you import a person's certificate from a file. Certificate files have the .p7c or .cer extension.

- **Export:** This option lets you export the certificate to a file. Doing so can be useful when you want to transfer a contact's certificate to another computer.

- **Remove:** This option deletes the certificate from the contact information.

Encrypting and digitally signing messages

It's important to understand that encrypting a message and signing a message are two different things, as follows:

- **Encrypting:** Encrypting uses the recipient's public key to encrypt the message and attachments so that only the recipient can read them.

- **Signing:** Signing uses your digital ID to mark a message so that recipients can verify that it really came from you.

A message can be signed, encrypted, or both.

28

FIGURE 28.20

Viewing a contact's digital certificates

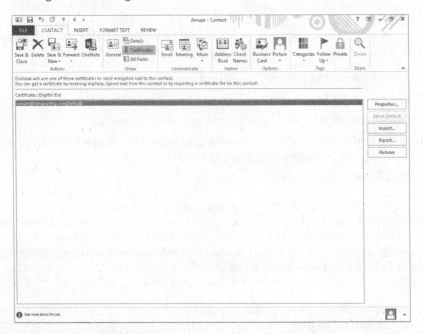

Encrypting messages

You can send an encrypted message to anyone for whom you have the public key — in other words, you have that recipient's certificate as part of his or her contact information. You can encrypt single messages or specify that all messages be encrypted (when possible).

To encrypt a single message:

1. **Create the new message.**
2. **In the message window, click the File tab on the Ribbon, click Info, and click Properties to display the Properties dialog box.**
3. **Click the Security Settings button to open the Security Properties dialog box (Figure 28.21).**

FIGURE 28.21

The Security Properties dialog box

4. **Select the Encrypt message contents and attachments option.**

5. **Click OK; then, click Close to return to the message.**

6. **Compose and send the message as usual.**

Of course, messages can be encrypted only when they are going to one or more recipients for whom you have a certificate. If you request encryption for a message going to people for whom you do not have a certificate, Outlook displays a message and gives you the option of sending the message without encryption.

You can also tell Outlook to encrypt all outgoing messages and attachments. Of course, this capability affects only messages that you send to people whose public key you have. To tell Outlook to encrypt all outgoing messages and attachments, follow these steps:

1. **In the main Outlook window, click the File tab, click Options, and then click Trust Center in the list at the left.**

2. **Click the Trust Center Settings button.**

3. **Select E-mail Security from the list on the left.**

4. **Check the Encrypt contents and attachments for outgoing messages check box.**

5. **Close the open dialog boxes.**

28

Digitally signing messages

As with encryption, you can apply digital signatures to individual outgoing messages or to all of them.

To add a digital signature to an individual message:

1. **Create, compose, and address a new e-mail message as usual.**
2. **In the message window, click the File tab on the Ribbon, click Info, and click Properties to display the Properties dialog box.**
3. **Click the Security Settings button to open the Security Properties dialog box (shown previously in Figure 28.21).**
4. **Select the Add digital signature to the message check box.**
5. **Click OK; then, click Close to return to the message.**

To add a digital signature to all outgoing messages:

1. **In the main Outlook window, click the File tab, click Options, and then click Trust Center in the list at the left.**
2. **Click the Trust Center Settings button.**
3. **Click E-mail Security.**
4. **In the Encrypted E-mail tab, select the Add digital signature to outgoing messages check box.**
5. **Click OK twice.**

HTML Message Dangers

Because HTML messages can contain script and ActiveX controls, they are a potential source of virus attacks. Outlook blocks links (depending on system settings) and a lot of functionality automatically, and may move a message to the Junk E-mail folder, as well. As shown in Figure 28.22, Outlook displays a notification in the message header when there is blocked content. The notification tells you how to restore the content. For example, you may be instructed to click the notification to download and view blocked pictures.

To guard against HTML viruses that make it past your anti-virus software, you can tell Outlook to display HTML messages as plain text. Because scripts and ActiveX controls are not activated until the HTML is displayed, this prevents them from doing harm.

FIGURE 28.22

Many features in HTML messages are automatically disabled.

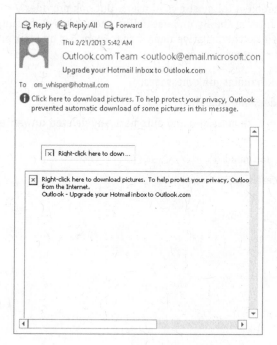

To guard against malicious HTML messages:

1. **In the main Outlook window, click the File tab, click Options, and then click Trust Center in the list at the left.**

2. **Click the Trust Center Settings button.**

3. **Click E-mail Security.**

4. **Under Read as Plain Text, select Read all standard mail in plain text (this means unsigned messages).**

5. **If you want to include digitally signed messages, select Read all digitally signed mail in plain text.**

TIP

Click Automatic Download in the list at the left to work with settings for other types of downloaded content.

---

6. **Click OK twice.**

Summary

Spam, or junk e-mail, is a serious problem for most e-mail users. Outlook provides you with some powerful tools to detect and filter spam. By understanding these tools and using them efficiently, you can greatly reduce the negative impact that spam has on your productivity. You should now know how to protect your system by:

- Understanding how Outlook handles junk messages.
- Blocking and allowing senders and domains.
- Creating e-mail rules to organize messages and automatically deleted unwanted junk.
- Adding virus protection if you need it.
- Getting and using digital certificates.

Working with Contacts

O utlook's Contacts feature is much more than a simple address book. It provides you with powerful tools not only to store but also to find and use information about your business and personal contacts.

Understanding Outlook Contacts (People)

Outlook's Contacts feature is one of its most powerful features. At heart, the Contacts feature is just an address book, but what an address book! Of course, it covers the basics of organizing names, addresses, and phone numbers, but it can do so much more. Many people use Contacts primarily as a way to store people's e-mail addresses for ease of sending e-mails. This is important, but if that's all you use Contacts for, you are really missing out. For example, you should know that you can use Outlook Contacts to:

- Create electronic business cards so that you can send your or other people's contact information by e-mail.

- Store multiple phone numbers, e-mail addresses, and postal addresses for an individual.

- Perform an automated mail merge, creating a mailing to some or all of your contacts.
- Store a photograph as part of a contact's information.
- Define custom fields to store whatever information you need as part of a contact.
- Communicate via Lync or Skype.
- View a map of the location of a contact's address.

After you understand all the power of Outlook Contacts, you can use as many or as few of its features as you like.

> **NOTE**
>
> Personal Address Books, a feature available in earlier versions of Outlook, is no longer supported.

The Contacts Window

When you click the People choice in the Navigation Bar at the bottom of Outlook and make sure that the Folder Pane is expanded at the left (click the Expand the Folder Pane arrow button at the top if it's collapsed), the pane displays the available contact lists (Address Books), grouped under *My Contacts*. If you have more than one address book, they are all displayed here.

By default, Contacts appear in People view, as shown in Figure 29.1. Use the Change View button in the Current View group of the View tab on the Ribbon to select how information will be displayed in the Contacts window. You have five view choices:

- People
- Business Card
- Card
- Phone
- List

Simply click on the view that you want, and the Contacts window changes immediately.

You can create groups to further organize your contacts or customize the view. The next sections look at these.

Adding a new contact group

By default, an Address Book is not subdivided. As the number of contacts grows, you may find it useful to define groups to organize contacts in a way that makes them easier to find and use.

Note that Contacts groups are different from the folder groups introduced in Chapter 27. A folder group enables you to store a completely separate list of contacts. You create the folder group and drag contacts from the list into the group.

FIGURE 29.1

The new default People view is one of several different ways to view contacts.

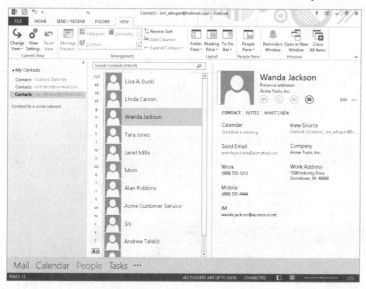

You create a Contact group, in contrast, so that you can easily send a message to the list of recipients defined in the group. You might have Family and Work Team groups, for example. You could then choose the Family group to send an e-mail to all your family members, and use the Work Team group to e-mail messages to your team members at work.

To define a group, follow these steps:

1. **Make sure that Contacts is selected in the Navigation Bar.**

2. **In the New group of the Home tab on the Ribbon, click the New Contact Group button.** The Contact Group window opens.

> **NOTE**
>
> If the New Contact button described in Step 2 is unavailable, that means you can't create groups for the contacts list selected in the Folder Pane. This is likely to be true of many accounts. Click the Outlook Data File list of contacts to create the group there.

3. **Type the name for the group in the Name text box.**

4. **In the Members group of the Contact Group tab of the Ribbon, click the Add Members button, and then click From Outlook Contacts.** The Select Members window opens.

29

5. **Select the contact(s) to add to the group in the list, and click the Members button.** You can select another list from the Address Book drop-down if needed, and then use Shift+click and Ctrl+click to select multiple contacts as needed. The members appear in the text box beside the button, as shown in Figure 29.2.

FIGURE 29.2

Adding contacts to a new group

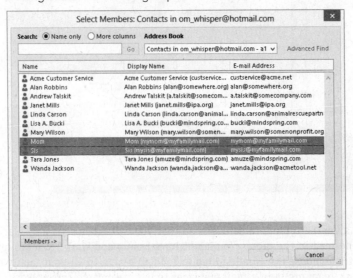

6. **After you finish adding all members as desired, click OK.**

7. **In the Actions group of the Contact Group tab of the Ribbon, click Save & Close.** Outlook adds the new group in the list of contacts (Figure 29.3).

The contacts you add to the group continue to appear in the overall list of contacts, as before.

After you have created one or more additional groups, you can simply double-click on a group to reopen it to change its name or add and remove group members.

Customizing a contacts view

The different views that Outlook provides for contacts can be customized to suit your needs. You cannot, however, create a new view from scratch. To customize a view:

1. **Click the View tab on the Ribbon, click Change View in the Current View group, and then click the name of the view to customize.**

FIGURE 29.3

The list of contacts now includes a group called *Family*.

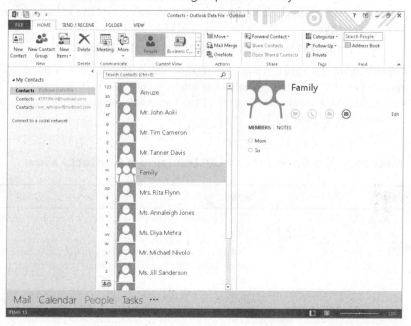

2. **Click the View tab on the Ribbon, and click View Settings in the Current View group.** Outlook displays the Advanced View Settings dialog box (Figure 29.4).

FIGURE 29.4

Customizing a List view

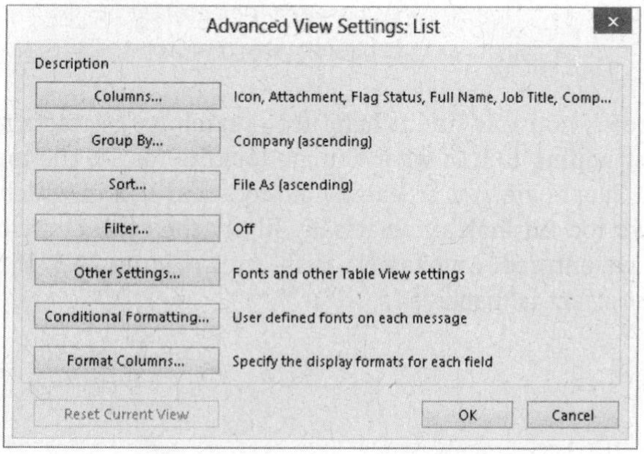

3. **Click on one of the buttons to change related view settings (explained in more detail in the text).** The text next to each button describes the purpose of each.

4. **If necessary, click Reset Current View to return the view to its original default settings.**

5. **Click OK to save your changes and close the dialog box.**

Depending on the view you are customizing, you may have only some of the buttons in the Advanced View Settings dialog box available because certain aspects of a view are not relevant to some views. The aspects of the view that you change with the different buttons are described in Table 29.1.

TABLE 29.1   Components of Customizing a Contacts View

Button	Action
Columns	Specify which fields (items of information) are included in the view.
Group By	Define grouping for the displayed contacts based on one or more fields. For example, you can group contacts by company or state.
Sort	Define how contacts are sorted. You can sort by last name, for example.
Filter	Display only those contacts that meet your defined criteria.
Other Settings	Specify fonts, grid lines, and other details of the Contact View layout.
Conditional Formatting	Define special formatting for contacts that meet certain conditions, such as for a contact associated with an overdue task or one that has been flagged.
Format Columns	Define formatting for columns in the view.

Finding contacts

As your Contacts list grows, you may find it helpful to search for contacts rather than simply look through the list hoping to find what you are looking for. At the top of the contacts list (the middle pane in People view) is a Search Contacts text box in which you type the text that you are looking for. Outlook automatically filters the contacts to show only those that match what you have entered. An example is shown in Figure 29.5. If no matches occur, a message to that effect is displayed.

FIGURE 29.5

Searching for contacts

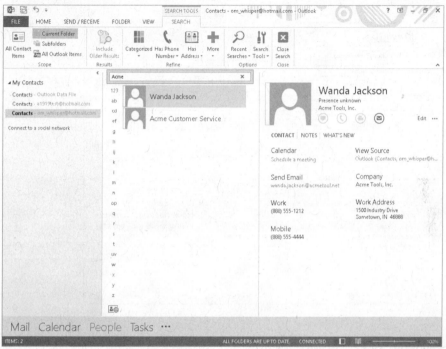

After conducting a search, click the X next to the Search box to clear the search and return to displaying all contacts.

The search just described searches all the contact fields for the text you entered. If you want to search in specific fields, you can perform an Advanced Search by clicking in the Search Contacts text box, clicking the Search Tools button in the Options group of the Search Tools ⇨ Search tab that appears, and then clicking Advanced Find. Outlook displays the Advanced Find window, as shown in Figure 29.6.

29

FIGURE 29.6

Performing an Advanced Search in Contacts

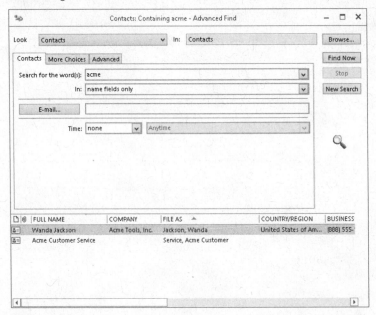

Following are ways to use these tools.

- On the Contacts tab, type the text to search for in the Search for the word(s) text box, and then use the In drop-down list to select the field to search.

- Click the More Choices tab to add additional criteria, such as selecting a category to search by.

- To include more fields in the search, click the Advanced tab and use the Field and Add to List buttons to select the desired fields.

- Click Find Now to perform the search. The search results appear at the bottom of the window. Close the window when you finish with the search.

Click Search Tools ⇨ Search ⇨ Close ⇨ Close Search when you finish working with the search feature.

Adding Contacts

Outlook provides you with several ways to add information to the Contacts list.

Adding a contact manually

To add a new contact to the list currently selected in the Folder Pane in Contacts, click the New Contact button in the New group of the Ribbon.

Outlook displays a new, blank contact window, as shown in Figure 29.7. Type in the information — only a name is required, and you can use or not use the other fields as you desire — and then click Save & Close in the Actions group on the Contact tab on the Ribbon. If you want to save this contact and enter another, click Save & New. Most of the fields on the contact form are self-explanatory, but I provide full details about the form later in this chapter.

FIGURE 29.7

A blank Contact window

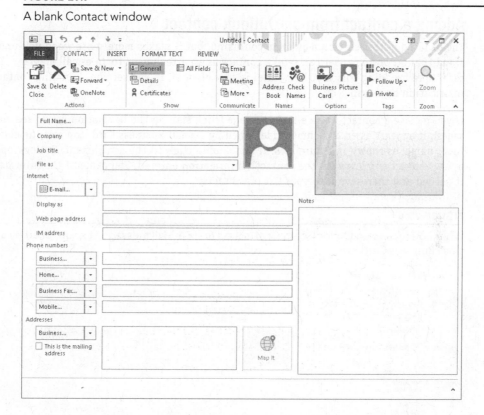

Adding a contact from a received e-mail

When you have opened a received e-mail (with Mail selected in the Navigation Bar), the From field displays the name or the e-mail address (or both) of the sender in the Reading

Pane. It also displays any other recipients — other than you, that is — in the To and Cc fields. You can add the From person or any of the other To or Cc people to your Contacts list by right-clicking on them and choosing Add to Outlook Contacts from the shortcut menu. Outlook opens a new Contact window with the available information filled in. This information includes only the person's e-mail address and perhaps name. You can add additional information to the Contact form, if desired, and then click Save.

By default, the new contact is saved to your Outlook Data File contacts. You can move the contact to another list by clicking it in the center contacts list, and then clicking Move in the Actions group of the Home tab. Click Other Folder to open the Move Items dialog box that you saw in Chapter 27. Select the contacts folder under another e-mail account, and then click OK to finish moving the contact.

Adding a contact from an Outlook contact

The heading of this section may seem confusing, but it makes more sense when you understand that an Outlook user can send a contact as an attachment to an e-mail message. The technique for doing this is covered later in this chapter, in the section, "Sending contact information by e-mail."

If you receive a contact in an e-mail message (click Mail on the Navigation Bar to see messages), it appears as an attachment identified by a small Business Card icon and the contact's name, as shown in Figure 29.8. If you double-click on the attachment, Outlook opens a new Contact window with the contact's information entered. You can edit the information if needed and then save it to your list of contacts.

FIGURE 29.8

When you receive an Outlook contact attached to an e-mail message, it is identified by a small Business Card icon.

A *vCard file* is a special file format designed to send contact information. Outlook can read vCard files that you may receive from people using other e-mail software.

Adding contacts from your social network

Outlook 2013 can connect directly to your Facebook and LinkedIn accounts so you can add the contacts you've made in those services to your Outlook contacts. To start the process, click People in the Navigation Bar, open the Folder Pane if needed, and click Connect to a social network in the pane. In the Connect Office to your social networks window that opens, click Next. In the next window that prompts you for Social Network Accounts information, click the check box beside any network you want to connect with, as shown in Figure 29.9. Enter your sign on information, click Connect, and then click Finish and Close.

FIGURE 29.9

Select a social network, and then enter your sign-on information.

Once you've added your social contacts, the Folder Pane includes a folder for the social network, such as LinkedIn, in the My Contacts group. Click the folder to see your social network contacts and work with them as for any other contacts. If some of your social network contacts are also in one of your other Outlook contacts lists, their social network information will show up in the Outlook contact information as well.

How you see some of the social contact information depends on if you're working in People view or one of the other views. In People view, if you click a contact in the center contacts list to display the contact in the Reading Pane, you can click What's New under the contact name in the Reading Pane to see updates for the contact. Figure 29.10 shows an example.

29

> **NOTE**
> If you double-click a contact in the middle list in People view, the "window" that opens is sometimes called the People Pane.

FIGURE 29.10

View social information and updates for a contact.

In the other views, if you double-click a contact, it opens in a full blown Contact window rather than a People Pane. To see the social network updates for the contact, click the up arrow Click to expand the People Pane button in the lower-right corner of the window, then use the tabs that appear at the left side of the pane to see information and social network updates about the contact.

To disconnect from the social network in any view, click the View tab, click People Pane in the People Pane group, and click Account Settings in the menu. Click the X (delete) icon to the far right of the social network you want to disconnect from, click Yes to confirm the deletion, and then click Finish.

Sending an E-mail to a Contact or Group

Part of the point of developing the list of contacts and creating groups is to make it even easier to make sure you're addressing e-mail to the correct person(s). To create an e-mail message from Contacts:

1. **With the desired account Contacts selected under My Contacts in the Folder Pane, In the list of contacts, click on the contact or group to which you want to send an e-mail.** You can Ctrl+click to select multiple contacts that are not in a group.

2. **On the Home tab, click E-mail in the Communicate group.** Outlook opens a new message window, as shown in Figure 29.11.

3. **Complete and send the message as you normally would.**

When you address an e-mail message to a group, the group name is displayed in the To or Cc field of the message with an adjacent + sign, as shown in Figure 29.11. If you click this + sign, the list is expanded to display its individual members just as though you had added them individually to the To or Cc field. This feature can be useful if you want to send a message to everyone on the list except one or two people; you can expand the Distribution list and delete those few individuals from the To or Cc field of the message.

FIGURE 29.11

A group in the To field of an e-mail message

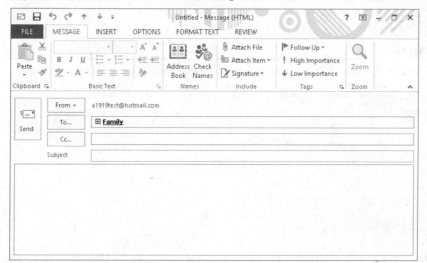

More about Contacts

Outlook Contacts function as much more than as the contents of a simple address book. This section covers additional details and capabilities of Outlook Contacts.

The Contact window

The Contact window (refer to Figure 29.7) that appears when you create a contact or that you can reopen at any time by double-clicking on the contact (except in People view) provides places for you to enter many different kinds of information about a contact. The only field that is required is the name; you can use all, some, or none of the other fields, as you like. Some of the elements on the Contacts window may deserve an explanation, as provided in the following sections.

> **TIP**
>
> When a contact is open, click the E-mail button in the Communicate group of the Contact tab on the Ribbon to create a new e-mail message addressed to the contact.

Full Name

You can simply enter a contact's name in the Full Name field in the usual way, for example, **John Q. Public**. You can also click the adjacent Full Name button to bring up the Check Full Name dialog box, shown in Figure 29.12. Here you can specify a title such as *Dr.* or *Mrs.* and a suffix such as *Jr.* or *Sr.*

FIGURE 29.12

The Check Full Name dialog box lets you enter more details for a contact's name.

Note the option in this dialog box: Show this again when name is incomplete or unclear. When this option is on (the default), Outlook opens this dialog box automatically when you enter an incomplete name such as *Fred* in the Full Name field.

The File As field determines how a contact will be filed in the Address Book. The default is last name first ("Public, John Q."), but you can also choose to file a contact first name first.

Phone Numbers

The Phone Numbers section of the Contacts window provides spaces for four numbers. By default, these are labeled as Business, Home, Business Fax, and Mobile, but you can change which numbers are displayed in a particular Phone Number text box by clicking the adjacent down-arrow and selecting from the list. Some of the choices available are Home Fax, Pager, and Assistant. Outlook can save a phone number for each designation, but only four numbers are displayed on the Contacts window at one time. When you open the list of designations, those for which you have entered a phone number are checked.

Next to each Phone Number field is a button with the field's designation on it. If you click on one of these buttons, Outlook opens the Check Phone Number dialog box, shown in Figure 29.13. Here you can enter additional details for the phone number if desired.

FIGURE 29.13

The Check Phone Number dialog box lets you enter more details for a contact's phone number.

Addresses

The Addresses section of the Contacts window can store up to three addresses designated as Home, Business, and Other. Select the one to display by clicking the down-arrow adjacent to the Address box. Click the adjacent button to open the Check Address dialog box (Figure 29.14), in which you can enter or edit address details. By default, Outlook displays this dialog box automatically if you enter an address that appears to be incomplete or unclear.

FIGURE 29.14

The Check Address dialog box lets you enter more details for a contact's address.

One of the addresses for a contact can be designated as the mailing address by selecting the corresponding option. Outlook uses this address when you are doing a mail merge using Outlook contact data. Mail merge is discussed later in this chapter.

Picture

You can associate a picture with a contact by clicking the Picture button in the Options group of the Contact tab in the Contacts window and then clicking Add Picture. Outlook displays a dialog box that lets you browse for the picture file. The picture file can be the person's picture, a company logo, or just a unique image that you want to use to identify the person. When you have associated a picture with a contact, it displays on the picture button and on the contact's Business Card, as shown in Figure 29.15. (If you are using a Windows phone, you will also see the photo when the contact calls you.) To remove or change the picture, right-click on it and choose from the shortcut menu.

FIGURE 29.15

You can associate a picture with a contact.

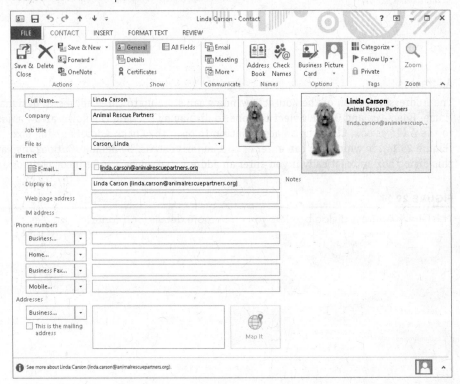

E-mail Addresses

Outlook can store as many as three e-mail addresses for a contact, designated as *E-mail*, *E-mail 2*, and *E-mail 3*. You select which one to display on the Contact window using the arrow adjacent to the E-mail button under Internet.

If you create an e-mail message to a contact by clicking the E-mail button on the Contact tab of the Ribbon in a Contact window, Outlook creates a message addressed to all the e-mail addresses for that contact. If you click the To button on an e-mail message, the list of contacts displays each e-mail address separately, and you can choose the one to use.

The Display As field determines how the contact is displayed in a message's To or Cc field. By default, Outlook displays the contact's name followed by the e-mail address in parentheses, but you can edit this to display as desired — for example, just the person's name.

Other contact displays

The default display for an open contact, called *General*, has been shown in the figures throughout this chapter so far. This is the display that you will probably use most often. Several other displays, or views, are available; you select the display to view from the Show group on the Contact tab of the Ribbon in the Contact message window.

Details view

The Details view gives you access to secondary information about a contact. This view is shown in Figure 29.16. This information includes fields such as Department, Office, Nickname, and Spouse/Partner. You may never use this view, but it's available if you need it.

FIGURE 29.16

The Details view for a contact

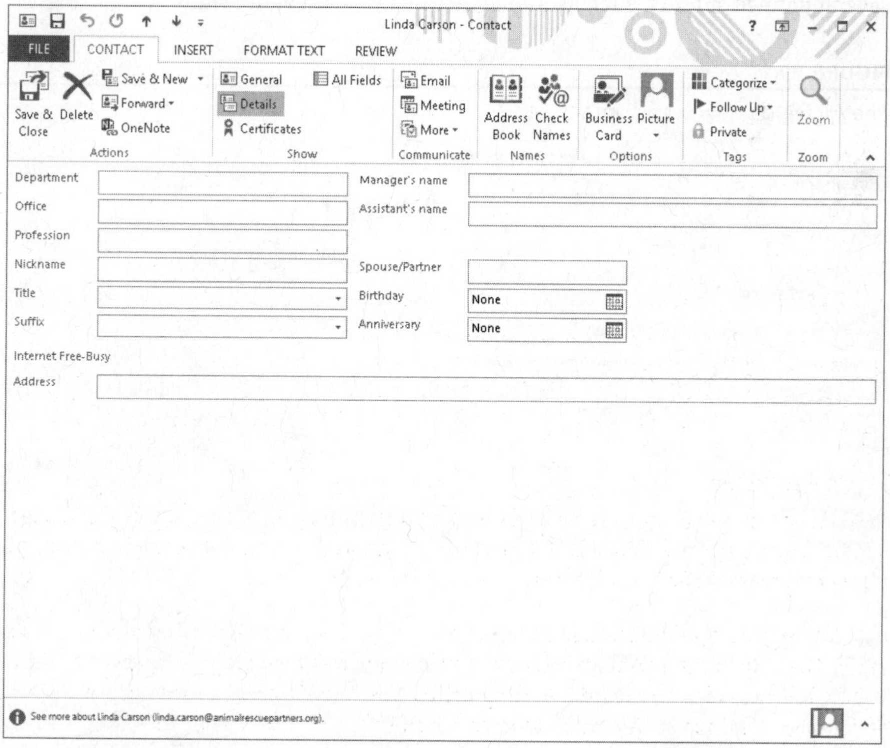

Activities view

When you use the Activities view in the Contact window, it displays all items pertaining to the contact, such as e-mails and tasks.

Certificates view

One of the security features available in Outlook is digital certificates. A contact can send you a certificate, and you can then use this certificate to send encrypted mail to that person. The Certificates display lets you view and work with the certificate(s) that you have for a contact. Digital certificates are covered in Chapter 28.

All Fields view

The All Fields view lets you view all or selected subsets of the data associated with a contact. The amount of information — number of fields — that an individual contact can hold is quite impressive and is way too much to display fully in any other contact view. The All Fields display also lets you define your own custom fields for a contact and to change the properties of some fields.

The All Fields display is shown in Figure 29.17. Near the top is the Select From list, in which you choose which fields to display in the window. You can display all fields as well as one of several defined subsets, such as All Contact Fields or All Mail Fields.

FIGURE 29.17

The All Fields view for a contact

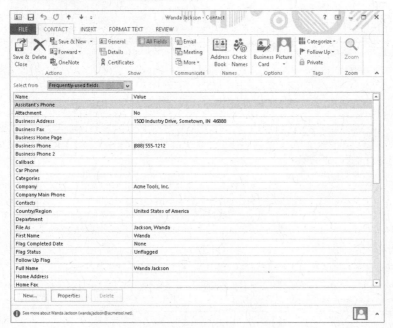

Some fields can be edited in this view by clicking in the Value column and making the desired changes. Other fields are generated internally by Outlook and cannot be edited.

You can add a custom field to the contact by clicking the New button at the bottom of the window. Outlook displays the New Column dialog box (Figure 29.18), in which you enter a name for the field (which cannot duplicate an existing field name). You also select the data type for the field. Your choices are Text, Number, Percent, Currency, Yes/No, and Date/Time. For certain data types, you can also select a format from the Format list. When you are finished, click OK, and the custom field will be added to the All Fields display.

FIGURE 29.18

Defining a new field for a contact

You can change the properties of a field by clicking on it in the list and then clicking the Properties button. This is relevant only for user-defined fields; the properties of Outlook's built-in fields are locked.

Editing the Business Card

Outlook creates a Business Card for each contact based on a default template. As you have seen in previous examples in the chapter, this template includes name, company, title, phone numbers, e-mail and postal addresses, and a photo (assuming that these elements are part of the contact).

To edit the Business Card for a contact, first double-click on the contact in a view other than People view to open its Contact window. Then, click the Business Card button in the Options group of the Contact tab on the Ribbon. Outlook opens the Edit Business Card dialog box, shown in Figure 29.19.

The top-left section of this dialog box previews how the Business Card will look with your edits. The top-right section defines the overall layout of the card:

- **Layout:** Specifies the image location. You can also omit the image or use it as the card background.
- **Background:** Lets you select a background color for the card.
- **Image:** Lets you specify a different image when you click the Change button.

29

FIGURE 29.19

Editing the Business Card for an individual contact

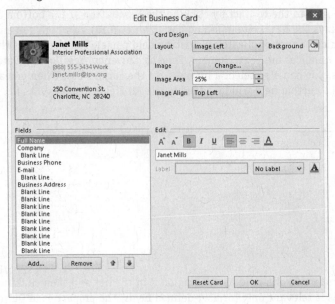

- **Image Area:** Determines how much of the card is occupied by the image. The maximum is 50 percent.
- **Image Align:** Determines how the image is positioned within the image area.

The lower-left section of the Edit Business Card dialog box lets you specify the data fields that are included on the card and their order. You can do the following:

- Click Add and then select from the menu to add a field to the card.
- Click Remove to remove the selected field from the card.
- Click the up- or down-arrow to change the position of the selected field.

The lower-right section of this dialog box is for text formatting. When a field is selected in the Fields list, use the tools here to do the following:

- Increase or decrease font size.
- Make font bold, italic, or underlined.
- Align text left, center, or right.
- Change font color.

Oddly enough, you cannot change the font used on a Business Card; you can change only its size.

The Label section lets you add a label to any data field. You can specify the text of the label, its color, and whether it is displayed to the left or right of the item.

Click the Reset Card button to undo any edits you have made and return the card to the default appearance. Click OK to save your changes and close the dialog box.

Sending contact information by e-mail

Sending contact information attached to an e-mail message can be very useful. Doing so lets recipients enter the information in their address books quickly and without errors. If you keep an entry for yourself in your Address Book, you can easily send your own information as well. You saw in Chapter 27 how to send Business Cards from Mail in Outlook. You also can send a contact directly in an open Contact window.

When you have a contact open in a Contacts window, the Actions group of the Contact tab of the Ribbon includes a Forward button. You can use this button to create a new e-mail message and send the open contact in one of three ways by selecting the corresponding command:

- **As a Business Card:** Outlook creates a new message with the contact inserted in the message body as a Business Card and attached to the message as a vCard file.

- **In Internet Format (vCard):** Outlook creates a new message with the contact attached to the message as a vCard file.

- **As an Outlook Contact:** Outlook creates a new message with the contact attached to the message as an Outlook item. This sends the contact information in Outlook's native format, so the recipient can open it and save it to his or her Contacts.

Contacts, and Lync and Skype

Outlook 2013 now integrates with *VoIP (Voice over IP)* calling capabilities, which means you can make calls over the Internet rather than a landline or mobile network. Outlook integrates with two separate services that support VoIP calling as well as instant messaging, and video calling: Skype and Lync 2013. For these features to work, you have to have the Skype and Lync 2013 client software installed; Skype is a separate download, while Lync is included with some Office versions, particularly Office 365 subscription versions of Office. To be able to work online with your Skype and Lync contacts via your Outlook contacts, you have to meet three basic conditions:

- The Skype or Lync software must be installed.

- The Outlook contact must also be one of your Skype or Lync contacts (or for Lync, within your organization's Office 365-allowed federated calling setup).

- The Skype or Lync application must be running, and you must be signed in to your account.

29

When all of the above are true, the buttons for initiating messaging, calls, and video calls are enabled in the Reading pane as shown in Figure 29.20. Click the button to start the desired activity, and then use the Skype or Lync window that appears to continue.

FIGURE 29.20

Messaging and calling features enabled for a contact

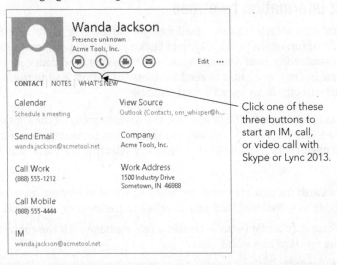

Click one of these three buttons to start an IM, call, or video call with Skype or Lync 2013.

TIP

If you're working in Mail, Calendar, or Tasks in Outlook, you can point to People in the Navigation Bar to see a pop-up list of online contacts that you can call or message.

Other contact actions

This section describes some of the other actions you can perform with contacts.

Viewing a map of the contact's address

If a contact has a valid address entered, you can click the Map It button to the right of the contact's address in the Contact window to open a web browser and view a map of the specified location. This feature is powered by the Bing Maps feature, which provides other services such as driving directions and business search.

Inviting the contact to a meeting

To invite the contact to a meeting, click the Meeting button in the Communicate group of the Contact tab on the Ribbon. Outlook creates a new meeting request addressed to the contact, as shown in Figure 29.21. You can specify the subject and location, enter the date and start and end times, and include a message. You can also add other recipients to the request. You can click Lync Meeting in the Lync Meeting group to set up the meeting via Lync.

FIGURE 29.21

Sending a meeting request to a contact

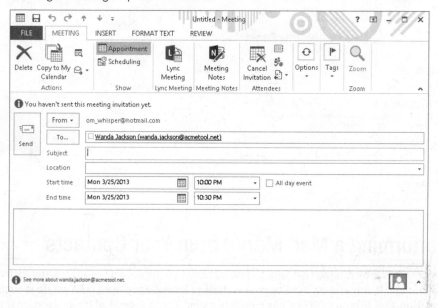

Assigning a task to a contact

To assign a new task to a contact, click the More button in the Communicate group on the Contact tab in the Contact window, and then click Assign Task. Outlook opens a Task window, as shown in Figure 29.21, in which you can enter details of the task and save it. You learn more about tasks, including assigning an existing task to a contact, in Chapter 30.

Viewing the contact's web page

If you have entered a web page URL for a contact, clicking the More button in the Communicate group of the Contact tab and then clicking Web Page launches your default web browser and displays the web page.

FIGURE 29.22

Assigning a task to a contact

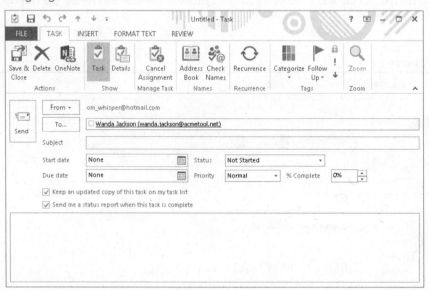

Performing a Mail Merge from Your Contacts

Mail merge is a technique that lets a form letter be addressed and sent to many different individuals. It can also be used to create mailing labels, envelopes, and catalogs such as a mailing list. Microsoft Office has merge tools built into several of its applications, most notably Word and Outlook.

When would you use Outlook to perform a mail merge? Only when the names and addresses that you want to use are in your Outlook Address Book. In this situation, using Outlook is often the simplest approach. Even so, some factors may mitigate against using Outlook for a merge and instead using the more advanced mail merge tools available in other Office applications. For example, Outlook cannot separate documents by zip code to get reduced mailing rates, and it would not be a good choice for a large merge that will create thousands of documents.

> **NOTE**
> You need to have Microsoft Word installed on your system to perform a mail merge.

The first step in performing a mail merge is usually to filter your contacts so that only the ones you want included are shown. You can do this by using Outlook's search capability or by customizing the Contacts view, both of which are covered earlier in this chapter. However, you can skip this step and select the contacts to include later. Then, follow these steps:

1. **In the main Outlook window, click People in the Navigation Bar.**
2. **Click Mail Merge in the Actions group of the Home tab.** Outlook displays the Mail Merge Contacts dialog box, as shown in Figure 29.23.

FIGURE 29.23

Performing a mail merge with Outlook contacts

3. **Make entries in this dialog box as described in the list that follows these steps.**
4. **Click OK to open Word to complete the merge.**

The options in the Mail Merge Contacts dialog box are as follows:

- **Contacts.** Select All Contacts in Current View to include all displayed contacts in the merge. Select Only Selected Contacts to select contacts to include later.

- **Fields to merge:** Specifies whether only visible contact fields or all contact fields will be available for the merge. These options may or may not be available depending on the current Contacts view.

- **Document file:** Specifies whether the merge will use a new or an existing Word document. If you choose the latter option, use the Browse button to locate the document to use.

29

- **Contact data file:** You can select this option to save the merge contact data in a separate Word document. Typically, this option is used to create a record of the people who were included in the mailing.

- **Document type:** You can merge to form letters, mailing labels, envelopes, or a catalog.

- **Merge to:** Specify whether the merge output goes to a Word document, to the printer, or to e-mail, as follows:

  - **New Document:** Merge creates a Word document that you can edit as needed before creating the final output.

  - **Printer:** The merged document is created and sent directly to the default printer.

  - **E-mail:** The merged documents are created as e-mail messages and placed in your Outbox.

In most situations, the remainder of the merge process is carried out in Word. Please consult your Word documentation for more information.

Setting Contact Options

Outlook has some global options that affect the way contacts work. To view and change these options:

1. **In the main Outlook window, click File, and then click Options.** The Outlook Options dialog box opens.

2. **Click the People tab in the list at the left to display the Outlook Options dialog box (Figure 29.24).**

3. **Set options as described in the list that follows these steps.**

4. **Click OK.**

The options that are available for contacts are as follows:

- **Default "Full Name" order:** Specifies how contacts are sorted when you order them based on full name. You can choose First Middle Last, Last First, or First Last1 Last2.

- **Default "File As" Order:** Specifies how contacts are sorted when you order them based on the File As field. Your choices are Last First, First Last, Company, Last First (Company), Company (Last, First).

- **Check for duplicate when saving new contacts:** Outlook warns you if you try to enter a new contact with the same name as an existing contact.

- **Show an additional index:** Outlook displays a second set of index buttons at the right edge of the Contacts window using the language you select from the list.

FIGURE 29.24

Setting global options for contacts

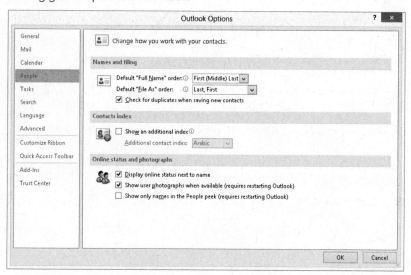

Summary

The Outlook Contacts feature is a powerful tool for managing and using information about people. It goes way beyond the basic Address Book to store just about any kind of information about a person you can imagine. What's more, it makes it easy to find and use that information in various ways. Many people find the Contacts feature to be one of Outlook's most useful tools. You can now take advantage of Contacts in the following ways:

- Display contacts in the default People view using the Navigation Bar, and change views from there.
- Add and edit contact information, including adding multiple phone numbers and other detailed information.
- Open a contact in the Contact window for additional commands.
- Organize contacts in groups, and e-mail a single contact or group.
- Add contacts from your social networks and view updates from those networks.
- Change a contact's business card and share contact info by e-mail.
- Use Skype and Lync IM and calling features with contacts.
- Mail merge and more to your contacts.
- Set contact options.

Working with Appointments and Tasks

A calendar is something you usually hang on the wall. It has a page for each month and a picture of a puppy, lighthouse, or famous painting. If that's what you think, then you haven't used the Outlook Calendar! Outlook provides a sophisticated calendar that helps you manage your time efficiently. In today's busy world, few of us have any shortage of things to do. A list of tasks always seems to be waiting for our attention, particularly in a high-pressure business or professional environment. This chapter covers the Outlook Calendar and Task (To-Do list) features, which can help you stay on time and on track with whatever you do.

Understanding the Outlook Calendar

At its heart, the Outlook Calendar stores and displays *appointments*. An *appointment* is just what it sounds like — a scheduled event with a title and a time and date specified for the beginning and end of the event. Outlook distinguishes between two types of appointments:

- A regular appointment has a specific start time and stop time. It is usually on the same day but does not have to be.
- An all-day event does not have specific start and stop times but rather takes up all of one or more days.

Scheduling appointments may not sound so special, and in fact it's not. But it's the way that Outlook lets you organize, use, and share your appointments that makes the Calendar so useful.

Using the Calendar

To show the Calendar, click Calendar in the Navigation bar at the bottom of Outlook. The Calendar appears in Month view, by default, and you'll explore more views momentarily. The top section of the Folder Pane shows a small calendar of the current month and next month, called the *Date Navigator*, which has several useful features, as shown in Figure 30.1 and described in the following list:

- Today's date is enclosed in a box — the 26th in Figure 30.1.
- The day(s) that are displayed in the larger Calendar view are highlighted in the small calendar. In Figure 30.1, these encompass February 24 through April 6.
- Days on which there is at least one appointment are in bold.
- The left and right arrows beside the month and year can be clicked on to move to the previous or next month, updating the larger Calendar view, as well. (You also can click the left and right arrows beside the current month or other timeframe at the top of the main Calendar to display earlier or later dates.)
- You can click any day number to change the Calendar view accordingly.

FIGURE 30.1

In Calendar, the Folder Pane displays the Date Navigator and the My Calendars group.

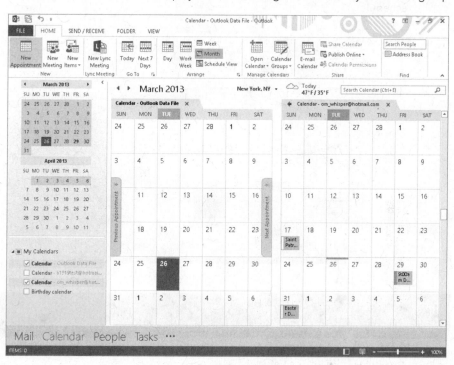

The Folder Pane includes the My Calendars Calendar group. It has a calendar for the Outlook Data file, plus a calendar for each additional e-mail account you set up. You can use the check boxes beside the listed calendars to determine which ones appear so that you can work with them. Make sure that you have selected the desired calendar in the Folder Pane when you start adding appointments. Also, by default, you will see multiple calendars side by side in the main Calendar window, as shown in Figure 30.1. The tab above each calendar identifies which account the calendar goes with; click the tab for the desired calendar to select that calendar.

If you prefer, you can open multiple calendars and *overlay* them for easier viewing. To turn overlay on or off (it's a toggle), choose View⇨Arrangement⇨Overlay. When you do this, the appointments from all the open calendars appear together in the main calendar pane, as shown in Figure 30.2. The information on each date is color coded to match its calendar tab, so that you can tell which calendar an appointment goes with. To select which calendar to work with, click its tab at the top of the overlaid schedule. The rest of the figures in this chapter will show the calendar with Overlay toggled on.

30

FIGURE 30.2

Toggle Overlay on to see the information from multiple calendars together on a single schedule.

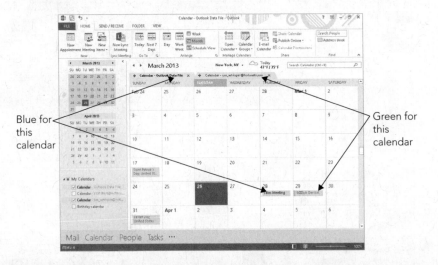

Blue for this calendar

Green for this calendar

> **TIP**
>
> You can use the View⇨Color⇨Color gallery to apply a different color coding color to the current calendar.

Working with Calendar views

When the Calendar is displayed, you can choose between viewing a single day (the default), a workweek, a week, or an entire month. Choose Week view to view the entire week or just the workweek (Monday–Friday). In Month view you can set the level of detail display to low, medium, or high. Plus you can use Schedule view to make it easier to find free time between two calendars to avoid scheduling conflicts. You select your view using either the View tab or the choices in the Arrange group on the Home tab. Outlook displays the date or date range displayed as well as buttons that move the calendar forward or backward by one of whatever unit (day, week, or month) is displayed above the calendar (see Figure 30.3).

> **TIP**
>
> No matter what day, week, or month you are viewing in the Calendar, you can always go directly to the current day by clicking the Today button in the Go To group on the Home tab of the Ribbon.

Using the Calendar Day view

When the Calendar is displaying a single day, it looks as shown in Figure 30.3. Times of the day are listed at the left edge of the schedule, and each appointment is displayed in its assigned time slot. Use the scroll bar to bring different times into view. Any all-day events for the day are displayed at the top of the schedule.

FIGURE 30.3

The Outlook Calendar displaying a single day's appointments

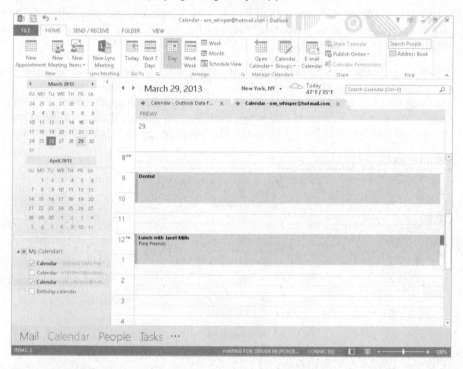

Click on an appointment to select it; it displays with a black border and small handles (boxes) on the top and bottom borders. You can:

- Drag the appointment to move it to a different time slot.
- Point at one of the handles at center top or bottom of the black border and drag it to change either the start or end time.

If you double-click on an appointment, it opens for editing, as explained later in this chapter.

TIP

You can use View ➪ Arrangement ➪ Time Scale to change the time intervals displayed in Day and Work Week views.

Using the Calendar Work Week and Week views

The Work Week view is shown in Figure 30.4. You can display the full seven-day week by selecting the Week view, instead.

In essence, the Week view consists of five or seven single-day views side-by-side, and you can perform the same actions as described for the Day view. You can also drag an appointment to a different day.

You can display the Reading pane with a view if you want to see details about a selected appointment, as shown at the right in Figure 30.4. This feature can be useful when the Calendar itself is too crowded to show these details for each appointment. To toggle the Reading pane on or off, click the View tab, click Reading Pane in the Layout group, and click the desired position. Clicking Off hides the Reading pane, which is the default setting.

FIGURE 30.4

The Outlook Calendar displaying an entire workweek's appointments

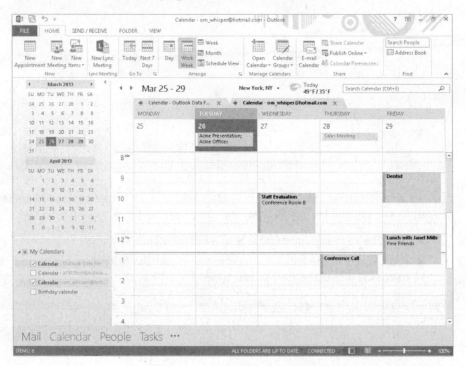

Using the Calendar Month view

The Month view shows an entire month of appointments, as shown in Figure 30.5. Appointments for each day are displayed in order but without time details. If an all-day event exists for the day, it is displayed with a white bar along the left — for example, the "Vacation Day" appointment on the 22nd, shown in Figure 30.5. If a day has more appointments than can be shown, a small down-arrow is displayed. Click on the arrow to open the single-day display, where you can view all appointments for that date.

Figure 30.5 shows the Month display with the High option selected for details, which is the default setting. You can also select Low or Medium details, as follows:

FIGURE 30.5

The Outlook Calendar displaying a month's appointments

NOTE

Note that the account calendar (note the Outlook Data File) shown in the examples in this chapter has holidays added. You can add holidays to a calendar using Outlook Options as noted later in the chapter. Also, many online services such as hotmail (now Outlook.com) enable you to sync with an online version of your calendar.

30

Using Schedule view

Schedule view, shown in Figure 30.6, lays out the currently open calendars along a horizontal timeline, giving you a way to compare timeframes and find open time slots available in all the calendars. In the example shown in Figure 30.6, the 1 to 2 P.M. timeframe is not open; the blue bar above that slot means the upper calendar has an all-day event, and the bottom calendar shows a conference call occurring at that time.

FIGURE 30.6

The Schedule view enables you to compare availability.

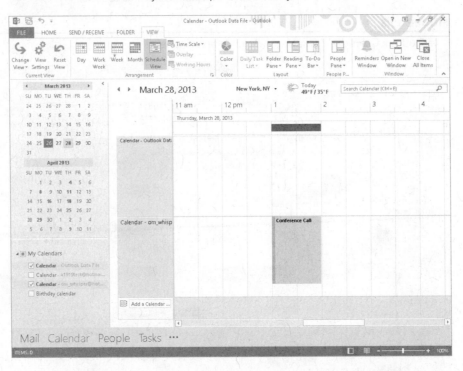

Using the To-Do Bar with appointments

Outlook's To-Do bar can be useful for working with Calendar items. To display the To-Do bar, click To-Do Bar in the Layout group of the View tab, then choose Normal. The To-Do bar is shown in Figure 30.7.

FIGURE 30.7

The To-Do bar can display the upcoming appointments, and more.

The To-Do bar can display three items:

- A list of Calendar appointments for the date you click in the calendar in the pane.

- A list of favorite People (Contacts), and a Search People text box for searching for contacts.

- A list of tasks. Tasks are not directly related to the Calendar and will be explained later in this chapter.

You can control what is displayed on the To-Do bar. You can display one, two, or all of the items in the preceding list. To change the To-Do bar display, choose View ➪ Layout ➪ To-Do bar, and then select or deselect the individual items — Calendar, People, and Tasks — on the shortcut menu as shown in Figure 30.7.

Controlling Which Calendar the To-Do Bar Displays

The Calendar and Tasks information is stored in the data file for the corresponding e-mail account. Features such as the To-Do Bar, sneak peek, and RSS feeds display the information from the default data file. Initially, the Outlook Data File is set as the default. To change this so that you see your account's schedule information, choose File ➪ Info ➪ Account Settings ➪ Account Settings. Click the Data Files tab, select the desired account in the list, and then click Set as Default above the list. In the Mail Delivery Location dialog box, click OK to confirm the change. Click Close, and then exit and restart Outlook so the change takes effect.

Note that if you make this change, however, Calendar only displays the calendar for the selected account and data file under My Calendars in the Folder Pane. The choice is a matter of whether its more important for you to work with scheduling between multiple calendars and perhaps put your calendar items and tasks in the Outlook Data File rather than your account's data file, noting that tasks sent from OneNote also will be put in the Outlook Data File. Or whether you want all your account information (except for e-mail messages, which are handled differently) stored in a single default file and be able to use the To-Do Bar and sneak peek effectively.

Getting a sneak peek

You don't have to be in Calendar in Outlook 2013 to see your appointments for an upcoming date. You can use a new feature, sometimes called *sneak peek*, that enables you to display a pop-up calendar from the Navigation Bar and click a date to preview. To use this feature from outside of Calendar, move the mouse pointer over Calendar in the Navigation Bar, then click the desired date in the pop-up calendar that appears. As shown in Figure 30.8, any appointments for the day are listed below the calendar. Move the mouse pointer off of the pop-up to close it.

FIGURE 30.8

Point to Calendar on the Navigation Bar and then click a date to see appointments.

Viewing the Weather Bar

You may have noticed in some of the earlier screen shots, such as Figure 30.6, that a little weather report appears above the calendar in some of the views. This Weather Bar automatically displays and hides itself depending on the current view settings. For example, there's no room for it to appear when you open the To-Do Bar. To change the location of the weather report provided, click the down arrow beside the displayed city, and then click Add Location. In the text box that appears, type a city and state or ZIP code, and then click the Search button.

Working with Appointments

An Outlook appointment can be very simple, or you can use Outlook's tools to add various features and options to an appointment. The following sections start with the basics of creating a simple appointment and then look at the various options.

Creating a simple appointment

To create a simple appointment, make sure that Outlook is displaying the Calendar, and that if multiple calendars are displayed, you have selected the one to which you want to add the appointment. Then do one of the following:

- Click the New Appointment button in the New Group of the Home tab on the Ribbon. Outlook opens a new appointment window for whatever day is selected in the Calendar.

- Double-click on a day on the Calendar. Outlook opens a new appointment window for that day.

- If working in Day, Work Week, or Week view, you can double-click on a specific time on a specific day to specify that the appointment should start at that time.

The Appointment window is shown in Figure 30.9 before any information has been entered. Then, follow these steps:

1. **At a minimum, you must enter a Subject for the appointment.** The Subject is the title of the appointment and is displayed in the Calendar — or at least part of it will be, depending on the length.

2. **Optionally, enter a Location for the appointment.** If you click on the arrow adjacent to the Location field, Outlook displays a list of previously used locations from which you can select. Otherwise, just type the location into the field. If space allows, the location displays along with the appointment subject in the Calendar.

30

FIGURE 30.9

An Outlook Appointment window

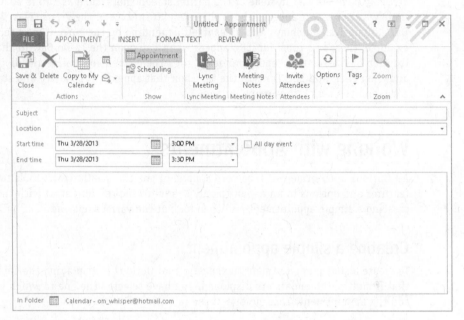

3. **If necessary, adjust the Start time or End time date (or both) by clicking on the arrow next to the displayed date and selecting from the calendar that Outlook displays.** An appointment can span two or more days, if needed.

4. **If the appointment is an all-day event, make sure that the All day event check box is checked.** An all-day event marks one or more entire days as Busy, with no specific start and stop times.

5. **If the appointment is not an all-day event, make sure that the All day event check box is not selected.** Outlook enables the fields for the start and stop times. If you double-clicked on a date in Month view, you will need to clear this check box before you can change times for the appointment.

6. **To select a Start time or End time, click on the adjacent arrow and select from the list that is displayed (Figure 30.10).**

FIGURE 30.10

Selecting the stop time for an appointment

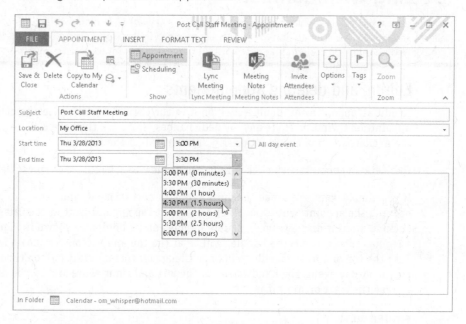

7. **Optionally, enter any desired notes in the field provided.**

8. **Click the Save & Close button in the Actions group of the Event or Appointment tab of the Ribbon.**

> **NOTE**
>
> If you've marked an appointment to be an all-day event, the first Ribbon tab in the Appointment window is the Event tab. When you have not marked an appointment as an all-day event, the first tab is the Appointment tab.

> **CAUTION**
>
> When you create an appointment that is an all-day event, Outlook does not mark the time as Busy but rather keeps it marked as Free. If you want an all-day event to display on the Scheduling page as either Tentative or Busy, you must explicitly select this option in the Options group of the Event tab of the Ribbon.

30

Dealing with Conflicts

You are free to schedule overlapping appointments if you want. When an overlap exists, Outlook displays a small message about it above the Subject text box in the Appointment window. So check that area carefully when you are creating new appointments if you want to avoid conflicts.

Editing and deleting appointments

To edit an appointment, double-click on it in the current Calendar view to open the Appointment window. Make any needed changes, and click the Save & Close button in the Actions group of the Event or Appointment tab of the Ribbon.

To delete an appointment, click it in Calendar view to select it; then, press Delete.

If you simply want to change the duration of an appointment, you can do so without opening the appointment form. When you select the appointment in the Calendar by clicking on it, it displays small, square handles on its border, as shown in Figure 30.11. For a regular appointment, the handles will be at the top and bottom, as shown in the figure. Drag the top or bottom handle to change the appointment's start or stop time, respectively. For an all-day event, the handles are on the left and right edges and can be dragged to change the start or stop time.

FIGURE 30.11

Drag a selected appointment's handles to change its duration.

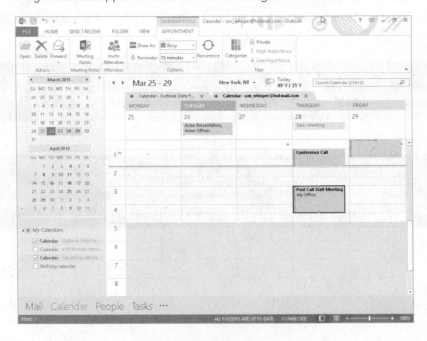

You can also change an appointment's time, date, or both without changing its duration; do so by pointing at the appointment and dragging it to the new position on the Calendar.

Appointment options

When you create an appointment, there are several optional features you may want to use. They are described in the following sections.

Scheduling recurring events

Some events occur on a regular basis. Perhaps you have a chiropractor appointment at 10:00 a.m. every Monday, or a company strategy meeting on the first Tuesday of each month. You can enter such appointments only once and have Outlook create all the recurrences automatically. Here's how:

1. **Use the techniques described earlier in this chapter to create an appointment for the first instance, but do not save and close it.**

2. **In the Appointment window, click the Recurrence button in the Options group of the Event or Appointment tab of the Ribbon.** (If necessary, click the Options button to display the group's options, and then click Recurrence.) Outlook displays the Appointment Recurrence dialog box, as shown in Figure 30.12.

FIGURE 30.12

Defining a recurring appointment

3. **In the Appointment time section of the dialog box, make sure that the Start time and End time are correct.**

4. **In the Recurrence pattern section, select Daily, Weekly, Monthly, or Yearly.**

30

5. **Depending on the option selected in the previous step, enter other recurrence details:**
   - **Daily:** Specify how often the appointment recurs (for example, every two days) or that it occurs every weekday.
   - **Weekly:** Specify how often the appointment recurs (for example, every week) and then on which day or days.
   - **Monthly:** Specify how often the appointment recurs (for example, every three months) and on which day. You can select a day by number, such as the 15th of every month. You can also select a day by the day of week, such as the second Tuesday of the month.

6. **Under Range of recurrence, enter the starting date and then specify when the recurrences end.** Your choices are the following:
   - No end date
   - End after a certain number of occurrences
   - End by a specified date

7. **Click OK to return to the Appointment window.**

8. **Complete any additional appointment details as needed.**

9. **Click Save & Close.**

When you double-click an existing recurring appointment for editing, you can click Open This Occurrence or Open the Series and then click OK to indicate whether to edit one or all of the appointments. You can then click the Recurrence button to open the Appointment Recurrence dialog box to modify the recurrence pattern. You can also remove the recurrence by clicking the Remove Recurrent button in this dialog box. Outlook removes all instances of the appointment from the Calendar except the next one. Note that changing the schedule for a single occurrence unlinks it from the overall recurring appointment.

If you try to delete a recurring appointment, Outlook gives you the option of deleting all occurrences of the appointment or just the current one.

Using appointment reminders

Outlook can remind you of an appointment by displaying a dialog box and playing a sound. You can specify how much advance notice you get and change the sound that is played. You can also turn reminders off. To set a reminder, follow these steps:

1. **Create the appointment, or open an existing one for editing.**

2. **Click the Reminder list in the Options group of the Event or Appointment tab of the Ribbon (Figure 30.13).** (Click the Options button first to expand the group's settings, if needed.)

FIGURE 30.13

Specifying the reminder interval for an appointment

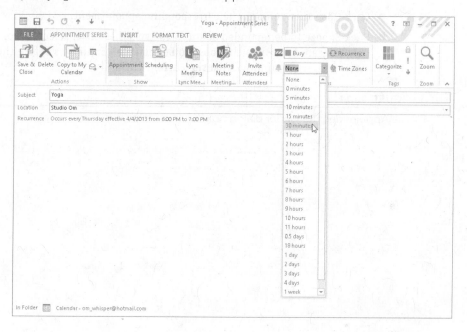

3. **Select the desired duration of the advance warning, from 0 minutes to 2 weeks.** The default is 15 minutes before the start time, although you can change this in Calendar Options (covered later in this chapter). Select None for no reminder.

4. **Reopen the menu and select Sound at the bottom to change the sound that is played when a reminder is displayed.** Deselect the Play This Sound option if you do not want a sound played (a dialog box is displayed).

5. **Click OK to return to the Appointment window.**

> **TIP**
>
> You also can point to an appointment on the calendar to see a pop-up note with more details such as the Start and End times.

When a reminder comes due, Outlook plays the sound (if one was specified for the appointment) and displays the dialog box shown in Figure 30.14. If more than one reminder is due, they will all be listed. The actions you can take are the following:

30

- Click Dismiss to dismiss the selected reminder.

- If more than one reminder is listed, click Dismiss All to dismiss all listed reminders.

- Click Open Item to open the corresponding appointment.

- Click Snooze to be reminded again in the specified time, selected from the adjacent list. You can, for example, choose to be reminded 5 minutes before the appointment start time, or 10 minutes from the current time.

FIGURE 30.14

The Appointment Reminder dialog box

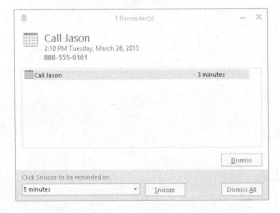

> **NOTE**
>
> Dismissing a reminder does not affect the appointment itself, which remains in your calendar.

Using other time zones

By default, Outlook appointments use the time zone that your system is set up to use. At times, you may want to use another time zone — for example, if you are in New York and your client says, "Call me at 8:00 A.M. my time." You may not know the number of hours difference, but as long as you know her time zone you are all set.

When you have the Appointment window open, click the Time Zones button in the Options group of the Event or Appointment tab of the Ribbon to display time zone selectors next to the start and end time fields (Figure 30.15); you may need to click an Options button first to display the group's options. Change either the start or end time zone to the desired setting; the other will change to the same thing. Now the start and stop times you enter will be interpreted as being in the selected time zone, and the appointment will be displayed in the correct local time slot. For example, if you are in the Eastern time zone and enter an appointment from 8:00 a.m. to 9:00 a.m. in the Pacific time zone, the appointment will display between 11:00 and 12:00 a.m. on your Calendar because the Pacific zone is three hours behind the Eastern zone.

FIGURE 30.15

Basing an appointment on a different time zone from the one you are in

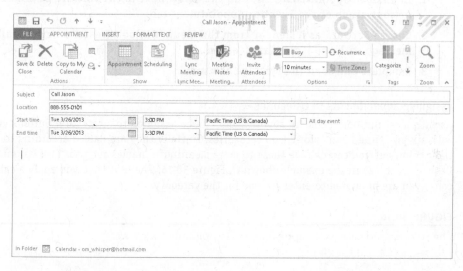

Forwarding an appointment

Outlook lets you forward an appointment to an e-mail recipient. Forwarding is different from inviting an attendee to a meeting (covered in the previous chapter). You have two ways to forward an Outlook appointment:

- Open the appointment, and click the Forward button in the Actions group of the Event or Appointment tab of the Ribbon.
- Right-click on the appointment in the Calendar, and select Forward from the shortcut menu.

In either case, Outlook creates a new e-mail message with the appointment attached as an Outlook item and the title of the appointment inserted in the Subject field. You then address and complete the e-mail message as usual. If you are using Outlook with an Exchange Server account, the appointment itself is forwarded without being attached to an e-mail message.

When the recipients receive a forwarded appointment, they can double-click on the attachment to open it. It opens in an Appointment window, and users can save it to their calendars or discard it as desired. Of course, recipients must be using Outlook or another program that supports the Outlook appointment format.

30

Another forwarding option for appointments is the iCalendar format. This is a widely supported format for calendar information and is supported by Outlook as well as many other scheduling programs. If you are not sure that all your recipients are using Outlook, using this format may be needed when forwarding an appointment. To do so, follow these steps:

1. **In an open appointment, click on the arrow next to the Forward button in the Actions group of the Event or Appointment tab.**

2. **Choose Forward as iCalendar from the menu. Outlook creates a new e-mail message with the iCalendar attached.**

3. **Complete and send the message as usual.**

Assigning appointments to categories

As with most Outlook items, an appointment can be assigned to a category. Outlook comes with six predefined and color-coded categories. Initially they are named according to their color, but you can change these to more meaningful names such as "Professional Development," as in the example shown in Figure 30.16. The first time you apply a category color, you are prompted to enter a name for the category.

FIGURE 30.16

The color-coded categories appear in the Appointment window.

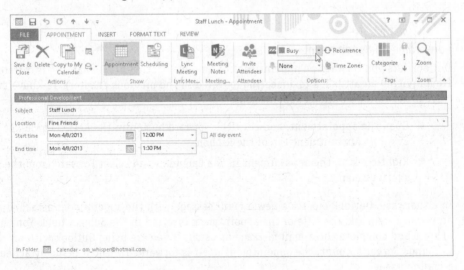

You have two ways to assign an appointment to a category:

- With the appointment open, click the Categorize button in the Tags group of the Event or Appointment tab of the Ribbon, and select the desired category from the list that is displayed. (You may need to click the Tags button first to display the group's choices.) Select Clear All Categories to remove any assigned categories from the appointment. Click All Categories to open the Color Categories dialog box where you can create and assign a custom color.

- In the Calendar, right-click on the appointment and select Categorize from the shortcut menu. Then, select the desired category.

An appointment, as is true of other Outlook items, can be assigned to more than one category. In the Calendar, a categorized appointment is displayed in the color of the assigned category.

Setting appointment importance

By default, all appointments that you create are assigned normal importance. You can assign either low or high importance to an open appointment by clicking on the corresponding button in the Tags group of the Event or Appointment tab of the Ribbon. (You may need to click the Tags button first to display the group's choices.) Then you can use this importance level as a criterion when using the Search feature in your Calendar, as discussed elsewhere in this chapter.

Marking an appointment as private

Outlook gives you the ability to publish your calendar so that other people can view your schedule. You may at times want to mark an appointment as Private so that other people viewing your calendar cannot see the details. They can still see that you are busy during the period of the appointment but will not have access to details about the appointment.

To mark an open appointment as Private, click the Private (padlock) button in the Tags group of the Event or Appointment tab of the Ribbon. Depending on the size of the Appointment window, you may need to click the Tags button to display the group's choices.

> **NOTE**
>
> You can use the E-mail calendar button in the Share group of the Home tab to share your calendar information for a particular timeframe. After you choose that command, it works just as described in the "Sending a calendar" section in Chapter 27. The Share group also includes a Share Calendar command, which is only available when you are using an Microsoft Exchange Server account, and a Publish Online ⇨ Publish to WebDAV command, which enables you to specify a World Wide Web Distributed Authoring and Versioning (WebDAV) server to publish to.

Determining how an appointment displays

An appointment in your calendar can display in one of several ways in the various views: Free, Working Elsewhere, Tentative, Busy, or Out of Office. This display affects your own calendar as well as that of other people with whom you are sharing your calendar. When you create an appointment, you can specify how it will display. (The default is Busy except for all-day events, as mentioned earlier in this chapter.) To do so, click the Show As list on the Options group of the Event or Appointment tab on the Ribbon (click the Options button first if needed), and select from the list (Figure 30.17).

30

FIGURE 30.17

Specifying how an appointment displays on the schedule

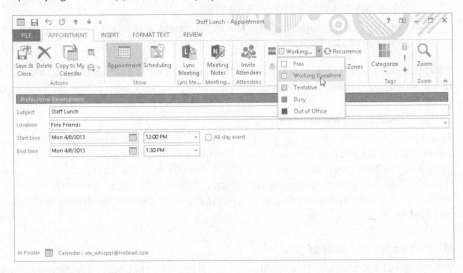

Why Display an Appointment as Free?

It may seem strange that Outlook gives you the option of displaying an appointment as Free on the schedule. It makes sense however, when you realize that some appointments are not critical and can easily be changed. You can just as easily get that haircut tomorrow as you can today. By displaying such appointments as Free, you do not prevent other people from scheduling a meeting at that time when they view your schedule.

Searching the Calendar

As your Calendar becomes filled with appointments past and future, it will become difficult if not impossible to find information by simply scrolling through the Calendar. You can use the Search feature to filter the Calendar to show just the information you want. For example, you can filter to show only appointments within a certain month assigned to a specific category.

For a basic search, enter your search term in the Search Calendar box at the top right of the Calendar display (Figure 30.18). You can also click on the down arrow to select from previously used search terms. Outlook automatically searches as you enter the term and displays only matching appointments (or a message, if it finds no matching entries). Click the X at the right end of the Search box to cancel the search and return to displaying all Calendar items.

FIGURE 30.18

Performing a basic search of the Calendar

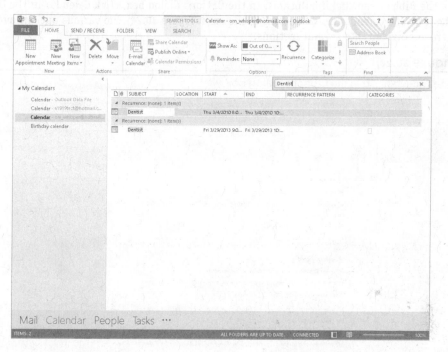

If you need more control over the search, click on the magnifying glass at the right end of the Search box without typing anything. Outlook displays the Search Tools ⇨ Search contextual tab, as shown in Figure 30.19. You can use one of the choices in the Refine group to narrow the search results. Or, you can click Search Tools in the Options group, and then click Advanced Find to open the Advanced Find dialog box. It works just like the one for Contacts described in Chapter 29. Click the Close Search button in the Close group at the right end of the tab to finish working with the search features.

FIGURE 30.19

Tools for performing an advanced search of the Calendar

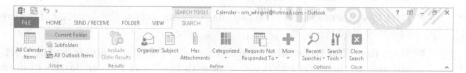

Setting Calendar Options

The Outlook Calendar comes with default settings for many aspects of its operation. As you become familiar with the Calendar, you may want to make changes to these settings to customize the Calendar for the way you work. You access Calendar Options by choosing File on the Ribbon and clicking Options. In the Options dialog box, click Calendar in the list at the left. The Calendar tab of options is shown in Figure 30.20. The various options available here are divided into several sections.

FIGURE 30.20

The Calendar tab in the Options dialog box

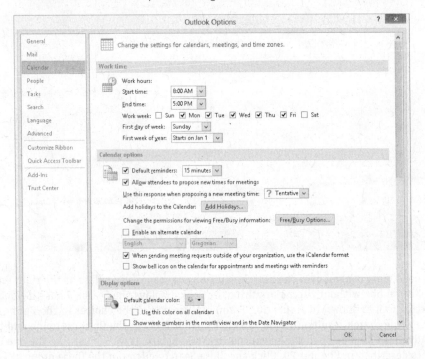

The first section of Calendar options has to do with how Outlook defines the workweek, as follows:

- **Work week:** Select days that you want to be considered part of the workweek, and deselect those that you do not.

- **First day of week:** Select the day that Outlook uses as the first day of the week for Calendar displays.

- **Start time/End time:** Select the times of day that Outlook uses for the start and stop of the workday. (If you work with Lync, you will see Outside of Normal Business Hours for times beyond the allowed work day for your organization.)

- **First week of year:** Select how Outlook determines the first week of the year. The options are Starts on Jan 1 (the week that contains Jan 1), the first week with four days in the new year, and the first week that is entirely in the new year.

The next section of the Calendar Options dialog box includes options for a variety of features:

- **Default reminders:** By default, Outlook reminds you of appointments 15 minutes before the start time (you can change this for individual appointments, of course). To change the default lead time, select it from the drop-down list. You can select any time from 0 minutes to two weeks. If you do not want a default reminder for messages, deselect the Default Reminder option.

- **Allow attendees to propose new times for meetings:** People you invite to meetings are allowed to respond by proposing a new time for the meeting.

- **Use this response when proposing a new meeting time:** Select from the list to specify whether new meeting times that you propose are marked as Tentative, Accept, or Decline.

- **Add holidays to calendar:** Lets you copy holidays for one or more specific countries onto your calendar. You select the country or countries from a list.

Finally, this dialog box has a few advanced options, as follows:

- **Enable an alternate calendar:** Lets you display an alternate calendar in parallel with the default one using the language and calendar structure you select.

- **When sending meeting requests...:** Sends meeting requests in the more widely supported iCalendar format instead of Outlook's proprietary format.

- **Free/Busy Options:** Sets options for publishing your calendar. These options were covered earlier in this chapter.

- **Default calendar color:** Select the color to use for the calendar display.

- **Time zones:** Sets the default time zone for your calendar and also permits you to display a second, alternate time zone in the Calendar.

- **Show weather on the calendar:** Enables you to control whether the new Weather Bar appears and whether it shows Fahrenheit or Celsius.

Understanding Tasks

A *task* is similar to an appointment in that it is something you must do. It is different in that it does not have a specific date or time associated with it, although it may well have a due date by which it is supposed to be completed. In this sense, Outlook tasks are pretty much like a paper to-do list that you stick on the fridge. When you look a little deeper, however, you'll find that tasks can do so much more:

- You can be reminded of a task at a specified time and date.

- You can specify different priorities for different tasks.

30

- You can assign a task to someone else and send that person a message with the required information.

- You can assign a status to a task (not started, in progress, and so on) as well as a percent completed value.

- You can send a status report on a task to other people.

Using the Tasks Feature

To switch to working with Tasks in Outlook, click the Tasks button on the Navigation bar. The list of tasks appears, using one of a variety of available views. The Simple List view, shown in Figure 30.21, displays active tasks — those not yet completed — as well as tasks checked off as complete. They are arranged by due date initially, although you can change the sort order by clicking the column headings (Subject, Due Date, and so on) at the top of the list.

If you want to view tasks differently, click the Change View button in the Current View group of the Home tab or the View tab, and click another view. Figure 30.22 shows the To-Do List view, which includes a pane at the right that provides more details about the selected task in the task list.

FIGURE 30.21

The Simple List view displays a list of all your tasks.

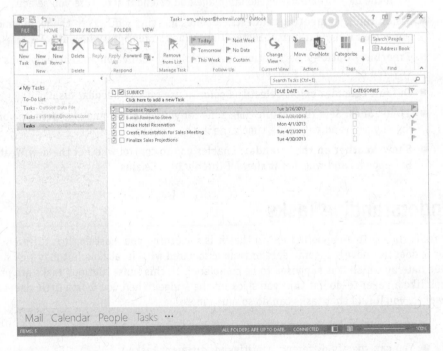

FIGURE 30.22

Task List view includes a pane with more details.

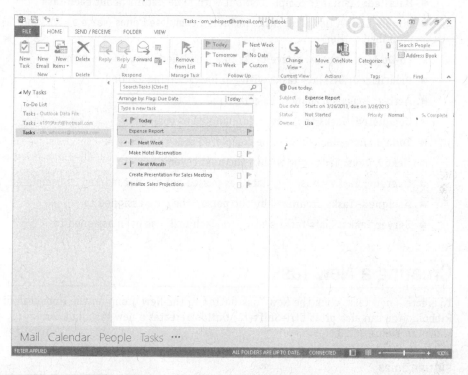

While you are viewing tasks, you can open a single task by double-clicking on it. You can also perform certain actions with the task by right-clicking on it in the task list and selecting from the shortcut menu. These actions are the following:

- Assign the task to someone.
- Add a follow-up to the task.
- Assign a category to the task.
- Delete the task.

You learn more about these actions later in this chapter when you learn how to create a new task.

30

The full list of available views is:

- **Detailed:** Similar to Simple List but with more details about each task
- **Simple List:** A list of all tasks including completed ones (same as clicking Tasks, as described earlier)
- **To-Do List:** Displays active tasks in a simplified, easy-to-use format
- **Prioritized:** Displays tasks with a priority setting applied
- **Active:** Tasks not marked as completed
- **Completed:** Tasks that have been marked as completed
- **Today:** Shows tasks due to be completed today
- **Next 7 Days:** Tasks due within the next seven days
- **Overdue:** Tasks whose due date has passed but are not marked as completed
- **Assigned:** Tasks organized by the person they are assigned to
- **Server Tasks:** Lists tasks and whom each task has been assigned to

Creating a New Task

To create a new task, click the New Task button in the New group on the Home tab of the Ribbon. (You can also press Ctrl+Shift+K.) Outlook creates a new task and displays it as shown in Figure 30.23.

FIGURE 30.23

Creating a new task

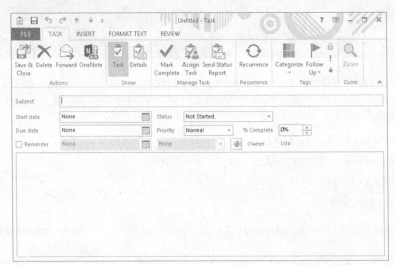

The only required entry in this window is the Subject, which will be the title of the task that is displayed in Task view. The other task information in the window is explained here and in the following sections:

- **Start date:** If you want to specify a start date for the task, click on the adjacent down-arrow, and select the date from the Calendar.

- **Due date:** Click on the adjacent down-arrow, and select the task's due date from the Calendar.

- **Status:** By default, this is set as Not Started. If necessary, you can open this list and select In Progress, Completed, Waiting on Someone Else, or Deferred.

- **Priority:** The default is Normal; you can also select Low or High.

- **% Complete:** If the task is already partially complete, use the up and down arrows to specify the correct value in this field.

- **Categorize:** Click on this button to assign the task to an Outlook category.

- **Follow Up:** Click on this button in the Tags group of the Task tab to assign a follow-up to the task.

- **Private:** Click on this button in the Tags group of the Task tab to make the task private so that it will not be viewable by other people when you share your calendar.

- **Reminder:** Check this check box if you want to be reminded of the task; then, use the adjacent fields to specify the date and time of the reminder. Click the speaker icon to change the sound that will be played at the reminder time.

- **Assign Task:** Click on this button in the Manage Task group of the Task tab to associate the task with one or more of your contacts.

- **Save & Close:** Click on this button on the Actions group of the Task tab of the Ribbon when you are finished defining the task.

Other aspects of creating a new task are explained in the following sections.

Entering task details

If you click the Details button in the Show group of the Task tab of the Ribbon, Outlook displays the Details window for the task. This window is shown in Figure 30.24.

The fields available in the Details window let you keep track of additional information related to a task. You can specify the completion date, enter information about the time spent on the task, identify a company associated with the task, track mileage, and enter billing information. Outlook does not track this information for you but just provides these detail fields for you to enter it in.

30

FIGURE 30.24

Entering details for a new task

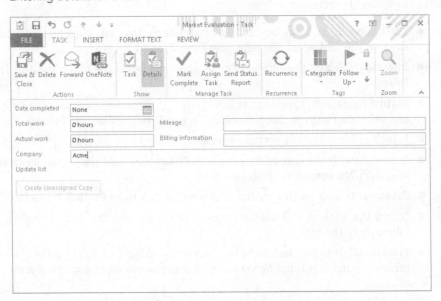

The lower section of the Details window is relevant only if the task has been assigned to someone as described shortly under "Assigning a task".

When you have finished entering details for the task, click the Task button in the Show group of the Task tab on the Ribbon to return to the regular Task window. You can also click Save & Close in the Actions group if you have finished defining the task.

Marking a task as complete

To mark a task as complete, click the check mark beside it in the current view. Or, double-click it to open it, and in the Manage Task group of the Task tab, click the Mark Complete button. You can then close the task window.

Assigning a task

Outlook lets you assign a task to someone else. Doing so can be useful in a variety of situations, such as when you are heading a committee and need to delegate various jobs to the committee members. By using Outlook's Assign Task command, you can track progress and be notified when each task has been completed.

To assign a task, create the task as described earlier in this chapter. You can also open an existing task and, as long as you are the owner of the task, assign it to someone else. Here's how:

1. **In the task window for the task to assign, click the Assign Task button in the Manage Task group of the Task tab of the Ribbon.** Outlook displays the window shown in Figure 30.25. This is actually just the regular Task window with a few extra elements.

FIGURE 30.25

Assigning a task to someone else

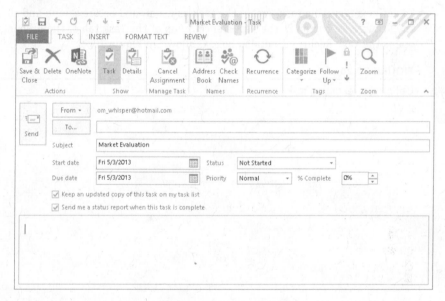

2. **In the To field, enter the e-mail address of the person to whom you are assigning the task.** You can also click the To button and select from your contacts.
3. **Enter additional information about the task, such as subject and due date, if it has not already been entered.**
4. **Select or deselect the two available options (explained next).**
5. **Click the Send button.**

Two options are available when you assign a task to someone else, as follows:

- **Keep an updated copy of this task on my task list:** You receive automatic updates when the person to whom you assign the task updates its status.
- **Send me a status report when this task is complete:** You receive an automatic notification when the person to whom you assign the task marks it as Completed.

30

When you send a task assignment, the recipient receives an e-mail message containing information about the assignment and permitting the recipient to either accept or decline the assignment. You learn more about this and other aspects of task assignments later in this chapter, in the section, "Working with Assigned Tasks."

Specifying task recurrence

Like appointments, tasks can have a defined recurrence. For example, you may have to review each month's sales figures by the end of the next month. Rather than enter a new task each month, you can define a task that recurs each month.

To define a recurring task, create the task as usual, and before saving and closing it, click the Recurrence button in the Recurrence group of the Task tab of the Ribbon. Outlook opens the Task Recurrence dialog box, as shown in Figure 30.26.

FIGURE 30.26

Defining a recurring task

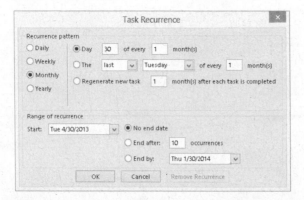

> **NOTE**
>
> When you assign a recurring task, a copy of the task remains in your Task List but cannot be updated automatically. However, if you requested a status report when the task is complete, you receive a status report for each occurrence of the task that is completed.

The four basic patterns of recurrence are Daily, Weekly, Monthly, and Yearly. When you choose the basic pattern in the top left of the dialog box, the remainder of the options change to reflect what's available:

- **Daily:** You can choose every so many days or every weekday.
- **Weekly:** You specify how often (every week, every two weeks, and so on) and the day or days of the week.

- **Monthly:** You specify which day of the month, either as a number (for example, the 25th of each month) or a day of the week (for example, the first Thursday).
- **Yearly:** You specify a specific date (for example, June 12) or a day of a month (for example, the first Monday in June).

In all cases, you also specify a start date and when the recurring task ends.

Working with Assigned Tasks

Working with assigned tasks, whether you are the person doing the assigning or the person accepting the assignment, can be a bit confusing. After you understand it, however, the tool can be very useful.

Receiving a task assignment

When someone sends you a task assignment, you receive an e-mail message asking you to respond to the assignment request. Select the message in the message list, and two choices appear above the task in the Reading Pane:

- **Accept:** Accepts the assignment, adds it to your Task List, and notifies the person who sent you the assignment that you have accepted.
- **Decline:** Declines the assignment and notifies the person who sent you the assignment that you have declined.

You also can open the task from your Task list, and use the Accept or Respond choice in the Respond group of the Task tab.

No matter which method you use, in the dialog box that appears, you can choose either Edit response before sending or Send response now and then click OK to proceed with the message in the desired fashion.

Receiving accept/decline notifications

When you send a task assignment to someone, one of three things will happen:

- **The person may accept the task:** You receive a message to that effect, and the task is automatically updated to reflect that the task was accepted and is now owned by that person.
- **The person may decline the task:** You receive an e-mail notification. When you open this e-mail, you can take one of the following two actions by clicking the corresponding button on the toolbar:
  - **Return the task to your Task list:** You regain ownership of the task.
  - **Assign task:** Assign the task to someone else.

30

About Task Ownership

A task has, at any given moment, one and only one owner. *Owning* a task means that you can assign it to someone else. Here's how ownership works:

- When you create a task, you are the original owner.
- When you assign the task to someone, that person becomes the temporary owner.
- The person who receives the assignment can do one of two things: (1) accept the task and become the owner; (2) decline the task and return ownership to the sender.

If you assign a task to someone and that person declines, ownership passes back to you only when you reclaim ownership by returning the task to your Task List. It does not happen automatically.

Assigning a Task to Multiple People

Although Outlook does not prevent you from assigning a task to two or more people, you cannot keep an updated copy of the task in your Task List. For this reason, it is better to divide a multiperson task into parts and assign each part, as a separate task, to an individual person.

Task status reports

When you have accepted a task assignment, you own that task and no one but you can change the task even though it may be on someone else's Task list. You can then, as you work on the task, open it and update the status and percentage completed of the task; you can also mark it as Completed. When you do so and save the modified task, an update is sent to the person who assigned you the task (assuming that the Keep an updated copy of this task on my task list option was selected when you were sent the assignment). By default, this update does not appear in the task assigner's Inbox but is processed automatically, and the updated information is available the next time the task assigner views the task.

Likewise, if the Send me a status report when this task is complete option was selected when you were sent the assignment, the person who assigned the task receives an automatic update when you mark the task as Completed. Although Task Complete updates are processed automatically, they appear in the person's Inbox.

A task can have more than one prior owner. Suppose, for example, that person A created the task and sent a task request to person B. Then, person B sent a task request to person C, who accepted the task. C is the owner of the task, and both A and B are prior owners and will receive status updates.

Sending a status report manually

Sometimes you may want to send a status report or comments about a task manually. Here are two situations in which doing so might be desirable:

- The original task request (when you were assigned the task) did not include a request for automatic status updates.

- You were not assigned the task; it is simply a task that you created but want to keep other people updated about.

To send a status report manually, open and save the task and click the Send Status Report button in the Manage Task group of the Task tab of the Ribbon. Outlook creates an e-mail message with information about the task status in the body of the message. You can add text as needed. If the task was assigned to you, the To field already contains the addresses of the task's prior owners. You can add additional recipients if desired.

Other Ways of Viewing Tasks

The most flexible way to view your tasks is by using the Task view, as explained earlier in this chapter. You can also have Outlook display tasks on the To-Do bar and in Calendar view.

Viewing tasks on the To-Do Bar

You can display active tasks on the To-Do bar along with the Date Navigator and upcoming appointments. They are displayed at the bottom, as shown in Figure 30.27. Use View⇨Layout⇨To-Do Bar⇨Tasks to toggle the task list on and off in the To-Do bar. When you're working with Tasks in Outlook and toggle on the task display in the To-Do Bar, it shows the tasks for all the folders (accounts) in the My Tasks group, unless you've changed to another default data file as described in an earlier note.

FIGURE 30.27

Viewing the daily Task List on the To-Do bar

Viewing tasks on the Calendar

The Outlook Calendar can display the daily Task list along with your appointments in some views such as Day view. The Daily Task List is displayed below the Appointment section of the Calendar, as shown in Figure 30.28. You have three options as to how the daily Task List is displayed:

- **Normal:** This is shown in the figure, with task subjects, categories, and follow-up flags.

- **Minimized:** This displays the number of active tasks for the displayed time period without any details.

- **Off:** This does not display the list.

FIGURE 30.28

Viewing the Daily Task List on the Outlook Calendar

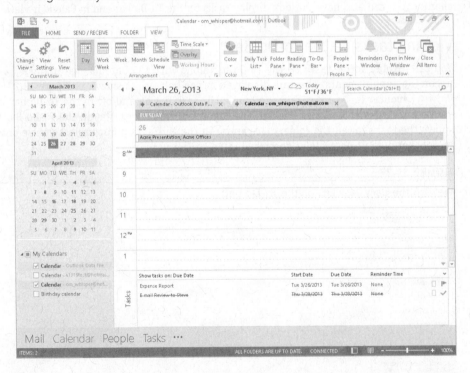

To switch between daily Task List views, display the Outlook Calendar, click the View tab, and then choose Daily Task List in the Layout group. Then, select the desired view from the next menu. The Arrange By choices on this menu also let you specify whether to display tasks by due date (the default) or start date, and whether to show completed tasks.

Setting Task Options

Outlook offers several options that relate to the way tasks and task assignments work. To view and change these options, select Options from the File to display the Outlook Options dialog box, then click Tasks at the left. The Tasks tab choices are shown in Figure 30.29. The first two options determine the colors used to display overdue tasks and completed tasks; the default colors are red and dark gray, respectively. The other options are as follows:

- **Set reminders on tasks with due dates:** If selected, Outlook automatically sets a reminder for all tasks that you create with a due date.

- **Keep my task list updated:** If selected, Outlook maintains updated copies of tasks you have assigned on your task list.

- **Send status report:** If selected, Outlook automatically sends a status report when you mark as Completed a task that you have been assigned.

FIGURE 30.29

The Tasks settings in Outlook Options

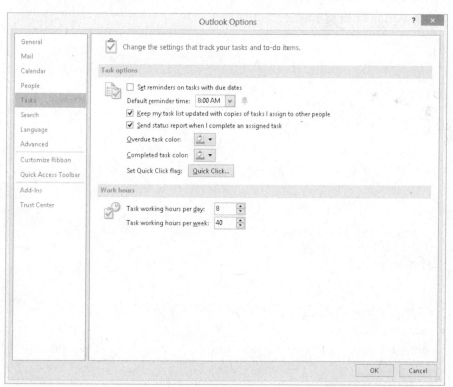

Summary

Outlook's Calendar is a powerful and flexible tool for keeping track of your appointments and other time commitments. Much more than a simple date book, the Outlook Calendar can do things such as remind you of an upcoming appointment. Outlook also provides some powerful tools for keeping track of your tasks. By listing your tasks and optionally reminding you of when they are due, Outlook can greatly reduce the chance that you'll forget to do something important. You should now be able to use Outlook to:

- Create appointments, including all day events and recurring appointments and events.
- Change your calendar view as needed, including viewing multiple calendars and overlaying calendars.
- Find appointments.
- Use the To-Do Bar and sneak peek.
- Build your list of tasks.
- Mark tasks as complete.
- Assign tasks to others.

Part VI

Designing Publications with Publisher

If you've tried designing more graphical documents in Word but have wanted more design help and different tools, then you might benefit from learning about Publisher 2013 in this part of the book. Chapter 31 shows you the basics of laying out information for a publication in Publisher. Chapter 32 then shows you how to apply more design flair and finalize a publication, concluding with an output option that's new in Publisher 2013.

Introducing Publisher

D esktop publishing made creating printed publications easier and faster, but for years it remained the bailiwick of graphic art and design superheroes. The software was expensive and difficult to master and provided little in the way of design help for mere mortals.

Microsoft Publisher was one of the first programs to make publication design affordable and doable for the average computer users. From its first version, Publisher offered an easy layout, simple tools, a variety of styles and graphics, and attractive templates for publication designs. This chapter shows you how to use Publisher 2013 to choose a publication template and add text and graphics to complete a publication.

The Publisher Workspace

Each time you start Publisher, the program prompts you to create a new publication file by selecting a template from the New template gallery. You can either create a new publication as described in the next section, click one of the choices under Recent to open a recently used document, or click the Open Other Publications command to open a publication you created previously. In any case, Publisher displays a publication and the Ribbon in its workspace (Figure 31.1).

FIGURE 31.1

The Publisher workspace offers a variety of tools for creating publications.

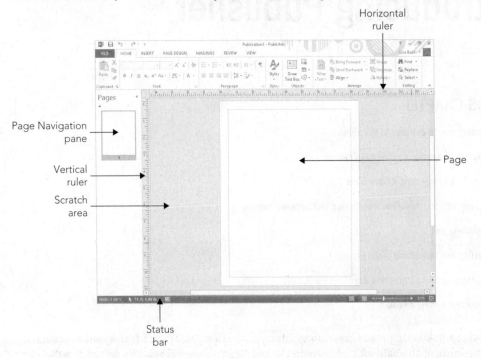

You can design your publications by adding text, graphic objects, and other elements to the white page area. When the publication has multiple pages, you can move between pages by pressing Ctrl+Page Up and Ctrl+Page Down, or by clicking on the icon for a page in the Page Navigation pane, on the left side of the workspace. The gray area that appears around the page is called the *scratch area*. This area serves as a holding space for any objects you might want to pull off the page and reuse elsewhere. For example, you can drag a graphic off one page to the scratch area, display another page, and then drag the graphic onto that page.

The *vertical* and *horizontal rulers* enable you to align objects on a page with precision. As you drag an object, a moving marker appears on each ruler to indicate the mouse position, and the position measurements appear in the status bar. By default, when you drag an object and release the mouse, the object will snap into alignment with any green ruler guides that you have displayed or added. You can turn this snap feature on or off using the Guides check box in the Layout group of the Page Design tab. You can display built-in ruler guides for arranging objects by clicking the Guides button in the Layout group of the Page Design tab, and then clicking one of the thumbnails under Built-In Ruler Guides on the gallery that appears. You can also create custom ruler guides by dragging them from either ruler, as shown in the example in Figure 31.2. Then, drag objects to align with your guides.

FIGURE 31.2

Drag from either ruler to create a guide.

Horizontal guide

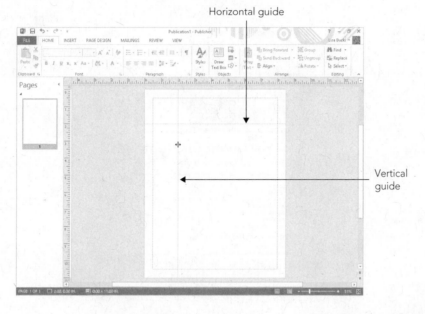

Vertical guide

NOTE

You also can use the Size settings, described later in the chapter, to size and position objects.

The Ribbon in Publisher offers a variety of buttons, galleries, and lists that you can use to add and work with publication content and publication files. Publisher displays these seven Ribbon tabs on-screen by default:

- **File:** As in the other Office 2013 applications, the File tab displays the Backstage view, with choices for creating, managing, sharing, and printing files.

- **Home:** This tab includes buttons for adding and formatting text, copying and pasting, working with object positioning, and finding and replacing.

- **Insert:** This tab enables you to insert pages, create tables, insert different types of illustrations such as online pictures, use building blocks to create content, add business information or insert text from another document, add hyperlinks, and work with headers and footers.

- **Page Design:** This tab enables you to change the page template, modify the margins, and set the color and font scheme. For example, Figure 31.3 shows a template applied to a previously blank document.

FIGURE 31.3

Use the Page Design tab to change templates and choose other page settings.

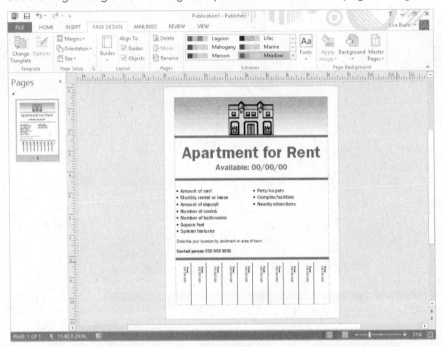

- **Mailings:** This tab enables you to merge data from a list to make custom copies of a document, as in Word 2013.

- **Review:** This tab offers choices for spell checking the document, performing content research, substituting words with the thesaurus, and changing language settings.

- **View:** This tab offers the options for changing how the document appears on-screen, including the settings for hiding and redisplaying specific screen elements such as guides and rulers.

> **TIP**
>
> Remember, to see the function of any Ribbon button or list, point to it with the mouse to display a pop-up ScreenTip identifying what the button or list does.

As in other Office applications, with Publisher one or more contextual tabs may appear depending on what item you've selected in the document. For example, you might see the Drawing Tools⇨Format or Text Box Tools⇨Format tabs. You can use the choices on contextual tabs as needed to format and edit the selected object.

Using a Template to Create a Publication

Any time you start Publisher or select the File⇨New command (Ctrl+N), Publisher displays the New template gallery choices in the Backstage view so that you can navigate to and select a template to use to create a new publication file. When your system is connected to the Internet and you are signed in to Publisher, you can click Featured above the template thumbnails and scroll down to see the suggested templates available for download, as shown in Figure 31.4. Click a template thumbnail to view a window with a preview and description, and then click Create to download the template and create a new publication based on it.

FIGURE 31.4

Publisher enables you to select a template from various publication types.

Featured selected

Scroll down to see templates available for download.

If you click Built-In above the template thumbnails, Publisher displays template categories including: Advertisements, Banners, Brochures, Business Forms, Flyers, and more. Scroll down, click a category thumbnail, and Publisher subcategories for that template type. You can click on the desired template to see a preview in the upper-right corner, as shown in Figure 31.5. Scroll down to see more subcategories, or click one of the folder icons at the far right of a subcategory to see even more templates for that subcategory. If you want to see more template subcategories, scroll down.

FIGURE 31.5

Browse, preview, and select a template.

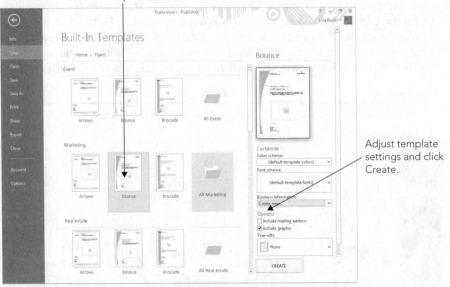

Click a template thumbnail to see a preview.

Adjust template settings and click Create.

NOTE

Some built-in template categories, such as the Newsletters category, do not include subcategories. You can just scroll down and click the desired template thumbnail.

When you've clicked the thumbnail for the template you'd like to use, you can set up the template by making choices in the Customize and Options areas below the template preview. The template settings are only available for installed templates. The window that appears when you download an online template does not display any options. After you've made the desired choices, click the Create button. The new publication based on the template will appear in the workspace, as in the example shown in Figure 31.6, so that you can begin replacing placeholder information with the unique information for your publication.

Notice that the new publication file has a placeholder name; the example in Figure 31.6 is named *Publication4*. Remember to use the File⇨Save As command (Ctrl+S) or click the Save button on the Quick Access Toolbar to name the publication and specify a save location for it. Press Ctrl+S periodically to save changes as you make them in the file, and use the File⇨Open command (Ctrl+O) or click the Open button on the Standard toolbar to reopen any existing publication.

FIGURE 31.6

The new publication based on the template appears.

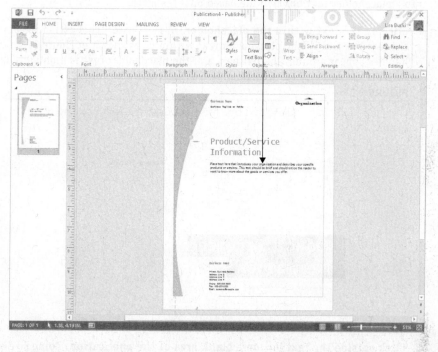

Text box with instructions

NOTE

After choosing File ⇨ Open, you can click Recent Publications under Open in the Backstage view and then click on one of the publications listed at right to reopen a recently used file.

Working with Text

In Publisher, you add text into a text box. When you move the mouse over a text box, a dashed boundary displays to define where the text will appear. (Clicking in the text box changes to a solid boundary with selection handles.) If you create your publication from a template, the template design provides placeholder text boxes within the publication, as in the example shown in Figure 31.6. In that case, you can simply use an existing text box to add the text. You also can create your own text boxes as required for your publication design.

Typing text in a placeholder

Adding text into a placeholder text box requires that you select the placeholder and then type the text within the placeholder to replace the example text. Use these steps to add text into a placeholder text box in a file based on a template:

1. **Click on the text within the placeholder.** In most cases, this action selects both the text box and all the placeholder text within it, as shown in Figure 31.7. Selection handles appear around the text box, and the placeholder text is highlighted.

FIGURE 31.7

Click the text in a template text box to select both the text box and the example text.

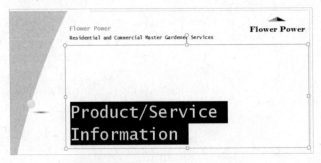

2. **Type the replacement text.** Your new text appears in the text box.
3. **Click outside the text box on a blank area of the publication.** Doing so deselects the text box, finishing your entry.

Text boxes do not resize automatically in Publisher, so if the text you add is too long to fit within the text box, you need to resize the text, as described later in the section, "Resizing, autoflow, and linked text boxes."

Many of the templates have automated placeholders that automatically insert business information stored in the business information set in Publisher. If you have not yet specified information for the business information set, choose File ⇨ Info ⇨ Edit Business Information. Enter the information in the Create New Business Information Set dialog box, click Save, and then click Update Publication. You can use the Business Information drop-down list in the Text group of the Insert tab to select a business information component and add that item to the publication at the insertion point. Business information items may have their own placeholders in publications. When you point to such an item, you can click on the option button that appears and then click on a choice in the shortcut menu to decide how to work with the information.

TIP

When you click in a text box, you can press the Del key to delete it from the publication.

Creating a placeholder and adding text

Whether you used a template as the basis for your publication or created the publication from scratch, you can add a new text box to place text in any location that you like in the publication. To add a text box, use the Draw Text Box tool, which is available on two of the Ribbon tabs.

1. **Click the Draw Text Box button in the Objects group of the Home tab or the Text group on the Insert tab.**

2. **Drag diagonally on the publication page to create a text box in the desired size and shape** (Figure 31.8). When you release the mouse button, the blinking insertion point appears within the text box.

FIGURE 31.8

Drag to define the size and shape for the text box.

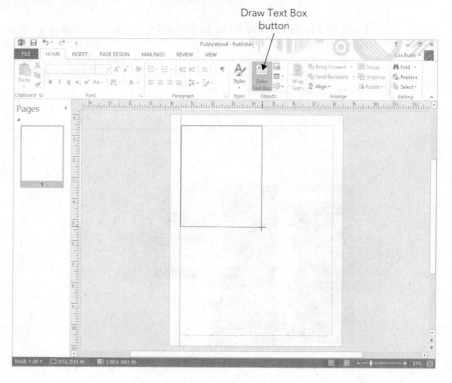

3. **Type the text.** Your new text appears in the text box.

4. **Click outside the text box on a blank area of the publication.** Doing so deselects the text box, finishing your entry.

Inserting a text file

Often, writing text and designing a publication are two separate activities assigned to two different people within an organization or group, especially for a publication that requires a lot of text, such as a newsletter or catalog. The person handling the writing assignment typically uses Word, WordPad, or another word processing program to write and edit the text, because a word processing program is the better tool for that purpose.

You need not worry about retyping text supplied by a colleague. Instead, you can insert word processing files [in popular formats including Word, WordPerfect, plain text (.txt), or Rich Text Format (.rtf)] directly into a text placeholder. The steps for doing so, which follow, combine the process for adding text into a text box and for opening a file:

1. **Click on the text within the placeholder.** If the text box is a template placeholder, this action selects both the text box and all the text within it. In the case of a placeholder for a newsletter story or other situation with linked text boxes, Publisher selects the entire placeholder story within all the linked boxes, as in the example shown in Figure 31.9.

FIGURE 31.9

Publisher selects the entire story in linked text boxes.

2. **Click the Insert tab, and click Insert File in the Text group.** The Insert Text dialog box appears.

3. **Navigate to the folder holding the word processing file to insert.** The dialog box lists the files with readable text formats stored in that folder, as depicted in Figure 31.10.

FIGURE 31.10

Insert a text file from a word processing program to avoid retyping the information.

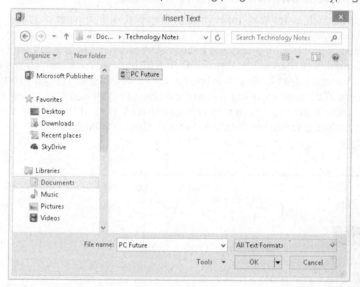

4. **Click on the name of the text file to insert, and then click OK.** The text from the inserted file appears in the placeholder you selected in Step 1. In some cases, such as when you have drawn your own text box in a blank document, Publisher may add another page text box if the inserted file doesn't fit in the selected placeholder. If that doesn't happen and the text doesn't all fit in the text box, you can link to another text box you create as described next.

Depending on the file format of the inserted file and whether any text and style formatting was applied in the original document, you may need to change the formatting of the text after inserting the file. The later section titled "Formatting Text" discusses some of the formatting methods you can use.

> **NOTE**
>
> If the writer for a publication that you're creating uses an older or unsupported word processing program that produces files in a format Publisher can't open, have the writer use the Save As or Export command in the program to save the file that you need to use as a plain-text or Rich Text Format file. Even PowerPoint can save files in RTF format.

Resizing, autoflow, and linked text boxes

In some cases, such as for text boxes in many templates, Publisher does not resize a text box if the text you type or a file you insert is too lengthy. When the number of words you've typed or placed into a text box exceeds the number the box can hold and you haven't allowed text to overflow into a linked text box, or there aren't any subsequent linked text boxes, a Text in Overflow button shown near the lower-right corner of the text box in Figure 31.11 appears. When you see that button, you can drag one of the handles on the text box to enlarge the box to display the text in its entirety. You also can flow the text into another text box, as described later in this section.

FIGURE 31.11

The Text in Overflow button cues you that the text doesn't fit in the text box.

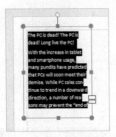

If you insert a file into a text box and the file's contents are too large for the text box, Publisher displays a message box like the one shown in Figure 31.12. If you click Yes, Publisher automatically flows the extra text into subsequent frames in the publication until all the text has been placed, a feature called *AutoFlow*. If you click No, you can handle the extra text by resizing the text box manually. Alternatively, you can link the text box to another of your choice, thus choosing exactly which text box will receive the flowed text. Linking text boxes enables you to control how a story flows from one text box to another.

FIGURE 31.12

Publisher enables you to AutoFlow extra text from an inserted file into other text boxes in the publication.

> **TIP**
>
> You can set up some text boxes to resize text so that it can, to some degree, fit itself within the existing boundary of a text box. To toggle this autofit feature on and off, right-click on the text box and click either Best Fit or Shrink Text on Overflow. If those options aren't active, click Format Text Box in the shortcut menu, instead. Click the Text Box tab in the Format Text Box dialog box, and then click Best fit or Shrink text on overflow under Text autofitting. Click OK to apply the change.

To link two text boxes so that the overflow text flows from one to the other:

1. **Click on the text box that holds the overflow text.** The Text in Overflow button appears below the text box.

2. **Click the Create Link button in the Linking group of the Text Box Tools ⇨ Format tab.** The mouse pointer changes to a pitcher appearance.

3. **Move the mouse pointer over the text box into which you want to flow the overflow text.** As shown in Figure 31.13, the mouse pointer changes to a "pouring" appearance to indicate that it is in position to add the overflow text into the text box.

FIGURE 31.13

Linking text boxes flows text between them.

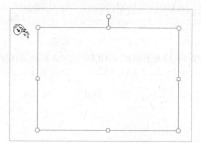

4. **Click on the text box to link.** The overflow text appears in the box. If a Text in Overflow button appears below the newly linked text box, it holds still more overflow text that you can display by resizing or linking to another text box.

> **NOTE**
>
> When text overflows the initial text box where you insert it, Publisher often creates a new page in the document and AutoFlows the text into it. If that's not the outcome you want, click the first text box where you added the text or file and click the Break button in the Linking group of the Text Box Tools ⇨ Format tab. Then link to the text box where you do want to place the overflow text as described above.

Other special buttons appear when you click on a linked text box. You may see the Go To Previous Text Box button above a linked text box. Clicking on that button selects the previous text box. When a Go To Next Text Box button appears below a linked text box, you can click on the button to select the next text box in sequence.

Formatting text

Some text formatting in Microsoft Publisher works similarly to Word and PowerPoint, and you can refer to earlier chapters about those programs to learn more about fonts, font sizes, alignments, and the type of text formats that you can apply. Click in the text box that has the text to format, drag over text within the text box to make a more specific selection to format or press Ctrl+A to select the entire story, and then use the choices in the Font and Paragraph groups of the Home tab to apply the desired changes. For example, you can click the Bold button to apply boldface or click the Bullets button to convert the text to a bulleted list.

Often, text that you've imported from another file will have its own formatting applied rather than adhere to the formatting established by the publication template. In this case, you can work with the Styles gallery to apply template formatting to the text:

1. **Click in the text box that holds the text to format.**
2. **Drag over text within the text box or press Ctrl+A to select the entire story.** The Ctrl+A shortcut even selects text in linked text boxes, making this a convenient shortcut when you need to reformat a larger volume of text distributed across multiple frames.
3. **Click Styles in the Styles group of the Home tab to open the drop-down gallery of styles.**
4. **Click on the desired style (Figure 31.14).** Publisher applies the style to the selected text.

FIGURE 31.14

Applying a template style saves formatting legwork.

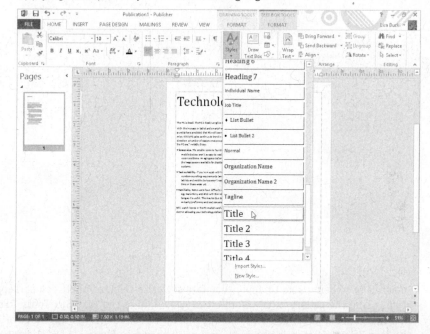

> **NOTE**
>
> Many of the body text styles automatically include spacing between paragraphs, so if you've pressed Enter to add space between paragraphs when creating your text—either in Publisher or in a word processing program—you may want to remove those extra hard returns after applying body text styles in Publisher.

One feature that Publisher 2013 shares with some other Microsoft Office 2013 applications is the ability to apply a new font scheme to the publication. Changing the font scheme changes the entire set of styles in the publication to styles that use different fonts, sizes, and so on. By making one choice in a task pane, you can update the look of all the text in the entire publication. Here's how to choose a new font scheme via the Format Publication task pane:

1. **Click the Page Design tab, and then click Fonts in the Schemes group.** The gallery of built-in font schemes appears.

2. **Scroll the list of schemes (Figure 31.15), and click on the new scheme to apply.** Publisher updates the fonts throughout the document for any text to which you've previously applied styles. If you want to return to the default font scheme for the template, choose the top font scheme choice.

FIGURE 31.15

Applying a font scheme updates all the document styles to use new formatting.

In addition to being able to apply template styles to selected text, you can apply WordArt styles using the gallery in the WordArt Styles group of the Text Box Tools ⇨ Format tab. New in Publisher 2013, you also can apply shadow, reflection, glow, and bevel effects using the Text Effects button in the same group. As shown in Figure 31.16, click the button, point to one of the effect types, and then move the mouse pointer over the gallery that appears to see a Live Preview of the effect on the selected text. When you see the effect you want to use, click it to apply it.

FIGURE 31.16

Publisher now enables you to apply four types of text effects.

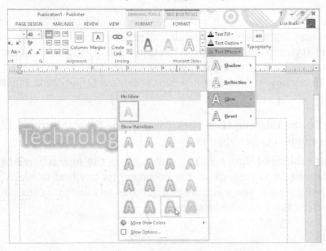

The Measurement pane

One nice benefit of Publisher's templates is that they have already been set up with great precision. All the text boxes, graphics, and other elements have been sized and aligned to exact dimensions. If you want to be as precise with your own publication — such as making sure that text boxes have the same width or sizing of certain types of graphics (for inserted objects or pictures, use the Format Object or Format Picture dialog box instead) to fit exactly within a column—you can use the Measurement pane (Figure 31.17).

FIGURE 31.17

View and change numerous dimensions for a selected object or text using the Measurement pane.

To display and hide the Measurement pane, select a graphic object or text box, click the Drawing Tools⇨Format tab, and then click Measurement in the Size group.

The Measurement pane displays the exact x (horizontal) and y (vertical) position of the upper-left corner of the selected text box or object. It also lists the object's width, height, and rotation angle (if any). If you've selected text within a text box, the Measurement pane also displays text settings including Tracking, Text Scaling, and Kerning.

To change any of the settings for the selected object or text, you can enter a new value in the applicable text box on the Measurement pane and press Enter, or you can use the spinner arrow buttons to change the entry. In this way, if you want three different text boxes in a publication to be exactly 2.205 inches wide, you can use the Measurement pane to set that width dimension.

Working with Graphics

Graphics bring publication stories to life. If you're a realtor creating a flyer to describe a terrific house that you have for sale, anyone who sees your flyer will *really* know how fabulous the house is if you include pictures of the granite countertops in the kitchen, the luxurious bathroom, and the gorgeous patio and landscaping in the backyard. Publisher makes it easy to add pictures and other graphic elements to punch up a story and really sell your message.

Inserting a picture file

Digital cameras and scanners are virtually as cheap as film cameras once were. Even the typical home or small business generally has a digital camera and users who take and transfer dozens of digital pictures to the computer's hard disk. Microsoft Publisher enables you to place pictures in formats commonly captured by digital cameras, such as JPEG and TIFF, as well as numerous other graphics formats created with drawing and painting programs, directly into a publication.

This process does not require a picture placeholder, so when you're ready to insert a digital picture file into a publication, follow this process:

1. **Display the page in the publication on which you'd like to insert the picture.** Clicking on a page icon in the status bar takes you there.

2. **Choose Insert ⇨ Illustrations ⇨ Pictures.** The Insert Picture dialog box appears.

3. **Navigate to the folder holding the file to insert.** The dialog box lists the files with readable graphics formats stored in that folder.

> **TIP**
> Click All Pictures and then select a particular format to list only picture files using that format.

4. **Click on the name of the text file to insert, and then click Insert.** The inserted picture file appears on the page.

After you insert the picture, you can resize and position it as needed. You can drag the handles that appear on the corners and sides of the picture (Figure 31.18) to resize it, or move the mouse within the picture and drag to move it. You also can use the Measurement pane as described earlier to set the picture's size and position. The Size group of the Picture Tools ⇨ Format tab also includes settings for sizing a picture precisely. As Figure 31.18 also illustrates, when you drag a picture to move it or drag a handle to resize it, alignment guides like those now also found in Word and PowerPoint appear to help you align the picture to the text dimensions or other objects with precision. When you finish sizing the picture, click outside it to deselect it.

FIGURE 31.18

Resize and move the inserted picture as needed.

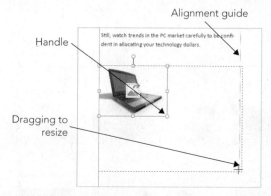

Alignment guide

Handle

Still, watch trends in the PC market carefully to be confident in allocating your technology dollars.

Dragging to
resize

31

> **CAUTION**
>
> If you plan to have your publication professionally printed, you need to use high-resolution pictures to get good results. If you crop a portion of a digital camera shot and then size it at a large size in the publication, those changes might result in a low-resolution graphic that prints with a fuzzy or blocky appearance. If you have any doubts about how an image might print, ask the print shop to inspect your publication file for such problems *before* proceeding with your print order.

Inserting an online image

If you don't have your own digital pictures but want to flesh out your publication with some images, you can take advantage of the royalty-free Clip Art available via Office.com. (You also can insert images from Bing Image Search or your SkyDrive; this process works just as it does in Word, so for more details, see "Adding an Online Picture" in Chapter 9.) You can search for the type of picture you want, such as a flower, boat, or person. Follow these steps when you want to insert an online picture into a publication:

1. **Display the page in the publication on which you'd like to insert the image.** Clicking on a page icon in the Page Navigation pane takes you to the page or two-page spread (in which case you need to then click on the page where you want to insert the picture).

2. **Select Insert ⇨ Illustrations ⇨ Online Pictures.** The Insert Pictures window appears.

3. **Type the descriptive word or phrase in the Search Office.com text box to the right of Office.com Clip Art and then click the Search button at the right end of the text box.** Thumbnail images of matching clip art appear in the window, as shown in Figure 31.19.

FIGURE 31.19

Find and insert online pictures for your publication.

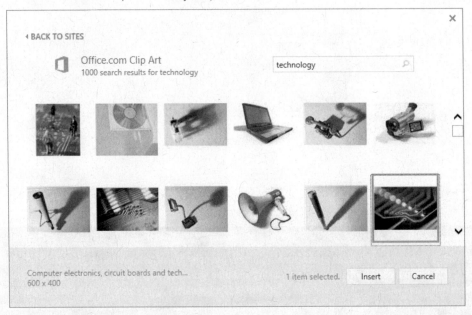

> **NOTE**
>
> The first time you search for clip art, a prompt may appear to ask whether you want to search online clips by default. Click Yes to do so.

4. **Scroll down to review all the available choices.**

5. **Click the clip art picture to place on the publication, and then click Insert.**
   It appears on the page you specified in Step 1. You can then resize the picture as needed to fit with the other contents in your publication, and click outside the picture to deselect it.

Inserting multiple pictures

Publisher 2013 also gives you the ability to insert multiple pictures into a publication at once. To do so, click the first picture in the Insert Picture dialog box or the online pictures search results, and then Ctrl+click additional pictures to select them before clicking Insert. Publisher places all the inserted pictures in the scratch area as shown in Figure 31.20. Drag a picture from the scratch area onto the desired page in your publication, and position and resize it from there as needed.

FIGURE 31.20

When you select multiple pictures before clicking Insert, Publisher places them on the scratch area so you can add them into the publication where needed.

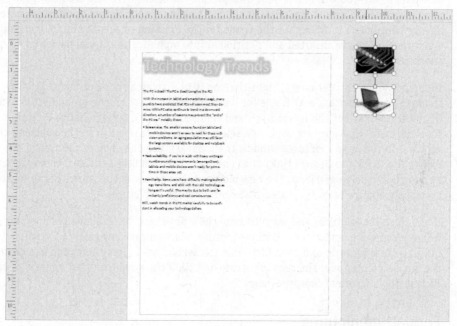

Swapping pictures

If you place a picture on a page but decide you'd prefer to insert a different one in the same position, right-click the picture, point to Change Picture, and then click Change Picture.

> **TIP**
>
> You now also can use a picture as the page background. Right-click the picture on the page, point to Apply to Background, and then click either Fill or Tile. Keep in mind that if your printer can't print all the way to the edge of the page (full bleed printing), then the printer will automatically leave an unprinted margin for the page. Be sure that you adjust text color as needed based on the background colors in the picture to ensure that the text in the document remains readable. To remove the background, choose Page Design ⇨ Page Background ⇨ Background, and then click the left white thumbnail under No Background.

Changing a placeholder picture or swapping pictures

Many publication templates include placeholder graphics that provide suggested sizes and locations where you can insert your own pictures or alternative clip art images. When you insert the replacement picture or clip art graphic, Publisher automatically resizes the replacement image to fit within the frame for the existing image. Similarly, you can replace a picture that you've inserted and positioned into a publication if you decide to go with another image.

To replace a placeholder image, right-click on it to display a shortcut menu. (If the picture frame is grouped with a text frame for a caption, right-click on the group first and click Ungroup. Then select the image itself and right-click on it.) Select Change Picture in the shortcut menu that appears, and then select Change Picture again in the submenu that appears. In the Insert Pictures window that appears, use the choices to insert a picture From a file (click the Browse link) or to choose Office.com Clip Art. From there, the steps work as previously described. The new picture takes on the styles and other formatting previously applied to the replaced placeholder image or picture.

If you have two pictures and want to *swap* their positions, for example placing picture A where picture B is and picture B where picture A is, you can now easily accomplish this. Click the first picture, and then Ctrl+click the second one. From there, you can either move the mouse pointer over the second picture and click the swap icon that appears or choose Picture Tools ⇨ Format Swap ⇨ Swap.

Formatting pictures

You can adjust numerous settings to fine-tune a picture and its placement, including settings such as an added fill color or outline, size and rotation, layout and text wrapping, and brightness and contrast. The available settings vary somewhat depending on whether the selected picture is a digital image file or clip art graphic, and whether the picture is inserted on its own or is within a frame that's grouped with other objects.

The settings for formatting a picture appear in the Format Picture dialog box. To display the dialog box, right-click on the picture (right-click on the grouped object first and click Ungroup, if needed, and then select the picture alone), and then select Format Picture. Change settings on the tabs in the Format Picture dialog box (Figure 31.21) as needed, and then click OK to apply your choices to the picture.

FIGURE 31.21

The tabs in this dialog box offer numerous settings for fine-tuning the appearance of a picture.

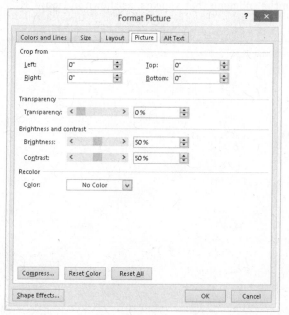

Adding picture effects

The Picture Tools ➪ Format tab includes a number of settings for jazzing up a picture in its Picture Styles group. You can not only apply an overall style that may include cropping, a frame, and a shadow or reflection from the Picture Styles gallery, but you also can use the choices that appear when you click the Picture Border or Picture Effects buttons in the Picture Styles group. Use the Caption button in Picture Styles to add a caption for a picture.

Drawing lines and shapes

You also can enhance a publication by drawing shapes using the Shapes choices in the Illustrations group of the Insert tab. For example, you might draw an arrow to point to an important piece of information or draw a banner AutoShape to layer behind headline text.

To draw the shape, click Insert, and then click the Shapes button in the Illustrations group. Click on the desired shape in the gallery that appears. If you click the AutoShapes button, a menu appears. Click on a shape category in the menu, and then click the specific AutoShape you want to draw in the submenu that appears, as shown in Figure 31.22.

FIGURE 31.22

You can select one of dozens of shapes to draw.

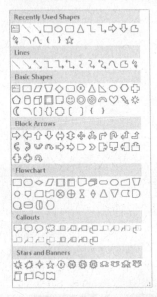

After you've selected the desired line or shape, drag on the publication page to draw the object. Keep these hints in mind when you draw and work with shapes:

- Drag in the desired direction to create a line or arrow. If you want to help the line snap to vertical, horizontal, or a 45-degree angle, press the Shift key when your line is close to the desired angle.

- Drag diagonally to draw an oval, rectangle, or other shape. Press and hold Shift as you drag to constrain the shape to proportional dimensions; doing so results in a perfect circle or square, or an AutoShape that fits within a perfect circle or square.

- Some shapes include a special yellow handle when selected. You can use this handle to reshape the object, such as dragging to increase the three-dimensional (3-D) angle of the shape.

- Right-click on a shape and then select Format AutoShape to display the Format AutoShape dialog box, where you can change shape settings, as for a picture. One cool thing you can do is insert a picture within a shape or AutoShape. To do so, click the Fill Effects in the Fill area of the Colors and Lines tab. Click the Picture tab in the Fill Effects dialog box that appears, and then use the Select Picture button to open the Select Picture dialog box. Navigate to and select the desired picture file, click Insert, and then click OK twice to fill the shape.

- Right-click on a shape, and click Add Text to insert text within it.

- To be able to reuse a shape that you've formatted, right-click on it and choose Save as Building Block. Specify the desired information in the Create New Building Block dialog box, and then click OK. You can then use the gallery you specified in the dialog box to insert the shape from the Building Blocks group of the Insert tab.

Working with Tables

When you need to organize information in a series of rows and columns, you don't have to draw and arrange a text box for each bit of data. You can instead create a table, which has cells formed by the intersections of rows and columns. When you create a table using these steps, you specify the number of rows and columns and pick the initial table design:

1. **Display the page in the publication on which you'd like to insert the table.** Clicking on a page thumbnail in the Page Navigation pane takes you to the page or two-page spread (in which case you need to then click on the page where you want to insert the picture).

2. **Click the Insert tab, and then click the Table button in the Tables group.** A table grid appears below the button.

3. **Drag diagonally on the grid to specify the table's size in rows and columns.** When you release the mouse button, the table appears on the page.

4. **Open the Table Formats gallery of the Table Tools ⇨ Design tab, and move the mouse pointer over a format.** As shown in Figure 31.23, moving the mouse pointer over one of the formats before clicking on it displays a live preview of the selected formatting on the table.

FIGURE 31.23

Create a table by specifying rows, columns, and format.

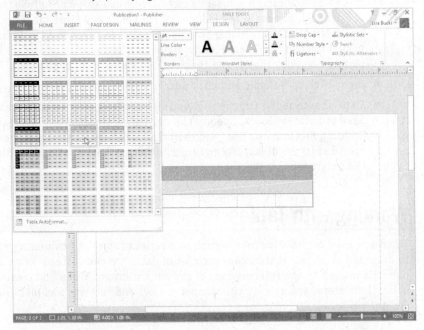

5. **Click on the format.** The formatting appears on the table. You can then move and resize the table as needed.

> **TIP**
> You also can create a table using the Create Table dialog box. Click the Insert tab, click Table in the Tables group, and then click Insert Table. After you make your choices and click OK, Publisher automatically places the table on the current publication page, where you can move and resize it as needed.

Entering and editing table data

When the new table appears, the insertion point appears in the upper-left cell. Simply type the entry for each cell, and press Tab to move on to the next cell. If you type more text than the cell can initially handle, Publisher wraps the text to the next line and increases the row height as needed. You can press Shift+Tab to back up to a previous cell as needed.

To edit the entry in any particular table cell, click on the cell and then make the desired changes by selecting and replacing text or using editing keys such as Backspace. When you finish entering and editing table text, click outside the table to deselect it.

You can then click on a table at any time to reselect it.

Working with the table format

As with other objects you've seen in this chapter, you can right-click on a table and then click Format Table to open the Format Table dialog box. Note that the settings on the Colors and Lines tab apply only to the selected cell—the cell upon which you right-clicked to open the dialog box. If you want to work with colors and fills for more than one cell, you have to select those cells before right-clicking and selecting Format Table. To select cells, first click on the table. Then drag over the cells to select. You also can move the mouse pointer outside the table boundary above a column or to the left of a row that you want to select. When the mouse pointer changes to a black arrow pointing to the row or column, clicking the mouse selects the entire row or column. Also note that the Format Table dialog box includes a Cell Properties tab, on which you can change the vertical text alignment, margins, and text rotation for the selected cells.

One last table skill that's handy to know is how to resize the width of a table column. To do so, point to the right border of the column until you see the resizing pointer, which appears in the Tuesday through Thursday row in Figure 31.24. Then drag left or right to fix the column width as desired.

FIGURE 31.24

Drag a divider to resize a table column.

Summary

Making it through this chapter provided you with the basic know-how for creating a publication in Microsoft Publisher. You learned to work with the features of the Publisher workspace, as well as how to:

- Create a blank file or a file based on a template supplied with Publisher or a featured template from Office.com.
- Add text into a text box supplied by a template or create a text box and type in text.
- Insert text from a word processing file.
- Format your text with formatting tools, styles, text effects, and a font scheme.
- Use the Measurement pane to format objects.
- Insert, create, and change graphics and tables to enhance the publication's appearance and supplement the message delivered in the text.

Designing Dazzling Publications with Publisher

S tarting your design with one of Publisher's templates virtually guarantees that you will create a nice-looking publication. You know your message and your audience best, so you can improve on a template by adding graphics and changing aspects of the overall document design. You can use special graphic features that emphasize or decorate text, add predesigned objects such as coupons, and work with page options such as the color scheme for the publication. From there, you can fine-tune objects and page settings and then wrap up and print the publication. This chapter shows you how to do all that to add your own razzle-dazzle to a publication.

Adding Special Effects

One of the advantages of using Publisher to design your publications is that Publisher makes laying out and designing document text easier. Linked text boxes give you much control over where information appears in a document. Beyond dealing with that aspect of text design, Publisher also provides you with tools to dress up text to catch your reader's eye—BorderArt, drop caps, WordArt, and special new text formatting choices and effects.

BorderArt

You learned in Chapter 31 that you can right-click on an inserted picture, clip art, or table object and select a format command that opens a formatting dialog box. Similarly, you can right-click on any text box in a publication and click Format Text Box to open the Format Text Box dialog box (Figure 32.1). You can use the tabs in this dialog box to add fills and outlines to the text box, and more. In addition, you can click the BorderArt button on the Colors and Lines tab to open the BorderArt dialog box.

FIGURE 32.1

Overall text box formatting settings appear in the Format Text Box dialog box.

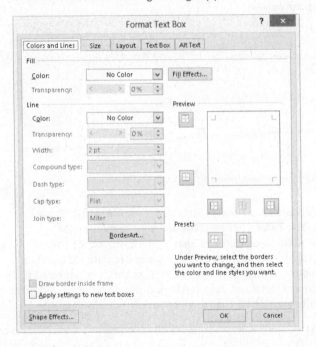

Rather than placing a plain-colored line around your text box, BorderArt applies a border made up of small graphics. The graphics range from geometric forms that apply a formal, decorative feel to items that set a fun mood or tone, such as ladybugs or candy corn. The available BorderArt designs fit any number of occasions, making them ideal to use in almost any of your publications, including invitations and greeting cards, for example.

As shown in Figure 32.2, you can preview any border by selecting it in the Available Borders list at the left side of the dialog box. The border design appears in the Preview area at the right, using its default settings. By default, Publisher stretches the border graphics to fill the border area a little more completely. If you prefer to turn off this feature, click the Don't stretch pictures option button near the lower-left corner of the dialog box. Each border has an automatic size, shown in the Preview. If you want to control the border width yourself, click to uncheck the Always apply at default size check box before continuing.

FIGURE 32.2

You can preview a border in the BorderArt dialog box.

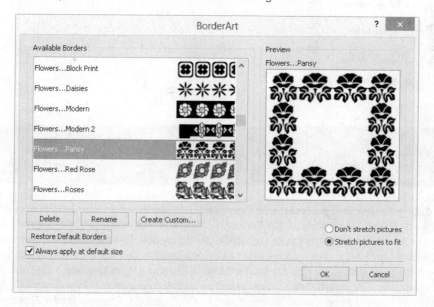

When you've selected the BorderArt and changed any settings as needed, click OK to close the BorderArt dialog box and return to the Format Text Box dialog box. Change the Width entry on the Colors and Lines tab to set the border width if needed. You also can modify the border color in the Line area, but you may not want to do so if the BorderArt graphics already include great colors. Click OK to close the dialog box and finish applying the BorderArt. As shown in the party invitation in Figure 32.3, the BorderArt can make even simple text pop from the page.

FIGURE 32.3

Party time! Seasonal or theme-oriented BorderArt works well for greeting cards and invitations.

> **TIP**
>
> To center text both horizontally and vertically as in Figure 32.3, select the text box. Click the Text Box Tools ⇨ Format tab, and click the Align Center button in the Alignment group.

You can create your own BorderArt using any graphic image stored on your hard disk or available as clip art. Click Create Custom in the BorderArt dialog box. To open a file from the hard disk, click the Select Picture in the Create Custom Border dialog box. Use the Insert Pictures window that appears to select a saved picture (use the Browse link beside from a file), to search for a clip art image on Office.com Clip Art (as described in Chapter 31), or to select a file from your SkyDrive; then click Insert. Publisher converts the picture into a border. Type a name for the new border into the Name Custom Border dialog box and click OK. The new border appears in the Available Borders list in the BorderArt dialog box until you select the border and click Delete.

> **TIP**
>
> Choose small, simple pictures to convert to custom border art. For example, you might want to crop a single flower out of a larger picture and use that small flower as your BorderArt graphic.

Drop caps

Formatting the first letter or word of a story or paragraph as a *drop cap* draws the eye to that spot in your publication. Setting up a letter or word as a drop cap increases its size, causing it to stand above the first line of text or have the first few lines wrap around it, or both. The drop cap style you choose might also use a contrasting color or other text formatting to give it a fancy appearance. Figure 32.4 shows a story with a drop cap applied.

FIGURE 32.4

Attract readers to a story by setting the first paragraph off with a drop cap.

Drop cap

Follow these steps to create a drop cap in a story:

1. **Select the text box and then click in the paragraph where you want to add the drop cap.**

2. **Click the Text Box Tools ⇨ Format tab, and then click Drop Cap in the Typography group.** The Drop Cap gallery appears, as shown in Figure 32.5. (Note that at a lower screen resolution, you may have to click the Typography button as shown in the Figure and then click Drop Cap.)

FIGURE 32.5

Make sure that the drop cap fits your text by checking the Preview.

Preview

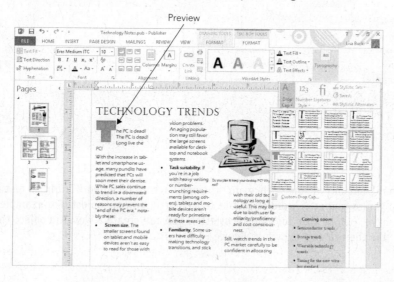

3. **Move the mouse pointer over the various drop cap styles.** Live Preview in the document shows how the drop cap will look when applied to the paragraph, as in the example in Figure 32.5.

4. **Click on a drop cap style to apply it.**

If none of the available drop cap styles is quite what you're looking for, you can click Custom Drop Cap at the bottom of the Drop Cap gallery to open the Drop Cap dialog box to display the settings for creating your own custom drop cap or for customizing a drop cap that you've already applied, as shown in Figure 32.6. You can work with the drop cap position, size, and text appearance. As you try on various setting combinations, the Preview at the right shows you how your paragraph will look with the custom drop cap. Click OK to apply the custom drop cap and close the dialog box.

FIGURE 32.6

For a truly custom drop cap, work with the settings here.

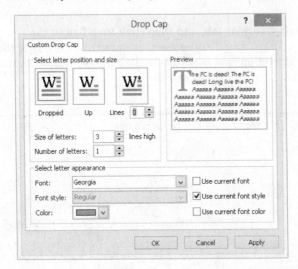

WordArt

The last several versions of some Office applications have all included *WordArt*, a feature that enables you to convert a word or phrase to a colorful graphic object. For example, rather than have "just" a title for your newsletter, you can create a WordArt object that really pops, like the example shown in Figure 32.7.

FIGURE 32.7

No mere text attracts attention the way that WordArt can.

To create a WordArt object in a publication, follow these steps:

1. **Display the page in the publication upon which you'd like to insert the WordArt.** Clicking on a page icon in the Page Navigation pane takes you there.
2. **Choose Insert ⇨ Text ⇨ WordArt.** The WordArt gallery (Figure 32.8) appears.

FIGURE 32.8

Give some text WordArt style — simple, wavy, shadowed, vertical, or 3-D.

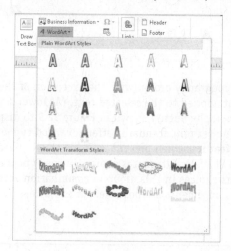

3. **Click on a WordArt style.** The Edit WordArt Text dialog box appears.
4. **Type the WordArt text, and adjust its font, size, and attributes as needed.**
5. **Click OK.** The WordArt object appears on the publication, where you can size and position it as desired.

TIP

Keep WordArt text brief. Decorative text created with WordArt can be difficult to read in large quantities.

When you select any WordArt object, the WordArt Tools ⇨ Format contextual tab appears. It offers buttons for editing the WordArt's text, changing the WordArt's style and shape, and more. Work with the settings here as needed to finish designing and positioning the WordArt object.

Text formatting and typography tools

The Text Box Tools ⇨ Format contextual tab, shown in Figure 32.9, offers some text enhancement settings that were not available in previous versions. The Effects group offers Shadow, Outline, Engrave, and Emboss treatments that you can add to selected text. These effects should be used sparingly because they can affect readability, so they are probably best reserved for headlines, advertisements, titles, and other situations in which you need to emphasize a word or phrase.

FIGURE 32.9

Use the settings in the WordArt Styles and Typography groups to enhance text.

The choices that become available in the Typography group (with the exception of the Drop Cap command) will depend on the font applied to the selected text. (At lower screen resolutions, you will have to click the Typography button shown in Figure 32.9 to display the group's choices.) Some fonts following newer font standards offer advanced typography features. You can take advantage of these features when present by using the Number Style, Ligatures, Stylistic Sets, Swash, and Stylistic Alternates choices in the Typography group. You can experiment with the various choices in this group in combination with different fonts to see what typographic enhancements are possible. For example, Figure 32.10 shows two ligatures.

FIGURE 32.10

The connections in the *ft* and *fi* letter pairs are ligatures.

daft fission

Using Building Blocks

Publications often include special elements not typically found in ordinary business documents. For example, a new product brochure might include a coupon. A flyer might need phone number tear-off tabs along the bottom. A newsletter might need a masthead with certain information or a volunteer sign-up form. Building these types of elements from scratch by layering graphics, text boxes, and borders could be time-consuming, but you don't have to bother. Instead, you can add any of a number of predesigned items from the building blocks galleries to your publication and then customize the item with your own text.

Follow these steps to add a building block object to a publication:

1. **Display the page in the publication upon which you'd like to insert the object.** Clicking on a page icon in the Page Navigation pane takes you there.

2. **Click the Insert tab on the Ribbon, and then click on the button for one of the galleries — Page Parts, Calendars, Borders & Accents, or Advertisements — in the Building Blocks group.** The specified gallery opens.

3. **Scroll down the gallery to review all the choices, and then click on the desired object.** The object appears on the publication page, where you can move and resize it, as well as update it with your own text if required. Figure 32.11 shows an example coupon building block from the Advertisements gallery.

FIGURE 32.11

Inspire your readers to action with building block objects.

Updating a Publication

Not only can you change settings for the text and objects in a publication, you also can make many changes to upgrade the publication itself. You can change the background fill for the pages, change how the page information is arranged, and choose another color scheme.

To make some publication-wide design changes, work with the Format Publication task pane. To make other publication-wide changes, use Page Design tab commands.

Changing the background

Many publication designs purposely do not have a background color. That's because for years few computer printers could print *bleeds*—in which color prints all the way to the edge of the page. Some color printers now can handle bleeds. If that applies in your case or if you're sending the publication for commercial printing (or you don't really care if your background doesn't print all the way to the edges of the page), you can apply a background to your publication. You also may want to add a background if you're using Publisher to design a web page.

> **CAUTION**
>
> Printing a bleed can add significantly to your costs because the printer will have to trim away paper stock around the edges of each page. Be sure you know whether your print shop charges more for bleeds.

To apply or remove a background, click the Page Design tab on the Ribbon, and then click Background in the Page Background group. The Background gallery appears (Figure 32.12). The available choices depend on the color scheme applied to the document. Click on a specific background choice to apply it. The publication immediately previews the background choice. To remove any applied background, redisplay the gallery and click the blank area directly below No Background at the top.

FIGURE 32.12

Pump up your pages with a background color or pattern.

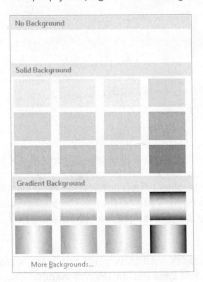

Changing page settings

The Page Design tab offers a variety of settings for changing the layout of the page or pages in your publication. For example, you can use the choices in the Page Setup group to specify Margins, Page Orientation, and Page Size. These choices now work the same as they do in Word, so you can refer to Chapter 8 to learn more.

Publications based on a template may have other page choices available. For a newsletter, for example, you might be able to specify the number of columns per page. To change the columns options for a publication page, first display the page to change. Click the Page Design tab, and then click the Options button in the Template group. In the Page Content dialog box that appears, select the options that you want and click OK.

Changing colors

In addition to an overall font scheme, every publication has an overall color scheme. The color scheme defines a main color and several accent colors for use throughout the publication. It's best to stick with the colors in the scheme for the text and objects as this helps keep the publication design coherent.

To choose another color scheme for your publication, click the Page Design tab on the Ribbon, and then click the More button in the Schemes group to open the Color Schemes gallery, as shown in Figure 32.13. Click on the desired color scheme. When you do so, Publisher automatically replaces the previous main and accent colors with those from the new scheme, so you can see the impact of the change on your publication. You can continue applying other color schemes until you've found one that suits your needs.

FIGURE 32.13

Bring new colors into your publication by choosing another color scheme here.

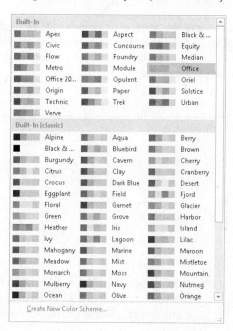

Fine-Tuning Objects

If you can't find just the right building block object or other object settings to meet your needs, or if you just like noodling around with design possibilities in your publications, you may find yourself creating and positioning many objects. Although you can drag with the mouse and use tools such as ruler guides to help you size and position objects, other shortcuts might be more appropriate in some cases. This section shows you some more tricks — aligning and grouping objects, and wrapping and hyphenating text.

Aligning objects

Aligning objects can be a little frustrating, especially if you have a finicky mouse or are working with a notebook touchpad to drag objects. You can use the arrow keys to move a selected object, but each press of a key merely nudges the object a very small distance in the indicated direction. Plus, if you're trying to do something trickier such as align multiple selected objects, you have no precise way to do it with the mouse.

Use the commands on the Arrange group of the Home tab to align multiple selected objects. After you Shift+click to select the desired objects, click Align in the Arrange group, and then select one of the commands on the menu that appears to align the objects' left, center, and right horizontal dimensions, or top, middle, and bottom vertical dimensions. You also can use the Distribute Horizontally or Distribute Vertically choice to space the objects equally.

Figure 32.14 shows an example of how you can use the Align menu commands to work with publication objects. After selecting both objects, both the Align Center and Align Middle commands were selected. These commands placed the center point of the mouse clip art image right over the center point of the beveled frame shape.

FIGURE 32.14

Move objects into position using alignment commands.

You also can keep your eyes peeled for pink alignment guidelines that may appear as you move around objects. These appear to indicate when you have reached an alignment point, such as centering an object on a column. For good alignment, release the object when you see one of these guides.

32

TIP

If you need to replace a picture that you've already formatted and positioned, select it, and then use the Change Picture button in the Adjust Group of the Picture Tools ⇨ Format tab.

TIP

To control how an object layers when positioned with other objects, right-click on the object, point to the Order command, and click one of the choices in the submenu that appears. For example, the Bring to Front command positions the selected object in front of (on top of) all other stacked objects.

Grouping objects

After you've placed multiple objects into the position you want, such as in the example in Figure 32.14, you should group the objects so that you can move them around as a unit without accidentally misaligning one or more of them. When you use Shift+click to select multiple objects, the Group choice in the Arrange group of the Home tab becomes active. You can use that button or right-click on the object and click Group, as shown in Figure 32.15. To ungroup a selected group, click the Ungroup button in the Arrange group of the Home tab, or right-click on the group and click Ungroup.

FIGURE 32.15

Use the Group command to make the selected objects stick together as a single unit.

NOTE

You can still select an individual object within a group, such as to work with the object's formatting settings. First click on the group and then click on the individual object. Selection handles with X marks in them appear around the selected object within the group.

Wrapping and hyphenating text

Your text will read much better if you make sure that you've chosen the right text-wrapping settings for objects and have chosen whether to use hyphenation in a story.

You can apply one of several text-wrapping styles to objects, typically shapes or picture objects that you want to appear within the text. Wrapping style options include Square, Tight, Through, Top and Bottom, and None. For example, Figure 32.16 illustrates the Tight wrapping style used for a grouped object. To choose a wrapping setting, click the Drawing Tools ⇨ Format tab or the Picture Tools ⇨ Format tab, click Wrap Text in the Arrange group, and then click on a wrapping option.

FIGURE 32.16

The right wrapping setting makes sure that text remains readable when it flows around the object.

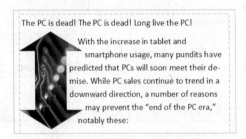

If you're wrapping text tightly around an object or have a narrow text box with large text, Publisher may by default hyphenate words to try to fill the space as well as possible. Many readers prefer not to see hyphens because they become tiring to read in longer stories. You can use these steps to turn the automatic hyphenation off in any story:

1. **Click in the story for which you'd like to change hyphenation settings.**
2. **Select Text Box Tools ⇨ Format ⇨ Text ⇨ Hyphenation (Ctrl+Shift+H).** The Hyphenation dialog box shown in Figure 32.17 opens.

FIGURE 32.17

Control hyphenation in any story by using this dialog box.

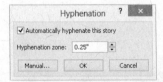

3. **Click the Automatically hyphenate this story check box to clear the check.**
4. **Click OK.** Publisher removes the hyphenation from the story you selected in Step 1.

Working with Pages

Many publications you create will be multipage documents, either to hold all the information that you want to present, as for a newsletter, or to come out in the proper format when folded, as for a greeting card. You can add any number of pages as needed to any publication.

Adding pages

The Page Navigation pane at the left side of Publisher shows a numbered icon for each page in the publication. To go to another page, just click on the icon for that page. You can insert more pages as needed to expand the contents of the publication.

If you want to insert a new page before or after a particular page that's already in the publication, click on the thumbnail for that page in the pane. Then click the Insert tab of the Ribbon, click the down arrow portion of the Page button in the Pages group, and click Insert Blank Page (Ctrl+Shift+N). This immediately inserts a blank page. However, if you want a bit more control, click Insert Page, instead.

NOTE

Using Ctrl+Shift+N will automatically insert a page after the currently selected page. It will not give you any additional options.

The Insert Page dialog box that appears after you click Insert Page varies depending on the type of publication you're working in. For example, when you're inserting a page in a file that was created as a blank publication, the dialog box looks like the one shown in Figure 32.18. Specify how many pages to insert and whether to insert before or after the current page; choose any other options you want, and then click OK. Publisher will choose the appropriate left-hand or right-hand layout for the inserted page.

FIGURE 32.18

If you started with a blank publication, Publisher assumes that you want to insert more blank pages.

If you are inserting a page in a file that was based on a more complicated template, such as a newsletter, Publisher assumes that you want to insert pages consistent with the layout of the existing pages and may even assume that you want to insert a pair of facing pages, so it displays a dialog box like the one shown in Figure 32.19. You can either use the drop-down list at the top of the dialog box to choose another type of page, as shown for Right-Hand Page at the top of Figure 32.19, or you can click the More button to display the Insert Page dialog box as shown in Figure 32.18. After you make your choice, click OK to insert the page(s).

FIGURE 32.19

In other types of publications, Publisher assumes that you want to insert pages that follow the template design.

To create an exact duplicate of the current page, use the Insert Duplicate Page command (Ctrl+Shift+U) on the Page menu in the Pages group of the Insert tab.

> **TIP**
> To delete a page, right-click on its thumbnail in the Page Navigation pane, and then click Delete in the shortcut menu.

Numbering pages

As a courtesy to your readers, you should always include page numbers for multipage documents. Including page numbers has the added benefit of giving anyone printing the document a heads-up about the order in which to place the pages. The process for adding page numbers places them in the header or footer area (above or below the rest of the text) in the position that you specify.

Select Page Number in the Header & Footer group of the Insert tab to open a gallery of page number position choices (Figure 32.20). Click on one of the choices to finish adding the page numbers.

FIGURE 32.20

You can add page numbers in the position you specify.

Checking and Printing

Printing your publication can be a thrilling moment—or an absolute dud if you discover that you've missed something and have to go back and fix it. So before you print, take the time to use the Design Checker. After that, it's off to the printer!

> **NOTE**
> Always remember to save your final changes to the publication before printing by pressing Ctrl+S or selecting File ⇨ Save.

Using the Design Checker

Publisher's Design Checker checks a publication for boo-boos such as empty text boxes and spacing errors. Running the Design Checker so that you can uncover and fix these errors saves you toner, paper, and printing time. Among the problems Design Checker looks for are text in overflow areas, disproportional pictures, empty frames, covered objects, objects partially off the page, objects in nonprinting regions, blank space at the top of the page, spacing between sentences, and (for websites) a page unreachable by hyperlinks.

Select File ⇨ Info ⇨ Run Design Checker to run Design Checker. When it finishes, results appear in the Design Checker pane, as shown in Figure 32.21. To correct each error, click on the error in the list. Publisher displays the location where the error occurs so that you can correct it.

FIGURE 32.21

Yep, Design Checker caught a number of errors in this publication.

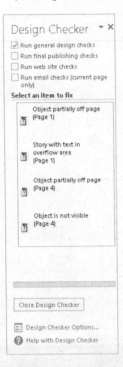

If you plan to have the document commercially printed, click the Run Commercial Printing Checks check box at the top of the Design Checker task pane to check that option. The Design Checker then immediately displays any errors that might cause a problem at a commercial printer, such as the publication's being in the wrong color mode. When you click on this type of error, a drop-down arrow appears beside it. Click on that error to display a drop-down menu with options for correcting or learning more about the error.

Printing

When you're satisfied that your publication is as near to perfect as you can make it, you're ready to print. Printing is pretty much the same as in any Office application, choose

File ➪ Print or press Ctrl+P. Review the preview in the Backstage view carefully, and then select a printer, a range of pages to print, and the number of copies you want. Click Print to finish and send the job to the printer.

Preparing for Outside Printing

Sometimes you want to be able to send your publication to a print shop for printing on a professional press rather than on your own printer. Publisher can help you prepare your files for that purpose.

Give Your Printer and Yourself a Break

Small print shops labor every day to deal with errors in Publisher files, from wrong output colors to unneeded spot colors to other poor document design and setup problems. If you're unwilling or unable to take the time to learn about and fix these types of issues, please be willing to pay your service bureau (print shop) a fair fee for fixing them. The following are always good practices for working with a print shop to get your publication file printed right:

- Know and adhere to the print shop's requirements.

- If you have questions but want to do the work yourself, consult Publisher's extensive help on this subject and ask the printer for tips.

- Most print shops will review a file for problems before printing it. Sending your file for such an advanced checkup provides time to fix problems.

- Be professional. A professional admits to errors and is willing to learn and change. If you keep submitting bad files to the print shop, you'll keep getting poorly printed materials.

To start preparing a publication for commercial printing, choose File ➪ Export ➪ Save for a Commercial Printer. At the right side of the Backstage view, make the choices you want from the top and bottom drop-down lists, which specify the overall type of printer and whether the preparation process will create just a Publisher file or both a Publisher file and a PDF file. (Some printers prefer that you submit your files as PDF files.) Generally speaking, you should choose either Commercial Press or High Quality Printing from the top drop-down list. If you choose Custom, Publisher opens a Publish Options dialog box (Figure 32.22), where you can choose more specific options, such as the resolution at which pictures should print. If you click Print Options in that dialog box, the Print Options dialog box offers even more choices, such as adding crop marks and whether to allow bleeds. Click OK after you make your choices in each of these dialog boxes.

FIGURE 32.22

The settings here are important for commercial printing and advanced print jobs of your own.

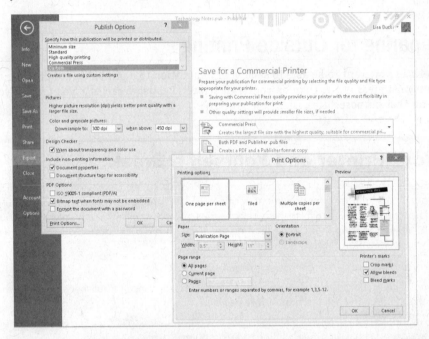

> **TIP**
>
> To create a more standard PDF file, say to e-mail to a colleague as a proof for the publication, click Create PDF/XPS Document after choosing File ⇨ Export.

Once you've selected the needed output settings, click the Pack and Go Wizard button. Specify where you want to save the file(s), click Next, and follow the prompts to finish the process of preparing your files for offsite professional printing, including embedding fonts, including linked graphics, creating links for embedded graphics, compressing your publication, and adding an unpacking utility for uncompressing it when it gets to its destination. In most cases, you will want to pack the files on a CD or DVD disc, unless your printer allows you to upload files to its location over the Internet or enables you to submit them on a USB flash drive.

Saving a Publication for Online Photo Center Printing

Publisher 2013 includes a new feature for saving publication as JPEG or TIFF files so that you can upload it to an online photo printing service, such as Snapfish or Shutterfly; the photo printing services offered by retailers such as Walgreens or CVS; or any number of local or regional online photo printing services. When you use this feature, Publisher saves each page of the publication as a separate JPEG or TIFF file, and places all the files in a single folder. You can choose the format you want based on the quality of output that you want. TIFF files are not compressed and retain more of the original image information, so they may be the best choice in situations such as when you want the pages printed as large format posters. You may choose JPEG for smaller jobs or to make the files faster to upload.

To save a publication for online photo printing, choose File ➪ Export ➪ Save for Photo Printing. At the right side of the Backstage view under Save for Photo Printing (Figure 32.23), choose the desired file format from the drop-down list. Click Save Image Set. In the Choose Location dialog box that appears, navigate to a folder and click it, and then click Select folder. Within the selected folder, Publisher creates a new folder with the same name as the publication file. Publisher then saves each page as a separate file within the new folder, naming the files sequentially (page01, page02, and so on) and adds the appropriate file name extension based on the format you selected. From there, you can rename the files if desired, and then upload them for printing.

FIGURE 32.23

The new options for saving a publication for online photo printing

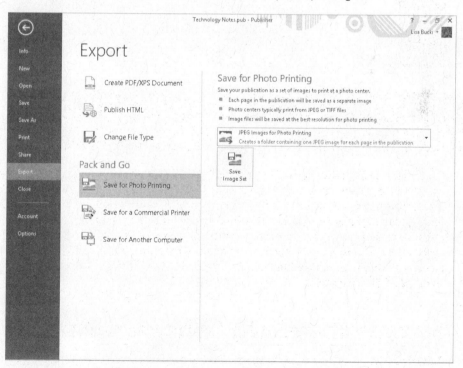

Summary

This final *Microsoft Office 2013 Bible* chapter about Microsoft Publisher gave you the information you need to improve the content and design for a publication, add missing elements, and finalize and print the publication. The chapter showed you how to:

- Use special effects such as BorderArt, drop caps, and WordArt.
- Add a building block object.
- Change overall page and publication design settings such as the color scheme.
- Better align objects and wrap text around them, as well as how to group them.
- Work with pages and page numbering before seeing how to check the design and print.
- Adhere to good practices for preparing a publication for commercial printing.
- Convert a publication to individual JPEG or TIFF files that you can send to an online photo printing service.

Part VII

Managing Information with Access and OneNote

Whether you need a very structured way to gather and manage business data or a more free form way to gather different types of information pertaining to your personal projects, Office has you covered. In this part, you learn the basics of using the powerful Access 2013 database program to organize data in tables, use forms to view and enter data, identify matching data with queries, and use reports to share data with team members and others. The part concludes with an introduction to OneNote, which functions as a virtual notebook to hold a variety of types of data organized by topic or as you otherwise please.

An Introduction to Database Development

D atabase development is unlike most other ways you work with computers. Unlike Microsoft Word or Excel, where the approach to working with the application is relatively intuitive, good database development requires prior knowledge. You have to learn a handful of fundamentals, including database terminology, basic database concepts, and database best practices.

Throughout this chapter, we cover the fundamentals of database development, especially as they pertain to Access 2013. If your goal is to get right into working with a database, you might want to skip to Chapter 34 and read about building tables.

The Database Terminology of Access

Access follows most, but not all, traditional database terminology. The terms *database, table, record, field,* and *value* indicate a hierarchy from largest to smallest. These same terms are used with virtually all database systems.

Databases

Generally, the word *database* is a computer term for a collection of information concerning a certain topic or business application. Databases help you organize this related information in a logical fashion for easy access and retrieval.

Databases aren't only for computers. There are also manual databases; we sometimes refer to these as *manual filing systems* or *manual database systems*. These filing systems usually consist of people, papers, folders, and filing cabinets — paper is the key to a manual database system. In manual database systems, you typically have in and out baskets and some type of formal filing method. You access information manually by opening a file cabinet, taking out a file folder, and finding the correct piece of paper. Users fill out paper forms for input, perhaps by using a keyboard to input information that's printed on forms. You find information by manually sorting the papers or by copying information from many papers to another piece of paper. You may use an Excel worksheet or calculator to analyze the data or display it in new and interesting ways.

An Access database is nothing more than an automated version of the filing and retrieval functions of a paper filing system. Access databases store information in a carefully defined structure. Access tables store a variety of different kinds of data, from simple lines of text (such as name and address) to complex data such as pictures, sounds, or video images. Storing data in a precise format enables a database management system (DBMS) like Access to turn data into useful information.

Tables serve as the primary data repository in an Access database. Queries, forms, and reports provide access to the data, enabling a user to add or extract data, and presenting the data in useful ways. Most developers add macros or Visual Basic for Applications (VBA) code to forms and reports to make their Access applications easier to use.

A relational database management system (RDBMS), such as Access, stores data in *related* tables. For example, a table containing employee data (names and addresses) may be related to a table containing payroll information (pay date, pay amount, and check number).

Queries allow the user to ask complex questions (such as "What is the sum of all paychecks issued to Jane Doe in 2012?") from these related tables, with the answers displayed as on-screen forms and printed reports.

In fact, one of the fundamental differences between a relational database and a manual filing system is that, in a relational database system, data for a single person or item may be stored in separate tables. For example, in a patient management system, the patient's name, address, and other contact information is likely to be stored in a different table from the table holding patient treatments. In fact, the treatment table holds all treatment information for all patients, and a patient identifier (usually a number) is used to look up an individual patient's treatments in the treatment table.

In Access, a *database* is the overall container for the data and associated objects. It's more than the collection of tables, however — a database includes many types of objects, including queries, forms, reports, macros, and code modules.

As you open an Access database, the objects (tables, queries, and so on) in the database are presented for you to work with. You may open several copies of Access at the same time and simultaneously work with more than one database, if needed.

Many Access databases contain hundreds, or even thousands, of tables, forms, queries, reports, macros, and modules. With a few exceptions, all the objects in an Access database reside within a single file with an extension of `.accdb`, `.accde`, `.mdb`, `.mde`, or `.adp`.

Tables

A table is just a container for raw information (called *data*), similar to a folder in a manual filing system. Each table in an Access database contains information about a single entity, such as a person or product, and the data in the table is organized into rows and columns. Chapter 34 will explain the rules governing table design and how to incorporate those rules into your Access databases. These rules and guidelines ensure that your applications perform well while protecting the integrity of the data contained within your tables.

In Access a table is an entity. As you design and build Access databases, or even when working with an existing application, you must think of how the tables and other database objects represent the physical entities managed by your database and how the entities relate to one another.

After you create a table, you can view the table in a spreadsheet-like form, called a datasheet, comprising rows and columns (known as records and fields, respectively — see the following section, "Records and fields"). Although a datasheet and a spreadsheet are superficially similar, a datasheet is a very different type of object. You'll learn even more about both fields and datasheets in the next chapter.

Records and fields

A datasheet is divided into rows (called *records*) and columns (called *fields*), with the first row (the heading on top of each column) containing the names of the fields in the database.

Each row is a single record containing fields that are related to that record. In a manual system, the rows are individual forms (sheets of paper), and the fields are equivalent to the blank areas on a printed form that you fill in.

Each column is a field that includes many properties that specify the type of data contained within the field, and how Access should handle the field's data. These properties include the name of the field (Company) and the type of data in the field (Text). A field may include other properties as well. For example, the Address field's Size property tells Access the maximum number of characters allowed for the address.

> **NOTE**
>
> When working with Access, the term *field* is used to refer to an attribute stored in a record. In many other database systems, including Microsoft SQL Server, *column* is the expression you'll hear most often in place of field. Field and column mean the same thing. The terminology used relies somewhat on the context of the database system underlying the table containing the record.

Values

At the intersection of a record and a field is a *value* — the actual data element. For example, if you have a field called Company, a company name entered into that field would represent one data value. Certain rules covered in Chapter 34 govern how data is contained in an Access table.

Relational Databases

Access is a relational database management system. Access data is stored in related tables, where data in one table (such as customers) is related to data in another table (such as orders). Access maintains the relationships between related tables, making it easy to extract a customer and all the customer's orders, without losing any data or pulling order records not owned by the customer.

Multiple tables simplify data entry and reporting by decreasing the input of redundant data. By defining two tables for an application that uses customer information, for example, you don't need to store the customer's name and address every time the customer purchases an item.

After you've created the tables, they need to be related to each other. For example, if you have a Customer table and a Sales table, you can relate the two tables using a common field between them. In this case, Customer Number would be a good field to have in both tables. This will allow you to see sales in the Sales table where the Customer Number matches the Customer table.

The benefit of this model is that you don't have to repeat key attributes about a customer (like customer name, address, city, state, zip) each time you add a new record to the Sales table. All you need is the customer number. When a customer changes address, for example, the address changes only in one record in the Customers table.

Separating data into multiple tables within a database makes a system easier to maintain because all records of a given type are within the same table. By taking the time to properly segment data into multiple tables, you experience a significant reduction in design and work time. This process is known as *normalization*.

Why Create Multiple Tables?

The prospect of creating multiple tables almost always intimidates beginning database users. Most often, beginners want to create one huge table that contains all the information they need — for example, a Customer table with all the sales placed by the customer and the customer's name, address, and other information. After all, if you've been using Excel to store data so far, it may seem quite reasonable to take the same approach when building tables in Access.

A single large table for all customer information quickly becomes difficult to maintain. You have to input the customer information for every sale a customer makes (repeating the name and address information over and over in every row). The same is true for the items purchased for each sale when the customer has purchased multiple items as part of a single purchase. This makes the system more inefficient and prone to data-entry mistakes. The information in the table is inefficiently stored — certain fields may not be needed for each sales record, and the table ends up with a lot of empty fields.

You want to create tables that hold a minimum of information while still making the system easy to use and flexible enough to grow. To accomplish this, you need to consider making more than one table, with each table containing fields that are related only to the focus of that table. Then, after you create the tables, you link them so that you're able to glean useful information from them. Although this process sounds extremely complex, the actual implementation is relatively easy.

Access Database Objects

If you're new to databases (or even if you're an experienced database user), you need to understand a few key concepts before starting to build Access databases. The Access database contains six types of top-level objects, which consist of the data and tools that you need to use Access:

- **Table:** Holds the actual data.
- **Query:** Searches for, sorts, and retrieves specific data.
- **Form:** Lets you enter and display data in a customized format.
- **Report:** Displays and prints formatted data.
- **Macro:** Automates tasks without programming.
- **Module:** Contains programming statements written in the VBA programming language.

Datasheets

Datasheets are one of the many ways by which you can view data in Access. Although not a permanent database object, a datasheet displays a table's content in a row-and-column format similar to an Excel worksheet. A datasheet displays a table's information in a raw form, without transformations or filtering. The Datasheet view is the default mode for displaying all fields for all records.

You can scroll through the datasheet using the arrow keys on your keyboard. You can also display related records in other tables while in a datasheet. In addition, you can make changes to the displayed data.

Queries

Queries extract information from a database. A query selects and defines a group of records that fulfill a certain condition. Most forms and reports are based on queries that combine, filter, or sort data before it's displayed. Queries are often called from macros or VBA procedures to change, add, or delete database records.

An example of a query is when a person at the sales office tells the database, "Show me all customers, in alphabetical order by name, who are located in Massachusetts and bought something over the past six months" or "Show me all customers who bought Chevrolet car models within the past six months and display them sorted by customer name and then by sale date."

Instead of asking the question in plain English, a person uses the query by example (QBE) method. When you enter instructions into the Query Designer window and run the query, the query translates the instructions into Structured Query Language (SQL) and retrieves the desired data. You'll learn more about queries in Chapter 36.

Data-entry and display forms

Data-entry *forms* help users get information into a database table quickly, easily, and accurately. Data-entry and display forms provide a more structured view of the data than what a datasheet provides. From this structured view, database records can be viewed, added, changed, or deleted. Entering data through the data-entry forms is the most common way to get the data into the database table.

Data-entry forms restrict access to certain fields within the table. Forms can also be enhanced with data validation rules or VBA code to check the validity of your data before it's added to the database table.

Most users prefer to enter information into data-entry forms rather than into Datasheet views of tables. Forms often resemble familiar paper documents and can aid the user with data-entry tasks. Forms make data entry easy to understand by guiding the user through the fields of the table being updated.

Read-only forms are often used for inquiry purposes. These forms display certain fields within a table. Displaying some fields and not others means that you can limit a user's access to sensitive data while allowing access to other fields within the same table.

Reports

Reports present your data in printed format. Access allows for an extraordinary amount of flexibility when creating reports. For instance, you can configure a report to list all records in a given table (such as a Customers table) or you can have the report contain only the records meeting certain criteria (such as all customers living in Arizona). You do this by basing the report on a query that selects only the records needed by the report.

Reports often combine multiple tables to present complex relationships among different sets of data. An example is printing an invoice. The customers table provides the customer's name and address (and other relevant data) and related records in the sales table to print the individual line-item information for each product ordered. The report also calculates the sales totals and prints them in a specific format. Additionally, you can have Access output records into an *invoice report,* a printed document that summarizes the invoice.

> **TIP**
>
> When you design your database tables, keep in mind all the types of information that you want to print. Doing so ensures that the information you require in your various reports is available from within your database tables.

Database objects

To create *database objects,* such as tables, forms, and reports, you first complete a series of design tasks. The better your design is, the better your application will be. The more you think through your design, the faster and more successfully you can complete any system. The design process is not some necessary evil, nor is its intent to produce voluminous amounts of documentation. The sole intent of designing an object is to produce a clear-cut path to follow as you implement it.

A Five-Step Design Method

The five design steps described in this section provide a solid foundation for creating database applications — including tables, queries, forms, reports, macros, and simple VBA modules.

The time you spend on each step depends entirely on the circumstances of the database you're building. For example, sometimes users give you an example of a report they want printed from their Access database, and the sources of data on the report are so obvious that designing the report takes a few minutes. Other times, particularly when the users' requirements are complex, or the business processes supported by the application require a great deal of research, you may spend many days on Step 1.

As you read through each step of the design process, *always* look at the design in terms of outputs and inputs.

33

Step 1: The overall design — from concept to reality

All software developers face similar problems, the first of which is determining how to meet the needs of the end-user. It's important to understand the overall user requirements before zeroing in on the details.

For example your users may ask for a database that supports the following tasks:

- Entering and maintaining customer information (name, address, and financial history)
- Entering and maintaining sales information (sales date, payment method, total amount, customer identity, and other fields)
- Entering and maintaining sales line-item information (details of items purchased)
- Viewing information from all the tables (sales, customers, sales line items, and payments)
- Asking all types of questions about the information in the database
- Producing a monthly invoice report
- Producing a customer sales history
- Producing mailing labels and mail-merge reports

When reviewing these eight tasks, you may need to consider other peripheral tasks that weren't mentioned by the user. Before you jump into designing, sit down and learn how the existing process works. To accomplish this, you must do a thorough needs analysis of the existing system and how you might automate it.

Prepare a series of questions that give insight to the client's business and how the client uses his data. For example, when considering automating any type of business, you might ask these questions:

- What reports and forms are currently used?
- How are sales, customers, and other records currently stored?
- How are billings processed?

As you ask these questions and others, the client will probably remember other things about the business that you should know.

A walkthrough of the existing process is also helpful to get a feel for the business. You may have to go back several times to observe the existing process and how the employees work.

As you prepare to complete the remaining steps, keep the client involved — let the users know what you're doing and ask for input on what to accomplish, making sure it's within the scope of the user's needs.

Step 2: Report design

Although it may seem odd to start with reports, in many cases, users are more interested in the printed output from a database than they are in any other aspect of the application. Reports often include every bit of data managed by an application. Because reports tend to be comprehensive, they're often the best way to gather important information about a database's requirements.

When you see the reports that you'll create in this section, you may wonder, "Which comes first — the chicken or the egg?" Does the report layout come first, or do you first determine the data items and text that make up the report? Actually, these items are considered at the same time.

It isn't important how you lay out the data in a report. The more time you take now, however, the easier it will be to construct the report. Some people go so far as to place gridlines on the report to identify exactly where they want each bit of data to be.

Step 3: Data design

The next step in the design phase is to take an inventory of all the information needed by the reports. One of the best methods is to list the data items in each report. As you do so, take careful note of items that are included in more than one report. Make sure that you keep the same name for a data item that is in more than one report because the data item is really the same item.

For example, you can start with all the customer data you'll need for each report, as shown in Table 33.1.

TABLE 33.1 Customer-Related Data Items Found in the Reports

Customers report	Invoice report
Customer Name	Customer Name
Street	Street
City	City
State	State
ZIP Code	ZIP Code
Phone Numbers	Phone Numbers
E-Mail Address	
Web Address	
Discount Rate	
Customer Since	
Last Sales Date	
Sales Tax Rate	
Credit Information (four fields)	

As you can see by comparing the type of customer information needed for each report, there are many common fields. Most of the customer data fields are found in both reports. Table 33.1 shows only some of the fields that are used in each report — those related to customer information. Because the related row and field names are the same, you can easily make sure that you have all the data items. Although locating items easily isn't critical for this small database, it becomes very important when you have to deal with large tables containing many fields.

After extracting the customer data, you can move on to the sales data. In this case, you need to analyze only the Invoice report for data items that are specific to the sales. Table 33.2 lists the fields in the report that contain information about sales.

TABLE 33.2   Sales Data Items Found in the Reports

Invoice report	Line item data
Invoice Number	Product Purchased
Sales Date	Quantity Purchased
Invoice Date	Description of Item Purchased
Payment Method	Price of Item
Salesperson	Discount for Each Item
Discount (overall for sale)	
Tax Location	
Tax Rate	
Product Purchased (multiple lines)	
Quantity Purchased (multiple lines)	
Description of Item Purchased (multiple lines)	
Price of Item (multiple lines)	
Discount for each item (multiple lines)	
Payment Type (multiple lines)	
Payment Date (multiple lines)	
Payment Amount (multiple lines)	
Credit Card Number (multiple lines)	
Expiration Date (multiple lines)	

As you can see when you examine the type of sales information needed for the report, a few items (fields) are repeating (for example, the Product Purchased, Quantity Purchased, and Price of Item fields). Each invoice can have multiple items, and each of these items needs the same type of information — number ordered and price per item. Many sales have more than one purchased item. Also, each invoice may include partial payments, and it's possible that this payment information will have multiple lines of payment information, so these repeating items can be put into their own grouping.

You can take all the individual items that you found in the sales information group and extract them to their own group for the invoice report. Table 33.2 shows the information related to each line item.

Step 4: Table design

Now for the difficult part: You must determine what fields are needed for the tables that make up the reports. When you examine the multitude of fields and calculations that make up the many documents you have, you begin to see which fields belong to the various tables in the database. (You already did much of the preliminary work by arranging the fields into logical groups.) For now, include every field you extracted. You'll need to add others later (for various reasons), although certain fields won't appear in any table.

It's important to understand that you don't need to add every little bit of data into the database's tables. For example, users may want to add vacation and other out-of-office days to the database to make it easy to know which employees are available on a particular day. However, it's very easy to burden an application's initial design by incorporating too many ideas during the initial development phases. Because Access tables are so easy to modify later on, it's probably best to put aside noncritical items until the initial design is complete. Generally speaking, it's not difficult to accommodate user requests after the database development project is under way.

After you've used each report to display all the data, it's time to consolidate the data by purpose (for example, grouped into logical groups) and then compare the data across those functions. To do this step, first look at the customer information and combine all its different fields to create a single set of data items. Then do the same thing for the sales information and the line-item information. Table 33.3 compares data items from these three groups of information.

TABLE 33.3 Comparing the Data Items

Customer data	Invoice data	Line items
Customer Company Name	Invoice Number	Product Purchased
Street	Sales Date	Quantity Purchased
City	Invoice Date	Description of Item Purchased
State	Payment Method	Price of Item
ZIP Code	Discount (overall for this sale)	Discount for Each Item
Phone Numbers (two fields)	Tax Rate	Taxable?

Continues

TABLE 33.3 *(continued)*

Customer data	Invoice data	Line items
E-Mail Address	Payment Type (multiple lines)	
Web Address	Payment Date (multiple lines)	
Discount Rate		
Customer Since	Payment Amount (multiple lines)	
Last Sales Date	Credit Card Number (multiple lines)	
Sales Tax Rate	Expiration Date (multiple lines)	
Credit Information (four fields)		

Consolidating and comparing data is a good way to start creating the individual table, but you have much more to do.

As you learn more about how to perform a data design, you also learn that the customer data must be split into two groups. Some of these items are used only once for each customer, while other items may have multiple entries. An example is the Sales column — the payment information can have multiple lines of information.

You need to further break these types of information into their own columns, thus separating all related types of items into their own columns — an example of the normalization part of the design process. For example, one customer can have multiple contacts with the company or make multiple payments toward a single sale. Of course, we've already broken the data into three categories: customer data, invoice data, and line items.

Keep in mind that one customer may have multiple invoices, and each invoice may have multiple line items on it. The invoice-data category contains information about individual sales and the line-items category contains information about each invoice. Notice that these three columns are all related; for example, one customer can have multiple invoices, and each invoice may require multiple line items.

The relationships between tables can be different. For example, each sales invoice has one and only one customer, while each customer may have multiple sales. A similar relationship exists between the sales invoice and the line items of the invoice.

Database table relationships require a unique field in both tables involved in a relationship. A unique identifier in each table helps the database engine to properly join and extract related data.

Only the Sales table has a unique identifier (Invoice Number), which means that you need to add at least one field to each of the other tables to serve as the link to other tables. For example, adding a Customer ID field to the Customer table, adding the same field to the Invoice table, and establishing a relationship between the tables through Customer ID in each table. The database engine uses the relationship between customers and invoices to connect customers with their invoices. Relationships between tables are done through key fields.

With an understanding of the need for linking one group of fields to another group, you can add the required key fields to each group. Table 33.4 shows two new groups and link fields created for each group of fields. These linking fields, known as *primary keys* and *foreign keys,* are used to link these tables together.

The field that uniquely identifies each row in a table is the *primary key*. The corresponding field in a related table is the *foreign key*. In our example, Customer ID in the Customers table is a primary key, while Customer ID in the Invoices table is a foreign key.

Let's assume a certain record in the Customers table has 12 in its Customer ID field. Any record in the Invoices table with 12 as its Customer ID is "owned" by Customer 12.

TABLE 33.4 Tables with Keys

Customers data	Invoice data	Line items data	Sales payment data
Customer ID	Invoice ID	Invoice ID	Invoice ID
Customer Name	Customer ID	Line Number	Payment Type
Street	Invoice Number	Product Purchased	Payment Date
City	Sales Date	Quantity Purchased	Payment Amount
State	Invoice Date	Description of Item Purchased	Credit Card Number
ZIP Code	Payment Method	Price of Item	Expiration Date
Phone Numbers (two fields)	Salesperson	Discount for Each Item	
E-Mail Address	Tax Rate		
Web Address			
Discount Rate			
Customer Since			
Last Sales Date			
Sales Tax Rate			

With the key fields added to each table, you can now find a field in each table that links it to other tables in the database. For example, Table 33.4 shows Customer ID in both the Customers table (where it's the primary key) and the Invoice table (where it's a foreign key).

You've identified the three core tables for your system, as reflected by the first three columns in Table 33.4. This is the general, or first, cut toward the final table designs. You've also created an additional fact table to hold the sales payment data. Normally, payment details (such as the credit card number) are not part of a sales invoice.

Taking time to properly design your database and the tables contained within it is arguably the most important step in developing a database-oriented application. By designing your database efficiently, you maintain control of the data — eliminating costly data-entry mistakes and limiting your data entry to essential fields.

Although this book is not geared toward teaching database theory and all its nuances, this is a good place to briefly describe the art of database normalization. As already mentioned, normalization is the process of breaking data down into constituent tables. Earlier in this chapter you read about how many Access developers add dissimilar information, such as customers, invoice data, and invoice line items, into one large table. A large table containing dissimilar data quickly becomes unwieldy and hard to keep updated. Because a customer's phone number appears in every row containing that customer's data, multiple updates must be made when the phone number changes.

Step 5: Form design

After you've created the data and established table relationships, it's time to design your forms. *Forms* are made up of the fields that can be entered or viewed in Edit mode. Generally speaking, your Access screens should look a lot like the forms used in a manual system.

When you're designing forms, you need to place three types of objects on-screen:

- **Labels and text-box data-entry fields:** The fields on Access forms and reports are called *controls*.
- **Special controls (multiple-line text boxes, option buttons, list boxes, check boxes, business graphs, and pictures).**
- **Graphical objects to enhance the forms (colors, lines, rectangles, and three-dimensional effects).**

Ideally, if the form is being developed from an existing printed form, the Access data-entry form should resemble the printed form. The fields should be in the same relative place on the screen as they are in the printed counterpart.

Labels display messages, titles, or captions. Text boxes provide an area where you can type or display text or numbers that are contained in your database. Check boxes indicate a condition and are either unchecked or checked. Other types of controls available with Access include list boxes, combo boxes, option buttons, toggle buttons, and option groups. Chapter 35 will cover how to create forms.

Summary

The chapter introduced the concepts and considerations driving database development. Think of the many ways that users value data. Most companies can't operate without their customer and product lists, accounts receivable and accounts payable, and payroll information. Even very small companies must efficiently manage business data. After reading this chapter you should understand:

- An Access database organizes information in tables comprised of records and fields.
- Access is a relational database system that enables you to create relationships between fields in separate tables. The process of breaking down data into properly simplified tables is called normalization.
- The most basic view for a table is the datasheet, which displays data in basic rows and columns.
- You can use queries to retrieve specific data and forms to enter and display data.
- You can develop reports to printed data from the database.
- One method of database design involves five steps: overall design, report design, data design, table design, and finally form design.

33

Creating Access Tables

I n this chapter, you learn how to create a new Access database and its tables. You establish the database container to hold your tables, forms, queries, reports, and code that you build as you learn Access. You learn how to design your table, add the fields, and enter the data next.

The Access Start Screen

If you open Access 2013 (via the Windows 8 Start screen or the Windows 7 Start menu), you'll see the default Access Start screen shown in Figure 34.1. The Start screen gives you several options for opening an existing Access database or creating a new database.

> **NOTE**
> If you open an Access database directly from Windows Explorer (by double-clicking it), you won't see the Start screen. Instead, you'll go directly to the database interface covered later in this chapter.

In the upper-left corner of the welcome screen, you'll notice the Recent section. The files listed here are databases that you've previously opened through Access 2013. You can click any of the database files listed there to open them.

> **NOTE**
>
> Access does not distinguish existing databases from deleted databases when populating the Recent section. This means you could see a database in the Recent list that you know for a fact you've deleted. Clicking an already deleted database in the Recent list will simply activate an error message stating that Access could not find the database.

FIGURE 34.1

The Access welcome screen provides a number of ways to start working with Access.

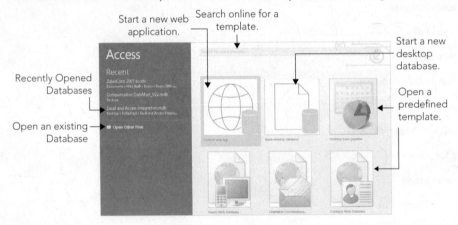

Below the Recent section, you'll see the Open Other Files choice. Click it to browse for and open databases on your computer or network.

At the top of the Start screen, you can search for Access database templates online. These templates are typically starter databases that have various purposes. Microsoft makes them available free of charge.

In the center of the Start screen, you'll see various predefined templates that you can click on to download and use. Microsoft established the online templates repository as a way to provide people with the opportunity to download partially or completely built Access applications. The template databases cover many common business requirements, such as inventory control and sales management. You may want to take a moment to explore the online templates, but they aren't covered in this book.

In the center of the Start screen, you'll also see two tiles: Custom web app and Blank desktop database. These two options allow you to create a database from scratch. If your aim is to create a new Access database that will be used on a PC (either yours or your users'), choose Blank Desktop Database. If you'll eventually be publishing your Access application via SharePoint, choose the Custom Web App database.

How to Create a Blank Desktop Database

To create a new blank database, you can click Blank desktop database option on the Start screen (refer to Figure 34.1). When you do, the dialog box shown in Figure 34.2 appears, allowing you to specify the name and location of your database. The default location of the new database will be your Documents folder. If you want to use a different folder, click the Browse button (it looks like a File Explorer folder) to the right of the File Name text box to browse to the location you want to use. After you specify the name and save location, click Create.

FIGURE 34.2

Enter the name of the new database in the File Name box.

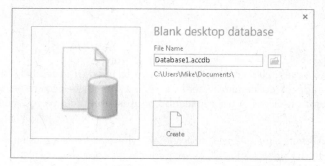

When the new database is created, Access automatically opens it for you. In Figure 34.3, notice that Access opens the new database with a blank table already added to the database, ready to be filled in with fields and other design details.

FIGURE 34.3

Your new database is created.

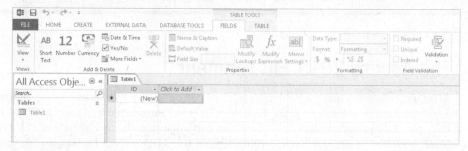

Access File Formats

Since Access 2007, the default file format for Access database files has been .accbd instead of .mdb. It's worth a moment of your time to understand why this changed and how it affects how Access 2013 works with older Access database files.

Since its inception, Access has used a database engine named Jet (an acronym for Joint Engine Technology). With Access 2007, the Access development team wanted to add significant new features to Access, such as multivariable and attachment fields. Because the new features were so significant, they couldn't retrofit Jet with the code necessary to support the new features. As a result, Microsoft developed an entirely new database engine, the Access Connectivity Engine (ACE).

Access 2013 supports several file formats, including the following:

- Access 2007–2013 .accbd format
- Access 2002–2003 .mdb format
- Access 2000 .mdb format
- Access 97 .mdb format

Earlier versions of Access (before Access 2007) cannot open nor link to the new .accbd file format. Also, the .accbd format doesn't support replication or user-level security. If you need to use an Access 2013 database with earlier versions of Access or use replication or user-level security, you must use the .mdb format.

The .accbd format should be used only in an Access environment where all users are using Access 2007 or higher versions. Stick with the Access 2002–2003 .mdb format for compatibility with a mixed environment of Access users (pre-Access 2007 and post-Access 2007). If your environment includes Access 2000 users, stay with the Access 2000 .mdb format.

In Access 2013, you can open Access 2002–2003 and Access 2000 .mdb files and make any desired changes to them, but you'll only be able to use features specific to those versions. Some of the new Access features won't be available, particularly those features that rely on the ACE database engine. You can open and even run Access 97 .mdb files, but you can't make any design changes in Access 97 .mdb files.

You can convert a database saved in a previous format by opening the database in Access 2013, choosing File ➪ Save As, and then, in the Save As dialog box, choosing any one of the different Access formats.

The Access 2013 Environment

After you create or open a new database, the Access screen will look similar to Figure 34.4. Across the top of the screen is the Ribbon, which was introduced in Access 2007. On the left, you see the Navigation pane. These two components make up the bulk of the Access interface. In addition, you have at your disposal the Quick Access Toolbar, which you can customize with the commands you use most frequently.

FIGURE 34.4

The Access interface includes the Ribbon at the top and the Navigation pane at the left.

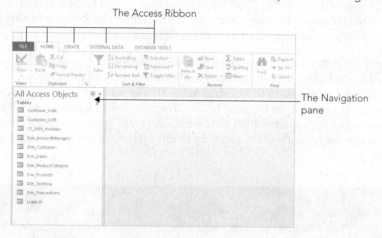

The Navigation pane

The Navigation pane, at the left of the screen, is your primary navigation aid when working with Access. The Navigation pane shows queries, forms, reports, and other Access object types. It can also display a combination of different types of objects.

Click the drop-down list in the Navigation pane's title bar to reveal the navigation options (see Figure 34.5).

FIGURE 34.5

Choosing an alternate display for the Navigation pane

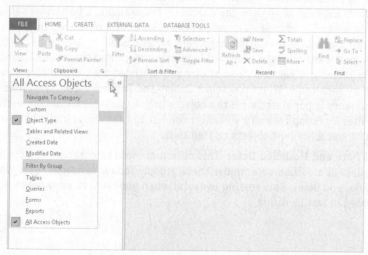

The navigation options are divided into two categories: Navigate to Category and Filter by Group. First, you choose an option under Navigate to Category, and then you choose an option under Filter by Group. The Filter By Group options you're presented with depend on the Navigate to Category option you select. We cover each of the Navigate to Category options in the following sections, along with the corresponding Filter by Group options.

- **Custom:** The Custom option creates a new tab in the Navigation pane. This new tab is titled *Custom Group 1* by default and contains objects that you drag and drop into the tab's area. Items added to a custom group still appear in their respective object type view, as described in the next bullet. When you select Custom, the Filter By Group category is populated with all the custom groups you've previously created. You can use the Filter By Group category to filter to any of the created custom groups.

> **TIP**
>
> Custom groups are a great way to group dissimilar objects (like tables, queries, and forms) that are functionally related. For example, you could create a Customers custom group and add all the database objects related to customer activities. Items contained in a custom group can appear in other groups as well.

- **Object Type:** The Object Type option is most similar to previous versions of Access. When you select Object Type, the following choices appear under Filter By Group: Tables, Queries, Forms, Reports, and All Access Objects. By default, the Navigation pane shows all objects in the current database. Select All Access Objects when you've been working with one of the filtered views and want to see every object in the database.

- **Tables and Related Views:** The Tables and Related Views option requires a bit of explanation. Access tries very hard to keep the developer informed of the hidden connections between objects in the database. For example, a particular table may be used in a number of queries or referenced from a form or report. In previous versions of Access, these relationships were very difficult to determine, and no effective tool was built into Access to help you understand these relationships. Selecting Tables and Related Views allows you to understand which objects are affected by each table. When you select Tables and Related Views, the Filter By Group category is populated with the objects in your database. Clicking each object in the Filter By Group category will filter the list to that object and all the other dependent and precedent objects related to it.

- **Created Date and Modified Date:** This option groups the database objects by the created date or modified date, under these groups: Today, Yesterday, Last Week, Two Weeks Ago, and Older. This setting is useful when you need to know when an object was created or last modified.

Tabbed Windows

A common complaint among some developers with earlier versions of Access was the fact that when multiple objects were simultaneously opened in the Access environment, the objects would often overlap and obscure each other, making it more difficult to navigate between the objects.

Microsoft has added a tabbed document interface to Access, preventing objects from obscuring other objects that are open at the same time. In the accompanying figure, multiple objects are open (one query and four tables). As you can see, switching between them is very easy — just select a tab associated with an object, and the object is brought to the top.

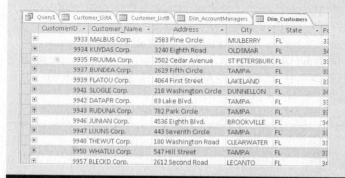

TIP

Don't like the new tabbed windows configuration? You can go back to the old overlapping windows by choosing File ➪ Options. In the Access Options dialog box, select the Current Database tab, and change the Document Window Options from Tabbed Documents to Overlapping Windows. You'll have to close and reopen your database to have the change take effect.

34

The Ribbon

The Ribbon occupies the top portion of the main Access screen and is divided into five tabs, each tab containing any number of controls and commands (refer to Figure 34.5):

- **File:** When you click the File tab, the Backstage view opens. Backstage view contains a number of options for creating databases, opening databases, saving databases, and configuring databases.

- **Home:** The theme of the Home tab is "frequently used." Here, you find generally unrelated commands that are repeatedly called upon during the course of working with Access.

- **Create:** The Create tab contains commands that create the various objects in Access. This tab is where you'll spend most of your time. Here, you can initiate the creation of tables, queries, forms, reports, and macros. As you read this part of the book, you'll be using the Create tab all the time.

- **External Data:** The External Data tab is dedicated to integrating Access with other sources of data. On this tab, you find commands that allow you to import and export data, establish connections to outside databases, and work with SharePoint or other platforms.

- **Database Tools:** The Database Tools tab contains the commands that deal with the inner workings of your database. Here, you find tools to create relationships between tables, analyze the performance of your database, document your database, and compact and repair your database.

In addition to the standard five tabs on the Access Ribbon, you'll also see contextual tabs. *Contextual tabs* are special types of tabs that appear only when a particular object is selected. For example, when you're working with the query builder, you'll see the Query Tools⇨Design tab shown in Figure 34.6.

FIGURE 34.6

Contextual tabs contain commands that are specific to whichever object is active.

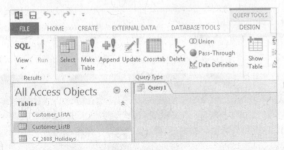

Creating a new table

Creating database tables is as much art as it is science. Acquiring a good working knowledge of the user's requirements is a fundamental step for any new database project.

It's always a good idea to plan tables on paper first, before you use the Access tools to add tables to the database. Many tables, especially small ones, really don't require a lot of forethought before adding them to the database. After all, not much planning is required to design a table holding lookup information, such as the names of cities and states. However, more complex entities, such as customers and products, usually require considerable thought and effort to implement properly.

Although you can create the table interactively without any forethought, carefully planning a database system is a good idea. You can make changes later, but doing so wastes time; generally, the result is a system that's harder to maintain than one that you've planned well from the beginning.

The importance of naming conventions

Most Access developers eventually adopt a naming convention to help identify database objects. Most naming conventions are relatively simple and involve nothing more than adding a prefix indicating an object's type to the object's name. For example, an employee's form might be named frmEmployees.

As your databases grow in size and complexity, the need to establish a naming convention for the objects in your databases increases. Even with the Name AutoCorrect option turned on (click File ➪ Options ➪ Current Database ➪ Name AutoCorrect), Access only corrects the most obvious name changes. Changing the name of a table breaks virtually every query, form, and report that uses the information from that table. Your best defense is to adopt reasonable object names, use a naming convention early on as you begin building Access databases, and stick with the naming convention throughout the project.

Access imposes very few restrictions on the names assigned to database objects. Therefore, it's entirely possible to have two distinctly different objects (for example, a form and a report, or a table and a macro) with the same name. (You can't, however, have a table and a query with the same name, because tables and queries occupy the same namespace in the database.)

Although simple names like Contacts and Orders are adequate, as a database grows in size and complexity, you might be confused about which object a particular name refers to. For example, when working with Visual Basic for Applications (VBA), the programming language built into Access, there must be no ambiguity or confusion between referenced objects. Having both a form and a report named Contacts might be confusing to you *and* your code.

The simplest naming convention is to prefix object names with a three- or four-character string indicating the type of object carrying the name. Using this convention, tables are prefixed with tbl and queries with qry. The generally accepted prefixes for forms, reports, macros, and modules are frm, rpt, mcr, and bas or mod, respectively.

In this book, most compound object names appear in *camel case*: tblBookOrders, tblCustomers, and so on. Most people find camel-case names easier to read and remember than names that appear in all-uppercase or all-lowercase characters (such as TBLBOOKORDERS or tblbookorders).

Also, at times, we use informal references for database objects. For example, the formal name of the table containing contact information in the previous examples is tblContacts. An informal reference to this table might be "the Contacts table."

In most cases, your users never see the formal names of database objects. One of your challenges as an application developer is to provide a seamless user interface that hides all data-management and data-storage entities that support the user interface. You can easily control the text that appears in the title bars and surfaces of the forms, reports, and other user-interface components to hide the actual names of the data structures and interface constituents.

34

Access allows table names up to 64 characters. Take advantage of this to give your tables, queries, forms, and reports descriptive, informative names. There is no reason why you should confine a table name to BkOrd when tblBookOrders is handled just as easily and is much easier to understand.

Descriptive names can be carried to an extreme, of course. There's no point in naming a form frmUpdateContactInformation if frmUpdateInfo does just as well. Long names are more easily misspelled or misread than shorter names, so use your best judgment when assigning names.

Although Access lets you use spaces in database object names, you should avoid spaces at all costs. Spaces don't add to readability and can cause major headaches, particularly when upsizing to client/server environments or using OLE automation with other applications. Even if you don't anticipate extending your Access applications to client/server or incorporating OLE or DDE automation into your applications, get into the habit of not using spaces in object names.

Finally, you can use some special characters, like an underscore, in your table names. Some developers use an underscore to separate words in a table name as part of a larger naming convention. Unless you use a specific convention that includes special characters, you should avoid them.

Designing tables

Designing a table is a multistep process. By following the steps in order, your table design can be created readily and with minimal effort:

1. **Create the new table.**
2. **Enter field names, data types, properties, and (optionally) descriptions.**
3. **Set the table's primary key.**
4. **Create indexes for appropriate fields.**
5. **Save the table's design.**

Generally speaking, some tables are never really finished. As users' needs change or the business rules governing the application change, you might find it necessary to open an existing table in Design view. This book, like most books on Access, describes the process of creating tables as if every table you ever work on is brand new. The truth is, however, that most of the work that you do on an Access application is performed on existing objects in the database. Some of those objects you've added yourself, while other objects may have been added by another developer at some time in the past. However, the process of maintaining an existing database component is exactly the same as creating the same object from scratch.

Adding a new table to the database

Begin by selecting the Create tab on the Ribbon. The Create tab (shown in Figure 34.7) contains all the tools necessary to create not only tables, but also forms, reports, and other database objects.

FIGURE 34.7

The Create tab contains tools necessary for adding new objects to your Access database.

There are two main ways to add new tables to an Access database from the Tables group on the Create tab:

- **Clicking the Table button:** Adds a table in Datasheet view to the database with one AutoNumber field named ID.

- **Clicking the Table Design button:** Adds a table in Design view to the database.

The later example was created using the Table Design button, but first, let's take a look at the Table button.

Clicking the Table button adds a new table to the Access environment. The new table appears in Datasheet view in the area to the right of the Navigation Pane. The new table is shown in Figure 34.8. Notice that the new table appears in Datasheet view, with an ID column already inserted and a Click to Add column to the right of the ID field.

FIGURE 34.8

The new table in Datasheet view

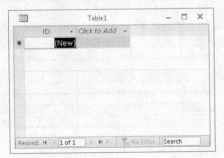

The Click to Add column is intended to permit users to quickly add fields to a table. All you have to do is begin entering data in the new column. You assign the field a name by right-clicking the field's heading, selecting Rename Field, entering a name for the field, and pressing Enter. In other words, building an Access table can be very much like creating a worksheet in Excel. This approach is usually referred to as "creating a table in Datasheet view."

Once you've added the new column, the tools on the Table Tools ⇨ Fields tab of the Ribbon (shown in Figure 34.9) allow you to set the specific data type for the field, along with its formatting, validation rules, and other properties.

FIGURE 34.9

Field design tools are located on the Table Tools ⇨ Fields tab of the Ribbon.

The second method of adding new tables is to click the Table Design button in the Tables group on the Create tab. Access opens a new table in Design view, allowing you to add fields to the table's design. Figure 34.10 shows a new table's design after a few fields have been added. Table Design view provides a somewhat more deliberate approach to building Access tables.

FIGURE 34.10

A new table added in Design view

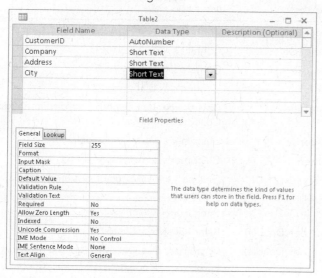

The Table Designer is quite easy to understand, and each column is clearly labeled. At the far left is the Field Name column, where you input the names of fields you add to the table. You assign a Data Type to each field in the table and (optionally) provide a Description for the field in the columns of those names.

For example, say you wanted to create the Customers table for a Collectible Mini Cars database. The basic field design for this table is outlined in Table 34.1. The "Creating an Example Table" section, later in this chapter, gives an overview of how to create a table, mentioning the fields in Table 34.1 as an example. If desired, you can practice creating a table using the fields listed in Table 34.1.

TABLE 34.1   The Collectible Mini Cars Customers Table Fields

Field name	Data type	Description
CustomerID	AutoNumber	Primary key
Company	Short Text	Contact's employer or other affiliation
Address	Short Text	Contact's address
City	Short Text	Contact's city
State	Short Text	Contact's state
ZipCode	Short Text	Contact's zip code

Continues

TABLE 34.1 *(continued)*

Field name	Data type	Description
Phone	Short Text	Contact's phone
Fax	Short Text	Contact's fax
Email	Short Text	Contact's e-mail address
WebSite	Short Text	Contact's web address
OrigCustDate	DateTime	Date the contact first purchased something from Collectible Mini Cars
CreditLimit	Currency	Customer's credit limit in dollars
CurrentBalance	Currency	Customer's current balance in dollars
CreditStatus	Short Text	Description of the customer's credit status
LastSalesDate	DateTime	Most recent date the customer purchased something from Collectible Mini Cars
TaxRate	Number (Double)	Sales tax applicable to the customer
DiscountPercent	Number (Double)	Customary discount provided to the customer
Notes	Long Text	Notes and observations regarding this customer
Active	Yes/No	Whether the customer is still buying or selling to Collectible Mini Cars

The Short Text fields in the preceding table use the default 255 character Field Size. While it's unlikely that anyone's name will occupy 255 characters, there's no harm in providing for very long names. Access only stores as many characters as are actually entered into a text field. So, allocating 255 characters doesn't actually *use* 255 characters for every name in the database.

Looking once again at Figure 34.10, you see that the Table Design window consists of two areas:

- **The Field Entry Area:** Use the field entry area, at the top of the window, to enter each field's name and data type. You can also enter an optional description. "Specifying a data type" later in this chapter explains the various data types.

- **The Field Properties Area:** The area at the bottom of the window is where the field's properties are specified. These properties include Field Size, Format, Input Mask, and Default Value, among others. The actual properties displayed in the properties area depend upon the data type of the field.

> **TIP**
>
> You can switch between the upper and lower areas of the Table Designer by pressing F6. The F6 key cycles through all open panes, such as the Navigation pane and the Property search, so you may have to press it multiple times to get where you're going.

Using the Table Tools ⇨ Design tab

The Table Tools ⇨ Design tab shown in Figure 34.11 contains many controls that assist in creating a new table definition.

FIGURE 34.11

The Design tab of the Ribbon

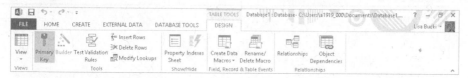

The controls on the Design tab affect the important table design considerations. Only a few of the controls shown in Figure 34.11 are described in the following sections. You'll learn much more about the other buttons in the "Creating an Example Table" section later in this chapter.

Primary Key

Click this button in the Tools group to designate which of the fields in the table you want to use as the table's primary key. Traditionally, the primary key appears at the top of the list of fields in the table, but it could appear anywhere within the table's design.

Although it makes very little difference to the database engine, many developers are fussy about the sequence of fields in a table. Many of the wizards in Access display the fields in the same order as the table. Keeping an address field above a city field, for example, can make development easier.

Clicking the Insert Rows button in the Tools group inserts a blank row just *above* the position occupied by the insertion point. For example, if the insertion point is currently in the second row of the Table Designer, clicking the Insert Row button inserts an empty row in the second position, moving the existing second row to the third position.

> **TIP**
>
> To move a field, simply left-click the selector to the left of the field's name to highlight the field in the Table Designer, and drag the field to its new position.

Delete Rows

Clicking the Delete Rows button in the Tools group removes a row from the table's design.

> **CAUTION**
>
> Access doesn't ask you to confirm the deletion before actually removing the row.

Property Sheet

Clicking the Property Sheet button in the Show/Hide group opens the table's Property Sheet (shown in Figure 34.12). These properties enable you to specify important table characteristics, such as a validation rule to apply to the entire table, or an alternate sort order for the table's data.

FIGURE 34.12

The Property Sheet

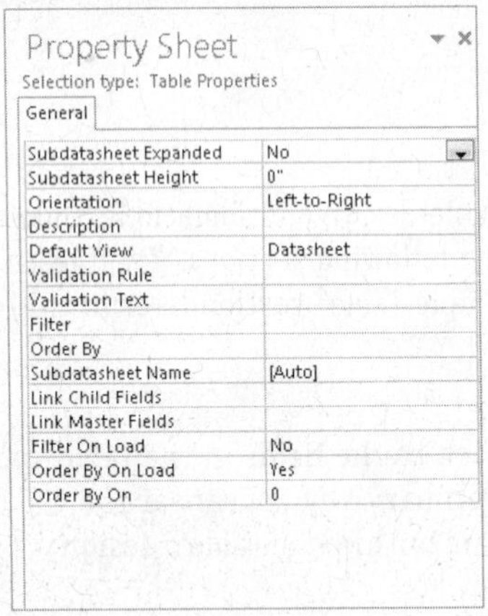

Indexes

Indexes are discussed in much more detail in the "Indexing Access Tables" section, later in this chapter. Clicking the Indexes button in the Show/Hide group opens the Indexes dialog box, which enables you to specify the details of indexes on the fields in your table.

Working with fields

You create fields by entering a field name and a field data type in the upper entry area of the Table Design window. The (optional) Description property indicates the field's purpose. The description appears in the status bar at the bottom of the screen during data entry and may be useful to people working with the application. After entering each field's name and data type, you can further specify how each field is used by entering properties in the property area.

Naming a field

A field name should be descriptive enough to identify the field to you as the developer, to the user of the system, and to Access. Field names should be long enough to quickly identify the purpose of the field, but not overly long. (Later, as you enter validation rules or use the field name in a calculation, you'll want to save yourself from typing long field names.)

To enter a field name, position the pointer in the first row of the Table Design window under the Field Name column. Then type a valid field name, observing these rules:

- Field names can be from 1 to 64 characters in length.
- Field names can include letters, numbers, and many special characters.
- Field names can include spaces. Spaces should be avoided in field names for some of the same reasons you avoid them in table names.
- Field names can't include a period (.), exclamation point (!), brackets ([ ]), or accent grave (`).
- You can't use low-order ASCII characters — for example Ctrl+J or Ctrl+L (ASCII values 0 through 31).
- You can't start with a blank space.
- You can't use a double quotation mark ("") in the name of a Microsoft Access project file.

You can enter field names in uppercase, lowercase, or mixed case. If you make a mistake while typing the field name, position the insertion point where you want to make a correction and type the change. You can change a field name at any time, even if the table contains data.

NOTE

Access is not case sensitive, so the database itself doesn't care whether you name a table tblCustomers or TblCustomers. Choosing uppercase, lowercase, or mixed case characters is entirely your decision and should be aimed at making your table names descriptive and easy to read.

CAUTION

After your table is saved, if you change a field name that is also used in queries, forms, or reports, you have to change it in those objects as well. One of the leading causes of errors in Access applications stems from changing the names of fundamental database objects such as tables and fields, but neglecting to make all the changes required throughout the database. Overlooking a field name reference in the control source of a control on the form or report, or deeply embedded in VBA code somewhere in the application, is far too easy.

34

Specifying a data type

When you enter a field, you must also decide what type of data each of your fields will hold. In Access, you can choose any of several data types. The available data types are shown in Table 34.2.

TABLE 34.2   **Data Types Available in Microsoft Access**

Data type	Type of data stored	Storage size
Short Text	Alphanumeric characters	255 characters or less
Long Text	Alphanumeric characters	1GB of characters or less
Number	Numeric values	1, 2, 4, or 8 bytes; 16 bytes for Replication ID (GUID)
Date/Time	Date and time data	8 bytes
Currency	Monetary data	8 bytes
AutoNumber	Automatic number increments	4 bytes; 16 bytes for Replication ID (GUID)
Yes/No	Logical values: Yes/No, True/False	1 bit (0 or –1)
OLE Object	Pictures, graphs, sound, video	Up to 1GB (disk space limitation)
Hyperlink	Link to an Internet resource	1GB of characters or less
Attachment	A special field that enables you to attach external files to an Access database	Varies by attachment
Lookup Wizard	Displays data from another table	Generally 4 bytes

Figure 34.13 shows the Data Type drop-down list used to select the data type for the field you just created.

FIGURE 34.13

The Data Type drop-down list

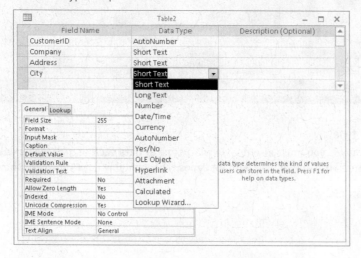

One of these data types must be assigned to each of your fields. Some of the data types have additional options, such as Field Size for Short Text fields and Number fields.

Here are the basic questions to consider when choosing the data type for new fields in your tables:

- **What is the data type?** The data type should reflect the data stored in the field. For example, you should select one of the numeric data types to store numbers like quantities and prices. Don't store data like phone numbers or Social Security numbers in numeric fields, however; your application won't be performing numeric operations like addition or multiplication on phone numbers. Instead, use text fields for common data, such as Social Security numbers and phone numbers.

NOTE

Numeric fields never store leading zeros. Putting a zip code such as 02173 into a numeric field means only the last four digits (2173) are actually stored.

- **What are the storage requirements of the data type you've selected?** Although you can use the Long Integer data type in place of Integer or Byte, the storage requirements of Long Integer (4 bytes) is twice that of Integer. This means that twice as much memory is required to use and manipulate the number and twice as much disk space is required to store its value. Whenever possible, use Byte or Integer data types for simple numeric data.

- **Will you want to sort or index the field?** Because of their binary nature, Long Text and OLE Object fields can't be sorted or indexed. Use Long Text fields sparingly. The overhead required to store and work with Long Text fields is considerable.

- **What is the impact of the data type on sorting requirements?** Numeric data sorts differently from sorting text data. Using the numeric data type, a sequence of numbers will sort as expected: 1, 2, 3, 4, 5, 10, 100. The same sequence stored as text data will sort like this: 1, 10, 100, 2, 3, 4, 5. If it's important to sort text data in a numeric sequence, you'll have to first apply a conversion function to the data before sorting.

TIP

If it's important to have text data representing numbers to sort in the proper order, you might want to prefix the numerals with zeros (001, 002, and so on). Then the text values will sort in the expected order: 001, 002, 003, 004, 005, 010, 100.

- **Is the data text or date data?** When working with dates, you're almost always better off storing the data in a Date/Time field than as a Short Text field. Text values sort differently from dates (dates are stored internally as numeric values), which can upset reports and other output that rely on chronological order.

34

- **Don't be tempted to store dates in one Date/Time field and time in another Date/Time field.** The Date/Time field is specifically designed to handle both dates and times, and, as you'll see throughout this book, it's quite easy to display only the date or time portion of a Date/Time value.

- **A Date/Time field is also meant to store a discrete date and time, and not a time interval.** If keeping track of durations is important, you could use two Date/Time fields — one to record the start and the other at the end of a duration — or one Long Integer field to store the number of elapsed second, minutes, hours, and so forth.

- **What reports will be needed?** You won't be able to sort or group memo or OLE data on a report. If it's important to prepare a report based on memo or OLE data, add a Tag field like a date or sequence number, which can be used to provide a sorting key, to the table.

Short Text data type

The Short Text data type holds information that is simply characters (letters, numbers, punctuation). Names, addresses, and descriptions are all text data, as are numeric data that are not used in a calculation (such as telephone numbers, Social Security numbers, and zip codes).

Although you specify the size of each Short Text field in the property area, you can enter no more than 255 characters of data in any Short Text field. Access uses variable length fields to store text data. If you designate a field to be 25 characters wide and you use only 5 characters for each record, then only enough room to store 5 characters is used in your database.

You'll find that the .accdb database file might quickly grow quite large, but text fields are not the usual cause. However, it's good practice to limit Short Text field widths to the maximum you believe is likely for the field. Names can be quite tricky because fairly long names are common in some cultures. However, it's a safe bet that a postal code will be less than 12 characters, while a U.S. state abbreviation is always 2 characters. By limiting a Short Text field's width, you also limit the number of characters users can enter when the field is used in a form.

Long Text data type

The Long Text data type holds a variable amount of data up to 1GB. Long Text fields use only as much memory as necessary for the data stored. So, if one record uses 100 characters, another requires only 10, and yet another needs 3,000, you use only as much space as each record requires.

You don't specify a field size for the Long Text data type. Access allocates as much space as necessary for the data.

Number data type

The Number data type enables you to enter *numeric* data — that is, numbers that will be used in mathematical calculations or represent scalar quantities such as inventory counts. (If you have data that will be used in monetary calculations, you should use the Currency data type, which performs calculations without rounding errors.)

The exact type of numeric data stored in a number field is determined by the Field Size property. Table 34.3 lists the various numeric data types, their maximum and minimum ranges, the decimal points supported by each numeric data type, and the storage (bytes) required by each numeric data type.

TABLE 34.3   Numeric Field Settings

Field size setting	Range	Decimal places	Storage size
Byte	0 to 255	None	1 byte
Integer	−32,768 to 32,767	None	2 bytes
Long Integer	−2,147,483,648 to 2,147,483,647	None	4 bytes
Double	-1.797×10^{308} to 1.797×10^{308}	15	8 bytes
Single	-3.4×10^{38} to 3.4×10^{38}	7	4 bytes
Replication ID	N/A	N/A	16 bytes
Decimal	1–28 precision	15	8 bytes

34

Design your tables very conservatively, and allow for larger values than you ever expect to see in your database. This is not to say that using the Double data type for all numeric fields is a good idea. The Double data type is very large (8 bytes) and might be somewhat slow when used in calculations or other numeric operations. Instead, the Single data type is probably best for most floating-point calculations, and Long Integer is a good choice where decimal points are irrelevant.

Date/Time data type

The Date/Time data type is a specialized number field for holding dates or times (or dates *and* times). When dates are stored in a Date/Time field, it's easy to calculate days between dates and other calendar operations. Date data stored in Date/Time fields sort and filter properly as well. The Date/Time data type holds dates from January 1, 100, to December 31, 9999.

Currency

The Currency data type is another specialized number field. Currency numbers are not rounded during calculations and preserve 15 digits of precision to the left of the decimal point and 4 digits to the right. Because Currency fields use a fixed decimal point position, they're faster in numeric calculations than doubles.

AutoNumber

The AutoNumber field is another specialized Number data type. When an AutoNumber field is added to a table, Access automatically assigns a long integer (32-bit) value to the field (beginning at 1) and increments the value each time a record is added to the table. Alternatively (determined by the New Values property), the value of the AutoNumber field is a random integer that is automatically inserted into new records.

Only one AutoNumber field can appear in a table. Once assigned to a record, the value of an AutoNumber field can't be changed programmatically or by the user. AutoNumber fields are stored as a Long Integer data type and occupy 4 bytes. The range of possible values for AutoNumber fields is from 1 to 4,294,967,296 — more than adequate as the primary key for most tables.

> **NOTE**
>
> An AutoNumber field is not guaranteed to generate a continuous, unbroken set of sequential numbers. For example, if the process of adding a new record is interrupted (such as the user pressing the Esc key while entering the new record's data) an AutoNumber field will "skip" a number. AutoNumber fields should not be used to provide a stream of sequential numbers. Instead, sequential numbers can be easily added to a table through a data macro or VBA code.

Yes/No fields accept only one of two possible values. Internally stored as 1 (Yes) or 0 (No), the Yes/No field is used to indicate yes/no, on/off, or true/false. A Yes/No field occupies a single bit of storage.

OLE Object

The OLE Object field stores OLE data, highly specialized binary objects such as Word documents, Excel spreadsheets, sound or video clips, and images. The OLE object is created by an application that Windows recognizes as an OLE server and can be linked to the parent application or embedded in the Access table. OLE objects can only be displayed in bound object frames in Access forms and reports. OLE fields can't be indexed.

Attachment

The Attachment data type was introduced in Access 2007. In fact, the Attachment data type is one of the reasons Microsoft changed the format of the Access data file. The older MDB format is unable to accommodate attachments.

The Attachment data type is relatively complex, compared to the other types of Access fields, and it requires a special type of control when displayed on Access forms. For details on this interesting type of field, turn to "Understanding Attachment Fields," later in this chapter.

Hyperlink data type

The Hyperlink data type field holds combinations of text and numbers stored as text and used as a hyperlink address. It can have up to three parts:

- The text that appears in a control (usually formatted to look like a clickable link)
- The Internet address — the path to a file or web page
- Any sub-address within the file or page. An example of a sub-address is a picture on a web page. Each part of the hyperlink's address is separated by the pound sign (#).

Access hyperlinks can even point to forms and reports in other Access databases. This means that you can use a hyperlink to open a form or report in an external Access database and display the form or report on the user's computer.

Lookup Wizard

The Lookup Wizard data type inserts a field that enables the end-user to choose a value from another table or from the results of a SQL statement. The values may also be presented as a combo box or list box. At design time, the Lookup Wizard leads the developer through the process of defining the lookup characteristics when this data is assigned to a field.

As you drag an item from the Lookup Wizard field list, a combo box or list box is automatically created on the form. The list box or combo box also appears on a query data sheet that contains the field.

Entering a field description

The field description is completely optional; you use it only to help you remember a field's uses or to let another developer understand the field's purpose. Often, you don't use the

Description column at all, or you use it only for fields whose purpose is not obvious. If you enter a field description, it appears in the status bar whenever you use that field in Access — in the datasheet or in a form. The field description can help clarify a field whose purpose is ambiguous or give the user a more complete explanation of the appropriate values for the field during data entry.

Specifying data validation rules

The last major design decision concerns data validation, which becomes important as users enter data. You want to make sure that only good data (data that passes certain defined tests) gets into your system. You have to deal with several types of data validation. You can test for known individual items, stipulating that the Gender field can accept only the values Male, Female, or Unknown, for example. Or you can test for ranges, specifying that the value of Weight must be between 0 and 1,500 pounds.

Creating an Example Table

Working with the different data types, you should be ready to create a first table. If you want, you can create the fields presented in Table 34.1 for the tblCustomers (Customers) table.

Using AutoNumber fields

Access gives special considerations to AutoNumber fields. You can't change a previously defined field from another type to AutoNumber if any data has been added to the table. If you try to change an existing field to an AutoNumber, you'll see an error that says:

```
Once you enter data in a table, you can't change the data type of any
field to AutoNumber, even if you haven't yet added data to that field.
```

You'll have to add a new AutoNumber field and begin working with it instead of changing an existing field to AutoNumber.

> **NOTE**
> Only one AutoNumber field can be added to an Access table. Generally speaking, it's better to use AutoNumber fields where their special characteristics are needed by an application.

Completing the table

Once you create a new table in Design view, you're ready to add its fields. Table 34.1, shown earlier in this chapter, lists the field definitions for the example tblCustomers table. If you want to work with those example fields, enter the field names and data types as shown in Table 34.1. The next few pages explain how to change existing fields (which includes rearranging the field order, changing a field name, and deleting a field).

Here are the steps for adding a field to a table structure in Design view:

1. **Click in the Field Name column in the row where you want the field to appear.**
2. **Enter the field name and press Enter or Tab to move to the Data Type column.**
3. **Select the field's data type from the drop-down list in the Data Type column.**
4. **If desired, add a description for the field in the Description column.**

Repeat each of these steps to create each of the data entry fields for your table (or the example tblCustomers table). You can press the Down Arrow key to move between rows, or use the mouse and click on any row. Pressing F6 switches the focus from the top to the bottom of the Table Design window, and vice versa.

Setting the Primary Key

Every table should have a *primary key* — one or a combination of fields with a unique value for each record. (This principle is called *entity integrity* in the world of database management.) In tblCustomers, the CustomerID field is the primary key. Each customer has a unique CustomerID value so that the database engine can distinguish one record from another. CustomerID 17 refers to one and only one record in the Contacts table. If you don't specify a primary key (unique value field), Access can create one for you.

Choosing a primary key

Without a field such as the CustomerID field in the example table, you'd have to rely on another field or combination of fields for uniqueness. You couldn't use the Company field because two customers could easily have the same company name. In fact, you couldn't even use the Company and City fields together (in a multi-field key), for the same reason — it's entirely possible that two customers with the same name exist in the same city. You need to come up with a field or combination of fields that makes every record unique.

The easiest way to solve this problem is to add an AutoNumber field to serve as the table's primary key. The primary key in tblCustomers is CustomerID, an AutoNumber field.

If you don't designate a field as a primary key, Access can add an AutoNumber field and designate it as the table's primary key. AutoNumber fields make very good primary keys because Access creates the value for you, the number is never reused within a table, and you can't change the value of an AutoNumber field.

34

Good primary keys:

- Uniquely identify each record
- Cannot be null
- Must exist when the record is created
- Must remain stable (You should never change a primary key value once it's established.)
- Should be simple and contain as few attributes as possible

In addition to uniquely identifying rows in a table, primary keys provide other benefits:

- A primary key is always an index.
- An index maintains a presorted order of one or more fields that greatly speeds up queries, searches, and sort requests.
- When you add new records to your table, Access checks for duplicate data and doesn't allow any duplicates for the primary key field.

By default, Access displays a table's data in the order of its primary key.

By designating a field such as CustomerID as the primary key, data is displayed in a meaningful order. In our example, because the CustomerID field is an AutoNumber, its value is assigned automatically by Access in the order that a record is put into the system.

The ideal primary key is, then, a single field that is immutable and guaranteed to be unique within the table. For these reasons, the example Collectible Mini Cars database uses the AutoNumber field exclusively as the primary key for all tables.

Creating the primary key

The primary key can be created in any of three ways. With a table open in Design view:

- Select the field to be used as the primary key and click the Primary Key button (the key icon) in the Tools group on the Design tab of the Ribbon.
- Right-click the field and select Primary Key from the shortcut menu.
- Save the table without creating a primary key, and allow Access to automatically create an AutoNumber field.

After you designate the primary key, a key icon appears in the gray selector area to the left of the field's name to indicate that the primary key has been created.

Creating composite primary keys

You can designate a combination of fields to be used as a table's primary key. Such keys are often referred to as *composite primary keys*. As indicated in Figure 34.14, select the fields that you want to include in the composite primary key; then click the Primary Key button in the Tools group of the Design tab of the Ribbon. It helps, of course, if the fields lie right next to each other in the table's design.

FIGURE 34.14

Creating a composite primary key

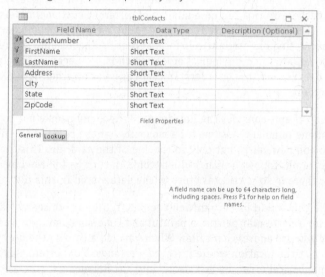

Composite primary keys are primarily used when the developer strongly feels that a primary key should be comprised of data that occurs naturally in the database. There was a time when all developers were taught that every table should have a *natural primary key* (data that occurs naturally in the table).

Composite primary keys are seldom used these days because developers have come to realize that data is highly unpredictable. Even if your users promise that a combination of certain fields will never be duplicated in the table, things have a way of turning out differently from planned. Using a *surrogate primary key* (a key field that does not naturally occur in the table's data, such as a Social Security Number or Employee ID), such as an AutoNumber, separates the table's design from the table's data. The problem with natural primary keys is that, eventually, given a large enough data set, the values of fields chosen as the table's primary key are likely to be duplicated.

34

Furthermore, when using composite keys, maintaining relationships between tables becomes more complicated because the fields comprising the primary key must be duplicated in all the tables containing related data. Using composite keys simply adds to the complexity of the database without adding stability, integrity, or other desirable features.

Indexing Access Tables

Data is rarely, if ever, entered into tables in a meaningful order. Usually, records are added to tables in random order (with the exception of time-ordered data). For example, a busy order-entry system will gather information on a number of different customer orders in a single day. Most often, this data will be used to report orders for a single customer for billing purposes or for extracting order quantities for inventory management. The records in the Orders table, however, are in chronological order, which is not necessarily helpful when preparing reports detailing customer orders. In that case, you'd rather have data entered in customer ID order.

To further illustrate this concept, consider the Rolodex card file many people use to store names, addresses, and phone numbers. Assume for a moment that the cards in the file were fixed in place. You could add new cards, but only to the end of the card file. This limitation would mean that "Jones" might follow "Smith," which would in turn be followed by "Baker." In other words, there is no particular order to the data stored in this file.

An unsorted Rolodex like this would be very difficult to use. You'd have to search each and every card looking for a particular person, a painful and time-consuming process. Of course, this isn't how you use address card files. When you add a card to the file, you insert it into the Rolodex at the location where it *logically* belongs. Most often, this means inserting the card in alphabetical order, by last name, into the Rolodex.

Records are added to Access tables as described in the fixed card file example earlier. New records are always added to the end of the table, rather than in the middle of the table where they may logically belong. However, in an order-entry system, you'd probably want new records inserted next to other records on the same customer. Unfortunately, this isn't how Access tables work. The *natural order* of a table is the order in which records were added to the table. This order is sometimes referred to as *entry order* or *physical order* to emphasize that the records in the table appear in the order in which they were added to the table.

Using tables in natural order is not necessarily a bad thing. Natural order makes perfect sense if the data is rarely searched or if the table is very small. Also, there are situations where the data being added to the table is highly ordered to start with. If the table is used to gather sequential data (like readings from an electric meter) and the data will be used in the same sequential order, there is no need to impose an index on the data.

But for situations where natural order doesn't suffice, Access provides *indexing* to help you find and sort records faster. You specify a *logical* order for the records in a table by creating an *index* on that table. Access uses the index to maintain one or more internal sort orders for the data in the table. For example, you may choose to index the LastName field that will frequently be included in queries and sorting routines.

Access uses indexes in a table as you use an index in a book: To find data, Access looks up the data's location in the index. Most often, your tables will include one or more *simple indexes*. A simple index is one that involves a single field in the table. Simple indexes may arrange the table's records in ascending or descending order. Simple indexes are created by setting the field's Indexed property to one of the following values:

- Yes (Duplicates OK)
- Yes (No Duplicates)

By default, Access fields are not indexed, but it's hard to imagine a table that doesn't require some kind of index. The next section discusses why indexing is important to use in Access tables.

The importance of indexes

Microsoft's data indicates that more than half of all tables in Access databases contain *no* indexes. This number doesn't include the tables that are improperly indexed — it includes only those tables that have no indexes at all. It appears that a lot of people don't appreciate the importance of indexing the tables in an Access database.

In a number of repeated tests, the indexed table consistently finds a word in less than 20 milliseconds, while the unindexed search takes between 200 and 350 milliseconds. It goes without saying that the actual time required to run a query depends very much on the computer's hardware, but performance enhancements of 500 percent and more are not at all uncommon when adding an index to a field.

Because an index means that Access maintains an internal sort order on the data contained in the indexed field, you can see why query performance is enhanced by an index. You should index virtually every field that is frequently involved in queries or is frequently sorted on forms or reports.

Without an index, Access must search each and every record in the database looking for matches. This process is called a *table scan* and is analogous to searching through each and every card in a Rolodex file to find all the people who work for a certain company. Until you reach the end of the deck, you can't be sure you've found every relevant card in the file.

As mentioned earlier in this chapter, a table's primary key field is always indexed. This is because the primary key is used to locate records in the table. Indexing the primary key

34

makes it much easier for Access to find the required tables in either the current table or a foreign table related to the current table. Without an index, Access has to search all records in the related table to make sure it has located all the related records.

Multiple-field indexes

Multiple-field indexes (also called *composite indexes*) are easy to create. In Design view, click the Indexes button in the Show/Hide group of the Design tab or choose View⇨Indexes. The Indexes dialog box (shown in Figure 34.15) appears, allowing you to specify the fields to include in the index.

FIGURE 34.15

Multiple-field (composite) indexes can enhance performance.

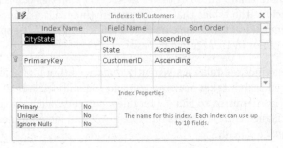

Enter a name for the index (CityState in Figure 34.15) and tab to the Field Name column. Use the drop-down list to select the fields to include in the index. In this example City and State are combined as a single index. Any row appearing immediately below this row that does not contain an index name is part of the composite index. Access considers both these fields when creating the sort order on this table, speeding queries and sorting operations that include both the City and State fields.

As many as ten fields can be included in a composite index. As long as the composite index is not used as the table's primary key, any of the fields in the composite index can be empty.

Figure 34.16 shows how to set the properties of an index. The insertion point is placed in the row in the Indexes dialog box containing the name of the index. Notice the three properties appearing below the index information in the top half of the Indexes dialog box.

FIGURE 34.16

It's easy to set the properties of an index.

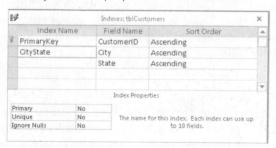

The index properties are quite easy to understand (these properties apply to single-field and composite indexes equally):

- **Primary:** When set to Yes, Access uses this index as the table's primary key. More than one field can be designated as the primary key, but keep the rules governing primary keys in mind, particularly those requiring each primary key value to be unique and that no field in a composite primary key can be empty. The default for the Primary property is No.

- **Unique:** When set to Yes, the index must be unique within a table. A Social Security number field is a good candidate for a unique index because the application's business rules may require one and only one instance of a Social Security number in the table. In contrast, a last name field should not be uniquely indexed, because many last names, like Smith and Jones, are very common, and having a unique index on the last name field will only cause problems.

  When applied to composite keys, the *combination* of field values must be unique — each field within the composite key can duplicate fields found within the table.

- **Ignore Nulls:** If a record's index field contains a null value (which happens in a composite index only if all fields in the composite index are null) the record's index won't contribute anything to the overall indexing. In other words, unless a record's index contains some kind of value, Access doesn't know where to insert the record in the table's internal index sort lists. Therefore, you might want to instruct Access to ignore a record if the index value is null. By default, the Ignore Nulls property is set to No, which means Access inserts records with a Null index value into the indexing scheme along with any other records containing Null index values.

You should test the impact of the index properties on your Access tables and use the properties that best suit the data handled by your databases.

A field can be both the primary key for a table and part of a composite index. You should index your tables as necessary to yield the highest possible performance without worrying about over-indexing or violating some arcane indexing rules. For example, in a database such as Collectible Mini Cars, the invoice number in tblSales is frequently used in forms and reports and should be indexed. In addition, there are many situations in which the invoice number is used in combinations with other fields, such as the sales date or salesperson ID. You should consider adding composite indexes combining the invoice number with sales date, and salesperson ID, to the sales table.

When to index tables

Depending on the number of records in a table, the extra overhead of maintaining an index may not justify creating an index beyond the table's primary key. Though data retrieval is somewhat faster than it is without an index, Access must update index information whenever you enter or change records in the table. In contrast, changes to nonindexed fields do not require extra file activity. You can retrieve data from nonindexed fields as easily (although not as *quickly*) as from indexed fields.

Generally speaking, it's best to add secondary indexes when tables are quite large and when indexing fields other than the primary key speeds up searches. Even with large tables, however, indexing can slow performance if the records in tables will be changed often or new records will be added frequently. Each time a record is changed or added, Access must update all indexes in the table.

Given all the advantages of indexes, why not index everything in the table? What are the drawbacks of indexing too many fields? Is it possible to over-index tables?

First, indexes increase the size of the Access database somewhat. Unnecessarily indexing a table that doesn't really require an index eats up a bit of disk space for each record in the table. More important, indexes extract a performance hit for each index on the table every time a record is added to the table. Because Access automatically updates indexes each time a record is added (or removed), the internal indexing must be adjusted for each new record. If you have ten indexes on a table, Access makes ten adjustments to the indexes each time a new record is added or an existing record is deleted, causing a noticeable delay on large tables (particularly on slow computers).

Sometimes changes to the data in records cause adjustments to the indexing scheme. This is true if the change causes the record to change its position in sorting or query activities. Therefore, if you're working with large, constantly changing data sets that are rarely searched, you may choose *not* to index the fields in the table, or to minimally index by indexing only those few fields that are likely to be searched.

As you begin working with Access tables, you'll probably start with the simplest one-field indexes and migrate to more complex ones as your familiarity with the process grows. Do keep in mind, however, the trade-offs between greater search efficiency and the overhead incurred by maintaining a large number of indexes on your tables.

It's also important to keep in mind that indexing does not modify the physical arrangement of records in the table. The natural order of the records (the order in which the records were added to the table) is maintained after the index is established.

> **NOTE**
>
> A compact and repair cycle on an Access database forces Access to rebuild the indexes in all the tables, and physically rearranges tables in primary key order in the `.accdb` file. The maintenance operations ensure that your Access databases operate at maximum efficiency.

Printing a Table Design

You can print a table design by clicking the Database Documenter button in the Analyze group on the Database Tools tab of the Ribbon. The Analyze group contains a number of tools that make it easy to document your database objects. When you click the Database Documenter button, the Documenter dialog box appears, letting you select objects to print. In Figure 34.17, tblCustomers is selected on the Tables tab of the Documenter dialog box.

FIGURE 34.17

The Documenter dialog box

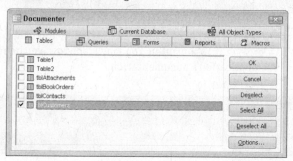

You can also set various options for printing. When you click the Options button, the Print Table Definition dialog box (shown in Figure 34.18) appears, enabling you to select which information from the Table Design to print. You can print the various field names, all their properties, the indexes, and even network permissions.

FIGURE 34.18

Printing options in the Print Table Definition dialog box

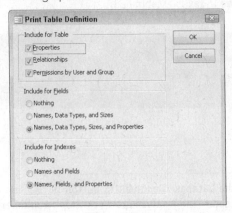

After you select which data you want to view, Access generates a report. You can view the report in a Print Preview window or send it to a printer. You may want to save the report within the database as part of the application's documentation.

Saving the Completed Table

You can save the completed table design by choosing File ➪ Save or by clicking the Save button on the Quick Access Toolbar in the upper-left corner of the Access window. If you're saving the table for the first time, Access asks for its name. Table names can be up to 64 characters long and follow standard Access object naming conventions — they may include letters and numbers, can't begin with a number, and can't include punctuation. You can also save the table when you close it.

If you've saved this table before and you want to save it with a different name, choose File⇨Save Object As and enter a different table name. This action creates a new table design and leaves the original table with its original name untouched. If you want to delete the old table, select it in the Navigation pane and press the Delete key.

Manipulating Tables

As you add many tables to your database, you may want to use them in other databases or make copies of them as backups. In many cases, you may want to copy only the table's design and not include all the data in the table. You can perform many table operations in the Navigation pane, including renaming, deleting, and copying tables. You perform these tasks by direct manipulation or by using menu items.

Renaming tables

Rename a table by right-clicking its name in the Navigation pane and selecting Rename from the shortcut menu; type the new name and press Enter. After you change the table name, it appears in the Tables list, which re-sorts the tables in alphabetical order.

> **CAUTION**
>
> If you rename a table, you must change the table name in any objects in which it was previously referenced, including queries, forms, and reports.

Deleting tables

Delete a table by right-clicking its name in the Navigation pane and selecting Delete from the shortcut menu or by selecting the table in the Navigation pane and pressing the Delete key. Like most delete operations, you have to confirm the delete by clicking Yes in a confirmation box.

> **CAUTION**
>
> Be aware that holding down the Shift key while pressing the Delete key deletes the table (or any other database object, for that matter) *without* confirmation. You'll find the Shift+Delete key combination useful for removing items but also dangerous if not carefully applied.

Copying tables in a database

The copy and paste options in the Clipboard group on the Home tab allow you to copy any table in the database. When you paste the table back into the database, the Paste Table As dialog box appears, asking you to choose from three options:

- **Structure Only:** Clicking the Structure Only button creates a new, empty table with the same design as the copied table. This option is typically used to create a temporary table or an archive table to which you can copy old records.

- **Structure and Data:** When you click Structure and Data, a complete copy of the table design and all its data is created.

- **Append Data to Existing Table:** Clicking the Append Data to Existing Table button adds the data of the selected table to the bottom of another table. This option is useful for combining tables, such as when you want to add data from a monthly transaction table to a yearly history table.

Follow these steps to copy a table:

1. **Right-click the table name in the Navigation pane and choose Copy from the shortcut menu, or click the Copy button in the Clipboard group on the Home tab.**

2. **Choose Paste from the shortcut menu, or click the Paste button in the Clipboard group on the Home tab.** The Paste Table As dialog box (shown in Figure 34.19) appears.

FIGURE 34.19

Pasting a table opens the Paste Table As dialog box

3. **Enter the name of the new table.** When you're appending data to an existing table (see the next step), you must type the name of an existing table.

4. **Choose one of the Paste options — Structure Only, Structure and Data, or Append Data to Existing Table — from the Paste Table As dialog box.**

5. **Click OK to complete the operation.**

Copying a table to another database

Just as you can copy a table within a database, you can copy a table to another database. There are many reasons why you may want to do this. Maybe you share a common table among multiple systems, or maybe you need to create a backup copy of your important tables within the system.

When you copy tables to another database, the relationships between tables are not copied. Access copies only the table design and the data to the other database. The method for copying a table to another database is essentially the same as for copying a table within a database:

1. **Right-click the table name in the Navigation pane and choose Copy from the shortcut menu, or click the Copy button in the Clipboard group on the Home tab.**

2. **Open the other Access database and choose Edit Paste from the shortcut menu, or click the Copy button in the Clipboard group on the Home tab.** The Paste Table As dialog box appears.

3. **Enter the name of the new table.**

4. **Choose one of the Paste options: Structure Only, Structure and Data, or Append Data to Existing Table.**

5. **Click OK to complete the operation.**

Adding Records to a Database Table

Adding records to a table is as simple as clicking the table in the Navigation pane to open the table in Datasheet view. Once the table is opened, enter values for each field. Figure 34.20 shows adding records in datasheet mode to the table. In the case of the example tblCustomers table shown in the figure, you can enter information into all fields except CustomerID. AutoNumber fields automatically provide a number for you.

FIGURE 34.20

Using Datasheet view to add records to a table

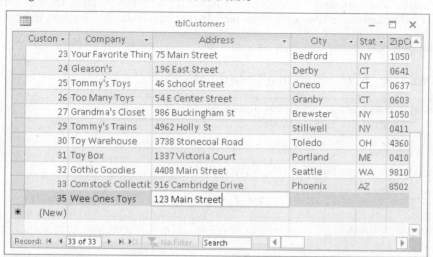

Although you can add records directly into the table through the Datasheet view, it isn't the most efficient way. (Nevertheless, you're going to learn a bit more about forms now so that you'll be comfortable working in them.) Adding records using forms is better because code behind a form can dynamically provide default values (perhaps based on data already added to the form) and communicate with the user during the data entry process.

Opening a Datasheet

Follow these steps to open a datasheet from the Database window:

1. **Click Tables in the Navigation pane if you don't see the table objects in the database.**
2. **Double-click the table name you want to open (in this example, tblProducts).**

An alternative method for opening the datasheet is to right-click a table in the Navigation pane and select Open from the shortcut menu.

> **TIP**
>
> If you're in any of the design windows, click the Datasheet View command in the View group of the Home tab to view your data in a datasheet.

Moving within a datasheet

You easily move within the Datasheet window using the mouse to indicate where you want to change or add to your data — just click a field within a record. In addition, the scroll bars and Navigation buttons make it easy to move among fields and records. Think of a datasheet as a worksheet without the row numbers and column letters. Instead, columns have field names, and rows are unique records that have identifiable values in each cell.

Table 34.4 lists the navigational keys you use for moving within a datasheet.

TABLE 34.4   Navigating in a Datasheet

Navigational direction	Keystrokes
Next field	Tab
Previous field	Shift+Tab
First field of current record	Home
Last field of current record	End
Next record	Down Arrow
Previous record	Up Arrow

First field of first record	Ctrl+Home
Last field of last record	Ctrl+End
Scroll up one page	PgUp
Scroll down one page	PgDn

Using the Navigation buttons

The *Navigation buttons* (shown in Figure 34.21) are the six controls located at the bottom of the Datasheet window, which you click to move between records. The two leftmost controls move you to the first record or the previous record in the datasheet. The three rightmost controls position you on the next record, last record, or new record in the datasheet. If you know the record number (the row number of a specific record), you can click the record-number box, enter a record number, and press Enter.

FIGURE 34.21

The Navigation buttons of a datasheet

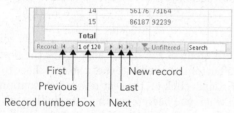

NOTE

If you enter a record number greater than the number of records in the table, an error message appears stating that you can't go to the specified record.

34

Entering New Data

All the records in your table are visible when you first open it in Datasheet view. If you just created your table, the new datasheet doesn't contain any data. Figure 34.22 shows an empty datasheet and the Table Tools ⇨ Fields tab of the Ribbon. When the datasheet is empty, the first row contains an asterisk (*) in the record selector — indicating it's a new record.

FIGURE 34.22

An empty datasheet. Notice that the first record is blank and has an asterisk in the record selector.

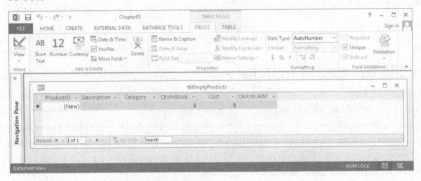

The Table Tools⇨Fields contextual tab includes virtually all the tools needed to build a complete table. You can specify the data type, default formatting, indexing, field and table validation, and other table construction tasks from the controls in the Table Tools⇨Fields tab.

The new row appears at the bottom of the datasheet when the datasheet already contains records. Click the New button in the Record group of the Home tab, or click the New Record button in the group of navigation buttons at the bottom of the datasheet to move the insertion point to the new row — or simply click on the last row, which contains the asterisk. The asterisk turns into a pencil when you begin entering data, indicating that the record is being edited. A new row — containing an asterisk — appears below the one you're entering data into. The new record pointer always appears in the last row of the datasheet. Figure 34.23 shows adding a new record to tblProducts.

FIGURE 34.23

Entering a new record in Datasheet view of a table

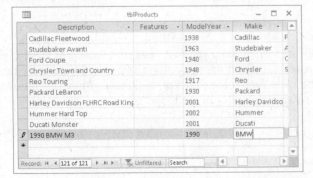

To add a new record to the open Datasheet view of a table, follow these steps:

1. **Click the New button in the Records group of the Home tab of the Ribbon.**
2. **Type in values for all fields of the table, moving between fields by pressing the Enter key or the Tab key.**

When adding or editing records, you might see three different record pointers:

- **Record being edited:** A pencil icon
- **Record is locked (multiuser systems):** A padlock icon
- **New record:** A pencil icon

> **CAUTION**
>
> If the record contains an AutoNumber field, Access shows the name (New) in the field. You can't enter a value in this type of field; instead, simply press the Tab or Enter key to skip the field. Access automatically puts the number in when you begin entering data.

Saving the record

Moving to a different record saves the record you're editing. Tabbing through all the fields, clicking on the Navigation buttons, clicking Save in the Record group of the Home tab, and closing the table all write the edited record to the database. You'll know the record is saved when the pencil disappears from the record selector.

To save a record, you must enter valid values into each field. The fields are validated for data type, uniqueness (if indexed for unique values), and any validation rules that you've entered into the Validation Rule property. If your table has a primary key that's not an AutoNumber field, you'll have to make sure you enter a unique value in the primary key field to avoid the error message shown in Figure 34.24. One way to avoid this error message while entering data is to use an AutoNumber field as the table's primary key.

FIGURE 34.24

The error message Access displays when attempting to save a record with a duplicate primary key value entered into the new record. Use an AutoNumber field as your primary key to avoid this error.

> **TIP**
> The Undo button in the Quick Access Toolbar reverses changes to the current record and to the last saved record.

> **TIP**
> You can save the record to disk without leaving the record by pressing Shift+Enter.

Now you know how to enter, edit, and save data in a new or existing record. In the next section, you learn how Access validates your data as you make entries into the fields.

Understanding automatic data-type validation

Access validates certain types of data automatically. Therefore, you don't have to enter any data validation rules for these data types when you specify table properties. The data types that Access automatically validates include:

- Number/Currency
- Date/Time
- Yes/No

Access validates the data type when you move off the field. When you enter a letter into a Number or Currency field, you don't initially see a warning not to enter these characters. However, when you tab out of or click on a different field, you get a warning like the one shown in Figure 34.25. This particular warning lets you choose to enter a new value or change the column's data type to Text. You'll see this message if you enter other inappropriate characters (symbols, letters, and so on), enter more than one decimal point, or enter a number too large for the specified numeric data type.

FIGURE 34.25

The warning Access displays when entering data that doesn't match the field's data type. Access gives you a few choices to correct the problem.

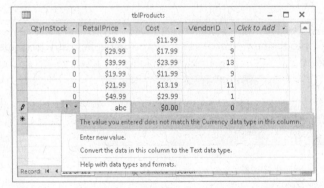

Access validates Date/Time fields for valid date or time values. You'll see a warning similar to the one shown in Figure 34.25 if you try to enter a date such as 14/45/05, a time such as 37:39:12, or an invalid character in a Date/Time field.

Yes/No fields require that you enter one of these defined values:

- **Yes:** Yes, True, On, –1, or a number other than 0 (which displays as –1)
- **No:** No, False, Off, or 0

Of course, you can define your own acceptable values in the Format property for the field, but generally these values are the only acceptable ones. If you enter an invalid value, the warning appears with the message to indicate an inappropriate value.

> **TIP**
>
> The default value of a Yes/No field's Display Control is Check Box. Displaying a check box in Yes/No fields prevents users from entering invalid data.

Navigating Records in a Datasheet

Wanting to make changes to records after you've entered them is not unusual. You might need to change records because you receive new information that changes existing values or you discover errors in existing values.

When you decide to edit data in a table, the first step is to open the table, if it isn't already open. From the list of tables in the Navigation pane, double-click the table object to open it in Datasheet view. If you're already in Design view for the table, click the Datasheet View button in the Views group of the Home tab to switch views.

When you open a datasheet in Access that has related tables, a column with a plus sign (+) is added to indicate the related records, or subdatasheets. Click a row's plus sign to open the subdatasheet for the row.

Moving between records

You can move to any record by scrolling through the records and clicking on the desired record. With a large table, scrolling through all the records might take a while, so you'll want to use other methods to get to specific records quickly.

Use the vertical scroll bar to move between records. The scroll bar arrows move one record at a time. To move through many records at a time, drag the scroll box or click the areas between the scroll thumb and the scroll bar arrows.

34

Use the five Navigation buttons (refer to Figure 34.21) to move between records. You simply click these buttons to move to the desired record. If you know the record number (the row number of a specific record), click the record number box, enter a record number, and press Enter.

Also, use the Go To command in the Find group of the Home tab to navigate to the First, Previous, Next, Last, and New records.

Finding a specific value

Although you can move to a specific record (if you know the record number) or to a specific field in the current record, usually you'll want to find a certain value in a record. You can use one of these methods for locating a value in a field:

- Select the Find command (a pair of binoculars) from the Find group of the Home tab.
- Press Ctrl+F.
- Use the Search box at the bottom of the Datasheet window.

The first two methods display the Find and Replace dialog box (shown in Figure 34.26). To limit the search to a specific field, place your insertion point in the field you want to search before you open the dialog box. Change the Look In combo box to Current Document to search the entire table for the value.

FIGURE 34.26

The Find and Replace dialog box. The fastest way to activate it is to simply press Ctrl+F.

The Find and Replace dialog box lets you control many aspects of the search. Enter the value you want to search for in the Find What combo box — which contains a list of recently used searches. You can enter a specific value or choose to use wildcard characters. Table 34.5 lists the wildcard characters available in the Find dialog box.

TABLE 34.5   Wildcard Characters

Character	Description	Example
* (asterisk)	Matches any number of characters	Ford* finds Ford Mustang
? (question mark)	Matches any single character	F?rd finds Ford
[ ] (brackets)	Matches one of a list of characters	19[67]1 finds 1961 and 1971
! (exclamation point)	With brackets, excludes a list of characters	19[!67]1 finds 1951 but not 1961
- (hyphen)	With brackets, matches a range of characters	196[2–8] finds 1962 to 1968
# (hash)	Matches one number	1:## finds 1:18 but not 1:9

You can combine wildcard characters for more robust searches. For example, 196[!2–8] will find 1961 and 1969, but nothing in between.

The Match drop-down list contains three choices that eliminate the need for wildcards:

- **Any Part of Field:** If you select Any Part of Field, Access searches to see whether the value is contained anywhere in the field. This search finds the Ford anywhere in the field, including values like Ford Mustang, 2008 Ford F-150, and Ford Galaxy 500.

- **Whole Field:** The default is Whole Field, which finds fields containing exactly what you've entered. For example, the Whole Field option finds Ford only if the value in the field being searched is exactly Ford, and nothing else.

- **Start of Field:** A search for Ford using the Start of Field option searches from the beginning of the field and returns all the rows containing Ford as the first four characters of the description.

34

In addition to these combo boxes, you can use two check boxes at the bottom of the Find and Replace dialog box:

- **Match Case:** Match Case determines whether the search is case sensitive. The default is not case sensitive (not checked). A search for SMITH finds smith, SMITH, or Smith. If you check the Match Case check box, you must then enter the search string in the exact case of the field value. (The data types Number, Currency, and Date/Time don't have any case attributes.)

  If you've checked Match Case, Access doesn't use the value Search Fields As Formatted (the second check box), which limits the search to the actual values displayed in the table. (If you format a field for display in the datasheet, you should check the box.)

- **Search Fields As Formatted:** The Search Fields As Formatted check box, the selected default, finds only text that has the same pattern of characters as the text specified in the Find What box. Clear this box to find text regardless of the formatting. For example, if you're searching the Cost field for a value of $16,500, you must enter the comma if Search Fields as Formatted is checked. Uncheck this box to search for an unformatted value (16500).

> **CAUTION**
> Checking Search Fields As Formatted may slow the search process.

The search begins when you click the Find Next button. If Access finds the value, Access highlights it in the datasheet. To find the next occurrence of the value, click the Find Next button again. The dialog box remains open so that you can find multiple occurrences. Choose one of three search direction choices (Up, Down, or All) in the Search drop-down list to change the search direction. When you find the value that you want, click Close to close the dialog box.

Use the search box at the bottom of the Datasheet window to quickly search for the first instance of a value. When using the search box, Access searches the entire datasheet for the value in any part of the field. If you enter **FORD** in the search box, the datasheet moves to the closest match as you type each letter. First, it finds a field with *F* as the first character, then it finds *FO*, and so on. Once it finds the complete value, it stops searching. To find the next instance, press the Enter key.

Changing Values in a Datasheet

If the field that you're in has no value, you can type a new value into the field. When you enter new values into a field, follow the same rules as for a new record entry.

Manually replacing an existing value

Generally, you enter a field with either no characters selected or the entire value selected. If you use the keyboard (Tab or Arrow keys) to enter a field, you select the entire value. (You know that the entire value is selected when it's highlighted) When you begin to type, the new content replaces the selected value automatically.

When you click in a field, the value is not selected. To select the entire value with the mouse, use any of these methods:

- Click just to the left of the value when the mouse pointer is shown as a large plus sign.
- Click to the left of the value, hold down the left mouse button, and drag the mouse to select the whole value.
- Click in the field and press F2.

> **TIP**
>
> You may want to replace an existing value with the value from the field's Default Value property. To do so, select the value and press Ctrl+Alt+Spacebar. To replace an existing value with that of the same field from the preceding record, press Ctrl+' (apostrophe). Press Ctrl+; (semicolon) to place the current date in a field.

> **CAUTION**
>
> Pressing Ctrl+– (minus sign) deletes the current record.

If you want to change an existing value instead of replacing the entire value, use the mouse and click in front of any character in the field to activate Insert mode; the existing value moves to the right as you type the new value. If you press the Insert key, your entry changes to Overstrike mode; you replace one character at a time as you type. Use the arrow keys to move between characters without disturbing them. Erase characters to the left by pressing Backspace, or to the right of the insertion point by pressing Delete.

Table 34.6 lists editing techniques.

TABLE 34.6   Editing Techniques

Editing operation	Keystrokes
Move the insertion point within a field.	Press the Right Arrow and Left Arrow keys.
Insert a value within a field.	Select the insertion point and type new data.
Toggle entire field and insertion point.	Press F2.
Move insertion point to the beginning of the field.	Press Ctrl+Left Arrow key or press the Home key.

Continues

34

TABLE 34.6   *(continued)*

Editing operation	Keystrokes
Move insertion point to the end of the field.	Press Ctrl+Right Arrow key or press the End key.
Select the previous character.	Press Shift+Left Arrow key.
Select the next character.	Press Shift+Right Arrow key.
Select from the insertion point to the beginning.	Press Ctrl+Shift+Left Arrow key.
Select from the insertion point to the end.	Press Ctrl+Shift+Right Arrow key.
Replace an existing value with a new value.	Select the entire field and type a new value.
Replace a value with the value of the previous field.	Press Ctrl+' (apostrophe).
Replace the current value with the default value.	Press Ctrl+Alt+Spacebar.
Insert a line break in a Short Text or Long Text field.	Press Ctrl+Enter.
Save the current record.	Press Shift+Enter or move to another record.
Insert the current date.	Press Ctrl+; (semicolon).
Insert the current time.	Press Ctrl+: (colon).
Add a new record.	Press Ctrl++ (plus sign).
Delete the current record.	Press Ctrl+− (minus sign).
Toggle values in a check box or option button.	Press Spacebar.
Undo a change to the current field.	Press Esc or click the Undo button.
Undo a change to the current record.	Press Esc or click the Undo button a second time after you undo the current field.

Fields that you can't edit

Some fields can't be edited, such as:

- **AutoNumber fields:** Access maintains AutoNumber fields automatically, calculating the values as you create each new record. AutoNumber fields can be used as the primary key.

- **Calculated fields:** Forms or queries may contain fields that are the result of expressions. These values are not actually stored in your table and are not editable.

- **Fields in multiuser locked records:** If another user is editing a record, it can be locked, and you can't edit any fields in that record.

Understanding Attachment Fields

Microsoft recognizes that database developers must deal with many different types of data. Although the traditional Access data types (Text, Currency, OLE Object, and so on) are able to handle many different types of data, until recently there was no way to accommodate *complete files* as Access data without performing some transformation on the file (such as conversion to OLE data).

Since Access 2010, Access has included the Attachment data type, enabling you to bring entire files into your Access database as "attachments" to a table. When you click an attachment field, a small Attachments dialog box (shown in Figure 34.27) appears, enabling you to locate files to attach to the table.

FIGURE 34.27

Managing attachments in an Attachment field

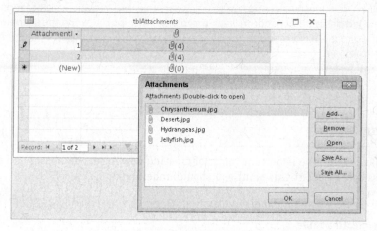

The Add button in Figure 34.27 opens the familiar Choose File dialog box, enabling you to search for one or more files to attach to the field. The selected files are added to the list you see in Figure 34.27. Notice also that the Attachments dialog box includes buttons for removing attachments from the field, and for saving attachments back to the computer's disk.

The significant thing to keep in mind about the Attachment data type is that a single attachment field in a table can contain multiple files of different types. It's entirely possible to store a Word document, several audio or video clips, and a number of photographs, within a single attachment field.

> **CAUTION**
>
> Obviously, because the attached data is incorporated into the database, the `.accdb` file will quickly grow if many attachments are added. You should use the Attachment data type only when its benefits outweigh the burden it places on an Access application.

A Brief Look at Relationships

As you recall from Chapter 33, normalization is the process of breaking down a database into numerous tables to decrease data repetition and errors. You can then create relationships between the tables to tell Access how the data fits together overall. To create a relationship between fields holding related data in multiple tables (such as a CustNo field in Customer and Orders tables), choose Database Tools ➪ Relationships ➪ Relationships. Choose Design ➪ Relationships ➪ Show Table, click each table to add and then click Add. Close the dialog box, and then drag a field from one table over the related field in another table. Use the Edit Relationships dialog box that appears to choose relationship settings, and then click Create. A detailed description of normalization and relationships is beyond the scope of this book, but if you want to learn more, you can see "Understanding Table Relationships," in Chapter 4 of *The Access 2013 Bible*.

Summary

This chapter has covered the important topics of creating new Access databases and adding tables to Access databases. At this point you should understand:

- How to create a database and move around Access.
- How to create a table.
- Which fields to use and how to add them in Table design view.
- How and why to set a primary key.
- How to add data and save the table.
- How to navigate the datasheet and edit table data.

Creating and Entering Data with Basic Access Forms

orms provide the most flexible way for viewing, adding, editing, and deleting your data. They're also used for *switchboards* (forms with buttons that provide navigation), for dialog boxes that control the flow of the system, and for messages. Controls are the objects on forms such as labels, text boxes, buttons, and many others. In this chapter, you learn how to create different types of forms and learn about the types of controls that are used on a form. This chapter also discusses form and control properties and how you determine the appearance and behavior of an Access interface through setting or changing property values.

The forms you add to an Access database are a critical aspect of the application you create. In most situations, users should not be permitted direct access to tables or query datasheets. It's far too easy for a user to delete valuable information or incorrectly input data into the table. Forms provide a useful tool for managing the integrity of a database's data. Because forms can contain VBA code or macros, a form can verify data entry or confirm deletions before they occur. Also, a properly designed form can reduce training requirements by helping the user understand what kind of data is required by displaying a message as the user tabs into a control. A form can provide default values or perform calculations based on data input by the user or retrieved from a database table.

Formulating Forms

Use the Forms group on the Create tab of the Ribbon to add forms to your database. The commands in the Forms group — shown in Figure 35.1 — let you create the following different types of forms and ways to work with Access forms:

FIGURE 35.1

Use the Forms group on the Create tab of the Ribbon to add new forms to your database.

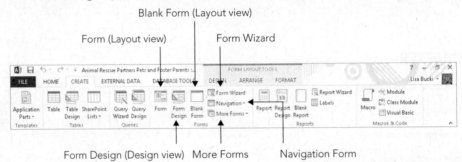

- **Form:** Creates a new form that lets you enter information for one record at a time. You must have a table, query, form, or report open or selected to use this command. When you click the Form button with a table or query highlighted in the Navigation pane, Access binds the new form to the data source and opens the form in Layout view.

- **Form Design:** Creates a new blank form and displays it in Design view. The form isn't bound to any data source. You must specify a data source (table or query) and build the form by adding controls from the data source's Field List.

- **Blank Form:** Instantly creates a blank form with no controls. Like Form Design, the new form is not bound to a data source, but it opens in Layout view.

- **Form Wizard:** Access features a simple wizard to help you get started building forms. The wizard asks for the data source, provides a screen for selecting fields to include on the form, and lets you choose from a number of very basic layouts for the new form.

- **Navigation Form:** The Access navigation form is a specialized form intended to provide user navigation through an application. Navigation forms are discussed in detail later in this chapter.

- **More Forms:** The More Forms button in the Forms group drops down a gallery containing a number of other form types.

- **Multiple Items:** This is a simple tabular form that shows multiple records bound to the selected data source.

- **Datasheet:** Creates a form that is displayed as a datasheet.

- **Split Form:** Creates a split form, which shows a datasheet in the upper, lower, left, or right area of the form, and a traditional form in the opposite section for entering information on the record selected in the datasheet.

- **Modal Dialog:** Provides a template for a modal dialog form. A modal dialog form (often called a *dialog box*) stays on the screen until the user provides information requested by the dialog or is dismissed by the user.

If any of the terminology in the preceding bullets is new to you, don't worry — each of these terms is discussed in detail in this chapter. Keep in mind that the Access Ribbon and its contents are very context dependent, so every item may not be available when you select the Create tab.

Creating a new form

Like many other aspects of Access development, Access provides multiple ways of adding new forms to your application. The easiest is to select a data source, such as a table, and click the Form command on the Create tab of the Ribbon. Another is to use the Form Wizard and allow the wizard to guide you through the process of specifying a data source and other details of the new form.

Using the Form command

Use the Form command in the Forms group of the Ribbon to automatically create a new form based on a table or query selected in the Navigation pane.

> **NOTE**
>
> This process was called *AutoForm* in previous versions of Access.

To create a form based on a table, follow these steps:

1. **Select the table in the Navigation pane.**
2. **Select the Create tab of the Ribbon.**
3. **Click the Form command in the Forms group.** Access creates a new form containing all the fields from the table displayed in Layout view, shown in Figure 35.2. Layout view lets you see the form's data while changing the layout of controls on the form.

The new form is opened in Layout view, which is populated with controls, each of which is bound to a field in the underlying data source. Layout view gives you a good idea how the controls appear relative to one another, but it provides only limited ability to resize controls or move controls on the form. Right-click the form's title bar and select Design View to rearrange controls on the form.

35

FIGURE 35.2

Use the Form command to quickly create a new form with all the fields from a table or query.

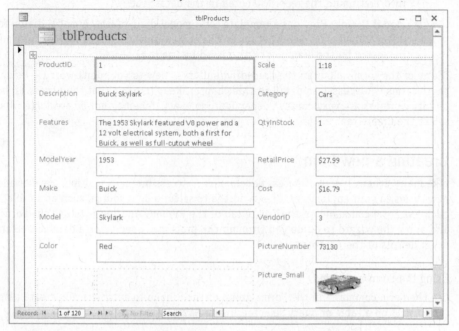

The Form Design button in the Forms group does essentially the same thing as the Form button, except that no controls are added to the form's design surface and the form is opened in Design view. Form Design is most useful when you're creating a new form that might not use all the fields in the underlying data source, and you want more control over control placement from the start.

Similarly, the Blank Form option opens a new empty form, but this time in Layout view. You add controls to the form's surface from the Field List, but you have little control over control placement. The Blank Form option is most useful for quickly building a form with bound controls with little need for precise placement. A new blank form can be produced in less than a minute.

Using the Form Wizard

Use the Form Wizard command in the Forms group to create a form using a wizard. The Form Wizard visually walks you through a series of questions about the form that you want to create and then creates it for you automatically. The Form Wizard lets you select which fields you want on the form, the form layout (Columnar, Tabular, Datasheet, Justified), and the form title.

To start the Form Wizard and use it create a form, follow these steps:

1. **Select the table in the Navigation pane.**
2. **Click the Create tab of the Ribbon.**
3. **Click the Form Wizard button in the Forms group.** Access starts the Form Wizard, shown in Figure 35.3.

FIGURE 35.3

Use the Form Wizard to create a form with the fields you choose.

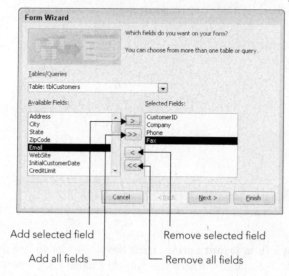

Add selected field

Add all fields

Remove selected field

Remove all fields

4. **Use the buttons in the middle of the form to add and remove fields to the Available Fields and Selected Fields list boxes.** The wizard is initially populated with fields from the selected table, but you can choose another table or query with the Tables/Queries drop-down list above the field selection area.

NOTE

You can also double-click any field in the Available Fields list box to add it to the Selected Fields list box.

CAUTION

If you click Next or Finish without selecting any fields, Access tells you that you must select fields for the form before you can continue.

35

5. **Click Next.** The second wizard dialog box (shown in Figure 35.4) appears so you can specify the overall layout and appearance of the new form. The Columnar layout is the wizard default, but you can also choose the Tabular, Datasheet, or Justified options.

FIGURE 35.4

Select the overall layout for the new form.

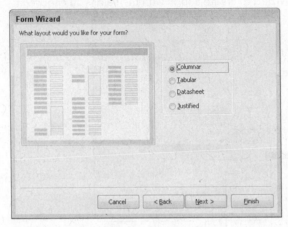

6. **After selecting a form layout option, click Next.** The last wizard dialog box shown in Figure 35.5 appears, where you provide a name for the new form.

7. **Edit the form name in the top text box if needed, and click Finish.**

FIGURE 35.5

Saving the new form

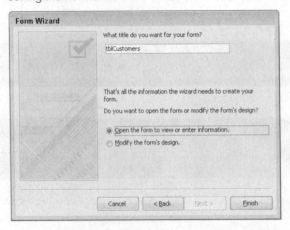

TIP

The main advantage of using the Form Wizard is that it binds the new form to a data source and adds controls for the selected fields. In most cases, however, you still have considerable work to do after the Form Wizard has finished.

Looking at special types of forms

When working with Access, the word *form* can mean any of several different things, depending on context. This section discusses several different ways that "forms" are used in Access and presents an example of each usage.

Navigation forms

Access 2010 introduced an entirely new form intended specifically as a navigation tool for users. Navigation forms include a number of tabs that provide instant access to any number of other forms in a form/subform arrangement. The Navigation button on the Ribbon offers a number of button placement options (shown in Figure 35.6). Horizontal Tabs is the default.

FIGURE 35.6

The Navigation button provides a number of tab placement options.

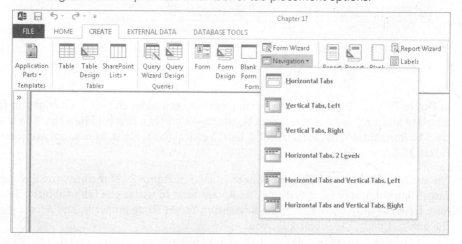

Selecting a tab placement in the Navigation drop-down list opens the new navigation form in Design view (see Figure 35.7). The new form includes a row of tabs along the top and a large area under the tabs for embedding subforms. You type the tab's label (like Products) directly into the tab, or add it through the tab's Caption property. As you complete the tab's label, Access adds a new, blank tab to the right of the current tab.

FIGURE 35.7

The Navigation form features a large area for embedding subforms.

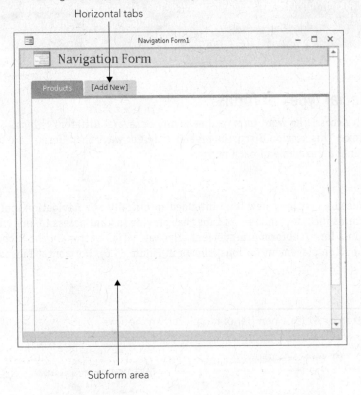

Horizontal tabs

Subform area

In Figure 35.7, the Horizontal Tabs option was selected when choosing a navigation form template and a tab was named Products, which generates a new Add New tab. The alternatives to Horizontal Tabs (Vertical Tabs, Left, Vertical Tabs, Right, and so on) are shown in Figure 35.6.

The example Product tab's Property Sheet (shown in Figure 35.8) includes the Navigation Target Name property for specifying the Access form to use as the tab's subform. Select a form from the drop-down list in the Navigation Target Name property, and Access creates the association to the subform for you.

The completed navigation form is shown in Figure 35.9. The auto-generated navigation form makes extravagant use of screen space. There are a number of things that could be done to enhance this form, such as removing the navigation form's header section and reducing the empty space surrounding the subform.

FIGURE 35.8

Use the Navigation Target Name property to specify the tab's subform.

Navigation Target Name property   List of all forms in database

FIGURE 35.9

A navigation form is a quick and easy way to provide basic navigation features.

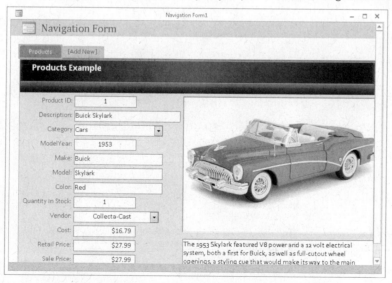

Multiple-items forms

Click the More Forms button in the Forms group of the Ribbon and then click the Multiple Items button to create a tabular form based on a table or query selected in the Navigation pane. A tabular form is much like a datasheet, but it's much more attractive than a plain datasheet.

Because the tabular form is truly an Access form, you can convert the default text box controls on the form to combo boxes, list boxes, and other advanced controls. Tabular forms display multiple records at one time, which makes them very useful when you're reviewing or updating multiple records. To create a multiple-items form based on a table, follow these steps:

1. **Select the table in the Navigation pane.**
2. **Select the Create tab on the Ribbon.**
3. **Click the More Forms button and click Multiple Items.** Access creates a new multiple-items form based on the table and displays it in Layout view (as shown in Figure 35.10).

FIGURE 35.10

Create a multiple-items form when you want to see data similar to Datasheet view.

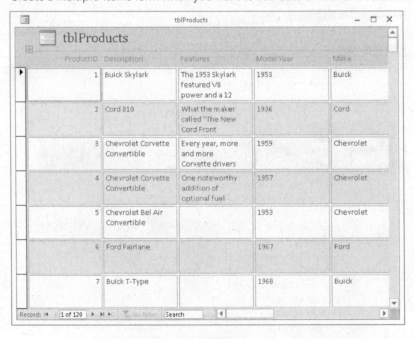

Split forms

Click the More Forms button in the Form group of the Ribbon and then click the Split Form button to create a split form based on a table or query selected in the Navigation pane. The split-form feature gives you two views of the data at the same time, letting you select a record from a datasheet in the lower section and edit the information in a form in the upper section.

To create a split form based on a table, follow these steps:

1. **Select the table in the Navigation pane.**
2. **Select the Create tab of the Ribbon.**
3. **Click the More Forms button and click Split Form.** Access creates a new split form based on the table and displays it in Layout view (shown in Figure 35.11). Resize the form and use the splitter bar in the middle to make the lower section completely visible.

FIGURE 35.11

Create a split form when you want to select records from a list and edit them in a form. Use the splitter bar to resize the upper and lower sections of the form.

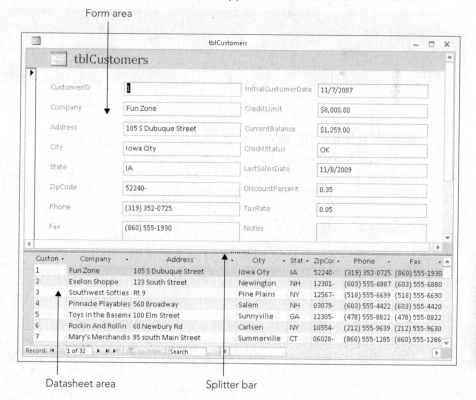

35

The Split Form Orientation property (on the Format tab of the form's Property Sheet) determines whether the datasheet is on the top, bottom, left, or right of the form area. The default is as shown in Figure 35.11, with the datasheet area on the bottom.

Datasheet forms

Click the More Forms button in the Forms group of the Ribbon and then click the Datasheet button to create a form that looks like a table or query's datasheet. A datasheet form is useful when you want to see the data in a row and column format, but you want to limit which fields are displayed and editable.

To create a datasheet form based on a table, follow these steps:

1. Select the table in the Navigation pane.
2. Select the Create tab of the Ribbon.
3. Click the More Forms button in the Forms group and then click Datasheet. You can view any form you create as a datasheet by selecting Datasheet View from the View drop-down menu in the Views group of the Home tab. A datasheet form appears in Datasheet View by default when you open it.

> **TIP**
> Some forms have their Allow Datasheet View property set to No by default. The View drop-down doesn't show a Datasheet View option for those forms. You'll learn more about form properties in the "Introducing Properties" section, later in this chapter.

Resizing the form area

The area with gridlines in the form is where you work. This is the size of the form when it's displayed. Resize the grid area of the form by dragging any of the area borders to make it larger or smaller. Figure 35.12 shows a blank form in Design view being resized.

Saving your form

You can save the form at any time by clicking the Save button in the Quick Access Toolbar. When you're asked for a name for the form, give it a meaningful name (for example, frmProducts, frmCustomers, or frmProductList.) Once you've given the form a name, you won't be prompted the next time you click Save.

When you close a form after making changes, Access asks you to save it. If you don't save a form, all changes since you opened the form (or since you last clicked Save) are lost. You should frequently save the form while you work if you're satisfied with the results.

FIGURE 35.12

Design view of a blank form. Resize the form area by dragging the bottom-right corner.

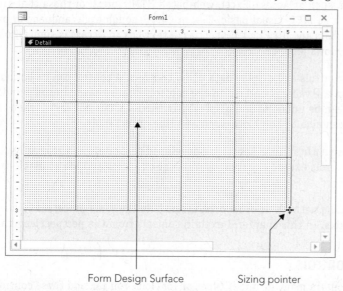

Form Design Surface   Sizing pointer

> **TIP**
>
> If you're going to make extensive changes to a form, you might want to make a copy of the form. For example, if you want to work on the form frmProducts, you can copy and then paste the form in the Navigation pane, giving it a name like frmProductsOriginal. Later, when you've completed your changes and tested them, you can delete the original copy.

Working with Controls

Controls and properties form the basis of forms and reports. It's critical to understand the fundamental concepts of controls and properties before you begin to apply them to custom forms and reports.

> **NOTE**
>
> Although this chapter is about forms, you'll learn that forms and reports share many common characteristics, including controls and what you can do with them. As you learn about controls in this chapter, you'll be able to apply nearly everything you learn when you create reports.

35

The term *control* has many definitions in Access. Generally, a control is any object on a form or report, such as a label or text box. These are the same sort of controls used in any Windows application, such as Access, Excel, web-based HTML forms, or those that are used in any language, such as .NET, Visual Basic, C++, or C#. Although each language or product has different file formats and different properties, a text box in Access is similar to a text box in any other Windows product.

You enter data into controls and display data using controls. A control can be bound to a field in a table (when the value is entered in the control, it's also saved in some underlying table field), or data can be unbound and displayed in the form but not saved when the form is closed. A control can also be an object, such as a line or rectangle.

Some controls that aren't built into Access are developed separately — these are ActiveX controls. ActiveX controls extend the basic feature set of Access and are available from a variety of vendors.

Whether you're working with forms or reports, essentially the same process is followed to create and use controls. In this chapter, I explain controls from the perspective of a form.

Categorizing controls

Forms and reports contain many different types of controls. You can add these controls to forms using the Controls group on the Form Design Tools⇨Design tab, or Form Layout Tools⇨Arrange tab shown in Figure 35.13. Hovering the mouse over the control displays a ScreenTip telling you what the control is.

FIGURE 35.13

The Design tab lets you add and customize controls in a form's Design view.

Table 35.1 briefly describes the basic Access controls.

TABLE 35.1　Controls in Access Forms

Control	What It Does
Text Box	Displays and allows users to edit data.
Label	Displays static text that typically doesn't change.
Button	Also called a command button. Runs macros or VBA code when clicked.

Combo Box	A drop-down list of values. Combo boxes include a text box at the top for inputting values that are not included in the drop-down list.
List Box	A list of values that is always displayed on the form or report.
Subform/ Subreport	Displays another form or report within the main form or report.
Line	A graphical line of variable thickness and color, which is used for separation.
Rectangle	A rectangle can be any color or size or can be filled in or blank; the rectangle is used to group related controls visually.
Image	Displays a bitmap picture with very little overhead.
Option Group	Holds multiple option buttons, check boxes, or toggle buttons.
Check Box	A two-state control, shown as a square that contains a check mark if it's on and an empty square if it's off. Before a Check Box's value is set, it appears as a grayed-out square.
Option Button	Also called a radio button, this button is displayed as a circle with a dot when the option is on.
Toggle Button	This is a two-state button — up or down — which usually uses pictures or icons instead of text to display different states.
Tab Control	Displays multiple pages in a file folder type of interface.
Page	Adds a page on the form or report. Additional controls are added to the page, and multiple pages may exist on the same form
Chart	Displays data in a graphical format.
Unbound Object Frame	Holds an OLE object or embedded picture that isn't tied to a table field and can include graphs, pictures, sound files, and video.
Bound Object Frame	Holds an OLE object or embedded picture that is tied to a table field.
Page Break	Usually used for reports and indicates a physical page break.
Hyperlink	Creates a link to a web page, a picture, an e-mail address, or a program.
Attachment	Manages attachments for the Attachment data type. Attachment fields provide a way to *attach* external files (such as music or video clips or Word documents) to Access tables.

The Use Control Wizards button, revealed by expanding the Controls group by clicking on the More button in the lower-right corner of the group, doesn't add a control to a form. Instead, the Use Control Wizards button determines whether a wizard is automatically activated when you add certain controls. The Option Group, Combo Box, List Box, Subform/ Subreport, Bound and Unbound Object Frame, and Command Button controls all have wizards to help you when you add a new control. You can also use the ActiveX Controls button (also found at the bottom of the expanded Controls group) to display a list of ActiveX controls, which you can add to Access.

There are three basic categories of controls:

- **Bound controls:** These are controls that are bound to a field in the data source underlying the form. When you enter a value in a bound control, Access automatically updates the field in the current record. Most of the controls used for data entry can be bound. Controls can be bound to most data types, including Text, Date/Time, Number, Yes/No, OLE Object, and Memo fields.

- **Unbound controls:** Unbound controls retain the entered value, but they don't update any table fields. You can use these controls for text label display, for controls such as lines and rectangles, or for holding unbound OLE objects (such as bitmap pictures or your logo) that are stored not in a table but on the form itself. Very often, VBA code is used to work with data in unbound controls and directly update Access data sources.

- **Calculated controls:** *Calculated controls* are based on expressions, such as functions or calculations. Calculated controls are unbound because they don't directly update table fields. An example of a calculated control is `=[SalePrice]-[Cost]`. This control calculates the total of two table fields for display on a form but is not bound to any table field. The value of an unbound calculated control may be referenced by other controls on the form, or used in an expression in another control on the form or in VBA in the form's module.

Adding a control

You add a control to a form in a number ways:

- **By clicking a button in the Controls group on the Design tab of the Ribbon and drawing a new unbound control on the form:** Use the control's ControlSource property to bind the new control to a field in the form's data source.

- **By dragging a field from the Field List to add a bound control to the form:** Access automatically chooses a control appropriate for the field's data type and binds the control to the selected field.

- **By double-clicking a field in the Field List to add a bound control to the form:** Double-clicking works just like dragging a field from the Field List to the form. The only difference is that, when you add a control by double-clicking a field, Access decides where to add the new control to the form. Usually the new control is added to the right of the most recently added control, and sometimes below it.

- **By right-clicking a field in the Field List and choosing Add Field to View:** Right-clicking places a bound control in the same location as if it were double-clicked.

- **By copying an existing control and pasting it to another location on the form:** Copying a control can be done in all the familiar ways: Click Copy on the Home tab of the Ribbon, right-click the control and choose Copy, or press Ctrl+C. Pasted controls are bound to the same field as the control that was copied.

Using the Controls group

When you use the buttons in the Controls group to add a control, you decide which type of control to use for each field. The control you add is *unbound* (not attached to the data in a table field) and has a default name such as Text21 or Combo11. After you create the control, you decide what table field to bind the control to, enter text for the label, and set any properties. You'll learn more about setting properties later in this chapter.

You can add one control at a time using the Controls group. To create three different unbound controls, for example, you would perform these steps:

1. **With the form created earlier open in Design view, click the Text Box button in the Controls group.**

2. **Move the mouse pointer to the Form Design window and drag on the form's surface to specify the Text Box control's initial size and position.**

3. **Click the Option button in the Controls group, and drag on the form to specify the Option button control's initial size and position.**

4. **Click the Check Box button in the Controls group and add it to the form as you added the other controls.** When you're done, your result would resemble Figure 35.14.

FIGURE 35.14

Unbound controls added from the Controls group

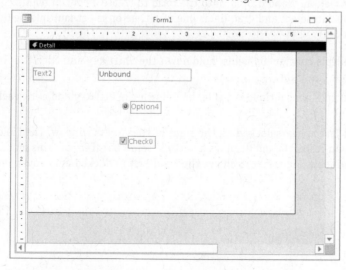

35

> **TIP**
>
> Clicking the Form Design window with a control selected creates a default-size control. If you want to add multiple controls of the same type, right-click the icon in the Controls group and choose Drop Multiple Controls, and then draw as many controls as you want on the form. Click the selector control (the arrow) to unlock the control and return to normal operation.

> **TIP**
>
> To remove the gridlines from the form's detail area, select Grid from the Size/Space control on the Form Design Tools ➪ Arrange tab of the Ribbon while the form is in Design view. Most of the figures in this section don't show the grid so the edges of the controls are easier to see.

Using the Field List

The Field List displays a list of fields from the table or query the form is based on. Open the Field List by clicking the Add Existing Fields button in the Tools group on the Form Design Tools ➪ Design tab of the Ribbon (refer to Figure 35.13).

If you created a form using a method that automatically binds the form to a table or query, the field list for that table or query will be displayed. For this example, we created a form using the Blank Form button, which does not automatically bind the form to a datasource. In this case, the Field List only shows a Show All Tables link. Click the Show All Tables link to get a list of tables. Then click the plus sign next to the desired table to show the fields in that table.

Drag a field from the Field List and drop it onto the form to create a control bound to that field on the form. You can select and drag fields one at a time or select multiple fields by using the Ctrl key or Shift key:

- To select multiple contiguous fields, hold down the Shift key and click the first and last fields that you want.
- To select multiple noncontiguous fields, hold down the Ctrl key and click each field that you want.

By default, the Field List appears docked on the right of the Access window. The Field List window is movable and resizable and displays a vertical scroll bar if it contains more fields than can fit in the window. Figure 35.15 shows the Field List undocked and moved on top of the form.

FIGURE 35.15

Click Add Existing Fields in the Tools group to show the Field List.

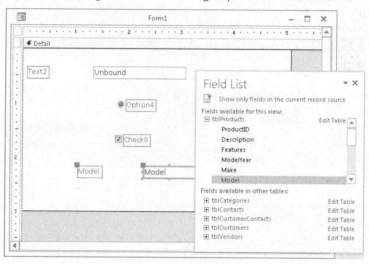

Most often, dragging a field from the Field List adds a bound text box to the Design window. If you drag a Yes/No field from the Field List window, Access adds a check box. Optionally, you can select the type of control by selecting a control from the Controls group and dragging the field to the Design window.

CAUTION

When you drag fields from the Field List window, the first control is placed where you release the mouse button. Make sure that you have enough space to the left of the control for the labels. If you don't have enough space, the labels slide under the controls.

You gain several distinct advantages by dragging a field from the Field List window:

- The control is automatically bound to the field.
- Field properties inherit table-level formats, status bar text, and data validation rules and messages.
- The label control and label text are created with the field name as the caption.
- The label control is attached to the field control, so they move together.

In the example in Figure 35.16, the Description, Category, RetailPrice, and Cost fields were selected in the Field List window and dragged to the form. Double-clicking a field also adds it to the form.

35

FIGURE 35.16

Drag fields from the Field List to add bound controls to the form.

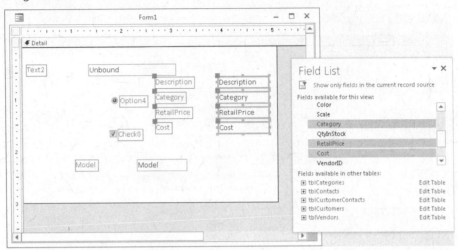

You can see four new pairs of controls in the form's Design view — each pair consists of a Label control and a Text Box control (Access attaches the Label control to the Text Box automatically). You can work with these controls as a group or independently, and you can select, move, resize, or delete them. Notice that each control has a label with a caption matching the field name, and the Text Box control displays the bound field name used in the text box. If you want to resize just the control and not the label, you must work with the two controls (label and associated text box) separately. You'll learn about working with labels attached to controls later in this chapter.

Close the Field List by clicking the Add Existing Fields command in the Tools group of the Design tab or by clicking the Close button on the Field List.

TIP

In Access, you can change the type of control after you create it; then you can set all the properties for the control. For example, suppose that you add a field as a Text Box control and you want to change it to a List Box. Right-click the control and select Change To from the shortcut menu to change the control type. However, you can change only from some types of controls to others. You can change almost any type of control to a Text Box control, while Option Button controls, Toggle Button controls, and Check Box controls are interchangeable, as are List Box and Combo Box controls.

In the "Introducing Properties" section, later in this chapter, you learn how to change the control names, captions, and other properties. Using properties speeds the process of naming controls and binding them to specific fields. If you want to see the differences between bound and unbound controls, switch to Form view using the View command in the View group of the Ribbon. Bound controls display data from the table that they're bound to. Unbound controls don't display data because they aren't bound to any data source.

Selecting and deselecting controls

After you add a control to a form, you can resize it, move it, or copy it. The first step is to select one or more controls. Depending on its size, a selected control might show from four to eight *handles* (small squares called *moving* and *sizing handles*) around the control — at the corners and midway along the sides. The move handle in the upper-left corner is larger than the other handles and you use it to move the control. You use the other handles to size the control. Figure 35.17 displays some selected controls and their moving and sizing handles.

FIGURE 35.17

Selected controls and their moving and sizing handles

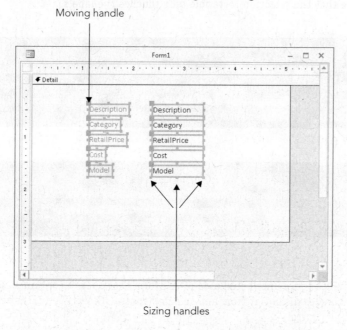

The Select command (which looks like an arrow) in the Controls group of the Design tab must be chosen in order for you to select a control. If you use the Controls group to create a single control, Access automatically reselects the pointer as the default.

Selecting a single control

Select any individual control by clicking anywhere on the control. When you click a control, the sizing handles appear. If the control has an attached label, the move handle for the label also appears in the upper-left corner of the control. If you select a label control that is associated with another control, all the handles for the label control are displayed, and only the move handle appears in the associated control.

Selecting multiple controls

You select multiple controls in these ways:

- By clicking each control while holding down the Shift key
- By dragging the pointer through or around the controls that you want to select
- By clicking and dragging in the ruler to select a range of controls

Figure 35.17 shows the result of selecting the multiple bound controls graphically. When you select multiple controls by dragging the mouse, a rectangle appears as you drag the mouse. Be careful to drag the rectangle only through the controls you want to select. Any control you touch with the rectangle or enclose within it is selected. If you want to select labels only, make sure that the selection rectangle only touches the labels.

> **TIP**
>
> If you find that controls are not selected when the rectangle passes through the control, you may have the global selection behavior property set to Fully Enclosed. This means that a control is selected only if the selection rectangle completely encloses the entire control. Change this option by choosing File ⇨ Options ⇨ Object Designers, and in the Form/Report design view section, click Partially enclosed under Selection behavior. Click OK.

> **TIP**
>
> By holding down the Shift or Ctrl key, you can select several noncontiguous controls. This lets you select controls on totally different parts of the screen. Click the form in Design view and then press Ctrl+A to select *all* the controls on the form. Press Shift or Ctrl and click any selected control to remove it from the selection.

Deselecting controls

Deselect a control by clicking an unselected area of the form that doesn't contain a control. When you do so, the handles disappear from any selected control. Selecting another control also deselects a selected control.

Manipulating controls

Creating a form is a multistep process. The next step is to make sure that your controls are properly sized and moved to their correct positions. The Form Design Tools ⇨ Arrange tab or Form Layout Tools⇨Arrange tab (shown in Figure 35.18) contains commands used to assist you in manipulating controls.

FIGURE 35.18

The Arrange tab lets you work with moving and sizing controls, as well as manipulate the overall layout of the form.

Resizing a control

You *resize* controls using any of the smaller handles in the upper, lower, and right edges of the control. The sizing handles in the control corners let you drag the control larger or smaller in both width and height — and at the same time. Use the handles in the middle of the control sides to size the control larger or smaller in one direction only. The top and bottom handles control the height of the control; the left and right handles change the control's width.

When the mouse pointer touches a corner sizing handle of a selected control, the pointer becomes a diagonal double arrow. You can then drag the sizing handle until the control is the desired size. If the mouse pointer touches a side handle in a selected control, the pointer changes to a horizontal or vertical double-headed arrow. Figure 35.19 shows the Description control after being resized. Notice the double-headed arrow in the corner of the Description control.

FIGURE 35.19

Resizing a control

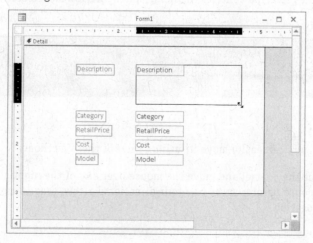

35

TIP

You can resize a control in very small increments by holding the Shift key while pressing the arrow keys (up, down, left, and right). This technique also works with multiple controls selected. Using this technique, a control changes by only 1 pixel at a time (or moves to the nearest grid line if Snap to Grid is selected in the Size/Space menu in the Sizing & Ordering group of the Arrange tab).

When you double-click on any of the sizing handles, Access resizes a control to best fit the text contained in the control. This feature is especially handy if you increase the font size and then notice that the text is cut off either at the bottom or to the right. For label controls, note that this best-fit sizing adjusts the size vertically and horizontally, though text controls are resized only vertically. This is because when Access is in Form Design view, it can't predict how much of a field to display — the field name and field contents can be radically different. Sometimes, Access doesn't correctly resize the label and you must manually change its size.

Sizing controls automatically

Clicking the Size/Space button in the Sizing & Ordering group of the Arrange tab opens a menu with several commands that help you arrange controls:

- **To Fit:** Adjusts control height and width for the font of the text they contain
- **To Tallest:** Makes selected controls the height of the tallest selected control
- **To Shortest:** Makes selected controls the height of the shortest selected control
- **To Grid:** Moves all sides of selected controls in or out to meet the nearest points on the grid
- **To Widest:** Makes selected controls the width of the widest selected control
- **To Narrowest:** Makes selected controls the height of the narrowest selected control

TIP

You can access many commands by right-clicking after selecting multiple controls. When you right-click on multiple controls, a shortcut menu displays choices to size and align controls.

Moving a control

After you select a control, you can easily move it, using either of these methods:

- Click once to select the control and move the mouse over any of the highlighted edges; when the mouse pointer turns to a four-directional arrow, drag to move the control to a new location.

- Select the control and use the arrow keys on the keyboard to move the control. Using this technique, a control changes by only 1 pixel at a time (or moves to the nearest grid line if Snap to Grid is selected in the Size/Space menu in the Sizing & Ordering group of the Arrange tab).

Figure 35.20 shows a Label control that has been separately moved to above a Text Box control.

FIGURE 35.20

Moving a control

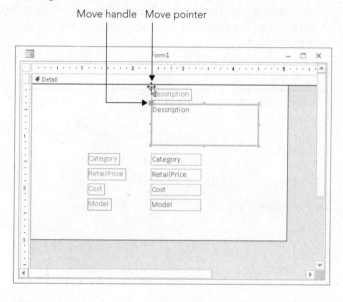

Press Esc before you release the mouse button to cancel a moving or a resizing operation. After a move or resizing operation is complete, click the Undo button on the Quick Access Toolbar to undo the changes, if needed.

Aligning controls

You might want to move several controls so that they're all aligned. The Sizing & Ordering group's Align menu choices on the Arrange tab contains the following alignment commands:

- **To Grid:** Aligns the top-left corners of the selected controls to the nearest grid point
- **Left:** Aligns the left edge of the selected controls with the leftmost selected control
- **Right:** Aligns the right edge of the selected controls with the rightmost selected control

35

- **Top:** Aligns the top edge of the selected controls with the topmost selected control
- **Bottom:** Aligns the bottom edge of the selected controls with the bottommost selected control

You can align any number of selected controls by selecting an align command. When you choose one of the align commands, Access uses the control that's the closest to the desired selection as the model for the alignment. For example, suppose that you have three controls and you want to left-align them. They're aligned on the basis of the control farthest to the left in the group of the three controls.

Figure 35.21 shows several sets of controls. The first set of controls is not aligned. The label controls in the middle set of controls have been left-aligned while the text box controls in the right-side set have been right-aligned.

FIGURE 35.21

An example of unaligned and aligned controls on the grid

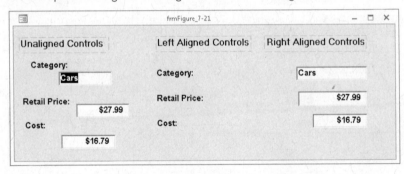

Each type of alignment must be done separately. In this example, you can left-align all the labels or right-align all the text boxes at once.

By default, Access displays a series of small dots across the entire surface of a form while it's in Design view. The grid can assist you in aligning controls. Hide or display the grid by selecting the Grid command from the Size/Space gallery under the Sizing & Ordering group on the Arrange tab of the Ribbon. You can also hide or display the ruler using the Ruler command in the same gallery.

Use the Snap to Grid command in the Size/Space menu to align controls to the grid as you draw or place them on a form. This also aligns existing controls to the grid when you move or resize them.

As you move or resize existing controls, Access lets you move only from grid point to grid point. When Snap to Grid is off, Access ignores the grid and lets you place a control anywhere on the form or report.

Click Size/Space in the Sizing & Ordering group on the Arrange tab to access commands to adjust spacing between controls. The spacing commands adjust the distance between controls on the basis of the space between the first two selected controls. If the controls are across the screen, use horizontal spacing; if they're down the screen, use vertical spacing. The commands in the Spacing group of the Size/Space menu are

- **Equal Horizontal:** Makes the horizontal space between selected controls equal. You must select three or more controls in order for this command to work.

- **Increase Horizontal:** Increases the horizontal space between selected controls by one grid unit.

- **Decrease Horizontal:** Decreases the horizontal space between selected controls by one grid unit.

- **Equal Vertical:** Makes the vertical space between selected controls equal. You must select three or more controls in order for this command to work properly.

- **Increase Vertical:** Increases the vertical space between selected controls by one grid unit.

- **Decrease Vertical:** Decreases the vertical space between selected controls by one grid unit.

Modifying the appearance of a control

To modify the appearance of a control, select the control and click commands that modify that control, such as the options in the Font or Controls group. Follow these steps to change the text color and font of an example label:

1. **Click the label on the form.**

2. **In the Font group on the Format tab, change Font Size to 14, click the Bold button, and change Font Color to blue.**

3. **Resize the Description label so the larger text fits.** You can double-click any of the sizing handles to size the label automatically.

35

To modify the appearance of multiple controls at once, select the controls and click commands to modify the controls, such as commands in the Font or Controls group. To change the text color and font for multiple labels and text boxes, for example, follow these steps:

1. **Select multiple labels and three text boxes by dragging over them.**

2. **In the Font group on the Format tab of the Ribbon, change the Font Size to 14, click the Bold button, and change Font Color to blue.**

3. **Resize the labels and text boxes so the larger text fits.** You can double-click any of the sizing handles to the controls automatically. As you click the commands, the controls' appearances change to reflect the new selections (shown in Figure 35.22). The fonts in each control increase in size, become bold, and turn blue. Any changes you make apply to all selected controls.

FIGURE 35.22

Changing the appearance of multiple controls at the same time

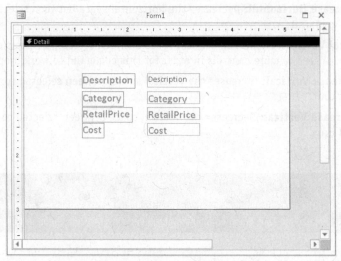

When multiple controls are selected, you can also move the selected controls together. When the mouse pointer changes to the four-directional arrow, drag to move the selected controls. You can also change the size of all the controls at once by resizing one of the controls in the selection. All the selected controls increase or decrease by the same number of units.

Grouping controls

If you routinely change properties of multiple controls, you might want to group them together. To group controls together, select the controls by holding down the Shift key and clicking them or dragging over them. After the desired controls are selected, select Arrange ➪ Sizing & Ordering ➪ Size/Space ➪ Group. Then, when one control in a group is selected, all controls in that group are automatically selected, as shown in Figure 35.23.

FIGURE 35.23

Grouping multiple controls together

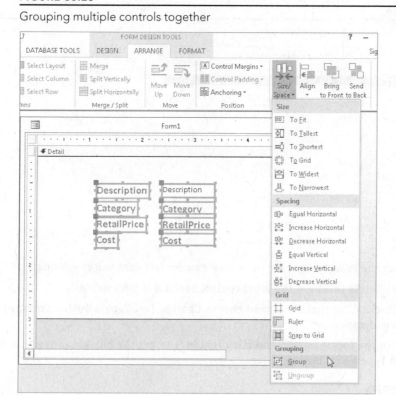

Double-click a control to select just one control in a group. After a single control in the group is selected, you can click any other control to select it.

To resize the entire group, point to the side you want to resize. After the double arrow pointer appears, drag until you reach the desired size. Every control in the group changes in size. To move the entire group, drag the group to its new location. With grouped controls, you don't have to select all the controls every time you change something about them.

To remove a group, select the group by clicking any field inside the group, and then select Arrange ➪ Sizing & Ordering ➪ Size/Space ➪ Ungroup.

35

Changing a control's type

Although there are times you may want to use a check box to display a Boolean (yes/no) data type, there are other ways to display the value, such as a toggle button, as shown in Figure 35.24. A toggle button is raised if it's true and pressed if it's false.

FIGURE 35.24

Turn a check box into a toggle button

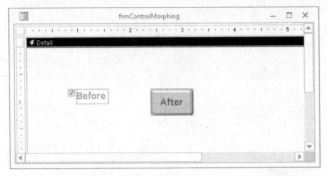

Use these steps to turn a check box into a toggle button:

1. **Select the label control for the check box control (not the check box).**
2. **Press Delete to delete the label control because it isn't needed.**
3. **Right-click the check box, and choose Change To ⇨ Toggle Button from the shortcut menu.**
4. **Resize the toggle button and click inside it to get the blinking insertion point; then type a new button name.**

Copying a control

You can create copies of any control by copying it to the Clipboard and then pasting the copies where you want them. If you have a control for which you've entered many properties or specified a certain format, you can copy it and revise only the properties (such as the control's name and bound field name) to make it a different control. This capability is useful with a multiple-page form when you want to display the same values on different pages and in different locations, or when copying a control from one form to another.

Deleting a control

You can delete a control by simply selecting it in the form's Design view and pressing the Delete key on your keyboard. The control and any attached labels will disappear. You can bring them back by immediately selecting Undo from the Quick Access Toolbar. You can also select Cut from the Clipboard group on the Home tab of the Ribbon, or Delete from the Records group on the Home tab of the Ribbon.

You can delete more than one control at a time by selecting multiple controls and pressing Delete. You can delete an entire group of controls by selecting the group and pressing Delete. If you have a control with an attached label, you can delete only the label by clicking the label itself and then selecting one of the delete methods. If you select the control, both the control and the label are deleted.

Reattaching a label to a control

If you accidentally delete a label from a control, you can reattach it. To create and then reattach a label to a control, follow these steps: Later in this chapter, in the "Naming control labels and their captions" section, you'll learn about the special relationship between a control and its label. By default, Access controls include a label when the control is added to a form; this label moves around with the control as you reposition the control on the form. The "Naming control labels and their captions" section describes these behaviors and how to work with control labels.

1. **Click Label in the Controls group of the Design tab.**
2. **Move the mouse pointer over the form in the Form Design window.** The mouse pointer becomes a capital A.
3. **Drag the mouse to draw the control at the desired size.**
4. **Type the desired label text in the new control, and then click outside the control.**
5. **Select the new label control.**
6. **Select Cut from the Clipboard group on the Home tab of the Ribbon.**
7. **Select the control to which you want to reattach the label, such as a text box control.**
8. **Select Paste from the Clipboard group on the Home tab of the Ribbon to attach the label control to the text box or other control.**

Another way to attach a label to a control is to select the label control and then click the information button next to the label, shown in Figure 35.25. This information button lets you know that the selected label is unassociated with a control. Select the Associate Label with a Control command from the menu, and then select the control you want to associate the label with.

FIGURE 35.25

Associating a label with a control

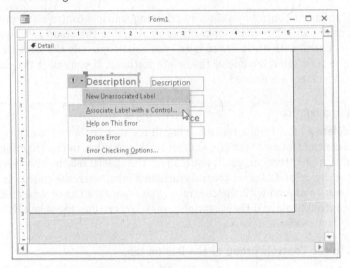

Introducing Properties

Properties are named attributes of controls, fields, or database objects that are used to modify the characteristics of a control, field, or object. Examples of these attributes are the size, color, appearance, or name of an object. A property can also modify the behavior of a control, determining, for example, whether the control is read-only or editable and visible or not visible.

Properties are used extensively in forms and reports to change the characteristics of controls. Each control on the form has properties. The form itself also has properties, as does each of its sections. The same is true for reports; the report itself has properties, as does each report section and individual control. The label control also has its own properties, even if it's attached to another control.

Everything that you do with the Ribbon commands — from moving and resizing controls to changing fonts and colors — can be done by setting properties. In fact, all these commands do is change properties of the selected controls.

Displaying the Property Sheet

Properties are displayed in a Property Sheet (sometimes called a Property window). To display the Property Sheet for a control in Form Design view, follow these steps:

1. **Click the control to select it.**
2. **Click the Property Sheet command in the Tools group on the Design tab of the Ribbon, or press F4 to display the Property Sheet.** The screen should look like the one shown in Figure 35.26. In Figure 35.26, the Description text box control has been selected and the Format tab in the Property Sheet is being scrolled to find the margin properties associated with a text box.

FIGURE 35.26

Change an object's properties with the Property Sheet.

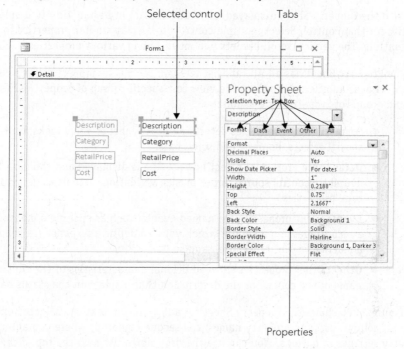

Because the Property Sheet is a window, it can be undocked, moved, and resized. It does not, however, have Maximize or Minimize buttons.

TIP

Double-click the title of an undocked Property Sheet to return it to its most recent docked location.

35

There are several ways to display a control's Property Sheet if it isn't visible:

- Select a control and click the Property Sheet command in the Tools group on the Design tab of the Ribbon.
- Double-click the edge of any control.
- Right-click any control and select Properties from the pop-up menu.
- Press F4 while any control is selected.

Getting acquainted with the Property Sheet

With the Property Sheet displayed, click any control in Design view to display the properties for that control. Select multiple controls to display similar properties for the selected controls. The vertical scroll bar lets you move among various properties.

The Property Sheet has an All tab that lets you see all the properties for a control. Or you can choose another tab to limit the view to a specific group of properties. The specific tabs and groups of properties are as follows:

- **Format:** These properties determine how a label or value looks: font, size, color, special effects, borders, and scroll bars.
- **Data:** These properties affect how a value is displayed and the data source it's bound to: control source, input masks, validation, default value, and other data type properties.
- **Event:** Event properties are named events, such as clicking a mouse button, adding a record, pressing a key for which you can define a response (in the form of a call to a macro or a VBA procedure), and so on.
- **Other:** Other properties show additional characteristics of the control, such as the name of the control or the description that displays in the status bar.

Figure 35.26 shows the Property Sheet for a Description text box selected on the form. The first column lists the property names; the second column is where you enter or select property settings or options. You can use the drop-down list near the top of the Property Sheet (displaying Description in Figure 35.26) to change which control's properties are shown. The drop-down list also enables you to select other objects on the form, like the Detail section, Form Header, or the Form itself.

Changing a control's property setting

There are many different methods for changing property settings, including the following:

- Enter or select the desired value in a Property Sheet.
- For some properties, double-clicking the property name in the Property Sheet cycles through all the acceptable values for the property.

- Change a property directly by changing the control itself, such as changing its size.
- Use inherited properties from the bound field or the control's default properties.
- Enter color selections for the control by using the Ribbon commands.
- Change label text style, size, color, and alignment by using the Ribbon commands.

You can change a control's properties by clicking a property and typing the desired value.

In Figure 35.27, you see a down arrow and a button with three dots to the right of the Control Source property entry area. Some properties display a drop-down arrow in the property entry area when you click in the area. The drop-down arrow tells you that Access has a list of values from which you can choose. If you click the down arrow in the Control Source property, you find that the drop-down list displays a list of all fields in the example data source — tblProducts. Setting the Control Source property to a field in a table creates a bound control.

FIGURE 35.27

Setting a control's Control Source property

Some properties have a list of standard values such as Yes or No; others display varying lists of fields, forms, reports, or macros. The properties of each object are determined by the control itself and what the control is used for.

A nice feature in Access is the ability to cycle through property choices by repeatedly double-clicking the choice. For example, double-clicking the Display When property alternately selects Always, Print Only, and Screen Only.

The Builder button contains an ellipsis (...) and opens one of the many builders in Access — including the Macro Builder, the Expression Builder, and the Code Builder. When you open a builder and make some selections, the property is filled in for you. You'll learn about builders later in this book.

Each type of object has its own Property window and properties. These include the form itself, each of the form sections, and each of the form's controls. You display each of the Property windows by clicking the object first or by selecting the object from the Property Sheet's combo box. The Property window will instantly change to show the properties for the selected object.

Naming control labels and their captions

You might notice that each of the data fields has a label control and a text box control. Normally, the label's Caption property is the same as the text box's Name property. The text box's Name property is usually the same as the table's field name — shown in the Control Source property. Sometimes, the label's Caption is different because a value was entered into the Caption property for each field in the table.

When creating controls on a form, it's a good idea to use standard naming conventions when setting the control's Name property. Name each control with a prefix followed by a meaningful name that you'll recognize later (for example, txtTotalCost, cboState, lblTitle). Table 35.2 shows the naming conventions for form and report controls. You can find a very complete, well-established naming convention online at www.xoc.net/standards.

TABLE 35.2   Form/Report Control Naming Conventions

Prefix	Object
frb	Bound object frame
cht	Chart (graph)
chk	Check box
cbo	Combo box
cmd	Command button
ocx	ActiveX custom control
det	Detail (section)
gft[n]	Footer (group section)
fft	Form footer section
fhd	Form header section
ghd[n]	Header (group section)
hlk	Hyperlink
img	Image
lbl	Label

lin	Line
lst	List box
opt	Option button
grp	Option group
pge	Page (tab)
brk	Page break
pft	Page footer (section)
phd	Page header (section)
shp	Rectangle
rft	Report footer (section)
rhd	Report header (section)
sec	Section
sub	Subform/subreport
tab	Tab control
txt	Text box
tgl	Toggle button
fru	Unbound object frame

The properties displayed in Figure 35.27 are the specific properties for the Description text box. The first two properties, Name and Control Source, are set to Description.

The Name is simply the name of the field itself. When a control is bound to a field, Access automatically assigns the Name property to the bound field's name. Unbound controls are given names such as Field11 or Button13. However, you can give the control any name you want.

With bound controls, the Control Source property is the name of the table field to which the control is bound. In this example, Description refers to the field with the same name in tblProducts. An unbound control has no control source, whereas the control source of a calculated control is the actual expression for the calculation, as in the example =[SalePrice]−[Cost].

Using Form View

Form view is where you actually view and modify data. The data in Form view is the same data shown in a table or query's Datasheet view, just presented a little differently. Form view presents the data in a user-friendly format, which you create and design. Double-click a form object in the Navigation pane to open the form in Form view.

35

Figure 35.28 shows the Access window with a newly created form displayed in Form view. This view has many of the same elements as Datasheet view. At the top of the screen, you see the Access title bar, the Quick Access Toolbar, and the Ribbon. The form in the center of the screen displays your data, one record at a time.

FIGURE 35.28

A form in Form view

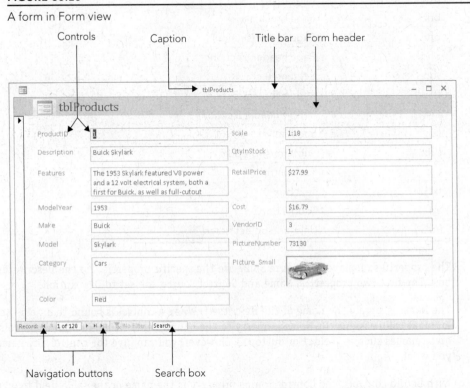

The status bar at the bottom of the Access window displays the active field's Status Bar Text property that you defined when you created the table (or form). If no Status Bar Text exists for a field, Access displays "Form View" in the status bar. Generally, error messages

---

TIP

If the form contains more fields than can fit onscreen at one time, Access automatically displays a horizontal and/or vertical scroll bar that you can use to see the remainder of the data. You can also see the rest of the data by pressing the Page Down key. If you're at the bottom of a form, or the entire form fits on the screen without scrolling, and you press Page Down, you'll move to the next record.

---

and warnings appear in dialog boxes in the center of the screen (rather than in the status bar). The navigation controls and search box are found at the bottom of the form's window and the view shortcuts are found in the status bar. These features let you move from record to record, quickly find data, or switch views.

Looking at the Home tab of the Ribbon

The Home tab of the Ribbon tab (shown in Figure 35.29) provides a way to work with the data. The Home tab has some familiar objects on it, as well as some new ones. This section provides an overview of the Home tab. The individual commands are described in more detail later in this chapter.

> **NOTE**
>
> Keep in mind that the Ribbon and its controls are very context sensitive. Depending on your current task, one or more of the commands may be grayed out or not visible. Although this behavior can be confusing, Microsoft's intent is to simplify the Ribbon as much as possible to allow you to focus on the task at hand, and not have to deal with irrelevant commands as you work.

FIGURE 35.29

The Home tab of the Ribbon in Form Design view.

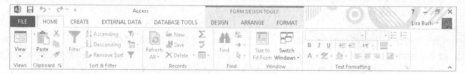

At the far left is the Views group, which enables you to switch among the following views, which you can see by clicking the button's drop-down arrow.

- **Form view:** Allows you to manipulate data on the form
- **Datasheet view:** Shows the data in the row-and-column format
- **Layout view:** Allows you to change the form's design while viewing data
- **Design view:** Allows you to make changes to the form's design

> **NOTE**
>
> All these commands may not be available on all forms. By setting the form's properties, you can limit which views are available.

The Clipboard group contains the Cut, Copy, Paste, and Format Paint commands. These commands work like the same commands in other applications (like Word and Excel). The Clipboard is a resource provided by Windows and shared by virtually all Windows applications. Items you copy or cut from Excel, for example, can be pasted into Access if the context is appropriate. For example, you could copy a VBA procedure from an Excel worksheet and paste it into an Access VBA code module because the contexts are the same. But you can't copy an Excel spreadsheet and paste it into an Access form in Form view, because Form view has no way of working with an Excel spreadsheet.

After you cut or copy a selection in Access, the Paste command's drop-down arrow gives you three choices:

- **Paste:** Inserts whatever item has been copied to the Windows Clipboard into the current location in Access. Depending on the task you're working on, the pasted item might be plain text, a control, a table or form, or some other object.
- **Paste Special:** Gives you the option of pasting the contents of the Clipboard in different formats (text, CSV, records, and so on).
- **Paste Append:** Pastes the contents of the Clipboard as a new record — as long as a record with a similar structure was copied to the Clipboard. Obviously, Paste Append remains disabled for any operation that doesn't involve copying and pasting a database table record.

The Sort & Filter group lets you change the order of the records, and, based on your criteria, limit the records shown on the form.

The Records group lets you save, delete, or add a new record to the form. It also contains commands to show totals, check spelling, freeze and hide columns, and change the row height and cell width while the form is displayed in Datasheet view.

The Find group lets you find and replace data and go to specific records in the datasheet. Use the Select command to select a record or all records.

The Window group contains two commands:

- **Size to Fit Form:** When you work with a form in Design view, Access "remembers" the size (height and width) of the form at the moment you save it. When working with the overlapping windows interface, a user may resize a form by dragging its borders to a new size and shape. The Size to Fit Form returns the form to the dimension set at design time.
- **Switch Windows:** Switch Windows provides a handy way to see all the objects (forms, reports, tables, and so on) that are currently open in the main Access windows. You can change to another object by selecting it from the drop-down list that appears when you click Switch Windows.

> **NOTE**
>
> When the current database's Document Window Options option is set to Tabbed Documents, the Home tab does not contain a Window group. With Tabbed Documents, all open Access objects are accessible through the tab interface, and the option to switch windows isn't necessary. To change the window style in Access options, choose File ➪ Options ➪ Current Database. In the Application Options section, click either Overlapping Windows or Tabbed Documents under Document Window Options, and then click OK.

The Text Formatting group lets you change the look of the datasheet in Datasheet view or Design view. Use these commands to change the font, size, bold, italic, color, and so on. Use the Align Left, Align Right, and Align Center commands to justify the data in the selected column. Click the Gridlines option to toggle gridlines on and off. Use Alternate Row Color to change the colors of alternating rows, or make them all the same. When modifying text in a Long Text field with the Text Format property set to Rich Text, you can use these commands to change the fonts, colors, and so on.

Navigating among fields

Navigating a form is nearly identical to moving around a datasheet. You can easily move around the form by clicking the control that you want and making changes or additions to your data. Because the form window displays only as many fields as can fit onscreen, you need to use various navigational aids to move within your form or between records.

Table 35.3 displays the navigational keys used to move between fields within a form.

TABLE 35.3   Navigating in a Form

Navigational Direction	Keystrokes
Next field	Tab, Right Arrow key, Down Arrow key, or Enter
Previous field	Shift+Tab, Left Arrow key, or Up Arrow key
First field of current record	Home
First field of first record	Ctrl+Home
Last field of current record	End
Last field of last record	Ctrl+End
Next page	Page Down or Next Record
Previous page	Page Up or Previous Record

35

Moving among records in a form

Although you generally use a form to display one record at a time, you still need to move between records. The easiest way to do this is to use the Navigation buttons, shown in Figure 35.30.

The Navigation buttons are the six controls located at the bottom-left corner of the Form window. The two leftmost controls move you to the first record and the previous record in the form. The three rightmost controls position you on the next record, last record, or new record in the form. If you know the record number (the row number of a specific record), you can click the Current Record box, enter a record number, and press Enter to go directly to that record.

FIGURE 35.30

The Navigation buttons of a form

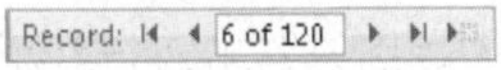

Record: ⏮ ◀ 6 of 120 ▶ ⏭ ▶*

The record number displayed in the Navigation controls is just an indicator of the current record's position in the recordset and may change when you filter or sort the records. To the right of the record number is the total number of records in the current view. The record count may not be the same as the number of records in the underlying table or query. The record count changes when you filter the data on the form.

Changing Values in a Form

Earlier in this book, you learned datasheet techniques to add, change, and delete data within a table. These techniques are the same ones you use on an Access form. Table 35.4 summarizes these techniques.

TABLE 35.4   Editing Techniques

Editing Technique	Keystrokes
Move insertion point within a control	Press the Right Arrow and Left Arrow keys
Insert a value within a control	Select the insertion point and type new data
Select the entire contents of a control	Press F2
Replace an existing value with a new value	Select the entire field and enter a new value
Replace a value with value of the preceding field	Press Ctrl+' (single quotation mark)
Replace the current value with the default value	Press Ctrl+Alt+Spacebar

Insert the current date into a control	Press Ctrl+; (semicolon)
Insert the current time into a control	Press Ctrl+: (colon)
Insert a line break in a Text control	Press Ctrl+Enter
Insert a new record	Press Ctrl++ (plus sign)
Delete the current record	Press Ctrl+– (minus sign)
Save the current record	Press Shift+Enter or move to another record
Toggle values in a check box or option button	Spacebar
Undo a change to the current control	Press Esc or click the Undo button
Undo a change to the current record	Press Esc or click the Undo button a second time after you Undo the current control

NOTE

The Right Arrow → and Left Arrow ← keys work differently in Navigation mode than they do in Edit mode. The F2 key switches between Navigation mode and Edit mode. The only visual cue for the mode that you're in is that the insertion point is displayed in Edit mode. The arrow keys navigate between controls in Navigation mode and are used to select text in Edit mode.

Knowing which controls you can't edit

Some controls, including the following, can't be edited:

- **Controls displaying AutoNumber fields:** Access maintains AutoNumber fields automatically, calculating the values as you create each new record.

- **Calculated controls:** Access may use calculated controls in forms or queries. Calculated values are not actually stored in your table.

- **Locked or disabled fields:** You can set certain form and control properties to prevent changes to the data.

- **Controls in multiuser locked records:** If another user locks the record, you can't edit any controls in that record.

Working with pictures and OLE objects

Object Linking and Embedding (OLE) objects are objects not part of an Access database. OLE objects commonly include pictures but may be any number of other data types, such as links to Word documents, Excel spreadsheets, and audio files. You can also include video files such as MPG or AVI files.

35

In Datasheet view, you can't view a picture or an OLE object without accessing the OLE server (such as Word, Excel, or the Windows Media Player). In Design view, however, you can size the OLE control area to be large enough to display a picture, chart, or other OLE objects in Form view. You can also size text box controls on forms so that you can see the data within the field — you don't have to zoom in on the value, as you do with a datasheet field.

The Access OLE control supports many types of objects. As with a datasheet, you have two ways to enter OLE fields into a form:

- Copy the object (such as an MP3 file) to the Clipboard and paste it from the controls in the Clipboard group of the Ribbon.
- Right-click the OLE control and click Insert Object from the shortcut menu to display the Insert Object dialog box, shown in Figure 35.31. Use the Insert Object dialog box to add a new object to the OLE field, or add an object from an existing file. The Create from File option button adds a picture or other OLE object from an existing file.

FIGURE 35.31

The Insert Object dialog box

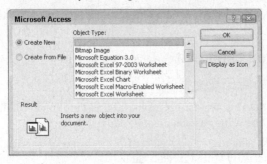

When displaying a picture in an OLE control, set the Size Mode property to control how the image representing the OLE object is displayed. The settings for this property are

- **Clip:** Keeps the image at its original size and cuts off parts of the picture that don't fit in the control.
- **Zoom:** Fits the image in the control and keeps it in its original proportion, which may result in extra white space.
- **Stretch:** Sizes an image to fit exactly between the frame borders. The stretch setting may distort the picture.

Entering data in the Long Text field

The Features field in the form shown in Figure 35.28 is a Long Text data type. This type of field contains up to 1GB of characters. The first three lines of data are visible in the text box. When you click in this text box, a vertical scroll bar appears, allowing you to view all the data in the control.

Better yet, you can resize the control in the form's Design view if you want to make it larger to show more data. Another method for viewing more text in a Long Text field's text box is to press Shift+F2 with the text box selected. A Zoom dialog box is displayed, as shown in Figure 35.32, allowing you to see more data. The text in the Zoom dialog box is fully editable. You can add new text or change text already in the control.

FIGURE 35.32

The Zoom dialog box

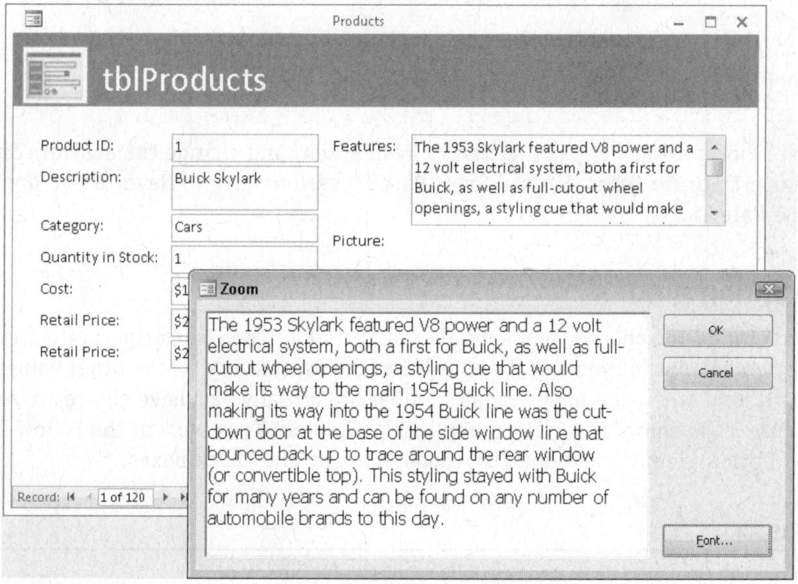

Entering data in the Date field

The SaleDate field in the frmSales_Layout form shown next in Figure 35.33 is a Date/Time data type. This field is formatted to accept and show date values. When you click in a Date/Time field on a form, a Date Picker icon automatically appears next to it, as shown in Figure 35.33. Click the Date Picker to display a calendar from which you can choose a date.

35

1275

FIGURE 35.33

Using the Date Picker control

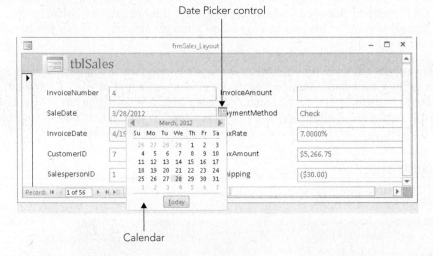

Calendar

If the Date Picker doesn't appear, switch to Design view and change the control's Show Date Picker property to For Dates. Set the Show Date Picker property to Never if you don't want to use the Date Picker.

Using option groups

Option groups let you choose from a number of option buttons (sometimes called radio buttons). Option buttons let you select one value while deselecting all the other values. Option groups work best when you have a small number of mutually exclusive choices to select from. Figure 35.34 shows an option group labeled Contact Type next to the Follow-Up Date text box. Option groups also work with toggle buttons and check boxes.

FIGURE 35.34

Using an option group to select a mutually exclusive value

The easiest and most efficient way to create option groups is with the Option Group Wizard. You can use it to create option groups with multiple option buttons, toggle buttons, or check boxes. When you're through, all your control's property settings are correctly set. To create an option group, switch to Design view and select the Option Group button from the Design tab's Controls group. Make sure the Use Control Wizards command is selected.

> **TIP**
>
> When creating an option group for a Yes/No field (which is actually stored as a number), set the Yes value to –1 and the No value to 0.

Using combo boxes and list boxes

Access has two types of controls — list boxes and combo boxes — for showing lists of data from which a user can select. The list box always displays as much of the list as possible, whereas the combo box has to be clicked to open the list. Also, the combo box enables you to enter a value that is not on the list and takes up less room on the form.

Because combo boxes are very efficient use of space on the surface of a form, you may want to use (for example) a combo box containing values from a table with customer or vendor names, as shown in Figure 35.35. The easiest way to do this is with the Combo Box Wizard. This wizard walks you through the steps of creating a combo box that looks up values in another table. To create a combo box, switch to Design view and select the Combo Box command from the Design tab's Controls group. Make sure the Use Control Wizards command is selected.

FIGURE 35.35

Using a combo box to select a value from a list.

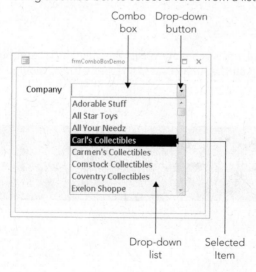

35

After you create the combo box, examine the Row Source Type, Row Source, Column Count, Column Heads, Column Widths, Bound Column, List Rows, and List Width properties. Once you become familiar with setting these properties, you can right-click a text box, choose Change To ⇨ Combo Box, and set the combo box's properties manually.

Switching to Datasheet view

With a form open, switch to Datasheet view by using one of these methods:

- Click the Datasheet View command in the Home tab's Views group.
- Click the Datasheet View button in the View Shortcuts section at the bottom-right of the Access window.
- Right-click the form's title bar — or any blank area of the form — and choose Datasheet View from the pop-up menu.

The datasheet is displayed with the cursor on the same field and record that it occupied while in the form. Moving to another record and field and then redisplaying the form in Form view causes the form to appear with the cursor on the field occupied in Datasheet view.

To return to Form view — or any other view — select the desired view from the Views group, the View Shortcuts, or the pop-up menu.

> **NOTE**
> By default, a new form's Allow Datasheet View property is set to No. To be able to switch to Datasheet View, set this property to Yes.

Saving a record

Access automatically saves each record when you move off it. Pressing Shift+Enter or selecting Save from the Records group on the Ribbon saves a record without moving off it. Closing the form also saves a record.

> **CAUTION**
> Because Access automatically saves changes as soon as you move to another record, you may inadvertently change the data in the underlying tables. And, because you can't undo changes to an Access database, there is no easy way to revert to the record's previous state.

Printing a Form

You can print one or more records in your form exactly as they appear onscreen. (You learn how to produce formatted reports in Chapter 37.) The simplest way to print is to use the keyboard shortcut Ctrl+P to show the Print dialog box. The Print dialog box has several options to customize your printout:

- **Print Range:** Prints the entire form or only selected pages or records
- **Copies:** Determines the number of copies to be printed
- **Collate:** Determines whether copies are collated

You can also click the Properties button and set options for the selected printer or select a different printer. The Setup button allows you to set margins and print headings.

Printing a form is like printing anything else. Windows is a WYSIWYG ("What You See Is What You Get") environment, so what you see on the form is what you get in the printed hard copy. If you added page headers or page footers, they would be printed at the top or bottom of the page. The printout contains any formatting that you specified in the form (including lines, boxes, and shading) and converts colors to grayscale if you're using a black-and-white printer.

The printout includes as many pages as necessary to print all the data. If your form is wider than a single printer page, you need multiple pages to print your form. Access breaks up the printout as necessary to fit on each page.

The Print command under the File menu provides additional printing options:

- **Quick Print:** Prints the active form using the default printer with no opportunity to change any options
- **Print:** Shows the Print dialog box
- **Print Preview:** Shows what the printout will look like based on the current settings

> **TIP**
>
> In Print Preview mode, the Print Preview tab of the Ribbon is displayed (and all other tabs are hidden). Use the Ribbon commands to select different views, change print settings, and zoom in and out. Click Print to print the form to the printer. Click the Close Print Preview command on the right side of the Ribbon to return to the previous view.

35

Summary

In this chapter, you learned how to add different types of forms to your database using the Create tab's Form group. At this point, you should be able to:

- Select a table and create a form for it using either the Form button or the Form Wizard.
- Add different types of controls to the form.
- Move, resize, and format controls.
- Display the Property Sheet, and use it to change properties for controls and other parts of the form.
- Display Form view, enter data, and navigate among records.
- Print a form.

Selecting Data with Queries

Queries are an essential part of any database application. Queries are the tools that enable you and your users to extract data from multiple tables, combine it in useful ways, and present it to the user as a datasheet, on a form, or as a printed report.

You may have heard the old cliché, "Queries convert data to information." To a certain extent, this statement is true — that's why it's a cliché. The data contained within tables is not particularly useful because, for the most part, the data in tables appears in no particular order. Also, in a properly normalized database, important information is spread out among a number of different tables. Queries are what draw these various data sources together and present the combined information in such a way that users can actually work with the data.

Introducing Queries

A database's primary purpose is to store and extract information. Information can be obtained from a database immediately after the data is added, or days, weeks, or even years later. Of course, retrieving information from database tables requires knowledge of how the database is designed.

For example, consider printed reports kept in a traditional filing cabinet, arranged by date and by a sequence number that indicates when the report was produced. To find a specific report, you must know its year and sequence number. In a good filing system, you might have a cross-reference book to help you find a specific report. This book might have all reports categorized alphabetically by type of report and, perhaps, by date. Such a book can be helpful, but if you know only the report's topic and approximate date, you still have to search through all the sections of the book to find out where to get the report.

Unlike manual filing systems, databases like Access quickly and easily retrieve information to meet virtually any criteria you specify.

This is the real power of a database — the capacity to examine the data in more ways than you can imagine. Queries, by definition, ask questions about the data stored in the database. Most queries are used to drive forms, reports, and graphical representations of the data contained in a database.

What queries are

Let's start with the basics. The word *query* comes from the Latin word *quaerere,* which means "to ask or inquire." Over the years, the word *query* has become synonymous with *quiz, challenge, inquire,* or *question.*

An Access query is a question that you ask about the information stored in Access tables. You build queries with the Access query tools, and then save it as a new object in the Access database. Your query can be a simple question about data in a single table, or it can be a more complex question about information stored in several tables. For example, you might ask your database to show you only trucks that were sold in the year 2012. After you submit the question in the form of a query, Access returns only the information you requested.

What queries can do

Queries are flexible. They allow you to look at your data in virtually any way you can imagine. Most database systems are continually evolving and changing over time. Very often, the original purpose of a database is very different from its current use.

Here's just a sampling of what you can do with Access queries:

- **Choose tables:** You can obtain information from a single table or from many tables that are related by some common data. Suppose you're interested in seeing the customer name along with the items purchased by each type of customer. When using several tables, Access combines the data as a single recordset.

- **Choose fields:** Specify which fields from each table you want to see in the recordset. For example, you can select the customer name, zip code, sales date, and invoice number from tblCustomers and tblSales.

- **Provide criteria:** Record selection is based on selection criteria. For example, you might want to see records for only a certain category of products.

- **Sort records:** You might want to sort records in a specific order. For example, you might need to see customer contacts sorted by last name and first name.

- **Perform calculations:** Use queries to perform calculations such as averages, totals, or counts of data in records.

- **Create tables:** Create a brand-new table based on data returned by a query.

- **Display query data on forms and reports:** The recordset you create from a query might have just the right fields and data needed for a report or form. Basing a report or form on a query means that, every time you print the report or open the form, you see the most current information contained in the tables.

- **Use a query as a source of data for other queries (subquery):** You can create queries that are based on records returned by another query. This is very useful for performing ad hoc queries, where you might repeatedly make small changes to the criteria. In this case, the second query filters the first query's results.

- **Make changes to data in tables:** Action queries modify multiple rows in the underlying tables as a single operation. Action queries are frequently used to maintain data, such as updating values in specific fields, archiving old records, or deleting obsolete information.

What queries return

Access combines a query's records and, when executed, displays them in Datasheet view by default. The set of records returned by a query is commonly called (oddly enough) a *recordset*. A recordset is a dynamic set of records. The recordset returned by a query is not stored within the database, unless you've directed Access to build a table from those records.

When you save a query, only the structure of the query is saved, not the returned records. That is to say, only the SQL syntax used to build the query is stored.

Consider these benefits of *not* saving the recordset to a physical table:

- A smaller amount of space on a storage device (usually a hard disk) is needed.
- The query uses updated versions of records.

Every time the query is executed, it reads the underlying tables and re-creates the recordset. Because recordsets themselves are not stored, a query automatically reflects any changes to the underlying tables made since the last time the query was executed — even in a real-time, multiuser environment. Depending on your needs, a query's recordset can be viewed as a datasheet, or in a form or report. When a form or report is based on a query, the query's recordset is re-created and bound to the form or report each time it's opened.

A query's recordset can also be used in macros and VBA procedures to help drive any number of automated tasks.

Creating a Query

After you create your tables and place data in them, you're ready to work with queries. To begin a query, select the Create tab on the Ribbon, and click the Query Design button in the Queries group. This opens the query designer shown in Figure 36.1.

Figure 36.1 shows two windows. The underlying window is the query designer. Floating on top of the designer is the Show Table dialog box. The Show Table dialog box is *modal,* which means that you must do something in the dialog box before continuing with the query. Before you continue, you add the tables required for the query. In this case, tblProducts is highlighted and ready to be added.

FIGURE 36.1

The Show Table dialog box and the query design window

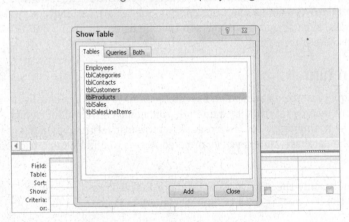

The Show Table dialog box (refer to Figure 36.1) displays the tables and queries in your database. Double-click a table on the Tables tab to add it to the query design, or click the table in the list and click the Add button. Close the Show Table dialog box after adding the table. Figure 36.2 shows an example table, tblProducts, added to the query.

FIGURE 36.2

The query design window with tblProducts added

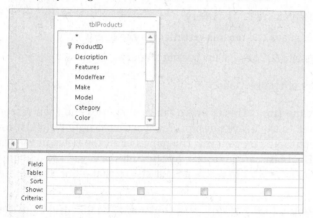

To add additional tables to the query, right-click anywhere in the upper portion of the query designer and select Show Table from the shortcut menu that appears. Alternatively, drag tables from the Navigation pane to the upper portion of the query designer. There is also a Show Table button on the Design tab of the Ribbon.

> **NOTE**
>
> Generally speaking, when you add multiple tables to a query, you should have previously created a relationship between the tables. For example, if you refer to the examples in Figure 36.1 and 36.2, notice that the tblProducts table has a ProductID field. The tblSalesLineItems table, which lists various sales transactions, also has a corresponding ProductID field. If you want to create a sales query using information from both tables, you would need to create a relationship between the ProductID fields in the two tables first. To create a relationship, click the Database Tools tab, and then click Relationships in the Relationships group. In the tools group of the Relationship Tools ⇨ Design tab, click Clear Layout and then Yes to clean any previously created relationships if they are not needed. In the Relationships group, click Show Table, Ctrl+click each table to add on the Tables tab of the Show Tables dialog box, and then click Add, and Close. Select the field for which you want to create a relationship in the first table, and drag it over the related field in the second table. The Edit Relationships dialog box opens, suggesting an appropriate relationship type based on the data in the specified fields. Verify the settings, and click Create to finish establishing the relationship. Click Close on the Relationship Tools ⇨ Design tab to hide the tab, clicking Yes when prompted to save the Relationships layout changes. You can then add the related tables to your query. For more about relationship types and creating relationships, see the Access Help topics "Guide to table relationships" and "Create, edit, or delete a relationship." You also can refer to the *Access 2013 Bible* for more on this subject. Later in the chapter, you'll see how to work with tables with overlapping data through ad hoc joins.

Removing a table from the query designer is easy. Just right-click the table in the query designer and select Remove Table from the shortcut menu.

The query design window has three primary views, accessible from the Results group of the Query Tools⇨Design tab or the Views group of the Home tab:

- **Design view:** Where you create the query
- **Datasheet view:** Displays the records returned by the query
- **SQL view:** Displays the SQL statement behind a query

The query designer consists of two sections:

- **The table/query pane (top):** This is where tables or queries and their respective Field Lists are added to the query's design. You'll see a separate Field List for each object you add. Each Field List contains the names of all the fields in the respective table or query. A Field List can be resized by clicking the edges and dragging it to a different size. You may want to resize a Field List so that all of a table's fields are visible.
- **The Query by Example (QBE) design grid (bottom):** The QBE grid holds the field names involved in the query and any criteria used to select records. Each column in the QBE grid contains information about a single field from a table or query contained within the upper pane.

The two window panes are separated horizontally by a pane splitter bar (refer to Figure 36.2). You can use the scroll bar above the splitter bar to shift the design grid left or right, or use the mouse to drag the splitter bar up or down to change the relative sizes of the upper and lower panes.

Switch between the upper and lower panes by clicking the desired pane or by pressing F6. Each pane has horizontal and vertical scroll bars to help you move around.

You actually build the query by dragging fields from the upper pane to the QBE grid.

Figure 36.2 displays an empty QBE grid at the bottom of the query designer. The QBE grid has six labeled rows:

- **Field:** This is where field names are entered or added.
- **Table:** This row shows the table the field is from. This is useful in queries with multiple tables.
- **Sort:** This row enables sorting instructions for the query.
- **Show:** This row determines whether to display the field in the returned recordset.
- **Criteria:** This row consists of the criteria that filter the returned records.
- **Or:** This row is the first of a number of rows to which you can add multiple query criteria.

You learn more about these rows as you create queries in this chapter.

The Query Tools ⇨ Design tab (shown in Figure 36.3) contains many different buttons specific to building and working with queries. Although each button is explained as it's used in the chapters of this book, here are the main buttons:

- **View:** Switches between the Datasheet view and Design view in the query design window. The View drop-down control also enables you to display the underlying SQL statement behind the query.

- **Run:** Runs the query. Displays a select query's datasheet, serving the same function as selecting Datasheet View from the View button. However, when working with action queries, the Run button performs the operations (append, make-table, and so on) specified by the query.

- **Select:** Clicking the Select button transforms the opened query into a Select query.

- **Make Table, Append, Update, Crosstab, and Delete:** Each of these buttons specifies the type of query you're building. In most cases, you transform a select query into an action query by clicking one of these buttons.

- **Show Table:** Opens the Show Table dialog box.

FIGURE 36.3

The Query Tools Design Ribbon

The remaining buttons are used for creating more-advanced queries, printing the contents of the query, and displaying a query's Property Sheet.

Adding fields to your queries

There are several ways to add fields to a query. You can add fields one at a time, select and add multiple fields, or select all the fields in a field list.

Adding a single field

You add a single field in several ways. One method is to double-click the field name in the table in the top pane of the query designer. The field name immediately appears in the first available column in the QBE pane. Alternatively, drag a field from a table in the top pane of the query designer, and drop it on a column in the QBE grid. Dropping a field between two fields in the QBE grid pushes other fields to the right.

In Figure 36.4 you can see that the Cost field was brought into the QBE grid. Once a field is added, you can simply add the next field you need to see in the query.

FIGURE 36.4

To add fields from your table to the QBE grid, simply double-click or drag the field.

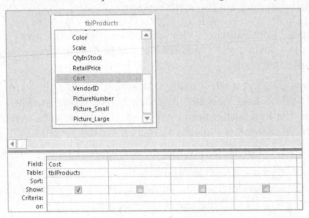

Each cell in the Table row of the QBE grid contains a drop-down list of the tables contained in the upper pane of the query designer.

Adding multiple fields

You can add multiple fields in a single action by selecting the fields from the Field List window and dragging them to the QBE grid. The selected fields don't have to be contiguous (one after the other). Hold down the Ctrl key while clicking additional fields. Figure 36.5 illustrates the process of adding multiple fields.

FIGURE 36.5

Selecting multiple fields to add to the QBE grid

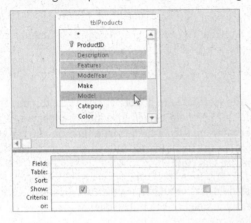

The fields are added to the QBE grid in the order in which they occur in the table.

You can also add all the fields in the table by double-clicking the Field List's header (where it says tblProducts in Figure 36.6) to highlight all the fields in the table. Then drag the highlighted fields to the QBE grid.

Alternatively, you can click the asterisk (*) in the Field List and then drag it to the QBE grid (or double-click the asterisk to add it to the QBE grid). Although this action doesn't add all the fields to the QBE grid, the asterisk directs Access to include all fields in the table in the query.

FIGURE 36.6

Adding the asterisk to the QBE grid selects all fields in the table.

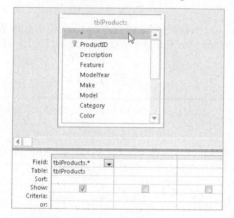

TIP

Unlike selecting all the fields, the asterisk places a reference to all the fields in a single column. When you drag multiple columns, as in the preceding example, you drag names to the QBE grid. If you later change the design of the table, you also have to change the design of the query. The advantage of using the asterisk for selecting all fields is that changes to the underlying tables don't require changes to the query. The asterisk means to select all fields in the table, regardless of the field names or changes in the number of fields in the table.

CAUTION

The downside of using the asterisk to specify all fields in a table is that the query, as instructed, returns all the fields in a table, regardless of whether every field is used on a form or report. Retrieving unused data can be an inefficient process. Very often, performance problems can be traced to the asterisk returning many more fields than necessary to a form or report.

Running your query

After selecting the fields, run the query by clicking the Run button in the Results group of the Query Tools⇨Design tab (see Figure 36.7).

FIGURE 36.7

Click the Run button to display the results of your query.

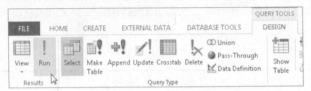

To return to the QBE grid, you can go up to the Home tab and choose View⇨Design View. Alternatively, you can right-click the tab header for the query (as shown in Figure 36.8) and select Design View.

FIGURE 36.8

Right-click on the queries tab header and select Design View to return to the QBE grid.

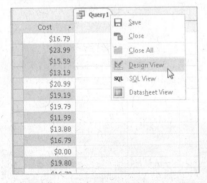

Working with Query Fields

Sometimes you'll want to work with the fields you've already selected — rearranging their order, inserting a new field, or deleting an existing field. You may even want to add a field to the QBE grid without showing it in the datasheet. Adding a field without showing it enables you to sort on the hidden field or to use the hidden field as criteria.

Selecting a field in the QBE grid

Before you can move a field's position, you must first select it. To select it, you will work with the field selector row.

The *field selector* is the thin gray area at the top of each column in the QBE grid at the bottom of the query designer. Each column represents a field. To select the Category field, move the mouse pointer until a small selection arrow (in this case, a dark downward arrow) is visible in the selector row and then click and drag the column. Figure 36.9 shows the selection arrow above the Category column just before it's selected.

FIGURE 36.9

Selecting a column in the QBE grid. The pointer changes to a downward-pointing arrow when you move over the selection row.

Field:	ProductID		Description	Category	QtyInStock	Cost
Table:	tblProducts		tblProducts	tblProducts	tblProducts	tblProducts
Sort:						
Show:		☑	☑	☑	☑	☑
Criteria:						

> **TIP**
>
> Select multiple contiguous fields by pointing to the field selector for the first field you want to select, and then when the down arrow pointer appears, dragging across the field selector bars of the other fields.

Changing field order

The left-to-right order in which fields appear in the QBE grid determines the order in which they appear in Datasheet view. You might want to move the fields in the QBE grid to achieve a new sequence of fields in the query's results. With the fields selected, you can move the fields on the QBE design by simply dragging them to a new position.

Left-click a field's selector bar, and, while holding down the left mouse button, drag the field into a new position in the QBE grid.

Figure 36.10 shows the Category field highlighted. As you move the selector field to the left, the column separator between the field's ProductID and Description changes (gets wider) to show you where Category will go.

FIGURE 36.10

Moving the Category field to between ProductID and Description. Notice the QBE field icon below the arrow near the Description column.

Field:	ProductID	Description	Category	QtyInStock	Cost
Table:	tblProducts	tblProducts	tblProducts	tblProducts	tblProducts
Sort:					
Show:	☑	☑	☑	☑	☑
Criteria:					

TIP

The field order in a query is irrelevant to how the data appears on a form or report. Normally, you'll arrange the controls on a form or report in response to user requirements.

Resizing columns in the QBE grid

The QBE grid generally shows five or six fields in the viewable area of your screen. The remaining fields are viewed by moving the horizontal scroll bar at the bottom of the window.

You might want to shrink some fields to be able to see more columns in the QBE grid. You adjust the column width to make them smaller (or larger) by moving the mouse pointer to the border between two fields in the field selector area, and dragging left or right (see Figure 36.11).

FIGURE 36.11

Resizing columns in the QBE grid

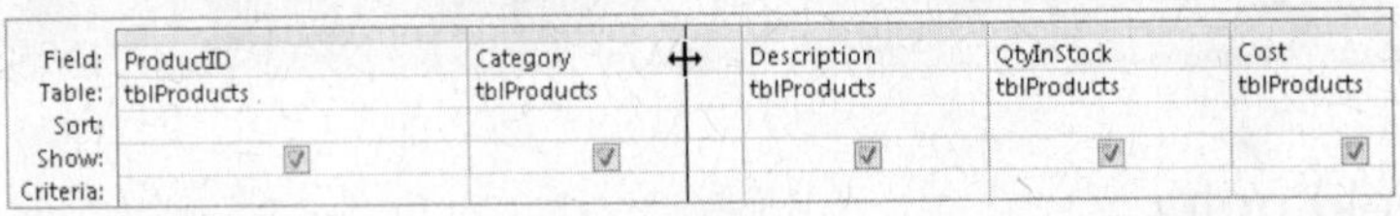
Field:
Table:
Sort:
Show:
Criteria:
ProductID
tblProducts
Category
tblProducts
Description
tblProducts
QtyInStock
tblProducts
Cost
tblProducts

TIP

An easier way to resize columns in the QBE grid is to double-click the line dividing two columns in the grid. Access auto-fits the column to fit the data displayed in the column.

The width of a column in the QBE grid has no affect on how the field's data is displayed in a datasheet, form, or report. The column width in the QBE grid is just a convenience to you, the developer. Also, QBE column width is not preserved when you save and close the query.

Removing a field

Remove a field from the QBE grid by selecting the field and pressing the Delete key. You can also right-click on a field's selector bar and choose Cut from the shortcut menu.

Inserting a field

Insert new fields in the QBE grid by dragging a field from a Field List window in the tables pane above the QBE grid and dropping it onto a column in the QBE grid. The new column is inserted to the left of the column on which you dropped the field. Double-clicking a field in a Field List adds the new column at the far-right position in the QBE grid.

Hiding a field

While you're performing queries, you might want to show only some of the fields in the QBE grid. Suppose, for example, you've chosen FirstName, LastName, Address, City, and State. Then you decide that you want to temporarily look at the same data, without the State field. Instead of completely removing the State field, you can simply hide it by unchecking the Show check box in the State column (see Figure 36.12).

FIGURE 36.12

The Show check box is unchecked for the State field so that field will not show in the results.

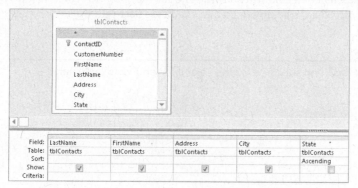

A common reason to hide a field in the query is because the field is used for sorting or as criteria, but its value is not needed in the query. For example, consider a query involving invoices. For a number of reasons, the users might want to see the invoices sorted by the order date, even though the actual order date is irrelevant for this particular purpose. You could simply include the OrderDate field in the QBE grid, set the sort order for the OrderDate field, and uncheck its Show box. Access sorts the data by the OrderDate field even though the field is not shown in the query's results.

> **NOTE**
>
> If you save a query that has an unused field (its Show box is unchecked and no criteria or sort order is applied to the field), Access eliminates the field from the query as part of the query optimization process. The next time you open the query, the field won't be included in the query's design.

Changing the sort order of a field

When viewing a recordset, you often want to display the data in a sorted order to make it easier to analyze the data. For example, you may want to review the results from the tblProducts table sorted by category.

Sorting places the records in alphabetical or numeric order. The sort order can be ascending or descending. You can sort on a single field or multiple fields.

You input sorting directions in the Sort row in the QBE grid. To specify a sort order on a particular field (such as LastName), perform these steps:

1. **Click the Sort cell in the column for the field you want to sort by.**

2. **Click the drop-down list arrow that appears in the cell, and select the sort order (Ascending or Descending) you want to apply.** Figure 36.13 shows the QBE grid with ascending sorts specified for the LastName and FirstName fields. Notice that the LastName field is still showing the sort options available. Also notice that the word *Ascending* is being selected in the field's Sort cell.

FIGURE 36.13

An ascending sort has been specified for the LastName and FirstName fields.

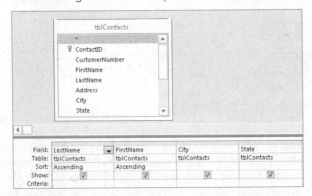

> **NOTE**
> You can't sort on a Memo or an OLE object field.

The left-to-right order in which fields appear in the QBE grid is important when sorting on more than one field. Not only do the fields appear in the datasheet in left-to-right order, but they're sorted in the same order; this is known as *sort order precedence*. The leftmost field containing sort criteria is sorted first, the first field to the right containing sort criteria is sorted next, and so on. In the example shown in Figure 36.13, the LastName field is sorted first, followed by the FirstName field.

Figure 36.14 shows the results of the query shown in Figure 36.13. Notice that the data is sorted by LastName and then by FirstName. This is why Ann Bond appears before John Bond, and John Jones appears before Kevin Jones in the query's data.

FIGURE 36.14

The order of the fields in the QBE grid is critical when sorting on multiple fields.

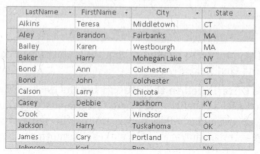

LastName	FirstName	City	State
Aikins	Teresa	Middletown	CT
Aley	Brandon	Fairbanks	MA
Bailey	Karen	Westbourgh	MA
Baker	Harry	Mohegan Lake	NY
Bond	Ann	Colchester	CT
Bond	John	Colchester	CT
Calson	Larry	Chicota	TX
Casey	Debbie	Jackhorn	KY
Crook	Joe	Windsor	CT
Jackson	Harry	Tuskahoma	OK
James	Cary	Portland	CT
Johnson	Karl	Rye	NY

Adding Criteria to Your Queries

Most often users want to work only with records conforming to some criteria. Otherwise, too many records may be returned by a query, causing serious performance issues. For example, you might want to look only at customers who haven't bought any products within the last six months. Access makes it easy for you to specify a query's criteria.

Understanding selection criteria

Selection criteria are filtering rules applied to data as they're extracted from the database. Selection criteria tell Access which records you want to look at in the recordset. A typical criterion might be "all sellers," or "only those vehicles that are not trucks," or "products with retail prices greater than $75."

Selection criteria limit the records returned by a query. Selection criteria aid the user by selecting only the records a user wants to see, and ignoring all the others.

You specify criteria in the Criteria row of the QBE grid. You designate criteria as an expression. The expression can be simple (like "trucks" or "not trucks"), or it can take the form of complex expressions using built-in Access functions.

Proper use of query criteria is critical to an Access database's success. In most cases, the users have no idea what data is stored in a database's tables and accept whatever they see on a form or report as truthfully representing the database's status. Poorly chosen criteria might hide important information from the application's users, leading to bad business decisions or serious business issues later on.

Entering simple string criteria

Character-type criteria are applied to Text-type fields. Most often, you'll enter an example of the text you want to retrieve. Here is a small example that returns only product records where the product type is "Cars":

1. **Add the desired fields to the query.** For example, from tblProducts, you could add the Description, Category, and Cost fields.

2. **Type the criterion into the Criteria cell in the column for the desired field.** For example, you could type CARS as the Category field Criteria entry as shown in Figure 36.15. Notice that Access adds double quotes around the value. Access, unlike many other database systems, automatically makes assumptions about what you want.

3. **Run the query.** In our example, only cars are displayed in the query's results.

FIGURE 36.15

Specifying Cars as the query's criteria

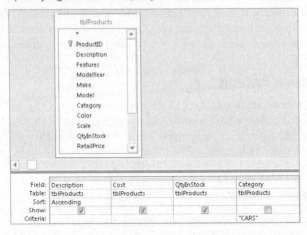

When looking at the results of the query, you may argue that there is no point in displaying Cars in every row. In fact, because this query only returns information about cars, the user can very well assume that every record references a car, and there's no need to display a product category in the query. Unchecking the Category field's Show box in the query's design removes Category from the datasheet, making the data easier to understand.

You could enter the criteria expression in any of these other ways:

CARS

= CARS

"CARS"

= "Cars"

By default, Access is *not* case sensitive, so any form of the word *cars* works just as well as this query's criteria.

Figure 36.15 is an excellent example for demonstrating the options for various types of simple character criteria. You could just as well enter **Not Cars** in the criteria column, to return all products that are not cars (trucks, vans, and so on).

Generally, when dealing with character data, you enter equalities, inequalities, or a list of acceptable values.

This capability is a powerful tool. Consider that you only have to supply an example, and Access not only interprets it but also uses it to create the query recordset. This is exactly what *Query by Example* means: You enter an example and let the database build a query based on the example.

To erase the criteria in the cell, select the contents and press Delete, or select the contents and right-click Cut from the shortcut menu that appears.

Entering other simple criteria

You can also specify criteria for Numeric, Date, and Yes/No fields. Simply enter the example data in the criteria field just as you did for text fields. In almost every case, Access understands the criteria you enter and adjusts to correctly apply the criteria to the query's fields.

It's also possible to add more than one criteria to a query. For example, suppose that you want to look only at contacts who live in Connecticut and have been customers since January 1, 2012 (where OrigCustDate is greater than or equal to January 1, 2012). This query requires criteria in both the State and OrigCustDate fields. To do this, it's critical that you place both examples on the same criteria row. Follow these steps to create a query like this:

1. **Create a new query, adding the desired table.** For example, you could create a new query based on tblCustomers.
2. **Add the desired fields to the QBE grid.** For example, you could add ContactType, FirstName, LastName, State, and OrigCustDate to the QBE grid.
3. **Enter the first criterion in the first field's Criteria row.** For our example, you would enter **ct** or **CT** in the Criteria cell in the State column.

4. **Enter the additional criterion in the Criteria row for another field.** For example, Enter **>= 01/01/2012** in the Criteria cell in the OrigCustDate column. Access adds pound sign characters (#) around the date in the criteria box. Figure 36.16 shows how the example query with multiple criteria should look.

5. **Run the query.**

FIGURE 36.16

Specifying text and date criteria in the same query

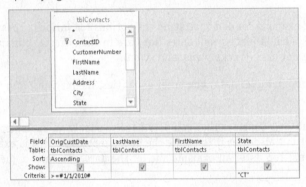

For our example query results, Access would display records of customers who live in Connecticut and who became customers on or after January 1, 2012.

Access uses comparison operators to compare Date fields to a value. These operators include less than (<), greater than (>), equal to (=), or a combination of these operators.

Notice that Access automatically adds pound sign (#) delimiters around the date value. Access uses these delimiters to distinguish between date and text data. The pound signs are just like the quote marks Access added to the "Cars" criteria. Because OrigCustDate is a DateTime field, Access understands what you want and inserts the proper delimiters for you.

Be aware that Access interprets dates according to the region and language settings in the Control Panel. For example, in most of Europe and Asia, #5/6/2012# is interpreted as June 5, 2012, while in the United States this date is May 6, 2012. It's very easy to construct a query that works perfectly but returns the wrong data because of subtle differences in regional settings.

Printing a Query's Recordset

After you create your query, you can easily print all the records in the recordset. Although you can't specify a type of report, you can print a simple matrix-type report (rows and columns) of the recordset created by your query.

You do have some flexibility when printing a recordset. If you know that the datasheet is set up just as you want, you can specify some options as you follow these steps:

1. **Open the query to print.**
2. **If you aren't in the Datasheet view, run the query** by clicking the Run button in the Results group of the Query Tools ➪ Design tab.
3. **Choose File ➪ Print.**
4. **Specify the print options that you want in the Print dialog box and click OK.**

The printout reflects all layout options in effect when you print the dataset. Hidden columns don't print, and gridlines print only if the Gridlines option is on. The printout reflects the specified row height and column width.

Saving a Query

To save your query, click the Save button on the Quick Access Toolbar at the top of the Access screen. Access asks you for the name of the query if this is the first time the query has been saved.

After saving the query, Access returns you to the mode you were working in. Occasionally, you'll want to save and exit the query in a single operation. To do this, click the Close Window button in the upper-right corner of the query designer. Access always asks you to confirm saving the changes before it actually saves the query.

Creating Multi-Table Queries

Using a query to get information from a single table is common; often, however, you need information from several related tables. For example, you might want to obtain a buyer's name and product purchased by the customer. This query requires four tables: tblCustomers, tblSales, tblSalesLineItems, and tblProducts.

After you create the tables for your database and decide how the tables are related to one another as described in a Note earlier in this chapter, you're ready to build multi-table queries to obtain information from several related tables. A multi-table query presents data as if it existed in one large table.

The first step in creating a multi-table query is to add the tables to the query design window:

1. **Create a new query by clicking the Query Design button in the Queries group of the Create tab.**

2. **Add the desired tables by double-clicking each table's name in the Show Table dialog box.** For example, you could double-click tblCustomers, tblSales, tblSalesLineItems, and tblProducts.

3. **Click the Close button.**

Figure 36.17 shows the top pane of the query design window with the four tables you just added. Because the relationships were set at table level, the join lines are automatically added to the query.

FIGURE 36.17

The query design window with four tables added. Notice that the join lines are already present.

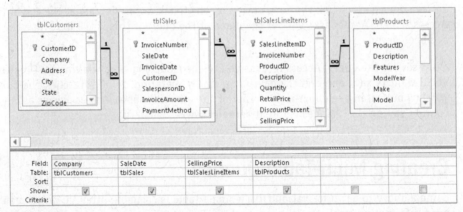

You add fields from more than one table to the query in exactly the same way as you do when you're working with a single table. You can add fields one at a time, multiple fields as a group, or all the fields from a table.

When you select a field that has a common name in multiple tables, Access adds the table's name, followed by a period and the field name. For example, if ProductID is a field found in more than one table used in the query design window (let's say tblProducts and tblSalesLineItems), adding the ProductID field from tblSalesLineItems will display that field in the design grid as tblSalesLineItems.ProductID. This helps you select the correct field name. Using this method, you can select a common field name from a specific table.

> **TIP**
>
> The easiest way to select fields is still to double-click the field names in the top half of the query designer. To do so, you might have to resize the Field List windows to see the fields that you want to select.

Viewing table names

When you're working with multiple tables in a query, the field names in the QBE grid can become confusing. You might find yourself asking, for example, just which table the Description field is from.

Access automatically maintains the table name that is associated with each field displayed in the QBE grid. Figure 36.18 shows the query designer with the name of each table displayed under the field name in the QBE grid.

FIGURE 36.18

The QBE grid with table names displayed. Notice that it shows all four table names.

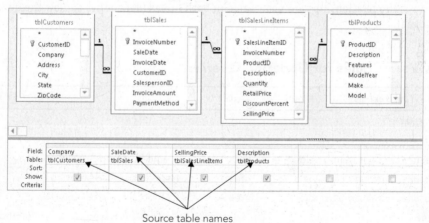

Source table names

Adding multiple fields

The process of adding multiple fields in a multi-table query is identical to adding multiple fields in a single-table query. When you're adding fields from several tables, you must add them from one table at a time. The easiest way to do this is to select multiple fields and drag them together down to the QBE grid.

Select multiple contiguous fields by clicking the first field of the list and then clicking the last field while holding down the Shift key. You can also select noncontiguous fields in the list by holding down the Ctrl key while clicking individual fields.

> **CAUTION**
>
> Using the asterisk (*) to add a table's fields has an additional drawback: You can't specify criteria on the asterisk column itself. You have to add an individual field from the table and enter the criterion. If you add a field for a criterion (when using the asterisk), the query displays the field twice — once for the asterisk field and a second time for the criterion field. Therefore, you might want to deselect the Show cell of the criterion field.

Recognizing the limitations of multi-table queries

When you create a query with multiple tables, there are limits to which fields can be edited. Generally, you can change data in a query's recordset, and your changes are saved in the underlying tables. The main exception is a table's primary key — a primary key value can't be edited if referential integrity is in effect and if the field is part of a relationship.

There may be instances when you will want to make manual edits to the resulting recordset of a query. In Access, the records in your tables might not always be updateable. Table 36.1 shows when a field in a table is updateable. As Table 36.1 shows, queries based on one-to-many relationships are updateable in both tables (depending on how the query was designed).

TABLE 36.1   Rules for Updating Queries

Type of Query or Field	Updateable	Comments
One table	Yes	
One-to-one relationship	Yes	
Results contains Memo field	Yes	Memo field updateable
Results contain a hyperlink	Yes	Hyperlink updateable
Results contain an OLE object	Yes	OLE object updateable
One-to-many relationship	Usually	Restrictions based on design methodology (see text)
Many-to-one-to-many relationship	No	Can update data in a form or data access page if Record Type = Recordset
Two or more tables with no join line	No	Must have a join to determine updateability
Crosstab	No	Creates a snapshot of the data

Totals query (Sum, Avg, and so on)	No	Works with grouped data creating a snapshot
Unique Value property is Yes	No	Shows unique records only in a snapshot
SQL-specific queries	No	Union and pass-through work with ODBC data
Calculated field	No	Will recalculate automatically
Read-only fields	No	If opened read-only or on read-only drive (CD-ROM)
Permissions denied	No	Insert, replace, or delete not granted
ODBC tables with no unique identifier	No	Unique identifier must exist
Paradox table with no primary key	No	Primary key file must exist
Locked by another user	No	Can't be updated while a field is locked by another

Overcoming query limitations

Table 36.1 shows that there are times when queries and fields in tables are not updateable. As a general rule, any query that performs aggregate operations or uses an ODBC data source is not updateable; most other queries can be updated. When your query has more than one table and some of the tables have a one-to-many relationship, some fields might not be updateable (depending on the design of the query).

Updating a unique index (primary key)

If a query uses two tables involved in a one-to-many relationship, the query must include the primary key from the "one" table. Access must have the primary key value so that it can find the related records in the two tables.

Replacing existing data in a query with a one-to-many relationship

Normally, all the fields in the "many" table (such as the tblSales table) are updateable in a one-to-many query. All the fields (*except* the primary key) in the "one" table (tblCustomers) can be updated. This is sufficient for most database application purposes. Also, the primary key field is rarely changed in the "one" table because it's the link to the records in the joined tables.

Updating fields in queries

If you want to add records to both tables of a one-to-many relationship, include the foreign key from the "many" table and show the field in the datasheet. After doing this, records can be added starting with either the "one" or "many" table. The "one" table's primary key field is automatically copied to the "many" table's join field.

If you want to add records to multiple tables in a form (covered in Chapter 35), remember to include all (or most) of the fields from both tables. Otherwise, you won't have a complete set of the record's data on your form.

Working with the Table Pane

The upper (table) pane of the query designer contains information that's important to your query. Understanding the table pane and how to work with Field Lists is critically important to building complex queries.

Looking at the join line

A *join line* connects tables in the query designer (refer to Figure 36.17). The join line connects the primary key in one table to the foreign key in another table. The join line represents the relationship between two tables in the Access database. In this example, a join line goes from tblSales to tblCustomers, connecting ContactID in tblCustomers to the Buyer field in tblSales. The join line is added by Access because relationships were set in the Relationship Builder.

If referential integrity is set on the relationship, Access uses a somewhat thicker line for the join connecting to the table in the query designer. A one-to-many relationship is indicated by an infinity symbol (∞) on the "many" table end of the join line.

Access auto-joins two tables if the following conditions are met:

- Both tables have fields with the same name.
- The same-named fields are the same data type (text, numeric, and so on). Note that the AutoNumber data type is the same as Numeric (Long Integer).
- One of the fields is a primary key in its table.

> **NOTE**
>
> After a relationship is created between tables, the join line remains between the two fields. As you move through a table selecting fields, the line moves relative to the linked fields. For example, if you scroll downward, towards the bottom of the window in tblCustomers, the join line moves upward with the customer number, eventually stopping at the top of the table window.

When you're working with many tables, these join lines can become confusing as they cross or overlap. As you scroll through the table, the line eventually becomes visible, and the field it's linked to becomes obvious.

Moving a table

Move the Field Lists by grabbing the title bar of a Field List window (where the name of the table is) with the mouse and dragging the Field List window to a new location. You may want to move the Field Lists for a better working view or to clean up a confusing query diagram.

You can move and resize the Field Lists anywhere in the top pane. Access saves the arrangement when you save and close the query. Generally speaking, the Field Lists will appear in the same configuration the next time you open the query.

Removing a table

You might need to remove tables from a query. Use the mouse to select the table you want to remove in the top pane of the query design window and press the Delete key. Or right-click the Field List window and choose Remove Table from the shortcut menu.

Removing a table from a query's design does not remove the table from the database, of course.

> **CAUTION**
>
> When you remove a table from a query design, join lines to that table are deleted as well. There is no warning or confirmation before removal. The table is simply removed from the screen, along with any of the table's fields added to the QBE grid. Be aware, however, that deleted tables referenced in calculated fields will not be removed. The "phantom" table references may cause errors when you try to run the query.

Adding more tables

You might decide to add more tables to a query or you might accidentally delete a table and need to add it back. You accomplish this task by clicking the Show Table button in the Query Setup group of the Design tab. The Show Table dialog box appears in response to this action.

Creating and Working with Query Joins

You'll often need to build queries that require two or more related tables be joined to achieve the desired results. For example, you may want to join an employee table to a transaction table in order create a report that contains both transaction details and information on the employees who logged those transactions. The type of join used will determine the records that will be output.

Understanding joins

There are three basic types of joins: inner joins, left outer joins, and right outer joins:

- **Inner joins:** An *inner join* operation tells Access to select only those records from both tables that have matching values. Records with values in the joined field that do not appear in both tables are omitted from the query results. Figure 36.19 represents the inner join operation visually.

FIGURE 36.19

An inner join operation will select only the records that have matching values in both tables. The arrows point to the records that will be included in the results.

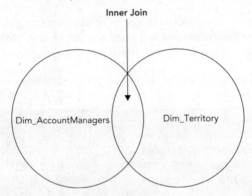

- **Left outer joins:** A *left outer join* operation (sometimes called a "left join") tells Access to select all the records from the first table regardless of matching *and* only those records from the second table that have matching values in the joined field. Figure 36.20 represents the left join operation visually.

FIGURE 36.20

A left outer join operation will select all records from the first table and only those records from the second table that have matching values in both tables. The arrows point to the records that will be included in the results.

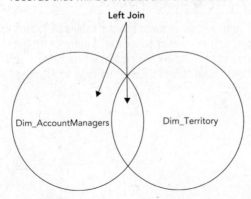

- **Right outer joins:** A *right outer join* operation (sometimes called a "right join") tells Access to select all the records from the second table regardless of matching *and* only those records from the first table that have matching values in the joined field (see Figure 36.21).

FIGURE 36.21

A right outer join operation will select all records from the second table and only those records from the first table that have matching values in both tables. The arrows point to the records that will be included in the results.

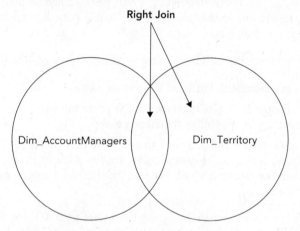

By default, an Access query returns only records where data exists on both sides of a relationship (inner join). For example, a query that extracts data from the Contacts table and the Sales table only returns records where contacts have actually placed sales and will not show contacts who haven't yet placed a sale. If a contact record isn't matched by at least one sales record, the contact data isn't returned by the query. This means that, sometimes, the query might not return all the records you expect.

Although this is the most common join type between tables in a query, users sometimes want to see all the data in a table (like tblCustomers in the preceding example), regardless of whether those records are matched in another table. In fact, users often want to specifically see records that are *not* matched on the other side of the join. Consider a sales department that wants to know all the contacts who have *not* made a sale in the last year. You must modify the default query join characteristics in order to process this type of query.

You can create joins between tables in these three ways:

- By creating relationships between the tables when you design the database.
- By selecting two tables for the query that have a field in common that has the same name and data type in both tables. The field is a primary key field in one of the tables.
- By modifying the default join behavior.

The first two methods occur automatically in the query design window. Relationships between tables are displayed in the query designer when you add the related tables to a query. It also creates an automatic join between two tables that have a common field, as long as that field is a primary key in one of the tables and the Enable Auto Join choice is selected (by default) in the Options dialog box.

If relationships are set in the Relationship Builder, you might not see the auto-join line if

- The two tables have a common field, but it isn't the same name.
- A table isn't related and can't be logically related to the other table (for example, tblCustomers can't directly join the tblSalesLineItems table).

If you have two tables that aren't related and you need to join them in a query, use the query design window. Joining tables in the query design window does *not* create a permanent relationship between the tables; instead, the join (relationship) applies only to the tables while the query operates.

Tables in a query have to be joined in some way. Including two tables with nothing in common (for example, a query based on tblCustomers and tblProducts) means that Access has no way to know which records in tblCustomers match which records in tblProducts. Unless there is some way to relate the tables to one another, the query returns unusable data.

Leveraging ad hoc table joins

Figure 36.22 shows a simple query containing tblSales, tblSalesLineItems, tblProducts, and tblCategories. This is an ad hoc join, formed when the Categories table was added to the query.

No direct relationship yet exists between tblProducts and tblCategories. However, Access found the Category field in both the tables, determined that the Category data type is the same in both tables, and determined that the Category field in tblCategories is the primary key. Therefore, Access added an ad hoc join between the tables.

FIGURE 36.22

An ad hoc join between tblProducts and tblCategories

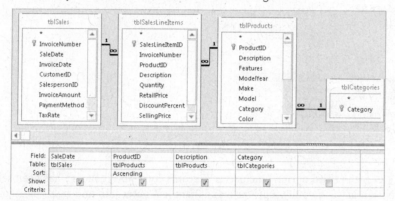

> **NOTE**
>
> Tables are not joined automatically in a query if they aren't already joined at the table level, if they don't have a common named field for a primary key, or if the AutoJoin option is off.

If Access hasn't auto-joined tblProducts and tblCategories (perhaps because the Category field was named differently in the tables), you can easily add an ad hoc join by dragging the Category field from one table and dropping it on the corresponding field in the other table.

Specifying the type of join

The problem with most joins is that, by default, they exhibit equi-join behavior as the query executes. In the case of the query in Figure 36.19, if a product record exists that doesn't have an assigned category (for example, a car that was never assigned to a category), the query doesn't return any records where a product record isn't matched by a category.

The problem is that you can't even tell records are missing. The only way you'd ever determine that there should be more records returned by this query is by carefully examining the sales records, by composing another query that counts all sales, or by performing some other audit operation.

You must modify the join characteristics between the two tables (such as tblProducts and tblCategories) to get an accurate picture of sales. Carefully right-click on the thin join line between the two tables (tblProducts and tblCategories), and select the Join Properties command from the shortcut menu. This action opens the Join Properties dialog box (see Figure 36.23), enabling you to specify an alternate join between the tables.

FIGURE 36.23

Selecting an outer join for the query

In Figure 36.23, the third option (Include All Records from 'tblProducts') has been selected (the first option is the default). Options 2 and 3 are left outer join and right outer join, respectively. These options direct Access to retrieve all records from the left (or right) table involved in the join, regardless of whether those records are matched on the other side of the join.

Figure 36.24 shows the result of the new join between the example tables. In the lower-right corner of this figure you see how an outer join appears in the Access query designer, while the rest of the figure shows the recordset returned by the query.

FIGURE 36.24

A right outer join corrects the "missing products" problem in Figure 36.23.

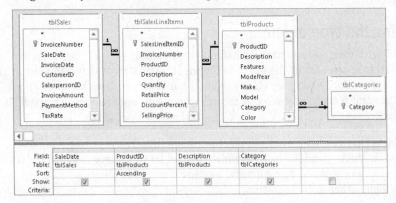

Of course, you can easily create joins that make no sense, but when you view the data, it'll be pretty obvious that you got the join wrong. If two joined fields have no values in common, you'll have a datasheet in which no records are selected.

You would never want to create a meaningless join. For example, you wouldn't want to join the City field from tblCustomer to the SalesDate field of tblSales. Although Access enables you to create this join, the resulting recordset will have no records in it.

Deleting joins

To delete a join line between two tables, select the join line and press the Delete key. Select the join line by placing the mouse pointer on any part of the line and clicking once.

> **CAUTION**
> If you delete a join between two tables and the tables remain in the query design window unjoined to any other tables, the solution will have unexpected results because of the Cartesian product that Access creates from the two tables. The Cartesian product is effective for only this query. The underlying relationship remains intact.

Access enables you to create multi-field joins between tables (more than one line can be drawn). The two fields must have data in common; if not, the query won't find any records to display.

Summary

This chapter has taken on the major topic of building Select queries. Without a doubt, query creation is a daunting task that takes a lot of practice. Queries are an integral and important part of any Access database application. Queries drive forms, reports, and many other aspects of Access applications. At this point, you should be familiar enough with query concepts to begin:

- Displaying Query Design view and adding tables.
- Finding the tools for establishing table relationships when a query needs to return related data from multiple tables.
- Adding, removing, and rearranging fields in the query design grid.
- Sorting query results or using criteria to filter the results.
- Saving and running a query, and printing the results from Datasheet view.
- Understanding how joins work (with and without relationships), and how to use an ad hoc join in a query.

Presenting Data with Access Reports

IN THIS CHAPTER

Looking at the different types of Access reports

Creating reports with a Report Wizard

Printing and saving the report

It's hard to underestimate the importance of reports in database applications. Many people who never work with an Access application in person use reports created by Access. A lot of maintenance work on database projects involves creating new and enhancing existing reports. Access is well known and respected for its powerful reporting features.

Reports provide the most flexible way of viewing and printing summarized information. They display information with the desired level of detail, while enabling you to view or print your information in many different formats. You can add multilevel totals, statistical comparisons, and pictures and graphics to a report.

In this chapter, you learn to use the Report Wizard as a starting point. You also learn how to create reports and what types of reports you can create with Access.

Introducing Reports

Reports present a customized view of your data. Report output is viewed onscreen or printed to provide a hard copy of the data. Very often, reports provide summaries of the information contained in the database. Data can be grouped and sorted in any order and can be used to create totals that perform statistical operations on data. Reports can include pictures and other graphics as well as memo fields in a report. If you can think of a report you want, Access probably supports it.

Identifying the different types of reports

Three basic types of reports are used by most businesses:

- **Tabular reports:** Print data in rows and columns with groupings and totals. Variations include summary and group/total reports.

- **Columnar reports:** Print data and can include totals and graphs.
- **Mailing label reports:** Create multicolumn labels or snaked-column reports.

Tabular reports

Tabular reports are similar to a table displaying data in rows and columns. Figure 37.1 is a typical tabular report (rptProductsSummary) displayed in Print Preview.

Unlike forms or datasheets, tabular reports often group data by one or more fields. Often, tabular reports calculate and display subtotals or statistical information for numeric fields in each group. Some reports include page totals and grand totals. You can even have multiple snaked columns so that you can create directories (such as telephone books). These types of reports often use page numbers, report dates, or lines and boxes to separate information. Reports may have color and shading and display pictures, business graphs, and memo fields. A special type of summary tabular report can have all the features of a detailed tabular report but omit record details.

FIGURE 37.1

An example tabular report displayed in Print Preview

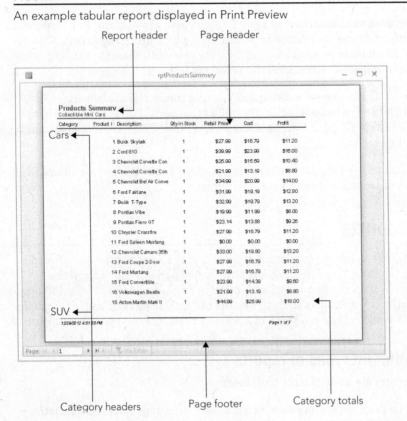

Columnar reports

Columnar reports generally display one or more records per page, but they do so vertically. Columnar reports display data very much as a data entry form does, but they're used strictly for viewing data and not for entering it. Figure 37.2 shows part of a columnar report (rptProducts) in Print Preview.

FIGURE 37.2

A columnar report showing report controls distributed throughout the entire page

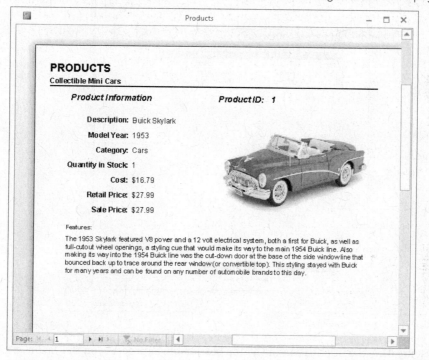

Another type of columnar report displays one main record per page (like a business form) but can show many records within embedded subreports. An invoice is a typical example. This type of report can have sections that display only one record and at the same time have sections that display multiple records from the "many" side of a one-to-many relationship — and even include totals.

Figure 37.3 shows an invoice report (rptInvoice) in Report view.

FIGURE 37.3

An invoice report

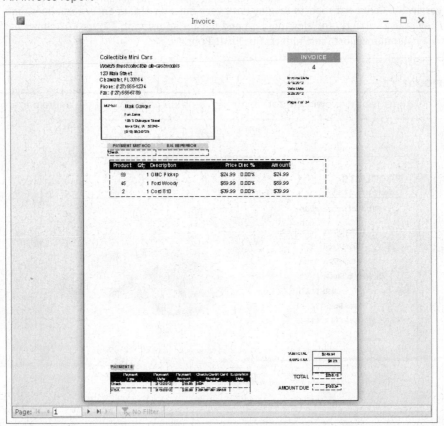

In Figure 37.3, the information in the top portion of the report is on the "main" part of the report, whereas the product details near the bottom of the figure are contained in a subreport embedded within the main report.

Mailing label reports

Mailing labels (shown in Figure 37.4) are also a type of report. Access includes a Label Wizard to help you create this type of report. The Label Wizard enables you to select from a long list of label styles. Access accurately creates a report design based on the label style you select. You can then open the report in Design view and customize it as needed.

FIGURE 37.4

A typical mailing label report

Distinguishing between reports and forms

The main difference between reports and forms is the intended output. Whereas forms are primarily for data entry and interaction with the users, reports are for viewing data (either onscreen or in hard-copy form). Calculated fields can be used with forms to display an amount based on other fields in the record. With reports, you typically perform calculations on groups of records, a page of records, or all the records included in the report. Anything you can do with a form — except input data — can be duplicated by a report. In fact, you can save a form as a report and then refine it in the report Design view.

Creating a Report, from Beginning to End

The report process begins with your desire to view data, but in a way that differs from a form or datasheet display. The purpose of the report is to transform raw data into a meaningful set of information. The process of creating a report involves several steps:

1. **Defining the report layout**
2. **Assembling the data**

3. **Creating the report with the Access Report Wizard**

4. **Printing or viewing the report**

5. **Saving the report**

Defining the report layout

You should begin by having a general idea of the layout of your report. You can define the layout in your mind, on paper, or interactively using the Report Wizard. When laying out a report, consider how the data should be sorted (for example, chronologically or by name), how the data should be grouped (for example, by invoice number or by week), and how the size of the paper used to print the report will constrain the data.

> **TIP**
>
> Very often, an Access report is expected to duplicate an existing paper report or form used by the application's consumers.

Assembling the data

After you have a general idea of the report layout, assemble the data needed for the report. Access reports use data from two primary sources:

- A single database table
- A recordset produced by a query

You can join many tables in a query and use the query's recordset as the record source for your report. A query's recordset appears to an Access report as if it were a single table.

As you learned in Chapter 36, you use queries to specify the fields, records, and sort order of the records stored in tables. Access treats a recordset data as if it were a single table (for processing purposes) in datasheets, forms, and reports. When the report is run, Access matches data from the recordset or table against the fields specified in the report and uses the data available at that moment to produce the report.

> **NOTE**
>
> Reports don't follow the sort order specified in an underlying query. Reports are sorted at the report level, either in the detail section or in a group section. It's a waste of time to sort data in a query that is used solely to populate a report because the data is re-sorted and rearranged by the report itself.

Creating a report with the Report Wizard

Access enables you to create virtually any type of report. Some reports, however, are easier to create than others, especially when a Report Wizard is used as a starting point. Like form wizards, the Report Wizard gives you a basic layout for your report, which you can then customize.

The Report Wizard simplifies laying out controls by stepping you through a series of questions about the report that you want to create. In this section, you use the Report Wizard to create tabular and columnar reports.

Creating a new report

The Ribbon contains several commands for creating new reports for your applications. The Create tab of the Ribbon includes the Reports group, which contains several options such as Report, Labels, and Report Wizard. To work through the report creation process in predefined steps, first select the table or query that has the data for the report in the Navigation pane, and then click the Report Wizard button. The first Report Wizard dialog box (shown in Figure 37.5) appears.

FIGURE 37.5

The Report Wizard dialog box after selecting a data source and fields

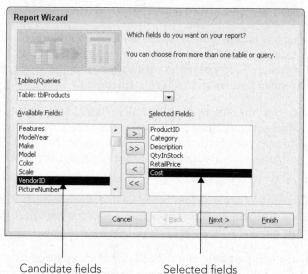

Candidate fields   Selected fields

In Figure 37.5, tblProducts has been selected as the data source for the new report. Under the Tables/Queries drop-down list is a list of available fields. When you click a field in this list and click the right-pointing arrow, the field moves from the Available Fields list to the report's Selected Fields list. The example in the figure shows the ProductID, Category, Description, QtyInStock, RetailPrice, and Cost fields added to the Selected Fields list.

You're limited to selecting fields from the original record source you started with. You can select fields from other tables or queries by using the Tables/Queries drop-down list in the Report Wizard. As long as you've specified valid relationships so that Access properly links the data, these fields are added to your original selection and you use them on the report. If you choose fields from unrelated tables, a dialog box asks you to edit the relationship and join the tables. Or you can return to the Report Wizard and remove the fields.

After you've selected your data, click Next to go to the next wizard dialog box.

Selecting the grouping levels

The next Report Wizard dialog box enables you to choose which field(s) to use for grouping data. Figure 37.6 shows the Category field selected as the data grouping field for the report. The field selected for grouping determines how data appears on the report, and the grouping fields appear as group headers and footers in the report.

Groups are most often used to combine data that are logically related. One example is grouping all products by product category. Another example is choosing to group on CustomerID so that each customer's sales history appears as a group on the report. You use the report's group headers and footers to display the customer name and any other information specific to each customer.

The Report Wizard lets you specify as many as four group fields for your report. You use the Priority buttons to change the grouping order on the report. The order you select for the group fields is the order of the grouping hierarchy.

Select the Category field as the grouping field and click the > button to specify a grouping based on category values. Notice that the picture changes to show Category as a grouping field, as shown in Figure 37.6. Each of the other fields (ProductID, Description, QtyInStock, RetailPrice, and SalesPrice in the example) selected for the report will appear in the Category group's details section.

FIGURE 37.6

Specifying the report's grouping

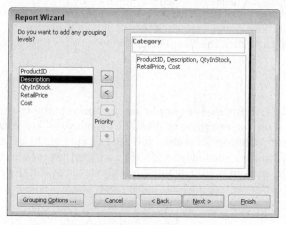

Defining the group data

After you select the group field(s), click the Grouping Options button at the bottom of the dialog box to display the Grouping Options dialog box, which enables you to further define how you want groups displayed on the report.

For example, you can choose to group by only the first character of the grouping field. This means that all records with the same first character in the grouping field are grouped. If you group a customers table on CustomerName, and then specify grouping by the first character of the CustomerName field, a group header and footer appears for all customers whose name begins with the same character. This specification groups all customer names beginning with the letter *A*, another group for all records with customer name beginning with *B*, and so on.

The Grouping Options dialog box enables you to further define the grouping. This selection can vary in importance, depending on the data type.

The Grouping Intervals list box displays different values for various data types:

- **Text:** Normal, 1st Letter, 2 Initial Letters, 3 Initial Letters, 4 Initial Letters, 5 Initial Letters
- **Numeric:** Normal, 10s, 50s, 100s, 500s, 1000s, 5000s, 10000s, 50000s, 100000s
- **Date:** Normal, Year, Quarter, Month, Week, Day, Hour, Minute

Normal means that the grouping is on the entire field. In this example, use the entire Category field.

Notice that the grouping options simplify creating reports grouped by calendar months, quarters, years, and so on. This means that you can easily produce reports showing sales, payroll, or other financial information needed for business reporting.

If you displayed the Grouping Options dialog box, click the OK button to return to the Grouping Levels dialog box, and then click the Next button to move to the Sort Order dialog box.

Selecting the sort order

By default, Access automatically sorts grouped records in an order meaningful to the grouping field(s). For example, after you've chosen to group by Category, Access arranges the groups in alphabetical order by Category. However, you can't be sure of the order of the records within the group, so it's a good idea to specify a sort within each group. As an example, your users might want to see the product records sorted by Retail Price in descending order so that the most expensive products appear near the top for each category group.

In this example, Access sorts data by the Category field. As Figure 37.7 shows, the data is also sorted by Description within each group.

FIGURE 37.7

Selecting the field sorting order

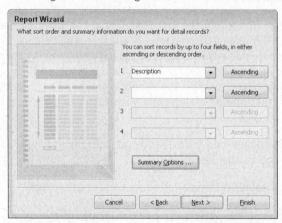

Sort fields are selected by the same method you use for selecting grouping fields. You can select sorting fields that haven't been chosen for grouping. The fields chosen in this dialog box affect only the sorting order in the data displayed in the report's Detail section. Select ascending or descending sort by clicking the button to the right of each sort field.

Selecting summary options

Near the bottom of the sorting screen of the Report Wizard is a Summary Options button. Clicking this button displays the Summary Options dialog box (shown in Figure 37.8), which provides additional display options for numeric fields. All the numeric and currency fields selected for the report are displayed and may be summed. Additionally, you can display averages, minimums, and maximums.

FIGURE 37.8

Selecting the summary options

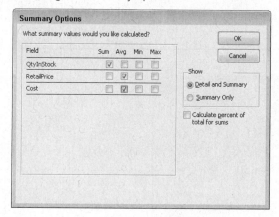

You can also decide whether to show or hide the data in the report's Detail section. If you select Detail and Summary, the report shows the detail data, whereas selecting Summary Only hides the Detail section and shows only totals in the report.

Finally, checking the Calculate percent of total for sums check box adds the percentage of the entire report that the total represents below the total in the group footer. If, for example, you have three products and their totals are 15, 25, and 10, respectively, 30%, 50%, and 20% shows below their total (that is, 50) — indicating the percentage of the total sum (100%) represented by their sum.

Clicking the OK button in this dialog box returns you to the sorting screen of the Report Wizard. There you can click the Next button to move to the next wizard screen.

Selecting the layout

The next step in the Report Wizard affects the look of your report. The Layout area enables you to determine the basic layout of the data. The Layout area provides three layout choices that tell Access whether to repeat the column headers, indent each grouping, and add lines or boxes between the detail lines. As you select each option, the picture on the left changes to show how the choice affects the report's appearance.

You choose between Portrait (up-and-down) and Landscape (across-the-page) layout for the report in the Orientation area. Finally, the Adjust the field width so all fields fit on a page check box enables you to cram a lot of data into a little area. (A magnifying glass may be necessary!)

For this example, choose Stepped and Portrait, as shown in Figure 37.9. Then click the Next button to move to the next dialog box.

FIGURE 37.9

Selecting the page layout

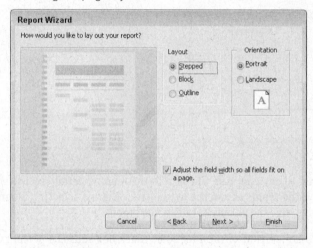

Opening the report design

The final Report Wizard dialog box contains an area for you to enter a title for the report. This title appears only once, at the very beginning of the report, not at the top of each page. The report title also serves as the new report's name. The default title is the name of the table or query you initially specified as the report's data source.

Next, choose one of the option buttons at the bottom of the dialog box:

- Preview the report
- Modify the report's design

For this example, leave the default selection intact to preview the report. Click Finish and the report displays in Print Preview (see Figure 37.10).

FIGURE 37.10

An example report displayed in Print Preview

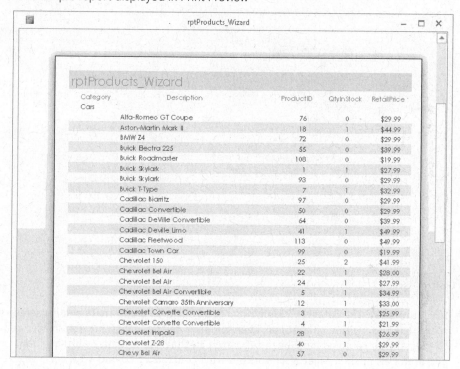

Adjusting the report's layout

There are a few small issues with the report you see in Figure 37.10. The Access Report Wizard has chosen the fonts and overall color scheme, which may not be what you had in mind. Also, the Retail Price column isn't quite wide enough to show the column heading.

The Report Wizard displays the new report in Print Preview. Right-click the report's title bar and select Layout View from the shortcut menu. Figure 37.11 shows a report in Layout view.

FIGURE 37.11

Layout view is useful for resizing controls in a columnar report.

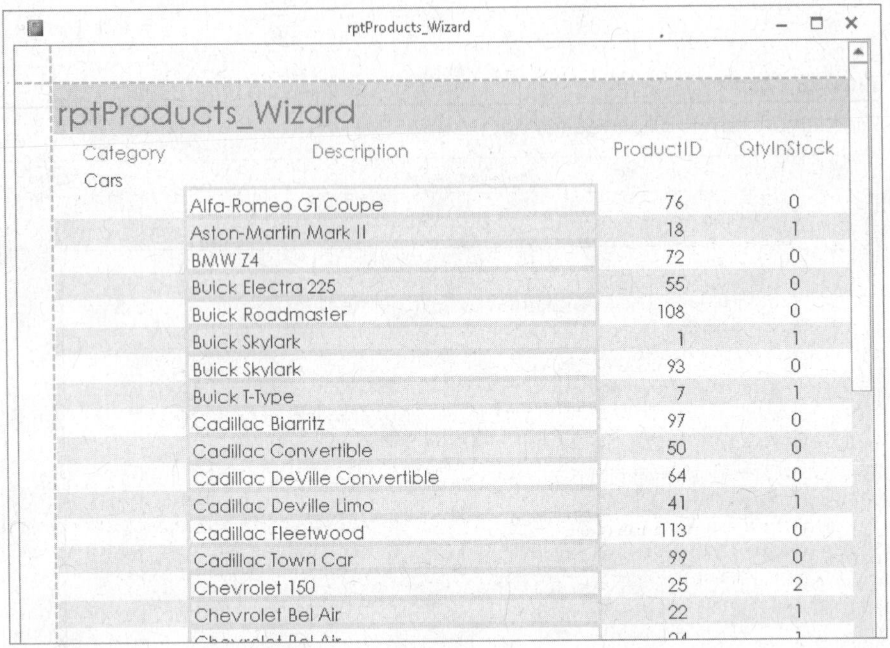

In Figure 37.11, the Category column has been shrunk to eliminate some wasted space, the Description column has been widened to the left to fill that space, and the remaining columns have been separated so that the column headings show and aren't all pushed together. Working with controls in Layout view for a report is identical to working with them in Layout view for a form. To shrink a column's width, for example, click one of its controls and drag the right edge of the control to the left.

Choosing a theme

After you adjust the layout, you can use controls in the Themes group of the Report Design Tools ⇨ Design tab to change the report's colors, fonts, and overall appearance. The Themes button opens a gallery containing several dozen themes (see Figure 37.12).

FIGURE 37.12

Choosing a theme for the report

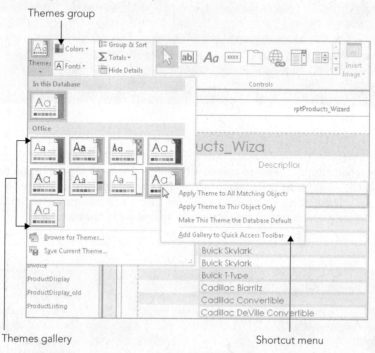

Themes group

Themes gallery

Shortcut menu

Themes are an important concept in Access 2013. A theme sets the color scheme, selected font face, font colors, and font sizes for Access 2013 forms and reports. As you hover the mouse over the theme icons in the gallery, the report open in Layout view behind the gallery instantly changes to provide a Live Preview of how the report would look with the selected theme.

Each theme has a name, like Office, Facet, Organic, and Slice. Theme names are useful when you want to refer to a particular theme in the application's documentation or in an e-mail or other correspondence. Themes are stored in a file with a THMX extension, in the Program Files\Microsoft Office\Document Themes 15 folder. Themes apply to all the Office 2013 documents (Word, Excel, and Access), making it easy to determine a style to apply to all of a company's Office output.

NOTE

Access 2007 users may be wondering what happened to the AutoFormat feature. For a number of reasons, Microsoft decided to replace AutoFormat with themes in later versions of Office. AutoFormat applied to individual controls, which meant a lot of work when building a complicated form or report. AutoFormat also tended to be all or nothing, making it difficult to apply an AutoFormat and then alter the colors and fonts to controls on a form or report. Themes are much more flexible. They even allow you to save a completed form or report as a new theme (see the Save Current Theme option at the bottom of the theme gallery in Figure 37.12). There was no way to create a custom AutoFormat in Access 2007.

As the shortcut menu in Figure 37.12 indicates, you can apply the selected theme just to the current report (Apply Theme to this Object Only), all reports (Apply Theme to All Matching Objects), or all forms *and* reports in the application (Make This Theme the Database Default). There's even an option to add the theme as a button to the Quick Access Toolbar, an extremely useful option for selectively applying the theme to other objects in the database.

TIP

It's very tempting to try out every reporting style and option when building Access forms and reports. Unfortunately, when carried too far, your Access application may end up looking like a scrapbook of design ideas rather than being a valuable business tool. Professional database developers tend to use a minimum of form and report styles and use them consistently throughout an application. Be considerate of your users and try not to overwhelm them with a lot of different colors, fonts, and other user interface and reporting styles.

Creating new theme color schemes

Access 2013 provides several default themes, with each theme consisting of a set of complementary colors, fonts, and font characteristics. In addition, you can set up entirely new color and font themes and apply them to your forms and reports. Creating a custom color theme is a great way to apply a company's corporate color scheme to the forms and reports in an application.

With a form or report open in Design view, follow these steps:

1. **Click the Colors button in the Themes group on the Report Design Tools⇨Design tab.** The color theme list opens.
2. **Select the Customize Colors command at the very bottom of the list of color themes.** The Create New Theme Colors dialog box (shown in Figure 37.13) appears, showing the currently selected color theme.

FIGURE 37.13

Setting up a custom color theme

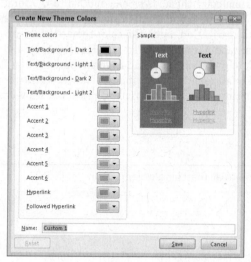

Modifying a color theme requires a considerable amount of work. As you can see from Figure 37.13, each color theme includes 12 different colors. Each of the 12 buttons on the Create New Theme Colors dialog box opens a color palette (shown in Figure 37.14) where you select a theme element's color, such as the color for the Text/Background – Light 2 element.

FIGURE 37.14

Selecting a theme element's color

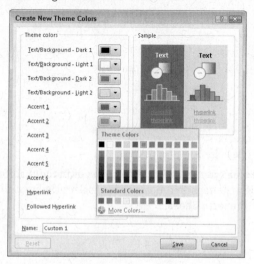

3. **When the color customization is complete, assign a name for the custom color theme and click Save.** When you close the Create New Theme Colors dialog box, you'll see that the custom color theme has been applied to the form or report currently open in Design view. If you want to apply the new color theme to all the forms or reports in the application, open the color theme list, right-click the name of a custom color theme at the top of the list (see Figure 37.15), and select Apply Color Scheme to All Matching Objects. If you have a report open in Design view, the theme will be applied to all reports in the application. If, on the other hand, you have a form open in Design view, all the forms in the application receive the new color theme.

FIGURE 37.15

Applying a color theme to all matching objects in an application

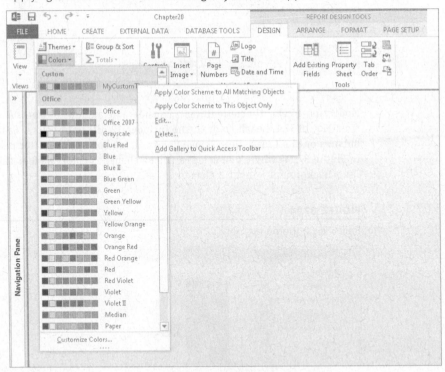

Even after applying a color theme, you can adjust the colors of individual items on a report (or form, for that matter). Open the report in Design view, select the item to change, and choose its new color(s) in the Property Sheet.

Although not described or shown here, a similar dialog box is available (Create New Theme Fonts) in the Fonts drop-down list in the Themes group on the Design tab. The Create New Theme Fonts dialog box enables you to set up a custom font theme (heading and body fonts, and so on) to apply to forms and reports. Creating custom fonts themes works just like adding your own color themes to an application. Save the theme with a name you'll recognize, and apply the font theme to forms and reports as needed.

Using the Print Preview view

Figure 37.16 shows a report in the Print Preview view. To change to this view, click the View down arrow (bottom half of the button) in the Views group of either the Home or Design tabs, and click Print Preview. This view displays your report with the actual fonts, shading, lines, boxes, and data that will be used on the report when printed to the default Windows printer. Clicking the left mouse button on the report's surface changes the view to a page preview that shows the entire page.

FIGURE 37.16

Displaying a report in the zoomed Print Preview view

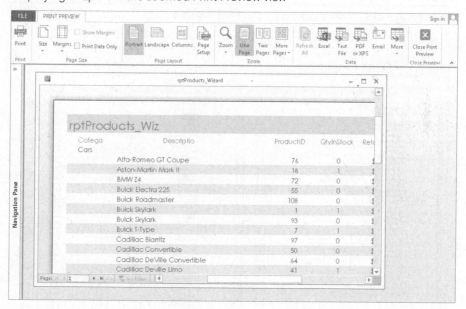

The Ribbon transforms to display controls relevant to viewing and printing the report. The Print Preview tab of the Ribbon includes controls for adjusting the size, margins, page orientation (Portrait or Landscape), and other printing options. The print options are stored with the report when you save the report's design. The Print Preview tab also includes a Print button for printing the report, and another button for closing Print Preview and returning to the report's previous view (Design, Layout, or Report view).

You can move around the page by using the horizontal and vertical scroll bars, or use the Page controls (at the bottom-left corner of the window) to move from page to page. The Page controls include DVD-like navigation buttons to move from page to page or to the first or last page of the report. You can also go to a specific page of the report by entering a value in the text box between the Previous and Next controls.

Right-clicking the report and selecting the Multiple Pages option, or using the controls in the Zoom group on the Print Preview tab of the Ribbon, lets you view more than one page of the report in a single view. Figure 37.17 shows a view of the report in the Print Preview's two-page mode. Use the navigation buttons (in the lower-left section of the Print Preview window) to move between pages, just as you would to move between records in a datasheet. The Print Preview window has a toolbar with commonly used printing commands.

FIGURE 37.17

Displaying multiple pages of a report in Print Preview

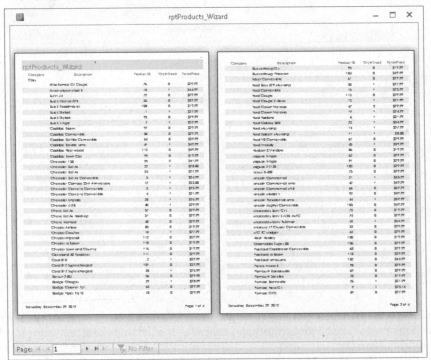

If, after examining the preview, you're satisfied with the report, click the Print button on the toolbar to print the report. If you're dissatisfied with the design, select the Close button to switch to the Design view and make further changes.

Publishing in alternate formats

An important feature of the Print Preview tab is the ability to output the Access report in a number of common business formats, including PDF, XPS (XML Paper Specification), HTML, and other formats.

Clicking the PDF or XPS button in the Data group on the Print Preview tab opens the Publish as PDF or XPS dialog box (shown in Figure 37.18). This dialog box provides options for outputting in standard PDF format or in a condensed version (for use in a web context). You also specify the destination folder for the exported file.

37

FIGURE 37.18

Access 2013 provides powerful options for publishing reports.

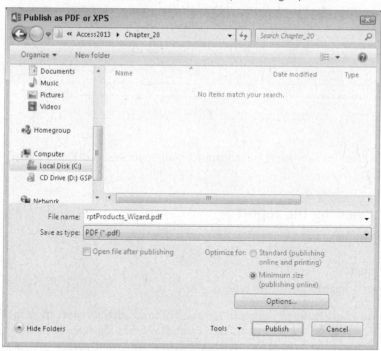

The PDF or XPS view of an Access report is indistinguishable from the report when viewed in Access. Either format is common in many business environments these days.

Viewing the Report in Design view

Right-click the report's title bar or tab and select Design View to show the report in Design view. As shown in Figure 37.19, the report design reflects the choices you made using the Report Wizard.

FIGURE 37.19

A report in Design view

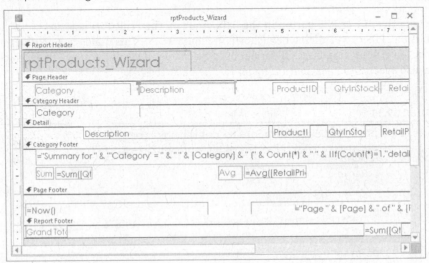

Return to the Print Preview mode by choosing Report Tools Design ⇨ Views ⇨ View arrow ⇨ Print Preview.

Printing or viewing the report

The final step in the process of creating a report is printing or viewing it.

Printing the report

There are several ways to print your report:

- **Choose File ⇨ Print in the main Access window (with a report highlighted in the Navigation pane).** The standard Print dialog box appears. You use this dialog box to select the print range, number of copies, and print properties.

- **Change to Print Preview view, and then click the Print button in the Print group of the Print Preview tab.** The report is immediately sent to the default printer without displaying a Print dialog box.

Viewing the report

You can view a report in four different views: Design, Report, Layout, and Print Preview using the View drop-down list choices in the Views group of the Home tab or Design tab. You can also print a report to the default Windows printer.

The report Design view is one of two places where you create and modify reports. You began working with a new report by selecting a table or query to serve as the new report's data source. Click the Blank Report button in the Reports group of the Create tab. By default, the new report appears in Layout view, as shown in Figure 37.20.

FIGURE 37.20

Layout view of a new blank report

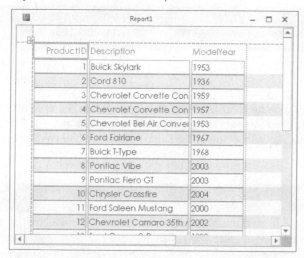

Layout view enables you to see the relative positions of the controls on the report's surface, as well as the margins, page headers and footers, and other report details.

The main constraint of Layout view is that you can't make fine adjustments to a report's design unless you put the report in Design view. Layout view is primarily intended to allow you to adjust the relative positions of controls on the report and is not meant for moving individual controls around on the report.

While in Layout view, you can also right-click any control and select Properties from the shortcut menu. The Property Sheet allows you to modify the default settings for the selected control.

Figure 37.21 shows the Ribbon while a report is open in Layout view. The Report Layout Tools offers four contextual tabs—Design, Arrange, Format, and Page Setup— that you can use to add and modify the controls for the reports. For example, use the Add Existing Fields button in the Tools group of the Design contextual tab to add the fields for the report.

FIGURE 37.21

The Ribbon offers four contextual tabs while a report is open in Layout view.

> **NOTE**
>
> Layout view first became available in Access 2007. Versions earlier than 2007 do not support Layout view.

Saving the report

Save the report design at any time by choosing File ⇨ Save, File ⇨ Save As, or File ⇨ Export in Design view, or by clicking the Save button on the Quick Access Toolbar. The first time you save a report (or any time you select Save As or Export), a dialog box enables you to select or type a name.

> **TIP**
>
> You might find it useful to save a copy of a report before beginning maintenance work on the report. Reports tend to be pretty complicated, and it's easy to make a mistake on a report's design and not remember how to return the report to its previous state. A backup provides a valuable safeguard against accidental loss of a report's design.

Summary

Reports are an important part of most Access applications. Reports enable you to share data from the database with colleagues who don't have access to the database itself or aren't proficient in using a database. At this point you should be able to:

- Use the Report Wizard to create a report based on a table or query.
- Change between different report views.
- Change the report theme and colors in Design view.
- Preview, print, and save the report.

Keeping Information at Hand with OneNote

One of the challenges in managing any project is how to bring together all the information so that it's at your fingertips. This typically includes making notes, tracking tasks, creating data files, looking at Web information, and handling other activities in different programs. Storing all the files or having many open program windows onscreen has never been a satisfactory way to manage your project's information. Microsoft OneNote 2013 provides that elusive solution, enabling you to bring together notes and other types of information in an accessible way. If you're ready to see how you can be better organized and more effective at anything you do, read this chapter and learn how to use OneNote.

Who Needs OneNote and Why

OneNote is designed to function as a digital three-ring binder. With a three-ring binder, you can add and rearrange pages, write on pages, paste clipped articles on a page, or even punch holes in a magazine or report page to add it to the binder. You also can add plastic sleeves that expand the notebook's versatility, enabling you to include non-paper materials in the notebook.

OneNote brings the same type of versatility to tracking all sorts of digital information in a centralized location. You can add a variety of information to a OneNote notebook — notes, Outlook tasks, pictures, files, screen clips, audio or video recordings, details about a meeting, information copied from a web page, and much more. But, the best part is that you can see and use *all* the information at the same time — you don't have to open multiple files and arrange multiple windows.

These capabilities make OneNote a perfect tool for managing information related to specific projects or clients, research or study subjects, or topical areas of interest. Although OneNote's versatility can make it useful to anyone, users in the following types of situations will find OneNote an especially valuable tool:

- If you attend many meetings that generate ideas and action items, OneNote can be perfect for tracking these. Because OneNote enables you to organize information quickly and flexibly, you can easily add the notes and tasks you need. You also can jump right to the information you need as a meeting discussion changes.

- If you often handle research projects in which you bring together information from a variety of sources, OneNote provides a great central storage location for statistics, citations, and useful documents.

- If you like to brainstorm or capture ideas about a topic over time, OneNote helps you keep the information together so that the big picture comes together. You can even capture your ideas as an audio recording so that you're not slowed down by your typing skills.

- If you're a student and need to keep together notes and information for each class, OneNote enables you to collect all the notes and schedule information that you need to stay prepared.

- If you need to use your notes on multiple computers or share them with other users, OneNote enables you to place a notebook on a shared network location or even a USB thumb drive. In this way, OneNote gives you the opportunity to take your work with you or keep others involved.

Touring OneNote

OneNote divides information into *notebooks*, *sections*, and *pages*. You can start OneNote by clicking its tile on the Windows 8 Start screen or by using the Windows 7 Start menu (Start⇨All Programs⇨Microsoft Office⇨OneNote 2013). If you don't see OneNote on the Windows 8 Start screen, you can use the Search charm to find the program's startup tile and then click it. When you store a notebook on your computer's hard disk, each notebook is set up as a separate subfolder within the `My Documents\OneNote Notebooks` folder within your Windows 7 or 8 user folder. The notebooks folder appears as the `OneNote Notebooks` folder within the Documents library.

Each section you add to a notebook appears as a file within the folder for the specific notebook, and that file stores the information for the pages in the section.

In the OneNote window, this arrangement translates to a Click to view other notebooks button at upper left, which shows the current notebook name; click it and then click on a listed notebook to change to that notebook and display its sections, as seen in Figure 38.1. Tabs for the sections within the selected notebook appear above the page area. Clicking a section tab selects that section, displaying page tabs for the pages in the section at the right. Click on a page tab to display the contents of that page. OneNote also includes a Ribbon with tabs and choices, just as in the other Office applications.

FIGURE 38.1

Clicking selects a notebook, section, or page.

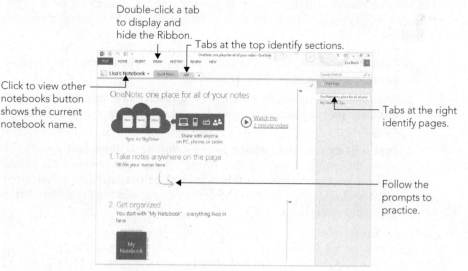

Double-click a tab to display and hide the Ribbon.

Tabs at the top identify sections.

Click to view other notebooks button shows the current notebook name.

Tabs at the right identify pages.

Follow the prompts to practice.

38

As Figure 38.1 also shows, by default, the first time you launch OneNote, the new notebook that you create includes a section named *Quick Notes* with descriptive instructions to help you get started. Scroll down the *OneNote: one place for all of your notes* page to read the useful information it offers. As shown in Figure 38.1, the first instruction on the page even prompts you to practice by writing or typing your name. The page also includes a variety of links to brief videos to help you learn more about using OneNote.

OneNote also now incorporates the Ribbon. The Ribbon is collapsed by default, as shown in Figure 38.1. To display it, double-click any Ribbon tab. Double-click a tab to re-collapse the Ribbon. The rest of the figures in this chapter will display the Ribbon uncollapsed so that you can see its tools and choices.

If you want to close any open notebook, click the Click to view other notebooks button, right-click the notebook name, and then click Close This Notebook. To close the current notebook, just click its name at upper left and click Close This Notebook. You can reopen a notebook at any time by choosing File ➪ Open, selecting a location from the Open from other locations list, clicking Browse, and navigating to and selecting the notebook folder in the Open Notebook dialog box, and then clicking Open.

Creating a Notebook

You can create a notebook for any project, client, subject, research topic, or purpose that you want. Because each notebook represents a folder, you can create as many notebooks as your system has storage to handle. Follow these steps to create a new notebook in OneNote:

1. **Choose File ➪ New.** The Backstage view prompts you to select the location where you would like to store the notebook.

2. **Click Computer under New Notebook to specify that you want to store the notebook on your local computer.** The Backstage view prompts you to name the notebook.

3. **Type a name for the notebook into the Notebook Name text box.** Figure 38.2 shows the notebook creation in progress. (If you want to create the notebook in a folder other than the default folder, such as a shared network folder, click Create in a different folder, navigate to the desired location in the Create New Notebook dialog box, and click Create.)

FIGURE 38.2

The Backstage view prompts you to name the new notebook.

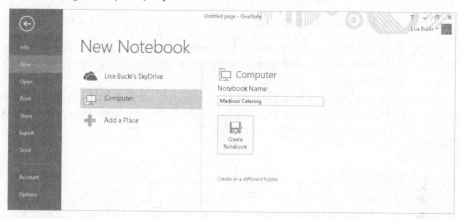

4. **Click Create Notebook.** The new notebook appears onscreen, ready for your use.

The new notebook will have a single section called *New Section 1* that contains a single blank page called *Untitled Page*.

> **NOTE**
> You can rename a notebook later by right-clicking on the notebook name on the upper-left, and clicking Rename. Change the contents of the Display Name text box as needed and then click OK.

Creating a Notebook in the Cloud

Rather than choosing to store the OneNote notebook on your computer, you can choose to store it in the cloud in Step 2 of the preceding section. Saving the notebook on the web in SkyDrive enables you to access it from anywhere, using a different computer or other devices, and optionally share it with other users. Leave your SkyDrive selected in Step 2, make an entry in the Notebook Name text box, and then click Create Notebook. See the section called "Working with Notes in the Cloud" for more about using SkyDrive online.

Creating a Section

Each new section in a notebook works much like a tabbed divider added into a three-ring binder. The section sets off the pages within and provides a label for them. If you create a notebook for client information, for example, you might create a new section for each client. If you create a notebook for school studies, you might create a section for each class during the current semester.

To add a new section to a notebook:

1. **Click the Click to view other notebooks button, and then click the name of the notebook to which you want to add a section.** The contents of the selected notebook appear.

2. **Click the Create a New Section tab (with the plus on it) to the right of the rightmost section tab.** The new Section tab appears, with the temporary name highlighted, as shown in Figure 38.3.

FIGURE 38.3

Type a name to replace the placeholder in the new section's tab.

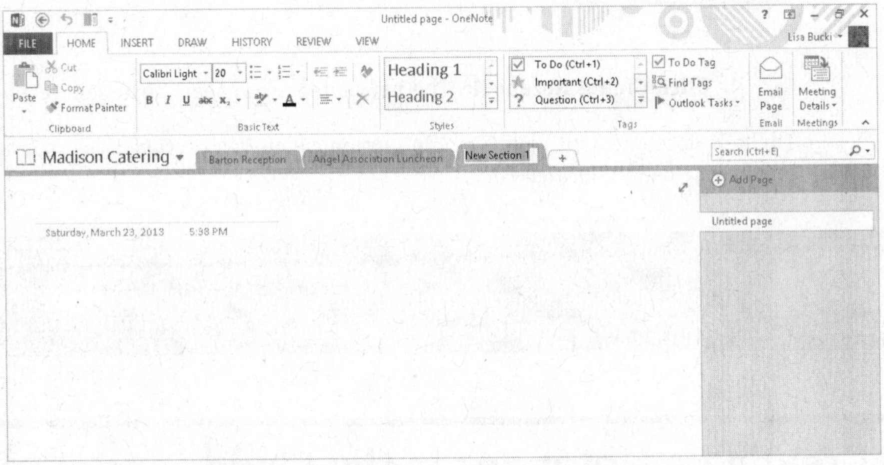

3. **Type the name for the new section and press Enter.** The finished section appears, waiting for you to add pages, notes, and other content.

Creating a Page

Each new section you create includes, by default, a new, blank page called *Untitled page*. You can add pages as needed to further organize the information in a notebook. For example, within a section for a client, you could have a page for each project you're handling for that client. Within a section for a class, you could have a page for each assignment, report, or exam. Because you can switch between pages simply by clicking a page tab, dividing your notes into more pages actually saves time because you can jump to the information you need by clicking a tab rather than having to scroll around in a lengthy document.

Use these steps to add a page:

1. **Click the Click to view other notebooks button, and then click on the name of the notebook to which you want to add a page.** The contents of the selected notebook appear.

2. **At the top of the notebook, click on the section tab for the section into which you want to add a page.** The tabs for the pages in the section appear at the right.

3. **Click the plus button beside Add Page button at the top of the page tabs area or press Ctrl+N; alternately, you can point to a location between two existing pages and click the plus button that appears to the left to insert the new page between the existing pages.** The new Page tab appears.

4. **Type a new name for the page and then press Enter.** As shown in Figure 38.4, the name you type appears on both the Page tab and in a title area on the new page.

FIGURE 38.4

The page name appears on the Page tab and as a page title.

> **NOTE**
>
> You don't have to save your work in OneNote. The program automatically saves it for you. You can use the Export command on the File tab to make a copy of the current notebook file.

You also can use a template to create a page. There are dozens of templates for special purposes from taking lecture notes to keeping meeting notes, to creating a planner, to simply applying a nice design to a page. Choose Insert ⇨ Pages ⇨ Page Templates ⇨ Page Templates. A Templates task pane appears. Click on the triangle beside any category to select it, and then click on a template. OneNote instantly inserts a page using that template design. You also can click Templates on Office.com in the page to search for a template online. Click the pane's Close (X) button to close it when you've finished.

Inserting Notes

Each new page you add to a notebook section is ready to go as a blank slate for your notes, doodles, tasks, and more. Adding notes to a notebook may be the feature you use the most. This section explains how OneNote trumps sticky notes in helping you capture key thoughts.

Plain notes

You can add a note anywhere on a page in OneNote. You're not bound by the tradition of starting at the top and working down to the bottom. Just click anywhere on the page, type the note text (see Figure 38.5), and click outside the note when you've finished. You can press Enter as needed within a note, and pressing Tab after you enter at least one character of text creates table cells within the note. You also can click back on the note to place the insertion point within it to make changes to the note at any time.

FIGURE 38.5

Click and type a note anywhere on a page.

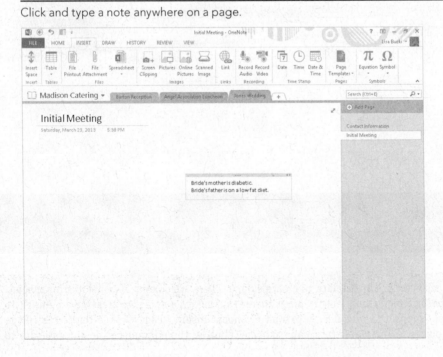

Tagged notes

Tagging a note assigns a category and icon to the note, such as the To Do tag, Important tag, Question tag, Phone number tag, or Idea tag. The tag icon appears beside the note so that you can determine what kind of information a note contains just by scanning the page. You also can view tagged notes by group, as described later in this chapter.

First click in the note to tag. On the Home tab of the Ribbon, click the More button for the Tag This Note gallery in the Tags group, and then click the tag to apply from the drop-down list. You can assign a tag when you create a note or at any later time. To assign the tag when you create the note, click in the page to position the insertion point where you want the note to appear, click the More button in the Tags group, and then click the desired tag type in the menu. A *note container* with the tag icon appears. Type your note text, and then click outside the boundaries to finish.

To assign a tag to an existing note, click the note to display its note container. Then click More on the Tag This Note gallery in the Tags group of the Home tab, and click the tag type in the drop-down list shown in Figure 38.6. (The Remove Tag command at the bottom removes a previously applied tag.) Then click outside the note.

FIGURE 38.6

Tagging a note identifies the type of information the note contains.

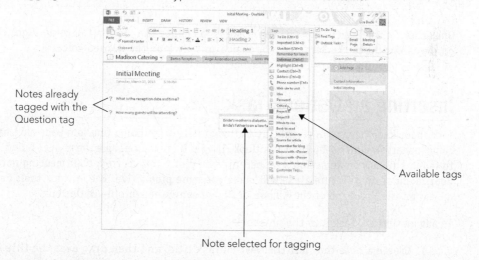

Notes already tagged with the Question tag

Available tags

Note selected for tagging

> **TIP**
>
> You also can convert a note into a To-Do item with a check box beside it. To do so, select the note container, and choose Home ⇨ Tags ⇨ To Do Tag. If the container holds a list of items, a check box appears beside each one. To mark an item as complete, click the empty check box to display a check mark in it.

Extra writing space

Even though you certainly can make room for more information by creating a new page in a section, you also have the option of extending the space available in a page so that it can accommodate more notes or larger items. To add more writing space, click the Insert tab of the Ribbon, and click the Insert Space button in the Insert group. Drag down the page until the down-arrow pointer changes from a single arrow to a layered arrow. Then click on the page. OneNote adds more space on the page. If you scroll back up without adding anything to the new space, the extra space disappears.

Formatting information

If you refer to Figure 38.6, you can see that the Home tab of the Ribbon includes a Basic Text group with a variety of formatting settings. These settings work just as they do in Word. You can drag over text within a note container and then apply formatting to only the selected text via the Mini Toolbar that pops up or the Home tab. Or, you can click the note container title bar to select all of the note text, and then apply the desired formatting.

> **NOTE**
>
> OneNote offers basic formatting styles like those found in Word. Select the note text to which you want to apply the style, open the Styles gallery in the Styles group of the Home tab, and click the style to apply.

One other formatting change you can make is to change the section tab color. Right-click on the tab, point to the Section Color choice, and click on the desired color.

Inserting an Outlook Task

Talk about keeping you on track! Any Outlook task you add on a OneNote page automatically appears in your To-Do list in Outlook. If you, like many people, have ever failed to follow through on an action item because you didn't copy it from your meeting notes to your calendar, this feature alone will make you more productive. The Outlook tools do not appear on the Home tab of the Ribbon until you configure a profile in Outlook.

To add an Outlook Task into the notebook:

1. **Create a note that has the desired task title, and then drag over the title in the note container.**
2. **Click the Outlook Tasks button in the Tags group of the Home tab.** A submenu or list of the flags that you can use to schedule the task — such as Today, Tomorrow, or This Week — appears.
3. **Click the desired flag.** The flag appears in the note container.

NOTE

If you click Custom, a Task window from Outlook opens so that you can enter a custom Start Date and Due Date to schedule the task in the Outlook To-Do List.

As shown in Figure 38.7, when you select the task in your Outlook To-Do list, Outlook identifies it as a task linked to OneNote. The two applications synchronize the task information. Marking the task as complete in Outlook, for example, identifies it as complete in OneNote, dimming the task flag for that note.

FIGURE 38.7

The selected task was created in OneNote and remains synchronized to the notebook.

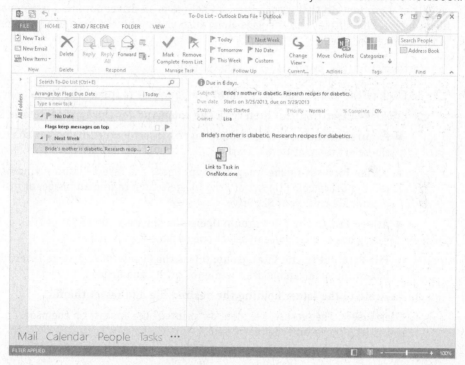

TIP

If you mark a task as complete in Outlook but want to reinstate it in OneNote, deselecting the task in Outlook won't work. You have to select the OneNote task, open the Outlook Tasks menu in the Tags group of the Home tab, and click Delete Outlook Task, and then use the drop-down list again to reapply a task flag. You can then delete the original task in Outlook.

Inserting a Picture or File

If the contents you want to capture already exist in a file outside OneNote, you can insert the information. Inserting information works much the same as opening a file: You give a command, navigate to the folder holding the file to insert, and select and insert the file.

When you insert a picture, the image appears on the OneNote page, where you can move or resize it as desired. You might insert a picture that shows a look or idea that you're after, or that you want to use to illustrate some other document at a later time. (You can copy-and-paste the picture from OneNote.)

There are two different ways in which you can insert a file. A regular insert operation displays a hyperlinked icon for the file on the page. Double-clicking the icon opens the file in its home application. Or, to display the file's contents on the OneNote page, insert the file as a printout. In that case, a special OneNote print driver outputs a version of the file's contents that displays on the page along with an icon for the file and a hyperlink to the original document.

To insert a picture, file, or printout, use these steps:

1. **Click in the page at the location where you want to insert the item.**
2. **Click the Insert tab and then click the command for the type of item to insert.**
   - **Pictures in the Images group:** Opens the Insert Picture dialog box so that you can select the picture to insert.
   - **Online Pictures in the Images group.** Opens the Insert Pictures window, so you can use Office.com Clip Art or Bing Image Search to find an image, or insert a picture file from your SkyDrive.
   - **Attach File in the Files group:** Opens the Choose a File or Set of Files to Insert dialog box so that you can select one or more files to insert.
   - **File Printout in the Files group:** Opens the Choose Document to Insert dialog box so that you can choose the file to "print" and display.
3. **Navigate to the folder holding the desired file and select the file.**
4. **Click Insert.** The picture, file icon, or "printed" file appears on the page. Figure 38.8 shows an example of each.

> **NOTE**
>
> For a hyperlink, click Link in the Links group of the Insert tab and enter Text to display, if any. Then use either the Browse the Web or Browse for File buttons to select the location or file to link to. Click OK to finish creating the hyperlink.

FIGURE 38.8

This page holds an icon for an inserted file, an inserted picture, and a "printout" of a file.

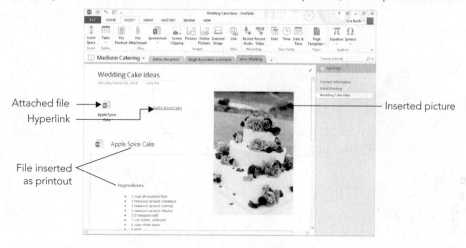

Attached file

Hyperlink

Inserted picture

File inserted as printout

Inserting a Screen Clipping

Adding a screen clipping to OneNote literally enables you to take a picture of something on your computer screen and place it on a OneNote page. You might use this feature to capture information that appears onscreen during a Webcast or shared online work session. Or you can capture information from a web page, such as grabbing the headline and lead photo from a news site so that you remember where you saw the information. When you take a screen clipping from a web page, OneNote also inserts a hyperlink to the web page.

Here's how to create a screen clip in OneNote:

1. **Click in the page at the location where you want to insert the item in OneNote.**
2. **Switch to the location from which you want to clip the screen.** For example, display the desktop or launch your web browser and browse to the page that holds the information to clip.
3. **Switch back to OneNote.**
4. **Choose Insert⇨Images⇨Screen Clipping.** OneNote minimizes, and the location you selected in Step 2 appears. The screen appears grayed out to indicate that OneNote is waiting for you to make your clip selection.
5. **Drag diagonally to make the selection.** When you release the mouse, the clip appears in a note container along with any hyperlink, as in the example in Figure 38.9.

FIGURE 38.9

The screen clip appears as a new note.

Roses
http://www.wilton.com/technique/Roses
Screen clipping taken: 3/23/2013 7:07 PM

> **NOTE**
>
> If you want to insert a plain hyperlink rather than a file or screen clipping, choose Insert ⇨ Links ⇨ Link. Type the URL to link to in the Address text box of the Hyperlink dialog box, or click the Browse for File button to select a file to link to. If you want the hyperlink to appear as a label or descriptive text rather than a URL or file path, make an entry in the Text to display text box. Then click OK. Use the Insert ⇨ Recording ⇨ Record Audio and Insert ⇨ Recording ⇨ Record Video commands to insert recorded content.

Writing on a Page

If you have a Tablet PC or a pen input device attached to your computer, you can choose a pen and then use the stylus to create a handwritten note, also called *ink*, like this:

1. **With the page on which you want to add the note selected, click the Draw tab on the Ribbon.**

2. **In the Tools group, click the More button for the pens gallery, and then click the desired pen.** The pen becomes active for the stylus.

3. **Write on the tablet with the stylus to create the note.** The note text appears on the page, as in the example in Figure 38.10.

FIGURE 38.10

Create handwritten notes on a Tablet PC or pen input device.

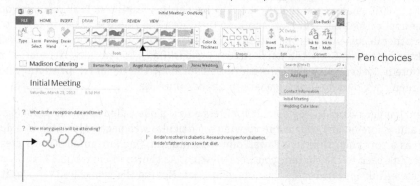

Pen choices

Handwritten text

4. **Click the Type button in the Tools group to turn off the pen (stylus) input.**
The stylus resumes working like a mouse.

> **NOTE**
>
> You also can use the ink feature with a regular mouse rather than a pen input device, but because writing with a mouse is rather difficult, you might change your mind after you try it.

If you want to convert the handwritten note to text, move the mouse over the note so that the note container appears. Click (or tap) the top edge of the note container to select all the note contents. Then choose Draw ⇨ Convert ⇨ Ink to Text. Figure 38.11 shows a selected note container with some handwriting and the same note with the ink converted to text. Converting the note to text in this way makes it easier to edit later, if needed.

FIGURE 38.11

You can select a handwritten note and convert it to text.

> **TIP**
>
> You also can create drawings on the page using a Tablet PC or pen input device.

38

Using Linked Note Taking

OneNote 2010 enables you to dock it to the side of the desktop so that you can work with other applications but still have access to OneNote. This makes it easier to take notes from other documents and the Internet. To dock or undock One Note, click the Dock to Desktop button on OneNote's Quick Access Toolbar (QAT). To redisplay the toolbar while OneNote is docked, click the bar with three dots along the top of the OneNote pane. You can then click Dock to Desktop again to undock OneNote.

When you dock OneNote, by default it enters a new mode called *Linked Note Taking*. When you add a note on any page while viewing a particular web page or location in a document such as a particular slide in a PowerPoint presentation, OneNote automatically creates a hyperlink back to the content you were viewing. As shown in Figure 38.12, an icon for the hyperlink appears beside the note container. Moving the mouse pointer over it displays information about the source, and clicking it redisplays the linked location.

FIGURE 38.12

Working with hyperlinked notes

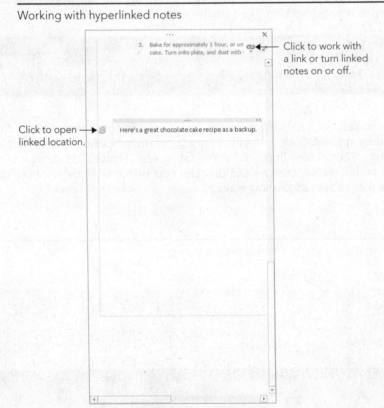

Click to work with a link or turn linked notes on or off.

Click to open linked location.

Here's a great chocolate cake recipe as a backup.

Using Send To OneNote

Another way to insert content into OneNote is to use the Send To OneNote feature, which has been enhanced in OneNote 2013. This feature starts automatically when you start OneNote and appears as a button on the taskbar. If it doesn't appear there, you can click View⇨Window⇨Send to OneNote Tool to display it. The tool works somewhat differently depending on what you're grabbing, so here are the overview steps:

1. **Go to the destination document, and if needed, select information in it.** For example, you could select an Excel chart.

2. **Click Send To OneNote on the taskbar.** Its pop-up appears as shown in Figure 38.13.

FIGURE 38.13

Using Send To OneNote

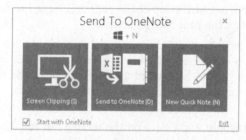

3. **Click the Send to OneNote button.**

4. **Select the Notebook, section, and page where you'd like to place the note in the Select Location in OneNote dialog box.**

5. **Click OK, and then respond to any other prompts that appear.** For example, if you're sending information from Excel, an Insert File window opens, and you have to click one of three choices: Attach File, Insert Spreadsheet, or Insert a Chart or Table.

> **NOTE**
> The New Quick Note choice in Figure 38.13 opens a quick note window that will enable you to type a note that will be inserted in your Quick Notes section. By default, this section appears in the first notebook you create in OneNote and will not function properly if copied or moved elsewhere. Go to your Quick Notes by clicking Quick Notes at the bottom of the Notebook list.

Organizing, Finding, and Sharing

Just as you can rearrange, change, and view pages in a three-ring binder, your OneNote notes remain flexible so that you can update, change, rearrange, and use them exactly as you need to. You can search for notes or even publish them for use by others. This section in the chapter explains how you can get the most out of all the content that you pile in to your OneNote notebooks.

Reorganizing

You can tackle any of a number of tasks to reorganize and rearrange information on a page, between sections, and between notebooks. These are the most common actions you will use to keep your notebook information up-to-date:

- **Rename a Section:** Right-click on the section tab, click Rename, type the new name, and press Enter.

- **Rename a Page:** Click in the title box at the top of the page and make the desired changes. The new name appears in the page tab, as well.

- **Move a Note on a Page:** Click the note, move the mouse pointer over the bar at the top of the note container until the four-headed arrow appears, and then drag. To move an icon, drag it. To move a picture or inserted file printout, place the mouse pointer over the picture or printout and click the select button that appears; then, drag the picture.

- **Move a section to another notebook:** Right-click on the section tab and click Move or Copy. In the Move or Copy Section dialog box that appears (Figure 38.14), click on the notebook into which you want to move the section, and then click the Move button.

- **Move a section within the notebook.** Drag the section tab left or right until the black triangle appears in the desired destination, and then release the mouse button.

- **Move or copy a page to another section:** Right-click on the page tab, and then click Move or Copy. Select the desired section in the Move or Copy Pages dialog box that appears (it resembles the Move or Copy Section dialog box in Figure 38.14), click the section into which you want to move or copy the page, and then click the Move or Copy button.

FIGURE 38.14

You can move a section into another notebook.

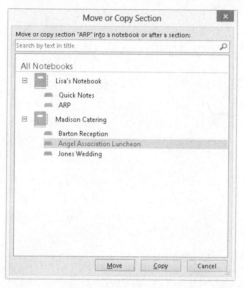

- **Move a page within its own section:** Drag the page tab until the black triangle appears at the desired destination location, and then release the mouse button.

- **Delete a note or other item from the page:** Move the mouse pointer over the item or note container, and then click the select button that appears. Press Delete.

- **Delete a page or section:** Right-click on the page or section tab, and then click Delete.

Viewing tagged notes

Taking the time to tag notes pays off when you need to view key note information later. OneNote can display a Tags Summary pane (Figure 38.15), which displays the tagged notes from all your open notebooks. To open the Tags Summary pane, click Find Tags in the Tags group of the Home tab. To change how the pane lists the notes, open the Group tags by drop-down list at the top of the task pane, and then click the desired grouping: Tag Name, Section, Title, Date, or Note Text. You can even add a new page listing the tagged notes to the current notebook by clicking the Create Summary Page button at the bottom of the pane. Click the pane's Close (X) button when you finish viewing the tagged notes.

FIGURE 38.15

Viewing tagged notes can help you find key information stored in your notebooks.

Searching notes

When you want to find a particular note, type a search word or phrase into the Search text box above the page tabs, and then press Enter. The Search feature highlights every item on the page that holds matching text. The search results also highlight the tab for every page that holds the matching text; click page tabs or the arrows in the Search textbox area to view additional matches. To close the search, click the X button at the right end of the Search text box to clear the search.

Saving note information for others

You can use the Export command to convert the current page, section, or notebook to another file format to share the information with others who need the information but don't necessarily need to have access to your OneNote notebook. You can select one of several formats: Single File Web Page (viewable with a Web browser), OneNote 2010-2013 Section or OneNote 2007 Section, Word Document (for Word 2013, 2010 and 2007 users), Word 97-2003 Document (for users of an older Word version), as well as the PDF and XPS formats.

Use this process to save information from the notebook in another file format:

1. **Select the notebook and section, and then select the pages to publish using the page tabs.** To select a single page, click on its tab. To select multiple pages, click on the first tab and then Ctrl+click to add other pages or Shift+click to select a range of pages.

2. **Choose File ⇨ Export.** The Export choices appear in Backstage view (Figure 38.16).

FIGURE 38.16

Saving notebook content in another format enables other users to view your notes.

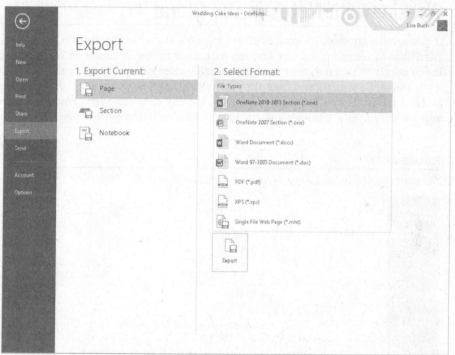

3. **Click the information you want to save in the 1. Export Current list.**

4. **Click the desired file type in the 2. Select Format list.**

5. **Click the Export button.** The Save As dialog box appears.

6. **Type a file name in the File name text box.**

7. **Select another folder to save to if needed.**

8. **Click Save.** OneNote creates the file, which you can then e-mail or otherwise provide to the desired recipients. The recipient can then double-click on the file in Windows to open the file in its associated application.

> **TIP**
>
> If you also have Microsoft Office Word 2013 installed, you can publish any page as a blog entry. Choose File ⇨ Send ⇨ Send to Blog. If you aren't already signed up with a blogging provider, you will be prompted to do so. Otherwise, the prompts help you configure Office to post to your blogging provider. If you're already set up with a blogging provider, the notes appear as a new blog post in Word, and you can edit them from there and then click the Publish button in the Blog group of the Blog Post tab to make the post. You also can use OneNote's File ⇨ Send command to e-mail the current page.

Working with Notes in the Cloud

If you saved a notebook to your SkyDrive as noted earlier in the chapter, you can choose File ⇨ Info to see commands for working with it, as shown in Figure 38.17. You can click Invite people to this notebook, enter the e-mail addresses of people you want to share with, add message text, and then click Share to share the notebook. If you click the Settings button beside the online notebook, you can click the Sync choice in the menu that appears to sync local changes and changes by sharers to the online copies.

FIGURE 38.17

You can sync, invite, and view an online notebook on the Info Page.

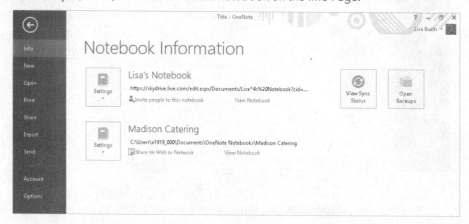

To view the notebook online, go to skydrive.live.com, sign in to your SkyDrive account, click the tile for the folder holding the notebook (usually Documents by default), and then click the tile for the notebook. The notebook opens in the OneNote Web App, as shown in the example in Figure 38.18. It offers a more limited number of tools than the full version of OneNote, but does enable you to keep up with your notes when you're away from your main working location.

FIGURE 38.18

Viewing and working with a notebook on SkyDrive

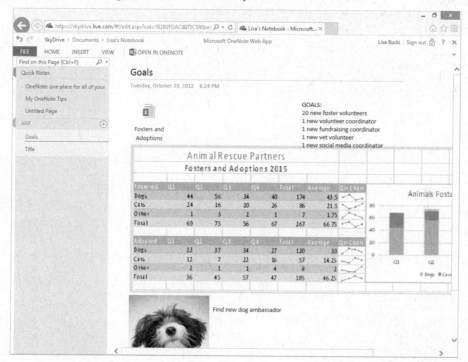

Summary

You're now well on your way to getting your life organized with Microsoft OneNote. This chapter explained the benefits of using OneNote and how OneNote organizes information. You should now be comfortable with:

- Creating a notebook, sections, and pages to arrange information in the way that suits your needs.
- Adding notes and tasks on a page, as well as how to insert a file, picture, or screen clipping and how to write on a page.
- Creating linked notes when OneNote is docked.
- Reorganizing and updating content.
- Saving information for others.
- Working with your notes in the cloud.

Part VIII

Sharing and Collaborating in the Cloud and Applications

The modern workplace demands more flexibility than ever before, including the flexibility to use your data where you want on the devices you want and to share it with the team members you want, as well as the flexibility to use data created by another person or in another application across a variety of documents. This part shows you how to use the flexibility built into Office to produce results and collaborate more quickly via the cloud and data sharing features.

Collaborating in the Cloud with SkyDrive

IN THIS CHAPTER

Learning the difference between SkyDrive and SkyDrive Pro

Saving to your SkyDrive and sharing files

Working with SkyDrive Pro

Using SkyDrive Pro with Office 365

Office 2013 includes features that integrate it into the cloud more than ever before, and this chapter serves as your roadmap for navigating them. The Microsoft account that you use to sign into Windows 8 and to Office applications includes free SkyDrive storage. You store files in your SkyDrive and share them from there directly, using the Save or Save As command on the File tab. If needed, you also can install client software to integrate SkyDrive with your Windows desktop file storage. Most versions of Office 2013 also include the SkyDrive Pro application. SkyDrive Pro works with a separate cloud-based service called Office 365 as well as SharePoint. It enables you to sync files from your online library to a local folder, as you'll learn near the conclusion of the chapter.

Understanding SkyDrive Pro and SkyDrive for Windows

SkyDrive is cloud-based service that offers you online storage and an online workspace. You automatically receive a SkyDrive account when you create a Microsoft account to sign into Windows 8 or Office 2013. Your free SkyDrive account includes 7 GB of free online storage space, accessed through your Microsoft account sign-in information. You can upgrade your SkyDrive account for a fee to include even more storage. But once your account is established you can share files and folders and use SkyDrive as your personal gateway for sharing files and folders.

> **NOTE**
>
> Previously, SkyDrive accounts offered 25 GB of free storage, but Microsoft reduced the free storage to 7 GB. If you established your Microsoft account prior to that change, as of this writing you should still enjoy 25 GB of free SkyDrive storage.

Most versions of Office 2013 include an application called *SkyDrive Pro*. SkyDrive Pro does not work with the SkyDrive account associated with your Microsoft account, but instead works with your library on your organization's *Office 365* site (as well as SharePoint and SharePoint online sites, but this book focuses on Office 365). Office 365 is a more team-oriented type of cloud-based sharing and requires a subscription. This is discussed further in the "Accessing Your SkyDrive Pro Library on Office 365" section later in this chapter.

You need to understand that SkyDrive syncing and SkyDrive Pro syncing are two distinct things. SkyDrive syncing uses the SkyDrive for Windows application. It sets up a copy of the cloud-based SkyDrive folders associated with your Microsoft account on your computer's hard disk, and keeps files synced between those local folders and your online SkyDrive. SkyDrive Pro syncing, in contrast, uses the SkyDrive Pro 2013 application included with some versions of Office, and syncs the online library associated with your Office 365 account with a location you specify on your computer's hard disk. You'll learn about each type of syncing later in the chapter.

Saving to the Cloud with SkyDrive

You can save to your SkyDrive storage directly from most Office 2013 applications. (Access and Outlook 2013 do not let you save to your SkyDrive, and OneNote 2013 notebooks sync to your SkyDrive using a different process as is covered in Chapter 38.) As long as you are signed into Office using the Microsoft account that has the same sign-in settings as the SkyDrive account that you want to use (some users have multiple accounts that include SkyDrive) you want to save to, the process should work seamlessly. If you have separate SkyDrive accounts for personal and work purposes, or if you are using a system where a colleague or family member is signed in, you could inadvertently upload sensitive files to the wrong account. In such instances you'll need to be a little more careful about saving your files.

The rest of this section covers the two SkyDrive operations you can perform within applicable Office applications: saving to your SkyDrive, and saving and sharing a file.

Saving

Saving to your SkyDrive is as easy as saving to your system's hard disk. SkyDrive has three top-level folders by default: Documents, Pictures, and Public. By default, the Documents and Pictures folders are not shared, but the Public folder is. So it's a good policy to save any file that you want to share with other users to the Public folder. Once you get comfortable working with your SkyDrive online, you'll learn how to create other folders and share them. Follow these steps to save a file to your SkyDrive:

1. **Open the file that you want to save to your SkyDrive, or save and name the current file.** While you can save a new file to the SkyDrive, chances are you will want both a local copy on your computer and a cloud copy, so saving is a manual way to make sure you have the local copy.

2. **Choose File ⇨ Save As.** The Save As choices appear in Backstage view.

> **NOTE**
>
> If you are not signed into Office with a Microsoft account, you will see a Sign In button. Click it, click Sign In in the Sign in to Office window that appears, enter your Microsoft account username and password, and sign in.

3. **In the middle pane, under Save As, click your SkyDrive if needed.** As shown in Figure 39.1, the right pane lists any Recent Folders you've used. You can click one to save to it and skip to Step 6, or go on to Step 4.

FIGURE 39.1

Choose your SkyDrive after clicking Save As.

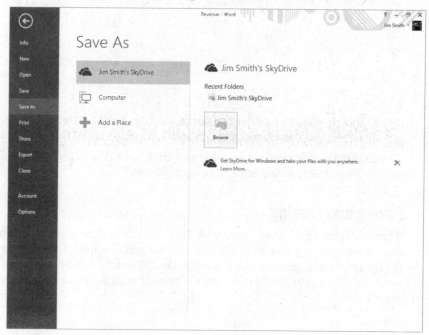

39

4. **Click Browse.** You may see a message that the application is contacting the (SkyDrive) server for information. After the connection is made, the Save As dialog box appears as shown in Figure 39.2. Note in the address bar that the current folder name is a series of letters and numbers. That's because the application (Word in this case) has prepared a virtual copy of the file to upload.

FIGURE 39.2

Specify a save location as you would for any file, and then click Save.

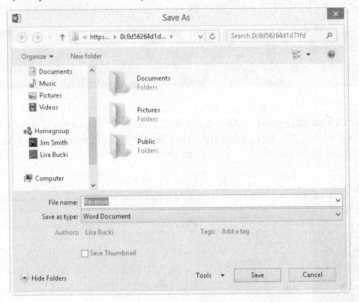

5. **Double-click the folder to save to, such as Public.** After contacting the SkyDrive server, the Save As dialog box displays the contents of that folder, if any.

6. **Edit the file name as desired, and click Save.** The Office application uploads the file to the specified folder on your SkyDrive.

Saving and sharing

When you *share* a file stored on your SkyDrive with other users, the process sends an email message with a link they can follow to see and download the file from your SkyDrive via a web browser. The process works differently depending on whether you've saved the file to your SkyDrive during the current work session in the Office application you're using.

If you've just saved the file to your SkyDrive using the preceding steps, follow these steps to share:

1. **Choose File ➪ Share.**

2. **In the middle pane, under Share, click Invite People.** As shown in Figure 39.3, the right pane enables you to enter recipient e-mail addresses and a message.

FIGURE 39.3

Sharing a file via SkyDrive

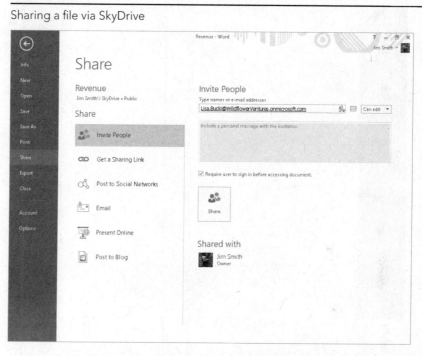

3. **In the Type names or e-mail addresses text box, enter or specify one or more e-mail addresses, separating addresses with a comma or semicolon (followed by an optional space).** As you type, a list of suggestions may appear.

4. **(Optional) To enable the user to view but not edit the file, click Can edit to open the drop-down list, and then click Can view to change the setting.**

5. **If enabled, type a personal message in the space provided.**

6. **To require the recipients to sign in with a Microsoft account to view the files, click the Require user to sign in before accessing document check box to check it.**

7. **Click Share.** SkyDrive sends the sharing e-mail message. After that, each recipient's name appears under Shared with on the Share page.

If you haven't just saved a file to your SkyDrive and choose File ⇨ Share ⇨ Invite People, you'll see the Save To Cloud button shown in Figure 39.4. Click it, and then follow the prompts that appear (which resemble the previously described processes to save and then share the file).

FIGURE 39.4

If you try to share a file before saving to your SkyDrive, the Save To Cloud button appears.

SkyDrive for Windows Application versus SkyDrive in Office

Using SkyDrive as described in the previous section has a limitation. The files you upload to SkyDrive exist independently of the copies on your hard disk. For example, if you or another user with whom you've shared a Word file (with Can edit enabled) makes changes to a file via Word Web App on your online SkyDrive, you may need to sync the files manually. As shown in Figure 39.5, the Save button on the QAT changes to include a refresh indicator. (If you want to be able to compare the changes that were made online to the local copy of the file, make a copy of the local file and rename the copy. Then, when you refresh the shared file with the changes from the SkyDrive version, you can use the Compare Documents feature to compare the two files. See the section called "Comparing Documents" in Chapter 11.)

FIGURE 39.5

Save a shared document from the QAT to update it with all user changes.

Microsoft has created another way to take your SkyDrive file syncing to a more secure and flexible level: the SkyDrive for Windows client application. And even limiting it to SkyDrive "for Windows" is not strictly accurate. You also can download a SkyDrive app for computers running the Mac OS X Lion operating system and mobile SkyDrive apps for Windows Phone, iOS, and Android. The various client apps will keep your files synced between your SkyDrive and any computer or mobile phone device where the app is installed. This means you have access to the latest version of your files from any device at any time.

Some versions of Windows 8 are now shipping with SkyDrive for Windows already installed. If you are running Office 2013 on Windows 7 or for some reason don't have it in Windows 8, you can install it. You can verify whether you have SkyDrive for Windows by opening a folder window from the desktop. As shown in Figure 39.6, expand the Favorites in the Navigation pane at the left and see if SkyDrive is listed. If it is, the SkyDrive client is installed and you can see the local copies of your SkyDrive folders and files.

FIGURE 39.6

When SkyDrive for Windows is installed, it appears under Favorites in File Explorer (Windows 8) or Windows Explorer (Windows 7).

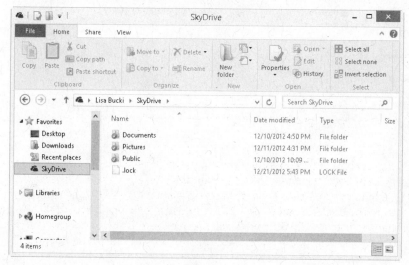

39

To download the SkyDrive desktop client (or to learn about and find the versions for the other platforms noted here), go to `http://windows.microsoft.com/en-US/skydrive/download` and click the Download button. You can then double-click the downloaded file to install it. The rest of this section assumes you have the client installed and are read to work with it.

> **TIP**
>
> In Windows 8, you also can access and work with files on your SkyDrive using the SkyDrive Windows 8 app on the Start screen. Display the Start screen and click the SkyDrive tile to start that app and connect with your SkyDrive.

Saving and viewing your files

Even with the SkyDrive client installed, the process for saving an Office file to your SkyDrive is the same as described earlier. The only difference is that when you click Browse, the Save As dialog box displays your local SkyDrive folders (see Figure 39.7), versus the virtual location shown earlier (see Figure 39.2). When you save to one of the online SkyDrive folders, the Office application again contacts the SkyDrive server and saves the file there, but it also saves a copy to the corresponding local SkyDrive subfolder.

FIGURE 39.7

Your local SkyDrive client folders are part of your user personal folders.

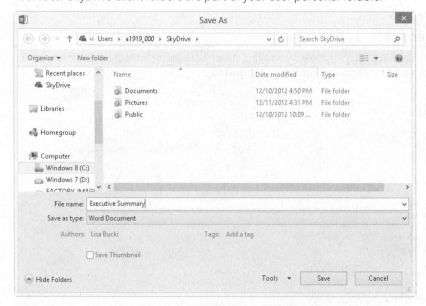

To view the files in a local SkyDrive folder, click SkyDrive under Favorites, and then double-click folders as needed to navigate to the desired location in the window. The files appear as in any folder window. Once you've navigated to a file, you can share it via the local SkyDrive folder. To share, right-click the file, point to SkyDrive, and click Share, as shown in Figure 39.8. After you do so, your SkyDrive opens in your web browser. Even though your SkyDrive and the file will appear, click Sign in to continue the sharing process. At that point, the screen shown in Figure 39.9 appears, so you can address and send an e-mail message sharing the file. Enter the desired recipient e-mail addresses and a message and click Share.

FIGURE 39.8

You also can share a file from your local SkyDrive client folder.

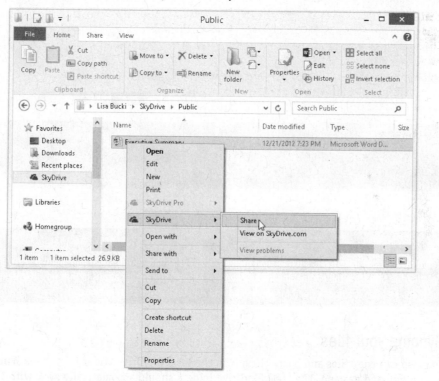

FIGURE 39.9

Finishing the share online on your SkyDrive

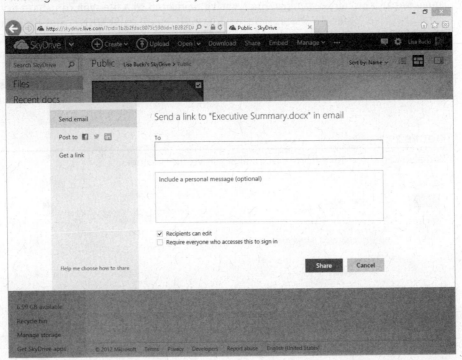

Syncing your files

You also can copy files and paste them into the local SkyDrive client folders via Windows by copying and pasting. The local SkyDrive folders should automatically sync with the SkyDrive folders in a matter of minutes. In Figure 39.10, the bottom file, Long Report, was copied within Windows. As shown by the check mark on its file icon, it has been automatically synced to the online SkyDrive. Assuming you are logged into Windows with the Microsoft account that corresponds to your SkyDrive, the syncing should occur automatically.

FIGURE 39.10

The Long Report file was copied to the local SkyDrive subfolder in Windows; the
check on the file icon shows that it has synced automatically with the online SkyDrive.

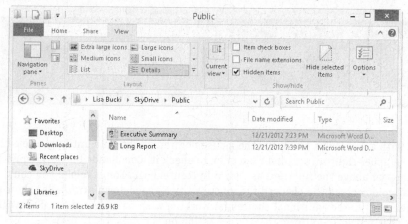

Viewing and working with SkyDrive files online

SkyDrive initially offered convenience because you could access your files via any web
browser and Internet connection. That holds true—the integration with the Office 2013
applications just adds another level of convenience. You can access your SkyDrive folders
via the web at any time.

There is one detail to be aware of at this point. Microsoft is in the process of rebranding
a number of its online services. Previously its hotmail.com domain provided e-mail and
file support. Then Microsoft moved on to the Windows Live branding, so you could sign on
for services at `home.live.com`, and it added `skydrive.live.com` from there. The new
branding is Outlook.com. Right now, there is legacy support for all of these. So if you go to
`hotmail.com`, `home.live.com`, `skydrive.live.com`, or `outlook.com` and sign in, you
should be taken to the main e-mail screen for Outlook.com.

> **NOTE**
>
> Even if you used a non-Microsoft (that is, not `live.com`, `hotmail.com`, or `outlook.com`) email address when
> creating your Microsoft account, you will still have a SkyDrive account and be able to log into it using the e-mail address
> for your Microsoft account.

After you sign in to your account, whatever its branding, click the down arrow icon to the
right of Outlook at the upper right to display the choices shown in Figure 39.11 (the down
arrow itself is not visible at this point), and then click SkyDrive. The Files section at the center
displays the folders in your SkyDrive. Double-click the tile for a folder to display its files.

FIGURE 39.11

At the main Outlook.com screen, click the arrow beside Outlook, and then click SkyDrive.

To work with a particular file, move the mouse pointer over its tile until you see a check box in the upper-right corner, and then click to check it. Commands for working with the file appear above the file tiles, as shown in Figure 39.12. For example, you could click Download to download the checked file, or click the Manage down arrow (also shown in Figure 39.12) to see additional choices for working with the selected file. Follow the prompts that appear to perform the desired action on the file.

FIGURE 39.12

Managing a file in your SkyDrive

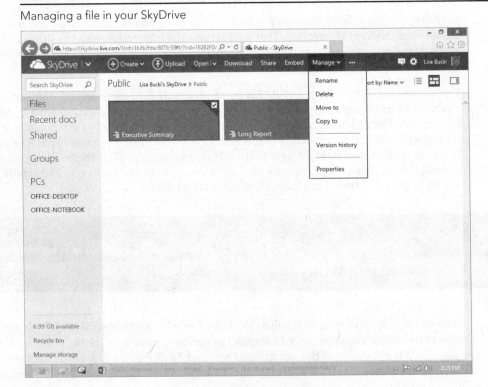

Touching up a document in the Web App

Your SkyDrive account also includes access to the Office Web Apps. These cloud-based versions of the Word, Excel, PowerPoint, and OneNote Office applications aren't fully featured, but they do allow you or your collaborators to make some of the most important types of edits—changes to the text—online without even needing to have Office installed. Here's how:

1. **Double-click the tile for a file when viewing it in SkyDrive via your web browser.** For example, you could double-click the tile for a Word file.

2. **In the Web App window that appears (such as Microsoft Word Web App), click Edit Document, and then click Edit in *Application* Web App.** (For example, you could click Edit in Word Web App as shown in Figure 39.13.)

FIGURE 39.13

Choose to edit a document stored in your SkyDrive using a Web App.

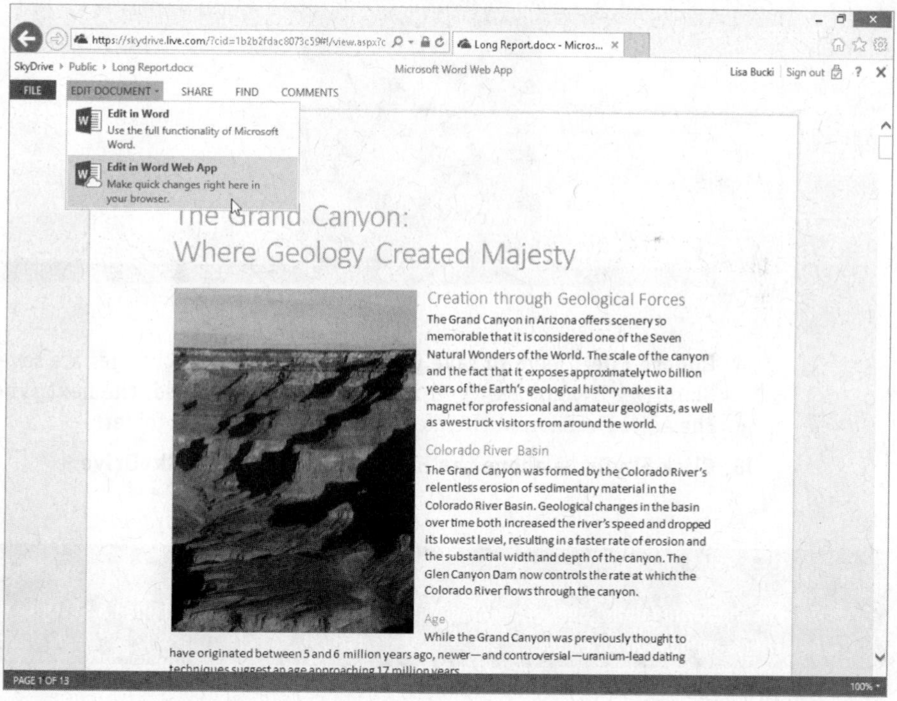

3. **Use the controls that appear (see Figure 39.14) to change the document as needed.**

FIGURE 39.14

The Web App Ribbon choices are a subset of the choices found in the full-blown version of the Office application.

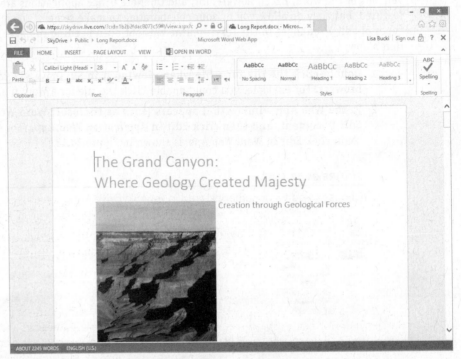

4. **Choose File ⇨ Save to save your changes.** The file changes are saved in your SkyDrive. If you have SkyDrive for Windows installed, the next sync will also place the edited version of the file in your local SkyDrive folder.

5. **Click SkyDrive above the Home tab to return to SkyDrive.**

TIP

Click Open In *Application* to the right of the main Web App tabs to download and open a SkyDrive file in the full-blown Office application for editing.

NOTE

Office 365, described next, also enables you to edit documents with Office Web Apps.

Accessing Your SkyDrive Pro Library on Office 365

Office 365 is a completely separate animal from SkyDrive. Office 365 is a licensed service that provides a platform for team members in an organization to access e-mail, share files, and more. The Office 365 file sharing capability is based on the SharePoint platform, an enterprise collaboration platform.

Office 2013 can interface directly with an Office 365 SharePoint-based team storage site, assuming the user is signed in to Office using the same sign-in information as for his or her Office 365 account. In addition, most Office versions include a SkyDrive Pro client by default. This client is specifically created to sync files between a file library on Office 365 and a local folder on your computer.

> **NOTE**
>
> SkyDrive Pro also works with SharePoint Online and proprietary organization SharePoint sites, but describing all the variations of using SkyDrive Pro with these various resources is beyond the scope of this book.

This final section of the chapter gives you an introduction to SkyDrive Pro and how it works with your Office 365 sign-in. To have an Office 365 sign-in, the administrator of an Office 365 account must add you as a user and provide your account sign-in information. If your Office 365 administrator has not added a private domain for the Office 365 setup, the sign-in e-mail addressed to you might be a variation of the onmicrosoft.com domain, as in mycompany.onmicrosoft.com.

Saving

Saving a file to your Office 365 account so that you can sync it via SkyDrive Pro in the future works much like saving to your SkyDrive:

1. **Open the file that you want to save to your Office 365 Library, or name and save the current file.**
2. **Choose File ⇨ Save As.** The Save As choices appear in Backstage view.
3. **In the middle pane, under Save As, click your Office 365 location (identified with a SharePoint icon).** As shown in Figure 39.15, the right pane lists any Recent Folders you've used. You can click one to save to it and then skip to Step 6, or go on to Step 4.

39

FIGURE 39.15

Saving to an Office 365 location

FIGURE 39.16

Save locations on an Office 365 team site

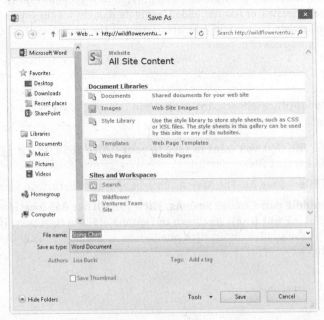

4. **Click Browse.** You may see a message that the application is contacting the server for information. After the connection is made, the Save As dialog box shows various libraries on the Office 365 team site, as shown in Figure 39.16.

5. **Double-click the location to save to, such as Documents.** After contacting the SkyDrive server, the Save As dialog box displays the contents of that library, if any.

6. **Click Save.** The Office application uploads the file to the specified Office 365 Library.

CAUTION

All these individual accounts can become confusing. To be able to save directly to an Office 365 location from an Office application, you must be signed in with your Office 365 sign-in information, which may be different than the Office account you sign in with every day. Click your username at the upper right, and click Switch account. In the window that appears, click Organizational account and follow the prompts that appear to sign in with your Office 365 account information provided by the system administrator.

Changing the sync folder, syncing files, and viewing local files

As you and other users view and edit your files via Office 365, you can use SkyDrive Pro 2013 to sync the files to a local folder and view the files. You can even change the local folder that you want to sync to. Here's the overview of how to accomplish all of that:

1. **While signed in to Windows using the same account information as your Office 365 account, start the SkyDrive Pro 2013 application.** In Windows 7, start it from the Start menu. In Windows 8, use the Search charm to start it under Microsoft Office 2013 if it doesn't appear on your Windows Start screen.

2. **If needed, click the Change sync folder link and specify another folder.**

3. **Enter the URL for the Office 365 team site to sync with.** If you don't know the URL, you can get it from your Office 365 system administrator.

4. **Click Sync.**

5. **As SkyDrive Pro is syncing files, it tells you, as shown in Figure 39.17.**

6. **To view the local copies of the synced files in a folder window, click Show my files.**

FIGURE 39.17

Use SkyDrive Pro to sync with Office 365 cloud storage.

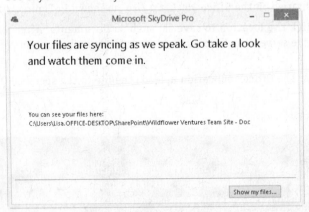

> **NOTE**
>
> If you click Show hidden icons in the Notification area of the taskbar, the choices that appear may include icons for SkyDrive for Windows and/or SkyDrive Pro when they are installed and running. The white cloud icon is for SkyDrive for Windows and the blue cloud icon is for SkyDrive Pro. Right-click either icon to see choices for working with its app.

Summary

In this chapter you've seen how Office integrates with cloud storage via SkyDrive and Office 365. You've learned that SkyDrive offers 7 GB of free online storage, when you sign in with your Microsoft account information, and that Office 365 is a separate team-based environment for sharing information in the cloud. You should now be able to do the following:

- Save a document to your SkyDrive from Office applications that allow you to do so (Word, Excel, PowerPoint, and Publisher).
- Use an Office application to share a document from your SkyDrive.
- Use the SkyDrive for Windows client to manage and sync files between your system and the cloud from your desktop.
- Understand the difference between Office 365 and SkyDrive.
- Use SkyDrive Pro to sync files from your Office 365 library to a local folder.

Integrating Office Application Information

I n some ways, using the Office suite is like using a single multipurpose program. Features from the different programs mesh together almost seamlessly. For example, when you create a chart in a Word 2013 document, the data also lives in Excel 2013, almost as if Excel were an extension of Word.

In this chapter, you explore the ways in which Excel, PowerPoint, Word, Outlook, and OneNote communicate with each other. Some things are perfectly intuitive, and others aren't. The casual PowerPoint user might never stumble on how to send outlines back and forth with Word. Do you ever wonder about the array of picture options available to you when copying images between Word and other programs? Which format should you use, and what are the consequences of using this one or that? How can pasting a 40K picture into a Word file add 900K to its size? In this chapter, the focus is on the less intuitive, to get you over some hurdles and stumbling blocks, and to make sense of some of those little mysteries that can make using Word seem like a struggle.

Excel

Although sharing work between Word and Excel often works well, differences in how the two programs operate can produce confusing results. This can be addressed by becoming aware of those differences, and working in a way that accommodates them and smoothes the way. This section looks at Word and Excel and ways to share text, data, tables, and graphics.

Using Excel content in Word

Word offers a variety of ways to share and exchange content with Excel:

- **Clipboard:** Copying content to the Clipboard, and then using Paste or Paste Special to insert the contents into Word or Excel. Commandment: When in doubt, use Paste Special.

- **Chart:** Using Office 2013's Chart feature to create a chart inside Word using Excel's facilities.

- **Object:** Using Insert ⇨ Text ⇨ Object ⇨ Create New or Create from File to embed all or part of an Excel worksheet into a Word document.

A common method that also works is drag and drop. You can select data or other content in Excel and drag it into Word. Make sure you press and hold the Ctrl key while dragging. If you do not see the plus with the mouse pointer as shown in Figure 40.1, the selection will be cut from Excel rather than copied. By default, the Excel data becomes an embedded object in the Word document, and you can double-click it there to display Excel tools for making changes. If you want the data to become a table in Word instead, use the Clipboard as described next.

FIGURE 40.1

Press Ctrl when dragging from Excel to Word to copy the range.

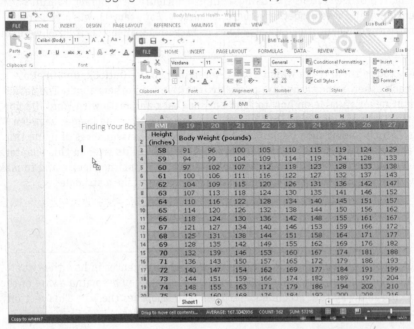

Read on to learn more about using the Clipboard, Chart, and Insert ⇨ Object features.

Clipboard

Excel's Clipboard works slightly differently from the Clipboard in most other Office programs. When you select cells in an Excel worksheet, they are highlighted. At this point, they are merely highlighted and cannot be moved or otherwise acted upon. You need to copy (or cut) the selection to the Clipboard, by pressing Ctrl+C or Ctrl+X, or right-clicking and choosing Copy or Paste. As in some other Office applications, you also can use the tools in the Clipboard group of Excel's Home tab to cut, copy, and paste a selection. After you cut or copy a selection of cells in Excel, an animated border appears around the selection, as shown in Figure 40.2.

FIGURE 40.2

The animated marquee around a selection in Excel shows you that you have cut or copied it.

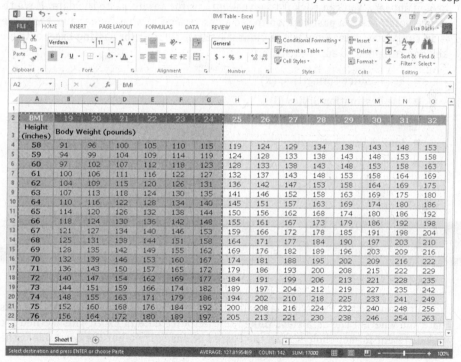

If you press Esc in Excel or double-click elsewhere (or perform any of a dozen or more other actions in Excel), the animated border disappears and you cannot paste the selection. Even if the data has actually been copied to the Clipboard, you still can't use the Paste button unless the animated border still appears in Excel. Dismissing the animated border also disables Paste Special, which is a helpful tool to use to determine how to paste Excel data.

40

> **TIP**
>
> There is one exception to this behavior. You can open the Clipboard pane in either Word or Excel by clicking the dialog box launcher in the Clipboard group of the Home tab. This will ensure that the Office Clipboard will collect the copied or cut data and keep it even if you press Esc or take another action that removes the animated border. (However, the Paste Special options still won't be available.) You can set the Office Clipboard to collect copied and cut selections in this way even if it is not open. To do so, click the Options button at the bottom of the Clipboard pane, and make sure that Collect Without Showing Office Clipboard is checked.

With the selection active in Excel, click where you want the data to appear in Word. If you simply click the Paste button in the Clipboard group of the Home tab, the cut or copied Excel selection pastes into Word as a Word table. As shown in Figure 40.3, the Paste Options button appears. You can click it to reveal options for how to paste the data. Move the mouse pointer over a paste option to see a description of what it does and a Live Preview of it on the pasted data. From left to right, the Paste Options for pasting Excel data and the key you can press to apply each are:

- Keep Source Formatting (K)
- Use Destination Styles (S)
- Link & Keep Source Formatting (F)
- Link & Use Destination Styles (L)
- Picture (U)
- Keep Text Only (T)

> **TIP**
>
> The Paste Options also are available when you click the Paste Special arrow, under Paste Options.

You also can use the Paste Special dialog box to paste and control how Word formats the data and whether the data stays linked to the source data in Excel. This method provides a few different format choices than the Paste Options button, but the downside is that you don't see a Live Preview of the pasted data. To use Paste Special, click the Paste button's down arrow (the bottom half of the button), and choose Paste Special (or press Ctrl+Alt+V). The Paste Special dialog box, shown in Figure 40.4, appears. Notice that the default is HTML format.

FIGURE 40.3

With a straight paste, the Excel data appears as a table, but you can use Paste Options to control how the pasted data appears.

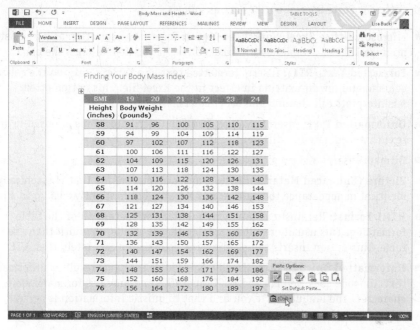

FIGURE 40.4

When using Paste Special to paste a selection of cells from Excel into Word, you'll have several options regarding how to paste.

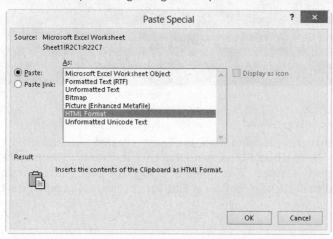

40

At the end of the day, both HTML and RTF retain both formatting and table structure, but there are differences. They might seem subtle, or they might seem substantial, depending on your needs. There also are differences among other options that might seemingly appear similar. Different Paste Special options are as follows:

- **Microsoft Office Excel Worksheet Object:** Inserts the selection as a complete mini-worksheet, complete with Excel editing if you double-click the object.
- **Formatted Text (RTF):** Inserts formatted text as a table, retaining the cell, column, and row formatting in effect in the Excel file. This option often misinterprets cell shading and other colors.
- **Unformatted Text:** Inserts plain text with no attributes. Tabs are used to separate text that originated in different cells.
- **Bitmap:** Inserts a `.bmp` picture file.
- **Picture (Enhanced Metafile):** Inserts an `.emf` picture file that is essentially identical in appearance to the Windows Metafile but is slightly smaller in size.
- **HTML Format:** Retains text formatting, but doesn't retain all of the table formatting. This usually results in a table that is smaller in width than the RTF table. This option inserts cell shading and colors more accurately than RTF.
- **Unformatted Unicode Text:** Usually, this yields the same result as unformatted text. Unicode goes well beyond ASCII and ANSI and provides for many more characters and languages. If you find that linguistic information is being lost when pasting as unformatted text, then switch to unformatted Unicode text.

Click the Paste link option button to the left of the list of formats if you want copied Excel data to be linked to its source. This means that any changes you make to the Excel data will appear in Word when you reopen the Word file. Click OK to finish the paste.

> **NOTE**
>
> Generally speaking, you can right-click linked data and click Update Link to refresh the data. Or in the shortcut menu, you can click the command for the linked object (such as Linked Worksheet Object for linked Excel data), and then click Links. The Links dialog that appears gives you options for working with the linked data, including a Break Link command for removing the link.

Chart

If you simply paste a chart from Excel to Word, the chart is pasted as an unlinked, embedded chart. Once the chart is in Word, when you click it, the Chart Tools contextual tabs — Design and Format — appear. If you need to change the data, choose the Chart Tools ⇨ Design tab, and then click Select Data or Edit Data in the Data group of the tab, as shown in Figure 40.5.

FIGURE 40.5

Clicking Edit Data in the Chart Tools ⇨ Design tab selects and opens the data in Excel.

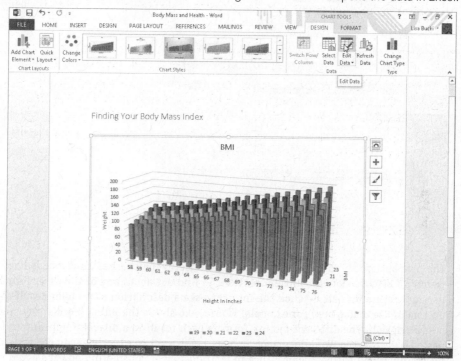

When you make changes to the data, the chart in Word is updated automatically to reflect the data changes. If there's a chance that you'll need to undo changes, leave the Excel window open. As long as it remains open, Ctrl+Z will work if you want to undo a change. If you close the Excel window with the data, changes to the chart and data are saved automatically, and Ctrl+Z will no longer undo changes you might have made.

When you copy graphics such as charts from Excel to Word with Paste Special, the rules change a bit. Right-click the chart or graphic and choose Copy. This time, you don't get the dashed selection because you're not copying cells — so it's a bit simpler, and once something has been copied to the Clipboard, the Paste Special options remain available. Switch to Word, click the Paste Special arrow or press Ctrl+Alt+V, and you'll see the options shown in Figure 40.6.

40

FIGURE 40.6

When you're copying graphics such as charts from Excel to Word, most of the formats presented are picture formats.

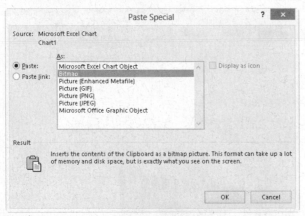

The first option, Microsoft Excel Chart Object, inserts the chart as an embedded object, which I'll discuss more in the next section. To find out about any of the other formats — various picture formats — click the format to see a description of it under Result at the bottom of the dialog box. For example, Figure 40.6 shows the Bitmap format selected and its description. The different picture formats each result in a different appearance for the pasted object in the Word document, so you might want to experiment to see which format gives you the best appearance in your document considering how it's going to be presented — online versus on paper.

> **NOTE**
>
> Even though you can use Paste Special to change a picture format when pasting into Word, for best results you should still use a dedicated graphics program for working with various file formats and other graphics modifications.

> **TIP**
>
> Some Office applications include an Insert ➪ Apps ➪ Apps for Office ➪ See All choice; after you select it click Find more apps at the Office Store. You can use it to download apps that are then added to the Apps for Office menu, adding new functionality and in some cases outside data and information within the application. For example, in Word you can add a dictionary for defining terms. In Excel, you can add apps for working with and visualizing data, such as presenting your data as a geographic heat map. If you can't do what you want to do simply by sharing between Office applications, check out the available Apps for Office.

Object

A third way to use Excel data in a Word document is as an object. In Word, choose
Insert ⇨ Text ⇨ Object. The Object dialog box appears. To use an existing Excel worksheet,
click the Create from File tab. To create a new Excel object, stay on the Create New tab.
Each tab is described next.

Create from File

On the Create from File tab, click the Browse button to navigate to the target file. Choose
Link to file and/or Display as icon, according to your needs, and click OK.

> **NOTE**
>
> Typically, you would use Display as icon when the purpose is to provide access to the contents of the Excel file rather
> than to display it. For example, suppose you have a number of tax tables that you want to provide to the reader. Some
> readers need one table, others need another, and so on. A document will be much less cluttered if users can click a
> link to open the data set of interest in Excel, rather than make all readers have to look through all of the data files to
> find the one they want.

Create New

In the Create New tab of the Object dialog box, select the desired type of Excel object,
as shown in Figure 40.7. Choose Display as icon, if desired (click Change Icon, if
appropriate), and then click OK. Use Excel's tools to create the desired object, as shown
in Figure 40.8, and then click outside the object (or close Excel, depending on the
object type).

FIGURE 40.7

The Change Icon button appears only if Display as icon is checked.

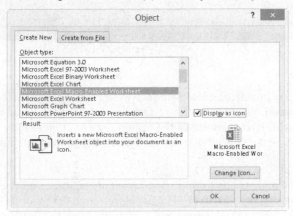

40

FIGURE 40.8

Creating an Excel worksheet object in Word

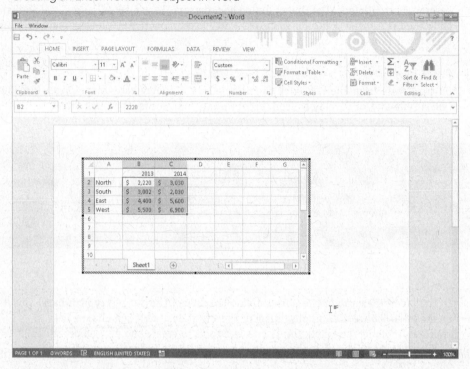

> **TIP**
>
> Notice that saving is controlled within the Word process. If you would like to have an independent version of the Excel object that is accessible from Excel without using Word, copy the contents of the "objectized" Excel worksheet to the Clipboard, open the full Excel application, paste your work into it, and save it.

From worksheet to table

As noted earlier, directly pasting formatted Excel data into Word creates a new table automatically. Sometimes, however, you need to insert data into a table that already exists. Typically, two problems can occur. First, sometimes the pasted cells don't go exactly where you want them to go. Second, no matter what you do, the formatting in the table never ends up exactly as you want.

To handle the first problem, the dimensions (rows and columns) of the source must be identical to the destination and the destination cells must be selected. For example, if you are pasting a selection of cells that contains 5 rows and 4 columns, then the destination must also be 5 × 4, and you must select the destination cells. If you try to paste in the top-left cell (which seems logical, right?), Word will paste the entire selection into that cell, so you end up with a table within a table.

TIP

If you are inserting new cells into an existing table (as opposed to replacing existing material), insert blank rows so you have empty cells that you can select and into which you can paste the incoming cells.

There is no perfect way to handle the second problem. Even if you choose the setting File ⇨ Options ⇨ Advanced ⇨ Pasting from other programs to Match Destination Formatting or Keep Text Only, *something* in the formatting will be messed up — usually the spacing.

Your best bet, assuming you're using a style, is to choose Keep Text Only from either Paste Options or the Paste Special button, and then reapply the style to the pasted cells. Alternatively, if there are table cells that contain the correct formatting, use the Format Painter to reformat the pasted cells as desired.

NOTE

The Paste Options differ slightly when pasting into an existing table. Nest Table (N) enables you to paste all the cells from the copied data into a single cell; or if you selected multiple cells before pasting, each of the selected cells receives a full copy of the pasted data. Insert as New Rows(s) creates new rows to hold the data for you and pastes beginning at the first column, which can lead to a ragged right side if the pasted selection has more or fewer columns than the destination table. Overwrite Cells (O) replaces any existing content in the selected destination but may alter the formatting. Keep Text Only (T), mentioned earlier, pastes without any text formatting but doesn't impact cell formatting.

Using Word content in Excel

Going from Word into Excel isn't quite as tricky as going from Excel into Word, although the setup of the Word content matters more in terms of how it pastes into the destination cells in Excel.

Clipboard

If you simply copy content from Word and paste it into Excel — using the Paste button or Ctrl+V — the setup of the original data controls how it is distributed in the destination cells in Excel. When you paste text that includes one or no paragraph marks, Excel inserts all of the text into the selected cell. If the selection contains multiple paragraphs, it is inserted into consecutive cells in the target column. For example, if the Clipboard contains three paragraphs and you paste into cell A1 (Row 1 Column 1), the three paragraphs are inserted into cells A1 (Row 1 Column 1), A2 (Row 2 Column 1), and A3 (Row 3 Column 1), respectively.

When pasting all or part of a table or text delimited with tabs into Excel, the cells are inserted into separate cells matching the original selection in Word. (Point to the table and then click the table move handle that appears to select the entire table or drag over cells to select them before clicking Copy or pressing Ctrl+C.) You only need to select the cell in the upper-left corner of the destination range. For example, to copy a 5 × 4 table from Word to Excel, select the table and copy or cut it to the Clipboard. In Excel, right-click in the upper-left cell of the 5 × 4 area where you want the table to appear and choose Paste or press Ctrl+V. By default, any formatting or shading from the original table appears when you paste to Excel.

Paste Options (also available via the Paste Special arrow) are a bit more limited, as shown in Figure 40.9. In this case, the two options are Keep Source Formatting (K) or Match Destination Formatting (M).

FIGURE 40.9

You also can choose Paste Options when pasting from Word to Excel.

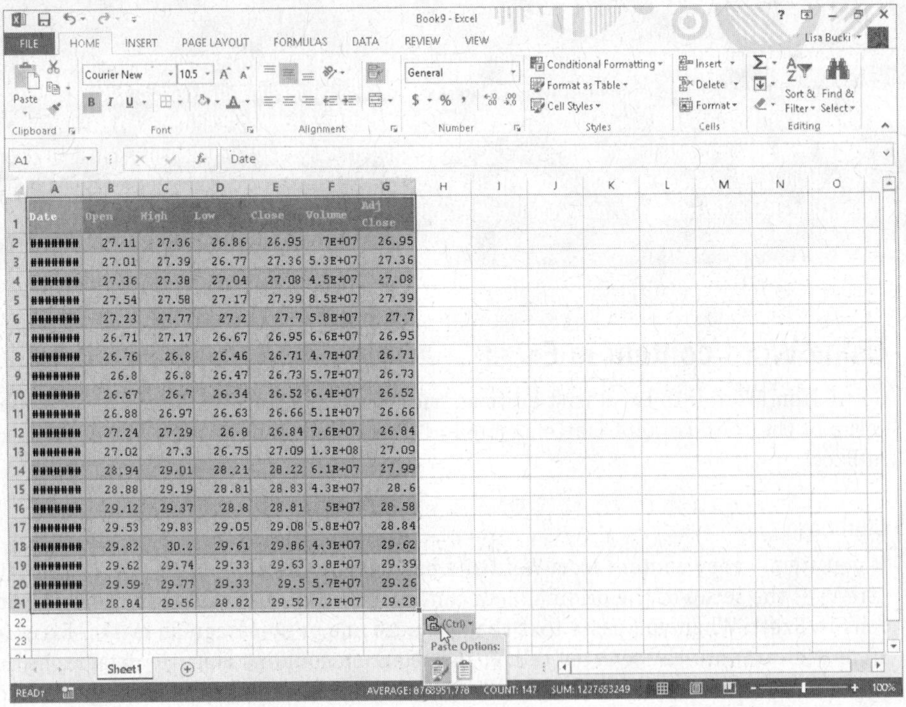

Notice in Figure 40.9 that you may need to make adjustments to column widths and number formatting. Columns A and F in the pasted data in the figure need to be widened. In the case of column A, the column is too narrow to display the date information, so pound signs appear instead. In the case of column F, the numeric values appear in scientific notation because the column is too narrow. Double-clicking the right border of the column heading (beside the column letter) AutoFits the column to the appropriate width. Also, the dollar values shown would have their decimal points vertically aligned with Accounting or Currency number formatting applied. Use the tools in the Number group of Excel's Home tab to work with the number formats for pasted data.

> **CAUTION**
>
> Note that even if you press Ctrl+A (Select All) to select the entire document and then copy, certain elements will not be copied. That's because Ctrl+A excludes content such as headers, footers, and footnotes. If you want to see the entire file, insert it as an object as described later.

When you paste a picture from Word into Excel, it is inserted into Excel's drawing layer rather than into cells. Note that Excel does not have text wrapping options for graphics, because cell text can't wrap around them.

Drag and drop

Unlike when copying via drag and drop from Excel to Word, when you do so from Word to Excel, you also need to press and hold Ctrl while dragging. Otherwise the text will be moved from Word. When dragging and dropping a table, drag from within the table; attempting to drag via the table move handle doesn't work. And if you drag and drop a table without using Ctrl, an empty table remains in Word after you move the contents to Excel.

> **NOTE**
>
> If you try dragging and dropping to Word and it doesn't work, make sure dragging and dropping is enabled in Word Options (File ⇨ Options ⇨ Advanced ⇨ Editing Options ⇨ Allow text to be dragged and dropped).

Object

You can insert a new or existing Word document into an Excel file as an object. In the destination file in Excel, click the cell where you want it to reside. Click the Insert tab, click the Text button to display the Text group if needed, and click Object. Click the Create from File tab and, as described earlier, use the Browse button to select the file to insert. Select Link to file and Display as icon, as needed, and then click OK. The inserted document looks like a picture object on the worksheet, but if you double-click it, you can edit its contents.

40

PowerPoint

In some ways even more than other Office applications, Word and PowerPoint were meant to work together. That's because PowerPoint uses heading levels that are similar to Word's Heading styles. When creating a PowerPoint presentation, for example, it's a simple matter to convert a Word outline into a PowerPoint presentation (or at least the basis for one), or to use a PowerPoint presentation as an outline for a Word document.

Converting a Word outline to a PowerPoint presentation

Converting a Word document outline into a PowerPoint presentation is simple — as long as you've used Word's Heading styles for your outline or created it in Outline view, which automatically applies the heading styles. Unfortunately, PowerPoint is not able to extract just the outline from a Word document with body text under the headings, so you would have to strip out the body text manually yourself if the document has already been written. Also keep in mind that you need to have saved and named the file. PowerPoint opens the outline from a saved file rather than using a copy type of process.

> **TIP**
>
> A quick way to strip body text from a Word document that was formatted using Heading styles is to copy the entire document to new blank file. Click a paragraph using the main style for body text. In the Editing group of the Home tab, click Select, and then click Select All Text with Similar Formatting. Press the Delete key to remove the text. Repeat the process to select and delete text formatted with other styles representing content not needed in the presentation. Save the file under a new name, and then create the PowerPoint presentation from it.

To convert a Word outline into a PowerPoint presentation, in PowerPoint start a new PowerPoint presentation (Ctrl+N). In the Slides group of the Home tab in PowerPoint, click the New Slide button arrow, and click Slides from Outline, as shown in Figure 40.10. In the Insert Outline dialog box, find the document containing your outline, select it, and click Insert.

> **NOTE**
>
> Once you've inserted an outline into a PowerPoint presentation, you'll often discover that stray or extra paragraph marks insinuate themselves prominently in the PowerPoint presentation, creating unsightly gaps. You can fix them in PowerPoint, or, if it's easier, press Ctrl+Z to undo the insert, clean up the outline in Word, and then try again. Or change to PowerPoint's Outline view by clicking the View tab and then clicking Outline View in the Presentation Views group. Note that Tab and Shift+Tab demote and promote outline levels in PowerPoint's Outline view as they do in Word's Outline view.

FIGURE 40.10

You can use a Word outline to create a PowerPoint presentation.

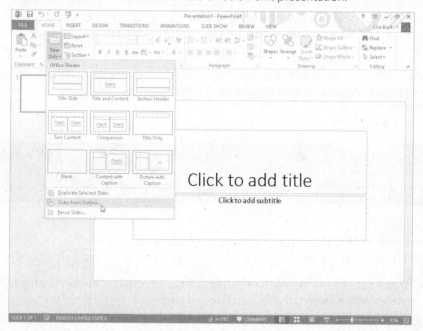

Converting a PowerPoint presentation to a Word document

You can also go in the other direction, using a PowerPoint presentation as a starting outline for a Word document. In PowerPoint, choose File⇨Save As. After selecting the save location from Backstage or clicking Browse and entering a name if needed in the File name text box, open the Save as type drop-down list and click Outline/RTF — near the bottom of the nonalphabetized list — and then click Save.

In Word, choose File⇨Open⇨Computer⇨Browse, navigate to the .rtf file you just created, and open it. Then switch to Outline view. The top level for each slide was assigned Heading 1, the next level Heading 2, and so on.

> **NOTE**
>
> You can export a PowerPoint presentation to a Word handout document that you can edit as needed. To do so, open the presentation in PowerPoint. Click the File tab⇨Export⇨Create Handouts⇨and Create Handouts. In the Send to Microsoft Word dialog box that appears, choose an option under Page layout in Microsoft Word, such as Notes below slides, and then click OK. The handout document gets sent to Word as a new document. From there, save, name, and format the new document as desired.

40

Using tables from Word

If a table already exists in Word, you can copy it into PowerPoint. PowerPoint will convert the Word table to a PowerPoint table. From that point on, it is a part of the presentation, and maintains no relationship to Word. You can edit its text directly in PowerPoint.

To paste a table from Word to PowerPoint, copy it to the Clipboard (Ctrl+C) in Word, and then paste it onto a slide in PowerPoint (Ctrl+V). The resulting table appears in the center of the slide.

> **NOTE**
>
> When you copy a table from Word to PowerPoint, you might need to increase the font size; Word's default size for body text is great for printed documents but too small for most PowerPoint slides.

A pasted Word table is placed into a content placeholder on the slide if an appropriate one is available. Here are the basic rules for what goes on:

- If the slide has an appropriate content placeholder that is empty, the table is placed into it but retains its own size and shape.
- If the slide does not have an appropriate empty content placeholder, the table is inserted as a free-floating object, unrelated to any placeholders.

Word's table feature is somewhat more robust than PowerPoint's. If you want to maintain all the Word capabilities in the table, paste the table as a Word object instead of doing a regular paste. Follow these steps:

1. **Copy the table in Word (Ctrl+C).**
2. **In PowerPoint, display the slide on which the table should be pasted.**
3. **On the Home tab, open the Paste button's menu and click Paste Special.** The Paste Special dialog box opens.
4. **Click the Paste option button.**
5. **In the As list, choose Microsoft Office Word Document Object.**
6. **Click OK.** The table appears as a free-floating object (not in any placeholder).

You can also use the Paste Options button that appears immediately after you paste the table. Click the third icon: Embed. The resulting table is an embedded object and cannot be edited directly using PowerPoint's table feature. To edit the object, you must double-click it to open it in Word.

Integrating Excel cells into PowerPoint

If you need calculating capabilities in a table, consider embedding Excel cells into the slide instead of using a traditional PowerPoint table:

1. **Display the slide on which you want to place the Excel cells.**
2. **If desired, select a placeholder into which the table should be placed.**
3. **On the Insert tab, click the Table button in the Tables group, and on its menu, choose Excel Spreadsheet.** A small frame with a few cells of an Excel spreadsheet appears, and the Ribbon changes to the tabs and tools for Excel.

4. **If desired, enlarge the Excel object by doing the following:**
   a. Click once on the Excel object's border to select it. Black selection handles appear around it.
   b. Drag a corner selection handle to enlarge the area of the object.
5. **Create the table using Excel's tools and features.**
6. **(Optional) If there are unused cells, resize the object again (using its selection handles) so that they are not visible.**
7. **Click away from the object to deselect it and return to PowerPoint.**

You've just created an embedded Excel object. It does not exist outside of this PowerPoint file; it's a mini-Excel spreadsheet that you use just for this one presentation. If you want to embed content from an existing Excel file, copy and paste it as in the previous section on Word tables.

Outlook

Outlook 2013 contains a number of tools for creating and formatting messages that greatly resemble the tools for creating and editing documents in Word 2013. This integration of functionality in both programs should make it comfortable for you to use both programs together. You've already seen in Chapter 10, "Data Documents and Mail Merge," how to use your Outlook Address Book contents for a mail merge. Read on to learn other ways that Word and Outlook interact.

Using the Outlook Address Book in Word

One of the more conspicuous relationships between Word and Outlook is in the use of the Outlook Address Book for addresses in Word documents — especially letters and envelopes. For example, in the Create group of the Mailings tab in Word, click Envelopes or Labels, and then click the Insert Address button (see Figure 40.11), which opens the Select Name dialog box.

FIGURE 40.11

You can access the Outlook Address Book using the Insert Address button.

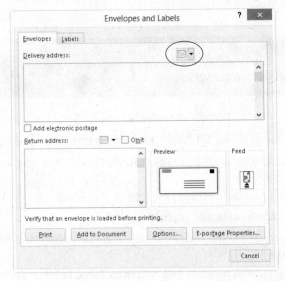

The Select Name dialog box appears, as shown in Figure 40.12. If you have multiple address books set up, click the Address Book drop-down arrow and choose the one you want. Note that the Search option enables you to search the Name only or More columns. When you use Name only, the dialog box displays only names that start with what you type.

FIGURE 40.12

Insert addresses for Word envelopes or labels via the Address Book.

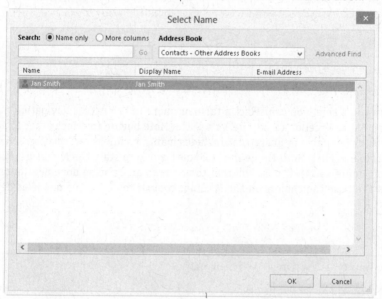

Alternatively, click More columns, type what you're looking for, and click Go. This search feature searches for occurrences of the search text anywhere in any contact field. If that still gives you too many hits, click Advanced Find. Use the Find dialog box to search for names containing text you type. When you find the person or business whose address you want, select it and click OK.

Once the address you need is selected in the Select Names dialog box, click OK, finish selecting settings in the Envelopes and Labels dialog box, and then click OK again.

Access Imports and Exports

The External Data tab in Access 2013 is divided into two groups (Figure 40.13): Import & Link and Export. You can easily import data from an Excel workbook file by choosing External Data➪Import & Link➪Excel, and then following the steps presented in the Get External Data dialog box. Use the Text File button in that group to import a delimited file that you've created in Word and saved as a plain text file.

40

FIGURE 40.13

Access by design can import and export a variety of file formats.

On the Export group side, you can select a table or query in the Access Navigation pane, and then export it as Excel or a Text File, or use the More button to select other Export formats. If you have a table or query that includes mailing address information selected in the Navigation pane, click Word Merge in the Export group to start the Microsoft Word Mail Merge Wizard (Figure 40.14). Choose whether to merge to an existing document or create a new one, and then use the choices on the Mailings toolbar to set up the merge as described in Chapter 10.

FIGURE 40.14

Use a mailing list from Access in a Word mail merge.

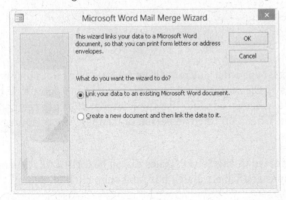

Other Access objects can be exported to differing formats. For example, if you've selected a report in the Navigation pane, you can use the PDF or XPS choice in the Export group to save to that file format to share information with other users.

OneNote

Until you get in the swing of using OneNote for note taking and project tracking, you might still do some of that work in Word. You also might have documentation previously generated in Word that you want to transfer to OneNote, or OneNote information that you want to incorporate in a more formal document in Word. Transferring information between the two applications is a breeze, making it easy for you to choose the note taking tool that's appropriate for any given situation.

Printing from Word to OneNote

When you want to incorporate information from a Word document into OneNote, you "print" from Word to OneNote. Start by opening the document to print in Word. To send only a portion of the document to OneNote, select the information to transfer.

Choose File ⇨ Print. In the Backstage view, open the Printer drop-down list, and click Send to OneNote 2013, the choice shown in Figure 40.15. If you selected part of the document to send, open the first Settings drop-down list, which initially shows Print All Pages, and click Print Selection. Then click the Print button near the top.

FIGURE 40.15

Printing a file from Word to OneNote

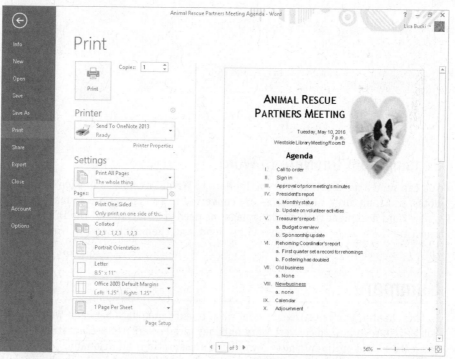

OneNote opens, and the Select Location in OneNote dialog box appears, as shown in Figure 40.16. Select one of the notebooks under Recent Picks, or use the folder tree under All Notebooks to choose a different destination. Then click OK. Word inserts the information as a page image on a new page tab in the specified notebook.

FIGURE 40.16

Selecting a Notebook destination for the "printed" Word information

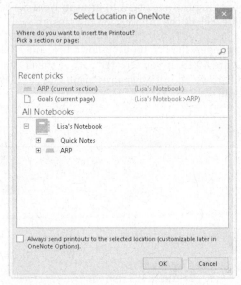

Sending from OneNote to Word

You can send a notebook page from OneNote to Word. The notebook page's information — notes, links, pictures, and more — are converted to an appropriate format and placed in a new Word document with as many pages as needed to include all the information. After selecting the page to send, choose File ➪ Send, and then click Send to Word.

Summary

In this chapter, you've learned several ways to exchange data between Word and Excel. You've also seen how to convert Word outlines into PowerPoint presentations, and how to create a Word outline using a PowerPoint presentation. Additionally, you've looked at several ways that Outlook and Word stay in contact. You should now be able to do the following:

- Insert Excel content in a Word document and vice versa using a variety of different methods.

- Use the Clipboard and drag and drop to copy or move content between Word and Excel.

- Exchange outlines between Word and PowerPoint.

- Paste a Word table or Excel cells into PowerPoint.

- Use the Outlook Address Book tool to insert a contact's address in Word envelopes or labels.

- Identify what file formats Access can import and export, including how to use a table or query of addresses in a merge.

- Print information from Word to OneNote or convert a OneNote page to a Word document.

40

Customizing Office

IN THIS APPENDIX

Finding program options

Using common options

Exploring top options from Word, Excel, PowerPoint, Access, and Outlook

Customizing the Ribbon and Quick Access Toolbar

Nearly every program has options that you can choose to customize the program to meet your working preferences. Each of the Office applications has numerous settings that you can tweak to adapt the program to your needs.

Finding Program Options

You can adjust Office program settings such as how often the program saves AutoRecover information, where to save files by default, how certain elements look onscreen, and on and on. Each of the Office programs offers dozens of settings for changing program appearance and behavior.

Opening the Options Dialog Box

Each Office application gathers its settings in an Options dialog box. The method for opening the Options dialog box is now the same across the Office applications:

1. **Click the File tab.** Backstage view appears.
2. **Click Options at the left.** As shown in Figure A.1, this button is near the bottom left of the Backstage view.

FIGURE A.1

Click Options near the bottom-left corner in Backstage view to choose options.

Navigating in the Dialog Box

The left side of the Options dialog box lists the categories of available settings. Figure A.2 shows the Word Options dialog box. To display the options in another category, click the category in the list at the left. For example, clicking Save, as shown in Figure A.2, will display Word's saving options.

FIGURE A.2

The left side of the Options dialog box lists categories of options.

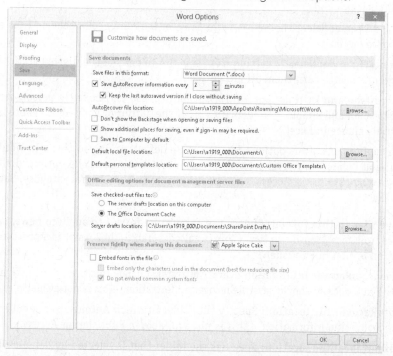

> **NOTE**
>
> The Advanced category typically has an extensive list of options, so you can use the scroll bar at the right side of the dialog box to move down and find the options you need.

Using Common Options

All the Office applications have some options in common. For example, each of the programs enables you to control how ScreenTips appear and what color scheme to use. The common options are found in the General category in the Options dialog box for each program. Here's a review of these common options:

- **Show Mini Toolbar on selection:** This check box controls whether the Mini Toolbar appears when you select text (with the exception of Access).

- **Enable Live Preview:** When this option is selected, pointing to a style, font, or other formatting choice in a gallery displays a preview of that formatting on the selected object.

- **Office Background:** Select a tattoo or pattern to appear at the top of the Office window, behind the title and Ribbon tabs. Choosing No Background results in a white background.
- **Office Theme:** Select the White, Light Gray, or Dark Gray color scheme from this drop-down list.
- **ScreenTip style:** Select a setting from this list to change the display style of ScreenTips or to turn them off altogether.
- **User name and Initials:** Enter information in these text boxes to personalize an application and enable it to identify you as the author of your files. (There is no Initials choice in Excel.)

Each of the applications offers options for setting up default saving settings. In Word, Excel, PowerPoint, and Publisher, you click the Save tab at the left side of the Options dialog box to find the saving choices; in Access, the options appear in the General category. Saving options include:

- **Save files in this format:** Choose the default file format to apply to newly saved files from this drop-down list. (This is called Default File Format in Access and is not an option in Publisher.)
- **Save AutoRecover information every _x_ minutes:** Change this value to specify how often AutoRecover should save file recovery information. (This is not available in Access.)
- **AutoRecover file location:** Specify the folder in which AutoRecover should store file recovering information. (This is not available in Publisher or Access.)
- **Default local file location:** Specifies the folder that is selected by default when you display the Save As or Open dialog boxes. This is sometimes referred to as your *default folder* or *working folder*. (This is called Default Database Folder in Access and is not found in Publisher.)

Note that the Save category for each application has additional choices that are specific to that application.

Some of the applications also include a Language category, where you can choose the default language used for display, editing, and help.

NOTE
Appendix C offers more information about language settings.

Top Word Options

Word's other options include settings that affect a document's appearance onscreen and when printed, how the proofing tools work, and how certain editing features behave. Here's a review of some of the most important features, identified by Options dialog box tab (category):

■ **Display:** Clicking this tab displays the settings shown in Figure A.3. The settings in the Always show these formatting marks on the screen section turn on marks that typically don't print, such as Tab character marks. If you need to check the formatting in your document, selecting the Show all formatting marks option to check its check box will display those marks so that you can eliminate such errors as double spaces. The settings in the Printing options section are also helpful. For example, if you are printing a document with a color printer, you may want to check the Print background colors and images choice to make sure that those decorative items print.

FIGURE A.3

Word's Display options.

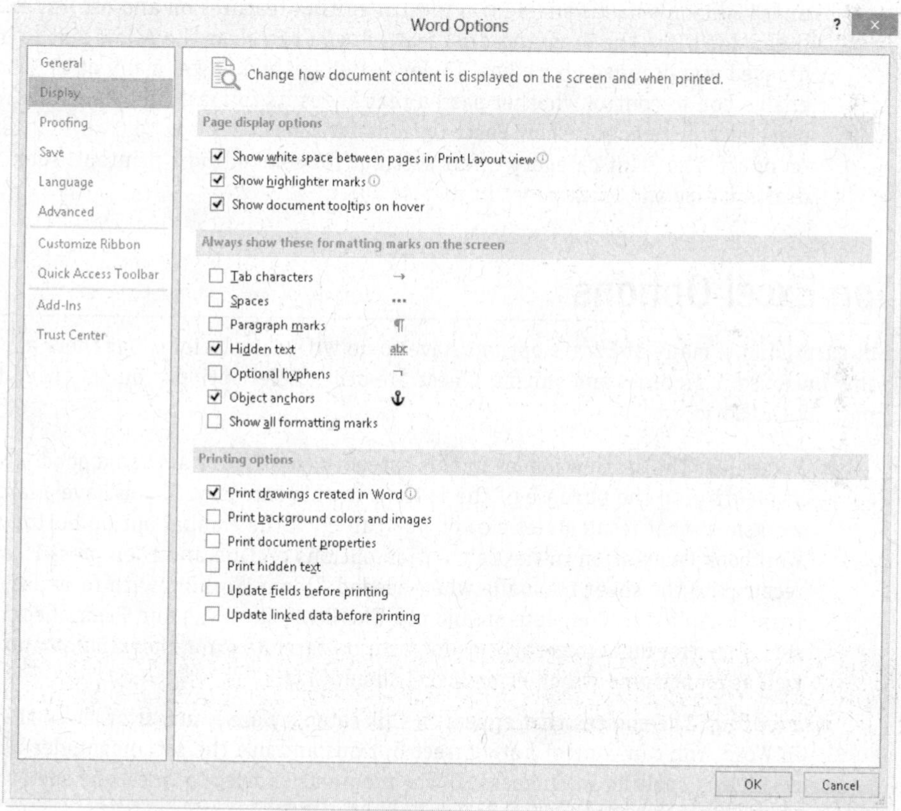

- **Proofing:** The settings in this category of the Word Options dialog box let you set up how the AutoCorrect, Spelling Check, and Grammar Check features work. Clicking the Auto-Correct Options button here opens a dialog box in which you can change AutoCorrect and AutoFormat settings. The choices under When correcting spelling in Microsoft Office programs enable you to turn certain corrections on and off; for example, clearing the Ignore words in UPPERCASE check box tells the Spelling Check feature to include words in all uppercase as possible misspellings. Under When correcting spelling and grammar in Word, the Check spelling as you type and Mark grammar errors as you type options control whether you see the wavy underlines under words that may be misspelled and grammar that may be incorrect.

- **Advanced:** Among the plethora of options here, you're likely to use those in the Editing Options; Cut, Copy, and Paste; and Print categories most often. The choices under Editing options enable you to turn editing features on and off. For example, if you don't like the drag-and-drop feature, you can clear the Allow text to be dragged and dropped check box. Under Cut, Copy, and Paste, many of the choices enable you to control whether pasted text keeps its formatting by default. You also can check or clear the Show Paste Options Buttons check box to turn that feature on or off. The Print category offers settings for controlling a printout, such as Use draft quality and Print pages in reverse order.

Top Excel Options

Not surprisingly, many of Excel's options have to do with calculations, but there are also other options for proofing and editing. These are other Excel options you may need to know, by category:

- **Formulas:** The section names in this category (see Figure A.4) do a good job of identifying the purpose of the options in this category. If you have a large worksheet that recalculates slowly, you can click the Manual option button under Workbook Calculation in the Calculation options section and then press F9 to recalculate the sheet manually when needed. Under Working with formulas, you can turn Formula AutoComplete on and off. The Error Checking and Error checking rules sections offer numerous settings for turning formula error checking on and off as well as identifying which errors Excel should flag.

- **Proofing:** The choices that appear in this category are a subset of those that appear in Word. You can control AutoCorrect Options and use the settings under When correcting spelling in Microsoft Office programs choices to fine-tune spell checking.

FIGURE A.4

Excel Formula options.

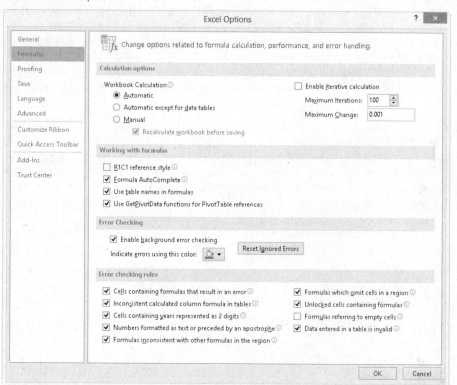

- **Advanced:** This category also includes Editing options for Excel, but they are different from those for Word. For example, with After pressing Enter, move selection selected, you can use the Direction drop-down list to specify which direction the cell selector will move. You can check the Enable automatic percent entry check box so that values you type with a percentage sign will be recognized as percentages, and you can also click Enable AutoComplete for cell values. The two sections of Display options settings are also important to many users. For example, you can clear the Show row and column headers check box if you want to hide the row numbers and column letters in a finished workbook. You can select Show page breaks if it's important for you to see page breaks onscreen, and you can control the appearance of gridlines using the Show gridlines and Gridline color options.

Top PowerPoint Options

PowerPoint offers additional options in the Proofing and Advanced categories. It includes many of the same Proofing options as in Word, such as the ability to ignore certain corrections and turn automatic spell checking on and off. Its Advanced category (Figure A.5) starts off with editing and pasting options. The most important settings appear in the Slide Show category, where you can choose Show menu on right mouse click, Show popup toolbar, Prompt to keep ink annotations when exiting, and End with black slide.

FIGURE A.5

PowerPoint Advanced options

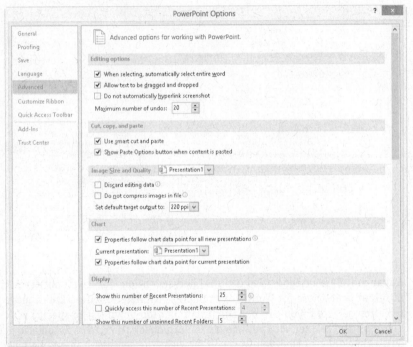

Top Access Options

Access's Options dialog box offers options to help you work more effectively with your databases, in these categories:

- **Current Database:** This tab (Figure A.6) offers settings for customizing the current database file, including entering an Application Title and selecting an Application Icon. You can choose a Display Form, set up Navigation options, and choose Ribbon and Toolbar Options for the finished database, among other choices.

FIGURE A.6

Access Current Database options

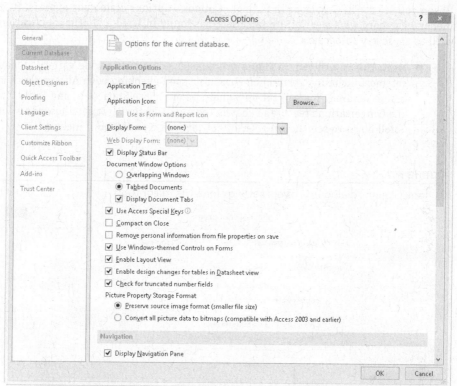

- **Datasheet:** This category offers formatting settings for any datasheet in Access. You can change settings for Gridlines and cell effects, and change the Default font settings.

- **Object Designers:** This tab offers choices for controlling appearance and behavior when you're using Table Design and Query Design views, as well as the design views for Forms/Reports. For example, you can choose a Default field type and Default text field size for the Table Design view, or choose whether to Show table names in Query Design view. This tab also has settings for controlling Error Checking.

- **Proofing:** As in the other applications, the settings here adjust AutoCorrect and Spelling Check.

- **Client Settings:** This tab offers various settings for editing in tables, such as whether pressing an arrow key moves to the next field or to the next character. You can specify margins for printing or turn on such features as Open last used database when Access starts under Advanced.

Top Outlook Options

When you select File ⇨ Options in Outlook, Outlook's Options dialog box appears. It offers a General category with most of the same settings found in Word and other applications, as well as these key categories:

- **Mail:** This tab, shown in Figure A.7, enables you adjust a wide variety of mail settings, including turning on automatic spell checking with Always check spelling before sending. You can set up Signatures or choose Stationery and Fonts, control the Conversations feature's behavior, change desktop alert settings, and a lot more. Scroll down to see the wide variety of settings this category includes.

FIGURE A.7

Outlook Options dialog box offers settings for all its major tools.

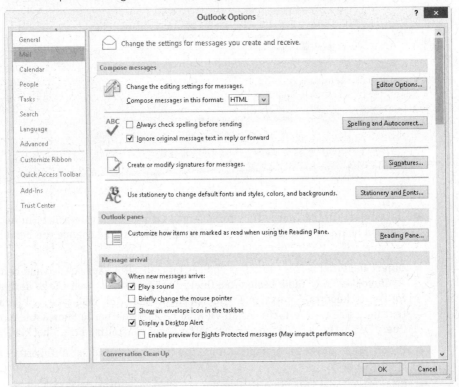

- **Calendar:** Choose a variety of Calendar defaults, such as the Start time and End time for work hours, adding holidays to the calendar, a Default calendar color, and more.

- **People:** Use this category to adjust Contacts settings such as Default "Full Name" order, Default "File As" order, and whether to Check for duplicates when saving new contacts.

- **Tasks:** Set up Tasks features such as Overdue task color and Completed task color here.

- **Search:** Use these categories to optimize search functionality.

- **Advanced:** This category enables you to customize the panes in Outlook. You can choose start and exit settings, AutoArchive settings, send and receive settings, and much more.

Customizing the Quick Access Toolbar

Even though certain commands you may have relied on in older menu-based versions of Office do not appear on the Ribbon in the current version of the applications, some of those commands remain available as buttons that you can add to the Quick Access Toolbar (QAT) above the File tab. You can find and add those "missing" buttons and others to the QAT using the Options dialog box, as follows:

1. **Click the Customize Quick Access Toolbar down-arrow button at the far-right end of the QAT and then click More Commands.** Doing so displays the program's Options dialog box, with the Quick Access Toolbar category already selected.

2. **Make a selection from the Choose commands from drop-down list.** If you're looking for a command from an earlier version, select Commands Not in the Ribbon.

3. **Click the command to add in the list at the left.**

4. **Click Add.** The command is added to the right list. For example, Figure A.8 shows the Strikethrough button added to the list of QAT commands at the right.

5. **Repeat Steps 2 through 4 to add buttons as needed.**

6. **To remove a button, click it in the right list, and then click Remove.**

7. **Click OK.** The QAT changes to reflect the buttons you added or removed.

FIGURE A.8

Use the Quick Access Toolbar category of the Options dialog box to add QAT buttons.

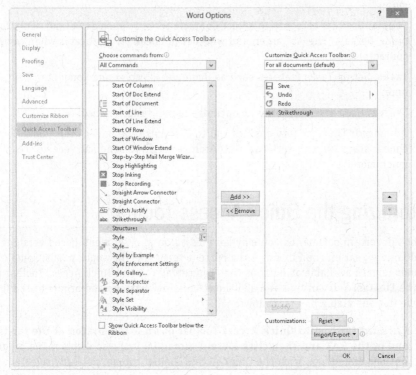

Customizing the Ribbon

Office 2013 now includes the ability to customize the Ribbon, a feature that will be welcomed by anyone who prefers to have frequently used commands all in one location. While you cannot add commands to any of the default Ribbon tabs, you can create a custom tab and fill it with the commands you need. Use the Options dialog box to customize the Ribbon, as follows:

1. **Choose File ⇨ Options in an Office application.**
2. **In the Options dialog box, click Customize Ribbon in the list at the left.**
3. **Click the New Tab button under the Main Tabs list.** The new tab and a new group appear in the Main Tabs list.
4. **Click New Tab (Custom), click the Rename button, type a new Name, and click OK.**
5. **Click New Group (Custom), click the Rename button, type a new Name, and click OK.** Make sure that the new group stays selected so that commands will be added to it.

6. **Make a selection from the Choose commands from drop-down list.** If you're looking for a command from an earlier version, select Commands Not in the Ribbon.

7. **Click the command to add in the list at the left.**

8. **Click Add.** The command in added to the tab in the Main Tabs list. For example, Figure A.9 shows three commands for applying headings added to a custom tab.

FIGURE A.9

Create a custom Ribbon tab.

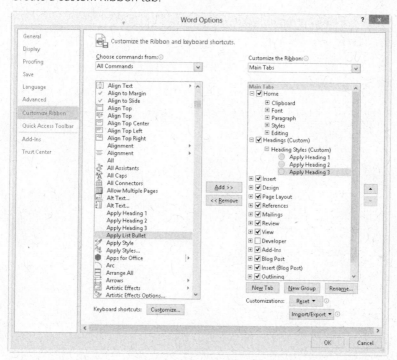

9. **Repeat Steps 2 through 4 to add commands as needed.**

10. **Use the Rename button as in Step 5 to rename any command or select an alternate display symbol.**

11. **To remove a command, click on it in the Main Tabs list, and then click Remove.**

12. **Click OK.** The Ribbon displays the new tab.

NOTE

Click the Developer choice in the Main Tabs list to display the Developer tab, which holds settings for creating and working with macros.

Optimizing Your Office Installation

IN THIS APPENDIX

Using the Setup disc

Activating Microsoft Office

Getting Office updates

Adding and removing programs and features

Running diagnostics

Repairing Microsoft Office

For many users, Office 2013 may already be installed on a company computer or pre-installed on a new system. Even if one of those situations applies to you, you may still need to adjust your Office installation at some point.

Using the Setup Disc

After you download the Office Setup files, it's a good practice to burn your own setup disc not only as a backup of the download, but also for maintenance purposes.

Many of the installation and repair tasks start with inserting the Microsoft Office 2013 disc into your DVD drive. In most cases, the setup program launches automatically. If it doesn't, open a folder window for the drive on the desktop and double-click the setup.exe file. If you downloaded the program, navigate to the folder where you saved the setup.exe file and launch it from there. If you are setting up Office for the first time, follow the onscreen prompts, entering your 25-character Product Key when prompted. Most users choose a typical install and install to the default location recommended by setup.

Activating Microsoft Office

One crucial action in keeping Office running well is to activate your Office installation. Microsoft requires activation as part of its system to verify users of properly acquired Office programs versus those who may have obtained the suite fraudulently.

When you start an Office application the first time, you will be prompted to activate your installation. If you decline to activate the software, Microsoft provides a grace period of 30 days of using Office, after which Office enters Reduced Functionality mode.

If you need to start the activation process manually, you can follow these steps from one of the Office programs:

1. **Choose File ⇨ Account.** The Backstage view appears.
2. **Click the Change Product Key link.**
3. **Type your product key and click Install, then OK.**
4. **Follow the prompts in the Microsoft Office Activation Wizard that appears.**

After Office has been activated, click the File tab and click Account again. The right portion of the screen displays a "Product Activated" message, as shown in Figure B.1.

FIGURE B.1

The Backstage view informs you that Office has been activated.

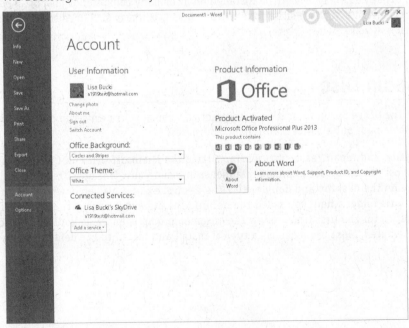

Getting Updates

Microsoft periodically releases updates to the Office programs that affect functionality and security. These should download automatically via the Windows Update feature. You can manually download and install updates at any time from the Control Panel. Start Control Panel from the desktop (Settings charm ⇨ Control Panel in Windows 8 or Start ⇨ Control Panel in Windows 7.) Click System and Security ⇨ Windows Update. If updates are already listed as available, click the link(s) to view important and optional updates to review them before installing. You can clear the check box beside any update you don't want to install. Then click the Install button. If you don't see any updates in the initial Windows Update screen, you can click Check for Updates.

Adding or Removing Office Features

You can add or remove Office applications and components as needed. Often in a business environment, systems are initially set up with a typical or minimal installation, and a user needs to add more components to tackle particular work tasks.

To add or remove programs and features in Office:

1. **Open Control Panel from the desktop (Settings charm ⇨ Control Panel in Windows 8 or Start ⇨ Control Panel in Windows 7), then click Uninstall a program under Programs.**

2. **Click Microsoft Office 2013 (the name will vary slightly depending on your version of Office), and then click Change.**

3. **Enter a User Account Control password, if prompted, and then click Yes.**

4. **Leave Add or Remove Features selected, and click Continue.** Note that at this point, you also could click Repair to repair the installation, Remove to uninstall Office, or Enter a Product Key if you need to change the product key.

5. **Choose options to install and uninstall in the Installation Options tab.** As shown in Figure B.2, you can choose to install (Run from My Computer) or uninstall (Not Available) by clicking the disk button for the option and then clicking the desired choice.

6. **Click Continue, and then respond to additional prompts as needed to finish adding and removing features.** You may be prompted to insert the Office install disk if adding features, so make sure that you have it handy.

FIGURE B.2

Add and remove features to your Office installation.

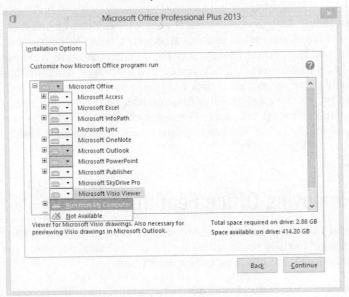

Running Microsoft Office Diagnostics

In Office 2013, you instead can enable an option that periodically downloads a file to diagnose problems. To enable this feature, click File, and then click Options. In the Options dialog box, click Trust Center at the left, and then click the Trust Center Settings button to open the Trust Center dialog box. Click Privacy Options at the left, click the Download a file periodically that helps determine system problems check box to check it, and then click OK twice to close the dialog boxes.

Repairing Your Installation

Repairing an installation generally takes care of any issues with missing or corrupted files. Repairing is a less drastic option than removing (uninstalling) and reinstalling Office, so it's always a good troubleshooting procedure to try to repair your install.

To repair Office (Windows 7 or Windows Vista):

1. **Open Control Panel from the desktop (Settings charm ⇨ Control Panel in Windows 8 or Start ⇨ Control Panel in Windows 7), then click Uninstall a program under Programs.**

2. **Click Microsoft Office 2013 (the name will vary slightly depending on your version of Office), and then click Change.**

3. **Enter a User Account Control password, if prompted, and then click Yes.**

4. **Click Repair in the dialog box shown in Figure B.3, and click Continue.**

FIGURE B.3

Repair your Office installation.

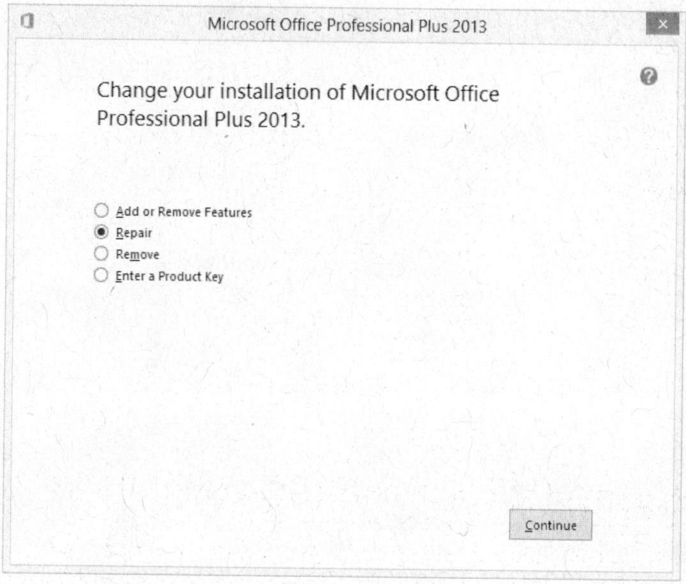

5. **Respond to additional prompts as needed to finish repairing the Office installation.**

International Support and Accessibility Features

IN THIS APPENDIX

Working with text encoding in Word

Enabling additional editing languages in Microsoft Office

Using translation and accessibility features

Today's global economy requires the ability to use documents with a variety of settings and also in different languages. You can be prepared for a wider variety of business situations if you know how to work with encoding, language, and accessibility features that affect Office.

Understanding and Choosing Text Encoding in Word

Behind the scenes, applications identify each character (letter, number, punctuation, or symbol) that you type as a numeric code. Each language uses its own encoding system, so character 232 in one language encoding system looks drastically different from character 232 in another language encoding system. The Unicode encoding system encompasses the characters in the most common language encoding systems in use. That means that as long as a document is saved with Unicode encoding, the default in Word, chances are you'll be able to open and view it.

If you have instances when Word documents open as funny, unreadable garbage characters, the document may be using an encoding scheme that Word doesn't recognize by default. In such a case, you can set up Word to prompt you to confirm encoding when you open a file. To do so:

1. **With an unreadable file open in Word, choose File ⇨ Options.**
2. **Click Advanced in the list at the left.**
3. **Scroll down and, under General, click the Confirm file format conversion on open check box.**
4. **Click OK to apply your changes.**

You can then close and reopen the file, and a Convert File dialog box should appear and prompt you to select the required encoding scheme.

If you need to apply particular encoding to a file that you're saving, you can do so to ensure that any recipient of the file will be able to open it and view its contents. To save a Word file with the specified encoding, follow these steps:

1. **Choose File ⇨ Save As.**

2. **Click Computer, and then Browse, and specify a save location in the Save As dialog box.**

3. **Select Plain Text from the Save as type drop-down list.**

4. **Click Save.** The File Conversion dialog box appears.

5. **Click Other encoding.** The list of encoding choices becomes active, as shown in Figure C.1.

FIGURE C.1

Save a Word file as text to choose encoding.

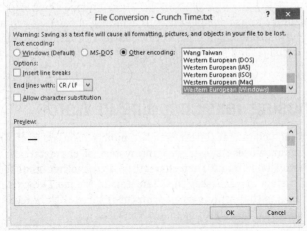

6. **Scroll through the Other Encoding list, and click the encoding set to apply.**

7. **Click OK.** Word saves the file with the proper encoding so that you can send it to recipients as needed.

Enabling Editing Languages for Office Programs

If you want to edit text in more than one language in Office, you have to install the appropriate language features. Some language features are specific to Office, whereas others are set in the Windows operating system.

FIGURE C.4

You can set up Windows to enable you to type in another language.

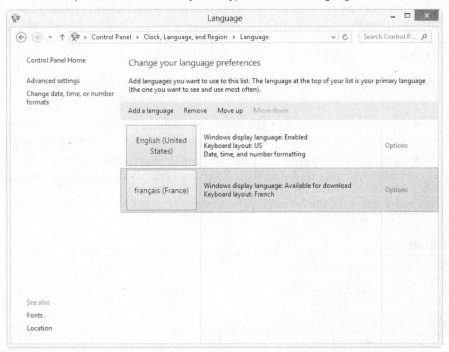

In Windows 7, choose Start ⇨ Control Panel. Then click Change display language under Clock, Language, and Region. The Region and Language Options dialog box appears.

First, click the Change Keyboards button on its Keyboards and Languages tab. Click the Add button in the dialog box that appears, and then use the tree in the Add Input Language dialog box to select the keyboard to install. Click OK.

Back in the Text Services and Input Language dialog box, choose the keyboard to use from the Default Input Language drop-down list at the top, and then click OK twice. You can then close the Control Panel.

> **TIP**
>
> To see the keyboard layout (characters) available for the selected keyboard, you can display the On-Screen keyboard, discussed later in the "Accessibility Features" section.

Language Translation Features

Even if you don't set up other editing languages, Office applications typically have the ability to translate at least a few languages, usually Arabic, English, French, and Spanish. These features can be helpful when you need to write or have received a limited amount of text in another language and you need a translation.

You can select text and translate it in several of the Office applications. Here are the methods you can use to start the translation in various Office 2013 applications:

- In Word or Outlook, select the text to translate, right-click, and then click Translate. If a submenu with languages appears, click the desired language.

- In Word, Excel, PowerPoint, Publisher, and OneNote, click the Review tab on the Ribbon and then click Translate. Select another translation option if needed.

Translations appear in the Research pane, shown in Figure C.5.

FIGURE C.5

Office can translate to French.

Accessibility Features

Working with some of the normal settings in Office applications can help a person with special needs to work more effectively. In other cases, you can call on settings in Windows to make a system easier to use.

Zoom

A neglected but simple way to convert onscreen documents to a "large print" version for people who are challenged by their eyesight is to zoom the document. For example, in Word, you can click the View tab on the Ribbon and then click the Zoom button in the Zoom group. Even a zoom setting of 125 percent makes many documents much more readable.

Ease of Access

Windows offers several features collectively called *Ease of Access Features*. Access some Ease of Access features by opening Control Panel (Settings charm⇨Control Panel in Windows 8 and Start⇨Control Panel in Windows 7), and then click Ease of Access⇨Ease of Access Center. The Ease of Access tools available via this Start menu group include:

- **Magnifier:** Opens a special pane that greatly magnifies a section of the current document for easier reading.

- **Narrator:** Starts the Narrator feature, which reads back onscreen text. This feature helps users with severe sight challenges.

- **On-Screen Keyboard:** As shown in Figure C.6, choosing this command opens a graphical keyboard. The user can then click with the mouse to type. Although it's a slower method of data entry, it may be preferable for users who have stiffness, soreness, or limited mobility in the fingers.

FIGURE C.6

Fingers too sore to type? Try clicking.

Scroll down and look under Explore all settings to see additional choices for setting up the system for greater comfort and ease of use.

Index